THE SOHO BIBLIOGRAPHIES
XX

EDMUND BLUNDEN

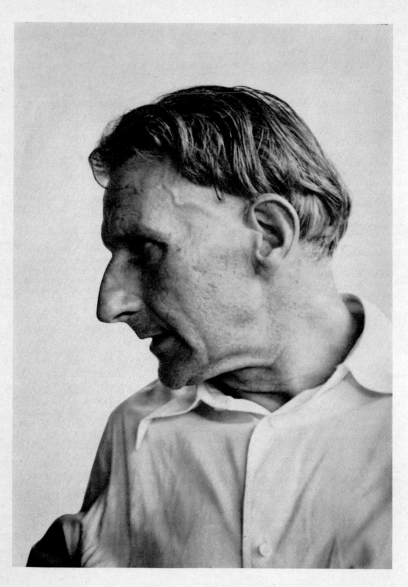

1. Edmund Blunden, *c.* 1955

A BIBLIOGRAPHY OF
EDMUND BLUNDEN

BY
B. J. KIRKPATRICK

With a Personal Introduction by
RUPERT HART-DAVIS

CLARENDON PRESS · OXFORD
1979

Oxford University Press, Walton Street, Oxford OX2 6DP

OXFORD LONDON GLASGOW NEW YORK
TORONTO MELBOURNE WELLINGTON CAPE TOWN
IBADAN NAIROBI DAR ES SALAAM LUSAKA ADDIS ABABA
KUALA LUMPUR SINGAPORE JAKARTA HONG KONG TOKYO
DELHI BOMBAY CALCUTTA MADRAS KARACHI

© *B. J. Kirkpatrick 1979*
Personal Introduction © *Rupert Hart-Davis 1979*

British Library Cataloguing in Publication Data

Kirkpatrick, Brownlee Jean
A bibliography of Edmund Blunden. — (Soho bibliographies).
1. Blunden, Edmund — Bibliography
I. Title II. Series
016.821'9'12   Z8105./   77-30460

ISBN 0-19-818170-1

*Set by Hope Services, Abingdon
and printed in Great Britain
at the Pitman Press, Bath*

CONTENTS

LIST OF ILLUSTRATIONS

Plate II is reproduced by kind permission of Professor Takeshi Saito.

PERSONAL INTRODUCTION

When I went up to Oxford in October 1926 I met again my prep-school friend Wyndham Ketton-Cremer. Always precocious in his reading, he introduced me to many unexpected delights such as Peacock's novels and the letters of Dorothy Osborne. One day he found me reading a book of poems by Humbert Wolfe. 'Don't waste your time with that rubbish,' he said; 'I'll give you a book of *real* poems,' and he presented me with a copy of *English Poems* by Edmund Blunden.

I read the book several times with ever-growing pleasure, marking as special favourites 'The Midnight Skaters', 'Pride of the Village' and 'The Still Hour' (which, to my lasting regret, I inadvertently overlooked when I was choosing the contents of *Poems of Many Years*). Without realising it I had picked on three poems that exemplified permanent preoccupations of the poet's muse—the mysterious if terrible beauty of nature, cricket and village life in the golden age of his youth, and the never-ending agony of the Great War.

In Blackwell's I excitedly found copies of *The Waggoner* and *The Shepherd*, and I bought each new book—*Leigh Hunt, Undertones of War* and the others—on publication, but it was only after my first meeting with the poet that the little shelf of his books began to turn into a Collection.

We met early in 1932, at a meeting of the Book Society selection committee, in Hugh Walpole's Piccadilly flat, and I was immediately struck by the exactitude of Robert Graves's description of the poet's appearance as 'a cross between Julius Caesar and a bird'. His tiny frame, his shyness, his quick-darting eyes and gestures, had all the grace and agility of a wren, while his noble nose suggested the dominance of the Latin poets he read and loved. Our friendship blossomed quickly, and soon I was fishing and playing cricket with him at his old home at Yalding in Kent. There followed many visits to his later homes, at Oxford (Merton and the Woodstock Road), Tonbridge, Virginia Water, and Long Melford, expeditions to Stratford and elsewhere, but mostly we met in London, where the book-barrows on the Farringdon Road were our constant quarry. He was the most accomplished book-hunter I have ever known—even more knowledgeable than my beloved Edward Garnett, since his range went further back. He knew every edition of every book, important or obscure, the handwriting of every writer and of many lesser individuals, and he had a diviner's instinct of where treasure might lurk.

Meanwhile I began to pick up secondhand copies of his Beaumont Press and other privately printed books (all quite cheap and available then), and he never failed to give me, or tell me of, any new item from his pen. Each time we met I would bring one of his books for him to inscribe, in prose or verse, with much wit and incredible facility. He was recovering from a painful operation when in November 1932 I visited him with a copy of the newly published *Halfway House*. He immediately sat up in bed, and in his exquisite hand wrote out these lines, without pause or erasure:

Horatian Ode to Rupert

While Hiems with his gelid griff
Doth Nature's pale persona biff,
   Thou Rupert unaffrighted
   Visit'st thy bard delighted.

While publishers i' th' haste divulge
Books which with W——p——e's praise refulge,
   Thou buy'st this lean and dim
   Item, from balance slim.

These amicable actions shall
Arouse thy friend from th' hospitall,
   Who as he marks thy fame
   Shall a just God proclaim.

My copy of *Undertones of War* he adorned with two of his own beautifully executed wartime maps, his edition of Wilfred Owen with a drawing of the Western Front, *Shells by a Stream* with topographical details concerning the poems in the book (see plate 10), and in his edition of the poems of William Collins he transcribed from memory these words of Dr Johnson's, which he liked to pretend described him too:

His morals were pure, and his opinions pious: in a long continuance of poverty, and long habits of dissipation, it cannot be expected that any character should be exactly uniform. There is a degree of want by which the freedom of agency is almost destroyed; and long association with fortuitous companions will at last relax the strictness of truth, and abate the fervour of sincerity. That this man, wise and virtuous as he was, passed always unentangled through the snares of life, it would be prejudice and temerity to affirm; but it may be said that at least he preserved the source of action unpolluted, that his principles were never shaken, that his distinctions of right and wrong were never confounded, and that his faults had nothing of malignity or design, but proceeded from some unexpected pressure, or casual temptation.

Edmund's many moves and incessant generosity made holes in the file of his own works, and he came to look on my collection as, so to speak, the official one, often giving me his only copy of some rare item, to fill up a gap. Thus he gave me the only known copy of A9 to make sure it was preserved. I had already acquired the corrected proofs —for five pounds—at the Esher sale in 1946, where I also bought some of the earlier pamphlets, even some duplicates, which went so cheaply that they were worth buying for the cloth cases Lord Esher had dressed them in.

My copy of A3 took some finding. E.B. told me that all six had been presented to 'the Great at Christ's Hospital', so I started with the children of the headmaster of E.B.'s day, Dr Upcott, and eventually his daughter Miss Gwen Upcott most generously exchanged her father's copy for other books. Except for the copy which belonged to Lord Carlow, and is now, I believe, in the possession of his son Lord Portarlington, I have never seen or heard of any of the other copies.

My Blunden researches brought me into touch with a

most engaging character called Major Trevor Moilliet. A retired soldier who had tried all sorts of jobs without success (he was for a time a greengrocer somewhere near Buckingham Palace), he was cheerfully undeterred by reverses, and when his vocal chords were removed because of cancer he quickly learned to breathe through a tube in his neck and to speak, clearly if a trifle huskily, by means of a system of controlled belches. He was a compulsive book-collector, but his reach so often exceeded his grasp that his small capital was always exhausted before his collection was complete, and he was forced to sell all he had and start off on some other author or period. When I met him he already had a considerable Blunden collection, and for some years we hunted in friendly competition, exchanging information and duplicates. Then his money ran out once again, and before selling his books he let me buy very reasonably a few items I lacked, in particular Copy B of *On Several Occasions* (A67b): goodness knows how he found it. He was a generous friend and a most likeable man. Peace to his shade.

My dear friend Simon Nowell-Smith most generously gave me the cloth-bound copy of *Pastorals* (A7b), which he had found in Blackwell's. When Edmund inscribed it for me in 1961 he declared it to be the first copy he had ever seen in this form. In more than forty years I have never heard of another, nor has one appeared in *Book Auction Records*. From Japan I have been greatly helped by Edmund's old friend Professor Takeshi Saito, and particularly by Professor Ichiro Niskizaki, who, after vainly scouring Japan for a second copy of Bret Harte's *Selected Poems* (B20), gave me his own precious copy, inscribed to him by Edmund. I have never seen another.

When Edmund went back to Japan, and later to Hong Kong, he faithfully posted me copies of everything of his that appeared there, so that I gradually accumulated a vast number of books, offprints and periodicals issued in those places. He also gave me all his surviving letters to his parents from the post-war years, and his letters to Philip and Kathleen Tomlinson, as well as some books and pamphlets from their collection. On the death of Edmund's old Japanese friend and pensioner Aki Hayashi I acquired more early items.

Besides almost everything in the bibliography (except a few minor items in Sections A and B and a good many of the periodicals in Section C), the collection contains a mass of miscellaneous material—hundreds of his letters to me; packets of manuscripts in prose and verse; corrected proofs; typescripts of lectures and broadcasts; photographs of Edmund at all ages, including my favourite one of the two of us setting out to open the batting in a cricket match; boxes of press-cuttings concerning the poet; reviews of his books; essays and books about him and his work; books dedicated to him; pamphlets and books that inspired poems of his, and the four-page pamphlet of which I had fifteen copies printed for his fiftieth birthday dinner. It contains the first printing of poems to Edmund by Siegfried Sassoon, Cecil Day-Lewis and William Plomer, and is signed by all the diners: Edmund, Day-Lewis, Plomer, T. S. Eliot, Walter de la Mare, Stanley Morison, Philip Tomlinson and myself.

My only serious lacuna in Sections A and B is the edition of eight copies of *Madrigals and Chronicles* (B14b). In 1936 I saw one of them in the New York shop of Mr Philip Duschnes, but he was asking the equivalent of twelve pounds for it, and I hadn't got the money. I sadly replaced the copy on his shelves and have never seen another.

I had always promised Edmund that I would compile his official bibliography, but when I retired to rural Yorkshire in 1964 I realized that I never should. In London I had always been too busy, and now I was too far from newspaper files and libraries. I therefore asked Miss Brownlee Kirkpatrick, who had compiled excellent Soho Bibliographies of Virginia Woolf and E. M. Forster, if she would undertake the task, basing her work on my collection. She agreed more readily perhaps than she would have done if she had been able to realise the appalling scope and complexity of the job. A glance at the 3370 entries in Section C will give some slight idea of the hundreds of hours she has spent in newspaper offices and the British Museum Library at Colindale. Her correspondence with publishers all over the world has been immense, her assiduity and exactitude most remarkable.

To avoid even more work, and to examine and check my unique copies and stacks of periodicals, she has made many visits to Yorkshire, which have given great pleasure. Suitcases full of Japanese periodicals have been carried to and fro, precious copies entrusted to the fickle post. She knows, as well as I do, that neither her bibliography nor my collection will ever be complete: vagrant items in Asia will elude us to the end, anonymous contributions will never be identified, but, to paraphrase Dr Johnson, when it shall be found that a few odds and ends are omitted, let it not be forgotten that a tremendous lot likewise is performed.

RUPERT HART-DAVIS

Marske-in-Swaledale
October 1978

PREFACE

Despite nine years' work, and its length, this bibliography must claim even less completeness than could have been anticipated at the outset. E.B. was a man of much generosity, and invariably responded to appeals from editors and others for poems or prose. This led to his work appearing in a number of little-known journals in this country, Japan, Hong Kong and elsewhere. The sheer volume of his published work is an indication of the great pressure under which he must have worked. Over 3000 contributions to periodicals and newspapers are an astonishing achievement, and, though a number of them are of no great significance, as part of his many-sided work they do reflect at least the wide range of his interests.

During these nine years when the end never seemed in sight, it was a great encouragement to become increasingly aware of the affection in which E.B. was held by his many friends from his school-days at Christ's Hospital, comrades of the Southdown Battalions Association from the 1914–1918 War, friends from his Oxford days after the War, and later as Fellow and Tutor of Merton College, from Japan and Hong Kong and elsewhere. All those who were approached seemed to welcome the opportunity of contributing to the record of his work.

STYLE

Full bibliographical details are given in Section A for all first editions. The 'degressive principle' has been adopted for later editions in this section, and for all entries in Section B, but not to the exclusion of essential information. Such a principle was almost a necessity in view of the volume of E.B.'s contributions to books other than his own. The titles of poems are indicated by small capitals throughout, except in the contents of E.B.'s own collections. First lines of poems are given in the bibliography only where either the poem is untitled, or there is more than one poem with the same title. There is, however, a First Line Index coupled with the title of the poem; the first lines also appear in the Index to the titles of poems. The General Index does not incorporate either of these categories. Items that I have not seen are marked by an asterisk.

NUMBER OF COPIES PRINTED OF EARLY BOOKS & OFFPRINTS

Evidence is available from several sources: notes made by EB in 1931 on a list of his publications covering the years 1913–1922, in letters and presentation copies to Sir Rupert Hart-Davis, and in letters from his brother, Mr Gilbert A. Blunden. Sometimes there is a discrepancy between figures recorded by E.B. himself and his brother, as for instance in *Old Homes*, where the latter in a letter dated 27 February 1923 refers to 50 copies printed; Blunden's figure is 100 copies (*see* A11). In such cases E.B.'s figure has been preferred. All these figures are confirmed, where recorded, in Professor Takeshi Saito's 'Bibliography of the Works of E.B.' in the *Study of English*, Tokyo, Vol. 20, No. 3, June 1927, pp. 226–7 (Edmund Blunden Number); the bibliography was brought up to date in *Today's Japan*, March/April 1960, Vol. 5, No. 3, pp. 63–8, and *Edmund Blunden: A Tribute from Japan*, 1974, pp. 193–212 (*see* B291). Professor Saito, in a letter to me dated 28 December 1969, wrote that he had obtained the figures from E.B. himself, and not from the publishers. Sir Rupert Hart-Davis was able to learn from Richard Cobden-Sanderson before his death that his firm's records no longer existed. Where print figures were not obtainable from the publishers, I tried the printers, and was particularly disappointed to find that the Kemp Hall Press, Oxford, printers of *Undertones of War*, ceased business in the Second World War. The Kemp Hall Bindery took over the name when occupying the Press's building at 33 St Aldates in 1946, but there was, in fact, no connection between them. The Shenval Press Ltd printed several of the books in the 1930s but their records do not extend so far back; unfortunately Mr James Shand, who had been intimately concerned with these publications, had died four years before my inquiry.

CHECK LISTS

In addition to Professor Saito's lists, the following are fuller than those generally appended to books on E.B.:

Muir, Percy H. *Points Second Series, 1866-1934*. London, Constable, 1934, pp. 83-94.

Hardie, Alec M. *Edmund Blunden*. London, Longmans, Green for the British Council, and the National Book League, 1958; revised edition, 1971.

A *Bibliography of Edmund Blunden*, by A. J. Gawsworth and J. Schwartz, Ulysses Bookshop, 1931 was announced but not published.

SOURCES NOT TRACED

As well as the untraced original appearance of some of the poems in papers such as the *Japan Advertiser* and the *Nippon Times*, the following sources have not been found:

The Mind's Eye, 1934 (A50)—the original publication of a few of the essays in this collection has not been found; the dates are noted as given:
A Battalion History, 1933
The Beauty of Vagueness, 1926
Line upon Line, 1926
Not Only Beautiful, 1926
Winter Comes to Tokyo, 1925
Yalding Bridges, 1931
Geographical Improvements, 1926
It is likely that at least five of these first appeared in Japanese journals.

The following have not been traced:

Letter on the death of a sentry in a Sussex newspaper, 1916—Blunden in a letter to John Gawsworth, dated

14 April 1931, now in the collection of Sir Rupert Hart-Davis, wrote 'A little later [i.e. probably after March 1916] I heard that a letter of mine on the death of one of my lucky lads in a fiery sap-head at Auchy was printed in a Sussex newspaper'; the *Crowborough & Uckfield Weekly*, *Horsham Times & West Sussex Courier*, *Southern Weekly News*, *Sussex County Herald*, *Sussex Express*, and the *West Sussex Gazette*, have been searched without success.

English Poetry. Review of *Lyrical Poetry from Blake to Hardy*, by H. J. C. Grierson; and *Phases of English Poetry*, by Herbert Read, both published in November 1928—seen in proof, signed Edmund Blunden; for the *Daily Telegraph*, and probably not published.

Ghosts [or Ghosts in Flanders], probably 1933—seen in proof, for a periodical.

Charles Lamb: An Appreciation of the Great Essayist, 1934—periodical, pp. 69–75; on the centenary of his death in December 1934.

The Housman Enigma, 1957 ⎫
Thomas Hardy's Best, 1959 ⎬ contributions to the British Council's Feature Articles Services for overseas publication.
On Keats's Letters, 1960 ⎭

The Poetry of Ignorance—periodical, pp. 149–50, signed E.B.

Midsummer Night's Dream—periodical, pp. 19–25, seen in proof in the collection of Sir Rupert Hart-Davis; inscribed by Blunden 'I hardly remember what this fragment of proofs belongs to, but *M.N.D.* was a magazine article originally. E.B.'

SERENITY—photograph of holograph, at foot: 'At Katori in June 1959 when the Reverend H. Nakaga kindly guided . . .'; seen in the collection of Sir Rupert Hart-Davis; probably not published.

Information on these and any other omissions will be welcomed. Contributions to periodicals which may be by E.B. are listed in the Appendix (*see* Eg).

MANUSCRIPTS

No attempt has been made to record the locations of E.B.'s manuscripts since they are so scattered, and for the most part in small holdings. Many remain in the hands of friends in the form of unpublished poems. The main collection is in the Humanities Research Center, University of Texas at Austin, and includes the manuscript of *Undertones of War*, poems and letters. There are also collections in the Berg Collection of the New York Public Library, the Department of Manuscripts of the British Library Reference Division, and the Charles Lamb Society at Edmonton Central Library. Reference should be made to the following for notes on the British Library collection: *Catalogue of an Exhibition of the Poetry Manuscripts in the British Museum, April–June 1967*, by Jenny Lewis, London, Turret Books, 1967 (title on cover: Poetry in the Making); *The Arts Council Collection of Modern Literary Manuscripts, 1963–1972: A Catalogue*, by Jenny Stratford, London, Turret Books, 1974: and *Modern Literary Manuscripts*, by W. H. Kelliher, London, British Museum Publications Ltd for the British Library Board [1974].

ACKNOWLEDGEMENTS

I am very grateful to Edmund Blunden for agreeing to Sir Rupert Hart-Davis's proposal that I should undertake his bibliography, and for the help he gave me, cut short, alas, all too soon by the ill-health of his last years, and to Mrs Blunden for all her assistance, which included the always pleasurable visits I made to Long Melford. These visits afforded me the added enjoyment of weeks and week-ends at Great Shelford with my old friend, the late Joan Greaves, who invariably accompanied me on these occasions.

Above all I owe an immeasurable debt to Sir Rupert Hart-Davis. The bibliography would hardly have been possible without recourse to his unique collection, and it has profited in every way from his knowledge of E.B. and all his works, and the kindly and meticulous way he has watched over its progress to the last stages of the type-script and proofs. My visits to Marske were always ones of relaxation despite a daily routine of work, and were all the more enjoyable for Lady Hart-Davis's warm hospitality.

From E.B.'s Christ's Hospital days, Mr A. H. Buck, who combed *The Blue* for contributions and provided some I had missed, as did Mr C. E. Escritt, and Mr Frank H. Smith, Editor of the Old Boys section of *The Blue*, gave me invaluable help with many points. I have also to thank Mr R. C. Horsnell, Miss Freda Lord, Mrs O. M. Peto, Librarian of Christ's Hospital, Mr Edwin Slade, and the Clerk of Christ's Hospital.

I am grateful to E.B.'s comrades in the Southdown Battalions Association, especially Mr A. J. Cosham, the Chairman, who ran to earth dinner-menus which I had not seen, and to Lt-Colonel E. G. Hollist, Royal Sussex Regimental Association.

Professor Takeshi Saito, E.B.'s oldest Japanese friend, gave me help with Japanese material without which the record of these publications would be far less complete. I am much indebted to Professor Saito's student, Mr Yuichi Mizunoe, for his lists of contributions to Japanese periodicals and newspapers unavailable in this country. Professor Ineko Kondo also gave me invaluable help in tracing E.B.'s contributions to the *Japan Advertiser* during his first visit to Japan in 1924–1927 of which I had seen clippings devoid of dates. I have also to thank Dr I. Inagaki of the School of Oriental and African Studies, University of London who transliterated and translated all material in Japanese; it was pleasant to learn that he had attended lectures by EB in 1949 at Kobe City University of Foreign Studies.

For help with Hong Kong material, I am grateful to Mr Geoffrey W. Bonsall, Director of Hong Kong University Press for his patience in answering many queries, and for drawing my attention to an unrecorded poem at the 'eleventh hour'; Professor Alec M. Hardie and Mr K. K.

Yung for the loan of items, some of which were unknown to me, and for helping me in other ways to complete details of publications; Mr Bernard Mellor for the information on his joint editorship with E.B.; Mrs Mary Visick for looking through *Eastern Horizon*, and checking other points; Mr T. C. Lai; Mr J. Llewellyn of the Faculty of Engineering and Architecture; Mr Paul Yeung, Manager, City Hall for information on E.B.'s two poems on the New City Hall; and St John's Cathedral Librarian; *South China Morning Post*; and the Urban Council Public Libraries.

E.B.'s vast number of contributions to the *Times Literary Supplement* could not have been identified without the help of Mr Arthur Crook, former Editor, and two of his assistants, if it had not been for their labours most of E.B.'s reviews must have remained in oblivion. I am also grateful to the Editor of the *New Statesman* for permission to identify contributions to the *Athenaeum* and the *Nation & Athenaeum*.

I am grateful to the following for help in various ways: The Revd Stephen Abbott; Miss C. Babington Smith; Mr F. W. Bateson; Mr Thomas Braun; Mr Neville Braybrooke; Mr W. P. Evans of May & Baker Ltd; Mr R. B. Gooch of the National Playing Fields Association; Dr Donald Gould; Mr Duff Hart-Davis; Dr C. R. Kirkpatrick; Mr K. C. S. Lea of the Kemp Hall Bindery; Mr R. G. C. Levens; Mr Jack Lively; Mr Simon Nowell-Smith; Professor Mamoru Osawa; Mr D. G. M. Owen; the Earl of Portarlington; Mrs Iris Pyves; Dr Margaret Ridley; Professor Neville Rogers; Mr and Mrs Philip Ross; Professor Moriaki Sakamoto; Miss E. M. Saunders, Headmistress of Channing School; the Revd Brocard Sewell; Mr W. J. J. Smillie, Catering Manager, House of Commons; Miss Janet Tomblin; Mr T. R. Tregear; Mr J. A. White; and Mr Peter Whittle.

Acknowledgements are also gratefully recorded to the archivists, curators and librarians of: Brighton Public Library; British Council, Portugal; Council for the Care of Churches; County Borough of Northampton; Dorset County Museum; Merton College, Oxford; National Book

League; New York Public Library; Nottinghamshire County Library; Poetry Library, Arts Council; The Queen's College, Oxford; Westfield College, University of London; Winchester College; to Mrs C. M. Gee, Archivist & Assistant Curator, Keats House; Mr Barry Hall, Peterborough Division, Cambridgeshire Libraries; Mr E. A. Harwood, *Daily Telegraph*; Mr D. G. Neill, Bodleian Library; Mr Gordon Phillips, Archivist, *The Times*; and Mr Patrick Strong, Keeper of College Library & Collections, Eton College.

I approached many publishers and printers, and most responded to what must have been troublesome questions. I should like to thank, in particular, the following for much information: Basil Blackwell, Publisher; Cambridge University Press; Jonathan Cape Ltd; Chatto & Windus Ltd; Harcourt Brace Jovanovich, Inc., New York; The Hokuseido Press Co. Ltd, Tokyo; Kenkyusha Ltd, Tokyo; Macmillan London Ltd; George Allen & Unwin Ltd; W. H. Allen & Co. Ltd; Archon Books, Hamden, Connecticut; J. W. Arrowsmith Ltd; Ernest Benn Ltd; B. T. Batsford Ltd; the late Mr Cyril Beaumont; The Bodley Head; Albert Bonniers Förlag AB, Stockholm; Bridge Books; British Council; C. K. Broadhurst & Co. Ltd; Mr J. L. Carr; Chappell & Co. Ltd; Wm Collins & Co. Ltd; Commonwealth War Graves Commission; Constable & Co. Ltd; Contemporary Arts Society; W. S. Cowell Ltd; Daedalus Press; Peter Davies Ltd; J. M. Dent & Sons Ltd; Librairie Marcel Didier, Paris; Dennis Dobson, Publishers; Doubleday & Company, Inc., New York; Gerald Duckworth & Co. Ltd; E. P. Dutton & Co. Inc., NewYork; Encyclopaedia Britannica International Ltd; The Encyclopedia Americana, New York; The English Association; Enitharmon Press; Faber and Faber Ltd; The Golden Head Press Ltd; Victor Gollancz Ltd; Hamish Hamilton Ltd; Harper & Row, Publisher, Inc., New York; George G. Harrap & Co. Ltd; The Harvill Press Ltd; Hazell Watson & Viney Ltd; Heinemann Educational Books Ltd; High Hill Press Ltd; Hilary Press; Hodder & Stoughton Ltd; Holmes, The Printers, Horsham; Hutchinson Publishing Group Ltd; International Learning Systems

Corporation Ltd; The Japan Society of London; Michael
Joseph Ltd; Kawade Shobo Shin-sha Publishing Co. Ltd,
Tokyo; Keats-Shelley Association of America; Keats-
Shelley Memorial Association; The Lavenham Press Ltd;
A. H. Leach & Co. Ltd; The Library Association; J. P.
Lippincott Company, Philadelphia; Longman Group Ltd;
Lund Humphries Publishers Ltd; David McKay Co. Inc.,
New York; The Macmillan Company, New York; Method-
ist Book Room; Methuen & Co. Ltd; National Education
Association, Washington, DC; Northamptonshire Natural
History Society & Field Club; Peter Owen Ltd; Pan Books
Ltd; Donald Parsons & Company Ltd; Pergamon Press Ltd;
The Poetry Book Society; G. P. Putnam's Sons, New York;
Routledge & Kegan Paul Ltd; The Royal Society of Litera-
ture; St Martin's Press Inc., New York; Charles Scribner's
Sons, New York; The Shakespeare Birthplace Trust; Shen-
val Press Ltd; Sidgwick & Jackson Ltd; G. F. Sims (Rare
Books); Southern Illinois University Press, Carbondale;
The Toucan Press; University of Michigan Press; University
of Toronto Press; The Viking Press, New York; and
Yuhodo Company Ltd, Tokyo.

Finally my thanks, with apologies, are due to those I
may have overlooked, including the staffs of the British
Library Reference Division, and the Newspaper Library,
Bodleian Library, Edmonton Public Library, University of
Hong Kong Libraries, and the University of London
Library.

B. J. KIRKPATRICK

A.

BOOKS AND PAMPHLETS

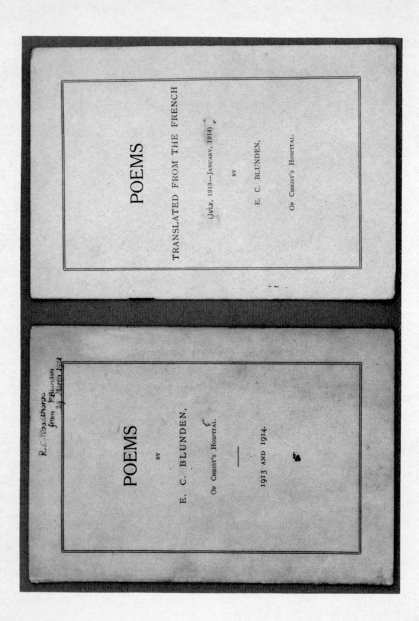

2. Wrappers of *Poems 1913 and 1914* (A1) and *Poems Translated from the French* (A2)

First edition:

POEMS | BY | E. C. BLUNDEN, | OF CHRIST'S HOSPI-
TAL. | [*short rule*] | 1913 AND 1914.

Small crown 8vo. 42 pp. 7¼ × 4¾ in.

P. [1] title; p. [2] at centre: HORSHAM: | PRICE & CO., PRIN-
TERS, WEST STREET. | [*short rule*] | 1914.; p. [3] at centre,
section-title: LONGER POEMS.; p. [4] blank; pp. [5]-13 text;
p. [14] blank; p. [15] at centre, section-title: SHORT POEMS.;
p. [16] blank; pp. [17]-30 text; p. [31] at centre, section-title:
SONNETS.; p. [32] blank; pp. [33]-41 text; p. [42] blank.

Pale grey paper wrappers; printed in black on upper wrapper: [*with-
in a double rule:*] POEMS | BY | E. C. BLUNDEN, | OF CHRIST'S
HOSPITAL. | [*short rule*] | 1913 AND 1914 | [*ornament*] ; edges
cut flush; sewn.

Issued October 1914; 100 copies printed. 6*d.*

Blunden has recorded that this was issued simultaneously with
Poems Translated from the French (*see* A2). *See also* A3, note.

Contents: *Longer Poems*: A Summer Idyll — The Runners — Kestrel
Farm — A Country Girl — Night Thunder in West Sussex — *Short
Poems*: Joy and Grief — Summer Peace (i) — Summer Peace (ii) —
"The Cool of the Day" — Dream City — Late Autumn — Christmas
Eve 1913 — The Old Churchyard — Song — The Streamside — April
— Before a Rainy Daybreak — The Dead Brother — The Old and
the New — The Mouth of the Medway — From the Hill-Top —
From the Cottage Garden — Idyll — The Nightingales — The Bourne
— Yews and a Brook — *Sonnets*: On the Medway: (i) Twyford
Bridge — (ii) The Deserted Mill — (iii) The River in Flood — (iv)
Bream Fishing — (v) Autumn Afternoon — The Silent Valley —
Melancholia — Plunder — Hopes and Harvests — On J. Blanco White
— January Evening Sussex, 1914 [incorporates Sonnet, C9] —
Sundown — The Marring — Vigil — Twyford Bridge — Oedipus at
Colonus — October 1914 — October Nightfall.

A2   POEMS TRANSLATED FROM   1914
                    THE FRENCH

First edition:

POEMS | TRANSLATED FROM THE FRENCH | (JULY,

1913 — JANUARY, 1914) | BY | E. C. BLUNDEN, | OF CHRIST'S HOSPITAL.

Small crown 8vo. 12 pp. $7\frac{1}{4} \times 4\frac{3}{4}$ in.

P. [1] title; p. [2] at centre: HORSHAM: | PRICE & CO., PRINTERS, WEST STREET. | [*short rule*] | 1914.; pp. [3]-12 text.

Pale grey paper wrappers; printed in black on upper wrapper: [*within a double rule:*] [*title as above*]; edges cut flush; stapled.

Issued October 1914; 100 copies printed. 6*d*.

Blunden has recorded that this was issued simultaneously with *Poems*, 1914 (*see* A1). *See also* A3, note.

Contents: Rondel (From the French of Guillaume de Machault, XIVth Century) (Come ye to my jubilee!) — Rondel (Eustache Deschamps, XIVth Century) (God hath made her wondrous fair,) — Rondel (Charles d'Orléans) (Lily-white and rosy-red,) — On Myself (Clement Marot) — Aubade (Pierre de Ronsard) (Come with your hat thrown on your long black hair) — Sonnet (Pierre de Ronsard) (If this our life be shorter than a day) — Sonnet (Joachim du Bellay) (Like as the rose upon the branch in May) — Sonnet (Joachim du Bellay) (Ye who through wood, through river and through lea) — Apparition (Victor Hugo) — The Winnower's Prayer to the Winds (Joachim du Bellay) — Spring Song (Jean-Antoine de Baif) — Ecstasy (Victor Hugo) — "I Picked This Flower." (Victor Hugo) — Never Again (Théodore de Banville) — Aubade (Théodore de Banville) (Marie, forth from your bed: my lady, wake!) — Autumn Song (Paul Verlaine) — Sweetest Melancholy (Paul Verlaine) — After Three Years (Paul Verlaine).

A3   POEMS [and] POEMS TRANSLATED   1914
                    FROM THE FRENCH

First edition — second issue:

[*title on upper cover: within a double rule:*] POEMS | BY | E. C. BLUNDEN, | OF CHRIST'S HOSPITAL. | [*short rule*] | 1913 AND 1914 | [*ornament*]

Small crown 8vo. 12, 42 pp. $7 \times 4\frac{3}{4}$ in.

A2 and A1 bound together without their wrappers.

Olive grey cloth boards; grey upper wrapper from A1 cut down and pasted on upper cover, printed as above; edges trimmed, speckled; white end-papers.

Issued probably November 1914; 6 or 12 copies bound. Not for sale.

Blunden has recorded in Sir Rupert Hart-Davis's copy: 'Six copies were bound in this way for presents to the Great at Christ's Hospital', and in Viscount Carlow's 'I think only six or twelve copies were so

3. Cover of A1 and A2 bound together (A3)

bound — for presents.' The Blunden collection formed by Viscount Carlow is now in the possession of his son, the Earl of Portarlington.

A4 THE BARN 1916

First edition:

[*within a rule*:] THE BARN, | : With : | CERTAIN OTHER POEMS. | [*ornament*] | THE AUTHOR, | E. C. BLUNDEN. | [*rule*] | [*four lines of quotation*:] "I hate your loathesome Poems." | *One Critic.* | "Surprisingly mature and original." | *Another Critic.* | [*rule*] | 1916. | To be had of J. BROOKER, High Street, Uckfield, | OR OF | G. A. BLUNDEN, Framfield, Uckfield.

Foolscap 8vo. [iv] , 44 pp. $5\frac{3}{8} \times 4\frac{1}{4}$ in.

P. [i] title, p. [ii] at centre, dedication: TO JAMES HENRY LEIGH HUNT, | NOW, ALAS, LONG DEAD, BUT ONE | OF THE MOST LOVELY-HEARTED | MEN THAT HAVE EVER BEEN.; p. [iii] [Preface] signed: E. C. Blunden, 10th Royal Sussex, Moore Park, Fermoy, Ireland, March 15th, 1916.; p. [iv] blank; pp. [1]–44 text.

Pale terra-cotta paper wrappers; printed in black on upper cover: [*within a triple rule*:] THE BARN. | [*device of a flower within a rule*, $1\frac{1}{8} \times \frac{7}{8}$ *in.*] | E. C. BLUNDEN. | 1916.; edges cut flush; sewn and gummed.

Published March 1916; 50 copies printed. 6*d.*

A copy in the collection of Sir Rupert Hart-Davis lacks pp. [iii–iv] . *See* note to A5.

Contents: Circe Penitent — The Barn — The River House — The Wicked Miller of Redlands.

A5 [THREE POEMS] 1916

First edition:

[*within a rule*:] THE SILVER BIRD OF HERNDYKE MILL, | STANE STREET, [*rule with loop*] | THE GODS OF THE WORLD BENEATH. | [*short rule*] | E. C. BLUN-DEN. | [*short rule*] | [*six lines of quotation*] | [*rule*] | 1916. | To be had of J. BROOKER, High Street, Uckfield, | or G. A. BLUNDEN, Framfield, Uckfield.

Foolscap 8vo. [28] pp. $5\frac{3}{8} \times 4\frac{1}{4}$ in.

5

P. [1] title; p. [2] at centre, dedication: INSCRIBED TO JOHN CLARE OF HELPSTONE; | BORN, IN A SMALL HOVEL THERE, IN 1793: | DIED, IN NORTHAMPTON COUNTY ASYLUM, | IN 1864. TRULY HE CAUGHT THE SOUL OF | VILLAGE AND FARM IN THE FINE | MESHED NET OF POETRY SUR- | -PRISINGLY BEAUTIFUL. - ; p. [3] Preface, signed: E. C. Blunden, 10th Royal Sussex, Moore Park, Fermoy, Ireland; p. [4] blank; pp. [5–27] text; p. [28] blank.

Pale terra-cotta paper wrappers; printed in black on upper wrapper: [*within a triple rule*:] THREE POEMS | [*device of a flower, within a rule*, 1⅛ × ⅞ *in.*] | E. C. BLUNDEN. | 1916.; edges cut flush; sewn and gummed.

Published April 1916; 50 copies printed. 6*d.*

'The Gods of the Earth Beneath' is erroneously printed as 'The Gods of the World Beneath' on the title-page.

Percy H. Muir in his *Points Second Series 1866–1934*, London, Constable, 1934, p. 83 notes: 'This book originally had an introduction. This was removed from most copies by the author.' The author has recorded in a note to Sir Rupert Hart-Davis: 'I intended, and this was probably in 1918, to tear out the preface from all copies; and yet I don't now remember how I could get at them all, or why I was so shamefaced.' No imperfect copy of [*Three Poems*] has been seen; however a copy of *The Barn* lacking pp. [iii–iv], i.e. the preface, is in the collection of Sir Rupert Hart-Davis. It seems as if the author and Muir may have confused these two works.

Contents: The Silver Bird of Herndyke Mill — Stane Street — The Gods of the Earth Beneath.

A6   THE HARBINGERS   1916
      [i.e. THE BARN and THREE POEMS]

First edition — second impression:

THE HARBINGERS. | [*long rule*] | POEMS | BY | E. C. BLUNDEN, | (*Late of Christ's Hospital*). | [*short rule*] | 1916.

Foolscap 8vo. [iv], 68 pp. 5¼ × 4¼ in.

P. [i] title; pp. [ii–iv] blank; pp. [1]–44 text of *The Barn*; pp. 45–67 text of [*Three Poems*] ; p. [68] blank.

Dark violet paper wrappers; printed in black on upper wrapper: [*within a triple rule*:] THE [*looped line*] | HARBINGERS. | POEMS. | [*short rule*] | E. C. BLUNDEN. | [*short rule*] | PRINTED 1916. | To be had of | G. A. BLUNDEN, | Framfield, | Uckfield.; edges cut flush; sewn and gummed.

Issued by 9 May 1916; 200 copies printed. Probably 1*s.*

The Barn and [*Three Poems*] (*see* A4, 5) bound together with a

6

cancel-title; pp. [i–iv] of *The Barn* and pp. [1–4] of [*Three Poems*] were removed, and [*Three Poems*] renumbered pp. 45–67. The deleted pages comprise the dedications and prefaces in both cases.

A7   PASTORALS   1916

a. First edition:

[*within a rule enclosing two vertical lines in pale turquoise:*] [*rule in pale turquoise*] | [*in black:*] Pastorals: | *A Book of* | Verses | *By* | E. C. Blunden | [*double rule in turquoise*] | London | Erskine Macdonald | Featherstone Buildings | Holborn, W.C.

Foolscap 8vo. 44 pp. $6\frac{1}{4} \times 3\frac{3}{4}$ in.

Pp. [1–2] blank; p. [3] half-title; p. [4] at foot: THE WILLIAM MORRIS PRESS LTD. | FORTY-TWO : : ALBERT STREET | MANCHESTER; p. [5] title; p. [6] at centre: *First Thousand : April, 1916* | *All rights reserved* | *Copyright by Erskine Macdonald in the* | *United States of America;* p. [7] Contents; p. [8] blank; p. [9] Editor's Note by S. Gertrude Ford; p. [10] at centre: IN-SCRIBED | TO S. E. WINBOLT, ESQ., M.A. | WHO HAS DONE MORE FOR | MY POETRY THAN ANY | ONE BESIDE; pp. 11–36 text; pp. [37–41] publisher's advertisements; p. [42] printer's monogram within a circle, $\frac{1}{2}$ in.; pp. [43–44] blank; pp. [37–44] integral.

Brown paper wrappers; printed in pastel blue in an ornamental design on upper wrapper; printed on upper wrapper in central panel: [*in pastel blue:*] THE LITTLE BOOKS | *of* GEORGIAN VERSE | : : (SECOND SERIES) : : | UNDER THE GENERAL EDIT- | ORSHIP *of* S. GERTRUDE FORD | [*in black letter:*] Pastorals | A Book of | [*ornament*] | Verses [*ornament*] | By E. C. Blunden | [*in pastel blue:*] ERSKINE MACDONALD | PUBLISHER | LONDON | 1916 | ● ; lower wrapper, verso printer's monogram within a circle, $\frac{1}{2}$ in.; top edges uncut, fore and bottom edges rough trimmed.

Published 16 June 1916 in the *Little Books of Georgian Verse*, Second Series; 1050 copies printed. 1s.

There was a second issue of ?50 copies, i.e. of the first impression (*see* A7*b*).

Contents: The Preamble — By Chanctonbury — A Song against Hope — Song of Summer Midnight — The Lane — The Twilight Farm — Holiday — Tragedy — Prayer of the Two Dead Foresters — Coats of Arms — The Memory of Kent — A Poem Dreamed — Three Sonnets: On the English Poets now Forgotten — Quam non sine amore video

— A Sacrilege — Asteropæa (i)–(ii) — The Fair Humanities of Old Religion — Hardham — The Dying of Michael Maye.

b. First edition — second issue. 1916:

[*title and imprint as above*]

Foolscap 8vo. 44 pp. 6¼ × 3¾ in.

Pale grey cloth boards; lettered in gold on upper cover on a dark green panel: [*within a double rule in gold*:] Pastorals | [*ornament*] | A Book of Verses | By E. C. Blunden; top edges uncut, fore and bottom edges rough trimmed; off-white end-papers.

Issued 16 June 1916; ?50 copies bound. 2*s*. 6*d*.

Though Blunden recorded 50 copies in cloth in a letter to Fytton Armstrong dated 14 April 1931, now in the collection of Sir Rupert Hart-Davis, and this is the figure given by both Saito and Muir, it is very doubtful that so many were in fact issued. Sir Rupert Hart-Davis's copy is the only one seen either by him or Blunden, and there is no record in *Book-Auction Records* or *Book-Prices Current* of a copy being sold at auction.

A8   THE WAGGONER   1920

a. First edition:

THE WAGGONER | AND OTHER POEMS | BY | EDMUND BLUNDEN | LONDON | SIDGWICK & JACKSON, LTD. | 1920

Crown 8vo. viii, 72 pp. 7½ × 5 in.

P. [i] half-title; p. [ii] blank; p. [iii] title; p. [iv] blank; pp. v–vi Contents; p. [vii] at centre, dedication: TO | MARY DAINES BLUNDEN; p. [viii] Acknowledgements; pp. 1–69 text; p. 70 Glossary of a Few Local or Dialect Words; p. [71] at centre: Printed by T. and A. CONSTABLE, Printers to His Majesty | at Edinburgh University Press; p. [72] blank.

Purple cloth boards; white paper label on spine, 2 × ½ in., printed in black: [*double rule, thick, thin*] | The | Waggon- | er and | other | Poems | [*short rule*] | Edmund | Blunden | [*short rule*] | Sidgwick | and | Jackson | [*double rule, thin, thick*] ; top edges trimmed, fore and bottom edges rough trimmed; white end-papers.

Published 15 August 1920; 500 copies printed. 5*s*.

Two hundred and fifty copies were bound in purple as above. One hundred copies in sheets were sent to Alfred A. Knopf, New York (*see* A8*c*). There was a second issue of 150 copies (*see* A8*b*). A spare

8

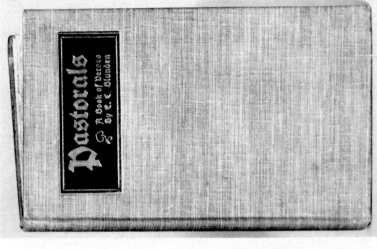

4. Cover of both issues of *Pastorals* (A7a and b)

spine-label is tipped-in the lower free end-paper of copies of the first and second issues. There was a second impression of 1000 copies in September 1920 issued in purple cloth boards; white paper label on spine; fore and bottom edges rough trimmed.

Contents: The Silver Bird of Herndyke Mill [*dedication*: For Siegfried Sassoon] — The Waggoner — Almswomen [*dedication*: For Nancy and Robert [Graves]] — On Turning a Stone [*dedication*: For Alan Porter] — The Pike (revised) — Sheepbells (revised and cut) [*formerly* An Evensong] — The Unchangeable (revised) — A Waterpiece — A Country God — The Sighing Time — In Festubert — Changing Moon — Mont de Cassel — The Barn — Sick-Bed — Leisure — Perch-Fishing [*dedication*: For G. W. Palmer] — Chinese Pond — Malefactors — Storm at Hoptime [*dedication*: For H. John Massingham] — The Estrangement (revised) [*formerly* Estrangement] — Wilderness [*dedication*: For Joy Blunden] — Clare's Ghost [*formerly*: Phantasies] — The Veteran [*dedication*: For G. H. Harrison] — The Gods of the Earth Beneath.

b. First edition — second issue. 1920:

[*title and imprint as above*]

Crown 8vo. viii, 72 pp. $7\frac{3}{8} \times 4\frac{7}{8}$ in.

Dark green cloth boards; white paper label on spine printed in green; edges trimmed. Pale dull green dust-jacket printed in black.

Issued August 1920; 150 copies bound. 5s.

c. First edition — American issue. 1920:

[*title as above*; *imprint*:] [*Borzoi device of a hound running,* $\frac{1}{2} \times 1$ *in.*] | NEW YORK | ALFRED A. KNOPF | 1920

Crown 8vo. viii, 72 pp. $7\frac{1}{2} \times 5$ in.

Claret cloth boards; white paper label on spine, $2\frac{1}{2} \times \frac{1}{2}$ in., printed in black: [*ornament*] | THE | WAG- | GONER | and | other | Poems | Edmund | Blunden | [*ornament*]; top edges dark grey, fore and bottom edges untrimmed; white end-papers. Maize yellow dust-jacket printed in dark green.

Issued December 1920. 100 copies bound. $1.50.

The sheets, with a cancel-title, were supplied by Sidgwick & Jackson in August 1920.

First edition:

THE APPRECIATION OF | LITERARY PROSE | BEING
ONE OF THE | SPECIAL COURSES OF | THE ART OF
LIFE | BY | EDMUND BLUNDEN | Author of "The Wag-
goner and Other Poems." | Assistant Editor of "The Athe-
naeum." Co-editor | of "Poems by John Clare," etc. |
[*publisher's device of a head and scales*, $1\frac{1}{2}$ × $1\frac{1}{8}$ *in.*] |
LONDON : | 28 JOHN STREET, BEDFORD ROW, W.C.

Small crown 8vo. 32pp. $7\frac{1}{4}$ × $4\frac{3}{4}$ in.

P. [1] title; p. [2] at centre: We issue this course in perfect faith |
that the Student's sense of Honour | and fair play will prevent the
peru- | sal of the Lessons by any who have | paid no Fees, . . . [*six
lines*] ; pp. 3–32 text.

Medium grey paper wrappers; printed in black on upper wrapper:
THE ART OF LIFE | CULTURAL COURSES | [*publisher's device
of a head and scales*, 3 × $2\frac{3}{8}$ *in.*] | THE APPRECIATION OF |
PROSE LITERATURE | LESSON I, and on lower wrapper, verso:
PRINTED BY J. EDWARD FRANCIS, | THE ATHENAEUM PRESS,
| 11 AND 13 BREAM'S BUILDINGS, LONDON, E.C.4.

Issued 1921; number of copies printed not ascertained. Available
on subscription.

Blunden has noted on a list of his publications prepared in 1931:
'F. C. Tilney projected, in a great hurry, a series of pamphlets on
the principle of Pelmanism or so, generally styled "The Art of Life",
& divided into various Arts. I was to furnish 6, on "The Appreciation of Prose Literature". I wrote 3; had proofs of 2, and an actual
copy of 1; the 3rd may never have been set up. As to the no of
copies printed, there w^d have been as many as required. Subscribers
were invited to pay for the whole course.' Galley proofs of *Lesson
II: The Logic of Reading* are in the collection of Sir Rupert Hart-
Davis, as is Blunden's own copy of *Lesson I*, the only copy known to
exist.

A10   **THE SHEPHERD**   1922

a. First edition:

THE SHEPHERD | AND OTHER POEMS | OF PEACE
AND WAR | BY EDMUND BLUNDEN | RICHARD |
COBDEN-SANDERSON | THAVIES INN | 1922

spine-label is tipped-in the lower free end-paper of copies of the first and second issues. There was a second impression of 1000 copies in September 1920 issued in purple cloth boards; white paper label on spine; fore and bottom edges rough trimmed.

Contents: The Silver Bird of Herndyke Mill [*dedication*: For Siegfried Sassoon] — The Waggoner — Almswomen [*dedication*: For Nancy and Robert [Graves]] — On Turning a Stone [*dedication*: For Alan Porter] — The Pike (revised) — Sheepbells (revised and cut) [*formerly* An Evensong] — The Unchangeable (revised) — A Waterpiece — A Country God — The Sighing Time — In Festubert — Changing Moon — Mont de Cassel — The Barn — Sick-Bed — Leisure — Perch-Fishing [*dedication*: For G. W. Palmer] — Chinese Pond — Malefactors — Storm at Hoptime [*dedication*: For H. John Massingham] — The Estrangement (revised) [*formerly* Estrangement] — Wilderness [*dedication*: For Joy Blunden] — Clare's Ghost [*formerly*: Phantasies] — The Veteran [*dedication*: For G. H. Harrison] — The Gods of the Earth Beneath.

b. First edition — second issue. 1920:

[*title and imprint as above*]

Crown 8vo. viii, 72 pp. $7\frac{3}{8} \times 4\frac{7}{8}$ in.

Dark green cloth boards; white paper label on spine printed in green; edges trimmed. Pale dull green dust-jacket printed in black.

Issued August 1920; 150 copies bound. 5*s*.

c. First edition — American issue. 1920:

[*title as above*; *imprint*:] [*Borzoi device of a hound running*, $\frac{1}{2} \times 1$ *in.*] | NEW YORK | ALFRED A. KNOPF | 1920

Crown 8vo. viii, 72 pp. $7\frac{1}{2} \times 5$ in.

Claret cloth boards; white paper label on spine, $2\frac{1}{2} \times \frac{1}{2}$ in., printed in black: [*ornament*] | THE | WAG- | GONER | and | other | Poems | Edmund | Blunden | [*ornament*]; top edges dark grey, fore and bottom edges untrimmed; white end-papers. Maize yellow dust-jacket printed in dark green.

Issued December 1920. 100 copies bound. $1.50.

The sheets, with a cancel-title, were supplied by Sidgwick & Jackson in August 1920.

9

First edition:

THE APPRECIATION OF | LITERARY PROSE | BEING
ONE OF THE | SPECIAL COURSES OF | THE ART OF
LIFE | BY | EDMUND BLUNDEN | Author of "The Wag-
goner and Other Poems." | Assistant Editor of "The Athe-
naeum." Co-editor | of "Poems by John Clare," etc. |
[*publisher's device of a head and scales*, $1\frac{1}{2}$ X $1\frac{1}{8}$ *in.*] |
LONDON : | 28 JOHN STREET, BEDFORD ROW, W.C.

Small crown 8vo. 32pp. $7\frac{1}{4}$ X $4\frac{3}{4}$ in.

P. [1] title; p. [2] at centre: We issue this course in perfect faith |
that the Student's sense of Honour | and fair play will prevent the
peru- | sal of the Lessons by any who have | paid no Fees, . . . [*six
lines*] ; pp. 3–32 text.

Medium grey paper wrappers; printed in black on upper wrapper:
THE ART OF LIFE | CULTURAL COURSES | [*publisher's device
of a head and scales*, 3 X $2\frac{3}{8}$ *in.*] | THE APPRECIATION OF |
PROSE LITERATURE | LESSON I, and on lower wrapper, verso:
PRINTED BY J. EDWARD FRANCIS, | THE ATHENAEUM PRESS,
| 11 AND 13 BREAM'S BUILDINGS, LONDON, E.C.4.

Issued 1921; number of copies printed not ascertained. Available
on subscription.

Blunden has noted on a list of his publications prepared in 1931:
'F. C. Tilney projected, in a great hurry, a series of pamphlets on
the principle of Pelmanism or so, generally styled "The Art of Life",
& divided into various Arts. I was to furnish 6, on "The Appreciation of Prose Literature". I wrote 3; had proofs of 2, and an actual
copy of 1; the 3rd may never have been set up. As to the no of
copies printed, there w^d have been as many as required. Subscribers
were invited to pay for the whole course.' Galley proofs of *Lesson
II: The Logic of Reading* are in the collection of Sir Rupert Hart-
Davis, as is Blunden's own copy of *Lesson I*, the only copy known to
exist.

A10 **THE SHEPHERD** **1922**

a. First edition:

THE SHEPHERD | AND OTHER POEMS | OF PEACE
AND WAR | BY EDMUND BLUNDEN | RICHARD |
COBDEN-SANDERSON | THAVIES INN | 1922

THE APPRECIATION OF

LITERARY PROSE

BEING ONE OF THE
SPECIAL COURSES OF

THE ART OF LIFE

BY
EDMUND BLUNDEN

Author of " The Waggoner and Other Poems."
Assistant Editor of " The Athenæum." Co-editor
of " Poems by John Clare," etc.

LONDON :
28 JOHN STREET, BEDFORD ROW, W.C.1

5. Title-page of *The Appreciation of Literary Prose* (A9)

Medium 8vo. 88 pp. 9 X 5¾ in.

P. [1] half-title; p. [2] list of works by the author; p. [3] title; p. [4] at head: Copyright 1922; p. 5 at head, dedication: Inscribed | to | SIEGFRIED SASSOON; p. 6 acknowledgements; pp. 7–8 Contents; pp. 9–86 text; p. [87] blank; p. [88] at head: Printed in Great Britain by Hazell, Watson & Viney, Ltd., | London and Aylesbury.

Egyptian-blue cloth boards; white paper label on spine, 1¼ X ½ in., printed in black: [rule] | THE | SHEP- | HERD | EDMUND | BLUN-DEN | [rule] ; edges untrimmed; white end-papers.

Published April 1922; 1000 copies printed. 6s.

There were reprints in May and December 1922; there was also probably a third reprint. Copies in sheets, probably 500, were sent to Alfred A. Knopf, New York (see A10b).

Contents: 11th R.S.R. — Shepherd — Forefathers — The Idlers — The March Bee — Gleaning — The Pasture Pond — November Morning — The Dried Millpond — Spring Night — The May Day Garland — Journey — High Summer — Evening Mystery — Sheet Lightning — Will o' the Wisp — Cloudy June — Mole Catcher [formerly Mole-catcher] — Water Sport — The Scythe Struck by Lightning — The Giant Buffball — First Snow — Village Green — The Poor Man's Pig — The Covert — The South-west Wind — The Watermill — The Forest — Behind the Line — The Avenue — Reunion in War — A Farm near Zillebeke — Festuberg, 1916 [later 1916 Seen From 1921] — The Troubled Spirit — The Late Stand-to — War Autobiography: Written in Illness — Third Ypres: A Reminiscence — 'The Earth hath Bubbles' — Death of Childhood Beliefs —The Canal — The Time is Gone — April Byeway — The Child's Grave — The Last of Autumn.

b. First edition — American issue. 1922:

[*title as above*; *imprint*:] [*Borzoi device of a hound running*, ⅝ X *1 in.*] | NEW YORK | ALFRED A. KNOPF | 1922

Small demy 8vo. 88 pp. 8½ X 5½ in.

Pale yellow patterned paper boards; printed in mauve, bright green, orange; oatmeal cloth spine, off-white paper label, 1½ X ½ in., printed in pale brown: [*ornament*] | THE | SHEP- | HERD | [*short rule*] | *Blunden* | [*ornament*] ; top edges brown, fore and bottom edges trimmed; cream end-papers.

Issued October 1922; probably 500 copies bound. $1.75.

The sheets were supplied by Cobden-Sanderson.

c. Second English edition. [*1928*] :

THE SHEPHERD | *And Other Poems of Peace and War* |
by | EDMUND BLUNDEN | DUCKWORTH | 3 HEN-
RIETTA STREET | LONDON, W. C. 2

Foolscap 8vo. 102 pp. 6¾ × 4½ in.

P. [1] half-title; p. [2] list of volumes in the series; p. [3] title; p.
[4] at head: *First Published by R. Cobden-Sanderson 1922* | *Revised
and issued in New Readers Library 1928*, at foot: *Made and Printed
in Great Britain by Burleigh Ltd.* | *at* THE BURLEIGH PRESS,
Bristol; p. [5] dedication; p. [6] acknowledgements; pp. 7–8 Contents; pp. 9–101 text; p. [102] blank. 4 pp. publisher's advertisements inserted.

Royal blue cloth boards; lettered in gold on spine: [*rule across head,
short vertical dashes, rule*] | THE | SHEPHERD | EDMUND | BLUN-
DEN | DUCKWORTH | [*rule across foot, short vertical dashes,
rule*] ; edges trimmed; white end-papers. Orange dust-jacket printed
in black.

Published 26 April 1928 as *The New Readers Library*, Vol. 31;
2000 copies printed. 3*s.* 6*d.*

Blunden notes on p. [6] 'Some corrections have been made in the
present edition, but with a sparing hand.'

A11   OLD HOMES   1922

First edition:

[*title on upper wrapper within a double rule*:] OLD
HOMES, | A Poem. | [*rule*] | By EDMUND BLUNDEN.
| [*double rule*] | CLARE | 1922. | [*outside double rule*:]
W. T. WARD. PRINTER & STATIONER, CLARE

Crown 8vo. [4] pp. 7⅝ × 5 in.

Pp. [1–4] text; p. [1] towards head, dedication: *TO G.* [i.e. *Gilbert Blunden*] .

Pale stone paper wrappers; printed in black as above; edges cut flush;
stapled.

Issued 20 June 1922; 100 copies printed. Not for sale.

(O happiest village! how I turned to you,). Reprinted in the *London
Mercury*, July 1922; *English Poems*, [1926] ; *The Poems*, 1930; and
Poems of Many Years, 1957 (*see* A20, 35, 135; C318).

12

UNDER NEW MANAGEMENT
To Rupert, however late, with
the Author's respects
~~20 June 1922~~
27 March 1946
"Sis in dies felicior."

OLD HOMES,

A Poem.

By EDMUND BLUNDEN.

CLARE
1922.

W. T. WARD. PRINTER & STATIONER, CLARE

6. Wrapper of *Old Homes* (A11)

a. First edition:

THE | BONADVENTURE | *A Random Journal of* | *an Atlantic Holiday* | By EDMUND BLUNDEN | [*five line quotation*] | LONDON | RICHARD COBDEN-SANDER-SON | 17 THAVIES INN

Crown 8vo. 192 pp. illus. on p. 192. $7\frac{1}{2} \times 5$ in.

P. [1] half-title; p. [2] list of works by the author; p. 3 [title]; p. [4] towards centre: *Copyright 1922*, at foot: *Printed in Great Britain by* Butler & Tanner, *Frome and London*; p. [5] at centre, dedication: To | H.W.M. [i.e. *H.W. Massingham*] | THIS | "ROUND TRIP"; p. [6] blank; pp. 7–8 Author's Note; pp. 9–10 letter from H. M. Tomlinson; pp. 11–192 text; p. 192 illustration by Ralph Hodgson.

Copenhagen blue cloth boards; white paper label on spine, $1\frac{5}{8} \times 1\frac{1}{4}$ in., printed in pale blue: [*double rule across head*] | THE BON- | ADVENTURE | EDMUND | BLUNDEN | [*double rule*]; top edges trimmed, fore and bottom edges rough trimmed; white end-papers. White pictorial dust-jacket printed in black.

Published 5 December 1922; 1000 copies printed. 6s.

There was a second impression in July 1923 issued at 6s. in binding similar to the first impression with cream pictorial dust-jacket printed in black. *See also* second impression, second issue (A12d).

Two poems appear on pp. 52–3 [untitled] (Mary, what news? –), and p. 172 THOUGHTS OF A ROMANTIC.

Chapters 4, 6, 12, 15, 19 and 31 were reprinted in *Edmund Blunden: A Selection of His Poetry and Prose*, 1950 (*see* A108).

b. First American edition. 1923:

The Bonadventure | A Random Journal of an Atlantic Holiday | By | Edmund Blunden | [*five line quotation*] | G. P. Putnam's Sons | New York & London | [*in black letter*:] The Knickerbocker Press | 1923

Small demy 8vo. [ii], 246 pp. $8\frac{1}{2} \times 5\frac{1}{2}$ in.

P. [i] half-title; p. [ii] list of works by the author; p. [1] title; p. [2] at centre: Copyright, 1923 | by | Edmund Blunden, towards foot: [*printer's device of a sailing ship*, $1 \times \frac{1}{2}$ *in.*] | Made in the United States of America; p. [3] at centre, dedication; p. [4] blank; pp. 5–10 Introduction by H. M. Tomlinson; pp. 11–12 Author's Note; pp. 13–14 letter from H. M. Tomlinson; p. 15 fly-title; p. [16] blank; pp. 17–245 text; p. 246 blank.

Porcelain blue cloth boards; lettered in gold on spine: The | Bon- | adventure | [*rule*] | Blunden | Putnam, and on upper cover: The | Bonadventure | [*long rule*] | Edmund Blunden; top edges gilt, fore and bottom edges trimmed; white end-papers.

Published 6 April 1923; 2500 copies printed. $2.

The illustration by Ralph Hodgson was omitted from this edition.

c. First edition — third printing — photo-offset reprint. 1927:

[*title as above*; *imprint*:] DUCKWORTH | 3 HENRIETTA STREET | LONDON, W.C.2

Foolscap 8vo. 192 pp. illus. on p. 192. $6\frac{3}{4} \times 4\frac{1}{2}$ in.

Royal blue cloth boards; lettered in gold on spine: [*rule across head, short vertical dashes, rule*] | THE | BONADVENTURE | EDMUND | DUCKWORTH | [*rule, short vertical dashes, rule*]; edges trimmed; white end-papers.

Issued 16 June 1927 as *The New Readers Library*, Vol. 7; 2000 copies printed. 3*s.* 6*d.*

P. [4] at head: *First published by R. Cobden-Sanderson December 1922* | *First Cheap Edition (Duckworth) May 1927*, at foot: PRINTED IN GREAT BRITAIN BY PHOTOTYPE LIMITED, BARNET, HERTS. [8] pp. publisher's advertisements inserted.

d. First edition — second impression — second issue. 1929:

[*title as above*; *imprint*:] DUCKWORTH | 3 HENRIETTA STREET, W.C.

Crown 8vo. 192 pp. illus. on p. 192. $7\frac{1}{2} \times 5$ in.

Ruby-red cloth boards; white paper label on spine similar to first printing but lettered in black; top edges trimmed; fore and bottom edges rough trimmed; white end-papers.

Issued October 1929; no record of the number of copies bound. 3*s.* 6*d.*

P. [4] at head: *First published (R. Cobden Sanderson). December 1922* | *Second Impression . . . July 1923* | *Cheap Edition (Duckworth) . . . 1929*, at foot: Printed in Great Britain by Butler & Tanner Ltd. Frome and London.

This issue is called a 'Cheap Edition' as is the issue of 1927 (*see* A12*c*).

14

a. First edition:

THE | BONADVENTURE | *A Random Journal of* | *an Atlantic Holiday* | By EDMUND BLUNDEN | [*five line quotation*] | LONDON | RICHARD COBDEN-SANDER-SON | 17 THAVIES INN

Crown 8vo. 192 pp. illus. on p. 192. $7\frac{1}{2} \times 5$ in.

P. [1] half-title; p. [2] list of works by the author; p. 3 [title]; p. [4] towards centre: *Copyright 1922*, at foot: *Printed in Great Britain by* Butler & Tanner, *Frome and London*; p. [5] at centre, dedication: To | H.W.M. [i.e. *H.W. Massingham*] | THIS | "ROUND TRIP"; p. [6] blank; pp. 7–8 Author's Note; pp. 9–10 letter from H. M. Tomlinson; pp. 11–192 text; p. 192 illustration by Ralph Hodgson.

Copenhagen blue cloth boards; white paper label on spine, $1\frac{5}{8} \times 1\frac{1}{4}$ in., printed in pale blue: [*double rule across head*] | THE BON- | ADVENTURE | EDMUND | BLUNDEN | [*double rule*]; top edges trimmed, fore and bottom edges rough trimmed; white end-papers. White pictorial dust-jacket printed in black.

Published 5 December 1922; 1000 copies printed. 6*s*.

There was a second impression in July 1923 issued at 6*s*. in binding similar to the first impression with cream pictorial dust-jacket printed in black. *See also* second impression, second issue (A12*d*).

Two poems appear on pp. 52–3 [untitled] (Mary, what news? –), and p. 172 THOUGHTS OF A ROMANTIC.

Chapters 4, 6, 12, 15, 19 and 31 were reprinted in *Edmund Blunden: A Selection of His Poetry and Prose*, 1950 (*see* A108).

b. First American edition. 1923:

The Bonadventure | A Random Journal of an Atlantic Holiday | By | Edmund Blunden | [*five line quotation*] | G. P. Putnam's Sons | New York & London | [*in black letter*:] The Knickerbocker Press | 1923

Small demy 8vo. [ii], 246 pp. $8\frac{1}{2} \times 5\frac{1}{2}$ in.

P. [i] half-title; p. [ii] list of works by the author; p. [1] title; p. [2] at centre: Copyright, 1923 | by | Edmund Blunden, towards foot: [*printer's device of a sailing ship*, $1 \times \frac{1}{2}$ *in*.] | Made in the United States of America; p. [3] at centre, dedication; p. [4] blank; pp. 5–10 Introduction by H. M. Tomlinson; pp. 11–12 Author's Note; pp. 13–14 letter from H. M. Tomlinson; p. 15 fly-title; p. [16] blank; pp. 17–245 text; p. 246 blank.

Porcelain blue cloth boards; lettered in gold on spine: The | Bon- | adventure | [*rule*] | Blunden | Putnam, and on upper cover: The | Bonadventure | [*long rule*] | Edmund Blunden; top edges gilt, fore and bottom edges trimmed; white end-papers.

Published 6 April 1923; 2500 copies printed. $2.

The illustration by Ralph Hodgson was omitted from this edition.

c. First edition — third printing — photo-offset reprint. 1927:

[*title as above*; *imprint*:] DUCKWORTH | 3 HENRIETTA STREET | LONDON, W.C.2

Foolscap 8vo. 192 pp. illus. on p. 192. $6\frac{3}{4} \times 4\frac{1}{2}$ in.

Royal blue cloth boards; lettered in gold on spine: [*rule across head, short vertical dashes, rule*] | THE | BONADVENTURE | EDMUND | DUCKWORTH | [*rule, short vertical dashes, rule*] ; edges trimmed; white end-papers.

Issued 16 June 1927 as *The New Readers Library*, Vol. 7; 2000 copies printed. 3*s*. 6*d*.

P. [4] at head: *First published by R. Cobden-Sanderson December 1922* | *First Cheap Edition (Duckworth) May 1927*, at foot: PRIN-TED IN GREAT BRITAIN BY PHOTOTYPE LIMITED, BARNET, HERTS. [8] pp. publisher's advertisements inserted.

d. First edition — second impression — second issue. 1929:

[*title as above*; *imprint*:] DUCKWORTH | 3 HENRIETTA STREET, W.C.

Crown 8vo. 192 pp. illus. on p. 192. $7\frac{1}{2} \times 5$ in.

Ruby-red cloth boards; white paper label on spine similar to first printing but lettered in black; top edges trimmed; fore and bottom edges rough trimmed; white end-papers.

Issued October 1929; no record of the number of copies bound. 3*s*. 6*d*.

P. [4] at head: *First published (R. Cobden Sanderson). December 1922* | *Second Impression . . . July 1923* | *Cheap Edition (Duck-worth) . . . 1929*, at foot: Printed in Great Britain by Butler & Tan-ner Ltd. Frome and London.

This issue is called a 'Cheap Edition' as is the issue of 1927 (*see* A12c).

7. Variant wrappers of *Dead Letters* (A13)

First separate edition:

[*two lines of ornaments*] | DEAD LETTERS | (T.L.H.)
[*i.e. Thornton Leigh Hunt*] | *by* | *Edmund Blunden* |
[*ornament*] | LONDON 1923 [*two lines of ornaments*]

Foolscap 8vo. [ii], 10 pp. 6 × 4¼ in.

Pp. [i–ii] blank; p. [1] title; p. 2 at head: [*line of ornaments*] | ¶ Of
fifty copies printed for HOLBROOK JACKSON | at the Pelican
Press, this is No. [*numbered in ink*], at foot: [*two ornaments*]; pp.
3–5 text; p. [6] blank; p. 7 at head: [*line of ornaments*] | ¶ DEAD
LETTERS first appeared in | *To-day*, December 1922, at foot:
[*two ornaments*]; pp. [8–10] blank.

Paper wrappers in various overall patterns and colours; white paper
label on upper wrapper, 1 × 2⅝ in. or 1½ × 3 in., printed in black:
[*within a frame*:] DEAD LETTERS | *by* EDMUND BLUNDEN;
some edges trimmed; sewn.

Issued February 1923; 50 copies printed. Not for sale.

(There lay the letters of a hundred friends). First published in
To-day, December 1922; and reprinted in *English Poems*, [1926];
The Poems, 1930; and *Poems of Many Years*, 1957 (*see* A20, 35,
135; C347).

a. First edition:

[*in dark brown*:] TO NATURE | [*in pale blue*:] NEW
POEMS BY | EDMUND BLUNDEN | [*circular illustra-
tion of a deer and pelican by a pool*, 2⅝ *in.*]

Medium 8vo. [xii], 52 pp. 9 × 5¾ in.

P. [i] blank; p. [ii] at centre, seven line certificate; p. [iii] half-
title; p. [iv] blank; p. [v] title; p. [vi] towards foot: *Printed in
Great Britain*; pp. [vii–x] Contents; p. [xi] fly-title; p. [xii] blank;
pp. 1–50 text; p. [51] blank; p. [52] HERE ENDS . TO NATURE .
A BOOK OF | Poems by Edmund Blunden The Cover Decora- |
tions and Initial Letters designed by Randolph | Schwabe The Typo-
graphy and Binding | arranged by Cyril William Beaumont Prin- |
ted on his Press at 75 Charing Cross | Road in the City of West-
minster Com- | pleted on the thirtieth day of June | in the year
MDCCCCXXIII | [*publisher's colophon*, 2⅞ × 2¼ *in.*] | THE BEAU-
MONT PRESS | [*rule*] | Pressman S. R. Minns | Compositor W.
Smith.

Grey pictorial paper boards; printed in apple green and orange in an overall pattern of leaves; oatmeal cloth spine; lettered up the spine: [*ornament*]TO NATURE · EDMUND BLUNDEN [*ornament*] ; some top edges uncut, fore and bottom edges rough trimmed; cream end-papers with nature scenes.

Published June 1923; 392 copies printed. £1. 5s.

Three hundred and ten copies, numbered 81–390, were printed on hand-made paper as above, and 80 numbered copies on Japanese vellum (*see* A14*b*). Two extra copies were printed for presentation; one is in the British Museum.

Contents: The Aftermath — "There is a Country" — The Eclogue — The Long Truce — A Fading Phantom — Blindfold — The River House — The Brook — The English Poets — Shooting Star at Harvest — The Old Year — Rural Economy (1917) — The Tune — To Nature — The Spell — A Village Knell — Water Moment — Time of Roses — Waste Ground — First Rhymes — In the Fens — Winter Piece [*later* Winter: East Anglia] — Night Piece — To Joy — To Clare — The Glimpse — Blue Butterfly — The Self-Imprisoned — In Helpston Churchyard (J.C.) [*later* To John Clare] — Rustic Wreath — Brook in Drought — Inheritance — The Still Hour — A Psalm.

b. First edition — Japanese vellum issue. 1923:

[*title and imprint as above*]

Medium 8vo. [xii] , 52 pp. 9 × 5¾ in.

Paper boards as above; vellum spine.

Issued June 1923; 80 copies bound. £2.10s.

Printed on Japanese vellum and numbered 1–80. P. [ii] below seven-line certificate: [*signed in ink*: Edmund Blunden | Randolph Schwabe | Cyril W. Beaumont.]

A15   **CHRIST'S HOSPITAL**   1923

First edition:

CHRIST'S HOSPITAL | A RETROSPECT | By | EDMUND BLUNDEN | AUTHOR OF "THE WAGGONERS," | ETC., ETC. | [*device of the arms of Christ's Hospital*, ⅞ × ¾ *in.*] | LONDON | CHRISTOPHERS | 22 BERNERS STREET, W.1

Crown 8vo. xvi, 208 pp. front., 7 plates facing pp. 30, 58, 70, 100, 124, 154, 176. 7½ × 4⅞ in.

P. [i] half-title; p. [ii] blank; p. [iii] title; p. [iv] at foot: PRINTED IN GREAT BRITAIN BY THE WHITEFRIARS PRESS, LTD., | LONDON AND TONBRIDGE.; p. [v] at centre: TO | H. S. GOODWIN | MY HOUSE MASTER : | WITH | GRATEFUL RESPECT; p. [vi] blank; p. vii Contents; p. viii List of Illustrations; pp. ix–xii Preface; pp. xiii–xvi Authorities; pp. 1–194 text; pp. 195–202 Appendix; pp. 203–206 Index of Persons; p. 206 at foot, printer's imprint; pp. [207–208] blank.

Navy-blue cloth boards; lettered in gold on spine: [*thick rule across head*] | CHRIST'S | HOSPITAL | [*short rule*] | BLUNDEN | [*thick rule*] | [*thick rule*] | CHRISTOPHERS | [*thick rule across foot*] , and in blind on upper cover: [*within a rule:*] CHRIST'S HOSPITAL | EDMUND BLUNDEN; top and fore edges trimmed, bottom rough trimmed, white end-papers. Buff dust-jacket printed in navy-blue.

Published November 1923; 1000 copies printed. 7s. 6d.

A16   THE DOOMED OAK   1925

First separate publication:

[*title at head of page* [2] :] THE DOOMED OAK | *From the French of Anatole France.*

Demy 8vo. An offprint of [4] pp. $8\frac{3}{4} \times 5\frac{3}{8}$ in.

P. [1] text preceding poem; pp. [2–3] text; p. [4] text of following poem.

No wrappers; edges trimmed; not secured.

Issued June 1925; number of copies printed not ascertained. Not for sale.

(In the warm wood bedipped with rosy day) [*later sub-title added*: AN IMITATION] . Reprinted from *Poetica*, Tokyo, June 1925; and reprinted in *Retreat*, 1928; and *The Poems*, 1930 (see A25, 35; C513).

A17   MASKS OF TIME   1925

a. First edition:

[*in dark brown*:] MASKS OF TIME | A NEW COLLECTION OF POEMS | PRINCIPALLY MEDITATIVE | BY EDMUND BLUNDEN | [*illustration of trees in brown and green*, $2\frac{5}{8} \times 1\frac{3}{4}$ *in.*]

Medium 8vo. [xvi] , 60 pp. 2 illus. on pp. [1] , [33] . $8\frac{7}{8} \times 5\frac{3}{4}$ in.

P. [i] blank; p. [ii] towards centre, seven-line certificiate; p. [iii] half-title; p. [iv] blank; p. [v] title; p. [vi] towards foot: *Printed and made in England.*, p. [vii] two-line quotation; p. [viii] blank; p. [ix] Note by the author; p. [x] blank; pp. [xi-xiv] Contents; p. [xv] section-title; p. [xvi] blank; p. [1] illustration; p. [2] blank; pp. 3-31 text; p. [32] blank; p. [33] illustration, section-title; p. [34] blank; pp. 35-58 text; p. [59] blank; p. [60] HERE ENDS · MASKS OF TIME · A BOOK | of Poems by Edmund Blunden The Cover Decora- | tions and Initial Letters designed by Randolph | Schwabe The Typography and Binding | arranged by Cyril William Beaumont Prin- | ted on his Press at 75 Charing Cross | Road in the City of Westminster Com- | pleted on the tenth day of January | in the year MXCCCCXXV | [*publisher's device of a fountain*, $2\frac{7}{8} \times 2\frac{1}{8}$ *in.*] | THE BEAUMONT PRESS | [*rule*] | Pressman S. R. Minns | Compositor W. Smith.

Brown pictorial paper boards printed in green and yellow in an over-all pattern of leaves; pale oatmeal cloth spine; lettered in gold up the spine; [*ornament*] MASKS OF TIME ● EDMUND BLUNDEN [*ornament*] ; top edges trimmed, fore and bottom edges untrimmed; white end-papers.

Published June 1925; 390 copies printed. £1. 5s.

Three hundred and ten copies, numbered 81-390, were printed on hand-made paper as above, and 80 numbered copies on Japanese vellum (*see* A17b).

Contents: A Yeoman — Interval — Masks of Time — Harvest — Rosa Mundi — Eras [*formerly* Epochs; *later* Achronos] — A Transcription — Village — "Art Thou Gone in Haste?" — A Dream — On the Death-Mask of John Clare [*later* The Death-Mask . . .] — "The Crown" [*later* The Crown Inn] — Intimations of Mortality — The Midnight Skaters — A Budding Morrow — Thus Far — Midnight — A Bridge — Strange Perspective — Omen — The Sentry's Mistake [*later* The Guard's Mistake; *and* The Sentry's Mistake] — Two Voices [*formerly* The Survivors (1916)] — Preparations for Victory — Escape — Zero [*later* Come On, My Lucky Lads; *and* Zero 1916] — At Senlis Once — The Zonnebeke Road — Battalion in Rest — E.W.T., On the Death of his Betty [i.e. Ernest W. Tice] — Pillbox — The Welcome — The Prophet — A Recognition [*later* Recognition] — II Peter ii, 22 — The Ancre at Hamel [*later* The Ancre at Hamel Afterwards] .

b. First edition — Japanese vellum issue. 1925:

[*title and imprint as above*]

Medium 8vo. [xvi] , 60 pp. 2 illus. on pp. [1] , [33] . $9 \times 5\frac{3}{4}$ in.

Paper boards as above; vellum spine.

Issued June 1925; 80 copies bound. £2.10s.

Printed on Japanese vellum and numbered 1–80. P. [ii] below seven-line certificate: [*signed in ink*: Edmund Blunden | Randolph Schwabe | Cyril W. Beaumont] .

A18   THE AUGUSTAN BOOKS   1925
OF MODERN POETRY

First edition:

[*title on p.* [i]: *within a double rule, within a border, within a rule*:] *THE AUGUSTAN BOOKS OF* | *MODERN POETRY* | [*rule*] | [*in open capitals*:] EDMUND | BLUN-DEN | [*rule*] | [*in italic*:] *LONDON : ERNEST BENN LTD.* | *8, BOUVERIE STREET, E.C.* 4

Demy 8vo. 32 pp. $8\frac{5}{8} \times 5\frac{1}{2}$ in.

P. [i] title; p. [ii] list of works in the series, at foot: MADE AND PRINTED IN GREAT BRITAIN BY | BILLING AND SONS, LTD., GUILDFORD AND ESHER; p. iii note on the author and acknowledgements; p. [iv] blank; p. v Contents; p. [vi] blank; p. vii Brief Bibliography; p. [viii] blank; pp. 9–30 text; p. [31] Sidgwick & Jackson advertisement; p. [32] at centre, publisher's circular device of a horse, $\frac{3}{4}$ in.

No wrappers; edges cut flush; stapled.

Published July 1925; 6000 copies printed. 6*d*.

There was more than one issue; p. [32] in some copies carries a publisher's advertisement in place of the device.

Contents: The Waggoner — Almswomen — The Pike — A Country God — Forefathers — Gleaning — Reunion in War — November Morning — Village Green — The Poor Man's Pig — Blindfold — A Fading Phantom — Rural Economy (1917) — A Village Knell — Water Moment — Winter Piece [*later* Winter: East Anglia] — The Midnight Skaters — Strange Perspective — At Senlis Once — A "First Impression" [*formerly* A "First Impression" Tokyo] — The Daimyo's Pond.

A19   FAR EAST   1925

First Edition:

[*title on p.* [2] *at head*:] FAR EAST

4to. [4] pp. $9\frac{1}{2} \times 6\frac{5}{8}$ in.

P. [1] towards centre: With the Compliments | of the Season, |

CHRISTMAS 1925 | from Edmund Blunden | TOKYO; pp. [2–3] text; p. [3] at foot: 1925 Edmund Blunden; p. [4] blank.

No wrappers; edges trimmed.

Issued December 1925; 200 copies printed. Not for sale.

(Old hamlets with your groves of flowers). Holograph facsimile. Privately printed by the author as a Christmas card. Reprinted in *London Mercury*, June 1926; *Japanese Garland*, 1928; *Near and Far*, 1929; *The Poems*, 1930; and *The Midnight Skaters*, [1968] (*see* A26, 31, 35, 174; C555).

A20   **ENGLISH POEMS**   1926

a. First edition:

ENGLISH POEMS | *By* EDMUND BLUNDEN | [*eight line quotation*] | RICHARD | COBDEN-SANDERSON | THAVIES INN

Medium 8vo. 128 pp. $8\frac{7}{8} \times 5\frac{3}{4}$ in.

P. [1] half-title; p. [2] list of works by the author; p. [3] title; p. [4] at head: Made and Printed in Great Britain by | Hazell, Watson & Viney, Ld., | London and Aylesbury., at centre: First Published: 1925; p. 5 at head, dedication: To | MARY [i.e. Mrs Blunden]; p. [6] blank; pp. 7–8 Preface; pp. 9–12 Contents; p. [13] section-title; p. [14] blank; pp. 15–40 text; p. [41] section-title; p. [42] blank; pp. 43–61 text; p. [62] blank; p. [63] section-title; p. [64] blank; pp. 65–97 text; p. [98] blank; pp. [99] section-title; p. [100] blank; pp. 101–127 text; p. [128] blank.

Reddish-brown cloth boards; white label on spine, $1\frac{3}{4} \times \frac{3}{4}$ in., printed in reddish-brown: [*double rule*] | ENGLISH | POEMS | ● | Edmund | Blunden | [*double rule*]; edges rough trimmed, some of top and fore edges uncut; white end-papers, spare spine label tipped-in the lower free end-paper.

Published January 1926; 1000 copies printed. 6s.

Five hundred copies in sheets were sent to Alfred A. Knopf (*see* A20*b*).

Contents: *Village*: Old Homes — Country Sale — The Long Truce — 'Very Jewels in their Fair Estate' — Winter: East Anglia [*formerly* Winter Piece] — A Yeoman — Village — The Crown Inn [*formerly* "The Crown"] — The Midnight Skaters — Midnight — The Baker's Van — Pride of the Village — Muffled — The Shop Door — Another Spring [*formerly* Shepherd's Calendar] — The Unknown Quantity — The Puzzle — No Continuing City — The Last Ray — *Field*: Augury — Shooting Star at Harvest — Water Moment — Time of Roses — Waste Ground — Blue Butterfly — Rustic Wreath — Brook in Drought — Rosa Mundi — Interval — The Masquerade — A Budding

Morrow — A Pastoral — The Embryo — Misunderstandings — Hawthorn [*formerly* Triune] — *Mind*: Dead Letters — The Eclogue — The Shadow [*formerly* The Warder] — A Fading Phantom — The English Poets — The Old Year — First Rhymes — Inheritance — The Still Hour — Thames Gulls — Masks of Time — Achronos [*formerly* Epochs; *and* Eras] — A Transcription — Harvest — A Dream — A Bridge — Strange Perspective — Omen — Elegy — Old Pleasures Deserted — Unteachable — The Daimyo's Pond — Bells — 'Thy Dreams Ominous' — Rue du Bois — Prodigal — Reliques — *Spirit*: 'There is a Country' — The Brook — The Spell — 'Art Thou Gone in Haste?' — To Joy — The Aftermath — To Nature — To Clare — A Psalm — The Death-Mask of John Clare [*formerly* On the Death-Mask . . .] — Intimations of Mortality — Thus Far — A 'First Impression' Tokyo [*later* "A First Impression"] — The Flower-Gatherers — The Deeps — Now or Never — Warning to Troops — To a Spirit [*formerly* To . . .] — The Message [*later* Prelusion; *and* The Message] — In a Country Churchyard — Byroad [*formerly* By Road] — Resentients.

b. *First edition — American issue. 1926*:

[*title as above*; *imprint*:] [*Borzoi device of a hound running*, $\frac{5}{8}$ × 1 *in*.] | ALFRED A. KNOPF | NEW YORK | 1926

Medium 8vo. 128 pp. $8\frac{5}{8}$ × $5\frac{3}{4}$ in.

Drab paper boards printed in mauve in an overall pattern of triangles; oatmeal cloth spine, off-white paper label on spine, 2 × $\frac{3}{4}$ in., printed in black: [*ornamental line*] | *English* | *Poems* | *by* | *Edmund* | *Blunden* | [*ornamental line*]; top edge mauve, fore edges untrimmed, bottom rough trimmed; white end-papers.

Issued October 1926; probably 500 copies bound. $2.50.

The sheets were supplied by Cobden-Sanderson.

c. *Second English edition. 1929*:

ENGLISH POEMS | by | EDMUND BLUNDEN | [*eight line quotation*] | DUCKWORTH | 3 HENRIETTA STREET | LONDON, W.C. 2

Foolscap 8vo. 144 pp. $6\frac{3}{4}$ × $4\frac{1}{2}$ in.

P. [1] half-title; p. [2] list of works in the series; p. [3] title; p. [4] at head: *First Published by R. Cobden-Sanderson* 1925 | *New and Revised Edition* (*New Readers Library*) 1929 | *All Rights Reserved*, at foot: *Printed in Great Britain* | *at the* BURLEIGH PRESS, *Lewin's*

Mead, BRISTOL.; pp. 5–8 Contents; pp. 9–10 Preface; p. [11] section-title; p. [12] blank; pp. 13–42 text; p. [43] section-title; p. [44] blank; pp. 45–66 text; p. [67] section-title; p. [68] blank; pp. 69–108 text; p. [109] section-title; p. [110] blank; pp. 111–144 text. 8 pp. publisher's advertisements inserted.

Navy-blue cloth boards; lettered in gold on spine: [*rule, short vertical dashes; rule across head*] | ENGLISH | POEMS | EDMUND | BLUNDEN | DUCKWORTH | [*rule, short vertical dashes, rule across foot*] ; edges trimmed; white end-papers.

Published 14 February 1929 as the *The New Readers Library*, Vol. 39; 2000 copies printed. 3s. 6d.

Some corrections have been made to a few of the poems.

A21   MORE FOOTNOTES TO   1926
                 LITERARY HISTORY

First separate publication:

[*title on upper wrapper*:] MORE FOOTNOTES TO | LITERARY HISTORY | BY | EDMUND BLUNDEN | REPRINTED FROM THE "STUDIES IN ENGLISH LITERATURE," | VOL. VI, NO. I, EDITED AND ISSUED BY THE ENGLISH | SEMINAR OF THE TOKYO IMPERIAL UNIVERSITY, | JAPAN | APRIL, 1926 . | TOKYO : KENKYUSHA

Small royal 8vo. An offprint of 22 pp. $8\frac{7}{8}$ × 6 in.

Pp. [1]–21 text; p. [22] blank.

Brownish-yellow paper wrappers; printed on upper wrapper as above; edges cut flush; stapled.

Issued April 1926; 20 copies printed. Not for sale.

Contents: 1, Free Thoughts on the Biography of John Keats — 2, John Clare: Notes and References.

Reprinted from *Studies in English Literature*, Vol. 6, No. 1; and reprinted in *Reprinted Papers*, 1950 (*see* A104; C545).

A22   ON RECEIVING FROM   1927
                 THE CLARENDON PRESS

First edition:

[*title on p.* [1]:] [*ornamental piece*, $2\frac{3}{8}$ × $\frac{3}{8}$ *in.*] | On

receiving from the | CLARENDON PRESS | the new Fac-
simile | edition of | CHRISTOPHER SMART'S | 'SONG
TO DAVID' | [ornament, $\frac{1}{2}$ X $\frac{3}{4}$ in.]

Imperial 8vo. [4] pp. $9\frac{1}{2}$ X $7\frac{1}{2}$ in.

P. [1] title as above; p. [2] blank; p. [3] text; p. [4] towards
head: *TWENTY copies of this leaflet have | been printed by John
Johnson | at the Clarendon Press | Oxford, England | 1927*

No wrappers; edges trimmed.

Issued probably early 1927; 20 copies printed. Probably unpriced.
(The Song itself! thus the majestic rhyme). The facsimile edition of
A Song to David was published on 11 November 1926. Reprinted as
SONNET ON RECEIVING FROM THE CLARENDON PRESS
[etc.] in *Retreat*, 1928; and SONNET ON SMART'S "SONG TO
DAVID" in *The Poems*, 1930 (*see* A25, 35). In a proof copy,
10 X $7\frac{5}{8}$ in., in the collection of Sir Rupert Hart-Davis, the certificate of limitation on p. [4] is scored through and corrected in ink:
Twelve^{NTY} copies of this leaflet have | . . . , from which it appears
as if it was originally intended to publish 12 copies.

Blunden has recorded 'the lines were printed without my having a
say in it'; the Clarendon Press has been unable to confirm this.

A23   ON THE POEMS OF   1927
                    HENRY VAUGHAN

First edition:

*ON THE POEMS OF | HENRY VAUGHAN | Character-
istics and Intimations | With his principal Latin poems |
carefully translated into | English verse | BY EDMUND
BLUNDEN | "O purer years of light and grace!" | LON-
DON | RICHARD COBDEN-SANDERSON | 17 THAVIES
INN*

Crown 8vo. 64 pp. front. $7\frac{1}{2}$ X 5 in.

P. [1] half-title; p. [2] list of works by the author; p. [3] title; p.
[4] at centre: *First published* 1927; at foot: *Made and Printed in
Great Britain by the | Botolph Printing Works, Gate Street, Kings-
way, W.C.* 2; p. [5] foreword: To the Reader; p. [6] blank; pp. 7–
56 text; p. [57] section-title; at centre: *TRANSLATIONS | FROM
| VAUGHAN'S LATIN*; p. [58] blank; pp. 59–64 Translations
from Vaughan's Latin; p. 64 spare spine label tipped-in.

Reddish-brown cloth boards; white paper label on spine, $2\frac{1}{8}$ X $\frac{5}{8}$ in.,
printed in reddish-brown: [*rule*] | Henry | Vaughan | [*ornament*] |

Edmund | Blunden | [*rule*] ; top edges trimmed, fore and bottom edges rough trimmed; white end-papers.

Published March 1927; 500 copies printed. 5*s.*

This essay is a revised version of that published in the *London Mercury*, November 1926 (*see* C585). Translations from Vaughan's Latin, p. 59 TO THE RIVER USK; p. 60 TO ECHO; p. 61 WITH A SALMON — to his excellent friend, Dr. Thomas Powell; pp. 62–63 THE FLASHING FLINT; p. 64 THE FATE OF SERVILIUS OR DIVINE VENGEANCE.

A24   LECTURES IN ENGLISH LITERATURE   1927

a. First edition:

LECTURES IN ENGLISH | LITERATURE | Given in the | IMPERIAL UNIVERSITY, TOKYO | BY | EDMUND BLUNDEN. | [*four line quotation*] | FIRST SERIES | Tokyo : Kodokwan | 1927

Crown 8vo. [vi] , 192 pp. $7\frac{3}{8} \times 5$ in.

P. [i] title, with tissue guard; p. [ii] blank; pp. [iii–iv] Preface; p. [v] Contents; p. [vi] blank; pp. [1]–189 text; p. [190] blank; p. [191] publisher's imprint; p. [192] publisher's advertisement; pp. [191–192] in Japanese.

Golden-brown paper limp boards; lettered in gold up the spine: LECTURES IN ENGLISH LITERATURE, and on upper cover on a panel: LECTURES IN ENGLISH | LITERATURE | BY | EDMUND BLUNDEN | [*below panel in blind*:] Tokyo | Kodokwan; top edges grey, fore and bottom edges trimmed; white end-papers. Grey dust-jacket printed in black.

Published 8 September 1927; number of copies printed not ascertained. 2 yen.

The second series was not published.

Contents: A First Address — Essayists of the Romantic Period: Introductory; Lamb; Coleridge; Hazlitt; Leigh Hunt; de Quincey; Landor — Poetry of Coleridge, Shelley and Keats — Poetry and Progress: Spenser to Thomson.

Essayists of the Romantic Period: Introductory; Lamb — Coleridge were reprinted in *Essayists of the Romantic Period* (*see* A117).

b. Second edition. 1952:

LECTURES IN ENGLISH | LITERATURE | *by* | EDMUND BLUNDEN | [*four line quotation*] | TOKYO : *Kodokwan* : MCMLII

Crown 8vo. 383 pp., the first 10 numbered [i]-[x] . front., 4 plates facing pp. 37, 148, 292, 340. 7¼ × 5 in.

P. [i] half-title; p. [ii] blank; p. [iii] title; p. [iv] towards centre: Copyright, 1952 | Bv KODOKWAN & CO., LTD. | 40 Nichome, Jimbocho, | Kanda, Tokyo. | foot: PRINTED IN JAPAN; pp. v-vi Preface; pp. vii-viii Preface to the Second Edition; p. [ix] Contents; p. [x] List of Illustrations; pp. 11-373 text; pp. 374-381 Index; p. [382] publisher's imprint etc. in Japanese.

Blue cloth boards; lettered on black imitation leather spine: LEC-TURES | IN | ENGLISH | LITERATURE | BY | E. BLUNDEN | KODOKAN [*sic*] ; gold rule down join of spine and cloth on upper cover; edges trimmed; pale turquoise blue end-papers.

Published 5 April 1952; number of copies printed not ascertained. 480 yen.

Rasselas and *The Vicar of Wakefield* — William Wordsworth: A Centenary Address — Robert Southey — Shelley and Keats, were added to this edition.

A25   **RETREAT**   1928

a. First edition:

RETREAT | *by* | EDMUND BLUNDEN | [*three line quotation*] | RICHARD | COBDEN-SANDERSON | THAVIES INN

Medium 8vo. 72 pp. 8⅞ × 5⅝ in.

P. [1] half-title; p. [2] list of works by the author; p. [3] title; p. [4] at head: Made and Printed in Great Britain by | Hazell, Watson & Viney Ld. | London and Aylesbury, at centre: First Published : 1928; p. [5] at head, dedication: *Dedicated* | *To Three* I *Love* | *Mary Clare* and John; p. [6] blank; p. [7] acknowledgements; p. [8] blank; pp. 9-10 Contents; p. [11] section-title; p. [12] blank; pp. 13-44 text; p. [45] section-title; p. [46] blank; pp. 47-70 text; pp. [71-72] blank.

Reddish-brown cloth boards; white paper label on spine, 1⅛ × ½ in., printed in reddish-brown: [*double rule*] | RETREAT | • | EDMUND | BLUNDEN | [*double rule*] ; edges rough trimmed; white end-papers, spare spine label tipped-in lower free end-paper. Buff dust-jacket printed in scarlet.

Published May 1928; no record of the number of copies printed. 6s.
One hundred and twelve copies were issued as a 'limited edition' (see A25b).

Contents: Poems: An Ancient Path [formerly Together] — Voices by a River — A Superstition Revisited [formerly A Superstition Revisited] — Girl With a Shawl — Nature Displayed — Solutions [formerly The Correct Solution] — Recollections of Christ's Hospital — A Morning Piece — The Age of Herbert and Vaughan — The Wartons and Other Early Romantic Landscape Poets [formerly The Wartons and Other Early Romantics; later The Wartons and Other Landscape Poets] — The Complaint — The Eccentric — The Charm — Ruin — The Passer-by — An Infantryman — The Resignation — Early and Late — Would You Return? — Village Lights — A Favourite Scene Recalled on Looking at Birket Foster's Landscapes — Sonnets and Occasional Stanzas: "For There is No Help in Them" [formerly 1919] — An Annotation — Trust — Night-wind [formerly Nightwind] — Ornithopolis — Cloud-Life — "Song to David," 1763 [formerly On Receiving from the Clarendon Press . . . ; later Sonnet on Smart's 'Song to David'] — The Unquiet Eye — On the Portrait of a Colonel [formerly Portrait of a Colonel] — The Chance [formerly Fragments] — The Doomed Oak — A Thought from Schiller — Entanglement — Release — Departure — The Escape — Libertine — To a Spirit — The Match [formerly The Prison] — The Storm — The Immolation — Chinese Picture — The Secret.

b. First edition — limited issue. 1928:

[in scarlet:] RETREAT [continues in black as above]

Medium 8vo. [iv], 72 pp. 9 × 5⅝ in.

Clay-brown cloth boards; lettered in gold on spine: RETREAT | EDMUND | BLUNDEN; edges rough trimmed; white end-papers.

Issued May 1928; 112 copies bound. £1. 5s.

P. [iv] at head: Of this edition on hand-made paper, signed | by the author, there are one hundred | and twelve copies only, of which | one hundred are for sale | This is No. [numbered in ink] | [signed: Edmund Blunden].

c. First American edition. 1928:

RETREAT | BY EDMUND BLUNDEN | [three line quotation] | DOUBLEDAY, DORAN | AND COMPANY, INC· GARDEN CITY, NEW YORK | 1928

Medium 8vo. [x], 62 pp. 8⅝ × 5⅝ in.

P. [i] half-title; p. [ii] list of works by the author; p. [iii] title; p. [iv] at foot: [*publisher's device of an anchor and fish*, $\frac{3}{4}$ × $\frac{1}{2}$ *in.*] | COPYRIGHT, 1928 | BY EDMUND BLUNDEN | ALL RIGHTS RESERVED | PRINTED IN THE UNITED STATES | AT THE COUNTRY LIFE PRESS | GARDEN CITY, N.Y. | FIRST EDITION; p. [v] dedication; p. [vi] blank; p. [vii] acknowledgements; p. [viii] blank; pp. [ix-x] Contents; p. [1] section-title; p. [2] blank; pp. 3-34 text; p. [35] section-title; p. [36] blank; p. 37-[60] text; pp. [61-62] blank.

Yellow paper boards; bright green cloth spine; lettered in gold on spine: [*rule*] | RETREAT | Edmund | BLUNDEN | DOUBLEDAY | DORAN; lettered in bright green on upper cover: [*in ornamental letters*:] RETREAT; top edges bright green, fore and bottom edges rough trimmed; white end-papers.

Published 21 September 1928; no record of the number of copies printed. $1.75.

A26   JAPANESE GARLAND   1928

a. First edition:

[*printed down in vertical lines on three panels*; *on pale grey panel*, $2\frac{1}{8}$ × $\frac{1}{2}$ *in.*:] EDMUND | BLUNDEN | [*on red panel*, 4 × 1 *in.*:] JAPANESE | GARLAND | [*on pale grey panel*, $1\frac{1}{2}$ × $\frac{1}{2}$ *in.*:] THE | BEAUMONT | PRESS

Medium 8vo. 40 pp. (including plates). 6 plates. $8\frac{7}{8}$ × $5\frac{5}{8}$ in.

P. [1] blank; p. [2] at centre, seven-line certificate; p. [3] half-title; p. [4] blank; p. [5] title; p. [6] at foot: *Printed and made in England*; p. [7] Contents; p. [8] blank; pp. 9-12 text; pp. [13-14] inserted plate; pp. 15-16 text; pp. [17-18] inserted plate; pp. 19-22 text; pp. [23-24] inserted plate; pp. 25-26 text; pp. [27-28] inserted plate; pp. 29-30 text; pp. [31-32] inserted plate; pp. 33-34 text; pp. [35-36] plate; pp. 37-39 text; p. [40] HERE ENDS • JAPANESE GARLAND • A | Book of Poems by Edmund Blunden. The | Cover and Decorations designed by Eileen | Mayo The Title-page written by A. J. | Vaughan The Typography and Binding | arranged and the book produced by Cyril | William Beaumont and printed at his | Press Completed on the fifth day of | June MCMXXVIII | [*publisher's device of an ornamental fountain*, $2\frac{7}{8}$ × $2\frac{1}{8}$ *in.*] | THE BEAUMONT PRESS | [*rule*] | Pressman S. R. Minns | Compositor W. Smith.

Silver paper boards printed in black and white in an overall bamboo pattern; royal blue cloth spine; lettered in black up the spine: [*figure of a Japanese*] JAPANESE GARLAND • EDMUND BLUNDEN [*figure of a Japanese*] ; top edges trimmed, fore and bottom edges untrimmed; white end-papers.

Published September 1928; 390 copies printed. £1. 1*s*.

Three hundred and ten copies, numbered 81–390, were printed on Japanese paper as above, and 80 numbered copies on Japanese paper with vellum spine (*see* A26*b*).

Contents: A "First Impression" (Tokyo) — The Daimyo's Pond — Oriental Ornamentations [*later* Ornamentations] — Far East — Tempest [*formerly* Eastern Tempest] — Inland Sea [*formerly* Japanese Nightpiece] — The Quick and the Dead — The Inviolate — Evening Music — Building the Library, Night Scene, Tokyo University — On a Small Dog, Thrust out in a Tokyo Street soon after his birth, and rescued in vain — The Author's Last Words to his Students.

b. First edition — vellum spine issue. 1928:

[*title and imprint as above*]

Medium 8vo. 40 pp. (including plates). 6 plates. $8\frac{7}{8} \times 5\frac{3}{4}$ in.

Paper boards as above; vellum spine; lettered in black.

Issued September 1928; 80 copies bound. £2. 2*s*.

Printed on Japanese paper and numbered 1–80. P. [2] below seven-line certificate: [*signed in ink*: Eileen Mayo | C. W. Beaumont | Edmund Blunden] .

A27   WINTER NIGHTS   1928

a. First edition:

[*title on upper wrapper*:] WINTER | NIGHTS | [*illustration of man and boy under a lamp*, $2\frac{1}{2} \times 2\frac{1}{4}$ *in.*] | A Reminiscence by | EDMUND BLUNDEN | Drawings by | ALBERT RUTHERSTON

Small crown 8vo. 8 pp. $7\frac{1}{4} \times 4\frac{3}{4}$ in.

Pp. [1–2] blank; p. [3] coloured illustration; pp. [4–5] text; p. [6] list of *Ariel Poems*; pp. [7–8] blank.

White paper wrappers printed in gentian blue; printed on upper wrapper as above, and on lower wrapper towards centre: This is No. 17 of | THE ARIEL POEMS | Published by Faber & Gwyer Limited | at 24 Russell Square, London, W.C. 1 | Printed at The Curwen Press, Plaistow; edges cut flush; sewn.

Published November 1928; no record of the number of copies printed. 1*s*.

Five hundred copies were printed on hand-made paper (*see* A27*b*).

(Strange chord! the weir-pool's tussling dance,). Reprinted in *The Poems*, 1930; and *Poems of Many Years*, 1957 (*see* A35, 135).

b. First edition — limited issue. 1928:

WINTER NIGHTS | A Reminiscence | by | EDMUND BLUNDEN | With drawings by | ALBERT RUTHERSTON | London: | FABER & GWYER LTD. | 1928

Small demy 8vo. [16] pp. 2 illus. on pp. [3, 7]. $8\frac{1}{2} \times 5\frac{3}{8}$ in.

P. [1] towards head: This large-paper edition, printed | on English hand-made paper, is | limited to five hundred copies | This is number | [*numbered in ink*] [*signed: Edmund Blunden*] ; p. [2] blank; p. [3] half-title and illustration; p. [4] blank; p. [5] title; p. [6] at head: PRINTED IN ENGLAND; p. [7] coloured illustration; p. [8] blank; p. [9] text; p. [10] blank; p. [11] text; p. [12] blank; p. [13] list of *Ariel Poems*; p. [14] at head: [*as lower wrapper above*] ; pp. [15–16] blank.

Pale blue paper boards; lettered in gold on upper cover: EDMUND BLUNDEN | [*three stars*] | WINTER NIGHTS; top edges trimmed, fore and bottom edges untrimmed; white end-papers.

Issued November 1928; 500 copies bound. 7*s*. 6*d*.

A28   **UNDERTONES OF WAR**   1928

a. First edition:

UNDERTONES OF WAR | BY | EDMUND BLUNDEN | LONDON | RICHARD COBDEN-SANDERSON | 17 THAVIES INN

Demy 8vo. xvi, 320 pp. map on p. [9]. $8\frac{3}{4} \times 5\frac{5}{8}$ in.

Pp. [i–ii] blank; p. [iii] title; p. [iv] at head: Made and Printed in Great Britain at the | Kemp Hall Press in the City of Oxford | 1928; p. [v] towards centre, dedication: *Dedicated to* | *PHILIP TOMLIN-SON* | *wishin him a lasting Peace and myself* | *his companshionship in Peace* | *or War*; p. [vi] blank; pp. vii–viii Preliminary; p. [ix] two quotations; p. [x] blank; pp. xi–xii Contents; pp. xiii–xiv A Supplement of Poetical Interpretations and Variations; p. [xv] fly-title; p. [xvi] blank; pp. 1–266 text; p. [267] section-title; p. [268] blank; pp. 269–317 A Supplement of Poetical Interpretations and Variations; p. [318] blank; pp. [319] list of works by the author; p. [320] blank.

Black cloth boards; lettered in gold on spine: UNDERTONES | OF |
WAR | EDMUND | BLUNDEN | COBDEN- | SANDERSON; top
edges trimmed, fore and bottom edges rough trimmed; white end-
papers. Buff dust-jacket printed in black.

Published *c.* 29 November 1928; number of copies printed not ascertained. 10*s.* 6*d.*

There were printings in December 1928 (three), in February, April
and September 1929; the eighth printing was revised (*see* A28*c*).

'The Cherry Orchard' was reprinted in *Edmund Blunden: A Selection of His Poetry and Prose*, 1950 (*see* A108).

Contents of 'A Supplement of Poetical Interpretations and Variations': A House in Festubert — The Guard's Mistake [*formerly and
later* The Sentry's Mistake] — Two Voices [*formerly* Survivors,
1916] — Illusions — Escape — Preparations for Victory — Come on,
My Lucky Lads [*formerly* Zero; *and later* Zero 1916] — At Senlis
Once — The Zonnebeke Road — Trench Raid near Hooge — Concert
Party: Busseboom — Rural Economy, 1917 — E.W.T.: On the Death
of his Betty [i.e. E. W. Tice] — Battalion in Rest — Vlamertinghe:
Passing the Château, July, 1917 — Third Ypres — Pillbox — The
Welcome — Gauzeaucourt: The Deceitful Calm — The Prophet — II
Peter ii 22 — Recognition [*formerly* A Recognition] — La Quinque
Rue — The Ancre at Hamel: Afterwards [*formerly* The Ancre at
Hamel] — "Trench Nomenclature" — A.G.A.V. [i.e. Arnold G. A.
Vidler] — Their Very Memory — On Reading that the Rebuilding of
Ypres Approached Completion — Another Journey from Béthune to
Cuinchy — Flanders Now [*formerly* Old Battlefields] — The Watchers.

b. *First American edition. 1929*:

UNDERTONES | OF WAR | BY EDMUND BLUNDEN |
[*publisher's device of an anchor and fish in orange* $\frac{3}{4}$ × $\frac{1}{2}$ *in.*]
| GARDEN CITY, NEW YORK | DOUBLEDAY, DORAN
& COMPANY, INC. | 1929

Royal 8vo. [2] , xvi, 344 pp. map on p. 10, illus. on p. 262. $9\frac{1}{8}$ × 6 in.
Pp. [1–2] blank; p. [i] half-title; p. [ii] list of works by the author;
p. [iii] title; p. [iv] at foot: COPYRIGHT, 1929 | BY EDMUND
BLUNDEN | ALL RIGHTS RESERVED | PRINTED IN THE
UNITED STATES AT | THE COUNTRY LIFE PRESS | GARDEN
CITY, N.Y. | FIRST EDITION; p. [v] two quotations; p. [vi] blank;
pp. vii–ix Preliminary; p. [x] blank; pp. xi–xiii Contents; p. [xiv]
blank; p. [xv] fly-title; p. [xvi] blank; pp. 1–276 text; p. [277]
section-title; p. [278] blank; pp. 279–342 A Supplement of Poetical
Interpretations and Variations; pp. [343–344] blank.

Black cloth boards; off-white paper label on spine, $2\frac{1}{4}$ × $1\frac{3}{8}$ in., printed in bright orange and black: UNDERTONES | [*illustration of helmeted soldiers*] | EDMUND | BLUNDEN; edges trimmed, top orange; white end-papers.

Published 22 March 1929; no record of the number of copies printed. $3.50.

'Zero', pp. 288–289, is the original title of 'Come on, My Lucky Lads' under which it appears in the first edition. The footnote and illustration on p. 262 do not appear in the first edition; there are slight variations in the text.

Copies in sheets were sent to Cobden-Sanderson in November 1934 and July 1940 (*see* A28*d*).

c. *First edition — eighth (revised) impression. 1930:*

[*title as above*; *imprint*:] [*publisher's device of an urn,* $\frac{7}{8} \times \frac{5}{8}$ *in.*] | LONDON | COBDEN-SANDERSON | 1930

Demy 8vo. xvi, 328 pp. map on p. 9. $8\frac{5}{8} \times 5\frac{5}{8}$ in.

Black cloth boards; lettered in dull orange on spine; top edges trimmed, fore and bottom edges untrimmed; white end-papers.

Issued June 1930; number of copies printed not ascertained. 5*s*.

In this, the eighth printing, called a 'Revised edition' or 'Second edition', the text was revised and repaged, the map on p. 9 redrawn on a reduced scale. There was a new preface, 'Preface to the Second Edition' pp. vii–viii, and the addition of 'Return of the Native' to 'A Supplement of Poetical Interpretations and Variations', pp. 325–326. There was a ninth printing in November 1930, called a 'Third and cheap edition (revised)'; p. viii '. . . Some slight corrections and additional observations are made on re-reading, in September 1930.' The tenth reprint in March 1935 was printed by photo-litho offset from the text of the ninth reprint by Lowe & Brydone, called a 'Fourth and cheap edition (revised)', and issued at 5*s*. *See* 'Blunden Revisions to *Undertones of War*' by Michael L. Turner in *The Warden's Meeting: A Tribute to John Sparrow*, Oxford University Society of Bibliophiles, 1977, pp. 72–76 for a description of the copy (issued June 1930) presented by Blunden to Richard Cobden-Sanderson.

d. *First American edition — English issue.* [*1934*]:*

[*title as above*; *imprint*: LONDON | COBDEN-SANDERSON | 1934]

Demy 8vo. 341 pp. 9 × 5 in.

Issued November 1934; no record of the number of copies bound. 3s. 6d.

The sheets were supplied by Doubleday, Doran. Further sheets were supplied by Doubleday, Doran in July 1940 and issued at 3s. 6d.

e. Japanese edition in English. [*1936*] :

KENKYUSHA GENDAI EIBUNGAKUSOSHO | [*rule*] | UNDERTONES OF WAR | BY | EDMUND BLUNDEN | *WITH INTRODUCTION AND NOTES* | BY | TAKESHI SAITO | PROFESSOR OF ENGLISH LITERATURE IN | THE UNIVERSITY OF TOKYO | AND | TORAO UEDA | PROFESSOR OF ENGLISH IN THE MILITARY ACADEMY | TOKYO | KENKYUSHA

Foolscap 8vo. [10], xlviii, iv, 520 pp. front. (port.), plans and 2 maps. $6\frac{7}{8} \times 4\frac{1}{2}$ in.

Black cloth boards; lettered in gold on spine with two rules and device; device in blind on upper cover; edges trimmed; white endpapers.

Published 30 May 1936 as *Kenkyūsha Modern English Literature Series*, Vol. 3; no record of the number of copies printed. Set of 26 volumes available at a subscription of 45 yen.

The text follows that of the first edition—eighth (revised) impression issued in June 1930 (*see* A28c). The plan on p. [xliii] was drawn by the author for this edition. Reprinted on 5 August 1948 in *Kenkyusha Modern English Classics* at 250 yen omitting pp. xx–xxxviii (part of the Introduction) and pp. [495]–514 (Index to Notes). Reprinted in full (500 copies) on 20 February 1954 at 400 yen; there were further reprints of 500 copies each of the complete text in 1956, 1959, 1964, 1966, and 1969.

f. German edition in English. [*1936*] :

NEUSPRACHLICHE LESEBOGEN | [*double rule, thick, thin*] | Nr. 236 | THE | SOMME BATTLE | SELECTED CHAPTERS AND POEMS | FROM | EDMUND BLUNDEN'S | UNDERTONES OF WAR | Herausgegeben | von | Dr. Erich Funke| Professor a. d. Universität Iowa (U.S.A.) | Mit einer Karte | [*double rule, thin, thick*] | VERLAG VON VELHAGEN & KLASING | BIELEFELD UND LEIPZIG

Crown 8vo. 36 pp. map. $7\frac{1}{2} \times 4\frac{7}{8}$ in.

Pale yellow paper wrappers; printed in black; edges cut flush; sewn.

Published 1936; number of copies printed not ascertained.

Contents: The Storm — A Home from Home — Very Secret — Two Voices — Illusions — Escape — The Ancre at Hamel: Afterwards.

g. Second English edition. [1937]:

[title as above; imprint:] PENGUIN BOOKS | London

Foolscap 8vo. 288 pp. map on p. 22. $7\frac{1}{8} \times 4\frac{3}{8}$ in.

White stiff paper wrappers; printed in pink and black; edges cut flush; sewn and gummed.

Published March 1937 (though dated 1936) as *Penguin Books*, Vol. 82; no record of the number of copies printed. 6d.

The text follows the ninth (revised) printing issued in November 1930.

h. Third English edition. 1956:

[title as above; imprint:] With a new Preface by the Author | [publisher's series device] | London | OXFORD UNIVERSITY PRESS | New York Toronto | 1956

Foolscap 8vo. xvi, 368 pp. map on p. 11. $5\frac{7}{8} \times 3\frac{1}{2}$ in.

Navy-blue cloth boards; lettered in gold on spine; publisher's device in blind on upper cover; edges trimmed; white end-papers. White pictorial dust-jacket printed in khaki and black, designed by Lynton Lamb.

Published 11 October 1956 as the *World's Classics*, Vol. 553; 5000 copies printed. 6s.

The text follows the eighth (revised) printing issued in June 1930; pp. vii–xi 'Preface to this Edition'.

i. Fourth English edition. [1962]:

[title as above; imprint:] THE NEW ENGLISH LIBRARY LTD BARNARD'S INN LONDON EC1

Foolscap 8vo. 256 pp. map on p. 11. $7\frac{1}{8} \times 4\frac{1}{4}$ in.

White stiff pictorial paper wrappers printed in dull gold and black; edges cut flush; gummed.

Published 4 January 1962 as *Four Square Books*, Vol. 609; no record of the number of copies printed. 3*s*. 6*d*.

The text follows the ninth (revised) printing issued in November 1930; 'Preliminary' and 'Preface to the Second Edition' were omitted.

j. Fifth English edition. [*1964*] :

[*title as above*; *imprint*:] COLLINS | ST JAMES'S PLACE | LONDON

Small demy 8vo. 256 pp. map on p. 27. $8\frac{3}{8} \times 5\frac{1}{2}$ in.

Oatmeal cloth boards; lettered in gold on a black panel on spine, and at foot; edges trimmed; white end-papers. White dust-jacket printed in orange, brown, brownish-red and black.

Published November 1964; 3500 copies printed. £1.10*s*.

Pp. 5–8 new Introduction. The text follows the first edition, first impression published in November 1928. There was a reprint in January 1965.

A29   NATURE IN ENGLISH LITERATURE   1929

a. First edition:

NATURE | IN | ENGLISH LITERATURE | EDMUND BLUNDEN | FORMERLY PROFESSOR OF ENGLISH LITERATURE IN THE | IMPERIAL UNIVERSITY AT TOKYO | [*nine line quotation*] | [*publisher's circular device of a wolf's head, $\frac{3}{4}$ in.*] | *Published by Leonard & Virginia Woolf at The* | *Hogarth Press, 52 Tavistock Square, London, W.C. 1* | 1929

Small crown 8vo. 160 pp. $7\frac{1}{4} \times 4\frac{3}{4}$ in.

P. [1] half-title; p. [2] list of works in series and forthcoming; p. [3] title; p. [4] at foot: Printed in Great Britain by | NEILL & CO., LTD., EDINBURGH.; p. 5 Note; p. [6] blank; p. 7 Contents; p. [8] blank; pp. 9–156 text; p. 156 at foot, printer's imprint; pp. [157–160] blank.

Orange cloth boards; lettered in red on spine: Nature | in | Literature | EDMUND | BLUNDEN | THE | HOGARTH | PRESS, and on upper cover: HOGARTH LECTURES | No. 9. | NATURE IN | LITERA-TURE | EDMUND BLUNDEN | [*publisher's circular device of a wolf's head, $\frac{3}{4}$ in.*] | THE HOGARTH PRESS; edges trimmed; white end-papers. Orange dust-jacket printed in orange.

Published June 1929 as *Hogarth Lectures*, No. 9; 3000 copies printed. 3*s*. 6*d*.

There was a reprint by photo-litho offset of 2500 copies issued in July 1949 in deep red cloth boards; lettered in gold on spine.

b. First edition — American photo-offset reprint. 1929:

[*title as above*; *imprint*:] [*publisher's device*] | [*rule*] | HARCOURT, BRACE AND COMPANY | NEW YORK

Small crown 8vo. [ii], 158 pp. $7\frac{1}{2} \times 5$ in.

Oxford blue cloth boards; lettered in orange on spine, and in blind on upper cover; top and bottom edges trimmed, fore edges rough trimmed; white end-papers.

Issued 3 October 1929; 1500 copies printed. $1.25.

A30   SHAKESPEARE'S SIGNIFICANCES   1929

First edition:

[*title on upper wrapper*:] THE SHAKESPEARE ASSOCIATION | SHAKESPEARE'S | SIGNIFICANCES | A PAPER READ BEFORE THE SHAKESPEARE | ASSOCIATION | BY | EDMUND BLUNDEN | LONDON | PUBLISHED FOR THE SHAKESPEARE ASSOCIATION | BY HUMPHREY MILFORD, OXFORD UNIVERSITY PRESS | AMEN HOUSE, WARWICK SQUARE, E. C. | 1929 | *Price One Shilling and Sixpence net*

Royal 8vo. 20 pp. $9\frac{5}{8} \times 6\frac{1}{4}$ in.

P. [1] at head: SHAKESPEARE'S SIGNIFICANCES | A PAPER READ BEFORE THE SHAKESPEARE | ASSOCIATION, 25th JANUARY, 1929, AT KING'S | COLLEGE, LONDON; p. [2] at centre: ALL RIGHTS RESERVED; pp. [3]-18 text; p. [19] blank; p. [20] at centre: THE DE LA MORE PRESS LIMITED | 2A CORK STREET, BOND STREET, W.1.

Grey paper wrappers; printed on upper wrapper as above; edges cut flush; sewn in white thread.

Published 29 August 1929; no record of the number of copies printed. 1*s*. 6*d*. (50 cents).

Reprinted in *The Mind's Eye*, 1934 (*see* A50). This essay was also included in *Shakespeare Criticism, 1919-35*, selected with an introduction by Anne Bradby, Oxford University Press (The World's Classics), 1936.

a. First edition:

NEAR AND FAR | *New Poems* | EDMUND BLUNDEN |
LONDON | COBDEN-SANDERSON | MCMXXIX

Medium 8vo. 68 pp. $8\frac{7}{8} \times 5\frac{3}{4}$ in.

P. [1] half-title; p. [2] list of works by the author; p. [3] title; p.
[4] at head: Made and Printed for R. Cobden-Sanderson Ltd. | in
Great Britain at the Botolph Printing | Works, Gate St., Kingsway,
W.C. 2; p. [5] at head, dedication: Dedicated | to that honest
friend | and admired poet, | William Force Stead; p. [6] Prefatory
Note; pp. [7–8] Contents; p. [9] section-title; p. [10] blank; pp.
11–16 text; p. [17] section-title; p. [18] blank; pp. 19–33 text;
p. [34] blank; p. [35] section-title; p. [36] blank; pp. 37–67 text;
p. [68] blank; spare spine label tipped-in.

Dull green cloth boards; white paper label on spine, $2 \times \frac{1}{2}$ in., prin-
ted in green: [*double rule*] | NEAR | AND | FAR | *New* | *Poems* |
EDMUND | BLUNDEN | [*double rule*] ; edges untrimmed; white
end-papers. Buff dust-jacket printed in green.

Published 26 September 1929; number of copies printed not ascertained. 6s.

One hundred and sixty copies were printed on hand-made paper
(*see* A31*b*).

Contents: The Geographer's Glory, or, the Globe in 1730 [*formerly*
The Geographer's Glory, or, the World in 1730] — *Japanese Garland*: The Visitor — Ornamentations [*formerly* Oriental Ornamenta-
tions] — Far East — Eastern Tempest [*later* Tempest] — Inland Sea
[*formerly* Japanese Nightpiece] — The Quick and the Dead — The
Inviolate — Building the Library, Tokyo University — On a Small
Dog, thrust out in a Tokyo Street soon after his birth, and rescued
in vain — The Author's Last Words to his Students — *Moods, Con-
jectures, and Fancies*: Familiarity — Inaccessibility in the Battlefield — War's People — Dream Encounters — Parable — A Sunrise
in March — Fragment — Summer Rainstorm [*formerly* The Summer
Rainstorm] — The Kiln — The Correlation — Autumn in the Weald
— Return — The Deeper Friendship — The Blind Lead the Blind —
Report on Experience — Epitaph — On a Biographical Dictionary —
A Quartet — A Connoisseur — Sir William Treloar's Dinner for
Crippled Children — The Study — Values.

b. First edition — limited issue. 1929:

[*in poppy-red*:] NEAR AND FAR | [*continues in black as
above*]

Medium 8vo. [iv] , 68 pp. 9 × 5¾ in.

Pale olive-green buckram boards; lettered in gold on spine: NEAR | AND | FAR | EDMUND | BLUNDEN; edges untrimmed; white endpapers. Buff dust-jacket printed in moss-green.

Issued 26 September 1929; 160 copies bound. £1. 5s.

Pp. [i–iii] blank; p. [iv] at head: *Of this edition on hand-made paper, signed | by the author, there are one hundred | and sixty copies only, of which one | hundred and fifty are for sale | This is No. [numbered in in ink] | [signed: Edmund Blunden]* .

c. First American edition. 1930:

NEAR AND FAR | *New Poems by* | EDMUND BLUNDEN | *[illustration of a tree in peacock blue]* | *Harper & Brothers Publishers* | *New York and London* | 1930

Small royal 8vo. [2] , x, 68 pp. 9½ × 6¼ in.

Pp. [1–2] blank; p. [i] half-title; p. [ii] list of works by the author; p. [iii] title; p. [iv] at foot: C-E | COPYRIGHT, 1930, BY EDMUND CHARLES BLUNDEN | PRINTED IN THE UNITED STATES; p. [v] at head, dedication; p. [vi] blank; pp. vii–viii Prefatory Note; pp. [ix–x] Contents; p. [1] section-title; p. [2] blank; pp. 3–9 text; p. [10] blank; p. [11] section-title; p. [12] blank; pp. 13–27 text; p. [28] blank; p. [29] section-title; p. [30] blank; pp. 31–64 text; p. [65] at head: C *Hand-set in Deepdene type by Elaine & Arthur Rushmore at | the Golden Hind Press in Madison, New Jersey. One hundred | and five copies have been printed on special mould-made paper from | Holland and signed by the author. Harper & Brothers, Publishers, | New York and London. Anno Domini* MDCCCCXXX; pp. [66–68] blank.

Pale blue paper boards; navy-blue cloth spine, lettered in gold: NEAR | & | FAR | *[ornament]* | Edmund | Blunden | *[rule at foot]* | HARPERS; printed in peacock-green on upper cover: NEAR AND FAR *[ornament]* | New Poems by EDMUND BLUNDEN | *[at foot:]* *[circular device of a ship, 1 in.]* ; edges trimmed; white end-papers. Grey dust-jacket printed in navy-blue.

Published 22 March 1930; 1315 copies printed. $2.

Seven hundred and fifty copies were bound as above, and 115 copies issued as a 'limited edition' (*see* A31*d*). The publishers write 'Apparently the remaining 450 sheets were later destroyed'.

d. First American edition — limited issue. 1930:

[*title as above*; *imprint*:] [*publisher's device of a ship in peacock blue*] | The GOLDEN HIND Press | New York and London | [*in peacock blue*:] *1930*

Small royal 8vo. [6], x, 68 pp. front. $9\frac{1}{2} \times 6\frac{1}{4}$ in.

Rust or royal-blue paper boards with overall pattern; black label on spine, $1\frac{5}{8} \times \frac{5}{8}$ in., lettered in gold; publisher's circular device in gold, 1 in., on upper cover; top edges uncut, fore and bottom edges rough trimmed; white end-papers.

Issued 22 March 1930; 115 copies bound.

Printed on 'special mould-made paper from Holland' and numbered 1–115. P. [i] below seven-line certificate: [*signed in ink: Edmund Blunden*]. The book may have been issued in other coloured paper boards.

A32   LEIGH HUNT   1930

a. First edition:

LEIGH HUNT | [*double rule, thick, thin*] | A BIOGRAPHY | [*double rule, thin, thick*] | BY | EDMUND BLUNDEN | [*short double rule, thin, thick*] | LONDON | [*double rule, thin, thick*] | COBDEN-SANDERSON | 1 MONTAGUE STREET | 1930

Demy 8vo. [2], xiv, 404 pp. front. (port.) and 7 plates facing pp. 8, 54, 96, 152, 264, 276, 328. $8\frac{5}{8} \times 5\frac{5}{8}$ in.

P. [1–2] blank; p. [i] half-title; p. [ii] blank; p. [iii] title; p. [iv] at foot: *Printed in Great Britain for* | R. COBDEN-SANDERSON, LTD. | *by* WALTER LEWIS, M.A., *at* | *the Cambridge University Press*; p. [v] towards centre, dedication: *To* | *The Secretary of the Elian Society* | F. A. DOWNING | This Life of his admired Friend of | Elia is affectionately dedicated | by his unalterable Brother | E. BLUNDEN; p. [vi] blank; pp. [vii]–viii Contents; p. [ix] Illustrations; p. [x] blank; pp. [xi]–xiii Preface; p. [xiv] blank; pp. [1]–351 text; pp. [352]–357 Appendix 1: Books by Leigh Hunt; pp. [358]–367 Appendix 2: A View of Leigh Hunt's Intimate Circle, by Thornton Hunt; pp. [368]–373 Appendix 3: Leigh Hunt's Collection of Locks of Hair; pp. [374]–378 Appendix 4: Some Authorities on Leigh Hunt, Biographical and Critical; pp. [379]–402 Index; p. 402 at foot, printer's imprint; pp. [403–404] blank.

Ruby-red cloth boards; lettered in gold on spine: LEIGH | HUNT | EDMUND | BLUNDEN | COBDEN- | SANDERSON; top edges ruby-red, fore and bottom edges rough trimmed; white end-papers.

White pictorial dust-jacket printed in black and pale pink, designed by Rex Whistler.

Published 29 May 1930; no record of the number of copies printed. £1. 1s.

There was a second issue in November 1932 at 7s. 6d., and a third in November 1934 at 5s. Copies in sheets were probably sent to Harper & Brothers, New York (*see* A32b).

b. First edition — American photo-offset reprint. 1930:

[*title varies*:] LEIGH HUNT | [*double rule, thick, thin*] | AND HIS CIRCLE | [*double rule, thin, thick*] | [*four lines*; *imprint*:] NEW YORK ★ LONDON | [*double rule, thin, thick*] | HARPER & BROTHERS | PUPLISHERS [*sic*] | 1930

Demy 8vo. xiv, 402 pp. front. (port.) and 15 plates facing pp. 8, 12, 32, 54, 76, 96, 130, 152, 180, 254, 264, 276, 306, 328, 350. $8\frac{1}{2} \times 5\frac{3}{4}$ in.

Red cloth boards; lettered in gold on spine with ornament; top edges orange, fore edges untrimmed, bottom trimmed; white end-papers. White pictorial dust-jacket printed in black and pink.

Issued 29 October 1930; 1500 copies printed. $4.

It is probable that 255 copies in sheets were supplied by Cobden-Sanderson, possibly in 1932 or 1934.

c. First edition — American photo-offset reprint. 1970:

[*title as above*; *imprint*:] Archon Books, Hamden, Connecticut*

xiv, 404 pp.

Issued 27 February 1970; 1000 copies printed. $12.50.

A33   DE BELLO GERMANICO   1930

a. First edition:

[*in black letter*:] De Bello Germanico | [*in roman*:] A FRAGMENT | OF | TRENCH HISTORY | [*short double rule, thick, thin*] | WRITTEN IN 1918 | BY THE AUTHOR OF | UNDERTONES OF WAR. | [*short double rule, thin, thick*] | [*in black letter:*] Hawstead : | [*in roman:*] G. A. BLUNDEN. | 1930

Crown 8vo. [ii] , 86 pp. plan on p. 12. $7\frac{1}{2}$ × 5 in.

P. [i] blank; p. [ii] towards centre: OF THIS BOOK | 250 Copies on ordinary paper | and | 25 Signed Copies on Special paper | are for sale.; p. [1] title; p. [2] towards centre: PAWSEY, LTD., BURY ST. EDMUND'S.; pp. [3-4] The Publisher's Preface; pp. 5-83 text; pp. [84-86] blank, integral.

Pale slate paper boards; white paper label on spine. $2\frac{7}{8}$ × $\frac{3}{8}$ in., printed in black letter up the spine: De Bello Germanico . [*rule at head and foot of label*] ; pale slate paper label on upper cover, $5\frac{5}{8}$ × $3\frac{5}{8}$ in., printed in black within a frame with an ornament in each angle as title above; edges untrimmed; white end-papers.

Published November 1930; 275 copies printed. 15*s.*

Twenty-five numbered copies were printed on 'special paper', i.e. in a larger format (*see* A33*b*).

b. First edition — limited issue. 1930:

[*title and imprint as above*]

Small demy 8vo. [ii] , 86 pp. plan on p. 12. $8\frac{3}{8}$ × $5\frac{1}{2}$ in.

Grey marbled paper boards; maroon leather spine and corners; lettered in gold on spine: [*double rule across head*] | [*on a black panel,* $1\frac{5}{8}$ × $\frac{5}{8}$ *in.:*] [*double rule*] | DE BELLO | GERMANICO | [*double rule*] | [*below panel: four sets of double rules*]; edges trimmed, mottled; white end-papers.

Issued November 1930; 25 copies bound. £2. 2*s.*

P. [ii] as above, then continues: [*numbered in ink*] | [*signed: Edmund Blunden*] .

A34   A SUMMER'S FANCY   1930

a. First edition:

A | SUMMER'S | [*ornament*] FANCY [*ornament*] | by | Edmund Blunden | [*circular illustration of a bridge with tree, 2 in.*] | LONDON | The Beaumont Press | 1930

Medium 8vo. 56 pp. 6 illus. on pp. [6], 11, [13], [28], [46], [54]. $8\frac{7}{8}$ × $5\frac{3}{4}$ in.

P. [1] blank; p. [2] at centre, seven-line certificate; p. [3] half-title; pp. [4-5] blank; p. [6] frontispiece; p. [7] title; p. [8] at foot:

8. Some bindings

Printed and made in England; p. [9] Preface; p. [10] blank; pp. 11–12 text; p. [13] illustration of a church; p. [14] blank; pp. 15–26 text; p. [27] blank; p. [28] illustration of a fair; pp. 29–44 text; p. [45] blank; p. [46] illustration of guns in a village; pp. 47–[54] text; p. [54] at centre, circular illustration of a village scene, 2¼ in.; p. [55] blank; p. [56] HERE ENDS · A SUMMER'S FANCY · By | Edmund Blunden The Cover, Title-page, Illus- | trations and Decorations designed by Randolph | Schwabe The Typography and Binding | arranged and the book produced by Cyril | William Beaumont and printed at his | Press Completed on the twenty-first | day of October MDCCCCXXX | [*publisher's colophon*, 2⅞ × 2⅛ *in.*] | THE BEAUMONT PRESS | [*rule*] | Pressman Arthur Foster | Compositor J. Spillett.

Off-white pictorial paper boards printed in dark green, paler green and yellow in an overall pattern of flower-heads and leaves; oatmeal cloth spine; lettered up the spine: [*ornament*] A SUMMER'S FANCY · EDMUND BLUNDEN [*ornament*]; top and bottom edges trimmed, fore edges untrimmed; white end-papers.

Published November 1930; 405 copies printed. £1. 1s.

Three hundred and twenty-five copies, numbered 81–405, were printed on hand-made paper as above, and 80 numbered copies on hand-made parchment vellum (*see* A34b).

This poem was reprinted in *Halfway House*, 1932; and *Poems 1930–1940*, [1941] (*see* A45, 68).

b. *First edition — hand-made parchment vellum issue. 1930*:

[*title and imprint as above*]

Medium 8vo. 56 pp. 6 illus. 8⅞ × 5⅝ in.

Paper boards as above; vellum spine.

Issued November 1930; 80 copies bound. £2. 2s.

Printed on hand-made parchment vellum and numbered 1–80. P. [2] below seven-line certificate: [*signed in ink: Edmund Blunden* | *Randolph Schwabe*].

A35   **THE POEMS**   **1930**

a. *First edition*:

THE POEMS OF | EDMUND BLUNDEN | [*five line quo-*

tation] | COBDEN-SANDERSON | 1 MONTAGUE
STREET | LONDON | 1930

Demy 8vo. [2] , xviii, 336 pp. $8\frac{5}{8}$ X $5\frac{5}{8}$ in.

Pp. [1–2] blank; p. [i] half-title; p. [ii] blank; p. [iii] title; p. [iv] at foot: *Printed in Great Britain for* | R. COBDEN-SANDERSON, LTD. *by* | THE SHENVAL PRESS *and bound by* | THE LEIGHTON-STRAKER BOOKBINDING | COMPANY, LTD.; pp. v–viii Preface; pp. ix–xvii Contents; p. [xviii] blank; p. [1] section-title; p. [2] blank; pp. 3–50 text; p. [51] section-title; p. [52] blank; pp. 53–136 text; p. [137] section-title; p. [138] blank; pp. 139–194 text; p. [195] section-title; p. [196] blank; pp. 197–292 text; p. [293] section-title; p. [294] blank; pp. 295–305 text; p. [306] blank; p. [307] section-title; p. [308] blank; pp. 309–329 text; pp. 330–336 Index to First Lines.

Off-white buckram boards; lettered in gold on spine: POEMS | 1914–30 | EDMUND | BLUNDEN | COBDEN- | SANDERSON; top edges dark grey, fore and bottom edges rough trimmed; white endpapers. Royal blue dust-jacket printed in black.

Published December 1930; no record of the number of copies printed. 10s. 6d.

Two hundred and ten copies were issued as a 'limited edition' (*see* A35*b*). Three hundred and fifty copies in sheets (i.e. the third issue) were sent to Harper & Brothers, New York (*see* A35*c*). There was what was probably a fourth issue rather than a second printing issued as a 'cheap edition' in March 1935 at 5s. possibly in off-white buckram boards as above, lettered in navy-blue on spine.

Contents: *Some Early Poems*: Afterwards — The Sunken Lane — Watching Running Water — "A View of the Present State of Ireland" — A Day Remorseful — Uneasy Peace — The Yellowhammer — The Festubert Shrine — Festubert: The Old German Line — In Festubert — Sheepbells [*formerly* An Evensong] — The New Moon — On Turning a Stone — Thiepval Wood — The Barn — The River House — The Bird of Herndyke Mill — Stane Street — The Gods of the Earth Beneath — "Transport Up" at Ypres — January Full Moon, Ypres — Les Halles d'Ypres — Clear Weather — Zillebeke Brook — Trees on the Calais Road — Bleue Maison — The Pagoda — Mont de Cassel — The Sighing Time — Clare's Ghost [*formerly* Phantasies] — The Unchangeable — Wild Cherry Tree — A Vignette — A Country God — *The English Scene*: Leisure — Wilderness — Changing Moon — The Waggoner — Malefactors — The Veteran — Almswomen — A Waterpiece — The Pike — Perch Fishing — Shepherd — Forefathers — The Idlers — The March Bee — Gleaning — The Pasture Pond — November Morning — The Dried Millpond — Spring Night — The May Day Garland — Journey — High Summer — Evening Mystery — Sheet Lightning — Will o' the Wisp — Cloudy June — Mole Catcher [*formerly* Molecatcher] — Water Sport — The Scythe Struck by Lightning [*formerly* The Scythe] — The Giant Puffball — First Snow —

Village Green — The Poor Man's Pig — The Covert — The Last of Autumn — Old Homes — Country Sale — The Long Truce — "Very Jewels in their Fair Estate" — Winter: East Anglia [*formerly* Winter Piece] — A Yeoman — Village — The Crown Inn [*formerly* "The Crown"] — The Midnight Skaters — Midnight — The Baker's Van — Pride of the Village — Muffled — Another Spring [*formerly* Shepherd's Calendar] — The Unknown Quantity — The Puzzle — No Continuing City — The Last Ray — Augury — Shooting Star at Harvest — Water Moment — Time of Roses — Waste Ground — Blue Butterfly — Rustic Wreath — Brook in Drought — Rosa Mundi — Interval — The Masquerade — A Budding Morrow — A Pastoral — The Embryo — Misunderstandings — Hawthorn [*formerly* Triune] — An Ancient Goddess — The Passer-By — Early and Late — Departure — Libertine — Winter Nights — Epitaph — Kingfisher — *War*: Impacts and Delayed Actions: A House in Festubert — The Sentry's Mistake [*later* The Guard's Mistake; *and* The Sentry's Mistake] — Illusions — Two Voices [*formerly* Survivors (1916)] — Premature Rejoicing — Escape — Preparations for Victory — Zero [*later* Come On, My Lucky Lads; *and* Zero 1916] — At Senlis Once — Into the Salient — The Zonnebeke Road — Trench Raid near Hooge — Concert Party: Busseboom — Rural Economy (1917) — Battalion in Rest [*later* Battalion in Rest, July 1917; *and* Battalion in Rest] — E.W.T.: On the Death of his Betty — Vlamertinghe: Passing the Chateau — Third Ypres — The Welcome — Pillbox — Gouzeaucourt: The Deceitful Calm — The Prophet — An Infantryman — Reunion in War — A Farm near Zillebeke — 1916 seen from 1921 [*formerly* Festubert, 1916] — The Troubled Spirit — The Late Stand-to — War Autobiography: Written in Illness — 11th R.S.R. — II Peter ii 22 — La Quinque Rue — "Trench Nomenclature" — The Ancre at Hamel: Afterwards [*formerly* The Ancre at Hamel] — Recognition [*formerly* A Recognition] — The Still Hour — The Avenue — Behind the Line — Their Very Memory — A.G.A.V. — Another Journey from Bethune to Cuinchy — On Reading that the Rebuilding of Ypres Approached Completion — Flanders Now [*formerly* Old Battlefields] — Inaccessibility in the Battlefield — War's People — The Watchers — Return of the Native — *Experience and Soliloquy*: The Estrangement [*formerly* Estrangement] — Sick Bed — The South-West Wind — The Watermill — The Forest — "The Earth Hath Bubbles" — Death of Childhood Beliefs — The Canal — The Time is Gone — April Byeway — The Child's Grave — Dead Letters — The Eclogue — The Shadow [*formerly* The Warder] — The Fading Phantom — The English Poets — The Old Year — First Rhymes — Inheritance — Thames Gulls — Masks of Time — Achronos [*formerly* Epochs; *and* Eras] — A Transcription — Harvest — A Dream — A Bridge — Strange Perspective — Omen — Elegy — Old Pleasures Deserted — Unteachable — Bells — "Thy Dreams Ominous" — Rue du Bois — Prodigal — Reliques — "There is a Country" — The Brook — The Spell — "Art thou gone in Haste?" — To Joy — The Aftermath — To Nature — To Clare — A Psalm — The Death-Mask of John Clare [*formerly* On

the Death-Mask . . .] — Intimations of Mortality — Thus Far —
The Flower-Gatherers — The Deeps — Now or Never — Warning
to Troops — To a Spirit [*formerly* To . . .] — The Message [*later*
Prelusion; *and* The Message] — In a Country Churchyard — Byroad
[*formerly* By Road] — Resentients — An Ancient Path [*formerly*
Together] — Voices by a River — A Superstition Revisited [*formerly*
. . . Re-visited] — Nature Displayed — A Morning Piece: Written
in Absence — The Age of Herbert and Vaughan — The Wartons
and Other Landscape-Poets [*formerly* The Wartons and Other
Early Romantics; *and* The Wartons and Other Early Romantic
Landscape Poets] — The Complaint — The Eccentric — The Charm
— Ruin — The Resignation — Would you return? — Village Lights —
A Favourite Scene: Recalled on looking at Birket Foster's Land-
scape — For There is no Help in Them [*formerly* 1919] — An Anno-
tation — Trust — Night-wind [*formerly* Nightwind] — Ornithopolis
— Cloud-life — The Unquiet Eye — On the Portrait of a Colonel
[*formerly* Portrait of a Colonel] — The Chance [*formerly* Frag-
ments] — Release — Entanglement — The Escape — To a Spirit —
The Match [*formerly* The Prison] — The Storm — The Immolation
— Chinese Picture — The Secret — Familiarity — Dream Encounters
— Parable — A Sunrise in March — Fragment — Summer Rainstorm
[*formerly* The Summer Rainstorm] — The Kiln — The Correlation
— Autumn in the Weald — Return — The Deeper Friendship — The
Blind Lead the Blind — Report on Experience — On a Biographical
Dictionary — A Quartet: "The Mikado" at Cambridge — A Connois-
seur — Sir W. Treloar's Dinner for Crippled Children [*formerly* Sir
William . . .] — The Study — Values — Chances of Remembrance —
In Wiltshire — Seen in Twilight — The Survival — My Window —
Japanese Garland: The Visitor — The Daimyo's Pond — A 'First
Impression', Tokyo — Ornamentations [*formerly* Oriental Orna-
mentations] — Far East — Eastern Tempest [*formerly* Tempest;
and Eastern Tempest] — Evening Music — Inland Sea [*formerly*
Japanese Nightpiece] — The Quick and the Dead — The Inviolate
— Building the Library, Tokyo University — On a Small Dog [sub-
title omitted] — The Author's Last Words to his Students — *Occasional Pieces*: A Japanese Evening — Recollections of Christ's Hospital — Sonnet on Smart's "Song to David" [*formerly* On Receiving
. . . ; *and* Sonnet on Receiving . . .] — Solutions [*formerly* The Correct Solution] — Under a Thousand Words — The Author of "The
Great Illusion" — On Mr. Frederick Porter's Pictures, 1930 — Old
Remedies — The Meadow Stream — The Doomed Oak: an Imitation [sub-title varies or omitted] — A Thought from Schiller — The
Geographer's Glory [sub-title varies] — The Nun at Court — The
Sunlit Vale [*formerly* The Failure].

b. First edition — limited issue. 1930:

[*title and imprint as above*]

Demy 8vo. [2], xviii, 336 pp. 9 × 5⅝ in.

Navy-blue cloth boards; lettered in gold on spine; edges untrimmed; pale grey end-papers. White dust-jacket printed in powder blue and black.

Issued December 1930; 210 copies bound. £3. 3s.

P. [2] at head: *This Edition is limited to 210 copies* | *of which* 200, *numbered* 1 *to* 200, *and* | *signed by the Author, are for sale.* | *This is No.* [*numbered in ink*] | [*signed: Edmund Blunden*].

c. First edition — American issue. [*1932*]:

[*title as above*; *imprint*:] [*publisher's device of a torch,* ⅞ × ⅝ *in.*] | HARPER AND BROTHERS | NEW YORK AND LONDON

Small royal 8vo. [2], xviii, 336 pp. 8⅝ × 5½ in.

Dark blue cloth boards; white paper label on flat spine, 2¼ × 1⅜ in., printed in blue within a double rule; edges trimmed; white end-papers.

Issued 1932; 350 copies bound. $3.

The sheets were supplied by Cobden-Sanderson.

A36   A POET ON THE OXFORD POETS   1930

First separate edition:

[*title at head of p.* [1]:] A POET ON | THE OXFORD POETS | EDMUND BLUNDEN | in *The Nation & Athenaeum* | 6 December 1930

Crown 8vo. [4] pp. 7½ × 5 in.

Pp. [1–4] text.

No wrappers; top and bottom edges trimmed, upper fore edge untrimmed.

Issued December 1930; no record of the number of copies printed. Not for sale.

On the *Oxford Poets* series published by Oxford University Press, and published as an advertisement for the series probably by the publishers who have been unable to trace any record. Blunden has recorded that he was not consulted. First published as 'A Masterly Series' in the *Nation & Athenaeum*, 6 December 1930 (*see* C1073).

P. [4] in some copies reads, at foot: *Printed on fine white paper,*
large crown 8vo. 6s. net, | *and on Oxford India paper, crown 8vo,*
7s. 6d. net, | *and in leather bindings*; the price 7s. 6d. is blacked out,
and 8s. 6d. is printed below, or the 7 changed to an 8 by hand.

A37   THE WEATHERCOCK – LA GIROUTTE   1931

First edition:

[*title on p.* [1]:] The Weathercock – La Girouette |
Edmund Blunden | 1917 | Ulysses Bookshop | 1931

Crown 4to. [4] pp. $9\frac{1}{2}$ X $6\frac{5}{8}$ in.

P. [1] title as above; pp. [2-3] text; p. [4] at centre: [*These verses*
were written by way of recreation in the | *Ypres salient towards the*
end of 1917. *At that time a* | *habit of reading French verse charac-*
terized the author and | *explains these stanzas! If any apology be*
required as well, | *let it be recalled that "there was a war on" – and*
such | *relics as this have their own value to those who remember it.* |
– E.B.] | [*at foot:*] *This entire edition is limited to* | 45 *numbered*
copies. | *This is No.* [*numbered in ink*] .

No wrappers; edges trimmed. Matching envelope printed as p. [1]
above.

Issued 1931; 45 copies printed.

Pp. [2-3] holograph facsimiles. (The turret's leaden carapace) (Sous
la lune le plomb de la tourelle). 'The Weathercock' was reprinted in
Known Signatures, 1932 (*see* B57).

A38   KEATS'S LETTERS, 1931   1931

First separate publication:

[*title on upper wrapper*:] KEATS'S LETTERS, 1931; |
MARGINALIA | BY | EDMUND BLUNDEN | From the
Studies in English Literature, Vol. XI, No. 4, Oct. 1931. |
Tokyo.

Medium 8vo. An offprint of [32] pp. $8\frac{3}{4}$ X $6\frac{1}{8}$ in.

Pp. [1-31] numbered [475]-507 text; p. [32] blank.

White stiff paper wrappers; printed on upper wrapper as above; edges
cut flush; sewn and gummed.

Issued October 1931; 50 copies printed. Not for sale.

Reprinted from *Studies in English Literature*, October 1931; and reprinted in *Reprinted Papers*, 1950 (*see* A104; C1150).

a. First edition:

VOTIVE TABLETS | Studies Chiefly Appreciative | of English Authors | and Books | BY | EDMUND BLUNDEN | [*four line quotation*] | LONDON | COBDEN-SANDER-SON | 1 MONTAGUE STREET

Demy 8vo. 368 pp. $8\frac{5}{8} \times 5\frac{5}{8}$ in.

P. [1] half-title; p. [2] blank; p. [3] title; p. [4] at foot: PRINTED IN GREAT BRITAIN FOR | R. COBDEN-SANDERSON LTD AT | THE CAMELOT PRESS LTD, LONDON | AND SOUTHAMPTON MCMXXXI; p. [5] dedication: TO | BRUCE RICHMOND Esq. | [*seventeen lines*]; p. [6] blank; p. [7] Note; p. [8] blank; pp. [9]–10 Contents; pp. 11–367 text; p. [368] blank.

Blue cloth boards; lettered in gold on spine: VOTIVE | TABLETS | o | EDMUND | BLUNDEN | COBDEN- | SANDERSON; top edges trimmed, fore and bottom edges untrimmed; white end-papers. Cream dust-jacket printed in pale blue.

Published *c.* 19 November 1931; number of copies printed not ascertained. 10*s*. 6*d*.

Sixty copies were issued as a 'limited edition' (*see* A39*b*). Two hundred and fifty copies in sheets (i.e. the third issue) were sent to Harper & Brothers, New York (*see* A39*c*). There was what was probably a fourth issue rather than a second printing issued as a 'cheap edition' in November 1934 at 5*s*.

Contents: John Skelton — Nicholas Breton's Prose — The Happy Island — Thomas Randolph — The Knight's Story — The Spirit of Bunyan — Herrick — "A Wedding or a Funeral" — Daniel Defoe April 26, 1731 — Defoe's Great Britain — Richard Steele — Pope and Theobald — "The Gentleman's Magazine" — Elton on the Johnson Era [*formerly* The Age of Johnson] — Charles Churchill 1731 — Goldsmith's Bicentenary [*formerly* Goldsmith, Poet, Novelist, Essayist: A Quiet Conquest] — A Boswellian Error — An Inherent Illusion — Selborne Day by Day — An Infantry Officer: Edward Gibbon [*formerly* Captain Gibbon] — Henry Mackenzie — Southey's "Doctor" — The "Rejected Addresses" — Leigh Hunt's Poetry [*formerly* Leigh Hunt] — The Biography of Shelley — The Lover and the Poet — Trelawny interpreted — Friends of Keats — The Country Tradition — Rural Rides — Lamb's Select Criticism — Hood's Literary Reminiscences — Beddoes and his Contemporaries — Coleridge the Less — George Darley and his Latest Biographer [*formerly* George Darley] — On Childhood in Poetry — The Laureates, 1922 [*formerly* The Laureates] — The Preservation of England — Fallen Englishmen.

b. First edition — limited issue. 1931:

[*title and imprint as above*]

Demy 8vo. 368 pp. 8¾ × 5⅝ in.

Ruby buckram boards; lettered in gold on spine; edges untrimmed; white end-papers.

Issued *c.* 19 November 1931; 60 copies bound. £3. 3*s.*

P. ⌈4⌉ at head: *This edition is limited to* 60 *copies, of which* 50, | *numbered* 1–50, *and signed by the Author,* | *are for sale.* | *This is No.* [*numbered in ink*] | [*signed: Edmund Blunden*].

c. First edition — American issue. 1932:

[*title as above*; *imprint*:] [*device*] | HARPER AND BROTHERS | New York and London | 1932

Demy 8vo. 368 pp. 8½ × 5¾ in.

Red-brown cloth boards; pale grey mottled paper label, 2⅜ × 1⅜ in., on spine printed in black: [*within a double rule, thick, thin*:] VO-TIVE | TABLETS | *by* | Edmund | Blunden | [*short rule*] | HARPERS; edges trimmed; white end-papers.

Issued 1932; 250 copies bound. $3.50.

The sheets were supplied by Cobden-Sanderson.

A40   **TO THEMIS**   **1931**

a. First edition:

TO | THEMIS | Poems on Famous Trials | *With Other Pieces* | BY | EDMUND BLUNDEN | [*illustration of a judge in court,* 2½ × 1⅝ *in.*] | LONDON | The Beaumont Press | 1931

Demy 8vo. 60 pp. illus. 8¾ × 5⅝ in.

P. [1] blank; p. [2] at centre, seven-line certificate; p. [3] half-title; pp. [4–5] blank; p. [6] frontispiece; p. [7] title; p. [8] at foot: *Printed in Great Britain*; pp. [9–10] Contents; p. [11] section-title; p. [12] blank; pp. 13–36 text; p. [37] section-title; p. [38] blank; pp. 39–58 text; p. [59] blank; p. [60] HERE ENDS · TO THEMIS · BY EDMUND | BLUNDEN The Cover, Frontispiece, and Title- | page designed by Randolph Schwabe The | Typography and Binding arranged and | the book produced by Cyril William | Beaumont and printed at his Press | Completed on the twenty-fourth day | of November MDCCCCXXXI | [*publisher's colophon,* 2⅞ × 2⅛ *in.*] | THE BEAUMONT PRESS | [*rule*] | Pressman Arthur Foster | Compositor J. Spillett.

Cream pictorial paper boards printed in black and yellow in an over-all pattern of scales and swords; oatmeal cloth spine; lettered in gold up the spine: [*ornament*] TO THEMIS · EDMUND BLUNDEN [*ornament*]; white end-papers; top and bottom edges trimmed, fore untrimmed.

Published December 1931; 405 copies printed. £1. 1s.

Three hundred and twenty-five copies, numbered 81–405, were prin-ted on hand-made paper as above, and 80 numbered copies on hand-made parchment vellum (*see* A40*b*).

Contents: *Sketches of Trials*: Mr. Charles Defends Himself; or, the Days of the Five-Mile Act — After the Forty-Five [*formerly* End of the Forty-Five] — Incident in Hyde Park, 1803 — The Atheist: Lord Eldon thinks over Shelley v. Westbrooke [*later* The Atheist, 1817] — *On Several Occasions*: Winter Stars — The Kiss — The Last Word [*formerly* The Memorial] — A Shadow by the Barn — An Aside — The Ballast-hole — The Recovery — A Night-piece — To the Cicada — 'Suitable Advice' — Epitaph for Sophocles.

b. First edition — hand-made parchment vellum issue. 1931:

[*title and imprint as above*]

Demy 8vo. 60 pp. illus. $8\frac{3}{4} \times 5\frac{3}{4}$ in.

Paper boards as above; vellum spine.

Issued December 1931; 80 copies bound. £2. 2s.

Printed on hand-made parchment vellum and numbered 1–80. P. [2] below seven-line certificate: [*signed: Edmund Blunden* | *Randolph Schwabe*].

A41   CONSTANTIA AND FRANCIS   1931

First edition:

[*title on p.* [1]:] CONSTANTIA | AND | FRANCIS | *An Autumn Evening* | BY | EDMUND BLUNDEN | PRI-VATELY PRINTED | FOR THE FRIENDS OF ELKIN MATHEWS LTD | DECEMBER | 1931

Demy 8vo. [8] pp. $9 \times 6\frac{1}{8}$ in.

P. [1] title; p. [2] at foot: [*rule*] | PRINTED IN GREAT BRITAIN | BY R. & R. CLARK LIMITED EDINBURGH; pp. [3–5] text; p. [6] blank; p. [7] at head: EDMUND BLUNDEN'S POEM |

CONSTANTIA AND FRANCIS │ IS HERE PRINTED FOR THE FIRST TIME │ TWO HUNDRED COPIES ONLY │ THIS IS NUM-BER │ [*numbered in ink*] ; p. [8] blank.

No wrappers; edges untrimmed; sewn in white thread.

Issued 23 December 1931; 200 copies printed. Not for sale.

(Here we have found our goddess; moor the boat). Reprinted in *Halfway House*, 1932; and *Poems 1930–1940*, [1941] (*see* A45, 68).

A42   **IN SUMMER**   1931 [i.e. 1932]
a. First edition:

[*within a double rule*:] *IN SUMMER* │ *The Rotunda of the Bishop of Derry* │ *by* │ *EDMUND BLUNDEN* │ [*long rule*] │ [*illustration of a rotunda, 2 × 2¾ in.*] │ *With decorations by* │ *EDWARD CARRICK* │ [*long rule*] │ *IN LONDON* │ *PRIVATELY PRINTED* │ MCMXXXI

Royal 8vo. [8] pp. 2 illus. on pp. [5–6]. 9⅛ × 6 in.

P. [1–2] blank; p. [3] title; p. [4] at head: *Of this book* 290 *numbered copies printed on Basingwerk* │ *Parchment have been issued, all signed by the author,* 250 │ *copies for sale only. There is also a special edition of* 15 │ *copies, lettered A–O,* 10 *copies for sale only.*, at centre: *Copy* [*numbered in ink*] │ [*signed: Edmund Blunden*] ; pp. [5–6] text; p. [7] at head: *Here ends In Summer, a poem by Edmund Blunden,* │ *the second of the seasons, celebrated in* │ *a privately printed edition for* │ *Terence Fytton Armstrong* │ 18 *Dean Street* │ *London* │ *W*.I; p. [8] at centre: *Made and printed in Great Britain by Charles Mitchell Ltd., London, E.C.* 4.

Pale grey paper boards; printed in green on upper cover: [*within a triple rule, thin, thick, thin*:] *IN SUMMER* │ *EDMUND BLUNDEN*; edges trimmed; paste-down end-papers; sewn in white thread. Transparent dust-jacket.

Published January 1932; 305 copies printed. 6*s*.

Fifteen lettered copies were issued as a 'special edition' (*see* A42*b*).

(Out of the sparkling flood of green) [*later* THE ROTUNDA]. Reprinted in *Known Signatures*, 1932; *Halfway House*, 1932; and *Poems 1930–1940*, [1941] (*see* A45, 68; B57).

The volumes on the other seasons, *In Spring* by Edith Sitwell, *In Autumn* by Herbert Palmer, and *In Winter* by W. H. Davies were published uniformly.

b. First edition —special issue. 1931 [i.e. 1932] :

[*title, with coloured illustration, and imprint as above*]

Royal 8vo. [8] pp. 2 illus. on pp. [5-6] . $9\frac{1}{8}$ × 6 in.

Paper boards as above; cream paper label.

Issued January 1932; 15 copies bound. £1. 1s.

Lettered A–O. P. [4] below line 4: [*signed: Edmund Blunden | Edward Carrick*].

A43   THE FACE OF ENGLAND   1932

a. First edition:

[*within a compartment:*] THE | FACE OF ENGLAND | IN A SERIES OF OCCASIONAL SKETCHES | *by* | EDMUND BLUNDEN | [*device of trees*, $\frac{5}{8}$ × $\frac{5}{8}$ *in.*] | LONGMANS, GREEN AND CO. | LONDON • NEW YORK • TORONTO | 1932

Foolscap 8vo. xiv, 178 pp. $6\frac{3}{4}$ × $4\frac{5}{8}$ in.

P. [i] half-title; p. [ii] list of works in the series; p. [iii] title; p. [iv] towards head, name and address of publisher, at foot: *Made in Great Britain*; pp. v–vii Introduction by J. C. Squire; p. [viii] blank; pp. ix–xi Preface, signed E.B.; p. [xii] towards head, quotation from Priscilla Wakefield's *Family Tour*; pp. xiii–xiv Contents; pp. 1–178 text; p. 178 at foot: PRINTED BY J. AND J. GRAY, EDINBURGH.

Dark green cloth boards; lettered in gold on spine: [*rule across head*] | *The* | *Face of* | *England* | *Edmund* | *Blunden* | [*device of trees*, $\frac{5}{8}$ × $\frac{5}{8}$ *in.*] | *English* | *Heritage* | [*rule across foot*] ; circular device of trees, $1\frac{3}{8}$ in., in gold and blind on upper cover; edges trimmed; white end-papers. Cream dust-jacket printed in black and scarlet; illustration of trees on upper jacket and spine.

Published 17 March 1932 in the *English Heritage Series*; no record of the number of copies printed. 3s. 6d. ($1.25).

There was a reprint in 1933, and a second reprint in October 1949 issued in the *Clifford Library* at 5s. in black cloth boards; lettered in gold on spine.

Contents: Janus — To Twelfth Night — Jasmine — Trouble at Twilight — Expressions at the Market — The Jays — The British School — The Fan Tod — Young February — WINTER PROUD — Lent Passes — Wills and Testaments — THE STARLING'S NEST — "There's Nought but Winning and Losing" — No Hurry — Great Hurry — The Hop Leaf — EVENING WALKS — An Ancient Holiday

— The Sigh — A CORNER OF THE MEADOW — Summer and the Poets — "While Fields Shall Bloom, Thy Name Shall Live" — Imaginary Work — THE TOWER — Pastoral No Fable — ART AND NATURE [*formerly* DOES THE SAME CAUSE ALWAYS PRODUCE THE SAME EFFECT?] — Just a Victorian — Floodland — Urn Burial — YOUNG TRAVELLERS — The Winter Moth — Fireside Collaboration — Mists and Fogs — The Village Chimneys — The Find — An Ex-Footballer — Battlefield — A COUNTRY PRAYER — National Biography.

b. *Japanese edition in English. 1938*:

[*title as above*; *followed by*:] SELECTED | WITH INTRODUCTION AND NOTES | *by* | G.S.I. KISHIMOTO, B.A. (OXON) | KAIRYUDO | TOKYO | 1938

Crown 8vo. xliv, iv, 206 pp. front. (port.), and map. $7\frac{3}{8} \times 5$ in.

Dark pink cloth boards; lettered in gold on spine with ornament; blind rule round upper cover; edges trimmed; white end-papers.

Published 20 January 1938; number of copies printed not ascertained. 1.50 yen.

Dedicated to, and with foreword by, Takeshi Saito. All the poems were omitted from this edition except The Starling's Nest, and the following additional ones included: The Waggoner — Almswomen — Thames Gulls — Byroad [*formerly* By Road] — The South-West Wind — At Senlis Once — To Joy — The Child's Grave — A Tale not in Chaucer not even in Dryden's Chaucer — The Excellent Irony.

A44   FALL IN, GHOSTS   1932

a. First edition:

FALL IN, GHOSTS | AN ESSAY ON | *A BATTALION REUNION* | BY | EDMUND BLUNDEN | THE WHITE OWL PRESS | LONDON | 1932

Crown 8vo. 32 pp. $7\frac{1}{2} \times 5$ in.

P. [1] towards head: *CONTEMPORARY ESSAYS* — *No.* 1 | (Edited by SYLVA NORMAN) | [*ornament*] | FALL IN, GHOSTS; p. [2] blank; p. [3] title; p. [4] blank; pp. [5–7] Editor's Preface; p. [8] blank; pp. 9–30 text; p. [31] blank; p. [32] note on the essay.

Stiff white paper wrappers; edges cut flush; sewn. Canary yellow dust-jacket printed in black on upper jacket: CONTEMPORARY |

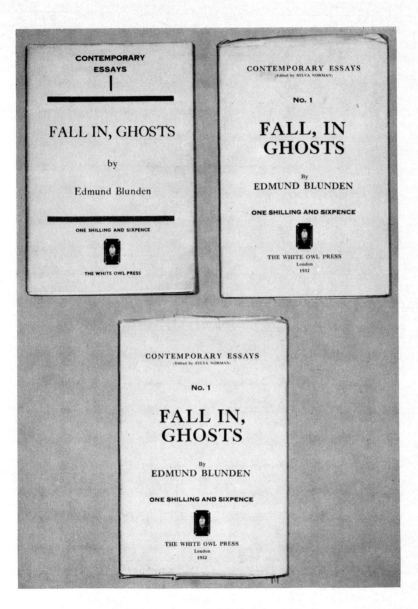

9. Variant wrappers of *Fall In, Ghosts* (A44)

ESSAYS | 1 | [*green band*] | FALL IN, GHOSTS | by | Edmund Blunden | [*green band*] | ONE SHILLING AND SIXPENCE | [*publisher's device of an owl,* $\frac{7}{8}$ × $\frac{1}{2}$ *in.*] | THE WHITE OWL PRESS.

Published June 1932 as *Contemporary Essays*, No. 1; number of copies printed not ascertained. 1*s.* 6*d.*

The dust-jacket appeared in three states (*see* plate 9). Fifty numbered copies were issued as a 'limited edition' (*see* A44*b*).

This essay was reprinted in *Contemporary Essays*, 1933; and *Edmund Blunden: A Selection of His Poetry and Prose*, 1950 (*see* A108; B60).

b. First edition — limited issue. 1932:

[*title, with the addition of a twelve-line quotation following the author's name, and imprint as above*]

Foolscap 4to. 32 pp. 8$\frac{1}{2}$ × 5$\frac{3}{8}$ in.

Grey paper boards marbled in black, pale blue, white and grey in a box pattern; imitation vellum spine; edges trimmed; off-white endpapers.

Issued June 1932; 50 copies bound. £1. 1*s.*

P. [1] towards head: This edition is limited to 50 copies. | No. [*numbered in ink*] | [*signed: Edmund Blunden*]. The Editor's Preface is omitted.

A45 **HALFWAY HOUSE** **1932**

a. First edition:

HALFWAY HOUSE | *A Miscellany of New Poems* | by | EDMUND BLUNDEN | [*five line quotation*] | London | COBDEN-SANDERSON | 1932

Demy 8vo. xii, 96 pp. 8$\frac{3}{4}$ × 5$\frac{1}{2}$ in.

Pp. [i–ii] blank; p. [iii] half-title; p. [iv] blank; p. [v] title; p. [vi] at foot: *Printed in England for* | R. COBDEN-SANDERSON LTD. | *by* THE SHENVAL PRESS; pp. vii–viii Preface; pp. ix–x Contents; p. [xi] section-title; p. [xii] blank; pp. 1–24 text; p. [25] section-title; p. [26] blank; pp. 27–43 text; p. [44] blank; p. [45] section-title; p. [46] blank; pp. 47–[95] text; p. [96] blank.

Brown cloth boards; off-white printed label, 1$\frac{7}{8}$ × $\frac{5}{8}$ in., on spine: [*triple rule, two thick, one thin*] | HALF- | WAY | HOUSE | [*ornament*] | Edmund | Blunden | [*triple rule, one thin, two thick*]; top edges trimmed, fore and bottom edges rough trimmed; white end-papers. Cream dust-jacket printed in brown.

Published probably 4 November 1932; no record of the number of copies printed. 6s.

Seventy copies were issued as a 'special edition' (see A45b). Copies in sheets (i.e. the third issue) were sent to Macmillan, New York (see A45c).

Contents: A Summer's Fancy — *To Themis*: Sketches of Famous Trials: Mr. Charles Defends Himself — After the Forty-Five [*formerly* End of the Forty-Five] — Incident in Hyde Park, 1803 — The Atheist: Lord Eldon thinks over Shelley v. Westbrooke [*later* The Atheist, 1817] — *Occasion and Mood*: Winter Stars — The Kiss — The Last Word [*formerly* The Memorial] — A Shadow by the Barn — The Rotunda [*formerly* In Summer] — Summer Hieroglyphs [*formerly* Apparitions in Summer] — An Aside — Constantia and Francis — The Ballast-Hole — Fancy and Memory — Mental Hospital: I, Two in a Corner; II, Poor Tom's Welcome — The Memorial, 1914–1918 — Inscribed in War-Books, I; II [*formerly* An Inscription] — November 1, 1931 — The Recovery — Segrave's Death: A Market-Town Reminiscence — Another Altar — A Calm Rain — Desire and Delight [*formerly* In Disappointment] — The Excellent Irony — On Some Crocuses: At Trinity College — Argument in Spring — Verses in Reminiscence and Delight — A Night-Piece — To the Cicada — 'Suitable Advice' — Epitaph for Sophocles — The Dog from Malta — A Tale not in Chaucer — An Ancient, but Jubilant Ballad, 1696.

b. First edition — limited issue. 1932:

[*title and imprint as above*]

Demy 8vo. xii, 96 pp. $8\frac{3}{4} \times 5\frac{5}{8}$ in.

Brownish-red buckram boards; lettered in gold on spine: HALF | WAY | HOUSE | EDMUND | BLUNDEN | COBDEN- | SANDER-SON; top edges gilt, fore and bottom edges untrimmed; white end-papers. Buff dust-jacket printed in black.

Issued probably 4 November 1932; 60 copies bound.

P. [iv] at head: *This special edition, signed by the | Author, is limited to 70 copies, of | which 60 are for sale. This is | No. [numbered in ink] | [signed: Edmund Blunden]*.

c. First edition — American issue. 1933:

[*title as above*; *imprint*:] The Macmillan Company, New York, 1933*

Demy 8vo. xii, 96 pp.
Issued January 1933; no record of the number of copies bound. $2.
The sheets were supplied by Cobden-Sanderson.

A46 THE CAMBRIDGE HISTORY 1933
OF ENGLISH LITERATURE

First separate publication:

[*title at head of leaf*:] *The* CAMBRIDGE HISTORY *of* |
ENGLISH LITERATURE | By EDMUND BLUNDEN* |
(from THE BOOK SOCIETY NEWS)

Imperial 8vo. [1] leaf. 10 × 7½ in.

Leaf [1] text, with advertisement for *The Cambridge History* within
a triple rule at centre; at foot: [*long rule*] | *Reprinted from the
issue of *The Book Society News* for January 1933 by The Phoenix
Book Company Ltd., | 3 & 4 King Street, Covent Garden, London
W.C.2.

No wrappers; off-white leaf; edges trimmed.

Issued January 1933; no record of the number of copies printed.
Not for sale.

Review of *The Cambridge History of English Literature*, reissue. Reprinted by photo-offset as an advertisement from the *Book Society
News*, January 1933. The advertisement on Leaf [1] replaces the
photograph of Margaret Kennedy in the *Book Society News*'s original printing (*see* C1253).

A47 WE'LL SHIFT OUR GROUND 1933

First edition:

WE'LL SHIFT OUR GROUND | *or* | TWO ON A TOUR |
almost | A NOVEL | *by* | EDMUND BLUNDEN | *and* |
SYLVA NORMAN | [*publisher's device of an urn*, ⅞ × ⅝ *in.*]
| LONDON: *Cobden-Sanderson* : MCMXXXIII

Small crown 8vo. xii, 320 pp. 7⅜ × 4¾ in.

Pp. [i–ii] blank; p. [iii] half-title; p. [iv] blank; p. [v] title-page; p.
[vi] at head: *First published in 1933*, at foot: *Printed in Great
Britain for* | R. COBDEN-SANDERSON LTD. | *by* THE SHENVAL
PRESS; p. [vii] at head, dedication: *To* | M. AND MME. LOUIS
BONNEROT | *and* | THE FRANCE THAT IS; pp. viii–x Contents;
pp. xi–xii A Preface; p. [1] section-title; p. [2] blank; pp. 3–23 text;

p. [24] blank; p. [25] section-title; p. [26] blank; pp. 27–144 text; p. [145] section-title; p. [146] blank; pp. 147–196 text; p. [197] section-title; p. [198] blank; pp. 199–231 text; p. [232] blank; p. [233] section-title; p. [234] blank; pp. 235–305 text; p. [306] blank; p. [307] section-title; p. [308] blank; pp. 309–316 text; p. [317] section-title; p. [318] blank; pp. 319–[320] text.

Cornflower-blue cloth boards; lettered in gold on spine: WE'LL SHIFT | OUR GROUND | EDMUND | BLUNDEN | AND | SYLVA | NORMAN | COBDEN- | SANDERSON; edges trimmed; white end-papers.

Published January 1933; no record of the number of copies printed. 7s. 6d.

A48   THE EPILOGUE FOR KING JOHN   1933

First edition:

[*title on p.* [*1*] : *in open letters*:] THE EPILOGUE | for | KING JOHN | [*in roman*:] presented by the O.U.D.S. | February 25th, 1933 | on the occasion | of the closing of | [*in open letters*:] THE NEW THEATRE | OXFORD | *Theatre Manager: President, O.U.D.S.:* | [*in roman*:] S. C. DORRILL, ESQ. H. S. HUNT, ESQ. | Magdalen

Crown 8vo. [4] pp. $7\frac{5}{8} \times 5$ in.

P. [1] title as above; pp. [2–3] text; p. [4] at foot: HOLYWELL PRESS, ALFRED STREET, OXFORD.

No wrappers; top, bottom and lower fore edges trimmed, upper fore edge rough trimmed.

Issued 25 February 1933; number of copies printed not ascertained. (So the fierce beauty of this princely play).

A49   CHARLES LAMB AND HIS   1933
                 CONTEMPORARIES

a. First edition:

CHARLES LAMB | AND HIS CONTEMPORARIES | [*double rule, thick, thin*] | BEING THE CLARK LEC-TURES | DELIVERED AT TRINITY COLLEGE | CAM-BRIDGE 1932 | BY | *EDMUND BLUNDEN* | A Fellow of Merton College, Oxford | and formerly Professor of English

Literature in | the Imperial University of Tokyo | [*double rule, thin, thick*] | CAMBRIDGE | AT THE UNIVERSITY PRESS | 1933

Large crown 8vo. [2], x, 216 pp. 8 × 5⅛ in.

Pp. [1–2] blank; p. [i] half-title; p. [ii] towards centre: LONDON | Cambridge University Press | FETTER LANE | NEW YORK · TORONTO | BOMBAY · CALCUTTA · MADRAS | Macmillan | TOKYO | Maruzen Company Ltd | *All rights reserved*; p. [iii] title; p. [iv] at foot: PRINTED IN GREAT BRITAIN; p. [v] Contents; p. [vi] blank; pp. [vii]–ix Preface, signed E.B. 1933; p. [x] blank; pp. [1]–206 text; pp. [207]–215 Index; p. 215 at foot: *Cambridge: Printed by W. Lewis, M.A., at the University Press*; p. [216] blank.

Pale blue cloth boards; lettered in gold on spine: BLUNDEN · | [*double rule, thin, thick*] | *Charles* | *Lamb* | [*publisher's device*] | CAMBRIDGE; edges trimmed, top blue; white end-papers. Mid-green dust-jacket printed in pale blue and black.

Published 5 April 1933; 2000 copies printed. 7*s.* 6*d.*

Copies in sheets were sent to Macmillan, New York (*see* A49*b*). There was a reprint of 1250 copies in December, some of which were probably reissued in May 1937 at 3*s.* 6*d.* as *The Cambridge Miscellany*, Vol. 19 in maroon cloth boards; lettered in gold on spine with double rule across head, centre and foot; edges trimmed, top pale grey, lower end-papers only.

b. First edition — American issue. 1933:

[*title as above*; *imprint*:] The Macmillan Company, New York, 1933*

Crown 8vo. x, 216 pp.
Issued June 1933; no record of the number of copies bound. $2.50.
The sheets were supplied by Cambridge University Press. There was a second issue in 1937.

c. First edition — American photo-offset reprint. 1967:

[*title as above*; *imprint*:] ARCHON BOOKS | 1967

Small crown 8vo. x, 218 pp. 7¼ × 4⅝ in.
Royal blue cloth boards; lettered in gold down the spine; edges trimmed; white end-papers. Pale blue dust-jacket printed in black.
Issued 25 August 1967; 1000 copies printed. $5.50.

First edition:

THE MIND'S EYE │ *Essays by* │ EDMUND BLUNDEN │ [*publisher's circular device of a vase of flowers,* $\frac{5}{8}$ *in.*] │ JONATHAN CAPE │ THIRTY BEDFORD SQUARE │ LONDON

Large crown 8vo. 288 pp. $7\frac{7}{8} \times 5\frac{1}{4}$ in.

Pp. [1–2] blank; p. [3] half-title; p. [4] list of works by the author; p. [5] title; p. [6] at head: FIRST PUBLISHED 1934 │ JONATHAN CAPE LTD. 30 BEDFORD SQUARE, LONDON │ AND 91 WELLINGTON STREET WEST, TORONTO, at foot: PRINTED IN GREAT BRITAIN IN THE CITY OF OXFORD │ AT THE ALDEN PRESS │ BOUND BY A. W. BAIN & CO., LTD. │ PAPER MADE BY JOHN DICKINSON & CO., LTD.; pp. 7–8 Contents; p. [9] at head, dedication: *To* │ SYLVA [i.e. *Sylva Norman*] │ who does these things better; p. [10] blank; p. 11 Author's Note; p. [12] blank; p. [13] section-title; p. [14] blank; pp. 15–85 text; p. [86] blank; p. [87] section-title; p. [88] blank; pp. 89–142 text; p. [143] section-title; p. [144] blank; pp. 145–192 text; p. [193] section-title; p. [194] blank; pp. 195–284 text; pp. [285–288] blank, integral.

Green cloth boards; lettered in scarlet on spine: [*in open capitals*:] THE │ MIND'S │ EYE │ EDMUND │ BLUNDEN │ [*in roman*:] JONATHAN │ CAPE, and on upper cover: [*in open capitals*:] THE MIND'S EYE; publisher's device of a vase of flowers in scarlet on lower cover at centre; top and fore edges trimmed, top green, bottom rough trimmed; white end-papers. Cream dust-jacket printed in black and red.

Published 30 April 1934; 1500 copies printed. 7s. 6d.

There was a reprint of 1000 copies in July 1934. Most of them were issued in February 1938 at 4s. 6d. as *The Life & Letters Series*, Vol. 80 in dark green cloth boards; lettered in gold on spine, and on upper cover; top and fore edges trimmed, bottom rough trimmed; white end-papers; white dust-jacket printed in green.

Contents: 1, Flanders: War and Peace — Aftertones [*formerly* A Postscript] — The Somme Still Flows — We Went to Ypres — The Extra Turn — A Battalion History — 2, Japan: Japanese Moments — A Tokyo Secret — Winter Comes to Tokyo — On Some Humorous Prints of Hiroshige [*formerly* Hiroshige as Humorist: A Little Known Aspect of the Famous Artist] — Buddhist Paintings — Atami of the Past — Ghosts and Grotesques — The Beauty of Vagueness — 'Not Only Beautiful' — 3, England: Bells on the Breeze — Miss Warble — The English Countryside — A Lost Leader — Yalding Bridges — On Preservation — Lord's, June 27th, 1930 — Life aboard a 'Tramp' — 4, The World of Books: Shakespeare's Significances —

The Ideal Laureate — Again, What is Poetry? — Bringing them Home — Children as Readers — Subject in Poetry — Geographical Improvements — Siegfried Sassoon's Poetry.

A51   GEORGE HERBERT'S LATIN POEMS   1934

First separate publication:

[*title at head of p.* [*1*]:] GEORGE HERBERT'S LATIN POEMS

Demy 8vo. An offprint of [12] pp. $8\frac{5}{8} \times 5\frac{1}{2}$ in.

Pp. [1–11] numbered [29]–39 text; p. [12] numbered 40 text of following article; blank leaf pasted over p. [12].

Pale brown paper wrappers; edges cut flush; stapled and gummed.

Issued June 1934; no record of the number of copies printed. Not for sale.

Reprinted from *Essays and Studies by Members of the English Association*, 1933 [i.e. June 1934] (*see* C1376).

A52   CHOICE OR CHANCE   1934

a. First edition:

CHOICE OR CHANCE | *New Poems by* | EDMUND BLUNDEN | [*publisher's device of an urn,* $1\frac{1}{2} \times 1$ *in.*] | *London* | COBDEN-SANDERSON | *1 Montague Street*

Demy 8vo. viii, 64 pp. $8\frac{3}{4} \times 5\frac{5}{8}$ in.

P. [i] half-title; p. [ii] blank; p. [iii] title; p. [iv] at foot: *Printed in England for* | R. COBDEN-SANDERSON LTD. | *by* THE SHENVAL PRESS | 1934; p. v Author's Note, signed E.B.; p. [vi] blank; pp. vii–viii Contents; pp. 1–60 text; pp. [61–64] blank, integral.

Pink cloth boards; white paper label on spine, $1\frac{3}{4} \times \frac{3}{8}$ in., printed in pink: [*triple rule, two thick, one thin*] | CHOICE | OR | CHANCE | [*ornament*] | *Edmund* | *Blunden* | [*triple rule, one thin, two thick*]; top edges trimmed, fore and bottom edges rough trimmed; cream end-papers. Cream dust-jacket printed in scarlet.

Published November 1934; no record of the number of copies printed. 6*s.*

Forty-five copies were issued as a 'special edition' (*see* A52*b*).

Contents: To Sylva — Full Bloom — Spirit-Wind [*formerly* The Unexpected Victory] — The Hill — Grown Up — Into the Distance — Long Moments — The Surprise — Afternoon in Japan [*formerly*

Somewhere East] — The Cottage at Chigasaki — South Atlantic — Reflections — The Toad — Lark Descending — 'Sentimental' — Anonymous Donors — Fur Coat — Theology Over the Gate — Unlucky Allusions — A Thought of the Downs — A Prologue [*later* The Country Round Christ's Hospital] — The Branch Line — Housing Questions [*later* Housing Question] — Some Talk of Peace — The Lost Battalion — From Age to Age [*formerly* The Only Answer] — To the Southdowns, on their dining again together, 1934 — At Rugmer — Experience Teaches . . . — Stormy Night [*formerly* The Voice of the Past] — Carfax — A Nature — To One Long Dead [Written on reading *Harriet*, by Elizabeth Jenkins] — A Touchstone [*formerly* Think of Shelley] — Country Conversation — In a Library — An Ominous Victorian [*formerly* An Eminent Victorian] — To Dr. I. Lettsom — Arcadian Law; A Notice in Cheltenham — The March of Mind — Chapters of Literary History — Oriental Tale [*formerly* Thoughts on Books] — The Art of Poetry: [i] Epitaph; [ii] Satire; [iii] Slogan; [iv] Pastoral; [v] Epic; [vi] Another — Fable.

b. First edition — limited issue. [*1934*] :

[*title and imprint as above*]

Demy 8vo. viii, 64 pp. $8\frac{3}{4} \times 5\frac{5}{8}$ in.

Cherry-red buckram boards; lettered in gold on spine: CHOICE | OR | CHANCE | EDMUND | BLUNDEN | COBDEN- | SANDERSON; top edges gilt, fore and bottom edges rough trimmed; white endpapers.

Issued November 1934; 45 copies bound.

P. [ii] at head: *This Special Edition signed by* | *the Author is limited to 45 copies* | *of which 35 are for sale* | *This is number* [*numbered in ink*] | [*signed: Edmund Blunden*] .

A53   EDWARD GIBBON AND HIS AGE   1935

First edition:

EDWARD GIBBON | AND HIS AGE | EDMUND BLUNDEN | *Arthur Skemp* | *Memorial Lecturer* | 1935 | [*device of the University of Bristol,* $\frac{3}{4} \times \frac{5}{8}$ *in.*] | *Printed for the* | UNIVERSITY OF BRISTOL | *by* J. W. ARROWSMITH LTD., 12 SMALL STREET

Small demy 8vo. 40 pp. $8\frac{1}{8} \times 5\frac{1}{4}$ in.

P. [1] half-title; p. [2] blank; p. [3] title; p. [4] blank; p. [5] The

Lecturer's Note; p. [6] blank; pp. 7–38 text; p. [39] blank; p. [40] at centre, printer's device.

Pale grey stiff paper wrappers, $8\frac{1}{2} \times 5\frac{5}{8}$ in., printed in black on upper wrapper: [*within a double rule, thick, thin:*] EDWARD GIBBON │ AND HIS AGE │ *being the* │ ARTHUR SKEMP │ MEMORIAL LEC-TURE │ *delivered in the* │ *University of Bristol* │ 15*th* February, 1935 │ *By* │ EDMUND BLUNDEN │ [*device of the University of Bristol, with motto,* $1 \times \frac{3}{4}$ *in.*] │ [*outside double rule:*] PRICE ONE SHILLING AND SIXPENCE; edges trimmed; sewn and gummed.

Published July 1935; no record of the number of copies printed. 1*s*. 6*d*.

A54   KEATS'S FRIEND MATHEW   1936

First separate publication:

[*title on p.* [2] *at head*:] (46) KEATS'S FRIEND MATHEW │ *By* EDMUND BLUNDEN

Imperial 8vo. An offprint of [12] pp. illus. (port.) on p. [2]. $9\frac{3}{4} \times 7\frac{3}{8}$ in.

P. [1] blank; pp. [2–11] numbered 46–55 text; p. [12] blank.

Grey paper wrappers; printed on upper wrapper: [*double rule, thick, thin*] │ *REPRINTED FROM* │ ENGLISH │ THE MAGAZINE OF THE │ ENGLISH ASSOCIATION │ VOLUME I NUMBER I │ [*double rule, thin, thick*], and on lower wrapper: PRINTED IN GREAT BRITAIN AT THE UNIVERSITY PRESS, OXFORD │ BY JOHN JOHNSON, PRINTER TO THE UNIVERSITY; edges cut flush; sewn and gummed.

Issued February 1936; no record of the number of copies printed. Not for sale.

On George Felton Mathew. Reprinted from *English*, [January] 1936 (*see* C1499).

A55   PROLOGUE TO 'SAVONAROLA'   1936

First edition:

[*title on p.* [1]:] Prologue to 'Savonarola' │ *Written by* Mr. BLUNDEN │ *Spoken by* Mr. MURE

Royal 8vo. [2] leaves. $10 \times 6\frac{1}{4}$ in.

Leaf [1] title as above; leaf [2] text, at foot: MERTON, │ *March 3rd, 1936.*

No wrappers; edges trimmed.

Issued 3 March 1936; number of copies printed not ascertained. 6d.
(From gaunt A.B.'s, and dialogue marine). *Savonarola* by Ladbroke
Brown from Max Beerbohm's *Seven Men* and *In the Zone* by Eugene
O'Neill were staged by the Merton Floats at Merton College. The
'Prologue' was spoken by Geoffrey Mure. No copy has been seen of
'*In the Zone* and *"Savonarola" Brown* including a "Preface to
'Savonarola'" by Blunden', printed by the Potter Press which was
advertised in G. F. Sims (Rare Books) Catalogue No. 78. It is not in
the British Library, Bodleian Library or Merton College Library.

A56   **THE NOVEMBER HOUR**   1936

First edition:

[*title on leaf* [1]:] THE NOVEMBER HOUR | by | ED-
MUND BLUNDEN | Set in 12 pt. "Dolphin", and 200
copies made by S. M. Rich.

Foolscap 4to. [2] leaves. 8 × 6½ in.

Leaf [1] title as above; leaf [2] text, at foot: [*dotted line*] | *Supple-
ment to No 10 of the Bulletin of the Charles Lamb Society, April,
1936.* | [*line of ornaments*].

No wrappers; edges trimmed.

Issued 1 April 1936; 200 copies printed. Available on subscription.

(Pausing in the churchyard here, I feel anew); dated St Andrew's,
Holborn, 23rd November 1934.

A57   **A NORTHAMPTONSHIRE POETESS**   1936

First separate publication:

[*title on upper wrapper: within a double rule*:] A | North-
amptonshire Poetess: | MARY LEAPOR. | By | EDMUND
BLUNDEN. | *NORTHAMPTON,* | *1936.*

Demy 8vo. An offprint of [16] pp. 8⅝ × 5½ in.

Pp. [1–16] numbered [59]–74 text.

Pale grey paper wrappers; printed on upper wrapper as above; edges
cut flush; stapled.

Issued June 1936; no record of the number of copies printed. Not
for sale.

Reprinted from the *Journal of the Northamptonshire Natural History Society and Field Club*, June 1936 (*see* C1534).

62

First edition:

KEATS'S PUBLISHER: | *A Memoir of* | John Taylor | (*1781-1864*) | by | EDMUND BLUNDEN | [*publisher's circular device of a bowl of flowers*, $\frac{5}{8}$ *in.*] | [*four line quotation*] | JONATHAN CAPE | THIRTY BEDFORD SQUARE | LONDON

Large crown 8vo. 256 pp. front. (port.) and 7 plates facing pp. 34, 54, 86, 136, 198, 224, 236. 8 × 5$\frac{1}{4}$ in.

Pp. [1-2] blank; p. [3] half-title; p. [4] list of works by the author; p. [5] title; p. [6] at head: FIRST PUBLISHED 1936 | JONATHAN CAPE LTD. 30 BEDFORD SQUARE, LONDON | AND 91 WELLINGTON STREET WEST, TORONTO, at foot: PRINTED IN GREAT BRITAIN IN THE CITY OF OXFORD | AT THE ALDEN PRESS | ˋPAPER MADE BY JOHN DICKINSON & CO. LTD. | BOUND BY A. W. BAIN & CO. LTD.; p. 7 Contents; p. [8] blank; p. 9 Illustrations; p. [10] blank; p. [11] at head, dedication: *Dedicated | with very much affection | to* | RUPERT HART-DAVIS; p. [12] blank; pp. 13-15 Preface; p. [16] blank; p. [17] fly-title; p. [18] blank; pp. 19-242 text; pp. 243-248 Notes; pp. 249-251 John Taylor's Writings; pp. 252-256 Index.

Claret cloth boards; lettered in gold on spine: KEATS'S | PUBLISHER | EDMUND | BLUNDEN | [*publisher's device of a bowl of flowers*, $\frac{1}{4}$ × $\frac{1}{4}$ *in.*] ; top and fore edges trimmed, top claret, bottom rough trimmed; white end-papers. Cream dust-jacket printed in reddish-brown.

Published 23 October 1936; 1500 copies printed. 8*s.* 6*d.*

One thousand and fifteen copies were reissued in May 1940 at 4*s.* 6*d.* as *The Life and Letters Series*, Vol. 97 in dark green cloth boards; lettered in silver on spine, and on upper cover; edges trimmed; lower end-paper; white dust-jacket printed in green.

First separate edition:

[*title at head of p.* [2] :] A City on a Hill

Crown 8vo. [4] pp. 6$\frac{3}{4}$ × 5$\frac{1}{4}$ in.

P. [1] blank; pp. [2-3, p. 3 numbered 2] text; p. [4] blank.

No wrappers; edges trimmed.

Issued December 1936; 150-200 copies printed. Not for sale.

(We climbed the hill and passed the mill,). Holograph facsimile.

On Mount Cassel. Printed privately for the author as a Christmas card. First published in the *Book Society Annual*, December 1936; and reprinted in *An Elegy*, 1937; and *Poems 1930–1940*, [1941] (*see* A64, 68; C1580).

A60   VERSES TO H.R.H.   1936 [i.e. 1937]
                        THE DUKE OF WINDSOR

First edition:

[*title on upper wrapper*: *first word in open capitals*:]
VERSES | TO H.R.H. | THE DUKE OF | WINDSOR |
MCMXXXVI

Medium 8vo. 4 pp. 8¾ × 6 in.

Pp. 1–4 text; p. 4 at foot: *December* 1936 EDMUND BLUNDEN.

White paper wrappers; printed in black on upper wrapper as above, and inside lower wrapper: *One hundred copies only of these Verses | have been printed in the | City of Oxford at the | Alden Press | for | [signed in ink: Edmund Blunden] | Copy number: | [numbered in ink]*; edges cut flush; bottom edges of wrappers rough trimmed in some copies; stapled.

Issued January 1937; 100 copies printed. Not for sale.

(These, then have triumphed. You have broken). Reprinted in *Edmund Blunden: A Selection of His Poetry and Prose*, 1950 (*see* A108).

A61   UNEASY QUIET   [1937]

First edition:

[*title on leaf* [1]:] UNEASY | QUIET

Small royal 8vo. [4] leaves. 9⅜ × 6¼ in.

Leaf [1] title as above; leaves [2–3] text; leaf [4] This edition is limited to 35 copies | numbered and signed by the | author. The type has been set | by hand in 14=pt. Marathon and | printed on a hand press. The | copies numbered 1 to 30 have | been printed on "Strathmore" | Silverflake blue paper. The re= | maining 5 copies lettered A to E | for the exclusive use of the | printer are on various papers. | *[numbered in ink]* | *[signed in ink: Edmund Blunden]* | Printed at the Corvinus Press on | December 31, 1936 and January | 1, 1937. Laus Deo.

No wrappers; sky-blue paper flecked with silver; top and bottom edges trimmed, some fore edges untrimmed; sewn in blue thread.

Published February 1937; 35 copies printed. 7*s.* 6*d.*

Fourteen copies were given to the author, and 16 were for sale. The remaining 5 copies printed for the printer were printed on (a) blue-tinted white paper with a blue hair; (b) green paper with a green hair; (c) white paper with a grey hair; (d) on 'goldflake' paper; (e) on 'silverflake' paper. None of these 5 copies has been seen; all are in Lord Portarlington's collection.

(The moon seems creeping with retarded pace). Reprinted as 'TOWN END' in *An Elegy*, 1937; and *Poems 1930-1940*, [1941] (A64, 68).

A62   THE KLOSTERHAUS READINGS,   1937
1937

First separate publication:

[*title on p.* [*1*]:] THE KLOSTERHAUS READINGS, 1937 | *by* EDMUND BLUNDEN

Royal 8vo. An offprint of [6] pp. $9\frac{5}{8}$ × 6 in.

P. [1] title as above at head of text; pp. [1-6] numbered 33-38 text.

No wrappers; edges trimmed; stapled.

Issued October 1937; number of copies printed not ascertained. Not for sale.

Reprinted from *German Life and Letters*, October 1937 (*see* C1645).

A63   LINES TO CHARLES LAMB   1937

First separate edition:

[*title at head of leaf*: *in maroon*:] LINES TO CHARLES LAMB | *Who for some seven years heard the Bible read every day* | *in Christ Church, Greyfriars.*

Demy 4to. [1] leaf. $10\frac{1}{2}$ × 4 in.

Leaf [1] text; towards foot: *Written for the Dedication of the Centenary* | *Memorial at Christ Church, Greyfriars on* | *November 5th., 1935.* | [*rule*] | Supplement to No. 24 of the Monthly Bulletin *of* the Charles | Lamb Society, October, 1937.

No wrappers; edges trimmed.

Issued October 1937; probably 200 copies printed. Available on subscription.

(Among all houses in haunted London). First published in the *Christ Church, Greyfriars* programme of service, 1935; and reprinted as 'AT CHRIST CHURCH, GREYFRIARS' in *An Elegy*, 1937; *Poems 1930-1940*, [1941]; and *Poems of Many Years*, 1957 (*see* A64,68, 135; B72).

First edition:

AN ELEGY | *and other Poems* | EDMUND BLUNDEN |
[*publisher's device of an urn,* $\frac{3}{4}$ × $\frac{1}{4}$ *in.*] | *London* |
COBDEN-SANDERSON | *One Montague Street*

Demy 8vo. [ii], 98 pp. 8$\frac{3}{4}$ × 5$\frac{5}{8}$ in.

P. [i] half-title; p. [ii] blank; p. [1] title; p. [2] at foot: PRINTED
IN GREAT BRITAIN FOR | COBDEN-SANDERSON LTD BY
| JOHN BELLOWS LTD, GLOUCESTER | 1937; p. [3] at head,
dedication: *To* | *Henry Donner* | *with great regard*; pp. [4–5]
Contents; p. [6] blank; p. [7] Preface; p. [8] blank; p. [9] section-
number; p. [10] blank; pp. 11–12 text; p. [13] section-number;
p. [14] blank; pp. 15–55 text; p. [56] blank; p. [57] section-
number; p. [58] blank; pp. 59–70 text; p. [71] section-number; p.
[72] blank; pp. 73–91 text; p. [92] blank; p. [93] section-number;
p. [94] blank; pp. 95–96 text; pp. [97–98] blank, integral.

Black cloth boards; cream paper label on spine, 1$\frac{3}{4}$ × $\frac{5}{8}$ in., printed in
poppy-red: [*triple rule, thick to thin*] | AN | ELEGY | [*ornament*]
| *Edmund* | *Blunden* [*triple rule, thin to thick*]; top edges trimmed,
fore and bottom edges rough trimmed; white end-papers. Cream
dust-jacket printed in scarlet.

Published early November 1937; number of copies printed not ascertained. 6*s.*

Contents: Elegy on His Majesty King George V [*formerly* Elegy;
later An Elegy] — Past and Present: A Hymn; A Second Hymn —
Woe to Drunkards: A Jacobean Sermon — The Subtle Calm — A City
on a Hill — The Spell of France — Late Light — Personal Survivals —
Writing a Sketch of a Forgotten Poet — At Christ Church, Greyfriars
[*formerly* Lines to Charles Lamb] — Near Sunset — The Ambush —
Invitation [*formerly* Poetry's Invitation] — And Then — From the
Branch Line — 'A Musique, Soldier' — In My Time — Cabaret Tune
— Town End [*formerly* Uneasy Quiet] — An International Football
Match — Minority Report — Anti-Basilisk — Fresh Thoughts on an
Old Poem — Present Discontents — The Spire — 'Can You Remem-
ber?' — Rue des Berceaux — Nights Before Battle — Nearing the
Ancre Battlefield 1916 — Marching Back to Peace 1916 — On a
Picture by Dürer — Monts de Flandre — The Inaccessible House —
Recurrence — Tell Your Fortune — Not So Dead — A Tune —Winter
Ending — Pasture — In Berkshire — Village Sketch — Market Town —
Cricket, I Confess — Cleave's Garden — Lonely Love — Looking
Eastward [*formerly* A Song] — Sixpence to the River — Departed
or, 'tis Twenty Years Since — Chaffinch on Suburban Growths —
Ask Old Japhet — Waiting the Word — Stanzas: Midsummer.

First separate edition:

[*title at head of p.* [*1*]:] [*in black letter*:] A Ballad of Titles | [*ornament*]

Small crown 8vo. [4] pp. 6⅞ X 5 in.

Pp. [1–3] text; p. [3] at foot: [*in black letter*:] Christmas 1937; p. [4] blank.

No wrappers; edges trimmed.

Issued December 1937; 150–200 copies printed. Not for sale.

(Lord Randall started up in's bed,). Unsigned. Printed privately for the author as a Christmas card. First published in the *Book Society Annual*, December 1937 (*see* C1661).

First edition:

[*title on p.* [*1*]:] THE | HURRYING | BROOK

Royal 4to. [4] pp. 9¼ X 5⅞ in.

P. [1] title as above; p. [2] [*in Blunden's autograph*: Best wishes, 1938 | [*in Sylva Norman's autograph*: from Edmund & Sylva]; p. [3] text, [*signed in ink: Edmund Blunden*]; p. [4] blank.

No wrappers; top edges trimmed, fore and bottom edges untrimmed.

Issued December 1938; 150–200 copies printed. Not for sale.

(With half a hundred sudden loops and coils). Privately printed for the author as a Christmas card. Reprinted in *On Several Occasions*, 1939; *Poems 1930–1940*, [1941]; and *Poems of Many Years*, 1957 (*see* A67–8, 135).

a. First edition:

ON | SEVERAL | OCCASIONS | By | A Fellow of | Merton College

Royal 8vo. [vi, 32] leaves. 10¼ X 6½ in.

Leaves [i–ii] form paste-down and free end-papers; leaves [iii–v] blank; leaf [vi] title; leaves [1–27] text; leaf [28] 60 copies of these poems by Edmund Blunden have | been hand set in 18-pt. Corvinus light italic type and | printed on an Arnold and Foster hand-made paper. | All copies are numbered and signed by the Author. | 3 copies lettered 'A', 'B' and 'C', have been | reserved for the author and printer. 'A' has been | printed on a hand-made tissue made by Sweetapple | in 1827. 'B' and 'C' have been printed on a | hand-made straw paper watermarked GWP and | made about 1800. | This copy is number [*numbered in ink*] | [*signed: Edmund Blunden*] | Completed at the Corvinus Press during December, | 1938. Laus Deo.; leaves [29–30] blank; leaves [31–32] form free and paste-down end-papers.

Off-white cloth boards, with an overall pattern of small flowers and dots in navy-blue; navy-blue cloth spine, lettered in gold up the spine: *ON SEVERAL OCCASIONS*; top edges gilt, fore and bottom edges untrimmed; no end-papers.

Published April 1939; 60 copies printed. £1.15*s*.

Three lettered copies were issued for the author and printer (*see* A67*b*).

Contents: *all poems untitled* [In the Margin] — [The Hurrying Brook] — [Railway Note] — [The Dreamer] — [In West-Flanders] — [Beauty in the Mountain] — [Jim's Mistake] — [To W.O. and his Kind; i.e. Wilfred Owen] — [Victorians] — [The Scientists] — [I Just Noticed . . .] — [At My Writing Table] — [The Kind Star] — [The Hippodrome] — [Spring and Criticism] — [The Same Englishman] — [You Never Stay] — [To Our Catchment Board] — [untitled (Soon we shall know; and soon we shall not know)] — [Let Joe do it].

b. First edition — lettered issue. [*1939*] :

[*in rust:*] ON | SEVERAL | OCCASIONS | [*in black as above*]

Royal 8vo. [vi, 32] leaves. $11\frac{3}{4} \times 7\frac{7}{8}$ in.

Pale mottled brown leather boards; lettered in gold up the spine: [*raised band*] ON SEVERAL OCCASIONS BY A FELLOW OF MERTON COLLEGE [*raised band*]; gold rule round upper and lower covers, publisher's device of a bird in gold on upper cover, $1\frac{3}{4} \times 1\frac{3}{4}$ in.; top and bottom edges trimmed, fore edges rough trimmed; end-papers. Dull green slip case.

Issued April 1939; 3 copies bound. Not for sale.

Transcribed from copy 'B' which varies from *a* above: (a) title-page with lines 1–3 in rust; (b) page size $11\frac{3}{4} \times 7\frac{7}{8}$ in.; (c) collation: Leaves [i–ii] blank; leaf [iii] title; leaves [1–27] text; leaf [28] at centre: This copy has been printed for | EDMUND BLUNDEN | on a paper water-marked GWP and | made about 1800.; leaf [29] as leaf [28] above for lines 1–10 followed by: This is number [*lettered in ink: B*] [*signed: Edmund Blunden Carlow*], continues as leaf [28] above; leaves [30–32] blank; lower paste-down end-paper printed in gold at foot: BOUND BY S[angorski] & S[utcliffe] LONDON. Copies 'A' and 'C' have not been seen; they are in Lord Portarlington's collection. Copy B is in Sir Rupert Hart-Davis's.

a. First edition:

POEMS | 1930-1940 | *by* | EDMUND BLUNDEN | [*three line quotation*] | LONDON | MACMILLAN & CO. LTD | 1940

Demy 8vo. [2], xiv, 264 pp. $8\frac{1}{2} \times 5\frac{3}{8}$ in.

Pp. [1-2] blank; p. [i] half-title; p. [ii] blank; p. [iii] title; p. [iv] at centre: COPYRIGHT, at foot: PRINTED IN GREAT BRITAIN | BY R. & R. CLARK, LIMITED, EDINBURGH; p. [v] at centre, dedication: *Gratefully dedicated | to* | H. W. GARROD | A MASTER OF CRITICAL ENCOURAGEMENT; p. [vi] blank; pp. vii–viii Preface; pp. ix–xiv Contents; p. [1] section-title; p. [2] blank; p. [3] sub-section-title; p. [4] blank; pp. 5–26 text; p. [27] section-title; p. [28] blank; pp. 29–46 text; p. [47] section-title; p. [48] blank; pp. 49–82 text; p. [83] section-title; p. [84] blank; pp. 85–122 text; p. [123] section-title; p. [124] blank; pp. 125–180 text; p. [181] section-title; p. [182] blank; pp. 183–197 text; p. [198] blank; p. [199] section-title; p. [200] blank; pp. 201–221 text; p. [222] blank; p. [223] section-title; p. [224] blank; pp. 225–258 text; pp. 259–[264] Index of First Lines; p. [264] at foot: *Printed in Great Britain by* R. & R. CLARK, LIMITED, *Edinburgh*.

Green cloth boards; lettered in gold on spine: [*double rule, wavy rule, double rule across head*] | POEMS | 1930-1940 | [*double rule, wavy rule, double rule*] | EDMUND | BLUNDEN | MAC-MILLAN; edges trimmed, top green; white end-papers. Buff dust-jacket printed in green.

Published 21 January 1941; 2000 copies printed. 10*s. 6d.*

Five hundred copies in sheets were sent to The Macmillan Company, New York (*see* A68*b*).

Contents: *Halfway House*: A Summer's Fancy: A Summer's Fancy; *To Themis: Sketches of Trials*: Mr. Charles Defends Himself — The Deist — After the 'Forty-Five [*formerly* End of the Forty-Five] — Incident in Hyde Park, 1803 — The Atheist, 1817 [*formerly* The Atheist: Lord Eldon Thinks Over Shelley v. Westbrooke] — *Occasion and Mood*: Winter Stars — The Kiss — The Last Word [*formerly* The Memorial] — A Shadow by the Barn — The Rotunda [*formerly* In Summer] — Summer Hieroglyphs [*formerly* Apparitions in Summer] — An Aside — Constantia and Francis — The Ballast-Hole — Fancy and Memory — Mental Hospital [*formerly* Mental Hospital: I, Two in a Corner; II, Poor Tom's Welcome] — The Memorial, 1914–1918 — Inscribed in War-Books [*formerly* An Inscription i.e. War-Books II] — November 1, 1931 — The Recovery — Another Altar — A Calm Rain — Desire and Delight [*formerly* In Disappointment] — The Excellent Irony — On Some Crocuses [sub-title omitted] — Argument in Spring — Verses in Reminiscence and Delight —

A Night-Piece — To the Cicada — 'Suitable Advice' — Epitaph for Sophocles — The Dog from Malta — A Tale Not in Chaucer — An Ancient, but Jubilant Ballad, 1696 — *Choice and Chance*: To Sylva — Full Bloom — Spirit — Wind [*formerly* The Unexpected Victory] — The Hill — Grown Up — Into the Distance — Long Moments — The Surprise — Afternoon in Japan [*formerly* Somewhere East] — The Cottage at Chigasaki — South Atlantic — Reflections — The Toad — Lark Descending — 'Sentimental' — Anonymous Donors — Fur Coat — Theology over the Gate — Unlucky Allusions —A Thought of the Downs — A Prologue [*later* The Country Round Christ's Hospital] — The Branch Line — Housing Question [*formerly* Housing Questions] — Some Talk of Peace — The Lost Battalion — From Age to Age [*formerly* The Only Answer] — To the Southdowns on their dining again together, 1934 — At Rugmer — Experience Teaches — Stormy Night [*formerly* The Voice of the Past] — Carfax — A Nature — To One Long Dead — A Touchstone [*formerly* Think of Shelley] — Country Conversation — In a Library — An Ominous Victorian [*formerly* An Eminent Victorian] — To Dr. I. Lettsom — Arcadian Law; A Notice in Cheltenham — The March of Mind — Oriental Tale [*formerly* Thoughts on Books] — Fable — *An Elegy, and Other Poems*: Elegy [*later* An Elegy; and Elegy on His Majesty King George V] — Past and Present: A Hymn — A Second Hymn [*formerly* Past and Present: A Second Hymn] — Woe to Drunkards — The Subtle Calm — A City on a Hill — The Spell of France — Late Light — Personal Survivals — Writing a Sketch of a Forgotten Poet — At Christ Church, Greyfriars [*formerly* Lines to Charles Lamb] — Near Sunset — The Ambush — Poetry's Invitation [*formerly* Invitation] — And Then — From the Branch Line — 'A Musique, Soldier' — In My Time — Cabaret Tune — Town End [*formerly* Uneasy Quiet] — An International Football Match — Minority Report — Anti-Basilisk — Fresh Thoughts on an Old Poem — Present Discontents — The Spire — 'Can You Remember?' — Rue des Berceaux — Nights Before Battle — Nearing the Ancre Battlefield 1916 — Marching Back to Peace 1916 — On a Picture by Dürer — Monts de Flandre — The Inaccessible House — Recurrence — Tell Your Fortune — Not So Dead — A Tune — Winter Ending — Pasture — In Berkshire — Village Sketch — Market Town — Cricket, I Confess — Lonely Love — Looking Eastward [*formerly* A Song] — Sixpence to the River — Departed [*sub-title omitted*] — Chaffinch [*subtitle omitted*] — Ask Old Japhet — Waiting the Word — Stanzas: Midsummer, 1937 — *Later Poems*: In West Flanders — Weserland, 1939 [*formerly* Weserland] — The Dreamer — Chance Pleasures — Beauty in the Mountain — The Kind Star — To J.A. [i.e. Joan Appleton] — After a Masque — Godstow — Country Characters — A Window in Germany — You Never Stay — To Sylva on the Mountainside — London: A December Memory — At Warnham — *Échoes from the Great War*: In May 1916: Near Richbourg St. Vaast — Rhymes on Bethune, 1916 — Near Albert-sur-Ancre, 1916 — The Camp in the Wood — To a Nature-Lover [*formerly* Echoes from 1914–18] —

70

Ruins — Farm Behind Battle Zone — Company Commander, 1917 —
War Cemetery — In the Margin — To W. O. and his Kind [i.e. Wil-
fred Owen] — Exorcized — To the Southdowns: At the Yearly
Reunion, 1939 — War Talk: Winter 1938 — The Same Englishmen
— By the Belgian Frontier [later Dikkebusch] — Varia: These Prob-
lems — About These Germans — A Recollection in a Far Year [for-
merly Some Said . . .] — Railway Note — Development — To Our
Catchment Board — A Chronomachy [formerly Chronomachy or
One of Us Is Not Tired Yet] — Strolling Players — The Hippodrome
— The Scientists — At My Writing Table — Spring and Criticism —
The Winners — Let Joe Do It — Jim's Mistake — 'Age Zoo' — Serious
Call [formerly Sam'l Pepys: His Plaint . . .] — Freddy Flail Proves
his Point — Village Song — In Childhood — The Hurrying Brook —
Horse and Cows — After Any Occasion — A Pastoral to Madeline —
Victorians — To the Earl of Surrey — In Memoriam, A.R.-I. [i.e.
Arthur Rose-Innes] — I Just Noticed — A Not Unusual Case — To a
Friend — A Change — The Sum of All.

b. First edition — American issue. 1940 [i.e. 1941] :

[*title as above*; *imprint*:] NEW YORK | THE MACMILLAN
COMPANY | 1940

Demy 8vo. [2] , xiv, 264 pp. $8\frac{1}{2} \times 5\frac{1}{2}$ in.

Pale dull green cloth boards; lettered in gold on spine: POEMS |
1930- | 1940 | Edmund | Blunden | MACMILLAN | [*short rule*] ;
edges trimmed; white end-papers.

Issued probably Spring 1941; 500 copies bound. $2.50.

The sheets were supplied by Macmillan, London.

A69   ENGLISH VILLAGES   1941

a. First edition:

ENGLISH VILLAGES | [*swelled rule*] | EDMUND BLUN-
DEN | [*short swelled rule*] | *WITH* | *12 PLATES IN*
COLOUR | *AND* | *25 ILLUSTRATIONS IN* | *BLACK &*
WHITE | [*publisher's device of a colonnade*, $\frac{7}{8} \times 1\frac{1}{4}$ *in*.] |
WILLIAM COLLINS OF LONDON | MCMXXXXI

Foolscap 4to. 48 pp. 12 plates (col.) between pp. 8-9, 12-13, 20-
21, 24-25, 32-33, 40-41, and 24 illus. and map. $8\frac{3}{4} \times 6\frac{1}{4}$ in.

P. [1] half-title; p. [2] at head: GENERAL EDITOR | W. J. TUR-
NER | [*ornament*] , at foot, Editor's acknowledgements; p. [3]

71

title; p. [4] at head: PRODUCED BY | ADPRINT LIMITED LON-
DON | [*ornament*] | PRINTED | IN GREAT BRITAIN BY | WM.
COLLINS SONS AND CO. LTD. GLASGOW; pp. [5–6] List of Illustrations; pp. 7–18 text; p. [19] illustration; pp. 20–29 text; p.
[30] illustration; pp. 31–41 text; p. [42] illustration; pp. 43–[48]
text.

White paper boards printed in yellow ochre; lettered in white up the
spine: [*triple rule across foot*] EDMUND BLUNDEN — ENGLISH
VILLAGES [*triple rule across head*] , and on upper cover: [*within
a triple rule*:] ENGLISH | VILLAGES | [*illustration of an inn sign,
$3\frac{1}{4}$ X $4\frac{1}{4}$ in.*] | EDMUND BLUNDEN; triple rule in white round
lower cover; edges trimmed; white end-papers. Cream matching
dust-jacket.

Published September 1941; no record of the number of copies printed. 3s. 6d.

The publishers note that sales amounted to 'many, many thousands'.
The essay was reprinted in *The Englishman's Country*, edited by
W. J. Turner (*see* B113).

b. First edition — American issue. 1941:

[*title as above*;*imprint*:] Hastings House, New York, 1941*

4to. 48 pp.

Issued late 1941; number of copies bound not ascertained. $1.25.

A70   [HARDY OF WESSEX]   1941

First separate publication:

[*title at head of leaf* [1]:] Hardy of Wessex. His Life and
Literary Career. By CARL J. | WEBER [*publisher's im-
print, pagination, and price*]

Medium 8vo. An offprint of [4] leaves. $8\frac{3}{4}$ X $5\frac{3}{4}$ in.

Leaves [1–4] numbered [368]–371 text.

No wrappers; edges trimmed.

Issued probably September 1941; no record of the number of copies
printed. Not for sale.

Review of *Hardy of Wessex: His Life and Literary Career*, by Carl J.
Weber. Reprinted from the *Review of English Studies*, July 1941
(*see* C1871). *See also* A172.

First separate edition:

[*title at head of leaf*: *in brown*:] THE TWO BOOKS | A
NEW POEM by EDMUND BLUNDEN

Crown 8vo. [1] leaf. $7\frac{1}{4} \times 4\frac{7}{8}$ in.

Leaf [1] text; at foot: CHRISTMAS, 1941.

No wrappers; edges trimmed.

Issued December 1941; 150–200 copies printed. Not for sale.

(Come, tell me: of these two books lying here,). Privately printed by
the author as a Christmas card. First published in the *Book Society
Annual*, December 1941; and reprinted in *Shells by a Stream*, 1944;
and *Poems of Many Years*, 1957 (*see* A77, 135; C1896).

A72   **THOMAS HARDY**   1941 [i.e. 1942]

a. First edition:

THOMAS HARDY | BY | EDMUND BLUNDEN | [*twelve
line quotation*] | MACMILLAN AND CO., LIMITED |
ST. MARTIN'S STREET, LONDON | 1941

Crown 8vo. x, 286 pp. $7\frac{3}{8} \times 5$ in.

P. [i] half-title; p. [ii] work by the author listed; p. [iii] title; p.
[iv] at centre: COPYRIGHT, at foot: PRINTED IN GREAT BRI-
TAIN | BY R. & R. CLARK, LIMITED, EDINBURGH; p. [v] at
centre, dedication: TO | SIEGFRIED SASSOON | REMEMBERING
OTHER DAYS | IN THE HOMES OF | WILLIAM BARNES AND
THOMAS HARDY; p. [vi] blank; pp. vii–[v]iii Preface; p. ix Contents; p. [x] blank; pp. 1–280 text; pp. 281–286 Index; p. 286 at
foot, printer's imprint.

Claret cloth boards; lettered in gold on spine: [*rule across head*]
THOMAS | HARDY | [*ornament*] | EDMUND | BLUNDEN |
MACMILLAN | [*rule across foot*] ; rule in blind round upper cover;
top edges claret, fore and bottom edges rough trimmed; white end-
papers.

Published 17 February 1942 in the *English Men of Letters* series;
2280 copies printed. 7*s.* 6*d.*

Copies in sheets were sent to Macmillan, New York (*see* A72*b*).
There was a reprint of 2020 copies in September 1942. The next
four reprints were issued at 5*s.* in *Macmillan's Pocket Library* in
sky-blue cloth boards; lettered in gold on spine with three sets of
triple rules; blind rule round upper cover; series device in blind on
upper cover; 2012 copies in July 1951, 1000 copies in 1954, 1040

copies in 1958, and 2012 copies in 1960. The seventh reprint of 10,000 copies was issued in 1967 at 8*s.* 6*d.* as *Papermac*, Vol. 183 in white pictorial paper wrappers printed in black, scarlet and yellow; 1150 bound copies were sent to St Martin's Press, New York (*see* A72*c*).

b. First edition — American issue. 1942:

[*title as above*; *imprint*:] The Macmillan Company, New York, 1942*

Crown 8vo. x, 286 pp.

Issued 1942; no record of the number of copies bound. $2.

The sheets were supplied by Macmillan, London. Copies in sheets were probably also supplied in 1952 and issued in the *Pocket Library* at $1.35.

c. First edition — seventh reprint — American issue. 1967:

[*title as above*; *imprint*:] St. Martin's Press, New York, 1967*

Crown 8vo. x, 286 pp.

Issued 2 October 1967; 500 copies bound.

The sheets were supplied by Macmillan, London. A further 650 copies in sheets were supplied during 1968–1969.

A73   VERSES IN MEMORY OF   1942
CATHERINE MACKENZIE HARDIE

First edition:

[*title at head of leaf*:] Verses | in memory of | Catherine MacKenzie Hardie

Foolscap 4to. [1] leaf. $8\frac{1}{2} \times 6\frac{1}{2}$ in.

Leaf [1] text.

No wrappers; edges trimmed.

Issued April 1942; 40 copies printed. Not for sale.

(To live in quietness, yet be the clear). Holograph facsimile. Privately printed for the author by Alden, Oxford. Also recorded on the grave of Mrs Catherine MacKenzie Hardie at Forfar cemetery, Angus.

First separate publication:

[*title at the head of p.* [1]:] LEIGH HUNT'S ELDEST SON. | BY PROFESSOR EDMUND BLUNDEN, F.R.S.L. | [Read October 29th, 1941.]

Small demy 8vo. An offprint of [24] pp. $8\frac{1}{2} \times 5\frac{1}{2}$ in.

Pp. [1-23] numbered [53]-75 text; p. [24] blank.

No wrappers; edges trimmed; stapled and gummed.

Issued probably May 1942; no record of the number of copies printed. Not for sale.

On Thornton Hunt. Read before the Royal Society of Literature on 29 October 1941. Reprinted from *Essays by Divers Hands*, 1942 (*see* C1898).

A75   ROMANTIC POETRY AND   1942
                    THE FINE ARTS

First separate publication:

ROMANTIC POETRY | AND | THE FINE ARTS | by | EDMUND BLUNDEN | WARTON LECTURE | ON ENGLISH POETRY | BRITISH ACADEMY | 1942 | FROM THE PROCEEDINGS OF THE | BRITISH ACA-DEMY. VOLUME XXVIII | LONDON : HUMPHREY MILFORD | AMEN HOUSE, E.C.

Small royal 8vo. 20 pp. $9\frac{7}{8} \times 6\frac{1}{4}$ in.

P. [1] title; p. [2] at foot: PRINTED IN GREAT BRITAIN; pp. 3-20 text; p. 20 at foot: PRINTED IN GREAT BRITAIN AT THE UNIVERSITY PRESS, OXFORD | BY JOHN JOHNSON, PRINTER TO THE UNIVERSITY.

Pale grey paper wrappers; printed on upper wrapper: [*as title above with the addition of:*] Price 1s. 6d. net [*following line nine*] ; list of Warton Lectures on English Poetry on lower wrapper, verso; edges cut flush; sewn.

Issued October 1942 as *Warton Lecture on English Poetry*, No. 33; 508 copies printed. 1s. 6d.

Reprinted from *Proceedings of the British Academy*, 1942 (*see* C1899).

First edition:

CRICKET COUNTRY | *by* | EDMUND BLUNDEN |
[*publisher's device of a fountain*, $\frac{3}{4}$ × $\frac{3}{4}$ *in.*] | COLLINS |
48 PALL MALL LONDON | 1944

Crown 8vo. 224 pp. $7\frac{1}{2}$ × 5 in.

P. [1] half-title; p. [2] list of works by the author; p. [3] title; p.
[4] at centre, dedication: TO | F. W. WAGNER | IN GRATITUDE
FOR OUR | MANY TALKS, at foot: COPYRIGHT | PRINTED IN
GREAT BRITAIN | COLLINS CLEAR-TYPE PRESS : LONDON
AND GLASGOW | 1944; pp. 5–8 Preface; p. 9 Contents; p. [10]
blank; pp. 11–224 text.

Brownish-orange cloth boards; lettered in gold on spine: CRICKET |
COUNTRY | Edmund | Blunden | COLLINS; top and fore edges
trimmed, bottom edges rough trimmed; cream end-papers. White
pictorial dust-jacket printed in green, grey, brown, dull yellow and
black.

Published 27 April 1944; no record of the number of copies printed. 8*s*. 6*d*.

The publishers note the book 'was a big seller'. The Reprint Society,
London issued a reprint in 1945 in dark green cloth boards; lettered
in gold on a black panel on spine; edges trimmed, top yellow; white
end-papers. Collins issued a reprint of 6000 copies at 6*s*. as *St
James's Library*, Vol. 13 on 5 March 1951 in royal-blue cloth
boards; lettered in gold on spine with ornament and two double
rules; top and fore edges trimmed, top royal-blue, bottom edges
rough trimmed; white end-papers; grey dust-jacket printed in black
and peacock blue.

The poem A CRICKET ADVICE appeared on pp. 179–180, and was
reprinted with a Latin translation in *Versions and Diversions*, 1964
(*see* D41). *An Index to "Cricket Country"*, compiled by J. N. Goldsmith, [i], 9 leaves (typescript), 1944, records under 'Anonymous,
E. Blunden' reference to information communicated by the author.
A copy is in the British Library.

A77 **SHELLS BY A STREAM** 1944

a. First edition:

SHELLS BY | A STREAM | *New Poems* | *by* | EDMUND
BLUNDEN | LONDON | MACMILLAN & CO. LTD |
1944

Perhaps my dear Rupert you would like
a note here of the geography of some of these
pieces. The title-poem comes from the meadows
by the Beult at Yalding; and the stream in the next
piece is that which sneaks along from Marston into
the Cherwell. "What is Winter?" occurred on looking
out of F. H. Bradley's old rooms with the oriel windows at
Merton. "A Patrol" was made by Claire and me round
the park boundaries at Thame. In "The Gift" memory
returned to Cheveney on the Beult; the slaughtered tree
in "Timber" was seen at Toyford on the Medway. (It
looks as though there are usually rivers in the author's
system.)   "A Prospect of Swans" was found near the
gasworks on the Thames past Folly Bridge.
    The church intended to be characterized next is at
Kirtling, Suffolk, where the child Joy is buried; the
neglected lake on p. 15 and the nameless stream are near
Osmaston in Derbyshire, where too at Markeaton Claire
admired the roses. The imagined scene of "Thomasine"
was called up from 30 years ago at Heaven's Mill, Framfield
in Sussex, but "The Winter Walk" is Port Meadow, Oxford;
and the other little walk is in Squitchey Lane near there.
Lastly we come to the cathedral at Derby.
    Maybe each Bard should be compelled by act
of parliament to express his acknowledgements to
the Parishes which have supplied his scenery.
    Wishing you a golden age among English poems
and parishes after all these war years,
                                    Ever your affect⁻ᵉ friend
                                            Edmund

Oct. 20, 1945.

10. Topographical inscription in *Shells by a Stream* (A77)

Demy 8vo. viii, 60 pp. $8\frac{1}{2} \times 5\frac{1}{2}$ in.

P. [i] half-title; p. [ii] works by the author listed; p. [iii] title; p. [iv] at centre: COPYRIGHT, at foot: PRINTED IN GREAT BRI-TAIN | BY R. & R. CLARK, LIMITED, EDINBURGH; p. [v] at centre, dedication: *To* | CLAIRE. | WITH DEVOTION; p. [vi] blank; pp. vii-viii Contents; pp. 1-[60] text; p. [60] at foot: *Printed in Great Britain by* R. & R. CLARK, LIMITED, *Edinburgh.*

Bright green cloth boards; lettered in gold down the spine: SHELLS BY A STREAM [*ornament*] EDMUND BLUNDEN MACMILLAN, and on upper cover: SHELLS | BY A [*ornament*] | STREAM | EDMUND | BLUNDEN; edges trimmed; cream end-papers. Cream dust-jacket printed in navy-blue.

Published 27 October 1944; 4000 copies printed. 5s.

There was a reprint of *c.* 2000 copies in early 1945. Copies in sheets were sent to Macmillan, New York (*see* A77b).

Contents: The Home of Poetry — Shells by a Stream — October Comes — What is Winter? [*formerly* A Day in December] — A Patrol — The Gift: For C.M.P. [i.e. Claire M. Poynting] — Timber — To Teise, a Stream in Kent — Triumph of Autumn [*formerly* To Autumn] — For the Country Life [*formerly* The Means] — A Prospect of Swans — A Church — On a Journey, 1943 — The Ornamental Water — The Nameless Stream — A Country Character: *Homo Unius Libri* — Dovedale on a Spring Day — Thoughts of Thomas Hardy — Gibbon: In the Margin [*formerly* Man Grown Safe] — To the Memory of Coleridge — Lascelles Abercrombie [*formerly* L.A.] — One Kind of Artist — The Two Books — The Florilegium — A Painted Window: Stored Underground for the Period of War — Travellers, 193– [*formerly* Travellers — 1938] — A Remembrance — Octogenarian — Alumnus in Luck (1940) — Morning in March 1943 — The Vanishing Land — The Unfortunate Shipmate — Tigranes (*Suggested by Bacon's Essay, "Of the True Greatnesse of Kingdome and Estates"*) — The Man in the Street — Nature and the Lost — The Lost Name — Aircraft — The Boy on Leave — The Victor — Lovelight — The Fine Nature — Fulfilment — The Flowers — The Waterfall [*formerly* A Song] — The Happiest — Time Together — Among All These — Claire's Birthday in 1940 — The Spring Gale — One Among the Roses [*formerly* Among the Roses] — Thomasine — The Winter Walk — God's Time — At a Cathedral Service.

b. First edition — American issue. 1945:

[*title as above*; *imprint*:] The Macmillan Company, New York, 1945*

Demy 8vo. viii, 60 pp.

Issued early 1945; no record of the number of copies bound. $1.75.

The sheets were supplied by Macmillan, London.

a. First edition:

SHELLEY | A Life Story | *by* | EDMUND BLUNDEN |
[*publisher's device of a fountain,* $\frac{3}{4}$ × $\frac{3}{4}$ *in.*] | [*nine line
quotation*] | COLLINS ST. JAMES'S PLACE LONDON

Demy 8vo. 320 pp. front. (port.). $8\frac{1}{2}$ × $5\frac{1}{4}$ in.

P. [1] half-title; p. [2] list of works by the author; p. [3] title; p.
[4] towards head, dedication: *Inscribed* | TO MY CLAIRE, at foot:
COPYRIGHT | PRINTED IN GREAT BRITAIN | COLLINS
CLEAR-TYPE PRESS : LONDON AND GLASGOW | 1946; p. 5
Contents; p. [6] blank; pp. 7–9 Preface; p. [10] blank; pp. 11–315
text; pp. 316–320 Index.

Reddish-brown cloth boards; lettered in gold on spine: SHELLEY |
Edmund | Blunden | COLLINS; top and fore edges trimmed, bottom
edges untrimmed; cream end-papers. White dust-jacket printed in
pale blue and black, with portrait of Shelley on upper jacket.

Published 29 April 1946; no record of the number of copies printed.
12*s.* 6*d.*

The Readers Union issued a reprint in 1948 in bright yellow cloth
boards; lettered in green down the spine with two long rules, and
oval device at foot; edges trimmed; white end-papers. The chapter
'Geneva' was reprinted as 'Shelley and Byron at Geneva' in *Profiles
from Notable Biographies*, introduced by Leonard Gribble, London,
Sampson Low, Marston, [1946], pp. [145]–157. *See also* A80;
C2418.

Blunden wrote the description of the book in *Collins Autumn Book
List*, 1945, p. 4.

b. First American edition. 1947:

Shelley | A LIFE STORY | BY EDMUND BLUNDEN |
[*nine line quotation*] | 1947 | NEW YORK • THE VIKING
PRESS

Demy 8vo. xii, 388 pp. $8\frac{1}{4}$ × $5\frac{1}{2}$ in.

P. [i] half-title; p. [ii] blank; p. [iii] title; p. [iv] towards head:
COPYRIGHT, 1946, 1947, BY EDMUND BLUNDEN | PUBLISHED
BY THE VIKING PRESS IN JANUARY 1947, at foot: PRINTED
IN U.S.A. | BY VAIL-BALLOU PRESS, INC., BINGHAMTON,
N.Y.; p. [v] dedication; p. [vi] blank; pp. vii–viii Contents; pp. ix–
xii Preface; p. [1] fly-title; p. [2] blank; pp. 3–368 text; p. [369]
section-title: Appendix: Some Shelleyana; p. [370] blank; pp.
371–379 text; p. [380] blank; p. [381] section-title; p. [382]
blank; pp. 383–388 Index.

Pale blue cloth boards; lettered in navy-blue on spine: EDMUND |
BLUNDEN | [*device of a bird*] | Shelley | VIKING, and on upper
cover: [*device of a bird*] | Shelley; edges trimmed, top pink; white
end-papers.
Published 6 January 1947; 6500 copies printed. $3.75.
Pp. 371–379 'Some Shelleyana' are not included in the English editions.

c. Second English edition. 1965:

[*title as above*; *imprint*:] LONDON | OXFORD UNIVER-
SITY PRESS | NEW YORK TORONTO | 1965

Crown 8vo. x, 310 pp. $7\frac{3}{4} \times 5$ in.
Pink pictorial paper wrappers printed in black and white; Curran
portrait of Shelley on upper cover; edges cut flush; gummed.
Published 17 June 1965 as *Oxford Paperbacks*, No. 95; 7600 copies
printed. 12*s*. 6*d*.
The last two sentences of the Preface are omitted.

A79   THE MAKING OF A NOVELIST   1946

First separate publication:

[*title at head of leaf*:] THE MAKING OF A NOVELIST
[1] leaf. $25 \times 9\frac{1}{4}$ in.
Leaf [1] text.
No wrappers; edges trimmed.
Issued *c*. 29 June 1946; 7 copies printed. Not for sale.
Review of *The Letters and Private Papers of William Makepeace
Thackeray*, Vols. 1–2, edited by Gordon N. Ray. Unsigned. Reprin-
ted from the *TLS*, 29 June 1946 (*see* C2247).

A80   HARRIET SHELLEY   1946

First separate publication:

[*title at head of leaf*:] *Letters to the Editor* | HARRIET
SHELLEY
An offprint of [1] leaf. $14 \times 4\frac{7}{8}$ in.
Leaf [1] text.

No wrappers; edges trimmed.

Issued *c.* 13 July 1946; 12 copies printed. Not for sale.

Letter to the Editor of the *TLS*, signed E. Blunden. Reprinted from the *TLS*, 13 July 1946 (*see* C2257). *See also* A78.

A81   MILTON REGAINED   1946

First separate publication:

[*title at head of leaf:*] THE TIMES LITERARY SUPPLE-MENT SATURDAY AUGUST 17 1946 | MILTON RE-GAINED

An offprint of [1] leaf. 25 × $9\frac{1}{4}$ in.

Leaf [1] text.

No wrappers; edges trimmed.

Issued *c.* 17 August 1946; 12 copies printed. Not for sale.

Review of *Paradise Lost in Our Time: Some Comments*, by Douglas Bush; *John Milton's Complete Poetical Works*, compiled and edited by Harris Francis Fletcher. Unsigned. Reprinted from the *TLS*, 17 August 1946 (*see* C2272).

A82   BOOK FORGERIES   1946

First separate publication:

[*title at head of leaf:*] BOOK FORGERIES: "AN EN-QUIRY" RE-READ | By EDMUND BLUNDEN

An offprint of [1] leaf. $10\frac{5}{8}$ × $9\frac{5}{8}$ in.

Leaf [1] text.

No wrappers; edged trimmed.

Issued *c.* 28 September 1946; 12 copies printed. Not for sale.

On the forgeries by T. J. Wise. Reprinted from the *TLS*, 28 September 1946 (*see* C2284).

A83   THE LAST ENGLISH SOCIALIST?   1948

First separate publication:

[*title at head of leaf:*] 232 THE TIMES LITERARY

SUPPLEMENT SATURDAY APRIL 24 1948 | THE LAST
ENGLISH SOCIALIST?

An offprint of [1] leaf. $18\frac{3}{8} \times 15\frac{3}{8}$ in.

Leaf [1] text.

No wrappers; edges trimmed.

Issued *c.* 24 April 1948; probably 12 copies printed. Not for sale.

Review of *On Art and Socialism: Essays and Lectures*, by William
Morris, selected with an introduction by Holbrook Jackson; *Portrait
of William Morris*, by Esther Meynell; and *Warrior Bard: The Life of
William Morris*, by Edward and Stephani Godwin. Unsigned. Reprinted from the *TLS*, 24 April 1948 (*see* C2428).

A84   SHAKESPEARE TO HARDY   1948

First edition:

SHAKESPEARE TO HARDY | Short Studies of Charac-
teristic | English Authors | *Given in a Series of Lectures* |
at Tokyo University by | EDMUND BLUNDEN | TOKYO
| KENKYUSHA | 1948

Demy 8vo. x, 216 pp. front. (port.). $8\frac{1}{4} \times 5\frac{7}{8}$ in.

P. [i] half-title; p. [ii] blank; p. [iii] title; p. [iv] blank; p. [v]
towards centre, dedication: DEDICATED TO | THE SUCCESSORS
OF | SANKI ICHIKAWA AND TAKESHI SAITO· | AND THEIR
STUDENTS; p. [vi] blank; pp. [vii]–viii Preface; p. [ix] Contents;
p. [x] blank; pp. [1]–212 text; pp. [213–214] blank; p. [215] publisher's imprint, in Japanese; p. [216] blank.

Paper boards marbled in blue and grey; white paper spine; lettered in
gold on spine: SHAKE- | SPEARE | TO | HARDY | EDMUND |
BLUNDEN | KENKYUSHA; edges trimmed; off-white end-papers.
Buff dust-jacket printed in brown.

Published 1 September 1948; 500 copies printed. 250 yen.

There were reprints of 500 copies in August 1949, November 1950,
August 1952, late 1952, May 1955, May 1956, June 1958, July
1959, June 1962, May 1964, February 1966, January 1967, May
1969, and September 1970.

Contents: Shakespeare to Hardy: I, William Shakespeare — II, Fran-
cis Bacon — III, John Milton — IV, Thomas Gray — V, William
Wordsworth — VI, Samuel Taylor Coleridge — VII, Charles Lamb —
VIII, Thomas Love Peacock — IX, Percy Bysshe Shelley — X, John
Keats — XI, Charles Dickens — XII, Thomas Hardy — Portrait of
Shakespeare.

First edition:

EDMUND BLUNDEN | TWO LECTURES | ON | ENGLISH
LITERATURE | [*following five lines in Japanese*:]
Edomando Buranden | EIBUNGAKU NO SHURYÛ | ABE
TOMOJI | OGAMI MASAJA | YAKU | OSAKA KYOIKU
TOSHO CO. LTD. | 1948

Crown 8vo. 98 pp. illus. (port.) on p. [3]. $7\frac{1}{4}$ × 5 in.

P. [1] title; p. [2] blank; p. [3] portrait of the author with autograph facsimile of signature; p. [4] blank; pp. [5–9] text of four
poems in holograph facsimile; p. [10] at foot, in Japanese, note on
portrait and the poems; pp. [11]–15 Preface, in Japanese; p. [16]
Contents; p. [17] section-title; p. [18] blank; pp. 19–54 text; p.
[55] section-title; p. [56] blank; pp. [57]–74 Japanese translation
of 'The Growth of English Literature' by Tomoji Abe, with notes;
pp. [75]–96 Japanese translation of 'Contemporary Writing' by
Masaja Ogami, with notes; p. [97] publisher's imprint, in Japanese;
p. [98] blank.

Off-white pictorial wrappers, printed in black, rust, yellow and
green; edges trimmed; off-white end-papers; sewn and gummed.

Published 30 October 1948; number of copies printed not ascertained. 60 yen.

Contents: OSAKA IN RECONSTRUCTION — THE TOURIST
(NEAR KOMORO) — VOICES IN TOKYO — WILLIAM ADAMS AT
ITO [*later* TO THE CITIZENS OF ITO] — The Growth of English
Literature — Contemporary Writing.

First edition:

[*title at head of leaf*:] MATSUSHIMA. | [*illustration of
the islands on both sides of poem*]

Foolscap 8vo. [1] leaf. $3\frac{5}{8}$ × $6\frac{3}{4}$ in.

Leaf [1] text; at foot; Christmas Greetings | 1948 Tokyo
No wrappers; edges trimmed.

Issued December 1948; 150–200 copies printed. Not for sale.

(Melodious is that name Matsushima;). Unsigned. Privately printed
for the author as a Christmas card. Reprinted in *Eastward*, [1950];
The Shikai, October 1950, and *Contemporary Verse*, 1955 (*see* A97;
B178; C2563; D8).

First edition:

[*title on p.* [1]:] 1. They Died Young | 2. Poetry And Science | Edmund Blunden | Manuscript of Lectures given at Kyusha Gakuin | on February 18, 1949.

Oblong crown 4to. [ii, 14] pp. portrait. $10\frac{1}{8} \times 7\frac{1}{4}$ in.

P. [i] title; p. [ii] portrait of the author and his wife; pp. 1-6 text; pp. [7-12] numbered 1-6 text; pp. [13-14] blank. Errata slip inserted.

No wrappers; edges trimmed; stapled; tissue guard between pp. 6-[7].

Issued 1949; probably 200 copies printed. Not for sale.

Unauthorised publication for the use of students. 'Poetry and Science' was reprinted in *Poetry and Science and Other Lectures*, 1949 (*see* A93).

Contents: They Died Young — Poetry and Science.

A88 **THE MUSICAL MISCELLANY** **1949**

First separate publication:

[*title on upper wrapper*:] THE MUSICAL MISCELLANY | *A Fragmentary Appreciation* | *with Some Selections* | By | EDMUND BLUNDEN | (Reproduced from *The Rising Generation*, Vol. XCV. — No. 7.) | TOKYO | KENKYUSHA | 1949

Imperial 8vo. An offprint of [12] pp. $10\frac{1}{8} \times 7\frac{1}{8}$ in.

P. [i] half-title; p. [ii] blank; pp. 1-10 text.

Cream paper wrappers; printed in black on upper wrapper as above; edges cut flush; stapled.

Issued July 1949; no record of the number of copies printed. Not for sale.

Reprinted from the *Rising Generation*, 1 July 1949 (*see* C2470).

A89 **AFTER THE BOMBING** **1949**

a. First edition:

AFTER | THE BOMBING | *and other short poems* | BY | EDMUND BLUNDEN | LONDON | MACMILLAN & CO. LTD | 1949

Demy 8vo. viii, 56 pp. $8\frac{1}{4} \times 5\frac{1}{2}$ in.

P. [i] half-title; p. [ii] list of works by the author; p. [iii] title; p. [iv] at centre: COPYRIGHT, at foot: PRINTED IN GREAT BRITAIN; p. [v] at centre, dedication: To | A. D. PETERS | in gratitude for a friendship of many | years, this later collection of verses is | dedicated; p. [vii] blank; pp. vii–viii Contents; pp. 1–[51] text; p. [52] at centre: PRINTED BY R. & R. CLARK, LTD., EDINBURGH; pp. [53–56] blank.

Crimson cloth boards; lettered in gold on spine: AFTER | THE | BOMBING | ○ | EDMUND | BLUNDEN | MACMILLAN; edges trimmed; white end-papers. Cream dust-jacket printed in crimson and pale blue.

Published 14 October 1949; 3000 copies printed. 6s.

Copies in sheets were sent to Macmillan, New York (see A89b).

Contents: Half a Century — Nature's Beauty: During a Crisis of War — Nature's Adornings [formerly Nature's Daring] — Butterfly Dance — Flowers Walking — The Boy on the Waggon — Station Road — The Tree in the Goods Yard — The Ivy Bush in Autumn [formerly The Ivy Bush] — The Blackthorn Bush in Spring — Farm Bailiff [with Part II added] — Two Small Elegies: (i) The Hedgehog killed on the Road; (ii) The Snail — A Prayer for the Birds — After the Bombing — Night-Sounds — To the New Japan [formerly Walking in Tokyo 1948] — Voices in Tokyo — From the Flying-Boat — "For the Fallen" — Joy and Margaret — Children Passing — The Halted Battalion [formerly The Halted Battalion: 1916] — Homes and Haunts — Byroniana: (i) Kirke White at Wilford; (ii) Newstead [formerly Newstead Abbey] — High Elms, Bracknell — At Mapledurham [formerly At Mapledurham in War-Time] — Buxted — On Reading a Magazine edited by Oscar Wilde — A Greek Deity: Inscribed to the Apollo Society — The Blueprint — To a Planner — Inter Arma — The Evil Hour — Invocation Written in Spring 1944 — Southern England in 1944 [formerly South-East England in 1944] — To the Memory of Viscount Carlow — The Portrait — Serena — The Dell — Harbour Sketch: Written in Absence — The Tower [revised] — Rival Feasts [formerly Rival Appetites] — Hammond, England: A Cricketer [formerly Hammond of England] — William Lily's Rules for Schoolboys [formerly Qui Mihi] — When the Statue Fell: A Grandfather's Tale.

b. First edition — American issue. 1949:

[title as above; imprint:] The Macmillan Company, New York*

Demy 8vo. viii, 52 pp.

Issued late 1949; no record of the number of copies bound. $1.25.

The sheets were supplied by Macmillan, London.

a. First separate edition:

[*title at head of leaf in holograph facsimile*:] A SONG FOR KWANSEI

Royal 4to. [1] leaf. $11\frac{1}{8} \times 8\frac{1}{8}$ in.

Leaf [1] text.

No wrappers; edges untrimmed.

Issued 14 October 1949; number of copies printed not ascertained. Not for sale.

(That we may both receive and give,). Holograph facsimile. Reprinted in *Sixtieth Anniversary Kwansei Gakuin University: The Diamond Jubilee*, 1949; and *Poems on Japan*, 1967 (*see* A171; B134).

b. Second separate edition. [*195-*] :

[*title at head of leaf*:] A SONG FOR KWANSEI

[1] leaf. $8\frac{3}{8} \times 6$ in.

Leaf [1] text in English and Japanese.

No wrappers; edges trimmed.

Issue date not ascertained.

Japanese translation by Bunshō Jugaku.

A91   ADDRESSES ON GENERAL SUBJECTS   1949

First edition:

ADDRESSES | on General Subjects | connected with English Literature | *Given at Tokyo University and* | *elsewhere in 1948 by* | EDMUND BLUNDEN | TOKYO | KENKYUSHA | 1949

Demy 8vo. viii, 320 pp. $8\frac{1}{2} \times 5\frac{3}{4}$ in.

P. [i] half-title; p. [ii] blank; p. [iii] title; p. [iv] blank; pp. v–vi Preface; p. [vii] Contents; p. [viii] blank; pp. 1–318 text; p. [319] publisher's imprint in Japanese; p. [320] blank.

Paper boards marbled in blue and grey; white paper spine; lettered in gold on spine: ADDRESSES | ON | GENERAL | SUBJECTS | EDMUND | BLUNDEN | KENKYUSHA; edges trimmed; pale biscuit end-papers. Buff dust-jacket printed in brown.

Published 30 October 1949; probably 500 copies printed. 350 yen.

There were reprints of 500 copies in August 1955, June 1958, June 1962, July 1964, May 1966, May 1969 and October 1969.

Contents: The Poets' Universe — Imagination and Society — Man and Nature — The Religious Side of the Romantic Movement — Goethe and the English Romantics — Poetry: Chaucer to Meredith — Fiction: Chaucer to Dickens — Criticism: Sidney to Arnold — Shorter Poems — Shakespeare Characters — Some English Characters — The English Mind — English Life — English Literature — English Poetry — Experience and Record.

A92   SONS OF LIGHT   1949

a. First edition:

[*first three words in open capitals:*] SONS OF LIGHT | A SERIES OF LECTURES | ON | ENGLISH WRITERS | BY | EDMUND BLUNDEN | THE HOSEI UNIVERSITY RRESS [*sic*] | 1949

Demy 8vo. viii, 144 pp. $8\frac{1}{8} \times 5\frac{3}{4}$ in.

P. [i] half-title; p. [ii] blank; p. [iii] title; p. [iv] blank; pp. [v]–vi Preface; p. [vii] Contents; p. [viii] blank; pp. [1]–136 text; pp. [137]–139 Postscript on Mr. Blunden and his Lectures in this Country, by Makoto Sangu; pp. [140]–142 Brief Record of Life and Works of Edmund Blunden; p. [143] publisher's imprint in Japanese; p. [144] blank.

Buff paper boards; white paper spine; off-white paper label on upper cover, $2\frac{3}{8} \times 3\frac{5}{8}$ in., printed in rust: [*within a rule:*] SONS OF LIGHT | A SERIES OF LECTURES | ON | ENGLISH WRITERS | BY | EDMUND BLUNDEN; edges trimmed; off-white end-papers. Transparent dust-jacket.

Published 25 November 1949; number of copies printed not ascertained. 180 yen.

There was a 'de-luxe edition' (*see* A92*b*).

Contents: Sir Philip Sidney — John Clare — Henry Vaughan — William Cowper — William Blake — Charles and Mary Lamb —Robert Bridges — Postscript: On Mr Blunden and his Lectures in this Country — Brief Record of Life and Works of Edmund Blunden.

b. First edition — de-luxe issue. 1949:

[*title and imprint as above*]

Demy 8vo. viii, 144 pp. front. (port.). $8\frac{1}{8} \times 5\frac{3}{4}$ in.

Grey paper boards; white paper spine; white paper label on spine, $2\frac{1}{4} \times \frac{5}{8}$ in., printed in black: [*double rule, thick, thin*] | SONS | OF | LIGHT | EDMUND | BLUNDEN | [*double rule, thin, thick*] ; edges trimmed; off-white end-papers.

Issued 25 November 1949; number of copies bound not ascertained. 300 yen.

P. [143] Publisher's imprint in Japanese pasted on.

A93   POETRY AND SCIENCE   1949

First edition:

[*in black letter*:] Contemporary English Series | [*in roman*:] [3] | POETRY AND SCIENCE | AND OTHER LECTURES | BY | EDMUND BLUNDEN | WITH INTRO-DUCTION AND NOTES | BY | K. ISHIDA | *Professor of Kyoto University* | OSAKA KYOIKU TOSHO CO. | 1949

Crown 8vo. [2] , [viii] , 160 pp. $7\frac{1}{8} \times 5$ in.

P. [1] title; p. [2] blank; pp. [1-2] tipped-in; p. [i] Preface by Blunden; p. [ii] blank; pp. [iii–v] numbered [i]–iii Introduction in Japanese; p. [vi] blank; p. [vii] Contents; p. [viii] blank; pp. [1]–105 text; p. [106] blank; pp. [107]–158 Notes in Japanese; p. [159] publisher's imprint in Japanese; p. [160] list of the volumes in the series.

Chocolate-brown paper boards; lettered in gold on spine: [*rule across head*] | POETRY | *and* | SCIENCE | [*rule*] ; publisher's name, in Japanese, in blind on lower cover; edges trimmed; off-white end-papers. Off-white dust-jacket printed in brown and black.

Published 30 November 1949; number of copies printed not ascertained. 100 yen.

Contents: Poetry and Science — Popularity in Literature — Shakespeare's Great Tragedies — The Growth of English Literature — Contemporary Writing.

A94   FROM THE JAPANESE INN WINDOW   1949

First edition:

[*title at head of leaf*:] From the Japanese Inn Window

[1] leaf. $4\frac{1}{8} \times 5$ in.

Leaf [1] text; at foot: With Christmas greetings and wishes. | Edmund and Claire Blunden. Tokyo. | 1949

No wrappers; edges trimmed.

Issued December 1949; probably 100 copies printed. Not for sale.

(Fierce came the snow — and is gone like a dream). Holograph facsimile. Privately printed for the author as a Christmas card. Reprinted as THE INN WINDOW, FUKUOKA in *Eastward*, [1950]; as FROM THE JAPANESE INN WINDOW in *Rising Generation*, 1 April 1950 and *Records of Friendship*, 1950 and as THE EARLY YEAR, FUKUOKA in *Contemporary Verse*, 1955 (*see* A97, 106; B178; C2513).

A95   SAKURAJIMA, A VOLCANO   1949

First edition:

[*title at head of leaf*:] SAKURAJIMA, A VOLCANO

[1] leaf. $4\frac{1}{8}$ × 5 in.

Leaf [1] text; at foot: — With greetings from Claire and Edmund | Blunden. Tokyo. Christmas 1949.

No wrappers; edges trimmed.

Issued December 1949; probably 100 copies printed. Not for sale.

(Before us, the stone basin and its fountain.). Holograph facsimile. Privately printed for the author as a Christmas card. Reprinted as THE VOLCANO in *The Spectator*, 6 January 1950; and as SAKURAJIMA, A VOLCANO in *Records of Friendship*, 1950 (*see* A106; C2494).

A96   HAMLET, AND OTHER STUDIES   1950

First edition:

[*title on plate, recto*: *within a rule*:] Hamlet, and Other Studies | *by* | *Edmund Blunden* | Notes by S. Tomiyama | [*illustration of a castle*, $1\frac{1}{2}$ × $2\frac{3}{8}$ *in.*] | Allington Castle | *The Student's Library*

Crown 8vo. [ii] , 54 pp. plate. $7\frac{1}{8}$ × 5 in.

Plate, recto, title as above; verso, portrait of the author; p. [i] Preface in Japanese by S. Tomiyama; p. [ii] blank; pp. [1]–45 text; p. [46] blank; pp. 47–54 Notes.

White pictorial paper wrappers printed in dark green, pale orange and black; lettered on upper wrapper: HAMLET, AND OTHER STUDIES | [*following two lines in Japanese*:] Gendai Bei-Ei Bungaku Tampenshû | Hamuret, Manatsu no yo no yume, Gendai sakkaron | THE STUDENT'S LIBRARY, and on lower wrapper, at centre:

[*within an oval: publisher's monogram*]; publisher's imprint in Japanese, pasted inside lower wrapper.

Published 30 January 1950 by Yūhōdō, Tokyo; no record of the number of copies printed. 40 yen.

Contents: Hamlet — Midsummer Night's Dream — Contemporary English Writers.

A97   EASTWARD   1950

First edition:

[*in holograph facsimile*:] EASTWARD | A SELECTION OF VERSES | ORIGINAL AND TRANSLATED | by Edmund Blunden | [*ornament*]

Imperial 8vo. 48 pp. 11 × 7⅝ in.

P. [1] half-title; p. [2] blank; p. 3 title; p. [4] blank; p. [5] Preface; p. [6] blank; pp. 7–44 text; pp. [45–46] Contents; p. [47] at head: The edition of this book is limited to 250 copies, all | signed and numbered by the author. | This is number [*numbered*]; p. [48] at head: HERE — ENDS — *EASTWARD*, | a collection of poems by Edmund Blunden, printed by subscription | for "English Poetry" edited by T. Sone, Y. Sakai, I. Nishi- | zaki and S. Oshima. The hand-made text paper was | specially made by Zenzo Oikawa of Rikuchu, the | paper used on the binding by Saichiro Naruko | of Omi, and the style of the volume | was designed by Bunsho Jugaku. | Completed on the twelfth | of December, | 1949., at foot: Printed at the Benrido, Kyoto, Japan; p. [48] spare spine label tipped-in; two leaves bound round the pages to form paste-down and free end-papers.

Cream paper boards; off-white paper label, 3½ × ⅜ in., printed in brown down the spine: *EASTWARD* by EDMUND BLUNDEN; circular ornament, ¾ in., in blind on upper cover; top and fore edges trimmed, bottom untrimmed.

Published March 1950; 250 copies printed. 3000 yen; 1300 yen to subscribers.

Pp. 3, [5], 7–44 holograph facsimiles.

Contents: *Occasional Poems*: Change and Song — "Know'st thou the Land . . . ?" — Time for New Leaves — Running Stream — The Beloved River — A Survivor from One War Reflects during Another — A Christmas Tale from "The Golden Legend" — Fairy Gifts — Clairissima — Decorations — Liberty — After a Discussion — Shelley is Drowned [1822] — On Chaˢ Lamb's Birthday [*formerly* On Charles Lamb's Birthday 1945] — An Ode for St. Cecilia's Day — "Thou" — The Lawn: A Fragment of Family History at a House in Tokyo — A Woodland Holiday: Karuizawa — Matsushima — The

Mountain [*formerly* The Mountain One November Morning] — A First Visit to Yashima [*later* Yashima in Winter; *and* A First Visit to Yashima] — Moments [*title in Contents* Moment]: In a Park at Kyoto; The Inn Window, Fukuoka [*formerly* From the Japanese Inn Window; *later* The Early Year, Fukuoka; *and* The Inn Window, Fukuoka]; A House in Ushigome — To Japanese Students — Impromptu upon Reading Dr. Julian Huxley on Progress [*formerly* Impromptu After [*etc.*]] — Appeal — *Translated Poems*: At the Shrine of Apollo — A Girl's Invocation — Horace Renounces Love — Spring-time, Death [*title in Contents* Springtime and Death] — The Triumph of the Poet — My Room — Chimney-Smoke.

A98   COLLEGE SONG   1950

a. First edition:

[*title at head of p.* [1]:] COLLEGE SONG | [*holograph facsimile*, 5¼ × 3½ *in., double vertical rule at each side*:] For Tokyo Joshi Daigaku. | A Hymn | "And when they had sung a hymn" | Come, all who love the way of truth, | [*nineteen lines*] | 31 March 1950 Edmund Blunden | [*at foot*:] TOKYO WOMAN'S CHRISTIAN COLLEGE | 1950

Crown 4to. [4] pp. 10⅜ × 7½ in.

P. [1] title, holograph facsimile of poem; pp. [3–4] music score, English tune, 17th century arranged by K. Kurosawa; p. [4] notes in Japanese.

No wrappers; edges trimmed.

Issued April 1950; *c.* 1000 copies printed. Not for sale.

(Come, all who love the way of truth,). Reprinted as FOR TOKYO JOSHI DAIGAKU: A HYMN in *Bulletin, Tokyo Woman's Christian College*, May 1950; and in *Poems on Japan*, 1967 (*see* A171; C2520). The poem was also printed in a number of Tokyo Woman's Christian College publications including *A Handbook of Information*.

b. Second edition:

[*title on p.* [1]: *in brown*:] COLLEGE SONG | [*illustration in white of crossed wavy lines*, ⅝ × ⅝ *in.*] | TOKYO WOMAN'S CHRISTIAN COLLEGE

Crown 8vo. 8 pp. illus. on p. [8]. 7⅛ × 5 in.

P. [1] title; p. 2 music score, text in English; p. 3 text; p. 4 music score; p. 5 explanation of the poem by Takeshi Saitō in Japanese; pp. 6-7 notes on the author in Japanese; p. [8] at head: KOKA | [*illustration of college tower*, 4⅝ X 3 *in*.] | TOKYO JOSHI DIAGAKU | ¥30.

No wrappers; pp. [1] and [8] printed in sky-blue and brown; edges trimmed; stapled.

Published April 1950; no record of the number of copies printed. 30 yen.

A99   INFLUENTIAL BOOKS   1950

First edition:

INFLUENTIAL BOOKS | Lectures given at Waseda University | in | 1948 and 1949 | by | EDMUND BLUNDEN | [*four line quotation*] | THE HOKUSEIDO PRESS

Crown 8vo. [viii], 176 pp. front. (port.), 2 plates facing pp. [40] and [125]. 7⅞ X 5 in.

P. [i] half-title; p. [ii] blank; p. [iii] title; p. [iv] blank; p. [v] Preface; p. [vi] blank; p. [vii] Contents; p. [viii] blank; p. [1]-176 text.

Dull green cloth boards; lettered in gold on spine: Influential | Books | By | Edmund | Blunden | HOKUSEIDO, and on upper cover: [*within a rule in blind*:] INFLUENTIAL | BOOKS | [*at foot*: *in blind*:] THE HOKUSEIDO PRESS; publisher's device of a bird, 1⅛ X 1⅛ in., on lower cover; edges trimmed; grey end-papers.

Published in Tokyo 5 April 1950; 2000 copies printed. 100 yen.

Contents: White's "Selborne" — Darwin's "Origin of Species" — Shelley's "Prometheus Unbound" — Keats's "Lamia, Isabella and Other Poems" — Byron's "Childe Harold" — Thomas Hardy's "The Dynasts" — Gibbon's "Decline and Fall of the Roman Empire" — Milton's "Paradise Lost" — Shakespeare: How to Read Him — Shakespeare: Tragedies: "Hamlet" — Shakespeare: Comedies: "A Midsummer Night's Dream" — Contemporary English Literature, 1 — Contemporary English Literature, 2.

A100   VERSES BY THE WAY   1950

First separate publication:

[*title at head of leaf* 1:] Verses By The Way | by EDMUND BLUNDEN

An offprint of 4 leaves. 10¼ X 7¼ in.

Leaves 1–4, also numbered [147]–150, text.

No wrappers; edges trimmed; stapled.

Issued July 1950; number of copies printed not ascertained. Not for sale.

Reprinted from *English Poetry*, Tokyo, July 1950 (*see* C2529-33).

Contents: Age — Tokyo Lawn [*later* From a Tokyo Lawn; *and* Tokyo Lawn (1948)] — Two Village Minstrels — Tomkins — Ode to an Ink-Jar (Stephens' Ink) [*later* To a British Jar Containing Stephen's Ink].

A101   FAVOURITE STUDIES IN ENGLISH   1950
LITERATURE

First edition:

FAVOURITE STUDIES | IN | ENGLISH LITERATURE | Lectures given at Keio University | in | 1948 and 1950 | by | EDMUND BLUNDEN | KEIO UNIVERSITY SPECIAL PUBLICATION | PRINTED BY | THE HOKU-SEIDO PRESS | 1950 | TOKYO, JAPAN

Crown 8vo. [viii], 100 pp. front., 2 plates facing pp. [v], [83]. $7\frac{1}{8} \times 4\frac{7}{8}$ in.

P. [i] half-title; p. [ii] blank; p. [iii] title; p. [iv] at head: All of Prof. Edmund Blunden's lectures given at Keio | University are collected in this volume except "Contemporary | Literature", which is contained in his "Influential Studies."; p. [v] A Note by the author; p. [vi] blank; p. [vii] Contents; p. [viii] blank; pp. [1]-99 text; p. [100] blank.

Green cloth boards; lettered in gold up the spine: E. BLUNDEN: FAVOURITE STUDIES IN ENGLISH LITERATURE, and on upper cover: [*within a blind rule*:] FAVOURITE STUDIES | IN | ENGLISH LITERATURE | [*in blind*:] THE HOKUSEIDO PRESS; publisher's device of a bird in blind, $1\frac{1}{4} \times 1\frac{1}{4}$ in., on lower cover; edges trimmed; grey end-papers.

Published 10 July 1950; 2000 copies printed. 70 yen.

Plate facing p. [v] holograph facsimile of Blunden's entries in Keio Guest Book.

There was a reprint of 2000 copies issued on 3 February 1970 at 350 yen; an introduction by Isao Sato and thirty pages of notes were added, and the plates omitted.

Contents: John Milton: Areopagitica (1644) — P. B. Shelley: Essays (Collected, 1840) — William Hazlitt: The Spirit of the Age (1825) — Charlotte Brontë: Jane Eyre (1847) — John Milton: Minor Poems —

Alexander Pope: An Essay on Man (1731–4) — William Blake: Songs of Innocence (1789) — W. Wordsworth and S. Taylor Coleridge: Lyrical Ballads (1798) — Alfred Tennyson: In Memoriam (1850).

A102   A WANDERER IN JAPAN   1950

First edition:

[*within a rule in brown*: *in holograph facsimile*:] "A Wanderer in Japan." | by | Edmund Blunden. | [*below rule in roman*:] Sketches and reflections, | in prose and verse. | [*device of a bowl on a teacloth in brown*, $\frac{3}{4}$ × $\frac{3}{4}$ *in.*] | Asahi-shimbun-sha

Small demy 8vo. [iv] , 6, 122 pp. front. (holograph); Japanese text 10, 142 pp. front. (port.). $8\frac{1}{4}$ × $5\frac{3}{4}$ in.

P. [i] half-title; p. [ii] at foot: Cover Design by | KOSHIRO ONJI; p. [iii] title; p. [iv] blank; pp. 1–2 Preface; p. [3] section-title; pp. [4–5] Contents; p. [6] blank; pp. 1–119 text; pp. [120–121] blank; p. [122] title in English and Japanese; Japanese text (printed in usual Japanese style but paginated left to right): pp. 1–3 Preface; p. [4] blank; p. [5] section-title; pp. [6–9] Contents; p. [10] blank; p. [1] section-title; p. [2] blank; pp. 3–141 text; p. [142] blank.

Mustard-yellow paper boards; lettered on spine: [*on a scarlet panel, in mustard-yellow*:] A | WANDERER | IN JAPAN | [*outside panel, in orange*:] [*rule*] | Edmund | Blunden | [*rule*] | [*following lines in Japanese on a scarlet panel, in mustard-yellow*:] NIHON HEN- REKI | EDOMANDO BRUNDEN CHO | [*outside panel, in orange*:] [*rule*] | TOMIYAMA | SHIGERU YAKU | [*rule*] | [*publisher's device of a horse in scarlet*, $\frac{5}{8}$ × $\frac{1}{2}$ *in.*] | ASAHI SHIMBUN-SHA; on upper cover: [*on a scarlet panel, in mustard-yellow*:] A WAN- DERER | IN JAPAN | [*outside panel, in orange*:] Edmund Blun- den | [*circle in red*] ; and on lower cover: [*following lines in Japa- nese on a scarlet panel, in mustard-yellow*:] NIHON HENREKI EDOMANDO BRUNDEN CHO | [*outside panel in orange*:] TOMI- YAMA SHIGERU YAKU | [*circle in red*] ; edges trimmed; white end-papers. White dust-jacket printed in garnet brown and black. White slip case printed in garnet brown and mustard-yellow. Garnet brown book marker.

Published in Tokyo on 15 July 1950; number of copies printed not ascertained. 320 yen.

Frontispiece, holograph facsimile of the first $2\frac{1}{2}$ paragraphs of 'The Sea Speaking'. Text in English and Japanese; translated by Shigeru Tomiyama. A reprint of the English text was issued on 15 April 1951 at 150 yen in white paper boards printed in blue and brown, with a new frontispiece (port.) and the omission of the final sentence of the Preface.

Contents: Arrival — Agricultural Japan — English Studies: A Paradox — Among the Ruins — Points of Progress — Landscape and Temperament: SUMMER STORM [*later* SUMMER STORM IN JAPANESE HILLS] — In Passing: Tokyo in 1948 — Culture: A Little Dialogue — The Sea Speaking — AMONG THE HILLS — Stranger in Asahigawa — Sounkyo — Far Away and Long Ago — Daydream in Hokkaido — AINU CHILD — Treaty Port — John Saris's Journal — The Japanese Student, 1949 — THE TEMPLE — Pictures in the Wind — Tokyo Seclusion — A Party at the Palace — Art Gallery — Some of the Wonders — Jpapnese [*sic*] Food — "Judgments".

A103   **SOME WOMEN WRITERS**   1950

First separate publication:

[*title on upper wrapper*:] SOME WOMEN WRITERS | Three Lectures Given at Tokyo Woman's Christian College, 1949 | BY | EDMUND BLUNDEN | From the ESSAYS and STUDIES, Vol. 1, No. 1. September, 1950 | TOKYO WOMAN'S CHRISTIAN COLLEGE

Small demy 8vo. An offprint of 36 pp. $8\frac{1}{4} \times 5\frac{7}{8}$ in.

Pp. [1]-35 text; p. [36] blank.

White paper wrappers; printed on upper wrapper as above; edges cut flush; stapled.

Issued September 1950; 20 copies printed. Not for sale.

Contents: 1, Poetry — 2, Novels — 3, Miscellany.

Reprinted from *Ronshu: Essays and Studies*, September 1950 (*see* C2550).

A104   **REPRINTED PAPERS**   1950

First edition:

REPRINTED PAPERS | Partly concerning | Some English Romantic Poets | *With a few postscripts by* | EDMUND BLUNDEN | Published for | THE ENGLISH LITERARY SOCIETY OF JAPAN | by Kenkyusha, Tokyo | 1950

Crown 8vo. [vi], 268 pp. $7\frac{1}{8} \times 5$ in.

P. [i] title; p. [ii] blank; pp. [iii-iv] Preface, signed E.B.; p. [v]

94

Contents; p. [vi] blank; pp. 1–266 text; p. [267] publisher's imprint; p. [268] blank.

Green cloth boards; lettered in gold up the spine: REPRINTED PAPERS *by E. Blunden*; edges trimmed; white end-papers. Grey dust-jacket printed in black and dull red.

Published 5 September 1950; no record of the number of copies printed. 280 yen.

First published in *Studies in English Literature* (*see* C545, 564, 593, 609, 622, 809, 1150). 'Keats's Letters, 1931; Marginalia' was also issued separately as an offprint (*see* A38).

Contents: More Footnotes to Literary History: 1, Free Thoughts on the Biography of John Keats; 2, John Clare: Notes and References — Coleridge, Shelley and Keats (*see also* A24) — Physicians and Poetry: A Brief Record — A.D. 1827 in English Literature — Fragmentary Notes on the Painter-Poets — Westminster Abbey and English Writers — Keats's Letters, 1931; Marginalia.

A105   THE SWINBURNE LABYRINTH   1950

First separate publication:

[*title at head of leaf*:] 564 THE TIMES LITERARY SUPPLEMENT FRIDAY SEPTEMBER 8 1950 | THE SWINBURNE LABYRINTH

An offprint of [1] leaf. 24 $\frac{7}{8}$ × 15 in.
Leaf [1] text.
No wrappers; edges trimmed.
Issued *c*. 8 September 1950; 6 copies printed. Not for sale.

Review of *Selected Poems*, by A. C. Swinburne, edited with an introduction by Edward Shanks. Unsigned. Reprinted from the *TLS*, 8 September 1950 (*see* C2552).

A106   RECORDS OF FRIENDSHIP   1950

First edition:

RECORDS | OF | FRIENDSHIP | [*rule*] | Occasional & Epistolary Poems | Written during Visits to Kyushu | [*rule*] | by | EDMUND BLUNDEN | Compiled & Edited by | T. Nakayama | Kyushu University | 1950 | KYUSHU UNIVERSITY PRESS

Crown 8vo. [2], iv, 34 leaves. plate facing p. [1]. 7 × 5 in.

Leaf [1] title; leaf [2] blank; leaves i–ii Prologue by Edmund Blunden; leaves iii–iv Contents; leaves [1]–30 text; leaves 31–33 Editor's Word; leaf [34] at centre: PRINTED AND BOUND BY | S. HORIKAWA, OF KYUSHU | UNIVERSITY PRESS, FUKUOKA: | PAPER MADE AT FUKUSHIMA | TECHNICAL LABORATORY OF FUKUOKA PREFECTURE | This edition is limited to two | hundred copies, of which this | is No. [*number stamped*].

Pink and pale blue mottled paper boards; white paper label, $1\frac{7}{8}$ × $3\frac{1}{4}$ in., on upper wrapper: [*within a double rule, thick, thin:*] RECORDS | OF | FRIENDSHIP | Edmund Blunden; edges trimmed; white endpapers; errata-slip tipped-in on upper free end-paper in some copies.

Published probably 14 September 1950; 200 copies printed.

Leaves [1–2] holograph facsimiles of the first two poems.

Contents: To Claire — Sakurajima, A Volcano [*later* The Volcano; *and* Sakurajima, A Volcano] — Moji on the Sea — To a Waltonian in Kyusha — A Modest Scholar — On a Fly-Leaf of Chaucer's *Wyf of Bathe* — To Mrs Hirai of Kikusui Hotel — From the Japanese Inn Window [*later* The Inn Window, Fukuoka; *and* The Early Year, Fukuoka] — To Kikue-san — A Scholar — Evening on the River — Nature Rebels — Lecturing — The Dean — And Still, the Dean — Railway Journey — Saga Memory — A Signature: A. Mizunoe — Nagasaki Old and New — In Nagasaki Harbour — "English Studies" — The Teacher — The Art Student's Other Career — A Sabbath — Symposium — The Soldier's Burden — Rinkotei — To Chieko-san — The Autumn Moment — At the Departure from Kyusha.

A107   JOHN KEATS   1950

First edition:

JOHN | KEATS | *By* EDMUND BLUNDEN | PUBLISHED FOR | THE BRITISH COUNCIL | and the NATIONAL BOOK LEAGUE | BY LONGMANS, GREEN & CO., LONDON, NEW YORK, TORONTO

Small demy 8vo. 38 pp. front. (port.). $8\frac{3}{8}$ × $5\frac{3}{8}$ in.

P. [1] half-title; p. [2] blank; p. [3] title; p. [4] at head: LONGMANS, GREEN & CO. LTD. | 6 & 7 Clifford Street, London, W.1 | Also at Melbourne and Cape Town | [*six lines of addresses*], at centre: *First Published in 1950*, at foot: *Printed in Great Britain by Benham and Company Limited* | *Colchester*; p. [5] Contents; p. [6] blank; pp. 7–34 text; pp. 35–37 A Select Bibliography; p. [38] blank.

Buff paper wrappers; printed on upper wrapper: Supplement to *British Book News* | [*in burnt sienna:*] JOHN | KEATS | *By* EDMUND BLUNDEN | PUBLISHED FOR | THE BRITISH COUNCIL

| and the NATIONAL BOOK LEAGUE | by LONGMANS, GREEN & CO. | LONDON. NEW YORK. TORONTO; edges cut flush; stapled.

Published 25 September 1950 as a Supplement to *British Book News*; 15,000 copies printed. 1*s.*

There were reprints of 8000 copies in September 1954 with a new bibliography 'John Keats: Bibliography' pp. 35–40, and issued as *Writers and Their Work*, No. 6 at 2*s.* (half-title: *Bibliographical Series of Supplements to* 'British Book News' *on Writers and Their Work* . . .); 6000 copies in 1959 (revised); in 1963; in 1966, and 7000 copies in 1969.

A108   EDMUND BLUNDEN: A SELECTION OF   1950
HIS POETRY AND PROSE

a. First edition:

EDMUND | BLUNDEN | *A Selection of his Poetry and Prose* | *Made by Kenneth Hopkins* | [*publisher's device of a fox,* $1\frac{7}{8}$ × $1\frac{5}{8}$ *in.*] | *London* | RUPERT HART-DAVIS | 1950

Large crown 8vo. 376 pp. prelims numbered [i]–[xviii]; front. (port.) $8\frac{1}{8}$ × 5 in.

P. [i] half-title; p. [ii] blank; p. [iii] title; p. [iv] at head: First published 1950, at foot: Printed in Great Britain by Richard Clay and Company, Ltd., | Bungay, Suffolk; pp. v–vii Contents; p. [viii] blank; pp. ix–xv Introduction, with Note by Edmund Blunden, p. xv; p. xvi Acknowledgements; p. [17] section-title; p. [18] blank; pp. 19–71 text; p. [72] blank; p. [73] section-title; p. [74] blank; pp. 75–179 text; p. [180] blank; p. [181] section-title; p. [182] blank; pp. 183–218 text; p. [219] section-title; p. [220] blank; pp. 221–260 text; p. [261] section-title; p. [262] blank; pp. 263–281 text; p. [282] blank; p. [283] section-title; p. [284] blank; pp. 285–324 text; p. [325] section-title; p. [326] blank; pp. 327–367 text; p. [368] blank; p. [369] section-title; p. [370] blank; p. 371 text; p. [372] blank; pp. 373–374 Check-List of Books by Edmund Blunden; pp. [375–376] blank.

Green cloth boards; lettered in gold on spine: EDMUND | BLUNDEN | [*ornament*] | POETRY | AND PROSE | RUPERT | HART-DAVIS; edges trimmed, top brown; white end-papers. Pastel-green dust-jacket printed in rust and black.

Published 20 October 1950; 3000 copies printed. 15*s.*

Copies with a cancel-title were sent to Horizon Press, New York (*see* A108*b*).

Contents: *England*: THE KISS — Sussex — FOREFATHERS — The Rural Tradition — THE VETERAN — Miss Warble — THE NAMELESS STREAM — National Biography — THE TOWER — Home Thoughts on Kent — THE SUNLIT VALE [*formerly* THE FAILURE] — *Literature*: IN A LIBRARY — The Creed of the Book — Memorials and Forgettings — THE AGE OF HERBERT AND VAUGHAN — The Much Tried Silurist — A Study of William Collins — A Word for Kirke White — A TOUCHSTONE [*formerly* THINK OF SHELLEY] — Wills and Testaments — John Clare — CLARE'S GHOST [*formerly* PHANTASIES] — The Cowden Clarkes — *Cricket*: CRICKET, I CONFESS — Is It Still Our National Game? — An Ancient Holiday — PRIDE OF THE VILLAGE — "Cricket Won't be Druv" — Lord's, June 27th, 1930 — HAMMOND (ENGLAND) A CRICKETER [*formerly* HAMMOND OF ENGLAND] — Some Cricket Books — *War*: CAN YOU REMEMBER? — "TRANSPORT UP" AT YPRES — The Cherry Orchard — AT SENLIS ONCE — Aftertones [*formerly* A Postscript] — THE STILL HOUR — Fall In, Ghosts — REPORT ON EXPERIENCE — FROM AGE TO AGE [*formerly* THE ONLY ANSWER] — *Occasions*: TO JOY — THE MIDNIGHT SKATERS — INCIDENT IN HYDE PARK, 1803 — The Find — Notes on Visits to Thomas Hardy [*formerly* Thomas Hardy] — VERSES TO H.R.H. THE DUKE OF WINDSOR — *Contemporaries*: THE HOME OF POETRY — Writers and Readers — Walter de la Mare [*formerly* The Friend of Life] — H. M. Tomlinson — LASCELLES ABERCROMBIE [*formerly* L.A.] — Siegfried Sassoon's Poetry — *Travel*: THE BRANCH LINE — Six Chapters from *The Bonadventure* — A Tokyo Secret — "Line upon Line" — Winter Comes to Tokyo — THE AUTHOR'S LAST WORDS TO HIS STUDENTS — *Envoi*: THE SUM OF ALL — Check-List of Books by Edmund Blunden.

b. *First edition — American issue.* [*1961*] :

[*title as above*; *imprint*:] HORIZON PRESS | NEW YORK

Large crown 8vo. 376 pp. preliminary pages numbered [i]–[xviii]. front. (port.) 8 × 5 in.

Green cloth boards; lettered in gold on spine with ornament; edges trimmed, top brown; white end-papers.

Issued 1961; no record of number of copies bound. $4.95.

Copies with a cancel-title were supplied by Rupert Hart-Davis, London.

First separate publication:

[*title at head of leaf*:] 660 THE TIMES LITERARY SUP-
PLEMENT FRIDAY OCTOBER 20 1950 | MR. HUNT AT
THE PLAY

An offprint of [1] leaf. $25\frac{1}{8} \times 13\frac{1}{4}$ in.

Leaf [1] text.

No wrappers; edges trimmed.

Issued *c.* 20 October 1950; probably 12 copies printed. Not for sale.

Review of *Dramatic Criticism, 1808-1931*, by Leigh Hunt, edited
by Lawrence Huston Houtchens and Carolyn Washburn Houtchens.
Unsigned. Reprinted from the *TLS*, 20 October 1950 (*see* C2567).

First edition:

CHAUCER TO "B.V." | With an additional paper on |
Herman Melville | *A Selection of Lectures given chiefly* |
at Tokyo University by | EDMUND BLUNDEN | TOKYO
| KENKYUSHA | 1950

Demy 8vo. viii, 268 pp. $8\frac{1}{4} \times 5\frac{3}{4}$ in.

P. [i] half-title; p. [ii] blank; p. [iii] title; p. [iv] blank; pp. v-vi
Preface; p. [vii] Contents; p. [viii] blank; pp. 1-265 text; p. [266]
blank; p. [267] publisher's imprint in Japanese; p. [268] blank.

Paper boards marbled in blue and grey; white paper spine; lettered
in gold on spine: CHAUCER | TO | "B.V." | EDMUND | BLUN-
DEN | KENKYUSHA; edges trimmed; pale biscuit flecked end-
papers. Pale green dust-jacket printed in pale brown.

Published 15 December 1950; no record of the number of copies
printed. 300 yen.

There was a reprint of 500 copies in April 1967.

Contents: Geoffrey Chaucer — Edmund Spenser: and especially "The
Faery Queen" — Christopher Marlowe — John Donne — John
Webster — Robert Herrick — John Bunyan — Jonathan Swift —
Samuel Johnson — Thomas Chatterton — Thomas Hood —Robert
Browning — Matthew Arnold — "B.V.": James Thomson the Second
— Herman Melville.

First separate publication:

[*title at head of leaf:*] 826 THE TIMES LITERARY SUP-
PLEMENT FRIDAY DECEMBER 29 1950 | SMART
AND HIS EDITORS

An offprint of [1] leaf. 25 × 13½ in.

Leaf [1] text.

No wrappers; edges trimmed.

Issued *c.* 29 December 1950; probably 12 copies printed. Not for
sale.

Review of *Poems*, by Christopher Smart, edited with an introduction
and notes by Robert Brittain. Unsigned. Reprinted from the *TLS*, 29
December 1950 (*see* C2597).

First separate publication:

[*title at head of leaf* [2]:] Plays and Poems of Thomas
Lovell Beddoes

Royal 8vo. [3] leaves. 9¼ × 6¼ in.

Leaf [1] at head, half-title; leaves [2–3] numbered [193]–194 text.

No wrappers; edges trimmed; stapled.

Issued April 1951; number of copies printed not ascertained. Not for
sale.

Review of *Plays and Poems of Thomas Lovell Beddoes*, edited with
an introduction by H. W. Donner. Reprinted from the *Review of
English Studies*, April 1951 (*see* C2647).

First edition:

TODAY AND TOMORROW SERIES | SKETCHES AND
REFLECTIONS | by | Edmund Blunden | with Notes by |
Shigeru Tomiyama | [*publisher's device of a vase*, ⅞ × ⅞ *in.*]
| EIBUNSHA

Crown 8vo. [iv] , 46 pp. 7⅛ × 5 in.

P. [i] title; p. [ii] blank; p. [iii] Contents; p. [iv] blank; pp. 1–36 text; pp. 37–43 Notes; p. [44] blank; p. [45] publisher's imprint in Japanese; p. [46] note on the series in Japanese and English.

White paper wrappers; printed in black down the spine: SKETCHES AND REFLECTIONS BY E. BLUNDEN, and on upper wrapper: TODAY AND TOMORROW SERIES | [*within a double rule in navy-blue, and on a navy-blue panel,* $1\frac{1}{2}$ X $3\frac{7}{8}$ *in., in white:*] SKETCHES | AND | REFLECTIONS | [*illustration of flowers on right of panel*] | [*below panel, in black: illustration of triangles with leaves at centre*] | [*in navy-blue:*] by | EDMUND BLUNDEN | [*in black:*] TOKYO | EIBUNSHA; edges cut flush; white end-papers; stapled and gummed.

Published 1 September 1951 as *Today and Tomorrow Series*, Vol. 2; number of copies printed not ascertained. 50 yen.

Advertisement for series inserted. There were reprints on 10 September 1952, and 10 September 1953.

Contents: Coming East: Glimpses of a Voyage in 1947 — The Post-War Student — Books of Today: 1, Poems of Gerard Manley Hopkins; 2, Sassoon's Life of Meredith.

The transcription is taken from the second reprint.

A114   THE POEMS OF CLOUGH   1951

First separate publication:

[*title at head of leaf:*] 748 THE TIMES LITERARY SUPPLEMENT FRIDAY NOVEMBER 23 1951 | THE POEMS OF CLOUGH

An offprint of [1] leaf. $18\frac{1}{2}$ X $12\frac{1}{2}$ in.

Leaf [1] text.

No wrappers; edges trimmed.

Issued *c.* 23 November 1951; probably 12 copies printed. Not for sale.

Review of *The Poems of Arthur Hugh Clough*, edited by H. F. Lowry, A. L. P. Norrington and F. L. Mulhauser. Unsigned. Reprinted from the *TLS*, 23 November 1951 (*see* C2736).

A115   CHARLES EDMUND BLUNDEN   1951

First separate publication:

[*title at head of leaf:*] Charles Edmund Blunden. | [*rule*]

Medium 8vo. An offprint of [1] leaf. 9 × 5 in.

Leaf [1] text; at foot: EDMUND BLUNDEN.

No wrappers; edges trimmed.

Issued December 1951; number of copies printed not ascertained. Not for sale.

On Blunden's father. Reprinted from SS. *Peter & Paul, Yalding with S. Mary, Laddingford* [*Parish Magazine*], December 1951 (*see* C2744).

A116   A LOVER OF BOOKS   1952

First separate publication:

[*title at head of p.* [1]:] Vᵉ ANNÉE NUMERO 3 AOÛT 1952 | ETUDES | ANGLAISES | GRANDE-BRETAGNE • ETATS-UNIS | [*long double rule*] | A LOVER OF BOOKS, J.-W. DALBY | (1799–1880)

Royal 8vo. An offprint of [9] pp. $9\frac{7}{8}$ × $6\frac{1}{2}$ in.

Pp. [1–9] numbered [193]–201 text.

Cream wrappers printed in brown and black; fore and bottom edges trimmed, top rough trimmed or uncut; stapled.

Issued August 1952; number of copies printed not ascertained. Not for sale.

Reprinted from *Etudes anglaises*, août 1952 (*see* C2863).

A117   ESSAYISTS OF THE ROMANTIC   1952
                    PERIOD

First edition:

EDMUND BLUNDEN | ESSAYISTS OF THE | ROMAN-TIC PERIOD | *First Series* | [*rule*] | Edited with Notes | by | Ichiro Nishizaki | TOKYO | AT THE KODOKWAN PRESS

Crown 8vo. 122 pp. plate. $7\frac{1}{8}$ × 5 in.

P. [1] half-title; p. [2] blank; plate numbered pp. [3–4] tipped-in; p. [5] title; p. [6] blank; p. [7] Contents; p. [8] blank; pp. 9–10 Preface in Japanese; pp. 11–92 text; pp. [93]–120 Notes in Japanese and English; p. [121] publisher's imprint in Japanese; p. [122] publisher's list of books in series.

Pale grey paper wrappers; printed in crimson up the spine: E.

BLUNDEN ESSAYISTS OF THE ROMANTIC PERIOD, on upper wrapper: ESSAYISTS | OF | THE ROMANTIC PERIOD | (FIRST SERIES) | *EDMUND BLUNDEN*, and on lower wrapper at foot: KODOKWAN; holograph facsimiles of essayists printed in pale brown over upper and lower wrappers; edges cut flush; sewn and gummed.

Published 15 September 1952; number of copies printed not ascertained. 90 yen.

Contents: Essayists of the Romantic Period: Introductory — Charles Lamb — Samuel Taylor Coleridge. Reprinted from *Lectures in English Literature* (*see* A24).

A118   THE DEDE OF PITTIE   1953

First edition:

THE | DEDE OF PITTIE | *Dramatic Scenes* | *reflecting the History of* | CHRIST'S HOSPITAL | *and offered in celebration of* | *the Quatercentenary* | *1953* | *at the Fortune Theatre* | [*four line quotation*]

Demy 8vo. 44 pp. 8¾ × 5⅝ in.

P. [1] title; p. [2] Contents; p. [3] Preface; pp. 4–42 text; pp. [43–44] blank.

Grey paper wrappers; printed on upper wrapper: CHRIST'S [*device of the arms of Christ's Hospital*] HOSPITAL | [*as title-page to 1953, followed by:*] *Written by Edmund Blunden and published by* | *Christ's Hospital, London.* | *Price 2s.6d.*, and on lower wrapper, verso, at centre: [*short rule*] | HOLMES | *The Printers* | HORSHAM | [*short rule*] ; edges cut flush; stapled.

Issued probably May 1953; no record of the number of copies printed. 2*s.* 6*d.*

The Preface, p. [3], is a revised version of the preface to *The Dede of Pittie Theatre Programme* (*see* B154). Details of the production of the play, 'Old Blues' Quatercentenary Production', were published in *The Blue*, March 1953, Vol. 80, No. 2, pp. 109–110, September 1953, Vol. 80, No. 3, p. 195, and 'The Dede of Pittie' by Edmund Blunden, pp. 196–200.

A118.1 CHRIST'S HOSPITAL CELEBRATIONS   1953

First separate publication:

[*title at head of leaf:*] CHRIST'S HOSPITAL CELEBRA- TIONS | [*swelled rule*] | "A UNIQUE FOUNDATION"

An offprint of [1] leaf. 5 illus. $21\frac{5}{8} \times 14\frac{1}{4}$ in.

Leaf [1] text.

No wrappers; edges trimmed.

Issued *c.* 15 May 1953; no record of the number of copies printed. Not for sale.

On the quatercentenary celebrations. Signed By a Special Correspondent. Reprinted from the *Times Educational Supplement*, 15 May 1953 (*see* C3025). *See also* C2853, 2929, 3027.

A119   BOOK SOCIETY CHOICE FOR   1953
                            NOVEMBER

First separate publication:

Reprinted from | [*illustration of an issue of The Bookman*] | [*rule across page*] | *The Selection Committee's Review* | *of the* | BOOK SOCIETY CHOICE | for November | *together with the abridged review* | *of the alternative choice* | [*rule across page*] | DESCRIPTIVE NOTES of the volumes recommended | by the Book Society's Selection Committee | for October are given on the back page. | [*ornament*]

Small crown 8vo. [4] pp. $7\frac{1}{4} \times 4\frac{3}{4}$ in.

P. [1] title; pp. [2–3] text; p. [4] list of Recommended Books for October.

No wrappers; edges trimmed.

Issued November 1953; number of copies printed not ascertained. Not for sale.

Review of *The Reason Why*, by Cecil Woodham-Smith. Reprinted from *The Bookman*, October 1953 (*see* C3090).

A120   KEATS'S ODES : FURTHER NOTES   1954

First separate publication:

[*title at head of p.* [1] :] Keats's Odes: Further Notes | By EDMUND BLUNDEN

Crown 4to. An offprint of [8] pp. $10 \times 6\frac{7}{8}$ in.

Pp. [1–8] numbered [39]–46 text.

Primrose-yellow stiff paper wrappers; printed on upper wrapper: [*in*

104

brown:] A REPRINT FROM | Keats- | Shelley | Journal | VOLUME
III WINTER 1954 | *Published by* | THE KEATS-SHELLEY ASSO-
CIATION OF AMERICA, INC.; edges cut flush; stapled.

Issued April or May 1954; 25 copies printed. Not for sale.

Reprinted from the *Keats-Shelley Journal*, Winter 1954 [*i.e.* April or
May 1954] (*see* C3106).

A121   "I FOUND THE POEMS IN   1954
                    THE FIELDS"

First separate publication:

[*title at head of leaf*:] 688 THE TIMES LITERARY SUP-
PLEMENT FRIDAY OCTOBER 29 1954 | "I FOUND
THE POEMS IN THE FIELDS"

An offprint of [1] leaf. $18\frac{5}{8} \times 12\frac{3}{4}$ in.

Leaf [1] text.

No wrappers; edges trimmed.

Issued *c.* 29 October 1954; probably 12 copies printed. Not for sale.

Review of *The Rural Muse: Studies in the Peasant Poetry of England*,
by Rayner Unwin. Unsigned. Reprinted from the *TLS*, 29 October
1954 (*see* C3120).

Reprinted [*as* Country Poets] in *English Critical Essays: Twentieth
Century, Second Series*, selected by Derek Hudson (*see* B209).

A122   A FIRST VISIT TO YASHIMA   1954

First separate edition:

[*title at head of leaf*:] A First Visit to | Yashima

[1] leaf. $10\frac{1}{8} \times 7\frac{5}{8}$ in.

Leaf [1] text.

Enclosed within a white paper wrapper, $12\frac{1}{8} \times 15\frac{3}{8}$ in., folded in
three; multi-coloured pictorial upper fold printed in black: [*in Japa-
nese*:] YASHIMA O TAZUNETE | EDOMANDO BURANDEN;
edges of leaf, trimmed or rough trimmed; edges of wrapper trimmed.
Printed leaf, size varies $5 \times 7\frac{1}{2}$ in., or $4\frac{1}{2} \times 7\frac{5}{8}$ in., an anonymous
Japanese translation, inserted.

Issued 1 November 1954; number of copies printed not ascertained.
Not for sale.

(Like a long roof, men say, and well they say,). Holograph facsimile.
Published by the English Education Society in Kagawa Prefecture.

Some copies appear to have been published without the paper wrapper. First published in *Eastward*, [1950] ; and reprinted as YASHIMA IN WINTER in *The Month*, March 1950 (*see* A97; C2501).

A stone with a holograph facsimile of the poem reproduced on a panel, and dated Feb. 7 1949, was unveiled to commemorate Blunden's visit; an account, in Japanese, of the visit is also on the stone.

A123   **VERSES ON BEHALF OF THE**   1954
          UNIVERSITY OF HONG KONG

First edition:

[*title at head of leaf*:] VERSES | on behalf of the UNIVERSITY OF HONG KONG | in honour of the Vice-Chancellor Dr. L. T. RIDE'S | marriage with Miss Violet May WITCHELL on | 12 November 1954

[1] leaf. $9\frac{3}{4} \times 6\frac{1}{2}$ in.

Leaf [1] text.

No wrappers; edges trimmed.

Issued 12 November 1954; probably 200–250 copies printed. Not for sale.

(Assemble, all you paragons of learning,). Signed E.B. Holograph facsimile. Reprinted in *Malayan Undergrad*, 22 January 1955 (*see* C3128).

A124   **CHARLES LAMB**   1954

First edition:

CHARLES | LAMB | *By* EDMUND BLUNDEN | PUBLISHED FOR | THE BRITISH COUNCIL | and the NATIONAL BOOK LEAGUE | BY LONGMANS, GREEN & CO., LONDON, NEW YORK, TORONTO

Demy 8vo. 40 pp. front. (port.). $8\frac{3}{8} \times 5\frac{1}{2}$ in.

P. [1] half-title; p. [2] blank; p. [3] title; p. [4] at head: LONGMANS, GREEN & CO. LTD. | 6 & 7 Clifford Street, London W.1 | Also at Melbourne and Cape Town | [*six lines of addresses*], at centre: *First published in 1954*, at foot: *Printed in Great Britain by Benham and Company Limited* | *Colchester*; p. [5] Contents; p. [6] at head, Lamb's dates of birth and death; pp. 7–36 text; pp. 37–40 Charles Lamb: A Select Bibliography.

Buff paper wrappers; printed on upper wrapper: [*within an*

ornamental border in burnt sienna:] Writers and Their Work: No.
56 | [*in burnt sienna:*] CHARLES | LAMB | [*in black:*] *by* |
EDMUND BLUNDEN | PUBLISHED FOR | THE BRITISH COUN-
CIL | and the NATIONAL BOOK LEAGUE | *by* LONGMANS,
GREEN & CO. | *Two shillings net*; and on lower wrapper inside
ornamental border in sienna, and inside wrappers; edges cut flush;
stapled.

Published 29 November 1954 as *Writers and Their Work*, No. 56;
10,000 copies printed. 2*s*.

There was a reprint of 6000 copies in 1964 (revised).

A125   ENGINEERING AND POETRY   1954

First separate publication:

[*title at head of p.* [2]:] 18 HONG KONG UNIVERSITY
JOURNAL | [*long rule*] | Engineering and Poetry

Imperial 8vo. An offprint of [6] pp. $10\frac{1}{4} \times 7\frac{1}{8}$ in.

P. [1] numbered 17 end of preceding matter; pp. [2-6] numbered
18-22 text.

No wrappers; edges trimmed; pages unsecured.

Issued December 1954; 5 copies printed. Not for sale.

Reprinted from the *Hong Kong University Engineering Journal*,
December 1954 (*see* C3122).

A126   A FRAGMENT OF BYRONISM   1955

First separate publication:

[*title at head of p.* [2]:] A FRAGMENT OF BYRONISM

Small royal 8vo. An offprint of [12] pp. $9\frac{1}{2} \times 6$ in.

P. [1] cancel leaf pasted over text; pp. [2-12] numbered [32]-42
text.

Salmon paper wrappers; printed in brown on upper wrapper:
ETUDES | ANGLAISES | GRANDE-BRETAGNE · ETATS-UNIS |
Directeurs: | A. KOSZUL | M. LE BRETON F. MOSSÉ | [*swelled
rule*] | [*in black:*] ARTICLES | [*list of articles and authors, seven-
teen lines*] | [*in brown: swelled rule*] | [*in black:*] VIIIe année
JANVIER-MARS N° 1 | [*in brown:*] DIDIER | 4 & 6 RUE DE LA
SORBONNE PARIS | [*in black:*] *Publié avec le Concours du Centre
National de la Recherche Scientifique*; edges cut flush; stapled.

Issued probably March 1955; number of copies printed not ascertained. Not for sale.

Reprinted from *Etudes anglaises*, janvier/mars 1955 (*see* C3129).

First separate publication:

[*title on p.* 1:] The Family Physician | in the 17th Century

Crown 4to. An offprint of 6 pp. 5 illus. $9\frac{5}{8} \times 7\frac{1}{4}$ in.

Pp. 1–5 text; p. 5 following text: (*The decorations are by Prudence Rowe-Evans*), at foot: *Reprinted from ELIXIR, Journal of the Hong Kong University | Medical Society, Spring, 1955*.; p. [6] blank.

Issued probably June 1955; 100 copies printed. Not for sale.

Reprinted from *Elixir*, Spring 1955. *See also* ' "Signals" ' in the issue of Autumn, 1955 (*see* A129; C3132, 3147).

A128   SOME SEVENTEENTH-CENTURY   1955
LATIN POEMS

First separate publication:

[*title at head of p.* [2]:] Some Seventeenth-Century | Latin Poems | by English Writers [*thick vertical rule at right of last three lines*] Edmund Blunden

Small royal 8vo. An offprint of [16] pp. $9\frac{1}{4} \times 6\frac{1}{4}$ in.

P. [1] blank; pp. [2–14] numbered 10–22 text; pp. [15–16] blank.

Salmon paper wrappers; printed on upper wrapper: Reprint from | *UNIVERSITY OF* | *Toronto Quarterly* | *A CANADIAN JOURNAL OF THE HUMANITIES* | University of Toronto Press | Printed in Canada; edges cut flush; stapled.

Issued October 1955; no record of the number of copies printed. Not for sale.

Includes English translations by Blunden of Latin poems by Donne, Herbert, Crashaw and Milton.

Reprinted from the *University of Toronto Quarterly*, October 1955 (*see* C3150).

A129   "SIGNALS"   1955

First separate publication:

[*title at head of p.* [1] *between an illustration of a manuscript book and a mortar and pestle, within an oval black panel*, $1 \times 5\frac{1}{2}$ *in.*:] "SIGNALS"

Crown 4to. An offprint of [2] pp. 4 illus. $9\frac{5}{8} \times 7\frac{1}{4}$ in.

Pp. [1–2] text; p. [2] towards foot: EDMUND BLUNDEN. |
(*The decorations are by Prudence Rowe-Evans*).

No wrappers; edges trimmed.

Issued probably November 1955; probably 100 copies printed. Not
for sale.

On medical recipes. Reprinted from *Elixir*, Autumn 1955. *See also*
'The Family Physician in the 17th Century' in the issue of Spring
1955 (*see* A127; C3132, 3147).

A130　　　　　"THE HAPPY MORN"　　　　　1955

First edition:

[*title at head of leaf*: *in scarlet*:] "THE HAPPY MORN"

Small demy 8vo. [1] leaf. $8\frac{3}{8} \times 5\frac{5}{8}$ in.

Leaf [1] text; at foot: [*in scarlet*:] Hong Kong, 1955 Edmund
Blunden.

No wrappers; top, fore, and bottom edges trimmed, left edge rough
trimmed.

Issued December 1955; 150–200 copies printed. Not for sale.

(Then: then the days were dark,). Holograph facsimile. Privately
printed for the author as a Christmas card. There is a variant issue
with [4] pp., pp. [2–4] are blank; copies are in the collections of
Sir Rupert Hart-Davis and Mr K. K. Yung. Reprinted in *A Hong
Kong House*, 1962 (*see* A156).

A130.1　　　　ON A PORTRAIT BY　　　　1955
　　　　　　　MRS. LEIGH HUNT

First separate publication:

[*title at head of p.* [1]:] ON A PORTRAIT BY MRS.
LEIGH HUNT | *by Edmund Blunden*

Foolscap 4to. An offprint of [6] pp. 2 illus. on pp. [2–3]. $8\frac{1}{4} \times 6\frac{1}{2}$
in.

Pp. [1–6] numbered 7–12 text.

White paper wrappers; edges cut flush; gummed and stapled.

Issued probably December 1955; probably 20 copies printed. Not
for sale.

Reprinted from the *Keats-Shelley Memorial Bulletin*, *Rome*,
[December] 1955 (*see* C3155).

First separate publication:

[*title at head of p.* [2]:] THE HEAD MASTER'S ALBUM | EDMUND BLUNDEN

Demy 8vo. An offprint of [12] pp. 8¼ × 5⅞ in.

P. [1] numbered 401 end of previous article pasted to inside upper wrapper; pp. [2-12] numbered 402-412 text.

White paper wrappers; edges cut flush; gummed.

Issued *c.* 9 January 1956; 30 copies printed. Not for sale.

On James Boyer, Charles Lamb's master at Christ's Hospital. Reprinted from *Fukhara Rintarō Sensei Kanreki Kinen Rombunshū Kindai No Eibungaku*, a collection of essays presented to Professor Rintarō Fukuhara on his sixtieth birthday entitled *Modern English Literature* (*see* B182).

A132   A RETIRED NAVAL MAN   1956

First separate publication:

[*title on p.* [1]:] A RETIRED NAVAL MAN | by | EDMUND BLUNDEN | *Reprinted from ELIXIR, Journal of the Hong Kong University* | *Medical Society, Christmas, 1955.*

Crown 4to. An offprint of 6 pp. 5 illus. 9⅝ × 7¼ in.

P. [1] title; pp. [2]-6 text.

No wrappers; edges trimmed; gummed.

Issued February 1956; 100 copies printed. Not for sale.

On William Vane. Illustrated by Prudence Rowe-Evans. Reprinted from *Elixir*, Christmas 1955 (*see* C3154).

A133   COLERIDGE'S FELLOW-GRECIAN   1956

First separate publication:

[*title on upper wrapper:*] COLERIDGE'S FELLOW-GRECIAN | Some Account of Charles Valentine Le Grice | *Edmund Blunden* | [*in Japanese:*] SAITÔ TAKESHI HAKASE KOKI SHUKUGA ROMBUNSHÛ "EIBUN-GAKU KENKYÛ" NUKIZURI

Demy 8vo. An offprint of [36] pp. $8\frac{1}{4}$ X $5\frac{7}{8}$ in.

Pp. [1–35] numbered 47–81 text; p. [36] blank.

White paper wrappers; printed on upper wrapper as above; edges cut flush; sewn and gummed.

Issued *c.* 10 May 1956; 50 copies printed. Not for sale.

Reprinted from *Saitô Takeshi Hakase Koki Shukuga Rombunshû: Eibungakukenkyû*, a collection of essays in commemoration of Professor Takeshi Saito's seventieth birthday entitled *Studies in English Literature* (*see* B186).

A134   LORD BYRON: SOME EARLY   1956
               BIOGRAPHIES

First separate publication:

[*title at head of p.* 1:] LORD BYRON : SOME EARLY BIOGRAPHIES | *by Edmund Blunden*

Foolscap 4to. An offprint of 4 pp. plate facing p. 1. $8\frac{1}{8}$ X $6\frac{5}{8}$ in.

Pp. 1–3 text; p. 4 commencement of following article pasted to lower inside wrapper.

White paper wrappers; edges cut flush; stapled.

Issued December 1956; 20 copies printed. Not for sale.

Reprinted from the *Keats-Shelley Memorial Bulletin, Rome*, [December] 1956 (*see* C3183).

A135   POEMS OF MANY YEARS   1957

First edition:

Edmund Blunden | [*swelled rule*] | POEMS OF | MANY YEARS | COLLINS | ST JAMES'S PLACE, LONDON | 1957

Demy 8vo. 312 pp. $8\frac{5}{8}$ X $5\frac{1}{2}$ in.

P. [1] half-title; p. [2] list of works by the author; p. [3] title; p. [4] at foot: [publisher's device of a fountain, $\frac{1}{4}$ X $\frac{1}{4}$ in.] | PRINTED IN GREAT BRITAIN | COLLINS CLEAR-TYPE PRESS : LONDON AND GLASGOW; p. [5] towards head, dedication: *To* | *A.C.W. EDWARDS* | *of Christ's Hospital*; p. [6] acknowledgements; pp. 7–14 Contents; pp. 15–17 Preface; p. [18] blank; pp. 19–299 text; p. [300] blank; pp. 301–305 Index of Titles; pp. 306–312 Index of First Lines.

Pink cloth boards; lettered in gold on spine: POEMS | OF | MANY

| YEARS | [*swelled rule*] | EDMUND | BLUNDEN | COLLINS; edges trimmed; white end-papers. White dust-jacket printed in greyish-green and black.

Published 17 June 1957; 3000 copies printed. 18*s*.

Selected and arranged by Rupert Hart-Davis.

Contents: Early Poems from *Poems 1914–1930*: The Yellowhammer — The Festubert Shrine — Festubert: The Old German Line — "Transport" up at Ypres — Les Halles d'Ypres — Trees on the Calais Road — Bleue Maison — From *The Waggoner*: The Silver Bird of Herndyke Mill — The Waggoner — Almswomen —The Pike — Sheepbells [*formerly* An Evensong] — The Unchangeable — A Waterpiece — A Country God — The Sighing Time — In Festubert — Mont de Cassel — The Barn — Leisure — Malefactors — Clare's Ghost [*formerly* Phantasies] — The Veteran — From *The Shepherd*: 11th R.S.R. — Shepherd — Forefathers — Gleaning — The Pasture Pond — November Morning — High Summer — Evening Mystery — Sheet Lightning — Cloudy June — Mole Catcher [*formerly* Molecatcher] — The Scythe Struck by Lightning [*formerly* The Scythe] — The Poor Man's Pig — The Covert — The Watermill — Reunion in War — A Farm near Zillebeke — 1916 Seen from 1921 [*formerly* Festubert, 1916] — War Autobiography: Written in Illness — Third Ypres — The Child's Grave — The Last of Autumn — From *English Poems*: Old Homes — Country Sale — Winter: East Anglia [*formerly* Winter Piece] — The Crown Inn [*formerly* "The Crown"] — The Midnight Skaters — Pride of the Village — Muffled — The Puzzle — No Continuing City — The Last Ray — Augury — Hawthorn [*formerly* Triune] — Dead Letters — Thames Gulls — Masks of Time — Achronos [*formerly* Epochs; *and* Eras] — Harvest — Strange Perspective — Rue du Bois — To Joy — A Psalm — The Death-Mask of John Clare [*formerly* On the Death-Mask . . .] — Intimations of Mortality — A "First Impression", Tokyo — Warning to the Troops — In a Country Churchyard — Byroad [*formerly* By Road] — From *Retreat*: An Ancient Path [*formerly* Together] — Solutions [*formerly* The Correct Solution] — The Age of Herbert and Vaughan — The Wartons and Other Landscape-Poets [*formerly* The Wartons and Other Early Romantics; *and* The Wartons and Other Early Romantic Landscape-Poets] — The Complaint — An Infantryman — The Resignation — Would You Return? — An Annotation — Ornithopolis — On the Portrait of a Colonel [*formerly* Portrait of a Colonel] — Departure — Libertine — From *Undertones of War*: A House in Festubert — The Sentry's Mistake [*later* The Guard's Mistake; *and* The Sentry's Mistake] — Two Voices [*formerly* Survivors, 1916] — Illusions — Preparations for Victory — Zero [*later* Come On, My Lucky Lads; *and* Zero, 1916] — At Senlis Once — Zonnebeke Road — Concert Party: Busseboom — Rural Economy, 1917 — E.W.T.: On the Death of his Betty — Battalion in Rest — Vlamertinghe: Passing the Chateau — Recognition [*formerly* A Recognition] — La Quinque Rue — A.G.A.V. — Their Very Memory — On Reading that the Rebuilding of Ypres Approached Completion — Flanders Now [*formerly*

112

113

The Halted Battalion: 1916] — Homes and Haunts — Byroniana:
(i) Kirke White at Wilford; (ii) Newstead [*formerly* Newstead
Abbey] — High Elms, Bracknell — On Reading a Magazine Edited
by Oscar Wilde — The Blueprint — Invocation Written in Spring —
The Portrait — Serena — Rival Feasts [*formerly* Rival Appetites] —
Hammond, England: A Cricketer [*formerly* Hammond of England]
— From *Eastward*: Change and Song — Running Stream — *New
Poems*: Twenty Miles from Town — The Season Reopens [*later* The
Season Opens] — Assaulting Waves — Water-Meadow Evening —
Young Fieldmouse — Those Who First Encouraged Us — The Fond
Dream [*formerly* A Dream] — Early Ideas Reawakened [*formerly*
Early Ideas Remembered] — The Farmhouse Family — H-Bomb —
The Sussex Downs — In Memory of Robert Nichols — C.E.B. Ob.
November 1951 — Frank Worley, D.C.M., July 1954 — Collins of
Chichester — Unrecorded — As Boswell Records — At the Great Wall
of China — Chimes at Midnight — Vision.

A136   PROLOGUE [AS YOU LIKE IT]   1958

First separate publication:

[*title at head of leaf*:] PROLOGUE

Small royal 8vo. [1] leaf. $9\frac{1}{4} \times 6$ in.
Leaf [1] text.
No wrappers; edges trimmed.
Issued *c.* 12 March 1958; 20 copies printed. Not for sale.

(Our company is met once more, and you,). Holograph facsimile.
Preprinted from the programme for the production of *As You Like
It*, by The Masquers, University of Hong Kong (*see* B206).

A137   WAR POETS 1914-1918   1958

First edition:

WAR POETS | 1914-1918 | *by* | EDMUND BLUNDEN |
PUBLISHED FOR | THE BRITISH COUNCIL | and the
NATIONAL BOOK LEAGUE | *by* LONGMANS, GREEN
& CO.

Small demy 8vo. 44 pp. 4 plates between pp. 22-23. $8\frac{1}{2} \times 5\frac{1}{2}$ in.
P. [1] half-title; p. [2] blank; p. [3] title; p. [4] at head: LONG-
MANS, GREEN & CO. LTD. | [*ten lines of addresses*], at centre:
First published in 1958 | © Edmund Blunden, 1958, at foot: *Printed
in Great Britain by Unwin Brothers Limited* | *Woking and London*;

p. [5] Contents; p. [6] blank; p. [7] Illustrations; p. [8] blank; pp. 9–39 text; pp. 40–43 A Select Bibliography; p. [44] blank.

Pale greenish-yellow paper wrappers; printed on upper wrapper: WRITERS AND THEIR WORK NO. 100 | [*ornament*] | [*in red*:] War Poets | 1914–1918 | By EDMUND BLUNDEN | [*in black*: *ornament*] | Published for The British Council | and The National Book League | by Longmans, Green & Co. | *Two shillings and six-pence net*; note on the pamphlet inside upper wrapper; list of titles in the series inside lower wrapper; quotation from the *TLS* outside lower wrapper; edges cut flush; stapled. Inserted 4 pp. leaflet on the series by the editor, Bonamy Dobrée.

Published 28 July 1958 as *Writers and their Work*, No. 100; 8000 copies printed. 2*s*. 6*d*.

There were reprints of 6000 copies in 1964 (revised), and 7000 copies in 1969.

A138   MARY SHELLEY'S ROMANCES   1958

First separate publication:

[*title on upper wrapper*:] MARY SHELLEY'S ROMANCES | EDMUND BLUNDEN

Medium 8vo. An offprint of 4 pp. 9 × 6⅛ in.

Pp. [1]–4 text.

White paper wrappers; printed on upper wrapper as above; edges trimmed; stapled.

Issued 25 September 1958; 10 copies printed. Not for sale.

Reprinted from *Yasuo Yamato's Sixtieth Birthday Festschrift* (*see* B210).

A139   LOVE AND FRIENDSHIP   1958

First separate publication:

[*title at head of leaf*:] 688 THE TIMES LITERARY SUP-PLEMENT FRIDAY NOVEMBER 28 1958 | LOVE AND FRIENDSHIP

An offprint of [1] leaf. 18½ × 12½ in.

Leaf [1] text.

No wrappers; edges trimmed.

Issued *c.* 28 November 1958; 10 copies printed. Not for sale.

Review of *Edward Thomas: The Last Four Years*, Book 1 of the

Memoirs of Eleanor Farjeon. Unsigned. Reprinted from the *TLS*, 28 November 1958 (*see* C3218).

A140   GODWIN'S LIBRARY CATALOGUE   1958

First separate publication:

[*title at head of p.* [1]:] GODWIN'S LIBRARY CATA-LOGUE | *by Edmund Blunden*

Foolscap 4to. An offprint of [4] pp. 2 plates facing pp. [1] and [2]. 8¼ × 6⅝ in.

Pp. [1-3] numbered 27-29 text; p. [4] numbered 30 commencement of following article pasted to inside lower wrapper.

White paper wrappers; edges cut flush; stapled.

Issued probably December 1958; probably 20 copies printed. Not for sale.

Reprinted from the *Keats-Shelley Memorial Bulletin*, [December], 1958 (*see* C3219).

A141   A TOURIST TO TOURISTS   1959

First separate publication:

[*title at head of p.* [1]:] XIIᵉ ANNÉE N°. 2 AVRIL-JUIN 1959 | ETUDES | ANGLAISES | GRANDE-BRETAGNE ○ ETATS-UNIS [*long double rule*] | A TOURIST TO TOURISTS

Small royal 8vo. An offprint of [3] pp. 9¼ × 6 in.

Pp. [1-3] numbered [97]-99 text.

Salmon paper wrappers; printed in brown and black; edges cut flush; stapled.

Issued probably June 1959; number of copies printed not ascertained. Not for sale.

Reprinted from *Etudes anglaises*, avril-juin 1959 (*see* C3225).

A142   THREE YOUNG POETS   1959

First edition:

THREE YOUNG POETS | Critical Sketches of Byron, |

Shelley and Keats | *By* | EDMUND BLUNDEN | *Some-time Professor English Literature* | *in the Imperial University of Tokyo* | KENKYUSHA LTD | TOKYO : 1959

Demy 8vo. [vi] , 70 pp. 8⅜ × 5¾ in.

P. [i] title; p. [ii] at head: © 1959, by Edmund Blunden, at foot: *Manufactured in Japan. Printed at* | THE KENKYUSHA PRESS | *Ushigome, Tokyo.*; p. iii Preface; p. [iv] blank; p. [v] Contents; p. [vi] blank; pp. 1–68 text; p. [69] publisher's imprint in Japanese; p. [70] blank.

Pale blue paper wrappers; printed down the spine: THREE YOUNG POETS *by Edmund Blunden* KENKYUSHA, and on upper wrapper as title above with the omission of place of publication and date; end-papers; edges cut flush. Pale yellow dust-jacket printed in brown.

Published 10 June 1959; 2000 copies printed. 180 yen.

A143   FLOWERS OF THE ROCK   1959

First separate publication:

[*title at head of p.* [1]: *in open capitals*:] FLOWERS OF THE ROCK

Medium 8vo. An offprint of [2] pp. 8⅞ × 5⅝ in.

P. [1] text, towards centre: *With the author's best wishes to C. D. Narasimhaiah on his visiting us* | in Hong Kong, on *1 June 1959.* | Edmund Blunden; p. [2] 'Poem' by E. E. Cummings.

No wrappers; edges trimmed.

Issued after 1 June 1959; number of copies printed not ascertained. Not for sale.

(Upon that cliff, that rock upright). Reprinted from an unidentified journal; first published in *Rising Generation*, 1 April 1950; and reprinted in *A Hong Kong House*, 1962; *Poems on Japan*, 1967; and *Kyōin Zuihitsu*, [1967] (*see* A156, 171; D12).

A144   SHAKESPEARE'S "TEMPEST"   1959

First separate publication:

[*title on upper wrapper*:] Shakespeare's "Tempest" | By | EDMUND BLUNDEN | [*following line in Japanese*:] Tôkyô Joshi Daigaku RONSHŪ Dai-jukkan Dai-nigô bessatsu | From the Essays and Studies, Vol. X, No. 2.

Octover [*sic*] 1959 | TOKYO WOMAN'S CHRISTIAN COLLEGE

Medium 8vo. An offprint of 12 pp. $8\frac{1}{4}$ X $5\frac{3}{4}$ in.

Pp. 1–12 text; original pagination [43]–54 also printed.

White paper wrappers; printed on upper wrapper as above; edges cut flush; stapled and gummed.

Issued October 1959; *c.* 20 copies printed. Not for sale.

Reprinted from *Ronshu: Essays and Studies*, Tokyo Woman's Christian College, October 1959 (*see* C3231).

A145   A HONG KONG HOUSE   1959

First separate edition:

[*title on upper wrapper*:] A HONG KONG HOUSE |
[*illustration of warehouses*, 3 X $4\frac{1}{4}$ *in.*] | Edmund Blunden

Small demy 8vo. [4] pp. $8\frac{1}{4}$ X $5\frac{1}{2}$ in.

P. [1] half-title; pp. [2–3] text; p. [4] blank.

White paper wrappers; upper wrapper printed in pale pink and black as above; outside lower wrapper: 'A Hong Kong House' by Edmund Blunden | is the second of a series of facsimile holograph | poems to be published by the Poetry Book | Society Limited, 4 St James's Square | London SW1 | The booklet was printed by | the Westerham Press and published in | August 1959 in an edition | of 1,100 copies, of which 1,000 are | for sale to members of the | Poetry Book Society and to the | public; edges cut flush; sewn. Matching envelope.

Published probably November 1959; 1100 copies printed. 1s.

(And now a dove and now a dragon-fly). Holograph facsimile. A variant state, proof copies of which two are in the collection of Sir Rupert Hart-Davis, and one in that of Mr K. K. Yung, lacks on the outside lower wrapper the word 'facsimile'; between lines 5 and 6 is inserted: The cover was designed by Ichabod Caxton, and after the final line: PRICE ONE SHILLING. This poem was first published in *The Quill*, Vol. 1, 1955; reprinted in *A Hong Kong House*, 1962; and *The Midnight Skaters*, [1968] (*see* A156, 174, C3159). The facsimile was reprinted in *Edmund Blunden Sixty-Five*, 1961, pp. [193–197] (*see* B234).

First separate publication:

[*title at head of p.* [2]:] MARIANNE HUNT : A LETTER AND FRAGMENT | OF A DIARY | *by Edmund Blunden*

Foolscap 4to. An offprint of [4] pp. plate pasted on inside lower wrapper. 8¼ X 6½ in.

P. [1] numbered 31 end of previous article pasted on inside upper wrapper; pp. [2-4] numbered 30-32 text.

White paper wrappers; edges cut flush; stapled.

Issued probably December 1959; probably 20 copies printed. Not for sale.

Reprinted from the *Keats-Shelley Memorial Bulletin*, [December] 1959 (*see* C3232).

First separate publication:

[*title at head of leaf*:] THE OBSCURE WEBB(E) | By EDMUND BLUNDEN

An offprint of [1] leaf. 21¼ X 13½ in.

Leaf [1] text.

No wrappers; three edges trimmed, fourth untrimmed.

Issued *c*. 18 December 1959; 12 copies printed. Not for sale.

On Cornelius Webb. Reprinted from the *TLS*, 18 December 1959 (*see* C3234).

First separate publication:

[*title on leaf tipped on p.* [1]:] ON COLERIDGE AS A THINKER, | AND SOME OF | HIS CONTEMPORARIES | EDMUND BLUNDEN

Demy 8vo. An offprint of [14] pp. 8¼ X 5⅞ in.

Pp. [1-13] numbered [139]-151 text; leaf tipped on p. [1] with title as above; p. [14] blank.

No wrappers; edges trimmed; gummed.

Issued February 1960; no record of the number of copies printed. Not for sale.

Reprinted from *Takahashi Genji Hakase Kanreki Kinen Eibungaku Rombunshū: Kotoba to Bungaku*, 1960, a collection of essays on English language and literature in honour of Dr Genji Takahashi's sixtieth birthday entitled *Language and Literature* (*see* B223).

A149   THE ROMANTICS AND OURSELVES   1960

First separate publication:

[*title at head of p.* [1]:] THE ROMANTICS AND OUR-SELVES* | [*rule*] | EDMUND BLUNDEN | [*rule*]

Demy 8vo. An offprint of [12] pp. 8¼ × 5⅞ in.

Pp. [1–12] numbered 217–228 text.

White paper wrappers; edges trimmed; stapled.

Issued *c.* 16 June 1960; 19 copies printed. Not for sale.

Address delivered at the Thirty-first General Meeting of the English Literary Society of Japan. Reprinted from *Studies in English Literature*, April 1960 (*see* C3241).

A150   MOMENTS IN A LIBRARY   1960

First separate publication:

[*title as head of p.* [1]:] *Reprinted from* The Library Association Record, *Vol. 62, No. 8, August 1960* | [*long rule*] | Moments in a Library* | *By* EDMUND BLUNDEN, *Professor of English, University of Hong Kong*

Crown 4to. An offprint of [6] pp. 9¾ × 7¼ in.

Pp. [1–5] numbered [243]–247 text; p. [6] blank.

No wrappers; edges trimmed; stapled.

Issued August 1960; *c.* 25 copies printed. Not for sale.

Reprinted from the *Library Association Record*, London, August 1960 (*see* C3246).

A151   A WESSEX WORTHY   1960

a. First separate publication:

A WESSEX WORTHY | THOMAS RUSSELL | *By* |

EDMUND BLUNDEN | BEAMINSTER, DORSET | At
The Toucan Press of J. Stevens Cox | 1960

Small crown 8vo. 12 pp. $7\frac{1}{4} \times 4\frac{3}{4}$ in.

P. [1] title; p. [2] at foot: Printed in Great Britain; pp. 3–6 text; pp.
7–11 Selections from Russell's Poems; p. 11 towards centre: A
hundred copies of this pamphlet | have been issued for sale. | It first
appeared in Stevens Cox's | Literary Repository, No. 2/1960; p.
[12] blank.

Dark green paper wrappers; printed on upper wrapper as lines 1–4
of title as above; edges cut flush; stapled.

Issued c. 19 September 1960; 112 copies printed. 7s.

On Thomas Russell. Twelve copies were printed on hand-made paper
(see A151b). Reprinted from the Literary Repository, [March]
1960 (see C3238).

b. *First separate publication — hand-made paper issue.
1960*:

[*title and imprint as above*] *

Small crown 8vo. 12 pp. $7\frac{3}{8} \times 4\frac{7}{8}$ in.

Wrappers as above.

Issued c. 19 September 1960; 12 copies bound. Not for sale.

Printed on hand-made paper for private circulation.

c. *First separate edition*:

[*title at head of p.* [1]:] *DORSET WORTHIES No. 2* |
[*rule*] | THOMAS RUSSELL 1762–1788 | By EDMUND
BLUNDEN

Demy 8vo. [4] pp. illus. (port.) on p. [1]. $8\frac{1}{2} \times 5\frac{1}{2}$ in.

Pp. [1–4] text; p. [4] at foot: *Published by the Dorset Archaeological and Natural History Society, Dorchester 1962*.

No wrappers; edges trimmed.

Published August 1962 as *Dorset Worthies*, No. 2; 2000 copies printed. 1s.

There were two issues. Pp. [2–3] of the first issue were transposed;
about 30 copies were distributed, and the remainder, about 1970,
were pulped when this was noted. The transposition was corrected,
and there was a second issue of 2000 copies.

First separate publication:

[*title at head of p.* [1]:] INDICATIONS OF KEATS | *by Edmund Blunden*

Foolscap 4to. An offprint of 6 pp. $8\frac{1}{4}$ × $6\frac{1}{2}$ in.

Pp. 1–5 text; p. 6 commencement of following article pasted on inside lower wrapper.

White paper wrappers; edges cut flush; stapled.

Issued *c.* 18 December 1960; probably 20 copies printed. Not for sale.

Reprinted from the *Keats-Shelley Memorial Bulletin*, [December] 1960 (*see* C3249).

A153   TO THE COMPANY MET FOR   1961
                MY BIRTHDAY, 1961

First edition:

[*title at head of leaf*:] To the Company | Met for my Birthday, 1961

Imperial 8vo. [1] leaf. $10\frac{3}{4}$ × $7\frac{1}{4}$ in.

No wrappers; edges trimmed.

Issued 1 November 1961; 700–1000 copies printed. Not for sale.

(When I was thirty-five, I think). Holograph facsimile, signed: Hong Kong, 1 xi 1961 Edmund Blunden. Reprinted in *A Hong Kong House*, 1962 (*see* A156).

A154   KEATS'S EDITOR   1961

First separate publication:

[*title at head of p.* [1]:] KEATS'S EDITOR | *by Edmund Blunden*

Foolscap 4to. An offprint of 2 pp. $8\frac{1}{4}$ × $6\frac{1}{2}$ in.

Pp. 1–2 text.

White paper wrappers; edges cut flush; gummed.

Issued probably 21 December 1961; 20 copies printed. Not for sale.

On H.W. Garrod. Reprinted from the *Keats-Shelley Memorial Bulletin*, [December] 1961 (*see* C3267).

a. First edition:

English Scientists | as | Men of Letters | EDMUND BLUN-
DEN | C.B.E., M.C., M.A. OXON., F.R.S.L. | *Jubilee
Congress Lecture | delivered on September eleventh, 1961
| in Loke Yew Hall, University of Hong Kong* | [*univer-
sity's device,* ½ × ½ *in.*] | HONG KONG UNIVERSITY
PRESS | OXFORD UNIVERSITY PRESS | 1961

Demy 8vo. [iv] , 12 pp. 8¼ × 5½ in.

P. [i] half-title; p. [ii] blank; p. [iii] title; p. [iv] at head: © *by the
Hong Kong University Press, 1961* | *Limited edition, 1000 copies,
December 1961*, at centre, Oxford University Press's addresses, at
foot: *Printed in Hong Kong by* | CATHAY PRESS | *31 Wong Chuk
Hang Road, Aberdeen*; pp. [1]-11 text; p. [12] blank.

Pale brown stiff paper wrappers; printed on upper wrapper as title
above; list of Hong Kong University Press publications on lower
wrapper; leaf pasted inside wrappers to form paste-down end-papers;
list of works by the author on paste-down end-papers; edges cut
flush; sewn.

Published 28 December 1961; 3000 copies printed. HK$1.50 (3s.).

One thousand copies were bound in wrappers as above, and 2000
as the *University of Hong Kong Supplement to the Gazette* (*see*
A155*b*).

b. First edition — second issue. [*1961*] :

[*title at head of p.* [1] :] ENGLISH SCIENTISTS AS |
MEN OF LETTERS | BY | EDMUND BLUNDEN

Demy 8vo. 12 pp. 8½ × 5½ in.

Pp. [1]-11 text; p. [1] at foot: Jubilee Congress Lecture, delivered
on Monday, September 11, 1961 | at 5.30 p.m., at Loke Yew Hall,
University of Hong Kong. | © *Hong Kong University Press, Hong
Kong, 1961*; p. [12] blank.

No wrappers; edges trimmed; stapled.

Issued 28 December 1961 as the *University of Hong Kong Supplement to the Gazette*; 2000 copies. Not for sale.

A155.1   "A SONG TO DAVID," 1763   1962

First separate publication:

[*title on upper wrapper*:] "A Song to David," 1763 | By |
Edmund Blunden | [*following line in Japanese*:] Tôkyô
Joshi Daigaku RONSHU Dai-jûshi-kan Dai-ni-gô betsu-
zuri | From the Essays and Studies, Vol. XIV, No. 2,
March 1962 | TOKYO WOMAN'S CHRISTIAN COLLEGE

Medium 8vo. An offprint of 8 pp. $8\frac{1}{4} \times 5\frac{3}{4}$ in.

Pp. 1–8 text.

White paper wrappers; printed on upper wrapper as above; edges cut
flush; stapled and gummed.

Issued March 1962; *c.* 20 copies printed. Not for sale.

Reprinted from *Ronshu: Essays and Studies*, Tokyo Woman's Christian College, March 1962 (*see* C3270.1).

A156   A HONG KONG HOUSE   1962

First edition:

Edmund Blunden | A HONG KONG | HOUSE | poems
1951–1961 | COLLINS · London, 1962

Demy 8vo. 104 pp. $8\frac{1}{2} \times 5\frac{1}{2}$ in.

P. [1] half-title; p. [2] list of works by the author; p. [3] title; p.
[4] note by the author, at foot: © Edmund Blunden 1962 | Printed
in Great Britain | Collins Clear-Type Press | London and Glasgow;
p. [5] towards head, dedication: *To the students of English who
have so* | *encouraged me for nearly a decade to share* | *life and
letters with them in the University* | *of Hong Kong, and to their
'pastors and* | *masters', my colleagues*; p. [6] blank; pp. [7–9] Con-
tents; p. [10] blank; pp. 11–102 text; pp. [103–104] blank, integral.

Turquoise cloth boards; lettered in gold on spine: A | HONG |
KONG | HOUSE | *Poems* | *1951–1961* | [*swelled rule*] | *Edmund* |
Blunden | COLLINS; edges trimmed; white end-papers. White pic-
torial dust-jacket printed in greyish-yellow, blue and black.

Published 3 September 1962; 1500 copies printed. £1. 1*s.*

Contents: View from the University of Hong Kong [*formerly* A
View from the Department of English; *and* A View from a Hong
Kong Office] — A Hong Kong House — On Lamma Island [To
S.G.D. *i.e.* S. G. Davis] — On the Air — The Sleeping Amah —The
Busy Fly — Chinese Paper-Knife [*formerly* A Chinese Paperknife] —
An Island Tragedy — To the Company Met for My Birthday, 1961 —
Arrival at a River, in Japan — Summer Storm in Japanese Hills

[*formerly* Summer Storm] — In Hokkaido — The Stone Garden
(Kyōto) [*title in Contents*: . . . in Kyōto] — Voice of Kyōto — The
Tea-House [*formerly* Japanese Inn] — Flowers of the Rock — Petals
— Tokyo Lawn (1948) [*formerly* Tokyo Lawn; *later* From a Tokyo
Lawn] — A Threefold Screen [*formerly* Japanese Glimpses] — Voice
of Autumn: A Theme for a Dance — Voice of Spring [*formerly* For
a Spring Dance by Tamami Gojo] — Japan Revived — Japan Beautiful — Nearing Yokohama, 15 August 1960 — Pine-Trees — A Storm:
1907 [*title in Contents*: Storm: 1907] — Once on a Hill — Appearances of the Season, May 1938 [*title in Contents*: . . . 1938] — Antiquities — Thorny Winter — The Young Mariners — A Life's Unity —
The Passer-By — The Beloved River — Millstream Memories — A
Southern Pilgrim — Autolycus's Country [*formerly* On Shakespeare's Winter's Tale] — The Recapture — Later Flowers — Christmas Invitation for 1756: pre-Telephone [*formerly* no sub-title] —
The Happy Morn [*formerly* "The Happy Morn"] — A Christmas
Tale — Christmas Eve, 1959 — A Vicar In Remembrance — An
Empty Chair [Chas. E. B.] [*title in Contents*: C.E.B. An Empty
Chair; *i.e.* the poet's father] — The Child in Church — Autolycus
Again: In Memory of B.D. [*i.e.* Bert Daines; *formerly* An Autoly-
cus] — Speech by a Hamlet in the Amiens District — Picardy Sunday
[*formerly* Picardy in Autumn] — Over the Valley — Cathedrals —
Seers — The Adorning [*formerly* The Adorned] — Wild Creatures
at Nightfall — Dog on Wheels — Reader, No Reader — To a British
Jar Containing Stephens' Ink [*formerly* Ode to an Ink-Jar (Stephens'
Ink)] — A Family Discourse — Catherine Sings — A New Song — An
Old Song — The Little Song — And Away — A Short Ode — An Ode
for Saint Cecilia's Day — A Variation — For a Musician's Monument:
G.F. [*i.e.* Gerald Finzi] — A March [*title in Contents*: The March] —
But at Last — Forsaken Memorials [*formerly* Nouvelles Littéraires,
or Inani Munere] — Ballad of the Sergeants of Other Days [*formerly*
Echo de l'Autre Guerre] — A Poet's Death, 1958 — W.S.: Last Plays
[*i.e.* William Shakespeare] — Seventeenth Century Fashion — James
Clarence Mangan — Two Tributes: (i) On Reading of Mahatma
Gandhi's Death [*formerly* To the Memory of Gandhi]; (ii) For the
Centenary of Rabindranath Tagore — On Tearing Up a Cynical Poem
— Sententiae: In Memoriam Samuel Williams, B.A.

A157   GEORGE EDWARD SHELLEY, M.B.E.   1962

First separate publication:

[*title at head of p.* 2:] GEORGE EDWARD SHELLEY,
M.B.E. | *by Edmund Blunden*

Foolscap 4to. An offprint of 4 pp. $8\frac{3}{8} \times 6\frac{5}{8}$ in.

P. 1 end of previous article pasted to inside upper wrapper; pp. 2–3 text; p. 4 commencement of following article pasted to inside lower wrapper.

White paper wrappers; edges cut flush; stapled.

Issued probably December 1962; 20 copies printed. Not for sale.

Reprinted from the *Keats-Shelley Memorial Bulletin*, [December] , 1962 (*see* C3281).

A158   **WILLIAM CROWE**   1963

a. First edition:

[*title on upper wrapper: within a double rule, thick, thin:*] WILLIAM CROWE | (1745-1829) | by EDMUND BLUN-DEN | [*publisher's device of a toucan,* $1\frac{1}{8} \times \frac{5}{8}$ *in.*] | Published by | J. Stevens Cox at The Toucan Press | Beaminster, Dorset. | 1963

Small demy 8vo. 4 pp. 2 illus. on pp. [1] and 4. $8\frac{5}{8} \times 5\frac{5}{8}$ in.

Pp. [1]-3 text; p. 4 Bibliography of the Works of William Crowe.

Pale green stiff paper wrappers; printed on upper wrapper as above, and publisher's advertisement on lower wrapper; edges trimmed; pages not secured.

Published 23 April 1963; 100 copies printed. 7s.

Fifty copies were published in pale green wrappers as above, and 50 in mid-blue wrappers. The Dorset Natural History and Archaeological Society issued a reprint (*see* A158*b*).

b. First edition — second printing. [*1963*] :

[*title at head of p.* [1]:] DORSET WORTHIES No. 5 | [*rule*] | WILLIAM CROWE B.C.L. (1745-1829) | By EDMUND BLUNDEN

Demy 8vo. An offprint of 4 pp. 2 illus. on pp. [1] and 4. $8\frac{5}{8} \times 5\frac{5}{8}$ in.

Pp. [1]-4 text; p. 4 at foot: Published by the Dorset Natural History and Archaeological Society, Dorchester, 1963.

No wrappers; edges trimmed.

Issued December 1963 as *Dorset Worthies*, No. 5; 2000 copies printed. 1s.

a. First edition:

A Corscombe Inhabitant | by | EDMUND BLUNDEN | [*publisher's device of a toucan*, 1⅛ × ⅝ *in*.] | Privately Printed at | The Toucan Press | of | J. Stevens Cox, | Beaminster, Dorset, England | May 1963

Large crown 8vo. [4] pp. 8 × 5 in.

P. [1] title; p. [2] 'A Note on Hollis and Corscombe' by J. Stevens Cox, at foot: Fifty three copies of this, the first edition of *A Cors-combe Inhabitant* have been printed: Fifty two for the friends of Edmund Blunden and J. Stevens Cox and one for the British Museum; p. [3] text; p. [4] blank.

Off-white paper wrappers; printed on upper wrapper: A | Corscombe | Inhabitant | by | EDMUND | BLUNDEN; edges cut flush; pages not secured.

Published May 1963; 53 copies printed. Not for sale.

(Wandering through time with Boswell, I arrived). Fifty copies were printed on hand-made paper as above, and 3 on vellum (*see* A159*b*). J. Stevens Cox originally intended to publish this poem as a broadsheet, and 53 copies were printed on a leaf, 14 × 8 in. As the result was not satisfactory, 50 copies were pulped. Three copies of this trial issue exist; 2 are in the collection of J. Stevens Cox, and one in Blunden's collection.

b. First edition — vellum issue. 1963:

[*title and imprint as above*]

Crown 8vo. [4] pp. 7 × 5 in.

Wrappers as above.

Issued May 1963; 3 copies. Not for sale.

Printed on vellum. Two copies are in the collection of J. Stevens Cox, and one in Blunden's collection.

A160   BARRY CORNWALL AND KEATS   1963

First separate publication:

[*title at head of p.* [2]:] BARRY CORNWALL AND KEATS | *by Edmund Blunden*

Foolscape 4to. An offprint of [6] pp. 8⅜ × 6 in.

P. [1] numbered 3 end of previous article pasted to inside upper wrapper; pp. [2–5] numbered 4–7 text; p. [6] numbered 8 commencement of following article pasted to inside lower wrapper.

White paper wrappers; edges cut flush; stapled.

Issued probably December 1963; probably 20 copies printed. Not for sale.

Reprinted from the *Keats-Shelley Memorial Bulletin*, [December], 1963 (*see* C3293).

A161   **CORDUROY COUNTRY**   1964

First separate publication:

[*title at head of leaf*:] 858 THE TIMES LITERARY SUPPLEMENT THURSDAY SEPTEMBER 17 1964 | CORDUROY COUNTRY

An offprint of [1] leaf. $25\frac{1}{8} \times 15$ in.

Leaf [1] text.

No wrappers; edges trimmed.

Issued *c.* 17 September 1964; 10 copies printed. Not for sale.

Review of *Apple Acre*, by Adrian Bell. Unsigned. Reprinted from the *TLS*, 17 September 1964 (*see* C3319).

A162   **GUEST OF THOMAS HARDY**   1964

First edition:

Monographs on the Life of Thomas Hardy: No. 10 | Edited by J. STEVENS COX, F.S.A. | GUEST OF | THOMAS HARDY | by | EDMUND BLUNDEN | With an introduction by Richard Curle | [*publisher's device of a toucan*, $1\frac{1}{8} \times \frac{5}{8}$ *in.*] | Published by | J. STEVENS COX | at The Toucan Press, Beaminster, Dorset, 1964.

Crown 8vo. 16 pp. 4 illus. on pp. [2], 8, 10 and 12. $7\frac{1}{2} \times 5$ in.

P. [1] blank; p. [2] photograph of the author; p. [3] title; p. [4] at foot: *Copyright © reserved by J. Stevens Cox, 1964* | Printed in Great Britain; pp. 5–6 Introduction by Richard Curle; p. 7 text; p. 8 photograph of Thomas Hardy; p. 9 text; p. 10 photograph of the author; p. 11 text; p. 12 photograph of the author; pp. 13–14 text; pp. [15–16] blank.

White paper wrappers; printed in green on upper wrapper as title above within a double rule, thick, thin; list of 'Monographs on the

Life of Thomas Hardy' printed in green on outside lower wrapper; note on the series printed in black on inside upper wrapper; list of publications printed in black on inside lower wrapper; edges cut flush; stapled.

Published *c.* 17 September 1964; 2000 copies printed. 3*s.*

There was a trial issue of 6 copies with wrappers printed in black as above; the list of 'Monographs on the Life of Thomas Hardy' is printed in black on the outside of the lower wrapper; the inside of both wrappers is blank.

A163   JOHN TAYLOR, 1781–1864   1964

First separate publication:

[*title at head of p.* [1]:] JOHN TAYLOR, 1781–1864 |
by Edmund Blunden

Foolscap 4to. An offprint of [4] pp. $8\frac{1}{8} \times 6\frac{5}{8}$ in.

Pp. [1–4] numbered 21–24 text.

White paper wrappers; edges cut flush; stapled.

Issued probably December 1964; probably 20 copies printed. Not for sale.

Reprinted from the *Keats-Shelley Memorial Bulletin*, [December] 1964 (*see* C3328).

A164   THE GREAT CHURCH OF   1965
          THE HOLY TRINITY LONG MELFORD

a. First edition:

[*title on upper wrapper*: *within a double rule*:] A BRIEF GUIDE TO | [*in garnet brown*:] The Great Church | of the | Holy Trinity | Long Melford | [*in black*:] [*illustration of the cross,* $2\frac{3}{8} \times 1\frac{3}{8}$ *in.*] | By Edmund Blunden, C.B.E., M.C., D. Litt., C. Lit. | 1965 | PRICE 2/-

Demy 8vo. 16 pp. 5 illus. on pp. [2], 4, 6, [9] and [11]. $8\frac{1}{2} \times 5\frac{1}{2}$ in.
Pp. 1–10 text; p. [11] illustration; p. 12 text; p. 13 poem by John Press; pp. 14–15 List of Rectors; p. 15 towards centre: Some Books Consulted; p. 16 plan.

White stiff paper wrappers; printed on upper cover as above, and inside lower wrapper: [*at centre*: *acknowledgement to photographer*;

at foot:] Printed by East Anglian Magazine Ltd., 6 Great Colman Street, Ipswich.; edges cut flush; stapled.

Published 1965; probably 20,200 copies printed. 2*s.*

b. *Second edition. 1966*:

[*title inside upper wrapper*: *in white*:] The Great Church | of the Holy Trinity | Long Melford | [*in black*:] by ED-MUND BLUNDEN, CBE, MC, D LITT, C LIT | 1966 | PRICE 2*s* 6*d*

Demy 8vo. 20 pp. 8 illus. on pp. [2], [4], [6], [8], [10], [12], [14], and [16]; plan on p. 19. $8\frac{1}{2} \times 5\frac{1}{2}$ in.

P. [1] text; p. [2] illustration; p. 3 text; p. [4] illustration; p. [5] text; p. [6] illustration; p. 7 text; p. [8] illustration; p. 9 text; p. [10] illustration; p. 11 text; p. [12] illustration; p. 13 text; p. [14] illustration; p. 15 text, and poem by John Press; p. [16] illustration; pp. 17–18 List of Rectors; p. 18 Some Books Consulted; p. 19 plan; p. [20] Acknowledgements, at foot: Designed and printed by | W. S. Cowell Ltd, Butter Market, Ipswich.

White stiff pictorial paper wrappers, designed by John Piper; printed outside wrappers in grey and black, and inside in dull rose; printed on upper wrapper: [*in white*:] LONG MELFORD CHURCH | [*at foot: autograph facsimile in black*:] John Piper; edges cut flush; stapled.

Published June 1966; 16,800 copies printed. 2*s.* 6*d.*

The text is revised; all the illustrations are new.

There was a reprint of 25,000 copies in December 1968.

A165   PROLOGUE [THE TAMING   1965
OF THE SHREW]

First separate publication:

[*title at head of leaf*:] Prologue

Royal 4to. An offprint of [1] leaf. $11\frac{7}{8} \times 8\frac{7}{8}$ in.

Leaf [1] text, towards foot: May 1965 from an old contributor | Edmund Blunden.

No wrappers; edges trimmed.

Issued May 1965; number of copies printed not ascertained. Not for sale.

(Japanese friends and others all,). Holograph facsimile. Reprinted from the programme to the Mad Masters' production of *The Taming of the Shrew*. Reprinted in *Poems on Japan*, 1967 (*see* A171; B261).

A166   T. J. HOGG'S LIBRARY   1965

First separate publication:

[*title at head of p.* [1]:] T. J. HOGG'S LIBRARY | *by Edmund Blunden*

Foolscap 4to. An offprint of [2] pp. $8\frac{1}{4} \times 6\frac{5}{8}$ in.

Pp. [1–2] numbered 45–46 text; p. [2] numbered 46 lower half pasted over.

White paper wrappers; edges cut flush; gummed.

Issued probably September 1965; probably 20 copies printed. Not for sale.

Reprinted from the *Keats-Shelley Memorial Bulletin*, [September] 1965 (*see* C3341).

A167   FREEDOM OF POPERINGE   1965

First separate publication:

[*title at head of leaf*:] *Freedom of Poperinge* | [These few stanzas refer to the "Jubileum Toc H" at Poperinge, | June 19–20, 1965. The King of the Belgians and his subjects | [*seven lines on the reunion signed E.B.*]]

Small crown 8vo. [1] leaf. $7\frac{1}{4} \times 4\frac{3}{8}$ in.

Leaf [1] text.

No wrappers; edges trimmed.

Issued December 1965; 250 copies printed. Not for sale.

(Shall we not also join the friends). Reprinted from *Toc H Journal*, December 1965 (*see* C3347).

A168   ELEVEN POEMS   1965 [i.e. 1966]

a. First edition:

ELEVEN POEMS | by | Edmund Blunden | THE GOLDEN HEAD PRESS | CAMBRIDGE | 1965

Demy 8vo. [ii] , 22 pp. plate facing p. [4] . $8\frac{3}{8} \times 5\frac{1}{2}$ in.

Pp. [i-ii] blank; p. [1] half-title; p. [2] blank; p. [3] title; p. [4] at foot: EDMUND BLUNDEN © 1965 | The Golden Head Press | Abbey Road, Cambridge | Printed by Crampton and Sons, Ltd. | Sawston, Cambridge; p. [5] Contents; p. [6] blank; p. [7] Preface; p. [8] blank; pp. 9-20 text; p. 21 at centre: *Eleven Poems* | Twenty impressions on Hodomura paper, | specially bound. Signed by the author. | Two hundred impressions on Glastonbury | Antique paper, in wrappers. | This is number [*numbered in ink over a row of dots*] ; p. [22] blank.

White stiff paper wrappers covered by pastel green thin paper wrappers; white paper label on upper wrapper, $2\frac{5}{8}$ × $3\frac{1}{2}$ in., printed in black: [*within a border:*] ELEVEN POEMS | [*short rule*] | EDMUND BLUNDEN; edges cut flush; sewn. Celophane envelope.

Published 5 March 1966; 246 copies printed. £1.

Twenty-one copies were issued as an Hodomura paper issue (*see* A168*b*). The 26 copies printed in addition to the number recorded on p. 21 include review and copyright copies; 25 copies were bound as above, and one as the Hodomura paper issue.

Contents: A Swan, a Man — Gone — Ancre, 1916 — Armistice: A March — Darkness — From our Corner in Hong Kong — Written in the Woman's Christian College, Tokyo — A Sonnet after Listening to B.B.C. News 12 November 1963 — Modern Times — L. C. [*i.e.* Lily Chan] — Andrew Marvell's Hortus Translated [*formerly* Marvell's "Hortus"] .

b. First edition — Hodomura paper issue. 1965 [*i.e. 1966*] :

[*title and imprint as above*]

Demy 8vo. [48] pp. plate facing p. 16. $8\frac{5}{8}$ × $5\frac{1}{2}$ in.

P. [i] half-title; pp. [ii-iv] blank; p. [v] title; pp. [vi-vii] blank; p. [viii] as p. [4] above; p. [ix] Contents; pp. [x-xii] blank; p. [xiii] Preface; pp. [xiv-xvi] blank; pp. 9-20 [*i.e.* 17-40] text printed on the first and last pages of each 4 pp.; p. 21 [*i.e.* 41] Certificate, signed by the author; pp. [42-46] blank.

Grey pictorial paper boards; printed in yellow, dark brown, green and red; white paper label, $1\frac{3}{4}$ × 3 in., on upper cover: ELEVEN POEMS | by | Edmund Blunden; fore and bottom edges trimmed; top untrimmed; white end-papers.

Issued 5 March 1966; 21 copies bound. £5.

First edition:

A SELECTION OF THE | SHORTER POEMS | OF |
EDMUND BLUNDEN | PRICE TWO SHILLINGS | [*long
rule*] | (Profits from the sale of this book will aid the work
of | restoring the Great Church of the Holy Trinity, | Long
Melford) | [*long rule*]

Foolscap 8vo. [24] pp. $6 \times 4\frac{3}{8}$ in.

P. [1] title; pp. [2-24] text.

White stiff paper wrappers; printed on upper wrapper: [*photograph
of the author*] | EDMUND BLUNDEN, and outside lower wrapper
at foot: Published by J. A. White, Long Melford. | Printed at the
Lavenham Press. | This selection is produced by the generous permis-
sion of | the poet and his publishers, Messrs. William Collins.; inside
lower wrapper, note on the author; edges cut flush; stapled.

Published July 1966; 2000 copies printed. 2s.

Contents: The Western Front: A Farm near Zillebeke — Illusions —
Report on Experience — Some Talk of Peace — The English Land-
scape, (with figures): Winter, East Anglia [*formerly* Winter Piece] —
Muffled — A Storm: 1907 — The Passer-By — Cathedrals — Wild
Creatures at Nightfall — Half a Century — The Orient: Voice of
Kyoto — The Stone Garden (Kyoto) — The Tea-House [*formerly*
Japanese Inn] — Summer Storm in Japanese Hills [*formerly* Summer
Storm] — The Cottage at Chigasaki — At the Great Wall of China —
The Sleeping Amah — Cricket: Cricket, I Confess — From Hammond
(England) A Cricketer [*formerly* Hammond of England] — Reflec-
tions: Reflections — Minority Report — Values.

A170   HORACE WALPOLE'S YOUNG POET   1966

First separate publication:

[*title towards head of p*. [1]:] Horace Walpole's Young
Poet | EDMUND BLUNDEN

Small demy 8vo. An offprint of [6] pp. $8\frac{3}{8} \times 5\frac{1}{2}$ in.

Pp. [1-5] numbered 95-99 text; p. [6] blank.

Pale grey paper wrappers; printed in black on upper wrapper:
RENAISSANCE | AND MODERN | ESSAYS | [*long rule*] | Presen-
ted to Vivian de Sola Pinto | on the occasion of his seventieth birth-
day | [*long rule*] | EDITED BY G. R. HIBBARD | *with the assist-
ance of* | *George A. Panichas and Allan Rodway* | [*within a heavy*

black rule:] OFFPRINT | [*below rule*:] [*publisher's device*] |
Routledge and Kegan Paul | LONDON; edges cut flush; stapled.

Issued September 1966; 4 copies printed. Not for sale.

On Thomas Pentycross. Reprinted from *Renaissance and Modern Essays*, edited by G. R. Hibbard (*see* B266).

A171   POEMS ON JAPAN   1967

First edition:

EDMUND BLUNDEN | POEMS ON JAPAN | HITHERTO
UNCOLLECTED AND | MOSTLY UNPRINTED | Compiled and Edited in Honour of | His Seventieth Birthday
by | TAKESHI SAITO | 1967

Foolscap 8vo. viii, 80 pp. $6\frac{3}{4} \times 4\frac{1}{4}$ in.

P. [i] half-title; p. [ii] blank; p. [iii] title; p. [iv] at head: Copyright © Edmund Blunden 1967; pp. v–viii Contents; pp. 1–69 text; p. [70] blank; pp. 71–75 Edmund Blunden by Takeshi Saito; p. [76] blank; p. [77] These poems of Edmund Blunden were compiled | by one of his admirers, one who is proud of | their friendship of more than forty years' | standing. This edition printed on handmade | Japanese paper is limited to 150 copies, | of which 50 were presented to the author | and the rest have been reserved for | distribution in this country by | the Blunden Society in Japan. | This copy is No. [*numbered*] | Printed in Japan | at the Kenkyusha Press, Tokyo.; pp. [78–80] blank, integral.

Pale cream paper boards; white paper label on spine, $2\frac{1}{2} \times \frac{1}{4}$ in., printed in black down the spine: BLUNDEN : POEMS ON JAPAN; edges trimmed; pale cream end-papers. Pale cream dust-jacket printed in black.

Issued May 1967; 150 copies printed. Not for sale.

There was a reprint of 500 copies issued in June 1967 at 350 yen in pale mottled cream and rust paper boards; printed in black down the spine, and on upper cover; edges trimmed; cream end-papers; transparent dust-jacket.

Contents: Up, Up! — Torao Taketomo — untitled (The same divinity that gnarls) — untitled (The way was long, the church was cold,) — untitled (To see my scribbled pages thus enshrined,) — Yukichi — untitled (The rhyme shall yet again relate) — untitled (Too soon for us more happy days must end,) — To Jojun Deguchi — Shindo-san — untitled (Here Bunyan finds a home, a house of learning,) — untitled (Another war has thundered through those plains,) — In Zuiganji Temple — For the Education Institute of Aichi Prefecture — Takamatsu Countryside — Return to Japan — To Koichi Nakane — Going to a Lecture — For a Water-Colour by Y. Noguchi — untitled

(Among the lakes the Painter finds his bliss,) — untitled (So have you lived, that finer life may be;) — untitled (This is a scene that from my early years) — For the Engish Group in Asahigawa — A Song for Kwansei — untitled (Forget the winter's tooth; the merry flames leap) — The Flowers of the Rock — At Harihan — A Glimpse — untitled (Outside, the night, the lamps of distant farms) — To T. Kitamura — Gate to Poetry — untitled (There may be nights to come when I shall need) — To Mr and Mrs Hani — For Tokyo Joshi Daigaku : A Hymn [*formerly* College Song] — The King's Arms, Kobe — For Takeshi and Fumiko — For Yukuchi Nakamura — untitled (The children cannot stay) — untitled (How soon these little girls run round the lovely lake) — A Thought of H.I.H. Prince Chichibu — On a Picture of H.I.H. Prince Chichibu — untitled (Many words may never find) — In Honour of Royal Couple, To Akihito, Michiko [*formerly* In Honor of Royal Couple; *later* In Honor of Crown Prince Akihito and Miss Michiko Shoda] — untitled (On a rainy June morning) — untitled (A. Mitsuoka's verse should be) — untitled (If Robert Burns were in Japan) — Books — untitled (Even Many Years have now become still More;) — June 1959, To the English Department of Hiroshima University — Michio Masui — Mr Collins at Miyajima 1959 — For Yoshitaka Sakai — untitled (It shall be written:) — Translated from the Japanese of H. M. Empress Nagako [*formerly* On Blood Transfusion] — untitled (Yours is the modern Castle of Osaka.) — A Small Offering — Captaincy — Otani Women's College — untitled (The sea hath its pearls,) — untitled (What rarities you set before us) — untitled (Keiko commanded, and we met) — Written in the Woman's Christian College, Tokyo — To Yukichi Nakamura — untitled (As my kind Prologue yesterday) — To Mr Ito, Mayor of Matsushima — Seigo Shiratori at Matsushima — The Summer Journey — Prologue to *The Taming of the Shrew* — untitled (Here is Charles Lamb's first church, which modern war).

A172   [HARDY OF WESSEX]   1967

First separate publication:

[*title at centre of leaf* [2] :] Hardy of Wessex. His Life and Literary Career. By CARL J. WEBER. | [*publisher's imprint, pagination and price in two lines*] | Thomas Hardy. The Will and the Way. by ROY MORRELL. Pp. xvi + 188. | [*publisher's imprint and price*]

Small royal 8vo. An offprint of [3] leaves. $9\frac{3}{8} \times 6\frac{1}{4}$ in.

Leaves [1-3] numbered 223-225 text.

No wrappers; leaf printed in black forms upper covering; edges trimmed.

Issued probably July 1967; no record of the number of copies printed. Not for sale.

Review of *Hardy of Wessex: His Life and Literary Career*, [revised edition], by Carl J. Weber; and *Thomas Hardy: The Will and the Way*, by Roy Morrell. Reprinted from the *Review of English Studies*, May 1967 (*see* C3362). *See also* A70.

A173   A FEW NOT QUITE FORGOTTEN   1967
WRITERS?

First edition:

THE ENGLISH ASSOCIATION | *Presidential Address* | 1967 | A FEW | NOT QUITE FORGOTTEN | WRITERS? | BY | EDMUND BLUNDEN | C.B.E., M.C., C.LIT., LITT.D. | JULY 1967

Royal 8vo. 16 pp. $9\frac{3}{4} \times 6\frac{1}{4}$ in.

P. [1] title; p. [2] at head: © *The English Association 1967*, at foot: PRINTED IN GREAT BRITAIN; pp. [3]–14 text; pp. [15–16] blank, integral.

Pale grey paper wrappers printed in black; printed on upper wrapper: THE ENGLISH ASSOCIATION | 8 CROMWELL PLACE, LONDON, S.W.7 | [*as title above*; *at foot*:] *Price* 7s. 6d.; list of pamphlets and presidential addresses inside upper wrapper, and on lower wrapper; outside lower wrapper, at foot: Printed in Great Britain at the University Press, Oxford, by Vivian Ridler | and published by Oxford University Press, Ely House, London, W.1; edges cut flush; sewn in white thread.

Published 7 September 1967; 2500 copies printed. 7s. 6d.

A174   THE MIDNIGHT SKATERS   1968
First edition:

EDMUND BLUNDEN | The Midnight | Skaters | *Poems for young readers chosen* | *and introduced* | *by* | C. Day Lewis | [*illustration of a tree*, 2 × 3 *in.*] | ILLUSTRATIONS BY | David Gentleman | THE BODLEY HEAD | LONDON SYDNEY | TORONTO

Demy 8vo. 96 pp. 38 illustrations on pp. [5], [17], 19, [21], 23, [24]–26, [28], 30, 33, [35]–36, 40, 44, 46, [49], 51–[52], 54, 59,

[61], [63], 66-67, 70, 72, [75]-76, 79, [81]-[83], 85, 87, 91, [93]-[94]. 8½ × 5½ in.

P. [1] half-title; p. [2] blank; p. [3] title; p. [4] at head: OTHER POETRY SELECTIONS | FOR YOUNG READERS | [*five line list of other selections*] , towards foot: [*publisher's device of a deer and two trees*, 1 × ⅝ *in.*] | This collection © Edmund Blunden 1968 | Foreword © The Bodley Head Ltd 1968 | Illustrations © The Bodley Head Ltd 1968 | Printed and bound in Great Britain for | The Bodley Head Ltd | 9 Bow Street, London WC2 | by William Clowes & Sons Ltd, Beccles | Set in Monotype Baskerville | *This collection first published 1968*; p. [5] illustration; p. [6] blank; pp. 7-12 Introduction by C. Day Lewis; pp. 13-15 Contents; p. [16] blank; p. [17] section-title; pp. 18-47 text; p. [48] blank; p. [49] section-title; pp. 50-62 text; p. [63] section-title; pp. 64-74 text; p. [75] section-title; pp. 76-82 text; p. [83] section-title; pp. 84-[94] text; pp. 95-96 Index of First Lines.

Powder-blue cloth boards; lettered in gold down the spine: The Midnight Skaters [*ornament*] *Edmund Blunden* BODLEY HEAD; edges trimmed, top rose-pink; rose-pink end-papers. White pictorial dust-jacket printed in black and powder-blue.

Published 11 July 1968; 7500 copies printed. 18*s*.

Contents: *Country Things and People*: Forefathers — Farm Bailiff (Part II) — Almswomen — The Idlers — The Waggoner — Mole Catcher [*formerly* Molecatcher] — The Poor Man's Pig — The Pike — Cloudy June — The May Day Garland — Blue Butterfly — Hawthorn [*formerly* Triune] — What is Winter? [*formerly* A Day in December] — The South-West Wind — A Prospect of Swans — Nature's Adornings [*formerly* Nature's Daring] — Country Sale — No Continuing City — The Child's Grave — For the Country Life [*formerly* The Means] — *War Remembered*: The Zonnebeke Road — At Senlis Once — An Infantryman — The Late Stand-to — The Ancre at Hamel: Afterwards [*formerly* The Ancre at Hamel] — Their Very Memory — 1916 Seen from 1921 [*formerly* Festubert, 1916] — Illusions — The Branch Line — *Far East*: Far East — Elegy — Petals — A Japanese Evening — A Hong Kong House — To the New Japan [*formerly* Walking in Tokyo 1948] — Chinese Paper-Knife [*formerly* A Chinese Paperknife] — *Poetry and Poets*: The English Poets — Clare's Ghost [*formerly* Phantasies] — High Elms, Bracknell — Thoughts of Thomas Hardy — First Rhymes — *Mysteries*: The Brook — A Bridge — Death of Childhood Beliefs — The Time is Gone — Timber — The Midnight Skaters — The Sunlit Vale [*formerly* The Failure] — Report on Experience.

137

First separate publication:

[*title on upper wrapper*:] WORDSWORTH'S LATER
POEMS | *By* | EDMUND BLUNDEN, C.B.E., M.C., C.LIT.,
LITT.D., F.R.S.L. | *Reprinted from* | ESSAYS BY
DIVERS HANDS | VOLUME XXXV

Demy 8vo. An offprint of [6] pp. $8\frac{1}{2} \times 5\frac{1}{2}$ in.

P. [1] blank; pp. [2-6] numbered [18]-22 text.

Dull blue paper wrappers; printed in black on upper wrapper as
above, and on outside lower wrapper: PRINTED IN GREAT
BRITAIN | AT THE UNIVERSITY PRESS, OXFORD | BY
VIVIAN RIDLER | PRINTER TO THE UNIVERSITY; edges cut
flush; stapled.

Issued 8 February 1969; 25 copies printed. Not for sale.

Reprinted from *Essays by Divers Hands*, Vol. 35 (*see* C3370). *See
also* E*b*32.

First edition:

A SELECTION FROM | THE POEMS | OF | EDMUND
BLUNDEN | [*long rule*] | TWO SHILLINGS – TEN
NEW PENCE | [*long rule*] | Proceeds from the sale of this
book will aid the restoration | of the Great Church of the
Holy Trinity, Long Melford | [*long rule*]

Foolscap 8vo. 24 pp. $6 \times 4\frac{1}{4}$ in.

P. [1] title; pp. [2-24] numbered 1-23 text.

White stiff paper wrappers; printed on upper wrapper: [*photograph
of the author by J. A. White*] | A SELECTION FROM THE POEMS
OF | EDMUND BLUNDEN, and outside lower wrapper at centre:
[*rule*] | This limited edition is produced by the generous permission
| of the poet and his publishers, Messrs William Collins. | Selected by
Jim White, published by the Restoration Fund | Committee and
printed by The Lavenham Press Limited. | [*rule*] ; inside lower wrap-
per, note on the author; edges cut flush; stapled.

Published late June 1969; 5000 copies printed. 2*s*.

Contents: *The Western Front*: Report on Experience – Illusions –
A Farm near Zillebeke – *From* Third Ypres [Verses 6-7 in part] –
Some Talk of Peace – *From* 11th R.S.R. [Verse 2] – *The English
Landscape*: A Storm: 1907 – Village Sketch – The Poor Man's Pig

— The Midnight Skaters — Winter: East Anglia [*formerly* East Anglia] — Half a Century — Reflections — *The Villager*: *From* Farm Bailiff [Part 1, Verses 4-5; Part II, Verses 2-3] — *From* A Yeoman [Verse 1] — *From* The Barn [Verses, last two] — *The Orient*: The Sleeping Amah — The Tea-House [*formerly* Japanese Inn] — Summer Storm in Japanese Hills [*formerly* Summer Storm] — At the Great Wall of China — The Cottage at Chigasaki — *Cricket*: Cricket, I Confess — *From* Farm Bailiff [Part II, Verse 5] — *From* Hammond, England [*formerly* Hammond of England] [Verse 1] — *Reflections*: [Seers; Verse 1] — In a Library — Appeal — Chimes at Midnight — Minority Report — Values.

A177   JOHN CLARE : BEGINNER'S LUCK   1971

First edition:

JOHN CLARE: | BEGINNER'S LUCK | by | EDMUND BLUNDEN | [*publisher's monogram*, $\frac{1}{2}$ × $\frac{1}{4}$ *in.*] | BRIDGE BOOKS | KENT EDITIONS | 1971

Small crown 8vo. 16 pp. $7\frac{1}{4}$ × $4\frac{7}{8}$ in.

P. [1] half-title; p. [2] blank; p. [3] title; p. [4] at head: This talk, prepared in 1964, is first published on the | occasion of the author's 75th birthday | by Bridge Books | in an edition of 250 copies | of which This is copy No. [*numbered in ink*], at foot: W & J Mackay & Co Ltd, Chatham; pp. 5-14 text; pp. [15-16] blank.

Cream pictorial paper wrappers printed in tan and black, with illustration of the poet Clare on upper wrapper; edges cut flush; stapled.

Published 1 November 1971; 260 copies printed. £1.

The 10 copies printed in addition to the number recorded on p. [4] were for review and copyright purposes. The essay was prepared for the centenary of Clare's death in 1964.

B.

CONTRIBUTIONS TO BOOKS AND PAMPHLETS

THE OXFORD & CAMBRIDGE
MISCELLANY

First edition:

THE | Oxford & Cambridge | Miscellany. | [*towards foot at left*:] *Oxford Editors*: | HERBERT BAXTER (New College). | ALAN PORTER (Queen's). | [*at right*:] *Cambridge Editors*: | L. DE G. SIEVEKING (S. Catherine's). | ALEC MACDONALD (Corpus Christi).

4to. [iv] , 64 pp. 1 illus., 3 plates, and [4] pp. music scores. $10\frac{3}{4} \times 7\frac{1}{4}$ in.

Stiff white paper wrappers; printed in grey or dark maroon and green in an overall pattern; white paper label on upper wrapper printed in black; edges rough trimmed; sewn.

Published June 1920; no record of the number of copies printed. 6s.

The wrappers may have been printed in other colours.

P. [1] ON TURNING A STONE; reprinted in *The Waggoner*, 15 August 1920; and *The Poems*, 1930 (*see* A8, 35) — pp. 19–20 "THE MIGHTY FALLEN.", dated 1916 — pp. 24–29 The Lost Leader; reprinted in *The Mind's Eye*, 1934 (*see* A50).

B2   **A QUEEN'S COLLEGE MISCELLANY**   **1920**

First edition:

A | *Queen's* | *College* | *Miscellany* | *Published at the* | *Queen's College, Oxford* | *1920*

8vo. [viii] , 52 pp. plates. $8\frac{1}{2} \times 6\frac{5}{8}$ in.

White paper wrappers; printed in navy-blue; top and fore edges trimmed, bottom edges untrimmed; upper paste-down end-paper; pp. [49–52 pp.] form lower end-papers; sewn and gummed.

Published June 1920; no record of the number of copies printed. 3s. 6d.

Pp. 1–3 LEISURE; reprinted in *The Waggoner*, [August] 1920; *The Poems*, 1930; and *Poems of Many Years*, 1957 (*see* A8, 35, 135) — pp. 4–5 PERCH FISHING; reprinted in *The Waggoner*, [August] 1920; and *The Poems*, 1930 (*see* A8, 35) — pp. 19–21 Miss Warble; reprinted in *The Mind's Eye*, 1934; and *Edmund Blunden: A Selection of His Poetry and Prose*, 1950 (*see* A50, 108).

a. First edition:

JOHN CLARE | POEMS | CHIEFLY FROM MANU-
SCRIPT | LONDON | RICHARD COBDEN-SANDERSON
| 17 THAVIES INN

Small demy 8vo. 256 pp. front. (port.). $8\frac{3}{4} \times 5\frac{1}{2}$ in.

Navy-blue cloth boards; white paper label on spine printed in navy-
blue; top and fore edges trimmed, bottom rough trimmed; white
end-papers.

Published November 1920; 2000 copies printed. 10*s.* 6*d.*

Two hundred and fifty copies in sheets were sent to G. P. Putnam's
(*see* B3*b*). There was a 'cheap edition' in Cobden-Sanderson's *Blue
Series* in 1934, issued at 5*s.*; it is probable that this was a third issue
rather than a third impression.

Pp. 5–6 Note by Blunden and Alan Porter. Pp. 9–45 Biographical
signed B.; reprinted in *Edmund Blunden: A Selection of His Poetry
and Prose*, 1950 (*see* A108).

b. First edition — American issue. 1921:

[*title as above*; *imprint*:] G. P. PUTNAM'S SONS | NEW
YORK | 1921

Small demy 8vo. 256 pp. front. (port.) $8\frac{1}{2} \times 5\frac{3}{8}$ in.

Navy-blue cloth boards; white paper label on spine printed in navy-
blue; white end-papers; top and fore edges trimmed, bottom rough
trimmed.

Issued 15 April 1921; 250 copies bound. $3.75.

The sheets were supplied by Cobden-Sanderson.

First edition:

OXFORD POETRY | 1920 | EDITED BY | V.M.B.,
C.H.B.K., A.P. | OXFORD | BASIL BLACKWELL |
1920

Crown 8vo. vi, 58 pp. $7\frac{1}{2} \times 5$ in.

Navy-blue paper wrappers; white paper label on upper wrapper printed in navy-blue with floral ornament; edges rough trimmed; sewn.

Published 19 November 1920; 2300 copies printed. 2s.

Edited by Vera M. Brittain, C. H. B. Kitchen and Alan Porter.

Also issued in navy-blue paper boards; imitation vellum spine with white paper label printed in navy-blue; white paper label on upper cover printed in navy-blue with floral ornament.

Pp. 1-2 SHEET LIGHTNING; first published in *Voices*, June 1920; and reprinted in *The Shepherd*, 1922; *The Poems*, 1930; and *Poems of Many Years*, 1957 (*see* A10, 35, 135; C46) — pp. 3-4 FORE-FATHERS; first published in *The Nation*, 12 June 1920; and reprinted in *The Shepherd*, 1922; *The Augustan Books*, 1925; *The Poems*, 1930; *Edmund Blunden: A Selection of His Poetry and Prose*, 1950; *Poems of Many Years*, 1957; and *The Midnight Skaters*, [1968] (*see* A10, 18, 35, 108, 135, 174; B23; C48).

B5   THE NEW KEEPSAKE FOR   1920
THE YEAR 1921

a. First edition:

THE NEW [*double vertical rule*] LE NOUVEAU | KEEP-SAKE | FOR POUR | THE YEAR L'ANNEE | [*double vertical rule separates last two lines*] 1921 | EDITED BY | X. M. BOULESTIN | WITH PLATES SELECTED BY | J. E. LABOUREUR | Published for X. M. BOULESTIN, 102, George Street | Portman Square, W., by the Chelsea Book Club | 65, Cheyne Walk, S.W. | LONDON [*double vertical rule*] PARIS

Large crown 8vo. 128 pp. illus., plates and music scores. $7\frac{1}{2} \times 5\frac{1}{2}$ in. Bright yellow cloth boards; illustration in black on spine; lettered in black on upper cover with illustration; top edges trimmed, fore and bottom edges rough trimmed; white end-papers.

Published December 1920; 651 copies printed. 18s. 6d.

Five hundred and fifty copies, numbered 71-620, were issued as above. Fifty copies, numbered 1-50, were printed on Japanese vellum, and 20 copies, numbered 51-70, on azure vellum; a further 31 copies, numbered I-XXXI, were printed (*see* B5b).

Pp. 55-56 FESTUBERT, 1916 [*later* 1916 SEEN FROM 1921]; reprinted in *A Queen's College Miscellany*, 1921; *The Shepherd*, 1922; *The Poems*, 1930; *Poems of Many Years*, 1957; and *The Midnight Skaters*, [1968] (*see* A10, 35, 135, 174; B6).

b. First edition — *Japanese vellum issue. 1920*:

[*title and imprint as above*] *

Large crown 8vo. 128 pp. illus., plates and music scores.

Issued December 1920; 50 copies bound.

Numbered 1–50. In addition 20 copies, numbered 51–70, were printed on azure vellum; a further 31 copies, numbered I–XXXI, were issued.

B6   **A QUEEN'S COLLEGE MISCELLANY**   1921

First edition:

A | Queen's | College | Miscellany | Published at the | Holywell Press, Oxford | 1921

8vo. [viii], 64 pp. $8\frac{1}{2}$ × $6\frac{5}{8}$ in.

Blue paper wrappers; printed in navy-blue; edges trimmed; pp. [i–iv] form upper end-papers; lower end-papers; sewn and gummed.

Published June 1921; no record of the number of copies printed. 3*s.* 6*d.*

Pp. 12–14 REUNION IN WAR; first published in *The Nation*, 20 November 1920; and reprinted in *The Shepherd*, 1922; *The Augustan Books*, [1925]; *The Poems*, 1930; and *Poems of Many Years*, 1957 (*see* A10, 18, 35, 135; C165) — pp. 15–16 FESTUBERT, 1916 [*later* 1916 SEEN FROM 1921] (*see* A10, 35, 135, 174; B5) — p. 17 THE DRIED MILL POND; reprinted in *The Shepherd*, 1922; and *The Poems*, 1930 (*see* A10, 35) — pp. 18–20 APRIL BYEWAY; first published in *The Nation*, 14 August 1920; and reprinted in *The Shepherd*, 1922; and *The Poems*, 1930 (*see* A10, 35; C82).

B7   **OXFORD POETRY**   1921

First edition:

OXFORD POETRY | 1921 | EDITED BY | ALAN PORTER RICHARD HUGHES | ROBERT GRAVES | OXFORD BASIL BLACKWELL | MCMXXI

Crown 8vo. [viii], 64 pp. $7\frac{5}{8}$ × 5 in.

Navy-blue paper wrappers; white paper label on upper wrapper printed in black; edges rough trimmed; sewn.

Published 21 November 1921; 1500 copies printed. 2*s.*

Also issued in navy-blue paper boards; imitation vellum spine with white paper label printed in black; white paper label on upper cover printed in black.

Pp. 2-3 THE WATERMILL; first published in *The Nation*, 29 January 1921; and reprinted in *The Shepherd*, 1922; *The Poems*, 1930, and *Poems of Many Years*, 1957 (*see* A10, 35, 135; C232) — pp. 4-6 THE SCYTHE [*later* THE SCYTHE STRUCK BY LIGHTNING]; first published in *Oxford Outlook*, January 1921; *London Mercury*, February 1921; and reprinted in *The Shepherd*, 1922; *The Poems*, 1930; and *Poems of Many Years*, 1957 (*see* A10, 35, 135; C206) — p. 7 THE TIME IS GONE [*title in Contents*: THAT TIME IS GONE]; reprinted in *The Shepherd*, 1922; *The Poems*, 1930; and *The Midnight Skaters*, [1968] (*see* A10, 35, 174) — p. 8 THE SOUTH-WEST WIND; first published in *The Nation*, 1 January 1921; and reprinted in *The Shepherd*, 1922; *The Poems*, 1930; *The Face of England*, 1932; and *The Midnight Skaters*, [1968] (*see* A10, 35, 43*b*, 174; C207) — pp. 9-10 THE CANAL; first published in *The Athenaeum*, 24 December 1920; and reprinted in *The Shepherd*, 1922; and *The Poems*, 1930 (*see* A10, 35; C195) — p. 11 THE MARCH BEE; first published in the *London Mercury*, July 1921; and reprinted in *The Shepherd*, 1922; and *The Poems*, 1930 (*see* A10, 35; C275).

B8   **POEMS ABOUT BIRDS**   1922

First edition:

POEMS ABOUT BIRDS | *From the Middle Ages to the Present* | *Day Chosen and Edited, with an Introduction* | *and Notes by* H. J. MASSINGHAM | WITH A PREFACE BY | J. C. SQUIRE | T. FISHER UNWIN LTD | LONDON: ADELPHI TERRACE

Crown 8vo. 416 pp. 7¾ × 5 in.

Mid-green paper boards; pale brown cloth spine lettered in gold; edges trimmed, top gilt; white end-papers.

Published October 1922; no record of the number of copies printed. 10*s*. 6*d*.

Pp. 349-350 AUGURY; reprinted in *English Poems*, [1926]; *The Poems*, 1930; and *Poems of Many Years*, 1957 (*see* A20, 35, 135).

B9   **GEORGIAN POETRY 1920-1922**   1922

First edition:

GEORGIAN | POETRY | 1920-1922 | [*six ornaments*] |

Crown 8vo. [xiv], 210 pp. 7⅜ × 5 in.

Red cloth boards; lettered in gold on spine, and on a black panel at foot, and on upper cover; top edges gilt, fore and bottom edges untrimmed; white end-papers.

Published November 1922; number of copies printed not ascertained. 6s.

Pp. 25-34 THE POOR MAN'S PIG (*see* A10, 18, 35, 135, 174, 176; C236) — ALMSWOMEN (*see* A8, 18, 35, 43*b*, 135, 174; B23; C37) — PERCH-FISHING (*see* A8, 35; B2) — THE GIANT PUFFBALL (*see* A10, 35; C233) — THE CHILD'S GRAVE (*see* A10, 35, 43*b*, 135, 174) — APRIL BYEWAY (*see* A10, 35; B6; C82).

B10   A MISCELLANY OF POETRY   1922

a. First edition:

A Miscellany of Poetry | 1920-1922 | *Edited by* | *William Kean Seymour* | *London* | JOHN G. WILSON | 350 *Oxford Street,* | *W.* 1

Crown 8vo. [2], x, 212 pp. 7⅜ × 5 in.

Dull blue paper boards; yellow cloth spine; lettered in gold on spine; white paper label on upper cover printed in black; top edges trimmed, fore and bottom edges rough trimmed; white end-papers.

Published December 1922; 1500 copies printed. 6s.

Copies in sheets were sent to Thomas Seltzer, New York (*see* B10*b*).

Pp. 29-30 THE ECLOGUE; first published in the *Nation & Athenaeum*, 3 June 1922; and reprinted in *To Nature*, [1923]; *English Poems*, [1926]; and *The Poems*, 1930 (*see* A14, 20, 35; C314) — pp. 31-32 THRESHOLD; first published in the *Yale Review*, July 1922 (*see* C320) — pp. 33-34 COUNTRY SALE; first published in the *Yale Review*, July 1922; and reprinted in *English Poems*, [1926]; *The Poems*, 1930; *Poems of Many Years*, 1957; and *The Midnight Skaters*, [1968] (*see* A20, 35, 135, 174; C321).

b. First edition — American issue. 1924:

[*title as above*; *imprint*:] [*monogram*] | *New York* | THOMAS SELTZER | 1924

Crown 8vo. [2], x, 212 pp. 7⅜ × 5 in.

Dark blue paper boards; buff linen spine; off-white paper label on spine printed in black; off-white paper label on upper cover printed in black; top edges trimmed, fore and bottom edges untrimmed; white end-papers.

Issued 1924; number of copies bound not ascertained.

The sheets, with a cancel-title, were supplied by John G. Wilson, London.

B11   A SONG TO DAVID   1924

Eighth edition:

A SONG TO DAVID | WITH OTHER POEMS | *By* CHRIS-TOPHER SMART | CHOSEN WITH BIOGRAPHICAL | AND CRITICAL PREFACE AND | NOTES BY EDMUND BLUNDEN | [*six line quotation*] | LONDON | RICHARD COBDEN-SANDERSON | 17 THAVIES INN

Crown 8vo. 108 pp. front. (port.) $7\frac{1}{2} \times 5$ in.

Reddish-brown cloth boards; white paper label on spine printed in pale brown; top edges trimmed, fore and bottom edges rough trimmed; white end-papers.

Published March 1924; 1000 copies printed. 6*s*.

Pp. 7–23 Address; pp. 97–[99] Notes.

B12   THE BIRTH, LIFE AND DEATH   1924
OF SCARAMOUCH

a. First edition:

[*within a compartment*:] The *BIRTH, LIFE and* Death *of* | [*in orange*:] SCARAMOUCH | [*in black*:] BY | *Master* ANGELO CONSTANTINI | Known as MEZZETIN, *Comedian in Ordinary, of the* | *Italian* Company of Players in the service of the | King of *France* | [*long rule*] | *Translated from the* FIRST EDITION *published at* PARIS, 1695 | BY | CYRIL W. BEAUMONT | [*long rule*] | *Together with* MEZZETIN'S *dedicatory Poems and* LORET'S | *rhymed News-letters concerning* SCARAMOUCH, *now first* | *rendered into* ENGLISH *Verse* | BY | EDMUND BLUNDEN | [*long rule*] | *Embellished with four illustrations* |

149

[*device*] | LONDON | Published by C. W. BEAUMONT |
at the *Sign* of the *Harlequin's Bat* | 75, Charing Cross Road
| [*rule*] | MDCCCCXXIV

Medium 8vo. [2], xliv, [18], 88 pp. front. (p. [iv]) and 3 illus.
$8\frac{7}{8} \times 5\frac{3}{4}$ in.

Buff paper boards; printed in orange and green in an overall pattern;
white vellum spine lettered in gold up the spine with two ornaments;
white paper label on upper cover printed in black; top edges
trimmed, fore and bottom edges untrimmed; white end-papers.

Published April 1924; 393 copies printed. £1. 1*s*.

Three hundred and ten copies, numbered 81–390, were issued as
above; a further three were printed for presentation. Eighty copies,
numbered 1–80, were printed on hand-made parchment vellum (*see*
B12*b*).

Pp. [4–7] THE COMIC MUSE and STANZAS — pp. [12–13]
[LORET'S ODE] — pp. 15–17 EPITAPH, VERSES, EPIGRAM ON
THE PORTRAIT OF SCARAMOUCH.

b. First edition — hand-made parchment issue. 1924:

[*title and imprint as above*]

Medium 8vo. [2], xliv, [18], 88 pp. front. (p. [iv]) and 3 illus.
$8\frac{7}{8} \times 5\frac{3}{4}$ in.

Binding as above.

Issued April 1924; 80 copies bound.

Numbered 1–80 of which 5 were not for sale. P. [ii] signed: Cyril W.
Beaumont | Edmund Blunden.

B13   THE BOOK OF THE QUEEN'S   1924
                      DOLLS' HOUSE
                        [VOL. 2]

Limited edition:

[*in scarlet*:] THE BOOK OF THE | QUEEN'S DOLLS'
HOUSE | LIBRARY | [*in black*:] EDITED BY | E. V.
LUCAS | WITH TWENTY-FOUR PLATES | OF WHICH
EIGHT ARE IN COLOUR | METHUEN & CO. LTD. | 36
ESSEX STREET W.C. | LONDON | [*in scarlet*:] BY PER-
MISSION OF H. M. THE QUEEN

Crown 4to. [2], xiv, 384 pp. front. (col.) and 23 plates (some col.) $10\frac{1}{4} \times 7\frac{3}{4}$ in.

Royal blue paper boards; oatmeal linen spine with white label printed in black within a double rule, and below rule; crown, royal initials and date in gold on upper cover; edges untrimmed; white endpapers.

Published June 1924; 1500 copies printed. £3. 3s.

Pp. 34–36 BEHIND THE LINE (*see* A10, 35) — COUNTRY SALE (*see* A20, 35, 135, 174; B10; C321) — p. 36 THE WARDER [*formerly and later* THE SHADOW]; first published in the *Yale Review*, July 1922; and reprinted in *English Poems*, [1926]; and *The Poems*, 1930 (*see* A20, 35; C319) — p. 37 TO JOHN CLARE [*formerly* IN HELPSTON CHURCHYARD] (*see* A14).

B14 MADRIGALS & CHRONICLES 1924

a. First edition:

[*in olive green*:] MADRIGALS & | CHRONICLES | *Being newly found Poems written* | *by* JOHN CLARE | *Edited with a Preface and Commentary* | *by* EDMUND BLUNDEN | [*woodcut*] | LONDON | *THE BEAUMONT PRESS* | *75 Charing Cross Road* | MDCCCCXXIV

Medium 8vo. xxiv, 104 pp. 5 illus., and 3 plates. $9 \times 5\frac{3}{4}$ in.

Pale grey pictorial paper boards; printed in yellow and olive in an overall pattern of flower heads and leaves; oatmeal cloth spine lettered in gold up the spine with two ornaments; top edges trimmed, fore and bottom edges rough trimmed; white end-papers.

Published August 1924; 401 copies printed. £1. 5s.

Three hundred and ten copies, numbered 89–398, were issued as above. Eight copies, numbered 1–8, were printed on vellum; and 83 copies, numbered 9–88, and 3 lettered A, B and C, were printed on Japanese vellum (*see* B14*b–c*).

Pp. vii–[xiv] Preface; p. [xv] Note; and pp. 99–102 Commentary.

b. First edition — vellum issue. 1924:

[*title and imprint as above*]

Medium 8vo. xxiv, 104 pp. 5 illus., and 3 plates. $9 \times 5\frac{3}{4}$ in.

Binding as above; vellum spine.

Issued August 1924; 8 copies bound.

Numbered 1–8 of which 2 copies were not for sale. P. [ii] signed: Edmund Blunden | Randolph Schwabe | Cyril W. Beaumont.

151

c. First edition — Japanese vellum issue. 1924:

[*title and imprint as above*]

Medium 8vo. xxiv, 104 pp. 5 illus., and 3 plates. $8\frac{7}{8} \times 5\frac{3}{4}$ in.

Binding as above; vellum spine.

Issued August 1924; 83 copies bound.

Numbered 9–88 of which 5 were not for sale, and 3 lettered A, B and C for Blunden, Schwabe (illustrator) and Beaumont (publisher). P. [ii] signed as above.

B15   **THE BEST POEMS OF 1924**   **1925**

a. First edition:

The | BEST POEMS | *of* 1924 | [*device*] | *Selected by* | THOMAS MOULT | & *decorated by* | PHILIP HAGREEN | *Jonathan Cape, Ltd., Thirty Bedford Square* | LONDON

Crown 8vo. xvi, 128 pp. illus. $7\frac{3}{8} \times 5$ in.

Paper boards marbled in pale bluish-green and navy-blue; white paper label on spine printed in black; top edges trimmed, fore and bottom edges untrimmed; white pictorial end-papers printed in black.

Published June 1925; 2700 copies printed. 6s.

One thousand, two hundred and fifty copies in sheets were sent to Harcourt, Brace, New York (*see* B15*b*).

Pp. 108–109 A "FIRST IMPRESSION" [*formerly* A "FIRST IMPRESSION" TOKYO] ; first published in *London Mercury*, October 1924; and reprinted in *Japan Times*, 4 December 1924; *The Augustan Books*, [July 1925] ; *English Poems*, [1926] ; *Japanese Garland*, [1928] ; *The Poems*, 1930; and *Poems of Many Years*, 1957 (*see* A18, 20, 26, 35, 135; C481).

b. First edition — American issue. 1925:

[*title as above*; *imprint*:] Harcourt, Brace, New York*

Crown 8vo. xvi, 128 pp.

Issued 26 June 1925; 1250 copies bound. $2.

The sheets were supplied by Jonathan Cape, London.

a. First edition:

[*within a border*:] *Shelley and Keats* | *As they struck their Contemporaries* | Notes partly from Manuscript Sources | *Edited by* | Edmund Blunden | [*illustration*] | London | Published by C. W. BEAUMONT | *at the Sign of the Harlequin's Bat* | 75, Charing Cross Road | 1925

Medium 8vo. [xii], 96 pp. $8\frac{7}{8} \times 5\frac{3}{4}$ in.

Cream pictorial paper boards; printed in orange and green in an overall pattern of roses; vellum spine lettered in gold up the spine with two ornaments; top edges trimmed, fore and bottom edges rough trimmed; white end-papers.

Published September 1925; 390 copies printed. £1. 1*s*.

Three hundred and ten copies, numbered 81–390, were issued as above. Eighty copies, numbered 1–80, were printed on hand-made parchment vellum (*see* B16*b*).

Pp. [vii–viii] Preface — pp. 9–10 notes *et passim*.

b. First edition — hand-made parchment vellum issue.
1925:

[*title and imprint as above*]

Medium 8vo. [xii], 96 pp. $8\frac{3}{4} \times 5\frac{3}{4}$ in.

Binding as above.

Issued September 1925; 80 copies bound.

Numbered 1–80 of which 5 copies were not for sale. P. [ii] signed: Edmund Blunden | Wyndham Payne | C. W. Beaumont.

B17   **THE TALK OF THE TOWN**   **1926**

a. First edition:

The Talk of the Town, Tokyo, 1926*

Published probably January 1926.

A Word Beforehand.

See also A Complete Guide to English Conversation (B232), and *First Steps in English Conversation* (B233).

b. Second edition. 1951:

[*in brown, within a frame*: *first line in Japanese*:] KÔTÔ
EIGO SHAKÔKAIWA | [*in open letters*:] The | Talk of
the Town | [*in roman*:] A Volume of Real English Con-
versation | *by* | Eishiro Hori | [*illustration*] | [*triple rule*]
| *Taishukan* | *Tokyo*

Foolscap 8vo. xxii, 4, 220 pp. illus. 6¾ × 4 in.

Brownish-yellow cloth boards; lettered in gold up the spine with two
stars, and on upper cover; device in blind on lower cover; edges
trimmed, brown; cream end-papers flecked with white. White pictorial dust-jacket printed in green and black.

Published 25 September 1951; number of copies printed not ascertained. 230 yen.

Pp. [v–vi] A Word Beforehand, holograph facsimile dated 14
January 1926 — pp. [xi–xii] Introduction, holograph facsimile dated
September 1948 — pp. [xiii–xxii] Dialogue I: Education, dialogue
between Blunden and Hori, holograph facsimile.

B18   **GREAT NAMES**   **1926**

First edition:

[*within a compartment*; *within a rule*:] GREAT NAMES |
[*rule*] | [*within vertical rules*:] *Being an* Anthology *of*
English | & American Literature *from* | CHAUCER *to*
FRANCIS THOMPSON | *With* Introductions *by Various* |
Hands & Drawings *by* J. F. HOR- | RABIN *after* Original
Portraits | *The* Whole Edited *by* WALTER J. | TURNER
for THE NONESUCH | PRESS & *here* First Published | *by*
Special Arrangement | [*device*] | [*rule*] *Lincoln Mac
Veagh* [*rule*] | NEW YORK : THE DIAL PRESS :
MCMXXVI

Crown 4to. xii, 284 pp. illus. 10 × 7½ in.

Navy-blue cloth boards; lettered in gold on spine with double rules,
thick, thin at head and foot, and on upper cover; device in gold on
upper cover; edges trimmed, top navy-blue; white end-papers.

Published 1926; number of copies printed not ascertained. $3.

The book was not published by the Nonesuch Press, or any other
English publisher.

Pp. 9–13 Edmund Spenser 1552–1599; first published in the *Daily*

Herald, 16 August 1922 (*see* C329) — pp. 141-144 William Hazlitt 1778-1830; first published in the *Daily Herald*, 10 November 1920 (*see* C156) — pp. 145-148 Leigh Hunt 1784-1859; first published in the *Daily Herald*, 22 December 1920 (*see* C193) — pp. 149-152 Thomas de Quincey 1785-1859; first published in the *Daily Herald*, 20 April 1921 (*see* C257) — pp. 195-199 Tennyson 1809-1892 [title in contents: Alfred, Lord Tennyson]; first published in the *Daily Herald*, 26 October 1921 (*see* C298).

B19   **BRET HARTE**   **1926**

First edition:

BRET HARTE | SELECTED POEMS | EDITED WITH AN INTRODUCTION AND NOTES | BY | EDMUND BLUNDEN AND BENJAMIN BRADY | Department of English | TOKYO IMPERIAL UNIVERSITY | *WITH ILLUSTRA-TIONS* | KODO-KWAN | TOKYO | [*short rule*] | 1926

Crown 8vo. [2], xvi, 108 pp. front. (port.) and 8 plates. $7\frac{3}{8}$ × 5 in. Dark red cloth boards; white paper label on upper cover printed in black; edges gilt; white end-papers.

Published 6 May 1926; number of copies printed not ascertained. 1 yen.

Pp. [i]-xiv Introduction — pp. 79-101 Notes.

B20   **THE PYRAMID**   **1926**

First edition:

THE PYRAMID | *By* SHERARD VINES | *With Prefatory Verses* | *by* | EDMUND BLUNDEN | *and* | YONE NOGU-CHI | LONDON | RICHARD COBDEN-SANDERSON | 17 THAVIES INN

Crown 8vo. xii, 64 pp. $7\frac{1}{2}$ × 5 in. Dull green cloth boards; white paper label on spine printed in green; top edges trimmed, fore and bottom edges rough trimmed; white end-papers.

Published November 1926; no record of the number of copies printed. 5s.

P. v TO SHERARD VINES, OF HIS INGENIOUS POEMS.

a. First edition:

[*within a proscenium in gold, ruby and black*:] The |
ACTOR | A Poem by | ROBERT LLOYD | [*rule*] | To
which is Prefix'd | AN ESSAY | By EDMUND BLUNDEN
| [*rule*] | The whole embellish'd with | THEATRICAL
FIGURES | By RANDOLPH SCHWABE | [*double rule*] |
LONDON | Published by C. W. Beaumont | At 75 Charing
Cross Road | [*rule*] | MDCCCCXXVI

Small royal 8vo. [2], 46 pp. 6 illus. $9\frac{1}{8} \times 5\frac{3}{4}$ in.

Pale grey-blue pictorial paper boards; blue cloth spine lettered in
gold up the spine with two ornaments; edges trimmed; white end-
papers. Off-white dust jacket.

Published December 1926; 270 copies printed. 15s.

Two hundred and ten copies, numbered 61–270, were issued as
above. Sixty copies, numbered 1–60, were printed on Japanese vellum (*see* B21b).

Pp. vii–xix On Familiar Poetry and Robert Lloyd.

b. First edition — Japanese vellum issue. 1926:

[*title and imprint as above*]

Small royal 8vo. [2], 46 pp. 6 illus. $9\frac{1}{8} \times 5\frac{3}{4}$ in.

Binding as above; vellum spine.

Issued December 1926; 60 copies bound.

Numbered 1–60 of which 5 copies were not for sale. P. [2] signed:
Edmund Blunden | Randolph Schwabe | C. W. Beaumont.

B22   **A HUNDRED ENGLISH POEMS**   **1927**

a. First edition:

A HUNDRED ENGLISH | POEMS | from the ELIZA-
BETHAN Age to the VICTORIAN: | TO WHICH ARE
ADDED | Specimens of SONNETS, BALLADS, EPI-
GRAMS, | &c.; and of the | PRINCIPAL AMERICAN
POETS | Selected by EDMUND BLUNDEN, | with notes
and illustrations. | [*ten line quotation*] | TOKYO : KEN-
KYUSHA | 1927

Small crown 8vo. xii, 250 pp. front., and 7 plates. $7\frac{3}{8} \times 4\frac{5}{8}$ in.

Navy-blue cloth boards; white paper label on spine printed in black with scarlet rule at head and foot; edges trimmed; white end-papers.

Published 25 March 1927; 2000 copies printed. 2 yen.

There was a second printing in May 1927, and two further printings.

Pp. [ix]–xii Introduction, signed E. B. – p. [1] *et passim* notes.

b. *Second edition. 1949*:

A HUNDRED | ENGLISH POEMS | from the XIVth Century to the XIXth | With supplements containing | SONNETS, BALLADS, EPIGRAMS, | and examples of AMERICAN POETRY. | *Chosen and annotated by* | EDMUND BLUNDEN | A NEW AND REVISED EDITION | TOKYO | KENKYUSHA

Crown 8vo. x, 280 pp. front. (col.) and 7 plates. $7\frac{1}{8} \times 5$ in.

Apple green cloth boards; lettered in gold on spine with three double rules; edges trimmed; white end-papers. Cream dust-jacket printed in black.

Published 15 December 1949; 1000 copies printed. 250 yen.

There were 17 further printings between November 1950 and October 1971.

Pp. iii–iv Preface signed E. B.; the Preface is new.

B23   EDMUND BLUNDEN   1927
HIS PROFESSORSHIP AND HIS WRITINGS

First separate publication:

[*title on upper wrapper*; *within a double rule*:] *Edmund Blunden* | *His Professorship and His Writings* | APPRECIATIONS | *by* | *Some of His Students and Friends* | [*ornament*] | KENKYUSHA, TOKYO | 1927

Small royal 8vo. 96 pp. front. (port.), and illus. $9\frac{3}{8} \times 6\frac{3}{8}$ in.

Off-white paper wrappers; printed in black as above; untrimmed; gummed.

Issued June 1927; 450 copies printed. Price not known.

This was a special issue of the *Study of English*, June 1927, the 'Edmund Blunden Number', of which 10,000 copies were printed. The text is in Japanese except for Blunden's poems.

Pp. 12-13 EASTERN TEMPEST [*later* TEMPEST; *and* EASTERN TEMPEST], holograph facsimile; first published in the *Study of English*, June 1927; and reprinted in *Japanese Garland*, 1928; *Near and Far*, 1929; and *The Poems*, 1930 (*see* A26, 31, 35; C620) — pp. 79–88 ALMSWOMEN (*see* A8, 18, 35, 43*b*, 135, 174; B9; C37) — THE BARN (*see* A4, 6, 8, 35, 135, 176; C929) — FOREFATHERS (*see* A10, 18, 35, 108, 135, 174; B4; C48) — EVENING MYSTERY (*see* A10, 35, 135; C283) — MIDNIGHT (*see* A17, 20, 35) — HAW-THORN [*formerly* TRIUNE] (*see* A20, 35, 135, 174; C557) — THUS FAR (*see* A17, 20, 35; C472) — BYROAD [*formerly* BY ROAD] (*see* A20, 35, 43*b*, 135; C515) — THE DAIMYO'S POND (*see* A18, 20, 26, 35; C480) — pp. 88–89 TRUST; reprinted in *Retreat*, 1928; and *The Poems*, 1930 (*see* A25, 35) — p. 89 ORNI-THOPOLIS; first published in *Adelphi*, November 1926, and reprin-ted in *Retreat*, 1928; *The Poems*, 1930, and *Poems of Many Years*, 1957 (*see* A25, 35, 135; C584).

B24   AUTOBIOGRAPHY OF   1927
            BENJAMIN ROBERT HAYDON

World's Classics edition:

AUTOBIOGRAPHY OF | BENJAMIN ROBERT HAY-DON | *With an Introduction* | *and Epilogue by* | EDMUND BLUNDEN | [*device*] | OXFORD UNIVERSITY PRESS | HUMPHREY MILFORD

Foolscap 8vo. xxii, 426 pp. 6 × 3⅝ in.

Olive-green cloth boards; lettered in gold on spine with a double rule at head and foot; design in blind, and a triple rule in blind round upper and lower covers; edges trimmed; white end-papers. White pic-torial dust-jacket printed in navy-blue.

Published December 1927 as the *World's Classics*, Vol. 314; no record of the number of copies printed. 2*s*.

Pp. [ix]–xvi Editor's Introduction — pp. 393–400 Epilogue.

B25   THE BEST POEMS OF 1927   1927

a. First edition:

The | BEST POEMS | *of* 1927 | [*device*] | *Selected by* | THOMAS MOULT | *& decorated by* | JOHN AUSTEN | LONDON | *Jonathan Cape, Limited* | 1927

Crown 8vo. xiv, 104 pp. front., and illus. 7⅜ X 5 in.

Dull pink cloth boards patterned in putty; white paper label on spine printed in black; top edges trimmed, fore and bottom edges untrimmed; white pictorial end-papers printed in black.

Published December 1927; 3750 copies printed. 6s.

One thousand, two hundred and fifty copies in sheets were sent to Harcourt, Brace, New York (*see* B25*b*). There was a reprint of 500 copies.

P. 15 WOULD YOU RETURN?; first published in the *Nation & Athenaeum*, 11 December 1926; and reprinted in *Retreat*, 1928; *The Poems*, 1930; and *Poems of Many Years*, 1957 (*see* A25, 35, 135; C591).

b. First edition — American issue. 1928:

[*title as above*; *imprint*:] Harcourt, Brace, New York*

Crown 8vo. xiv, 104 pp.

Issued 12 January 1928; 1250 copies bound. $2.

The sheets were supplied by Jonathan Cape, London.

B26   THE BEST POEMS OF 1927   1928

First edition:

THE BEST POEMS | OF 1927 | EDITED BY | L. A. G. STRONG | [*device*] | DODD, MEAD & COMPANY | NEW YORK 1928*

8vo. 269 pp.

Published March 1928; number of copies printed not ascertained. $2.

Pp. 66–68 A SUPERSTITION RE-VISITED [*later* ... REVISITED]; first published in the *London Mercury*, June 1926; and reprinted in *Retreat*, 1928, and *The Poems*, 1930 (*see* A25, 35; C560).

**B27   LEIGH HUNT'S "EXAMINER"   1928
EXAMINED**

a. First edition:

LEIGH HUNT'S | "EXAMINER" EXAMINED | *Comprising* | SOME ACCOUNT of that CELEBRATED | NEWS-

PAPER'S CONTENTS, &c. 1808–25 │ AND │ SELEC-
TIONS, by or concerning LEIGH HUNT, │ LAMB, KEATS,
SHELLEY, and BYRON, │ Illustrating the Literary History
of that Time, │ for the most part previously unreprinted │
By EDMUND BLUNDEN │ [*two line quotation*] │ LON-
DON │ COBDEN-SANDERSON │ THAVIES INN

Demy 8vo. [2], xii, 266 pp. front. (port.) 8¾ × 5⅝ in.

Claret cloth boards; white paper label on spine printed in claret and
black with two rules in claret; top edges trimmed, fore and bottom
edges rough trimmed; white end-papers. Cream dust-jacket printed
in scarlet.

Published July 1928; no record of the number of copies printed. 15*s.*
Two hundred and fifty copies in sheets were sent to Harper &
Brothers, New York (*see* B27*b*).

Pp. v–vi Preface — pp. ix–xi Introductory — pp. 3–122 commentary.

b. First edition — American issue. [*1931*] :

[*title as above*; *imprint*:] [*device*] │ HARPER & BRO-
THERS, PUBLISHERS │ NEW YORK & LONDON

Demy 8vo. [2], xii, 266 pp. front. (port.) 8⅝ × 5⅝ in.

Pale blue and white grained cloth boards; cream paper label on spine
printed in pale brown with a double rule at head and foot; top edges
trimmed, fore and bottom edges rough trimmed; white end-papers.

Issued 1931; 250 copies bound. $4.

The sheets were supplied by Cobden-Sanderson.

c. First edition — American photo-offset reprint. 1967 :

[*title as above*; *imprint*:] ARCHON BOOK │ 1967

Demy 8vo. xiv, 266 pp. (incl. front.) 8½ × 5⅜ in.

Red cloth boards; lettered in gold down the spine; edges trimmed;
white end-papers. Cream dust-jacket printed in navy-blue.

Issued 19 May 1967; 1000 copies printed. $7.

The preliminary pages were renumbered; the pagination in the Contents is unaltered.

Pp. vii–viii Preface, 1967; the original Preface is included, and the
former is not noted in the Contents.

World's Classics edition:

THE AUTOBIOGRAPHY OF | LEIGH HUNT | WITH AN
INTRODUCTION BY | EDMUND BLUNDEN | [*device*] |
OXFORD UNIVERSITY PRESS | HUMPHREY MILFORD

Foolscap 8vo. xii, 572 pp. $5\frac{7}{8} \times 3\frac{5}{8}$ in.

Olive-green cloth boards; lettered in gold on spine with a double rule
at head and foot, and ornamental design in blind; quadruple rule in
blind round upper and lower covers; edges trimmed; white end-
papers.

Published September 1928 as the *World's Classics*, Vol. 329; no
record of the number of copies printed. 2s.

Also issued in red leather.

Pp. [v]–xi Editor's Introduction.

B29   THE POEMS OF WILLIAM COLLINS   1929

a. Etchells & Macdonald edition:

The POEMS | *of* | [*in open capitals*:] WILLIAM COLLINS
| [*in roman*:] EDITED | WITH AN INTRODUCTORY
STUDY | BY | EDMUND BLUNDEN | [*ornament*] |
LONDON | FREDERICK ETCHELLS & HUGH MAC-
DONALD | 1a KENSINGTON PLACE, W.8 | 1929

Medium 8vo. [8], viii, 192 pp. front. $9 \times 6\frac{1}{4}$ in.

Blue-grey paper boards; white paper label on spine printed in black;
pp. [1–4] and [189–192] form end-papers; p. [190] spare spine
label tipped-in; edges rough trimmed. Pale grey dust-jacket printed
in black.

Published *c.* 22 June 1929 in the *Haslewood Books* series; 550
copies printed. 18s.

Five hundred copies, numbered 51–550, were printed on all-rag
paper as above, and 50 numbered copies on Van Gelders' Japon
paper (*see* B29b). Some copies were also issued in pale navy-blue
cloth boards, white paper label on spine, pale grey dust-jacket printed in black.

Pp. v–vi Preface, signed E.B. — pp. 3–38 A Study of William Collins, reprinted in *Edmund Blunden: A Selection of His Poetry and
Prose*, 1950 (*see* A108) — pp. 161–179 Notes. *See also* C882 for the
review in the *TLS*, 18 July 1929, p. 573, and Blunden's replies.

b. Limited issue. 1929:

[*title and imprint as above*]

Medium 8vo. [8], viii, 192 pp. front. 9 × 6¼ in.

Grey paper boards; rust leather spine; lettered in gold on spine; ornamental design in gold on upper cover; edges rough trimmed; pp. [1–4] and [189–192] form end-papers.

Issued *c.* 22 June 1929; 50 copies bound. £2. 2s.

Numbered 1–50. P. [ii] signed Edmund Blunden.

B30   **THE LEGION BOOK**   1929

a. First edition:

THE LEGION BOOK | EDITED BY CAPTAIN H. COTTON MINCHIN | [*long rule*] | CASSELL AND COMPANY LTD. | LA BELLE SAUVAGE, LONDON. E.C. 4

Demy 4to. [xii], 236 pp. 4 illus., and 12 plates. 11⅛ × 8¾ in.

Maroon cloth boards; lettered in gold on spine; top edges trimmed, maroon, fore and bottom edges rough trimmed; white end-papers.

Published September 1929; no record of the number of copies printed. £1. 1s.

Six hundred copies were issued as a 'limited edition' (*see* B30*b*).

Pp. [134]–144 A Postscript [*later* Aftertones]; reprinted in *The Mind's Eye*, 1934; and *Edmund Blunden: A Selection of His Poetry and Prose*, 1950 (*see* A50, 108).

b. First edition — limited issue. [*1929*] :.

[*title and imprint as above*]

Demy 4to. [10], xiv, 242 pp. 8 illus., and 12 plates. 12½ × 9⅜ in.

Brownish-red cloth boards; lettered in gold on spine; top edges gilt, fore and bottom edges untrimmed; preliminary pp. [1–4] form upper end-papers, lower end-papers.

Issued September 1929; 600 copies bound.

The text was repaginated, with the initial paragraph of each contribution partly reset to accommodate an ornamental initial letter; there are 5 additional illustrations, and 1 in the ordinary issue lacking.

Pp. 136–146 A Postscript.

c. First American edition. 1929:

Legion, The Book of the British Legion by Britain's Foremost Writers in Prose and Verse. New York, Doubleday, Doran*

viii, 290 pp.

Published 22 November 1929; no record of the number of copies printed. $3.

B31   THE NEW FORGET-ME-NOT   1929

a. First edition:

[*within a double rule in pale blue; in open capitals*:] THE NEW FORGET-ME-NOT | *A CALENDAR* | [*rule in pale blue*] | [*three columns divided by vertical rules in pale blue; columns one and three list contributors' names; centre column*:] Decorated | by | Rex Whistler | [*illustration in blue*] | MCMXXIX | [*rule in pale blue*] | COBDEN-SANDERSON | 1 MONTAGUE STREET | LONDON

Demy 8vo. xii, 148 pp. illus., and 4 plates. $8\frac{1}{2} \times 5\frac{5}{8}$ in.

Cream pictorial paper boards; printed in pale blue and pale green; blue cloth spine lettered in gold between two double rules; edges trimmed, top pale blue; white end-papers.

Published October 1929; no record of the number of copies printed. 6s.

Three hundred and sixty copies were issued as a 'limited edition' (*see* B31*b*).

Pp. 94–95 Fishing.

b. First edition — limited issue. 1929:

[*title and imprint as above*]

Demy 8vo. xii, 148 pp. illus., and 4 plates. $8\frac{7}{8} \times 5\frac{5}{8}$ in.

Cream pictorial paper boards as above; blue vellum corners and spine lettered in gold; top edges uncut, fore and bottom edges rough trimmed; white end-papers.

Issued October 1929; 360 copies bound. £2. 2s.

Three hundred and fifty numbered copies were for sale.

P. [ii] signed by the artist, Rex Whistler.

Oxford University Press edition:

THE | LAST ESSAYS OF ELIA | BY | CHARLES LAMB | EDITED WITH AN INTRODUCTION | BY | EDMUND BLUNDEN | AND NOTES BY | FREDERICK PAGE | OXFORD UNIVERSITY PRESS | LONDON : HUMPHREY MILFORD | 1929

Small crown 8vo. xx, 236 pp. $7\frac{1}{4} \times 4\frac{3}{4}$ in.

Olive-green cloth boards; lettered in gold on spine with rule at head and foot; rule in blind round upper and lower covers; edges trimmed; white end-papers.

Published 10 October 1929; 3000 copies printed. 3*s*. 6*d*. ($1.25).

There were further reprints of 7500 copies in May 1932, 5000 in September 1932, 10,000 in February 1933, and 10,000 in January 1935.

Blunden did not edit the work as indicated on the title-page, the text used being that of *The Works of Charles and Mary Lamb*, edited by Thomas Hutchinson as noted on p. [v].

Pp. [ix]–xix Introduction.

First English edition:

KEATS' VIEW OF POETRY | BY TAKESHI SAITO, D. Lit., Tokyo | Assistant Professor in the Imperial University of Tokyo | To which is prefixed an Essay on | ENGLISH LITERATURE IN JAPAN | BY EDMUND BLUNDEN | Professor in that University from 1924 to 1927 | LONDON | COBDEN-SANDERSON | MONTA-GUE STREET

Crown 8vo. 144 pp. $7\frac{1}{2} \times 4\frac{7}{8}$ in.

Maroon cloth boards; lettered in gold on spine; top and fore edges trimmed, bottom rough trimmed; cream end-papers.

Published November 1929; no record of the number of copies printed. 6*s*.

Pp. 9–19 English Literature in Japan.

First edition:

TRADITION AND | EXPERIMENT | IN PRESENT-DAY
LITERATURE | ADDRESSES DELIVERED | AT THE
CITY LITERARY | INSTITUTE | 1929 | OXFORD UNI-
VERSITY PRESS | LONDON: HUMPHREY MILFORD

Crown 8vo. [viii], 216 pp. $7\frac{1}{2} \times 5$ in.

Green cloth boards; lettered in gold on spine, and on upper cover;
some top edges uncut, fore and bottom edges rough trimmed; white
end-papers.

Published 25 November 1929; 2028 copies printed. 7s. 6d. ($2.50).
There was a second printing of 2015 copies.

Pp. 54–73 Tradition in Poetry; reprinted in *The Bookman*, New
York, December 1929 (*see* C919).

First separate publication:

[*title on upper wrapper*; *in navy-blue*:] THE WAR | 1914-
1916 | [*ornament*] | A BOOKLIST | COMPILED BY
EDMUND BLUNDEN | CYRIL FALLS, H. M. TOMLIN-
SON | and R. WRIGHT | INTRODUCTION BY | EDMUND
BLUNDEN | PUBLISHED BY | THE READER, 16 RUS-
SELL SQUARE, LONDON, W.C.1

Foolscap 4to. An offprint of 12 pp. $9\frac{3}{8} \times 6\frac{3}{8}$ in.

Green paper wrappers; printed in navy-blue; edges cut flush; sewn or
stapled.

Issued January 1930; number of copies printed not ascertained.
6d.

Pp. [1]–3 Introduction; reprinted from *The Reader*, October-
November 1929 (*see* C900).

a. First edition:

[*title on p.* [1]:] THE LONDON | ARTISTS' ASSOCIA-
TION | *Guarantors*: | Samuel Courtauld Esq. J. Maynard
Keynes Esq. C.B. | L. H. Myers Esq. F. Hindley Smith Esq.
| [*ornaments*] | RECENT PAINTINGS BY | FREDERICK
PORTER | with a Foreword by | EDMUND BLUNDEN |
March 18th to April 17th 1930 | [*ornaments*] | 92 NEW
BOND STREET | Telephone : Mayfair 5224 Secretary :
Angus Davidson

Crown 8vo. [4] pp. $7\frac{1}{2}$ × 5 in.

No wrappers; edges trimmed.

Issued 18 March 1930; number of copies printed not ascertained.
Not for sale.

P. [2] ON MR. PORTER'S ROOM OF PICTURES [*later* ON MR.
FREDERICK PORTER'S [etc.]]; reprinted in *The Poems*, 1930
(*see* A35).

b. Second separate edition. 1945:

[*title on upper wrapper*:] MEMORIAL EXHIBITION | of
| PAINTINGS & WATERCOLOURS | by | [*in scarlet*:]
FREDERICK J. PORTER | [*in black*:] WITH A FORE-
WORD BY | [*in scarlet*:] JAMES BOSWELL | [*in black*:]
POEM BY | [*in scarlet*:] EDMUND BLUNDEN | [*in
black*:] SEPTEMBER, 1945 | THE LEFEVRE GALLERY
| (ALEX REID & LEFEVRE, LTD.) | 131–134 NEW
BOND STREET | LONDON, W.1 | (FIRST FLOOR) |
CATALOGUE – – – PRICE SIXPENCE

Demy 16mo. 8 pp. $5\frac{3}{4}$ × $4\frac{1}{2}$ in.

Off-white stiff paper wrappers; printed in black and scarlet; edges
trimmed; stapled.

Issued September 1945; number of copies printed not ascertained.
6*d*.

Pp. 4–5 ON MR. PORTER'S ROOM OF PICTURES.

First edition:

[*title on p.* [1]:] [*head of Norman Angell with wings*] |
AN ANGELL- | [*in script*:] though he's a | perfect devil
on | horseback. | [*illustrator's autograph facsimile*:] W. K.
HASELDEN. [*illustration to right of last four lines*] |
LUNCHEON | TO | Mr. NORMAN ANGELL | *HOUSE
OF COMMONS* | *March 20th*, 1930

Small crown 8vo. [4] pp. 7 × 4½ in.

No wrappers; gilt edges with round corners.

Issued 20 March 1930; probably 1 menu per person. Not for sale.

A luncheon on the occasion of the twenty-first anniversary of the
publication of *The Great Illusion*.

P. [2] THE AUTHOR OF "THE GREAT ILLUSION"; reprinted in
The Poems, 1930 (*see* A35).

B38   A BOOK OF NARRATIVE VERSE   1930

a. World's Classics edition:

A BOOK OF | NARRATIVE VERSE | *Compiled by* |
V. H. COLLINS | *With an Introduction by* | EDMUND
BLUNDEN | [*device*] | OXFORD UNIVERSITY PRESS
| LONDON : HUMPHREY MILFORD

Foolscap 8vo. [2], xxii, 468 pp. 5⅞ × 3⅝ in.

Olive-green cloth boards; lettered in gold on spine with a double rule at
head and foot, and a design in blind; quadruple rule in blind on upper
and lower covers; edges trimmed, top olive-green; white end-papers.

Published April 1930 as the *World's Classics*, Vol. 350; no record of
the number of copies printed. 2*s*.

Reprinted 13 times between 1930 and 1950.

Pp. [xi]–xxi Remarks on Narrative Poetry.

b. Second edition. 1954:

[*title and imprint as above*]

Foolscap 8vo. xx, 412 pp. $5\frac{7}{8} \times 3\frac{5}{8}$ in.

Navy-blue cloth boards; lettered in gold on spine; device in blind on upper cover; edges trimmed; white end-papers. White dust-jacket printed in mid-blue and black.

Published 1954; no record of the number of copies printed.

There were 6 reprints between 1954 and 1961, and further reprints with revisions in 1963 (3 times), and in 1966, 1968, 1969 and 1970.

Pp. [xi]–xix Remarks on Narrative Poetry.

B39   MEMOIRS OF THE LATE MRS. ROBINSON 1930

Cobden-Sanderson edition:

MEMOIRS OF | *The Late* | MRS. ROBINSON | [*double rule, thick, thin*] | *WRITTEN BY HERSELF* | [*double rule, thin, thick*] | A NEW EDITION | *with an Introduction* | [*double rule, thick, thin*] | [*in black letter*:] London | [*in roman*:] COBDEN-SANDERSON | 1, Montague Street | 1930

Large crown 8vo. xvi, 200 pp. front. (port.) and 1 plate. $8\frac{3}{8} \times 5\frac{1}{8}$ in.

Oatmeal paper boards; magenta cloth spine; oatmeal paper label on spine printed in black; top edges trimmed, fore and bottom edges untrimmed; white end-papers. Grey dust-jacket printed in black.

Published April 1930; no record of the number of copies printed. 7s. 6d.

Pp. vii–xv Notices of the Authoress, unsigned.

The original title-page designed by Stanley Morison included Blunden's name; it is inserted in Sir Rupert Hart-Davis's copy.

B40   GREAT SHORT STORIES OF THE WAR   1930

a. First edition:

GREAT SHORT STORIES | OF THE WAR | ENGLAND, FRANCE, GERMANY | AMERICA | With an Introduction | by | EDMUND BLUNDEN | [*ornamental design*] | 1930 | EYRE & SPOTTISWOODE | Publishers | LONDON

Large crown 8vo. [2], [a]–[j], 984 pp., the first 18 numbered i–xviii. $7\frac{7}{8} \times 5\frac{1}{4}$ in.

Orange cloth boards; lettered in black on spine; edges trimmed; white end-papers.

Published September 1930; 10,250 copies printed. 8s. 6d.

Two hundred and fifty copies, printed on India paper, were issued as a 'limited edition' (*see* B40b). A 'cheap edition' was issued in June 1933 at 5s.

Pp. i–vii Introduction.

b. First edition – limited issue. 1930:

[*title and imprint as above*]

Large crown 8vo. [2], [a]–[j], 984 pp., the first 18 numbered i–xviii. $7\frac{5}{8} \times 5\frac{3}{8}$ in.

Paper boards marbled in grey, green and dark red; black cloth spine lettered in gold; edges trimmed, top gilt; white end-papers. Mottled black slip-clase.

Issued September 1930; 250 copies bound. £1.10s.

P. [b] signed Edmund Blunden.

B41   THE BEST POEMS OF 1930   1930

a. First edition:

The | BEST POEMS | *of* 1930 | [*device*] | *Selected by* | THOMAS MOULT | *& decorated by* | ELIZABETH MONTGOMERY | LONDON | *Jonathan Cape, Limited* | TORONTO

Crown 8vo. xiv, 104 pp. front., and illus. $7\frac{3}{8} \times 5$ in.

Grey cloth boards patterned in mauve; white paper label on spine printed in black; top edges trimmed, fore and bottom edges rough trimmed; white pictorial end-papers printed in black.

Published 22 September 1930; 3500 copies printed. 6s.

One thousand, three hundred copies in sheets were sent to Harcourt, Brace, New York (*see* B41b).

P. 100 THE SURVIVAL; first published in *London Mercury*, June 1930; and reprinted in *The Poems*, December 1930 (*see* A35; C992).

b. First edition — American issue. 1930:

[*title as above*; *imprint*:] Harcourt, Brace, 1930*

Crown 8vo. xiv, 104 pp.

Issued 23 October 1930; 1300 copies bound. $2.50.

The sheets were supplied by Jonathan Cape, London.

B42   **ENGLISH LITERATURE IN THE**   **1930**
    EARLY NINETEENTH CENTURY 1789-1837

First edition:

ENGLISH LITERATURE | IN THE | EARLY NINE-
TEENTH CENTURY | [*swelled rule*] | 1789-1837 |
[*swelled rule*] | With an Introduction | by | EDMUND
BLUNDEN | [*long swelled rule*] | ELKIN MATHEWS
LIMITED | 33 CONDUIT STREET | LONDON | 1930

Small demy 8vo. 248 pp., the first 6 numbered i-vi. $8\frac{1}{2} \times 5\frac{1}{2}$ in.

Pale grey paper wrappers; printed in black on spine with triple rule
at head and foot, and on upper wrapper within a triple rule; edges
cut flush; sewn.

Published October 1930 as *Catalogue*, No. 32; number of copies
printed not ascertained.

Pp. v-vi Introduction.

B43   **THE SIGNATURE OF PAIN**   **1930**

First edition:

THE SIGNATURE | OF PAIN | AND OTHER POEMS |
ALAN PORTER | LONDON | COBDEN-SANDERSON |
1930

Medium 8vo. 88 pp. $8\frac{7}{8} \times 5\frac{5}{8}$ in.

Rust cloth boards; cream paper label on spine printed in rust with a
double rule at head and foot; edges rough trimmed; white end-
papers.

Published October 1930; no record of the number of copies printed.
6*s.*

P. 12 DIALOGUE: VIATORES, AND A FRIEND OF ALAN POR-
TER, ESQ.

a. First edition:

AN ANTHOLOGY | OF WAR POEMS | *Compiled by* | FREDERICK BRERETON | *Introduction by* | EDMUND BLUNDEN | [*device*] | LONDON 48 PALL MALL | W. COLLINS & CO LTD | GLASGOW SYDNEY AUCKLAND

Crown 8vo. 192 pp. $7\frac{5}{8} \times 5\frac{1}{2}$ in.

Biscuit cloth boards; white paper label on spine printed in black; top edges trimmed, fore and bottom rough trimmed; white end-papers.

Published November 1930; no record of the number of copies printed. 6s.

Two hundred copies were issued as a 'limited edition' (*see* B44*b*).

Pp. 13–24 Introduction: The Soldier Poets of 1914–1918 — pp. 41–49 THIRD YPRES (*see* A10, 28, 35, 135, 176) — THE ZONNEBEKE ROAD (*see* A17, 28, 35, 135, 174; C829).

b. First edition — limited issue on hand-made paper. [*1930*]:

[*title and imprint as above*]

Medium 8vo. 192 pp. $9 \times 5\frac{3}{4}$ in.

Slate cloth boards; oatmeal cloth spine; olive green panel on spine lettered in gold within a double rule, and at foot of spine; top edges gilt, fore and bottom edges untrimmed; white end-papers.

Issued November 1930; 200 copies bound. £2. 2s.

P. [2] signed Edmund Blunden.

B45   **CATALOGUE OF THE EXHIBITIONS**   **1930**

First edition:

CATALOGUE OF THE EXHIBITIONS | (1) Pastorals-Water-Colours | by ETHELBERT WHITE | (2) Paintings | by MARK GERTLER | ERNEST BROWN & PHILLIPS | THE LEICESTER GALLERIES | LEICESTER SQUARE, LONDON | NOVEMBER, 1930 | EXHIBITIONS Nos. 502–503

Medium 16mo. 16 pp.; [1] leaf tipped-in p. [6]. $5\frac{5}{8} \times 4\frac{3}{8}$ in.

Pale grey paper wrappers; printed in black; edges untrimmed; stapled.

Issued November 1930; number of copies printed not ascertained.

Leaf tipped-in p. [6] TO ETHELBERT WHITE (There comes a day, —). *See also* poem of same title (B116).

B46   **OTHER RANKS**   **1931**

First edition:

OTHER RANKS | W. V. TILSLEY | WITH AN INTRO-
DUCTION BY | EDMUND BLUNDEN | [*device*] | LON-
DON | COBDEN-SANDERSON | 1 MONTAGUE STREET

Crown 8vo. xiv, 270 pp. $7\frac{1}{2} \times 4\frac{7}{8}$ in.

Black cloth boards; lettered in gold on spine; top and fore edges trimmed, bottom untrimmed; white end-papers. Sky-blue dust-jacket printed in black.

Published March 1931; number of copies printed not ascertained. 7s. 6d.

Pp. vii–xiii Introduction.

B47   **THE POEMS OF WILFRED OWEN**   **1931**

a. Second edition:

THE POEMS OF | WILFRED OWEN | A NEW EDITION |
INCLUDING MANY PIECES NOW | FIRST PUBLISHED,
AND NOTICES | OF HIS LIFE AND WORK | BY | ED-
MUND BLUNDEN | LONDON | Chatto & Windus | 1931

Large crown 8vo. viii, 136 pp. front. (port.) 8×5 in.

Dark purple cloth boards; lettered in gold on spine; top edges trimmed, fore and bottom edges rough trimmed, some uncut; white end-papers. Cream dust-jacket printed in black and dark red.

Published March 1931; 2200 copies printed. 6s.

One hundred and sixty copies were issued as a 'limited edition', and 520 copies in sheets were sent to the Viking Press, New York (*see* B47*b–c*). There were reprints of 4000 copies in July 1933, and 2000 copies in April 1939 in the *Phoenix Library*, and twenty-one reprints totalling 96,782 copies between April 1946 and February 1971 including 2350 copies in *New Directions*, and 33,820 copies in the *Queen's Classics*.

Pp. 3–41 Memoir; pp. 121–129 Notes.

b. Second edition — limited issue. 1931:

[*title and imprint as above*]

Demy 8vo. [4], viii, 136 pp. front. (port.) 9 × 5⅝ in.

Grey-brown buckram boards; lettered in gold on spine; top edges gilt, fore edges rough trimmed, bottom untrimmed; white end-papers.

Issued March 1931; 160 copies bound. £1. 5s.

P. [i] at head: 160 COPIES OF THIS SPECIAL │ EDITION HAVE BEEN PRINTED; │ 150 ARE FOR SALE │ NO. [*numbered in ink*].

c. Second edition — American issue. 1931:

[*title as above*; *imprint*:] [*ornament*] │ [*device*] │ THE VIKING PRESS │ NEW YORK — 1931

Large crown 8vo. viii, 136 pp. front. (port.) 8 × 5 in.

Dark purple cloth boards; lettered in gold on spine with triple gold band, and on upper cover within a double band; edges rough trimmed; white end-papers.

Issued probably June 1931; 520 copies bound. $2.

The sheets were supplied by Chatto & Windus.

d. Third edition. 1963:

THE │ COLLECTED POEMS │ OF │ [*in open capitals*:] WILFRED OWEN │ *Edited with an Introduction* │ *and Notes by* │ C. DAY LEWIS │ *and with a Memoir by* │ EDMUND BLUNDEN │ 1963 │ CHATTO & WINDUS │ LONDON

Demy 8vo. 196 pp., the first 10 numbered [i]–x, illus. 8½ × 5⅜ in.

Yellow cloth boards; lettered in gold on spine on a crimson oval panel, and in gold at foot; edges trimmed, top dark pink; white end-papers. Yellow dust-jacket printed in black and dark pink.

Published 12 September 1963; 4500 copies printed. £1. 1s.

There were eleven reprints totalling 101,450 copies between October 1963, and June 1974 including 2160 copies in *New Directions* in October 1963 and July 1964, and 75,900 copies in paperback.

Pp. 147–180 Memoir (1931); reprint 'with a few minor alterations'.

a. First edition:

SKETCHES IN THE LIFE OF | JOHN CLARE | WRIT-
TEN BY HIMSELF | NOW FIRST PUBLISHED, WITH |
AN INTRODUCTION, NOTES | AND ADDITIONS |
BY | EDMUND BLUNDEN | LONDON | COBDEN-
SANDERSON | 1931

Demy 8vo. [ii], 122 pp. $8\frac{3}{4} \times 5\frac{1}{2}$ in.

Navy-blue cloth boards; white paper label on spine printed in navy-
blue; top edges trimmed, fore and bottom edges rough trimmed;
white end-papers. Pale grey dust-jacket printed in black.

Published March 1931; no record of the number of copies printed.
6*s.*

Errata slip tipped-in p. [108]; spare spine label tipped-in p. [122].
Copies in sheets were sent to Oxford University Press, New York.
See B48*b.*

Pp. [9]–42 Introduction — pp. 93–99 Notes; *see also* p. 101, paragraph 1, and pp. 109–121 *passim.*

b. First edition — American issue. 1931:

[*title as above*; *imprint:*] OXFORD UNIVERSITY PRESS
| NEW YORK | 1931

Demy 8vo. [ii], 122 pp. $8\frac{3}{4} \times 5\frac{1}{2}$ in.

Navy-blue cloth boards as above.

Issued 1931; no record of the number of copies bound. $2.50.

Copies in sheets were supplied by Cobden-Sanderson.

B49   THE RIME OF THE ANCIENT MARINER   1931

Cheshire House edition:

[*within a rule in green, across an illustration of a ship in
brown and green:*] THE RIME OF | THE ANCIENT
MARINER | *by* | Samuel Taylor Coleridge | *INTRODUC-
TION BY* | EDMUND BLUNDEN | *ILLUSTRATIONS BY*

| *H. CHARLES TOMLINSON* | NEW YORK : CHESHIRE
HOUSE | 1931

[2], xviii, 56 pp. illus. 13 X 9 in.

Green pictorial paper boards; printed in darker green, and white;
lettered in green down the spine; top edges trimmed, slight mottling
in green, fore and bottom edges untrimmed; cream end-papers. Pale
brown slip case.

Published *c.* 20 April 1931; 1200 copies printed. $13.50.

Pp. iii–xvi An Introduction.

B50   **TRAGICAL CONSEQUENCES**   **1931**

First separate edition:

[*title on p.* [1]; *within a double rule*:] TRAGICAL |
CONSEQUENCES | *OR* | A DISASTER AT DEAL | [*long
rule*] | *being an unpublished letter of* | WILLIAM GOD-
WIN | Dated Wednesday, November 18th, 1789 | and Re-
marks thereon by | *EDMUND BLUNDEN* | [*long rule*] |
[*three line quotation*] | [*long rule*] | *LONDON* | Printed
for Fytton Armstrong at | Sixty, Frith Street, Soho Square
| *MCMXXXI*

4to. [8] pp. $11\frac{7}{8}$ X $9\frac{1}{4}$ in.

No wrappers; edges trimmed; sewn in white thread.

Issued May 1931; probably 51–56 copies printed.

These were issued (a) twenty-five to thirty numbered copies as above;
(b) 12 unnumbered copies on cartridge paper, $11\frac{7}{8}$ X $8\frac{3}{8}$ in., for
presentation; (c) 10 lettered copies in cream paper boards marbled in
grey, brown and dark yellow, $11\frac{7}{8}$ X $9\frac{1}{4}$ in., white paper label on
upper cover, p. [4] signed by Blunden, spare label inserted; (d) 4
numbered proof copies, p. [7] ... Proof Copy: | hand printed ... ,
12 X $9\frac{1}{8}$ in. Some of these details were noted by Bertram Rota in a
letter to Sir Rupert Hart-Davis, 11 April 1946, following a conversation between the former and Fytton Armstrong, *i.e.* John Gawsworth, who may have printed more copies than indicated.

Pp. [3–4] Remarks, on the death of Thomas Holcroft's son William;
reprinted as Death of a Youth in *Backwaters: Excursions in the
Shades*, by John Gawsworth, London, Denis Archer, [1932], pp. 13–
17.

First edition:

ESSAYS OF | THE YEAR | 1930–1931 | [*monogram*] |
Published at the Offices of | The ARGONAUT PRESS |
175, PICCADILLY, LONDON

Crown 8vo. xx, 236 pp. $7\frac{1}{4}$ × $4\frac{7}{8}$ in.

Grey cloth boards; lettered in navy-blue with two triple rules on
spine; illustration on upper cover; edges trimmed; end-papers.

Published November 1931; number of copies printed not ascertained. 5s.

Pp. 78–85 Lord's, June 27th, 1930; first published in the *Nation &
Athenaeum*, 5 July 1930; and reprinted in *The Mind's Eye*, 1934;
and *Edmund Blunden: A Selection of His Prose and Poetry*, 1950
(*see* A50, 108; C1006).

a. First edition:

[*in open capitals*:] THE NEW KEEPSAKE | *Contributions
by* | MAURICE BARING H. J. MASSINGHAM | [*contri-
butors' names in two columns, eleven further lines*] |
Decorated by | REX WHISTLER | COBDEN-SANDERSON
| 1 MONTAGUE STREET | LONDON

Demy 8vo. [x], 150 pp. $8\frac{1}{2}$ × $5\frac{5}{8}$ in.

White cloth boards; lettered in black on spine; illustration on spine
and upper cover in pink and black; edges trimmed; white end-papers.
Cream pictorial dust-jacket printed in pink and black.

Published November 1931; no record of the number of copies printed. 6s.

Sixty copies were issued as a 'limited edition' (*see* B52*b*).

Pp. 7–13 The Extra Turn [on the Western Front of the 1914–1918
war] ; reprinted in *The Mind's Eye*, 1934 (*see* A50).

b. First edition — limited issue. [*1931*] :

[*title and imprint as above*]

Demy 8vo. [x] , 150 pp. illus. $8\frac{1}{2}$ × $5\frac{1}{2}$ in.

Pink cloth boards; lettered in gold on spine; illustration on spine and upper cover in gold; edges gilt; white end-papers.

Issued November 1931; 60 copies bound.

P. [iv] signed by the artist, Rex Whistler.

B53   **NEW ENGLISH POEMS**   **1931**

First edition:

NEW ENGLISH POEMS | *A MISCELLANY OF CONTEM-PORARY VERSES* | *NEVER BEFORE PUBLISHED* | [*double rule, thick, thin*] | The Collection Made | by LASCELLES ABERCROMBIE | LONDON | VICTOR GOLLANCZ LTD | 14 Henrietta Street Covent Garden

Crown 8vo. 352 pp. $7\frac{1}{4} \times 4\frac{7}{8}$ in.

Blue cloth boards; lettered in gold on spine with two double rules; edges trimmed; off-white end-papers.

Published 9 November 1931; probably 2500 copies printed. 6s.

There was a reprint of probably 2500 copies in the same month.

Pp. 78-79 THE MEMORIAL (1914-1918); reprinted in *Halfway House*, 1932; *Poems 1930-1940*, [1941]; and *Poems of Many Years*, 1957 (*see* A45, 68, 135).

B54   **THE CITY OF DREADFUL NIGHT**   **1932**

Methuen edition:

THE CITY OF | DREADFUL NIGHT | AND OTHER POEMS | BY | JAMES THOMSON | ('B. V.') | WITH AN INTRODUCTION BY | EDMUND BLUNDEN | WITH A FRONTISPIECE BY | JAMES McBEY | [*device*] | METHUEN & CO. LTD. | 36 ESSEX STREET W.C. | LONDON

Crown 8vo. 96 pp. front. ([p. 2]) $7\frac{3}{8} \times 5$ in.

Purple cloth boards; lettered in gold on spine with a double rule at head and foot, and on upper cover; rule in blind round upper cover; top edges trimmed, fore edges uncut, bottom rough trimmed; white end-papers.

Published June 1932; no record of the number of copies printed. 5s.

Pp. 5-14 Introduction.

First edition:

CRITICAL ESSAYS | OF TO-DAY | SELECTED BY | EDWARD PARKER | M.A., PH.D., DIP. ED. | MACMILLAN AND CO., LIMITED | ST. MARTIN'S STREET, LONDON | 1932

Small crown 8vo. xxxvi, 176, [4] pp. $7\frac{3}{8} \times 4\frac{3}{4}$ in.

Pale blue cloth boards; lettered in blue on spine; edges trimmed; white end-papers.

Published July 1932; 3000 copies printed. 2s. 6d.

Pp. 128–135 Keats and his Predecessors (A Note on the "Ode to a Nightingale."); first published in the *London Mercury*, July 1929 (*see* C869).

a. First edition:

[*rule*] | THE GREAT | VICTORIANS | [*quadruple rule*] | IVOR NICHOLSON & WATSON, LTD. | 44 ESSEX STREET, STRAND, LONDON, W.C. | [*double rule*]

Demy 8vo. xx, 556 pp. $8\frac{1}{2} \times 5\frac{1}{2}$ in.

Orange cloth boards; lettered in black on spine, and on upper cover with illustration; edges trimmed; white end-papers.

Published August 1932; no record of the number of copies printed. 8s. 6d.

There were reprints in September and December 1932.

Pp. 1–16 Matthew Arnold; partly reprinted as Introductory Note to *The Scholar-Gipsy*, by Matthew Arnold, London, Ivor Nicholson & Watson, 1933 — pp. 245–250 Thomas Hardy, Part II [*later* Notes on Visits to Thomas Hardy]; reprinted in *Edmund Blunden: A Selection of His Poetry and Prose*, 1950 (*see* A108).

b. First American edition. 1932:

[*title as above*; *imprint*:] Garden City, New York, Doubleday, Doran & Company, Inc. 1932*

xxi, 507 pp.

Published 9 November 1932; no record of the number of copies printed. $3.

c. Second English edition. [*1938*]:

PELICAN BOOKS | THE GREAT VICTORIANS | EDITED BY H. J. MASSINGHAM | AND HUGH MASSINGHAM | *In two volumes* | I | [*device*] | PUBLISHED BY | PENGUIN BOOKS LIMITED | HARMONDSWORTH MIDDLESEX ENGLAND

Small crown 8vo. 288 pp. $7\frac{1}{8} \times 4\frac{1}{2}$ in.

White stiff paper wrappers; printed in sky-blue and black; edges cut flush; sewn and gummed.

Published October 1938 as *Pelican Books*, Vol. A11; number of copies printed not ascertained. 6*d.*

Vol. 1, pp. 24-37 Matthew Arnold 1822-1888 — pp. 236-242 Thomas Hardy 1840-1928, Part II.

B57   **KNOWN SIGNATURES**   **1932**

First edition:

[*in green*:] KNOWN | SIGNATURES | [*in black*:] *NEW POEMS BY* | [*contributors' names in nine lines of two columns*] | *EDITED WITH AN INTRODUCTION BY* | [*in green*:] JOHN GAWSWORTH | [*device*] | [*in black*:] RICH & COWAN LTD. | MAIDEN LANE STRAND | LONDON

Crown 8vo. 80 pp. $7\frac{3}{8} \times 5$ in.

Opaline green cloth boards; lettered in red up the spine; cream paper label let into upper cover, printed in red and green within a wavy rule; top edges green, fore and bottom edges rough trimmed; white pictorial end-papers printed in green, designed by Edward Carrick.

Published October 1932; no record of the number of copies printed. 5*s.*

Pp. 23-24 IN SUMMER, THE ROTUNDA OF THE BISHOP OF DERRY [*later* THE ROTUNDA]; first published in a separate edition, [1932]; and reprinted in *Halfway House*, 1932; and in *Poems 1930-1940*, [1941] (*see* A42, 45, 68) — pp. 25-26 THE WEATHERCOCK; first published in a separate edition, 1931 (*see* A37).

First edition:

LITTLE | INNOCENTS | CHILDHOOD REMINISCENCES | *by* | [*contributors' names in thirty lines*] | *Preface by* | ALAN PRYCE-JONES | [*long swelled rule*] | *London*: COBDEN-SANDERSON : *Mcmxxxii*

Demy 8vo. viii, 128 pp. $8\frac{1}{2} \times 5\frac{3}{8}$ in.

Opaline green cloth boards; lettered in gold on spine with ornament; edges trimmed, top green; white end-papers. Cream pictorial dust-jacket printed in opaline green.

Published November 1932; no record of the number of copies printed. 6*s*.

Pp. 23–26 Bells on the Breeze; reprinted in *The Mind's Eye*, [1934] (*see* A50).

B59   **SPECTATOR'S GALLERY**   1933

First edition:

SPECTATOR'S GALLERY | *ESSAYS, SKETCHES, SHORT* | *STORIES & POEMS* | *from* | *The Spectator* | *1932* | [*device*] | Edited by | PETER FLEMING | and DEREK VERSCHOYLE | JONATHAN CAPE | THIRTY BEDFORD SQUARE | LONDON

Crown 8vo. 416 pp. $7\frac{5}{8} \times 5$ in.

Buff cloth boards; lettered in red on spine; top and fore edges trimmed, bottom rough trimmed; white end-papers. Off-white dust jacket printed in black and red.

Published 19 June 1933; 2000 copies printed. 7*s*. 6*d*.

Pp. 22–26 The English Countryside; first published in *The Spectator*, 18 November 1932; and reprinted in *The Mind's Eye*, [1934] (*see* A50; C1241).

B60   **CONTEMPORARY ESSAYS 1933**   1933

First edition:

CONTEMPORARY ESSAYS | 1933 | [*long double rule, thick, thin*] | EDITED | WITH AN INTRODUCTION | BY | SYLVA NORMAN | LONDON [*device*] 1933 | [*double*

rule, thick, thin] | ELKIN MATHEWS & MARROT, LTD
| 44 ESSEX STREET, STRAND

Demy 8vo. [2], xxvi, 204 pp. $8\frac{3}{4} \times 5\frac{3}{8}$ in.

Reddish-brown cloth boards; lettered in gold on spine; top and fore edges trimmed, top reddish-brown, bottom untrimmed; white endpapers.

Published October 1933; number of copies printed not ascertained. 10*s.* 6*d.*

Pp. 187–203 Fall In, Ghosts, including Note on its derivation; first published in a separate edition, 1932; and reprinted in *Edmund Blunden: A Selection of His Poetry and Prose*, 1950 (*see* A44, 108).

**B61   CHARLES LAMB HIS LIFE   1934
RECORDED BY HIS CONTEMPORARIES**

First edition:

CHARLES LAMB | His Life Recorded by his | Contemporaries | Compiled by | EDMUND BLUNDEN | [*device*] | LONDON, 1934 | PUBLISHED BY LEONARD AND VIRGINIA WOOLF AT | THE HOGARTH PRESS, 52 TAVISTOCK SQUARE, W.C.1

Demy 8vo. 256 pp. $8\frac{1}{2} \times 5\frac{1}{2}$ in.

Scarlet cloth boards; lettered in white on spine; edges trimmed; white end-papers. Off-white pictorial dust-jacket printed in black and pale pink, designed by Vanessa Bell.

Published March 1934 as *Biographies through the Eyes of Contemporaries*, Vol. 1; 1500 copies printed. 7*s.* 6*d.*

Pp. 11–14 Preface; p. 15 note *et passim.*

B62   NIL

**B63   SOUTHDOWN BATTALIONS'   1934
ASSOCIATION ANNUAL DINNER**

First edition:

[*title on p.* [1]: *in blue*:] The Southdown Battalions'

Association | (11th, 12th and 13th BATTALIONS) | The Royal Sussex Regiment. | [*double rule, long, short*] | [*regimental badge with battle honours on both sides*] | [*within a compartment: in open letters*:] [*double rule*] The Ninth [*double rule*] | ANNUAL DINNER | [*outside compartment*:] AT THE | AQUARIUM RESTAURANT, | BRIGHTON, | *On Saturday, March 24th, 1934.* | [*name of chairman etc. in three lines*]

Small crown 8vo. [4] pp. $7\frac{1}{4} \times 4\frac{1}{2}$ in.
No wrappers; edges trimmed.
Issued 24 March 1934; no record of the number of copies printed. Not for sale.

P. [4] TO THE SOUTHDOWNS; reprinted (revised) in *Choice or Chance*, 1934; and in *Poems 1930–1940*, [1941] (*see* A52, 68).

B64   **THE COUNTRY AROUND**   1934
              CHRIST'S HOSPITAL

First edition:

THE COUNTRY AROUND | CHRIST'S HOSPITAL | This handbook is a tribute by Old Blues and masters of | Christ's Hospital to the memory of L. H. White, priest | and master, who in 1903 founded the Natural History | Society and for twenty-four years made it his pleasure | to interpret Nature to the boys of this City Foundation. | CONTENTS. | [*titles and contributors' names in twelve lines*], and published by | the Christ's Hospital Natural History Society, 1934.

Demy 8vo. 24 pp. front. (map) and 2 maps. $8\frac{3}{8} \times 5\frac{1}{2}$ in.
Buff pictorial paper wrappers; printed in black on upper wrapper; edges cut flush; stapled.
Issued 19 April 1934; 1000 copies printed. Either not for sale or available to subscribing members of the Natural History Society.
P. 3 A PROLOGUE [*later* THE COUNTRY ROUND CHRIST'S HOSPITAL]; reprinted in *Choice or Chance*, 1934; *Poems 1930–1940*, [1941]; and *The Christ's Hospital Book*, 1953 (*see* A52, 68; B153).

First edition:

MISCELLANY | Edited by | Robert Daubney | and | Harold Cooper | Published at | The Queen's College | Oxford 1934

8vo. 52 pp. $9\frac{3}{4} \times 7\frac{3}{8}$ in.

Grey paper wrappers; printed in black; edges cut flush; sewn and gummed.

Published July 1934; no record of the number of copies printed.

P. 6 THE UNEXPECTED VICTORY [*later* SPIRIT-WIND] (*see* A52, 68) — pp. 32–36 Emile Jacot: An Old Contributor — pp. 51–52 HOUSING QUESTIONS [*later* HOUSING QUESTION] (*see* A52, 68).

First edition:

COLERIDGE | STUDIES BY SEVERAL HANDS | ON THE HUNDREDTH ANNIVERSARY | OF HIS DEATH | *Edited by* | EDMUND BLUNDEN | AND | EARL LESLIE GRIGGS | [*four line quotation*] | LONDON | CONSTABLE & CO LTD | 1934

Demy 8vo. viii, 244 pp. front. (port.) $8\frac{5}{8} \times 5\frac{1}{2}$ in.

Navy-blue cloth boards; lettered in gold on spine; edges trimmed, top pale navy-blue; white end-papers. White dust-jacket printed in navy-blue.

Published 26 July 1934; no record of the number of copies printed. 10*s.* 6*d.*

P. v Preface signed E.B./E.L.G. — pp. 53–69 Coleridge and Christ's Hospital. *See also* C1438 for letter by Blunden on the frontispiece.

First edition:

ENGLISH COUNTRY | *Fifteen Essays* | by | *Various Authors* | EDITED WITH AN INTRODUCTION | BY |

H. J. MASSINGHAM | WISHART & CO. 9 JOHN STREET
ADELPHI | 1934

Crown 8vo. xviii, 274 pp. 15 plates. $7\frac{1}{4} \times 4\frac{7}{8}$ in.

Grey-green cloth boards; lettered in gold on spine; edges trimmed,
top dark green; white end-papers.

Published September 1934; number of copies printed not ascertained. 7s. 6d.

Pp. 43–60 Sussex; reprinted in *Edmund Blunden: A Selection of His
Poetry and Prose*, 1950 (*see* A108).

B68 **CHALLENGE TO DEATH** **1934**

a. First edition:

CHALLENGE TO DEATH | *By* | PHILIP NOEL BAKER |
GERALD BARRY | VERNON BARTLETT | EDMUND
BLUNDEN | [*contributors' names in eleven further lines*]
| *and* | *with a Foreword by* | VISCOUNT CECIL | CON-
STABLE & CO LTD | LONDON

Crown 8vo. xvi, 344 pp. $7\frac{1}{4} \times 4\frac{7}{8}$ in.

Coral red cloth boards; lettered in black on spine, and on upper
cover; edges trimmed, top red; white end-papers.

Published 19 November 1934; no record of the number of copies
printed. 5s.

Pp. 333–337 WAR CEMETERY; reprinted in *Poems 1930–1940*,
[1941]; and *Poems of Many Years*, 1957 (*see* A68, 135).

b. First edition — American photo-offset reprint. 1935:

[*title as above*; *imprint*:] [*device*] | NEW YORK | E. P.
DUTTON & CO., INC.

Crown 8vo. xx, 344 pp. $7\frac{1}{2} \times 5\frac{1}{8}$ in.

Pale blue cloth boards; lettered in red on spine, and on upper cover;
top edges trimmed, fore and bottom edges rough trimmed; white
end-papers.

Issued 9 May 1935; 2000 copies printed. $1.

Foreword by Vera Brittain.

B69 THE YEAR'S POETRY 1934

First edition:

THE YEAR'S POETRY | A REPRESENTATIVE SELEC-
TION | ● | Compiled by | DENYS KILHAM ROBERTS |
GERALD GOULD ● JOHN LEHMANN | JOHN LANE
THE BODLEY HEAD | LONDON

Crown 8vo. 144 pp. 7⅜ × 4⅞ in.
Cream cloth boards; lettered in red on spine; edges trimmed, top
pink; white end-papers.
Published 4 December 1934; probably 3000 copies printed. 6s.
P. 68 THE RIPPLE; first published in the *Spectator*, 29 December
1933 (*see* C1334).

B70 SOUTHDOWN BATTALIONS' 1935
ASSOCIATION ANNUAL DINNER

First edition:

[*title on p.* [1]; *yellow band with royal blue edging top
and left margins with battle honours; in royal blue*:] [*regi-
mental badge at left; at right*:] The Southdown | Battalions'
Association | (11th, 12th and 13th | BATTALIONS) |
The Royal | Sussex Regiment. | [*double rule, thick, thin*]
| [*double rule in yellow, thick, thin*] | The Tenth .. .. .. |
ANNUAL DINNER | *Saturday, March 30th, 1935* | AT
THE | AQUARIUM RESTAURANT, BRIGHTON. |
[*double rule in yellow, thin, thick*] | [*at left*: *name of
chairman etc., in nine lines*] | [*at right*: *illustration*]

Small crown 8vo. [4] pp. 7⅜ × 4⅝ in.
No wrappers; edges trimmed.
Issued 30 March 1935; no record of the number of copies printed.
Not for sale.
P. [4] FATHER WILLIAM AGAIN, signed E. Blunden.

185

a. First edition:

THE PILGRIMS' LIBRARY | [*wavy line*] | THE LEGACY | OF ENGLAND | AN ILLUSTRATED SURVEY OF | THE WORKS OF MAN IN THE | ENGLISH COUNTRY | [*wavy line*] | *With Contributions by* | Adrian Bell, George A. Birmingham, Edmund | Blunden, Ivor Brown, Bernard Darwin, Charles | Bradley Ford, R. H. Mottram, G. M. Young | *and 114 Illustrations* | *from Photographs* | [*two stars*] | LONDON | B. T. BATSFORD LTD | 15 NORTH AUDLEY STREET, W.1

Crown 8vo. viii, 248 pp. front., and 47 plates. 7⅜ × 5 in.

Bright green cloth boards; lettered in brown on spine, and on upper cover; edges trimmed; white end-papers. White pictorial dust-jacket printed in brown, black, blue, pink and green.

Published November 1935; *c.* 10,000 copies printed. 5*s.*

Copies in sheets were sent to Charles Scribner's, New York (*see* B71*b*). There were reprints in the winters of 1941–1942 and 1946–1947.

Pp. 1–33 The Landscape.

b. First edition – American issue. 1936:

South of England: An Illustrated Survey of the Works of Man in the English Country. New York, Scribner's*

viii, 248 pp.

Issued March 1936 in the *English Countryside Series*; no record of the number of copies bound. $2.

The sheets were supplied by B. T. Batsford.

B72   CHRIST CHURCH, GREYFRIARS   1935

First edition:

[*title on p.* [1]; *within a double rule*:] Christ Church, Greyfriars | [*illustration*] | CHARLES LAMB | *by Sir William Reynolds-Stephens* | [*illustration*] | DEDICATION

| OF THE | CENTENARY MEMORIAL | Tuesday, 5th November, 1935, at 3.30 p.m.

Crown 8vo. [8] pp. 7 × 4⅞ in.

No wrappers; edges trimmed; sewn.

Issued 5 November 1935; number of copies printed not ascertained. Not for sale.

Order of service.

P. [8] LINES TO CHARLES LAMB, WHO FOR SOME SEVEN YEARS HEARD THE BIBLE READ EVERY DAY IN CHRIST CHURCH, GREYFRIARS [*later* AT CHRIST CHURCH, GREY-FRIARS]; first published in a separate edition, 1937; and reprinted in *An Elegy*, 1937; *Poems 1930–1940*, [1941]; and *Poems of Many Years*, 1957 (*see* A63–4, 68, 135).

B73   **GRAND TOUR**   1935

a. First edition:

GRAND TOUR | A Journey in the Tracks of the | Age of Aristocracy | *conducted by* | Mona Wilson | Douglas Woodruff | Edmund Blunden | Janet Adam Smith | Richard Pyke | Sacheverell Sitwell | Malcolm Letts | *and edited by* | R. S. Lambert | *London* | Faber and Faber Limited | *24 Russell Square*

Demy 8vo. 168 pp. front., 28 plates, and map. 8⅝ × 5⅝ in.

Buckram boards patterned in browns and dark red; black buckram spine lettered in gold with illustration; top edges trimmed, pale brown, fore and bottom edges rough trimmed; white end-papers. Mauve pictorial dust-jacket printed in black.

Published 7 November 1935; no record of the number of copies printed. 10s. 6d.

Pp. 55–69 From Paris to Geneva; first published in *The Listener*, 17 July 1935 (*see* C1464).

b. First edition — American photo-offset reprint. [*1937*]:

[*title as above*; *imprint*:] *New York* | E. P. Dutton & Co., Inc. | *Publishers*

Demy 8vo. [iv], 174 pp. 8½ × 5⅝ in.

Magenta paper boards patterned in navy-blue; black cloth spine let-

187

tered in yellow; top and bottom edges trimmed, top magenta, fore rough trimmed; pp. [i–iv] and 171–174 form end-papers.

Issued 22 January 1937; 1250 copies printed. $2.50.

B74   **SOUTHDOWN BATTALIONS'**   1936
ASSOCIATION ANNUAL DINNER

First edition:

[*title on p.* [1]: *in blue*:] The Southdown Battalions' Association | (11th, 12th and 13th BATTALIONS) | [*in black letter*:] The Royal Sussex Regiment | [*in roman*:] [*battle honours in four lines*] | [*ornaments*] | THE ELEVENTH | [*in black letter*:] Annual Dinner | [*double rule, long, short*] | [*in roman*:] AT | THE AQUARIUM RESTAURANT, | BRIGHTON, | *On Saturday, March 28th, 1936* | [*ornaments*] | [*names of chairman etc., in two lines*]

Small crown 8vo. [4] pp. $7\frac{1}{4} \times 4\frac{1}{2}$ in.

No wrappers; edges trimmed.

Issued 28 March 1936; no record of the number of copies printed. Not for sale.

P. [4] TELL YOUR FORTUNE, signed E. B.; reprinted in *An Elegy*, 1937; and *Poems 1930–1940*, [1941] (*see* A64, 68).

B75   **THE WAR OF THE GUNS**   1936

a. First edition:

THE WAR OF | THE GUNS | *Western Front, 1917 &* *1918* | *By* | AUBREY WADE | *With an Introduction by* | EDMUND BLUNDEN | *Illustrated from Photographs* | LONDON | B. T. BATSFORD LTD. | 15 NORTH AUDLEY STREET, W. 1

Demy 8vo. xviii, 142 pp. front., 96 plates, and 2 maps. $8\frac{5}{8} \times 5\frac{3}{8}$ in.

Black cloth boards; lettered in red on spine, and on upper cover; edges trimmed, top red; pictorial end-papers.

Published May 1936; no record of the number of copies printed. 7s. 6d.

Copies in sheets were sent to Charles Scribner's, New York (*see* B75*b*). There was a reprint in 1959 entitled *Gunner on the Western Front* from which Blunden's Introduction was omitted despite a quotation from it on the dust-jacket.

Pp. ix–xvii Introduction From an Infantryman of those Days.

b. First edition – American issue. 1936:

New York, Scribner's*

xvii, 142 pp.

Issued 10 September 1936; no record of the number of copies bound. $3.

The sheets were supplied by B. T. Batsford.

B76   **MISCELLANY**   **1936**

First edition:

MISCELLANY | edited by George Haslam | Allan Plowman | Victor Ruse | published at The Queen's College | Oxford 1936

8vo. 64 pp. 9¾ × 7¼ in.

Blue-grey paper wrappers; printed in black; edges cut flush; gummed and sewn.

Published August 1936; no record of the number of copies printed.

P. 6 ON A PICTURE BY DÜRER; reprinted in *An Elegy*, 1937; and *Poems 1930–1940*, [1941] (*see* A64, 68) – p. 6 IN BERKSHIRE; reprinted in *An Elegy*, 1937; and *Poems 1930–1940*, [1941] (*see* A64, 68).

B77   **SOUTHDOWN BATTALIONS'**   **1937**
            ASSOCIATION ANNUAL DINNER

First edition:

[*title on p.* [1]: *in blue*:] [*regimental badge*] | [*in black letter*:] The Royal Sussex Regiment | [*in roman*:] The Southdown Battalions' Association | (11th, 12th and 13th BATTALIONS) | [*battle honours in four lines*] | [*ornaments*] | THE TWELFTH | [*in black letter*:] Annual

Dinner | [*double rule, long, short*] | [*in roman:*] AT | THE AQUARIUM RESTAURANT | BRIGHTON | *On Saturday, April 3rd, 1937* | [*ornaments*] | [*name of chairman etc., in two lines*]

Small crown 8vo. [4] pp. $7\frac{1}{4} \times 4\frac{1}{2}$ in.

No wrappers; edges trimmed.

Issued 3 April 1937; no record of the number of copies printed. Not for sale.

P. [4] "SUSSEX AND FLANDERS", signed E. Blunden.

**B78   THE M[ARYLEBONE]. C[RICKET].   1937
C[LUB]. 1787–1937**

First separate edition:

The M.C.C. | 1787–1937 | REPRINTED FROM | THE TIMES M.C.C. NUMBER | MAY 25, 1937 | [*monogram*] | PRICE 1s. NET | LONDON | THE TIMES PUBLISHING COMPANY LTD. | PRINTING HOUSE SQUARE | 1937

Royal 8vo. [viii], 136 pp. front., and 28 plates. $9\frac{5}{8} \times 5\frac{3}{4}$ in.

White paper boards printed in navy-blue, yellow and scarlet; edges trimmed; white end-papers, lower printed in black.

Published 25 June 1937; no record of the number of copies printed. 1*s*.

Pp. 112–118 Some Cricket Books; first published in *The Times*, M.C.C. Number, 25 May 1937; and reprinted in *Edmund Blunden: A Selection of His Poetry and Prose*, 1950 (*see* A108; C1617).

B79   THE IMMORTAL HERITAGE   1937

First edition:

THE IMMORTAL HERITAGE | *An Account of the Work and Policy* | *of The Imperial War Graves Commission* | *during twenty years* | *1917–1937* | by | FABIAN WARE | with an Introduction by | EDMUND BLUNDEN | and | thirty-two photographs | CAMBRIDGE | AT THE UNIVERSITY PRESS | 1937

Medium 8vo. 82 pp. illus., and 25 plates. $7\frac{7}{8} \times 5\frac{7}{8}$ in.

Pale blue grained cloth boards; lettered in gold on spine, and on upper cover within a double rule; edges trimmed; white end-papers.

Published 1 October 1937; 5000 copies printed. 2s. 6d.

Pp. [15]–21 Introduction.

B80   **AUTHORS TAKE SIDES**   1937

First edition:

AUTHORS TAKE SIDES | ON THE SPANISH WAR | LEFT REVIEW | 2 Parton Street | London | W.C.1

Royal 8vo. [32] pp. 9¾ × 6⅛ in.

Yellow wrappers; printed in scarlet; edges cut flush; stapled.

Published December 1937; number of copies printed not ascertained. 6d.

P. [31] contribution to the section Against the Government. *See also Authors Take Sides on Vietnam* (B274).

B81   **THE MERTON FLOATS**   1937

First edition:

[*title on upper wrapper*:] THE MERTON FLOATS | *present* | The Ascent of F6 | *by* | W. H. AUDEN | *and* | CHRISTOPHER ISHERWOOD | [*ornament*] | *Produced by* | W. ROBERTSON-DAVIES

Royal 8vo. [4] pp. 9⅞ × 6¼ in.

Pale blue wrappers; printed in black; edges trimmed; stapled.

Issued *c.* 4 December 1937; number of copies printed not ascertained. Not for sale.

Outside lower wrapper, at centre: The Potter Press | 29 St. Giles, Oxford.

P. [1] ANTHEM PRELIMINARY TO THE MASSACRE.

B82   **SOUTHDOWN BATTALIONS'**   1938
ASSOCIATION ANNUAL DINNER

First edition:

[*title on p.* [1]: *in blue*:] [*regimental badge*] | [*in black letter*:] The Royal Sussex Regiment | [*in roman*:] The Southdown Battalions' Association | (11th, 12th, and 13th BATTALIONS) | [*battle honours in four lines*] | THIRTEENTH | Annual Dinner | AT | THE AQUARIUM | RESTAURANT | BRIGHTON | On Saturday, March 5th, 1938 | [*name of chairman etc., in two lines*]

Small crown 8vo. [4] pp. 7¼ × 4½ in.

No wrappers; edges trimmed.

Issued 5 March 1938; no record of the number of copies printed. Not for sale.

P. [4] "AGE 200.", signed E. Blunden; reprinted in *Poems 1930-1940*, [1941] (*see* A68).

B83   **ON SHELLEY**   1938

First edition:

[*within a triple rule*:] On Shelley | [*ornament*] | Oxford University Press | 1938

Crown 8vo. viii, 100 pp. front. 7½ × 5 in.

White paper boards; lettered in black on spine; four rules in blind on upper and lower covers; top and fore edges trimmed, bottom rough trimmed; white end-papers.

Published 21 April 1938; 500 copies printed. 5s. ($2).

Pp. [v]–vi Preface signed E. B., G[avin]. de B[eer]., and S[ylva]. N[orman]. – pp. [1]–33 Shelley is Expelled.

B84   **THE BEST POEMS OF 1938**   1938

a. First edition:

The | BEST POEMS | *of* 1938 | [*device*] | *Selected by* | THOMAS MOULT | *with drawings by* | HANS AUFSEE-SER | LONDON | *Jonathan Cape Limited* | TORONTO

Crown 8vo. 128 pp. (incl. front.). front., and illus. 7¼ × 5 in.

Off-white cloth boards mottled in green and pink; white paper label on spine printed in black; illustration in green on upper cover; top edges trimmed, fore and bottom edges untrimmed; white pictorial end-papers printed in green.

Published 21 October 1938; 2554 copies printed. 6s.

One thousand, one hundred and forty-four copies in sheets were sent to Harcourt, Brace, New York (*see* B84*b*).

P. 79 IN THE MARGIN; first published in *The Listener*, 26 January 1938; and reprinted in *On Several Occasions*, 1939; *Poems 1930–1940*, [1941]; and *Poems of Many Years*, 1957 (*see* A67, 68, 135; C1677).

b. First edition – American issue. 1938:

[*title as above*; *imprint*:] Harcourt, Brace, New York*

Crown 8vo. 128 pp.
Issued 8 December 1938; 1144 copies bound. $2.
The sheets were supplied by Jonathan Cape, London.

B85   SOUTHDOWN BATTALIONS'   1939
             ASSOCIATION ANNUAL DINNER

First edition:

[*title on p.* [1]: *in blue*:] [*regimental badge*] | [*in black letter*:] The Royal Sussex Regiment | [*in roman*:] The Southdown Battalions Association | (11th, 12th and 13th BATTALIONS) | [*battle honours in four lines*] | FOURTEENTH | ANNUAL DINNER | AT | THE REGENT RESTAURANT | BRIGHTON | On Saturday, March 4th, 1939 | [*name of chairman etc., in two lines*]

Small crown 8vo. [4] pp. $7\frac{1}{4} \times 4\frac{1}{2}$ in.
No wrappers; edges trimmed.
Issued 4 March 1939; no record of the number of copies printed. Not for sale.
P. [4] "TO THE SOUTHDOWNS!", signed E. B.; reprinted in *Poems 1930–1940*, [1941] (*see* A68).

B86   KEATS HOUSE AND MUSEUM   1939

a. Third Edition (revised):

[*title on upper wrapper*:] *Keats House* | *AND MUSEUM* |

Wentworth Place, Hampstead | *Historical and Descriptive Guide* | *THIRD EDITION, REVISED*

Demy 8vo. 34 pp. front. 8½ × 5½ in.

Pale buff wrappers printed in black; edges cut flush; stapled.

Published April 1939; 3000 copies printed. 6*d.*

Pp. 1–2 Introduction, autograph facsimile signature on p. 2; reprinted in the fourth edition, fourth edition (revised), and the fifth edition of which 3000 copies each were printed.

b. Sixth edition. [*1966*]:

[*title on upper wrapper:*] [*illustration*] | [*on bright blue; in white:*] Keats House | [*in black:*] A GUIDE TO | THE HOUSE AND MUSEUM | Sixth Edition, 2s. 6d.

Small demy 8vo. 36 pp. 8 plates, and plan. 8⅜ × 5⅞ in.

White pictorial paper wrappers; printed in bright blue, grey and black; lower wrapper, verso, at foot: Printed in England by Battley Brothers Printers Clapham Park London SW4.

Published 31 August 1966; 3000 copies printed. 2*s.* 6*d.*

There were reprints (revised) of 3000 copies in November 1968, and 5000 copies in 1971.

Pp. 1–2 Introduction, autograph facsimile on p. 2; the Introduction is revised.

B87   POEMS AMONG SHAPES AND SHADOWS   1939

First edition:

[*ornament*] POEMS [*ornament*] | AMONG SHAPES AND SHADOWS | *by* | Shotaro Oshima | THE HOKUSEIDO PRESS | TOKYO

Demy 8vo. 90 pp. front. 8¾ × 5⅝ in.

Pale brown cloth boards; lettered in black down the spine with two stars in red; device in blind on lower cover; top edges trimmed, fore and bottom edges rough trimmed; cream end-papers.

Published 14 September 1939; 350 copies printed. 2 yen.

The publisher's records show a printing of 500 copies; it is, therefore possible that either 500 copies were printed and not 350, or that there was a second printing of 150 copies.

P. [4] tipped-in label: [*in black letter:*] Limited Edition | *350* copies of this book have been | issued, and the present copy is | No. [numbered] — p. 5 TO THE AUTHOR, signed E. Blunden.

B88   **ROSE WINDOW**   **1939**

a. First edition:

ROSE WINDOW | *a tribute offered to* | *St. Bartholomew's Hospital* | *by Twenty-Five Authors* | WITH A FOREWORD BY | THE LORD HORDER | G.C.V.O., M.D., F.R.C.P. | [*device*] | WILLIAM HEINEMANN LTD | LONDON :: TORONTO

Crown 8vo. [2], xii, 386 pp. illus. $7\frac{1}{2} \times 5$ in.

Orange cloth boards; lettered in gold on spine on three black panels; device in blind on lower cover; edges trimmed; buff end-papers.

Published 27 November 1939; number of copies printed not disclosed. 7*s.* 6*d.*

Pp. 245–246 NATURE'S DARING [*later* NATURE'S ADORNINGS] ; reprinted in *After the Bombing*, 1949; *Poems of Many Years*, 1957; and *The Midnight Skaters*, [1968] (*see* A89, 135, 174).

b. First edition — American issue. 1939:

New York, Transatlantic*

xii, 386 pp.

Issued 1939; number of copies bound not ascertained. $2.50.

B89   **THE MERTON FLOATS**   **1939**

First edition:

With the permission of Mr. Vice-Chancellor and the Rt. Worshipful the Mayor | *By members of* MERTON FLOATS DRAMATIC SOCIETY | *and* UNIVERSITY COLLEGE DRAMATIC SOCIETY *in the* | CLARENDON PRESS INSTITUTE, WALTON STREET | *on* DECEMBER 5*th and* 7*th*, 1939, *at* 8.15 *p.m.* | *and on* DECEMBER, 7*th*, *also at* 2.15 *p.m.* | [*in scarlet*:] The Secular Masque | [*in black*:] *By* John Dryden | *and* | [*in scarlet*:] Tom Thumb the Great | [*in black*:] *By* Henry Fielding | With musical settings for both pieces newly composed | by Kenneth Brooks | [*in scarlet*:] Proceeds to be given to the Red Cross | [*in black*:] Price of the Programme — *Sixpence* | A COLLECTION WILL BE MADE AT EACH PERFORM-ANCE

Demy 4to. [4] pp. 10$\frac{1}{2}$ × 8$\frac{1}{8}$ in.
No wrappers; edges trimmed.
Published 5 December 1939; no record of the number of copies printed. 6*d*.
P. [2] PROLOGUE to the Plays — p. [4] at foot: The Potter Press, 29 St Giles'.

B90   **AUGURY**   **1940**

First edition:

AUGURY | *An* Oxford Miscellany *of* | Verse & Prose | *Edited by* ALEC M. HARDIE | *and* KEITH C. DOUGLAS | OXFORD : BASIL BLACKWELL | 1940

Large crown 8vo. xvi, 64 pp. 7$\frac{7}{8}$ × 5$\frac{3}{8}$ in.
Pale grey paper boards; printed in black on spine, and on upper cover; illustration in scarlet on upper cover; edges trimmed; white end-papers.
Published 27 April 1940; 500 copies printed. 4*s*. 6*d*.
P. 30 TO WILFRED OWEN; first published in *Cherwell*, 3 February 1940 (*see* C1798) — p. 31 RESTORATION — pp. 31–32 THE MEANS [*later* FOR THE COUNTRY LIFE]; reprinted in *Shells by a Stream*, 1944; and *The Midnight Skaters*, [1968] (*see* A77, 174) — pp. 62–63 A RECOLLECTION IN A FAR YEAR [*formerly* SOME SAID . . .]; reprinted in *Poems 1930–1940*, [1941] (*see* A68).

B91   **FEAR NO MORE**   **1940**

First edition:

FEAR NO MORE | A Book of Poems | for the Present Time by | living English Poets | [*illustration*] | CAM-BRIDGE | AT THE UNIVERSITY PRESS | 1940

Crown 8vo. [2], x, 96 pp. 7⅜ × 4⅞ in.

Ruby paper boards, grey cloth spine; lettered in ruby up the spine; edges trimmed; white end-papers. White pictorial dust-jacket printed in brown.

Published 5 July 1940; 2500 copies printed. 3s. 6d.

There were reprints of 750 copies each in November and December 1940, and 1000 copies in July 1941. The Readers' Union Limited issued a reprint of 2000 copies in April 1941 in white pictorial paper boards, printed in blue and maroon; edges trimmed; white end-papers; there was a further reprint of 1000 copies in July 1941.

P. 12 WESERLAND [later WESERLAND, 1939]; reprinted in *Poems 1930-1940*, [1941] (*see* A68) — p. 19 GODSTOW; reprinted in *Poems 1930-1940*, [1941] (*see* A68) — p. 76 DIKKEBUSCH [*formerly and later* BY THE BELGIAN FRONTIER]; first published in *Kingdom Come*, December/January 1939/1940; and reprinted in *Poems 1930-1940*, [1941] (*see* A68; C1787). All the poems are unsigned.

B92   THE BEST POEMS OF 1940   1940

a. First edition:

The | BEST POEMS | *of* 1940 | *Selected by* | THOMAS MOULT | *& Decorated by* | ELIZABETH MONTGOMERY | LONDON | *Jonathan Cape Limited* | TORONTO

Crown 8vo. 128 pp. (incl. front.). front., and illus. 7¼ × 5 in.

Bright green cloth boards; white paper label on spine printed in black; top edges trimmed, fore and bottom edges untrimmed; white pictorial end-papers printed in pale blue.

Published 2 November 1940; 2500 copies printed. 6s.

One thousand and forty copies in sheets were sent to Harcourt, Brace, New York (*see* B92b).

P. 42 A WINDOW IN GERMANY AUGUST 1939; first published in the *TLS*, 16 September 1939; and reprinted in *Poems 1930-1940*, [1941] (*see* A68; C1775).

b. First edition — American issue. 1941:

[*title as above*; *imprint*:] Harcourt, Brace, New York*.

Crown 8vo. 128 pp.

Issued 3 April 1941; 1040 copies bound. $2.

The sheets were supplied by Jonathan Cape, London.

B93   THE CAMBRIDGE BIBLIOGRAPHY   1940
OF ENGLISH LITERATURE

a. First edition:

THE | CAMBRIDGE BIBLIOGRAPHY | OF | ENGLISH
LITERATURE | Edited by | F. W. BATESON | VOLUME
III | 1800-1900 | [*device*] | CAMBRIDGE | AT THE
UNIVERSITY PRESS | 1940

Small royal 8vo. xxii, 1100 pp. $9\frac{1}{4} \times 6\frac{3}{8}$ in.

Mid-brown cloth boards; lettered in gold on spine with device; edges trimmed, top brown; white end-papers.

Published 15 November 1940; 5000 copies printed. £7. 7s. the set of 4 volumes.

There were reprints of 1000 copies in January 1967, and 1500 copies in July 1969.

Pp. 218-219 John Clare (1793-1864) — pp. 631-637 Charles Lamb (1775-1834) — pp. 643-648 Leigh Hunt (1784-1859); all signed E.BL. Blunden is erroneously listed as a contributor to Volume I.

b. First edition — American issue. 1941:

[*title as above*; *imprint*:] The Macmillan Company, New York*

xxii, 1100 pp.

Issued 1941; no record of the number bound. $32.50 the set of 4 volumes.

c. Second edition. 1969:

The New | Cambridge Bibliography | of English Literature | [*swelled rule*] | *Edited by* | GEORGE WATSON | Volume 3 | 1800-1900 | [*device*] | CAMBRIDGE | AT THE UNIVERSITY PRESS | 1969

Crown 4to. xxiv pp., 1948 columns, [10] pp. $9\frac{7}{8} \times 6\frac{7}{8}$ in.

Dull green cloth boards; lettered in gold on spine, with device; edges trimmed, top green; white end-papers.

Published 23 October 1969; 7500 copies printed.

Columns 356–358 John Clare 1793–1864, signed E.B.; the bibliography is revised. The entries for Charles Lamb and Leigh Hunt are not by Blunden.

B94   THE BEST POEMS OF 1941   1942

a. First edition:

The | BEST POEMS | *of* 1941 | *Selected by* | THOMAS MOULT | LONDON | *Jonathan Cape Limited* | TORONTO

Crown 8vo. 128 pp. (incl. front.). front., and illus. 7¼ × 5 in.

Yellow cloth boards; white paper label on spine printed in black; illustration in red on upper cover; edges trimmed; white pictorial end-papers printed in red.

Published 16 January 1942; 3680 copies printed. 6s.

One thousand, three hundred copies in sheets were sent to Harcourt, Brace, New York (*see* B94*b*).

P. 60 THE FINE NATURE; first published in the *TLS*, 7 December 1940; and reprinted in *Shells by a Stream*, 1944 (*see* A77; C1842).

b. First edition — American issue. 1942:

[*title as above*; *imprint*:] Harcourt, Brace, New York*

Crown 8vo. 128 pp.

Issued 23 July 1942; 1300 copies bound. $2.

The sheets were supplied by Jonathan Cape, London.

B95   MODERN ESSAYS 1939–1941   1942

First edition:

MODERN ESSAYS | 1939–1941 | Selected and Edited by | A. F. SCOTT, M.A. | *Senior English Master at Taunton School* | MACMILLAN AND CO., LIMITED | ST. MARTIN'S STREET, LONDON | 1942

Foolscap 8vo. x, 262 pp. 6⅞ × 4¼ in.

Bottle green cloth boards; lettered in gold on spine with a triple

rule at head and foot and device; edges trimmed; white end-papers.
Published July 1942 in the *Scholar's Library*; no record of the number of copies printed. 3s.

Pp. 36–44 The Spirit of England; first published in the *World Review*, September 1940 (*see* C1829).

B96   **POEMS OF THIS WAR**   1942

a. First edition:

[*within a black rule across head and foot, and a red rule down each side of the title*:] POEMS | OF THIS WAR | By Younger Poets | [*in red*: *star*] | *Edited by* | *Patricia Ledward* | *and Colin Strong* | [*in red*: *star*] | *With an Introduction by* | *Edmund Blunden* | [*in red*: *star*] | CAMBRIDGE | AT THE UNIVERSITY PRESS | 1942

Large crown 8vo. xii, 100 pp. 8 × 5⅛ in.

Cerise cloth boards; grey label on spine printed in cerise up the spine; top and fore edges trimmed, bottom rough trimmed; white end-papers. Grey dust-jacket printed in cerise.

Published 17 July 1942; 2500 copies printed. 5s.

There was a reprint of 1500 copies in October 1942. The rights were transferred to the Falcon Press in 1945 who issued a reprint in 1947 under the title of *Retrospect 1939–1942*.

Pp. vii–[xii] Introduction.

b. First edition — American issue. 1942:

New York, Macmillan*

xii, 100 pp.

Issued 1942; no record of the number of copies bound. $1.75.

B97   **LONDON CALLING**   1942

First edition:

London Calling, edited by Storm Jameson. New York, Harper & Brothers*

vi, 322 pp.

Published 13 November 1942; 2000 copies printed. $2.50.

There was a reprint of 750 copies.

Pp. 114–115 THE TOWER; reprinted (revised) in *After the Bombing*, 1949 (*see* A89).

B98   THE BEST POEMS OF 1942   1943

a. First edition:

The | BEST POEMS | *of* 1942 | *Selected by* | THOMAS MOULT | JONATHAN CAPE | THIRTY BEDFORD SQUARE | LONDON

Crown 8vo. 112 pp. (incl. front.). front., and illus. $7\frac{5}{8} \times 5\frac{1}{4}$ in.

Bright yellow cloth boards; pale blue cloth spine; white paper label on spine printed in black; illustration in blue on upper cover; top edges trimmed, fore and bottom edges untrimmed; white pictorial end-papers printed in blue.

Published 15 March 1943; 4000 copies printed. 6*s*.

One thousand, three hundred copies in sheets were sent to Harcourt, Brace, New York (*see* B98*b*).

P. 109 SHELLS BY A STREAM; first published in *Queen's Quarterly*, Summer 1942; and reprinted in *Shells by a Stream*, 1944 (*see* A77; C1916).

b. First edition – American issue. 1943:

[*title as above*; *imprint*:] Harcourt, Brace, New York*

Crown 8vo. 112 pp.

Issued 19 August 1943; 1300 copies bound. $2.

The sheets were supplied by Jonathan Cape, London.

B99   RETURN TO HUSBANDRY   1943

First edition:

RETURN TO HUSBANDRY | An Annotated List of Books dealing with | the History, Philosophy and Craftsmanship of | Rural England, and intended to suggest alterna- | tives to Commercialism and Mechanization. | With four preliminary Essays | EDITED BY | EDMUND BLUNDEN | J. M. DENT AND SONS LIMITED

Small crown 8vo. 32 pp. $7\frac{1}{4} \times 4\frac{3}{4}$ in.

Stiff white pictorial wrappers; printed in bottle-green; edges cut flush; sewn.

Published 15 April 1943; 2000 copies printed. 6*d.*

There was a reprint of 3000 copies later in April 1943.

P. [3] Note.

B100   **AN ENGLISH LIBRARY**   1943

First edition:

AN | ENGLISH LIBRARY | AN ANNOTATED LIST OF 1300 CLASSICS | By | F. SEYMOUR SMITH, F.L.A. | CHIEF LIBRARIAN FINCHLEY PUBLIC LIBRARIES | Foreword by | EDMUND BLUNDEN | LONDON | NATIONAL BOOK COUNCIL

Crown 8vo. 88 pp. $7\frac{1}{4} \times 4\frac{3}{4}$ in.

Oatmeal cloth boards; lettered in green down the spine; edges trimmed; white end-papers. Cream pictorial dust-jacket printed in dark green.

Published August 1943; no record of the number of copies printed. 2*s.*

Reprinted (revised) in November 1943, January 1944, later in 1944, and in 1950.

Pp. 5–6 Foreword; first published in the *National Book Council News Sheet*, June 1943 (*see* C1966). *See also* C2549 for review by Blunden.

B101   **THE BEST POEMS OF 1943**   1944

a. First edition:

The | BEST POEMS | of 1943 | *Selected by* | THOMAS MOULT | JONATHAN CAPE | THIRTY BEDFORD SQUARE | LONDON

Crown 8vo. 128 pp. (incl. front.). front., and illus. $7\frac{1}{4} \times 5\frac{1}{8}$ in.

Bright green cloth boards; white paper label on spine printed in black; illustration in red on upper cover; top edges trimmed, fore and bottom edges untrimmed; white pictorial end-papers printed in black.

Published 8 August 1944; 4000 copies printed. 6*s.*

One thousand, three hundred copies in sheets were sent to Harcourt, Brace, New York (see B101b).

P. 88 A SONG [later THE WATERFALL]; first published in the *Queen's Quarterly*, Spring 1943; and reprinted in *Shells by a Stream*, 1944; and *Poems of Many Years*, 1957 (see A77, 135; C1961).

b. First edition — American issue. 1944:

[*title as above*; *imprint*:] Harcourt, Brace, New York*

Crown 8vo. 128 pp.
Issued 29 November 1944; 1300 copies bound. $2.
The sheets were supplied by Jonathan Cape, London.

B102   **PERSUASION**   **1944**

a. Book Society edition:

PERSUASION | JANE AUSTEN | [*ornament*] | *Intro-duction by* EDMUND BLUNDEN | *Illustrations by* JOHN AUSTEN | THE BOOK SOCIETY | LONDON NINETEEN FORTY-FOUR

Demy 8vo. x, 230 pp. front. (col.), illus., and 7 plates (col.), $8\frac{1}{2} \times 5\frac{1}{4}$ in.
Rose pink cloth boards; lettered in gold across and up the spine, with device, and on upper cover; edges trimmed, top pale grey; cream pictorial end-papers printed in brown.
Published 25 December 1944; number of copies printed not ascertained. 9s.
Distributed as the Book Society's members' book for Christmas.
Pp. v–ix [Introduction]: Jane Austen.

b. Second printing. 1946:

[*title as above*; *imprint*:] [*device*] | AVALON PRESS : LONDON

Small demy 8vo. x, 230 pp. front. (col.), illus., and 7 plates (col.). $8\frac{1}{2} \times 5\frac{1}{4}$ in.
Green cloth boards; lettered in gold up and across the spine, and in blind on upper cover; edges trimmed, top pink; cream pictorial end-

papers printed in brown. Cream pictorial dust-jacket printed in pink, blue, green and grey.

Issued 1946; number of copies printed not ascertained.

Pp. v–ix Introduction.

B103   **EASTES & LOUD LTD**   1944
             CENTENARY SOUVENIR   [i.e. 1945]

First edition:

EASTES & LOUD LTD. | DIRECTORS: | J. E. HOSKING
T. R. SHAXSON W. S. HOLLIWELL | [*short rule*] | 1944

Small demy 8vo. [vi], 26 pp. 2 plates. $8\frac{1}{2}$ × $5\frac{1}{2}$ in.

Navy-blue cloth boards; lettered in gold on upper cover; edges trimmed; pp. [i–iv] and [23–26] form end-papers.

Issued 4 January 1945; 1000 copies printed. Not for sale.

Pp. 5–19 Home Thoughts on Kent, 1844–1944; reprinted in *Edmund Blunden: A Selection of His Poetry and Prose*, 1950 (*see* A108) — p. 20 "SOUTHERN ENGLAND" IN 1944 [*formerly* SOUTH-EAST ENGLAND IN 1944]; first published in the *TLS*, 28 October 1944; and reprinted in *After the Bombing*, 1949 (*see* A89; C2056).

B104   **THE NATURAL ORDER**   1945

First edition:

THE NATURAL ORDER | *Essays in* | THE RETURN TO HUSBANDRY | *by* | EDMUND BLUNDEN J. E. HOS-KING | [*contributors' names in six further lines*] | *Illustrated by* | THOMAS HENNELL | Edited with an Introduction and Notes | *by* | H. J. MASSINGHAM | LONDON | J. M. DENT & SONS LTD.

Small crown 8vo. vi, 178 pp. illus. $7\frac{1}{4}$ × $4\frac{3}{4}$ in.

Rust cloth boards; lettered in gold on spine; edges trimmed, top rust; white pictorial end-papers printed in black. Pale blue dust-jacket printed in darker blue and black.

Published 1 February 1945; 5000 copies printed. 7*s.* 6*d.*

There was a reprint (revised) of 5000 copies in April 1946.

Pp. 21–30 The Rural Tradition; reprinted in *Edmund Blunden: A Selection of His Poetry and Prose*, 1950 (*see* A108).

First edition:

FOLLY BRIDGE | [*within wavy dashes:*] A Romantic Tale | by | [*outside dashes:*] D. L. MURRAY | [*illustration*] | London | Hodder and Stoughton Limited | and The Book Society

Large crown 8vo. 336 pp. illus. $7\frac{3}{4} \times 5\frac{1}{4}$ in.

Lobster red cloth boards; lettered in black on spine; illustration on upper cover; edges trimmed, top dark grey; white end-papers, with map on upper end-papers.

Published 2 July 1945; *c.* 60,000 copies printed. 10*s.* 6*d.*

P. 133 DISTRESS; p. 218 untitled poem (" 'One fell a'roaring lyke a bull,); both unsigned.

B106   THE LIFE OF GEORGE S. GORDON   1945

First edition:

The Life of | GEORGE S. GORDON | 1881–1942 | *by* | M.C.G. | *With an Introduction by* | LORD HALIFAX | OXFORD UNIVERSITY PRESS | *London New York Toronto* | 1945

Crown 8vo. xii, 172 pp. front. (port.) and 8 plates. $7\frac{3}{8} \times 4\frac{7}{8}$ in.

Peacock green cloth boards; lettered in gold on spine; top and fore edges trimmed, bottom rough trimmed, top peacock green; white end-papers.

Published 30 August 1945; 1506 copies printed. 10*s.* 6*d.*

Pp. 90–92 reminiscences on his association with the Book Society.

B107   ESSAYS ON THE EIGHTEENTH   1945
CENTURY

First edition:

ESSAYS ON THE | EIGHTEENTH CENTURY | *Presented to* | DAVID NICHOL SMITH | *in honour of* | *his seventieth birthday* | OXFORD | AT THE CLARENDON PRESS | 1945

Demy 8vo. viii, 288 pp. front. (port.) $8\frac{3}{4} \times 5\frac{1}{2}$ in.

Navy-blue cloth boards; lettered in gold on spine with device and a rule at head and foot; top and fore edges trimmed, bottom rough trimmed; white end-papers.

Published 27 September 1945; 1250 copies printed. £1. 1s. ($6.50).

Pp. [225]–237 Elegant Extracts; on *Elegant Extracts*, edited by Vicesimus Knox.

B108   **WHEN ALL IS DONE**   1945

First edition:

WHEN ALL IS DONE | by | ALISON UTLEY | [*five line quotation*] | FABER AND FABER LTD | 24 Russell Square | London

Crown 8vo. 256 pp. $7\frac{1}{4} \times 4\frac{7}{8}$ in.

Crimson cloth boards; lettered in gold down the spine; edges trimmed; white end-papers.

Published 19 October 1945; no record of the number of copies printed. 8s. 6d.

P. [5] untitled poem [*i.e.* HOMES AND HAUNTS]; first published in the *TLS*, 22 July 1944; and reprinted in *After the Bombing*, 1949; and *Poems of Many Years*, 1957 (*see* A89, 135; C2041; *see also* B224).

B109   **TRANSLATION (LONDON)**   1945

First edition:

TRANSLATION (LONDON) | EDITED BY NEVILLE BRAYBROOKE & ELIZABETH KING | LONDON | PHOENIX PRESS | 1945

Small demy 8vo. [48] pp. $8\frac{3}{8} \times 5\frac{1}{2}$ in.

Crimson paper wrappers; printed in black on upper wrapper; edges cut flush; sewn.

Published November 1945; 4000 copies printed. 2s.

There was a reprint of 1000 copies in March 1946 with an errata slip on Blunden's poem.

Pp. [5–6] AT THE SHRINE OF APOLLO, HORACE 65–8 B.C.; reprinted in *Eastward*, [1950] (*see* A97).

First edition:

VOICES | on the | GREEN | [*star*] | *Edited by* | A.R.J. WISE | and | REGINALD A. SMITH | [*three line quotation*] | [*device*] | MICHAEL JOSEPH LTD. | 26 *Bloomsbury Street, London, W.C.* 1

Small crown 8vo. 224 pp. front. (p. [1]), and illus. $7\frac{1}{4} \times 4\frac{3}{4}$ in.

Mid-blue cloth boards; lettered in silver down and across the spine with device, and on upper cover; edges trimmed, top blue; off-white end-papers.

Published December 1945; no record of the number of copies printed. 10*s.* 6*d.*

Pp. 123–124 VOICES I HEARD.

First edition:

Spring | PIE | *The Pocket* | *Miscellany* | *All profits from this* PIE POCKET | SPECIAL *will be given to* TOC H, *in* | *aid of its Service welfare work in* | *Occupied Europe and the Far East* | Hutchinson

Small crown 8vo. 192 pp. (including plates). illus., and 16 plates. $7\frac{1}{8} \times 4\frac{1}{2}$ in.

White pictorial paper wrappers; printed in blue, pink, scarlet, yellow and black; edges cut flush; stapled.

Published 14 January 1946; 185,000 copies printed. 2*s.*

Pp. 49–53 Country Mysteries.

First edition:

[*title on upper wrapper*:] [*illustration*] | OCCASIONAL PAPER | PLOUGH SUNDAY | 1946 | *Published by* | THE COUNCIL FOR THE CHURCH AND COUNTRYSIDE, | ST. ANNE'S HOUSE, 57A DEAN STREET, W.1 | PRICE ONE SHILLING

Small demy 8vo. 32 pp. $8\frac{3}{8} \times 5\frac{1}{2}$ in.

Buff paper wrappers; printed in black; edges cut flush; stapled.

Published *c.* 16 February 1946; number of copies printed not ascertained. 1*s.*

Pp. 10–11 Poets of the Land.

B113   **THE ENGLISHMAN'S**   **1945**
             COUNTRY   **[i.e. 1946]**

a. First edition:

THE | ENGLISHMAN'S COUNTRY | INTRODUCTION
BY EDMUND BLUNDEN | EDITED BY W. J. TURNER |
[*swelled rule*] | *WITH* | *48 PLATES IN COLOUR* | *AND*
| *137 ILLUSTRATIONS IN* | *BLACK & WHITE* | [*device*]
COLLINS • 14 ST. JAMES'S PLACE • LONDON |
MCMXXXXV

Medium 8vo. 320 pp. (including plates). illus., 47 plates and 3 maps.
$8\frac{3}{4} \times 6\frac{3}{8}$ in.

Pale moss green cloth boards; lettered in gold on spine with illustration; edges trimmed; white end-papers.

Published March 1946; no record of the number of copies printed.
£1. 1*s.*

The publishers write that sales amounted to 'tens of thousands'.

Pp. 5–8 Introduction — pp. 11–52 English Villages; first published in a separate edition, 1941 (*see* A69).

b. First edition — American issue. 1946:

Panorama of Rural England. New York, Hastings House*
316 pp.

Issued 1946; number of copies bound not ascertained. $5.

B114   **POEMS BY C. W. BRODRIBB**   **1946**
First edition:

POEMS | BY | C. W. BRODRIBB | WITH AN INTRO-
DUCTION | BY | EDMUND BLUNDEN | LONDON |
MACMILLAN & CO. LTD | 1946

Small crown 8vo. xviii, 102 pp. front. (port.) $7\frac{1}{4} \times 4\frac{5}{8}$ in.

Navy-blue cloth boards; lettered in gold down the spine, and on upper cover; edges trimmed; white end-papers. Cream dust-jacket printed in black and pale blue.

Published 28 May 1946; 1900 copies printed. 6s.

Published on commission from *The Times*, and probably designed by Stanley Morison.

Pp. v–xiii Introduction.

B115   **A SENTIMENTAL JOURNEY**   **1946**

Pan Books edition:

LAURENCE STERNE | [*rule*] | A SENTIMENTAL | JOURNEY | through France and Italy | WITH A NEW INTRODUCTION BY | EDMUND BLUNDEN | [*publisher's device*] | [*broken rule*] | *Pan Books Ltd*

Small crown 8vo. [ii], 126 pp. $7 \times 4\frac{5}{8}$ in.

Grey paper wrappers; printed in rust and black; edges cut flush; sewn and gummed.

Published July 1946; no record of the number of copies printed. 1s.

The first book published by Pan Books.

Pp. 5–9 Introduction.

B116   **POSE & POISE**   **1946**

First edition:

[*title on upper fold of card: in brown*:] [*illustration*] | POSE & POISE | Exhibition of Drawings | *by* | ETHELBERT | WHITE | PRIVATE VIEW | Monday, 8th July, 1946 | St. George's Gallery | 81 Grosvenor Street, W.1

Folded card. $4 \times 8\frac{1}{2}$ in. (open); 4×5 in. (closed).

Buff card printed in dark brown; edges trimmed.

Published 8 July 1946; number of copies printed not ascertained. Not for sale.

Lower fold, recto TO ETHELBERT WHITE. *See also* poem of same title (B45).

First edition:

[*illustration*] | *The* | [*in pink open letters*:] Saturday
Book | [*in black*:] SIXTH YEAR | *edited by* | *LEONARD
RUSSELL* | *with illustrations by Laurence Scarfe* |
Hutchinson

Medium 8vo. 288 pp. (incl. plates). illus., and plates. 9 × 6 in.

Orange buckram boards; lettered in gold across and down the spine;
edges trimmed; white pictorial end-papers printed in rust.

Published October 1946; probably 10,000 copies printed. £1. 1*s.*

Pp. 128–134 Coventry Patmore 1823–1896; above title: After Fifty
Years.

First edition:

[*title on upper wrapper*; *lines* 1-3 *in open letters*:] B. |
B.C. | pamphlets | [*in red*:] No. 2 | [*rule*] | BOOKS |
AND | AUTHORS | [*rule*] | PRICE | 12 as.

Crown 8vo. 32 pp. plate. $7\frac{3}{8}$ × 5 in.

Buff paper wrappers; printed in navy-blue and crimson; inside lower
wrapper, at foot: PRINTED IN INDIA BY W. T. JENKINS AT THE
WESLEY | PRESS AND PUBLISHING HOUSE, MYSORE CITY
AND | PUBLISHED BY GEOFFREY CUMBERLEGE, BOMBAY;
edges cut flush; sewn.

Published 29 October 1946 as *BBC Pamphlets*, No. 2; 2500 copies
printed. 12 annas.

Two thousand, one hundred and three copies were pulped in February 1949.

Pp. 11–15 Thomas Hardy.

First separate publication:

[*title at head of leaf*:] HARDY'S EARLIEST VERSE

An offprint of [1] leaf. $14\frac{3}{8}$ × $6\frac{3}{4}$ in.

No wrappers; edges trimmed.

Issued *c.* 23 August 1947; 14 copies printed. Not for sale.

Introductory note, unsigned; reprinted from the *TLS*, 23 August 1947 (*see* C2394).

B120   THE LIFE OF GEORGE CRABBE   1947

Cresset Library edition:

THE LIFE OF | [*in open capitals*:] GEORGE | CRABBE | [*in roman*:] BY HIS SON | WITH | AN INTRODUCTION BY | EDMUND BLUNDEN | [*ornamental rule*] | LONDON | THE CRESSET PRESS | MCMXLVII

Crown 8vo. [2], xxx, 288 pp. $7\frac{3}{4}$ X 5 in.

Navy-blue cloth boards; lettered in gold on spine, and on upper cover, with an ornamental design on spine and upper cover; edges trimmed; white end-papers. White dust-jacket printed in pale green, brown and black.

Published October 1947; number of copies printed not ascertained. 8*s.* 6*d.*

Pp. [vii]–xxv Father and Son.

B121   ST. CECILIA'S DAY FESTIVAL   1947
CONCERT

First edition:

[*title on upper wrapper; within a rule in grey, within a pictorial frame*:] UNDER THE GRACIOUS PATRONAGE | OF THEIR MAJESTIES THE KING AND QUEEN | [*in ornamental script*:] St. Cecilia's | Day | Festival | Concert | [*in roman*:] IN AID OF THE MUSICIANS' BENEVOLENT FUND | *Sponsored by the* | DAILY HERALD | ROYAL ALBERT HALL | (Manager: C. S. Taylor) | SATURDAY, 22 November, 1947

Demy 4to. [20] pp. illus. $10\frac{3}{8}$ X $8\frac{3}{8}$ in.

White pictorial paper wrappers; printed in pale blue, black, yellow, brown, red, mauve and green; outside lower wrapper, at foot: Produced and printed by ODHAMS PRESS LTD., Long Acre, London, W.C.2; edges trimmed; stapled.

Published 22 November 1947; number of copies printed not ascertained.

P. [2] AN ODE FOR ST. CECILIA'S DAY; reprinted in *Eastward*,

[1950]; and *A Hong Kong House*, 1962 (*see* A97, 156). Also re-printed in the programme for *St. Cecilia's Festival Concert* on 22 November 1950, p. 11.

B122   HYMNS FOR   1947 [i.e. 1948]
           THE AMUSEMENT OF CHILDREN

Luttrell Society edition:

HYMNS | FOR THE AMUSEMENT | OF CHILDREN | BY CHRISTOPHER SMART | *OXFORD,* | Printed for the Luttrell Society | by Basil Blackwell | MCMXLVII

Small crown 8vo. xvi, [4], ii, 86 pp. illus. $7\frac{1}{8} \times 4\frac{7}{8}$ in.

Grey paper wrappers; printed in navy-blue; edges trimmed; sewn and gummed.

Published 1 March 1948 as the *Luttrell Society Reprint*, No. 5; 400 copies printed. £1. 5s.

Pp. iii–xvi Introduction, signed E. B.

B123   TRIBUTE TO WALTER DE LA MARE   1948

First edition:

TRIBUTE TO | WALTER DE LA MARE | on his | Seventy-fifth Birthday | [*decorated rule*] | FABER AND FABER LIMITED | 24 Russell Square | London

Medium 8vo. 196 pp. front., and 5 plates. $8\frac{5}{8} \times 5\frac{1}{2}$ in.

Mid-blue cloth boards; lettered in gold on spine on a pink panel and at foot; monogram in blind on upper cover; edges trimmed, top gilt; white end-papers.

Published 26 April 1948; no record of the number of copies printed. 15s.

Pp. 142–148 Without Tears.

B124   SHELLEY'S DEFENCE OF POETRY   1948

a. First edition:

SHELLEY'S | DEFENCE OF POETRY | *Edited* | *with Introduction and Notes* | *by* | EDMUND BLUNDEN | THE HOKUSEIDO PRESS | 1948

Crown 8vo. [iv], 88 pp. 7⅛ × 5 in.

Pale grey paper wrappers; printed in black; off-white end-papers; edges cut flush; stapled and gummed.

Published 27 May 1948; no record of the number of copies printed. 35 yen.

There were two reprints. The number of copies printed of both editions total 8500. *See also* B124*b–c*.

P. [1] Preface, signed E. B. — pp. [3]–11 Introduction — pp. 69–86 Notes.

b. First edition — fourth reprint (revised). [*1952*] :

SHELLEY'S | DEFENCE OF POETRY | AND | BLUNDEN'S | LECTURES ON "DEFENCE" | THE HOKUSEIDO PRESS

Crown 8vo. [ii], 134 pp. 7⅛ × 5 in.

Pale green paper wrappers; printed in black; white end-papers; edges cut flush; stapled and gummed.

Issued 10 April 1952; no record of the number of copies printed. 80 yen.

There was a reprint in April 1958. *See* B124*a* for note on the number of copies printed.

P. [1] Preface, signed E. B. — pp. 3–11 Introduction — pp. 71–116 Lectures Founded on Shelley's "Defence of Poetry" — pp. 117–134 Notes.

c. Second edition. [*1959*] :

[*title and imprint as above*]

Crown 8vo. [iv], 140 pp. 7¼ × 5 in.

Pale slate wrappers; printed in black; white end-papers, publisher's advertisements on lower end-papers; edges cut flush; gummed.

Published 18 April 1959; no record of the number of copies printed. 90 yen.

There were reprints in October 1963 and September 1970. *See* B124*a* for note on the number of copies printed.

P. [1] Preface, signed E. B. — pp. 3–13 Introduction — pp. [73]–120 Lectures Founded on Shelley's "Defence of Poetry" — pp. 121–139 Notes.

First edition:

CHA-NO-YU | Head Quarters of | the Ura Senke School | of Tea Ceremonials. | Sen Soshitsu | 14th Generation from Sen Rikyu | Published by the International Association for the Advancement | of the Japanese Tea Cult. | Kogawa-Kashira, Kyoto, Japan | 1948

[vi], [52] pp. illus. 7 × 7⅜ in.

Pale blue paper boards; lettered in black on spine, and upper and lower covers; coloured illustration on upper cover; edges trimmed; off-white end-papers.

Published *c.* June 1948; number of copies printed not ascertained.

P. [3] untitled poem (Some day in England), holograph facsimile dated 23 May 1948; p. [4] Japanese translation of poem.

B126   CULTURE THROUGH ENGLISH   1948

First edition:

[*within a compartment*:] CULTURE THROUGH | ENGLISH | BOOK II | COMPILED | BY | THE CHRISTIAN EDUCATION | ASSOCIATION IN JAPAN | KANDA ° AI-IKU-SHA ° TOKYO

Crown 8vo. [ii], 78 pp. illus., and music score. 7⅛ × 5 in.

White pictorial paper wrappers; printed in dark and pale brown; edges cut flush; lower end-papers, upper paste-down end-paper formed by pp. [i–ii], no upper free end-paper; stapled and gummed.

Published 15 June 1948; number of copies printed not ascertained. 40 yen.

Pp. 49–53 An Impression of Thomas Hardy.

B127   JANE EYRE   1948

a. Phoenix Library edition:

[*title on upper wrapper*:] The Phoenix Library — No. 2 | [*row of dots with an ornament at centre*] | CHARLOTTE BRONTË: | JANE EYRE | An Abridgement | by Ichiro Nishizaki | WITH INTRODUCTION | BY EDMUND BLUNDEN | TOKYO | THE SASAKI TYPE | 1948

40 pp. (mimeo.). $9\frac{7}{8} \times 7\frac{1}{4}$ in.

Buff paper wrappers; printed in black; edges cut flush; gummed and stapled.

Published 28 June 1948; number of copies printed not ascertained. 32 yen.

Pp. 1–6 Introduction, dated 5 July 1948 [*sic*].

b. Hokuseido Press edition. [*1956*] :

[*title as above*; *continues*:] Abridged and Edited with Notes by | Ichiro Nishizaki & Nobuko Suto | *With an Introduction by* | Edmund Blunden | THE HOKUSEIDO PRESS

Crown 8vo. xii, 196 pp. front. (port.). $7\frac{1}{4} \times 5\frac{1}{8}$ in.

Limp grey rexine wrappers; printed in navy-blue; white end-papers; edges trimmed; gummed and stapled.

Published 10 May 1956; no record of the number of copies printed of the first impression. 150 yen.

There were 13 reprints; the total number of copies printed is 14,000.

Pp. [iii]–ix Introduction.

B127.1   **NEW CAMPUS**   1948

First edition:

[*within a double broken rule with first and last lines in the gaps*:] NEW CAMPUS | *Series For High School Folks* | VOL. II | [*six line quotation*] | TIENHSIN-SHA

Crown 8vo. [ii], 78 pp. $7\frac{1}{8} \times 5\frac{1}{8}$ in.

White paper wrappers; printed in brown and black; edges cut flush; stapled.

Published 1 October 1948; number of copies printed not ascertained. 45 yen.

Pp. 56–60 The Dilemma of Progress; first published in *Youth's Companion*, April 1948 (*see* C2426).

First edition:

[*title on verso of card, towards head*:] LEIGH HUNT. | 1784–1859.

Postcard. port. $3\frac{1}{8} \times 5\frac{3}{8}$ in.

Edges trimmed.

Published probably 1949; probably 500 copies printed. 3*d.*

Portrait of James Henry Leigh Hunt from a painting of 1837 by Samuel Laurence published by the National Portrait Gallery, London as card 2508.

Verso of card text signed E. Blunden; the text was dropped from the card in 1970 when the National Portrait Gallery began to change the format of their cards.

First edition:

SATURDAY MORNINGS | *ESSAYS* | REPRINTED FROM | THE [*ornament*] TIMES | LITERARY SUPPLE- MENT | [*double rule, thick, thin*] | LONDON | THE TIMES PUBLISHING COMPANY, LIMITED | PRINTING HOUSE SQUARE | 1949

Crown 8vo. [viii], 208 pp. $7\frac{1}{4} \times 4\frac{3}{4}$ in.

Dull pink cloth boards; lettered in gold on spine, and on upper cover; edges trimmed, top dark pink; white end-papers.

Published 1949; no record of the number of copies printed.

Pp. 14–21 Poets in the Storm; first published in the *TLS*, 11 August 1945 (*see* C2135).

First edition:

KEATS SHELLEY & ROME | *An Illustrated Miscellany* | [*swelled rule*] • [*swelled rule*] | *Compiled by* | NEVILLE ROGERS | *Postscript by* | FIELD MARSHALL EARL WAVELL | P.C., G.C.B., G.C.S.I., G.C.I.E., M.C. | *Published on behalf of the* | KEATS SHELLEY MEMORIAL

ASSOCIATION | [*swelled rule*] • [*swelled rule*] | CHRIS-
TOPHER JOHNSON | 109 GREAT RUSSELL STREET |
LONDON | 1949

Demy 8vo. 76 pp. illus., and 8 plates. $8\frac{1}{2}$ × $5\frac{3}{8}$ in.

Mid-brown cloth boards; lettered in gold on upper cover; edges
trimmed; white end-papers. Cream pictorial dust-jacket printed in
brown.

Published January 1949; no record of the number of copies printed.
7s. 6d.

The Keats Shelley Memorial Association write that 5500 copies were
sold by May 1971.

Pp. 50–58 The Fame of Shelley 1947. *See also* C2465.

B131   RABBEY IN THE WOODS   1949

First edition:

EIGO EBANASHI SŌSHO | *Rabbey in the Woods* | S.
TOMIYAMA | [*illustration*] | YUHODO

Crown 8vo. [vi], 52, 8 pp. illus. $7\frac{1}{8}$ × 5 in.

White pictorial paper wrappers; printed in primrose, green and black;
edges trimmed; off-white pictorial end-papers printed in orange.

Published 25 January 1949 in Tokyo; 10,000 copies printed. 40 yen.
There were 20 further printings totalling 100,000 copies.

Pp. [i–iii] Introduction, and Japanese translation; English in holograph facsimile. The holograph facsimile and the translation were
reprinted in *A Magic Wand & Other Stories, Kappa & Other Stories*,
both published in 1949; *Shojoji no Tanuki, Dicky Bear*, both published in 1950; *Lucy and the Flowers* and *Hagoromo* both published
in 1951; all children's books by Shigeru Tomiyama.

B132   NIL

B133   TO THE LIGHTHOUSE   1949

First Japanese edition:

[*in Japanese*:] VIRGINIA WOOLF | TŌDAI E | [*transla-
ted by*] | ŌZAWA MINORU | [*illustration*] | ONDORISHA

Crown 8vo. [ii], 302 pp. front. (port.) and plate. $7\frac{1}{8}$ × 5 in.

White pictorial paper wrappers; printed in pale, royal and turquoise blue; edges trimmed; gummed.

Published 30 July 1949 in Tokyo; number of copies printed not ascertained. 100 yen.

A translation by Minoru Ōzawa of *To the Lighthouse*.

Plate facing p. [i] foreword, holograph facsimile, and Japanese translation.

B134   SIXTIETH ANNIVERSARY KWANSEI   1949
GAKUIN UNIVERSITY

First edition:

[*device*] | *Sixtieth Anniversary* | *Kwansei Gakuin University* | *The Diamond Jubilee* | *1949* | *Nishinomiya, Japan*

Crown 4to. [ii], 34 pp. illus. $10\frac{1}{8} \times 7\frac{3}{8}$ in.

Off-white paper wrappers; printed in black and dark turquoise; edges trimmed; stapled.

Issued 14 October 1949; number of copies printed not ascertained.

P. [33] A SONG FOR KWANSEI, holograph facsimile; first published in a separate edition, 1949; and reprinted in *Poems on Japan*, 1967 (*see* A90, 171).

B135   THE HISTORY OF MOJI   1949

First edition:

[*title on upper wrapper; in open capitals*:] THE AB-STRACT FROM THE | HISTORY OF MOJI | *Edited and published* | by | [*in open capitals*:] MOJI CITY HALL | MOJI, KYUSHU | JAPAN

Foolscap 4to. [x], 14 pp. illus., and map. $8\frac{5}{8} \times 6$ in.

White paper wrappers; printed in black as above, and on lower wrapper: PRINTED BY | RYUBUNDO PRINTING CO. | MOJI; edges cut flush; purple ribbon.

Issued probably November 1949; number of copies printed not ascertained. Not for sale.

P. [iii] MOJI ON THE SEA, dated 20 May 1949; reprinted in *Records of Friendship*, 1950 (*see* A106).

First edition:

In His Bosom | — Songs in War-ruined Tokyo — | by |
Jose Civasaqui | 1950 | SHINKYO SHUPPANSHA |
Tokyo

vi, 68 pp. plate. 8 × 5¾ in.

Pale brown mottled paper wrappers; pale brown label printed in
green on upper wrapper; edges trimmed; buff mottled paste-down
end-papers; two blue ribbons.

Published early 1950; number of copies printed not ascertained.

Plate facing p. [iv] Introduction, holograph facsimile, dated December 1949.

First edition:

[*title on upper wrapper*:] TWO BLIND MICE | [*illustration*] | THE EXCHANGE HOTEL THEATRE | Tokyo,
Japan | March 28 — April 2, 1950

12 pp. 9⅛ × 6⅝ in.

Buff paper wrappers; printed in black; edges cut flush; stapled.

Issued 28 March 1950; number of copies printed not ascertained.

Programme for *Two Blind Mice*, by Samuel Spewack, directed by
Vaughn Baggerly, and presented by the Tokyo International Players.

Pp. 1, 9 Dreadful Note.

First edition:

ADVENTURES | AMONG BOOKS | *First Selection* |
Edited by | EDMUND BLUNDEN | & | ICHIRO NISHI-
ZAKI | THE HOKUSEIDO PRESS

Crown 8vo. [viii], 104 pp. front., and plate. 7⅛ × 5 in.

Buff pictorial stiff paper wrappers; printed in black and greenish
yellow; off-white end-papers; edges cut flush; stapled and gummed.

Published 15 April 1950 in Tokyo; no record of the number of copies printed. 60 yen.

There was a reprint in August 1950; 9500 copies of the three *Selections* were printed (*see* below).

P. v Preface Concerning the Series, by the Editors; reprinted in the *Second Selection* and the *Third Selection* published on 25 July and 7 September 1953 respectively.

A mimeograph specimen edition entitled *The Renaissance Readers*, 3 vols. was prepared by The Hokuseido Press for examination by the Department of Education but was not accepted.

B139   VOICE OF AUTUMN   1950

First separate edition:

[*title on upper wrapper*; *in red*:] VOICE of AUTUMN | by | EDMUND BLUNDEN | [*in sky-blue*:] AKINOKOE

Crown 4to. 12 pp. (including wrappers). illus. $10\frac{1}{8} \times 7\frac{1}{8}$ in.

White pictorial paper wrappers; printed in blue, pale orange and red; edges cut flush; stapled.

Published 26 November 1950; number of copies printed not ascertained. Not for sale.

Ballet programme; performed 26 November 1950 in Tokyo.

P. [5] VOICE OF AUTUMN: a theme for a dance offered with admiration to TAMAMI GOJŌ; holograph facsimile in English, and Japanese translation by Saiko Tomita; first published in *Shûkan Asahi*, 5 August 1950; and reprinted in *A Hong Kong House*, 1962 (*see* A156; C2542). *See also* B171.

B140   THE KING'S ARMS HOTEL   1951

First edition:

[*title towards head of p.* [1]:] [*in black letter*:] The King's Arms Hotel | Kobe Japan

[4] pp. illus. $10\frac{1}{2} \times 7\frac{3}{8}$ in.

No wrappers; edges trimmed.

Issued probably 1951; number of copies printed not ascertained. Not for sale.

Hotel brochure; a reprint carried Blunden's poem on p. [2] in holograph facsimile.

P. [1] THE KING'S ARMS HOTEL, KOBE JAPAN [*later* THE

KING'S ARMS, KOBE]; reprinted in *Poems on Japan*, 1967 (*see* A171).

B141   ENGLISH FOR EVERYMAN   1951

First edition:

NOTTINGHAMSHIRE EDUCATION COMMITTEE | [*rule*] | ENGLISH FOR EVERYMAN | [*rule*] | LECTURES | given at the course for teachers at | Eaton Hall, Retford, from | 14th to 19th July, 1950.

Large crown 8vo. 72 pp. 8 × 5¼ in.

Cream paper wrappers; printed in black; edges cut flush; stapled.

Published March 1951; 400 copies printed. 3*s*. 7*d*.

Pp. 9–19 Our English Heritage.

**B142   THE M.C.C. BOOK FOR THE YOUNG   1951
                    CRICKETER**

First edition:

[*in pale brown*:] *The* | M.C.C. BOOK | [*in black*:] *for the Young Cricketer* | [*in pale brown*: *monogram*] | [*in black*:] THE NALDRETT PRESS 29 GEORGE STREET LONDON W1 | [*in pale brown*:] 1951

Crown 4to. 192 pp. illus. 9½ × 7¼ in.

Bright green paper boards; lettered in navy-blue down the spine; monogram in navy-blue on upper cover; edges trimmed; white endpapers.

Published June 1951; no record of the number of copies printed. 10*s*. 6*d*.

Pp. 57–61 Cricket Verses: an introduction to a few of the many poets who have found inspiration in cricket.

B143   JIYU GAKUEN   1952

First edition:

[*title on p.* [1]:] [*illustration*] | JIYU GAKUEN
40 pp. illus. 10⅛ × 7⅛ in.

No wrappers; edges trimmed; stapled.

Issued 1952; number of copies printed not ascertained.

P. 40 at foot: WRITTEN AND EDITED BY GIRLS JUNIOR COL-LEGE GRADUATES OF 1952. | AND PRINTED IN JIYU GAKUEN PRINTINIG [*sic*] OFFICE. | JIYU GAKUEN | MINA-MISAWA | TOKYO.

P. 6 TO MR AND MRS HANI, signed: from Claire and Edmund Blunden, March 25, 1950; holograph facsimile; reprinted in *Poems on Japan*, 1967 (*see* A171).

Mr and Mrs Y. Hani were founders and presidents of the school.

B144   **NEW POEMS 1952**   1952

First edition:

New Poems | [*swelled rule*; *within a decorated oval*:] 1952 [*swelled rule*] | *A P.E.N. Anthology* | *Edited by* | CLIF-FORD DYMENT, ROY FULLER | & MONTAGU SLATER | *Introduction by* | C.V. WEDGWOOD | PRESIDENT OF THE P.E.N. | [*device*] | *London* | MICHAEL JOSEPH

Large crown 8vo. 168 pp. 8 × 5¼ in.

White patterned paper boards; printed in powder blue and black; buff cloth spine lettered in blue with device and four swelled rules; edges trimmed; white end-papers.

Published 26 May 1952; no record of the number of copies printed. 10*s*. 6*d*.

P. 26 A LIFE'S UNITY; first published in *The Listener*, 5 April 1951; and reprinted in *A Hong Kong House*, 1962 (*see* A156; C2648).

B145   **NAVAL MEMORIALS IN THE**   1952
                        UNITED KINGDOM

First edition:

1939–1945 | NAVAL MEMORIALS | IN THE | UNITED KINGDOM | Introduction to the Registers | [*device*] | LONDON: COMPILED AND PUBLISHED BY ORDER OF | THE IMPERIAL WAR GRAVES COMMISSION | 1952

8vo. [ii], 22 pp. 6 plates, and maps. 10 × 8 in.

Grey paper wrappers; printed in black; edges cut flush; sewn and gummed.

Published August 1952 as *Memorial Register*, No. 1; 4000 copies printed. 7s. 6d.

Blunden's contribution also appeared in the Registers to the 5 other Naval Memorials at Plymouth, Portsmouth, Lee-on-Solent, Liverpool and Lowestoft; of these 9125 copies were printed.

Pp. 1-14 I, The War at Sea, 1939-1945 — II, The Naval Memorials in the United Kingdom — III, Conclusion; edited by Blunden. *See also* C2965.

Blunden was Honorary Literary Adviser to the Commission and gave 'literary supervision to the writing of the Introductions'. His offer to give assistance was reported at a meeting of the Commission on 17 April 1952.

B146   **THE SATURDAY BOOK**   1952

First edition:

[*pictorial title within a rose-pink frame*:] *Twelfth Issue of* | [*in green*:] The | [*in dark pink*:] *SATURDAY BOOK* | [*in sage green*:] *Founded by Leonard Russell* | [*in dark pink*:] *Edited by John Hadfield* | [*in black*:] PUBLISHED BY HUTCHINSON

Medium 8vo. 296 pp. (incl. plates). illus., and plates. 9 X 6 in.

Rose-pink buckram boards; lettered in gold across and down the spine; edges trimmed; white pictorial end-papers printed in chocolate brown.

Published September 1952; probably 10,000 copies printed. £1. 5s.

Pp. 286-296 L'Ennuyée; above title: A Young Lady of the Eighteen-Twenties. On Georgina Beet; with illustrations by Philip Gough.

B147   **IMPRESSIONS OF JAPAN**   1952

First edition:

[*within a rule in green*:] IMPRESSIONS | OF JAPAN | AND OTHER ESSAYS | BY G. S. FRASER | [*illustration in green*] | ASAHI-SHIMBUN-SHA

Small demy 8vo. [ii], 8[*] , 2, 140 pp. English text; [ii], 10, 174 pp. front., and plate Japanese text. 8½ X 5¾ in.

White paper boards printed in sky-blue and grey; lettered in sky-blue and grey on spine, and on upper and lower covers in sky-blue, white and grey; edges trimmed; white end-papers.

Published 25 September 1952; number of copies printed not ascertained. 400 yen.

The English text was also issued separately on 10 March 1953 at 180 yen, omitting pp. 137–140, in white paper covered boards printed in sky-blue and pale brown; edges trimmed; white end-papers. Pp. 1[*]–3[*] Foreword.

B148   EXHIBITION DEDICATED TO YOUTH   1952

First edition:

ALL ARTS COMMITTEE | OF | THE NATIONAL PLAY- ING FIELDS ASSOCIATION | [*four lines*] | EXHIBITION | Dedicated to Youth | FROM | "Elizabeth to Elizabeth" | A BIOGRAPHY OF THE BRITISH PEOPLE IN OUT- LINE | TO BE HELD AT | HUTCHINSON HOUSE, | STRATFORD PLACE, W.1 | [*three lines*] | NOVEMBER 24th | [*six lines*]

28 pp. illus. 9 × 7 in.

Buff pictorial stiff paper wrappers; printed in brown; edges cut flush; stapled.

Issued 24 November 1952; no record of the number of copies printed.

P. 23 The Poets.

B149   A KEATS-SHELLEY DIVERSION   1953

First separate publication:

[*at head of p.* [1] :] News Notes

Imperial 8vo. An offprint of [8] pp. numbered [115]–122. plate. 10 × 6$\frac{7}{8}$ in.

Pale green stiff paper wrappers; printed in pale green; edges cut flush; stapled.

Issued March 1953; 24 copies printed. Not for sale.

P. [7] numbered 121 A Keats–Shelley Diversion; on a match between the Hampstead Cricket Club and a Keats–Shelley Eleven; reprinted from the *Keats–Shelley Journal*, January 1953 [*i.e.* March 1953] (*see* C2984).

B150   THE BOOK OF CRICKET VERSE   1953

First edition:

THE BOOK OF | [*in open capitals*:] CRICKET | VERSE | [*in roman*:] AN ANTHOLOGY | EDITED BY | GERALD BRODRIBB | [*illustration*] | RUPERT HART-DAVIS | 36 SOHO SQUARE LONDON W1 | 1953

Small crown 8vo. 216 pp. illus. $7\frac{1}{4} \times 4\frac{3}{4}$ in.

Green paper boards; lettered in silver on spine; edges trimmed; white end-papers.

Published 27 March 1953; 5000 copies printed. 10s. 6d.

Pp. 18–19 THE SEASON OPENS [*formerly* and *later* THE SEASON REOPENS] ; first published in the *Medical Bulletin*, July 1952; and reprinted in *Poems of Many Years*, 1957 (*see* A135; C2856).

B151   EDDIE MARSH   1953

First edition:

Eddie Marsh | SKETCHES FOR A COMPOSITE LITER-ARY PORTRAIT OF | SIR EDWARD MARSH, K.C.V.O., C.B., C.M.G. | *Compiled by* | CHRISTOPHER HASSALL | *and* | DENIS MATHEWS | *Published by* LUND HUM-PHRIES *for the* | CONTEMPORARY ART SOCIETY | *The Tate Gallery, London SW1*

Demy 8vo. 52 pp. 12 plates. 9×6 in.

White paper wrappers; edges cut flush; sewn and gummed. White pictorial dust-jacket printed in olive green and black.

Published May 1953; 2500 copies printed. 7s. 6d.

Pp. 26–17 untitled contribution.

B152   GAME OF A LIFETIME   1953

First edition:

Game of a Lifetime | [*swelled rule*] | *by* | *Denzil Batchelor*

| Werner Laurie : London W.C.1

Demy 8vo. 216 pp. front., and 8 plates. $8\frac{1}{2} \times 5\frac{1}{2}$ in.

Navy-blue cloth boards; lettered in gold on spine with three swelled rules; edges trimmed; white end-papers. White pictorial dust-jacket printed in green, yellow and black.

Published May 1953; number of copies printed not ascertained. 12s. 6d.

Pp. 203–207 A View of Woolley.

B153   THE CHRIST'S HOSPITAL BOOK   1953

First edition:

THE | [*in sky-blue*:] CHRIST'S HOSPITAL | [*in black*:] BOOK | WITH A FOREWORD BY | H.R.H. THE DUKE OF GLOUCESTER | PUBLISHED FOR A | COMMITTEE OF OLD BLUES | BY | HAMISH HAMILTON | [*double rule, thick, thin*] | LONDON

Demy 8vo. xxxiv, 426 pp. front., and 52 plates. $8\frac{3}{4} \times 5\frac{1}{2}$ in.

Navy-blue cloth boards with bevilled edges; lettered in silver on spine with device and coat of arms on upper cover; edges trimmed, top yellow; white end-papers. Pale blue dust-jacket with coat of arms in red, yellow and peacock blue.

Published 22 May 1953; 4000 copies printed. £1. 5s.

There was a reprint (revised) of 1500 copies in 1958 issued as a 'New and revised edition'.

Pp. xxvii–xxxiii Introduction – pp. 282–284 RECOLLECTIONS OF CHRIST'S HOSPITAL (*see* A25, 35; C589) – pp. 300–301 THE COUNTRY ROUND CHRIST'S HOSPITAL [*formerly* A PROLOGUE] (*see* A52, 68; B64).

B154   THE DEDE OF PITTIE – THEATRE   1953
                    PROGRAMME

First edition:

[*title on p.* 1:] 1553 [*device*] 1953 | THE | DEDE OF PITTIE | *Dramatic Scenes* | *reflecting the History of* | CHRIST'S HOSPITAL | *in celebration of* | *the Quater-centenary* | *by* | *EDMUND BLUNDEN* | *FORTUNE*

226

THEATRE, LONDON, W.C. 2 | *Friday, May 22nd &*
Saturday, May 23rd, 1953

Large crown 8vo. 12 pp. 8 X 5 in.

No wrappers; edges cut flush; stapled.

Issued 22 May 1953; no record of the number of copies printed.
6d.

Page Two [Preface], signed E. B.; a revised version was published in
The Dede of Pittie, 1953 (*see* A118).

**B155   HIS IMPERIAL HIGHNESS THE   1953
CROWN PRINCE OF JAPAN IN BRITAIN**

First separate publication:

[*title on upper wrapper*:] HIS IMPERIAL HIGHNESS |
THE CROWN | PRINCE OF JAPAN | IN BRITAIN |
[*double rule*] | APRIL TO JUNE, 1953 | *Reprinted from
Bulletin No. 10 (June, 1953), of The Japan Society of
London.*

Crown 4to. An offprint of [12] pp. $9\frac{3}{4}$ X $7\frac{3}{8}$ in.

Buff paper wrappers; printed in black; edges cut flush; stapled.

Issued June 1953; no record of the number of copies printed. Not
for sale.

P. [1] TO WELCOME PRINCE AKIHITO [*formerly* PRINCE
AKIHITO POEM READ], signed E.B.; first published in the *Daily
Telegraph*, 5 May 1953; and reprinted from the *Bulletin of the
Japan Society*, June 1953 (*see* C3020).

B156   HUMANITY   [1953]

First edition:

HUMANITY | *A Poem of the Atomic Age* | *by* | JOHN
ROBSON WATSON | *with an Appreciation by* | THE
RIGHT HONOURABLE R. A. BUTLER, P.C., M.P. |
President of the Royal Society of Literature | *and a Fore-
word by* | EDMUND BLUNDEN | *London* | THE EP-
WORTH PRESS

Foolscap 8vo. [32] pp. $6\frac{7}{8}$ X $4\frac{7}{8}$ in.

Grey paper wrappers; printed in red; edges cut flush; stapled.
Published June 1953; 900 copies printed. 2s.
Pp. [11–12] Foreword.

B157   A GARLAND FOR THE QUEEN   1953

First edition:

[*illustration*] | [*ornament*; *in script*: E ₁₁ R; *ornament*] | [*within a compartment, within a rule, ornaments on three sides*; *in open capitals*:] A | GARLAND | FOR | THE | QUEEN | [*outside compartment*:] *Songs for Mixed Voices* | *Stainer & Bell Limited, 69 Newman Street, London, W. 1* | *Made in England*

Imperial 8vo. xii, 88 pp. music scores. 11 × 7½ in.
White paper wrappers printed in bluish-green and gold; edges cut flush; gummed.
Published 28 May 1953; number of copies printed not ascertained.
P. xi THE WHITE FLOWERING DAYS, and pp. 68–74 text and music score by Gerald Finzi; first published in the *Sunday Times*, 24 May 1953 (*see* C3029). This poem was reprinted in the Royal Festival Hall Programme for 'Music for the Eve of Coronation Day' on 1 June and in other Coronation commemorative programmes such as *The Coronation and Cirencester*, p. [4] issued by the Urban District of Cirencester.

B158   THE RUNNYMEDE MEMORIAL   1953

First edition:

1939–1945 | THE | RUNNYMEDE MEMORIAL | to Airmen who have no known Grave | Introduction to the Register | [*device*] | LONDON : COMPILED AND PUBLISHED BY ORDER OF | THE IMPERIAL WAR GRAVES COMMISSION | 1953

8vo. [ii], 22 pp. 10 plates, map, and plan. 10 × 8 in.
Grey paper wrappers; printed in black; edges cut flush; sewn and gummed.

Published October 1963 as *Memorial Register*, No. 7; no record of the number of copies printed. 7*s.* 6*d.*

Pp. 1–18 I, The War in the Air Over North-West Europe — II, The Men Who Served — III, The Memorial; edited by Blunden (*see* note to B145).

B159   **A BIBLIOGRAPHICAL STUDY OF**   **1953**
WILLIAM BLAKE'S NOTE-BOOK

First edition:

A | BIBLIOGRAPHICAL | STUDY OF WILLIAM BLAKE'S | NOTE-BOOK | BY | BUNSHO JUGAKU | *Tokyo* | THE HOKUSEIDO PRESS | MCMLIII

Imperial 8vo. [xiv], 178 pp. 4 plates. 10¼ × 7¼ in.

Dark green cloth boards; lettered in gold on spine; device in blind on lower cover; edges trimmed; white end-papers. White dust-jacket printed in navy-blue.

Published 5 November 1953; 1000 copies printed. 1000 yen.

P. [v] Foreword.

B160   **CEMETERIES IN ITALY**   **1953**

First edition:

THE WAR DEAD OF | THE BRITISH COMMONWEALTH | AND EMPIRE | The Register of the names of those who fell | in the 1939–1945 War and are buried | in Cemeteries in Italy | AGIRA CANADIAN WAR CEMETERY | SICILY | [*device*] | LONDON : COMPILED AND PUB-LISHED BY ORDER OF | THE IMPERIAL WAR GRAVES COMMISSION | 1953

8vo. 30 pp. front. (map), and plan. 10 × 8 in.

Grey paper wrappers; printed in black; edges cut flush; sewn and gummed.

Published *c.* December 1953 as part of *War Graves in Italy*, Vol. 1; no record of the number of copies printed. 7*s.* 6*d.*

Pp. 3–6 The Campaign in Sicily, edited by Blunden. The introduction also appeared in the three other parts of the Register for Sicily (*see* note to B145). *See also* B170.

B161   KINDAISHI NO SHITEKI TEMBO   1954

First edition:

[*in Japanese*:] KINDAISHI NO SHITEKI TEMBÔ |
SANGŪ MAKOTO KYŌJU KATŌ KINEN BUNSHŪ
HENSANKAI HEN | KAWADE SHOBŌ KAN

Crown 8vo. vi, 460 pp. front. (port.). 7⅛ × 5 in.

Bluish-grey cloth boards; lettered in gold on spine; edges trimmed;
white end-papers.

Published 5 March 1954 in Tokyo; 2000 copies printed. 450 yen.

Festschrift in honour of Professor Makoto Sangū's sixtieth birthday.

Pp. 435–443 English Literature: The Circumstances in 1949.

B162   THEIR NAME LIVETH   1954

First edition:

THEIR NAME LIVETH | VOLUME I | SOME PICTURES
OF | COMMONWEALTH WAR CEMETERIES | 1914-
1918 1939-1945 | *With a message from* | HER MAJESTY
THE QUEEN | PUBLISHED FOR THE IMPERIAL WAR
GRAVES COMMISSION BY | METHUEN & CO. LTD.,
36 ESSEX STREET, LONDON, W.C.2

Royal 4to. xiv, 32 pp. front., 64 plates, and tables. 11⅝ × 10 in.

Crimson cloth boards; lettered in gold down the spine; device in gold
on upper cover; edges trimmed, top crimson; white end-papers.

Published 22 April 1954; 5000 copies printed. 15*s*.

Pp. 5–9 War Cemeteries in Italy (revised) [*formerly* War Graves in
Italy] ; first published in *The Times*, 8 November 1952 (*see* C2925).
See also B254.

B163   THE ALAMEIN MEMORIAL   1954

First edition:

1939-1945 | THE | ALAMEIN MEMORIAL | Introduc-
tion to the Register | [*device*] | LONDON : COMPILED
AND PUBLISHED BY ORDER OF | THE IMPERIAL
WAR GRAVES COMMISSION | 1954

8vo. front. (map), 8 plates, and plan. 10 × 8 in.

Grey paper wrappers; printed in black; edges cut flush; sewn and gummed.

Published *c.* May 1954 as *Memorial Register*, No. 10; no record of the number of copies printed. 7*s.* 6*d.*

Pp. 3–24 I, The Campaigns in North-East Africa and the Middle East — II, The Men Who Served — III, The Memorial; edited by Blunden (*see* note to B145).

B164   **SELECTED POEMS [OF]**   1954
PERCY BYSSHE SHELLEY

Collins edition:

SELECTED POEMS | PERCY BYSSHE SHELLEY | [*swelled rule*] | *Edited with an Introduction* | *and Notes by* | EDMUND BLUNDEN | [*device*] | COLLINS | LONDON AND GLASGOW

Small crown 8vo. 640 pp. front. (port. on p. 2). $7\frac{1}{8} \times 4\frac{1}{4}$ in.

Dark ruby cloth boards; lettered in gold on spine; two stars in blind on lower cover; edges trimmed, top ruby; white end-papers printed in pale grey in an overall design. White dust-jacket printed in bright yellow and black.

Published May 1954; no record of the number of copies printed. 6*s.*

Also issued in various styles of red and blue leather. There were *c.* 9 reprints; sales amounted to approximately 40,000 copies.

Pp. 11–58 Shelley's Life and Writings — p. [59] On the Selection — notes pp. 63–64, 124 *et passim.*

B165   **THE MALTA MEMORIAL**   1954

First edition:

THE WAR DEAD OF | THE BRITISH COMMONWEALTH | AND EMPIRE | The Register of the names of Airmen who fell | in the 1939–1945 War and have no | known Grave | THE MALTA MEMORIAL | PART I | [*device*] | LONDON : COMPILED AND PUBLISHED BY ORDER OF | THE IMPERIAL WAR GRAVES COMMISSION | 1954

8vo. xxii, 54 pp. 4 plates (incl. front.), and maps. 10×8 in.

Grey paper wrappers; printed in black; edges cut flush; sewn and gummed.

Published *c.* June 1954 as *Memorial Register*, No. 8; no record of the number of copies printed. 7*s.* 6*d.*

Pp. iii–xxi I, The War in the Air: Western Mediterranean — II, The Men Who Served — III, The Memorial; edited by Blunden. The introduction also appeared in Part II of the *Memorial Register* (*see* note to B145).

B165.1   ESSAYS & STUDIES PRESENTED TO   1954
DR. SANKI ICHIKAWA

First edition:

[*first two lines in Japanese*:] ICHIKAWA HAKASE | KANREKI SHUKUGA RONBUNSHŪ | Essays & Studies Presented to Dr. Sanki Ichikawa | in Honour of His Six- tieth Birthday | VOLUME VI | [*publisher's device*] | [*following line in Japanese*:] KENKYŪSHA | 1954*

Crown 8vo. Vol. 6. 7 × 5 in.

Published 1 July 1954; 1000 copies printed. 150 yen the set of 6 volumes.

Pp. 1–6 "The New World of Words"; on *The New World of English Words*, 1658 by Edward Phillips, Milton's nephew.

B166   SOUTHDOWN BATTALIONS'   1954
ASSOCIATION 40TH ANNIVERSARY CELEBRATION

First edition:

[*title on p.* [1]; *in blue*:] "LOWTHERS" [*regimental badge in dull gold*] "LAMBS" | SOUTHDOWN BATTALIONS ASSOCIATION | 11th, 12th, and 13th THE ROYAL SUSSEX REGIMENT | [*rule*] | [*battle honours in two lines*] | [*rule*] | 40th | Anniversary Celebration | [*orna- ment*] | ~ Souvenir Programme ~ | [*ornament*] | at BEXHILL-ON-SEA & COODEN CAMP | SUNDAY, SEP- TEMBER 19th, 1954 | [*ornament*] | [*name of chairman etc. in five lines*] | Price One Shilling

Small crown 8vo. [8] pp. 7¼ × 4⅝ in.
No wrappers; edges trimmed; stapled.

Issued 19 September 1954; 100 copies printed. 1s.
Pp. [2–3] [on the Association], signed E. B.

B167   **POEMS BY IVOR GURNEY**   **1954**

a. First edition:

POEMS | BY | IVOR | GURNEY | Principally selected
from | unpublished manuscripts | *With a memoir by* |
Edmund Blunden | HUTCHINSON | STRATFORD PLACE
| LONDON

Medium 8vo. 104 pp. 9 × 5¾ in.

Red paper boards; lettered in gold down the spine, and on upper
cover; top edges uncut, fore and bottom edges rough trimmed; white
end-papers. Cream dust-jacket printed in black and scarlet.

Published 20 September 1954; 1000 copies printed. 7s. 6d.

Pp. 9–19 Concerning Ivor Gurney; pp. 23 *et passim* brief notes.

b. Second edition. 1973:

POEMS OF | [*in open capitals*:] IVOR GURNEY | 1880–
1937 | *With an Introduction by* | EDMUND BLUNDEN |
and a Bibliographical Note by | LEONARD CLARK |
1973 | CHATTO & WINDUS | LONDON

Demy 8vo. 136 pp. front. (port.). 8½ × 5¼ in.

Red cloth boards; lettered in gold down the spine; edges trimmed;
white end-papers. White dust-jacket printed in black and red.

Published 12 July 1973; 1250 copies printed. £2.

Pp. 15–26 Introduction [*formerly* Concerning Ivor Gurney] (*see*
B167*a*).

B168   **NEW POEMS 1954**   **1954**

First edition:

New Poems | [*swelled rule*; *within a decorated oval*:] 1954
[*swelled rule*] | *Edited by* | REX WARNER | CHRISTO-
PHER HASSALL | LAURIE LEE | *with an introduction* |
[*device*] | *London* | MICHAEL JOSEPH

Large crown 8vo. 180 pp. $7\frac{7}{8}$ × 5 in.

Cream paper boards; printed in dull pink; oatmeal cloth spine lettered in dull pink with device and four swelled rules; edges trimmed; cream end-papers.

Published 27 September 1954; no record of the number of copies printed. 10s. 6d.

A P.E.N. Anthology.

P. 32 THE OLD SCHOOL MASTER (C.E.B., d. November 1951) [*formerly* and *later* C.E.B.]; first published in *South China Morning Post*, 22 September 1953; and reprinted in *Poems of Many Years*, 1957 (*see* A135; C3088).

B169   THE FLASHING STREAM –   1954
              THEATRE PROGRAMME

First edition:

[*within a frame*:] THE HONG KONG STAGE CLUB | presents | THE FLASHING STREAM | by | CHARLES MORGAN | at the | CHINA FLEET CLUB THEATRE | on | THURSDAY, 14th OCTOBER, at 9.00 p.m. | FRIDAY, 15th OCTOBER, at 7.30 p.m. | SATURDAY, 16th OCTOBER, at 9.00 p.m.

Demy 8vo. [8] pp. $8\frac{1}{2}$ × $5\frac{1}{2}$ in.

Pale dull blue paper wrappers; printed in navy-blue; edges cut flush; stapled.

Issued 14 October 1954; number of copies printed not ascertained.

P. [3] Morganiana, signed E. Blunden.

B170   CEMETERIES IN ITALY   1954

First edition:

THE WAR DEAD OF | THE BRITISH COMMONWEALTH | AND EMPIRE | The Register of the names of those who fell | in the 1939–1945 War and are buried | in Cemeteries in Italy | BARI WAR CEMETERY | Part I | [*device*] | LONDON : COMPILED AND PUBLISHED BY ORDER

8vo. 62 pp. front. (map), map, and plans. 10 X 8 in.

Grey paper wrappers; printed in black; edges cut flush; sewn and gummed.

Published *c*. November 1954 as *War Graves in Italy*, Vol. 1, Part I; no record of the number of copies printed. 7*s*. 6*d*.

Pp. 3–10 The Campaign in Southern Italy: From Reggio to Rome, edited by Blunden. The introduction also appeared in the other parts of the Register for Italy, Vol. 1, and Vol. 2, Parts 10–14/16 (*see* note to B145). *See also* B160.

B171   COMMEMORATIVE PERFORMANCE   1954
ON THE OCCASION OF TAMAMI GOJO'S
EUROPEAN TOUR

First edition:

[*title on upper wrapper*; *in pale yellow*:] COMMEMORA-
TIVE | PERFORMANCE | ON THE OCCASION | OF
TAMAMI GOJO'S | EUROPEAN TOUR | [*in black*:]
GOJÔ TAMAMI TOÔ KINEN KÔEN | [*in pale yellow*:]
Sponsored by | THE TAMAMI GOJO SUPPORTERS'
ASSOCIATION | Supported by | TOKYO METROPOLI-
TAN OFFICE | KOKUSẠI BUNKA SHINKOKAI | [*in*
black:] SHUSAI · GOJÔ˙ TAMAMI TOÔ KÔENKAI
KÔEN · TÔKYÔTO · KOKUSAI BUNKA SHINKÔKAI
[*illustration at right of lines* 1–5]

24 pp. illus. 9⅞ X 10 in.

White paper wrappers; printed in orange, pale yellow and black; edges cut flush; stapled.

Issued 11 November 1954; number of copies printed not ascertained. Probably not for sale.

P. 2 letter to Tamami Gojo dated 27 October 1954, with Japanese translation.

Pp. 8–9 FOR A SPRING DANCE BY TAMAMI GOJO [*later* VOICE OF SPRING]; first published in *Evening News*, Tokyo, 8 November 1954; and reprinted in *Elixir*, December 1954; and *A Hong Kong House*, 1962 (*see* A156; C3121) — pp. 10–11 VOICE OF AUTUMN, and Japanese translation (*see* A156; B139; C2542).

First edition:

THE WAR DEAD OF | THE BRITISH COMMONWEALTH | AND EMPIRE | The Register of the names of those who fell | in the 1939–1945 War and are buried | in Cemeteries in France | BANNEVILLE-LA-CAMPAGNE WAR CEME-TERY | Part I | [*device*] | LONDON: COMPILED AND PUBLISHED BY ORDER OF | THE IMPERIAL WAR GRAVES COMMISSION | 1954

8vo. xxii, 46 pp. front. (map), and plan. 10 × 8 in.

Grey paper wrappers; printed in black; edges cut flush; sewn and gummed.

Published *c.* December 1954; no record of the number of copies printed. 7*s.* 6*d.*

Pp. iii–xx The War in France, edited by Blunden. The introduction also appeared in the other parts of the Register for France (*see* note to B145).

B173   "HIAWATHA'S WEDDING FEAST"   1954

First edition:

[*title on p.* [1]:] HONG KONG SCHOOLS MUSIC ASSOCIATION | "HIAWATHA'S WEDDING FEAST" | *Presented by* | THE HONG KONG SINGERS | (Under the distinguished patronage of H. E. the Governor, | Sir Alexander Grantham, G.C.M.G., LL.D.) | [*at left*:] *THE GREAT* ○ *HALL* | *THE UNIVERSITY* | [*at right*:] *TUES-DAY, 14th DEC.* | *1954*

Demy 8vo. 16 pp. $8\frac{5}{8}$ × $5\frac{1}{2}$ in.

No wrappers; edges trimmed; stapled.

Issued 14 December 1954; number of copies printed not ascertained. Probably not for sale.

Pp. 4–6 A Word on Longfellow and "Hiawatha", signed E. B.

B174 CEMETERIES IN NORWAY AND SWEDEN 1955

First edition:

THE WAR DEAD OF | THE BRITISH COMMONWEALTH
| AND EMPIRE | The Register of the names of those who
fell | in the 1939–1945 War and are buried | in Cemeteries
in Norway | and Sweden | [*device*] | LONDON: COM-
PILED AND PUBLISHED BY ORDER OF | THE IM-
PERIAL WAR GRAVES COMMISSION | 1955

8vo. xiv, 62 pp. front. (map), and plans. 10 × 8 in.

Grey paper wrappers; printed in black; edges cut flush; sewn and gummed.

Published *c*. March 1955; no record of the number of copies printed. 7*s*. 6*d*.

Pp. v–xi British Operations in Norway, edited by Blunden (*see* note to B145).

B175   ADVANCED ENGLISH COURSE   1955

First edition:

[*in Japanese*:] SHŌWA NIJŪKUNEN SHICHIGATSU
SANJŪNICHI MOMBUSHŌ KENTEIZUMI KŌTŌGAKKŌ
GAIKOKUGOKAYŌ | KŌGAKISHA'S | ADVANCED
| ENGLISH COURSE | III | [*in two columns of eight and
four lines in Japanese except last line*:] [*Prof. Dr*] NISHI-
WAKI JUNZABURŌ | [*Prof.*] NAKAJIMA FUMIO |
[*Prof. Dr*] TAKAHASHI GENJI | J. O. GAUNTLETT |
KŌGAKUSHA

100 pp. illus. 8¼ × 5¾ in.

White pictorial stiff paper boards; printed in pale grey, dark grey, yellow and maroon; edges trimmed; end-papers.

Published 1 March 1955 in Tokyo; number of copies printed not ascertained. 50 yen.

The book was approved on 30 July 1954 by the Ministry of Education for use in foreign language courses in high schools.

Pp. 32–39 Memories; reprinted from the manuscript of a lecture with adaptations.

SELECTED POEMS | JOHN KEATS | [*swelled rule*] | *Edited with an Introduction* | *and Notes by* | EDMUND BLUNDEN | [*device*] | COLLINS | LONDON AND GLASGOW

Small crown 8vo. 416 pp. front. (port. on p. [2]). $7\frac{1}{8} \times 4\frac{1}{4}$ in.

Dark ruby cloth boards; lettered in gold on spine; star in blind on lower cover; edges trimmed, top ruby; white end-papers printed in grey in an overall design.

Published May 1955; no record of the number of copies printed. 5s.

Also issued in various styles of red and blue leather. There were *c.* 9 reprints; sales amounted to approximately 40,000 copies.

Pp. 11–50 Introduction: John Keats, His Life and Writings — pp. 51–52 Addendum: *Blackwood's Magazine* — pp. 55, 57–59 *et passim* notes.

**B177   CEMETERIES IN DENMARK,   1955
        ICELAND AND THE FAROE ISLANDS**

First edition:

THE WAR DEAD OF | THE BRITISH COMMONWEALTH | AND EMPIRE | The Register of the names of those who fell | in the 1939–1945 War and are buried | in Cemeteries in Denmark, Iceland | and the Faroe Islands | [*device*] | LONDON : COMPILED AND PUBLISHED BY ORDER OF | THE IMPERIAL WAR GRAVES COMMISSION | 1955

8vo. x, 88 pp. front. (map), and plans. 10×8 in.

Grey paper wrappers; printed in black; edges cut flush; sewn and gummed.

Published *c.* September 1955; no record of the number of copies printed. 7s. 6d.

Pp. vii–viii War Graves in Denmark, edited by Blunden (*see* note to B145).

First edition:

CONTEMPORARY VERSE: | AN ANTHOLOGY | *Poems and Translations* | Japan Poets' Club | 1955

Crown 8vo. 40, [ii], 200 pp. $7\frac{1}{8} \times 5$ in.

Buff paper wrappers; printed in olive brown, grey and black; edges trimmed; white end-papers.

Published 25 September 1955; number of copies printed not ascertained. 250 yen.

Pp. 5-6 Some Short Poems on Japanese Subjects: MATSUSHIMA (*see* A86, 97; C2563) — IN A PARK AT KYOTO (*see* A97; C2564) — THE EARLY YEAR, FUKUOKA [*formerly* FROM THE JAPANESE INN WINDOW; and THE INN WINDOW, FUKUOKA] (*see* A94, 97, 106; C2513) — AT HARIHAN; first published in the *Nippon Times*, 17 January 1950; and reprinted in *Poems on Japan*, 1967 (*see* A171; C2497) — BOOKS; first published in *Kansai University Bulletin*, 15 May 1950; and reprinted in *Poems on Japan*, 1967 (*see* A171; C2523).

B179 **THE EAST AFRICA MEMORIAL** **1955**

First edition:

THE WAR DEAD OF | THE BRITISH COMMONWEALTH | AND EMPIRE | Register of the names of those who fell | in the 1939-1945 War and have no | known Grave | THE EAST AFRICA MEMORIAL | NAIROBI | Part I | (Aba-Kye) | [*device*] |LONDON : COMPILED AND PUBLISHED BY ORDER OF | THE IMPERIAL WAR GRAVES COMMISSION | 1955

8vo. xx, 48 pp. front. 10×8 in.

Grey paper wrappers; printed in black; edges cut flush; sewn and gummed.

Published *c*. December 1955 as *Memorial Register*, No. 18; no record of the number of copies printed. 7*s*. 6*d*.

Pp. iii-xvii I, The War in East Africa — II, The Men Who Served — III, The Memorial; edited by Blunden. The introduction also appeared in the other parts of the *Memorial Register* (*see* note to B145).

First edition:

THE WAR DEAD OF | THE BRITISH COMMONWEALTH | AND EMPIRE | The Register of the names of those who fell | in the 1939-1945 War and are buried | in Cemeteries in Hong Kong | SAI WAN BAY WAR CEMETERY | THE SAI WAN BAY CREMATION MEMORIAL | [*device*] | LONDON: COMPILED AND PUBLISHED BY ORDER OF | THE IMPERIAL WAR GRAVES COMMISSION | 1956

8vo. xx, 58 pp. front. (map), and plan. 10 X 8 in.

Grey paper wrappers; printed in black; edges cut flush; sewn and gummed.

Published *c*. January 1956; no record of the number of copies printed. 7*s*. 6*d*.

Pp. iii–vii The Battle for Hong Kong, edited by Blunden. The introduction also appeared in the second part of the Register for Hong Kong (*see* note to B145).

First separate publication:

[*title on wrapper*; *within a double rule, thick, thin*:] JOURNAL OF | ORIENTAL STUDIES | [*long rule*] | REPRINTED FROM Vol. II. No. 2 July 1955 | [*long rule*] | REVIEWS | FAR EASTERN BIBLIOGRAPHY | [*two lines in Chinese*] | UNIVERSITY OF HONG KONG

Imperial 8vo. An offprint of [92] pp. numbered [323]–[414]. $10\frac{3}{8} \times 7\frac{5}{8}$ in.

Buff paper wrappers; printed in black; edges cut flush; sewn and gummed.

Issued January 1956; 50 copies printed. Not for sale.

Title at head of pp. 371, 373 Japanese Colour Prints.

Pp. 371–373 review of *Japanese Masters of the Colour Print*, by J. Hillier; *Japanese Colour Prints from Harunobu to Utamaro*, introduction by William Blunt; and *Pageant of Japanese Art: Painting 2*, Vol. 2, edited by Staff Members of the Tokyo National Museum — pp. 385–386 review of *A Story of Ukiyo-e*, by Ichitaro Kondō; and

Utamaro, by Ichitaro Kondō, signed E. B. — p. 387 review of *Japanese Folk Tales*, by Kunio Yanagita, signed E. B.

Reprinted from the *Journal of Oriental Studies*, July 1955 (*see* C3161-3).

B182   RINTARŌ FUKUHARA   1955 [i.e. 1956]

First edition:

[*in Japanese*:] FUKUHARA RINTARŌ SENSEI KAN-REKI KINEN ROMBUNSHŪ | KINDAI NO EIBUNGAKU | KENKYUSHA | 1955

Small royal 8vo. viii, 516 pp. $8\frac{3}{4} \times 6\frac{1}{4}$ in.

Title-page transcribed from a xerox copy; binding not seen.

Published 9 January 1956; 1000 copies printed. 700 yen.

A collection of essays presented to Professor Rintarō Fukuhara on his sixtieth birthday entitled *Modern English Literature*. For review by Blunden *see* C3197.

Pp. 402-412 The Head Master's Album; on James Boyer, Charles Lamb's master at Christ's Hospital. Also issued separately as an offprint (*see* A131).

B183   HONG KONG FESTIVAL   1956
              OF THE ARTS

First edition:

[*title on upper wrapper in brown*; *within a double rule, thick, thin*:] [*circular device*; *round the circle*:] HONG KONG FESTIVAL OF THE ARTS | [*outside device*:] Souvenir | Programme | THIRD TO TWENTY-FIFTH MARCH | 1956

64, [36] pp. 12 plates. $9\frac{1}{2} \times 6\frac{3}{4}$ in.

White paper wrappers; printed in brown; edges trimmed; stapled.

Issued 3 March 1956; probably 3000 copies printed. HK$1.

P. 19 The Masquers, unsigned.

First edition:

[*title on upper wrapper*; *within a rule*; *in holograph fac-simile*:] COMUS | A Masque | by | John Milton: | 1634. | [*long rule*] | Preceded by | THE SECULAR MASQUE | of | John Dryden: | 1700. | [*long rule*] | Presented | by The Masquers, | HONG KONG | 1956

[4] pp. $10\frac{1}{2} \times 7\frac{5}{8}$ in.

White paper wrappers; printed in black; edges cut flush; pale mauve ribbon tied in left margin.

Published 24 March 1956; 1000 copies printed. Probably HK$1.

P. [1] PROLOGUE, holograph facsimile.

B185 SSU LANG T'AN MU – **1956**
THEATRE PROGRAMME

First edition:

[*title on upper wrapper*; *in brown*:] COLLEGE OF | ST. JOHN THE EVANGELIST | University of Hong Kong | Ssu Lang T'an Mu | (Ssu Lang Visits His Mother) | King's Theatre, 9.30 p.m. | HONG KONG 18th APRIL 1956

[ii], 30 pp. illus. $9\frac{5}{8} \times 7\frac{1}{2}$ in.

Buff paper wrappers; printed in brown and black; brown ribbon on upper wrapper; inside lower wrapper at foot: PRINTED BY YE OLDE PRINTERIE LTD., HONG KONG; edges trimmed; stapled.

Published 18 April 1956; number of copies printed not ascertained.

Pp. 1–2 Foreword: Past, Present, Future, signed E.C.B.

B186 TAKESHI SAITO **1956**

First edition:

[*in Japanese*:] SAITO TAKESHI HAKASE KOKI SHUKUGA ROMBUNSHŪ | EIBUNGAKUKENKYŪ | KENKYŪSHA | 1956

Demy 8vo. x, 748 pp. front. (port.), 2 plates, and 6 diagrs. $8\frac{1}{4} \times 5\frac{3}{4}$ in.

Navy-blue cloth boards; lettered in gold on spine; edges trimmed; white end-papers.

Published 10 May 1956; *c.* 1000 copies printed. 700 yen.

A collection of essays in commemoration of Professor Takeshi Saito's seventieth birthday entitled *Studies in English Literature.*

P. 38 letter to Professor Saito, dated Hong Kong, 5 May 1955, signed E. Blunden; holograph facsimile — pp. 47–81 Coleridge's Fellow-Grecian: Some Account of Charles Valentine Le Grice. Also issued separately as an offprint (*see* A133).

A187   'WE' AND ME   1956

First edition:

'WE' AND ME | *Memories of four eminent Editors I worked with,* | *a discussion by Editors of the future of Editing,* | *and a candid account of the founding and the* | *editing, for twenty-one years, of my own magazine* | *by* | J. W. ROBERTSON SCOTT | C.H., Hon. M.A. (Oxon) | [*device*] | W.H. ALLEN | LONDON | 1956

Demy 8vo. 240 pp. front., illus., and 5 plates. $8\frac{1}{2} \times 5\frac{1}{2}$ in.

Scarlet cloth boards; lettered in gold on spine with monogram; edges trimmed; white end-papers.

Published 14 May 1956; *c.* 2000 copies printed. £1. 1*s.*

Pp. 157–158 contribution on H. W. Massingham; pp. 72–73 are not by Blunden as stated.

B188   THE INTEGRATION OF POETRY   1956

First edition:

THE | *INTEGRATION* | *OF POETRY* | *by* | *Bryn Jones* | [*device*] | HONG KONG UNIVERSITY PRESS | *London:* *Geoffrey Cumberlege* | OXFORD UNIVERSITY PRESS | 1956

Crown 8vo. x, 88 pp. $7\frac{3}{8} \times 5$ in.

Stiff white paper wrappers; printed in pale grey and dark green; edges cut flush; sewn and gummed.

Published 5 July 1956; 1000 copies printed. HK$10 (12*s.* 6*d.*)

Pp. [v]–vii Introduction, signed E. Blunden.

First edition:

The First Englishman | *in Japan* | THE STORY OF | WILL
ADAMS | by | P. G. ROGERS | Foreword by | EDMUND
BLUNDEN | *LONDON* | THE HARVILL PRESS

Demy 8vo. xvi, 144 pp. 8 plates, and map. $8\frac{1}{2} \times 5\frac{1}{2}$ in.

Brown cloth boards; lettered in blue on spine; edges trimmed; white
end-papers.

Published 23 July 1956; 4000 copies printed. 12s. 6d.

Pp. vii–x Foreword – plate facing p. 108 TO THE CITIZENS OF
ITO [*formerly* WILLIAM ADAMS AT ITO], photograph of the
poem incised on the Ito memorial stone, and dated 8 July 1948 (*see*
A85; C2506). Several other poems by Blunden were also incised on
memorial stones in Japan including MATSUSHIMA (*see* A86, 97;
C2563; D8) and FIRST VISIT TO YASHIMA [*later* YASHIMA IN
WINTER; *and* A FIRST VISIT TO YASHIMA] (*see* A97, 122;
C2501).

B190 **THE CASTLE OF INDOLENCE** 1956

JAMES THOMSON | The Castle of Indolence | *Introduc-*
tion by | Edmund Blunden | *Edited with notes by* | Alec
M. Hardie | [*device*] | HONG KONG UNIVERSITY
PRESS | *London: Geoffrey Cumberlege* | OXFORD UNI-
VERSITY PRESS | 1956

Foolscap 8vo. xxii, 82 pp. $6\frac{7}{8} \times 4\frac{1}{2}$ in.

White paper boards; edges cut flush; white end-papers; sewn and
gummed. White pictorial dust-jacket printed in mid-green.

Published 3 August 1956; 1500 copies printed. HK$10 (12s. 6d.).

Also issued in pale rust cloth boards; lettered in silver down the
spine; edges trimmed; white end-papers.

Pp. [vii]–xi Introduction, signed E.B.

First edition:

[*at left*: *holograph facsimile of poem by Blunden*] | [*at centre*: *crest in red, green, navy-blue and black*] | TO | THE CHANCELLOR AND MEMBERS | OF THE | UNIVERSITY OF MELBOURNE | [*in black letter*:] Greetings | [*ten-line greeting*] | Dated | Vice-Chancellor | [*at right*: *anonymous poem in Chinese*]

[1] leaf. 12 × 17⅞ in.

Edges trimmed.

Issued 15 August 1956; probably 5–6 copies printed. Not for sale. Address presented by the Vice-Chancellor of the University of Hong Kong at the centenary celebrations of the University of Melbourne.

At left of leaf FOR THE CENTENARY OF MELBOURNE UNIVERSITY [*later* untitled] ; reprinted in the *University of Hong Kong Gazette*, 1 September 1956 (*see* C3181).

B192   THE TOWER   1955 [i.e. 1956]
              HILL MEMORIAL

First edition:

THE WAR DEAD OF | THE BRITISH COMMONWEALTH | AND EMPIRE | 1939–1945 | THE TOWER HILL MEMORIAL | Introduction to the Register | [*device*] | LONDON: COMPILED AND PUBLISHED BY ORDER OF | THE IMPERIAL WAR GRAVES COMMISSION | 1955

8vo. 32 pp. 4 plates, and plan. 10 × 8 in.

Grey paper wrappers; printed in black; edges cut flush; sewn and gummed.

Published *c.* October 1956 as *Memorial Register*, No. 22; no record of the number of copies printed. 7*s.* 6*d.*

Pp. 3–11 I, The Merchant Navy and Fishing Fleets at War — II, The Men Who Served — III, The Memorial; edited by Blunden (*see* note to B145).

First edition:

THE WAR DEAD OF | THE BRITISH COMMONWEALTH
| AND EMPIRE | The Register of the names of those who
fell | in the 1939–1945 War and are buried | in Cemeteries
in Tunisia | BÉJA WAR CEMETERY | OUED ZARGA
WAR CEMETERY | [*device*] | LONDON: COMPILED
AND PUBLISHED BY ORDER OF | THE IMPERIAL
WAR GRAVES COMMISSION | 1956

8vo. xiv, 34 pp. front. (map), and plans. 10 × 8 in.

Grey paper wrappers; printed in black; edges cut flush; sewn and
gummed.

Published *c.* November 1956; no record of the number of copies
printed. 7*s.* 6*d.*

Pp. iii–xi The Campaign in North-West Africa, edited by Blunden.
The introduction also appeared in the other parts of the Register for
Tunisia (*see* note to B145).

First edition:

[*title on p.* [1] *at head*:] QUEEN ELIZABETH SCHOOL
| [*coat of arms*] | SECOND | ANNUAL SPEECH DAY |
ON | FRIDAY 9th NOVEMBER | at 5.30 p.m.

[14] pp. (mimeo.) 13⅛ × 8⅜ in.

No wrappers; edges trimmed; stapled.

Issued 9 November 1956; number of copies printed not ascertained.
Not for sale.

Queen Elizabeth School was a government school in Kowloon.
P. [2] SCHOOL SONG.

First edition:

THE WAR DEAD OF | THE BRITISH COMMONWEALTH
| AND EMPIRE | The Register of the names of those who
fell | in the 1939–1945 War and are buried | in Cemeteries

in Germany | REICHSWALD FOREST WAR CEMETERY | Part I | (Abb-Byt) | [*device*] | LONDON: COMPILED AND PUBLISHED BY ORDER OF | THE IMPERIAL WAR GRAVES COMMISSION | 1957

8vo. x, 48 pp. front. (map), plan, and table. 10 X 8 in.

Grey paper wrappers; printed in black; edges cut flush; sewn and gummed.

Published *c*. January 1957; no record of the number of copies printed. 7*s*. 6*d*.

Pp. iii–ix The Advance into Germany, edited by Blunden. The introduction also appeared in the other parts of the Register for Germany (*see* note to B145).

B196   HONG KONG BUSINESS SYMPOSIUM   1957

First edition:

HONG KONG | BUSINESS SYMPOSIUM | [*short rule*] | A COMPILATION OF AUTHORITATIVE VIEWS | on the | ADMINISTRATION, COMMERCE AND RESOUR-CES | of | BRITAIN'S FAR EASTERN OUTPOST | COMPILED BY | J. M. BRAGA | PRINTED BY | SOUTH CHINA MORNING POST, LTD. | HONG KONG

Demy 4to. 592 pp. illus., tables, and maps. 11 X 8⅜ in.

White pictorial paper boards; printed in blue; edges trimmed; endpapers (maps).

Published 1957; 1020 copies printed. HK$35.

P. 23 HONG KONG: VIEW FROM A HONG KONG OFFICE [*formerly* A VIEW FROM THE DEPARTMENT OF ENGLISH; A VIEW FROM A HONG KONG OFFICE; and *later* VIEW FROM THE UNIVERSITY OF HONG KONG]; first published in *The Union*, Hong Kong, [Summer 1954]; and reprinted in *A Hong Kong House*, 1962 (*see* A156; C3114).

B197   THE MASQUERS   1957

First edition:

THE MASQUERS | UNIVERSITY OF HONG KONG | TWELFTH NIGHT | by | William Shakespeare | at | LEE THEATRE | February 25th and 26th 1957

Demy 4to. [20] pp. 11 × 8½ in.

Cream paper wrappers; printed in maroon and grey; outside lower wrapper at foot: PRINTED BY YE OLDE PRINTERIE, LTD., HONG KONG; edges cut flush; stapled.

Issued 25 February 1937; probably 500 copies printed. Probably HK$1.

P. [9] PROLOGUE, signed E. B.; holograph facsimile.

B198   **CEMETERIES IN BELGIUM**   1957

First edition:

THE WAR DEAD OF | THE BRITISH COMMONWEALTH | AND EMPIRE | The Register of the names of those who fell | in the 1939–1945 War and are buried | in Cemeteries in Belgium | CEMETERIES IN WEST FLANDERS – I | [*device*] | LONDON : COMPILED AND PUBLISHED BY ORDER OF | THE IMPERIAL WAR GRAVES COMMIS-SION | 1957

8vo. xviii, 62 pp. front. (map), and plans. 10 × 8 in.

Grey paper wrappers; printed in black; edges cut flush; sewn and gummed.

Published *c*. April 1957; no record of the number of copies printed. 7*s*. 6*d*.

Pp. v–xv The War in Belgium and Holland, edited by Blunden. The introduction also appeared in the other parts of the Register for Belgium, and the Register for the Netherlands (*see* note to B145).

B199   **JOURNAL OF**   1956 [i.e. 1957]
        ORIENTAL STUDIES

First separate publication:

[*title on upper wrapper*; *within a double rule, thick, thin*:] JOURNAL OF | ORIENTAL STUDIES | [*long rule*] | REPRINTED FROM Vol. III. No. 1. JUNE 1956 | [*long rule*] | REVIEWS | [*one line in Chinese*] | UNIVERSITY OF HONG KONG

Imperial 8vo. An offprint of [68] pp. numbered [83]–148, [2]. 10⅝ × 7⅝ in.

Buff paper wrappers; printed in black; edges cut flush; sewn and gummed.

Issued August 1957; 50 copies printed. Not for sale.

P. 147 review of *Modern English Literature in Honour of Professor Rintaro Fukuhara*; and *Where Two Cultures Meet*, by Junesay Iddittie — pp. 147-148 review of *Hokusai (1760-1849)*, by Ichitaro Kondo.

Reprinted from *Journal of Oriental Studies*, June 1956 [*i.e.* August 1957] (*see* C3197-8).

B200 TWO MASTERS OF IRONY 1957

First edition:

[*within a double rule*:] M. S. YÜ | Two Masters | of Irony | *Annotations on three essays by* | OSCAR WILDE | AND | LYTTON STRACHEY | *with Special Reference to their* | *manner of writing* | [*device*] | HONG KONG UNIVERSITY PRESS | 1957

Small crown 8vo. [viii], 42 pp. $7\frac{1}{8} \times 4\frac{3}{8}$ in.

Cream stiff paper wrappers; printed in black and royal blue; edges cut flush; sewn.

Published 8 October 1957; 1000 copies printed. HK$2.90 (4*s.* 6*d.*).

P. [v] Foreword. The Foreword also appeared in the publisher's prospectus for the book.

B201 NEW POEMS 1957 1957

First edition:

New Poems | [*swelled rule*; *within a decorated oval*:] 1957 [*swelled rule*] | *Edited by* | KATHLEEN NOTT | C. DAY LEWIS | THOMAS BLACKBURN | [*device*] | *London* | MICHAEL JOSEPH

Large crown 8vo. 144 pp. $8 \times 5\frac{1}{4}$ in.

White patterned paper boards; printed in dark grey; lemon yellow cloth spine lettered in black with device and four swelled rules; edges trimmed.

Published 21 October 1957; no record of the number of copies printed. 15*s.*

A P.E.N. Anthology.

P. 25 OVERHEARD; reprinted in *The Chimes*, Hong Kong, August 1964 (*see* C3305) — pp. 25-26 CATHEDRALS; reprinted in *A Hong Kong House*, 1962; and *A Selection of the Shorter Poems*, [1966] (*see* A156, 169).

B202   THE BALLAD OF READING GAOL   1957

First separate publication:

THE BALLAD OF READING GAOL | *by* | [*in rose pink*:] OSCAR WILDE | [*in black*:] With Seventeen Illustrations | *by* | [*in rose pink*:] DOUGLAS BLAND | [*in black*:] And An Introduction | *by* | [*in rose pink*:] EDMUND BLUNDEN

Crown 4to. An offprint of [iv], xliv pp. illus. $9\frac{3}{4} \times 7\frac{3}{8}$ in.

Oatmeal cloth boards; lettered in black on upper cover; edges trimmed; white end-papers printed in a brown mottled pattern.

Issued Winter 1957; 100 copies printed. HK$20.

P. [iii] Introduction. Reprinted from *Elixir*, Winter 1957 (*see* C3202).

B203   ANDREW YOUNG   1957

First edition:

ANDREW YOUNG | *PROSPECT OF A POET* | *Essays and tributes by fourteen writers* | *edited by* | LEONARD CLARK | [*device*] | RUPERT HART-DAVIS | SOHO SQUARE LONDON | 1957

Small crown 8vo. 112 pp. front. (port.). $7\frac{1}{4} \times 4\frac{3}{8}$ in.

Pale grey paper boards; printed in black and pale green; edges trimmed; white end-papers.

Published 15 November 1957; 1000 copies printed. 12*s.* 6*d.*

P. 107 A SOUTHERN PILGRIM; reprinted in *A Hong Kong House*, 1962 (*see* A156).

B204   JOURNAL OF   1956 [i.e. 1958]
ORIENTAL STUDIES

First separate publication:

[*title on upper wrapper; within a double rule, thick, thin*:]
JOURNAL OF | ORIENTAL STUDIES | [*long rule*] |
REPRINTED FROM Vol. III, No. 2. JULY 1956 | [*long rule*] | REVIEWS | [*one line in Chinese*] | UNIVERSITY OF HONG KONG

Imperial 8vo. An offprint of [10] pp. numbered [2], [325]–434 pp. $10\frac{5}{8} \times 7\frac{5}{8}$ in.

Buff paper wrapper; printed in black; edges cut flush; sewn and gummed.

Issued January 1958; 50 copies printed. Not for sale.

Pp. 362–363 review of *Hokusai: Paintings, Drawings and Woodcuts*, by J. Hillier. Reprinted from the *Journal of Oriental Studies*, July 1956 [*i.e.* January 1958] (*see* C3207).

B205   THE GENESIS OF   1958
WUTHERING HEIGHTS

First edition:

The Genesis of | Wuthering Heights | BY | MARY VISICK | INTRODUCTION BY EDMUND BLUNDEN | [*device*] | HONG KONG UNIVERSITY PRESS | OXFORD UNIVERSITY PRESS | 1958*

Crown 8vo. xiv, 90 pp. $7\frac{1}{4} \times 5$ in.

Transcription composed from '2nd edition', 1967, and wrappers.

White stiff paper wrappers; edges cut flush; sewn and gummed. Pale green pictorial dust-jacket printed in brown.

Published 12 March 1958; 1000 copies printed. HK$10 (12*s*. 6*d*.).

There was a reprint, with an 'Author's Note to Second Edition' and a Select Bibliography added, of 1000 copies in April 1965, and 1000 copies in February 1967.

Pp. [v]–vii Foreword.

First edition:

THE MASQUERS | UNIVERSITY OF HONG KONG | AS
YOU LIKE IT | by | William Shakespeare | at | LOKE
YEW HALL | March 20th to 24th 1958

Demy 4to. [44] pp. 11¼ × 8⅝ in.

Cream pictorial paper wrappers; printed in bright green and maroon;
outside lower wrapper, at foot: Printed by South China Morning
Post, Ltd., H.K.; edges cut flush; stapled.

Issued 20 March 1958; probably 500 copies printed. Probably
HK$1.

Pp. [14–15] As You Like It – p. [21] PROLOGUE, unsigned, holograph facsimile – pp. [28–29] Meditation, signed B. THE PRO-
LOGUE was also issued separately as an offprint (*see* A136).

B207 **SHIROYAMA** 1958

a. First English edition:

[*title on upper wrapper*:] The English Version of the Biwa
Song | SHIROYAMA | and | A Brief Account of Takamori
Saigo | by | Moriaki Sakamoto | (The Japanese translations
and | the original Japanese Biwa song | included) |
Satsuma Biwa Players' Association

8vo. [ii], 14, 10, [ii] pp. 8⅜ × 6 in.

Pale turquoise paper wrappers; printed in black; errata slips tipped-in
inside upper and lower wrappers; edges trimmed; stapled.

Published April 1958; 300 copies printed. Not for sale.

Published under the auspices of the Department of English, Kagoshima University.

Blunden assisted the translator.

b. Second English edition. 1963:

THE FALL OF SHIROYAMA | (The Last Phase of Saigo
the Humanist) | PART II | Chapter VII- | Conclusion |
SAIGO AND FUKUZAWA: DEATH AND VINDICATION
| by | Moriaki Sakamoto | [*four lines*] | KAGOSHIMA
UNIVERSITY | (1963)

8vo. [ii], 48 pp. 2 plates. $8\frac{3}{8}$ X 6 in.

White pictorial paper wrappers; printed in black and scarlet; edges cut flush; stapled.

Published 30 October 1963; 1000 copies printed. Not for sale.

Published by the Faculty of Literature and Science, Kagoshima University.

B207.1   AICHIKEN KYŌIKU BUNKA   1958
                       KENKŸUSHO

First edition:

[*in Japanese*:] AICHIKEN KYŌIKU BUNKA KENKYŪ-SHO | JŪENSHI

178 pp. 8 X 6 in.

Dark blue cloth boards; lettered in gold on spine, and on upper cover; edges trimmed; white end-papers.

Published 27 June 1958 in Nagoya; number of copies printed not ascertained.

Published by Mineharu Asai, President of the Aichi Kyōiku Bunka Kenkyūsho (Aichi Prefecture Educational and Cultural Institute).

P. 23 FOR THE EDUCATION INSTITUTE OF AICHI PREFEC-TURE, dated January 1949, holograph and autograph facsimiles, and Japanese translation by Gorō Katayama; reprinted in *Poems on Japan*, 1967 and *Nihon no asu yobu chikara*, 1969 (*see* A171; B283.1).

B208   SHELLEY AT WORK   1958

First separate publication:

[*at head of p.* [1] :] *The Critical Forum*

Demy 8vo. An offprint of [22] leaves numbered 325–346. $8\frac{5}{8}$ X $5\frac{3}{8}$ in.

Pale green stiff paper wrappers; printed in black on upper wrapper; edges cut flush; stapled.

Issued July 1958; number of copies printed not ascertained. Not for sale.

Leaves [12-13] numbered 336–337 [Shelley at Work, Note 1]; on the review of *Shelley at Work*, by Neville Rogers in the issue of October 1957 — leaves [14-15] numbered 338–339 Note II by the reviewer G. M. Matthews, and Note III by D. M. Davin. Reprinted from *Essays in Criticism*, July 1958 (*see* C3212). *See also* C3196.

First edition:

ENGLISH | CRITICAL ESSAYS | *TWENTIETH CEN-*
TURY | [*double rule, thin, thick*] | *SECOND SERIES* |
SELECTED | WITH AN INTRODUCTION | BY | DEREK
HUDSON | LONDON | OXFORD UNIVERSITY PRESS
| 1958

Demy 16mo. xvi, 368 pp. $5\frac{7}{8}$ X $3\frac{5}{8}$ in.

Navy-blue cloth boards; lettered in gold on spine; device in blind
on upper cover; edges trimmed; white end-papers.

Published 25 September 1958 as *The World's Classics*, Vol. 567;
7500 copies printed. 7s.

There were reprints of 5000 copies each in 1960 and 1963, and
3500 copies in 1968.

Pp. 114–122 Country Poets [*formerly* "I Found the Poems in the
Fields"] ; reprinted from the *TLS*, 29 October 1954; and issued
separately as an offprint (*see* A121; C3120).

B210   YASUA YAMATO   **1958**

First edition:

[Essays in honour of Dr Yasua Yamato's Sixtieth Birth-
day] . Osaka Kyoiku Tosho Shuppan, Osaka*

Published 25 September 1958; 2000 copies printed. 600 yen.

Pp. — Mary Shelley's Romances. Also issued separately as an offprint
(*see* A138).

B211   HONG KONG FESTIVAL OF   **1958**
                THE ARTS

First edition:

FOURTH | *HONG KONG FESTIVAL OF THE ARTS* |
1958 | *OCTOBER 11th* — *NOVEMBER 8th* | *Published*
for the | *Central Committee* | *Hong Kong* | *1958*

[ii], 80, xxxx, [54] pp. illus. $9\frac{1}{2}$ X $6\frac{3}{4}$ in.

White pictorial paper wrappers; printed in black and scarlet; edges
cut flush; gummed.

Published 11 October 1958; 3000 copies printed.

P. 52 BRING YOUR MUSIC, composition competition sponsored by the Music Society of Hong Kong for part song to words by Blunden, and the authorized Chinese translation of the poem; first published in *Music Magazine*, September 1958 (*see* C3215).

B212   **NEW POEMS 1958**   1958

First edition:

New Poems | [*swelled rule*; *within a decorated oval*:] 1958 [*swelled rule*] | *Edited by* | BONAMY DOBRÉE | LOUIS MacNEICE | PHILIP LARKIN | [*device*] | London | MICHAEL JOSEPH

Large crown 8vo. 128 pp. $7\frac{7}{8} \times 5\frac{1}{4}$ in.

White patterned paper boards; printed in red, sage green and dark grey; red buckram spine lettered in white with device and four swelled rules; edges trimmed.

Published 10 November 1958; no record of the number of copies printed. 13s. 6d.

A P.E.N. Anthology.

P. 23 ON TEARING UP A CYNICAL POEM; reprinted in *A Hong Kong House*, 1962 (*see* A156) — p. 24 SENTENTIAE; reprinted in *A Hong Kong House*, 1962 (*see* A156).

B213   **THE WOMAN AT ST. LÔ**   1959

First edition:

[*within a wavy rule*:] [*illustration*] | *by* MAURICE SCHNEPS | [*in open letters*:] The Woman at St. Lô [*in roman*:] ILLUSTRATED BY THE AUTHOR | INTRODUCTION BY [*in script*:] Edmund Blunden | [*in roman*:] CROSS CONTINENT CO., LTD., Tokyo

Small demy 8vo. xviii [*i.e.* xvi], 108 pp. illus. $8\frac{1}{4} \times 5\frac{3}{4}$ in.

Dull green cloth boards; lettered in gold down the spine; illustration in gold on upper cover; edges trimmed; dull greenish-grey endpapers.

Published 1959; number of copies printed not ascertained. 900 yen (paper 600 yen).

Pp. xiii–xvi [*i.e.* xi–xiv] Introduction.

255

First edition:

A BRIEF SURVEY OF | QUAKER WORK CAMPS | IN HONG KONG FROM | 1954–1959.

Large crown 8vo. [8] pp. illus. $7\frac{3}{4} \times 5\frac{3}{8}$ in.

No wrappers; edges trimmed; sewn.

Issued early 1959; probably 500 copies printed. Not for sale.

Publication was arranged by Peter and Margaret Whittle who organised the work camps in an attempt to raise money and local support.

P. [1] ON READING "A BRIEF SURVEY".

B215   **BY A LONELY SEA**   1959

First edition:

By a lonely Sea | Translations and Poems | by | John Cairncross | Foreword by | Edmund Blunden | [*device*] | Hong Kong University Press | Oxford University Press | 1959

Crown 8vo. viii, 94 pp. front. $7\frac{1}{4} \times 5\frac{1}{4}$ in.

White paper boards; printed in black down the spine; edges trimmed; white end-papers. Off-white pictorial dust-jacket.

Published 25 February 1959; 500 copies printed. HK$10 (12*s*. 6*d*.).

P. v Foreword. The Foreword first appeared in the publisher's prospectus for the book.

B216   **FIRST ASIAN STUDENT SALON**   1959
OF PHOTOGRAPHY

First edition:

[*title on upper wrapper*; *in open capitals*:] FIRST | ASIAN STUDENT SALON | OF PHOTOGRAPHY | 1959 | [*in roman*:] THE PHOTOGRAPHIC SOCIETY | UNIVERSITY OF HONG KONG [*device*]

Royal 8vo. [40] pp. illus. $9\frac{3}{4} \times 6\frac{1}{4}$ in.

White pictorial stiff paper wrappers; printed in pale grey, black and green; edges cut flush; stapled.

Published 6 April 1959; number of copies printed not ascertained.

P. [1] at foot: *Published by*: │ Acme Advertising Agency │ 614 Man Yee Building, Hong Kong.

Pp. [6–8] Foreword, holograph facsimile.

B217   THE DICTIONARY OF NATIONAL   1959
BIOGRAPHY

First edition:

THE │ DICTIONARY │ OF │ NATIONAL BIOGRAPHY │ [*rule*] │ 1941–1950 │ Edited by L. G. Wickham Legg │ and │ E. T. Williams │ [*rule*] │ With an Index covering the years 1901–1950 │ in one alphabetical series │ OXFORD UNIVERSITY PRESS │ 1959

Small royal 8vo. [2], xxii, 1032 pp. $9\frac{1}{4} \times 6$ in.

Navy-blue cloth boards; lettered in gold on spine with device and rule at head and foot; edges trimmed; white end-papers.

Published 21 May 1959; 8180 copies printed. £5. 5s.

There were reprints of 2000 copies in 1968, and 1500 copies in 1972.

Pp. 92–93 Bottomley, Gordon (1874–1948) — pp. 626–627 Nichols, Robert Malise Bowyer (1893–1944).

B218   EASTERN WESTERN   1959

First edition:

[*title on upper wrapper*:] [*in grey*:] EASTERN [*in pale blue*:] WESTERN │ [*in navy-blue: illustration*] │ Compiled by The National │ Education Association of the │ United States for the Eighth │ Annual WCOTP Assembly │ in Washington, D.C., 1959 │ [*at right of last five lines in pale blue*:] a symposium │ [*up left side in pale blue*:] CULTURAL VALUES

Small royal 8vo. 40 pp. $8\frac{7}{8} \times 5\frac{7}{8}$ in.

Pale blue paper wrappers; printed in navy-blue and grey; edges cut flush; stapled.

Published June 1959; 3000 copies printed. Not for sale.

Pp. 3–9 Common Moral Concepts in Eastern and Western Cultures.

B219   WINCHESTER COLLEGE LIBRARY   1959

First edition:

[*title on p.* [1]:] [*in navy-blue*:] WINCHESTER COL-
LEGE | LIBRARY | [*in black*:] JUNE–JULY, 1959 |
WILLIAM COLLINS (1721–1759)

Crown 4to. 16 pp. $9\frac{7}{8} \times 7\frac{1}{2}$ in.

No wrappers; top and bottom edges trimmed, fore edges untrimmed;
sewn in white thread.

Issued June 1959; probably 500 copies printed. Not for sale.

Pp. 2–3 Introduction.

B220   THE PERSONAL VISION   1959

First edition:

[*title on p.* [1]:] *The Personal Vision* | *POETRY* |
SUPPLEMENT | *edited by* | *JAMES REEVES* | *for the* |
POETRY BOOK | *SOCIETY* | *CHRISTMAS 1959*

Crown 8vo. [12] pp. $7\frac{3}{8} \times 5$ in.

No wrappers; edges trimmed; stapled.

Published December 1959; probably 1500 copies printed. 2*s.* 6*d.* to
members of the Poetry Book Society.

P. [3] THE SLEEPING AMAH; reprinted in *A Hong Kong House*,
1962; *A Selection of the Shorter Poems*, [1966]; and *A Selection
from the Poems*, [1969] (*see* A156, 169, 176).

B221   CEMETERIES   1959 [i.e. 1960]
IN GREECE

First edition:

THE WAR DEAD OF | THE BRITISH COMMONWEALTH
| AND EMPIRE | The Register of the names of those who
fell | in the 1939–1945 War and are buried | in Cemeteries
in Greece | PHALERON WAR CEMETERY, ATHENS |
Part I | (Aar-Lyo) | [*device*] | LONDON: COMPILED

AND PUBLISHED BY ORDER OF | THE IMPERIAL
WAR GRAVES COMMISSION | 1959

8vo. xvi, 42 pp. front. (map), map, and plan. 10 × 8 in.

Grey paper wrappers; printed in black; edges cut flush; sewn and
gummed.

Published *c.* January 1960; no record of the number of copies printed. 7*s.* 6*d.*

Pp. v–x The War in Greece, edited by Blunden. The introduction also
appeared in Part II of the Register for Greece (*see* note to B145).

B222   **CEMETERIES IN CRETE**   1960
              AND THE DODECANESE

First edition:

THE WAR DEAD OF | THE BRITISH COMMONWEALTH
| AND EMPIRE | The Register of the names of those who
fell | in the 1939–1945 War and are buried | in Cemeteries
in Crete and the Dodecanese | CEMETERIES IN CRETE
AND THE DODECANESE | [*device*] | LONDON: COM-
PILED AND PUBLISHED BY ORDER OF | THE IM-
PERIAL WAR GRAVES COMMISSION | 1960

8vo. xii, 62 pp. front. (map), maps, and plans. 10 × 8 in.

Grey paper wrappers; printed in black; edges cut flush; sewn and
gummed.

Published *c.* February 1960; no record of the number of copies printed. 7*s.* 6*d.*

Pp. v–vii The Battle for Crete, edited by Blunden (*see* note to B145).

B223   **GENJI TAKAHASHI**   1960

First edition:

[*in Japanese*:] TAKAHASHI GENJI HAKASE KANREKI
KINEN | [*short rule*] EIGO EIBUNGAKU ROMBUNSHŪ
[*short rule*] | KOTOBA TO BUNGAKU | SHINOSAKI
SHOBŌ | 1960

Small demy 8vo. [4], ii, 442 pp. front. (port.) $8\frac{3}{8} \times 5\frac{7}{8}$ in.

Navy-blue cloth boards; lettered in gold on spine; initial letter S in blind on lower cover; edges trimmed; white end-papers. Buff slip case.

Published 25 February 1960 in Tokyo; c. 1000 copies printed. 500 yen.

A collection of essays on English language and literature in honour of Dr Genji Takahashi's sixtieth birthday entitled *Language and Literature.*

Pp. 137–151 On Coleridge as a Thinker, and Some of his Contemporaries. Also issued separately as an offprint (*see* A148).

B224　　　GEMS FROM ENGLISH POETRY　　　1960

First edition:

GEMS FROM | ENGLISH POETRY | *Read by* | EDMUND BLUNDEN | *Translated by* | TAKESHI SAITO | JOSÉ CIVASAQUI | TOKYO | KENKYUSHA

Small crown 8vo. vi, 30 pp. $6\frac{7}{8}$ × $4\frac{1}{2}$ in.

White pictorial stiff paper wrappers; printed in pale green, and black on upper wrapper; edges cut flush; gummed.

Published 30 April 1960; probably 500 copies printed. 600 yen, including E.P. record.

P. 1 [Foreword], holograph facsimile — pp. 20–29 THE TREE IN THE GOODS YARD (*see* A89, 135) — VOICES IN TOKYO (*see* A85, 89; C2445) — FROM THE FLYING-BOAT (*see* A89, 135) — HOMES AND HAUNTS (*see* A89, 135; B108; C2041).

There are Japanese translations by Takeshi Saito of all the above poems. *See also* Ed3.

B225　　　SELECTED CHINESE SAYINGS　　　1960

First edition:

[*line in Chinese*] | Selected Chinese Sayings | Translated and Annotated | by | T. C. Lai, M.A. | University Book Store | University of Hong Kong | 1960

Crown 8vo. viii, 192 pp. $7\frac{3}{8}$ × 5 in.

White rexine boards; lettered in gold down the spine, and across foot; edges trimmed; white end-papers.

Published June 1960; 2000 copies printed. HK$3.50 (£1).

Errata slip inserted. There were 3 reprints.

P. vi note on the proverbs. The note first appeared in the publisher's prospectus for the book.

B226   THE MASQUERS   **1960**

First edition:

THE MASQUERS | UNIVERSITY OF HONG KONG | THE DUCHESS OF MALFI | (1612) | by | John Webster | at | LOKE YEW HALL | (*By kind persmission of the Vice-Chancellor of the University of Hong Kong*) | July 6th to 9th, 1960

Demy 4to. [52] pp. $11\frac{1}{8} \times 8\frac{5}{8}$ in.

Off-white paper wrappers; printed in mauve and olive green; outside lower wrapper, at foot: PRINTED BY YE OLDE PRINTERIE, LTD., HONG KONG; edges cut flush; stapled.

Issued 6 July 1960; probably 500 copies printed. Probably HK$1.

P. [25] PROLOGUE, unsigned; holograph facsimile.

This and three earlier The Masquers programmes (B184, 197, 206) were bound together in dark red leather; lettered in gold on upper cover; pale blue end-papers patterned in turquoise and gold; edges trimmed.

B227   TWO JAPANESE SONGS ON   **1960**
                  BLOOD TRANSFUSION

First edition:

[*title on envelope*:] [*six lines in Japanese*] | TWO JAPA-NESE SONGS | ON BLOOD TRANSFUSION | by | H.I.M. Empress Nagako | on the Occasion of | The 8th Congress of the International Society of | Blood Transfusion, Tokyo, 1960 | Translated by | Professor Edmund Blunden

[3] leaves. $8\frac{1}{4} \times 7\frac{1}{8}$ in. (2 leaves); $7\frac{1}{8} \times 10\frac{1}{8}$ in. (1 leaf).

White envelope, $9\frac{7}{8} \times 7\frac{3}{4}$ in.; printed in black; [3] leaves inserted, leaves [1-2] grey and pale yellow; edges trimmed.

Issued September 1960; number of copies printed not ascertained.

Leaf [3] Japanese text with translation by Blunden entitled ON BLOOD TRANSFUSION [*later* TRANSLATED FROM THE JAPA-NESE OF H. M. EMPRESS NAGAKO]; reprinted in *Poems on Japan*, 1967 (*see* A171).

261

a. Heinemann edition:

SELECTED POEMS OF | TENNYSON | *Edited with an Introduction* | *and Notes* | *by* | EDMUND BLUNDEN | [*device*] | HEINEMANN | LONDON MELBOURNE TORONTO

Crown 8vo. vi, 162 pp. front. (port.). $7\frac{1}{4} \times 4\frac{7}{8}$ in.

Rose-pink cloth boards; lettered in gold down the spine; edges trimmed; white end-papers.

Published 26 September 1960; no record of the number of copies printed. 8*s*. 6*d*.

Pp. 1–24 Introduction — pp. 149–158 Notes.

b. American issue. 1960:*

New York, Macmillan

vi, 162 pp. front. (port.).

Issued 1960; no record of the number of copies bound.

B229   SEASON'S GREETINGS   1960

First edition:

[*title inside leaf; in brown*:] SEASON'S GREETINGS | [*autograph facsimile of proprietor's signature*] | The International House of Japan

[1] leaf (folded). illus. $7\frac{1}{4} \times 11\frac{1}{4}$ in. (open); $3\frac{3}{8} \times 5\frac{5}{8}$ in. (folded).

No wrappers; edges trimmed.

Issued December 1960 in Tokyo; number of copies printed not ascertained. Not for sale.

Verso of lower fold untitled poem (It shall be written:). This publication was unauthorized.

B230   EXHIBITION OF PAINTINGS   1961
                         BY PANSY NG

First edition:

[*title on upper fold*:] exhibition of paintings | by | pansy ng | JAN. 17–21, 1961 | AT U.S. CULTURAL CENTER, H.K.

[1] leaf (folded). 8 × 15⅛ in. (open); 8 × 5⅜ in. (folded).
No wrappers; edges trimmed.
Issued 17 January 1961 in Hong Kong; number of copies printed not ascertained.
Upper fold Foreword.

B231   **THE MASQUERS**   1961

First edition:

THE MASQUERS | UNIVERSITY OF HONG KONG | ROMEO & JULIET | by | William Shakespeare | at | LOKE YEW HALL | (*By kind permission of the Vice-Chancellor of the University of Hong Kong*) | March 23rd to 27th, 1961

Demy 4to. [52] pp. 11⅛ × 8⅝ in.
Cream paper wrappers; printed in maroon and olive; outside lower wrapper, at foot: PRINTED BY YE OLDE PRINTERIE, LTD., HONG KONG; edges cut flush; stapled.
Issued 23 March 1961; probably 500 copies printed. Probably HK$1.
Pp. [19–20] Romeo and Juliet: Some Notes, by Professor E. Blunden -- p. [25] PROLOGUE, unsigned, holograph facsimile.

B232   **A COMPLETE GUIDE TO**   1961
          ENGLISH CONVERSATION

Second edition:

[*triple rule in blue*] | A COMPLETE GUIDE TO | ENGLISH CONVERSATION | WITH TONE SYMBOLS | BY EISHIRO HORI | [*triple rule in blue*] | [*in Japanese:*] SHINTEI | TADASHII EIGOKAIWA | YOKUYŌKIGŌ TSUKI | HORI EISHIRŌ CHO | [*triple rule in blue*] | TAISHŪKAN SHOTEN

Demy 16mo. [2], xxiv, 554 pp. illus. 5¾ × 3⅝ in.
Maroon rexine soft boards; lettered in gold down the spine, and upper cover; device in blind on lower cover; edges speckled pale maroon; white end-papers, map on upper and tables on lower. Clear plastic dust-jacket.

Published 15 May 1961; number of copies printed not ascertained. 450 yen.

There was a reprint in July 1961.

Pp. [i–ii] Foreword, dated November 1960, holograph facsimile, and Japanese translation; reprinted in *First Steps in English Conversation*, [1961] (*see* B233) — pp. [iii–vi] note on the author, dated 10 November 1950, holograph facsimile, and Japanese translation.

B233 **FIRST STEPS IN** 1961
ENGLISH CONVERSATION

Second edition:

FIRST STEPS | IN | ENGLISH | CONVERSATION | [*row of stars in scarlet*] | [*in Japanese*:] SHINTEI | HAJIMETE MANABU HITONO | EIGOKAIWA | KANA-HATSUON TO YOKUYŌKIGŌ TSUKI | [*row of stars in scarlet*] | KEIŌ DAIGAKU MOTOKYŌJU HORI EISHIRŌ | NHK KOKUSAIKYOKU HORI NAOYUKI | KYŌDŌ-TSŪSHIN GAISHINBU HORI YOSHIAKI | TAISHŪKAN SHOTEN

Foolscap 8vo. [2], xviii, 312 pp. 6¾ × 4 in.

Bottle green rexine limp boards; lettered in gold down the spine, and upper cover; device in blind on lower cover; edges faintly speckled green; white end-papers. Clear plastic dust-jacket.

Published 25 May 1961; number of copies printed not ascertained. 300 yen.

There was a reprint in July 1961.

Pp. [i–ii] Foreword, dated November 1960, holograph facsimile, and Japanese translation; first published in *A Complete Guide to English Conversation*, [1961] (*see* B232) — pp. [iii–iv] note in honour of Naoyuki and Yoshiaki (*i.e.* Kiyoshi) Hori, the author and the illustrator, holograph facsimile, and Japanese translation.

B234 **EDMUND BLUNDEN SIXTY-FIVE** 1961

First edition:

EDMUND BLUNDEN | SIXTY-FIVE | NOVEMBER 1961 | HONG KONG

214 pp. (incl. plates). plates. 9 × 6½ in.

White paper boards; printed in gold and rust; top and fore edges untrimmed, bottom trimmed; white end-papers. White matching dust-jacket.

Published 1 November 1961 by Hong Kong Cultural Enterprise Co. for the English Society, University of Hong Kong; probably 1000 copies printed. HK$10.

P. [59] THE MIDNIGHT SKATERS, holograph facsimile (*see* A17-18, 20, 35, 108, 135, 174, 176) — p. [72] LATE LIGHT (*see* A64, 68, 135) — pp. [194-195] A HONG KONG HOUSE, holograph facsimile; first published in *The Quill*, 1955; and in a separate edition, 1959; and reprinted in *A Hong Kong House*, 1962; and *The Midnight Skaters*, [1968] (*see* A145, 156, 174; C3159).

B235   MEMOIR OF THOMAS BEWICK   1961

a. First edition:

MEMOIR OF | THOMAS BEWICK | WRITTEN BY HIMSELF | 1822-1828 | WITH AN INTRODUCTION BY | EDMUND BLUNDEN | [*woodcut*] | LONDON CENTAUR PRESS 1961

Demy 8vo. [xx], 274 pp. illus. $8\frac{1}{2} \times 5\frac{3}{8}$ in.

Black cloth boards; lettered in gold on spine; edges trimmed, top black; white end-papers.

Published 30 November 1961 in the *Centaur Classics* series; number of copies printed not ascertained. £3. 3s.

Seven hundred and twenty-six copies, with a cancel-title, were sent to Southern Illinois University Press (*see* B235b).

Pp. [vii-xix] Introduction.

b. First edition — American issue. 1962:

[*title as above*; *imprint*:] Southern Illinois University Press, Carbondale*

Demy 8vo. [xx], 274 pp. illus. $8\frac{3}{4} \times 5\frac{5}{8}$ in.

Issued 12 March 1962; 726 copies bound. $12.

Copies, with a cancel-title, were supplied by the Centaur Press, London.

B236   THE POEMS   1961
         OF SIR FRANCIS HUBERT   [i.e. 1962]

First edition:

The Poems of | *Sir Francis Hubert* | EDITED WITH AN
INTRODUCTION, | COMMENTARIES, AND GLOS-
SARY | *by* | BERNARD MELLOR | *Foreword by
Edmund Blunden* | [*device*] | HONG KONG UNIVER-
SITY PRESS | OXFORD UNIVERSITY PRESS | 1961

Demy 8vo. xlviii, 360 pp. $8\frac{5}{8} \times 5\frac{1}{2}$ in.

Dark blue cloth boards; lettered in gold on spine with device, and on
upper cover; edges trimmed; white end-papers. Cream pictorial dust-
jacket printed in brown.

Published 9 February 1962; 1000 copies printed. HK$42 (£3. 3s.).

Pp. [vii]–x Foreword. An extract from the final paragraph of the
Foreword also appeared in the publisher's prospectus for the book.

B237   STUDENTS RALLY   1962

First edition:

[*title on wrapper*:] STUDENTS RALLY | *sponsored by
the* | *Organising Committee of the Proposed Federation of*
| *Hong Kong Post-Secondary Arts and Commerce Students*
| [*in a circle*; *in yellow*:] UNIVERSITY OF HONG KONG
– NEW ASIA COLLEGE – BAPTIST COLLEGE –
HOUNG [*sic*] KONG COLLEGE – UNITED COLLEGE. |
[*in black*:] *Loke Yew Hall* | *15th Feb., 1962.*

Small royal 8vo. [8] pp. $9 \times 6\frac{1}{8}$ in.

Pale green paper wrappers; printed in black and yellow; edges cut
flush; stapled.

Issued 15 February 1962; number of copies printed not ascertained.

Inside lower wrapper Foreword, signed Edmund C. Blunden.

B238   ENCYCLOPEDIA AMERICANA   1962

1962 impression:

VOLUME 22 Photography to Pumpkin | [*illus.*] | EN-

CYCLOPEDIA | AMERICANA | INTERNATIONAL EDITION | COMPLETE IN THIRTY VOLUMES FIRST PUBLISHED IN 1829 | AMERICANA CORPORATION International Headquarters: 575 Lexington Avenue, New York, New York 10022

2 vols. $10\frac{1}{8} \times 7\frac{3}{8}$ in.

Royal blue cloth boards; lettered in gold on spine with eight rules and two black panels, and on upper cover with illustration; edges trimmed; blue end-papers.

Issued *c.* 21 March 1962; number of copies printed not disclosed. $329.50 for the set of 30 volumes.

Line 1 of Volume 24 reads: Russia to Silius | [*then as above*].

Volume 22, p. 654 Prometheus Unbound. Volume 24, pp. 688–691 Shelley, Percy Bysshe.

B239   **THE MASQUERS**   1962

First edition:

Harry Odell | *presents* | THE MASQUERS | UNIVERSITY OF HONG KONG | in | A MIDSUMMER NIGHT'S DREAM | by | William Shakespeare | in | THE CITY HALL (Concert Hall) | March 26th to 28th, 1962

Demy 4to. [39] pp. $11 \times 8\frac{5}{8}$ in.

Pale green paper wrappers; printed in crimson and olive green; out-side lower wrapper, at foot: PRINTED BY YE OLDE PRINTERIE, LTD., HONG KONG; edges cut flush; stapled.

Issued 26 March 1962; probably 500 copies printed. Probably HK$1.

Pp. [14–15] Through the Years, unsigned – p. [17] PROLOGUE, unsigned, holograph facsimile.

B240   **CHANNING SCHOOL**   1962

First edition:

[*title on p.* [1]:] CHANNING SCHOOL | FOUNDER'S DAY SERVICE | *14th July, 1962, 3.00 p.m.*

[4] pp. $8\frac{5}{8} \times 5\frac{1}{2}$ in.

No wrappers; edges trimmed.

Issued 14 July 1962; *c.* 1000 copies printed. Not for sale.

267

Pp. [1] and [4] in some copies, probably proof copies, are blank.
Founder's Day Order of Service. Blunden's grand-daughter, Caroline
Ross, attended the school.
P. [2] HYMN.

B241   **UNIVERSITY OF HONG KONG**   **1962**
               THE FIRST 50 YEARS

First edition:

UNIVERSITY OF HONG KONG | THE | FIRST [*in scar-
let*:] 50 [*in black*:] YEARS | 1911-1961 | *Edited by* |
BRIAN HARRISON | [*device*] | [*in scarlet*:] HONG
KONG UNIVERSITY PRESS

Royal 8vo. xvi, 248, [2], vi pp. front. (col.), 46 plates and end-paper
maps. $9\frac{1}{2} \times 6\frac{1}{4}$ in.
Green cloth boards; lettered in gold on spine; edges trimmed; white
end-papers printed in green.
Published 3 August 1962; 1000 copies printed. HK$35 (£2. 7s.).
Pp. [1]–4 The Setting — pp. [38]–44 Sir Charles Eliot.

B242   **SOME ENGLISH POEMS**   **1962**
First edition:

SOME ENGLISH POEMS | CHOSEN AND ANNOTATED
BY | EDMUND AND CLAIRE BLUNDEN | [*three line
quotation*] | HONG KONG CULTURAL ENTERPRISE |
HONG KONG

Crown 8vo. [2], x, 164 pp. 7 × 5 in.
White stiff paper wrappers; printed in bright blue; edges cut flush;
gummed.
Published *c.* 16 September 1962; 600 copies printed. HK$3.
Pp. [iii]–iv Introduction — p. [1] *et passim* annotations.

B243   **LEE LAN FLIES THE DRAGON KITE**   **1962**
First English edition:

Lee Lan flies the | dragon kite | RALPH HERRMANNS |

ENGLISH VERSION BY EDMUND BLUNDEN | COL-
LINS | ST JAMES'S PLACE · LONDON | 1962

Demy 4to. [48] pp. illus. (col.). $11\frac{3}{8} \times 8\frac{1}{4}$ in.

White pictorial paper boards; printed in many colours; edges
trimmed; white end-papers. White pictorial dust-jacket printed in
many colours.

Published 24 September 1962; 15,000 copies printed. 15s.

There were reprints of 10,000 copies in 1964, and 5000 copies in
1965.

B244   GRASS WIDOW   1962

a. First edition:

Grass Widow | by | CONSTANCE HALE | CITIZEN

Crown 8vo. 24 pp. $7\frac{1}{4} \times 4\frac{7}{8}$ in.

Dark red stiff paper wrappers; printed in black; edges cut flush;
stapled.

Published late September or early October 1962; 250 copies printed.
2s.

P. [2] at foot: Printed in England by | The Unicorn Press, Southend-
on-Sea, Essex.

P. [5] Foreword.

b. Second edition (revised). [1963] :

[*title and imprint as above*]

Crown 8vo. 24 pp. $7\frac{1}{4} \times 4\frac{3}{4}$ in.

Pale yellow stiff paper wrappers; printed in black; edges cut flush;
stapled.

Published 1963; number of copies printed not ascertained. 2s.

P. [2] at foot: Printed in England by | The Nore Press Ltd., 245
Sutton Road, Southend-on-Sea.

P. [5] Foreword.

B244.1   POET'S CHOICE   1962

First edition:

POET'S | CHOICE | [*ornamental rule*] | EDITED BY |

Paul Engle and Joseph Langland | [*device*] | THE DIAL
PRESS NEW YORK 1962

Medium 8vo. [2], xx, 306 pp. 9 × 5⅞ in.

Brownish-red cloth boards; lettered in gold down and across the
spine; edges trimmed; reddish-brown end-papers.

Published October 1962; number of copies printed not ascertained.
$6.95.

P. 31 THOUGHTS OF THOMAS HARDY (*see* A77, 135, 174;
C1856) — pp. 31–32 note by Blunden on his choice of the poem,
signature in autograph facsimile.

B245   **THE MASQUERS**   1963

First edition:

THE MASQUERS | UNIVERSITY OF HONG KONG |
present | OTHELLO | by | William Shakespeare | as a
tribute to | EDMUND BLUNDEN | THE CITY HALL
THEATRE | January 8th to 13th, 1963

Demy 4to. [38] pp. 11⅛ × 8⅝ in.

Pale grey paper wrappers; printed in copper red; outside lower
wrapper, at foot: PRINTED BY YE OLDE PRINTERIE, LTD.,
HONG KONG; edges cut flush; stapled.

Issued 8 January 1963; probably 500 copies printed. Probably
HK$1.

P. [17] PROLOGUE, unsigned, holograph facsimile.

B246   **MOTHER INDIA**   1963

First edition:

[*title on upper wrapper*:] [*in royal blue*:] UNDER THE
DISTINGUISHED PATRONAGE OF | HIS EXCELLENCE
THE GOVERNOR | THE TAGORE CENTENARY CELE-
BRATION COMMITTEE | PRESENTS | [*in scarlet*:]
"MOTHER INDIA" | [*illustration in royal blue edged with
gold*] | [*in royal blue*:] AT THE ROXY THEATRE | ON
THURSDAY, 10th JANUARY, 1963 | AT 9.20 P.M. |
[*in scarlet*:] ENTIRE PROCEEDS TO BE DONATED TO
TAGORE SCHOLARSHIPS | FOR NEEDY SCHOOL
CHILDREN IN THE COLONY.

[68] pp. illus. $9\frac{1}{4}$ × 7 in.

White pictorial paper wrappers; printed in royal blue, scarlet and gold; edges cut flush; gummed.

Issued 10 January 1963 in Hong Kong; number of copies printed not ascertained. Not for sale.

P. [5] TAGORE'S PAINTINGS.

B247   **ENGLISH POETRY**   1963

a. First edition:

English Poetry | A SHORT HISTORY | Kenneth Hopkins | [*six line quotation*] | [*device*] | PHOENIX HOUSE LTD | *LONDON*

Demy 8vo. 568 pp. $8\frac{5}{8}$ × $5\frac{1}{2}$ in.

Royal-blue cloth boards; lettered in gold on spine, with a rule and device; edges trimmed, top pale yellow; white end-papers.

Published 28 February 1963; number of copies printed not ascertained. £2. 2s.

P. 246 DR. JOHNSON REVISITS A MILL STREAM AT LICHFIELD, Blunden's 'version of Johnson's Latin lines on Stowe Mill, Lichfield'; first published in *Everybody's*, December 1951 (*see* C2745).

b. First edition — American issue. [*1963*] :

[*title as above*; *imprint*:] J. B. LIPPINCOTT COMPANY | PHILADELPHIA & NEW YORK

Demy 8vo. [ii], 574 pp. $8\frac{1}{4}$ × $5\frac{3}{4}$ in.

Peacock blue cloth boards; lettered on spine in dark peacock blue, and in silver on a dark peacock blue panel edged at top and bottom with ornaments in silver; top and bottom edges trimmed, fore edges rough trimmed; peacock blue end-papers.

Issued 3 September 1963; number of copies printed not disclosed. $5.95.

B248   **WAYSIDE POEMS**   1963

First edition:

Wayside Poems | OF THE | *Seventeenth Century* | [*illustration in pink*] | AN ANTHOLOGY GATHERED BY |

Edmund Blunden | AND | *Bernard Mellor* | HONG KONG
UNIVERSITY PRESS

Crown 8vo. xiv, 138 pp. 7⅜ × 4⅞ in.

Reddish-brown cloth boards; lettered in black down the spine with
device; edges trimmed; white end-papers. Off-white dust-jacket printed in black and pinkish-brown.

Published 5 November 1963; 2000 copies printed. HK$15 (£1. 1s.).

P. [vi] note on the origin of the volume, holograph facsimile — pp.
vii–[ix] Preface by Blunden and Bernard Mellor — pp. 101–128
Commentary for which the Editors were jointly responsible.

B249   A MOST RARE VISION   1964

First edition:

THE MASQUERS | *Humbly and Gratefully offer* | their
Tribute | TO | ALEC M. HARDIE | *On the Occassion*
[*sic*] *of His Joining* | the International Christian Univer-
sity, Japan | April, 1964 | *Hong Kong*

Small demy 8vo. [iv], 56 pp. illus. 8¼ × 5½ in.

Pale blue paper wrappers, printed in dark purple; illustration on
upper wrapper; edges cut flush; gummed and stapled. Leaf, List of
Masquers' Productions, inserted.

Issued April 1964; 500 copies printed. Not for sale.

P. [iii] A.M.H. OUR LEADER AND INSPIRER, signed E. B.
absente vate R. B., dated 29 iii 1964; holograph facsimile.

B250   THE RECOGNITION OF   1964
              EMILY DICKINSON

First edition:

[*in ornamental capitals*:] *THE RECOGNITION* | *OF* |
EMILY | *DICKINSON* | [*short rule*] | [*in roman*:] SELEC-
TED CRITICISM SINCE 1890 | [*short rule*] | EDITED
BY | *Caesar R. Blake* | AND | *Carlton F. Wells* | Ann
Arbor / The University of Michigan Press

Medium 8vo. [2], xviii, 316 pp. front. (port.). 9⅛ × 6 in.

Rust cloth boards; lettered in gold on spine; edges trimmed; end-
papers.

Published 29 April 1964; 3000 copies printed. $7.50.

There were reprints of 2000 copies in January 1965; and 5098 copies (paper-back) in June 1968.

Pp. 134–137 An Unguessed Poetry [*formerly* Emily Dickinson]; first published in the *Nation & Athenaeum*, 22 March 1930 (*see* C956).

B251   **JOHN CLARE 1793–1864**   **1964**

First edition:

[*title on upper fold*:] [*in white on a green ground*:] JOHN CLARE | 1793–1864 | [*portrait of Clare*] | [*in green*:] CENTENARY | COMMEMORATIONS | AT | NORTH-AMPTON | 1964

[1] sheet (folded twice). $8\frac{3}{4}$ × $11\frac{1}{8}$ in. (open); $8\frac{3}{4}$ × $3\frac{3}{4}$ in. (folded). No wrappers; edges trimmed.

Issued May 1964; 5000 copies printed. Not for sale.

Programme of events.

Verso of upper fold The Poet. *See also* E*b*28.

B252   **15 POEMS FOR**   **1964**
WILLIAM SHAKESPEARE

a. First edition:

[*within a double rule*:] 15 *Poems* | *for William* | *Shakespeare* | [*rule*] | *edited by* Eric W. White | *with an introduction by* | Patrick Garland | John Lehmann & | William Plomer | [*rule*] | 1964: *Stratford-upon-Avon* | The Trustees & Guardians | of Shakespeare's Birthplace

Royal 8vo. [vi, 18] pp. $9\frac{7}{8}$ × $5\frac{7}{8}$ in.

Pale grey paper wrappers; printed in black and dark green; edges trimmed; sewn.

Published June 1964; 1100 copies printed. 3*s.* 6*d.*

One hundred copies were issued as a 'special edition' (*see* B252*b*).

P. [1] TWO SONNETS; reprinted in *Review of English Literature*, October 1964 (*see* C3321).

b. First edition — limited issue. 1964:

[*title and imprint as above*]

Small royal 8vo. [vi, 18] pp. $9\frac{3}{4} \times 5\frac{7}{8}$ in.

Cream paper boards; lettered in gold on upper cover with illustration; edges trimmed; paste-down end-papers.

Issued June 1964; 100 copies bound. 10*s.* 6*d.*

Errata-slip referring to Blunden tipped-in p. [vi].

B253   **WAYSIDE POEMS**   **1964**

First edition:

Wayside Poems | OF THE | *Early Eighteenth Century* | [*illustration in bright green*] | AN ANTHOLOGY GATHERED BY | *Edmund Blunden* | AND | *Bernard Mellor* | HONG KONG UNIVERSITY PRESS

Crown 8vo. xiv, 160 pp. $7\frac{3}{8} \times 4\frac{7}{8}$ in.

Green cloth boards; lettered in gold down the spine with device; edges trimmed; white end-papers. Pale pink dust-jacket printed in green and black.

Published 1 June 1964; 2000 copies printed. HK$15 (£1. 1*s.*).

Pp. vi–vii Preface, signed E. B. and B. M., holograph facsimile — pp. 115–152 Commentary for which the Editors were jointly responsible.

B254   **THEIR NAME LIVETH**   **1964**

First edition:

THEIR NAME LIVETH | VOLUME V, PART II | SOME PICTURES OF | COMMONWEALTH WAR CEMETERIES | 1914–1918 1939–1945 | PUBLISHED BY ORDER OF THE COMMONWEALTH WAR GRAVES COMMISSION | 1964.

[ii], 30 pp. 24 plates. $11\frac{5}{8} \times 10$ in.

Crimson paper wrappers; printed in gold on upper wrapper, with device; 5 small squares in gold on spine; edges cut flush.

Published *c.* August 1964; no record of the number of copies printed.

Pp. 5–6 Monument of Mercy. *See also* B162.

a. Second edition — photo-offset reprint:

FREDERIC MANNING | (PRIVATE 19022) | Her
Privates We | Introduction by | EDMUND BLUNDEN |
[*four line quotation*] | [*monogram*] | LONDON: PETER
DAVIES

Large crown 8vo. xii, 276 pp. $7\frac{3}{4} \times 5\frac{1}{8}$ in.
Brown cloth boards; lettered in gold on spine; edges trimmed; white
end-papers. White dust-jacket printed in olive green, scarlet and
yellow.
Issued 4 August 1964; 4000 copies printed. £1. 1s.
There were reprints of 1500 copies in October 1964, 2000 copies in
November 1964, and 1600 copies in 1970.
Pp. [vii–viii] Introduction.

b. Third edition. 1967:

[*title as above*; *imprint*:] UNABRIDGED | PAN BOOKS
LTD : LONDON

Small crown 8vo. 304 pp. $7 \times 4\frac{3}{8}$ in.
White pictorial paper wrappers; printed in olive green, red, black and
yellow; edges cut flush; gummed.
Published 6 January 1967 as *Pan Books*, Vol. M179; 28,000 copies
printed. 5s.
Pp. 9–11 Introduction.

B256   EDWARDIAN ENGLAND 1901–1914   1964

First edition:

EDWARDIAN | ENGLAND | 1901–1914 | [*ornament*] |
EDITED BY | SIMON NOWELL-SMITH | LONDON |
OXFORD UNIVERSITY PRESS | NEW YORK TORONTO
| 1964

Small royal 8vo. [2], xxvi, 620 pp. front., illus., and 57 plates.
$9\frac{1}{4} \times 5\frac{7}{8}$ in.
Crimson cloth boards; lettered in gold on spine on a green panel
within a border and a rule, and at foot; edges trimmed; white end-
papers. White pictorial dust-jacket printed in rose pink, pale grey
and dark grey.

Published 8 October 1964; 6000 copies printed. £3. 15s.

There was a reprint of 3000 copies in 1965.

Pp. [547]–573 Country Childhood.

B257   **CHRIST CHURCH MEADOW**   1965

a. First edition:

CHRIST CHURCH | MEADOW | [*ornament*] | E.G.W.
BILL | PRINTED AT THE | UNIVERSITY PRESS ·
OXFORD | 1965

Small royal 8vo. 40 pp. front. (p. 2), and 12 illus. $9\frac{1}{4}$ X $6\frac{5}{8}$ in. *and*
1 leaf inserted $9\frac{1}{8}$ X 6 in.

Pale grey paper wrappers; printed in black with two rules and two
lines of ornaments on upper wrapper; edges cut flush; stapled.

Published 16 January 1965; 700 copies printed. Distributed free;
also on sale in Oxford bookshops at 5s.

Prepared with the help of Thomas F. R. G. Braun and Stephen E.
Medcalf in defence of the Meadow at the forthcoming Road Enquiry
starting on 19 January 1965.

Inserted leaf THE MEADOWS FOR EVER, holograph facsimile.

b. First edition — photo-offset reprint. 1968:

[*title as above*; *imprint*:] . . . | This second edition repro-
duced by | photolithography by | HALL THE PRINTER,
Oxford, 1968 | and published by | DONALD PARSONS
& CO. LTD. | Oxford, 1968

Oblong demy 4to. 20 pp. 12 illus., and 3 plans. $8\frac{1}{8}$ X 11 in.

Stiff pictorial white paper wrappers; printed in black; edges cut
flush; stapled.

Issued September 1968; 1000 copies printed. 7s. 6d.

Outside lower wrapper THE MEADOWS FOR EVER, holograph
facsimile.

B258   **WRITING BETWEEN THE LINES**   1965

First edition:

WRITING BETWEEN | THE LINES | *An Autobiography* |
BY | DEREK HUDSON | HIGH HILL BOOKS

Small demy 8vo. [x], 214 pp. front. (port.), and 10 plates. $8\frac{1}{2} \times 5\frac{1}{2}$ in.

Scarlet cloth boards; lettered in gold on spine; edges trimmed, top grey; white end-papers.

Published 15 February 1965; 1000 copies printed. £1. 15s.

P. 113 [untitled sonnet] (When from Pagani's painted palace freed, –).

B259   JOURNAL   1959/60 [i.e. 1965]
              OF ORIENTAL STUDIES

First separate publication:

[*title on upper wrapper*; *within a double rule, thick, thin*:] JOURNAL OF | ORIENTAL STUDIES | [*long rule*] | REPRINTED FROM Vol. V, Nos. 1-2 1959/60 | [*long rule*] | REVIEWS | [*one line in Chinese*] | UNIVERSITY OF HONG KONG

Imperial 8vo. An offprint of [151] pp. numbered [175]-[330]. $10\frac{5}{8} \times 7\frac{5}{8}$ in.

Buff paper wrappers; printed in black; edges cut flush; sewn and gummed.

Issued March 1965; 50 copies printed. Not for sale.

Pp. 252-253 Review of *Modern Japanese Novels and the West*, by Donald Keene; *Modern Japanese Stories: An Anthology*, edited by Ivan Morris; *Folk Legends of Japan*, by Richard M. Dorson; and *The Road to Inamura*, by Lewis Bush.

Reprinted from the *Journal of Oriental Studies*, 1959/60 [*i.e.* March 1965] (*see* C3334).

B260   UP THE LINE TO DEATH   1965

First edition:

UP THE LINE TO DEATH | *THE WAR POETS 1914– 1918* | [*long rule*] | AN ANTHOLOGY | *selected and arranged, with* | *an introduction and notes by* | BRIAN GARDNER | FOREWORD BY EDMUND BLUNDEN | [*long rule*] | METHUEN & CO LTD | 11 NEW FETTER LANE LONDON EC4

Large crown 8vo. xxvi, 190 pp. $7\frac{7}{8} \times 5\frac{1}{8}$ in.

Charcoal paper boards; lettered in gold on spine; edges trimmed, top pale yellow; white end-papers. White dust-jacket printed in black and olive-yellow.

Published April 1965; number of copies printed not disclosed. 18s.

Pp. vii–viii Foreword — pp. 42–43 COME ON, MY LUCKY LADS [*formerly* ZERO; *and later* ZERO 1916] (*see* A17, 28, 35, 135) — pp. 90–92 'TRENCH NOMENCLATURE' (*see* A28, 35); PREMATURE REJOICING (*see* A35, 135); PILL-BOX [*i.e.* PILLBOX] (*see* A17, 28, 35; C830) — pp. 125–126 VLAMERTINGHE: PASSING THE CHATEAU, JULY 1917 (*see* A28, 35, 135); CONCERT PARTY: BUSSEBOOM (*see* A28, 35, 135) — p. 150 THE WATCHERS (*see* A28, 35, 135; C632).

B261 **THE MAD MASTERS** 1965

First edition:

THE MAD MASTERS | E.D.D.C. | INTERNATIONAL CHRISTIAN UNIVERSITY | THE TAMING OF THE SHREW | (1594) | by | William Shakespeare | May 27th and 28th, 1965 | THE KOSEINENKIN KAIKAN | TOKYO | – I –

16 pp. 12 × 8½ in.

White paper wrappers; printed in black and scarlet; edges cut flush; stapled.

Issued 27 May 1965; 500 copies printed. 50 yen.

P. 5 PROLOGUE, holograph facsimile; also issued separately as an offprint; reprinted in *Poems on Japan*, 1967 (*see* A165, 171).

B262 **COMMONWEALTH LITERATURE** 1965

First edition:

COMMONWEALTH LITERATURE | Unity and Diversity in a Common Culture | Extracts from | the proceedings of a Conference | held at Bodington Hall, Leeds | 9–12 September 1964 | under the auspices of the | University of Leeds | Edited by | JOHN PRESS | [*device*] | HEINEMANN

Small demy 8vo. 224 pp., the first 18 numbered i–xviii. 8½ × 5½ in. Black paper boards; lettered in gold down the spine with device;

edges trimmed, top brown; white end-papers. White dust-jacket printed in pale brown and black.

Published 6 September 1965; no record of the number of copies printed. £1. 5s.

Pp. 179–185 The Cultural Rôle of the University.

B263　CRITICS WHO HAVE INFLUENCED　1965
TASTE

First edition:

CRITICS WHO HAVE | INFLUENCED TASTE | (*From "The Times"*) | BEN JOHNSON JOHN DRYDEN [*names of critics in two columns of eleven further lines each*] | Preface by Elizabeth Bowen | Edited by A. P. Ryan | GEOFFREY BLES LIMITED | PUBLISHERS

Small demy 8vo. [2] , xii, 98 pp. $8\frac{1}{2} \times 5\frac{3}{8}$ in.

Khaki cloth boards; lettered in gold on spine, and on upper cover; edges trimmed, top dark pink; pale brown end-papers.

Published *c.* 16 November 1965; number of copies printed not ascertained. 16s.

Pp. 27–29 Leigh Hunt; first published in *The Times*, 30 May 1963 (*see* C3285).

B264　MUCH ADO ABOUT NOTHING –　1966
THEATRE PROGRAMME

First edition:

[*on an olive-yellow page in dark green*:] William Shakespeare MUCH ADO | ABOUT NOTHING [*illustration at right and above first two lines*] | THE MISFITS | THE DRAMA CLUB | The International Christian University | APRIL : 11TH, 12TH, 13TH | THE KOSEINENKIN-KAIKAN SMALL THEATRE

[ii], 20 pp. illus. (port.). $9\frac{1}{4} \times 9\frac{1}{4}$ in.

White paper wrappers; printed in black on upper and lower wrappers; edges cut flush; stapled and gummed.

Issued 11 April 1966; 500 copies printed. 50 yen.

Inserted PROLOGUE SPOKEN BY BENEDICK, holograph facsimile.

Selections from Clare:

JOHN CLARE | The Wood is Sweet | *Poems for young readers chosen by* | David Powell | *Introduced by* | Edmund Blunden | [*illustration*] | ILLUSTRATED BY JOHN O'CONNOR | THE BODLEY HEAD | LONDON

Small demy 8vo. 96 pp. illus. $8\frac{1}{2} \times 5\frac{1}{2}$ in.

Pale brown cloth boards; lettered in gold down the spine; edges trimmed, top royal blue; bright blue end-papers. White pictorial dust-jacket printed in black and royal blue.

Published 16 June 1966; 6000 copies printed. 18*s*.

There was a reprint of 3000 copies in 1971.

Pp. 9–12 Introduction.

B266   RENAISSANCE AND MODERN ESSAYS   1966

First edition:

RENAISSANCE | AND MODERN | ESSAYS | [*rule*] | Presented to Vivian de Sola Pinto | in celebration of his seventieth birthday | [*rule*] | EDITED BY G.R. HIBBARD | *with the assistance of* | George A. Panichas and Allan Rodway | [*device*] | Routledge and Kegan Paul | LONDON

Demy 8vo. viii, 236 pp. front., and 3 illus. $8\frac{5}{8} \times 5\frac{1}{2}$ in.

Black cloth boards; lettered in gold on spine; edges trimmed; white end-papers.

Published 7 July 1966; number of copies printed not disclosed. £2.

Pp. 95–99 Horace Walpole's Young Poet; on Thomas Pentycross. Also issued separately as an offprint (*see* A170).

B267   A SELECTION FROM THE POEMS   1966
OF ROBERT BLOOMFIELD

First edition:

A selection from the Poems | of | ROBERT BLOOMFIELD | *Edited by* J. L. CARR | *with a Foreword* by

EDMUND BLUNDEN | THE NORTHANTS CAM-
PAIGNER | 27 MILL DALE ROAD, KETTERING

Small crown 8vo. [ii], 26 pp. plate. $7\frac{1}{4} \times 4\frac{3}{8}$ in.

Mid-brown paper boards; printed in black on upper cover; edges
trimmed; pp. [i–ii and 25–26] form paste-down end-papers.

Published 1 September 1966; 25 copies printed. 5s.

P. 6 Foreword, holograph facsimile.

B268   THE SATURDAY BOOK   1966

First edition:

The Saturday Book | EDITED BY JOHN HADFIELD |
[*within a decorated circle in blue*:] 26 | HUTCHINSON
OF LONDON

Medium 8vo. 256 pp. (incl. front., and plates). front., illus., and
plates. 9×6 in.

Buff cloth boards; lettered in gold on spine on a scarlet panel with
two double and two ornamental rules, and at foot with device; and
on upper cover on a scarlet panel within a double and decorated
rule; edges trimmed; pale grey end-papers with decorations printed
in red.

Published October 1966; probably 10,000 copies printed. £2.

Pp. 10–14 RANDOM TRIBUTES TO BRITISH PAINTERS.

B269   KEITH DOUGLAS COLLECTED   1966
POEMS

First edition:

[*in open letters*:] Keith Douglas | [*in roman*:] COLLEC-
TED POEMS | EDITED BY | JOHN WALLER, G. S.
FRASER AND J. C. HALL | WITH AN INTRODUCTION
BY | EDMUND BLUNDEN | FABER AND FABER | 24
Russell Square | London

Demy 8vo. 168 pp. front. (port.), 5 illus., and plate. $8\frac{1}{2} \times 5\frac{3}{8}$ in.

Green cloth boards; lettered in gold on spine, with ornamental rule;
edges trimmed; white end-papers. White dust-jacket printed in
mauve, green, brown and black.

Published 10 November 1966; no record of the number of copies printed. £1.10s.

Pp. 17–20 Introduction.

B270   CHAMBERS'S ENCYCLOPAEDIA   1966

Revised edition:

CHAMBERS'S | ENCYCLOPAEDIA | *NEW REVISED EDITION* | Volume VI | FREE CHURCH-HEINE | [*device*] | PERGAMON PRESS | OXFORD · LONDON · EDINBURGH · NEW YORK · TORONTO | PARIS · BRAUNSCHWEIG · SYDNEY · WELLINGTON · TOKYO

Imperial 8vo. 15 vols. illus., and plates. $10\frac{5}{8} \times 7\frac{1}{2}$ in.

Dark crimson cloth boards; lettered in gold on spine with nine rules and rectangular boxes, monogram in gold within a double rule on upper cover; edges trimmed, top pale red; white end-papers.

Published 14 November 1966; 15,000 copies printed. £135 (£165 de luxe) the set of 15 volumes.

Lines 4–5 in Vols. 7–8 read: Volume VII | HEINRICH DER GLICKEZAERE-IZVOLSKY; Volume VIII | J-MALATESTA.

Vol. VI, pp. 749–750 Hardy, Thomas (1840–1928); Vol. VII, p. 309 Hunt, James Henry Leigh (1784–1859); Vol. VIII, pp. 318–319 Lamb, Charles (1775–1834). Blunden is noted as a contributor to Vol. XII (Rosk-Spah) in the contributors' list; his article has not been traced.

B271   THE LIFE OF A POET   1967

First edition:

THE LIFE OF A POET | *A Biographical Sketch of* | WILLIAM COLLINS | *by* | P. L. CARVER, Ph.D. | *With a Foreword by* | Edmund Blunden | LONDON | SIDGWICK & JACKSON

Demy 8vo. xiv, 210 pp. $8\frac{1}{2} \times 5\frac{1}{2}$ in.

Sky-blue paper boards; lettered in gold on spine with two double rules; edges trimmed, top blue; white end-papers. White dust-jacket printed in bright blue, green and black.

Published 23 February 1967; 3000 copies printed. £1.10s.

Pp. xi–xii Foreword — p. 181, footnote 5 quotation from a private letter to the author.

First edition:

THE UNENDING | VIGIL | A history of the Common-
wealth | War Graves Commission | 1917–1967 | *by* |
PHILIP LONGWORTH | *with an introduction by* | ED-
MUND BLUNDEN | [*eight line quotation*] | CONSTABLE
LONDON

Demy 8vo. xxvi, 254 pp. front. (col.) 40 plates, and end-paper maps.
8½ × 5½ in.

Dark green cloth boards; scarlet panel on spine and on upper cover;
lettered in gold and white within a gold rule on spine, and on upper
cover within a double gold rule; device in white within two gold
circles on upper cover; edges trimmed; white end-papers printed in
olive green.

Published 15 May 1967; 4000 copies printed. £2. 2s. 6d.

Pp. xvii–xxv Introduction. *See also* C3363.

[*title on p.* [1]:] LIFE, BE KIND | for solo or unison
voices | and piano | by | DANIEL PURCELL | Edited by
Percy Young | Words by | EDMUND BLUNDEN | with
the original words | adapted from Henry Carey | Price 1/6
net | [*within a rule*:] 20/273 [*outside rule*:] CHAPPELL
Made in England

Crown 4to. 8 pp. 10 × 7 in.

No wrappers; edges trimmed; unsewn, no staples.

Published 19 June 1967; 1000 copies printed. 1s. 6d.

P. [2] quotation from a letter to Percy Young on the poem, and
holograph facsimile of the poem — pp. 3–7 text in music.

First edition:

[*each line between a rule in olive green*:] MUSIC AND
FINE ARTS | IN HONG KONG 1967 | PRESENTED BY
THE URBAN COUNCIL | TO CELEBRATE THE 5TH

ANNIVERSARY | OF THE OPENING OF THE CITY HALL | [*two lines in Chinese*] | [*geometrical design in olive green*] | [*line in Chinese*] | 14TH JULY TO 13TH AUGUST, 1967

104 pp. illus. 8 X 8 in.

White paper wrappers; printed in bright green and orange in a geometrical design; edges cut flush; gummed.

Published July 1967; 7500 copies printed. HK$2.50.

Five thousand copies were for sale; the balance of 2500 were complimentary copies.

P. [5] ON THE FIFTH ANNIVERSARY OF THE OPENING OF THE CITY HALL, HONG KONG, holograph facsimile; p. [4] Chinese translation by Lo King Man and Cheung Man Yee.

The poem also appeared on p. [1] of the [12] pp. brochure issued by the City Hall in July 1967.

B274   **AUTHORS TAKE SIDES ON**   1967
                        VIETNAM

First edition:

[*vertical rule towards left margin*] AUTHORS | TAKE SIDES ON VIETNAM | Two questions on the war in Vietnam | answered by the authors of several nations | EDITED BY | CECIL WOOLF AND JOHN BAGGULEY | [*device*] | PETER OWEN · LONDON

Demy 8vo. [iv], 236 pp. 8½ X 5⅜ in.

Black cloth boards; lettered in silver down the spine; edges trimmed; pp. [i–iv] and 233–236 form end-papers. White dust-jacket printed in black and scarlet.

Published *c.* 14 September 1967; over 2000 copies printed. £1.17*s.* 6*d.*

P. 19 contribution in the section Against the War. *See also Authors Take Sides on the Spanish War* (B80).

B275   **ONE HUNDRED AND ONE**   1967
                   CHINESE POEMS

First edition:

ONE HUNDRED | AND ONE | CHINESE POEMS | *With*

English Translations and Preface | *by* | SHIH SHUN LIU |
[*illustration*] | INTRODUCTORY BY | EDMUND BLUN-
DEN | FOREWORD BY | JOHN CAIRNCROSS | with
seven additional translations

Small crown 8vo. xxxviii, 174 pp. $7\frac{3}{8} \times 4\frac{7}{8}$ in.

Buff cloth boards; lettered in pale blue down the spine, with device
at foot; edges trimmed; white end-papers. Cream dust-jacket printed
in mauve and maroon.

Published 13 October 1967 in the *UNESCO Collection of Repre-
sentative Works, Chinese Series*; 1500 copies printed. HK$25
(£1.17s. 6d.).

Published by Hong Kong University Press. There was a reprint (with
corrections) of 2000 copies in May 1968 in pale blue cloth boards,
lettered in navy-blue.

Pp. [vi–vii] Introductory, holograph facsimile.

B276   **KEATS HOUSE, ROME**   **1967**

First edition:

[*title at head of p.* [1] : *within a double rule, thick, thin,
an ornamental border, and a double rule*:] Keats House,
Rome

[4] pp. illus. 8 × 5 in.

No wrappers; edges trimmed.

Issued 6 November 1967; 5000–5500 copies printed. Not for sale.

The poem was written specially for the Keats-Shelley Memorial
House Appeal. *See also* letter to *The Times*, 6 November 1967, p. 9,
and the earlier appeal (E*f*8, 10). Reference is made to the appeal in
the *Keats-Shelley Memorial Association Bulletin*, Vol. 18 (1967), p.
iv, and Vol. 19 (1968), p. iv. Blunden was president of the Association from 1968–1972.

P. [1] KEATS HOUSE, ROME, holograph facsimile.

B277   **TWELVE POEMS**   **1968**

a. First edition:

TWELVE POEMS | With a dedicatory poem by | EDMUND
BLUNDEN | & illustrations by Rigby Graham | R. H.
MOTTRAM | Daedalus Press 1968

Small royal 8vo. [28] pp. illus. $9\frac{1}{2} \times 6$ in.

Yellowish-grey pictorial paper wrappers; lettered in gold on upper wrapper; edges trimmed; sewn in white thread.

Published 1 January 1968; 312 copies printed. 12s. 6d.

Twelve lettered copies were bound by Trevor Hickman (see B277b).

P. [9] R. H. MOTTRAM, holograph facsimile.

b. *First edition — limited issue. 1968*:

[*title and imprint as above*]

Small royal 8vo. [28] pp. illus. $9\frac{1}{2}$ × 6 in.

Dull green cloth boards; upper cover as B 277a; edges trimmed; pale mustard-yellow end-papers.

Issued 1 January 1968; 12 copies bound. Not for sale.

Copies signed by the author and the artist, and lettered A–L.

B278   LIVING HISTORY: 1914   1968

First edition:

Living History: | 1914 | EDITED BY | JOHN CANNING | [*device*] | ODHAMS BOOKS LIMITED | LONG ACRE, LONDON, W.C. 2

Demy 8vo. 272 pp. 32 plates. $8\frac{3}{4}$ × $5\frac{3}{4}$ in.

Bright yellow paper boards; lettered in maroon on spine; edges trimmed; white pictorial end-papers printed in blue and black. White pictorial dust-jacket printed in kakhi, orange and black.

Published February 1968; number of copies printed not ascertained. £1.10s.

Pp. 7–9 Introduction.

B279   GARLAND   1968

First edition:

[*in garnet-brown*:] Garland | [*in black*:] A LITTLE AN-THOLOGY OF | POETRY AND ENGRAVINGS | THE GOLDEN HEAD PRESS | CAMBRIDGE

Medium 8vo. 24 pp. 6 illus. $9\frac{5}{8}$ × $5\frac{1}{2}$ in.

White stiff paper wrappers; edges cut flush; sewn. Bright green dust-jacket printed in black.

Published 24 May 1968; 310 copies printed. £1. 5s.

The number of copies printed include 35 for review and copyright purposes; 275 were for sale. Edited by Francis Warner.

P. 12 ANCRE SUNSHINE, dated 3 September 1966.

B280   **PROMISE OF GREATNESS**   **1968**

First edition:

PROMISE | OF GREATNESS | [*ornamental rule*] | THE WAR OF 1914–1918 | Edited by George A. Panichas | Foreword by Sir Herbert Read | THE JOHN DAY COMPANY | NEW YORK

Small royal 8vo. xxxvi, 572 pp. map. 9 × 6 in.

Kakhi cloth boards; lettered in gold on spine, and upper cover; edges trimmed; mustard-yellow end-papers. White dust-jacket printed in kakhi, scarlet and black.

Published November 1968; number of copies printed not ascertained. $12.

Published in commemoration of the fiftieth anniversary of the Armistice, 11 November 1918.

Pp. 24–37 Infantryman Passes By.

B281   **STUDIES IN THE ARTS**   **1968**

First edition:

Studies in the Arts | [*double rule, thick, thin*] | PROCEEDINGS OF | THE ST. PETER'S COLLEGE | LITERARY SOCIETY | EDITED BY | FRANCIS WARNER | *Fellow and Tutor of St. Peter's College, Oxford* | OXFORD | BASIL BLACKWELL · 1968

Medium 8vo. [2], viii, 182 pp. 3 plates. $8\frac{1}{4} \times 5\frac{1}{2}$ in.

Apple green cloth boards; lettered in gold down the spine, and numbered on lower cover; edges trimmed; white end-papers. Grey dust-jacket printed in apple green and black.

Published 3 December 1968; 2000 copies printed. £1.15s.

Pp. 1–9 The Other Coleridges, on Coleridge's relations.

First edition:

RUTH PITTER : | HOMAGE TO A POET | Edited by
Arthur Russell | With an introduction | by | David Cecil |
[*illustration*] | rapp + whiting

Demy 8vo. 128 pp. port. $8\frac{1}{2} \times 5\frac{1}{2}$ in.

Blue and white mottled paper boards; lettered in gold down the
spine, with a triple rule at head and foot and circular device, and on
upper cover; edges trimmed; white end-papers. Pale blue dust-jacket
printed in darker blue and black.

Published September 1969; number of copies printed not ascertained. £1.15s.

P. 11 Two Blessings, the first from Blunden, the second from
Andrew Young.

B283   SEIGFRIED SASSOON :   1969
     A MEMORIAL EXHIBITION

First edition:

SIEGFRIED SASSOON: | A MEMORIAL EXHIBITION
| *Catalogue compiled by* | DAVID FARMER | *With an
introductory note by* | EDMUND BLUNDEN | THE
ACADEMIC CENTER LIBRARY | *September–December
1969* | HUMANITIES RESEARCH CENTER • THE UNI-
VERSITY OF TEXAS AT AUSTIN [*initials* SS, *and also
down centre of page*]

Royal 8vo. 72 pp. 17 illus. $9\frac{3}{4} \times 6\frac{3}{8}$ in.

White paper wrappers; printed in mid-brown and black; edges cut
flush; gummed.

Published 18 September 1969; 2100 copies printed.

Pp. [9–10] Introduction; first published in *The Observer*, 3 September 1967 (*see* C3364).

B283.1 NIHON NO ASU YOBU CHIKARA 1969

First edition:

[*title on upper wrapper in Japanese*: *in black*:] Nihon no
asu yobu chikara | [*in red and black*:] Sen-kyūhyaku-

rokujū-kyū-nen jūni-gatsu Shakai Kyōiku Kyōkai hakkō
Nukizuri

Foolscap 8vo. 14 pp. illus. 7 × 4¼ in.

White paper wrappers; printed as above; edges cut flush; stapled.

Published December 1969; number of copies printed not ascertained.

The Power which calls Japan's Tomorrow, published by the Association of Social Education.

P. 2 FOR THE EDUCATION INSTITUTE OF AICHI PREFECTURE, holograph facsimile (*see* A171) — p. 3 untitled verse (In Goro Katayama's page), holograph facsimile — p. 5 Mr. Blunden's Message: [1] Message for the Young Japanese, [2] Message for Old Pupils in Japan, dated 3 August 1968 — pp. 3, 9, 13 notes, holograph facsimiles; p. 1 Japanese translation of Professor Blunden's Message, by Gorō Katayama.

B284   **THE SOLITARY SONG**   **1970**

First edition:

WILLIAM WORDSWORTH | The Solitary | Song | *Poems for young readers chosen* | *and introduced by* | Edmund Blunden | [*illustration*] | ILLUSTRATED BY | David Gentleman | THE BODLEY HEAD | LONDON SYDNEY | TORONTO

Small demy 8vo. 96 pp. 28 illus. 8½ × 5½ in.

Sage-green cloth boards; lettered in gold down the spine with an ornament; edges trimmed, top mustard-yellow; mustard-yellow endpapers. White pictorial dust-jacket printed in black and apple green.

Published 7 May 1970; 7500 copies printed. 90*p*.

Pp. 5-6 About William Wordsworth, signed E.B. — 7-9 Introduction.

B285   **POEMS OF WRENNE JARMAN**   **1970**

First edition:

POEMS OF | WRENNE | JARMAN | With a Foreword by Edmund Blunden | HILARY PRESS | 12 Blithfield Street, London, W.8 | 1970

Small demy 8vo. 176 pp. port. 8½ × 5⅝ in.

Putty cloth boards; lettered in black down the spine; edges trimmed;

white end-papers. White pictorial dust-jacket printed in black and mauve.

Published 15 November 1970; 300 copies printed. £1.10s.

Pp. 13–14 Foreword; first published in the *Aylesford Review*, Winter 1960/61; and *Poetry Review*, July/September 1961 (*see* C3248). The Foreword first appeared as a review in a prospectus for *Nymph in Thy Orisons*, by Wrenne Jarman and published by St Albert's Press, Aylesford, Kent in November 1960.

B286   THE DICTIONARY OF   1971
                 NATIONAL BIOGRAPHY

First edition:

THE | DICTIONARY | OF | NATIONAL BIOGRAPHY | [*double rule, thick, thin*] | 1951–1960 | EDITED BY | E. T. WILLIAMS | AND | HELEN M. PALMER | With an Index covering the years 1901–1960 | in one alphabetical series | OXFORD UNIVERSITY PRESS | 1971

Small royal 8vo. [2], xxvi, 1152 pp. $9\frac{3}{8} \times 6$ in.

Navy-blue cloth boards; lettered in gold on spine with device and a rule at head and foot; edges trimmed; white end-papers. Cream dust-jacket printed in scarlet and black.

Published June 1971; 8012 copies printed. £9.50.

There was a reprint of 4000 copies in 1973.

Pp. 916–917 Squire, Sir John Collings (1884–1958).

B287   WAYSIDE SONNETS   1971

First edition:

Wayside Sonnets | *1750–1850* | [*illustration*] | AN ANTHOLOGY GATHERED BY | *Edmund Blunden* | AND | *Bernard Mellor* | HONG KONG UNIVERSITY PRESS

Small crown 8vo. xxii, 162 pp. $7\frac{3}{8} \times 4\frac{7}{8}$ in.

Cobalt blue cloth boards; lettered in gold across and down the spine with device at foot; edges trimmed; pale blue end-papers. White dust-jacket printed in pale blue and black.

Published 4 November 1971; 1500 copies printed. HK$20 (£1.75).

Pp. [vii]–viii Preface by Blunden and Bernard Mellor — pp. [111]–148 Commentary for which the Editors were jointly responsible.

B288   **SINGING IN THE STREETS**   1972

First edition:

Singing in the Streets | POEMS | FOR | CHRISTMAS | [*autograph facsimile*:] Leonard Clark | London | Dennis Dobson

Foolscap 8vo. [iv] , 44 pp. 6 × 4⅜ in.

Maroon paper boards; lettered in silver down the spine; edges trimmed; lower end-papers, pp. [i–iv] form upper end-papers. White dust-jacket printed in mauve.

Published 30 November 1972; *c*. 3000 copies printed. 60*p*.

P. 5 Introduction.

B289   **LET THE POET CHOOSE**   1973

First edition:

[*in olive green*:] *Let the* | *Poet Choose* | edited by | JAMES GIBSON | [*device*] | HARRAP LONDON

Small demy 8vo. 192 pp. 8½ × 5⅜ in.

Bright orange paper boards; lettered in grey down the spine; edges trimmed; white end-papers. White dust-jacket printed in brown and pale orange.

Published 14 May 1973; number of copies printed not disclosed. £1.70.

Also issued in dark brown stiff paper wrappers printed in pale orange and white with all the authors' signatures in pale orange.

P. 37 Note by Blunden on his choice of poems − pp. 37–39 'CAN YOU REMEMBER?' (*see* A64, 68, 108, 135; C1501) − GOD'S TIME (*see* A77, 135; C1999).

B290   **TRIBUTE TO WALTER DE LA MARE**   1974

First edition:

TRIBUTE | TO | WALTER | DE LA MARE | BY | EDMUND BLUNDEN | AND | LEONARD CLARK | ENITHARMON PRESS · LONDON | 1974

[x], 14 pp. 8⅜ × 5⅞ in.

White stiff paper wrappers; cream pages; edges cut flush; pp. [i–ii] and [13–14] form paste-down end-papers; sewn. White pictorial dust-jacket printed in brown.

Published 15 November 1974; 225 copies printed. £2.25.

Centenary tribute.

Pp. 1–2 on Walter de la Mare [*formerly* Long Friendships. 3]; first published in *Books*, April/May 1956 (*see* C3171).

B291   EDMUND BLUNDEN : A TRIBUTE   1974
                FROM JAPAN

First edition:

EDMUND BLUNDEN | A TRIBUTE FROM JAPAN | Edited by | MASAO HIRAI | and | PETER MILWARD | KENKYUSHA | TOKYO

Demy 8vo. xiv, 214 pp., front. (port.), and 2 plates. $8\frac{1}{4} \times 5\frac{5}{8}$ in.

Reddish-brown cloth boards; lettered in gold down the spine; edges trimmed; brown end-papers. White dust-jacket printed in blue and black.

Published 30 November 1974; 1000 copies printed. 2500 yen.

P. 29 untitled poem (At Tsuruya in Kobe,) — pp. 31–32 *et passim* quoted speech and notes — p. 48 CHRISTMAS EVE, 1959 (*see* A156); *see also* p. 50 for corrections — p. 71 untitled poem ("The Last of the Fancy!" In Sendai!) — pp. 74, 176 WILLIAM ADAMS AT ITO (*later* TO THE CITIZENS OF ITO) (*see* A85; B189; C2506) — pp. 91–92 NEARING YOKOHAMA, 14 [*i.e.* 15] AUGUST 1960 (*see* A156) — p. 169 LOOKING EASTWARD (*formerly* A SONG) (*see* A64, 68; C1472) — pp. 170–171 THE DAIMYO'S POND (*see* A18, 20, 26, 35; B23; C480); *see also* pp. 108–109 for quoted revisions — p. 171 BUILDING THE LIBRARY, TOKYO UNIVERSITY (*formerly* BUILDING THE LIBRARY, NIGHT SCENE, TOKYO UNIVERSITY) (*see* A26, 31, 35; C604) — pp. 172–173 THE AUTHOR'S LAST WORDS TO HIS STUDENTS (*see* A26, 31, 35, 108, 135; D6, 20) — p. 173 IN THE MARGIN (*see* A67–8, 135; B84; C1677) — pp. 173–174 TO THE NEW JAPAN (*formerly* WALKING IN TOKYO, 1948) (*see* A89, 174) — pp. 174–175 THE STONE GARDEN (KYOTO) (*see* A156, 169; C3291; D13) — p. 175 VOICE OF KYOTO (*see* A156, 169) — pp. 176–177 MATSUSHIMA (*see* A86, 97; C2563; D8) — pp. 177–178 FOR TOKYO JOSHI DAIGAKU (*formerly* COLLEGE SONG) (*see* A98, 171; C2520) — pp. 178–179 JAPAN BEAUTIFUL (*see* A156; C3251; D38) — pp. 180–183 Fourth Visit: or, Japan up-to-date; first published in *Albion*, Tokyo, 1 August 1959 (*see* C3229) — pp. 184–187 A Fifth Visit to Japan — pp. 188–192 [On] Seeing More of Japan; *see also* D39.

B292   [GREETINGS FOR NEVILLE   1974
             ROGERS, 1954]

First edition:

[*title on p.* [2]:] EDMUND BLUNDEN | (1896–1974) |
Greetings for Neville Rogers, 1954 | *Reproduced in*
affectionate commemoration by permission of Mrs.
Blunden

[4] pp. 5½ × 4 in.

No wrappers; edges trimmed.

Issued December 1974; 300 copies printed. Not for sale.

Privately printed by the Favil Press of Kensington for Neville Rogers
as a Christmas card.

P. [1] [GREETINGS FOR NEVILLE ROGERS, 1954], holograph
facsimile within an ornamental frame.

B293   THE LIBRARY OF THE LATE   1975
             SIEGFRIED SASSOON

First edition:

The Library of | the late | Siegfried Sassoon | Comprising
a large collection of his own | original manuscripts and
printed books, | together with books (many presentation
| copies), manuscripts and autograph letters | from other
important writers | The Property of GEORGE SASSOON,
Esq. | *which will be sold at Auction by* | CHRISTIE,
MANSON & WOODS LTD. | [*twelve lines*] | On Wednes-
day, June 4, 1975 | [*five lines and three rules*]

100 pp. front., and 6 plates. 9½ × 7⅛ in.

Dull rose pink paper wrappers; printed in black; edges cut flush;
gummed.

Published *c.* 16 May 1975; *c.* 1300 copies printed. 30*p.*

P. 11, Item 40 untitled dedication ('Of old, this sweet domestic
touch); p. 13, Item 49 untitled verse ('Tis said, & I believe the
Tale,); p. 16, Item 63 quotation from letter dated 6 February 1942.
See also Items 29–69, 159, 356–364.

C.

CONTRIBUTIONS TO PERIODICALS AND NEWSPAPERS

All articles are signed: Edmund Blunden, unless stated otherwise.

Reference should be made to the General Index for place of publication.

The following abbreviation is used:

TLS, The Times Literary Supplement, London

1913

C1   "THE FIRST WINTER." *The Blue*, February 1913, Vol. 40, No. 4, p. 86. A Sonnet. Signed E.C.B.

C2   JOY AND GRIEF. *The Blue*, April 1913, Vol. 40, No. 6, p. 143. Signed ὀλολυγὰν [Any Loud Cry].
Reprinted (revised): *Poems*, 1914.

C3   "SUMMER PEACE." *The Blue*, May 1913, Vol. 40, No. 7, p. 173. Unsigned.
Reprinted (revised): *Poems*, 1914.

C4   THE COOL OF THE DAY. *The Blue*, June 1913, Vol. 40, No. 8, pp. 201-202. Unsigned.
Reprinted (revised): *Poems*, 1914.

C5   A SUMMER IDYLL. *The Blue*, July 1913, Vol. 40, No. 9, pp. 224-225. Unsigned.
Reprinted (revised): *Poems*, 1914.

C6   THE RUNNERS. *The Blue*, November 1913, Vol. 41, No. 2, pp. 34-35. Signed γείτων [A Neighbour].
Reprinted (revised): *Poems*, 1914.

C7   THE DESERTED MILL. *The Blue*, December 1913, Vol. 41, No. 3, p. 63. Signed B.
Reprinted: *Poems*, 1914.

1914

C8   KESTREL FARM, 1796. *The Blue*, March 1914, Vol. 41, No. 5, pp. 122-124. Signed B.
Reprinted (revised): *Poems*, 1914.

C9   SONNET [*later* JANUARY EVENING, SUSSEX, 1914]. *The Blue*, June 1914, Vol. 41, No. 8, p. 207. Signed B.
Reprinted: *Poems*, 1914.

C10   SUNDOWN. *The Blue*, July 1914, Vol. 41, No. 9, p. 233. Signed B.
Reprinted: *Poems*, 1914.

C11   Editorial. *The Blue*, October 1914, Vol. 42, No. 1, pp. 9-10. Unsigned. On assuming the editorship.

1915

C12   Delightes of the Schollar. *The Blue*, February 1915, Vol. 42, No. 4, pp. 94-97. Unsigned.

C13   COATS OF ARMS. *The Blue*, May 1915, Vol. 42, No. 7, p. 164. Unsigned.

Reprinted: *Pastorals*, 1916.

C14   A POEM DREAMED. *The Blue*, June 1915, Vol. 42, No. 8, p. 187. Unsigned.

Reprinted: *Pastorals*, 1916.

C15   Editorial. *The Blue*, July 1915, Vol. 42, No. 9, pp. 205-206. Unsigned. On his year's editorship, October 1914-July 1915.

1916

C16   LATE AUTUMN. *The Blue*, November 1916, Vol. 44, No. 2, p. 28. Unsigned.

First published: *Poems*, 1914.

C17   THE DANCER IN THRALL (THIEPVAL WOOD.). *The Blue*, December 1916, Vol. 44, No. 3, p. 52. Signed E. C. Blunden.

1917

C18   THE COOK'S STORY, OR NEVER NO MORE! *The Blue*, March 1917, Vol. 44, No. 5, pp. 91-93. Signed 1106 Pte. Alf Maconochie (E.C.B.).

C19   "The Feast of Five." *The Blue*, July 1917, Vol. 44, No. 8, pp. 162-163. Letter noted as from E. C. Blunden on the five Old Blues in the 11th Royal Sussex Regiment, B.E.F. France.

C20   A Tribute from the Field. *The Blue*, October 1917, Vol. 45, No. 1, pp. 10-11. Letter, signed E.B., on the death of W.J. Collyer and E. W. Tice. *See also* A17, 28, 35, 135.

C21   PHANTASIES [*later* CLARE'S GHOST]. *The Blue*, October 1917, Vol. 45, No. 1, p. 12. Signed E.B.

Reprinted: *The Waggoner*, 1920; *The Poems*, 1930; *Edmund Blunden: A Selection of his Poetry and Prose*, 1950; *Poems of Many Years*, 1957; and *The Midnight Skaters*, [1968].

1919

C22   Trees and Birds under Fire. *The Observer*, 12 January 1919, p. 3. Letter, signed E. Blunden, Lt., on the Ypres salient. *See also* letters from W. P. K. Neale in the issue of 5 January, p. 5, and Sherwood Forester in that of 19 January, p. 3.

C23   THE CONDEMNATION (HAMEL MILL). *Blighty*, 12 February 1919, Vol. 3, No. 138, p. 10. Signed Lieut. E. C. Blunden.

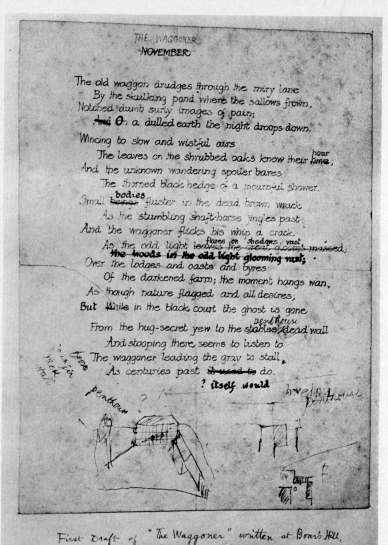

11. First draft of 'The Waggoner'

C24   Epicedium. *The Blue*, March 1919, Vol. 46, No. 3, pp. 67-68. Signed E.B. Obituary of A. R. Creese.

C25   GAVOTTE. *The Graphic*, 29 March 1919, Vol. 99, No. 2574, p. 422. Signed E. Blunden.

C26   A COUNTRY GOD. *The Owl*, October 1919, No. 2, pp. 22-23. Dated On leaving France, Feb. 25th, 1918.

Reprinted (revised): *The Waggoner*, 1920; *The Augustan Books*, [1925]; *The Poems*, 1930; and *Poems of Many Years*, 1957.

C27   Dr. Upcott and Christ's Hospital. *The Blue*, November 1919, Vol. 47, No. 1, pp. 8-10. Signed B. On the retirement of the Headmaster of Christ's Hospital.

C28   THE VETERAN. *The Nation*, 1 November 1919, p. 148.

Reprinted: *The Waggoner*, 1920; *The Poems*, 1930; *Edmund Blunden: A Selection of his Poetry and Prose*, 1950; and *Poems of Many Years*, 1957.

C29   THE PIKE. *Coterie*, December 1919, No. 3, pp. 15-16. Signed E. C. Blunden.

Reprinted (revised): *The Waggoner*, 1920; *The Augustan Books* [1925]; *The Poems*, 1930; *Poems of Many Years*, 1957; and *The Midnight Skaters*, [1968].

C30   AN EVENSONG [*later* SHEEPBELLS]. *Coterie*, December 1919, No. 3, pp. 16-17. Signed E. C. Blunden, dated Trenches, 1916.

Reprinted (revised): *The Waggoner*, 1920; *The Poems*, 1930; and *Poems of Many Years*, 1957.

C31   THE UNCHANGEABLE. *Coterie*, December 1919, No. 3, p. 17. Signed E. C. Blunden, Looking out from Larch Wood Tunnels on the railway cutting.

Reprinted (revised): *The Waggoner*, 1920; *The Poems*, 1930; and *Poems of Many Years*, 1957.

C32   A WATERPIECE. *Coterie*, December 1919, No. 3, p. 18. Signed E. C. Blunden.

Reprinted: *The Waggoner*, 1920; *The Poems*, 1930; and *Poems of Many Years*, 1957.

1920

C33   THE WAGGONER. *The Nation*, 3 January 1920, p. 478.

Reprinted: *The Waggoner*, 1920; *The Augustan Books*, [1925]; *The Poems*, 1930; *The Face of England*, 1932; *Poems of Many Years*, 1957; and *The Midnight Skaters*, [1968].

C34   ESTRANGEMENT [*later* THE ESTRANGEMENT]. *Voices*, February 1920, Vol. 3, No. 1, p. 5.

Reprinted (revised): *The Waggoner*, 1920; and *The Poems*, 1930.

C35   John Clare. *The Athenaeum*, 5 March 1920, pp. 297–299. Review article on *Poems by John Clare*, edited with an introduction by A. Symons. *See also* C39.

C36   WILDERNESS [*dedication*: For Joy Blunden]. *The Athenauem*, 12 March 1920, p. 332.

Reprinted: *The Waggoner*, 1920; and *The Poems*, 1930.

C37   ALMSWOMEN. *The Nation*, 13 March 1920, p. 808.

Reprinted (revised): *London Mercury*, March 1920, Vol. 1, No. 5, pp. 525–526; *The Waggoner*, 1920; *The Augustan Books*, [1925]; *The Poems*, 1930; *The Face of England*, 1932; *Poems of Many Years*, 1957; and *The Midnight Skaters*, [1968].

This poem was translated into Latin hexameter verse and recited by Edwin Slade on Christ's Hospital Speech Day, 1 July 1922 when it was awarded the Dr Richard's Prize Composition. Though the event was recorded in the Speech Day Programme and in *The Blue*, July 1922, p. 258, the Latin version does not appear to have been published.

C38   Ernest Hartley Coleridge. *The Athenaeum*, 19 March 1920, p. 370. Signed E.B. *See also* brief obituary in the issue of 12 March, p. 345.

C39   John Clare. *The Athenaeum*, 19 March 1920, pp. 379–380. Letter in reply to one by Alan Porter in the issue of 12 March, pp. 349–350. *See also* C35.

C40   New Discoveries about John Clare: The Helpston Poet ... *Peterborough Citizen*, 23 March 1920, p. 5. *See also* More Clare Discoveries at Peterborough, by Alan Porter in the issue of 30 March, p. 3.

C41   BROCELIANDE. *Voices*, April 1920, Vol. 3, No. 3, p. 102.

C42   Unpublished Writings of John Clare. *The Athenaeum*, 9 April 1920, pp. 470–471.

C43   CHANGING MOON. *Oxford Outlook*, May 1920, Vol. 2, No. 7, p. 194.

Reprinted: *The Waggoner*, 1920; and *The Poems*, 1930.

C44   CHINESE POND. *The Athenaeum*, 7 May 1920, p. 598.

Reprinted: *The Waggoner*, 1920.

C45   NOVEMBER MORNING. *To-day*, June 1920, Vol. 7, No. 40, p. 138.

Reprinted (revised): *The Shepherd*, 1922; *The Augustan Books*, [1925]; *The Poems*, 1930; and *Poems of Many Years*, 1957.

C46   SHEET LIGHTNING. *Voices*, June 1920, Vol. 3, No. 5/6, pp. 171–172.

Reprinted: *Oxford Poetry*, 1920; *The Shepherd*, 1922; *The Poems*, 1930; and *Poems of Many Years*, 1957.

C47 The Poetry of Leigh Hunt. *The Athenaeum*, 4 June 1920, pp. 727–729. Signed E. B.

C48 FOREFATHERS. *The Nation*, 12 June 1920, p. 343.

Reprinted: *Oxford Poetry*, 1920; *The Shepherd*, 1922; *The Augustan Books*, [1925]; *The Poems*, 1930; *Edmund Blunden: A Selection of His Poetry and Prose*, 1950; *Poems of Many Years*, 1957; and *The Midnight Skaters*, [1968].

C49 The Golden Answer. *The Nation*, 12 June 1920, pp. 346, 348. Review of *Enslaved, and Other Poems*, by John Masefield. Signed E. B.

C50 SICK-BED. *The Athenaeum*, 18 June 1920, p. 791.

Reprinted: *The Waggoner*, 1920; and *The Poems*, 1930.

C51 GLEANING. *London Mercury*, July 1920, Vol. 2, No. 9, pp. 263–264.

Reprinted (revised): *The Shepherd*, 1922; *The Augustan Books*, [1925]; *The Poems*, 1930; and *Poems of Many Years*, 1957.

C52 Manuscripts of John Clare. *London Mercury*, July 1920, Vol. 2, No. 9, pp. 316–326. On the collection in the Peterborough Museum.

C53 BLINDFOLD. *To-day*, July 1920, Vol. 7, No. 41, p. 169.

Reprinted (revised): *To Nature*, [1923]; and *The Augustan Books*, [1925].

C54 MOLECATCHER [*later* MOLE CATCHER]. *The Athenaeum*, 9 July 1920, p. 40.

Reprinted: *The Shepherd*, 1922; *The Poems*, 1930; *Poems of Many Years*, 1957; and *The Midnight Skaters*, [1968].

C55 [Paragraph commencing:] Many will welcome the re-opening of the Tate Gallery. *The Athenaeum*, 16 July 1920, p. 76. Unsigned.

C56 [Review of] *War Diary of the Fifth Seaforth Highlanders*, by Sullivan. *The Athenaeum*, 16 July 1920, p. 76. Unsigned.

C57 Our Library Table. *The Athenaeum*, 16 July 1920, p. 79. Review of *Burford Past and Present*, by M. Sturge Gretton; *Who Was Who, 1879–1916*; *The Great War, 1914–1918*, by C. R. L. Fletcher; and *Evening Memories*, by William O'Brien. Unsigned.

C58 [Paragraph commencing:] The first number of *Shama'a*, a quarterly published at Madras. *The Athenaeum*, 16 July 1920, p. 82. Unsigned.

C59 [Paragraph commencing:] A passage in Lamb's letters to Coleridge. *The Athenaeum*, 16 July 1920, p. 83. Unsigned.

C60 [Paragraph commencing:] The sexcentenary of the death of Dante. *The Athenaeum*, 16 July 1920, p. 85. Unsigned.

C61   [Review of] *Books in Manuscript*, by Falconer Madan. *The Athenaeum*, 23 July 1920, p. 108. Unsigned.

C62   [Review of] *The Literature of the Restoration: [Catalogue]*, by P. J. Dobell. *The Athenaeum*, 23 July 1920, p. 110. Unsigned.

C63   [Review of] *A Scavenger in France*, by William Bell. *The Athenaeum*, 23 July 1920, p. 112. Unsigned.

C64   [Paragraphs commencing:] The following is another entry in the catalogue: "History of Pickwick . . ."; Dickens immediately replied:; But the question. *The Athenaeum*, 23 July 1920, p. 115. Unsigned.

C65   [Review of] *Selections from the 'Historia Rerum Anglicarum' of William of Newburgh*, by Charles Johnson. *The Athenaeum*, 30 July 1920, p. 143. Unsigned.

C66   [Paragraph commencing:] The *Bodleian Quarterly Record*. *The Athenaeum*, 30 July 1920, p. 144. Unsigned.

C67   [Review of] *Anniversaries, and Other Poems*, by Leonard Huxley. *The Athenaeum*, 30 July 1920, p. 145. Unsigned.

C68   [Paragraph commencing:] There is, says the *Revue Bleue*, a Defoe fashion. *The Athenaeum*, 30 July 1920, p. 149. Unsigned.

C69   CLOUDY JUNE. *To-day*, August 1920, Vol. 7, No. 42, p. 214.

       Reprinted: *The Shepherd*, 1922; *The Poems*, 1930, *Poems of Many Years*, 1957; and *The Midnight Skaters*, [1968].

C70   A Proud Title. *The Athenaeum*, 6 August 1920, p. 170. Review of *The Cream of Curiosity*, by Reginald L. Hine. Unsigned.

C71   [Paragraph commencing:] Reims and her Cathedral. *The Athenaeum*, 6 August 1920, p. 171. Unsigned.

C72   [Review of] *Pioneers of Progress: Women*, series on Florence Nightingale, Dorothea Beale and Elsie Inglis. *The Athenaeum*, 6 August 1920, p. 175. Unsigned.

C73   [Review of] *Verd Antique: Poems*, by William Force Stead. *The Athenaeum*, 6 August 1920, p. 177. Unsigned.

C74   [Review of] *In Wild Rhodesia*, by Henry and Walter E. Masters. *The Athenaeum*, 6 August 1920, p. 177. Unsigned.

C75   Literary Gossip [paragraphs 8-11]. *The Athenaeum*, 6 August 1920, p. 181. Unsigned.

C76   [Paragraph commencing:] The *New Republic* . . . prints an article on "Wilfrid Blunt". *The Athenaeum*, 13 August 1920, p. 202. Unsigned.

C77   The Land Worker. *The Athenaeum*, 13 August 1920, p. 207. Review of *A History of the English Agricultural Labourer, 1870-1920*, by F. E. Green. Unsigned.

C78   [Review of] *Poems*, by G. H. Luce. *The Athenaeum*, 13 August 1920, p. 211. Unsigned.

C79   [Review of] *Universal Art* series published by Chapman and Hall. *The Athenaeum*, 13 August 1920, p. 213. Unsigned.

C80   Literary Gossip [paragraphs 1-2, 4, 7-13]. *The Athenaeum*, 13 August 1920, p. 214. Unsigned.

C81   [Paragraph commencing:] The Department of Scientific and Industrial Research. *The Athenaeum*, 13 August 1920, p. 216. Unsigned.

C82   APRIL BYEWAY. *The Nation*, 14 August 1920, p. 613.
       Reprinted: *A Queen's College Miscellany*, 1921; *The Shepherd*, 1922; and *The Poems*, 1930.

C83   [Review of] *The Royal Exchange*, by A. E. W. Mason. *The Athenaeum*, 20 August 1920, p. 235. Unsigned.

C84   [Review of] *The Charm of Oxford*, by J. Wells. *The Athenaeum*, 20 August 1920, p. 242. Unsigned.

C85   [Review of] *The Chapbook*, June-July 1920. *The Athenaeum*, 20 August 1920, p. 242. Unsigned.

C86   [Paragraph commencing:] It is expected . . . the first award will be made of the J. Tait Black memorial prizes. *The Athenaeum*, 20 August 1920, p. 243. Unsigned.

C87   Literary Gossip. *The Athenaeum*, 20 August 1920, p. 245. Unsigned.

C88   [Paragraph commencing:] An article in *Drama* . . . discusses the British Rhine Army Dramatic Society. *The Athenaeum*, 20 August 1920, p. 250. Unsigned.

C89   Charles Lamb, 1775-1834. *Daily Herald*, 25 August 1920, p. 7. One of a series entitled 'Great Names'.

C90   [Paragraph commencing:] In the August *Dial* Mr. Stuart Davies. *The Athenaeum*, 27 August 1920, p. 269. Unsigned.

C91   [Review of] *Books on History*, a catalogue issued by Bolton Public Libraries. *The Athenaeum*, 27 August 1920, p. 272. Unsigned.

C92   Literary Gossip [paragraphs 7-12]. *The Athenaeum*, 27 August 1920, p. 277. Unsigned.

C93   [Note on] the forthcoming London production by Ethel Irving of *La Tosca*. *The Athenaeum*, 27 August 1920, p. 282. Unsigned.

C94   [Paragraph commencing:] Words, says Professor Drennan of University College, Johannesburg. *The Athenaeum*, 27 August 1920, p. 286. Unsigned.

C95   Countryside. *The Athenaeum*, 3 September 1920, p. 303. Review of *Wild Creatures of Garden and Hedgerow*, by Frances Pitt. Signed E.B.

C96   [Review of] *About Others and Myself, 1745 to 1920*, by Major-General Sir Archibald Anson. *The Athenaeum*, 3 September 1920, p. 305. Unsigned.

C97   [Review of] *Essays on Early Ornithology and Kindred Subjects*, by James R. McClymont. *The Athenaeum*, 3 September 1920, p. 305. Unsigned.

C98   Literary Gossip [paragraphs 4–12]. *The Athenaeum*, 3 September 1920, p. 309. Unsigned.

C99   [Note on] the forthcoming production of Chaucer's *Canterbury Tales* by the People's Theatre Society and Everyman Theatre. *The Athenaeum*, 3 September 1920, p. 313. Unsigned.

C100   [Paragraph commencing:] The most illuminating passage in an essay on Thomas Hardy. *The Athenaeum*, 3 September 1920, p. 314. Unsigned.

C101   [Review of] *Michelin Guide to the Somme*, Vol. 1. *The Athenaeum*, 10 September 1920, p. 328. Unsigned.

C102   [Review of] *Ludvig Holberg*, by S. C. Hammer. *The Athenaeum*, 10 September 1920, p. 330. Unsigned.

C103   [Review of] *Old Village Life*, by P. H. Ditchfield. *The Athenaeum*, 10 September 1920, p. 333. Unsigned.

C104   Literary Gossip [paragraphs 5, 8–11]. *The Athenaeum*, 10 September 1920, p. 336. Unsigned.

C105   On the Norwich School. *The Athenaeum*, 10 September 1920, pp. 338–339. Review of *The Norwich School*, with articles by H. M. Cundall.

C106   Elegant Extracts. *The Athenaeum*, 10 September 1920, pp. 348–349. Review of *The New Literary Series*, Sixth Book; *The New World English Course*, Second Book; *Nisbet's English Class Books*, by M. Jones; *The New Era Literary Reader*, edited by M. J. O'Mullane; and *Passages for English Repetition*, selected by Masters at Uppingham School. Unsigned.

C107   [Review of] *Technical Writing*, by T. A. Rickard. *The Athenaeum*, 10 September 1920, p. 352. Unsigned.

C108   [Review of] *The Way of Poetry*, Books I–IV, edited by John Drinkwater. *The Athenaeum*, 10 September 1920, p. 352. Unsigned.

C109   WATER-SPORT. *The Nation*, 11 September 1920, p. 724.
        Reprinted: *The Shepherd*, 1922; and *The Poems*, 1930.

C110   A Christ's Hospital Book. *Daily Herald*, 22 September 1920, p. 7. Review of *The Poetry and Prose of Coleridge, Lamb, and Leigh Hunt*, edited by S. E. Winbolt. *See also* C239.

C111   St. Matthew's Day. *The Athenaeum*, 24 September 1920, p. 397. On Christ's Hospital. Unsigned.

C112   An Old Topic. *The Athenaeum*, 24 September 1920, pp. 404-405. Review of *Life in a Sussex Windmill*, by Edward A. Martin; and *The Book of Sussex Verse*, edited by C. F. Cook. Signed E.B.

C113   [Review of] *Five Years' Hell in a Country Parish*, by The Rev. E. F. Synnott. *The Athenaeum*, 24 September 1920, p. 408. Unsigned.

C114   [Review of] *Poems: 1912-1919*, by Gilbert Thomas. *The Athenaeum*, 24 September 1920, p. 408. Unsigned.

C115   [Review of] *Flashlights from Afar*, by R. Gordon Canning. *The Athenaeum*, 24 September 1920, p. 408. Unsigned.

C116   Bibliographical Notes [paragraph 1]. *The Athenaeum*, 24 September1920, p. 411. Unsigned.

C117   Literary Gossip [paragraphs 11-13]. *The Athenaeum*, 24 September 1920, p. 412. Unsigned.

C118   [Note on] *Oscar Wilde in America*, by Martin Birnbaum. *The Athenaeum*, 24 September 1920, p. 418. Unsigned.

C119   [Note on] *Outward Bound*, the first monthly issue. *The Athenaeum*, 24 September 1920, p. 418. Unsigned.

C120   SHEPHERD. *London Mercury*, October 1920, Vol. 2, No. 12, pp. 652-654.

        Reprinted: *The Shepherd*, 1922; *The Poems*, 1930; and *Poems of Many Years*, 1957.

C121   Bibliographical Notes & News. *London Mercury*, October 1920, Vol. 2, No. 12, pp. 722-726.

C122   SPRING NIGHT. *Voices*, October 1920, Vol. 4, No. 4, p. 124.

        Reprinted: *The Shepherd*, 1922; and *The Poems*, 1930.

C123   Lamb's Schoolmaster: A Forgotten Essay. *The Athenaeum*, 1 October 1920, p. 432. Signed E.B.

C124   [Review of] *Desiderum, MCMXV-MCMXVIII*, by Norman Davey. *The Athenaeum*, 1 October 1920, p. 441. Unsigned.

C125   Literary Gossip [paragraphs 5-7, 9-11]. *The Athenaeum*, 1 October 1920, p. 443. Unsigned.

C126   DEATH OF CHILDHOOD BELIEFS. *The Athenaeum*, 8 October 1920, p. 465.

        Reprinted: *The Shepherd*, 1922; *The Poems*, 1930; and *The Midnight Skaters*, [1968].

C127   [Paragraph commencing:] The sudden death of Mr. William Heinemann. *The Athenaeum*, 8 October 1920, p. 467. Unsigned.

C128   [Paragraph commencing:] The committee of the Coventry Public Libraries. *The Athenaeum*, 8 October 1920, p. 467. Unsigned.

C129   Orbilius non plagosus. *The Athenaeum*, 8 October 1920, p. 469. Review of *From a Common-Room Window*, by Orbilius, *i.e.* Edward Miall Johnstone. Signed E.B.

C130   [Review of] *Tales of the Ridings*, by F. W. Moorman. *The Athenaeum*, 8 October 1920, p. 473. Unsigned.

C131   Bibliographical Notes [paragraph 1]. *The Athenaeum*, 8 October 1920, p. 476. On *Amenities of Book-Collecting*, by A. E. Newton. Unsigned.

C132   Literary Gossip [paragraph 6]. *The Athenaeum*, 8 October 1920, p. 477. Unsigned.

C133   [Paragraph commencing:] The Sixty-Fifth Annual Exhibition of the Royal Photographic Society. *The Athenaeum*, 8 October 1920, p. 481. Unsigned.

C134   [Paragraph commencing:] An experiment in municipal drama . . . "Once a Week Players". *The Athenaeum*, 8 October 1920, p. 483. Unsigned.

C135   [Paragraph commencing:] After a long illness Mr. C. N. Williamson died at Bath. *The Athenaeum*, 15 October 1920, p. 530. Unsigned.

C136   [Paragraph commencing:] Messrs. Macmillan kindly inform us that the novels by Mr. Hardy. *The Athenaeum*, 15 October 1920, p. 531. Unsigned.

C137   Verse. *The Athenaeum*, 22 October 1920, p. 547. Review of *Richard Plantagenet, and Other Poems*, by David Davenport; *Poems*, by J. H. McEwen; *Dawn and Sunset Gold*, by Samuel J. Looker; *Wayside Poems*, by Gerald Bull; and *Chains*, by S. Winsten. Signed E.B.

C138   Tailpieces. *The Athenaeum*, 22 October 1920, p. 549. Review of *Neighbours*, by Wilfrid Wilson Gibson. Signed E.B.

C139   [Paragraph commencing:] When we mention the name "Crockford's". *The Athenaeum*, 22 October 1920, p. 551. Unsigned.

C140   [Review of] *Poems*, by Lady Gerald Wellesley. *The Athenaeum*, 22 October 1920, p. 553. Unsigned.

C141   Literary Gossip [paragraphs 1–10]. *The Athenaeum*, 22 October 1920, p. 556. Unsigned.

C142   Bibliographical Notes [paragraphs 1–2]. *The Athenaeum*, 22 October 1920, p. 556. Unsigned.

C143   [Paragraph commencing:] New exhibits in the Department of Woodwork at the Victoria and Albert Museum. *The Athenaeum*, 22 October 1920, p. 560. Unsigned.

C144   [Paragraph commencing:] M. Claude Monet. *The Athenaeum*, 22 October 1920, p. 561. Unsigned.

C145   [Paragraph commencing:] Rooms II. and XXIX. at the National Gallery. *The Athenaeum*, 22 October 1920, p. 565. Unsigned.

C146   [Review of] *Lines in Pleasant Places*, by William Senior. *The Athenaeum*, 29 October 1920, p. 585. Unsigned.

C147   [Review of] *Memories of Four-score Years*, by H. Harrington Roberts. *The Athenaeum*, 29 October 1920, p. 585. Unsigned.

C148   Literary Gossip [paragraphs 1–10]. *The Athenaeum*, 29 October 1920, p. 588. Unsigned.

C149   Bibliographical Notes [paragraphs 1–8]. *The Athenaeum*, 29 October 1920, p. 588. Unsigned.

C150   [Paragraph commencing:] In a striking letter . . . Col. J. C. Somerville, Commandant of the Royal Military School of Music. *The Athenaeum*, 29 October 1920, p. 593. Unsigned.

C151   Belles-Lettres and Criticism. *London Mercury*, November 1920, Vol. 3, No. 13, pp. 116–118. Review of *A Philosophical View of Reform*, by Percy Bysshe Shelley; *Naturalism in English Poetry*, by Stopford A. Brooke; *Shakespeare's Fight with the Pirates*, by A. W. Pollard; *Some Seventeenth-Century Allusions to Shakespeare and His Works*, published by Dobell; *The Life and Death of King John* (Variorum Shakespeare), edited by H. H. Furness; and *Norwegian Life and Literature: English Accounts and Views*, by C. B. Burchardt.

C152   Guy and his Followers. *The Athenaeum*, 5 November 1920, pp. 609–610. On fireworks. Signed E. B.

C153   [Paragraph commencing:] Messrs. Chatto & Windus announce . . . "The Twelve," by M. Alexander Blok. *The Athenaeum*, 5 November 1920, p. 620. Unsigned.

C154   Bibliographical Notes [paragraphs 1–4]. *The Athenaeum*, 5 November 1920, p. 620. Unsigned.

C155   [Paragraph commencing:] The October *Architectural Review*. *The Athenaeum*, 5 November 1920, p. 625. Unsigned.

C156   William Hazlitt 1778–1830. *Daily Herald*, 10 November 1920, p. 7. One of a series entitled 'Great Names'.

        Reprinted: *Great Names*, 1926.

C157   Below the Surface. *The Athenaeum*, 12 November 1920, p. 646. Review of *The Tunnellers of Holzminden*, by H. G. Durnford. Signed E.B.

C158   [Review of] *Belgium and the Western Front*, edited by Findlay Muirhead. *The Athenaeum*, 12 November 1920, p. 653. Unsigned.

C159   Literary Gossip [paragraphs 2–7]. *The Athenaeum*, 12 November 1920, p. 657. Unsigned.

C160   Bibliographical Notes [paragraphs 1-2]. *The Athenaeum*, 12 November 1920, p. 657. Unsigned. *See also* letter, 'Lamb Bibliography', by S. Butterworth in the issue of 19 November, pp. 706-707, with reply by 'The Writer of "Bibliographical Notes"', *i.e.* Blunden. *See also* 'Literary Gossip' in the issue of 13 August, p. 214 (C80).

C161   Mr. Masefield's Steeplechase. *The Athenaeum*, 19 November 1920, p. 692. Review of *Right Royal*, by John Masefield. Signed E. B.

C162   [Review of] *A Thousand and One Notes on "A New English Dictionary"*, by George G. Loane. *The Athenaeum*, 19 November 1920, p. 696. Unsigned.

C163   Literary Gossip [paragraphs 2-10]. *The Athenaeum*, 19 November 1920, p. 699. Unsigned.

C164   Bibliographical Notes [paragraphs 1-5]. *The Athenaeum*, 19 November 1920, p. 699. Unsigned.

C165   REUNION IN WAR. *The Nation*, 20 November 1920, p. 278.

    Reprinted: *A Queen's College Miscellany*, 1921, *The Shepherd*, 1922; *The Augustan Books*, 1925; *The Poems*, 1930; and *Poems of Many Years*, 1957.

C166   Among Many. *The Athenaeum*, 26 November 1920, p. 725. Review of *Two Foemen*, by H. E. Palmer; *Poems*, by Edward L. Davison; *Poems*, by G. P. Bird; and *Half-Way*, by H. S. Vere Hodge. Signed E.B.

C167   [Review of] *An Angler's Garland*, compiled by Eric Parker. *The Athenaeum*, 26 November 1920, p. 729. Unsigned.

C168   Literary Gossip [paragraphs 1-9]. *The Athenaeum*, 26 November 1920, p. 732. Unsigned.

C169   Bibliographical Notes [paragraphs 1-4]. *The Athenaeum*, 26 November 1920, p. 732. Unsigned.

C170   [Paragraph commencing:] An International Council . . . has been compiling an international catalogue of scientific literature. *The Athenaeum*, 26 November 1920, p. 733. Unsigned.

C171   THE PASTURE POND. *London Mercury*, December 1920, Vol. 3, No. 14, pp. 136-138.

    Reprinted: *The Shepherd*, 1922; *The Poems*, 1930; and *Poems of Many Years*, 1957.

C172   Literary History and Criticism. *London Mercury*, December 1920, Vol. 3, No. 14, pp. 227-229. Review of *Personal Aspects of Jane Austen*, by Mary A. Austen-Leigh; *Jane Austen*, by O. W. Firkins; *The Good Englishwoman*, by Orlo Williams; and *Some Contemporary Novelists (Women)*, by R. Brimley Johnson.

C173   The Annuals [of the early nineteenth century]. *To-day*, December 1920, Vol. 8, No. 44, pp. 72-74.

C174   [Review of] *Essex Dialect Dictionary*, Supplement, by E. Gepp. *The Athenaeum*, 3 December 1920, p. 756. Unsigned.

C175   Literary Gossip [paragraphs 3-6]. *The Athenaeum*, 3 December 1920, p. 764. Unsigned.

C176   Bibliographical Notes [paragraphs 1-5]. *The Athenaeum*, 3 December 1920, p. 764. Unsigned.

C177   The Annuals. *The Athenaeum*, 3 December 1920, p. 781. Review of *Tiny Folks' Annual; Blackie's Children's Annual*, [and others]. Unsigned.

C178   Stories of the War. *The Athenaeum*, 3 December 1920, p. 781. Review of *Lads of the Lothians*, by Escott Lynn; *The Story of the Great War*, by Donald A. Mackenzie; and *The Mastery of the Air*, by William J. Claxton. Unsigned.

C179   [Review of] *Habits and Characters of British Wild Animals*, by H. Mortimer Batten. *The Athenaeum*, 3 December 1920, p. 784. Unsigned.

C180   Animal Stories. *The Athenaeum*, 3 December 1920, pp. 788, 790. Review of *Baby Mishook: The Adventures of a Siberian Cub*, translated by Leon Golschmann; *The Wise Beasts of Hindustan*, by Harry W. Pike; and *Nero, An African Mongrel*, by Jane Spettigue. Unsigned.

C181   [Review of] *The Birds of the British Isles and their Eggs*, Series II, by T. A. Coward. *The Athenaeum*, 3 December 1920, p. 790. Unsigned.

C182   [Review of] *More Plants We Play With*, by H. R. Robertson. *The Athenaeum*, 3 December 1920, p. 790. Unsigned.

C183   The Real War. *The Athenaeum*, 10 December 1920, p. 807. Review of *Poems*, by Wilfred Owen. Signed E.B.

C184   [Review of] *The 51st Division: War Sketches*, by Fred A. Farrell. *The Athenaeum*, 10 December 1920, p. 811. Unsigned.

C185   Literary Gossip [paragraphs 2-8]. *The Athenaeum*, 10 December 1920, p. 814. Unsigned.

C186   Bibliographical Notes [paragraphs 1-5, 7]. *The Athenaeum*, 10 December 1920, p. 814. Unsigned.

C187   [Review of] *The Art of Arthur Streeton*, edited by Sydney Ure Smith, Bertram Stevens, and C. Lloyd Jones. *The Athenaeum*, 10 December 1920, p. 817. Unsigned.

C188   Poetry Overseas. *The Athenaeum*, 17 December 1920, p. 833. Review of *Merchants from Cathay*, by W. R. Benét; *Don Folquet, and Other Poems*, by Thomas Walsh; *The Plainsman*, by Rhys Carpenter; *Spring in New Hampshire*, by Claude McKay; *Poems*, by Frederick T. Macartney; *A*

Flagon of Song, by E. J. R. Atkinson; and *A Pagoda of Jewels*, by Moon Kwan. Signed E. B.

C189 [Review of] *The Goldfinches*, by Sylvia Lynd. *The Athenaeum*, 17 December 1920, p. 837. Unsigned.

C190 [Review of] *More Tales of the Ridings*, by F. W. Moorman. *The Athenaeum*, 17 December 1920, p. 838. Unsigned.

C191 Literary Gossip [paragraphs 1-5]. *The Athenaeum*, 17 December 1920, p. 840. Unsigned.

C192 Bibliographical Notes [paragraphs 1-4]. *The Athenaeum*, 17 December 1920, p. 840. Unsigned.

C193 Leigh Hunt (1784-1859). *Daily Herald*, 22 December 1920, p. 7. One of a series entitled 'Great Names'.

Reprinted: *Great Names*, 1926.

C194 [Paragraph commencing:] A recent incident . . . concerns a still-life painted by a M. Sassy. *The Athenaeum*, 24 December 1920, p. 857. Unsigned.

C195 THE CANAL. *The Athenaeum*, 24 December 1920, pp. 860-861.

Reprinted: *Oxford Poetry*, 1921; *The Shepherd*, 1922; and *The Poems*, 1930.

C196 [Review of] *The Immortal Caravel*, by Arthur Lynch. *The Athenaeum*, 24 December 1920, p. 866. Unsigned.

C197 [Review of] *The Essays of Elia*, with introduction by E. V. Lucas. *The Athenaeum*, 24 December 1920, p. 868. Unsigned.

C198 Literary Gossip [paragraphs 1-10]. *The Athenaeum*, 24 December 1920, p. 869. Unsigned.

C199 Bibliographical Notes [paragraphs 1-4]. *The Athenaeum*, 24 December 1920, p. 869. Unsigned.

C200 [Paragraph commencing:] Professor J. A. Thomson's course of Christmas Lectures . . . "The School of the Shore." *The Athenaeum*, 24 December 1920, p. 871. Unsigned.

C201 Revenge as a Literary Art. *The Athenaeum*, 31 December 1920, p. 886. Review of *Nollekens and his Times*, by John Thomas Smith, edited by Wilfred Whitten. Signed E.B.

C202 [Paragraph commencing:] The first number of *The Cherwell. The Athenaeum*, 31 December 1920, p. 887. Unsigned.

C203 Literary Gossip [paragraphs 1-9]. *The Athenaeum*, 31 December 1920, p. 894. Unsigned.

C204 Bibliographical Notes [paragraphs 1-4]. *The Athenaeum*, 31 December 1920, p. 894. Unsigned.

C205   Literary History and Criticism. *London Mercury*, January 1921, Vol. 3, No. 15, pp. 339–341. Review of *The Elder Edda and Ancient Scandinavian Drama*, by Bertha S. Phillpotts; *The Story of Early Gaelic Literature*, by Douglas Hyde; *King Alfred's Books*, by G. F. Browne; *John Dryden*, by Mark van Doren; *The Bibliography of Walt Whitman*, by Frank Shay; *The English Ode to 1660*, by Robert Shafer; *Flaubert and Maupassant*, by Agnes Rutherford Riddell; and *Transactions of the Royal Society of Literature*, 1919.

C206   THE SCYTHE [*later* THE SCYTHE STRUCK BY LIGHTNING]. *Oxford Outlook*, January 1921, Vol. 3, No. 11, pp. 6–7.
Reprinted: *London Mercury*, February 1921; *Oxford Poetry*, 1921; *The Shepherd*, 1922; *The Poems*, 1930; and *Poems of Many Years*, 1957.

C207   THE SOUTH-WEST WIND. *The Nation*, 1 January 1921, p. 482.
Reprinted: *Oxford Poetry*, 1921; *The Shepherd*, 1922; *The Poems*, 1930; *The Face of England*, 1938; and *The Midnight Skaters*, [1968].

C208   Was it darker? *Daily Herald*, 5 January 1921, p. 7. Review of *A History of Everyday Things in England, 1066–1799*, by Marjorie and C. H. B. Quennell.

C209   [Review of] *A Captive at Carlsruhe*, by Joseph Lee; and *Behind Boche Bars*, by Ernest Warburton. *The Athenaeum*, 7 January 1921, p. 15. Unsigned.

C210   [Note on] *Anne of Geierstein*, edited by C. B. Wheeler. *The Athenaeum*, 7 January 1921, p. 16. Unsigned.

C211   [Review of] *Men and Tanks*, by J. C. Macintosh. *The Athenaeum*, 7 January 1921, p. 18. Unsigned.

C212   Literary Gossip [paragraphs 1-6]. *The Athenaeum*, 7 January 1921, p. 19. Unsigned.

C213   [Note on] *Winter's Pie*. *The Athenaeum*, 7 January 1921, p. 22. Unsigned.

C214   [Note on] *American and English Genealogies in the Library of Congress*. *The Athenaeum*, 7 January 1921, p. 25. Unsigned.

C215   A Mystery. *Daily Herald*, 12 January 1921, p. 7. Review of *A Case in Camera*, by Oliver Onions. Signed E.B.

C216   [Paragraph commencing:] By the bequest of Mr. John Kirkhope. *The Athenaeum*, 14 January 1921, p. 33. Unsigned.

C217   Poetry in Public. *The Athenaeum*, 14 January 1921, p. 41. Review of *Twentieth Century Reciter's Treasury*, edited by

Ernest Guy Pertwee; and *The Boy's Own Reciter*, revised edition edited by A. L. Haydon. Signed E. B.

C218   Literary Gossip [paragraphs 1-6]. *The Athenaeum*, 14 January 1921, p. 46. Unsigned.

C219   [Review of] *A Book of Dovecotes*, by A. O. Cooke. *The Athenaeum*, 14 January 1921, p. 49. Unsigned.

C220   [Note on the forthcoming production of *Antony and Cleopatra* at Oxford]. *The Athenaeum*, 14 January 1921, p. 51. Unsigned.

C221   [Review of] *With the Walnuts and the Wine*, by Joe Miller. *The Athenaeum*, 14 January 1921, p. 53. Unsigned.

C222   Notes and Comments [paragraphs 1-3]. *The Athenaeum*, 21 January 1921, p. 61. Unsigned.

C223   [Note on Canadian memorials on the Western Front battlefields]. *The Athenaeum*, 21 January 1921, p. 71. Unsigned.

C224   Literary Gossip [paragraphs 1-8]. *The Athenaeum*, 21 January 1921, p. 74. Unsigned.

C225   [Paragraph commencing:] At the age of sixty-eight Mr. F. W. Bourdillon . . . has died. *The Athenaeum*, 28 January 1921, p. 89. Unsigned.

C226   [Review of] *The Princess Zoubaroff*, by Ronald Firbank. *The Athenaeum*, 28 January 1921, p. 102. Unsigned.

C227   [Review of] *The Broads, 1919*, by Hugh Money-Coutts. *The Athenaeum*, 28 January 1921, p. 102. Unsigned.

C228   [Paragraph commencing:] Mrs. Luther S. Livingston has issued . . . notes on the bibliography of Swinburne [*i.e. Swinburne's Proofsheets and American First Editions*, by Flora V. Livingston]. *The Athenaeum*, 28 January 1921, p. 103. Unsigned.

C229   Bibliographical Notes. *The Athenaeum*, 28 January 1921, p. 103. Unsigned.

C230   [Note on The Book House, Norwich pamphlet on the Norwich Players]. *The Athenaeum*, 28 January 1921, p. 108. Unsigned.

C231   [Note on Bernard Shaw's lecture 'The Need for the Political Organization of Mental Workers']. *The Athenaeum*, 28 January 1921, p. 108. Unsigned.

C232   THE WATERMILL. *The Nation*, 29 January 1921, p. 604.

Reprinted: *Oxford Poetry*, 1921; *The Shepherd*, 1922; *The Poems*, 1930; and *Poems of Many Years*, 1957.

C233   THE GIANT PUFFBALL. *London Mercury*, February 1921, Vol. 3, No. 16, p. 362. Second of Six Poems; for the First *see* C206.

Reprinted: *The Shepherd*, 1922; and *The Poems*, 1930.

C234   FIRST SNOW. *London Mercury*, February 1921, Vol. 3, No. 16, p. 363. Third of Six Poems.

Reprinted: *The Shepherd*, 1922; and *The Poems*, 1930.

C235   VILLAGE GREEN. *London Mercury*, February 1921, Vol. 3, No. 16, p. 364. Fourth of Six Poems.

Reprinted: *The Shepherd*, 1922; *The Augustan Books*, [1925]; and *The Poems*, 1930.

C236   THE POOR MAN'S PIG. *London Mercury*, February 1921, Vol. 3, No. 16, p. 364. Fifth of Six Poems.

Reprinted: *The Shepherd*, 1922; *The Augustan Books*, [1925]; *The Poems*, 1930; *Poems of Many Years*, 1957; *The Midnight Skaters*, [1968]; and *A Selection from the Poems*, [1969].

C237   THE AVENUE. *London Mercury*, February 1921, Vol. 3, No. 16, pp. 365–366. Last of Six Poems.

Reprinted: *The Shepherd*, 1922; and *The Poems*, 1930.

C238   [Paragraph commencing:] That important international journal *La Revue de Genève. The Athenaeum*, 4 February 1921, p. 119. Unsigned.

C239   Estese, Elia, Indicator. *The Athenaeum*, 4 February 1921, p. 124. Review of *The Poetry and Prose of Coleridge, Lamb, and Leigh Hunt*, edited by S. E. Winbolt. Signed E. B. *See also* C110.

C240   [Paragraph commencing:] One or two reprints. *The Athenaeum*, 4 February 1921, p. 125. Unsigned.

C241   [Review of] *Handlist of English and Welsh Newspapers, Magazines and Reviews. The Athenaeum*, 4 February 1921, p. 128. Unsigned.

C242   [Paragraph commencing:] "Whitaker's" has reached. *The Athenaeum*, 4 February 1921, p. 129. Unsigned.

C243   Literary Gossip [paragraphs 1–7]. *The Athenaeum*, 4 February 1921, p. 130. Unsigned.

C244   A Splendid Survey. *Daily Herald*, 9 February 1921, p. 7. Review of *The Glory that Was Greece*; and *The Grandeur that Was Rome*, by J. C. Stobart. Signed E. B.

C245   Unpublished Poems by John Clare. *Eton College Chronicle*, 10 February 1921, No. 1759, p. 967. Poems by Clare appeared in this issue, and those for 17 and 24 February, and 3 March, Nos. 1760–1762.

C246   [Review of] *The Chapbook (A Monthly Miscellany)*, January 1921. *TLS*, 10 February 1921, p. 94. Unsigned.

C247   [Review of] *The Blue Ship*, by Herbert Jones. *TLS*, 10 February 1921, p. 94. Unsigned.

C248   [Review of] *Kirkcudbrightshire and Wigtonshire*, by William Learmonth; and *Caithness and Sutherland*, by H. F. Campbell. *The Athenaeum*, 11 February 1921, p. 153. Unsigned.

C249   Dorset Biographies. *The Athenaeum*, 11 February 1921, p. 153. Review of *Wessex Worthies*, by J. J. Foster with an introductory note by Thomas Hardy. Signed E. B.

C250   Literary Gossip [paragraphs 1–6]. *The Athenaeum*, 11 February 1921, p. 158. Unsigned.

C251   Bibliographical Notes. *The Athenaeum*, 11 February 1921, p. 158. Unsigned.

C252   Keats and Shelley. *The Athenaeum*, 11 February 1921, p. 164. Letter in reply to one by John L. Gray in the same issue p. 164 on Blunden's review of *The Poetry and Prose of Coleridge, Lamb and Leigh Hunt*, edited by S. E. Winbolt (*see* C239).

C253   [Review of] *Passions*, by Russell Green. *TLS*, 17 February 1921, p. 111. Unsigned.

C254   The Poets of the War. *Nation & Athenaeum*, 26 February 1921, pp. 738–739. Letter on J. Middleton Murry's review of *Poems*, by Wilfred Owen in the issue of 19 February, pp. 705–707. *See also* letters in the issues of 12 March, p. 816 by Edith Sitwell, and 26 March, p. 910 by C. K. Scott Moncrieff.

C255   Lure of the Past. *Daily Herald*, 23 March 1921, p. 7. Review of *Old World Essays*, by R. L. Gales. Signed E. B.

C256   Leigh Hunt: An Annotation. *London Mercury*, April 1921, Vol. 3, No. 18, pp. 618–626.

C257   Thomas de Quincey (1785–1859). *Daily Herald*, 20 April 1921, p. 7. One of a series entitled 'Great Names'.
        Reprinted: *Great Names*, 1926.

C258   A Local Painter. *Nation & Athenaeum*, 23 April 1921, pp. 134–135. Review of *Crome*, by C. H. Collins Baker. Unsigned.

C259   Mr. Tomlinson's Triumph. *Daily Herald*, 27 April 1921, p. 7. Review of *London River*, by H. M. Tomlinson.

C260   Charles Lamb Once More. *TLS*, 28 April 1921, p. 273. Review of *The Life of Charles Lamb*, fifth edition revised, by E. V. Lucas. Unsigned. *See also* C264.

C261   The Case for the Archdeacon. *Nation & Athenaeum*, 30 April 1921, pp. 164–165. On the proceedings against Archdeacon Wakeford. *See also* 'A London Diary' comment by 'A Wayfarer' in the same issue p. 161; and letters in the issues of 7 May, pp. 209–210 by W.D.T., H. G. Barclay, May Sinclair; and 21 May, p. 284 by Mary Blunden and Alf. A. Toms.

C262 THE MAY DAY GARLAND. *Daily Herald*, May Day Annual 1921, p. 13.
Reprinted: *The Shepherd*, 1922; *The Poems*, 1930; and *The Midnight Skaters*, [1968].

C263 Thought in Verse. *TLS*, 19 May 1921, p. 318. Review of *Domesday Book*, by Edgar Lee Masters. Unsigned.

C264 Charles Lamb. *Daily Herald*, 25 May 1921, p. 7. Review of *The Life of Charles Lamb*, fifth edition revised, by E. V. Lucas. Signed E. B. *See also* C260.

C265 New Sidelights on Keats, Lamb, and Others from Letters to J. Clare. *London Mercury*, June 1921, Vol. 4, No. 20, pp. 141-149. *See also* C282.

C266 Literary History and Criticism. *London Mercury*, June 1921, Vol. 4, No. 20, pp. 217-218. Review of *Shelley and Calderón*, by Salvador de Madariaga; *Sidelights on Shakespeare*, by H. Dugdale Sykes; *The Early Life and Education of John Evelyn*, with commentary by H. Maynard Smith; *Ruskin the Prophet, and Other Centenary Studies*, by John Masefield and others; and *Johnson Club Papers*, Second Series.

C267 John Clare. *To-day*, June 1921, Vol. 8, No. 46, pp. 142-144.

C268 Mr. Gosse's Reviews. *TLS*, 2 June 1921, p. 347. Review of *Books on the Table*, by Edmund Gosse. Unsigned.

C269 [Review of] *Women in Love*, by D. H. Lawrence. *TLS*, 9 June 1921, p. 371. Unsigned.

C270 Strict and Free in Verse. *TLS*, 23 June 1921, p. 400. Review of *The Journey: Odes and Sonnets*, by Gerald Gould; and *Sonnets from Hafez, and Other Verses*, by Elizabeth Bridges. Unsigned.

C271 THE FOREST. *Nation & Athenaeum*, 25 June 1921, p. 469.
Reprinted: *The Shepherd*, 1922; and *The Poems*, 1930.

C272 The Early Prose of Henry James. *TLS*, 30 June 1921, p. 417. Review of *Notes and Reviews*, by Henry James. Unsigned.

C273 Literary Recreations. *TLS*, 30 June 1921, p. 417. Review of *Signs and Wonders*, by J. D. Beresford. Unsigned. *See also* C284.

C274 THE IDLERS. *London Mercury*, July 1921, Vol. 4, No. 21, p. 231.
Reprinted: *The Shepherd*, 1922; *The Poems*, 1930; and *The Midnight Skaters*, [1968].

C275   THE MARCH BEE. *London Mercury*, July 1921, Vol. 4, No. 21, pp. 231–232.

Reprinted: *Oxford Poetry*, 1921; *The Shepherd*, 1922; and *The Poems*, 1930.

C276   A PARAPHRASE. *The Outlook*, July 1921, Vol. 1, No. 1, p. 3 [*i.e.* 4]

C277   Nimphidia Reprinted. *TLS*, 7 July 1921, p. 433. Review of *Nimphidia: The Court of Fayrie*, by Michael Drayton. Unsigned.

C278   [Review of] *Pugs and Peacocks*, by Gilbert Cannan. *TLS*, 7 July 1921, p. 435. Unsigned.

C279   John Clare. *TLS*, 14 July 1921, p. 452. Letter. *See also* the issue of 30 June, p. 421.

C280   A Lillyputian Fantasy. *TLS*, 28 July 1921, p. 481. Review of *Memoirs of a Midget*, by Walter de la Mare. Unsigned.

C281   The Return of John Clare, the Northamptonshire Peasant Poet. *Discovery*, August 1921, Vol. 2, No. 20, pp. 198–200.

C282   Taylor and Keats. *London Mercury*, August 1921, Vol. 4, No. 22, p. 412. *See also* C265.

C283   EVENING MYSTERY. *Nation & Athenaeum*, 6 August 1921, p. 679.

Reprinted: *The Shepherd*, 1922; *The Poems*, 1930; and *Poems of Many Years*, 1957.

C284   Gay and Grave. *Daily Herald*, 10 August 1921, p. 7. Review of *The Holidays: A Book of Gay Stories*, translated from the French of Henri Duvernois, introduction by Alys Eyre Macklin; and *Signs and Wonders*, by J. D. Beresford. *See also* C273.

C285   Herrick. *TLS*, 18 August 1921, p. 528. Review of *The Poetical Works of Robert Herrick*, edited by F. W. Moorman. Unsigned.

Reprinted: *Votive Tablets*, 1931.

C286   THE RIVER HOUSE. *The Spectator*, 20 August 1921, p. 236.

Reprinted: *To Nature*, 1923.

C287   First Poems. *TLS*, 25 August 1921, p. 544. Review of *Poems*, by Frank Prewett. Unsigned.

C288   HIGH SUMMER. *To-day*, September 1921, Vol. 8, No. 47, p. 190.

Reprinted: *The Shepherd*, 1922; *The Poems*, 1930; and *Poems of Many Years*, 1957.

C289   [Review of] *One Woman*, by Alfred Ollivant. *TLS*, 1 September 1921, p. 563. Unsigned.

C290   Playing at Plays. *TLS*, 8 September 1921, p. 577. Review of *Antique Pageantry: A Book of Verse Plays*, by Clifford Bax. Unsigned.

C291   JOURNEY. *Nation & Athenaeum*, 10 September 1921, p. 826.

Reprinted: *The Shepherd*, 1922; and *The Poems*, 1930.

C292   Nature Displayed. *Daily Herald*, 14 September 1921, p. 7. Review of *Some Birds of the Countryside: The Art of Nature*, by H. J. Massingham; and *A Philosopher with Nature*, by Benjamin Kidd.

C293   THE AWAKENING. *Form*, October 1921 [New Series], Vol. 1, No. 1, p. 25.

C294   On Childhood in Poetry. *TLS*, 6 October 1921, pp. 633–634. Review of *A Book of English Verse on Infancy and Childhood*, chosen by C. S. Wood. Unsigned.

Reprinted: *Votive Tablets*, 1931.

C295   [Review of] *The Singing Captives*, by E. B. C. Jones. *TLS*, 6 October 1921, p. 641. Unsigned.

C296   "THE EARTH HATH BUBBLES". *Nation & Athenaeum*, 8 October 1921, p. 51.

Reprinted: *The Shepherd*, 1922; and *The Poems*, 1930.

C297   The Same War. *Nation & Athenaeum*, 22 October 1921, p. 148. Review of *Three Soldiers*, by John Dos Passos. Signed E. B.

C298   Tennyson (1809–1892). *Daily Herald*, 26 October 1921, p. 7. One of a series entitled 'Great Names'.

Reprinted: *Great Names*, 1926.

C299   Poets and Philosophy. *TLS*, 10 November 1921, p. 731. Review of *Three Studies in Shelley, and an Essay on Nature in Wordsworth and Meredith*, by Archibald T. Strong. Unsigned. *See also* C305.

C299   Mr. Freeman's Poems. *TLS*, 1 December 1921, p. 784. Re-
.1   view of *Music: Lyrical and Narrative Poems*, by John Freeman. Unsigned.

C300   Anthologies and Claimants. *TLS*, 8 December 1921, pp. 793-794. Review of *An English Anthology*, compiled and arranged by Sir Henry Newbolt. Unsigned.

C301   Village Character. *TLS*, 8 December 1921, p. 807. Review of *Old England: A God's-Eye View of a Village*, by Bernard Gilbert. Unsigned.

C302   [Review of] *Mr. Paul*, by Gertrude Bone. *TLS*, 22 December 1921, p. 859. Unsigned.

C303   THE LATE STAND-TO. *London Mercury*, January 1922, Vol. 5, No. 27, pp. 231-232.

Reprinted: *The Shepherd*, 1922; *The Poems*, 1930; and *The Midnight Skaters*, [1968].

C304   WILL-O'-THE-WISP. *London Mercury*, January 1922, Vol. 5, No. 27, p. 233.

Reprinted: *The Shepherd*, 1922; and *The Poems*, 1930.

C305   Literary History and Criticism. *London Mercury*, January 1922, Vol. 5, No. 27, pp. 320-322. Review of *Edgar A. Poe: A Study*, by John W. Robertson; *Three Studies in Shelley, and an Essay on Nature in Wordsworth and Meredith*, by A. T. Strong (*see also* C299); *Sikes and Nancy: A Reading*, by Charles Dickens, edited by J. H. Stonehouse; *David Copperfield: A Reading in Five Chapters*, by Charles Dickens, with a note by J. H. Stonehouse; and *Matthew Prior: A Study of his Public Career and Correspondence*, by L. G. Wickham Legg.

C306   The Laureates [*later* The Laureates (1922).] *TLS*, 26 January 1922, pp. 49-50. Review of *The Laureateship: A Study of the Office of Poet Laureate in England, with some accounts of the poets*, by Edmund Kemper Broadus. Unsigned.

Reprinted: *Votive Tablets*, 1931.

C307   WAR AUTOBIOGRAPHY (WRITTEN IN ILLNESS). *London Mercury*, February 1922, Vol. 5, No. 28, pp. 343-344.

Reprinted: *The Shepherd*, 1922; *The Poems*, 1930; and *Poems of Many Years*, 1957.

C308   Literary History and Criticism. *London Mercury*, March 1922, Vol. 5, No. 29, pp. 544-546. Review of *A Short History of English Literature*, by A. T. Strong; *Le Morte d'Arthur of Sir Thomas Malory*, by Vida D. Scudder; *Early Tudor Poetry, 1485-1547*, by John M. Berdan; *Peacock's Four Ages of Poetry, Shelley's Defence of Poetry, Browning's Essay on Shelley*, edited by H. F. B. Brett-Smith; *The Year's Work in English Studies*, edited by Sir Sidney Lee; *Behind my Library Door*, by G. C. Williamson (*see also* C335); and *Carols: Their Origin, Music, and Connection with Mystery-Plays*, by W. J. Phillips.

C309   THE BROOK. *Nation & Athenaeum*, 25 March 1922, p. 944.

Reprinted: *To Nature*, [1923]; *English Poems*, [1926]; *The Poems*, 1930; and *The Midnight Skaters*, [1968].

C310   THE ENGLISH POETS. *Nation & Athenaeum*, 22 April 1922, p. 119.

Reprinted: *To Nature*, [1923]; *English Poems*, [1926]; *The Poems*, 1930; and *The Midnight Skaters*, [1968].

C311   Landscape in Verse: 18th Century Poets. *The Times*, 17 May 1922, p. 16.

C312   Poems of the East. *TLS*, 18 May 1922, p. 319. Review of *Via Triumphalis*, by Edward J. Thompson. Unsigned.

C313   Tranquility. *TLS*, 1 June 1922, p. 359. Review of *The Sweet Miracle and Other Poems*, by W. Force Stead. Unsigned.

C314   THE ECLOGUE. *Nation & Athenaeum*, 3 June 1922, p. 341.

Reprinted: *A Miscellany of Poetry*, [1922]; *To Nature*, [1923]; *English Poems*, [1926]; and *The Poems*, 1930.

C315   Tales and Poems. *TLS*, 8 June 1922, p. 379. Review of *Clorinda Walks in Heaven: Tales*, by A. E. Coppard; and *Hips and Haws: Poems*, by A. E. Coppard. Unsigned.

C316   A Mirror of the May-Day Age [*later* "A Wedding or a Funeral" (first part)]. *TLS*, 22 June 1922, p. 409. Review of *A Pepsyian Garland: Blackletter Broadside Ballads of the Years, 1595-1693*, edited by Hyder E. Rollins. Unsigned.

Reprinted: *Votive Tablets*, 1931.

C317   Anti-Antimacassar: Where William Morris Failed. *Daily News*, 30 June 1922, p. 7. Review of *The Life of William Morris*, by J. W. Mackail.

C318   OLD HOMES. *London Mercury*, July 1922, Vol. 6, No. 33, pp. 232-235. Dedication: To G. [*i.e. Gilbert Blunden*].

First published in a separate edition, 1922. Reprinted: *English Poems*, [1926]; *The Poems*, 1930; and *Poems of Many Years*, 1957.

C319   THE SHADOW [*later* THE WARDER; *and* THE SHADOW]. *Yale Review*, July 1922, New Series, Vol. 11, No. 4, p. 699.

Reprinted: *The Book of the Queen's Dolls' House*, [1924]; *English Poems*, [1926], and *The Poems*, 1930.

C320   THRESHOLD. *Yale Review*, July 1922, New Series, Vol. 11, No. 4, pp. 699-700.

Reprinted: *A Miscellany of Poetry*, [1922].

C321   COUNTRY SALE. *Yale Review*, July 1922, New Series, Vol. 11, No. 4, pp. 700-702.

Reprinted: *A Miscellany of Poetry*, [1922]; *The Book of the Queen's Dolls' House*, [1924]; *English Poems*, [1926]; *The Poems*, 1930; *Poems of Many Years*, 1957; and *The Midnight Skaters*, [1968].

C322 Shelley After a Hundred Years. *Daily News*, 7 July 1922, p. 4. On the centenary of his death.

C323 Shelley and his Friends. *Nation & Athenaeum*, 8 July 1922, pp. 506-507.

C324 Towards the English Anthology. *TLS*, 13 July 1922, p. 457. Review of *Some Contributions to the English Anthology*, by John Drinkwater; and *Byways Round Helicon: A Kind of Anthology*, by Iola A. Williams. Unsigned.

C325 Antique Verse. *TLS*, 27 July 1922, p. 488. Review of *Voyage of Ass*, by E. H. W. Meyerstein; and *In Merlin's Wood*, by E. H. W. Meyerstein. Unsigned.

C326 Miss Stuart's Poems. *TLS*, 3 August 1922, p. 504. Review of *Poems*, by Muriel Stuart. Unsigned.

C327 Careless Raptures: What the Birds Say. *Daily News*, August 1922, p. 7. Review of *Songs of the Birds*, by Walter Garstang.

C328 A Courteous Indictment. *TLS*, 10 August 1922, p. 518. Review of *The Realistic Revolt in Modern Poetry*, by A. M. Clark. Unsigned.

C329 Edmund Spenser (1552-1599). *Daily Herald*, 16 August 1922, p. 7. One of a series entitled 'Great Names'.
Reprinted: *Great Names*, 1926.

C330 The Happy Island. *TLS*, 17 August 1922, pp. 525-526. On *Polyolbion*, by Michael Drayton. Unsigned.
Reprinted: *Votive Tablets*, 1931.

C331 In Defence of Wild Flowers. *Daily News*, 22 August 1922, p. 7. Review of *The Call of the Wild Flower*, by Henry S. Salt.

C332 THE BLUE BUTTERFLY [*later* BLUE BUTTERFLY]. *To-day*, September 1922, Vol. 9, No. 51, p. 18.
Reprinted: *To Nature*, [1923]; *English Poems*, [1926]; *The Poems*, 1930; and *The Midnight Skaters*, [1968].

C333 SHOOTING STAR AT HARVEST. *Nation & Athenaeum*, 2 September 1922, p. 738.
Reprinted: *To Nature*, [1923]; *English Poems*, [1926]; and *The Poems*, 1930.

C334 Where Shakespeare Planted a Tree. *Daily News*, 20 September 1922, p. 7. Review of *Shakespeare's Garden*, by Ernest Law.

C335 Literary History and Criticism. *London Mercury*, October 1922, Vol. 6, No. 36, pp. 661-663. Review of *Pages from the Works of Thomas Hardy*, arranged by Ruth Head; *Thomas Hardy: Poet and Novelist*, by Samuel C. Chew; *Thomas Hardy's Dorset*, by R. Thurston Hopkins; *John Masefield: A Critical Study*, by W. H. Hamilton; *The Uncollected Poetry and Prose of Walt Whitman*, edited by

Emory Holloway; *Michael Field*, by Mary Sturgeon; *Shakespeare to Sheridan*, by Alwin Thaler; and *Behind My Library Door*, by G. C. Williamson (*see also* C308).

C336   Flecker. *Nation & Athenaeum*, 21 October 1922, p. 126. Review of *Hassan*, by James Elroy Flecker; *Collected Prose of James Elroy Flecker*; and *James Elroy Flecker: An Appreciation*, by Douglas Goldring. Unsigned.

C337   A "Spasmodic". *TLS*, 26 October 1922, p. 683. Review of *Broken Shade*, by John Helston. Unsigned.

C338   Dishevelled Reveries. *Nation & Athenaeum*, 28 October 1922, p. 164. Review of *The Hundred- and- One Harlequins*, by Sacheverell Sitwell. Unsigned.

C339   Mr. Davies' "Album Verses". *TLS*, 2 November 1922, p. 699. Review of *The Hour of Magic, and Other Poems*, by W. H. Davies. Unsigned.

C340   RURAL ECONOMY (1917). *Nation & Athenaeum*, 4 November 1922, p. 195.

Reprinted: *To Nature*, [1923]; *The Augustan Books*, [1925]; *Undertones of War*, 1928; *The Poems*, 1930; and *Poems of Many Years*, 1957.

C341   Simplicity. *TLS*, 9 November 1922, p. 722. Review of *Preludes, 1921-1922*, by John Drinkwater. Unsigned.

C342   THE TUNE. *The Challenge*, 10 November 1922, New Series, Vol. 1, No. 7, p. 133.

Reprinted: *To Nature*, [1923].

C343   Leigh Hunt [*later* Leigh Hunt's Poetry]. *TLS*, 16 November 1922, pp. 733-734. Review of *The Poetical Works of Leigh Hunt*, edited by H. S. Milford. Unsigned. *See also* C351, 355.

Reprinted: *Votive Tablets*, 1931.

C344   A Veteran. *TLS*, 16 November 1922, p. 743. Review of *A Hundred Poems*, by Sir William Watson. Unsigned.

C345   "Hic et Ubique?". *The Challenge*, 24 November 1922, New Series, Vol. 1, No. 9, pp. 175-176. Review of *A Hind in Richmond Park*, by W. H. Hudson.

C346   Dedicated to Elia. *The Blue*, December 1922, Vol. 50, No. 1, pp. 4-8. On *Recollections of a Blue-Coat Boy; or a View of Christ's Hospital*, by W. P. Scargill, published in 1829. Signed E. B.   P. [1] of issue dated November 1922.

C347   DEAD LETTERS (T.L.H.) [*i.e.* Thornton Leigh Hunt]. *To-day*, December 1922, Vol. 9, No. 52, pp. 53-54.

Reprinted: separate edition, 1923; *English Poems*, [1926]; *The Poems*, 1930; and *Poems of Many Years*, 1957.

C348   Paradise of Birds. *Nation & Athenaeum*, 2 December 1922, pp. 360, 362. Review of *Poems About Birds*, edited by H. J. Massingham. Unsigned. *See also* B8.

C349   A Vision of Faith. *TLS*, 7 December 1922, p. 797. Review of *The Holy City: A Tragedy and Allegory*, by Dorothy St Cyres. Unsigned.

C350   The Child's Parnassus. *TLS*, 7 December 1922, p. 801. Review of *Down-Adown-Derry: A Book of Fairy Poems*, by Walter de la Mare; *Youngster: Collected Poems of Childhood*, by Burges Johnson; *Nursery Lyrics*, by Lady Strachey; *The Bower Book of Simple Poems*, edited by Letty and Ursula Littlewood; and *Christmas Poems*, selected by T. H. Darlow. Unsigned.

C351   Leigh Hunt's Poems: The Amazing Industry of Last Century. *Daily News*, 21 December 1922, p. 7. Review of *The Poetical Works of Leigh Hunt*, edited by H. S. Milford. *See also* C343, 355.

C352   The Diarist. *TLS*, 21 December 1922, p. 857. Review of *Blake, Coleridge, Wordsworth, Lamb, &c.: Being Selections from the Remains of Henry Crabb Robinson*, edited by Edith J. Morley. Unsigned. *See also* C364.

C353   An Independent. *TLS*, 28 December 1922, p. 870. Review of *Well Shone Moone: Poems*, by Alan Sims. Unsigned.

1923

C354   TO NATURE. *Empire Review*, January 1923, Vol. 37, No. 264, p. 55.

Reprinted: *To Nature*, [1923]; *English Poems*, [1926]; and *The Poems*, 1930.

C355   "The Indicator's" Verse. *The Spectator*, 20 January 1923, pp. 106–107. Review of *The Poetical Works of Leigh Hunt*, edited by H. S. Milford. *See also* C343, 351.

C356   Mr. Fausset's Poems. *TLS*, 25 January 1923, p. 53. Review of *The Condemned* and *The Mercy of God: Two Poems of Crisis*, by Hugh l'Anson Fausset. Unsigned.

C357   WATER MOMENT. *London Mercury*, February 1923, Vol. 7, No. 40, p. 345.

Reprinted: *To Nature*, [1923]; *The Augustan Books*, [1925]; *English Poems*, [1926]; and *The Poems*, 1930.

C358   TIME OF ROSES. *London Mercury*, February 1923, Vol. 7, No. 40, p. 345.

Reprinted: *To Nature*, [1923]; *English Poems*, [1926]; and *The Poems*, 1930.

C359 WASTE GROUND. *London Mercury*, February 1923, Vol. 7, No. 40, p. 346.

Reprinted: *To Nature*, [1923]; *English Poems*, [1926]; and *The Poems*, 1930.

C360 THE SPELL. *London Mercury*, February 1923, Vol. 7, No. 40, p. 347.

Reprinted: *To Nature*, [1923]; *English Poems*, [1926]; and *The Poems*, 1930.

C361 Clare on the "Londoners". *London Mercury*, February 1923, Vol. 7, No. 40, pp. 393–398.

C362 An Independent Quartet. *TLS*, 22 February 1923, p. 119. Review of *Poems by Four Authors* [J. R. Ackerley, Archibald Y. Campbell, Edward Davison, and Frank Kendon]. Unsigned.

C363 Mr. Montague's Short Stories. *Nation & Athenaeum*, 24 February 1923, p. 788. Review of *Fiery Particles*, by C. E. Montague.

C364 Crabb Robinson. *The Spectator*, 24 February 1923, pp. 331–332. Review of *Blake, Coleridge, Wordsworth, Lamb, &c.: Being Selections from the Remains of Henry Crabb Robinson. See also* C352.

C365 Mr. Hewlett's Maypole. *TLS*, 1 March 1923, p. 139. Review of *Extemporary Essays*, by Maurice Hewlett. Unsigned.

C366 War. *Outlook*, 17 March 1923, Vol. 51, No. 1311, pp. 212–214. On *A Soldier's Diary*, by Ralph Scott.

C367 The Author's Workshop. *Cassell's Weekly*, 21 March 1923, p. 7.

C368 A POET'S LETTERS. *Cassell's Weekly*, 21 March 1923, p. 13. Signed E. B. On being invited to contribute to *Cassell's Weekly*.

C369 "Holla, My Fancy . . .". *TLS*, 22 March 1923, p. 195. Review of *Whipperginny*, by Robert Graves. Unsigned.

C370 The Author's Workshop. *Cassell's Weekly*, 28 March 1923, p. 40. Unsigned; inset photograph of Blunden.

C371 Prose and Poetry. *TLS*, 29 March 1923, p. 213. Review of *Selected Poems*, by Robert Frost. Unsigned. *See also* C1579.

C372 The Author's Workshop. *Cassell's Weekly*, 4 April 1923, p. 80.

C373 The Author's Workshop. *Cassell's Weekly*, 11 April 1923, p. 112. 'The Author's Workshop' in the issue of 18 April, p. 148 is unsigned; it is probably by Blunden.

C374 A Voice Apart. *TLS*, 12 April 1923, p. 245. Review of *Collected Poems: Second Series*, by W. H. Davies. Unsigned.

C375   Books You May Have Missed: Treasures from Coleridge's Note-Books. *Cassell's Weekly*, 18 April 1923, pp. 165–166. On *Anima Poetae*, by S. T. Coleridge.

C376   "Old England". *TLS*, 19 April 1923, p. 263. Review of *The Rural Scene*, by Bernard Gilbert. Unsigned.

C377   On the Keeping of Diaries. *Cassell's Weekly*, 25 April 1923, pp. 185–186. Review of *English Diaries*, by Arthur Ponsonby. One of a series entitled 'The Book of the Week'. *See also* C382.

C378   The Author's Workshop. *Cassell's Weekly*, 25 April 1923, p. 188.

C379   The Moorland Spirit. *TLS*, 26 April 1923, p. 285. Review of *The Lowery Road*, by L. A. G. Strong. Unsigned.

C380   Mr. Kipling Reconstructs. *Nation & Athenaeum*, 28 April 1923, pp. 122–123. Review of *The Irish Guards in the Great War*, by Rudyard Kipling. Signed E. Blunden.

C381   The Author's Workshop. *Cassell's Weekly*, 2 May 1923, p. 235.

C382   Diarists in Honour. *TLS*, 3 May 1923, p. 301. Review of *English Diaries*, by Arthur Ponsonby. Unsigned. *See also* C377.

C383   The Author's Workshop. *Cassell's Weekly*, 9 May 1923, p. 248.

C384   The Five Greatest Novels. *Cassell's Weekly*, 9 May 1923, p. 259.

C385   Folk-Songs of the Thames. *TLS*, 10 May 1923, p. 312. Review of *Folk Songs of the Upper Thames*, collected and edited by Alfred Williams. Unsigned.

C386   The Author's Workshop. *Cassell's Weekly*, 16 May 1923, p. 280.

C387   Poets I Have Known. *Cassell's Weekly*, 16 May 1923, pp. 291, 306.

C388   The Author's Workshop. *Cassell's Weekly*, 19 May 1923, p. 321.

C389   Siegfried Sassoon: A Singer of the Truth. *Cassell's Weekly*, 19 May 1923, p. 325.

C390   Wessex Revised. *TLS*, 24 May 1923, p. 352. Review of *The Left Leg*, by T. F. Powys. Unsigned.

C391   A Poet's Appreciation of a Critic: Mr. J. Middleton Murry and His Work [*later* Mr. J. M. Murry and His Work]. *Cassell's Weekly*, 26 May 1923, p. 352.

Reprinted: *Ceylon Observer*, 17 June 1923, p. 12.

C392   The Author's Workshop. *Cassell's Weekly*, 26 May 1923, p. 359.

C393   Difficult Dimension. *TLS*, 31 May 1923, p. 369. Review of *Bucolic Comedies*, by Edith Sitwell. Unsigned.

C394   Upon Literary Centenaries. *The Writer*, June 1923, Vol. 4, No. 9, pp. 205–206. Cover title: Literary Centenaries.

C395   The Author's Workshop. *Cassell's Weekly*, 2 June 1923, p. 385.

C396   Lamb's Black Sheep, Wainewright: Artist, Forger, and Poisoner. *Cassell's Weekly*, 2 June 1923, p. 392. On T. G. Wainewright.

C397   "Commercial Candour". *TLS*, 7 June 1923, p. 384. Review of *An Autobiography*, by Anthony Trollope. Unsigned.

C398   Mr. Masefield's "King Cole". *TLS*, 7 June 1923, p. 385. Review of *King Cole and Other Poems*, by John Masefield. Unsigned.

C399   Life and Letters of a Great Russian. *Cassell's Weekly*, 9 June 1923, p. 409. Review of *Dostoevsky: Letters and Reminiscences*, translated by S. S. Koteliansky and J. Middleton Murry. One of a series entitled 'The Book of the Week'.

C400   The Author's Workshop. *Cassell's Weekly*, 9 June 1923, p. 417.

C401   [Review of] *Landscape of Cytherea: Record of a Journey into a Strange Country*, by W. J. Turner. *TLS*, 14 June 1923, p. 401. Unsigned. *See also* C406.

C402   A Poet as Purser: Mr. Edmund Blunden's Adventures at Sea. *Cassell's Weekly*, 20 June 1923, p. 444.

C403   The Author's Workshop. *Cassell's Weekly*, 20 June 1923, p. 457.

C404   The Wanted Book: A Peep Behind the Scenes. *Cassell's Weekly*, 20 June 1923, p. 460. On the Library of Congress's 'want lists' for 1922.

C405   The Author's Workshop: Masters of the Arts of Binding and Printing. *Cassell's Weekly*, 27 June 1923, p. 481.

C406   The Poetry of W. J. Turner. *Cassell's Weekly*, 27 June 1923, p. 488. Review of *Landscape of Cytherea*, by W. J. Turner. Signed E. Blunden. *See also* C401.

C407   Mr. Squire's New Verse. *TLS*, 28 June 1923, p. 436. Review of *American Poems and Others*, by J. C. Squire. Unsigned.

C408   The Author's Workshop: Reviewers who are Troubled by a Conscience. *Cassell's Weekly*, 4 July 1923, p. 510.

C409   The Author's Workshop: Coming Biographies of Note. *Cassell's Weekly*, 11 July 1923, p. 543.

C410　"England, My England": An Accession to the Selbornian Family. *Cassell's Weekly*, 11 July 1923, p. 551. Review of *Untrodden Ways*, by H. J. Massingham.

C411　Fantasies and Satires. *TLS*, 12 July 1923, p. 466. Review of *Out of the Flame*, by Osbert Sitwell. Unsigned.

C412　"The Delusive Fly." *Nation & Athenaeum*, 14 July 1923, pp. 492–493. Review of *Salmon and Trout Angling*, by Joseph Adams. Signed E. Blunden.

C413　Summer and the Poets. *Cassell's Weekly*, 18 July 1923, p. 578. On S. T. Coleridge and John Clare.
　　　Reprinted: *The Face of England*, 1932.

C414　The Author's Workshop: The Perseverance of the Biographer. *Cassell's Weekly*, 18 July 1923, p. 588.

C415　The Author's Workshop: New Books About Art. *Cassell's Weekly*, 25 July 1923, p. 620.

C416　A Pre-Georgian. *TLS*, 26 July 1923, p. 500. Review of *Selected Poems*, by Francis Coutts. Unsigned. *See also* C419.

C417　The Author's Workshop. *Cassell's Weekly*, 1 August 1923, p. 648.

C418　Marvell Triumphant. *TLS*, 2 August 1923, p. 515. Review of *Miscellaneous Poems*, by Andrew Marvell. Unsigned.

C419　Luck and Minor Poets. *Nation & Athenaeum*, 4 August 1923, pp. 577–578. Review of *The Posthumous Poems of C. F. Keary; Selected Poems*, by Francis Coutts (*see also* C416); and *Sublunary*, by Nancy Cunard. Signed E. Blunden.

C420　The Water Finder: Wonders of the Diving Rod. *Cassell's Weekly*, 8 August 1923, p. 664. Signed E. B.

C421　The Author's Workshop: Unpublished Letters of Keats. *Cassell's Weekly*, 8 August 1923, p. 677. On the forthcoming *Life of John Keats*, by Amy Lowell.

C422　The Author's Workshop. *Cassell's Weekly*, 15 August 1923, p. 705. Unsigned. *See also* letter 'Living Englishmen Barred: The Bitter Wail of a Poor Reader' signed 'A Poor Reader' in the issue of 25 July, p. 602 on the price of books; it is probably by Blunden.

C423　Cotton's Poems. *TLS*, 16 August 1923, p. 543. Review of *Poems of Charles Cotton 1630–1687*, edited by John Beresford. Unsigned.

C424　Andrew Marvell as a Prose Writer. *Cassell's Weekly*, 22 August 1923, p. 716.

C425　A Dramatic Fragment. *TLS*, 23 August 1923, p. 554. Review of *The Feather Bed*, by Robert Graves. Unsigned.

C426　Lamb's Select Criticism. *TLS*, 23 August 1923, p. 555. Review of *Lamb's Criticism: A Selection from the Literary Criticism*, edited by E. M. W. Tillyard. Unsigned.

Reprinted: *Votive Tablets*, 1931.

C427　Strange and Stranger. *Nation & Athenaeum*, 25 August 1923, pp. 666–667. Review of *El Supremo*, by Edward Lucas White; *The Murder of M. Fualdès*, by Armand Praviel; *Nordenholt's Million*, by J. J. Connington; *The Astonishing Adventure of Jane Smith*, by Patricia Wentworth; and *A Chandala Woman*, by Lucian de Zilwa.

C428　The Author's Workshop: Printing and the Making of Books. *Cassell's Weekly*, 29 August 1923, p. 761.

C429　The Hero of "In Memoriam": "Whom the Gods Love Die Young". *Cassell's Weekly*, 29 August 1923, p. 762. On Arthur Henry Hallam. Signed E. B.

C430　The Author's Workshop: An Oxford Book of English Prose. *Cassell's Weekly*, 5 September 1923, p. 789.

C431　In Many Fields. *Nation & Athenaeum*, 8 September 1923, pp. 717–718. Review of *The Log of a Sportsman*, by E. H. D. Sewell.

C432　The Author's Workshop: A Varied Parcel of Books. *Cassell's Weekly*, 12 September 1923, p. 817.

C433　The Author's Workshop: First Leaves of Autumn. *Cassell's Weekly*, 19 September 1923, p. 21.

C434　A Bookseller's Memories. *TLS*, 20 September 1923, p. 614. Review of *Forty Years in My Bookshop*, by Walter T. Spencer, edited by Thomas Moult. Unsigned.

C435　The Author's Workshop: An Autumn Olla Podrida. *Cassell's Weekly*, 26 September 1923, p. 51.

C436　From Grave to Gay. *TLS*, 4 October 1923, p. 647. Review of *Beasts Royal*, by Dorothy Margaret Stuart. Unsigned.

C437　"Prime Old Tusser": Five Hundred Points of Good Husbandry. *Cassell's Weekly*, 17 October 1923, p. 138. On *Five Hundred Points of Good Husbandry*, by Thomas Tusser, Gentleman. Signed E. B.

C438　Two Travellers. *Nation &Athenaeum*, 27 October 1923, pp. 156–157. Review of *Equatoria, the Lado Enclave*, by C. H. Stigand; and *Sea-Tracks of the Speejacks Round the World*, by Dale Collins.

C439　A YEOMAN. *To-day*, November 1923, Vol. 10, No. 57, p. 84.

Reprinted (revised): *Masks of Time*, [1925]; *English Poems*, [1926]; *The Poems*, 1930; and *A Selection from the Poems*, [1969], Verse 1.

C440   Emotion and Sentiment. *TLS*, 1 November 1923, p. 724. Review of *Poems*, by Edna St Vincent Millay. Unsigned. *See also* C448.

C441   The Eleventh of November. *TLS*, 8 November 1923, p. 746. Review of *Cenotaph: A Book of Remembrance*, compiled and edited by Thomas Moult. Unsigned.

C442   Phases and Phantoms. *Nation & Athenaeum*, 10 November 1923, pp. 254, 256. Review of *Thomas de Cobham, Bishop of Worcester, 1317-1327*, by E. H. Pearce; *Hervey, First Bishop of Ely, and Some Others of the Same Name*, Suffolk Green Books, No. 19; *Bernard Vaughan, S.J.* by C. C. Martindale; *An Independent Parson: Autobiography of Alfred Rowland; A Victorian Schoolmaster: Henry Hart of Sedbergh*, by G. C. Coulton; *Lord Guthrie: A Memoir*, by Robert Low Orr; *The World of Fashion, 1837-1922*, by Ralph Nevill; *Fellow-Travellers*, by Horace Annesley Vachell; *The Sands of Time*, by Walter Sichel; *Things I Know about Kings, Celebrities, and Crooks*, by William Le Queux; *Ventures in Book-Collecting*, by William Harris Arnold; *Exits and Entrances*, by Eva Moore; *Stray Recollections*, by C. E. Callwell; *Social and Diplomatic Memories, 1894-1901*, Second Series, by Sir J. Rennell Rodd; and *From Immigrant to Inventor*, by Michael Pupin.

C443   Mr. Masefield's Poems, 1902-1923. *TLS*, 29 November 1923, p. 818. Review of *The Collected Poems of John Masefield*. Unsigned.

C444   THE STILL HOUR. *The Adelphi*, December 1923, Vol. 1, No. 7, pp. 581-583.

Reprinted: *To Nature*, [1923]; *English Poems*, [1926]; *The Poems*, 1930; and *Edmund Blunden: A Selection of His Poetry and Prose*, 1950.

C445   Stray Notes in Lockhart's "Exhibitioners". *The Blue*, December 1923, Vol. 51, No. 1, pp. 4-5. On subscribers to *Translations of the Psalms of David*, by Christopher Smart listed in *List of Exhibitioners*, by A. W. Lockhart. Signed E.B.

C446   FIRST RHYMES. *Winter Owl*, 1923, p. 26.

First published: *To Nature*, [1923]. Reprinted: *English Poems*, [1926]; *The Poems*, 1930; and *The Midnight Skaters*, [1968].

C447   "After Noise, Tranquility". *TLS*, 6 December 1923, p. 848. Review of *April and Rain: Poems*, by Geoffrey Winthrop Young. Unsigned.

C448   New and Old. *Nation & Athenaeum*, 8 December 1923, pp. 404-406. Review of *Days and Nights*, by Arthur Symons; *Love's Cruelty*, by Arthur Symons; *Shores of Lyonesse*, by James Dryden Hosken; *New Idyllia*, by Morton Luce;

Parentalia, by J. D. C. Pellow; *The Secret Flowers*, by Cyril G. Taylor; *Little Journeys into the Heavenly Country*, by W. R. Hughes; *Crown of Nothing*, by F. H. Shephard; *Poet's Light*, by Ian Kelway; *Sea Songs and Ballads, 1917-1922*, by C. Fox Smith; *Poems*, by Camilla Doyle; *Poems*, by Edna St Vincent Millay (*see also* C440); *Roman Bartholow*, by Edwin Arlington Robinson; *Oxford Poetry, 1923*, edited by D. C. Thomson and F. W. Bateson; *A Miscellany of Current Verse*, edited by E. Guy Pertwee; *Valour and Vision: Poems of the War*, edited by Jacqueline Trotter; *Contemporary German Poetry*, chosen and translated by Babette Deutsch and Avrahm Yarmolinsky; *Every Man's Book of Sacred Verse*, edited by Gordon Crosse; and *Come Hither: A Collection of Rhymes and Poems for the Young of All Ages*, made by Walter de la Mare.

C449   Fantasy. *TLS*, 13 December 1923, p. 871. Review of *Pages from the History of Zachy Trenoy*, by Ruth Manning-Saunders. Unsigned.

C450   A Devon Worthy. *Nation & Athenaeum*, 15 December 1923, p. 435. Review of *Life of General the Right Hon. Sir Redvers Buller, V.C.*, by C. H. Melville. Signed E.B.

C451   A Novelist-Poet. *TLS*, 27 December 1923, p. 906. Review of *Cherry-Stones*, by Eden Philpotts. Unsigned.

1924

C452   EPITAPH (There was a ship, no lady, it was said,). *The Lifeboat*, Centenary Number 1924, p. 48. Signature in holograph facsimile.

C453   "A Man So Various". *Nation & Athenaeum*, 5 January 1924, pp. 521-522. Review of *The Story of My Life*, by Sir Harry Johnston. Signed E.B.

C454   Childhood's Mirror. *TLS*, 24 January 1924, p. 50. Review of *Childhood in Verse and Prose: An Anthology*, chosen by Susan Miles. Unsigned.

C455   VILLAGE. *Nation & Athenaeum*, 26 January 1924, p. 606. Reprinted: *Masks of Time*, [1925]; *English Poems*, [1926]; and *The Poems*, 1930.

C456   A Prose-Writer's Poems. *Nation & Athenaeum*, 26 January 1924, p. 609. Review of *Poems*, by Katherine Mansfield.

C457   A Luckier Lycidas. *TLS*, 31 January 1924, p. 63. Review of *An Offering of Swans*, by Oliver Gogarty. Unsigned.

C458   Wanted, A Catechist. *Nation & Athenaeum*, 2 February 1924, p. 638. Review of *A Popular History of English Poetry*, by T. Earle Welby.

C459 A Lesser Elizabeth. *The Spectator*, 16 February 1924, pp. 248-249. Review of *Mrs. Montagu: "Queen of the Blues": Her Letters and Friendships from 1762-1800*, edited by Reginald Blunt.

C460 Night Thoughts. *TLS*, 21 February 1924, p. 109. Review of *Nightcaps: The Gentle Art of Reading in Bed*, by E. B. Osborn. Unsigned.

C461 The Roman Rake. *TLS*, 28 February 1924, p. 125. Review of *Ovid: The Lover's Handbook*, a complete translation of the *Ars Amatoria*, by F. A. Wright. Unsigned.

C462 Arnold George Alexander Vidler, Peele A, 1902-1908. *The Blue*, March 1924, Vol. 51, No. 3, pp. 87-88. Obituary. Signed E.B.

C463 THE OPERA—A HYMN OF PRAISE. *The Blue*, March 1924, Vol. 51, No. 3, pp. 95-96. Signed E.B. (with apologies to W.W.B.). No. 4 of 'Four Points of View' on the production of *H.M.S. Pinafore*.

C464 Susan Miles and Others. *Weekly Westminster*, 1 March 1924, p. 564. Review of *Little Mirrors*, by Susan Miles (*see also* C469); *Narcotics*, by C. A. Renshaw; *Songs of Many Days*, by Nina Salaman; *The Conflict*, by Elsie Paterson Cranmer; *Poems*, Part II, by Malcolm Taylor (*see also* C715); *Kent Ways*, by George H. Vallins; *At Dawn*, by Evan Morgan; *Windows*, by George Montagu, Earl of Sandwich; *The Knights of Dee*, by D.A.S.; *Our Brave Boys*, by William Brantom; *Various Verses*, by William Brantom; and *Poems Satirical and Miscellaneous*, by Charles Richard Cammell.

C465 Australian Anthologies. *TLS*, 6 March 1924, p. 141. Review of *A Book of Australian Verse*, chosen by Walter Murdoch; and *Poetry in Australia, 1923*, preface by Norman Lindsay. Unsigned.

C466 A TRANSCRIPTION. *Nation & Athenaeum*, 8 March 1924, p. 797.

Reprinted: *Masks of Time*, [1925]; *English Poems*, [1926]; and *The Poems*, 1930.

C467 Epigram and Poetry. *Weekly Westminster*, 15 March 1924, p. 630. Review of *Kensington Gardens*, by Humbert Wolfe (*see also* C469).

C468 And Still They Come. *Weekly Westminster*, 22 March 1924, pp. 649-650. On modern poetry.

C469 On the Borders of Prose. *TLS*, 27 March 1924, p. 188. Review of *Little Mirrors*, by Susan Miles (*see also* C464); *Kensington Gardens*, by Humbert Wolfe (*see also* C467); and *Poems and Sonnets*, by Frank Kendon. Unsigned.

C470 An Experiment in Epic. *TLS*, 10 April 1924, p. 220. Review of *The Book of the Beloved: A Modern Epic Poem*, by J. C. Johnston. Unsigned.

C471 INTIMATIONS OF MORTALITY. *Weekly Westminster*, 3 May 1924, p. 12.

Reprinted: *Masks of Time*, [1925] ; *English Poems*, [1926] ; *The Poems*, 1930; and *Poems of Many Years*, 1957.

C471 .1 A BUDDING MORROW. *The Torchbearer*, Summer 1924, p. —.*

Reprinted: *Masks of Time*, [1925]; *English Poems*, [1926]; and *The Poems*, 1930.

C472 THUS FAR. *The Adelphi*, June 1924, Vol. 2, No. 1, p. 30.

Reprinted: *Masks of Time*, [1925] ; *English Poems*, [1926] ; and *The Poems*, 1930.

C473 ROSA MUNDI. *The Adelphi*, July 1924, Vol. 2, No. 2, p. 129.

Reprinted (revised): *Masks of Time*, [1925]; *English Poems*, [1926]; and *The Poems*, 1930.

C474 THE ANCRE AT HAMEL [*later* THE ANCRE AT HAMEL: AFTERWARDS]. *New Statesman*, 12 July 1924, p. 410.

Reprinted: *Masks of Time*, [1925]; *Undertones of War*, 1928; *The Poems*, 1930; and *The Midnight Skaters*, [1968].

C475 THE SURVIVORS (1916) [*later* TWO VOICES]. *Weekly Westminster*, 2 August 1924, p. 422.

Reprinted: *Masks of Time*, [1925]; *Undertones of War*, 1928; *The Poems*, 1930; and *Poems of Many Years*, 1957.

C476 INTERVAL. *Weekly Westminster*, 16 August 1924, p. 471.

Reprinted: *Masks of Time*, [1925]; *English Poems*, [1926]; and *The Poems*, 1930.

C477 A First Address: "The Richness of English Literature". *Rising Generation*, 1 September 1924, Vol. 51, No. 11, pp. 322-323; and 15 September, Vol. 51, No. 12, pp. 354-355.*

Reprinted: *Lectures in English Literature*, 1927.

C478 ELEGY. *Nation & Athenaeum*, 27 September 1924, p. 777.

Reprinted: *Poetica*, May 1925, Vol. [1], No. 4, p. [7]; *English Poems*, [1926]; *The Poems*, 1930; and *The Midnight Skaters*, [1968].

C479 TOKYO: AN UNPUBLISHED PASSAGE FROM GOLDSMITH'S *THE TRAVELLER*? *The Blue*, October 1924, Vol. 52, No. 1, p. 15. Signed B.

C480 THE DAIMYO'S POND. *London Mercury*, October 1924, Vol. 10, No. 60, pp. 574-575.

Reprinted: *Japan Advertiser*, 2 November 1924, p. 6; *The Augustan Books*, [1925]; *English Poems*, [1926]; *Japanese Garland*, [1928]; and *The Poems*, 1930.

C481   A "FIRST IMPRESSION" TOKYO [*later* A "FIRST IMPRESSION"]. *London Mercury*, October 1924, Vol. 10, No. 60, pp. 575-576.

Reprinted: *Japan Times*, 4 December 1924, p. —; *The Best Poems of 1924*, [1925]; *The Augustan Books*, [1925]; *English Poems*, [1926]; *Japanese Garland*, [1928]; *The Poems*, 1930; and *Poems of Many Years*, 1957.

C482   UNTEACHABLE. *Nation & Athenaeum*, 11 October 1924, p. 53.

Reprinted: *Japan Advertiser*, 9 December 1924, p. 4*; *English Poems*, [1926]; and *The Poems*, 1930.

C483   HARVEST. *The Adelphi*, November 1924, Vol. 2, No. 6, p. 473.

Reprinted: *Masks of Time*, [1925]; *English Poems*, [1926]; *The Poems*, 1930; and *Poems of Many Years*, 1957.

C484   Modern Biography. *The Adelphi*, November 1924, Vol. 2, No. 6, pp. 519-522.

C485   Two Travelers: From Italy and From England to Japan. *Japan Advertiser*, 7 December 1924, p. 6. Review of *Sunward*, by Louis Golding; and *In Praise of England*, by H. J. Massingham.

C486   THAMES GULLS. *Japan Advertiser*, 21 December 1924, p. 6.*

Reprinted: *English Poems*, [1926]; *The Poems*, 1930; *The Face of England*, 1938; and *Poems of Many Years*, 1957.

C487   The Christmas Tradition. *Tokyo Nichinichi*, 25 December 1924, Christmas and New Year Number, p. 2.*

1925

C488   Argument of "The Dynasts" by Thomas Hardy. *Rising Generation*, 1 January 1925, Vol. 54, No. 7, pp. 194-195; and 15 January, Vol. 54, No. 8, pp. 230-232.

C489   John Masefield. *Oriental Literary Times*, 15 January 1925, Vol. 1, No. 1, pp. 9-13. First in a series entitled 'Literary England'.

C490   The Pedlar's Pack. *Oriental Literary Times*, 15 January 1925, Vol. 1, No. 1, pp. 27-30. Signed Quince.

C491   PRIDE OF THE VILLAGE. *The Adelphi*, February 1925, Vol. 2, No. 9, pp. 743-744.

Reprinted: *English Poems*, [1926]; *The Poems*, 1930; *Edmund Blunden: A Selection of His Poetry and Prose*, 1950; and *Poems of Many Years*, 1957.

C492   A BRIDGE. *Poetica*, February 1925, Vol. [1], No. 1, p. [6].

Reprinted: *Masks of Time*, [1925] ; *English Poems*, [1926] ; *The Poems*, 1930; and *The Midnight Skaters*, [1968].

C493   "ART THOU GONE IN HASTE?". *Poetica*, February 1925, Vol. [1], No. 1, p. [7].

Reprinted: *The Masks of Time*, [1925]; *English Poems*, [1926] ; and *The Poems*, 1930.

C494   BURIAL IN SPRING: FROM THE FRENCH OF BRIZEUX. *Oriental Literary Times*, 1 February 1925, Vol. 1, No. 2, p. 12.

C495   In the Footsteps of Charles Lamb. *Oriental Literary Times*, 1 February 1925, Vol. 1, No. 2, pp. 14-17. Signed B.

C496   OMEN. *Weekly Westminster*, 14 February 1925, p. 467.

Reprinted: *Masks of Time*, [1925] ; *English Poems*, [1926] ; and *The Poems*, 1930.

C497   Vivat! *Oriental Literary Times*, 15 February 1925, Vol. 1, No. 3, pp. 70-72. On Charles Chaplin. Signed E.

C498   A Literary Criticism: Power and Gentleness, A Certain Mysticism. *Japan Advertiser*, 27 February 1925, p. 4; and 28 February, p. 4.* An address to the Tokyo Women's Club.

C499   EPOCHS [*later* ERAS; *and* ACHRONOS]. *Poetica*, March 1925, Vol. [1], No. 2, p. [6].

Reprinted: *Masks of Time*, [1925] ; *English Poems*, [1926] ; *The Poems*, 1930; and *Poems of Many Years*, 1957.

C500   THE FLASHING FLINT: FROM THE LATIN OF HENRY VAUGHAN [*later* THE FLASHING FLINT]. *Oriental Literary Times*, 1 March 1925, Vol. 1, No. 4, pp. 110-111. Signed B.

Reprinted: *On the Poems of Henry Vaughan*, [1927].

C501   H. M. Tomlinson. *Oriental Literary Times*, 15 March 1925, Vol. 1, No. 5, pp. 139-144. Second in a series entitled Literary England.

Reprinted: *Edmund Blunden: A Selection of His Poetry and Prose*, 1950.

C502   FROM VERLAINE: LE CIEL EST, PAR-DESSUS LE TOIT. *Oriental Literary Times*, 15 March 1925, Vol. 1, No. 5, p. 145. Unsigned.

C503   Letters to the Editor. *The Blue*, April 1925, Vol. 52, No. 3, p. 140. On 'Charles Lamb' in the issue of December 1924, p. 49. Signed Azure. At head: From a Distinguished Professor of Literature in Tokio.

C504 ILLUSIONS. *Poetica*, April 1925, Vol. [1], No. 3, p. [6].
Above title: Three Scenes from the European War: Flanders
(1914-1918).

Reprinted (revised): *Undertones of War*, 1928; *The Poems*,
1930; *Poems of Many Years*, 1957; *A Selection of the Shorter
Poems*, [1966]; *The Midnight Skaters*, [1968]; and *A
Selection from the Poems*, [1969].

C505 TRENCH RAID NEAR HOOGE. *Poetica*, April 1925, Vol.
[1], No. 3, p. [7]. Above title: Three Scenes from the European War: Flanders (1914-1918).

Reprinted (revised): *Undertones of War*, 1928; and *The
Poems*, 1930.

C506 BATTALION IN REST [*later* BATTALION IN REST,
JULY 1917]. *Poetica*, April 1925, Vol. [1], No. 3, p. [8].
Above title: Three Scenes from the European War: Flanders
(1914-1918).

Reprinted (revised): *The Adelphi*, November 1925, Vol. 3,
No. 6, pp. 417-418; *Masks of Time*, [1925]; *Undertones of
War*, 1928; *The Poems*, 1930; and *Poems of Many Years*,
1957.

C507 SPLEEN: FROM BAUDELAIRE. *Oriental Literary Times*,
1 April 1925, Vol. 1, No. 6, pp. 185-196. Unsigned.

C508 Selling Up the Old House: Its Many Treasures and its Historic Associations Under the Auctioneer's Hammer. *The
Sphere*, 16 May 1925, p. 220b.

C509 [UNTITLED (Omicron, who with just and vigorous wit)].
Nation & Athenaeum, 23 May 1925, p. 237. Verse in reply
to Omicron's note [*i.e.* Leonard Woolf's note] on 'the
English have lost their skill with bat and ball'. Signed
Revenant. *See also* the issue of 21 February, p. 715, 'From
Alpha to Omega', paragraph 1.

C510 PERHAPS. *The Blue*, June 1925, Vol. 52, No. 4, p. 169.
Signed B.

C511 TO . . . . [*later* TO A SPIRIT]. *London Mercury*, June
1925, Vol. 12, No. 68, pp. 119-120.

Reprinted: *English Poems*, [1926]; and *The Poems*, 1930.

C512 IN A COUNTRY CHURCHYARD. *London Mercury*, June
1925, Vol. 12, No. 68, pp. 120-121.

Reprinted: *English Poems*, [1926]; *The Poems*, 1930; and
Poems of Many Years, 1957.

C513 THE DOOMED OAK FROM THE FRENCH OF ANATOLE
FRANCE [*later* THE DOOMED OAK; *and* with sub-title:
AN IMITATION OF ANATOLE FRANCE]. *Poetica*, June
1925, Vol. [1], No. 5, pp. 6-7. Also issued separately as an
offprint (*see* A16).

Reprinted: *Retreat*, 1928; and *The Poems*, 1930.

C514   THE PUZZLE. *Saturday Review*, 27 June 1925, p. 711.

Reprinted: *English Poems*, [1926] ; *The Poems*, 1930; and *Poems of Many Years*, 1957.

C515   BY ROAD [*later* BYROAD]. *Calendar of Modern Letters*, July 1925, Vol. 1, No. 5, pp. 343–344.

Reprinted: *English Poems*, 1926; *The Poems*, 1930; *The Face of England*, 1938; and *Poems of Many Years*, 1957.

C516   "THY DREAMS OMINOUS". *Calendar of Modern Letters*, July 1925, Vol. 1, No. 5, p. 345.

Reprinted: *English Poems*, 1926; and *The Poems*, 1930.

C517   SHEPHERD'S CALENDAR [*later* ANOTHER SPRING]. *Calendar of Modern Letters*, July 1925, Vol. 1, No. 5, p. 345.

Reprinted: *English Poems*, 1926; and *The Poems*, 1930.

C518   MISUNDERSTANDINGS. *Calendar of Modern Letters*, July 1925, Vol. 1, No. 5, p. 346.

Reprinted: *English Poems*, 1926; and *The Poems*, 1930.

C519   Anthologies. *The Adelphi*, August 1925, Vol. 3, No. 3, pp. 203–206.

C520   FRAGMENTS [*later* THE CHANCE]. *Poetica*, August 1925, Vol. 2, No. 1, p. 6.*

Reprinted: *Retreat*, 1928; and *The Poems*, 1930.

C521   1919 [*later* "FOR THERE IS NO HELP IN THEM"]. *Nation & Athenaeum*, 8 August 1925, p. 570.

Reprinted: *Retreat*, 1928; and *The Poems*, 1930.

C522   THE FLOWER-GATHERERS. *London Mercury*, September 1925, Vol. 12, No. 71, p. 463.

Reprinted: *English Poems*, 1926; and *The Poems*, 1930.

C523   THE EMBRYO. *London Mercury*, September 1925, Vol. 12, No. 71, pp. 463–464.

Reprinted: *English Poems*, 1926; and *The Poems*, 1930.

C524   THE DEEPS. *London Mercury*, September 1925, Vol. 12, No. 71, p. 464.

Reprinted: *English Poems*, 1926; and *The Poems*, 1930.

C525   Human and Divine: A Decade of Inspirations and an English Poet. *Japan Advertiser*, 13 September 1925, p. 4. Review of *Selected Poems*, by Siegfried Sassoon. *See also* C565.

C526   Literary Impostures: Two Famous Attempts that Were Exposed. *Japan Advertiser*, 20 September 1925, pp. 4–5.*

C527   Gleanings from our Post Bag. *The Blue*, October 1925, Vol. 53, No. 1, pp. 33–34. From Kikufuji Hotel, Tokyo. Extract from letter.

C528   Railway Centenary: The Early Poets of the Age of Steam. *Japan Advertiser*, 4 October 1925, p. 4.

C529   The World of Books: A Problem Picture localized in Fleet Street. *Japan Advertiser*, 18 October 1925, p. 4.*

C530   Buddhist Paintings: Free Thoughts on the Exhibition at Ueno. *Japan Advertiser*, 1 November 1925, pp. 6–7.*

        Reprinted: *The Mind's Eye*, 1934.

C531   On "Japanese English": A New Poet's Accomplishment is Evaluated. *Japan Advertiser*, 15 November 1925, p. 6. On *Twelve Poems*, by Haxon Ishii.

C532   British Literature of 1925 contrasted with [the] Victorian Age. *Japan Times*, 29 November 1925, p. 11.*

C533   LANDSCAPE. *Poetica*, December 1925, Vol. 2, No. 5, p. 7.*

C534   A Doubtful Activity: The Unfortunate "King Lear" When Abroad. *Japan Advertiser*, 6 December 1925, pp. 4, 12. On a French translation of *King Lear*.

C535   Coming of Alexandra: The Poetic Welcome Accorded Her in 1863. *Japan Advertiser*, 13 December 1925, p. 6. On the death of Queen Alexandra and her treatment by the poets.

C536   Herman Melville, Poet: Poems of the Man Who Wrote "Moby Dick". *Japan Advertiser*, 27 December 1925, p. 6. Review of *Works of Herman Melville*, Standard Edition, Constable.

1926

C537   Days Before the War: Recollections of a Village in the Garden of England. *Japan Advertiser*, 17 January 1926, p. 8.*

C538   Japan's English Poets: Transplanting the Cherry Tree—Today and the Future. *Japan Advertiser*, 7 February 1926, pp. 8–9.

C539   THE CORRECT SOLUTION [*later* SOLUTIONS]. *Nation & Athenaeum*, 13 February 1926, p. 681.

        Reprinted: *Japan Advertiser*, 10 May 1926, p. 2*; *Retreat*, 1928; *The Poems*, 1930; and *Poems of Many Years*, 1957.

C540   "Subject in Poetry": Vagaries and Changes of Topic and Title. *Japan Advertiser*, 21 February 1926, pp. 8–9.*

        Reprinted: *The Mind's Eye*, 1934.

C541   Correspondence. *The Blue*, March 1926, Vol. 53, No. 4, p. 159. At head: From E.B., Kikufugi Hotel, Tokyo. Extract from letter.

C542   NIGHTWIND [*later* NIGHT-WIND]. *The Spectator*, 13 March 1926, Literary Supplement, p. 455.

        Reprinted: *Retreat*, 1928; and *The Poems*, 1930.

C543 Concerning Old Maps: Some Notes in the Margin made More Recently. *Japan Advertiser*, 14 March 1926, pp. 4, 15.*

C544 More Hearn Letters: Some of His Epistles to Japanese Correspondents. *Japan Advertiser*, 29 March 1926, p. 2. Review of *Some New Letters and Writings of Lafcadio Hearn*, edited by Sanki Ichikawa.

C545 More Footnotes to Literary History. *Studies in English Literature*, April 1926, Vol. 6, No. 1, pp. 1–21. Part 1, Free Thoughts on the Biography of John Keats—Part 2, John Clare, Notes and References. Also issued separately as an offprint (*see* A21).
Reprinted: *Reprinted Papers*, 1950.

C546 A Notable Memorial. *Studies in English Literature*, April 1926, Vol. 6, No. 1, pp. 111–112. Review of *The Letters of Thomas Manning to Charles Lamb*, edited by G. A. Anderson. Signed E. Blunden.

C547 Portrait of a Modest Man. *Studies in English Literature*, April 1926, Vol. 6, No. 1, p. 113. Review of *The Translator of Dante: H. F. Cary*, by R. W. King. Signed E. Blunden.

C548 Two on a Tower. *Studies in English Literature*, April 1926, Vol. 6, No. 1, pp. 114–116. Review of *Human Shows*, by Thomas Hardy; and *New Verse*, by Robert Bridges. Signed E. Blunden.

C549 Sweet Seriousness. *Studies in English Literature*, April 1926, Vol. 6, No. 1, pp. 116–117. Review of *Night Fears*, by L. P. Hartley; and *Simonetta Perkins*, by L. P. Hartley. Signed E. Blunden.

C550 New Textbooks. *Studies in English Literature*, April 1926, Vol. 6, No. 1, pp. 117–118. Review of *The Tide of Time in English Poetry*, edited by Henry Newbolt; *Tennyson*, edited by S. S. Sopwith; and *Hamlet*, edited by George Sampson. Signed E. Blunden.

C551 Art of Handwriting: Some Notes on a Neglected History. *Japan Advertiser*, 4 April 1926, pp. 4–5.

C552 From a Book-Fancier: Treasure Troves Found in Curious Corners. *Japan Advertiser*, 25 April 1926, p. 6.

C553 "Japan" and its Group: Following the Word Through the Dictionary. *Japan Advertiser*, 2 May 1926, p. 6.

C554 Poets' Ample Corner: Poems Gathered from a Year's Periodicals. *Japan Advertiser*, 9 May 1926, p. 6. Review of *The Best Poems of 1925*, Boston, 1926.

C555 FAR EAST. *London Mercury*, June 1926, Vol. 14, No. 80, pp. 122–123.

First published: separate edition, 1925; reprinted: *Japanese Garland*, 1928; *Near and Far*, 1929; *The Poems*, 1930; and *The Midnight Skaters*, [1968].

C556   THE COMPLAINT. *London Mercury*, June 1926, Vol. 14, No. 80, pp. 123-124.

Reprinted (revised): *Retreat*, 1928; *The Poems*, 1930; and *Poems of Many Years*, 1957.

C557   TRIUNE [*later* HAWTHORN]. *London Mercury*, June 1926, Vol. 14, No. 80, p. 124.

Reprinted: *English Poems*, 1925; *The Poems*, 1930; *Poems of Many Years*, 1957; and *The Midnight Skaters*, [1968].

C558   VOICES BY A RIVER. *London Mercury*, June 1926, Vol. 14, No. 80, p. 125.

Reprinted (revised): *Retreat*, 1928; and *The Poems*, 1930.

C559   TOGETHER [*later* AN ANCIENT PATH]. *London Mercury*, June 1926, Vol. 14, No. 80, pp. 125-126.

Reprinted (revised): *Retreat*, 1928; *The Poems*, 1930; and *Poems of Many Years*, 1957.

C560   A SUPERSTITION RE-VISITED [*later* A SUPERSTITION REVISITED]. *London Mercury*, June 1926, Vol. 14, No. 80, pp. 126-127.

Reprinted (revised): *Retreat*, 1928; and *The Poems*, 1930.

C561   PRELUSION [*formerly; and later* THE MESSAGE]. *London Mercury*, June 1926, Vol. 14, No. 80, p. 128.

First published: *English Poems*, 1926. Reprinted: *The Poems*, 1930.

C562   Bacon's Tercentenary: "The Father of the English Essay". *Japan Advertiser*, 6 June 1926, pp. 6, 15.

C563   A Counter-Attack on Mencken: England Replies to the Indictment Voiced by the Most Facile Critic of New York and Baltimore. *Japan Advertiser*, 27 June 1926, p. 7. On H. L. Mencken.

C564   Coleridge, Shelley and Keats. *Studies in English Literature*, July 1926, Vol. 6, No. 2, pp. 161-179; and October 1926, Vol. 6, No. 3, pp. 325-343. Based on lectures given at the University of Tokyo during the summer of 1926.

Reprinted: *Lectures in English Literature*, 1927; and *Reprinted Papers*, 1950.

C565   Sassoon in Selection. *Studies in English Literature*, July 1926, Vol. 6, No. 2, pp. 288-289. Review of *Selected Poems*, by Siegfried Sassoon (*see also* C525); and *Augustan Books of Modern Poetry: Siegfried Sassoon*. Signed E.B.

C566   A Fragment of Truth. *Studies in English Literature*, July 1926, Vol. 6, No. 2, p. 290. Review of *In Retreat*, by Herbert Read. Signed E.B.

C567   "Points". *Studies in English Literature*, July 1926, Vol. 6, No. 2, pp. 290–291. Review of *Bibliographies of Modern Authors (Second Series)*, compiled and edited by C. A. and H. W. Stonehill. Signed E.B.

C568   Hardy, Gosse and Bridges Fifty Years Ago. *Study of English*, July 1926, Vol. 19, No. 4, pp. 353–360.

C569   The Oxford Group of 1919–1920: When Many Literary Lights Gathered on Boar's Hill—Who They Were and What They May Become. *Japan Advertiser*, 1 August 1926, p. 7.

C570   Shakespeare's Witches and Some Others. *Rising Generation*, 15 August 1926, Vol. 55, No. 10, pp. 326–328*; 1 September 1926, Vol. 55, No. 11, pp. 362–364; and 15 September 1926, Vol. 55, No. 12, pp. 398–399.

C571   Hiroshige as Humorist: A Little Known Aspect of the Famous Artist [*later* On Some Humorous Prints of Hiroshige]. *Japan Advertiser*, 22 August 1926, p. 6.

Reprinted: *The Mind's Eye*, 1934.

C572   London Salesroom: 'Christie's' Auctions Reflected a Nation's History. *Japan Advertiser*, 5 September 1926, p. 6.

C573   Our Curious Present: An English Poet Satirizes Our Well-Known Age. *Japan Advertiser*, 12 September 1926, p. 6. Review of *Satirical Poems*, by Siegfried Sassoon.

C574   Life Aboard a "Tramp": Some Brief Glimpses of Seafaring Character. *Japan Advertiser*, 26 September 1926, p. 6.*

Reprinted: *The Mind's Eye*, 1934.

C575   The Casual Cavalier. *Studies in English Literature*, October 1926, Vol. 6, No. 3, pp. 429–431. Review of *The Poems of Richard Lovelace*, edited by C. H. Wilkinson. Signed E.B. *See also* C989.

C576   The Load of Fame. *Studies in English Literature*, October 1926, Vol. 6, No. 3, pp. 431–433. Review of *The Pilgrim of Eternity: Byron, A Conflict*, by John Drinkwater. Signed E.B.

C577   "Is This the Mighty Ocean". *Studies in English Literature*, October 1926, Vol. 6, No. 3, pp. 434–435. Review of *Samuel Taylor Coleridge*, by Hugh I'Anson Fausset. Signed E.B.

C578   Gibson for Schools. *Studies in English Literature*, October 1926, Vol. 6, No. 3, pp. 436–437. Review of *Sixty-Three Poems*, by Wilfrid Gibson, edited by E. A. Parker. Signed E.B.

C579   Ideals and Achievements. *Studies in English Literature*, October 1926, Vol. 6, No. 3, pp. 437–439. Review of *The Journals of Thomas James Cobden-Sanderson*. Signed E.B.

C580   America Collects Art: Tribute Levied Upon England and Its Effect. *Japan Advertiser*, 10 October 1926, p. 6. On the export of books and art treasures.

C581   A Palace of Art. *Nation & Athenaeum*, 16 October 1926, p. 90. Review of *Christie's, 1766 to 1925*, by H. C. Marillier. Signed E. Blunden.

C582   Ghosts-Grotesques: The Curious Color Prints of Kuniyoshi. *Japan Advertiser*, 17 October 1926, p. 6.

Reprinted: *The Mind's Eye*, 1934.

C583   English in Japan: The Fine Record of Several Japanese Scholars. *Japan Advertiser*, 31 October 1926, p. 6.

C584   ORNITHOPOLIS [*later* sub-title added]. *The Adelphi*, November 1926, Vol. 4, No. 5, p. 278. Arising from 'Starlings in London' by Eric Parker in *The Spectator*, 6 March 1926, p. 412.

Reprinted: *Edmund Blunden: His Professorship and His Writing*, 1927; *Retreat*, 1928; *The Poems*, 1930; and *Poems of Many Years*, 1957.

C585   On the Poems of Henry Vaughan. *London Mercury*, November 1926, Vol. 15, No. 85, pp. 59–75.

Reprinted (revised): in a separate edition, [1927].

C586   War and Peace. *Nation & Athenaeum*, 6 November 1926, pp. 181–182.

Reprinted: *The Mind's Eye*, 1934.

C587   ORIENTAL ORNAMENTATIONS [*later* ORNAMENTATIONS]. *Japan Advertiser*, 14 November 1926, p. 6.*

Reprinted (revised): *Japanese Garland*, 1928; *Near and Far*, 1929; *The Bookman*, London, November 1929, Vol. 77, No. 458, p. 127; and *The Poems*, 1930.

C588   A Tokyo Secret: The Tokugawa Mausoleums at Shiba. *Japan Advertiser*, 23 November 1926, p. 4.

Reprinted: *The Mind's Eye*, 1934; and *Edmund Blunden: A Selection of His Poetry and Prose*, 1950.

C589   RECOLLECTIONS OF CHRIST'S HOSPITAL. *The Blue*, December 1926, Vol. 54, No. 2, pp. 53–54.

Reprinted: *Retreat*, 1928; *The Poems*, 1930; and *The Christ's Hospital Book*, [1953].

C590   Dreams of Great Writers. *Rising Generation*, 1 December 1926, Vol. 56, No. 5, pp. 153–154; and 15 December 1926, Vol. 56, No. 6, pp. 182–183.

C591   WOULD YOU RETURN? *Nation & Athenaeum*, 11 December 1926, p. 387.

Reprinted: *The Best Poems of 1927*, 1927; *Retreat*, 1928; *The Poems*, 1930; and *Poems of Many Years*, 1957.

C592   Atami of the Past: An Old Guide-Book Throws Light on Resort. *Japan Advertiser*, 12 December 1926, p. 8.
Reprinted: *The Mind's Eye*, 1934.

1927

C593   Physicians and Poetry: A Brief Record. *Studies in English Literature*, January 1927, Vol. 7, No. 1, pp. 1–16.
Reprinted: *Reprinted Papers*, 1950.

C594   A Person of Importance in Our Day. *Studies in English Literature*, January 1927, Vol. 7, No. 1, pp. 127–130. Review of *Christopher Smart: Sa Vie et ses Oeuvres*, by K. A. McKenzie.

C595   A Master-Key. *Studies in English Literature*, January 1927, Vol. 7, No. 1, pp. 130–132. Review of *A Register of Bibliographies of the English Language and Literature*, by Clark Sutherland Northup. Signed E.B.

C596   Chiefly Coleridge. *Studies in English Literature*, January 1927, Vol. 7, No. 1, pp. 132–134. Review of *German Influence in the English Romantic Period, 1788–1818*, by F. W. Stokoe. Signed E.B.

C597   Verse and the Attention. *Studies in English Literature*, January 1927, Vol. 7, No. 1, p. 134. Review of *On the Relation of Poetry to Verse*, by Sir Philip Hartog. Signed B.

C598   A Friend of Liberty. *Studies in English Literature*, January 1927, Vol. 7, No. 1, pp. 135–136. Review of *Memoirs of Thomas Holcroft*, written by himself and continued by William Hazlitt. Signed B.

C599   An Uncollected Poem by Thomas Hood. *Studies in English Literature*, January 1927, Vol. 7, No. 1, pp. 140–142. Signed E.B.

C600   On a Map of London in 1797. *Studies in English Literature*, January 1927, Vol. 7, No. 1, pp. 143–145. On *A New Pocket Plan of the Cities of London and Westminster, with the Borough of Southwark*. Signed E.B.

C601   The Essential de la Mare. *Study of English*, January 1927, Vol. 19, No. 10, pp. 1036–1041.

C602   C.H. and the Press in Japan. *The Blue*, February 1927, Vol. 54, No. 3, p. 111. Signed E.B.

C603   Leigh Hunt or Thornton? *The Blue*, February 1927, Vol. 54, No. 3, p. 113. Letter signed John Middleton Murry, Edmund Blunden. *See also* letters signed Leigh Hunt [*sic*] and W. G. Poskitt in the issue of April 1927, pp. 137–140.

C604　BUILDING THE LIBRARY, NIGHT SCENE, TOKYO UNIVERSITY [*later* BUILDING THE LIBRARY, TOKYO UNIVERSITY]. *Japan Advertiser*, 6 February 1927, p. 6.*
Reprinted: *Japanese Garland*, 1928; *Near and Far*, 1929; and *The Poems*, 1930.

C605　Wordsworthian Topics. *The Adelphi*, March 1927, Vol. 4, No. 9, pp. 559–560. On Sneyd Davies, Archdeacon of Derby, Canon-Residentiary of Lichfield.

C606　OLD BATTLEFIELDS [*later* FLANDERS NOW]. *Harper's Monthly Magazine*, March 1927, Vol. 154, p. 497.
Reprinted: *Undertones of War*, 1928; *The Poems*, 1930; and *Poems of Many Years*, 1957.

C607　The Oldest English Publishers: Oxford University Press Approaches its 500th Birthday. *Japan Advertiser*, 27 March 1927, p. 4.

C608　[Extract from a letter to the Editor]. *The Blue*, April 1927, Vol. 54, No. 4, p. 173. Letter dated 18 February 1927, Tokyo.

C609　A.D. 1827 in English Literature. *Studies in English Literature*, April 1927, Vol. 7, No. 2, pp. 169–190.
Reprinted: *Reprinted Papers*, 1950.

C610　Lectures on Keats. *Studies in English Literature*, April 1927, Vol. 7, No. 2, pp. 288–291. Review of *Keats*, by H. W. Garrod. Signed E.B.

C611　More about E. A. Poe. *Studies in English Literature*, April 1927, Vol. 7, No. 2, pp. 292–295. Review of *Edgar Allan Poe: Letters till Now Unpublished* . . . edited by Mary Newton Stanard; *Edgar Allan Poe: The Man*, by Mary E. Phillips; and *Edgar Allan Poe: A Study in Genius*, by Joseph Wood Krutch. Signed E.B.

C612　Autographic Gleanings. *Studies in English Literature*, April 1927, Vol. 7, No. 2, pp. 295–298. Review of *A Book for Bookmen*, by John Drinkwater. Signed E.B.

C613　A Double Anthology. *Studies in English Literature*, April 1927, Vol. 7, No. 2, pp. 298–299. Review of *Great Names, Being an Anthology of English & American Literature from Chaucer to Francis Thompson*, edited by W. J. Turner. Signed E.B. *See also* B18.

C614　Miscellanies. *Studies in English Literature*, April 1927, Vol. 7, No. 2, pp. 305–309. Signed E.B.

C615　Discovering a Poet: The Story of a Literary Treasure Hunt is Told by a Hunter. *Japan Advertiser*, 10 April 1927, p. 5.* On John Clare.

C616　Man and His Chances: "The Pyramid", A Book of Remarkable New Poetry by a Keio Professor. *Japan Advertiser*, 24 April 1927, p. 4. Review of *The Pyramid*, by Sherard Vines. *See also* B20.

C617   The Writers of the War: Mr. Churchill's "Flamboyant and Inflated" Book, and Some Others. *Japan Advertiser*, 8 May 1927, p. 4. Review of *The World Crisis, 1916–1918*, by Winston S. Churchill, and on Wilfrid Owen, Siegfried Sassoon and others.

C618   [Letter on *The Christ's Hospital (or, Blue-Coat School)*, by William Frederick Mylius, London, 1811]. *The Blue*, June 1927, Vol. 54, No. 5, pp. 204–206. Signed E.B. *See also* letter from J. Middleton Murry in the issue of October 1927, p. 39.

C619   TO JOY. *Study of English*, June 1927, No. 3, upper wrapper, recto. Issued as an Edmund Blunden Number.

       First published: *To Nature*, 1923; and *English Poems*, 1926; reprinted: *The Poems*, 1930; *The Face of England*, 1938; *Edmund Blunden: A Selection of His Poetry and Prose*, 1950; and *Poems of Many Years*, 1957.

C620   EASTERN TEMPEST [*later* TEMPEST; *and* EASTERN TEMPEST]. *Study of English*, June 1927, No. 3, pp. 236–237. Holograph facsimile.

       Reprinted: *The Observer*, 18 September 1927; *Edmund Blunden: His Professorship and His Writing*, 1927; *Japanese Garland*, 1928; *Near and Far*, 1929; and *The Poems*, 1930.

C621   RUIN. *Nation & Athenaeum*, 4 June 1927, p. 306.

       Reprinted: *Retreat*, 1928; and *The Poems*, 1930.

C622   Fragmentary Notes on the Painter-Poets. *Studies in English Literature*, July 1927, Vol. 7, No. 3, pp. 329–348. On Thomas Flatman, Alexander Pope, John Dyer and others.

       Reprinted: *Reprinted Papers*, 1950.

C623   Moments of Revision. *Studies in English Literature*, July 1927, Vol. 7, No. 3, pp. 452–461. On Laurence Binyon's addition of a fifth book to Palgrave's *Golden Treasury; Oxford Book of Eighteenth Century Verse*, edited by D. Nichol Smith; and *Poetical Works of William Cowper*, edited by D. Nichol Smith. Signed E.B.

C624   Benn's Sixpenny Library. *Studies in English Literature*, July 1927, Vol. 7, No. 3, pp. 461–462. Review of No. 53, *Italian Literature*, by Edmund G. Gardner; and No. 54, *Shakespeare*, by G. B. Harrison. Signed E.B.

C625   Newton's Poet. *Studies in English Literature*, July 1927, Vol. 7, No. 3, pp. 475–478. On James Thomson. Signed E.B.

C626   Hardy and his American Publishers, 1882. *Studies in English Literature*, October 1927, Vol. 7, No. 4, pp. 635–636. Signed E.B.

C627   Without Pepys. *TLS*, 6 October 1927, p. 687. Review of *More English Diaries*, by Arthur Ponsonby; and *Scottish and Irish Diaries*, by Arthur Ponsonby. Unsigned.

C628   The Fourteenth Volume. *TLS*, 20 October 1927, p. 734. Review of *Leaves and Fruit*, by Sir Edmund Gosse. Unsigned.

C629   "The Temple" Restored. *TLS*, 20 October 1927, p. 735. Review of *The Temple*, by George Herbert. Unsigned.

C630   [Review of] *An Introduction to the Reading of Shakespeare*, by Frederick S. Boas. *TLS*, 20 October 1927, p. 745. Unsigned.

C631   "Haig Strikes Again". *Nation & Athenaeum*, 29 October 1927, p. 160. Review of *A Subaltern on the Somme*, by Mark VII [*i.e.* Mark Plowman].

C632   THE WATCHERS. *St Martin's Review*, November 1927, No. 441, p. 568.

    Reprinted: *Undertones of War*, 1928; *The Poems*, 1930; and *Poems of Many Years*, 1957.

C633   Leigh Hunt Prologizes. *TLS*, 3 November 1927, p. 785. Review of *Prefaces by Leigh Hunt: Mainly to his Periodicals*, edited by R. Brimley Johnson. Unsigned.

C634   [Review of] *The Blessing of Pan*, by Lord Dunsany. *TLS*, 3 November 1927, p. 785. Unsigned.

C635   JAPANESE NIGHTPIECE [*later* INLAND SEA]. *The Observer*, 6 November 1927, p. 24.

    Reprinted: *Japanese Garland*, 1928; *Near and Far*, 1929; and *The Poems*, 1930.

C636   The Tradition of L'Allegro. *TLS*, 10 November 1927, p. 809. Review of *The Joy of Life*, edited by E. V. Lucas. Unsigned.

C637   [Review of] *Letters from the Cape*, by Lady Duff Gordon. *TLS*, 10 November 1927, p. 811. Unsigned.

C638   One Soldier's Faith. *TLS*, 10 November 1927, p. 816. Review of *Religio Militis*, by Austin Hopkinson. Unsigned.

C639   [Review of] *Mediocrity*, by Futubatei Shimei. *TLS*, 10 November 1927, p. 820. Unsigned.

C640   [Review of] *The Poet and the Flowers*, by Mary A. Johnstone. *TLS*, 10 November 1927, p. 823. Unsigned.

C641   John Philips Revived. *TLS*, 17 November 1927, p. 835. Review of *The Poems of John Philips*, edited by M. G. Lloyd Thomas. Unsigned.

C642   Blake Selected and Revealed. *TLS*, 24 November 1927, p. 858. Review of *Selected Poems of William Blake*, with an introduction by Basil de Sélincourt. Unsigned.

C643   The Ariel Poems. *TLS*, 24 November 1927, p. 873. Review of *Yuletide in a Younger World*, by Thomas Hardy; *The Linnet's Nest*, by Sir Henry Newbolt; *The Wonder Night*, by Laurence Binyon; *Alone*, by Walter de la Mare; *Gloria in Profundis*, by G. K. Chesterton; *The Early Whistler*, by Wilfrid Gibson; *Nativity*, by Siegfried Sassoon; and *Journey of the Magi*, by T. S. Eliot. Unsigned.

C644   Scottish Victorians. *Nation & Athenaeum*, 26 November 1927, p. 330. Review of *Brother Scots*, by Donald Carswell.

C645   A Conrad Repository. *London Mercury*, December 1927, Vol. 17, No. 98, pp. 179–186. Review of *Joseph Conrad: Life & Letters*, by G. Jean-Aubry.

C646   The Biography of Shelley. *TLS*, 1 December 1927, pp. 893–894. Review of *Shelley: His Life and Work*, by Walter Edwin Peck; and *The Narrative Poems of Percy Bysshe Shelley*, with introduction by C. H. Herford.

        Reprinted: *Votive Tablets*, 1931.

C647   The Language Test. *Nation & Athenaeum*, 3 December 1927, p. 368. Review of *Collected Essays, Papers, &c., of Robert Bridges, First Part* (*see also* C1084); *The Prospects of Literature*, by Logan Pearsall Smith; and *Castles in Spain*, by John Galsworthy.

C648   A Rural Interpreter. *TLS*, 8 December 1927, p. 929. Review of *A Small Boy in the Sixties*, by George Sturt. Unsigned.

C649   Estimates and Reminders. *TLS*, 8 December 1927, p. 932. Review of *Lectures on Dead Authors*, by Lacon Watson. Unsigned.

C650   [Review of] *John Bunyan*, by Gwilym O. Griffith. *TLS*, 8 December 1927, p. 935. Unsigned.

C651   [Review of] *Social Currents in Japan* . . . by Harry Emerson Wildes. *TLS*, 15 December 1927, p. 967. Unsigned.

C652   Herrick in Honour. *TLS*, 29 December 1927, p. 987. Review of *Delighted Earth: A Selection from Herrick's "Hesperides"*, edited by Peter Meadows. Unsigned.

C653   Mr. Stead's New Poems. *TLS*, 29 December 1927, p. 988. Review of *Festival in Tuscany*, by William Force Stead. Unsigned. *See also* C673.

C654   Book-Pastime and Book Science. *Nation & Athenaeum*, 31 December 1927, pp. 519–520. Review of *The Elements of Book-Collecting*, by Iolo Williams; and *An Introduction to Bibliography for Literary Students*, by Ronald B. McKerrow.

1928

C655 Tracts for All Times. *TLS*, 5 January 1928, p. 9. Review of *A Miscellany of Tracts and Pamphlets* . . . edited by A. C. Ward. Unsigned.

C656 [Review of] *Some Strange English Literary Figures of the Eighteenth and Nineteenth Centuries in a Series of Lectures*, by Lafcadio Hearn, edited by R. Tanabé. *TLS*, 5 January 1928, p. 14. Unsigned.

C657 The Two Japans. *Nation & Athenaeum*, 7 January 1928, p. 542. Review of *Glimpses of Unfamiliar Japan*, by Lafcadio Hearn; and *The Civilization of Japan*, by J. Ingram Bryan.

C658 VILLAGE LIGHTS. *The Observer*, 8 January 1928, p. 11.

Reprinted: *Retreat*, 1928; and *The Poems*, 1930.

C659 Defoe's Great Britain. *TLS*, 12 January 1928, p. 25. Review of *A Tour Thro' the Whole Island of Great Britain*, by Daniel Defoe. Unsigned.

Reprinted: *Votive Tablets*, 1931.

C660 Some Early Glories. *Nation & Athenaeum*, 21 January 1928, pp. 602–603. On the centenary of *The Athenaeum*.

C661 Rambles Round Camelot. *Nation & Athenaeum*, 21 January 1928, p. 618. Review of *Le Mort d'Arthur*, by Sir Thomas Malory with Beardsley's designs; *Le Morte d'Arthur*, illustrated by W. Russell Flint; and *Arthur of Britain*, by E. K. Chambers. Signed E.B. in contents, Edmund Blunden on article.

C662 Men and Trees. *TLS*, 26 January 1928, p. 53. Review of *The Book of the Tree*, edited by Georgina Mase. Unsigned.

C663 [Review of] *John Bunyan*, by R. H. Coats. *TLS*, 26 January 1928, p. 65. Unsigned.

C664 A Town With a Past. *Nation & Athenaeum*, 28 January 1928, pp. 658, 660. Review of *The History of Hitchin*, Vol. 1, by Reginald L. Hine.

C665 A Pattern for Intellectuals. *London Mercury*, February 1928, Vol. 17, No. 100, pp. 413–417. Review of *The Correspondence of Henry Crabb Robinson with the Wordsworth Circle (1808–1866)*, edited with introduction, notes and index by Edith J. Morley.

C666 The Country Tradition. *TLS*, 2 February 1928, pp. 69–70. Unsigned. On Gilbert White, J. L. Knapp and other nature writers.

Reprinted: *Votive Tablets*, 1931.

C667 Scotland Yet. *Nation & Athenaeum*, 4 February 1928, p. 694. Review of *Old Scotch Songs and Poems*, phonetically spelt and translated by Sir James Wilson. Signed E.B.

C668   CHINESE PICTURE. *The Observer*, 5 February 1928, p. 16.

Reprinted: *Retreat*, 1928; and *The Poems*, 1930.

C669   The True Aristocracy. *TLS*, 9 February 1928, p. 93. Review of *Poems by Anne, Countess of Winchilsea, 1661–1720*, selected . . . by John Middleton Murry. Unsigned.

C670   The Cool of the Day. *Nation & Athenaeum*, 11 February 1928, pp. 722, 724. Review of *The Pleasures of Princes*, by Gervase Markham; *The Experienced Angler*, by Robert Venables; *A New Orchard and Garden*, by William Lawson; and *The Countrie Housewife's Garden*, by William Lawson. Signed E.B.

C671   Japan, Ancient and Modern. *Nation & Athenaeum*, 18 February 1928, p. 758. Review of *An Outline History of Japan*, by Herbert H. Gowen; and *Modern Japan and its Problems*, by G. C. Allen.

C672   Mr. George Moore and Shakespeare-Bacon: The Case of Richard II. *Daily Telegraph*, 24 February 1928, p. 6. Review of *The Making of an Immortal*, by George Moore.

C673   Satire, Pantheism and Jewellery. *Nation & Athenaeum*, 25 February 1928, pp. 788, 790. Review of *The Wayzgoose: A South African Satire*, by Roy Campbell; *Festival in Tuscany, and Other Poems*, by William Force Stead (*see also* C653); *Black Armour*, by Elinor Wylie; and *Nets to Catch the Wind*, by Elinor Wylie. Unsigned.

C674   NATURE DISPLAYED. *London Mercury*, March 1928, Vol. 17, No. 101, p. 510.

Reprinted: *Retreat*, 1928; and *The Poems*, 1930.

C675   THE AGE OF HERBERT AND VAUGHAN. *London Mercury*, March 1928, Vol. 17, No. 101, p. 511.

Reprinted: *Retreat*, 1928; *The Poems*, 1930; *Edmund Blunden: A Selection of His Poetry and Prose*, 1950; and *Poems of Many Years*, 1957.

C676   THE WARTONS AND OTHER EARLY ROMANTICS [*later* THE WARTONS AND OTHER EARLY ROMANTIC LANDSCAPE POETS; *and* THE WARTONS AND OTHER LANDSCAPE POETS]. *London Mercury*, March 1928, Vol. 17, No. 101, pp. 511-512.

Reprinted: *Retreat*, 1928; *The Poems*, 1930; and *Poems of Many Years*, 1957.

C677   New England Relics. *TLS*, 1 March 1928, p. 147. Review of *Handkerchiefs from Paul: Being Pious and Consolatory Verses of Puritan Massachusetts*, edited by Kenneth B. Murdock. Unsigned.

C678   [Review of] *The Loyalists of New Jersey: Their Memorials, Petitions* . . . by E. Alfred Jones. *TLS*, 1 March 1928, p. 153. Unsigned.

C679   Hardyana. *Nation & Athenaeum*, 3 March 1928, p. 816. Review of *Talks With Thomas Hardy, 1920–1922*, by Vere H. Collins; and *Thomas Hardy and His Philosophy*, by Patrick Braybrooke.

C680   DEPARTURE. *Saturday Review*, 3 March 1928, p. 256.

Reprinted: *Retreat*, 1928; *The Poems*, 1930; and *Poems of Many Years*, 1957.

C681   THE STORM. *The Observer*, 4 March 1928, p. 18.

Reprinted: *Retreat*, 1928; and *The Poems*, 1930.

C682   Novels and Sketches. *Nation & Athenaeum*, 10 March 1928, pp. 852, 854. Review of *The Ring Fence*, by Eden Phillpotts; *The Key of Life*, by Francis Brett Young; *The Lame Duck*, by Maude G. Pease; *Wife to John*, by Barnaby Brook; *The Plough*, by Naomi Jacob; *The Axe*, by Sigrid Undset; *Cavalleria Rusticana*, by Giovanni Verga; *Chains*, by Theodore Dreiser; *The Irish R.M.*, by E. Œ. Somerville and Martin Ross; and *The Fast Gentleman*, by Keble Howard.

C683   Vanbrugh, The Restoration Spirit: Its Saving Qualities. *Daily Telegraph*, 13 March 1928, p. 15. Review of *The Complete Works of Sir John Vanbrugh*, edited by Bonamy Dobrée and Geoffrey Webb.

C684   England's Theophrastus. *TLS*, 15 March 1928, p. 185. Review of *Micro-Cosmographie*, by John Earle. Unsigned.

C685   At St. Helena, Napoleon in Exile: Sir Hudson Lowe and his Enemies. *Daily Telegraph*, 20 March 1928, p. 18. Review of *Napoleon in Captivity: Reports and Letters of Count Balmain*, translated and edited by Julian Park.

C686   Another Convention. *TLS*, 22 March 1928, p. 210. Review of *Etched in Moonlight*, by James Stephens. Unsigned.

C687   [Review of] *John Bunyan: His Life and Times*, by R. Winboult Harding. *TLS*, 22 March 1928, p. 223. Unsigned.

C688   [Review of] *John Bunyan (1628–1688): His Life, Times and Work*, by John Brown. *TLS*, 22 March 1928, p. 227. Unsigned. *See also* C799.

C689   War's Environments. *Nation & Athenaeum*, 24 March 1928, pp. 946, 948. Review of *Passchendaele and the Somme*, by Hugh Quigley. Signed E.B. *See also* complaint by the author in the issue of 14 April, p. 42, and reply by E. B. (*see* C695).

C690   A Letter from England. *Studies in English Literature*, April 1928, Vol. 8, No. 2, pp. 311–318. *See also* C740, 781, 870.

C691   Haydon Outside his "Autobiography". *Nation & Athenaeum*, 7 April 1928, pp. 13–14.

C692   Editorial Superfluity. *TLS*, 12 April, 1928, p. 268. Review of *Washington Irving's Notes While Preparing Sketch Book, &c, 1817* . . . edited by Stanley T. Williams. Unsigned.

C693   The Prince of Privateers: George Walker. *Daily Telegraph*, 13 April 1928, p. 18. Review of *The Voyages and Cruises of Commodore Walker*, edited by H. S. Vaughan.

C694   [Paragraph commencing] A large circle of readers will regret the death of Stanley Weyman. *Nation & Athenaeum*, 14 April 1928, p. 33. Unsigned.

C695   Passchendaele and the Somme. *Nation & Athenaeum*, 14 April 1928, p. 42. Reply following letter from Hugh Quigley complaining of the review of his book in the issue of 24 March, pp. 946, 948, signed E.B. (*see* C689).

C696   A Crime and its Echo. *TLS*, 19 April 1928, p. 285. Review of *The Mysterious Murder of Maria Marten*, by J. Curtis; and *Maria Marten, or, The Murder in the Red Barn*, edited by Montagu Slater. Unsigned.

C697   A Romantic Miscellany. *TLS*, 26 April 1928, p. 312. Review of *Essays in Petto*, by Montague Summers. Unsigned.

C698   [Review of] *John Bunyan, Pilgrim and Dreamer*, by William Henry Harding. *TLS*, 26 April 1928, p. 317. Unsigned.

C699   "Q" in Thirty Volumes. *Nation & Athenaeum*, 28 April 1928, p. 116. Review of *Dead Man's Rock; Troy Town; Noughts and Crosses;* and *The Splendid Spur*, by Sir Arthur Quiller-Couch.

C700   GIRL WITH SHAWL. *English Review*, May 1928, Vol. 46, p. 598.

Reprinted: *Retreat*, 1928.

C701   AN INFANTRYMAN. *English Review*, May 1928, Vol. 46, p. 599.

Reprinted (revised): *Retreat*, 1928; *The Poems*, 1930; *Poems of Many Years*, 1957; and *The Midnight Skaters*, [1968].

C702   A MORNING PIECE: WRITTEN IN ABSENCE. *London Mercury*, May 1928, Vol. 18, No. 103, pp. 15–16.

Reprinted: *Retreat*, 1928; and *The Poems*, 1930.

C703   THE CHARM. *London Mercury*, May 1928, Vol. 18, No. 103, pp. 16–17.

Reprinted: *Retreat*, 1928; and *The Poems*, 1930.

C704   AN ANNOTATION. *London Mercury*, May 1928, Vol. 18, No. 103, p. 17.

Reprinted: *Retreat*, 1928; *The Poems*, 1930; and *Poems of Many Years*, 1957.

C705   PORTRAIT OF A COLONEL [*later* ON THE PORTRAIT OF A COLONEL]. *London Mercury*, May 1928, Vol. 18, No. 103, pp. 17–18.

Reprinted (revised): *Retreat*, 1928; *The Poems*, 1930; and *Poems of Many Years*, 1957.

C706   THE PRISON [*later* THE MATCH]. *London Mercury*, May 1928, Vol. 18, No. 103, p. 18.

Reprinted (revised): *Nation & Athenaeum*, 17 November 1928, p. 256; *Retreat*, 1928; and *The Poems*, 1930.

C707   [Review of] *Veld Verse*, by Kingsley Fairbridge. *TLS*, 3 May 1928, p. 330. Unsigned.

C708   Charles Darwin, the Growth of a Great Idea: Earlier Evolutionists. *Daily Telegraph*, 4 May 1928, p. 6. Review of *The Evolution of Charles Darwin*, by George A. Dorsey.

C709   Elia's G.D. *Nation & Athenaeum*, 5 May 1928, pp. 138–139. On George Dyer.

C710   The Poetic Privacy. *TLS*, 10 May 1928, p. 352. Review of *Dedication*, by Viola Garvin; and *The Secret Meadow and Other Poems*, by C. Henry Warren. Unsigned. *See also* C726.

C711   THE SECRET. *Saturday Review*, 12 May 1928, p. 596.

Reprinted: *Retreat*, 1928; and *The Poems*, 1930.

C712   Arnold of Rugby: Education and Character. *Daily Telegraph*, 15 May 1928, p. 8. Review of *Dr. Arnold of Rugby*, by Arnold Whitridge.

C713   Mechanisms of Poetry. *TLS*, 17 May 1928, p. 375. Review of *Poetic Diction: A Study in Meaning*, by Owen Barfield (*see also* C2802); and *The Laws of Verse*, by J. C. Andersen. Unsigned.

C714   [Review of] *The Last Sheaf: Essays*, by Edward Thomas. *Nation & Athenaeum*, 19 May 1928, pp. 218, 220. Unsigned.

C715   Rarity of the Phoenix. *Nation & Athenaeum*, 19 May 1928, pp. 228–229. Review of *Different Days*, by Frances Cornford; *It Was Not Jones*, by R. Fitzurse; *Matrix*, by Dorothy Wellesley; *Reflections*, by R.Q. [*i.e.* Robert Hope Case] (*see also* C735); *Poems*, by Reginald Rowe; *Poems*, by Malcolm Taylor (*see also* C464); *Brother Beast*, by Eden Phillpotts (*see also* C815); *The Vortex*, by J. Redwood Anderson; and *Poems from the Divan of Hafiz*, translated by Gertrude L. Bell. Unsigned.

C716   Bioscope. *Nation & Athenaeum*, 19 May 1928, pp. 232, 234. Review of *Black Majesty*, by John W. Vandercook; *Genghis Khan*, by Harold Lamb; *Commodore Vanderbilt*, by A. D. Howden Smith; *Tombstone, an Epic of Arizona*, by W. N. Burns; *Gentleman Johnny Burgoyne*, by F. J. Hudleston; *The Eighth Earl of Elgin*, by J. L. Morison; *Earl Haig*, by Ernest Protheroe; *Herbert Edward Ryle*, by M. H. Fitzgerald; *Days in Doorn*, by the Empress Hermine; *The Ruler of Baroda*, by P. W. Sergeant; *Richard Baxter and Margaret Charlton*, by John T. Wilkinson; *Josephine E. Butler*, edited by G. W. and L. A. Johnson; *Harrison of Ightham*, by Sir Edward R. Harrison; *Jörgensen: an Autobiography*; and *A Final Burning of Boats*, by Ethel Smyth. Unsigned.

C717   Japan in 19—. *TLS*, 24 May 1928, p. 390. Review of *Yuki San*, by Ellen Forest, translated . . . by Jacobine Menzies Wilson. Unsigned. *See also* C722.1.

C718   Popular Literary History. *TLS*, 24 May 1928, p. 393. Review of *English Literature*, by Margharita Widdows. Unsigned.

C719   A Famous Case, The Trial of Jean Calas: A Judge's Study. *Daily Telegraph*, 25 May 1928, p. 6. Review of *The Case of Jean Calas*, by F. H. Maugham.

C720   An Expensive Vision. *Nation & Athenaeum*, 26 May 1928, p. 259. Review of *The Uncensored Dardanelles*, by E. Ashmead-Bartlett. Signed E.B.

C721   A QUARTET ("THE MIKADO" AT CAMBRIDGE). *The Observer*, 27 May 1928, p. 16.

    Reprinted: *Near and Far*, 1929; and *The Poems*, 1930.

C722   [Review of] *The Pilgrim's Progress*, by John Bunyan. *TLS*, 31 May 1928, p. 415. Unsigned. *See also* C744, 799, 826.

C722   [Review of] *Yuki-San: A Japanese Mystery*, by Ellen .1   Forest. *Now & Then*, Summer 1928, No. 28, pp. 13–15. *See also* C717.

C723   Campbell's Political Poetry. *English Review*, June 1928, Vol. 46, pp. 703–706.

C724   Some Remarks on Hudibras. *London Mercury*, June 1928, Vol. 18, No. 104, pp. 172–177.

C725   Literary England Month by Month. *Study of English*, June 1928, Vol. 21, No. 3, pp. 270–274. Dated 'London, March 16, 1928'.*

C726   Is it Poetry? *Nation & Athenaeum*, 2 June 1928, p. 304. Review of *This Blind Rose*, by Humbert Wolfe; *New Poems*, by W. J. Turner (*see also* C815); *Dedication*, by Viola Garvin (*see also* C710); *Tristram*, by Edwin Arlington

Robinson; *The Secret Meadow*, by C. Henry Warren (*see also* C710); and *Mary of Huntingdon*, by Gilbert Thomas. Unsigned.

C727   Fruits of Solitude. *TLS*, 7 June 1928, p. 426. Review of *Midsummer Eve*, by A.E. [*i.e.* G. W. Russell] . Unsigned.

C728   [Review of] *John Bunyan: The Man and his Work*, by A. R. Buckland. *TLS*, 7 June 1928, pp. 431–432. Unsigned.

C729   [Review of] *The Gardens of Japan*, by Jiro Harada, edited by Geoffrey Holme. *TLS*, 7 June 1928, p. 433. Unsigned.

C730   Dr. Johnson: Light on his Oxford Life. *Daily Telegraph*, 12 June 1928, p. 17. Review of *Johnsonian Gleanings*, Part V, *The Doctor's Life, 1728–1735*, by A. L. Reade.

C731   "Orion" Horne. *TLS*, 14 June 1928, p. 447. Review of *Orion*, by R. H. Horne. Unsigned. *See also* C773.

C732   [Review of] *The Legacy of Bunyan*, by W. Y. Fullerton. *TLS*, 14 June 1928, p. 455. Unsigned.

C733   A Tercentenary Issue: Harvey's Exercises: A Great Detective Story. *Daily Telegraph*, 15 June 1928, p. 9. Review of *The Anatomical Exercises of Dr. William Harvey*.

C734   A SUNRISE IN MARCH. *Nation & Athenaeum*, 16 June 1928, p. 361.

Reprinted: *Near and Far*, 1929; *The Poems*, 1930; and *Poems of Many Years*, 1957.

C735   Taste and Feeling. *TLS*, 21 June 1928, p. 464. Review of *Reflections: In Verse*, by R.Q. [*i.e.* Robert Hope Case] . Unsigned (*see also* C715).

C736   The Antarctic Continent, Life and Adventure: An Enthusiast's Survey. *Daily Telegraph*, 22 June 1928, p. 6. Review of *Antarctica: A Treatise on the Southern Continent*, by J. Gordon Hayes.

C737   Where Are the Others? *Nation & Athenaeum*, 23 June 1928, pp. 400, 402. Review of *A Story Without a Tail*, by William Maginn. Signed E.B.

C738   [Review of] *Memories*, by Harry Preston. *Nation & Athenaeum*, 23 June 1928, p. 404. Unsigned.

C739   The Knight's Story. *TLS*, 28 June 1928, p. 481. Review of *The Autobiography of Edward, Lord Herbert of Cherbury*, with an introduction by C. H. Herford. Unsigned.

Reprinted: *Votive Tablets*, 1931.

C740   A Letter from England, II. *Studies in English Literature*, July 1928, Vol. 8, No. 3, pp. 441–447. *See also* C690, 781, 870.

C741   Literary England Month by Month. *Study of English*, July 1928, Vol. 21, No. 4, pp. 378–385. Dated 'London, April 12, 1928'.

C742   The Roman Slave: Light on a Difficult Problem. *Daily Telegraph*, 3 July 1928, p. 15. Review of *Slavery in the Roman Empire*, by R. H. Barrow.

C743   The Madness of Lear. *Nation & Athenaeum*, 7 July 1928, pp. 458–459.

C744   Realising Bunyan. *Nation & Athenaeum*, 7 July 1928, pp. 472, 474. Review of *The Pilgrim's Progress*, by John Bunyan; and *John Bunyan*, by G. B. Harrison. Unsigned. *See also* C722, 799, 826.

C745   [Review of] *Incredible Adventures of Rowland Hern*, by Nicholas Olde. *Daily Telegraph*, 10 July 1928, p. 8. Signed E.C.B.

C746   With Cannibals: Adventures in the South Seas. *Daily Telegraph*, 13 July 1928, p. 6. Review of *Cannibal Nights*, by H. E. Raabe.

C747   Sir Edmund Gosse in Selection. *Sunday Times*, 15 July 1928, p. 8. Review of *Selected Essays: First and Second Series*, by Sir Edmund Gosse. One of a series entitled 'The World of Books' to which Gosse had contributed regularly. *See also* C756.

C748   [Review of] *The English Literary Library*, Group 1, *The Novel*. Vol. 1, *The Birth of Romance from Euphues*, Sidney's *Arcadia, Romantics and Pastorals*; Vol. 2, *Some Little Tales, from Steele, Addison* [etc.], selected with introductions by R. Brimley Johnson. *TLS*, 19 July 1928, p. 539. Unsigned.

C749   Ireland To-day: Achievements of the Free State. *Daily Telegraph*, 24 July 1928, p. 16. Review of *The Irish Free State, 1922–1927*, by Denis Gwynn.

C750   The Augustans Out of Town. *TLS*, 26 July 1928, p. 549. Review of *Nature and the Country in English Poetry of the First Half of the Eighteenth Century*, by C. de Haas. Unsigned. *See also* C766.

C751   Science of the Ancients: Early Discoveries. *Daily Telegraph*, 27 July 1928, p. 6. Review of *From Magic to Science*, by Charles Singer.

C752   British Sport. *Nation & Athenaeum*, 28 July 1928, pp. 565–566. Review of *Fair Play*, by Rudolf Kircher; *Training for Athletes*, by H. M. Abrahams and A. Abrahams; and *Tennis*, by Helen Wills.

C753   Literary England Month by Month. *Study of English*, August 1928, Vol. 21, No. 5, pp. 486–492. Dated 'May 17, 1928'.*

C754   Our Lost Leader. *Study of English*, August 1928, Vol. 21, No. 5, pp. 518–519.*

C755   The Philosophy of Reading. *Rising Generation*, 1 August
        1928, Vol. 59, No. 9, pp. 294–295; and 15 August 1928,
        Vol. 59, No. 10, pp. 330–331.*

C756   Edmund Gosse's Essays. *TLS*, 2 August 1928, p. 565. Re-
        view of *Selected Essays, First and Second Series*, by Sir
        Edmund Gosse. Unsigned. *See also* C747.

C757   Genius and Merit. *Nation & Athenaeum*, 4 August 1928,
        pp. 594–595. Review of *Triforium*, by Sherard Vines;
        Poems, by Ronald Ross; *Goodwill*, by Eden Phillpotts (*see
        also* C770); *High Road and Lonning*, by John Helston;
        Tristram's Tomb, by James Ormerod; *The Child*, by J. L.
        Bagshawe; *First Poems*, by Betty Askwith; *A Flying Scroll*,
        by Stanley Snaith; and *Poems*, by G. Turquet-Milnes.

C758   Henry Mackenzie. *TLS*, 9 August 1928, p. 579. Review of
        The Men of Feeling, by Henry Mackenzie. Unsigned. *See
        also* C2136.

        Reprinted: *Votive Tablets*, 1931.

C759   Mary Tighe: Influence on Keats's Verse. *Daily Telegraph*,
        14 August 1928, p. 5. Review of *Keats and Mary Tighe*,
        edited by Earle Vonard Weller.

C760   [Paragraph commencing] The Menin Gate commemora-
        tions. *Nation & Athenaeum*, 18 August 1928, p. 637. Un-
        signed.

C761   A XVth-Century Bestiary: Nature & Allegory. *Daily Tele-
        graph*, 24 August 1928, p. 13. Review of *Physiologus*, by
        Bishop Theobald, translated by A. W. Rendell.

C762   Poetic Tours. *Nation & Athenaeum*, 25 August 1928, p.
        684. Review of *The New Argonautica*, by W. B. Drayton
        Henderson; *Rhymes of the Road*, by David Emrys; and *The
        Second Voyage*, by Carla Lanyon Lanyon. Unsigned.

C763   Ruskin on Letters. *TLS*, 30 August 1928, p. 615. Review of
        Ruskin as Literary Critic: Selections, edited by A. H. R.
        Ball. Unsigned.

C764   Literary England Month by Month. *Study of English*, Sep-
        tember 1928, Vol. 21, No. 6, pp. 595–601. 'Dated June 23,
        1928'.*

C765   The Triumphant Captive. *Nation & Athenaeum*, 1 Septem-
        ber 1928, p. 708. Review of *The Enormous Room*, by E. E.
        Cummings.

C766   [Review of] *Nature and the Country in English Poetry*, by
        C. E. de Haas. *Nation & Athenaeum*, 1 September 1928,
        p. 712. Unsigned. *See also* C750.

C767   [Review of] *The King's Regiment (Liverpool), 1914–1919*,
        Vol. 1, by Everard Wyrall. *Nation & Athenaeum*, 1 Septem-
        ber 1928, p. 712. Unsigned.

C768   Andrew Marvell, Poet, Puritan and Patriot. *Daily Telegraph*, 4 September 1928, p. 7. Review of *Andrew Marvell: Poete, Puritain, Patriote, 1621–1678*, by Pierre Legouis.

C769   An Inherent Illusion. *TLS*, 6 September 1928, p. 629. Review of *The Noble Savage: A Study in Romantic Naturalism*, by Hoxie Neale Fairchild. Unsigned.

Reprinted: *Votive Tablets*, 1931.

C770   Towards the New Race. *TLS*, 6 September 1928, p. 631. Review of *Goodwill*, by Eden Phillpotts. Unsigned. *See also* C757.

C771   [Review of] *Christ's Hospital from a Boy's Point of View 1864–1870*, by W. M. Digues Le Touche, edited by his brother. *TLS*, 6 September 1928, p. 634. Unsigned. *See also* C774.

C772   [Paragraph commencing] 'Goldsmith certainly'. *Nation & Athenaeum*, 15 September 1928, p. 760. Dramatic review of *She Stoops to Conquer* at the Lyric Theatre, Hammersmith. Unsigned.

C773   "Orion" Refreshed. *Nation & Athenaeum*, 15 September 1928, pp. 768, 770. Review of *Orion*, by R. H. Horne. Signed E.B. *See also* C731.

C774   [Review of] *Christ's Hospital from a Boy's Point of View*, by W. M. Digues La Touche. *Nation & Athenaeum*, 15 September 1928, p. 772. Unsigned. *See also* C771.

C775   Goethe's Life & Amours: Herr Ludwig's Study. *Daily Telegraph*, 18 September 1928, p. 6. Review of *Goethe: The History of a Man*, by Emil Ludwig.

C776   Lamb's "Mr. Sea-Gull". *TLS*, 20 September 1928, p. 667. Letter signed Edmund Blunden. *See also* letter in the issue of 6 September, p. 632 by John M. Turnbull. On William Pitt Scargill.

C777   RETURN. *The Observer*, 23 September 1928, p. 18.

Reprinted: *Near and Far*, 1929; *The Poems*, 1930; and *Poems of Many Years*, 1957.

C778   A "Thrill" Anthology. *Daily Telegraph*, 28 September 1928, p. 6. Review of *Great Short Stories of Detection, Mystery and Horror*, edited by Dorothy L. Sayers. Signed E.C.B.

C779   The Belgian Rabelais. *Nation & Athenaeum*, 29 September 1928, p. 828. Review of *The Legend of Ulenspiegel*, by Charles de Coster, translated by F. M. Atkinson; and *The Legend of the Glorious Adventures of Tyl Ulenspiegel*, by Charles de Coster, translated by Geoffrey Whitworth. Signed E.B.

C780   A CONNOISSEUR. *English Review*, October 1928, Vol. 47, p. 480.

Reprinted: *Near and Far*, 1929; *The Poems*, 1930; and *Poems of Many Years*, 1957.

C781   A Letter from England, III. *Studies in English Literature*, October 1928, Vol. 8, No. 4, pp. 635-641. *See also* C690, 740, 870.

C782   Literary England Month by Month. *Study of English*, October 1928, Vol. 21, No. 7, pp. 730-735. 'Dated July 20, 1928'.*

C783   Goldsmith's Letters: A Bundle of Scraps, the Early Years. *Daily Telegraph*, 5 October 1928, p. 17. Review of *The Collected Letters of Oliver Goldsmith*, edited by Katherine C. Balderston.

C784   Good Gardeners. *Nation & Athenaeum*, 6 October 1928, pp. 22, 24. Review of *Nature in the Age of Louis XIV*, by Phyllis E. Crump. Signed E.B.

C785   A Monument to Montrose. *Nation & Athenaeum*, 13 October 1928, p. 58. Review of *Montrose*, by John Buchan. Signed E.B.

C786   The Friend of Keats [*later* Friends of Keats]. *TLS*, 18 October 1928, p. 753. Review of *John Hamilton Reynolds: Poetry and Prose*, edited by G. L. Marsh; and *The Life and Letters of John Keats*, by Lord Houghton. Unsigned.

Reprinted: *Votive Tablets*, 1931.

C787   About Poets: A Wordsworthian's Leisure. *Daily Telegraph*, 19 October 1928, p. 16. Review of *Spirit of Delight*, by George McLean.

C788   The Enslavement of Cowper. *TLS*, 25 October 1928, p. 776. Review of *William Cowper*, by Hugh l'Anson Fausset. Unsigned.

C789   Literary England Month by Month. *Study of English*, November 1928, Vol. 21, No. 8, pp. 822-827. 'Dated Aug. 27, 1928'.*

C790   [Review of] *England from Wordsworth to Dickens*, by R. W. King. *TLS*, 1 November 1928, p. 811. Unsigned.

C791   Romance and Modernism. *TLS*, 8 November 1928, p. 827. Review of *Midsummer Night*, by John Masefield. Unsigned.

C792   What Are Those Golden Builders Doing? *Nation & Athenaeum*, 10 November 1928, p. 216. Review of *Collected Poems of D. H. Lawrence; Roan Stallion*, by Robinson Jeffers; *John Brown's Body*, by Stephen Vincent Benét; and *The Golden Room*, by Wilfrid Gibson. Signed E.B.

C793   Goldsmith, Poet, Novelist, Essayist: A Quiet Conquest [*later* Goldsmith's Bicentenary]. *The Times*, 12 November 1928, pp. 17–18. On the bicentenary of his birth.

Reprinted: *Votive Tablets*, 1931.

C794   A Companion to "Selborne". *TLS*, 15 November 1928, p. 852. Review of *Gilbert White: Pioneer, Poet and Stylist*, by Walter Johnson. Unsigned.

C795   Literature: What Goes to Making It. *Daily Telegraph*, 16 November 1928, p. 8. Review of *The Making of Literature*, by R. A. Scott-James.

C796   ON A BIOGRAPHICAL DICTIONARY. *The Observer*, 18 November 1928, p. 18.

Reprinted: *Near and Far*, 1929; and *The Poems*, 1930.

C797   [Review of] *Ballads and Poems*, by Alfred Noyes. *TLS*, 22 November 1928, p. 881. Unsigned.

C798   Katherine Mansfield's Evolution. *Nation & Athenaeum*, 24 November 1928, pp. 296, 298. Review of *The Letters of Katherine Mansfield*, edited by J. Middleton Murry. Signed E.B.

C799   The Spirit of Bunyan. *TLS*, 29 November 1928, pp. 917–918. Review of *John Bunyan (1628–1688), His Life, Times, and Work*, by John Brown, revised by Frank Mott Harrison (*see also* C688); *The Pilgrim's Progress and The Life and Death of Mr. Badman*, introduction by G. B. Harrison, Nonesuch Press; and *Pilgrim's Progress*, Noel Douglas [Press]. Unsigned. *See also* C722, 744, 826.

Reprinted: *Votive Tablets*, 1931.

C800   [Review of] *The Church Book of Bunyan Meeting, 1656–1821*, with an introduction by G. B. Harrison. *TLS*, 29 November 1928, p. 941. Unsigned.

C801   Swinburne, The Poet and a Commentator. *Daily Telegraph*, 30 November 1928, p. 9. Review of *Selected Poems of Algernon Charles Swinburne*, with an introduction by Humbert Wolfe. *See also* C2552.

C802   Literary England Month by Month. *Study of English*, December 1928, Vol. 21, No. 9, pp. 942–947. Dated 'Sept. 28, 1928'.*

C803   Notes for Poems. *New Adelphi*, December 1928/February 1929, Vol. 2, No. 2, pp. 167–168. Review of *Toulemonde*, by Christopher Morley; and *Notes for Poems*, by William Plomer.

C804   Japanese Drama: Classic and Modern Theatres. *Daily Telegraph*, 4 December 1928, p. 8. Review of *An Outline History of Japanese Drama*, by Frank Alanson Lombard.

C805   Beddoes and His Contemporaries. *TLS*, 13 December 1928, pp. 973-974. Review of *The Complete Works of Thomas Lovell Beddoes*, edited with a memoir, by Sir Edmund Gosse; *The Oxford Book of Regency Verse, 1798-1837*, chosen by H. S. Milford; and *Lyrical Poetry from Blake to Hardy*, by H. J. C. Grierson (*see also* C837). Unsigned.

Reprinted: *Votive Tablets*, 1931.

C806   The Poems of Mary Webb. *TLS*, 27 December 1928, p. 1022. Review of *Poems, and The Spring of Joy*, by Mary Webb, with an introduction by Walter de la Mare. Unsigned.

C807   Anthology Not Extinct. *Nation & Athenaeum*, 29 December 1928, p. 469. Review of *A Book of Poetry from Spenser to Bridges*, compiled by A. Watson Bain; *Apes and Parrots: An Anthology of Parodies*, collected by J. C. Squire; *An Anthology of "Nineties" Verse*, edited by A. J. A. Symons; *Poems of Revolt*, chosen by Joan Beauchamp; *The Best Poems of 1928*, selected by Thomas Moult; *The Tramp's Anthology*, edited by Stephen Graham; *The Bath Anthology*, edited by Charles Whitby; and *The Mindes Delight: A Fanciful Anthology*, by Hedley Hope-Nicholson. Signed E.B.

1929

C808   Literary History & Criticism—1. *London Mercury*, January 1929, Vol. 19, No. 111, pp. 324-326. Review of *The Colvins and their Friends*, by E. V. Lucas; *Matthew Arnold*, by Hugh Kingsmill; *The Brownings*, by Osbert Burdett; *Theodore Hook and His Novels*, by Myron F. Brightfield (*see also* C811); and *The Gothic Revival: An Essay in the History of Taste*, by Kenneth Clark. Part II is by Alan Pryce-Jones.

C809   Westminster Abbey and the English Writers. *Studies in English Literature*, January 1929, Vol. 9, No. 1, pp. 1-11.

Reprinted: *Reprinted Papers*, 1950.

C810   Literary England Month by Month. *Study of English*, January 1929, Vol. 21, No. 10, pp. 1048-1053. Dated 'Oct 23, 1928'.*

C811   Theodore Hook Reconsidered. *TLS*, 3 January 1929, p. 9. Review of *Theodore Hook and his Novels*, by Myron F. Brightfield. *See also* C808.

C812   Soul of a Race: England's Spirit in the Ages, A Masterly Survey. *Daily Telegraph*, 4 January 1929, p. 14. Review of *The History of British Civilisation*, by Esmé Wingfield-Stratford.

C813　The Promise of May. *Nation & Athenaeum*, 12 January 1929, pp. 528-529. Review of *The Complete Poems of Lord Alfred Douglas; Forty-Nine Poems*, by W. H. Davies; *Ezra Pound: Selected Poems*, edited by T. S. Eliot; *Invocations to Angels*, by Edgell Rickword; *Trivial Breath*, by Elinor Wylie; *The Buck in the Snow*, by Edna St Vincent Millay; *Love as Love, Death as Death*, by Laura Riding; *Oxford Poetry, 1928*, edited by Clere Parsons and B.B. Signed E.B.

C814　The Age of Johnson [*later* Elton on the Johnson Era]. *TLS*, 17 January 1929, p. 41. Review of *A Survey of English Literature, 1730-1780*, by Oliver Elton. Unsigned.

　　　Reprinted: *Votive Tablets*, 1931.

C815　Two Modern Poets. *TLS*, 24 January 1929, p. 59. Review of *Brother Beast*, by Eden Phillpotts (*see also* C715); and *New Poems*, by W. J. Turner (*see also* C726). Unsigned.

C816　Literary England Month by Month. *Study of English*, February 1929, Vol. 21, No. 11, pp. 1184-1189. Dated 'London, Nov. 29, 1928.'

C817　In Central Asia: An Archaeologist's Story. *Daily Telegraph*, 1 February 1929, p. 17. Review of *Buried Treasures of Chinese Turkestan*, by Albert von Le Coq, translated by Anna Barwell.

C818　William Collins. *TLS*, 7 February 1929, p. 95. Review of *The Poetry of Collins*, by H. W. Garrod; and *Collins*, by H. W. Garrod. Unsigned.

C819　[Review of] *John Bunyan in Relation to His Times*, by Edmund Arbuthnott Knox. *TLS*, 7 February 1929, p. 101. Unsigned.

C820　Two Books on Napoleon: A Russian's Curious Study, Great Man's Sayings. *Daily Telegraph*, 8 February 1929, p. 18. Review of *Napoleon: A Study*, by Dmitri Merezhkovsky; and *Memoirs of Napoleon I*, compiled from his own writings by F. M. Kircheisen, translated by Frederick Collins.

C821　George Darley [*later* George Darley and his Latest Biographer]. *TLS*, 14 February 1929, pp. 105-106. Review of *The Life and Letters of George Darley, Poet and Critic*, by Claude Colleer Abbott. Unsigned.

　　　Reprinted: *Votive Tablets*, 1931.

C822　Swift's Verses: Clearing up their History. *Daily Telegraph*, 15 February 1929, p. 17. Review of *Swift's Verse: An Essay*, by F. Elrington Ball.

C823　Among the Ghosts. *Nation & Athenaeum*, 16 February 1929, p. 690. Review of *A Fatalist at War*, by Rudolf Binding.

C824   Oakham School. *TLS*, 21 February 1929, p. 131. Review of *The Book of Oakham School*, by W. L. Sargant. Unsigned.

C825   [Review of] *Gold Coast Customs*, by Edith Sitwell. *TLS*, 21 February 1929, p. 137. Unsigned.

C826   A Definitive Text. *TLS*, 28 February 1929, p. 159. Review of *The Pilgrim's Progress*, by John Bunyan, edited by James Blanton Wharey. Unsigned. *See also* C722, 744, 799.

C827   [Review of] *The Strong City*, by Alfred Noyes. *TLS*, 28 February 1929, p. 166. Unsigned.

C828   AT SENLIS ONCE. *The Bookman*, March 1929, Vol. 69, No. 1, p. 12.

First published: *Masks of Time*, 1925; *The Augustan Books*, 1925; *Undertones of War*, 1928; reprinted: *The Poems*, 1930; *The Face of England*, 1938; *Edmund Blunden: A Selection of His Poetry and Prose*, 1950; *Poems of Many Years*, 1957; and *The Midnight Skaters*, [1968].

C829   THE ZONNEBEKE ROAD. *The Bookman*, March 1929, Vol. 69, No. 1, pp. 12–13.

First published: *Masks of Time*, 1925; *Undertones of War*, 1928; reprinted: *The Poems*, 1930; *An Anthology of War Poems*, [1930]; *Poems of Many Years*, 1957; and *The Midnight Skaters*, [1968].

C830   PILLBOX. *The Bookman*, March 1929, Vol. 69, No. 1, p. 13.

First published: *Masks of Time*, 1925; *Undertones of War*, 1928. Reprinted: *The Poems*, 1930.

C831   The Preservation of England. *TLS*, 7 March 1929, pp. 169–170. Review of *Must England's Beauty Perish?: A Plea on Behalf of the National Trust*, by George Macauley Trevelyan; *The Changing Face of England*, new edition, by Anthony Collett; and *The Oxford Preservation Trust*, Second Annual Report. Unsigned.

Reprinted: *Votive Tablets*, 1931.

C832   [Review of] *The Thracian Stranger*, by Edward Thompson. *TLS*, 14 March 1929, p. 202. Unsigned.

C833   A War Diary: Memories of Life in the Trenches. *Daily Telegraph*, 19 March 1929, p. 17. Review of *A Soldier's Diary of the Great War*, with an introduction by Henry Williamson.

C834   Japanese Intuitions. *TLS*, 21 March 1929, p. 228. Review of *Paper Houses*, by William Plomer. Unsigned.

C835   Celtic Unities. *TLS*, 21 March 1929, p. 229. Review of *Pilgrimage*, by Austin Clarke. Unsigned.

C836   The "Rejected Addresses". *TLS*, 28 March 1929, p. 257. Review of *Rejected Addresses*, edited . . . by Andrew Boyle. Unsigned.

Reprinted: *Votive Tablets*, 1931.

C837   Ancient and Modern. *New Adelphi*, March/May 1929, Vol. 2, No. 3, pp. 278-279. Review of *Lyrical Poetry from Blake to Hardy*, by H. J. C. Grierson (*see also* C805); and *Phases of English Poetry*, by Herbert Read.

C838   Literary England Month by Month. *Study of English*, April 1929, Vol. 22, No. 1, pp. 62-67. Dated 'London, Jan. 12, 1929'.*

C839   Goethe and his Circle, Crabb Robinson's Notes: A Giant of Character. *Daily Telegraph*, 2 April 1929, p. 4. Review of *Crabb Robinson in Germany, 1800-1805: Extracts from his Correspondence*, edited by Edith J. Morley.

C840   [Review of] *The Immortal Nine: An Introduction to the Poetry of Last Century*, by J. M. Stuart-Young. *TLS*, 18 April 1929, p. 318. Unsigned.

C841   Early Sterne Writings: Yorick & Politics. *Daily Telegraph*, 19 April 1929, p. 19. Review of *The Politicks of Laurence Sterne*, by Lewis Perry Curtis. See also C848.

C842   EPITAPH. *Nation & Athenaeum*, 20 April 1929, p. 76.

Reprinted: *Near and Far*, 1929; *The Poems*, 1930; and *Poems of Many Years*, 1957.

C843   Adventures on Sea & Land: Lure of the East Indies. *Daily Telegraph*, 26 April 1929, p. 6. Review of *The Great Horn Spoon*, by Eugene Wright, with an introduction by Rosita Forbes.

C844   THE KILN. *London Mercury*, May 1929, Vol. 20, No. 115, p. 10. Two Poems [1].

Reprinted: *Near and Far*, 1929; and *The Poems*, 1930.

C845   THE CORRELATION. *London Mercury*, May 1929, Vol. 20, No. 115, pp. 10-11. Two Poems [2].

Reprinted: *Near and Far*, 1929; and *The Poems*, 1930.

C846   Literary England Month by Month. *Study of English*, May 1929, Vol. 22, No. 2, pp. 170-175. Dated 'London, Feb. 4, 1929'.

C847   A Young Poet. *TLS*, 2 May 1929, p. 357. Review of *Prose Pieces and Poems*, by Anthony Abbott. Unsigned.

C848   A Piece of Sterne. *Nation & Athenaeum*, 4 May 1929, pp. 164, 166. Review of *The Politicks of Laurence Sterne*, by Lewis Perry Curtis. Signed E.B. See also C841.

C849   DREAM ENCOUNTERS. *The Observer*, 5 May 1929, p. 18.

Reprinted: *Near and Far*, 1929; *The Poems*, 1930; and *Poems of Many Years*, 1957.

C850   The Muse in Mourning [*later* "A Wedding or a Funeral" (second half)] . *TLS*, 16 May 1929, p. 399. Review of *The Funeral Elegy and the Rise of English Romanticism*, by John W. Draper. Unsigned.

Reprinted: *Votive Tablets*, 1931.

C851   Ethiopic Texts and Marvels, Christianity and Magic: The Sacred Names. *Daily Telegraph*, 17 May 1929, p. 8. Review of *The Bandlet of Righteousness: An Ethiopian Book of the Dead*, edited with an English translation, by Sir E. A. Wallis Budge.

C852   A Boswellian Error, More Talks with Johnson: Mrs. Le Noir's Notes. *The Times*, 20 May 1929, pp. 11–12.

Reprinted: *Votive Tablets*, 1931.

C853   Charlotte Mew and Others. *Nation & Athenaeum*, 25 May 1929, pp. 277–278. Review of *The Rambling Sailor*, by Charlotte Mew; *Angels and Earthly Creatures*, by Elinor Wylie; *Poems*, by Russell George Alexander; *The Passionate Neatherd*, by Jack Lindsay; and *Moods Cadenced and Declaimed*, by Theodore Dreiser. Signed E.B.

C854   A Poet's Characteristics. *TLS*, 30 May 1929, p. 433. Review of *Walter de la Mare: A Critical Study*, by Forrest Reid. Unsigned.

C855   The Eastern Empire: A New Reading of History. *Daily Telegraph*, 31 May 1929, p. 17. Review of *The Byzantine Achievement, A.D. 330–1453*, by Robert Byron.

C856   Siegfried Sassoon's Poetry. *London Mercury*, June 1929, Vol. 20, No. 116, pp. 156–166.

Reprinted: *The Mind's Eye*, 1934; and *Edmund Blunden: A Selection of His Poetry and Prose*, 1950.

C857   DOES THE SAME CAUSE ALWAYS PRODUCE THE SAME EFFECT? [*later* ART AND NATURE] . *Oxford Outlook*, June 1929, Vol. 10, No. 49, pp. 304–305. At head of title: Two translations. 1, Translated from *Carmina Quadragesimalia ab Aedis Christi Oxon. Alumnis Composita*. 1723. *See also* C858.

Reprinted: *The Face of England*, 1932.

C858   WHETHER LIVING BODIES HAVE ULTIMATE AIMS? *Oxford Outlook*, June 1929, Vol. 10, No. 49, p. 305. At head of title: Two translations. [2] . *See also* C857.

C859   Literary England Month by Month. *Study of English*, June 1929, Vol. 22, No. 3, pp. 302–307. Dated 'London, March 1, 1929'.

C860   No Connection with Herbert. *Nation & Athenaeum*, 1 June 1929, pp. 308–309. Review of *Retrospections of Dorothea Herbert, 1770–1789*. Unsigned.

C861   VALUES. *The Observer*, 2 June 1929, p. 18.

Reprinted: *Near and Far*, 1929; *The Poems*, 1930; *Poems of Many Years*, 1957; *A Selection of the Shorter Poems*, 1966; and *A Selection from the Poems*, [1969].

C862   Captain Gibbon [*later* An Infantry Officer: Edward Gibbon]. *TLS*, 6 June 1929, pp. 441–442. Review of *Gibbon's Journal to January 28th, 1763*, with introductory essays by D. M. Low. Unsigned.

Reprinted: *Votive Tablets*, 1931.

C863   Not What It Was. *Nation & Athenaeum*, 8 June 1929, pp. 334–335. On a sheep fair.

C864   A Parodist of 1816. *TLS*, 13 June 1929, p. 470. Review of *The Poetical Mirror*, by James Hogg, edited . . . by T. Earle Welby. Unsigned. *See also* letter entitled 'Wordsworth's "Flying Tailor" ' by John M. Turnbull in the issue of 24 October, p. 846. *See also* C868.

C865   [Review of] *The Defendant Soul*, by Charles Forrest. *TLS*, 13 June 1929, p. 476. Unsigned.

C866   To Which Generation? *Nation & Athenaeum*, 15 June 1929, p. 369. Review of *The Crater of Mars*, by Ferdinand Tuohy; *The Storm of Steel*, Ernst Jünger, translated by Basil Creighton; and *War*, by Ludwig Renn, translated by Willa and Edwin Muir.

C867   John Skelton. *TLS*, 20 June 1929, pp. 481–482. On the quatercentenary of his death. Unsigned.

Reprinted: *Votive Tablets*, 1931.

C868   Miscellanies. *Nation & Athenaeum*, 22 June 1929, pp. 401–402. Review of *The Latin Portrait: An Anthology*, by George Rostrevor; *The Tree of Life: An Anthology*, by Vivian de Sola Pinto and George Neill Wright; *The Stratford Anthology*, compiled by Ronald Petrie; and *The Poetical Mirror, Parodies*, by James Hogg, edited by T. Earle Welby (*see also* C864). Unsigned.

C869   Keats and his Predecessors: A Note on the *Ode to the Nightingale*. *London Mercury*, July 1929, Vol. 20, No. 117, pp. 289–292.

Reprinted: *Critical Essays of To-day*, 1932.

C870   A Letter from London [*formerly* A Letter from England]. *Studies in English Literature*, July 1929, Vol. 9, No. 3, pp. 453–460. The last of four letters. *See also* C690, 740, 781.

C871   Shelley, J. W. Dalby, and Other Shelleians. *Studies in English Literature*, July 1929, Vol. 9, No. 3, pp. 460–462. Signed An Old Correspondent.

C872   Literary England Month by Month. *Study of English*, July 1929, Vol. 22, No. 4, pp. 398–403. Dated 'London, March 27, 1929'.*

C873   THE GEOGRAPHER'S GLORY: OR, THE WORLD IN 1730 [*later sub-title:* OR, THE GLOBE IN 1730; *or is omitted*]. *Fortnightly Review*, 1 July 1929, N.S. Vol. 126, pp. 70–73.

Reprinted (revised): *Near and Far*, 1929; and *The Poems*, 1930.

C874   The Somme Still Flows. *The Listener*, 10 July 1929, pp. 41–43. A broadcast on 1 July.

Reprinted: *The Mind's Eye*, 1934.

C875   Thomas Randolph. *TLS*, 11 July 1929, p. 555. Review of *The Poems of Thomas Randolph*, edited by G. Thorn-Drury. Unsigned.

Reprinted: *Votive Tablets*, 1931.

C876   Courtier-Poet's Music: The Lyric Verse of Wyatt. *Daily Telegraph*, 12 July 1929, p. 18. Review of *The Poetry of Sir Thomas Wyatt: A Selection and a Study*, by E. M. W. Tillyard.

C877   THE SUMMER RAINSTORM [*later* SUMMER RAINSTORM]. *The Observer*, 14 July 1929, p. 18.

Reprinted (revised): *Near and Far*, 1929; *The Poems*, 1930; and *Poems of Many Years*, 1957.

C878   Moulded Masks of the Dead: A Peculiar Mystery. *Daily Telegraph*, 16 July 1929, p. 17. Review of *Undying Faces: A Collection of Death Masks*, by Ernst Benkard.

C879   The Rev. William Jones. *TLS*, 18 July 1929, p. 573. Review of *The Diary of the Revd. William Jones, 1777–1821*, edited by O. F. Christie. Unsigned.

C880   The Progress of Poetry. *Nation & Athenaeum*, 20 July 1929, pp. 539–540. Review of *Collected Poems*, by Richard Aldington; *The Wall of Weeping*, by Edmond Fleg, translated by Humbert Wolfe; *Earth*, by Frank Townshend; *Wild Garden*, by Bliss Carman; *In Quiet Fields*, by Robert Crawford; *Some Poems*, by Rupert Croft-Cooke; and *A Collection of Poems*, by Eleanor Farjeon. Unsigned.

C881   THE VISITOR. *New Statesman*, 20 July 1929, p. 470.

Reprinted: *Near and Far*, 1929; *The Poems*, 1930; and *Poems of Many Years*, 1957.

C882   William Collins. *TLS*, 25 July 1929, p. 592, and 29 August, p. 668. Letters signed Edmund Blunden. On the review of *The Poems of William Collins*, edited by Edmund Blunden in the issue of 18 July, p. 573. *See also* letters in the issues of 8 August, p. 624 and 29 August, p. 668, by H. W. Garrod (*and* B29).

C883   AUTUMN IN THE WEALD. *New Statesman*, 27 July 1929, p. 498.

Reprinted: *Near and Far*, 1929; *The Poems*, 1930; and *Poems of Many Years*, 1957.

C884   Literary England Month by Month. *Study of English*, August 1929, Vol. 22, No. 5, pp. 498–503. Dated 'London, April 14, 1929'.*

C885   Thinking as a Fine Art: False Impressions and Beliefs. *Daily Telegraph*, 2 August 1929, p. 6. Review of *The Art of Thinking*, by Ernest Dimnet.

C886   Mystery at the Mill. *Nation & Athenaeum*, 3 August 1929, p. 598. Review of *Rod and Line*, by Arthur Ransome. Signed E.B.

C887   KINGFISHER. *The Observer*, 11 August, 1929, p. 17.

Reprinted: *The Poems*, 1930; and *Poems of Many Years*, 1957.

C888   Forty Miles from London: A Quiet Old Village in Sunshine. *T.P.'s and Cassell's Weekly*, 17 August 1929, p. 470. One of a series entitled 'In the Days of My Youth'; title in Contents: A Poet's Boyhood.

C889   Nicholas Breton's Prose. *TLS*, 22 August 1929, pp. 641–642. Review of *A Mad World My Masters, and Other Prose Works*, by Nicholas Breton, edited by Ursula Kentish-Wright. Unsigned.

Reprinted: *Votive Tablets*, 1931.

C890   [Review of] *The Compleat Walton*, edited by Geoffrey Keynes. *TLS*, 29 August 1929, p. 665. Unsigned.

C891   Richard Steele: Debt of English Letters, A Lively Moralist. *The Times*, 31 August 1929, pp. 11–12. On the bicentenary of his death.

Reprinted: *Votive Tablets*, 1931.

C892   Literary England Month by Month. *Study of English*, September 1929, Vol. 22, No. 6, pp. 620–625. 'Dated London, May 22, 1929'.*

C893   INACCESSIBILITY IN THE BATTLEFIELD. *Fortnightly Review*, 2 September 1929, N.S. Vol. 126, p. 377.

Reprinted: *Near and Far*, 1929; and *The Poems*, 1930.

C894   The County Anthologies. *Nation & Athenaeum*, 7 September 1929, pp. 738–739. Review of *Yorkshire in Prose and Verse: An Anthology*, by G. F. Wilson; *Lanarkshire*, by Hugh Quigley; and *Derbyshire*, by Thomas Moult. Signed E. Blunden.

C895   IN WILTSHIRE (SUGGESTED BY POINTS OF SIMILARITY WITH THE SOMME COUNTRY). *The Observer*, 15 September 1929, p. 18.

Reprinted: *The Poems*, 1930.

C896   The War Generation. *TLS*, 19 September 1929, p. 713. Review of *Death of a Hero*, by Richard Aldington. Unsigned.

C897   New War-Books. *Nation & Athenaeum*, 21 September 1929, p. 799. Review of *The Worcestershire Regiment in the Great War*, by H. FitM. Stacke; *Crusader's Coast*, by Edward Thompson; and *One Man's War*, by Bert Hall and J. J. Niles.

C898   FRAGMENT. *Bermondsey Book*, Sept./Oct./Nov., 1929, Vol. 6, No. 4, p. 51.

Reprinted: *Near and Far*, 1929; and *The Poems*, 1930.

C899   THE FAILURE [*later* THE SUNLIT VALE]. *London Mercury*, October 1929, Vol. 20, No. 120, pp. 555-556.

Reprinted: *The Poems*, 1930; *Edmund Blunden: A Selection of His Poetry and Prose*, 1950; *Poems of Many Years*, 1957; and *The Midnight Skaters*, [1968].

C900   A Booklist on the War, 1914-1918. *The Reader*, October-November 1929, Vol. 5, Nos. 1-2, pp. 25-31, 79-83. Compiled by Blunden, Cyril Falls, H. M. Tomlinson and R. Wright; introduction pp. 25-28, by Blunden. Also issued separately as an offprint (*see* B35).

C901   Literary England Month by Month. *Study of English*, October 1929, Vol. 22, No. 7, pp. 678-682. 'Dated London, June 27, 1929'.*

C902   Boswell's Friend. *TLS*, 3 October 1929, p. 763. Review of *Diaries of William Johnston Temple*, 1780-1796, edited with a memoir by Lewis Bettany. Unsigned.

C903   Heine's Poetic Work: English Lack of Recognition, Creator of Clear-Cut Forms. *Daily Telegraph*, 11 October 1929, p. 19. Review of *Heine*, by H. G. Atkins.

C904   "Q" as a Poet. *TLS*, 17 October 1929, p. 814. Review of *The Poems of "Q"*, *i.e.* Sir Arthur Quiller-Couch. Unsigned.

C905   Studies of the Coleridges, Their Writings and Lives: Intellect Joined with Innocence. *Daily Telegraph*, 18 October 1929, p. 18. Review of *Coleridge the Sublime Somnambulist*, by John Charpentier, translated by M. V. Nugent; and *Hartley Coleridge, His Life and Work*, by Earle Leslie Griggs (*see also* C912).

C906   [Review of] *The Book of Beauty*, by H. M. Green. *TLS*, 24 October 1929, p. 851. Unsigned.

C907   A Poet's Prophecy. *Everyman*, 31 October 1929, p. 347. On *Night Thoughts*, by Edward Young; and *The Universe Around Us*, by Sir James Jeans.

C908   Seventeenth-Century English. *TLS*, 31 October 1929, p. 872. Review of *Colloquial Language of the Commonwealth and Restoration*, by Margaret Williamson. Unsigned.

C909　RETURN OF THE NATIVE. *St. Martin's Review*, November 1929, No. 465, p. 541.

Reprinted: *Undertones of War*, 8th (revised) impression, 1930; and *The Poems*, 1930.

C910　Literary England Month by Month. *Study of English*, November 1929, Vol. 22, No. 8, pp. 834–839. Dated 'London, July 18, 1929'.*

C911　Spirit of the Classics, Greek Ideal and Romance: The Limiting Power of Perfection. *Daily Telegraph*, 1 November 1929, p. 17. Review of *Classical Studies*, by G. M. Sargeaunt.

C912　Coleridge the Less. *TLS*, 7 November 1929, pp. 881–882. Review of *Hartley Coleridge, His Life and Work*, by Earle Leslie Griggs. Unsigned. *See also* C905.

Reprinted: *Votive Tablets*, 1931.

C913　Living Poets. *TLS*, 7 November 1929, p. 892. Review of *King's Daughter*, by V. Sackville-West; and *The Family Tree*, by William Plomer. Unsigned.

C914　A Pathetic Library. *Time and Tide*, 8 November 1929, pp. 1339–1340. On John Clare's Library.

C915　A Dictionary of Proverbs. *TLS*, 21 November 1929, p. 952. Review of *English Proverbs and Proverbial Phrases: A Historical Dictionary*, by G. L. Apperson. Unsigned. *See also* letter entitled "Mad as a Hatter", by Austen Chamberlain in the issue of 5 December, p. 1032.

C916　A Follower of the Humanities: Prof. John Burnet. *Daily Telegraph*, 22 November 1929, p. 6. Review of *Essays and Addresses*, by John Burnet, with a memoir by Lord Charnwood.

C917　A Window on England. *TLS*, 28 November 1929, p. 989. Review of *The Way In*, by John Gore. Unsigned.

C918　The Older Poetry. *TLS*, 28 November 1929, p. 996. Review of *English Verse: Campion to the Ballads*, edited by W. Peacock; and *An Anthology of English Poetry, Sixteenth to Seventeenth Centuries*, by Kathleen Campbell. Unsigned.

C919　Tradition in Poetry. *The Bookman*, N.Y., December 1929, Vol. 70, No. 4, pp. 360–368.

First published: *Tradition and Experiment in Present-Day Literature*, 1929.

C920　Literary England Month by Month. *Study of English*, December 1929, Vol. 22, No. 9, pp. 946–951. Dated 'London, Aug. 27, 1929'.*

C921　The Public and the War Book. *Manchester Guardian*, 5 December 1929, Supplement, p. iii.

C922   Bury St. Edmunds. *TLS*, 5 December 1929, p. 1011.
       Review of *The History of King Edmund the Martyr and of
       the Early Years of his Abbey*, edited by Lord Francis
       Hervey. Unsigned.

C923   The Months. *TLS*, 5 December 1929, p. 1023. Review of
       Leigh Hunt's "The Months", edited by R.H.B. with preface
       by Brimley Johnson. Unsigned.

C924   The Soldier's Farewell. *Time and Tide*, 6 December 1929,
       pp. 1477–1478. Review of *Goodbye to All That: An Auto-
       biography*, by Robert Graves.

C925   Children as Readers. *Nation & Athenaeum*, 7 December
       1929, pp. 367–368.
       Reprinted: *The Mind's Eye*, 1934.

C926   The Advent. *Saturday Review*, 7 December 1929, p. 667.
       On winter in the country.

C927   Southey on Holiday. *TLS*, 12 December 1929, p. 1053.
       Review of *Journal of a Tour in Scotland in 1819*, by Robert
       Southey, with an introduction and notes by C. H. Herford.
       Unsigned.

C928   Studies by "Q". *TLS*, 26 December 1929, p. 1094. Review
       of *Studies in Literature, Third Series*, by Sir Arthur Quiller-
       Couch. Unsigned.

1930

C929   THE BARN. *Rising Generation*, January 1930, Vol. 62, No.
       9, p. 309.
       First published: *The Barn*, 1916; *The Harbingers*, 1916; and
       The Waggoner, 1920. Reprinted: *Poems*, 1930; *Poems of
       Many Years*, 1957; and *A Selection from the Poems*,
       [1969] (Part IV, verses 7–8).

C930   Current Notes. *Studies in English Literature*, January 1930,
       Vol. 10, No. 1, pp. 26–34.

C931   Literary England Month by Month. *Study of English*,
       January 1930, Vol. 22, No. 10, pp. 1060–1065. Dated
       'London, Sept. 23, 1929'.

C932   Shelley's Critics. *TLS*, 2 January 1930, p. 9. Review of *The
       Early Reviews of Shelley*, by G. L. North. Unsigned.

C933   Japanese Moments. *Time and Tide*, 3 January 1930, pp.
       16–17.
       Reprinted: *The Mind's Eye*, 1934.

C934   "This Crystal". *TLS*, 9 January 1930, p. 24. Review of *Two
       Poems, Ten Songs*, by Sacheverell Sitwell. Unsigned.

C935   The Light Reading of the Elizabethans. *TLS*, 30 January
       1930, p. 74. Review of *The Palace of Pleasure*, by William
       Painter, with introduction by Hamish Miles. Unsigned.

C936   [Review of] *No Man's Land*, by Vernon Bartlett. *TLS*, 30 January 1930, p. 76. Unsigned.

C937   [Review of] *Fables and Satires*, by Sir Ronald Ross. *TLS*, 30 January 1930, p. 76. Unsigned.

C938   Keats and C. A. Brown. *TLS*, 30 January 1930, p. 78. Letter signed E. Blunden.

C939   Lafacadio Hearn. *The Bookman*, London, February 1930, Vol. 77, No. 461, pp. 281-282. Review of *Lectures on Shakespeare*, by Lafcadio Hearn, edited by Iwao Inagaki; and *Essays on American Literature*, by Lafcadio Hearn, edited by Sanki Ichikawa.

C940   Literary England Month by Month. *Study of English*, February 1930, Vol. 22, No. 11, pp. 1180-1185. Dated 'London, Oct. 17, 1929'.

C941   The Storm of Battle. *Fortnightly Review*, 1 February 1930, N.S. Vol. 127, pp. 275-276. Review of *All Our Yesterdays*, by H. M. Tomlinson; and *Retreat, A Story of 1918*, by C. R. Benstead.

C942   CHANCES OF REMEMBRANCE. *The Observer*, 2 February 1930, p. 18.

        Reprinted: *The Poems*, 1930; and *Poems of Many Years*, 1957.

C943   [Review of] *From Gretna Green to Land's End: A Literary Journey to England*, by Katherine Lee Bates. *TLS*, 6 February 1930, p. 107. Unsigned.

C944   We Went to Ypres. *Time and Tide*, 7 February 1930, pp. 169-170.

        Reprinted: *The Mind's Eye*, 1934.

C945   Odes and Songs. *TLS*, 13 February 1930, p. 119. Review of *Collected Poems of Ronald Campbell Macfie*. Unsigned.

C946   News of Alfred Tennyson. *Nation & Athenaeum*, 22 February 1930, p. 705. One of a series entitled 'The World of Books'. On *The Devil and the Lady*, by Alfred Tennyson.

C947   Literary England Month by Month. *Study of English*, March 1930, Vol. 22, No. 12, pp. 1288-1293. Dated 'London, Nov. 20, 1929.'*

C948   Poets of the Golden Age. *Fortnightly Review*, 1 March 1930, N.S. Vol. 127, p. 421. Review of *The Jade Mountain: A Chinese Anthology*, translated by Witter Bynner from the texts of Kiang Kang-hu.

C949   The British in Flanders. *Nation & Athenaeum*, 1 March 1930, p. 734. One of a series entitled 'The World of Books'. On *Flemish Influence in Britain*, by J. A. Fleming; *Memories of the Artists' Rifles*, by H. A. R. May; *War is War; Postscript to Adventure*, by Ashley Gibson; *Pass Guard at Ypres*, by Ronald Gurner; and *The Men in the Line*, by V. Walpole.

C950　The Soldier Speaks Out. *Everyman*, 6 March 1930, Vol. 3, No. 58, p. 163. Arising from *Everyman at War*, edited by C. B. Purdom.

C951　Coleridge, or Sixty Years in a Balloon. *Nation & Athenaeum*, 8 March 1930, p. 766. One of a series entitled 'The World of Books'. On *Coleridge on Logic and Learning*, by Alice Snyder.

C952　Hood's Literary Reminiscences. *TLS*, 13 March 1930, p. 208. Review of *Thomas Hood and Charles Lamb: The Story of a Friendship*, edited by Walter Jerrold. Unsigned.
Reprinted: *Votive Tablets*, 1931.

C953　An Old Dramatist. *Nation & Athenaeum*, 15 March 1930, p. 803. One of a series entitled 'The World of Books'. On *Tourneur's Writings*, edited by Allardyce Nicoll.

C954　The Lover and the Poet. *TLS*, 20 March 1930, p. 239. Review of *Shelley's Lost Letters to Harriet*, with an introduction by Leslie Hotson; and *The Shelley Notebook in the Harvard College Library* . . . with notes by George Edward Woodberry. Unsigned.

C955　And for Delight. *Time and Tide*, 21 March 1930, pp. 375–376. Review of *A Writer's Notes on his Trade*, by C. E. Montague.

C956　Emily Dickinson [*later* An Unguessed Poetry]. *Nation & Athenaeum*, 22 March 1930, p. 863. One of a series entitled 'The World of Books'. On *Emily Dickinson: The Human Background of her Poetry*, by Josephine Pollitt; *The Complete Poems of Emily Dickinson*; and *Further Poems of Emily Dickinson*.
Reprinted: *The Recognition of Emily Dickinson*, edited by Caesar R. Blake and Carlton F. Wells, [1964].

C957　An Away Match. *Time and Tide*, 28 March 1930, pp. 402–403. On a local football match.

C958　Eleanor in the North. *Nation & Athenaeum*, 29 March 1930, p. 894. One of a series entitled 'The World of Books'. On *John Franklin's Bride*, by the Hon. Mrs Gell.

C959　Literary England Month by Month. *Study of English*, April 1930, Vol. 23, No. 1, pp. 5–9. Dated 'London, January 3, 1930'.*

C960　[Review of] *The Magic of the Stars*, by Maurice Maeterlinck, translated by Alfred Sutro. *Fortnightly Review*, 1 April 1930, N.S. Vol. 127, pp. 565–566.

C961　The Footsteps of Evelina. *Nation & Athenaeum*, 5 April 1930, p. 17. One of a series entitled 'The World of Books'. On *Evelina*, by Fanny Burney, edited by Sir F. D. Mackinnon.

C962   A Literary Pocket-Book [paragraphs 1-3]. *Nation & Athenaeum*, 5 April 1930, p. 26. Unsigned.

C963   Mr. Gould's Poems. *TLS*, 10 April 1930, p. 314. Review of *The Collected Poems of Gerald Gould.* Unsigned.

C964   The Horrible Example. *Nation & Athenaeum*, 12 April 1930, p. 50. One of a series entitled 'The World of Books'. On *Johann Faust: The Man and the Myth*, by H. G. Meek.

C965   Pope and Theobald. *TLS*, 17 April 1930, p. 332. Review of *The Dunciad Variorum*, by Alexander Pope, with an introductory essay by Robert Kilburn Root. Unsigned.

        Reprinted: *Votive Tablets*, 1931.

C966   Annals of the Fine Arts. *Nation & Athenaeum*, 19 April 1930, p. 84. One of a series entitled 'The World of Books'. On *Art in England, 1821-1837*, by William T. Whitley.

C967   A Literary Pocket-Book [paragraphs 1-2, 5]. *Nation & Athenaeum*, 19 April 1930, p. 92. Unsigned.

C968   An Anonymous Table-Talker. *TLS*, 24 April 1930, p. 349. Review of *Characters and Observations: An Eighteenth Century Manuscript*, with a foreword by Lord Gorell. Unsigned. *See also* C975.

C969   The Ideal Laureate. *Nation & Athenaeum*, 26 April 1930, p. 106. On Robert Bridges.

        Reprinted: *The Mind's Eye*, 1934.

C970   [Review of] The film *Journey's End*, by R. C. Sherriff. *Nation & Athenaeum*, 26 April 1930, p. 112. Unsigned.

C971   Milton and the New Consciousness. *Nation & Athenaeum*, 26 April 1930, p. 113. One of a series entitled 'The World of Books'. On *Milton*, by E. M. W. Tillyard.

C972   A Literary Pocket-Book [paragraphs 1-2, 5-6]. *Nation & Athenaeum*, 26 April 1930, pp. 118, 120. Unsigned.

C973   Literary England Month by Month. *Study of English*, May 1930, Vol. 23, No. 2, pp. 107-111. Dated 'London, January 24, 1930'.*

C974   Mr. Thompson's Poems. *TLS*, 1 May 1930, p. 366. Review of *The Collected Poems of Edward Thompson.* Unsigned.

C975   A Quiet Mind. *Time and Tide*, 2 May 1930, p. 567. Review of *Characters and Observations: An Eighteenth Century Manuscript*, with a foreword by Lord Gorell. *See also* C968.

C976   Freedom and Duty. *Nation & Athenaeum*, 3 May 1930, p. 143. One of a series entitled 'The World of Books'. On *Liberty in the Modern State*, by H. J. Laski.

C977   [Review of] *Sober Truth: A Collection of Nineteenth-Century Episodes*, compiled and edited by Margaret Barton and Osbert Sitwell. *Nation & Athenaeum*, 3 May 1930, p. 150. Unsigned.

C978   Gay Goes to Town. *TLS*, 8 May 1930, p. 388. Review of *Rural Sports*, by John Gay, with an introduction by Owen Culbertson. Unsigned.

C979   The Phenomenon of Defoe. *TLS*, 8 May 1930, p. 389. Review of *The Life and Strange and Surprising Adventures of Daniel Defoe*, by Paul Dottin, translated . . . by Louise Ragan. Unsigned.

C980   Mrs. Hardy's Second Volume. *Nation & Athenaeum*, 10 May 1930, p. 174. One of a series entitled 'The World of Books'. On *The Later Years of Thomas Hardy, 1892-1928*, by Mrs. Hardy.

C981   A Literary Pocket-Book [paragraphs 1-4]. *Nation & Athenaeum*, 10 May 1930, p. 184. Unsigned.

C982   Mr. Campbell's Poetry. *TLS*, 15 May 1930, p. 410. Review of *Adamastor, Poems*, by Roy Campbell. Unsigned.

C983   The Figure of Shelley. *TLS*, 15 May 1930, p. 411. Review of *Mad Shelley*, by James Ramsey Ullman. Unsigned.

C984   [Paragraph commencing] After the usual amount of speculation . . . in John Masefield . . . the laureateship. *Nation & Athenaeum*, 17 May 1930, p. 205. Unsigned.

C985   Another Victorian. *Nation & Athenaeum*, 17 May 1930, p.218. One of a series entitled 'The World of Books'. On the poet T. E. Brown.

C986   [Note on] *What is a Journalist? Do's and Don'ts*, by R. D. Blumenfeld. *Nation & Athenaeum*, 17 May 1930, p. 228. Unsigned.

C987   The Story of a Surgeon. *Nation & Athenaeum*, 24 May 1930, p. 249. One of a series entitled 'The World of Books'. On *Story of a Surgeon*, by Sir John Bland-Sutton.

C988   Among these Rocks. *TLS*, 29 May 1930, p. 452. Review of *Ash Wednesday*, T. S. Eliot. Unsigned.

C989   Mr. Wilkinson's Lovelace. *Nation & Athenaeum*, 31 May 1930, p. 291. One of a series entitled 'The World of Books'. On *The Poems of Richard Lovelace*, edited by C. H. Wilkinson. *See also* C575.

C990   A Literary Pocket-Book [paragraphs 5-7]. *Nation & Athenaeum*, 31 May 1930, pp. 294, 296. Unsigned.

C991   With Roberts to Hagley Park. *The Bookman*, London, June 1930, Vol. 78, No. 465, pp. 162-163. Review of *An Eighteenth Century Gentleman, and Other Essays*, by S. C. Roberts.

C992   THE SURVIVAL. *London Mercury*, June 1930, Vol. 22, No. 128, p. 106.

        Reprinted: *The Best Poems of 1930*, [1930]; and *The Poems*, 1930.

C993   Literary England Month by Month. *Study of English*, June 1930, Vol. 23, No. 3, pp. 207–211. Dated 'London, March 3, 1930'. Final paragraph in holograph facsimile.

C994   Nature's God. *TLS*, 5 June 1930, p. 474. Review of *The House on the Wold, and Other Poems*, by William Force Stead. Unsigned.

C995   The Grecian Urn. *Nation & Athenaeum*, 7 June 1930, p. 321. One of a series entitled 'The World of Books'. On the *Oxford Book of Greek Verse*.

C996   Messrs. Chapman & Hall. *Nation & Athenaeum*, 14 June 1930, p. 349. One of a series entitled 'The World of Books'. On *A Hundred Years of Publishing*, by Arthur Waugh.

C997   A Literary Pocket-Book [paragraphs 1–3, 5]. *Nation & Athenaeum*, 14 June 1930, p. 356. Unsigned.

C998   Indian Village. *Nation & Athenaeum*, 21 June 1930, p. 379. One of a series entitled 'The World of Books'. On *Rusticus Loquitur, or the Old Light and the New in the Punjab Village*, by Malcolm Lyall Darling.

C999   Plays and Pictures [paragraphs 3, 6]. *Nation & Athenaeum*, 28 June 1930, p. 409. Unsigned.

C1000   Anti-Babel. *Nation & Athenaeum*, 28 June 1930, p. 410. One of a series entitled 'The World of Books'. On *Babel, or the Past, Present, and Future of Human Speech*, by Sir Richard Paget.

C1001   [Review of] *The Place-Names of Sussex*, by A. Mawer and F. M. Stenton. *Nation & Athenaeum*, 28 June 1930, p. 418. Unsigned.

C1002   Mr. Editor. *The Blue*, July 1930, Vol. 57, No. 6, pp. 290–291. Letter on *Haunting Years*, by W. L. Andrews. *See also* review in the issue of June 1930, Vol. 57, No. 5, p. 245, signed A.C.W.E.

C1003   Literary England Month by Month. *Study of English*, July 1930, Vol. 23, No. 4, pp. 309--313. Dated 'London, April 1, 1930'.*

C1004   OLD REMEDIES. *The Window*, July 1930, Vol. 1, No. 3, p.5. There were 10 signed copies of this issue signed by all the contributors.

       Reprinted: *The Poems*, 1930.

C1005   A County Anthology. *TLS*, 3 July 1930, p. 551. Review of *Middlesex in Prose and Verse: An Anthology*, by T. Michael Pope. Unsigned.

C1006   Lord's, June 27th, 1930. *Nation & Athenaeum*, 5 July 1930, pp. 439–440.

       Reprinted: *Essays of the Year*, [1931]; *The Mind's Eye*, 1934; and *Edmund Blunden: A Selection of His Poetry and Prose*, 1950.

C1007   The Younger Son. *Nation & Athenaeum*, 5 July 1930, p. 443. One of a series entitled 'The World of Books'. On *The Friend of Shelley: A Memoir of Edward John Trelawny*, by H. J. Massingham. *See also* C1008.

C1008   Trelawny Interpreted. *TLS*, 10 July 1930, p. 571. Review of *The Friend of Shelley: A Memoir of Edward John Trelawny*, by H. J. Massingham. Unsigned. *See also* C1007.

        Reprinted: *VotiveTablets*, 1931.

C1009   R. L. Gales as a Poet. *TLS*, 10 July 1930, p. 574. Review of *Richard Lawson Gales: Poems*, selected and introduced by Anthony C. Deane. Unsigned.

C1010   Sea Anthologies. *Nation & Athenaeum*, 12 July 1930, p. 473. One of a series entitled 'The World of Books'.

C1011   A Kind of Allegory. *TLS*, 17 July 1930, p. 590. Review of *Doctor Donne and Gargantua, The First Six Cantos*, by Sacheverell Sitwell. Unsigned.

C1012   Ruskin and Kate Greenaway. *Nation & Athenaeum*, 19 July 1930, p. 501. Unsigned.

C1013   The Japanese Pilgrimage. *Nation & Athenaeum*, 19 July 1930, p. 502. One of a series entitled 'The World of Books'. On *History of Japanese Religion*, by Masaharu Anesake.

C1014   A Literary Pocket-Book [paragraph 6]. *Nation & Athenaeum*, 19 July 1930, p. 512. Unsigned.

C1015   Fading Voices. *TLS*, 24 July 1930, p. 609. Review of *Songs and Slang of the British Soldier, 1914-1918*, edited by John Brophy and Eric Partridge. Unsigned. *See also* C1045, 1173.

C1016   "The Roll of Thespis". *Nation & Athenaeum*, 26 July 1930, p. 533. One of a series entitled 'The World of Books'. On *The Life of Michael Kelly, 1762-1826*, by S. M. Ellis.

C1017   A Literary Pocket-Book [paragraph 5]. *Nation & Athenaeum*, 26 July 1930, p. 542. Unsigned.

C1018   Mr. Bennett in 1929. *TLS*, 31 July 1930, p. 624. Review of *Journal, 1929*, by Arnold Bennett. Unsigned.

C1019   [Review of] *The Wipers Times*, with a foreword by Field-Marshall Lord Plumer. *TLS*, 31 July 1930, p. 626. Unsigned.

C1020   Literary England Month by Month. *Study of English*, August 1930, Vol. 23, No. 5, pp. 406-410. Dated 'London, April 29, 1930'.*

C1021   Miss Sitwell's Work. *Fortnightly Review*, 1 August 1930, N.S. Vol. 128, pp. 271-272. Review of *The Collected Poems of Edith Sitwell*.

C1022   Twenty Years After. *Nation & Athenaeum*, 2 August 1930, p. 566. One of a series entitled 'The World of Books'. On *A Modern Symposium*, by G. Lowes Dickinson in the form of an imaginary conversation.

C1023 A Literary Pocket-Book [paragraphs 2-3, 6-7]. *Nation &*
Athenaeum, 2 August 1930, p. 571. Unsigned.

C1024 Mr. Squire's Reviews. *TLS*, 7 August 1930, p. 638. Review
of *Sunday Mornings*, by J. C. Squire. Unsigned.

C1025 Shakespeare's Transmissions. *Nation & Athenaeum*, 9
August 1930, p. 593. One of a series entitled 'The World of
Books'. On *The Wheel of Fire: Essays in Interpretation of
Shakespeare's Sombre Tragedies*, by G. Wilson Knight.

C1026 Keats, G. F. Mathew and others. *TLS*, 14 August 1930, p.
651. Review of *Studies in Keats*, by John Middleton Murry.
Unsigned.

C1027 Where Things Are. *Nation & Athenaeum*, 16 August 1930,
p. 622. One of a series entitled 'The World of Books'. On
reference books.

C1028 A Golden Legend. *Nation & Athenaeum*, 23 August 1930,
p. 650. One of a series entitled 'The World of Books'. On
Writing for Profit, by Donald Wilhelm.

C1029 On Going to the Wars. *Nation & Athenaeum*, 30 August
1930, p. 677. One of a series entitled 'The World of Books'.
On *War Letters of Fallen Englishmen*, edited by Laurence
Housman. *See also* C1032.

C1030 THE MEADOW STREAM. *London Mercury*, September
1930, Vol. 22, No. 131, pp. 393-395.

Reprinted: *The Poems*, 1930.

C1031 Literary England Month by Month. *Study of English*,
September 1930, Vol. 23, No. 6, pp. 510-513. Dated
'London, June 2, 1930'.*

C1032 Fallen Englishmen. *TLS*, 4 September 1930, p. 693. Review
of *War Letters of Fallen Englishmen*, edited by Laurence
Housman. Unsigned. *See also* C1029.

Reprinted: *Votive Tablets*, 1931.

C1033 Select Victorianism. *Nation & Athenaeum*, 6 September
1930, p. 706. One of a series entitled 'The World of Books'.
On *England Under Victoria*, edited by H. V. Routh. *See
also* C1040.

C1034 A Literary Pocket-Book [paragraph 1]. *Nation & Athenaeum*, 6 September 1930, p. 711. Unsigned.

C1035 [Review of] *Roads to Glory*, by R. Aldington. *TLS*, 11
September 1930, p. 714. Unsigned.

C1036 Mr. Murry Edits Keats. *Nation & Athenaeum*, 13 September 1930, p. 734. One of a series entitled 'The World of
Books'. On *The Poems and Verses of John Keats*, edited by
John Middleton Murry. *See also* letters signed E. Blunden
in the issues of 27 September, pp. 786-787 and 18 October, pp. 99-100; letters from J. Middleton Murry in the
issues of 20 September, pp. 757-758, 4 October, pp. 10-11,

with reply by Blunden, 11 October, pp. 41-42; and from Eyre & Spottiswoode (Publishers) Ltd., 1 November, pp. 161-162, with reply by Blunden.

C1037   Mr. Sassoon's Reminiscences. *TLS*, 18 September 1930, p. 731. Review of *Memoirs of an Infantry Officer*, by Siegfried Sassoon. Unsigned.

C1038   The Decline of Puritanism. *Nation & Athenaeum*, 20 September 1930, p. 765. One of a series entitled 'The World of Books'. On *The Decline of Merry England*, by Storm Jameson.

C1039   A Literary Pocket-Book [paragraphs 1-2]. *Nation & Athenaeum*, 20 September 1930, pp. 769-770. Unsigned.

C1040   Victorian England. *TLS*, 25 September 1930, p. 747. Review of *England Under Victoria*, edited by H. V. Routh. Unsigned. *See also* C1033.

C1041   "Will You Come to the Camp?" *Nation & Athenaeum*, 27 September 1930, p. 794. One of a series entitled 'The World of Books'. On *The Wind on the Heath*, a gypsy anthology edited by John Sampson.

C1042   A Literary Pocket-Book [paragraphs 3-4]. *Nation & Athenaeum*, 27 September 1930, pp. 802, 804. Unsigned.

C1043   Literary England Month by Month. *Study of English*, October 1930, Vol. 23, No. 7, pp. 610-613. Dated 'London, June 16, 1930.'

C1044   [Review of] *Queensland Poets*, by Henry Arthur Kellow. *TLS*, 2 October 1930, p. 786. Unsigned.

C1045   [Review of] *Songs and Slang of the British Soldier, 1914-1918*, second edition revised, edited by John Brophy and Eric Partridge. *TLS*, 2 October 1930, p. 786. Unsigned. *See also* C1015, 1173.

C1046   Hewitt on the Alphabet. *Nation & Athenaeum*, 4 October 1930, p. 17. One of a series entitled 'The World of Books'. On *Lettering*, by Graily Hewitt.

C1047   Rural Rides. *TLS*, 9 October 1930, pp. 789-790. Review of *Rural Rides, Together with Tours in Scotland and Letters from Ireland*, by William Cobbett, edited . . . by G. D. H. Cole and Margaret Cole. Unsigned.

Reprinted: *Votive Tablets*, 1931.

C1048   From Gay to Grave. *TLS*, 9 October 1930, p. 799. Review of *The Glance Backward*, by Richard Church. Unsigned.

C1049   Two Books on Tennyson. *TLS*, 9 October 1930, p. 803. Review of *Tennyson*, by Humbert Wolfe; and *The Poetry of Alfred Tennyson: An Essay in Appreciation*, by C. H. O. Scaife. Unsigned.

C1050   Improved Newspapers. *Nation & Athenaeum*, 11 October 1930, p. 47. One of a series entitled 'The World of Books'.

C1051 A Novelist's Poems. *TLS*, 16 October 1930, p. 830. Review of *Poems New and Old*, by R. H. Mottram. Unsigned.

C1052 Super-Playfair. *Nation & Athenaeum*, 18 October 1930, p. 106. One of a series entitled 'The World of Books'. On *Secret Service*, by Sir George Aston.

C1053 A Letter from Mr. E. Brunden [*sic*]. *Kitsune to Suisen*, 20 October 1930, Vol. 3, pp. 28–30.

C1054 Coleridge and Opium. *TLS*, 23 October 1930, p. 866. Letter on the review of *Coleridge as Philosopher*, by John H. Muirhead in the issue of 16 October, p. 830.

C1055 [Review of] *The Wattlefold: Unpublished Poems*, by Michael Field, collected by Emily C. Fortey. *TLS*, 23 October 1930, p. 870. Unsigned.

C1056 Improved Education. *Nation & Athenaeum*, 25 October 1930, p. 137. One of a series entitled 'The World of Books'. On *English Education, 1789–1902*, by J. W. Adamson.

C1057 Literary England Month by Month. *Study of English*, November 1930, Vol. 23, No. 8, pp. 809–811. Dated 'London, July 25, 1930'.*

C1058 An Unlucky Romantic. *Nation & Athenaeum*, 1 November 1930, p. 165. One of a series entitled 'The World of Books'. On *A Life of Thomas Chatterton*, by E. H. W. Meyerstein. *See also* C1066.

C1059 [Review of] *The Grave of Arthur*, by G. K. Chesterton; *Elm Angel*, by Harold Monro; *In Sicily*, by Siegfried Sassoon; *The Triumph of the Machine*, by D. H. Lawrence; *Marina*, by T. S. Eliot; *The Gum Trees*, by Roy Campbell; and *News*, by Walter de la Mare (The Ariel Poems). *TLS*, 6 November 1930, p. 923. Unsigned.

C1060 Fermented Liquors. *Nation & Athenaeum*, 8 November 1930, p. 195. One of a series entitled 'The World of Books'. On *The Savoy Cocktail Book*, by Harry Craddock; *Whisky*, by Aeneas Macdonald; *Gentlemen, I Give You Wine*, by Warner Allen; *French Wines*, by Paul de Cassagnac; and *What We Drink*, edited by H. W. Bayly.

C1061 The Oldest Profession? *Nation & Athenaeum*, 15 November 1930, p. 237. One of a series entitled 'The World of Books'. On *Publishing and Bookselling*, by F. A. Mumby.

C1062 Surviving Customs. *TLS*, 20 November 1930, p. 967. Review of *The Folklore Calendar*, by George Long. Unsigned. *See also* letter from F. White, Hon. Secretary of the English Folk Cookery Association in the issue of 27 November, p. 1014.

C1063 Southey's "Doctor". *TLS*, 20 November 1930, p. 972. Review of *The Doctor, &c.*, by Robert Southey, newly edited and abridged from John Wood Warter's edition (1848) by Maurice Fitzgerald. Unsigned.

Reprinted: *Votive Tablets*, 1931.

C1064   The Oracular Poets. *Nation & Athenaeum*, 22 November 1930, p. 267. One of a series entitled 'The World of Books'. On *Seven Types of Ambiguity*, by William Empson.

C1065   Glimpses of Immortals. *TLS*, 27 November 1930, p. 1005. Review of *Unpublished Letters from the Collection of John Wild*, selected and edited by R. N. Carew Hunt. Unsigned.

C1066   Thomas Chatterton. *TLS*, 27 November 1930, p. 1009. Review of *A Life of Thomas Chatterton*, by E. H. W. Meyerstein. Unsigned. *See also* C1058.

C1067   A Poem of Action. *TLS*, 27 November 1930, p. 1011. Review of *The Pursuit (Hauran, Autumn, 1918)*, by P. P. Graves. Unsigned.

C1068   Difficulties of Biography. *Nation & Athenaeum*, 29 November 1930, p. 297. One of a series entitled 'The World of Books'. On *Psychiatry in Relation to Biography and History*, by Hubert Norman.

C1069   Observation Posts. *The Adelphi*, December 1930, N.S. Vol. 1, No. 3, pp. xxii–xxv. Review of *Verdun*, by Marshal Pétain, authorised translation by Margaret MacVeagh; *Salute of Guns*, by Donald Boyd; and *Mars, or, the Truth About War*, by Alain, translated by Doris Mudie and Elizabeth Hill.

C1070   Progress? *The Blue*, December 1930, Vol. 58, No. 2, p. 67. On the despoilation of the countryside. Signed E. Blunden.

C1071   Bringing Them Home. *Book-Collector's Quarterly*, December 1930, No. 1, pp. 1–8.

Reprinted: *The Mind's Eye*, 1934.

C1072   Literary England Month by Month. *Study of English*, December 1930, Vol. 23, No. 9, pp. 707–711. Dated 'London, Aug. 20, 1930'.*

C1073   A Masterly Series. *Nation & Athenaeum*, 6 December 1930, p. 327. One of a series entitled 'The World of Books'. On the *Oxford Poets* series published by Oxford University Press. Also published separately as an advertisement by the publishers (*see* A36).

C1074   [Review of] *The Torch-Bearers*, Volume 3, *The Last Voyage*, by Alfred Noyes. *TLS*, 11 December 1930, p. 1060. Unsigned. *See also* letter from Alfred Noyes in the issue of 25 December, p. 1101.

C1075   [Review of] *Three Short Plays*, by Laurence Binyon. *TLS*, 11 December 1930, p. 1067. Unsigned.

C1076   Subject to Alteration. *Nation & Athenaeum*, 13 December 1930, p. 378. One of a series entitled 'The World of Books'. On *Cancels*, by R. W. Chapman.

C1077   [Review of] *The Pleasures of Poetry: A Critical Anthology, First Series, Milton and the Augustan Age*, by Edith Sitwell. *TLS*, 18 December 1930, p. 1083. Unsigned.

C1078   The Turbulent Priest. *Nation & Athenaeum*, 20 December 1930, p. 409. One of a series entitled 'The World of Books'. On *The Development of the Legend of Thomas Becket*, by Paul A. Brown.

C1079   Power and Serenity. *TLS*, 25 December 1930, p. 1099. Review of *Nine Poems*, by T. Sturge Moore. Unsigned.

C1080   Hanging No Remedy. *Nation & Athenaeum*, 27 December 1930, p. 436. One of a series entitled 'The World of Books'. On *Report from the Select Committee on Capital Punishment.*

1931

C1081   Literary England Month by Month. *Study of English*, January 1931, Vol. 23, No. 10, pp. 910–913. Dated 'London, Sept. 21, 1930'.*

C1082   AE's New Poems. *TLS*, 1 January 1931, p. 9. Review of *Enchantment and Other Poems*, by AE [*i.e.* G. W. Russell]. Unsigned.

C1083   Mr. Abercrombie's Dramatic Poems: His Miltonic Power. *Daily Telegraph*, 2 January 1931, p. 4. Review of *The Poems of Lascelles Abercrombie.*

C1084   Some Pamphlets. *Nation & Athenaeum*, 3 January 1931, p. 460. One of a series entitled 'The World of Books'. On *Collected Essays, Papers &c., of Robert Bridges* (*see also* C647); *Poetical Intoxication*, by W. N. Bates, Jr (*see also* C1087); and other pamphlets of verse.

C1085   WINTER STARS. *The Observer*, 4 January, 1931, p. 14. Reprinted: *To Themis*, 1931; *Halfway House*, 1932; and *Poems 1930–1940*, [1941].

C1086   Nature-Pictures. *TLS*, 8 January 1931, p. 24. Review of *Winter Movement and Other Poems*, by Julian Bell. Unsigned.

C1087   [Review of] *Poetical Intoxication*, by William Nickerson Bates, Jr. *TLS*, 8 January 1931, p. 30. Unsigned. *See also* C1084.

C1088   [Review of] *As Between Friends: Criticism of Themselves and One Another in the Letters of Coleridge, Wordsworth and Lamb*, by Barbara Birkhoff. *TLS*, 8 January, 1931, p. 30. Unsigned.

379

C1089   Discovering England. *Nation & Athenaeum*, 10 January 1931, p. 484. One of a series entitled 'The World of Books'. On *Rediscovering England*, by Charlotte A. Simpson.

C1090   [Review of] *Selected Poems of Alice Meynell*, with an introductory note by W.M. [i.e. Wilfrid Meynell] *TLS*, 15 January 1931, p. 47. Unsigned.

C1091   Another Problem. *Nation & Athenaeum*, 17 January 1931, p. 511. One of a series entitled 'The World of Books'. On *History of Applied Entomology*, by L. O. Howard.

C1092   Coleridge, Hazlitt, Scott. *Nation & Athenaeum*, 24 January 1931, p. 543. One of a series entitled 'The World of Books'. On *Coleridge's Shakespearian Criticism*, edited by T. M. Raysor; *William Hazlitt and Hackney College*, by H. W. Stephenson; and *Bibliography of the Waverley Novels*, by Greville Worthington.

C1093   Nineteenth-Century Poetry. *Nation & Athenaeum*, 31 January 1931, p. 574. One of a series entitled 'The World of Books'. On *A Hundred Years of English Poetry*, edited by E. B. Powley.

C1094   Literary England Month by Month. *Study of English*, February 1931, Vol. 23, No. 11, pp. 1006–1009. Dated 'London, October 24, 1930.'*

C1095   Charles Churchill. *TLS*, 5 February 1931, pp. 85–86. On the bicentenary of his birth. Unsigned.

   Reprinted: *Votive Tablets*, 1931.

C1096   [Review of] *W. A. Way, Headmaster and Poet*, by A. H. J. Bourne. *TLS*, 5 February 1931, p. 100. Unsigned.

C1097   Some Book Catalogues. *Nation & Athenaeum*, 7 February 1931, p. 603. One of a series entitled 'The World of Books'. On catalogues published by the Rosenbach Company, and P. J. Dobell.

C1098   Three Autobiographies. *Nation & Athenaeum*, 14 February 1931, p. 634. One of a series entitled 'The World of Books'. On *Memories of Sixty Years*, by Lord Sanderson; *My Eighty Years*, by Robert Blatchford; and *After Sixty Years*, by Shan F. Bullock.

C1099   The Publications of 1930. *Nation & Athenaeum*, 21 February 1931, p. 668. One of a series entitled 'The World of Books'. On *The English Catalogue of Books*.

C1100   THE KISS. *New Statesman & Nation*, 28 February 1931, p. 17.

   Reprinted: *To Themis*, 1931; *Halfway House*, 1932; *Poems 1930–1940*, [1941]; *Edmund Blunden: A Selection of His Poetry and Prose*, 1950; and *Poems of Many Years*, 1957.

C1101 INCIDENT IN HYDE PARK, 1803. *London Mercury*, March 1931, Vol. 23, No. 137, pp. 408–410.

Reprinted: *To Themis*, 1931; *Halfway House*, 1932; *Poems 1930–1940*, [1941]; *Edmund Blunden: A Selection of His Poetry and Prose*, 1950; and *Poems of Many Years*, 1957.

C1102 Literary England Month by Month. *Study of English*, March 1931, Vol. 23, No. 12, pp. 1102–1105. Dated 'London, Dec. 1, 1930.'

C1103 [Review of] *The Frozen Ocean and Other Poems*, by Viola Meynell. *TLS*, 5 March 1931, p. 172. Unsigned.

C1104 A Soldier Poet. *TLS*, 5 March 1931, p. 172. Review of *The Poems of Sidney Godolphin*, edited by William Dighton, with a preface by John Drinkwater. Unsigned.

C1105 Blake's Poetry. *TLS*, 12 March 1931, p. 194. Review of *Poems of Blake*, chosen and edited by Laurence Binyon. Unsigned.

C1106 Nature Spiritualized. *TLS*, 12 March 1931, p. 197. Review of *Sunflower and Elm*, by Gertrude Woodthorpe, with an introduction by Walter de la Mare. Unsigned.

C1107 [Review of] *Heroes and Kings*, by Charles Williams. *TLS*, 12 March 1931, p. 203. Unsigned.

C1108 London in Queen Elizabeth's Spacious Days. *Daily Telegraph*, 20 March 1931, p. 7. Review of *A Second Elizabethan Journal: Being a Record of Those Things most Talked of During the Years 1595–1598*, by G. B. Harrison.

C1109 English Aphorisms. *TLS*, 26 March 1931, p. 248. Review of *A Treasury of English Aphorisms*, edited with an introduction by Logan Pearsall Smith; *Afterthoughts*, by Logan Pearsall Smith; and *Aphorisms*, by F. H. Bradley. Unsigned.

C1110 Literary England Month by Month. *Study of English*, April 1931, Vol. 24, No. 1, pp. 20–22. Dated 'London, January 11, 1931.'

C1111 Horace Walpole's Verse. *TLS*, 16 April 1931, p. 302. Review of *Horace Walpole's Fugitive Verse*, edited by W. S. Lewis. Unsigned.

C1112 Sheridan and his Biographers. *TLS*, 16 April 1931, p. 303. Review of *Sheridan: A Ghost Story*, by E. M. Butler. Unsigned.

C1113 The Editing of Keats: Work of a Father and Son. *Daily Telegraph*, 17 April 1931, p. 7. Review of *The Letters of John Keats*, edited by Maurice Buxton Forman.

C1114 Japan Opened: The Process of Transition. *Daily Telegraph*, 21 April 1931, p. 17. Review of *Yofuku, or Japan in Trousers*, by Sherard Vines; and *Realism in Romantic Japan*, by Miriam Beard.

C1115 Daniel Defoe, April 26, 1731. *TLS*, 23 April 1931, pp. 313-314. On the bicentenary of his death. Unsigned.

Reprinted: *Votive Tablets*, 1931.

C1116 Shelley's Scientific Allusions. *TLS*, 23 April 1931, p. 326. Review of *A Newton Among Poets*, by Carl Grabo. Unsigned.

C1117 Selborne Day by Day. *TLS*, 30 April 1931, p. 337. Review of *Journals of Gilbert White*, edited by Walter Johnson. Unsigned.

Reprinted: *Votive Tablets*, 1931.

C1118 Literary England Month by Month. *Study of English*, May 1931, Vol. 24, No. 2, pp. 112-114. Dated 'London, Jan. 23, 1931.'

C1119 The Terrible Gifford. *TLS*, 7 May 1931, p. 361. Review of *William Gifford, Tory Satirist, Critic, and Editor*, by Roy Benjamin Clark. Unsigned.

C1120 Lamb and Lear. *The Spectator*, 9 May 1931, p. 739. Letter on 'Two Lears' by Peter Fleming in the issue of 25 April, pp. 658-659. Signed E. Blunden.

C1121 Anna Seward. *TLS*, 14 May 1931, p. 382. Review of *The Singing Swan: An Account of Anna Seward*, by Margaret Ashmun, with a preface by Frederick A. Pottle. Unsigned.

C1122 [Review of] *Vale and Other Poems*, by AE, [*i.e.* G. W. Russell]. *TLS*, 14 May 1931, p. 383. Unsigned.

C1123 An Early Baedeker. *TLS*, 14 May 1931, p. 390. Letter signed E. Blunden. *See also* letter in the issue of 11 June, p. 467 by Hans Baedeker.

C1124 A Sheaf of Essays by Mr. Tomlinson. *Daily Telegraph*, 15 May 1931, p. 7. Review of *Out of Soundings*, by H. M. Tomlinson.

C1125 A Young Man's Journey: Modern Outlook. *Daily Telegraph*, 26 May 1931, p. 4. Review of *The Spring Journey*, by Alan Pryce-Jones.

C1126 Miss Sitwell's Anthology. *TLS*, 28 May 1931, p. 422. Review of *The Pleasures of Poetry: A Critical Anthology, Second Series, The Romantic Revival*, by Edith Sitwell. Unsigned.

C1127 Mrs. Lynd's Poems. *TLS*, 28 May 1931, p. 426. Review of *The Yellow Placard*, by Mrs. S. Lynd. Unsigned.

C1128 The Book of the Month. *English Review*, June 1931, Vol. 53, pp. 63-68. Review of *The Mercury Book of Verse: Being a Selection of Poems Published in the London Mercury, 1919-30*, with an introduction by Sir Henry Newbolt.

C1129 Literary England Month by Month. *Study of English*, June 1931, Vol. 24, No. 3, pp. 210-213. Dated 'London, March 1, 1931.'

C1130 Literary Periodicals. *TLS*, 4 June 1931, p. 442. Review of *English Literary Periodicals*, by Walter Graham. Unsigned.

C1131 The Gentleman's Magazine, 1731-1907. *TLS*, 11 June 1931, pp. 453-454. Unsigned.

Reprinted (omitting dates): *Votive Tablets*, 1931.

C1132 A Practical Wordsworthian. *New Statesman & Nation*, 27 June 1931, p. 652. Review of *Hartley Coleridge, Poet's Son and Poet*, by Herbert Hartman. *See also* C1134.

C1133 Literary England Month by Month. *Study of English*, July 1931, Vol. 24, No. 4, pp. 312-315. Dated 'London, March 28, 1931.'*

C1134 Hartley Coleridge. *TLS*, 2 July 1931, p. 525. Review of *Hartley Coleridge, Poet's Son and Poet*, by Herbert Hartman (*see also* C1132); and *Hartley Coleridge* (The Augustan Books of Poetry). Unsigned.

C1135 SEGRAVE'S DEATH: A MARKET TOWN REMINISCENSE. *The Observer*, 5 July 1931, p. 18.

Reprinted: *Halfway House*, 1932.

C1136 English Lectures in Japan: A Reply to Miss West. *Daily Telegraph*, 6 July 1931, p. 9. Letter on the review by Rebecca West of *Landscape in English Art and Poetry*, by Laurence Binyon in the issue of 3 July, p. 15. Signed E. Blunden.

C1137 Mr. Graves's Poems. *TLS*, 23 July 1931, p. 578. Review of *Poems, 1926-1930*, by Robert Graves; and *To Whom Else*, by Robert Graves. Unsigned.

C1138 Lafcadio Hearn, the Mystic. *Daily Telegraph*, 31 July 1931, p. 15. Review of *Blue Ghost: A Study of Lafcadio Hearn*, by Jean Temple.

C1139 THE MEMORIAL [*later* THE LAST WORD]. *English Review*, August 1931, Vol. 53, p. 295.

Reprinted: *To Themis*, 1931; *Halfway House*, 1932; and *Poems 1930-1940*, [1941].

C1140 Literary England Month by Month. *Study of English*, August 1931, Vol. 24, No. 5, pp. 414-418. Dated 'London April 22, 1931.'*

C1141 Charles Lamb's Executor. *TLS*, 13 August 1931, p. 618. Review of *Seven Letters from Charles Lamb to Charles Ryle of the East India House, 1828-1832*. Unsigned.

C1142 [Review of] *Sissinghurst*, by V. Sackville-West. *TLS*, 13 August 1931, p. 623. Unsigned.

C1143　Literary England Month by Month. *Study of English*, September 1931, Vol. 24, No. 6, pp. 517–521. Dated 'London May 25, 1931.'

C1144　Nelson: His Heroic Life an "Ode to Duty". *Daily Telegraph*, 11 September 1931, p. 16. Review of *Nelson*, by Clennell Wilkinson.

C1145　The Living Past. *TLS*, 17 September 1931, p. 697. Review of *Englishmen at Rest and Play: Some Phases of English Leisure, 1558–1714*, by Members of Wadham College, edited by Reginald Lennard. Unsigned.

C1146　THE BALLAST-HOLE. *The Observer*, 20 September 1931, p. 22.

　　　　Reprinted: *To Themis*, 1931; *Halfway House*, 1932; and *Poems 1930–1940*, [1941].

C1147　Skelton Modernized. *TLS*, 24 September 1931, p. 725. Review of *The Complete Poems of John Skelton, Laureate*, edited by Philip Henderson. Unsigned.

C1148　Scots Queen of Romance: Judge Parry States the Case for Mary Stewart. *Daily Telegraph*, 25 September 1931, p. 6. Review of *The Persecution of Mary Stewart, The Queen's Cause: A Study in Criminology*, by Sir Edward Parry.

C1149　END OF THE FORTY-FIVE [*later* AFTER THE FORTY-FIVE]. *London Mercury*, October 1931, Vol. 24, No. 144, pp. 487–488. Title in index: The End of the 'Forty-Five.

　　　　Reprinted: *To Themis*, 1931; *Halfway House*, 1932; and *Poems 1930–1940*, [1941].

C1150　Keats's Letters, 1931; Marginalia. *Studies in English Literature*, October 1931, Vol. 11, No. 4, pp. 475–507. Also issued separately as an offprint (*see* A38).

　　　　Reprinted: *Reprinted Papers*, 1950.

C1151　Literary England Month by Month. *Study of English*, October 1931, Vol. 24, No. 7, pp. 614–616. Dated 'London June 23, 1931.'

C1152　THE RECOVERY. *Fortnightly Review*, 1 October 1931, N.S. Vol. 130, p. 477.

　　　　Reprinted: *To Themis*, 1931; *Halfway House*, 1932; and *Poems 1930–1940*, [1941].

C1153　Mr. Guedalla's Wellington: A Brilliant Study of a Long Life of Service. *Daily Telegraph*, 2 October 1931, p. 19. Review of *The Duke*, by Philip Guedalla.

C1154　[Review of] *The King of the Beggars: Bampfylde Moore Carey*, edited by C. H. Wilkinson. *TLS*, 8 October 1931, p. 767. Unsigned.

C1155 Four Cavaliers Assembled. *TLS*, 8 October 1931, p. 777. Review of *Minor Poets of the 17th Century: Sir John Suckling, Richard Lovelace, Thomas Carew, Lord Herbert of Cherbury*, by R. G. Howarth. Unsigned.

C1156 Foch: A Vivid Portrait, the Man Who Became the Symbol of Invincibility. *Daily Telegraph*, 9 October 1931, p. 7. Review of *Foch: The Man of Orleans*, by B. H. Liddell Hart.

C1157 A Bronte Extravaganza. *TLS*, 15 October 1931, p. 796. Review of *The Spell: An Extravaganza, An Unpublished Novel*, by Charlotte Bronte, edited with an introduction by George Edwin MacLean. Unsigned.

C1158 Mr. Masefield's New Poems. *TLS*, 22 October 1931, p. 817. Review of *Minnie Maylow's Story, and Other Tales*, and *Other Tales and Scenes*, by John Masefield. Unsigned.

C1159 AN INSCRIPTION [*later* INSCRIBED IN WAR-BOOKS II]. *The Observer*, 25 October 1931, p. 16.

Reprinted: *Halfway House*, 1932; and *Poems 1930-1940*, [1941].

C1160 An Institution and a Moral. *Oxford Outlook*, November 1931, Vol. 11, No. 56, pp. 190-198. On *Oxford Poetry*, 1931.

C1161 Literary England Month by Month. *Study of English*, November 1931, Vol. 24, No. 8, pp. 719-721. Dated 'London, July 20, 1931.'*

C1162 Augustan Poetry. *TLS*, 5 November 1931, p. 861. Review of *An Anthology of Augustan Poetry*, compiled and edited by Frederick T. Wood. Unsigned.

C1163 [Review of] *Plays and Pageants*, by Edward Thompson. *TLS*, 12 November 1931, p. 884. Unsigned.

C1164 William Cowper, Harmonist of the Countryside: The Companionable Poet. *The Times*, 13 November 1931, pp. 15-16. On the bicentenary of his birth.

C1165 Power and Gentleness. *TLS*, 19 November 1931, pp. 901-902. Review of *The Poems of William Cowper*, edited by H. I'A. Fausset. Unsigned.

C1166 Snatches of Cheerful Song: "Evoe's" Entertaining Anthology of Humorous Verse. *Daily Telegraph*, 20 November 1931, p. 7. Review of *Humorous Verse: An Anthology*, chosen by E. V. Knox.

C1167 Ariel Poems. *TLS*, 26 November 1931, p. 944. Review of *A Child is Born*, by Henry Newbolt; *To Lucy*, by Walter de la Mare; *To the Red Rose*, by Siegfried Sassoon; *Triumphal March*, by T. S. Eliot; *Jane Barston, 1719-1746*, by Edith Sitwell; *Invitation to Cast Out Care*, by V. Sackville-West; and *Choosing a Mast*, by Roy Campbell (Ariel Poems, Nos 32-38). Unsigned.

C1168   Literary England Month by Month. *Study of English*, December 1931, Vol. 24, No. 9, pp. 824-825. Dated 'London, Aug. 25, 1931.'*

C1169   Friends of Elia. *TLS*, 3 December 1931, p. 977. Review of *The Elian Miscellany: A Charles Lamb Anthology*, compiled and edited by S. M. Rich. Unsigned.

C1170   Against Mediocrity. *TLS*, 3 December 1931, p. 980. Review of *The Georgiad: A Satirical Fantasy in Verse*, by Roy Campbell. Unsigned.

C1171   Dr. Darwin, born December 12, 1731. *TLS*, 10 December 1931, pp. 989-990. On the centenary of Erasmus Darwin's birth. Unsigned.

C1172   A Goldsmith Discovery. *TLS*, 17 December 1931, p. 1022. Review of *The Grumbler: An Adaptation*, by Oliver Goldsmith, with an introduction and notes by Alice I. Perry Wood. Unsigned.

C1173   [Review of] *Songs and Slang of the British Soldier, 1914-1918*, third edition . . . much enlarged, edited by John Brophy and Eric Partridge. *TLS*, 17 December 1931, p. 1030. Unsigned. *See also* C1015, 1045.

C1174   FANCY AND MEMORY. *The Observer*, 27 December 1931, p. 10.

       Reprinted: *Halfway House*, 1932; *Poems 1930-1940*, [1941]; and *Poems of Many Years*, 1957.

C1175   On Preservation. *Council for the Preservation of Rural England, Fifth Annual Report*, 1931, pp. 11-13.

       Reprinted: *The Mind's Eye*, 1934.

1932

C1176   Literary England Month by Month. *Study of English*, January 1932, Vol. 24, No. 10, pp. 916-919. Dated 'London, Sept. 24, 1931.'*

C1177   Fantastics. *TLS*, 7 January 1932, p. 9. Review of *Elynour Rummynge*, by John Skelton; and *Tom of Bedlam's Song*, with an introduction and notes by David Greenhood. Unsigned.

C1178   The Year's Essays. *Time and Tide*, 30 January 1932, pp. 125-126. Review of *Essays of the Year 1930-1931*. Signed E.B.

C1179   [Review of] *The Poems of T. Sturge Moore: Collected Edition*, Vol. 1, and *Collected Poems of Laurence Binyon*, 2 vols. *English Review*, February 1932, Vol. 54, pp. 223, 225-226.

C1180 A TALE NOT IN CHAUCER. *Queen's Quarterly*, February 1932, Vol. 39, No. 1, pp. 81–82.

Reprinted: *Halfway House*, 1932; *The Face of England*, 1938; and *Poems 1930–1940*, [1941]. The poem appeared as 'A Tailwagger' in catalogue 21 of C. K. Broadhurst & Co. Ltd., Southport in October 1971.

C1181 Literary England Month by Month. *Study of English*, February 1932, Vol. 24, No. 11, pp. 1022–1025. Dated 'London Oct. 23, 1931.'*

C1182 George Crabbe, February 3, 1832. *TLS*, 4 February 1932, pp. 65–66. On the Centenary of Crabbe's death. Unsigned.

C1183 George Crabbe's Centenary, the Poet and his Works: A Successor to Chaucer. *The Observer*, 7 February 1932, p. 11.

C1184 [Review of] *Studies in English*, by Members of University College, Toronto, collected by Malcolm W. Wallace. *TLS*, 11 February 1932, p. 91. Unsigned.

C1185 *Westfront* at the Oxford Film Society. *New Statesman & Nation*, 13 February 1932, pp. 198–199. Review of the film. *See also* Eb2.

C1186 Poems by Geoffrey Scott. *TLS*, 18 February 1932, p. 109. Review of *Poems*, by Geoffrey Scott. Unsigned.

C1187 Poems from the Dutch. *TLS*, 25 February 1932, p. 131. Review of *The Flute, with Other Translations and a Poem*, by H. J. C. Grierson. Unsigned.

C1188 Youth and Age. *The Cherwell*, 27 February 1932, Vol. 34, No. 6, p. 130. Review of *Of Unsound Mind*, by E. Tangye Lean.

C1189 [Review of] *The Spanish Omnibus*, translated by Warre B. Wells. *Book Society News*, March 1932, pp. nine–ten.

C1190 [Review of] *The Blecheley Diary of the Rev. William Cole, 1765–1767*, edited from the original MS. by Francis Griffin Stokes. *English Review*, March 1932, Vol. 54, pp. 334–335.

C1191 Literary England Month by Month. *Study of English*, March 1932, Vol. 24, No. 12, pp. 1115–1117. Dated 'London, Nov. 28, 1931.'*

C1192 Mr. Rylands' Poems. *TLS*, 10 March 1932, p. 169. Review of *Poems*, by George Rylands. Unsigned.

C1193 [Review of] *Lamb before Elia*, by F. V. Morley. *TLS*, 17 March 1932, p. 193. Unsigned.

C1194 [Review of] *Sons of Singermann*, by Myron Brinig. *Book Society News*, April 1932, pp. three–four. *See also* C1199.

C1195 [Review of] *Wold Without End*, by H. J. Massingham. *Book Society News*, April 1932, pp. seven–eight. *See also* C1251.

C1196   Literary England Month by Month. *Study of English*, April 1932, Vol. 25, No. 1, pp. 18–21. Dated 'London, Dec. 28, 1931.'*

C1197   [Review of] *Shrove Tuesday Football*, by Francis Peabody Magoun, Jr. *TLS*, 21 April 1932, p. 294. Unsigned.

C1198   [Review of] *Satires and Personal Writings*, by Jonathan Swift, edited with introduction and notes by William Alfred Eddy. *TLS*, 21 April 1932, p. 295. Unsigned. *See also* C2162.

C1199   [Review of] *Sons of Singermann*, by Myron Brinig. *The Cherwell*, 30 April 1932, Vol. 35, No. 1, p. 17. Signed E.B. *See also* C1194.

C1200   [Review of] *The Soldier and the Gentlewoman*, by Hilda Vaughan. *Book Society News*, May 1932, pp. one–two.

C1201   [Review of] *New Signatures: Poems by Several Hands*, collected by Michael Roberts. *Book Society News*, May 1932, p. eight.

C1202   APPARITIONS IN SUMMER [*later* SUMMER HIEROGLYPHS]. *Oxford Outlook*, May 1932, Vol. 12, No. 58, p. 100.

Reprinted: *Halfway House*, 1932; and *Poems 1930–1940*, [1941].

C1203   A CALM RAIN. *St. Martin's Review*, May 1932, No. 495, p. 259.

Reprinted: *Halfway House*, 1932; *Poems 1930–1940*, [1941]; and *Poems of Many Years*, 1957.

C1204   Literary England Month by Month. *Study of English*, May 1932, Vol. 25, No. 2, pp. 114–117. Dated 'London, January 18, 1932.'

C1205   [Letter] To the Editor of The Cherwell. *The Cherwell*, 7 May 1932, Vol. 35, No. 2, p. 41. On the quotation in 'Very special Saying of the Week' in the issue of 30 April, p. 5. Signed The author of *The Face of England*.

C1206   The Conflicts of Shelley. *TLS*, 12 May 1932, p. 346. Review of *Desire and Restraint in Shelley*, by Floyd Stovall. Unsigned.

C1207   IN DISAPPOINTMENT [*later* DESIRE AND DELIGHT]. *New Statesman & Nation*, 14 May, p. 619.

Reprinted: *Halfway House*, 1932; *Poems 1930–1940*, [1941]; and *Poems of Many Years*, 1957.

C1208   AN ANCIENT BUT JUBILANT BALLAD (1696). *The Isis*, 19 May 1932, No. 848, p. 10.

Reprinted: *Halfway House*, 1932; and *Poems 1930–1940*, [1941].

C1209 [Review of] *Nymph Errant*, by James Laver. *Book Society News*, June 1932, p. four.

C1210 [Review of] *Fifty Years: Memories and Contrasts, A Composite Picture of the Period 1882-1932*, by twenty-seven contributors to *The Times*. *Book Society News*, June 1932, pp. five-six.

C1211 Literary England Month by Month. *Study of English*, June 1932, Vol. 25, No. 3, pp. 216-219. Dated 'London, February 26, 1932.'*

C1212 New Country Conversations. *The Spectator*, 4 June 1932, pp. 805-806. Review of *The Labouring Life*, by Henry Williamson.

C1213 The Life of Clare. *TLS*, 9 June 1932, pp. 413-414. Review of *John Clare: A Life*, by J. W. and Anne Tibble. Unsigned. *See also* C1214.

C1214 "The Samson of Northamptonshire". *The Spectator*, 18 June 1932, pp. 867-868. Review of *John Clare: A Life*, by J. W. and Anne Tibble. *See also* 1213.

C1215 Warburton and Hurd. *TLS*, 23 June 1932, pp. 453-454. Review of *Warburton and the Warburtonians: A Study in some Eighteenth-Century Controversies*, by A. W. Evans; and *The Correspondence of Richard Hurd and William Mason*, edited by Leonard Whibley. Unsigned.

C1216 [Review of] *People in the South*, by Alan Pryce-Jones. *Book Society News*, July 1932, pp. four-five.

C1217 [Review of] *Criticism*, by Desmond MacCarthy. *Book Society News*, July 1932, pp. six-eight.

C1218 Literary England Month by Month. *Study of English*, July 1932, Vol. 25, No. 4, pp. 316-319. Dated 'London, March 28, 1932.'

C1219 Wither's Plague-Poem. *TLS*, 21 July 1932, p. 529. Review of *The History of the Pestilence (1625)*, by George Wither, edited with an introduction and notes by J. Milton French. Unsigned.

C1220 Mr. Read's Wordsworth. *The Spectator*, 23 July 1932, p. 126. Review of *Wordsworth*, by Herbert Read.

C1221 [Review of] *A Superficial Journey through Tokyo and Peking*, by Peter Quennell. *Book Society News*, August 1932, pp. four-five.

C1222 Dilemma in the Library. *Book Society News*, August 1932, pp. ten-eleven.

C1223 ANOTHER ALTAR. *Queen's Quarterly*, August 1932, Vol. 39, No. 3, pp. 423-424.

Reprinted: *Halfway House*, 1932; *Poems 1930-1940*, [1941]; and *Poems of Many Years*, 1957.

C1224 Literary England Month by Month. *Study of English*, August 1932, Vol. 25, No. 5, pp. 417–419. Dated 'London, May 19.'

C1225 An Icelandic Saga. *Time and Tide*, 6 August 1932, p. 870. Review of *Heimskringla*, by Snorre Sturlason, edited by Erling Monsen. Signed E.B.

C1226 Travel Books for the Pocket. *Time and Tide*, 27 August 1932, p. 933. Review of *On Foot in the Highlands*, by Ernest A. Baker; *Orkney*, by J. Gunn; *Venice*, by Arnold Lunn; and *The Pyrenees*, by E. Allison Peers. Signed E.B.

C1227 [Review of] *South America*, by Kasimir Edschmid. *Book Society News*, September 1932, p. five.

C1228 [Review of] *The Elegant Woman*, by Gertrude Aretz. *Book Society News*, September 1932, p. six.

C1229 The Wordsworths and Coleridges. *Scrutiny*, September 1932, Vol. 1, No. 2, pp. 168–172. Review of *An Estimate of William Wordsworth, by his Contemporaries, 1793–1822*, by Elsie Smith; *Dorothy Wordsworth: The Early Years*, by Catherine Macdonald Maclean; and *Unpublished Letters of Samuel Taylor Coleridge*, edited by Earl Leslie Griggs.

C1230 THOUGHTS ON BOOKS: A SATIRE IN VERSE [*later* ORIENTAL TALE]. *Book Society News*, October 1932, Vol. 4, No. 10, p. 1.

Reprinted: *Choice or Chance*, 1934; and *Poems 1930–1940*, [1941].

C1231 [Review of] *Talleyrand*, by Duff Cooper. *Book Society News*, October 1932, Vol. 4, No. 10, p. 6.

C1232 Literary England Month by Month. *Study of English*, October 1932, Vol. 25, No. 7, pp. 614–617. Dated 'London, June 1, 1932.'

C1233 Preternatural History. *The Spectator*, 8 October 1932, p. 448. Review of *Animal Lore in English Literature*, by P. Ansell Robin.

C1234 Miss Sitwell's Anthology. *TLS*, 13 October 1932, p. 729. Review of *The Pleasures of Poetry, Third Series, The Victorian Age*, by Edith Sitwell. Unsigned.

C1235 A Victorian Muse. *TLS*, 13 October 1932, p. 731. Review of *Jane Hollybrand, and Other Original Poems*, by Edward Edwin Foot, edited and illustrated by James Thorpe. Unsigned.

C1236 [Review of] *The Common Reader: Second Series*, by Virginia Woolf. *Book Society News*, November 1932, Vol. 4, No. 11, p. 4.

C1237 [Review of] *Small Vehicles: A Painter's Baggage*, by Walter Bayes; and *Robino and Other Stories*, by Umberto Fracchia. *Book Society News*, November 1932, Vol. 4, No. 11, p. 4. Signed E.B.

C1238 The Poetry of Scott. *Queen's Quarterly*, November 1932, Vol. 39, No. 4, pp. 593–602.

C1239 Literary England Month by Month. *Study of English*, November 1932, Vol. 25, No. 8, pp. 720–723. Dated 'London, July 23, 1932.'*

C1240 Scott as a Poet. *TLS*, 10 November 1932, p. 832. Review of *New Love Poems*, by Sir Walter Scott, edited by Davidson Cook; and *The Heart of Scott's Poetry*, selected by John Haynes Holmes. Unsigned.

C1241 The English Countryside. *The Spectator*, 18 November 1932, pp. 726, 728.

Reprinted: *Spectator's Gallery*, [1933]; and *The Mind's Eye*, 1934.

C1242 Authors on the Platform. *The News-Letter*, 26 November 1932, Vol. 2, No. 6, pp. 12–14.

C1243 THE MARCH OF MIND. *The Isis*, 30 November 1932, No. 860, p. 6.

Reprinted: *Choice or Chance*, 1934; *Poems 1930–1940*, [1941]; and *Poems of Many Years*, 1957.

C1244 [Review of] *Stamboul Train*, by Graham Greene. *Book Society News*, December 1932, Vol. 4, No. 12, p. 7.

C1245 [Review of] *The Oxford Book of Sixteenth Century Verse*, edited by Sir Edmund Chambers. *Book Society News*, December 1932, Vol. 4, No. 12, p. 10.

C1246 COUNTRY CONVERSATION. *Book Society Annual*, December 1932, p. 21.

Reprinted: *Choice or Chance*, 1934; *Poems 1930–1940*, [1941]; and *Poems of Many Years*, 1957.

C1247 Literary England Month by Month. *Study of English*, December 1932, Vol. 25, No. 9, pp. 814–817. Dated 'London, Aug. 25, 1932.'*

C1248 SOMEWHERE EAST [*later* AFTERNOON IN JAPAN]. *The Cherwell*, 3 December 1932, Vol. 36, No. 8, p. 172.

Reprinted: *Choice or Chance*, 1934; and *Poems 1930–1940*, [1941].

C1249 Mid-Winter's Antidote. *The Observer*, 4 December 1932, Christmas Literary Supplement, p. ii. Review of *The South Country*, by Edward Thomas, with an introduction by Helen Thomas.

C1250 Mr. Davies' New Lyrics. *The Spectator*, 9 December 1932, p. 840. Review of *Poems, 1930–31*, by W. H. Davies.

1933

C1251 The Bare Hills and Backcloths. *Architectural Review*, January 1933, Vol. 73, p. 30. Review of *Wold Without End*, by H. J. Massingham. *See also* C1195.

C1252 [Review of] *A Passionate Prodigality*, by Guy Chapman. *Book Society News*, January 1933, Vol. 5, No. 1, p. 4. *See also* C3338.

C1253 [Review of] *The Cambridge History of English Literature*. *Book Society News*, January 1933, Vol. 5, No. 1, p. 11. Also issued as an offprint (*see* A46).

C1254 A Note on Modern Poetry. *The Highway*, January 1933, Vol. 25, pp. 5–7. Title on wrapper: Modern Poetry.

C1255 Literary England Month by Month. *Study of English*, January 1933, Vol. 25, No. 10, pp. 920–923. Dated 'London, Sept. 30, 1932.'*

C1256 [Review of] *The Singing Caravan: A Sufi Tale*, by Robert Vansittart. *TLS*, 19 January 1933, p. 36. Unsigned.

C1257 [Review of] *England, their England*, by A. G. Macdonell. *Book Society News*, February 1933, Vol. 5, No. 2, p. 6.

C1258 [Review of] *Vagabond Flag*, by Essex Brooke. *Book Society News*, February 1933, Vol. 5, No. 2, p. 7.

C1259 Literary England Month by Month. *Study of English*, February 1933, Vol. 25, No. 11, pp. 1004–1007. Dated 'London, Oct 31, 1932.'

C1260 Ariadne's Lover. *TLS*, 2 February 1933, p. 72. Review of *Ariadne*, by F. L. Lucas. Unsigned.

C1261 Drunken Barnaby. *TLS*, 9 February 1933, p. 89. Review of *Barnabae Itinerarium: Barnabees Journall*, by Richard Brathwait. Unsigned.

C1262 [Review of] *The Arches of the Years*, by Halliday Sutherland. *Book Society News*, March 1933, Vol. 5, No. 3, p. 8.

C1263 [Review of] *The English Muse*, by Oliver Elton. *Book Society News*, March 1933, Vol. 5, No. 3, p. 9.

C1264 Literary England Month by Month. *Study of English*, March 1933, Vol. 25, No. 12, pp. 1108–1111. Dated 'London, November 26, 1932.'

C1265 Shelley Sees it Through. *The Spectator*, 3 March 1933, pp. 306, 308. Review of *The Life of Shelley: as Comprised in The Life of Shelley*, by T. J. Hogg; *The Recollections of Shelley and Byron*, by E. J. Trelawny; and *Memoirs of Shelley*, by T. L. Peacock; with an introduction by Humbert Wolfe, 2 vols. *See also* C1271.

C1266 Sandford and Merton. *TLS*, 9 March 1933, p. 162. Review of *The Author of Sanford and Merton: A Life of Thomas Day, Esq.*, by George Warren Gignilliat, Jr. Unsigned.

C1267 [Review of] *A Collection of English Poems, 1660-1800*, selected and edited by Ronald S. Crane. *TLS*, 16 March 1933, p. 185. Unsigned.

C1268 THE ONLY ANSWER [*later* FROM AGE TO AGE]. *The Spectator*, 17 March 1933, p. 373.

Reprinted: *Choice or Chance*, 1934; *Poems 1930-1940*, [1941]; *Edmund Blunden: A Selection of His Poetry and Prose, 1950*; and *Poems of Many Years*, 1957.

C1269 A New Poet. *The News-Letter*, 18 March 1933, Vol. 2, No. 14, p. 16. Review of *The Man of Gingerbread*, by Alastair Rowsell Miller.

C1270 [Review of] *Pond Hall's Progress*, by H. W. Freeman. *Book Society News*, April 1933, Vol. 5, No. 4, p. 7.

C1271 Lives of Shelley. *Book Society News*, April 1933, Vol. 5, No. 4, p. 12. Review of *The Life of Shelley*, by T. J. Hogg, E. J. Trelawny and T. L. Peacock. *See also* C1265.

C1272 THINK OF SHELLEY [*later* A TOUCHSTONE]. *Revue anglo-américaine*, Paris, avril 1933, 10e Année, No. 4, p. 289. Note: 'poème inédit.'

Reprinted: *Choice or Chance*, 1934; *Poems 1930-1940*, [1941]; *Edmund Blunden: A Selection of His Poetry and Prose*, 1950; and *Poems of Many Years*, 1957.

C1273 Literary England Month by Month. *Study of English*, April 1933, Vol. 26, No. 1, pp. 15-17. Dated 'London, December 29, 1932.'

C1274 Japanese Poems. *Fortnightly Review*, 1 April 1933, N.S. 133, pp. 527-528. Review of *An Anthology of Haiku*, translated and annotated by Asatarō Miyamori.

C1275 The Team Spirit. *The Spectator*, 7 April 1933, p. 506. Review of *New Country: Prose and Poetry by the Authors of New Signatures*, edited by Michael Roberts.

C1276 THE VOICE OF THE PAST [*later* STORMY NIGHT]. *Sunday Times*, 16 April 1933, p. 9.

Reprinted: *Choice or Chance*, 1934; and *Poems 1930-1940*, [1941].

C1277 Alexander. *Time and Tide*, 29 April 1933, pp. 501-502. Review of *The Macedonian*, by Mary Butts.

C1278 IN A LIBRARY. *Time and Tide*, 29 April 1933, Special Book Supplement, p. 513.

Reprinted: *Choice or Chance*, 1934; *Poems 1930-1940*, [1941]; *Edmund Blunden: A Selection of His Poetry and Prose*, 1950; *Poems of Many Years*, 1957; and *A Selection from the Poems*, [1969].

Read by the author at the Poetry Reading in the Wigmore Hall, 14 September 1943 and published with the other poems read by Clifford Bax, T. S. Eliot and S. I. Hsiung in

Poet's Choice, arranged by Dorothy Dudley Short on behalf of the Arts and Letters Sectional Committee of the National Council of Women of Great Britain, 1945.

C1279   [Review of] *The Private Life of Mrs. Siddons*, by Naomi Royde-Smith. *Book Society News*, May 1933, Vol. 5, No. 5, p. 12.

C1280   "Brush Up Your English!". *Book Society News*, May 1933, Vol. 5, No. 5, pp. 15–16. Review of *The Shorter Oxford Dictionary*, and *Universal Dictionary of the English Language*, by H. C. Wyld.

C1281   Literary England Month by Month. *Study of English*, May 1933, Vol. 26, No. 2, pp. 110–113. Dated 'London, January 20, 1933.'

C1282   Old Worlds and New. *TLS*, 11 May 1933, p. 326. Review of *The Next Volume*, by Edward James, with decorations by Rex Whistler. Unsigned.

C1283   Critical Voluntaries. *TLS*, 25 May 1933, p. 361. Review of *Essays and Studies*, Vol. 18, by Members of the English Association, collected by Hugh Walpole. Unsigned.

C1284   THE COTTAGE AT CHIGASAKI. *Now and Then*, Summer 1933, No. 45, p. 25.

Reprinted: *Choice or Chance*, 1934; *Poems 1930–1940*, [1941]; *Poems of Many Years*, 1957; *A Selection of the Shorter Poems*, [1966]; and *A Selection from the Poems*, [1969].

C1285   [Review of] *Hostages to Fortune*, by Elizabeth Cambridge. *Book Society News*, June 1933, Vol. 5, No. 6, p. 5.

C1286   [Review of] *The Fleeting*, by Walter de la Mare. *Book Society News*, June 1933, Vol. 5, No. 6, p. 9.

C1287   Literary England Month by Month. *Study of English*, June 1933, Vol. 26, No. 3, pp. 216–219. Dated 'London, Feb. 17, 1933.'

C1288   Realities of Poetry. *TLS*, 1 June 1933, pp. 369–370. Review of *The Name and Nature of Poetry*, by A. E. Housman (*see also* C1296); *Romantic and Unromantic Poetry*, by Humbert Wolfe; *Some Aspects of the Diction of English Poetry*, by Henry Cecil Wyld; and *English Poetry in the Later Nineteenth Century*, by B. Ifor Evans. Unsigned.

C1289   Cobbett, by Himself. *TLS*, 8 June 1933, p. 392. Review of *The Progress of a Ploughboy to a Seat in Parliament as Exemplified in the History of William Cobbett, M.P. for Oldham*, edited by William Reitzel. Unsigned.

C1290   Harold Monro's Poems. *TLS*, 8 June 1933, p. 393. Review of *The Collected Poems of Harold Monro*, edited by Alida Monro. Unsigned.

C1291　Works of the Learned. *The Spectator*, 9 June 1933, p. 840. Review of *University Studies: Cambridge, 1933*, edited by Harold Wright.

C1292　THE BRANCH LINE. *The Spectator*, 23 June 1933, p. 907. Reprinted: *Choice or Chance*, 1934; *Poems 1930-1940*, [1941]; *Edmund Blunden: A Selection of His Poetry and Prose*, 1950; *Poems of Many Years*, 1957; and *The Midnight Skaters*, [1968].

C1293　[Review of] *Spectator's Gallery*. *Book Society News*, July 1933, Vol. 5, No. 7, p. 4.

C1294　[Review of] *The Beauty of England*, by Thomas Burke. *Book Society News*, July 1933, pp. 8-9.

C1295　Literary England Month by Month. *Study of English*, July 1933, Vol. 26, No. 4, pp. 314-317. Dated 'London, April 2, 1933.'

C1296　Again, What is Poetry? *The Listener*, 12 July 1933, pp. 41-42, 73. A talk based on *The Name and Nature of Poetry*, by A. E. Housman. *See also* C1288.

　　　　Reprinted: *The Mind's Eye*, 1934.

C1297　Poetic Wisdom. *TLS*, 13 July 1933, p. 476. Review of *Verses, Third Book*, by Elizabeth Daryush. Unsigned.

C1298　A Pastoral Poet. *TLS*, 13 July 1933, p. 477. Review of *The Works of Thomas Purney*, edited by H. O. White. Unsigned. *See also* C1306.

C1299　[Review of] *Ordinary Families*, by Arnot Robertson. *Book Society News*, August 1933, Vol. 5, No. 8, p. 3.

C1300　THE TOAD. *Queen's Quarterly*, August 1933, Vol. 40, No. 3, p. 375.

　　　　Reprinted: *Choice or Chance*, 1934; and *Poems 1930-1940*, [1941].

C1301　Literary England Month by Month. *Study of English*, August 1933, Vol. 26, No. 5, pp. 410-412. Dated 'London, April 21, 1933.'*

C1302　An Autobiographical Classic. *The Spectator*, 25 August 1933, p. 255. Review of *The Prelude*, by William Wordsworth, edited by Ernest de Selincourt.

C1303　[Review of] *The Child of Queen Victoria*, by William Plomer. *Book Society News*, September 1933, Vol. 5, No. 9, p. 9.

C1304　[Review of] *Testament of Youth*, by Vera Brittain. *Book Society News*, September 1933, Vol. 5, No. 9, p. 10.

C1305　Literary England Month by Month. *Study of English*, September 1933, Vol. 26, No. 6, pp. 511-513. Dated 'London, May 26, 1933.'

C1306   One Purney, a Poet. *The Listener*, 13 September 1933, p. 404. Review of *The Works of Thomas Purney*, edited by H. O. White. *See also* C1298.

C1307   [Review of] *Trumpeter, Sound!* by D. L. Murray. *Book Society News*, October 1933, Vol. 5, No. 10, p. 10.

C1308   [Review of] *The Winding Stair: New Poems*, by W. B. Yeats. *Book Society News*, October 1933, Vol. 5, No. 10, p. 19.

C1309   Literary England Month by Month. *Study of English*, October 1933, Vol. 26, No. 7, pp. 610–612. Dated 'London, June 30, 1933.'

C1310   [Review of] *The Albatross Book of Living Verse, English and American Poetry from the Thirteenth Century to the Present Day*, edited by Louis Untermeyer. *TLS*, 12 October 1933, p. 692. Unsigned.

C1311   After Palgrave. *Time and Tide*, 14 October 1933, Literary Supplement, p. 1226. Review of *The English Galaxy of Shorter Poems*, chosen and edited by Gerald Bullett. *See also* C1322.

C1312   The Shopkeepers. *The Observer*, 22 October 1933, p. 9. Review of *The English Vision: An Anthology*, by Herbert Read. *See also* C1317.

C1313   A Quaker Physician. *TLS*, 26 October 1933, pp. 717–718. Review of *Lettsom: His Life, Times, Friends and Descendants*, by James Johnston Abraham. Unsigned.

C1314   [Review of] *Blessington-D'Orsay*, by Michael Sadleir. *Book Society News*, November 1933, Vol. 5, No. 11, p. 5. *See also* C2413.

C1315   [Review of] *The Augs*, by G. B. Stern. *Book Society News*, November 1933, Vol. 5, No. 11, p. 7.

C1316   Aspects of Modern Poetry. *Study of English*, November 1933, Vol. 26, No. 8, pp. 1006–1009. Dated 'London, Sept. 4, 1933.'*

C1317   The English Vision. *TLS*, 2 November 1933, pp. 737–738. Review of *The English Vision: An Anthology*, edited by Herbert Read (*see also* C1312); and *The Out-of-Doors Book*, selected and arranged by Arthur Stanley. Unsigned.

C1318   The Poems of Churchill. *TLS*, 9 November 1933, p. 769. Review of *Poems of Charles Churchill*, edited by James Laver. Unsigned.

C1319   AN EMINENT VICTORIAN [*later* AN OMINOUS VICTORIAN]. *The Spectator*, 17 November 1933, p. 698.

Reprinted: *Choice or Chance*, 1934; *Poems 1930–1940*, [1941]; and *Poems of Many Years*, 1957.

C1320   Trench Tour. *The Spectator*, 17 November 1933, p. 704. Review of *Twelve Days*, by Sidney Rogerson.

C1321   [Review of] *Selections from Cowper*, edited with an introduction by Lord David Cecil. *TLS*, 23 November 1933, p. 822. Unsigned.

C1322   Two Anthologies. *TLS*, 23 November 1933, p. 823. Review of *The English Galaxy of Shorter Poems*, edited by Gerald Bullett (*see also* C1311); and *Elizabethan Prose*, selected by Michael Roberts. Unsigned.

C1323   Biographical Dialogues. *TLS*, 30 November 1933, p. 852. Review of *As Their Friends Saw Them: Biographical Conversations*, by Bonamy Dobrée. Unsigned.

C1324   Miss Sackville-West's Poetry. *TLS*, 30 November 1933, p. 852. Review of *Collected Poems*, Volume One, by V. Sackville-West. Unsigned.

C1325   [Review of] *Dawn of Darkness*, by Balder Olden. *Book Society News*, December 1933, Vol. 5, No. 12, p. 15.

C1326   [Review of] *Samuel Johnson*, by Hugh Kingsmill. *Book Society News*, December 1933, Vol. 5, No. 12, p. 18.

C1327   CHAPTERS OF LITERARY HISTORY: VERY LITTLE KNOWN. *Book Society Annual*, December 1933, No. 3, p. 29. Libellous drawings by Tom Titt.

Reprinted: *Choice or Chance*, 1934.

C1328   Literary England Month by Month. *Study of English*, December 1933, Vol. 26, No. 9, pp. 1031–1033. Dated 'London, Aug. 5, 1933.'*

C1329   [Review of] *Essays and Characters: Montaigne to Goldsmith*, by Robert Withington. *TLS*, 7 December 1933, p. 881. Unsigned.

C1330   Miss Leighton's Georgics. *The Observer*, 10 December 1933, Christmas Literary Supplement, p. iii. Review of *The Farmer's Year*, written and engraved by Clare Leighton.

C1331   [Review of] *The Lovers' Song-Book*, by W. H. Davies. *TLS*, 21 December 1933, p. 906. Unsigned.

C1332   Mr. Drinkwater's New Poems. *TLS*, 28 December 1933, p. 918. Review of *Summer Harvest: Poems, 1924–1933*, by John Drinkwater. Unsigned.

C1333   [Review of] *The Pursuit of Death: A Study of Shelley's Poetry*, by Benjamin P. Kurtz. *TLS*, 28 December 1933, p. 923. Unsigned.

C1334   THE RIPPLE. *The Spectator*, 29 December 1933, p. 967.

Reprinted: *The Year's Poetry*, [1934].

C1335   The Wordsworths. *The Spectator*, 29 December 1933, p. 969. Review of *Dorothy Wordsworth: A Biography*, by Ernest de Selincourt; and *The Later Wordsworth*, by Edith C. Batho.

1934

C1336 [Review of] *Six Trials*, by Winifred Duke. *Book Society News*, January 1934, p. 7.

C1337 [Review of] *The Smith of Smiths*, by Hesketh Pearson. *Book Society News*, January 1934, p. 8.

C1338 SOUTH ATLANTIC. *The Seafarer*, January 1934, No. 1, p. 9.

Reprinted: *Choice or Chance*, 1934; and *Poems 1930-1940*, [1941].

C1339 Literary England Month by Month. *Study of English*, January 1934, Vol. 26, No. 10, pp. 1135-1137. Dated 'London, Sept. 27, 1933.'*

C1340 [Review of] *The Chronicle of Caroline Quellen*, by Seaton Peacey. *Book Society News*, February 1934, p. 6.

C1341 [Review of] *Napoleon and his Marshals*, by A. G. Macdonell. *Book Society News*, February 1934, p. 12.

C1342 Literary England Month by Month. *Study of English*, February 1934, Vol. 26, No. 11, pp. 1234-1237. Dated 'London, Oct. 21, 1933.'*

C1343 Miss Sitwell's Verse. *TLS*, 1 February 1934, p. 73. Review of *Five Variations on a Theme*, by Edith Sitwell. Unsigned.

C1344 The Nonesuch Coleridge. *The Spectator*, 9 February 1934, p. 204. Review of *Coleridge: Select Poetry and Prose*, edited by Stephen Potter.

C1345 Lamb in 1934: Birthday Gifts for Elia. *The Observer*, 11 February 1934, p. 4. Review of *At the Shrine of St. Charles*, by E. V. Lucas; and *The Frolic and the Gentle: A Centenary Study of Charles Lamb*, by A. C. Ward.

C1346 [Review of] *Sense and Poetry: Essays on the Place of Meaning in Contemporary Verse*, by John Sparrow. *TLS*, 15 February 1934, p. 104. Unsigned.

C1347 [Review of] *Matador*, by Marguerite Steen. *Book Society News*, March 1934, p. 5.

C1348 [Review of] *In the Dark Backward*, by H. W. Nevinson. *Book Society News*, March 1934, p. 10.

C1349 [Review of] *Looking Back*, by Norman Douglas. *Book Society News*, March 1934, p. 11.

C1350 Literary England Month by Month. *Study of English*, March 1934, Vol. 26, No. 12, pp. 1334-1335. Dated 'London, Nov. 20, 1933.'*

C1351 Symposia. *TLS*, 8 March 1934, p. 159. Review of *The Clubs of Augustan London*, by Robert J. Allen. Unsigned.

C1352 One Battalion's War. *The Observer*, 11 March 1934, p. 7. Review of *The Cambridgeshires, 1914-1919*, by E. Riddell and M. C. Clayton.

C1353 [Review of] *End and Beginning*, by John Masefield. *TLS*, 22 March 1934, p. 210. Unsigned.

C1354 On Spring and Poetry. *The Spectator*, 23 March 1934, pp. 443-444.

C1355 The Circling Year. *The Spectator*, 23 March 1934, p. 460. Review of *The Yeoman's England*, by Sir William Beach Thomas.

C1356 [Review of] *Entertaining the Islanders*, by Struthers Burt. *Book Society News*, April 1934, p. 6.

C1357 Satires and Diversions. *Book Society News*, April 1934, pp. 11-12. Review of *Squared Circle*, by William Montgomerie; *Satirical Poems*, by Siegfried Sassoon; *John Lord, Satirist*, by George Rostrevor Hamilton; *The Horoscope*, by Horace Horsnell; *Archy's Life of Mehitabel*, by Don Marquis; *Mandarin in Manhattan*, by Christopher Morley; *The Last Recollections of Captain Gronow*; *The Crimson Jester*, by H. H. Dunn; *These Hurrying Years*, by Gerald Heard; and *Modernismus*, by Sir Reginald Blomfield.

C1358 [Review of] *T. E. Lawrence: In Arabia and After*, by Liddell Hart. *Book Society News*, April 1934, p. 12.

C1359 THEOLOGY OVER THE GATE. *London Mercury*, April 1934, Vol. 29, No. 174, p. 487.

Reprinted: *Choice or Chance*, 1934; and *Poems 1930-1940*, [1941].

C1360 Literary England Month by Month. *Study of English*, April 1934, Vol. 27, No. 1, pp. 10-11. Dated 'London, December 31, 1933.'*

C1361 Charles Reade Jubilee, the Man and his Work: An Appreciation. *The Observer*, 8 April 1934, p. 21.

C1362 [Review of] *In Arcadia*, by W. Macneile Dixon. *TLS*, 12 April 1934, p. 259. Unsigned.

C1363 The Old Front Line. *The Observer*, 15 April 1934, p. 4. Review of *The History of the 7th Royal Sussex Regiment 1914-1919*, The Times Publishing Co.

C1364 Wilfred Owen: A War Poet's Manuscripts. *The Times*, 16 April 1934, p. 17. On the acquisition of his manuscripts by the British Museum.

C1365 Poetry and Progress. *TLS*, 26 April 1934, p. 300. Review of *Unheard Melodies*, by Lord Gorell. Unsigned.

C1366 [Review of] *Dark Hazard*, by W. R. Burnett. *Book Society News*, May 1934, p. 8.

C1367 [Review of] *Remembering Sion*, by Desmond Ryan. *Book Society News*, May 1934, p. 9.

C1368 [Review of] *Black Monastery*, by Alader Kuncz. *Book Society News*, May 1934, p.

C1369   Literary England Month by Month. *Study of English*, May 1934, Vol. 27, No. 2, pp. 112–115. Dated 'London, January 17, 1934.'*

C1370   The Mind's Eye. *New Statesman & Nation*, 19 May 1934, p. 763. Letter on the anonymous review in the issue of 12 May, pp. 724–725. *See also* A50.

C1371   Old and New Japan. *The Observer*, 20 May 1934, p. 4. Review of *A Tokyo Calendar*, by Frank H. Lee.

C1372   Nine Lives. *Now & Then*, Summer 1934, No. 48, pp. 32–33. Review of *Victorian Wallflowers*, by Malcolm Elwin. *See also* C1378.

C1373   [Review of] *Cheapjack*, by Philip Allingham. *Book Society News*, June 1934, p. 8.

C1374   [Review of] *Garibaldi*, by David Larg. *Book Society News*, June 1934, p. 9.

C1375   [Review of] *The Native's Return*, by Louis Adamic. *Book Society News*, June 1934, p. 10.

C1376   George Herbert's Latin Poems. *Essays and Studies*, 1933 [*i.e.* June 1934], Vol. 19, pp. 29–39. Also issued separately as an offprint (*see* A51).

C1377   Literary England Month by Month. *Study of English*, June 1934, Vol. 27, No. 3, pp. 210–211. Dated 'London, February 23, 1934.'

C1378   Past Celebrities. *The Spectator*, 1 June 1934, p. 861. Review of *Victorian Wallflowers*, by Malcolm Elwin. *See also* C1372.

C1379   A Narrative Poet. *TLS*, 7 June 1934, p. 406. Review of *The Return: A Tale in Verse*, by J. R. Young. Unsigned.

C1380   White's Selborne. *TLS*, 14 June 1934, p. 421. Review of *A Bibliography of Gilbert White*, with a biography and a descriptive account of the village of Selborne, by Edward A. Martin. Unsigned.

C1381   Anodyne or Stimulant? *The Observer*, 24 June 1934, p. 5. Review of *Toward the Flame*, by Hervey Allen.

C1382   [Review of] *The Fool of Love*, by Hesketh Pearson. *Book Society News*, July 1934, p. 9.

C1383   [Review of] *Cape Farewell*, by Harry Martinsson. *Book Society News*, July 1934, p. 12.

C1384   [Review of] *Journey to the End of the Night*, by Louis-Ferdinand Céline. *Book Society News*, July 1934, p. 12.

C1385   Literary England Month by Month. *Study of English*, July 1934, Vol. 27, No. 4, pp. 310–312. Dated 'London, March 29th, 1934.'*

C1386   By Mossy Stones. *TLS*, 5 July 1934, p. 473. Review of *The English Antiquaries of the Sixteenth, Seventeenth and Eighteenth Centuries*, by H. B. Walters. Unsigned.

C1387 A Poetic Partnership. *TLS*, 12 July 1934, p. 488. Review of *Whether a Dove or Seagull: Poems*, by Sylvia Townsend Warner and Valentine Ackland. Unsigned.

C1388 Shelley: Verse and Prose. *TLS*, 12 July 1934, p. 489. Review of *Verse and Prose from the Manuscripts of Percy Bysshe Shelley*, edited by Sir John C. E. Shelley-Rolls and Roger Ingpen. Unsigned.

C1389 From Chaucer to Bridges. *TLS*, 19 July 1934, p. 507. Review of *Oxford Lectures on Poetry*, by E. de Selincourt. Unsigned.

C1390 Coleridge: A Personal Thanksgiving. *Poetry Review*, July/August 1934, Vol. 25, No. 4, pp. 259–262. On the centenary of Coleridge's death.

C1391 Books on a Table. *Book Society News*, August 1934, pp. 11–12. Review of *Shelley: Verse and Prose; Shelley*, by Ruth Bailey; *After Shelley: Letters of T. J. Hogg*, edited by Sylva Norman; *Jack and Jill*, by W. J. Turner; *Variations on a Time Theme*, by Edwin Muir; *Tristram*, by Frank Kendon; *Modern Poetry, 1922–1934*, compiled by Maurice Wollman; *A Mad Lady's Garland*, by Ruth Pitter (*see also* C1410); *Trial of Guy Fawkes*, edited by Donald Carswell; *Scots Guard*, by Wilfrid Ewart; *A Holiday Fisherman*, by Maurice Headlam; *The Old School*, edited by Graham Greene; *The Tragedy of Gandhi*, by Glorney Bolton; *Understanding the Chinese*, by William Martin; *The Novels of Elinor Wylie; The Lonely Lady of Dulwich*, by Maurice Baring; *His Worship the Mayor*, by Walter Greenwood; and *Unfinished Cathedral*, by T. S. Stribling.

C1392 [Review of] *The Fire-Raisers*, by Harold Dearden. *Book Society News*, August 1934, p. 13.

C1393 [Review of] *Red Road Through Asia*, by Bosworth Goldman. *Book Society News*, August 1934, p. 13.

C1394 Literary England Month by Month. *Study of English*, August 1934, Vol. 27, No. 5, pp. 410–412. Dated 'London, April 28th, 1934.'*

C1395 A Poet Displayed. *TLS*, 23 August 1934, p. 575. Review of *W. H. Davies*, by Thomas Moult. Unsigned.

C1396 Whitmanism. *TLS*, 30 August 1934, p. 586. Review of *Walt Whitman in England*, by Harold Blodgett; and *Letters of William Michael Rossetti Concerning Whitman, Blake and Shelley, to Anne Gilchrist and her son Herbert Gilchrist*, edited by Clarence Gohdes and Paull Franklin Baum. Unsigned.

C1397 [Review of] *Altogether*, by W. S. Maugham. *Book Society News*, September 1934, p. 10.

C1398 [Review of] *James I*, by Charles Williams. *Book Society News*, September 1934, p. 13.

C1399 The Wilmot Russian Journals (1803-1808). *Book Society News*, September 1934, p. 14. Review of *The Russian Journals of Martha and Catherine Wilmot*.

C1400 Literary England Month by Month. *Study of English*, September 1934, Vol. 27, No. 6, pp. 510-511. Dated 'London, May 31, 1934.'*

C1401 Lady Gerald Wellesley's Poems. *TLS*, 6 September 1934, p. 600. Review of *Poems of Ten Years, 1924-1934*, by Dorothy Wellesley. Unsigned.

C1402 Elian Values. *TLS*, 20 September 1934, p. 633. Review of *Charles Lamb: A Study*, by J. Lewis May. Unsigned.

C1403 Escape. *The Observer*, 23 September 1934, p. 7. Review of *Condemned to Death*, by Louise Thuliez, translated from the French by Marie Poett-Velitchko.

C1404 A Reflective Poet. *TLS*, 27 September 1934, p. 650. Review of *Beyond the Sunrise, and Other Poems*, by James Bramwell. Unsigned.

C1405 [Review of] *Honeymoon and Other Stories*, by Malachi Whitaker. *Book Society News*, October 1934, p. 9.

C1406 [Review of] *The Collected Poems of W. H. Davies*. *Book Society News*, October 1934, p. 12.

C1407 Books on a Table. *Book Society News*, October 1934, pp. 15-16. Review of *Peace with Honour*, by A. A. Milne; *Methods of Revolution*, by Raymond Postgate; *English Country*, edited by H. J. Massingham; *Wisdom and Waste in the Punjab Village*, by M. L. Darling; *A Hope for Poetry*, by C. Day Lewis (*see also* C1443); *A Short History of English Words*, by Bernard Groom; *The Man of the Renaissance*, by Ralph Roeder; *Author Hunting, 1897-1925*, by Grant Richards; *Retreat from Glory*, by R. H. Bruce Lockhart; *Round the Corner*, by Percy Brown; *News from the Past*, compiled by Yvonne French; *How Like an Angel*, by A. G. Macdonell; *Stars Were Born*, by Barbara Lucas; *The Sun in Capricorn*, by Edward Sackville West; *Earthquake in the Triangle*, by Lewis Gibbs; *Tender is the Night*, by F. Scott Fitzgerald; *Thirsty Earth*, by F. Rhodes Farmer; *Island of Refuge*, by John Fisher; *The Dark Island*, by V. Sackville West; and *Treatise on Right and Wrong*, by H. L. Mencken.

C1408 DEPARTED: OR, 'TIS TWENTY YEARS SINCE. *London Mercury*, October 1934, Vol. 30, No. 180, p. 486.

Reprinted: *An Elegy*, 1937; *Poems 1930-1940*, [1941]; and *Poems of Many Years*, 1957.

C1409 Literary England Month by Month. *Study of English*, October 1934, Vol. 27, No. 7, pp. 610-611. Dated 'London, June 24th, 1934.'

C1410 Wit-Melancholy. *TLS*, 4 October 1934, p. 670. Review of *A Mad Lady's Garland*, by Ruth Pitter. Unsigned. *See also* C1391.

C1411 Keats and His Reviewers. *TLS*, 18 October 1934, p. 710. Review of *Keats and the Periodicals of his Time*, by George L. Marsh and Newman I. White. Unsigned.

C1412 John Galsworthy's Poems. *TLS*, 25 October 1934, p. 730. Review of *The Collected Poems of John Galsworthy*. Unsigned.

C1413 [Review of] *A History of the Great War*, by C. R. M. Crutwell. *Book Society News*, November 1934, p. 9.

C1414 [Review of] *Man of Aran*, by Pat Mullen. *Book Society News*, November 1934, p. 11.

C1415 A Poet's Reading. *The Fortnightly*, November 1934, N.S. Vol. 136, pp. 628–630. Review of *The Pleasures of Poetry: A Critical Anthology*, by Edith Sitwell.

C1416 Literary England Month by Month. *Study of English*, November 1934, Vol. 27, No. 8, pp. 712–714. Dated 'London, July 24, 1934.'*

C1417 Literary England Month by Month. *Study of English*, December 1934, Vol. 27, No. 9, pp. 806–807. Dated 'London, Aug. 29, 1934.'

C1418 [Review of] *The Collected Plays of W. B. Yeats*. *Book Society News*, December 1934, p. 12.

C1419 [Review of] *Prince Rupert the Cavalier*, by Clennell Wilkinson. *Book Society News*, December 1934, p. 12.

C1420 PROPHETIC BALLAD FOR MCMXXXV. *Book Society Annual*, Christmas 1934, No. 4, p. 29.

C1421 Gift Books, 1934. *Book Society Annual*, Christmas 1934, No. 4, pp. 41–42, 44. Review of *Victoria Regina*, by Laurence Housman; *Balletomania*, by Arnold L. Haskell; *The Black Prince*, by M. Coryn; *The Wandering Prince*, by L. Dumont-Wilden; *A Stuart Portrait*, by Alice Buchan; *The England of Charles II*, by Arthur Bryant; *King James the Second*, by F. M. G. Higham; *The Last Post*, by Sir J. W. Fortescue; *The Sailor's Way*, by A. R. Evans; *The Last of the Wind Ships*, by A. J. Villiers; *Commodore Anson's World Voyage*, by Boyle T. Somerville; *Northern Conquest*, by Jeanette Mirsky; *A Plant Hunter in Tibet*, by F. Kingdon-Ward; *Unending Battle*, by H. C. Armstrong; *Red Saunders*, by "Sinbad"; *Good Morning and Good Night*, by H. H. the Ranee Margaret of Sarawak; *Silent Hours*, by Robert de Traz; *The Story of Gardening*, by Richardson Wright; *Creation by Evolution*, edited by Frances Mason; *Biology for Everyman*, by Sir J. Arthur Thomson; *Good Days*, by Neville Cardus; *Pavlova*, by Walford Hyden; *The Young Joseph*, by Thomas Mann; *In the*

Last Coach, by Leonhard Frank; *The Tales of Elinor Mordaunt; Autobiography of Cornelis Blake*, by George R. Preedy; *The Stolen Expedition*, by L. E. O. Charlton; and *Dickens*, by André Maurois.

C1422 DETAILS FROM DECEMBRIA. *The Isis*, 5 December 1934, No. 907, p. 8.

C1423 "The English Poets". *TLS*, 6 December 1934, pp. 861-862. Unsigned.

C1424 CHAUCER'S CANTERBURY TALES. *The News-Letter*, 8 December 1934, Vol. 6, No. 6, p. 94. Verse of 'Additional Character'.

C1425 John Sampson's Byplay. *TLS*, 27 December 1934, p. 918. Review of *In Lighter Moments: A Book of Occasional Verse and Prose*, by John Sampson. Unsigned.

C1426 The Genius of Charles Lamb. *Yorkshire Post*, 27 December 1934, p. 6. On the centenary of his death.

1935

C1427 [Review of] *This Was Ivor Trent*, by Claude Houghton. *Book Society News*, January 1935, p. 3.

C1428 [Review of] *Pigeon Hoo*, by Franklin Lushington. *Book Society News*, January 1935, pp. 4-5.

C1429 [Review of] *Below London Bridge*, by H. M. Tomlinson. *Book Society News*, January 1935, p. 7.

C1430 Literary England Month by Month. *Study of English*, January 1935, Vol. 27, No. 10, pp. 908-909. Dated 'London, Sept. 20, 1934.'

C1431 Thomas Barnes. *The Blue*, February 1935, Vol. 42, No. 3, p. 112. On the first editor of *The Times*. Signed E.B.

C1432 B— W—'s Leg. *The Blue*, February 1935, Vol. 42, No. 3, p. 112. On the article ascribed to Charles Lamb, pp. 113-114. Signed B.

C1433 [Review of] *Experience*, by Desmond MacCarthy. *Book Society News*, February 1935, p. 8.

C1434 [Review of] *Monkey's Money*, by Mabel L. Tyrrell. *Book Society News*, February 1935, p. 8.

C1435 Wisdom From the East. *Book Society News*, February 1935, p. 15. Review of *The Wisdom of the East Series*, edited by L. Cranmer-Byng and S. A. Kapadia.

C1436 Fanny Kelly and Elia. *The Fortnightly*, February 1935, New Series, Vol. 137, pp. 241-242. Review of *Lamb's "Barbara S—": The Life of Frances Maria Kelly, Actress*, by L. E. Holman; and *Lamb Always Elia*, by Edith Christina Johnson.

C1437   Literary England Month by Month. *Study of English*, February 1935, Vol. 27, No. 11, pp. 1009-1011. Dated 'London, November 1, 1934.'

C1438   A Coleridge Portrait. *TLS*, 14 February 1935, p. 92. Letter on the frontispiece to *Coleridge: Studies by Several Hands*, edited by Blunden and E. L. Griggs (*see* B66). Signed E. Blunden. *See also* letters in the same issue, p. 92 by Walter H. Cam; and 7 February, p. 76 by Wensley Pithey.

C1439   John Arbuthnot, M.D. Died February 27, 1735. *TLS*, 28 February 1935, pp. 113-114. On the bicentenary of his death. Unsigned.

C1440   [Review of] *Between Two Worlds*, by J. Middleton Murry. *Book Society News*, March 1935, p. 9.

C1441   Books on a Table. *Book Society News*, March 1935, pp. 15-16. Review of *The Author's Handbook for 1935*, edited by D. Kilham Roberts; *The Growth of Stuart London*, by Norman G. Brett-James; *The Secret War*, by Frank C. Hanighen and Anton Zischka; *Arising Out of That*, by H. A. Vachell; *Good-by for the Present*, by Eleanor Acland; *Idle Warriors*, by Bertram Ratcliffe; *The Winter Garden*, by John Galsworthy; *Poems*, by John Clare, edited by J. W. Tibble (*see also* C1444, 1448); *The Lonely*, by Jules Romains; *Appointment in Samarra*, by John O'Hara; *Dusk at the Grove*, by Samuel Rogers; *Grammar of Love*, by Ivan Bunin; *Via Bodenbach*, by Ferenc Karmendi; *A Derbyshire Tragedy*, by F. C. Boden; *Khartoum Tragedy*, by Malcolm Maclaren; *Honey and Bread*, by Rhys Davies; *The Path of Glory*, by Edward Frankland; *One Light Burning*, by R. C. Hutchinson; *Morning Shows the Day*, by Helen Hull; and *Strangers Come Home*, by Ronald Macdonald Douglas.

C1442   Literary England Month by Month. *Study of English*, March 1935, Vol. 27, No. 12, pp. 1101-1103. Dated 'London, Nov. 25, 1934.'

C1443   On Post-War Poets. *TLS*, 7 March 1935, p. 139. Review of *A Hope for Poetry*, by Cecil Day Lewis. Unsigned. *See also* C 1407.

C1444   John Clare Comes into His Own. *The Bookmark*, Spring 1935, Vol. 11, No. 38, p. 19. Letter on the publication of *The Poems of John Clare*, edited by J. W. Tibble. Signed E. Blunden. *See also* C1441, 1448.

C1445   [Review of] *The Stars Look Down*, by A. J. Cronin. *Book Society News*, April 1935, p. 8.

C1446   [Review of] *John Nash*, by John Summerson. *Book Society News*, April 1935, p. 10.

C1447   [Review of] *Africa Dances*, by Geoffrey Gorer. *Book Society News*, April 1935, p. 11.

C1448   The Northamptonshire Peasant. *The Fortnightly*, April 1935, New Series, Vol. 137, pp. 497–498. Review of *The Poems of John Clare*, edited with an introduction by J. W. Tibble. *See also* C1441, 1444.

C1449   Literary England, 1934. *Rising Generation*, 1 April 1935, Vol. 73, No. 1, pp. 8–9; *and* 1 May 1935, Vol. 73, No. 3, pp. 82–83.*

C1450   [Review of] *In Search of History*, by Vincent Sheean. *Book Society News*, May 1935, p. 14.

C1451   Some More New Books. *Book Society News*, May 1935, pp. 17–18. Review of *Rats, Lice and History*, by Hans Zinsser; *Climbing Days*, by Dorothy Pilley; *The Blue Tunnyman*, by Andrew Andrews; *Greek Salad*, by Kenneth Matthews; *Coleridge and S.T.C.*, by Stephen Potter (*see also* C1452); *D. H. Lawrence*, by E.T.; *Playtime in Russia*, by Hubert Griffith; *The Lost Language of London*, by Harold Bayley; *The Letters of King Charles I*, edited by Sir Charles Petrie; *Love in Winter*, by Storm Jameson; *Victoria Glencairn*, by Glenda Spooner; *Nancy Brown*, by H. P. McGraw; *Lodgings for Twelve*, by H. H. Bashford; *Summervale*, by J. Kenward; and *Storm Song*, by Denis Johnston.

C1452   Messrs. Coleridge. *The Spectator*, 3 May 1935, p. 742. Review of *Coleridge and S.T.C.*, by Stephen Potter. *See also* C1451.

C1453   New Poems by Pope. *TLS*, 16 May 1935, p. 311. Review of *Pope's Own Miscellany*, edited by Norman Ault. Unsigned.

C1454   Paeans and Memorials. *TLS*, 16 May 1935, p. 311. Review of *The Odes of Ronald Campbell Macfie*. Unsigned.

C1455   Victorian Reading. *The Spectator*, 24 May 1935, p. 880. Review of *The Victorians and their Books*, by Amy Cruse.

C1456   War Letters, 1914–1918: Four Years as a Company Officer. *The Observer*, 26 May 1935, p. 4. Review of *An Infant in Arms: War Letters of a Company Officer, 1914–1918*, by Graham H. Greenwell.

C1457   [Review of] *We, the Accused*, by Ernest Raymond. *Book Society News*, June 1935, p. 8.

C1458   [Review of] *Beyond the Sunset*, by Charles Douie. *Book Society News*, June 1935, p. 10.

C1459   [Review of] *Portrait of Ianthe*, by E. M. Oddie. *Book Society News*, June 1935, p. 11.

C1460   [Review of] *Benthamite Reviewing: The First Twelve Years of the Westminster Review, 1824–1836*, by George Nesbitt. *TLS*, 20 June 1935, p. 395. Unsigned.

C1461   [Review of] *George the Fourth*, by Roger Fulford. *Book Society News*, July 1935, p. 5.

C1462 [Review of] *Captain Conan*, by Roger Vercel. *Book Society News*, July 1935, p. 7.

C1463 [Review of] *Early One Morning in the Spring*, by Walter de la Mare. *The Fortnightly*, July 1935, New Series, Vol. 138, pp. 121–122.

C1464 From Paris to Geneva. *The Listener*, 17 July 1935, pp. 99–102. Third in a series entitled Grand Tour. Other contributors to the series were Mona Wilson, Douglas Woodruff, Janet Adam Smith, Richard Pyke, Sacheverell Sitwell, and Malcolm Letts.

Reprinted: *Grand Tour*, 1935.

C1465 [Review of] *Polly Oliver*, by A. E. Coppard. *Book Society News*, August 1935, p. 6.

C1466 [Review of] *No Quarter Given*, by Paul Horgan. *Book Society News*, August 1935, p. 10.

C1467 Collins and Dodsley's "Museum". *TLS*, 8 August 1935, p. 501. Letter signed E. Blunden. *See also* letters in the issues of 4 July, p. 432 and 25 July, p. 477, by E. H. W. Meyerstein; and 11 July, p. 448, by Frederick Page. On the attribution of 'Of the Essential Excellencies in Poetry' to William Collins. *See also The Poems of William Collins* (B29).

C1468 The Coleridge Student. *TLS*, 29 August 1935, p. 535. Review of *Samuel Taylor Coleridge: A Selected Bibliography for Students and Teachers*, compiled by Virginia Wardlow Kennedy assisted by Mary Neill Barton. Unsigned.

C1469 [Review of] *The Beachcomber*, by William McFee. *Book Society News*, September 1935, p. 9.

C1470 [Review of] *Oliver Goldsmith*, by Stephen Gwynn. *Book Society News*, September 1935, p. 12. *See also* C1478.

C1471 Books on a Table. *Book Society News*, September 1935, p. 13. Review of *White Man's Country*, by Elspeth Huxley; *Sir George Alexander and the St. James's Theatre*, by A. E. W. Mason; *John Bailey, 1864–1931: Letters and Diaries*, edited by His Wife; *New Pathways in Science*, by Sir Arthur Eddington; *The Voyage of the Chelyuskin*, translated by Alec Brown; *The Last Flight*, by P. Barbara Hall; *Unknown Quantity*, by Hermann Broch; *Fool's Quarter Day*, by Louis Marlow; and *Men of Good Will: Book VIII: Provincial Interlude*, by Jules Romains.

C1472 A SONG [*later* LOOKING EASTWARD]. *The Fortnightly*, September 1935, New Series, Vol. 138, p. 338.

Reprinted: *An Elegy*, 1937; and *Poems 1930–1940*, [1941].

C1473 The Wordsworth Letters. *London Mercury*, September 1935, Vol. 32, No. 191, pp. 481–482. Review of *The Early Letters of William and Dorothy Wordsworth (1787–1805)*, arranged and edited by E. de Selincourt.

C1474   Lamb's Autobiography. *The Spectator*, 13 September 1935, p. 397. Review of *The Letters of Charles Lamb, to which are added those of his sister Mary Lamb*, edited by E. V. Lucas. 3 vols.

C1475   Shelley's Electrical Universe. *TLS*, 26 September 1935, p. 593. Review of *The Meaning of "The Witch of Atlas"*, by Carl Grabo. Unsigned.

C1476   Generals and Ghosts. *Book Society News*, October 1935, p. 13. Review of *Haig*, Vol. I, by Duff Cooper (*see also* C1525); and *The War Letters of General Monash*.

C1477   [Review of] *I Walked by Night*, by Lilias Rider Haggard. *Book Society News*, October 1935, p. 15.

C1478   Travels in Bohemia. *The Fortnightly*, October 1935, New Series, Vol. 138, pp. 501–502. Review of *Oliver Goldsmith*, by Stephen Gwynn. *See also* C1470.

C1479   A Victorian Adventure. *The Spectator*, 11 October 1935, p. 576. Review of *The Frozen Heart: A Victorian Adventure*, by Mrs St Loe Strachey.

C1480   [Review of] *Fire of Life*, by H. W. Nevinson. *Book Society News*, November 1935, p. 11.

C1481   [Review of] *Steady Drummer*, by Stanley Casson. *Book Society News*, November 1935, p. 13.

C1482   [Review of] *Dwight Morrow*, by Harold Nicolson. *Book Society News*, November 1935, p. 14.

C1483   On the Trail of Beddoes: Secrets from the Vanished Browning Box. *TLS*, 16 November 1935, pp. 729–730. Review of *Thomas Lovell Beddoes: The Making of a Poet*, by H. W. Donner; *The Browning Box, or, The Life and Works of Thomas Lovell Beddoes*, edited with an introduction by H. W. Donner; *The Works of Thomas Lovell Beddoes*, edited with an introduction by H. W. Donner; and *Bristols Bedeutung für die englische Romantik und die deutsch-englischen Beziehungen*, by Carl August Weber. Unsigned.

C1484   A Study of Cobbett. *TLS*, 16 November 1935, p. 737. Review of *Peter Porcupine: A Study of William Cobbett, 1762–1835*, by Marjorie Bowen. Unsigned.

C1485   The Watch-Tower. *The Listener*, 27 November 1935, p. 984. Review of *Vigils*, by Siegfried Sassoon.

C1486   [Review of] *Victorious Troy*, by John Masefield. *Book Society News*, December 1935, p. 10.

C1487   [Review of] *I Find Four People*, by Pamela Frankau. *Book Society News*, December 1935, p. 13.

C1488   [Review of] *English Fabric*, by Harvey Darton. *Book Society News*, December 1935, p. 14.

C1489   THE REJECTED'S REVENGE: A DRAMATIC FRAG-
MENT WITH A WILDLY IMPOSSIBLE PLOT. *Book
Society Annual*, Christmas 1935, pp. 28–29.

C1490   Gray's Letters Restored. *The Fortnightly*, December 1935,
New Series, Vol. 138, pp. 749–750. Review of *Correspondence of Thomas Gray*, edited by the late Paget Toyn-
bee and Leonard Whibley.

C1491   VILLAGE SKETCH. *The Listener*, 4 December 1935, p.
1018.

Reprinted: *An Elegy*, 1937; *Poems 1930–1940*, [1941];
Poems of Many Years, 1957; and *A Selection from the
Poems*, [1969].

C1492   An Essay on War. *Time and Tide*, 7 December 1935, pp.
1798, 1800. Review of *Mars His Idiot*, by H. M. Tomlinson.

C1493   "Extempore Effusion", Wordsworth's Dead Friends, 1835,
The Ettrick Shepherd. *TLS*, 14 December 1935, pp. 845–
846. On the centenary of the publication of Wordsworth's
'Extempore Effusion upon the death of James Hogg.' Unsigned.

C1494   Christ's Hospital. I, The Voice of the Past. *Country Life*,
21 December 1935, Vol. 78, No. 2031, pp. 656–662. *See
also* Part II, The Modern Blue, by Peter Sparks in the issue
of 28 December, pp. 680–685.

C1495   [Review of] *Petron*, by Hugh Sykes Davies. *TLS*, 21
December 1935, p. 88. Unsigned.

1936

C1496   [Review of] *The Pursuer*, by Louis Golding. *Book Society
News*, January 1936, p. 7.

C1497   [Review of] *The Tumult and the Shouting*, by George
Slocombe. *Book Society News*, January 1936, p. 8.

C1498   Mainly the Poets. *Book Society News*, January 1936, p. 12.
Review of *Selected Poems*, by A. E. [*i.e.* G. W. Russell];
Poems, 1919–1934, by Walter de la Mare; *The Year's
Poetry, 1935*, compiled by Gerald Gould, Denys Kilham
Roberts and John Lehmann; *Poems*, by William Empson;
Poems, by Archibald MacLeish; *The White Blackbird*, by
Andrew Young; *Anne Boleyn*, by Loyd Haberly; *The Win-
ter House*, by Norman Cameron; *First Day*, by Clifford
Dyment; *Michael and His Angels*, by Lewis Gibbs; and *Cage
Me a Peacock*, by Noel Langley.

C1499   Keats's Friend Mathew. *English*, [January] 1936, Vol. 1,
No. 1, pp. 46–55. On George Felton Mathew. Also issued
separately as an offprint (*see* A54).

C1500   Poetical Turnstiles. *English*, [January] 1936, Vol. 1, No. 1,
pp. 66–68. Review of *Poetry: Direct and Oblique*, by
E. M. W. Tillyard.

C1501 'CAN YOU REMEMBER – ?' *English*, [January] 1936, Vol. 1, No. 2, p. 135.

Reprinted (revised): *An Elegy*, 1937; *Poems 1930-1940*, [1941]; *Edmund Blunden: A Selection of His Poetry and Prose*, 1950; and *Poems of Many Years*, 1957.

C1502 [Review of] *Facing Two Ways*, by Baroness Shidzué Ishimoto. *The Fortnightly*, January 1936, N.S. Vol. 139, p. 117.

C1503 IN MY TIME. *London Mercury*, January 1936, Vol. 33, No. 195, p. 274.

Reprinted: *An Elegy*, 1937; and *Poems 1930-1940*, [1941].

C1504 A Garland of Verse. *TLS*, 4 January 1936, p. 11. Review of *Beelzebub and Other Poems*, by R. C. Trevelyan. Unsigned.

C1505 ELEGY [*later* AN ELEGY; *and* ELEGY ON HIS MAJESTY KING GEORGE V]. *TLS*, 25 January 1936, p. 61. On the death of George V.

Reprinted: *The Times*, 28 January 1936, Funeral Supplement, p. iii; *An Elegy*, 1937; *Poems 1930-1940*, [1941]; and *Poems of Many Years*, 1957.

C1506 Arbuthnot in Satire and Science. *TLS*, 25 January 1936, p. 71. Review of *John Arbuthnot: Mathematician and Satirist*, by Lester M. Beattie. Unsigned.

C1507 [Review of] *In the Second Year*, by Storm Jameson. *Book Society News*, February 1936, p. 7.

C1508 [Review of] *Agents and Patients*, by Anthony Powell. *Book Society News*, February 1936, p. 8.

C1509 After the City. *Time and Tide*, 8 February 1936, pp. 188, 190. Review of *John Freeman's Letters*, edited by Gertrude Freeman and Sir John Squire. *See also* C1515.

C1510 An Approach to Shakespeare. *Time and Tide*, 22 February 1936, p. 270. Review of *Shakespeare*, by John Middleton Murry.

C1511 [Review of] *Modern Chinese Poetry*, translated by Harold Acton and Ch'en Shih-hsiang. *TLS*, 22 February 1936, p. 154. Unsigned.

C1512 Poems by Mr. Coppard. *TLS*, 22 February 1936, p. 156. Review of *Cherry Ripe*, by A. E. Coppard; and *Cherry Ripe: Poems*, by A. E. Coppard; English and American editions. Unsigned.

C1513 [Review of] *So Long to Learn*, by Doreen Wallace. *Book Society News*, March 1936, p. 9.

C1514 [Review of] *Naval Odyssey*, by Thomas Woodrooffe. *Book Society News*, March 1936, p. 11.

C1515   Some More New Books. *Book Society News*, March 1936, pp. 15-16. Review of *Abraham: A Study of Hebrew Origins*, by Sir Leonard Woolley; *Mahommed, the Man and his Faith*, by Tor Andrae; *The Monks of Athos*, by R. M. Dawkins; *The Last of the Empresses*, by Daniele Vare; *The Exile*, by Pearl S. Buck; *Nanda Devi*, by E. E. Shipton; *England Have my Bones*, by T. H. White; *House of Orleans*, by M. Coryn; *Kings of Merry England*, by Philip Lindsay; *Letters of John Freeman (see also* C1509); *The Faber Book of Modern Verse*, edited by Michael Roberts; *Words for Tonight*, by George Buchanan; *Bread and Butter*, by Bechhofer Roberts; *The Double Quest*, by R. J. Cruikshank; *Pig and Pepper*, by David Footman; *Express to the East*, by A. den Doolard; *The Croatian Shirt*, by T. B. Marle; and *Thou Shell of Death*, by Nicholas Blake.

C1516   The Most Wonderful City. *Staniland*, Boston, March 1936, No. 22, pp. [13-14]. On Calais.

C1517   Two Poets. *TLS*, 21 March 1936, p. 243. Review of *Call to the Swan*, by L. A. G. Strong; and *Twelve Noon*, by Richard Church. Unsigned.

C1518   [Review of] *Wordsworth*, by Peter Burra. *TLS*, 28 March 1936, pp. 279-280. Unsigned.

C1519   [Review of] *Westward: A Collection of West Country Verses*, by Arthur L. Salmon. *TLS*, 28 March 1936, p. 281. Unsigned.

C1520   [Review of] *Ali the Lion*, by William Plomer. *Book Society News*, April 1936, p. 9.

C1521   [Review of] *The Sound Wagon*, by T. S. Stribling. *Book Society News*, April 1936, p. 11.

C1522   [Review of] *Salamina*, by Rockwell Kent. *Book Society News*, April 1936, p. 13.

C1523   "Legendary Monster". *The Spectator*, 17 April 1936, p. 711. Review of *A Flame in Sunlight: The Life and Work of Thomas de Quincey*, by Edward Sackville-West.

C1524   "Sea and Hill and Wood". *TLS*, 25 April 1936, p. 352. Review of *The Squirrel's Granary: A Countryman's Anthology*, by Sir William Beach Thomas. Unsigned.

C1525   [Review of] *Haig*, Vol. II, by Duff Cooper. *Book Society News*, May 1936, p. 6. *See also* C1476.

C1526   [Review of] *Labby*, by Hesketh Pearson. *Book Society News*, May 1936, p. 9.

C1527   Tribute to Edward Thomas. *TLS*, 2 May 1936, p. 373. Review of *These Things the Poets Said*, edited by Robert P. Eckart, Jr. Unsigned.

C1528   Leigh Hunt Under the Microscope: A French Critic's Survey. *TLS*, 9 May 1936, p. 394. Review of *Leigh Hunt, 1784-1859 . . .* , by Louis Landré. Unsigned.

C1529   A Realist in Europe: Sir Arnold Wilson's Diary. *The Observer*, 24 May 1936, p. 9. Review of *Walks and Talks Abroad: The Diary of a Member of Parliament in 1934-6*, by Sir Arnold Wilson.

C1530   A Scholar's Experience of Poetry. *TLS*, 30 May 1936, p. 454. Review of *The Study of Poetry*, by H. W. Garrod. Unsigned.

C1531   [Review of] *The General*, by C. S. Forester. *Book Society News*, June 1936, p. 8.

C1532   [Review of] *The Queen's Doctor*, by Robert Neumann. *Book Society News*, June 1936, p. 8.

C1533   [Review of] *Ramblin' Jack*, transcribed by R. Reynell Bellamy. *Book Society News*, June 1936, p. 11.

C1534   A Northamptonshire Poetess: Glimpses of an Eighteenth-Century Prodigy. *Journal of the Northamptonshire Natural History Society and Field Club*, June 1936, Vol. 28, No. 215, pp. 59-74. On Mary Leapor. Also issued separately as an offprint (*see* A57).

C1535   Mr. Mottram Returns. *The Spectator*, 12 June 1936, pp. 1090, 1092. Review of *Journey to the Western Front Twenty Years After*, by R. H. Mottram.

C1536   [Review of] *True Thomas*, by Thomas Wood. *Book Society News*, July 1936, p. 8.

C1537   [Review of] *Bird Alone*, by Sean O'Faolain. *Book Society News*, July 1936, p. 9.

C1538   [Review of] *The Gentle Savage*, by Richard Wyndham. *Book Society News*, July 1936, p. 11.

C1539   The Poet Laureate. *London Mercury*, July 1936, Vol. 34, No. 201, pp. 257-259. Review of *A Letter from Pontus and Other Verse*, by John Masefield.

C1540   The Volunteer Laureate. *The Spectator*, 24 July 1936, p. 150. Review of *The Poems of Sir William Watson, 1878-1935*.

C1541   English Lyrics by Irish Poets. *TLS*, 25 July 1936, p. 612. Review of *The Collected Poems of Austin Clarke*, with an introduction by Padraic Colum. Unsigned.

C1542   An Ancient Race: The English Countryman at Home. *TLS*, 25 July 1936, p. 614. Review of *The Open Air: An Anthology of English Country Life*, by Adrian Bell. Unsigned.

C1543   [Review of] *The Spleen*, by Matthew Green, edited . . . by W. H. Williams. *TLS*, 25 July 1936, p. 618. Unsigned.

C1544   [Review of] *Men in Arms*, by George Slocombe. *Book Society News*, August 1936, p. 7.

C1545   [Review of] *The Court of Fair Maidens*, by Wilhelm Speyer. *Book Society News*, August 1936, p. 8.

C1546 [Review of] *Peter the Great*, by Alexei Tolstoi. *Book Society News*, August 1936, p. 9.

C1547 Mr. Geoffrey Young's Poems. *TLS*, 1 August 1936, p. 629. Review of *Collected Poems of Geoffrey Winthrop Young*. Unsigned.

C1548 Mr. W. R. Childe's Poems. *TLS*, 8 August 1936, p. 643. Review of *Selected Poems of Wilfred Rowland Childe*. Unsigned.

C1549 WAITING THE WORD. *The Spectator*, 28 August 1936, p. 344.

Reprinted: *An Elegy*, 1937; and *Poems 1930-1940*, [1941].

C1550 THE AMBUSH. *The Spectator*, 28 August 1936, p. 344.

Reprinted: *An Elegy*, 1937; and *Poems 1930-1940*, [1941].

C1551 [Review of] *Masterpieces of Japanese Poetry Ancient and Modern*, translated and annotated by Miyamori Asatarō. *TLS*, 29 August 1936, p. 698. Unsigned.

C1552 [Review of] *Again, One Day*, by Matila Ghyka. *Book Society News*, September 1936, p. 9.

C1553 [Review of] *Summer Will Show*, by S. Townsend Warner. *Book Society News*, September 1936, p. 10.

C1554 [Review of] *Sherston's Progress*, by Siegfried Sassoon. *Book Society News*, September 1936, p. 11. *See also* C1556.

C1555 The Wordsworthian Community. *London Mercury*, September 1936, Vol. 34, No. 203, pp. 450-451. Review of *George and Sarah Green: A Narrative*, by Dorothy Wordsworth, edited by E. de Selincourt.

C1556 Mr. Sassoon's Trilogy. *TLS*, 5 September 1936, p. 709. Review of *Sherston's Progress*, by Siegfried Sassoon. Unsigned. *See also* C1554.

C1557 Essays in Retrospect: Some English Aphorists. *TLS*, 12 September 1936, p. 725. Review of *Reperusals and Recollections*, by Logan Pearsall Smith. Unsigned.

C1558 [Review of] *Crocus*, by Neil Bell. *Book Society News*, October 1936, p. 10.

C1559 [Review of] *Dance of the Quick and the Dead*, by Sacheverell Sitwell. *Book Society News*, October 1936, p. 11.

C1560 [Review of] *The Life of George Moore*, by Joseph Hone. *Book Society News*, October 1936, p. 13.

C1561 Satyrane Among the Authors. *London Mercury*, October 1936, Vol. 34, No. 204, pp. 543-545. Review of *Coleridge's Miscellaneous Criticism*, edited by Thomas M. Raysor. *See also* C1562.

C1562 Men and Books. *Time and Tide*, 10 October 1936, pp. 1391-1392. Review of *Coleridge's Miscellaneous Criticism*, edited by Thomas M. Raysor. *See also* C1561.

413

C1563   [Review of] *The Gold and the Grey: Some More Collected Verses, 1930–1935*, by Hilton Brown. *TLS*, 10 October 1936, p. 817. Unsigned.

C1564   [Review of] *The Birth of Song: Poems, 1935–36*, by W. H. Davies. *TLS*, 10 October 1936, p. 817. Unsigned.

C1565   INVITATION [*later* POETRY'S INVITATION]. *The Spectator*, 16 October 1936, p. 630.

Reprinted: *An Elegy*, 1937; *Poems 1930–1940*, [1941]; and *Poems of Many Years*, 1957.

Read by the author at the Poetry Reading in the Wigmore Hall, 14 September 1943, and published with the other poems read by Clifford Bax, T. S. Eliot and S. I. Hsiung in *Poet's Choice*, arranged by Dorothy Dudley Short on behalf of the Arts and Letters Sectional Committee of the National Council of Women of Great Britain, 1945.

C1566   Allurements to Serenity. *TLS*, 17 October 1936, p. 825. Review of *Storm and Peace*, by John Beresford. Unsigned.

C1567   [Review of] *Daily Meditations*, by Philip Pain . . . with introduction by Leon Howard. *TLS*, 17 October 1936, p. 842. Unsigned.

C1568   Housman and Housman. *Time and Tide*, 31 October 1936, p. 1520. Review of *More Poems*, by A. E. Housman (*see also* C1572); and *A. E. Housman: A Sketch*, by A. S. F. Gow.

C1569   [Review of] *The King Sees Red*, by Anthony Bertram. *Book Society News*, November 1936, p. 7.

C1570   [Review of] *The Friendly Tree*, by C. Day Lewis. *Book Society News*, November 1936, p. 8.

C1571   [Review of] *Of Mortal Love*, by William Gerhardi. *Book Society News*, November 1936, p. 9.

C1572   A. E. Housman's Poems. *Book Society News*, November 1936, p. 11. Review of *More Poems*, by A. E. Housman. *See also* C1568.

C1573   [Review of] *Through the Woods*, by H. E. Bates. *The Fortnightly*, November 1936, N.S. Vol. 140, p. 628.

C1574   PRESENT DISCONTENTS. *Oxford Magazine*, 12 November 1936, Vol. 55, No. 5, p. 153. Signed E.B.

Reprinted: *An Elegy*, 1937; and *Poems 1930–1940*, [1941].

C1575   [Review of] *The Poet's Way*, selected by E. W. Parker, edited by A. R. Moon; and *Ballads and Narrative Poems*, edited by T. W. Moles. *TLS*, 14 November 1936, p. 929. Unsigned.

C1576   Satire and Sensibility. *The Spectator*, 20 November 1936, Literary Supplement, p. 14. Review of *Fanny Burney*, by Christopher Lloyd.

C1577 Anthologies for Every Mood: New Quests in Old Fields. *TLS*, 21 November 1936, p. 943. Review of *Spiritual Songs from English MSS of Fourteenth to Sixteenth Centuries*, edited by Frances M. Comper; *The Locked Book: An Anthology*, made by Helen Granville-Barker; *The Poet's Walk: A Nature Anthology*, made by Viola Meynell (*see also* C1581); *The Way of a Man With a Maid* . . . compiled by Vernon Rendall; *Parents and Children: An Anthology*, edited by Hugh Kingsmill; *Toward Evening: An Anthology*, edited by Sir James Marchant; *The Testament of Man: An Anthology of the Spirit*, by Sir Arthur Stanley; and *Pick and Choose: A Gallimaufry*, composed by Daniel George. Unsigned.

C1578 [Review of] *Everyday Science*, by A. W. Haslett. *Book Society News*, December 1936, p. 19.

C1579 Robert Frost's Selected Poems. *Book Society News*, December 1936, p. 20. Review of *Selected Poems*, by Robert Frost. See also C371.

C1580 A CITY ON A HILL. *Book Society Annual*, [Christmas] 1936, p. 29. Holograph facsimile.

Reprinted: separate edition, 1936; *An Elegy*, 1937; and *Poems 1930-1940*, [1941].

C1581 "The Poetry Department". *Book Society Annual*, [Christmas] 1936, p. 53. Review of *Collected Poems of Sacheverell Sitwell; Mithraic Emblems*, by Roy Campbell; *Visiting the Caves*, by William Plomer; *Look, Stranger*, by W. H. Auden; *Bright Feather Fading*, by Lilian Bowes Lyon; *Devil's Dyke*, by Christopher Hassall; *The Emperor Heart*, by Laurence Whistler; *New Oxford Poetry, 1936*, edited by A. W. Sandford; *The Year's Poetry*, compiled by Denys Kilham Roberts and John Lehmann (*see also* C1604); and *The Poet's Walk: A Nature Anthology*, made by Viola Meynell (*see also* C1577).

C1582 Poems of 1936. *TLS*, 19 December 1936, p. 1048. Review of *The Best Poems of 1936*, selected by Thomas Moult. Unsigned.

C1583 [Review of] *An Anthology of the Seasons*, collected by Rhona Arbutnot Lane. *TLS*, 19 December 1936, p. 1053. Unsigned.

1937

C1584 Elia and Christ's Hospital. *Essays and Studies*, 1936, [*i.e.* 1937], Vol. 22, pp. 37–60.

C1585 [Review of] *The Four Winds of Love: The East Wind*, by Compton MacKenzie. *Book Society News*, January 1937, p. 6.

C1586 [Review of] *Low Company*, by Mark Benney. *Book Society News*, January 1937, p. 8.

C1587 [Review of] *Great Trade Route*, by Ford Madox Ford. *Book Society News*, January 1937, p. 10.

C1588 A First Draft. *The Fortnightly*, January 1937, N.S. Vol. 141, pp. 111-112. Review of *Boswell's Journal of a Tour to the Hebrides*, edited by Frederick A. Pottle and Charles H. Bennett.

C1589 Unpublished Letters. *The Spectator*, 22 January 1937, pp. 134-135. Review of *Letters of Fanny Brawne to Fanny Keats (1820-1824)*, edited by Fred Edgcumbe; *Some Letters and Miscellanea of Charles Brown*, edited by Maurice Buxton Forman (*see also* C1591); and *Letters of Hartley Coleridge*, edited by Grace Evelyn Griggs and Earl Leslie Griggs.

C1590 Spiritual Persistence. *TLS*, 30 January 1937, p. 72. Review of *Essays by Divers Hands, Transactions of the Royal Society of Literature*, N.S. Vol. 15, edited by Hugh Walpole. Unsigned.

C1591 Keats's Friends. *TLS*, 30 January 1937, p. 73. Review of *Some Letters and Miscellanea of Charles Brown*, edited by Maurice Buxton Forman. Unsigned. *See also* C1589.

C1592 [Review of] *The du Mauriers*, by Daphne du Maurier. *Book Society News*, February 1937, pp. 10-11.

C1593 [Review of] *The Unexpected Years*, by Laurence Housman. *Book Society News*, February 1937, p. 11.

C1594 [Review of] *Lucie Duff Gordon*, by Gordon Waterfield. *Book Society News*, February 1937, p. 12.

C1595 [Review of] *The Tricolour Sun . . .* by William K. Matthews. *TLS*, 6 February 1937, p. 93. Unsigned.

C1596 The Australian Microscope—Critical Eyes on English Poets. *TLS*, 20 February 1937, pp. 117-118. Review of *Modern Australian Literature*, by Nettie Palmer; *Hamlet: Two Popular Lectures*, by Sir Mungo MacCallum; *Hamlet: A Study in Critical Method*, by A. J. A. Waldock; *Chaucer's Debt to Italy*, by Sir Mungo MacCallum; *Donne's Influence on English Literature*, by R. C. Bald; *Thomas Hardy and The Dynasts*, by A. J. A. Waldock; *A Midsummer Night's Dream: A Popular Lecture*, by H. M. Green; and *Some Recent Developments in English Literature*, by A. J. A. Waldock, R. G. Howarth and E. J. Dobson. Unsigned.

C1597 [Review of] *Poems*, by Thomas Hennell. *TLS*, 20 February 1937, p. 133. Unsigned.

C1598 [Review of] *Present Indicative*, by Noel Coward. *Book Society News*, March 1937, p. 7.

C1599 [Review of] *Midnight on the Desert*, by J. B. Priestley. *Book Society News*, March 1937, p. 9.

C1600 [Review of] *Coronation Summer*, by Angela Thirkell. *Book Society News*, March 1937, p. 12.

C1601 Crabb Robinson by Himself. *The Spectator*, 5 March 1937, p. 420. Review of *Henry Crabb Robinson of Bury, Jena, "The Times", and Russell Square*, by John Milton Baker.

C1602 Georgics in Prose. *TLS*, 20 March 1937, p. 200. Review of *English Cavalcade*, by W. J. Blyton. Unsigned.

C1603 [Review of] *Lucid Intervals*, by Walter Murdoch. *TLS*, 27 March 1937, p. 241. Unsigned.

C1604 [Review of] *The Year's Poetry, 1936*, compiled by Denys Kilham Roberts and John Lehmann. *TLS*, 27 March 1937, p. 242. Unsigned. *See also* C1581.

C1605 [Review of] *The Honeysuckle and the Bee*, by Sir John Squire. *Book Society News*, April 1937, p. 9.

C1606 [Review of] *Unfinished Journey*, by Jack Jones. *Book Society News*, April 1937, p. 11.

C1607 [Review of] *Europe in Arms*, by Liddell Hart. *Book Society News*, April 1937, p. 12.

C1608 Wordsworth in Council. *London Mercury*, April 1937, Vol. 35, No. 210, pp. 631–633. Review of *The Letters of William and Dorothy Wordsworth: The Middle Years*, arranged and edited by Ernest de Selincourt.

C1609 THE SPELL OF FRANCE. *Études anglaises, avril/juin* 1937, Vol. 1, No. 2, pp. 97–98.

Reprinted: *An Elegy*, 1937; and *Poems 1930–1940*, [1941].

C1610 Collins Reconsidered. *TLS*, 3 April 1937, p. 252. Review of *Poor Collins: His Life, His Art and His Influence*, by Edward Gay Ainsworth, Jr. Unsigned.

C1611 [Review of] *The Muse of Monarchy: Poems by Kings and Queens of England. TLS*, 10 April 1937, p. 276. Unsigned.

C1612 [Review of] *T. E. Lawrence, by his Friends*, edited by A. W. Lawrence. *Book Society News*, May 1937, p. 8.

C1613 The Göttingen Celebrations: Oxford's Abstention. *The Times*, 1 May 1937, p. 12. Letter.

C1614 Everybody's Books: Popular Taste and Clever Enterprises. *TLS*, 1 May 1937, pp. 328–329. On the reading public, 1837–1937. Unsigned.

C1615 Very Old Blues: Tudor Foundlings at Christ's Hospital. *TLS*, 22 May 1937, p. 390. Review of *Christ's Hospital Admissions*, Vol. 1, *1554–1599*. Unsigned.

C1616 In Praise of Cricket: The Game and the Spectacle. *TLS*, 22 May 1937, p. 394. Review of *An ABC of Cricket*, by P. G. H. Fender; *In Search of Cricket*, by J. M. Kilburn; and *A Cricket Pro's Lot*, by Fred Root. Unsigned.

C1617   Some Cricket Books. *The Times*, M.C.C. Number, 25 May 1937, p. xxiv.

Reprinted: *The M.C.C. 1787–1937*, 1937; and *Edmund Blunden: A Selection of His Poetry and Prose*, 1950.

C1618   Keats: A Famous Document. *The Spectator*, 28 May 1937, p. 1002. Review of *Life of John Keats*, by Charles Armitage Brown, edited by Dorothy Hyde Bodurtha and Willard Bissell Pope. *See also* C1620.

C1619   The Charm of Oxford: An Aerial Annotation. *The Cherwell*, 29 May 1937, Vol. 50, No. 5, p. 103. Dialogue.

C1620   Armitage Brown's "Keats". *TLS*, 29 May 1937, p. 409. Review of *Life of John Keats*, by Charles Armitage Brown, edited by Dorothy Hyde Bodurtha and Willard Bissell Pope. Unsigned. *See also* C1618.

C1621   "This Knowledge": Mr. Ronald Fraser's New Novel. *The Observer*, 30 May 1937, p. 9. Review of *A House in the Park*, by Ronald Fraser.

C1622   [Review of] *Avalanche*, by Gordon Hayward. *Book Society News*, June 1937, p. 5.

C1623   [Review of] *St. Helena*, by Octave Aubry. *Book Society News*, June 1937, p. 7.

C1624   [Review of] *Sir Richard Grenville of the Revenge*, by A. L. Rowse. *Book Society News*, June 1937, p. 7.

C1625   [Review of] *Town and Country in Southern France*, by Francis Strang. *Book Society News*, June 1937, p. 8.

C1626   [Review of] *Jonathan Swift*, by Bertram Newman. *The Fortnightly*, June 1937, N.S. Vol. 141, pp. 755–756.

C1627   A TUNE. *St. Martin's Review*, June 1937, No. 556, p. 261.

Reprinted: *An Elegy*, 1937; and *Poems 1930–1940*, [1941].

C1628   [Review of] *Song of the Sun*, by Ernest Rhys. *TLS*, 12 June 1937, p. 442. Unsigned.

C1629   A Lamb Mystification. *TLS*, 12 June 1937, p. 447. Letter on a letter from Charles Lamb to Vincent Novello. Signed E. Blunden.

C1630   [Review of] *Act of God*, by F. Tennyson Jesse. *Book Society News*, July 1937, p. 8.

C1631   [Review of] *Britain and the Beast*, edited by Clough Williams-Ellis and others. *Book Society News*, July 1937, p. 10.

C1632   [Review of] *Defoe*, by James Sutherland. *Book Society News*, July 1937, p. 13.

C1633   Keats Day by Day. *London Mercury*, July 1937, Vol. 36, No. 213, pp. 302–303. Review of *Adonais: A Life of John Keats*, by Dorothy Hewlett.

C1634   Poets on Vacation: Parnassus and the Suitcase. *TLS*, 10 July 1937, p. 509. On books to be taken on holiday. Unsigned.

C1635   Edward Thomas in Detail. *The Spectator*, 23 July 1937, p. 156. Review of *Edward Thomas: A Biography and a Bibliography*, by Robert P. Eckert.

C1636   The Four Strange Years: Anthology of the Great War. *The Observer*, 25 July 1937, p. 4. Review of *Vain Glory: A Miscellany of the Great War, 1914-1918*, edited by Guy Chapman.

C1637   [Review of] *Musical Chains*, by Eugenia Wake. *Book Society News*, August 1937, p. 8.

C1638   [Review of] *Forbidden Journey*, by Ella Maillart. *Book Society News*, August 1937, p. 9.

C1639   [Review of] *Harvest Comedy*, by Frank Swinnerton. *Book Society News*, September 1937, p. 6.

C1640   [Review of] *They Seek a Country*, by Francis Brett Young. *Book Society News*, September 1937, p. 7.

C1641   [Review of] *A Date With a Duchess*, by Arthur Calder-Marshall. *Book Society News*, September 1937, p. 11.

C1642   [Review of] *The Complete Memoirs of George Sherston*, by Siegfried Sassoon. *Book Society News*, October 1937, p. 8.

C1643   [Review of] *For Us in the Dark*, by Naomi Royde-Smith. *Book Society News*, October 1937, pp. 10-11.

C1644   [Review of] *The Life and Death of a Spanish Town*, by Elliot Paul. *Book Society News*, October 1937, p. 13.

C1645   The Klosterhaus Readings, 1937. *German Life and Letters*, October 1937, Vol. 2, No. 1, pp. 33-38. Also issued separately as an offprint (*see* A62).

C1646   Cobbett in America. *TLS*, 2 October 1937, p. 710. Review of *Letters from William Cobbett to Edward Thornton* . . . edited . . . by G. D. H. Cole. Unsigned.

C1647   From Walthamstow to Madrid. *The Spectator*, 15 October 1937, p. 650. Review of *Fanny Keats*, by Marie Adami.

C1648   Poet on Dartmoor. *TLS*, 16 October 1937, p. 754. Review of *A Dartmoor Village*, by Eden Phillpotts. Unsigned.

C1649   [Review of] *Christ's Hospital*, by G. A. T. Allan. *TLS*, 16 October 1937, p. 761. Unsigned.

C1650   Pre-Plywood Carpenters. *TLS*, 30 October 1937, p. 795. Review of *The Village Carpenter*, by Walter Rose. Unsigned.

C1651   [Review of] *A Purse of Coppers*, by Seán O'Faoláin. *Book Society News*, November 1937, p. 8.

C1652　[Review of] *Augustus*, by John Buchan. *Book Society News*, November 1937, p. 10.

C1653　[Review of] *Red Star Over China*, by Edgar Snow. *Book Society News*, November 1937, p. 11.

C1654　Report of Social Evening on October 11th Inaugurating the Winter Session of 1937–1938. *Charles Lamb Society Monthly Bulletin*, November 1937, No. 25, p. 2. Greetings on the commencement of the new session.

C1655　Chinese Folk-Song. *London Mercury*, November 1937, Vol. 37, No. 217, pp. 80–81. Review of *The Book of Songs*, translated from the Chinese, by Arthur Waley.

C1656　Birds, Mostly Modern. *TLS*, 6 November 1937, p. 825. Review of *A Book of Birds*, by Mary Priestley. Unsigned.

C1657　Mr. Laurence Housman's Poems: A Harvest of Years. *TLS*, 6 November 1937, p. 832. Review of *The Collected Poems of Laurence Housman*. Unsigned.

C1658　[Review of] *Here's Flowers: An Anthology of Flower Poems*, compiled by Joan Rutter. *TLS*, 6 November 1937, p. 853. Unsigned.

C1659　Sketches from Nature. *The Spectator*, 19 November 1937, Literary Supplement, p. 26. Review of *Down the River*, by H. E. Bates, with wood-engravings by Agnes Miller Parker; and *Country Matters*, written and engraved by Clare Leighton.

C1660　Mr. Masefield's Sketch-Book. *TLS*, 27 November 1937, p. 907. Review of *The Country Scene in Poems*, by John Masefield. Unsigned.

C1661　A BALLAD OF TITLES. *Book Society Annual*, Christmas 1937, p. 17.

Reprinted: separate edition, December 1937.

C1662　[Review of] *Portrait of a Village*, by Francis Brett Young. *Book Society News*, December 1937, p. 55.

C1663　[Review of] *Paint and Prejudice*, by C. R. W. Nevinson. *Book Society News*, December 1937, p. 61.

C1664　[Review of] *Ludwig II of Bavaria*, by Ferdinand Mayr-Ofen. *Book Society News*, December 1937, p. 64.

C1665　[Review of] *The Best Poems of 1937*, selected by Thomas Moult; and *The Year's Poetry, 1937*, compiled by Denys Kilham Roberts and Geoffrey Grigson. *TLS*, 11 December 1937, p. 950. Unsigned.

C1666　Poems in Divers Humours. *TLS*, 18 December 1937, p. 960. Review of *A Kite's Dinner: Poems in Divers Humours*, by Eric N. Batterham. Unsigned.

C1667 Le Brave des Braves. *The Spectator*, 24 December 1937, pp. 1154-1155. Review of *Marshal Ney: A Play in Five Acts*, by J. C. Masterman.

C1668 King Coel. *TLS*, 25 December 1937, p. 976. Review of *Old King Coel: A Rhymed Tale in Four Books*, by Adam Fox. Unsigned.

C1669 Drinkwater's Poems. *TLS*, 25 December 1937, p. 977. Review of *The Collected Poems of John Drinkwater*, Vol. 3. Unsigned.

1938

C1670 [Review of] *The Summing Up*, by W. Somerset Maugham. *Book Society News*, January 1938, p. 4.

C1671 [Review of] *The Silver Land*, by J. M. Scott. *Book Society News*, January 1938, p. 5.

C1672 [Review of] *British Consul*, by Ernest Hambloch. *Book Society News*, January 1938, p. 8.

C1673 Another Poor Indian. *TLS*, 1 January 1938, p. 8. Review of *Inkle and Yarico Album*, selected and arranged by Lawrence Marsden Price. Unsigned.

C1674 Charles Brown. *TLS*, 8 January 1938, p. 28. Letter on the rarity of his *Narensky*. Signed E. Blunden.

C1675 Mary Shelley and Others. *The Spectator*, 21 January 1938, p. 94. Review of *Mary Shelley: A Biography*, by R. Glynn Grylls. *See also* C1676.

C1676 Shelley's Ideal Wife: A Portrait from Sources Old and New. *TLS*, 22 January 1938, p. 57. Review of *Mary Shelley: A Biography*, by R. Glynn Grylls. Unsigned. *See also* C1675.

C1677 IN THE MARGIN. *The Listener*, 26 January 1938, p. 186. Reprinted: *The Best Poems of 1938*, 1938; *On Several Occasions*, 1939; *Poems 1930-1940*, [1941]; and *Poems of Many Years*, 1957.

C1678 [Review of] *No News*, by Pamela Frankau. *Book Society News*, February 1938, p. 6.

C1679 [Review of] *Japan Over Asia*, by William Chamberlain. *Book Society News*, February 1938, p. 8.

C1680 [Review of] *Escape on Skis*, by Brian Meredith. *Book Society News*, February 1938, p. 10.

C1681 Poet of East Anglia. *TLS*, 5 February 1938, p. 88. Review of *A Boy of Clare*, by E. H.W. Meyerstein. Unsigned.

C1682 [Review of] *South Latitude*, by F. D. Ommanney. *Book Society News*, March 1938, p. 5.

C1683 [Review of] *Journalist's Wife*, by Lilian Mowrer. *Book Society News*, March 1938, p. 9.

C1684   [Review of] *Search for Tomorrow*, by Rom Landau. *Book Society News*, March 1938, p. 10.

C1685   THE DREAMER. *The Listener*, 30 March 1938, p. 701.
Reprinted: *On Several Occasions*, 1939; and *Poems 1930–1940*, [1941].

C1686   [Review of] *Dark Islands*, by John W. Vandercook. *Book Society News*, April 1938, pp. 19–20.

C1687   [Review of] *Looking Forward*, by Harold Anson. *Book Society News*, April 1938, pp. 21–22.

C1688   [Review of] *The World of Action*, by Valentine Williams. *Book Society News*, May 1938, pp. 18–19.

C1689   [Review of] *D'Annunzio*, by Tom Antongini. *Book Society News*, May 1938, pp. 20–21.

C1690   [Review of] *Edward Lear*, by Angus Davidson. *Book Society News*, May 1938, pp. 21–22.

C1691   A Late Victorian Boyhood. *London Mercury*, May 1938, Vol. 38, No. 223, pp. 72–74. Review of *The Childhood of Edward Thomas, A Fragment of Autobiography*, with a preface by Julian Thomas.

C1692   Thomas Wainewright the "Monster": Riddle of a Reputation. *TLS*, 14 May 1938, p. 330. Review of *Janus Weathercock*, by Jonathan Curling. Unsigned.

C1693   Legendary Monsters. *TLS*, 14 May 1938, p. 335. Third leader on Thomas Wainewright. Unsigned.

C1694   Yorick at the Bodleian. *TLS*, 21 May 1938, p. 353. Third leader on the exhibition of jest-books. Unsigned.

C1695   [Review of] *The Importance of Living*, by Lin Yutang. *Book Society News*, June 1938, pp. 16–17.

C1696   [Review of] *Brought Up and Brought Out*, by Mary Pakenham. *Book Society News*, June 1938, pp. 19–20.

C1697   [Review of] *Among Others*, by Lord Elton. *Book Society News*, June 1938, pp. 20–21.

C1698   Thomas Hardy Among His Books. *The Cherwell*, 11 June 1938, Vol. 53, No. 7, pp. 151–152. One of a series entitled 'Books in General'. Review of *Thomas Hardy: A Study of His Writings*, by William R. Rutland.

C1699   "The Byble in Englyshe". *TLS*, 11 June 1938, p. 400. On the quatercentenary of the publication of Thomas Cromwell's Bible. *See also* C1703.

C1700   [Review of] *An American Testament*, by Joseph Freeman. *Book Society News*, July 1938, pp. 16–17.

C1701   [Review of] *In Praise of Ulster*, by Richard Hayward. *Book Society News*, July 1938, pp. 17–18.

C1702   [Review of] *The Witnesses*, by Thomas Hennell. *Book Society News*, July 1938, p. 19.

C1703 "Re-opening the Bible". *TLS*, 2 July 1938, p. 450. Letter on the advertisement by Cambridge University Press in the issue of 25 June, p. 427 disclaiming authorship of quotations from the leader 'Re-opening the Bible' in the issue of 11 June, p. 401. *See also* C1699.

C1704 [Review of] *A Cabinet of Gems: Short Stories from the English Annuals*, edited with an introduction by Bradford Allen Booth. *TLS*, 30 July 1938, pp. 510-511. Unsigned.

C1705 [Review of] *In Search of the Gyr-Falcon*, by Ernest Lewis. *Book Society News*, August 1938, pp. 14-15.

C1706 [Review of] *Oscar Wilde*, by Frank Harris. *Book Society News*, August 1938, pp. 15-16.

C1707 [Review of] *Sir John Vanbrugh*, by Laurence Whistler. *Book Society News*, August 1938, pp. 16-17.

C1708 Novels of a Sentimental Age: The Minor Writer as a Mirror of Taste. *TLS*, 6 August 1938, p. 515. Review of *The Polite Marriage: Essays*, by J. M. S. Thompkins. Unsigned.

C1709 [Review of] *Some Still Live*, by F. G. Tinker. *Book Society News*, September 1938, p. 17.

C1710 [Review of] *The Universal Provider*, by R. S. Lambert. *Book Society News*, September 1938, p. 18.

C1711 [Review of] *Marlborough*, Vol. 4, by Winston Churchill. *Book Society News*, September 1938, p. 20. Signed E.B.

C1712 [Review of] *The Old Century and Seven More Years*, by Siegfried Sassoon. *Book Society News*, October 1938, pp. 10-11. *See also* C1715.

C1713 [Review of] *Ordeal at Lucknow*, by Michael Joyce. *Book Society News*, October 1938, pp. 16-17.

C1714 [Review of] *Shake Hands and Come Out Fighting*, by L. A. G. Strong. *Book Society News*, October 1938, p. 24.

C1715 Siegfried Sassoon—Early Years. *London Mercury*, October 1938, Vol. 38, No. 228, pp. 570-572. Review of *The Old Century and Seven More Years*, by Siegfried Sassoon. *See also* C1712.

C1716 EXORCIZED. *TLS*, 8 October 1938, p. 633. *See also* Latin poem, by C. W. B. in the issue of 15 October, p. 662.
Reprinted: *Poems 1930-1940*, [1941].

C1717 Crabb Robinson. *The Spectator*, 14 October 1938, pp. 622, 624. Review of *Henry Crabb Robinson on Books and Their Writers*, edited by Edith J. Morley.

C1718 [The Annual Orations in the Great Hall at Christ's Hospital on St. Matthew's Day]. *The Blue*, November 1938, Vol. 66, No. 1, p. 3. On the oil painting by Thomas Stothard.

C1719 [Review of] *The Gate is Open*, by Carl Fallas. *Book Society News,* November 1938, pp. 18-19.

C1720   [Review of] *Guns or Butter*, by R. H. Bruce Lockhart. *Book Society News*, November 1938, p. 19.

C1721   [Review of] *Collected Essays in Literary Criticism*, by Herbert Read. *Book Society News*, November 1938, pp. 22-23.

C1722   SONG FOR THE SECRETARY OF A PRESERVATION LEAGUE. *Oxford Magazine*, 17 November 1938, p. 173. Signed E.B.

C1723   SAM'L PEPYS: HIS PLAINT, A LAMENT FROM A NEGLECTED BOOKSHELF [*later* SERIOUS CALL]. *Book Society Annual* (incorporating the *Book Society News*), Christmas 1938, pp. 25-26.
        Reprinted: *Poems 1930-1940*, [1941].

C1724   [Review of] *Portrait of a Chef: The Life of Alexis Soyer*, by Helen Morris. *Book Society Annual* (incorporating the *Book Society News*), December 1938, p. 74.

C1725   [Review of] *I Know an Island*, by R. M. Lockley. *Book Society Annual* (incorporating the *Book Society News*), December 1938, pp. 75-76.

C1726   [Review of] *Listen! the Wind*, by Anne Morrow Lindbergh. *Book Society Annual* (incorporating the *Book Society News*), December 1938, p. 78.

C1727   Four Years of War. *London Mercury*, December 1938, Vol. 39, No. 230, pp. 220-222. Review of *The War the Infantry Knew, 1914-1919: A Chronicle of Service in France and Belgium*. An account by members of the 2nd Royal Welch Fusiliers.

1939

C1728   [Review of] *Katia*, by Princess Marthe Bibesco. *Book Society News*, January 1939, p. 16.

C1729   [Review of] *Travels in the North*, by Karel Capek. *Book Society News*, January 1939, pp. 17-18.

C1730   [Review of] *The Year's Poetry, 1938*, compiled by D. Kilham Roberts and Geoffrey Grigson. *Book Society News*, January 1939, p. 18. Signed E.B.

C1731   Coleridge, and about Him. *London Mercury*, January 1939, Vol. 39, No. 231, pp. 350-352. Review of *Samuel Taylor Coleridge: A Biographical Study*, by E. K. Chambers; and *The Life of S. T. Coleridge: The Early Years*, by Lawrence Hanson.

C1732   [Review of] *Indian Ink*, by Philip Steegman. *Book Society News*, February 1939, pp. 16-17.

C1733   [Review of] *The Lake of the Royal Crocodiles*, by Eileen Bigland. *Book Society News*, February 1939, pp. 17-18.

C1734   [Review of] *African Women*, by Sylvia Leith-Ross. *Book Society News*, February 1939, p. 18.

C1735   BRITISH MUSEUM BLUES (I WAIT FOR A BOOK). *Oxford Magazine*, 2 February 1939, Vol. 57, No. 11, p. 348. Signed E.B.

C1736   CHANCE PLEASURES. *The Listener*, 16 February 1939, p. 351.

Reprinted: *Poems 1930-1940*, [1941].

C1737   Genius and Insanity. *The Spectator*, 24 February 1939, pp. 312, 314. Review of *Rejoice in the Lamb: A Song from Bedlam*, by Christopher Smart. *See also* C1738.

C1738   An Eighteenth-Century Psalmist: Poet's Song from Bedlam. *TLS*, 25 February 1939, p. 122. Review of *Rejoice in the Lamb: A Song from Bedlam*, by Christopher Smart. Unsigned. *See also* C1737.

C1739   "London's Dove". *The Blue*, March 1939, Vol. 66, No. 4, pp. 162-163. Signed B. On Robert Dove, and his bequest to Christ's Hospital.

C1740   [Review of] *Leonardo da Vinci*, by Antonina Vallentin. *Book Society News*, March 1939, pp. 18-19.

C1741   [Review of] *The Horse and Buggy Doctor*, by Arthur E. Hertzler. *Book Society News*, March 1939, pp. 19-20.

C1742   [Review of] *Meet the Prisoner*, by John A. F. Watson. *Book Society News*, March 1939, pp. 21-22.

C1743   The Wordsworth Letters Completed. *London Mercury*, March 1939, Vol. 39, No. 233, pp. 542-543. Review of *The Letters of William and Dorothy Wordsworth: The Later Years*, edited by E. de Selincourt.

C1744   THE SUM OF ALL. *The Listener*, 16 March 1939, p. 572.

Reprinted: *Poems 1930-1940*, [1941]; *Edmund Blunden: A Selection of His Poetry and Prose*, 1950; and *Poems of Many Years*, 1957.

C1745   [Review of] *A Number of People*, by Sir Edward Marsh. *Book Society News*, April 1939, pp. 17-20.

C1746   [Review of] *English Captain*, by Tom Wintringham. *Book Society News*, April 1939, p. 20. Signed E.B.

C1747   [Review of] *James Ramsay MacDonald*, by Lord Elton. *Book Society News*, April 1939, pp. 23-24.

C1748   IN MEMORIAM A.R.–I. YOKOHAMA, NOVEMBER 1938 [*i.e.* Arthur Rose-Innes]. *London Mercury*, April 1939, Vol. 39, No. 234, p. 584.

Reprinted: *Poems 1930-1940*, [1941].

C1749   [Review of] *Indian Pilgrimage*, by Ranjee G. Shahani. *Book Society News*, May 1939, p. 13.

C1750 [Review of] *Voodoo Gods*, by Zora Hurston. *Book Society News*, May 1939, pp. 13–14.

C1751 [Review of] *Hell-Fire Francis*, by Ronald Fuller. *Book Society News*, May 1939, pp. 15–16. Signed E.B.

C1752 [Review of] *The English Miss*, by Alicia Percival. *Book Society News*, May 1939, pp. 18–19.

C1753 LYRICAL BALLAD. *Oxford Magazine*, 4 May 1939, Vol. 57, No. 18, p. 566. Signed E. B.

C1754 TO OUR CATCHMENT BOARD. *The Cherwell*, 20 May 1939, Vol. 56, No. 4, p. 76.

Reprinted: *On Several Occasions*, 1939; and *Poems 1930–1940*, [1941].

C1755 [Review of] *Education de Prince*, and *Jezebel*, at the Scala Cinema, Oxford. *Oxford Magazine*, 25 May 1939, Vol. 57, No. 21, pp. 656–657. Film review. Signed E.B.

C1756 [Review of] *Inside Asia*, by John Gunther. *Book Society News*, June 1939, pp. 13–14.

C1757 [Review of] *Behold, this Dreamer*, by Walter de la Mare. *Book Society News*, June 1939, pp. 21–22.

C1758 [Review of] *Happy Countryman*, by C. Henry Warren. *Book Society News*, June 1939, pp. 22–23.

C1759 Unveiling of a Plaque in Memory of Charles Lamb at Christ's Hospital, May 13th, 1939. *Charles Lamb Society Monthly Bulletin*, June 1939, No. 42, Supplement, p. 5. Message as a Vice President, regretting his inability to be present.

C1760 Ourselves and Germany: A Minority Retrospect. *The Fortnightly*, June 1939, N.S. Vol. 145, pp. 618–626.

Reprinted [sub-title: A Retrospect] : *Anglo-German Review*, July 1939, pp. 208–210.

C1761 [Review of] *The Girl Downstairs*, and *Going Places*, at the Ritz Cinema, Oxford. *Oxford Magazine*, 1 June 1939, Vol. 57, No. 22, p. 684. Film review. Signed E.B.

C1762 CHRONOMACHY OR ONE OF US IS NOT TIRED YET [*later* A CHRONOMACHY]. *The Cherwell*, 3 June 1939, Vol. 56, No. 6, p. 108.

Reprinted: *Poems 1930–1940*, [1941].

C1763 [Review of] *L'Homme à Abattre, Mother Goose Goes to Hollywood*, and *Horsefeathers*, at the Scala Cinema, Oxford. *Oxford Magazine*, 8 June 1939, Vol. 57, No. 23, p. 715. Film review. Signed E.B.

C1764 Keats: A Classic Edition. *The Spectator*, 30 June 1939, pp. 1138–1139. Review of *The Poetical Works of John Keats*, edited by H. W. Garrod.

C1765 [Review of] *The Child in the Crystal*, by Lady Sybil Lubbock. *Book Society News*, July 1939, pp. 17–18.

C1766 [Review of] *The Mirrors of Versailles*, by Elisabeth Kyle. *Book Society News*, July 1939, p. 20.

C1767 COUNTRY CHARACTERS. *TLS*, 15 July 1939, Summer Reading Section, p. i.
Reprinted: *Poems 1930–1940*, [1941].

C1768 [Review of] *The Defence of Britain*, by Liddell Hart. *Book Society News*, August 1939, pp. 14–15.

C1769 [Review of] *The Dear Monster*, by G. R. Halkett. *Book Society News*, August 1939, pp. 15–16.

C1770 [Review of] *Turn Left for England*, by Reginald Pound. *Book Society News*, August 1939, p. 17.

C1771 [Review of] *Ten Years Under the Earth*, by Norbert Casteret. *Book Society News*, August 1939, pp. 18–19.

C1772 [Review of] *The Arrogant History of White Ben*, by Clemence Dane. *Book Society News*, September 1939, pp. 13–14.

C1773 [Review of] *Apparitions and Haunted Houses*, by Sir Ernest Bennett. *Book Society News*, September 1939, pp. 21–22.

C1774 [Review of] *Love for a Country*, by Rom Landau. *Book Society News*, September 1939, p. 23.

C1775 A WINDOW IN GERMANY: AUGUST 1939. *TLS*, 16 September 1939, p. 539.
Reprinted: *The Best Poems of 1940*, [1940]; and *Poems 1930–1940*, [1941].

C1776 [Review of] *North Cape*, by F. D. Ommanney. *Book Society News*, October 1939, p. 14.

C1777 [Review of] *Wind, Sand and Stars*, by Antoine de Saint Exupery. *Book Society News*, October 1939, pp. 15–16.

C1778 [Review of] *The Jackdaw's Nest: An Anthology*, edited by Gerald Bullett. *Book Society News*, October 1939, p. 16.

C1779 Old Rural Crafts: Mr. Massingham's "Hermitage". *TLS*, 28 October 1939, p. 422. Review of *Country Relics*, by H. J. Massingham. Unsigned.

C1780 [Review of] *The Scrapbook of Katherine Mansfield*, edited by J.M.M. [i.e. John Middleton Murry]. *Book Society News*, November 1939, p. 18.

C1781 [Review of] *The Moores of Moore Hall*, by Joseph Hone. *Book Society News*, November 1939, pp. 18–19.

C1782 [Review of] *Caroline of England: An Augustan Portrait*, by Peter Quennell. *Book Society News*, November 1939, p. 19.

C1783　Romantic Poetry. *Études anglaises*, octobre/décembre 1939, Vol. 3, pp. 367–368. Review of *La poésie romantique anglaise*, by Louis Cazamian.

C1784　[Review of] *To-morrow is a New Day*, by Jennie Lee. *Book Society Annual* (incorporating the *Book Society News*), December 1939, p. 23.

C1785　[Review of] *The German Army*, by Herbert Rosinski. *Book Society Annual* (incorporating the *Book Society News*), December 1939, p. 25.

C1786　AN OCCULT ENCOUNTER. *Book Society Annual* (incorporating the *Book Society News*), December 1939, pp. 38–39.

C1787　BY THE BELGIAN FRONTIER [*later* DIKKEBUSCH; and BY THE BELGIAN FRONTIER]. *Kingdom Come*, December/January 1939/1940, Vol. 1, No. 2, p. 41.

　　　　Reprinted: *Fear No More*, 1940; and *Poems 1930–1940*, [1941].

1940

C1788　[Review of] *The Romanovs*, by William Gerhardi. *Book Society News*, January 1940, p. 8.

C1789　[Review of] *War and Soldier*, by Ashihei Hino. *Book Society News*, January 1940, pp. 10–11.

C1790　[Review of] *Edith Sitwell's Anthology*. *Book Society News*, January 1940, p. 13.

C1791　ABOUT THESE GERMANS. *St. Martin's Review*, January 1940, No. 587, pp. 17–18.

　　　　Reprinted: *Poems 1930–1940*, [1941].

C1792　THE UNFORTUNATE SHIPMATE. *The Cherwell*, 27 January 1940, Vol. 58, No. 2, p. 20.

　　　　Reprinted: *Shells by a Stream*, 1944.

C1793　John Randall. *New Statesman & Nation*, 27 January 1940, p. 107. Letter on his death.

C1794　[Review of] *The Provincial Lady in War-Time*, by E. M. Delafield. *Book Society News*, February 1940, pp. 7–9.

C1795　[Review of] *The Wandering Years*, by Weston Martyr. *Book Society News*, February 1940, p. 18.

C1796　[Review of] *Keeping Cool & Other Essays*, by J. B. S. Haldane; and *Philosophy for Our Times*, by C. E. M. Joad. *Book Society News*, February 1940, p. 20. Signed E.B.

C1797　[Review of] *Essays and Addresses*, by Oliver Elton. *Oxford Magazine*, 1 February 1940, Vol. 58, No. 11, pp. 178–179. Signed E.B.

C1798 TO WILFRED OWEN. *The Cherwell*, 3 February 1940, Vol. 58, No. 3, p. 42.

Reprinted: *Augury*, 1940.

C1799 OLD MERTONIAN. *Oxford Magazine*, 22 February 1940, Vol. 58, No. 14, pp. 221-222.

C1800 Old Christ's College: Great Names and Forgotten Records. *TLS*, 24 February 1940, p. 100. Review of *Christ's College in Former Days*, edited by H. Rackham. Unsigned.

C1801 [Review of] *My Life*, by Havelock Ellis. *Book Society News*, March 1940, pp. 16-18.

C1802 [Review of] *Yeats: Last Poems and Plays*. *Book Society News*, March 1940, p. 19.

C1803 [Review of] *Waltzing Matilda: A Background to Australia*, by Arnold L. Haskell. *Book Society News*, March 1940, p. 21.

C1804 How the Fens were Drained: Fighters Against Swamp and Bog. *TLS*, 9 March 1940, p. 119. Review of *The Medieval Fenland*, by H. C. Darby; and *The Draining of the Fens*, by H. C. Darby. Unsigned.

C1805 [Review of] *Masaryk*, by Paul Selver. *Book Society News*, April 1940, p. 14.

C1806 [Review of] *The Reign of Beau Brummell*, by Willard Connely. *Book Society News*, April 1940, pp. 16-17.

C1807 [Review of] *Mauretania*, by Sacheverell Sitwell. *Book Society News*, April 1940, p. 17.

C1808 Farm Labourer: Pictures of Rural England. *TLS*, 13 April 1940, p. 186. Review of *Brother to the Ox: The Autobiography of a Farm Labourer*, by Fred Kitchen. Unsigned.

C1809 Bombing of Cities. *The Times*, 16 April 1940, p. 4. Letter.

C1810 Miss Strickland and "The Queens": Life of a Victorian Bluestocking. *TLS*, 27 April 1940, p. 210. Review of *Agnes Strickland: Biographer of the Queens of England, 1796-1874*, by Una Pope-Hennessy. Unsigned. *See also* C1813.

C1811 [Review of] *Horace Walpole*, by R. W. Ketton-Cremer. *Book Society News*, May 1940, pp. 21-22. Signed E.B.

C1812 [Review of] *A Chinese Childhood*, by Chiang Yee. *Book Society News*, May 1940, pp. 22-23.

C1813 [Review of] *Agnes Strickland: Biographer of the Queens of England, 1796-1874*, by Una Pope-Hennessy. *Book Society News*, May 1940, p. 24. *See also* C1810.

C1814 Ephraim Chambers: Pedagogue of Millions. *TLS*, 18 May 1940, p. 244. Unsigned.

C1815 [Review of] *Christopher Marlowe: A Biographical and Critical Study*, by Frederick S. Boas. *Oxford Magazine*, 23 May 1940, Vol. 58, No. 21, p. 344. Signed E.B.

C1816   [Review of] *Private Road*, by Forrest Reid. *Book Society News*, June 1940, pp. 14-15.

C1817   [Review of] *I Believe: 23 Confessions of Faith*. *Book Society News*, June 1940, p. 15.

C1818   [Review of] *Ten Victorian Poets*, by F. L. Lucas. *Oxford Magazine*, 6 June 1940, Vol. 58, No. 23, pp. 374-375. Signed E.B.

C1819   [Review of] *Winter in Arabia*, by Freya Stark; and *Island Years*, by F. Fraser Darling. *Book Society News*, July 1940, pp. 14-15.

C1820   [Review of] *Another Time*, by W. H. Auden; and *The Oxford Book of Christian Verse*, edited by Lord David Cecil. *Book Society News*, July 1940, pp. 16-17.

C1821   [Review of] *Poltergeists*, by Sacheverell Sitwell. *Book Society News*, July 1940, p. 18.

C1822   Message from Mr. Edmund Blunden, Vice-President. *Charles Lamb Society Monthly Bulletin*, July 1940, No. 47, p. 1. On keeping the Society alive.

C1823   Mr. de la Mare's Speculations. *TLS*, 6 July 1940, p. 323. Review of *Pleasures and Speculations*, by Walter de la Mare. Unsigned.

C1824   [Review of] *The Pope Speaks*, by Charles Rankin; *Life on Other Worlds*, by H. Spencer Jones; and *Thomas E. Dewey*, by Rupert Hughes. *Book Society News*, August 1940, pp. 14-15.

C1825   TRAVELLERS – 1938 [*later* TRAVELLERS, 193–]. *TLS*, 31 August 1940, p. 424.

         Reprinted: *Shells by a Stream*, 1944; and *Poems of Many Years*, 1957.

C1826   [Review of] *Memory Hold-the-Door*, by John Buchan. *Book Society News*, September 1940, pp. 11-12.

C1827   [Review of] *Judge Jeffreys*, by H. Montgomery Hyde; and *An Epic of the Gestapo*, by Sir Paul Dukes. *Book Society News*, September 1940, pp. 13-14.

C1828   IN CHILDHOOD. *St. Martin's Review*, September 1940, No. 595, p. 423.

         Reprinted: *Poems 1930-1940*, [1941].

C1829   The Spirit of England. *World Review*, September 1940, pp. 10-14.

         Reprinted: *Modern Essays 1939-1941*, 1942.

C1830   [Review of] *H.M.S.: His Majesty's Ships and their Forebears*, by Cecil King. *Book Society News*, October 1940, p. 17.

C1831   TO AUTUMN [*later* TRIUMPH OF AUTUMN]. *The Cherwell*, 24 October 1940, Vol. 60, No. 1, p. 7.

Reprinted: *Shells by a Stream*, 1944; and *Poems of Many Years*, 1957.

C1832 [Review of] *Sons of Sindbad*, by Alan Villiers. *Book Society News*, November 1940, p. 13.

C1833 [Review of] *As I Remember Him*, by Hans Zinsser. *Book Society News*, November 1940, p. 14.

C1834 [Review of] *Memoirs of Madame Pilsudski. Book Society News*, November 1940, p. 15.

C1835 ECHOES FROM 1914–18 [*later* TO A NATURE-LOVER].
St. Martin's Review, November 1940, No. 597, p. 507.
Sub-title: 1. To a Nature-Lover.
Reprinted: *Poems 1930–1940*, [1941].

C1836 ZUDAUSQUES. *The Cherwell*, 7 November 1940, Vol. 60, No. 3, p. 37.

C1837 [Review of] *Sweet Thames Run Softly*, written and illustrated by Robert Gibbings. *Book Society Annual* (incorporating the *Book Society News*), December 1940, p. 13.

C1838 [Review of] *English Wits*, edited by Leonard Russell. *Book Society Annual* (incorporating the *Book Society News*), December 1940, pp. 14, 16.

C1839 [Review of] *Private and Official*, by Nourah Waterhouse; and *The Tide of Fortune*, by Stefan Zweig. *Book Society Annual* (incorporating the *Book Society News*), December 1940, p. 19.

C1840 TO TEISE, A STREAM IN KENT. *Book Society Annual* (incorporating the *Book Society News*), December 1940, pp. 34–35.
Reprinted (revised): *Shells by a Stream*, 1944; and *Poems of Many Years*, 1957.

C1841 AN ODE TO THE MEMORY OF S. T. COLERIDGE. *The Cherwell*, 5 December 1940, Vol. 60, No. 7, p. 108.

C1842 THE FINE NATURE. *TLS*, 7 December 1940, Christmas Books Section, p. iii.
Reprinted: *The Best Poems of 1941*, [1942] ; and *Shells by a Stream*, 1944.
Read by the author at the Poetry Reading in the Wigmore Hall, 14 September 1943, and published with the other poems read by Clifford Bax, T. S. Eliot and S. I. Hsiung in *Poets' Choice*, arranged by Dorothy Dudley Short on behalf of the Arts and Letters Sectional Committee of the National Council of Women of Great Britain, 1945.

1941

C1843 [Review of] *Modern Naval Strategy*, by Reginald Bacon and Francis E. McMurtrie. *Book Society News*, January 1941, pp. 10–12.

C1844   [Review of] *If I Laugh*, by Rupert Downing. *Book Society News*, January 1941, p. 14.

C1845   [Review of] *The Poetical Works of William Wordsworth: Poems Written in Youth, etc.*, edited by E. de Selincourt. *Oxford Magazine*, 23 January 1941, Vol. 59, No. 9, pp. 141-142. Signed E.B.

C1846   [Review of] *Spy and Counter-Spy*, by Emanuel Victor Voska and Will Irwin; and *Tinned Soldier*, by Alec Dixon. *Book Society News*, February 1941, pp. 12-13.

C1847   [Review of] *The Golden Treasury of Scottish Verse*, edited by Hugh MacDiarmid. *Book Society News*, February 1941, p. 14.

C1848   [Review of] *Poems*, by Dugald Sutherland MacColl. *Oxford Magazine*, 6 February 1941, Vol. 59, No. 11, p. 174. Signed E.B.

C1849   [Review of] *England's Hour*, by Vera Brittain. *Book Society News*, March 1941, pp. 14-16.

C1850   [Review of] *Truth on the Tragedy of France*, by Elie J. Bois. *Book Society News*, March 1941, p. 17.

C1851   [Review of] *A Bibliography of the Works of Edward Gibbon*, by J. E. Norton; and *The Library of Edward Gibbon*, with an introduction by Geoffrey Keynes. *Oxford Magazine*, 13 March 1941, Vol. 59, No. 16, pp. 255-256. Signed E.B.

C1852   [Review of] *Durham Company*, by Una Pope-Hennessy. *Book Society News*, April 1941, p. 10.

C1853   [Review of] *A Treasury of the World's Greatest Letters*, edited by M. Lincoln Schuster. *Book Society News*, April 1941, p. 12.

C1854   [Review of] *The Nine Days Wonder*, by John Masefield. *Book Society News*, April 1941, p. 13. Signed E.B.

C1855   [Review of] *The Wounded Don't Cry*, by Quentin Reynolds. *Book Society News*, April 1941, p. 13.

C1856   THOUGHTS OF THOMAS HARDY. *Kingdom Come*, Spring 1941, Vol. 2, No. 3, p. 83.

    Reprinted: *Shells by a Stream*, 1944; *Poems of Many Years*, 1957; and *The Midnight Skaters*, [1968].

C1857   [Review of] *The New Testament in Basic English*. *Book Society News*, May 1941, p. 8.

C1858   [Review of] *A Friend of France*, by Ian C. Black. *Book Society News*, May 1941, pp. 8-9. Signed E.B.

C1859   [Review of] *Italy Militant*, by Ernest Hambloch. *Book Society News*, May 1941, p. 9. Signed E.B.

C1860   [Review of] *Keats*, by Betty Askwith. *Book Society News*, May 1941, p. 10.

C1861 Two British Wars: A Comparison. *Britain To-day*, 2 May 1941, No. 52, pp. 8–11.

C1862 Thomas Barnes (1785–1841): Literary Diversions of an Editor. *TLS*, 10 May 1941, p. 226. Centre page article.

C1863 Two of the Coleridges. *Oxford Magazine*, 29 May 1941, Vol. 59, No. 21, pp. 333–334. Review of *Letters of Hartley Coleridge*, edited by Grace Evelyn Griggs; and *Coleridge Fille: A Biography of Sara Coleridge*, by Earl Leslie Griggs. Signed E.B.

C1864 [Review of] *Winged Words: Our Airmen Speak for Themselves. Book Society News*, June 1941, pp. 1–2.

C1865 [Review of] *Make Bright the Arrows*, by Edna St. Vincent Millay. *Book Society News*, June 1941, pp. 12–13.

C1866 [Review of] *New Year Letter*, by W. H. Auden. *Book Society News*, June 1941, p. 13. Signed E.B.

C1867 [Review of] *The Poetry of Matthew Arnold: A Commentary*, by C. B. Tinker and H. F. Lowry. *Oxford Magazine*, 19 June 1941, Vol. 59, No. 24, p. 382. Signed E. B.

C1868 [Review of] *Retrospective Adventures*, by Forrest Reid. *Book Society News*, July 1941, p. 9.

C1869 [Review of] *The Chestertons*, by Mrs. Cecil Chesterton. *Book Society News*, July 1941, p. 10.

C1870 [Review of] *Kabloona*, by Gontran de Poncins. *Book Society News*, July 1941, p. 12.

C1871 [Review of] *Hardy of Wessex: His Life and Literary Career*, by Carl J. Weber. *Review of English Studies*, July 1941, Vol. 17, No. 67, pp. 368–371. Also issued separately as an offprint (*see* A70). *See also* C3362.

C1872 [Review of] *Fishermen at War*, by Leo Walmsley. *Book Society News*, August 1941, pp. 6–7.

C1873 [Review of] *Democracy Marches*, by Julian Huxley; and *Remember Greece*, by Dilys Powell. *Book Society News*, August 1941, pp. 7–8.

C1874 [Review of] *Thus Spake Germany*, edited by W. W. Coole and M. F. Potter. *Book Society News*, August 1941, p. 8. Signed E.B.

C1875 Fred Edgcumbe. *TLS*, 2 August 1941, p. 373. Obituary. Unsigned.

C1876 [Review of] *Who Walk Alone*, by Percy Burgess. *Book Society News*, September 1941, p. 5.

C1877 [Review of] *War in the Air*, by David Garnett. *Book Society News*, September 1941, pp. 5–6.

C1878 [Review of] *Tudor Cornwall*, by A. L. Rowse. *Book Society News*, September 1941, p. 6.

C1879 A Seer Down the Street. *The Spectator*, 5 September 1941, p. 239. Review of *The Journals of George Sturt "George*

Bourne", *1890–1902*, edited with an introduction by Geoffrey Grigson. *See also* C1880.

C1880   Leaves from the Wheelwright's Shop: The Journals of George Sturt. *TLS*, 6 September 1941, p. 434. Review of *The Journals of George Sturt "George Bourne", 1890–1902*, edited with an introduction by Geoffrey Grigson. Unsigned. *See also* C1879.

C1881   A COUNTRY CHARACTER: HOMO UNIUS LIBRI. *TLS*, 6 September 1941, p. 434; illustrated by Bip Pares.

Reprinted: *Shells by a Stream*, 1944.

C1882   Philosopher at Home and Abroad, Arthur Young: 1741–1820, Traveller in Little Things and Great. *TLS*, 13 September 1941, p. 458. Unsigned.

C1883   [Review of] *Dawn Watch in China*, by Joy Homer. *Book Society News*, October 1941, p. 10.

C1884   [Review of] *Scum of the Earth*, by Arthur Koestler. *Book Society News*, October 1941, pp. 10–11.

C1885   [Review of] *Pack Clouds Away*, by Bernard Darwin. *Book Society News*, October 1941, p. 11. Signed E.B.

C1886   Rural Miscellany: Scenes and Characters. *TLS*, 25 October 1941, p. 532. Review of *Country Moods and Senses: A Non-Grammarian's Chap-Book*, by Edith Olivier. Unsigned.

C1887   ONE KIND OF ARTIST. *TLS*, 25 October 1941, p. 532.

Reprinted: *Shells by a Stream*, 1944.

C1888   Fred Edgcumbe (1885–1941). *C.L.S. Bulletin*, October 1941, No. 52, pp. [3–4]. Signed E.B. *See also* C1875.

C1889   [Review of] *Don't Think it Hasn't Been Fun*, by Quentin Reynolds. *Book Society News*, November 1941, p. 5.

C1890   [Review of] *The Life of Francis Drake*, by A. E. W. Mason. *Book Society News*, November 1941, pp. 6–7.

C1891   [Review of] *A House that was Loved*, by Katharine M. Kenyon. *Book Society News*, November 1941, pp. 7–8.

C1892   [Review of] *World of Birds*, by Eric Parker. *Oxford Magazine*, 6 November 1941, Vol. 60, No. 4, p. 62. Signed E.B.

C1893   [Review of] *Design for a Journey*, by M. D. Anderson. *Oxford Magazine*, 13 November 1941, Vol. 60, No. 5, pp. 77–78. Signed E.B.

C1894   [Review of] *Mr. Churchill: A Portrait*, by Philip Guedalla. *Book Society Annual* (incorporating the *Book Society News*), December 1941, p. 9.

C1895   [Review of] *Edward VII*, by Catherine Gavin; *Life Line*, by Charles Graves; and *Life's Little Oddities*, by Robert Lynd. *Book Society Annual* (incorporating the *Book Society News*), December 1941, pp. 13–14.

C1896   THE TWO BOOKS. *Book Society Annual* (incorporating the *Book Society News*), December 1941, p. 24.

Reprinted: separate edition, 1941; *Shells by a Stream*, 1944; and *Poems of Many Years*, 1957.

C1897 Oxford Poets. *Oxford Magazine*, 4 December 1941, Vol. 60, No. 8, pp. 117–118. [Review of] *The Buried Stream: Collected Poems, 1908 to 1940*, by Geoffrey Faber; and *Eight Oxford Poets*, selected by Michael Meyer and Sidney Keyes. Signed B.

1942

C1898 Leigh Hunt's Eldest Son. *Essays by Divers Hands*, 1942, New Series, Vol. 19, pp. 53–75. On Thornton Hunt. Read before the Royal Society of Literature on 29 October 1941. Also issued separately as an offprint (*see* A74).

C1899 Romantic Poetry and the Fine Arts. *Proceedings of the British Academy*, 1942, Vol. 28, pp. 101–118. Warton Lecture on English Poetry, read 4 March 1942. Also issued separately as an offprint (*see* A75).

C1900 [Review of] *Britain Against Napoleon*, by Carola Oman; *Glory Hill Farm*, by Clifton Reynolds; and *Housman, 1897–1936*, by Grant Richards. *Book Society News*, January 1942, pp. 7–8.

C1901 [Review of] *Ruins and Visions: Poems*, by Stephen Spender. *Book Society News*, February 1942, p. 11.

C1902 [Review of] *The Modern Short Story*, by H. E. Bates. *Book Society News*, February 1942, p. 12.

C1903 [Review of] *English Custom and Usage*, by Christina Hole. *Oxford Magazine*, 5 February 1942, Vol. 60, No. 11, p. 175. Signed E.B.

C1904 'The Wayward Somebody in All of Us'. *The Listener*, 19 February 1942, pp. 243–244. On 'The Scholar Gipsy' by Matthew Arnold. Title in contents: 'The Scholar Gipsy'. A talk broadcast on the Indian Service.

C1905 [Review of] *Australian Literature: A Descriptive and Bibliographical Survey*, by E. Morris Miller. *Oxford Magazine*, 19 February 1942, Vol. 60, No. 13, pp. 206–207. Signed E.B.

C1906 [Review of] *Report on France*, by Thomas Kernan. *Book Society News*, March 1942, pp. 8–9.

C1907 [Review of] *Catherine of Aragon*, by Garrett Mattingley; and *Walt Whitman*, by Hugh I'Anson Fausset. *Book Society News*, March 1942, p. 9.

C1908 On Pilgrimage in England: Voyages of Discovery. *TLS*, 28 March 1942, pp. 156, 161. Centre page article.

C1909 [Review of] *Collected Poems*, by Walter de la Mare. *Book Society News*, April 1942, p. 4.

C1910 [Review of] *Pictures in the Hallway*, by Sean O'Casey. *Book Society News*, April 1942, p. 7.

C1911 [Review of] *Volcanic Isle*, by Wilfrid Fleisher. *Book Society News*, April 1942, p. 8.

C1912 A Hartley Coleridge Windfall. *Oxford Magazine*, 30 April 1942, Vol. 60, No. 17, pp. 270-271. Review of *New Poems*, by Hartley Coleridge, edited by Earl Leslie Griggs. Signed B.

C1913 [Review of] *The Moon is Down*, by John Steinbeck. *Book Society News*, May 1942, p. 6.

C1914 [Review of] *Here's Richness*, by James Agate; and *In My Good Books*, by V. S. Pritchett. *Book Society News*, May 1942, p. 8.

C1915 [Review of] *Letters from Paris, 1870-1875*, edited by Robert Henrey. *Book Society News*, May 1942, p. 10.

C1916 SHELLS BY A STREAM. *Queen's Quarterly*, Summer 1942, Vol. 49, No. 2, p. 112.

Reprinted: *The Best Poems of 1942*, [1943]; and *Shells by a Stream*, 1944.

C1917 [Review of] *Phoenix*, by H. G. Wells. *Book Society News*, June 1942, p. 7.

C1918 [Review of] *The Death of the Moth*, by Virginia Woolf. *Book Society News*, June 1942, pp. 8-9.

C1919 [Review of] *Newspaper Days*, by H. L. Mencken. *Book Society News*, June 1942, p. 9.

C1920 [Review of] *The Poems of Lesbia Harford*. *Oxford Magazine*, 11 June 1942, Vol. 60, No. 23, p. 365. Signed E. B.

C1921 [Review of] *A Cornish Childhood*, by A. L. Rowse. *Book Society News*, July 1942, pp. 8-9.

C1922 [Review of] *H. R. L. Sheppard: Life and Letters*, by R. Ellis Roberts. *Book Society News*, July 1942, p. 9.

C1923 [Review of] *Auden and After*, by Francis Scarfe. *Book Society News*, July 1942, p. 10.

C1924 [Review of] *Murder for Pleasure*, by Howard Haycroft. *Book Society News*, July 1942, p. 10.

C1925 The Seeking Mind: Mr. H. J. Massingham's Pilgrimage. *TLS*, 20 June 1942, p. 310. Review of *Remembrance*, by H. J. Massingham. Unsigned.

C1926 THE BOY ON LEAVE. *TLS*, 18 July 1942, p. 356.

Reprinted: *Shells by a Stream*, 1944.

C1927 THE VICTOR. *The Observer*, 30 August 1942, p. 4.

Reprinted: *Shells by a Stream*, 1944; and *Poems of Many Years*, 1957.

C1928 [Review of] *War in the Sun*, by James Lansdale Hodson. *Book Society News*, September 1942, pp. 1-2.

C1929   [Review of] *The Unrelenting Struggle: War Speeches of Winston Churchill*, compiled by Charles Eade; *Spring Onions*, by Duncan McGuffie; and *Apple Acre*, by Adrian Bell (*see also* C3319). *Book Society News*, September 1942, pp. 8–9.

C1930   [Review of] *Sala*, by Ralph Strauss. *Book Society News*, September 1942, p. 10.

C1931   Good Words. *The Observer*, 6 September 1942, p. 3. Review of *A Word in Your Ear*, by Ivor Brown.

C1932   [Review of] *Retreat in the East*, by O. D. Gallagher. *Book Society News*, October 1942, pp. 6–7.

C1933   [Review of] *Brazil, Land of the Future*, by Stefan Zweig. *Book Society News*, October 1942, pp. 7–8.

C1934   [Review of] *Sword of Bone*, by Anthony Rhodes. *Book Society News*, November 1942, p. 8.

C1935   [Review of] *Country Ways*, edited by Esther Meynell. *Book Society News*, November 1942, p. 9.

C1936   [Review of] *Anglo-American Literary Relations*, by George Stuart Gordon. *Book Society News*, November 1942, pp. 10–11.

C1937   [Review of] *Palmyra of the North*, by Christopher Marsden. *Book Society News*, November 1942, p. 11.

C1938   OCTOBER COMES. *The Fortnightly*, November 1942, N.S. Vol. 152, p. 340.

Reprinted: *Shells by a Stream*, 1944.

C1939   Progress of Poesy. *The Spectator*, 6 November 1942, p. 436. Review of *The Weald of Youth*, by Siegfried Sassoon.

C1940   English Characters: The Tradition of Our People. *TLS*, 12 December 1942, p. 601. Review of *The English Countryman: A Study of the English Tradition*, by H. J. Massingham. Unsigned.

C1941   The Visionary Painters. *The Spectator*, 18 December 1942, pp. 580, 582. Review of *British Romantic Artists*, by John Piper.

C1942   [Review of] *Coming Down the Wye*, by Robert Gibbings. *Book Society Annual* (incorporating the *Book Society News*), Christmas 1942, p. 9.

C1943   [Review of] *The Years of Endurance*, by Arthur Bryant. *Book Society Annual* (incorporating the *Book Society News*), Christmas 1942, p. 10.

C1944   [Review of] *Crusader*, by Alexander Clifford; and *Recording Ruin*, by A. S. G. Butler. *Book Society Annual* (incorporating the *Book Society News*), Christmas 1942, p. 14.

C1945   Some New Poetry. *Book Society Annual* (incorporating the *Book Society News*), Christmas 1942, pp. 25–26.

Review of *Ode to France*, by Charles Morgan; *Little Gidding*, by T. S. Eliot; *The Night Watch for England*, by Edward Shanks; *Ode to the Sun*, by Laurence Whistler; *Victory for the Slain*, by Hugh Lofting; *Mother, What is Man*, by Stevie Smith; *Poetry in Wartime*, edited by M. J. Tambimuttu; and *Time Passes*, by Walter de la Mare.

C1946 Alan Porter. *TLS*, 26 December 1942, p. 636. Obituary. Unsigned.

1943

C1947 L.A. [*later* LASCELLES ABERCROMBIE]. *English*, 1943, Vol. 4, No. 24, p. 182.

Reprinted: *Shells by a Stream*, 1944; *Edmund Blunden: A Selection of His Poetry and Prose*, 1950; and *Poems of Many Years*, 1957.

C1948 [Review of] *Escape to Danger*, by François Nattages. *Book Society News*, January/February 1943, p. 6.

C1949 [Review of] *From Dusk till Dawn*, by A. G. Street. *Book Society News*, January/February 1943, p. 6.

C1950 [Review of] *Whereas I Was Blind*, by Sir Ian Fraser. *Book Society News*, January/February 1943, p. 8.

C1951 A DAY IN DECEMBER [*later* WHAT IS WINTER?]. *Poetry Review*, [January/February] 1943, Vol. 34, No. 1, p. 14.

Reprinted (revised): *Shells by a Stream*, 1944; and *The Midnight Skaters*, [1968].

C1952 [Review of] *The Romantics: An Anthology*, chosen by Geoffrey Grigson. *Oxford Magazine*, 4 February 1943, Vol. 61, No. 11, p. 171. Signed E.B.

C1953 AIRCRAFT. *The Observer*, 28 February 1943, p. 4.

Reprinted: *Shells by a Stream*, 1944.

C1954 [Review of] *The History of the Parson's Wife*, by Margaret H. Watt; and *Man and Boy*, by Sir Stephen Tallents. *Book Society News*, March 1943, pp. 9-10.

C1955 [Review of] *The Best Poems of 1942*, selected by Thomas Moult. *Book Society News*, March 1943, p. 10. Signed E.B.

C1956 [Review of] *The Land of the Great Image*, by Maurice Collis. *Book Society News*, March 1943, pp. 10-11.

C1957 [Review of] *The English People*, by D. W. Brogan. *Book Society News*, April 1943, p. 10.

C1958 [Review of] *Farming Adventure*, by J. Wentworth Day. *Book Society News*, April 1943, pp. 10-12.

C1959 [Review of] *India: An American View*, by Kate L. Mitchell. *Book Society News*, April 1943, p. 12.

C1960   [Review of] *A Witness Tree*, by Robert Frost; and *Twentieth Century Psalter*, by Richard Church. *Book Society News*, April 1943, p. 13.

C1961   A SONG [*later* THE WATERFALL]. *Queen's Quarterly*, Spring 1943, Vol. 50, No. 1, p. 36.

Reprinted: *The Best Poems of 1943*, [1944]; *Shells by a Stream*, 1944; and *Poems of Many Years*, 1957.

C1962   [Review of] *England is Here*, edited by W. Hanchant. *Book Society News*, May/June 1943, pp. 7–8.

C1963   [Review of] *Captain Smith and Company*, by Robert Henriques. *Book Society News*, May/June 1943, pp. 8–9.

C1964   British Craftsmanship. *TLS*, 6 May 1943, p. 117. Review of *British Craftsmen*, by T. Hennell. Unsigned.

C1965   Severn After Keats: Later Life of the Poet's Friend. *TLS*, 29 May 1943, p. 256. Review of *Against Oblivion: The Life of Joseph Severn*, by Sheila Birkenhead. Unsigned.

C1966   [Foreword to] *An English Library*. *National Book Council News Sheet*, June 1943, No. 165, p. [1].

Reprinted: *An English Library*, by F. Seymour Smith, August 1943.

C1967   OCTOGENARIAN. *The Observer*, 27 June 1943, p. 4.

Reprinted: *Shells by a Stream*, 1944.

C1968   [Review of] *Tattered Battlements: A Malta Diary*, by A Fighter Pilot. *Book Society News*, July 1943, p. 7.

C1969   [Review of] *Russia at War*, by Ilya Ehrenburg. *Book Society News*, July 1943, pp. 7–8.

C1970   [Review of] *Wind of Freedom*, by Compton Mackenzie. *Book Society News*, July 1943, p. 8.

C1971   [Review of] *The Triumphant Spirit: A Study of Depression*, by E. Graham Howe. *Book Society News*, July 1943, p. 9.

C1972   [Review of] *Here Comes Tomorrow*, by John Mansbridge. *The Seafarer*, July/August/September 1943, p. 69.

C1973   [Review of] *Letters of George Gordon*. *Book Society News*, August 1943, p. 11.

C1974   Behind the Poem: Students or Voluptuaries? *TLS*, 25 September 1943, pp. 462, 466. Centre page article.

C1975   [Review of] *William Nicholson*, by Marguerite Steen. *Book Society News*, September/October 1943, p. 8.

C1976   [Review of] *Born Under Saturn: A Biography of William Hazlitt*, by Catherine Macdonald Maclean. *Book Society News*, September/October 1943, pp. 10–11. *See also* C2001.

C1977   [Review of] *Love*, by Walter de la Mare. *Book Society News*, September/October 1943, pp. 11–12.

439

C1978 [Review of] *Norfolk Life*, by Lilias Rider Haggard and Henry Williamson. *Book Society News*, September/October 1943, p. 12. Signed E.B. *See also* C1980.

C1979 [Review of] *Charlotte Mary Yonge*, by Gina Battiscombe. *Book Society News*, September/October 1943, pp. 12–13.

C1980 Norfolk Scene: Record of a Rural Pen. *TLS*, 18 September 1943, p. 453. Review of *Norfolk Life*, by Lilias Rider Haggard and Henry Williamson. Unsigned. *See also* C1978.

C1981 A College Society in 1943. *Britain To-day*, October 1943, No. 90, pp. 20–23.

C1982 [Review of] *The Writings of Arthur Hallam*, now first collected and edited by T. H. Vail Motter. *Review of English Studies*, October 1943, Vol. 19, No. 76, pp. 437–438.

C1983 THE ORNAMENTAL WATER. *TLS*, 2 October 1943, p. 478.

Reprinted: *Shells by a Stream*, 1944.

C1984 Out of Town: Country Scene Round London. *TLS*, 9 October 1943, p. 488. Review of *The Home Counties: Middlesex, Surrey, Kent, Hertfordshire and Essex*, by S. P. B. Mais. Unsigned.

C1985 AMONG THE ROSES [*later* ONE AMONG THE ROSES]. *The Observer*, 10 October 1943, p. 3.

Reprinted: *Shells by a Stream*, 1944; and *Poems of Many Years*, 1957. *See also* Ed1.

C1986 Visionary Gleams: The Laureate on the Child's Wisdom. *TLS*, 23 October 1943, p. 512. Review of *Wonderings (Between One and Six Years)*, by John Masefield. Unsigned.

C1987 [Review of] *South Lodge*, by Douglas Goldring. *Book Society News*, November 1943, pp. 8–9.

C1988 [Review of] *More Diversions*, by C. H. Wilkinson. *Book Society News*, November 1943, p. 10.

C1989 [Review of] *Autobiography*, by Margiad Evans. *Book Society News*, November 1943, p. 11.

C1990 Rhythm of Earth: Rural Arts and Crafts. *TLS*, 6 November 1943, p. 536. Review of *Men of Earth*, by H.J. Massingham. Unsigned.

C1991 Editor-Statesman: Dedication of Thomas Barnes, Literature and Politics. *TLS*, 20 November 1943, p. 558. Review of *Thomas Barnes of The Times*, by Derek Hudson, edited by Harold Child.Unsigned. *See also* C2020, 2031.

C1992 Amateur and Idler: Observers of Rural Life. *TLS*, 20 November 1943, p. 562. Review of *Rural Amateur*, by Clifford Hornby; and *The Idle Countryman*, by "BB". Unsigned.

C1993 Love of Life. *The Observer*, 21 November 1943, p. 3. Review of *Double Lives: An Autobiography*, by William Plomer.

C1994 [Review of] *Journey Among Warriors*, by Eve Curie. *Book Society Annual* (incorporating the *Book Society News*), December 1943, pp. 10–11.

C1995 [Review of] *The Eagle and the Dove: A Study in Contrasts*, by V. Sackville West. *Book Society Annual* (incorporating the *Book Society News*), December 1943, p. 11.

C1996 [Review of] *One Eye on the Clock*, by Geoffrey Willans; and *The Little Ships*, by Gordon Holman. *Book Society Annual* (incorporating the *Book Society News*), December 1943, p. 12.

C1997 [Review of] *Darkness over Germany*, by E. Amy Buller. *Book Society Annual* (incorporating the *Book Society News*), December 1943, p. 13.

C1998 MAN GROWN SAFE: ON RE-READING A FAVOURITE PASSAGE IN EDWARD GIBBON [*later* GIBBON: IN THE MARGIN]. *Book Society Annual* (incorporating the *Book Society News*), December 1943, p. 29.

Reprinted: *Shells by a Stream*, 1944; and *Poems of Many Years*, 1957.

C1999 GOD'S TIME. *TLS*, 25 December 1943, p. 618.

Reprinted: *Shells by a Stream*, 1944; and *Poems of Many Years*, 1957.

C2000 The Living Landscape. *TLS*, 25 December 1943, p. 619. Leader on *Landmarks: A Book of Topographical Verse for England and Wales*, chosen by G. Rostrevor Hamilton and John Arlott. Unsigned.

1944

C2001 A Ghost of Soho. *Britain To-day*, January 1944, No. 93, pp. 25–26. Review of *Born Under Saturn: A Biography of William Hazlitt*, by Catherine Macdonald Maclean. *See also* C1976.

C2002 An Elian's Petition. *C.L.S. Bulletin*, January 1944, No. 61, p. [1]. On new editions of Lamb's essays and poems.

C2003 [Review of] *Pioneers! O Pioneers!* by Hilary St George Saunders. *Book Society News*, January/February 1944, p. 4.

C2004 [Review of] *Home Front*, by James Lansdale Hodson. *Book Society News*, January/February 1944, p. 8.

C2005 Thackeray at his Best. *The Listener*, 20 January 1944, pp. 76–77. A talk broadcast in the Eastern Service.

C2006　Gardens as Pictures: Horace Walpole's Inventions. *TLS*, 22 January 1944, p. 46. Review of *Horace Walpole: Gardenist* ... by Isabel Wakelin Urban Chase. Unsigned.

C2007　AT A CATHEDRAL SERVICE. *TLS*, 29 January 1944, p. 54.

Reprinted: *Shells by a Stream*, 1944; and *Poems of Many Years*, 1957.

C2008　The Dream Inn. *TLS*, 19 February 1944, p. 91. Second leader on *English Inns*, by Thomas Burke. Unsigned. *See also* letter from Enid Starkie in the issue of 26 February, p. 103.

C2009　[Review of] *The Way of a Countryman*, by Sir William Beach-Thomas. *Book Society News*, March 1944, p. 7. *See also* C2022.

C2010　[Review of] *We Fought Them in Gunboats*, by Robert Peverell Hichens. *Book Society News*, March 1944, p. 8.

C2011　[Review of] *Fine Building*, by Maxwell Fry. *Book Society News*, March 1944, p. 9.

C2012　Man and Machine: The Craftsman's Future. *TLS*, 4 March 1944, p. 117. Review of *British Handicrafts*, by Charles Marriott. Unsigned.

C2013　Fairfax's Tasso. *TLS*, 11 March 1944, p. 127. Leader on the quatercentenary of Tasso's birth. Unsigned.

C2014　TO A PLANNER. *TLS*, 25 March 1944, p. 146.

Reprinted: *After the Bombing*, 1949.

C2015　[Review of] *On Living in a Revolution*, by Julian Huxley. *Book Society News*, April 1944, pp. 7-8.

C2016　[Review of] *Gilbert K. Chesterton*, by Maisie Ward. *Book Society News*, April 1944, p. 8.

C2017　[Review of] *William the Silent*, by C. V. Wedgwood. *Book Society News*, April 1944, p. 9.

C2018　[Review of] *Collected Poems and Verses*, by Walter de la Mare. *Book Society News*, April 1944, p. 11.

C2019　Poets & Anthologists. *Book Society News*, April 1944, pp. 12-13. Review of *Plants and Glow-Worms*, by Edith Sitwell; *Introducing Modern Poetry*, edited by W. G. Bebbington; *Come In*, by Robert Frost; *Lorca*, by Arturo Barea; *Poems Chiefly Cornish*, by A. L. Rowse; *Ten Summers*, by John Pudney; *Poems, 1937-1942*, by David Gascoyne; *Chosen Poems*, by Frederic Prokosch; *The Cruel Solstice*, by Sidney Keyes (*see also* C2021); and *The Burning of the Leaves*, by Laurence Binyon.

C2020　The Fourth Estate. *Britain To-day*, April 1944, No. 96, p. 26. Review of *Thomas Barnes of The Times*, by Derek Hudson. *See also* C1991, 2031.

442

C2021 A Young Poet. *The Fortnightly*, April 1944, N.S. Vol. 155, No. 928, pp. 257-260. Review of *The Cruel Solstice*, by Sidney Keyes. *See also* C2019.

C2022 The Prevailing Paradise: Sir William Beach Thomas's Explorations. *TLS*, 1 April 1944, p. 157. Review of *The Way of a Countryman*, by Sir William Beach Thomas. Unsigned. *See also* C2009.

C2023 The Village To-Day. *TLS*, 15 April 1944, p. 190. Review of *Your Village and Mine*, by C. H. Gardiner. Unsigned.

C2024 Friends of Shelley: T. Jefferson Hogg's Claim to Fame, Light from a Long-Hidden Letter. *TLS*, 22 April 1944, p. 198. Review of *The Athenians: Being Correspondence between Thomas Jefferson Hogg and his Friends* . . . edited by Walter Sidney Scott. Unsigned.

C2025 Recovered Treasure. *TLS*, 22 April 1944, p. 199. Leader on a letter of Shelley's. Unsigned.

C2026 Blake's Revolutionary World. *TLS*, 22 April 1944, p. 200. Review of *A Man Without a Mask: William Blake, 1757–1827*, by J. Bronowski. Unsigned.

C2027 "Old Students" at War. *Britain To-day*, May 1944, No. 97, pp. 22-25.

C2028 [Review of] *Sing High! Sing Low!* by Osbert Sitwell. *Book Society News*, May/June 1944, p. 8.

C2029 [Review of] *I Married a Russian*, edited by Lucie Street. *Book Society News*, May/June 1944, p. 9.

C2030 [Review of] *Courts and Cabinets*, by G. P. Gooch; and *The Poisoned Crown*, by Hugh Kingsmill. *Book Society News*, May/June 1944, pp. 9-10.

C2031 [Review of] *Thomas Barnes of The Times*, by Derek Hudson, with selections from his critical essays, edited by Harold Child. *Oxford Magazine*, 11 May 1944, Vol. 62, No. 19, p. 241. Signed E. B. *See also* C1991, 2020.

C2032 [Review of] *English Gardens*, by Harry Roberts. *TLS*, 27 May 1944, p. 360. Unsigned.

C2033 A Religion in Action: Thoughts from a Garden Plot. *TLS*, 10 June 1944, p. 285. Review of *This Plot of Earth: A Gardiner's Chronicle*, by H. J. Massingham. Unsigned.

C2034 The English Portrait: From the Pages of Our Poets. *TLS*, 17 June 1944, p. 298. Review of *England: An Anthology*, with an introduction by Harold Nicolson. Unsigned.

C2035 [Review of] *Jefferies' Countryside: Nature Essays*, by Richard Jefferies, edited with an introduction and notes by Samuel J. Looker. *TLS*, 17 June 1944, p. 299. Unsigned.

C2036 THE BLUEPRINT. *TLS*, 24 June 1944, p. 308.

Reprinted: *After the Bombing*, 1949; and *Poems of Many Years*, 1957.

C2037   [Review of] *Red Letter Nights*, by James Agate. *Book Society News*, July 1944, p. 7.

C2038   [Review of] *Leningrad*, by Alexander Werth. *Book Society News*, July 1944, p. 9.

C2039   "S.E.W.": [Mr. S. E. Winbolt: Ward II, 1876–87, Master 1892–1926: died at Basingstoke in March 1944]. *The Blue*, June/July 1944, Vol. 71, No. 3, pp. 71–72. Obituary.

C2040   William Barnes. *TLS*, 1 July 1944, p. 319. Second leader. Unsigned.

C2041   HOMES AND HAUNTS. *TLS*, 22 July 1944, p. 356.
        Reprinted: *When All is Done*, by Alison Uttley, 1945; *After the Bombing*, 1949; and *Poems of Many Years*, 1957.

C2042   [Review of] *Pipeline to Battle*, by Peter W. Rainier. *Book Society News*, August 1944, p. 8.

C2043   [Review of] *Milton, Man and Thinker*, by Denis Saurat. *Book Society News*, August 1944, p. 8. Signed E.B.

C2044   New and Recent Poetry. *Book Society News*, August 1944, pp. 18–19. Review of *The Best Poems of 1943*, edited by Thomas Moult; *Modern Welsh Poetry*, edited by Keidrych Rhys; *Green Song*, by Edith Sitwell; *Such Liberty*, by John Buxton; *Five Rivers*, by Norman Nicholson; *Morning Songs*, by Eiluned Lewis; and *The Martyr*, by D. Page.

C2045   British Landscape: Poetry of River, Hill and Forest. *TLS*, 26 August 1944, p. 409. Review of *English, Scottish and Welsh Landscape, 1700–c.1860*, chosen by John Betjeman and Geoffrey Taylor. Unsigned.

C2046   [Review of] *Things Past*, by Michael Sadleir. *Book Society News*, September/October 1944, pp. 9–10.

C2047   [Review of] *The House in the Park*, by F. D. Ommanney. *Book Society News*, September/October 1944, p. 10. Signed E.B. *See also* C2054.

C2048   [Review of] *The American Problem*, by D. W. Brogan. *Book Society News*, September/October 1944, p. 11.

C2049   [Review of] *Unfinished Business*, by Stephen Bonsal. *Book Society News*, September/October 1944, pp. 11–12. Signed E.B.

C2050   [Review of] *Home from the Sea*, by Godfrey Winn. *Book Society News*, September/October 1944, p. 12.

C2051   What Next? *The Spectator*, 1 September 1944, p. 204. Review of *A Letter to My Son*, by Osbert Sitwell.

C2052   A Particular Dwelling. *TLS*, 2 September 1944, p. 427. Second leader on Thomas Hardy and Max Gate. Unsigned.

C2053   Francis Quarles: The Emblems of Mortality. *TLS*, 9 September 1944, p. 435. On the tercentenary of his death. Unsigned.

444

C2054 A House in Richmond Park: Childhood's Memories. *TLS*, 16 September 1944, p. 453. Review of *The House in the Park*, by F. D. Ommanney. Unsigned. *See also* C2047.

C2055 Village Secrets: Time Past in Norfolk. *TLS*, 21 October 1944, p. 512. Review of *Men of Branber*, by Edward G. Thompson. Unsigned.

C2056 SOUTH-EAST ENGLAND IN 1944 [*later* "SOUTHERN ENGLAND" IN 1944]. *TLS*, 28 October 1944, p. 525.

   Reprinted: Eastes & Loud Ltd. *Centenary Souvenir*, [1945]; and *After the Bombing*, 1949.

C2057 Shelley Secrets: Harriet, Mary and T. J. Hogg. *TLS*, 28 October 1944, p. 527. Review of *Harriet and Mary: Being the Relations Between Percy Bysshe Shelley, Harriet Shelley, Mary Shelley and Thomas Jefferson Hogg*, edited by Walter Sidney Scott. Unsigned.

C2058 The Man Wordsworth. *Britain To-day*, October 1944, No. 102, p. 25. Review of *A Study of Wordsworth*, by J. C. Smith.

C2059 [Review of] *Homage to Southey: Poems*, chosen and written by Harry Moreton Southey Edmonds, with an introduction by Henry Newnham. *TLS*, 28 October 1944, p. 528. Unsigned.

C2060 [Review of] *Elizabeth and Leicester*, by Milton Waldman. *Book Society News*, November 1944, pp. 8–9.

C2061 [Review of] *Part-time Countryman*, by Gerald Millar. *Book Society News*, November 1944, p. 9.

C2062 [Review of] *Valley of Graneen*, by Sean Dorman. *Book Society News*, November 1944, p. 11.

C2063 Brave Old World: A Novelist Reports on His Village. *TLS*, 4 November 1944, p. 529. Review of *Autumn Fields*, by Michael Home. Unsigned.

C2064 Through War-Time Britain. *TLS*, 25 November 1944, p. 572. Review of *A Literary Journey Through War-Time Britain*, by A. C. Ward. Unsigned.

C2065 [Review of] *Brenva*, by T. Graham Brown. *Book Society Annual*, Christmas 1944, pp. 10–11.

C2066 [Review of] *The Years of Victory*, by Arthur Bryant; *Remembering My Good Friends*, by Mary Agnes Hamilton; *Per Ardua*, by Hilary St George Saunders; and *Germany Between Two Wars*, by Lindley Fraser. *Book Society Annual*, Christmas 1944, pp. 13–15.

C2067 Some Recent Poetry. *Book Society Annual*, Christmas 1944, pp. 17–18. Review of *The Region of the Summer Stars*, by Charles Williams; *A World Within a War*, by Herbert Read; *Springboard*, by Louis MacNiece; *The Millstream*, by Ralph Lawrence; *Of Period and Place*, by John Arlott; and *The Island*, by Francis Brett Young.

445

C2068 ON READING A MAGAZINE EDITED BY OSCAR WILDE. *Horizon*, December 1944, Vol. 10, No. 60, pp. 370-371.

Reprinted: *After the Bombing*, 1949; and *Poems of Many Years*, 1957.

C2069 SERENA. *Horizon*, December 1944, Vol. 10, No. 60, p. 371.

Reprinted: *After the Bombing*, 1949; and *Poems of Many Years*, 1957.

C2070 Oxford Chinoiserie. *TLS*, 23 December 1944, p. 616. Review of *The Silent Traveller in Oxford*, by Chiang Yee. Unsigned.

1945

C2071 [Review of] *Middle East 1940-1942*, by Philip Guedalla. *Book Society News*, January/February 1945, p. 6.

C2072 [Review of] *Stand By to Beach!* by Gordon Holman. *Book Society News*, January/February 1945, pp. 6-7. Signed E.B.

C2073 [Review of] *A Prospect of Flowers*, by Andrew Young. *Book Society News*, January/February 1945, p. 7. *See also* C2088.

C2074 [Review of] *The Naval Heritage*, by David Mathew. *Book Society News*, January/February 1945, pp. 8-9.

C2075 The Idol of Completeness. *TLS*, 6 January 1945, p. 7. Second leader on *The Letters of Mary W. Shelley*, collected and edited by Frederick L. Jones. Unsigned. *See also* C2076.

C2076 Mary Shelley: The Years After the Tragedy. *TLS*, 6 January 1945, p. 8. Review of *The Letters of Mary W. Shelley*, collected and edited by Frederick L. Jones. Unsigned. *See also* C2075.

C2077 Goethe's Poems: New Commentary. *TLS*, 13 January 1945, p. 16. Review of *Notes to Goethe's Poems*, Vol. 1 (1749-1766), by James Boyd. Unsigned.

C2078 Annotation's Aid. *TLS*, 13 January 1945, p. 19. Second leader. Unsigned.

C2079 Scientist Squire. *TLS*, 20 January 1945, p. 33. Review of *Memories of Charles Davies Sherborn*, by J. R. Norman. Unsigned.

C2080 The Poet of Felicity. *Sunday Times*, 28 January 1945, p. 3. Review of *Thomas Traherne*, by Gladys I. Wade.

C2081 The English Scene. *Britain To-day*, February 1945, No. 106, pp. 11-14.

C2082 Farming Memoirs. *TLS*, 3 February 1945, p. 56. Review of *Farming Memoirs of a West Country Yeoman*, by S. G. Kendall.

C2083   The Mind's Eye. *TLS*, 24 February 1945, p. 92. Review of *Visionary Poems and Passages:, or the Poet's Eye*, chosen by Geoffrey Grigson. Unsigned.

C2084   [Review of] *Left Hand Right Hand!*, by Osbert Sitwell. *Book Society News*, March 1945, p. 4.

C2085   [Review of] *Southey*, by Jack Simmons. *Book Society News*, March 1945, pp. 8-9.

C2086   The Art of Bridges. *Britain To-day*, March 1945, No. 107, pp. 41-42. Review of *Robert Bridges, 1844-1930*, by Edward Thompson.

C2087   New Judgments. *TLS*, 3 March 1945, p. 103. Leader on Lord David Cecil's address to the Charles Lamb Society. Unsigned.

C2088   Led by Persephone. *TLS*, 3 March 1945, p. 105. Review of *A Prospect of Flowers*, by Andrew Young. Unsigned. *See also* C2073.

C2089   Is this the Mighty Ocean? *TLS*, 10 March 1945, p. 115. Leader on masterpieces of the sea. Unsigned.

C2090   On Sea and Shore. *TLS*, 10 March 1945, p. 116. Review of *Sea Poems*, chosen by Myfanwy Piper. Unsigned.

C2091   The Region of Fancy. *Sunday Times*, 11 March 1945, p. 3. Review of *Collected Poems of Sylvia Lynd*.

C2092   Rural Essays. *TLS*, 24 March 1945, p. 141. Review of *Green Tide*, by Richard Church. Unsigned.

C2093   Country Verses. *TLS*, 31 March 1945, p. 152. Review of *The Poems of a Countryman*, by Sir William Beach Thomas. Unsigned.

C2094   [Review of] *The Yogi and the Commissar*, by Arthur Koestler. *Book Society News*, April 1945, pp. 9-10.

C2095   [Review of] *Miles from Anywhere*, by C. Henry Warren; and *Four Years' Harvest*, by Frances Donaldson (*see also* C2096). *Book Society News*, April 1945, pp. 10-11.

C2096   In East Anglia. *TLS*, 7 April 1945, p. 166. Review of *Miles from Anywhere*, by C. Henry Warren. Unsigned. *See also* C2095.

C2097   The Scholar-Poet. *TLS*, 14 April 1945, p. 177. Review of *Alfred Williams: His Life and Work*, by Leonard Clark. Unsigned. *See also* C2107.

C2098   Young Visions and Reality. *TLS*, 14 April 1945, p. 177. Review of *The Sun in the Sands*, by Henry Williamson. Unsigned.

C2099   The Honest Soldier. *Britain To-day*, May 1945, No. 109, pp. 38-39. Review of *The Anatomy of Courage*, by Lord Moran.

C2100   KIRKE WHITE AT WILFORD. *New English Review*, May 1945, Vol. 11, No. 1, p. 58. Above title: Byroniana, I.

Reprinted: *After the Bombing*, 1949; and *Poems of Many Years*, 1957.

C2101   NEWSTEAD ABBEY [*later* NEWSTEAD]. *New English Review*, May 1945, Vol. 11, No. 1, pp. 58-59. Above title: Byroniana, II.

Reprinted: *After the Bombing*, 1949; and *Poems of Many Years*, 1957.

C2102   The Liberties of T. J. Hogg. *TLS*, 5 May 1945, p. 212. Review of *Shelley at Oxford: the Early Correspondence of P. B. Shelley with his Friend T. J. Hogg* . . . edited by Walter Sidney Scott. Unsigned.

C2103   [Review of] *Vintage Verse: An Anthology of Poetry in English*, compiled with commentary by Clifford Bax. *TLS*, 12 May 1945, p. 227. Unsigned.

C2104   The Cowden Clarkes. *Time and Tide*, 26 May 1945, pp. 436-437. On Mary and Charles Cowden Clarke.

Reprinted: *Edmund Blunden: A Selection of His Poetry and Prose*, 1950.

C2105   [Review of] *Maquis*, by George Millar. *Book Society News*, May/June 1945, pp. 4-5.

C2106   [Review of] *Chungking Diary*, by Robert Payne. *Book Society News*, May/June 1945, p. 11.

C2107   [Review of] *Alfred Williams: His Life and Work*, by Leonard Clark. *Book Society News*, May/June 1945, p. 11. Signed E.B. *See also* C2097.

C2108   ON CHARLES LAMB'S BIRTHDAY 1945 [*later* ON CHAS LAMB'S . . .]. *Decachord*, May/June 1945, Vol. 22, No. 111, p. 28. Dedication: To Ernest G. Crowsley Esq., Honorary Secretary and Founder of the Charles Lamb Society.

Reprinted: *English*, Hiroshima, April 1949; and *Eastward* [1950].

C2109   The Symbol of the Moon-Lover. *TLS*, 9 June 1945, p. 272. Review of *Keats and the Victorians: A Study of his Influence and Rise to Fame, 1821-1895*, by George H. Ford; and *Endymion in England: The Literary History of a Greek Myth*, by Edward S. Lecomte. Unsigned.

C2110   Leading Lights. *The Observer*, 10 June 1945, p. 3. Review of *English Public Schools*, by Rex Warner.

C2111   Classical Background. *TLS*, 23 June 1945, p. 295. Leader on *English in the Universities*, by James Sutherland. Unsigned.

C2112   Rural Affairs. *TLS*, 23 June 1945, p. 296. Review of *Jesse and His Friends*, by Fred Kitchen. Unsigned.

C2113   [Review of] *Modern Exploration*, by F. Kingdon Ward. *Book Society News*, July 1945, p. 8.

C2114   [Review of] *Wind Aloft, Wind Alow*, translated from the French of Marin-Marie. *Book Society News*, July 1945, pp. 9–10.

C2115   Is it Still Our National Game? a poet reconsiders cricket's place in the English scene. *Strand Magazine*, July 1945, Vol. 109, No. 655, pp. 48–51.
         Reprinted: *Edmund Blunden: A Selection of His Poetry and Prose*, 1950.

C2116   Horace Lends His Shield. *TLS*, 7 July 1945, p. 319. Leader on Lawrence Durrell's 'On First Looking into the 'Loeb' Horace'. Unsigned.

C2117   Literary Researches. *TLS*, 7 July 1945, p. 320. Review of *Mark Akenside: A Biographical and Critical Study*, by Charles Theodore Houpt; *More Essays on Greek Romances*, by Elizabeth Hazelton Haight; and *A Comparison Between the Two Stages: A Late Restoration Book of the Theatre*, edited by Staring B. Wells. Unsigned.

C2118   A Cairo Anthology. *TLS*, 7 July 1945, p. 320. Review of *Personal Landscape*, edited by Lawrence Durrell, Bernard Spencer, and Robin Fedden. Unsigned.

C2119   A Translator of Horace. *TLS*, 7 July 1945, p. 320. Review of *Twenty-Five Odes of Horace*, P.T. 15, *More Odes of Horace*, P.T. 20, rendered into English by J. S. Blake-Reed. Unsigned.

C2120   The Signature Tune. *TLS*, 14 July 1945, p. 331. Leading article on Charles Reade. Unsigned. *See also* letters in the issues of 28 July, p. 355 by John Wilson Baird; 4 August, p. 367 by E. H. Holthouse; and 25 August, p. 403 by J. H. Douglas Webster.

C2121   Poetry with History. *TLS*, 14 July 1945, p. 332. Review of *Poems of Our Time, 1900–1942*, chosen by Richard Church and M. M. Bozman. Unsigned.

C2122   The Embassy of Literature. *TLS*, 21 July 1945, p. 343. Leader on the tenth anniversary of the British Council. Unsigned.

C2123   English Literature in Brief. *TLS*, 21 July 1945, p. 344. Review of *English Literature*, by B. Ifor Evans. Unsigned.

C2124   Thoughts on Shelley. *TLS*, 21 July 1945, p. 344. Review of *Shelley and the Romantic Revolution*, by F. A. Lea. Unsigned.

C2125   The Master Journalists. *TLS*, 21 July 1945, p. 345. Review of *British Journalists and Newspapers*, by Derek Hudson. Unsigned.

C2126 Science into Aesthetics. *TLS*, 28 July 1945, p. 355. Leading article. Unsigned.

C2127 [Review of] *Imperial Commonwealth*, by Lord Elton. *Book Society News*, August 1945, p. 9.

C2128 [Review of] *Rudyard Kipling*, by Hilton Brown. *Book Society News*, August 1945, p. 10.

C2129 [Review of] *Bookman's Holiday: A Recreation for Booklovers*, by Holbrook Jackson. *Book Society News*, August 1945, p. 11. *See also* C2134, 2140.

C2130 [Review of] *Farming and Gardening for Health or Disease*, by Sir Albert Howard. *Book Society News*, August 1945, pp. 11-12.

C2131 Some New Poetry. *Book Society News*, August 1945, pp. 12-13. Review of *Vintage Verse*, by Clifford Bax; *Poetry London X*, edited by Tambimuttu; *Selected Poems and Epigrams*, by G. Rostrevor Hamilton; *The Dorking Thigh*, by William Plomer; *For the Time Being*, by W. H. Auden; *The Sphere of Glass and Other Poems*, by John Lehmann; *The Black Seasons*, by Henry Treece; *Poems*, by Harry Brown; and *Tonypandy*, by Idris Davies.

C2132 Blackbird Study. *TLS*, 4 August 1945, p. 368. Review of *The Blackbird: A Contribution to the Study of a Single Avian Species*, by A. F. C. Hillstead. Unsigned.

C2133 [Review of] *The Durham University Journal*, Vol. 38, No. 3, June 1945. *TLS*, 4 August 1945, p. 370. Unsigned.

C2134 Anatomy of Authorship. *Sunday Times*, 5 August 1945, p. 3. Review of *Bookman's Holiday: A Recreation for Booklovers*, designed by Holbrook Jackson. *See also* C2129, 2140.

C2135 Poets in the Storm: Sidney Keyes and Alun Lewis. *TLS*, 11 August 1945, p. 378. Review of *The Collected Poems of Sidney Keyes*, edited with a memoir and notes by Michael Meyer; and *Ha! Ha! Among the Trumpets: Poems in Transit*, by Alun Lewis. Unsigned.

Reprinted: *Saturday Mornings*, 1949.

C2136 The Man of Feeling. *TLS*, 11 August 1945, p. 379. Leader on *The Man of Feeling*, by Henry Mackenzie. Unsigned. *See also* C758.

C2137 Sewell of Radley. *TLS*, 18 August 1945, p. 392. Letter signed E.B. On the review of *A Forgotten Genius*, by Lionel James in the issue of 28 July, p. 354.

C2138 [Review of] *The Review of English Studies*, Vol. 21, No. 83, July 1945. *TLS*, 18 August 1945, p. 394. Unsigned.

C2139 Lectures on Ovid. *TLS*, 25 August 1945, p. 400. Review of *Ovid: A Poet Between Two Worlds*, by Hermann Fränkel. Unsigned.

C2140　Good Company. *TLS*, 25 August 1945, p. 403. Leader on *Bookman's Holiday: A Recreation for Booklovers*, by Holbrook Jackson. Unsigned. *See also* C2129, 2134.

C2141　Portraits in Prose. *Britain To-day*, September 1945, No. 113, p. 41. Review of *Four Portraits:Studies of the Eighteenth Century*, by Peter Quennell.

C2142　[Review of] *The Turn of the Tide*, by H. M. Tomlinson. *Book Society News*, September/October 1945, pp. 9–10. *See also* C2154.

C2143　[Review of] *Tales of a Devon Village*, by Henry Williamson. *Book Society News*, September/October 1945, p. 10.

C2144　[Review of] *Prospero's Cell*, by Lawrence Durrell. *Book Society News*, September/October 1945, p. 11. Signed E.B.

C2145　Poet-Journalist: The World Review of "Don Juan". *TLS*, 1 September 1945, p. 414. Review of *Byron's Don Juan: A Critical Study*, by Elizabeth French Boyd. Unsigned. *See also* letter by L. B. Namier in the issue of 14 September, p. 439.

C2146　Memorials and Forgettings. *TLS*, 1 September 1945, p. 415. Leading article. Unsigned.

Reprinted: *Edmund Blunden: A Selection of His Poetry and Prose*, 1950.

C2147　A New Zealand Essayist. *TLS*, 8 September 1945, p. 428. Review of *Timeless World: A Collection of Essays*, by M. H. Holcroft. Unsigned.

C2148　[Review of] *New Lyrical Ballads*, edited by Maurice Carpenter, Jack Lindsay, and Honor Arundel. *TLS*, 8 September 1945, p. 432. Unsigned.

C2149　Horatians. *Time and Tide*, 15 September 1945, pp. 774, 776. Review of *Horace and His Lyric Poetry*, by L. P. Wilkinson; and *Springs of Hellas and Other Essays*, by T. R. Glover.

C2150　A Milton Tercentenary. *TLS*, 22 September 1945, p. 451. Leader on *Poems of Mr. John Milton, both English and Latin, compos'd at several times*. Unsigned.

C2151　The Japanese Emperor. *TLS*, 29 September 1945, p. 459. Review of *The Son of Heaven: The Problem of the Mikado*, by Willard Price. Unsigned.

C2152　Astro-dramatic. *TLS*, 29 September 1945, p. 464. Review of *The Humors and Shakespeare's Characters*, by John W. Draper. Unsigned.

C2153　Hexapoda. *TLS*, 29 September 1945, p. 466. Review of *Insect Life in Britain*, by Geoffrey Taylor. Unsigned.

451

C2154 The Greater Tide. *Sunday Times*, 30 September 1945, p. 3. Review of *The Turn of the Tide*, by H. M. Tomlinson. *See also* C2142.

C2155 THE IVY BUSH [*later* THE IVY BUSH IN AUTUMN]. *Orion*, Autumn 1945, Vol. 2, p. 17.
Reprinted (revised): *After the Bombing*, 1949.

C2156 Autumn in Verse. *Strand Magazine*, October 1945, Vol. 110, No. 658, pp. 49–50. Above title: Autumn Panorama.

C2157 Beyond the Moment. *TLS*, 6 October 1945, p. 475. Leader on *The Coat of Many Colours*, by Herbert Read. Unsigned.

C2158 Merryman's Vision. *TLS*, 6 October 1945, p. 476. Review of *The Midnight Court: A Rhythmical Bacchanalia from the Irish of Bryan Merryman*, translated by Frank O'Connor. Unsigned.

C2159 "King Lear". *TLS*, 13 October 1945, p. 488. Review of *The True Text of King Lear*, by Leo Kirschbaum. Unsigned.

C2160 Homage to a Victorian. *Sunday Times*, 14 October 1945, p. 3. Review of *George Saintsbury: The Memorial Volume*.

C2161 The Heart of Swift. *The Times*, 19 October 1945, p. 5. Leader on Swift's bicentenary. Unsigned.

C2162 The Melancholy of Swift : Society and Solitude. *TLS*, 20 October 1945, p. 498. Review of *Satires and Personal Writings*, by Jonathan Swift, edited by William Alfred Eddy (*see also* C1198); and *Swift and His Circle: A Book of Essays*, by R. Wyse Jackson. Unsigned.

C2163 The Creed of the Book. *TLS*, 20 October 1945, p. 499. Leader. Unsigned.
Reprinted: *Edmund Blunden: A Selection of His Poetry and Prose*, 1950.

C2164 "The Cenci" on the Stage. *TLS*, 27 October 1945, p. 509. Review of *A Stage Version of Shelley's Cenci*, by Arthur C. Hicks and R. Milton Clarke. Unsigned.

C2165 Signed or Unsigned? *TLS*, 27 October 1945, p. 511. Leader on anonymous reviews. Unsigned.

C2166 [Review of] *Siegfried's Journey, 1916–1920*, by Siegfried Sassoon. *Book Society News*, November 1945, pp. 1–2. *See also* C2193, 2220.

C2167 [Review of] *An Autobiography*, by Frank Lloyd Wright. *Book Society News*, November 1945, pp. 9–10.

C2168 [Review of] *The Monastery*, by F. Majdalany. *Book Society News*, November 1945, p. 10.

C2169 [Review of] *Farewell Campo 12*, by James Hargest. *Book Society News*, November 1945, p. 12.

C2170   Reopening of Keats House. *TLS*, 3 November 1945, p. 528. Unsigned.

C2171   Keats and Ourselves. *TLS*, 10 November 1945, p. 535. Leader on the reopening of Keats House.

C2172   The Friend of Life: Mr. De la Mare's New Poems [*later* Walter de la Mare]. *TLS*, 17 November 1945, p. 546. Review of *The Burning Glass and Other Poems*, by Walter de la Mare. Unsigned. *See also* C2189, 2192.

Reprinted: *Edmund Blunden: A Selection of His Poetry and Prose*, 1950.

C2173   Substantial Language. *TLS*, 17 November 1945, p. 547. Leader on William Ellis of Little Gaddesden. Unsigned.

C2174   English Poetical Poetry. *Tribune*, 23 November 1945, pp. 13-14.

C2175   [On Joshua Barnes, the poet, 1654-1712]. *The Blue*, November/December 1945, Vol. 73, No. 1, pp. 15-16. Letter signed E. Blunden.

C2176   [Review of] *Things One Hears: Essays*, by Robert Lynd. *Book Society Annual*, Christmas 1945, pp. 17-18.

C2177   [Review of] *Livingstone's Last Journey*, by Sir Reginald Coupland. *Book Society Annual*, Christmas 1945, p. 18.

C2178   RIVAL APPETITES [*later* RIVAL FEASTS]. *Book Society Annual*, Christmas 1945, p. 25.

Reprinted: *Youth's Companion*, September 1948, Vol. 3, No. 6, pp. 2-5 (in English and Japanese, translated by Ichirô Nishizaki); *After the Bombing*, 1949; and *Poems of Many Years*, 1957. *See also* D30.

C2179   Songs from the Plays. *TLS*, 1 December 1945, p. 573. Review of *Songs and Lyrics from the English Playbooks*, collected by Frederick S. Boas. Unsigned.

C2180   A Famous Forest. *TLS*, 1 December 1945, p. 573. Review of *Epping Forest: Its Literary and Historical Associations*, by William Addison. Unsigned.

C2181   Among the English Poets. *TLS*, 8 December 1945, p. 583. Leader on William Broome, William Crowe, and William Hayley. Unsigned.

C2182   Analysts and Critics. *TLS*, 22 December 1945, p. 607. Leader on Samuel Johnson. Unsigned.

C2183   Anglers and Fellow-Creatures. *TLS*, 22 December 1945, p. 609. Review of *The Fisherman's Bedside Book*, compiled by "B.B."; and *These Also: An Anthology*, selected and arranged by M. M. Johnson, with an introduction by Walter de la Mare. Unsigned.

C2184 Voices from the Past. *TLS*, 22 December 1945, p. 609. Review of *The Vigil of Venus: Pervigilium Veneris*, Latin text, with an introduction and English translation by Allen Tate; and *The Philobiblon of Richard de Bury*, translated by Andrew Fleming West. Unsigned.

C2185 FARM BAILIFF. *The Observer*, 23 December 1945, p. 3. Reprinted (with the addition of Part II): *After the Bombing*, 1949; *Poems of Many Years*, 1957; *The Midnight Skaters*, [1968] (Part II); and *A Selection from the Poems*, [1969] (Part II, verses 2-3, 5).

C2186 A Follower of Cobbett. *Sunday Times*, 23 December 1945, p. 3. Review of *The Wisdom of the Fields*, by H. J. Massingham.

C2187 The Larger Entente. *TLS*, 29 Decmber 1945, p. 619. Leader on the retirement of Professor Louis Cazamian. Unsigned.

C2188 British Academy Papers. *TLS*, 29 December 1945, p. 620. Review of the *Proceedings of the British Academy*, 1942. Unsigned.

1946

C2189 Walter de la Mare's New Poems. *Britain To-day*, January 1946, No. 117, pp. 39-40. Review of *The Burning-Glass and Other Poems*, by Walter de la Mare. *See also* C2172, 2192.

C2190 [Review of] *Charity Man*, by Mark Benney. *Book Society News*, January/February 1946, p. 5.

C2191 [Review of] *The Story of Burma*, by Tennyson Jesse. *Book Society News*, January/February 1946, p. 6.

C2192 A Master Poet. *The Seafarer*, January/February/March 1946, No. 49, p. 15. Review of *The Burning-Glass and Other Poems*, by Walter de la Mare. *See also* C2172, 2189.

C2193 A Poet Reviews His Journey: Mr. Sassoon's Star. *TLS*, 5 January 1946, p. 6. Review of *Siegfried's Journey, 1916-1920*, by Siegfried Sassoon. Unsigned. *See also* C2166, 2220.

C2194 A British Envoy. *TLS*, 5 January 1946, p. 7. Leader on John Hookham Frere. Unsigned.

C2195 Mr. Betjeman's Work. *TLS*, 5 January 1946, p. 8. Review of *New Bats in Old Belfries*, by John Betjeman. Unsigned.

C2196 The Poet's Quotations. *TLS*, 12 January 1946, p. 19. Leader on *The Poetry of Thomas Gray*, by Lord David Cecil. Unsigned.

C2197 Ruskin and Morris: The Dream and the Business. *TLS*, 19 January 1946, p. 30. Review of *William Morris: Medievalist and Revolutionary*, by Margaret R. Grennan; and *Ruskin*, by R. W. Livingstone. Unsigned.

C2198 Keats with the Greeks. *TLS*, 19 January 1946, p. 31. Leader on *Potter and Printer in Ancient Athens*, by J. D. Beazley. Unsigned.

C2199 The Indigenous Pen. *TLS*, 26 January 1946, p. 43. Leader on *Creative Writing in Australia*, by John K. Ewers. Unsigned.

C2200 N. or M. *TLS*, 2 February 1946, p. 55. Leader on *Oxford Dictionary of Christian Names*, by E. G. Withycombe. Unsigned.

C2201 The Peacemakers. *TLS*, 9 February 1946, p. 67. Leader on Books Across the Sea. Unsigned.

C2202 'No Crabb, No Christmas'. *The Listener*, 14 February 1946, pp. 211-212. A talk on Henry Crabb Robinson broadcast on the Eastern Service. Title in contents: Henry Crabb Robinson.

C2203 Tidying Up. *TLS*, 23 February 1946, p. 91. Leader. Unsigned.

C2204 China's Wealth of Verse. *TLS*, 23 February 1946, p. 92. Review of *From the Chinese*, edited by R. C. Trevelyan. Unsigned.

C2205 John Townsend [1757-1826]. *The Blue*, March/April 1946, Vol. 73, No. 2, p. 61. Signed E.B.

C2206 Towpath and Track. *The Observer*, 3 March 1946, p. 3. Review of *English Rivers and Canals*, by Frank Eyre and Charles Hadfield (*see also* C2215); and *British Railways*, by Arthur Elton.

C2207 British Embassy, Tokyo. *TLS*, 9 March 1946, p. 112. Review of *Behind the Japanese Mask*, by Sir Robert Craigie. Unsigned.

C2208 No Moral. *TLS*, 9 March 1946, p. 115. Leader on *Tellers of Tales*, by R. L. Green. Unsigned.

C2209 The Zest of Stuart Drama. *TLS*, 9 March 1946, p. 116. Review of *An Introduction to Stuart Drama*, by Frederick S. Boas. Unsigned.

C2210 The Malory Enigma. *TLS*, 16 March 1946, p. 127. Leader on Sir Thomas Malory. Unsigned.

C2211 Myth and Form. *TLS*, 23 March 1946, p. 139. Leader on *George Macdonald: An Anthology*, selected by C. S. Lewis. Unsigned.

C2212 Illuminators. *TLS*, 23 March 1946, p. 140. Review of *Jean Fouquet und seine Zeit*, by Paul Wescher. Unsigned.

C2213 A Volume of Verses. *The Times*, 27 March 1946, p. 5. Leader on *A Shropshire Lad*, by A. E. Housman. Unsigned.

C2214 Captain of Industry. *TLS*, 30 March 1946, p. 151. Leader on Samuel Johnson. Unsigned.

C2215 Boat and Barge. *TLS*, 30 March 1946, p. 153. Review of *English Rivers and Canals*, by Frank Eyre and Charles Hadfield. Unsigned. *See also* C2206.

C2216 [Review of] *Cass Timberlane*, by Sinclair Lewis. *The Bookman*, April 1946, New Series, Vol. 1, No. 2, p. 3. *The Bookman* was a continuation of *Book Society News*.

C2217 [Review of] *Tooting Corner*, by Eric Bligh. *The Bookman*, April 1946, New Series, Vol. 1, No. 2, p. 9. *See also* C2264.

C2218 [Review of] *Reflections in a Mirror: Second Series*, by Charles Morgan. *The Bookman*, April 1946, New Series, Vol. 1, No. 2, pp. 9–10.

C2219 [Review of] *Industrial Research and Development*, by Sir H. Frank Heath and A. L. Hetherington. *The Bookman*, April 1946, New Series, Vol. 1, No. 2, pp. 10–11.

C2220 From War to Peace. *Britain To-day*, April 1946, No. 120, p. 39. Review of *Siegfried's Journey, 1916–1920*, by Siegfried Sassoon. *See also* C2166, 2193.

C2221 Supercargo. *TLS*, 6 April 1946, p. 163. Leader on editions of the classics. Unsigned.

C2222 Local Writers. *TLS*, 6 April 1946, p. 164. Review of *Monmouthshire Writers*, by W. J. Townsend Collins. Unsigned. *See also* C2237.

C2223 A Poet in the Storm. *TLS*, 13 April 1946, p. 176. Review of *The Note-Book of a Lieutenant in the Italian Campaign*, by Robert Dalzell Dillon Thomas. Unsigned.

C2224 Molière in England. *TLS*, 20 April 1946, p. 187. Leader on *Molière et la Comedie de Moeurs en Angleterre*, by André de Mandach. Unsigned.

C2225 English Studies. *TLS*, 20 April 1946, p. 189. Review of *The Year's Work in English Studies*, Vol. XXIV, 1943, edited by Frederick S. Boas; and *Essays by Divers Hands*, New Series, Vol. XXII, edited by the Marquess of Crewe. Unsigned.

C2226 Honour to the Swiss. *TLS*, 27 April 1946, p. 199. Leader on the Exhibition of the Books of Switzerland. Unsigned.

C2227 [Review of] *The Mind and Heart of Love*, by M. C. D'Arcy. *The Bookman*, May/June 1946, New Series, Vol. 1, No. 3, pp. 10–11.

C2228 [Review of] *A Texan in England*, by J. Frank Dobie. *The Bookman*, May/June 1946, New Series, Vol. 1, No. 3, pp. 11–12.

C2229 For the Record. *TLS*, 4 May 1946, p. 211. Leader on Wilfred Owen. Unsigned.

C2230 English Poets Abroad. *TLS*, 4 May 1946, p. 212. Review of *Ewiges England: Dichtung aus sieben Jahrhunderten*, by Hans Feist. Unsigned.

C2231 Imagined Dilemmas. *TLS*, 11 May 1946, p. 223. Leader on *Great French Romances*, selected with an introduction by Richard Aldington. Unsigned.

C2232 Critic's Commentary. *Time and Tide*, 18 May 1946, p. 474. Review of *Science and the Creative Arts*, by William Bowyer Honey. Signed E.B.

C2233 A Treasure Restored. *TLS*, 18 May 1946, p. 235. Leader on 'a curious piece of fraud in early Shakespeare publishing.' Unsigned.

C2234 Watching Cricket. *Sunday Times*, 19 May 1946, p. 3. Review of *To the Wicket*, by Dudley Carew.

C2235 World's Classics. *TLS*, 25 May 1946, p. 247. Leader on the Oxford University Press series. Unsigned.

C2236 The Mystery of Leonardo. *TLS*, 25 May 1946, p. 249. Review of *The Drawings of Leonardo da Vinci*, edited with an introduction and notes by A. E. Popham. Unsigned.

C2237 Father Augustine Baker [1575-1641]. *The Blue*, June/July 1946, Vol. 73, No. 3, pp. 124-125. Arising from *Monmouthshire Writers*, by W. J. Townsend Collins. Signed E.B. *See also* C2222.

C2238 Poemata. *TLS*, 1 June 1946, p. 259. Leader on Anglo-Latin poets. Unsigned.

C2239 Older Scottish. *TLS*, 1 June 1946, p. 260. Review of *A Dictionary of the Older Scottish Tongue from the Twelfth Century to the End of the Seventeenth*, Part X, *Dullit-Exercration*, by Sir William A. Craigie. Unsigned.

C2240 Chinese Georgics. *TLS*, 8 June 1946, p. 272. Review of *The Golden Year of Fan Cheng-ta: A Chinese Rural Sequence rendered into English Verse*, with notes and calligraphic decorations by Tsui Chi, by Gerald Bullett. Unsigned.

C2241 Mournful Numbers. *TLS*, 15 June 1946, p. 283. Leader on poetry and 'the arithmetical spirit'. Unsigned.

C2242 Elizabethan. *TLS*, 15 June 1946, p. 285. Review of *Sources for a Biography of Shakespeare*, E. K. Chambers. Unsigned.

C2243 In Praise of Alexander. *TLS*, 15 June 1946, p. 285. Review of *Alexander of Macedon*, by Viscount Mersey. Unsigned.

C2244 Plays: 1641-1700. *TLS*, 15 June 1946, p. 285. Review of *A Check List of English Plays, 1641-1700*, by Gertrude L. Woodward and James G. McManaway. Unsigned.

C2245   In Wordsworth's Study. *TLS*, 22 June 1946, p. 294. Review of *Poetical Works of William Wordsworth*, Vol. III, edited by E. de Selincourt and Helen Darbishire; and *Wordsworth's Interest in Painters and Pictures*, by Martha Hale Shackford. Unsigned.

C2246   Haydon's Tragedy. *TLS*, 22 June 1946, p. 295. Leader on the centenary of his death. Unsigned.

C2247   The Making of a Novelist. *TLS*, 29 June 1946, p. 306. Review of *The Letters and Private Papers of William Makepeace Thackeray*, Vols. 1-2, edited by Gordon N. Ray. Unsigned. *See also* letters in the issues of 6 July, p. 319, 13 July, p. 331, 20 July, p. 343, 27 July, p. 355, 10 August, p. 379, 17 August, p. 391, 7 September, p. 427, and 21 September, p. 451. *See also* C2374.

C2248   The Reader's Share. *TLS*, 29 June 1946, p. 307. Leader on the reading of poetry. Unsigned.

C2249   [Review of] *The Road of a Naturalist*, by Donald Culross Peattie. *The Bookman*, July 1946, New Series, Vol. 1, No. 4, pp. 11-12.

C2250   [Review of] *Country Things*, by Alison Uttley. *The Bookman*, July 1946, New Series, Vol. 1, No. 4, pp. 12-13. Signed E.B.

C2251   Poets and Poetry. *The Bookman*, July 1946, New Series, Vol. 1, No. 4, pp. 14-15. Review of *Thanks Before Going*, by John Masefield; *Collected Lyrical Poems*, by Vivian Locke Ellis; *The Sand Castle*, by C. C. Abbott; *Beowulf*, by Gavin Bone; *The Voyage and Other Poems*, by Edwin Muir; *A Map of Verona*, by Henry Reed; *Poems*, by Jonathan Wilson; *This Way to the Tomb*, by Ronald Duncan; *Peter Grimes and Other Poems*, by Montagu Slater; and *Old Man of the Mountains*, by Norman Nicholson.

C2252   Village Cricket is His Theme. *Strand Magazine*, July 1946, Vol. 111, No. 667, pp. 28-31. Above title: Poet's Prose.

C2253   Literary History. *TLS*, 6 July 1946, p. 319. Leader on Oliver Elton. Unsigned.

C2254   Charles Lamb in Literature and Life. *The Listener*, 11 July 1946, pp. 52-53. A talk broadcast on the Eastern Service.

C2255   The American Comment. *TLS*, 13 July 1946, p. 329. Review of *Transactions and Proceedings of the American Philological Association*, Vol. LXXV, 1944, edited by Warren E. Blake; and *Studies in Language and Literature*, edited by George R. Coffman. Unsigned.

C2256   Turbulent Skelton. *TLS*, 13 July 1946, p. 331. Leader on the pamphlet 'John Skelton's Contribution to the English Language', by F. M. Salter. Unsigned.

C2257   Harriet Shelley. *TLS*, 13 July 1946, p. 331. Letter signed E. Blunden. Also issued separately as an offprint (*see* A80).

C2258 Poetical Explorations. *TLS*, 20 July 1946, p. 341. Review of *Explorations: Essays in Criticism mainly on the Literature of the Seventeenth Century*, by L. C. Knights. Unsigned.

C2259 Hardy in America. *TLS*, 20 July 1946, p. 343. Leader on *Hardy in America*, by Carl J. Weber. Unsigned.

C2260 Literary Modes. *TLS*, 27 July 1946, p. 357. Review of *Studies in Literary Modes*, by Arthur Melville Clark. Unsigned.

C2261 [Review of] *The Scarlet Tree*, by Osbert Sitwell. *The Bookman*, August 1946, New Series, Vol. 1, No. 5, p. 3.

C2262 [Review of] *No Promise in Summer*, by Elizabeth Evelyn. *The Bookman*, August 1946, New Series, Vol. 1, No. 5, p. 6. Signed E.B.

C2263 [Review of] *Tolstoy and His Wife*, by Tikhon Polner. *The Bookman*, August 1946, New Series, Vol. 1, No. 5, p. 10.

C2264 Near London. *Britain To-day*, August 1946, No. 124, p. 42. Review of *Tooting Corner*, by Eric Bligh. *See also* C2217.

C2265 John Forster's Poet. *TLS*, 3 August 1946, p. 366. Review of *Owen Meredith: A Critical Biography of Robert, First Earl of Lytton*, by Aurelia Brooks Harlan. Unsigned.

C2266 Seen from Dublin. *TLS*, 3 August 1946, p. 367. Leader on *Postscript on Existentialism*, by Arland Ussher.Unsigned.

C2267 Thomas Barnes. *TLS*, 3 August 1946, p. 367. Letter signed E. Blunden. *See also* letters by Douglas Grant and M. D. George in the issues of 24 August, p. 403 and 5 October, p. 479.

C2268 Lord Keynes. *TLS*, 10 August 1946, p. 379. Second leader. Unsigned.

C2269 Classic Verse. *TLS*, 10 August 1946, p. 380. Review of *Flos Malvae*, by A. B. Ramsay. Unsigned.

C2270 A Lyrical Thinker. *TLS*, 10 August 1946, p. 380. Review of *Fire and Ice*, by T. W. Ramsey. Unsigned.

C2271 QUI MIHI [*later* WILLIAM LILY'S RULES FOR SCHOOLBOYS]. *Times Educational Supplement*, 17 August 1946, p. 391. 'Being a translation of the Latin poem prefixed by William Lily to the "Brevissima Institutio", 1513.'
Reprinted: *After the Bombing*, 1949.

C2272 Milton Regained. *TLS*, 17 August 1946, p. 390. Review of *Paradise Lost in Our Time: Some Comments*, by Douglas Bush; and *John Milton's Complete Poetical Works*, compiled and edited by Harris Francis Fletcher. Unsigned. Also issued separately as an offprint (*see* A81).

C2273 Medieval Sources. *TLS*, 17 August 1946, p. 391. Second leader. Unsigned.

C2274 A True Prince. *TLS*, 24 August 1946, p. 402. Review of *The New Shakespeare: Henry IV*, Parts I and II, edited by John Dover Wilson. Unsigned.

C2275 Dialect Poems. *TLS*, 24 August 1946, p. 403. Leader on William Barnes. Unsigned.

C2276 Homage to a Prince. *TLS*, 31 August 1946, p. 414. Review of *Prince Henry and English Literature*, by Elkin Calhoun Wilson. Unsigned.

C2277 [Review of] *The Perennial Philosophy*, by Aldous Huxley. *The Bookman*, September/October 1946, New Series, Vol. 1, No. 6, p. 14.

C2278 [Review of] *Comic Characters of Shakespeare*, by John Palmer. *The Bookman*, September/October 1946, New Series, Vol. 1, No. 6, p. 15. Signed E.B.

C2279 [Review of] *A Norfolk Notebook*, by Lilias Rider Haggard. *The Bookman*, September/October 1946, New Series, Vol. 1, No. 6, p. 15. Signed E.B.

C2280 Return to Goethe. *TLS*, 7 September 1946, p. 427. Second leader on the English Goethe Society. Unsigned.

C2281 A Literary Exchange. *TLS*, 7 September 1946, p. 429. Review of *The Percy Letters*, edited by David Nichol Smith and Cleanth Brooks; and *The Correspondence of Thomas Percy and Edmond Malone*, edited by Arthur Tillotson. Unsigned.

C2282 The Cheerful Poet. *TLS*, 14 September 1946, p. 439. Leader on the tercentenary of the publication of *Fragmenta aurea*, by Sir John Suckling. Unsigned.

C2283 The Ways of Shakespeare. *TLS*, 21 September 1946, p. 452. Review of *Shakespeare's Imagination*, by Edward A. Armstrong; and *A la Découverte de Shakespeare*, by Abel Lefranc. Unsigned.

C2284 Book Forgeries: "An Enquiry" Re-Read. *TLS*, 28 September 1946, p. 472. On the forgeries by T. J. Wise. Unsigned. Also issued separately as an offprint (*see* A82). *See also* letters by Alan Smith, Richard Curle and W. O. Raymond in the issues of 19 October, p. 507, 2 November, p. 535, and 14 December, p. 620; and 'T. J. Wise and H. Buxton Forman: Further Light on the 19th-Century Pamphlets' by John Carter and Graham Pollard in the issue of 1 June, p. 264.

C2285 THE HALTED BATTALION: 1916 [*later* sub-title omitted]. *Phoenix*, Autumn 1946, p. 20.

Reprinted: *English Poetry*, Tokyo, October 1948, Vol. 1, p. —; *After the Bombing*, 1949; and *Poems of Many Years*, 1957.

C2286   Critic and Poet. *TLS*, 5 October 1946, p. 479. Leader on *Robert Bridges*, by G. S. Gordon. Unsigned.

C2287   Hammond (England). *TLS*, 12 October 1946, p. 491. Review of *Cricket My Destiny*, by Walter R. Hammond, foreword by Sir Pelham Warner. Unsigned.

C2288   An Oxford Poet. *TLS*, 12 October 1946, p. 493. Leader on the gift by Sir John Shelley-Rolls to the Bodleian Library. Unsigned.

C2289   Caxton and After. *TLS*, 19 October 1946, p. 508. Review of *English Printed Books*, by Francis Meynell; and *Rowlandson and His Illustrations of Eighteenth Century English Literature*, by Edward C. J. Wolf. Unsigned.

C2290   A Poet's Collection. *TLS*, 19 October 1946, p. 508. Review of *Collected Poems*, by William Kean Seymour. Unsigned.

C2291   Shakespeare's Mind. *TLS*, 26 October 1946, p. 521. Leader on Shakespeare and modern pedantry. Unsigned.

C2292   Shelley: How Legends Are Made. *TLS*, 26 October 1946, p. 522. Review of *The Shelley Legend*, by Robert Metcalf Smith and others. Unsigned.

C2293   Arms and Men. *TLS*, 26 October 1946, p. 523. Review of *Thunderbolts*; and *Armaments and History*, by J. F. C. Fuller. Unsigned.

C2294   [Review of] *Brensham Village*, by John Moore. *The Bookman*, November 1946, New Series, Vol. 1, No. 7, pp. 1-2.

C2295   [Review of] *Ursa Major: A Study of Dr. Johnson and His Friends*, by C. E. Vulliamy. *The Bookman*, November 1946, New Series, Vol. 1, No. 7, pp. 9-10.

C2296   Off the Track. *TLS*, 2 November 1946, p. 535. Leader on *Essays and Studies*, by W. A. Osborne. Unsigned.

C2297   Old Homes. *TLS*, 2 November 1946, p. 536. Review of *Recording Britain*, Vol. 1, *London and Middlesex, Surrey, Berkshire, Buckinghamshire, Hertfordshire, Bedfordshire*. Unsigned.

C2298   An Excluded Angel. *TLS*, 9 November 1946, p. 549. Leader on Edward Irving and *The Catholic Apostolic Church sometimes called Irvingite* . . . by P. E. Shaw. Unsigned.

C2299   Other Words. *TLS*, 23 November 1946, p. 577. Leader on *The 'Q' Tradition*, by Basil Willey; *The Outlook in English Studies*, by Simeon Potter; and *The Critique of Pure English*, by Sir William Craigie. Unsigned.

C2300   [Review of] *Transformation Scene*, by Claude Houghton. *Bookman Annual*, Christmas 1946, p. 11.

C2301   [Review of] *The Hooked Hawk, or the Case of Mr. Boswell*, by D. B. Wyndham Lewis. *Bookman Annual*, Christmas 1946, pp. 14-15.

C2302   [Review of] *History of Western Philosophy*, by Bertrand Russell. *Bookman Annual*, Christmas 1946, p. 17.

C2303   [Review of] *When the Going Was Good*, by Evelyn Waugh. *Bookman Annual*, Christmas 1946, pp. 18–19.

C2304   [Review of] *Portraits in Prose*, by Hugh Macdonald. *Bookman Annual*, Christmas 1946, p. 19. Signed E.B.

C2305   [Review of] *Lord's, 1787–1945*, by Sir Pelham Warner. *Bookman Annual*, Christmas 1946, p. 20. *See also* C2307.

C2306   Recent New Poetry. *Bookman Annual*, Christmas 1946, pp. 43–45. Review of *A Sword in the Desert*, by Herbert Palmer; *Desert Wells*, by Dorothy Wellesley; *A Rough Walk Home*, by Lilian Bowes Lyon; *Consider the Years*, by Virginia Graham; *Fifty-One Poems*, by Mary Webb; *A Wreath for San Gemignano*, by Richard Aldington; *Seven Words and the Civilian*, by Adrian Head; and *The Lamp*, by Richard Church.

C2307   To Lord's and Further. *The Listener*, 5 December 1946, p. 812. Review of *Lord's, 1787–1945*, by Sir Pelham Warner. *See also* C2305.

C2308   Twenty Years with Aunt Judy. *TLS*, 7 Decmember 1946, Children's Book Section, p. i. On *Aunt Judy's Magazine*, 1866–1885. Unsigned.

C2309   Hakluyt Society. *TLS*, 7 December 1946, p. 603. Leader on the centenary. Unsigned.

C2310   White of Selborne. *TLS*, 14 December 1946, p. 614. Review of *White of Selborne and his Times*, by Walter S. Scott. Unsigned.

C2311   Translators. *TLS*, 14 December 1946, p. 615. Leader on UNESCO and the project for the advancement of translations. Unsigned.

C2312   Plough and Pen. *TLS*, 21 December 1946, p. 629. Leader on rural literature. Unsigned.

C2313   The Sphinx Smiles. *TLS*, 28 December 1946, p. 643. Leader on *Tennyson: An Introduction and Selection*, by W. H. Auden. Unsigned.

C2314   The Professor and the Poet. *TLS*, 28 December 1946, p. 645. Review of *The Discipline of Letters*, by George Gordon. Unsigned.

1947

C2315   The Microphone Essayist. *Britain To-day*, January 1947, No. 129, pp. 37–38. Review of *Mainly on the Air*, by Max Beerbohm.

C2316   HAMMOND OF ENGLAND [*later* HAMMOND (ENG-LAND): A CRICKETER]. *Strand Magazine*, January 1947, Vol. 112, No. 673, pp. 30–31.

Reprinted: *After the Bombing*, 1949; *Edmund Blunden: A Selection of His Poetry and Prose*, 1950; *Poems of Many Years*, 1957; and *A Selection of the Shorter Poems*, [1966].

C2317   [Review of] *C. P. Scott, 1846–1932*, by various authors. *The Bookman*, January/February 1947, New Series, Vol. 1, No. 9, pp. 8–9.

C2318   [Review of] *Hugh Dormer's Diaries*. *The Bookman*, January/February 1947, New Series, Vol. 1, No. 9, p. 10.

C2319   [Review of] *War in Val D'Orcia*, by Iris Origo. *The Bookman*, January/February 1947, New Series, Vol. 1, No. 9, p. 12.

C2320   Spenser: Legend and Learning. *TLS*, 11 January 1947, p. 22. Review of *The Life of Edmund Spenser*, by Alexander C. Judson. Unsigned.

C2321   Shakespeare's Bible. *TLS*, 11 January 1947, p. 23. Leader on William Whittingham. Unsigned.

C2322   Brief Elegies. *TLS*, 11 January 1947, p. 24. Review of *Epigrams*, by H. W. Garrod. Unsigned.

C2323   Italian Masterpieces. *TLS*, 18 January 1947, p. 35. Review of *La Pittura Veneziana del Cinquecento*, Vol. 1, by Rodolfo Pallucchini. Unsigned.

C2324   National Gallery Catalogue. *TLS*, 18 January 1947, p. 35. Review of *The British School*, by Martin Davies. Unsigned.

C2325   Surrey's Triumphs. *TLS*, 18 January 1947, p. 37. Leader on the quatercentenary of the Earl of Surrey's execution. Unsigned.

C2326   A Modern Devotional Poet. *TLS*, 18 January 1947, p. 39. Review of *Collected Poems, 1935–1946*, by Jack Gilbey. Unsigned.

C2327   [Review of] *The Dublin Magazine*, January–March 1947, edited by Seumas O'Sullivan. *TLS*, 18 January 1947, p. 42. Unsigned.

C2328   [Review of] *Publications of the Modern Language Association of America*, Vol. 61, No. 4, Part 1, December 1946, edited by Percy Waldron Long. *TLS*, 18 January 1947, p. 42. Unsigned.

C2329   [Review of] *The Friend's Quarterly*, January 1947. *TLS*, 18 January 1947, p. 42. Unsigned.

C2330   At 7, Albemarle St. *TLS*, 25 January 1947, p. 51. Leader on the National Book League's exhibition 'Victorian Fiction'. Unsigned.

C2331   An Old Inhabitant. *The Beacon*, February 1947, Vol. 1, No. 10, pp. 144–146. On boyhood days in the Uckfield district. Signed E. Blunden.

C2332   Webster's Women. *TLS*, 1 February 1947, p. 65. Leader on the one-volume edition of *The White Devil*, *The Duchess of Malfi*, and *The Devil's Law-Case*, by John Webster, Vision Press. Unsigned.

C2333   Boswell's Eye. *TLS*, 1 February 1947, p. 67. Review of *Boswell*, by Claude Colleer Abbott. Unsigned.

C2334   Editorial Charity. *TLS*, 15 February 1947, p. 91. Leader on Sir Walter Scott's *Journal*. Unsigned.

C2335   [Review of] *Collected Poems*, by Herbert Read. *The Bookman*, March 1947, New Series, Vol. 1, No. 10, p. 9.

C2336   [Review of] *The Poetic Image*, by C. Day Lewis. *The Bookman*, March 1947, New Series, Vol. 1, No. 10, p. 10.

C2337   Notes on New Poetry. *The Bookman*, March 1947, New Series, Vol. 1, No. 10, pp. 11–12. Review of *The Madness of Merlin*, by Laurence Binyon; *The Singing Vision*, by William A. Younger; *Beat Drum, Beat Heart*, by Sheila Wingfield; *A Soul for Sale*, by Patrick Kavanagh; *Voices in a Giant City*, by A. S. J. Tessimond; *Poems from New Writing 1936–1946*, foreword by John Lehmann; and *Collected Poems*, by Edgell Rickword.

C2338   THE HEDGEHOG KILLED ON THE ROAD. *Civic Hall Quarterly*, Wolverhampton, [March 1947], No. 1, p. 7. Above title: Two Small Elegies, [I].
         Reprinted: *After the Bombing*, 1949.

C2339   THE SNAIL. *Civic Hall Quarterly*, Wolverhampton, [March 1947], No. 1, p. 7. Above title: Two Small Elegies, [II].
         Reprinted: *After the Bombing*, 1949.

C2340   The Much Tried Silurist. *TLS*, 8 March 1947, p. 102. Review of *Henry Vaughan: A Life and Interpretation*, by F. E. Hutchinson. Unsigned.
         Reprinted (expanded): *Edmund Blunden: A Selection of His Poetry and Prose*, 1950.

C2341   Revival of Learning. *TLS*, 8 March 1947, p. 103. Leader on weekly journals. Unsigned.

C2342   Hope and Object. *TLS*, 8 March 1947, p. 103. Second leader on the *White Paper, Economic Survey for 1947*. Unsigned.

C2343   Fugitive Pieces. *TLS*, 22 March 1947, p. 127. Leader on reprints issued by the Percy Society, the Early English Text Society and others. Unsigned.

C2344   Milton Lost and Regained. *TLS*, 29 March 1947, p. 140. Review of *Milton's Paradise Lost: A Commentary on the Argument*, by John S. Diekhoff; and *Milton and the English Mind*, by F. E. Hutchinson. Unsigned.

C2345   Baconian Men. *TLS*, 29 March 1947, p. 141. Leader on *The Traveller's Eye*, by Dorothy Carrington. Unsigned.

C2346   The Essay Tradition. *TLS*, 29 March 1947, p. 143. Review of *English Essayists*, by Bonamy Dobrée. Unsigned.

C2347   Keats in America. *TLS*, 29 March 1947, p. 143. Review of *Keats' Reputation in America to 1848*, by Hyder E. Rollins. Unsigned.

C2348   [Review of] *Ciano's Diary 1939-1943*, edited by Malcolm Muggeridge. *The Bookman*, April 1947, New Series, Vol. 1, No. 11, pp. 7-8.

C2349   [Review of] *Westminster in War*, by William Sansom. *The Bookman*, April 1947, New Series, Vol. 1, No. 11, pp. 8-10. Signed E.B.

C2350   [Review of] *Sussex*, by Esther Meynell. *The Bookman*, April 1947, New Series, Vol. 1, No. 11, pp. 10-12.

C2351   My Horse and I. *Britain To-day*, April 1947, No. 132, pp. 40-41. Review of *The Traveller*, by Walter de la Mare.

C2352   Living Landscape. *TLS*, 5 April 1947, p. 157. Leader on *Chateaubriand's Natural Scenery*, by Thomas Capell Walker. Unsigned.

C2353   Publishers and Authors. *TLS*, 5 April 1947, p. 158. Review of *Of Making Many Books: A Hundred Years of Reading, Writing, and Publishing*, by Roger Burlingame. Unsigned.

C2354   Coleridge Catalogued. *TLS*, 5 April 1947, p. 159. Review of *Coleridge*, an excerpt from the General Catalogue of Printed Books in the British Museum. Unsigned.

C2355   Literary Explorers. *TLS*, 12 April 1947, p. 172. Review of *The Percy Letters: The Correspondence of Thomas Percy and Richard Farmer*, edited by Cleanth Brooks. Unsigned.

C2356   A Concourse of Poets. *TLS*, 19 April 1947, p. 183. Second leader on the exhibition of poetry at the National Book League. Unsigned.

C2357   Bewick's Legacy. *TLS*, 26 April 1947, p. 197. Leader on *Wood Engravings by Thomas Bewick*, King Penguin. Unsigned.

C2358   [Review of] *The Modern Language Review*, Vol. 42, No. 1. *TLS*, 26 April 1947, p. 201. Unsigned.

C2359   [Review of] *George Eliot*, by Gerald Bullett. *The Bookman*, May 1947, New Series, Vol. 1, No. 12, pp. 6-7.

C2360   A Gentle Pagan. *Britain To-day*, May 1947, No. 133, p. 41. Review of *Apostate*, by Forrest Reid.

C2361 Mary Lamb Memorial Address. *C.L.S. Bulletin*, May 1947, No. 77, pp. [1-2].

C2362 "Fastidious Brisk of Oxford". *TLS*, 10 May 1947, p. 226. Review of *Poems*, by Richard Leigh, reprinted with an introduction by Hugh Macdonald. Unsigned.

C2363 [Review of] *Theatre Note-Book: A Quarterly of Notes and Research*, April 1947, Vol. 1, No. 7. *TLS*, 10 May 1947, p. 229. Unsigned.

C2364 Johnson's Plan. *TLS*, 17 May 1947, p. 239. Leader on *Dr. Johnson and His English Dictionary*, by John E. W. Wallis. Unsigned.

C2365 Horace Walpole. *TLS*, 24 May 1947, p. 253. Second leader on Strawberry Hill. Unsigned.

C2366 Charles Lamb's Best Friend. *TLS*, 24 May 1947, p. 254. On Mary Lamb. Unsigned.

C2367 A Humane Geologist. *TLS*, 24 May 1947, p. 255. Review of *The Geology of Oxford*, by W. J. Arkell. Unsigned.

C2368 A Poet of South Africa. *TLS*, 31 May 1947, p. 269. Review of *Selected Poems of Francis Carey Slater*, introduction by R. C. K. Ensor. Unsigned.

C2369 The Pendulum. *TLS*, 7 June 1947, p. 281. Leader on *Before the Romantics*, edited by Geoffrey Grigson. Unsigned. *See also* C2379.

C2370 [Review of] *Rowlandson: The Life and Art of a British Genius*, by F. Gordon Roe. *TLS*, 7 June 1947, p. 284. Unsigned.

C2371 [Review of] *English*, Spring 1947, Vol. 6, No. 34, edited by F. B. Millett. *TLS*, 7 June 1947, p. 285. Unsigned.

C2372 Paper Shortage, and . . ? *Oxford Viewpoint*, 13 June 1947, Vol. 1, No. 2, pp. 2-4.

C2373 Oversights. *TLS*, 14 June 1947, p. 295. Leader on Thomas Hardy's poetry. Unsigned.

C2374 Thackeray's Letters. *TLS*, 14 June 1947, p. 297. Review of *The Letters and Private Papers of William Makepeace Thackeray*, Vol. 3, edited by Gordon N. Ray. Unsigned. *See also* C2247.

C2375 Rule and the Man. *TLS*, 21 June 1947, p. 309. Leader on *The Great Duke of Alba as a Public Servant*, by the Duke of Alba. Unsigned.

C2376 By Whom? *TLS*, 28 June 1947, p. 323. Leader on errors of ascription in literature. Unsigned.

C2377 [Review of] *Lord Cochrane*, by Christopher Lloyd. *The Bookman*, June/July 1947, New Series, Vol. 2, No. 1, pp. 8-10.

C2378   [Review of] *Once Only*, by Roy S. Neill. *The Bookman*, June/July 1947, New Series, Vol. 2, No. 1, p. 11. Signed E.B.

C2379   [Review of] *Before the Romantics*, edited by Geoffrey Grigson. *The Bookman*, June/July 1947, New Series, Vol. 2, No. 1, p. 13. *See also* C2369.

C2380   The Wordsworthian Spirit. *Britain To-day*, July 1947, No. 135, pp. 39–40. Review of *Wordsworthian and Other Studies*, by Ernest de Selincourt.

C2381   Canadian Prophet. *TLS*, 5 July 1947, p. 332. Review of *For the Time is at Hand*, by Richard S. Lambert. Unsigned.

C2382   After Gay. *TLS*, 5 July 1947, p. 339. Review of *The Illustrated Gorilla and Other Tales*, by Charles Ould. Unsigned.

C2383   Worcester History. *TLS*, 5 July 1947, p. 341. Review of *A History of the Worcester Royal Infirmary*, by William Henry McMenemy. Unsigned.

C2384   Readings of Earth. *TLS*, 12 July 1947, p. 349. Review of *Down to Earth*, by John Stewart Collis; and *Ploughshare and Pulpit*, together with a *Countryman's Creed*, by Philip A. Wright. Unsigned.

C2385   The Modern Book. *TLS*, 19 July 1947, p. 365. Leader on the National Book League's exhibition. Unsigned.

C2386   The Kennesswood Poet. *TLS*, 19 July 1947, p. 366. Review of *Michael Bruce, Shepherd-Poet of the Lomond Braes, 1746-1767*, by Thomas G. Snoddy. Unsigned.

C2387   [Review of] *Poseidon*, by Renalt Capes. *The Bookman*, August 1947, New Series, Vol. 2, No. 2, p. 6.

C2388   [Review of] *Irregular Adventure*, by Christie Lawrence. *The Bookman*, August 1947, New Series, Vol. 2, No. 2, p. 8.

C2389   [Review of] *The First Romantics*, by Malcolm Elwin. *The Bookman*, August 1947, New Series, Vol. 2, No. 2, p. 9. *See also* C2406.

C2390   [Review of] *Byzantine Legacy*, by Cecil Stewart. *The Bookman*, August 1947, New Series, Vol. 2, No. 2, p. 10.

C2391   Out of China. *TLS*, 2 August 1947, p. 391. Leader on *Chinese Poems*, by Arthur Waley. Unsigned.

C2392   John Ray's Forerunners. *TLS*, 16 August 1947, p. 414. Review of *English Naturalists from Neckam to Ray*, by Charles E. Raven. Unsigned.

C2393   Sussex Village. *TLS*, 23 August 1947, p. 425. Review of *The Story of Henfield*, by Henry de Candole. Unsigned.

C2394   Hardy's Earliest Verses. *TLS*, 23 August 1947, p. 432. Note on the illustration of Thomas Hardy's earliest poem. Also issued separately as an offprint (*see* B119). *See also* letters in the issues of 30 August, p. 439 by T. W. Hill, and 27 September, p. 497 by Bernard Rosenberg.

C2395   [Review of] *Collected Poems*, by Siegfried Sassoon. *The Bookman*, September 1947, New Series, Vol. 2, No. 3, p. 5. *See also* C2398.

C2396   [Review of] *Science in Transition*, by A. W. Haslett. *The Bookman*, September 1947, New Series, Vol. 2, No. 3, p. 9.

C2397   A Shelley Mystery. *John O'London's Weekly*, 19 September 1947, pp. 589–590. Review of *Shelley*, by Newman Ivey White.

C2398   A Poet's Variety. *The Spectator*, 19 September 1947, p. 374. Review of *Collected Poems*, by Siegfried Sassoon. *See also* C2395.

C2399   Machines and Men. *TLS*, 20 September 1947, p. 479. Second leader on reading aids for the infirm. Unsigned.

C2400   History at Alnwick Castle: The Percy Documents. *Times Educational Supplement*, 27 September 1947, p. 511. Signed From a Correspondent.

C2401   [Review of] *Nelson*, by Carola Oman. *The Bookman*, October 1947, New Series, Vol. 2, No. 4, p. 9.

C2402   [Review of] *The Steep Places*, by Sir Norman Angell. *The Bookman*, October 1947, New Series, Vol. 2, No. 4, p. 10.

C2403   [Review of] *Prose and Poetry*, by Alice Meynell. *The Bookman*, October 1947, New Series, Vol. 2, No. 4, p. 11.

C2404   [Review of] *Personality in Politics*, by Sir Arthur Salter. *The Bookman*, October 1947, New Series, Vol. 2, No. 4, pp. 12–13.

C2405   [Review of] *Albert Schweitzer*, by George Seaver. *The Bookman*, October 1947, New Series, Vol. 2, No. 4, pp. 13–14.

C2406   The Lake Poets. *Britain To-day*, October 1947, No. 138, pp. 42–43. Review of *The First Romantics*, by Malcolm Elwin. *See also* C2389.

C2407   Beautiful Handwriting: An Introduction. *Strand Magazine*, October 1947, Vol. 114, No. 682, pp. 70–78. Final sentence in holograph facsimile.

C2408   Shelley in the South. *TLS*, 11 October 1947, p. 523. Review of *Shelley in Italy: An Anthology*, selected by John Lehmann. Unsigned.

C2409   More of Mary Shelley. *TLS*, 1 November 1947, p. 560. Review of *Mary Shelley's Journal*, edited by Frederick L. Jones. Unsigned.

C2410 Ruskin at Oxford. *TLS*, 8 November 1947, p. 577. Leader on Sir Kenneth Clark's lectures. Unsigned.

C2411 An Eye for London. *TLS*, 8 November 1947, p. 580. Review of *Ned Ward of Grubstreet*, by Howard William Troyer. Unsigned.

C2412 An Album. *TLS*, 15 November 1947, p. 591. Leader on *Lost Treasures of Europe*, by Henry La Farge. Unsigned.

C2413 Lady and the Dandy. *Sunday Times*, 16 November 1947, p. 3. Review of *Blessington-D'Orsay: A Masquerade*, new edition, by Michael Sadleir. *See also* C1314.

C2414 [Review of] *Classical Landscape with Figures*, by Osbert Lancaster. *Bookman Annual*, Christmas 1947, p. 14.

C2415 [Review of] *Half-Time*, by Anthony Kimmins. *Bookman Annual*, Christmas 1947, p. 16.

C2416 Recent New Poetry. *Bookman Annual*, Christmas 1947, pp. 30-32. Review of *Poetry of the English-Speaking World*, edited by Richard Aldington; *The Green Man*, by Andrew Young; *The Drunken Sailor*, by Joyce Cary; *The Inn of the Birds*, by Anthony Rye; *The Prometheus Bound of Aeschylus*, translated by Rex Warner; *Paris Symphony*, by J. Redwood Anderson; *A Book of Both Sorts*, by John Masefield; and *A Marriage Song for the Princess Elizabeth*, by John Buxton.

C2417 The Age and After. *Britain To-day*, December 1947, No. 140, pp. 49-50. Review of *Letters to Malaya*, by Martyn Skinner.

C2418 Shelley: Some Gleanings, A Note Complementary to Next Month's Choice. *Readers News*, December 1947, Vol. 10, No. 7, pp. 2-6. Signed E.B. *Shelley* was the Readers Union choice for January 1948 (*see* A78).

1948

C2419 THE EVIL HOUR. *Penguin Parade*, 1948, Second Series, No. 2, p. 36.
Reprinted: *After the Bombing*, 1949.

C2420 Family Album. *TLS*, 24 January 1948, p. 48. Review of *John Henry Clive, 1781-1853, of North Staffordshire and His Descendants*, by Percy W. L. Adams. Unsigned.

C2421 [Review of] *John Martin: His Life and Works*, by Thomas Balston. *The Bookman*, February 1948, New Series, Vol. 2, No. 7, p. 9.

C2422 Changes in England's Countryside. *Fujin no Tomo*, February 1948, Vol. 42, No. 2, pp. 26-27. In English and Japanese; translated by Hikaru Saito; p. [3] first paragraph in holograph facsimile.

C2423 [Review of] *Two Quiet Lives*, by Lord David Cecil. *The Bookman*, April 1948, New Series, Vol. 2, No. 9, p. 7.

C2424 [Review of] *Our Partnership*, by Beatrice Webb. *The Bookman*, April 1948, New Series, Vol. 2, No. 9, pp. 8-9.

C2425 Charles Lamb, Reader: Some Notes. *Rising Generation*, April 1948, [Vol. 94], Jubilee Issue, pp. 3-25. In English and Japanese; p. 25 paragraphs 1-2 in holograph facsimile.

C2426 The Dilemma of Progress. *Youth's Companion*, April 1948, pp. 4-6. In English and Japanese.

Reprinted: *New Campus*, [1948].

C2427 THE CHILD'S GRAVE. *Current of the World*, 1 April 1948, Vol. 25, No. 4, pp. 30-32. In English and Japanese; translated by Kanau Nishimura; English in holograph facsimile. Note on the poem (*see* A10, 35, 43*b*, 135, 174).

C2428 The Last English Socialist? *TLS*, 24 April 1948, p. 232. Review of *On Art and Socialism*, by William Morris, selected with an introduction by Holbrook Jackson; *Portrait of William Morris*, by Esther Meynell; and *Warrior Bard: The Life of William Morris*, by Edward and Stephani Godwin. Unsigned. Also issued separately as an offprint (*see* A83). *See also* letters in the issues of 1 May, p. 247 by Sydney Cockerell, and 8 May, p. 261 by Roger Lancelyn Green.

C2429 [Review of] *The Middle Span*, by George Santayana. *The Bookman*, May 1948, New Series, Vol. 2, No. 10, p. 6.

C2430 AN OFFERING. *Oru Yomimono*, *Bijitto*, [May 1948], No. 2, p. 15. In English and Japanese; English in holograph facsimile.

Reprinted: *C.L.S. Bulletin*, July 1948, No. 84, p. [1].

C2431 A PRAYER FOR THE BIRDS. *World Literature*, Kyoto, May 1948, pp. 36-37.

Reprinted: *After the Bombing*, 1949; and *Poems of Many Years*, 1957.

C2432 Literary Occasions. *Nippon Times*, 5 May 1948, p. 4.

C2433 The Sigh. *Youth's Companion*, June 1948, pp. 42-43. In English and Japanese.

First published: *The Face of England*, 1932.

C2434 Charles Lamb and the Japanese. *C.L.S. Bulletin*, July 1948, No. 84, p. [1]. Letter signed E. Blunden.

C2435 "Annals of the Fine Arts". *Studies in English Literature*, July 1948, Vol. 25, No. 2, pp. 121-139. In English and Japanese. The first of three articles on periodicals. *See also* C2522, 2626.

C2436 Hartley Coleridge at Oxford. *Studies in English Literature*, July 1948, Vol. 25, No. 2, pp. 140-145. In English and Japanese.

C2437   TO THE MEMORY OF VISCOUNT CARLOW. *Waseda Guardian*, June/July 1948, Vol. 3, No. 15, p. 11.

Reprinted: *After the Bombing*, 1949.

C2438   INVOCATION WRITTEN IN SPRING 1944. *Waseda Guardian*, June/July 1948, Vol. 3, No. 15, p. 11.

Reprinted: *After the Bombing*, 1949; and *Poems of Many Years*, 1957.

C2439   American Literature in England. *World Literature*, Kyoto, August 1948, No. 24, pp. 22–23. In English and Japanese; translated by Kenji Ishida.*

C2440   Literary Notes. *Rising Generation*, 1 September 1948, Vol. 94, No. 9, p. 264.

C2441   Shelley's Two Friends. *Rising Generation*, 1 September 1948, Vol. 94, No. 9, p. 273. On Madame and Cornelia de Boinville.

C2442   AT MAPLEDURHAM IN WAR-TIME [*later* AT MAPLEDURHAM]. *English Poetry*, October 1948, No. 1, p. 1. For THE HALTED BATTALION, p. 2 (*see* C2285).

Reprinted: *After the Bombing*, 1949.

C2443   CHILDREN PASSING. *English Poetry*, October 1948, No. 1, p. 2.

Reprinted: *After the Bombing*, 1949.

C2444   Writers and Readers. *English Poetry*, October 1948, No. 1, pp. 17–20.

Reprinted: *Edmund Blunden: A Selection of His Poetry and Prose*, 1950.

C2445   VOICES IN TOKYO. *Study of English*, October 1948, Vol. 37, No. 1, p. 2. Title in contents: THE VOICES IN TOKYO.

Reprinted: *Two Lectures on English Literature*, 1948; *After the Bombing*, 1949; and *Adam International Review*, 1957, Year 25, No. 261, p. 4.

C2446   Literary Notes. *Rising Generation*, 1 October 1948, Vol. 94, No. 10, p. 296.

C2447   Phoenix and Rising Sun. *TLS*, 2 October 1948, p. 550. Review of *New Paths for Japan*, by Harold Wakefield. Unsigned.

C2448   [On an oration delivered by a Bluecoat boy, aged 12, before Queen Anne in 1706]. *The Blue*, November/December 1948, Vol. 76, No. 1, pp. 3–4. Letter signed E. Blunden.

C2449   A Midsummer-Night's Dream (Another Approach). *Aoyama Bungaku*, 15 November 1948, Vol. 21, No. 2, pp. 6–15.

C2450   Far Away and To-day. *TLS*, 27 November 1948, p. 667. Leader on Japanese studies of English language and literature. Unsigned.

C2451   Helps to Teachers of English Literature. *Foreign Language Teaching*, December 1948, No. 205, pp. 2–6.

C2452   Literary England. *Rising Generation*, 1 December 1948, Vol. 94, No. 12, pp. 358–359.

C2453   A Word for Kirke White. *Notes and Queries*, 11 and 24 December 1948, Vol. 193, Nos. 25–26, pp. 530–533, 564–566. *See also* the note by Sydney Race in the issue of 5 March 1949, Vol. 194, No. 5, p. 108.

Reprinted: *Edmund Blunden: A Selection of His Poetry and Prose*, 1950.

C2454   Japanese Reflections. *TLS*, 25 December 1948, p. 723. Review of *Mirror for Americans: Japan*, by Helen Mears; and *Via Tokyo*, by Christmas Humphreys. Unsigned.

1949

C2455   "And Japanese Scenery?" *Fujin no Tomo*, January 1949, Vol. 43, No. 1, pp. 12–14. In English and Japanese; translated by Hikaru Saito; pp. 12–13 in holograph facsimile.

C2456   A New Year Greeting. *Youth's Companion*, January 1949, Vol. 3, No. 10, pp. 4–6. In English and Japanese; translated by Ichirô Nishizaki.

C2457   IMPROMTU AFTER READING DR. JULIAN HUXLEY ON PROGRESS [*later* IMPROMTU UPON . . .]. *The Mainichi*, 1 January 1949, p. –. In English and Japanese; translated by Junzaburo Nishiwaki.*

Reprinted: *Eastward*, [1950].

C2458   TO JAPANESE STUDENTS: A SONNET. *New Age*, 1 January 1949, No. 1, p. 9. In English and Japanese; translated by Takeshi Saito.

Reprinted (revised): *Eastward*, [1950].

C2459   Literary Notes. *Rising Generation*, 1 January 1949, Vol. 95, No. 1, p. 7.

C2460   Japanese Culture, 1948: An Imaginary Conversation. *World News in Current English*, 1 January 1949, Vol. 5, No. 1, 68th Issue, pp. 4–5.

C2461   Literary Notes. *Rising Generation*, 1 February 1949, Vol. 95, No. 2, p. 37.

C2462   Popularity in Literature. *The Mainichi*, 13 February 1949, p. 3; and 20 February, 1949, p. –.*

Reprinted: *Poetry and Science*, 1949.

C2463   THE MOUNTAIN ONE NOVEMBER MORNING [*later* THE MOUNTAIN]. *Tô*, Tokyo, 1 March 1949, Vol. 1, No. 3, pp. 54–55. In English and Japanese; translated by Masaho Hirai; English in holograph facsimile.

Reprinted (revised): *Eastward*, [1950].

C2464   On Being Invited to Write about France. *Lumière*, Tokyo, April 1949, Vol. 1, No. 1, pp. 1-2.

C2465   Writ in Water. *TLS*, 13 May 1949, p. 313. Letter signed E. Blunden. Arising from *Keats, Shelley & Rome*, compiled by Neville Rogers (*see* B130). *See also* letters in the issues of 26 March, p. 201 by W. G. Bebbington; 2 April, p. 217 by H. A. Hammelmann; 9 April, p. 233 by J. C. Maxwell; 23 April, p. 265 by R. N. Green-Armytage; and 27 May, p. 353 by H. W. Garrod and R. W. Hunt.

C2466   Japanese Journey. *TLS*, 20 May 1949, p. 327. Review of *The First Voyage of the English to Japan*, by John Saris, edited by Takanobu Otsuka. Unsigned.

C2467   EMPIRE DAY. *Boon*, [Tokyo], 25 May 1949, Vol. 4, No. 39, p. 1.*

C2468   [On Christ's Hospital problems in *Notes and Queries*]. *The Blue*, July 1949, Vol. 76, No. 3, p. 152. Letter signed E. Blunden.

C2469   The Things Which Matter. *Gakusô*, July 1949, Vol. 2, No. 6, pp. 6-7. In English and Japanese; translated by Shigeru Toyama.

C2470   The Musical Miscellany: A Few Forgotten Songs of the Eighteenth Century with Prefatory Remarks. *Rising Generation*, 1 July 1949, Vol. 95, No. 7, pp. 243-252. Sub-title on cover: Prefatory Remarks and Selections with Notes. Also issued separately as an offprint with variant sub-title (*see* A88).

C2471   Literary Notes. *Rising Generation*, 1 July 1949, Vol. 95, No. 7, p. 265.

C2472   Kings of Thought. *TLS*, 19 August 1949, p. 538. Review of *The Philosophical Lectures*, by Samuel Taylor Coleridge, edited by Kathleen Coburn. Unsigned.

C2473   A DREAM [*later* THE FOND DREAM]. *Everybody's*, 17 September 1949, p. 20.

       Reprinted (revised): *Youth's Companion*, March 1950, p. 18; *Poems of Many Years*, 1957.

C2474   Literary Notes. *Rising Generation*, 1 October 1949, Vol. 95, No. 10, pp. 409-410.

C2475   FROM A STUDY TABLE [*later* FROM A STUDY WINDOW]. *The Spectator*, 14 October 1949, p. 493.

       Reprinted: *Youth's Companion*, March 1950, No. 3, p. 17. Signed E. Blunden.

C2476   After Many a Summer. *TLS*, 14 October 1949, p. 664. Review of *Alfred Tennyson*, by Charles Tennyson. Unsigned.

C2477   Friends of Keats. *Studies in English Literature*, November 1949, Vol. 26, No. 2, pp. 320-323. Review of *The Cowden Clarkes*, by Richard D. Altick.*

C2478 Some Recent Scholarly Works. *Studies in English Literature*, November 1949, Vol. 26, No. 2, pp. 323-324. Review of *The Best Books of the War.**

C2479 Literary Notes. *Rising Generation*, 1 November 1949, Vol. 95, No. 11, p. 451.

C2480 ONLY NOT INFINITE. *Notes and Queries*, 12 November 1949, Vol. 194, No. 23, p. 485. On the centenary of *Notes and Queries*. Holograph facsimile. Signed E.B.

C2481 SHELLEY IS DROWNED 1822. *English Poetry*, December 1949, No. 2, p. 1.

Reprinted: *Eastward*, [1950].

C2482 FAIRY GIFTS. *English Poetry*, December 1949, No. 2, p. 1.

Reprinted: *Eastward*, [1950].

C2483 "THOU". *English Poetry*, December 1949, No. 2, p. 1.

Reprinted: *Eastward*, [1950]; and *The Month*, March 1950, New Series, Vol. 3, No. 3, p. 165.

C2484 "Harriet Shelley Suicide Letter." *English Poetry*, December 1949, No. 2, p. 91.* Signed E.B.

C2485 Some English Characters. *English Poetry*, December 1949, No. 2, pp. 77-80.

First published: *Addresses on General Subjects*, 1949.

C2486 William Bell's "Elegy". *English Poetry*, December 1949, No. 2, p. 93.*

C2487 "The Keats Circle". *Rising Generation*, 1 December 1949, Vol. 95, No. 12, pp. 487-490. Review of *The Keats Circle: Letters and Papers, 1816-1878*, edited by Hyder Edward Rollins.

C2488 Literary Notes. *Rising Generation*, 1 December 1949, Vol. 95, No. 12, p. 490.

C2489 Versatile Victorian. *TLS*, 2 December 1949, p. 788. Review of *Concerning Andrew Lang:* [*Lectures*], by Andrew Lang. Unsigned.

1950

C2490 MAHATMA GANDHI. *Modern Review*, Calcutta, January 1950, Vol. 87, No. 1, p. 36. First of two poems composed as a birthday anniversary, and for the first memorial meeting of his death held in Tokyo. *See also* C2491.

C2491 TO THE MEMORY OF GANDHI [*later* ON READING OF MAHATMA GANDHI'S DEATH]. *Modern Review*, Calcutta, January 1950, Vol. 87, No. 1, p. 36. Second of two poems. *See also* C2490.

Reprinted: *A Hong Kong House*, 1962.

C2492 A Nineteenth-Century European. *Rising Generation*, 1 January 1950, Vol. 96, No. 1, pp. 38–39. Review of *Matthew Arnold*, by Louis Bonnerot.

C2493 The Japanese Student: 1949. *World News in Current English*, 1 January 1950, Vol. 6, No. 1, Issue 82, pp. 18–19.

Reprinted: *A Wanderer in Japan*, 1950.

C2494 THE VOLCANO [*formerly and later* SAKURAJIMA, A VOLCANO]. *The Spectator*, 6 January 1950, p. 8.

First published: separate edition, 1949; reprinted: *Rising Generation*, 1 April 1950, Vol. 96, No. 4, p. 179 (holograph facsimile); and *Records of Friendship*, 1950.

C2495 The New Japan. *TLS*, 6 January 1950, p. 11. Review of *Popcorn on the Ginza*, by L. Herndon Crockett. Unsigned.

C2496 AN AUTOLYCUS [*later* AUTOLYCUS AGAIN: IN MEMORY OF B.D.; *i.e.* Bert Daines]. *Everybody's*, 14 January 1950, p. 24.

Reprinted: *A Hong Kong House*, 1962.

C2497 AT HARIHAN. *Nippon Times*, 17 January 1950, p. —.*
One of four poems recorded on 27 December 1949, and broadcast from NHK in January 1950. *See also* C2513, 2563–4.

Reprinted: *Contemporary Verse*, 1955; and *Poems of Japan*, 1967.

C2498 NEW YEAR: OLD JAPAN. *The Spectator*, 17 February 1950, p. 210.

C2499 Bird and Beast. *TLS*, 17 February 1950, p. 107. Review of *The Old Knight: A Poem-Sequence for the Present Times*, by Herbert Palmer; and *Poems*, by Gerald Bullett. Unsigned.

C2500 THE CHILD IN CHURCH. *The Month*, March 1950, New Series, Vol. 3, No. 3, p. 165. For "THOU", p. 165 (*see* C2483).

Reprinted: *A Hong Kong House*, 1962.

C2501 YASHIMA IN WINTER [*formerly and later* A FIRST VISIT TO YASHIMA]. *The Month*, March 1950, New Series, Vol. 3, No. 3, p. 166.

First published: *Eastward*, [January 1950]; reprinted: separate edition, 1954.

C2502 THOSE WHO FIRST ENCOURAGED US. *The Month*, March 1950, New Series, Vol. 3, No. 3, p. 166.

Reprinted: *Poems of Many Years*, 1957.

C2503 Literary Notes. *Rising Generation*, 1 March 1950, Vol. 96, No. 3, pp. 112–113.*

C2504   Japanese Poetry. *TLS*, 3 March 1950, p. 138. Review of *Haiku*, Vol. 1; *Senryu: Japanese Satirical Verses*, translated and explained, by R. H. Blyth; and *Songs for Children, Sung in Japan*, by Yukus Uyehara. Unsigned.

C2505   Clubs. *Come Come Club*, Tokyo, April 1950, Vol. 3, No. 4, p. 5.

C2506   TO THE CITIZENS OF ITO [*formerly* WILLIAM ADAMS AT ITO]. *Rising Generation*, 1 April 1950, Vol. 96, No. 4, p.154. Issued as an Edmund Blunden Number.

First published: *Two Lectures on English Literature*, 1948; reprinted: *The First Englishman in Japan: The Story of Will Adams*, by P. G. Rogers, 1956.

C2507   [untitled; (Who first united England and Japan;)]. *Rising Generation*, 1 April 1950, Vol. 96, No. 4, p. 154. On Will Adams.

C2508   [untitled; (Here gathered in this kindly town)]. *Rising Generation*, 1 April 1950, Vol. 96, No. 4, p. 154. Written for Mr and Mrs Uchida of Ito, 8 July 1948.

C2509   [untitled; (Elia! and Edward Moxon! both together)]. *Rising Generation*, 1 April 1950, Vol. 96, No. 4, p. 155.

C2510   IN MEMORY OF ROBERT NICHOLS. *Rising Generation*, 1 April 1950, Vol. 96, No. 4, pp. 156–157. In English and Japanese. Edmund Blunden number.

Reprinted (revised): *The Listener*, 22 February 1951, p. 306; *Poems of Many Years*, 1957 (revised again); and *Kyôin Zuihitsu*, 1967 (as original).

C2511   THE FLOWERS OF THE ROCK [*later* FLOWERS . . .]. *Rising Generation*, 1 April 1950, Vol. 96, No. 4, p. 157. In English and Japanese. *See also* p. 151 for holograph facsimile of the poem.

Reprinted: separate edition, 1959; *A Hong Kong House*, 1962; *Poems on Japan*, 1967; and *Kyôin Zuihitsu*, [1967].

C2512   "First Catch Your Shakespeare". *Rising Generation*, 1 April 1950, Vol. 96, No. 4, pp. 158–164. Review of *Shakespeare's Sonnets Dated, and Other Essays*, by Leslie Hotson. In English and Japanese.

C2513   FROM THE JAPANESE INN WINDOW [*later* THE INN WINDOW, FUKUOKA; *and* THE EARLY YEAR, FUKUOKA]. *Rising Generation*, 1 April 1950, Vol. 96, No. 4, p. 164. Holograph facsimile.

First published: separate edition, 1949; reprinted: *Eastward*, [January 1950]; *Records of Friendship*, 1950; and *Contemporary Verse*, 1955. One of four poems recorded on 27 December 1949, and broadcast from NHK in January 1950. *See also* C2497, 2563–4.

C2514 Wordsworth: Occasional Thoughts on his Poetry and Characteristics. *Rising Generation*, 1 April 1950, Vol. 96, No. 4, pp. 165-179. In English and Japanese.

Reprinted: *Eikoku kindai sambunshû: Fukuhara Rintarô yaku-chû*, 1953.

C2515 Literary Notes. *Rising Generation*, 1 April 1950, Vol. 96, No. 4, p. 179. For SAKURAJIMA, A VOLCANO, p. 179 in holograph facsimile (*see* C2494).

C2516 TOWARDS THE FUTURE. *World News in Current English*, 5 April 1950, Vol. 6, No. 4, Issue 85, p. 26. In English and Japanese; translated by Takeshi Saito. English in holograph facsimile.

C2517 Popular Poetry. *TLS*, 14 April 1950, p. 229. Leader on *Phases of English Poetry*, by Herbert Read. Unsigned.

C2518 Wordsworth Grows Old. *TLS*, 21 April 1950, pp. 237-238. Front page article. Unsigned.

C2519 Education: The Student of English. *Current Thoughts in English Literature*, May 1950, Vol. 23, No. 1, pp. 4-11. *See also* E*b*15.

C2520 FOR TOKYO JOSHI DAIGAKU: A HYMN [*formerly* COLLEGE SONG]. *Bulletin, Tokyo Woman's Christian College*, May 1950, Vol. 3, No. 3, p. 1. Also in holograph facsimile.

First published: separate edition, 31 March 1950; reprinted: *Poems on Japan*, 1967.

C2521 Shakespeare and "Hamlet". *Gakusei*, May 1950, Vol. 35, No. 2, pp. 103-111.*

C2522 The Indicator. *Studies in English Literature*, May 1950, Vol. 27, No. 1, 36-45.* Second of three articles on periodicals. *See also* C2435, 2626.

C2523 BOOKS. *Kansai University Bulletin*, 15 May 1950, No. 231, inside upper wrapper. In English and Japanese; translated by Masato Hori. English in holograph facsimile.

Reprinted: *Contemporary Verse*, 1955; and *Poems on Japan*, 1967.

C2524 The Law of the Land. *TLS*, 16 June 1950, p. 373. Leader on the *National Parks and Access to the Countryside Act*, 1949. Unsigned. *See also* letters in the issues of 30 June, p. 405 by J. H. B. Andrews; and 21 July, p. 453, by Humphrey Baker.

C2525 A Victorian Editor. *TLS*, 23 June 1950, p. 384. Review of *The Story of the "Pall Mall Gazette", and of its First Editor, Frederick Greenwood, and of its Founder, George Murray Smith*, by J. W. Robertson Scott. Unsigned.

C2526 MacArthur's Japan. *The Observer*, 25 June 1950, p. 7. Review of *Kakemono: A Sketch Book of Post-War Japan*, by Honor Tracy. *See also* C2527.

C2527 Japanese Questions. *TLS*, 30 June 1950, p. 402. Review of *Kakemono: A Sketch Book of Post-War Japan*, by Honor Tracy. Unsigned. *See also* C2526.

C2528 A Cricket Festival. *TLS*, 30 June 1950, p. 412. On the exhibition at the National Book League. Unsigned.

C2529 AGE. *English Poetry*, July 1950, No. 3, p. 147. At head of title: Verses by the Way. First of five verses. *See also* C2530-3. Verses by the Way, Nos. [1-5] were also issued separately as a single offprint (*see* A100).

C2530 TOKYO LAWN [*later* FROM A TOKYO LAWN; *and* TOKYO LAWN (1948)]. *English Poetry*, July 1950, No. 3, p. 147. Second of five verses. *See also* C2529, 2531-3.

Reprinted: *The Adelphi*, May 1952, Vol. 28, No. 3, p. 629 (holograph facsimile); and *A Hong Kong House*, 1962.

C2531 TWO VILLAGE MINSTRELS, *English Poetry*, July 1950, No. 3, p. 148. Third of five verses. *See also* C2529-30, 2532-3.

C2532 TOMKINS. *English Poetry*, July 1950, No. 3, p. 148. Fourth of five verses. *See also* C2529-31, 2533.

C2533 ODE TO AN INK-JAR (STEPHENS' INK) [*later* TO A BRITISH JAR CONTAINING STEPHENS' INK]. *English Poetry*, July 1950, No. 3, pp. 149-150. Last of five verses. *See also* C2529-32.

Reprinted: *The Postmaster*, September 1952, Vol. 1, No. 1, pp. 31-32; and *A Hong Kong House*, 1962.

C2534 [To Praise Kenkyusha . . .]. *Kenkyûsha Geppô*, 20 July 1950, No. 6/7, p. 2. Holograph facsimile.

C2535 England and Japan. *TLS*, 21 July 1950, p. 448. Review of *Broken Thread*, by F. S. Piggott. Unsigned.

C2536 The Inward Light. *TLS*, 28 July 1950, p. 464. Review of *English Poetry and its Contribution to the Knowledge of a Creative Principle*, by Leone Vivante. Unsigned.

C2537 The Man of Letters. *TLS*, 28 July 1950, p. 468. Review of *A Last Vintage: Essays and Papers*, by George Saintsbury, edited by John W. Oliver. Unsigned.

C2538 Rosenberg's Poetry. *TLS*, 28 July 1950, p. 470. Review of *The Collected Poems of Isaac Rosenberg*, edited by Gordon Bottomley and Denys Harding; foreword by Siegfried Sassoon. Unsigned.

C2539 Japan Dreams of a Happy Future. *News Chronicle*, 29 July 1950, p. 2.

C2540 [Review of] *The Waters of Silence*, by Thomas Merton. *The Bookman*, July/August 1950, p. 12.

C2541 University Memories. *Study of English*, August 1950, Vol. 39, No. 8, pp. 4–7; *and* September 1950, Vol. 39, No. 9, pp. 4–5.

C2542 VOICE OF AUTUMN. *Shûkan Asahi*, 5 August 1950, Vol. 55, No. 34, Issue 1598, pp. 48–49. Sub-title: A theme for a dance, offered with admiration to Tamami Gojo. In English and Japanese; translated by Saika Tomita. English in holograph facsimile.

Reprinted: Ballet programme, Tokyo, 26 November 1950; *Elixir*, Hong Kong, December 1954, p. 37 [at head of title: Patterns for a Japanese Ballet; *see also* C3121]; and *A Hong Kong House*, 1962.

The first five lines were first published in *Asahi Shimbun*, Tokyo, 12 March 1950, p. 3. In English and Japanese. English in holograph facsimile.

C2543 Soldier Poet. *TLS*, 11 August 1950, p. 496. Review of *Here Comes She Home*, by Geoffrey Fyson. Unsigned.

C2544 "The Age of Brass". *TLS*, 11 August 1950, p. 501. Second leader on poetry and the future. Unsigned.

C2545 The Life and Work of James Thomson. *TLS*, 11 August 1950, p. 502. Review of *James Thomson (B.V.)*, by I. B. Walker. Unsigned.

C2546 Exchange of Ideas. *TLS*, 11 August 1950, p. 502. Review of *English Miscellany: A Symposium of History, Literature and the Arts*, edited by Mario Praz. Unsigned.

C2547 The Immediate View. *TLS*, 25 August 1950, [Special Issue:] A Critical & Descriptive Survey of Contemporary British Writing for Readers Oversea, p. ii. Unsigned.

C2548 PETALS. *TLS*, 25 August 1950, [Special Issue:] A Critical & Descriptive Survey of Contemporary British Writing for Readers Oversea, p. vii.

Reprinted: *A Hong Kong House*, 1962; and *The Midnight Skaters*, [1968].

C2549 [Review of] *An English Library*, 4th edition, by F. Seymour Smith. *Books*, September 1950, No. 252, pp. 190–191.

C2550 Some Women Writers. *Ronshu: Essays and Studies*, September 1950, Vol. 1, No. 1, pp. 1–35. Also issued separately as an offprint (*see* A103).

C2551 Cricketer Lucas. *TLS*, 8 September 1950, p. 561. Review of *Cricket All his Life: Cricket Writings in Prose and Verse*, by E. V. Lucas, assembled and arranged by Rupert Hart-Davis. Unsigned.

C2552   The Swinburne Labyrinth. *TLS*, 8 September 1950, p. 564. Review of *Selected Poems*, by A. C. Swinburne, edited by Edward Shanks. Unsigned. Also issued separately as an offprint (*see* A105). *See also* C801.

C2553   Proceedings. *TLS*, 8 September 1950, p. 565. Leader on the *Proceedings of the British Academy*, 1945. Unsigned.

C2554   A Cricket Master. *TLS*, 15 September 1950, p. 583. Review of *Cricketers' School*, by Walter Hammond. Unsigned.

C2555   The Japanese Language. *TLS*, 15 September 1950, p. 585. Review of *A.B.C. Japanese-English Dictionary*; and *Pictorial Chinese-Japanese Characters*, both by Oreste and Enko Elissa Vaccari. Unsigned.

C2556   Rhodesian Poetry. *TLS*, 22 September 1950, p. 595. Review of *Bronze Freize: Poems Mostly Rhodesian*, by N. H. Brettell. Unsigned.

C2557   Poets and Editors. *TLS*, 22 September 1950, p. 597. Leader on modern editorship. Unsigned.

C2558   [Review of] *The Review of English Studies*, New Series, Vol. 1, No. 3. *TLS*, 22 September 1950, p. 602. Unsigned.

C2559   [Review of] *England, Past, Present and Future*, by Douglas Jerrold. *The Bookman*, October 1950, pp. 16, 21. Signed E.B.

C2560   [Review of] *A Retrospect of Flowers*, by Andrew Young. *The Bookman*, October 1950, p. 21. *See also* C2565.

C2561   The Nature of Poetry. *Current Thoughts in English Literature*, October 1950, Vol. 23, No. 2, pp. 4-7.

C2562   Eastern Visitor. *National and English Review*, October 1950, Vol. 135, No. 812, pp. 368-370. Title in contents: Eastern Vision. On a visitor from Japan.

C2563   MATSUSHIMA. *The Shikai*, October 1950, No. 1, p. 1. Above title: Some Short Poems on Japanese Subjects. One of four poems recorded on 27 December 1949, and broadcast from NHK in January 1950. *See also* C2497, 2513, 2564.

First published: separate edition, 1948; reprinted: *Eastward*, [1950]; and *Contemporary Verse*, 1955.

C2564   IN A PARK AT KYOTO. *The Shikai*, October 1950, No. 1, p. 1. *See also* note to C2563.

First published: *Eastward*, [1950], and *Contemporary Verse*, 1955.

C2565   The Life of Flowers. *TLS*, 13 October 1950, p. 642. Review of *A Retrospect of Flowers*, by Andrew Young. Unsigned. *See also* C2560.

C2566 Crusade for Poetry. *TLS*, 13 October 1950, p. 645. Second leader on the series *Key Poets*. Unsigned. *See also* C2589.

C2567 Mr. Hunt at the Play. *TLS*, 20 October 1950, p. 660. Review of *Dramatic Criticism, 1808–1831*, by Leigh Hunt, edited by Lawrence Huston Houtchens and Carolyn Washburn Houtchens. Unsigned. Also issued separately as an offprint (*see* A109).

C2568 The Westernization of Japan. *TLS*, 27 October 1950, p. 671. Review of *The Western World and Japan*, by Sir George Sansom. Unsigned.

C2569 English Water-Colours. *TLS*, 27 October 1950, p. 672. Review of *Two Centuries of British Water-Colour Painting*, by Adrian Bury. Unsigned.

C2570 AMONG THE HILLS. *Everybody's*, 28 October 1950, p. 24.

First published: *A Wanderer in Japan*, 15 July 1950.

C2571 [Review of] *Boswell's London Journal, 1762–1763*. *The Bookman*, November 1950, pp. 3–4.

C2572 [Review of] *Stolen Journey*, by Oliver Philpot. *The Bookman*, November 1950, pp. 12–13.

C2573 [Review of] *Inward Companion: Poems*, by Walter de la Mare. *The Bookman*, November 1950, p. 14. *See also* C2593.

C2574 [Review of] *The Fuel of the Fire*, by Douglas Grant. *The Bookman*, November 1950, p. 21. *See also* C3118.

C2575 Researches. *TLS*, 3 November 1950, p. 693. Second leader on textual variants. Unsigned.

C2576 The Atlantic Awards. *TLS*, 10 November 1950, p. 709. Second leader on the Atlantic Awards in Literature. Unsigned.

C2577 Scholar-Poet. *TLS*, 17 November 1950, p. 729. Review of *Williams of Swindon*, by J. B. Jones. Unsigned.

C2578 Ironical Oddments. *TLS*, 17 November 1950, p. 731. Review of *A Short Trot with a Cultured Mind*, by Patrick Campbell. Unsigned.

C2579 Moonlight Fancies. *TLS*, 17 November 1950, Children's Book Section, p. ii. Review of *The Wandering Moon*, by James Reeves; and *The Tale of The Monster Horse*, by Ian Serraillier. Unsigned.

C2580 Penguins and Pelicans. *TLS*, 24 November 1950, p. 747. Second leader on the exhibition of Penguin Books. Unsigned.

C2581 Cricket Chroniclers. *TLS*, 24 November 1950, p. 751. Review of *J. M. Barrie's Allahakbarries C.C. 1899*, foreword by Don Bradman. Unsigned.

481

C2582 Keatsian Studies. *TLS*, 24 November 1950, p. 756. Review of *Harvard Library Bulletin*, Autumn 1950, Volume 4, No. 3. Unsigned.

C2583 'The Northamptonshire Peasant'. *Everybody's*, 25 November 1950, pp. 16–17. On John Clare.

C2584 [Review of] *The Tap on the Left Shoulder*, by Ricardo Sicre. *Bookman Annual*, Christmas 1950, pp. 6–7. Signed E.B.

C2585 [Review of] *The Forests of the Night*, by Jean-Louis Curtis. *Bookman Annual*, Christmas 1950, p. 7.

C2586 [Review of] *An Artist's Life*, by Sir Alfred Munnings. *Bookman Annual*, Christmas 1950, pp. 10–11.

C2587 [Review of] *The Bolshevik Revolution*, by Edward Hallett Carr. *Bookman Annual*, Christmas 1950, pp. 13, 15.

C2588 [Review of] *On Producing Shakespeare*, by Ronald Watkins. *Bookman Annual*, Christmas 1950, pp. 19–20.

C2589 Some Poetry, 1950. *Bookman Annual*, Christmas 1950, pp. 35–36. Review of *Collected Shorter Poems, 1939–1944*, by W. H. Auden; *Greek Poetry for Everyman*, translated by F. L. Lucas; *Seventy Cantos*, by Ezra Pound; *Mountains Beneath the Horizon*, by William Bell; *Underworlds*, by Francis Scarfe; and *Key Poets*, by Edith Sitwell, George Barker and others (*see also* C2566).

C2590 Letters from Charles and Mary Cowden Clarke to Alexander Main 1865–1886. *Keats-Shelley Memorial Bulletin, Rome*, [December] 1950, No. 3, pp. 35–53.

C2591 The Place of Clare. *TLS*, 8 December 1950, p. 782. Review of *Selected Poems of John Clare*, edited by Geoffrey Grigson; and *John Clare and Other Studies*, by John Middleton Murry. Unsigned.

C2592 Day by Day. *TLS*, 8 December 1950, p. 788. Review of *An English Almanac*, by Miles Hadfield. Unsigned.

C2593 Time and Eternity. *Time and Tide*, 16 December 1950, pp. 1282–1283. Review of *Inward Companion: Poems*, by Walter de la Mare. *See also* C2573.

C2594 The Lady Poverty. *TLS*, 22 December 1950, p. 815. Second leader on *The Pleasures of Poverty*, by Anthony Bertram. Unsigned.

C2595 French into German. *TLS*, 22 December 1950, p. 817. Review of *Bibliography of German Translations from the French, 1700–1848*, Volumes 1–2, by Hans Fromm. Unsigned.

C2596 Selected Lyrics. *TLS*, 29 December 1950, p. 822. Review of *Seventeenth Century Lyrics*, by Norman Ault. Unsigned.

C2597 Smart and His Editors. *TLS*, 29 December 1950, p. 826. Review of *Poems*, by Christopher Smart, edited with an introduction and notes by Robert Britain. Unsigned. Also issued separately as an offprint (*see* A111).

C2598 Shakespeare's Sonnets. *TLS*, 29 December 1950, p. 830. Review of *Thorpe's Edition of Shakespeare's Sonnets, 1609*, an explanatory introduction by C. Longworth de Chambrun; and *The Sonnets*, by William Shakespeare, illustrated by Steven Spurrier. Unsigned.

1951

C2599 [Review of] *The Mask and the Man*, by Alan Thomas. *The Bookman*, January/February 1951, pp. 6-7.

C2600 [Review of] *The Life of Mahatma Gandhi*, by Louis Fischer. *The Bookman*, January/February 1951, p. 11.

C2601 A Letter from London. *Bulletin, Tokyo Woman's Christian College*, January/February 1951, p. 1.

C2602 Concerning Chaucer. *TLS*, 5 January 1951, p. 8. Review of *Chaucer and the Canterbury Tales*, by William Witherle Lawrence. Unsigned.

C2603 Bibliotheca Phillippica. *TLS*, 5 January 1951, p. 12. Review of *A Selection of Precious Manuscripts, Historic Documents and Rare Books, the Majority from the Renowned Collection of Sir Thomas Phillipps, Bt. (1792-1872): Catalogue 81*. Unsigned.

C2604 English Water-Colour. *TLS*, 12 January 1951, p. 16. Review of *An Introduction to English Water-Colour Paintings*, by Graham Reynolds. Unsigned.

C2605 Fred Edgcumbe. *TLS*, 12 January 1951, p. 21. Letter in support of a memorial to Fred Edgcumbe at Keats House, Hampstead. *See also* letters in the issues of 18 August 1950, p. 517, by Willard B. Pope; and 10 November 1950, p. 709, by Ruth Draper. *See also* further letter by Blunden (C2840).

C2606 [Review of] *The Window*, No. 1. *TLS*, 19 January 1951, p. 42. Unsigned.

C2607 Home Counties. *TLS*, 26 January 1951, p. 55. Review of *Kent, Our Glorious Heritage*, by H. R. Pratt Boorman; and *Surrey*, by Ralph Lawrence. Unsigned.

C2608 Prophecy of War. *TLS*, 26 January 1951, p. 57. Review of *Of Fear and Freedom*, by Carlo Levi, translated by Adolphe Gourevitch. Unsigned.

C2609 [Review of] *The Goldfish of China in the XVIII Century*, by George Hervey, with a foreword by A. C. Moule. *TLS*, 26 January 1951, p. 58. Unsigned.

C2610 Poets of America. *TLS*, 2 February 1951, p. 63. Review of *The Oxford Book of American Verse*, edited by F. O. Matthiessen. Unsigned.

C2611 A Great Administrator. *TLS*, 2 February 1951, p. 72. Review of *Hart and the Chinese Customs*, by Stanley F. Wright. Unsigned.

C2612 Mary Shelley: Creator of Frankenstein. *Everybody's*, 3 February 1951, p. 20.

C2613 Three Titans. *TLS*, 9 February 1951, p. 86. Review of *Shelley, Trelawny, and Henley: The Worthing Cavalcade*, by Samuel Looker. Unsigned.

C2614 Brief Candle. *TLS*, 9 February 1951, p. 89. Review of *Twenty-Five Years, 1919-1944: Major Alastair Guy Spens Campbell*, by Alastair Buchan and Oliver Villiers. Unsigned.

C2615 [Review of] *British Newspapers and Periodicals, 1632-1800: A Descriptive Catalogue of a Collection at the University of Texas*, compiled by Stewart Powell. *TLS*, 9 February 1951, p. 90. Unsigned.

C2616 [Review of] *More Examples of English Handwriting*, compiled by Hilda E. P. Grieve. *TLS*, 16 February 1951, p. 106. Unsigned.

C2617 [Review of] *We Sang for England*, by Eehna Carbery, Seumas and Alice Milligan. *TLS*, 16 February 1951, p. 107. Unsigned.

C2618 [Review of] *Poems in Pamphlet*, by Charles Causley. *TLS*, 16 February 1951, p. 107. Unsigned.

C2619 [Review of] *Australian Poetry, 1949-1950*, edited by Rosemary Dobson. *TLS*, 16 February 1951, p. 107. Unsigned.

C2620 [Review of] *Poetry Awards, 1950. TLS*, 16 February 1951, p. 107. Unsigned.

C2621 [Review of] *World Within World*, by Stephen Spender. *The Bookman*, March 1951, pp. 1-2.

C2622 [Review of] *Moulded in Earth*, by Richard Vaughan. *The Bookman*, March 1951, pp. 6-7.

C2623 [Review of] *Mirabeau: Study of a Democratic Monarchist*, by Oliver J. G. Welch. *The Bookman*, March 1951, p. 13.

C2624 One Hundred. *C.L.S. Bulletin*, March 1951, No. 100, p. [2]. Letter on the centenary issue.

C2625 Literary Discoveries. *National and English Review*, March 1951, Vol. 136, No. 817, pp. 157-160.

C2626 The Liberal. *Studies in English Literature*, March 1951, Vol. 27, No. 2, pp. 143-152. The last of three articles on periodicals. *See also* C2435, 2522.

484

C2627   The Liberal Outlook in Japan. *United Nations News*, March/ April 1951, Vol. 6, No. 2, pp. 22–23, 32.

C2628   Professor and Poet. *TLS*, 2 March 1951, p. 133. Second leader on the election of C. Day Lewis as Professor of Poetry at Oxford. Unsigned.

C2629   Shaw's Village. *TLS*, 2 March 1951, p. 134. Review of *Bernard Shaw's Rhyming Picture Guide to Ayot Saint Lawrence*. Unsigned.

C2630   Occupation of Japan. *TLS*, 9 March 1951, p. 144. Review of *Time of Fallen Blossoms*, by Allan S. Clifton. Unsigned.

C2631   Keeping Wicket. *TLS*, 9 March 1951, p. 151. Review of *Behind the Stumps*, by Godfrey Evans. Unsigned.

C2632   [Review of] *Diodorus Siculus*, Vol. 5, Books XII 41–XIII, with an English translation by C. H. Oldfather. *TLS*, 9 March 1951, p. 154. Unsigned.

C2633   Poet Who Taught Shorthand. *Everybody's*, 10 March 1951, p. 25. On John Byrom.

C2634   A Portuguese Epic. *TLS*, 16 March 1951, p. 168. Review of *The Lusiads*, by Luiz de Camões, translated by Leonard Bacon. Unsigned.

C2635   [Review of] *The Durham University Journal*, Vol. 43, No. 2. *TLS*, 16 March 1951, p. 171. Unsigned.

C2636   [Review of] *Journal of the English Folk Dance and Song Society*, Vol. 6, No. 2. *TLS*, 16 March 1951, p. 171. Unsigned.

C2637   Acoustics of Poetry. *TLS*, 23 March 1951, p. 181. Second leader on Walter de la Mare. Unsigned.

C2638   A British Council Series. *TLS*, 30 March 1951, p. 197. Second leader on the *Supplements to British Book News*. Unsigned.

C2639   Back to Football. *TLS*, 30 March 1951, p. 200. Review of *Football*, by Percy M. Young. Unsigned.

C2640   [Review of] *Nature Interlude*, compiled by E. F. Linssen. *TLS*, 30 March 1951, p. 203. Unsigned.

C2641   [Review of] *To the Dyfrdwy, the River I Love*, by J. Redwood Anderson. *TLS*, 30 March 1951, p. 203. Unsigned.

C2642   [Review of] *Cricket in Fiction: A Bibliography*, by Gerald Brodribb. *TLS*, 30 March 1951, p. 203. Unsigned.

C2643   [Review of] *To Comfort the Signora*, by E. G. Cousins. *The Bookman*, April 1951, p. 5.

C2644   [Review of] *A Sailor's Odyssey*, by Admiral Viscount Cunningham of Hyndhope. *The Bookman*, April 1951, p. 7.

C2645   [Review of] *Samuel Butler's Notebooks*, edited by Geoffrey Keynes and Brian Hill. *The Bookman*, April 1951, p. 9.

C2646　[Review of] *The Liberal Imagination*, by Lionel Trilling. *The Bookman*, April 1951, p. 10.

C2647　[Review of] *Plays and Poems of Thomas Lovell Beddoes*, edited with an introduction by H. W. Donner. *Review of English Studies*, April 1951, New Series, Vol. 2, No. 6, pp. 193-194. Also issued separately as an offprint (*see* A112).

C2648　A LIFE'S UNITY. *The Listener*, 5 April 1951, p. 547.

Reprinted: *New Poems 1952*, [1952]; and *A Hong Kong House*, 1962.

C2649　A Village Diarist. *TLS*, 6 April 1951, p. 207. Review of *The Diary of Benjamin Rogers*, edited by C. D. Linnell. Unsigned.

C2650　London Borough. *TLS*, 6 April 1951, p. 217. Review of *Living in Lambeth, 1086-1914*, by Aileen Denise Nash. Unsigned.

C2651　Cricketing Sketches. *TLS*, 6 April 1951, p. 217. Review of *From the Boundary*, by Ray Robinson. Unsigned.

C2652　Facts and Fixtures. *TLS*, 6 April 1951, p. 217. Review of *The Playfair Book of Cricket Records*, compiled by Roy Webber; and *The Cricket Almanack of New Zealand*, edited by Arthur H. Carmen and Noel S. Macdonald. Unsigned.

C2653　Poetry and the Schools. *Public Opinion*, 13 April 1951, p. 22.

C2654　[Review of] *Trial—and Error*, by Herbert H. Marks. *TLS*, 27 April 1951, p. 267. Unsigned.

C2655　[Review of] *Aspects of Japan's Labor Problems*, by Miriam S. Farley. *TLS*, 27 April 1951, p. 267. Unsigned.

C2656　Modern Books and Writers. *TLS*, 27 April 1951, p. 268. On the exhibition at the National Book League. Unsigned.

C2657　Collected Thoughts. *TLS*, 27 April 1951, Religious Books Section, p. xi. Review of *Bedside Manna: A Book of Meditations*, by Frank W. Moyle. Unsigned.

C2658　[Review of] *Saints and Parachutes*, by John Miller. *The Bookman*, May 1951, pp. 9-10. Signed E.B.

C2659　[Review of] *My Six Convicts*, by Donald Powell Wilson. *The Bookman*, May 1951, p. 10.

C2660　[Review of] *William Cowper*, by Norman Nicholson. *The Bookman*, May 1951, p. 12. *See also* C2690.

C2661　The Care of Churches. *TLS*, 4 May 1951, p. 277. Second leader on the Eleventh Report of the Central Council for the Care of Churches. Unsigned.

C2662　Piety and Paradox. *TLS*, 4 May 1951, p. 278. Review of *Poems (1646)*, by Thomas Philipott, edited by L. C. Martin. Unsigned.

C2663 Poets Have a Future. *John O'London's Weekly*, 11 May 1951, p. 276.

C2664 Ears and No Ears. *TLS*, 11 May 1951, p. 293. Leader on *Reading and Listening*, by T. S. R. Boase. Unsigned.

C2665 Sussex in Pictures. *TLS*, 18 May 1951, p. 312. Review of *Sussex Views*, edited by Walter H. Godfrey and L. F. Salzman. Unsigned.

C2666 [Review of] *Pageantry on the Shakespearean Stage*, by Alice S. Venezy. *TLS*, 18 May 1951, p. 314. Unsigned.

C2667 [Review of] *The Beginnings of Political Democracy in Japan*, by Nobutaka Ike. *TLS*, 18 May 1951, p. 315. Unsigned.

C2668 Past, Present and Future. *TLS*, 25 May 1951, p. 325. Leader on the Pilgrim Trust. Unsigned.

C2669 221B, Baker Street. *TLS*, 25 May 1951, p. 325. Second leader on Sherlock Holmes. Unsigned.

C2670 Shelley and His Work. *TLS*, 25 May 1951, p. 326. Review of *Shelley: Selected Poetry, Prose and Letters*, edited by A. S. B. Glover; and *The Life of Percy Bysshe Shelley*, by Edward Dowden. Unsigned.

C2671 Cricketing Twins. *TLS*, 25 May 1951, p. 327. Review of *Our Cricket Story*, by Alec and Eric Bedser. Unsigned.

C2672 [Review of] *The Hinge of Fate*, by Winston S. Churchill. *The Bookman*, June 1951, pp. 4-5.

C2673 The American Shogun. *National and English Review*, June 1951, Vol. 136, No. 820, pp. 366-367. Review of *The Riddle of MacArthur: Japan, Korea and the Far East*, by John Gunther.

C2674 The Early Drama. *TLS*, 1 June 1951, p. 342. Review of *Gentleness and Nobility*; and *Law Tricks*, by John Day, The Malone Society Reprints. Unsigned.

C2675 With the M.C.C. in Australia. *TLS*, 1 June 1951, p. 345. Review of *In Quest of the Ashes, 1950-1951*, by B. Harris; *Elusive Victory*, by E. W. Swanton; *The Fight for the Ashes, 1950-1951*, by A. G. Moyes; and *No Ashes for England*, by E. M. Wellings. Unsigned.

C2676 County Club. *TLS*, 1 June 1951, p. 345. Review of *A History of Worcestershire County Cricket Club, 1844-1950*, by W. R. Chignell. Unsigned.

C2677 "And If We Fail —". *The Spectator*, 8 June 1951, p. 760. Review of *Ashes to Ashes: A Post-Mortem on the 1950-51 Tests*, by Rex Warner and Lyle Blair.

C2678 The Unsigned Review. *TLS*, 8 June 1951, p. 357. Leader. Unsigned.

C2679 THE ADORNED [*later* THE ADORNING]. *TLS*, 15 June 1951, p. 371.

Reprinted: *A Hong Kong House*, 1962.

C2680 Life-Lyrics. *TLS*, 15 June 1951, p. 373. Leader on *The Lyrical Poems of Thomas Hardy*, by C. Day Lewis. Unsigned.

C2681 T. E. Lawrence. *TLS*, 15 June 1951, p. 373. Letter on Lawrence's knowledge of Arabic. Signed E. Blunden. *See also* letters in the same issue, p. 373 by Lord Raglan; 8 June, p. 357 by O. G. S. Crawford; 22 June, p. 389 by David Carrington and C. F. Beckingham; 29 June, p. 405 by John Rothenstein; 13 July, p. 437 by Aubrey M. Zatman; and 20 July, p. 453 by O. G. S. Crawford.

C2682 [Review of] *Catch! An Account of Two Cricket Tours*, by Keith Miller and R. S. Whitington. *TLS*, 15 June 1951, p. 379. Unsigned.

C2683 Elizabethan Records. *TLS*, 29 June 1951, p. 405. Second leader on C. J. Sisson's address on the BBC Third Programme. Unsigned.

C2684 A Letter from Professor Edmond [*sic*] Blumden [*sic*]. *Aoyama Trojan*, 30 June 1951, p. 2. Letter to Shinichi Shimizu, Feature Editor of *Aoyama Trojan*. Signed E. Blunden. Autograph and 'yours sincerely' in holograph facsimile.

C2685 The Monthly Chronicle. *Studies in English Literature*, July 1951, Vol. 27, No. 3, pp. 282-290.*

C2686 Blake's Heavenly City. *Time and Tide*, 7 July 1951, pp. 648, 650. Review of *William Blake: Jerusalem*, A Facsimile, The Trianon Press. *See also* C2692.

C2687 [Review of] *Heavensent*, by Shu She-Yu. *The Bookman*, July/August 1951, pp. 6-7.

C2688 [Review of] *Blake's Hayley*, by Morchard Bishop. *The Bookman*, July/August 1951, p. 10.

C2689 [Review of] *Winged Chariot*, by Walter de la Mare. *The Bookman*, July/August 1951, p. 13. *See also* C2691.

C2690 Among the Evangelicals. *National and English Review*, July 1951, Vol. 137, No. 821, pp. 48, 50. Title in contents: Among the Evangelists. Review of *William Cowper*, by Norman Nicholson. *See also* C2660.

C2691 Meditation upon Time. *The Listener*, 19 July 1951, p. 113. Review of *Winged Chariot*, by Walter de la Mare. *See also* C2689.

C2692 England's Ezekiel. *TLS*, 20 July 1951, p. 453. Second leader on *Jerusalem*, by William Blake. Unsigned. *See also* C2686.

C2693   ASSAULTING WAVES. *TLS*, 27 July 1951, p. 462.

        Reprinted (revised): *Poems of Many Years*, 1957.

C2694   Beauty and Truth. *TLS*, 27 July 1951, p. 464. Review of *The Prefigurative Imagination of John Keats*, by Newell F. Ford. Unsigned.

C2695   Happy Voyager. *TLS*, 27 July 1951, p. 471. Review of *Long Innings: The Autobiography of Sir Pelham Warner*. Unsigned.

C2696   The Grecian Muse. *TLS*, 3 August 1951, p. 485. Leader on *Medieval and Modern Greek Poetry*, edited by C. A. Trypanis. Unsigned.

C2697   Advancing Science. *TLS*, 3 August 1951, p. 488. Review of *Francis Bacon*, by Benjamin Farrington. Unsigned.

C2698   JAPANESE GLIMPSES [*later* THREEFOLD SCREEN]. *Sunday Times*, 5 August 1951, p. 4.

        Reprinted: *A Hong Kong House*, 1962.

C2699   Alias Shakeshafte. *TLS*, 10 August 1951, p. 498. Review of *"In the Quick Forge and Working-House of Thought . . .": Lancashire and Shropshire and the Young Shakespeare*, by Alan Keen. Unsigned.

C2700   Caroline Poet. *TLS*, 10 August 1951, p. 501. Second leader on Robert Herrick. Unsigned.

C2701   The Fable of Comenius. *TLS*, 10 August 1951, p. 502. Review of *The Labyrinth of the World and the Paradise of the Heart*, by John Amos Komensky. Unsigned.

C2702   An English Type. *TLS*, 24 August 1951, p. 533. Leader on Sir Walter Raleigh. Unsigned.

C2703   [Review of] *Your Penmanship*, by K. U. Ockendon. *TLS*, 24 August 1951, p. 537. Unsigned.

C2704   [Review of] *The Year's Work in Literature, 1950*, edited by John Lehmann. *TLS*, 24 August 1951, p. 537. Unsigned.

C2705   DEPOSED. *TLS*, 24 August 1951, [Special Issue:] The Mind of 1951, p. xix.

C2706   The Far East. *TLS*, 24 August 1951, [Special Issue:] The Mind of 1951, p. xlvii. On English literature in Japan. Unsigned.

C2707   The Study of Hamlet. *TLS*, 31 August 1951, p. 550. Review of *Scourge and Minister*, by G. R. Elliott. Unsigned.

C2708   [Review of] *Letty Landon*, by Helen Ashton. *The Bookman*, September 1951, pp. 5–6.

C2709   [Review of] *Dead Men Rising*, by Seaforth Mackenzie. *The Bookman*, September 1951, p. 9. Signed E.B.

C2710   [Review of] *The Autobiography of an Unknown Indian*, by Nirad C. Chaudhuri. *The Bookman*, September 1951, pp. 10–11. Signed E.B.

C2711   [Review of] *Daughter of England*, by Dorothy Margaret Stuart. *The Bookman*, September 1951, p. 11.

C2712   [Review of] *The Young George du Maurier*, by Daphne du Maurier. *The Bookman*, September 1951, pp. 13–14.

C2713   Christianity in Japan. *TLS*, 14 September 1951, p. 585. Review of *The Christian Century in Japan, 1549–1650*, by C. R. Boxer. Unsigned.

C2714   Nature's Poet. *TLS*, 28 September 1951, p. 607. Review of *James Thomson, Poet of "The Seasons"*, by Douglas Grant. Unsigned.

C2715   Biographical Ways. *TLS*, 28 September 1951, p. 613. Leader on *Charles Dickens*, by Julian Symons. Unsigned.

C2716   Literary Talk. *TLS*, 28 September 1951, p. 614. Review of *Classical Influences on English Poetry*, by J. A. K. Thomson. Unsigned.

C2717   [Review of] *Henry Irving*, by his grandson Laurence Irving. *The Bookman*, October 1951, p. 3.

C2718   [Review of] *Leslie Stephen*, by Noel Annan. *The Bookman*, October 1951, p. 17. Signed E.B.

C2719   [Review of] *Sir Francis Drake*, by J. A. Williamson; and *Queen Victoria*, by Roger Fulford. *The Bookman*, October 1951, pp. 17–18.

C2720   [Review of] *Between Life and Death*, by Harley Williams. *The Bookman*, October 1951, p. 18. Signed E.B.

C2721   [Review of] *The Moods of London*, by R. J. Cruikshank. *The Bookman*, October 1951, pp. 21–22. Signed E.B.

C2722   [Review of] *A World Apart*, by Gustav Herling. *The Bookman*, October 1951, pp. 22–23.

C2723   [Review of] *The Letters of Private Wheeler*, edited by B. H. Liddell Hart. *The Bookman*, October 1951, pp. 23–24.

C2724   English Eccentric. *TLS*, 5 October 1951, p. 626. Review of *Salt and His Circle*, by Stephen Winston. Unsigned.

C2725   [Review of] *The Helen of Euripides*, a translation by Rex Warner. *TLS*, 19 October 1951, p. 666. Unsigned.

C2726   A Prose Election. *TLS*, 26 October 1951, p. 677. Leader on political poetry. Unsigned.

C2727   [Review of] *Tillotson*, by Philip Trower. *The Bookman*, November 1951, p. 6.

C2728   [Review of] *Nelson's Band of Brothers*, by Ludovic Kennedy. *The Bookman*, November 1951, p. 10.

C2729   [Review of] *The Life and Letters of David Beatty, Admiral of the Fleet*, by W. S. Chalmers. *The Bookman*, November 1951, pp. 11–12.

C2730   [Review of] *The Sea Around Us*, by Rachel L. Carson. *The Bookman*, November 1951, pp. 17–18.

C2731   [Review of] *Phantom Was There*, by R. J. T. Hills. *The Bookman*, November 1951, p. 19.

C2732   Old Papers. *TLS*, 2 November 1951, p. 693. Leader on the dispersal of John Nichols's papers. Unsigned.

C2733   Shakespeare's Integrity. *TLS*, 2 November 1951, p. 694. Review of *The Meaning of Shakespeare*, by Harold C. Goddard. Unsigned.

C2734   Youthful Idealism. *TLS*, 9 November 1951, p. 709. Review of *The Young Shelley: Genesis of a Radical*, by Kenneth Neill Cameron. Unsigned.

C2735   A Portion to Eight. *TLS*, 16 November 1951, p. 731. Leader on *Poems, 1951*, with introduction by John Hayward. Unsigned.

C2736   The Poems of Clough. *TLS*, 23 November 1951, p. 748. Review of *The Poems of Arthur Hugh Clough*, edited by H. F. Lowry, A. L. P. Norrington, and F. L. Mulhauser. Unsigned. Also issued separately as an offprint (*see* A114).

C2737   For the Young Person. *TLS*, 23 November 1951, p. 749. Second leader on *Children's Periodicals of the Nineteenth Century*, by Sheila Egoff. Unsigned.

C2738   Pursuits of Literature. *TLS*, 30 November 1951, p. 765. Leader on *The Year's Work in English Studies*, Vol. 30. Unsigned.

C2739   [Review of] *Maiden Voyage*, by Barnaby Dogbolt. *Bookman Annual*, Christmas 1951, p. 9.

C2740   [Review of] *Bernard Spilsbury*, by D. G. Browne and E. V. Tullett. *Bookman Annual*, Christmas 1951, pp. 13–14.

C2741   [Review of] *Wilkie Collins: A Biography*, by Kenneth Robinson. *Bookman Annual*, Christmas 1951, pp. 14–15.

C2742   [Review of] *Peninsular Cavalry General*, edited by T. H. McGuffie. *Bookman Annual*, Christmas 1951, p. 18.

C2743   Poetical Pieces. *Bookman Annual*, Christmas 1951, pp. 20–21. Comments on *Complete Poems of Robert Frost; Collected Poems*, by Marianne Moore; *The Lost River*, by Lawrence Spingarn; *The Visitor*, by Haro Hodson; *The Singing Earth*, by Douglas Gibson; *The Naked Mountain*, by Peter Leyland; *Every Star a Tongue*, by Margaret Willy; *This Starry Stranger*, edited by Jane Baird; and *Poetry and Drama*, by T. S. Eliot.

C2744   Charles Edmund Blunden. *SS. Peter & Paul, Yalding, with S. Mary, Laddingford [Parish Magazine]*, December 1951, Vol. 6, No. 12, pp. [4–5]. On Blunden's father. Also issued separately as an offprint (*see* A115).

C2745 DR. JOHNSON REVISITS A MILLSTREAM AT LICH-
FIELD. *Everybody's*, 1 December 1951, p. 24. Translated
from Johnson's Latin by Blunden.

Reprinted: *English Poetry: A Short History*, by Kenneth
Hopkins, 1962 (B247).

C2746 Literary Exchanges. *TLS*, 7 December 1951, p. 782. Review of *The Percy Letters*, edited by David Nichol Smith
and Cleanth Brooks, Vol. 3: *The Correspondence of
Thomas Percy and Thomas Warton*, edited by M. G. Robinson and Leah Dennis. Unsigned.

C2747 An Ancient School. *TLS*, 7 December 1951, p. 786. Review
of *A History of Worcester Royal Grammar School*, by F. V.
Follett. Unsigned.

C2748 Cricket History. *TLS*, 14 December 1951, p. 810. Review
of *Brown and Company: The Tour in Australia*, by J. H.
Fingleton; and *Pre-Victorian Sussex Cricket*, by H. F. and
A. P. Squire. Unsigned.

C2749 Japanese History. *TLS*, 21 December 1951, p. 815. Review
of *Japan in World History*, by G. B. Sansom; and *The Occupation of Japan: Second Phase, 1948–50*, by Robert A.
Fearey. Unsigned.

C2750 Hardy Annual. *TLS*, 28 December 1951, p. 837. Leader on
Whitaker's Almanack, 1952. Unsigned.

1952

C2751 [Review of] *The Struggle for Europe*, by Chester Wilmot.
The Bookman, January/February 1952, p. 5.

C2752 [Review of] *The Wilderness Voyage*, by Peter Grieve. *The
Bookman*, January/February 1952, pp. 12–13. Signed E.B.

C2753 [Review of] *Carl Linnaeus*, by Knut Hagberg. *The Bookman*, January/February 1952, p. 13. *See also* C2785.

C2754 [Review of] *Thomas Carlyle*, by Julian Symons. *The Bookman*, January/February 1952, p. 14. Signed E.B.

C2755 English Riddles. *TLS*, 4 January 1952, p. 10. Review of
English Riddles from Oral Traditions, by Archer Taylor.
Unsigned.

C2756 Signs and Spirits. *TLS*, 4 January 1952, p. 13. Review of
Pandaemonium, 1684, by Richard Bovet, with an introduction and notes by Montague Summers. Unsigned.

C2757 The Poet Revises. *TLS*, 11 January 1952, p. 25. Leader on
Poems in Process, by Phyllis Bartlett. Unsigned.

C2758 History and Reading. *TLS*, 25 January 1952, p. 77. Leader
on *English Literature and its Readers*, by G. M. Trevelyan.
Unsigned.

C2759 Constable's Letters. *TLS*, 25 January 1952, p. 79. Review of *Memoirs of the Life of John Constable*, by C. R. Leslie. Unsigned.

C2760 [Review of] *Oxford v. Cambridge: The Story of the University Rugby Match*, by Howard Marshall in collaboration with J. P. Jordan. *TLS*, 25 January 1952, p. 83. Unsigned.

C2761 Japan After the Occupation. *World Review*, February 1952, New Series, Vol. 36, pp. 9–12.

C2762 The Hardy Spirit. *TLS*, 1 February 1952, p. 93. Leader on *Thomas Hardy*, by R. A. Scott-James. Unsigned.

C2763 [Review of] *The Government College Miscellany*, Mangalore, March 1951, Vol. 28, Wordsworth Centenary Number, edited by M. I. Hashimi. *TLS*, 1 February 1952, p. 98.

C2764 [Review of] *The Worthing Parade: The First Collection of Sussex Articles Mainly Connected with Worthing*, Vol. 1. *TLS*, 1 February 1952, p. 99. Unsigned.

C2765 Penmanship. *TLS*, 1 February 1952, p. 100. Review of *Written by Hand*, by Aubrey West. Unsigned.

C2766 [Review of] *We Offer . . . Prose and Verse of the Poetry Guild*, Vol. 1, No. 1. *TLS*, 8 February 1952, p. 114. Unsigned.

C2767 [Review of] *Journal of the British Society of Master Glass-Painters*, Vol. 11, No. 1. *TLS*, 8 February 1952, p. 114.

C2768 [Review of] *The Life of Vice-Admiral William Bligh, R.N., F.R.S.*, by George Mackaness. *TLS*, 8 February 1952, p. 114. Unsigned.

C2769 [Review of] *Boyhood: An Autobiography*, by George Montagu, Earl of Sandwich. *TLS*, 8 February 1952, p. 114. Unsigned.

C2770 [Review of] *Three Romantic Countries: Reminiscences of Travel in Dalmatia, Ireland and Portugal*, by Douglas Goldring. *TLS*, 8 February 1952, p. 115. Unsigned.

C2771 England's Lucians. *TLS*, 15 February 1952, p. 125. Leader on the death of Norman Douglas. Unsigned.

C2772 A Rescued Poet. *The Spectator*, 22 February 1952, p. 240. Review of *The Complete Works of William Diaper*, edited with an introduction by Dorothy Broughton.

C2773 NOUVELLES LITTÉRAIRES, OR INANI MUNERE [*later* FORSAKEN MEMORIALS]. *TLS*, 22 February 1952, p. 135.

Reprinted (revised): *A Hong Kong House*, 1962.

C2774 Bacon to Pope. *TLS*, 22 February 1952, p. 143. Review of *The Seventeenth Century*, by Richard Foster Jones. Unsigned.

C2775 [Review of] *The Archaeological Journal*, Vol. 106 for the year 1949, Supplement: Memorial Volume to Sir Arthur Clapham. *TLS*, 22 February 1952, p. 146. Unsigned.

C2776 [Review of] *Voltaire: Man of Justice*, by Adolph Meyer. *TLS*, 22 February 1952, p. 146. Unsigned.

C2777 [Review of] *Proceedings of the British Academy*, 1948. *TLS*, 22 February 1952, p. 146. Unsigned.

C2778 [Review of] *This Unlikely Earth: Poems, 1946–51*, by F. Pratt Green. *TLS*, 22 February 1952, p. 146. Unsigned.

C2779 [Review of] *The Happy Valley*, by Jules Roy. *The Bookman*, March 1952, p. 11.

C2780 [Review of] *The Man Outside*, by Wolfgang Borchert. *The Bookman*, March 1952, p. 13.

C2781 [Review of] *Island of the Swan: Mauritius*, by Michael Malim. *The Bookman*, March 1952, p. 14. Signed E.B.

C2782 [Review of] *The Real Tripitaka*, by Arthur Waley. *The Bookman*, March 1952, pp. 15–16. Signed E.B.

C2783 [Review of] *Doctor in the House*, by Richard Gordon. *The Bookman*, March 1952, p. 16.

C2784 Leigh Hunt's "London Journal". *Studies in English Literature*, Tokyo, March 1952, Vol. 28, No. 1, pp. 1–16.*

C2785 Carl Linnaeus. *TLS*, 7 March 1952, p. 173. Second leader on *Carl Linnaeus*, by Knut Hagberg. Unsigned. *See also* C2753.

C2786 Canon Pym. *TLS*, 14 March 1952, p. 186. Review of *Tom Pym*, by Dora Pym. Unsigned.

C2787 William Langland. *TLS*, 14 March 1952, p. 189. Second leader. Unsigned.

C2788 Teller of Tales. *TLS*, 21 March 1952, p. 205. Second leader on *So Long to Learn*, by John Masefield. Unsigned.

C2789 Virginia in 1616. *TLS*, 21 March 1952, p. 209. Review of *A True Relation of the State of Virginia lefte by Sir Thomas Dale, Knight, in May last 1616*, printed from the original manuscript in the Private Library of Henry C. Taylor, Esq. Unsigned.

C2790 Contemplative Odes. *TLS*, 28 March 1952, p. 223. Review of *The Delphic Charioteer and Other Poems*, by E. H. W. Meyerstein. Unsigned.

C2791 [Review of] *Chinese Color-Prints from the Painting Manual of the Mustard Seed Garden*, with an introduction by Jan Tschichold. *TLS*, 28 March 1952, p. 226. Unsigned.

C2792 [Review of] *Gaelic Proverbs*, collected and translated into English with equivalents from other European languages, by Alexander Nicolson. *TLS*, 28 March 1952, p. 226. Unsigned.

C2793 [Review of] *The Desert in the Heart*, by Peter Gladwin. *The Bookman*, April 1952, p. 8.

C2794 [Review of] *Recalled to Service: Memoirs of General Maxime Weygand. The Bookman*, April 1952, pp. 11-12. Signed E.B.

C2795 [Review of] *In Place of Fear*, by Aneurin Bevan. *The Bookman*, April 1952, pp. 13-14. Signed E.B.

C2796 Coleridge's Letters. *The Spectator*, 4 April 1952, pp. 447-448. Review of *The Letters of Samuel Taylor Coleridge*, selected and with an introduction by Kathleen Raine.

C2797 Alias Southey. *TLS*, 4 April 1952, p. 231. Review of *Letters from England*, by Robert Southey, edited with an introduction by Jack Simmons. Unsigned.

C2798 About Donne. *TLS*, 4 April 1952, p. 238. Review of *The Poetry of John Donne*, by Doniphan Louthan and *The Prayers of John Donne*, selected and edited from the earliest sources with an essay on *Donne's Idea of Prayer*, by Herbert H. Umbach. Unsigned.

C2799 [Review of] *Bulletin of the Japan Society of London*, February 1952, Vol. 1, No. 6. *TLS*, 4 April 1952, p. 242. Unsigned.

C2800 [Review of] *The Literature of England, A.D. 500-1950: A Survey of British Literature from the Beginnings to the Present Day*, by William J. Entwistle and Eric Gillett. *TLS*, 4 April 1952, p. 242. Unsigned.

C2801 [Review of] *Hellenistic Civilization*, by W. W. Tarn, revised by the author and G.T. Griffith. *TLS*, 4 April 1952, p. 242. Unsigned.

C2802 [Review of] *Poetic Diction: A Study in Meaning*, by Owen Barfield. *TLS*, 4 April 1952, p. 243. Unsigned. *See also* C713.

C2803 [Review of] *Charles d'Orleans, and Other French Poets: Rondels*, chosen and translated by Cedric Wallis. *TLS*, 4 April 1952, p. 243. Unsigned.

C2804 [Review of] *The Vigil of Venus*, done into English, by Lewis Gielgud. *TLS*, 4 April 1952, p. 243. Unsigned.

C2805 [Review of] *Culture Worlds*, by Richard Joel Russell and Fred Bowerman Kniffen. *TLS*, 11 April 1952, p. 255. Unsigned.

C2806 Romance of Scholarship. *TLS*, 18 April 1952, p. 265. Second leader on the manuscript of *Beowulf*. Unsigned.

C2807 Merry & Co. *TLS*, 18 April 1952, p. 270. Review of *The Autobiography of Frank Richards*. Unsigned.

C2808 [Review of] *A Study in Writing: The Foundations of Grammatology*, by I. J. Gelb. *TLS*, 18 April 1952, p. 271. Unsigned.

C2809 Thomas Hardy and Miss Owen. *TLS*, 25 April 1952, p. 282. Review of *Hardy and the Lady from Madison Square*, by Carl J. Weber. Unsigned.

C2810 [Review of] *Index Verborum Iuvenalis*, by Lucile Kelling and Albert Suskin. *TLS*, 25 April 1952, p. 286. Unsigned.

C2811 [Review of] *James Joyce's Ulysses: A Study*, by Stuart Gilbert. *TLS*, 25 April 1952, p. 286. Unsigned.

C2812 [Review of] *Asia's Lands and Peoples . . . A Geography of One-Third the Earth and Two-Thirds Its People*, second edition, by George B. Cressey. *TLS*, 25 April 1952, p. 287. Unsigned.

C2813 A Poet Comes South. *The Adelphi*, May 1952, Vol. 28, No. 3, pp. 597-600. On James Thomson. For FROM A TOKYO LAWN, p. 629 *see* C2530.

C2814 [Review of] *A Many-Splendoured Thing: A Personal Narrative*, by Han Suyin. *The Bookman*, May 1952, pp. 1-2.

C2815 [Review of] *Black Vanguard*, by Edward Atiyah. *The Bookman*, May 1952, p. 8.

C2816 [Review of] *Southwards from China*, by Woodrow Wyatt. *The Bookman*, May 1952, pp. 12-13. Signed E.B.

C2817 [Review of] *The White Rabbit*, from the story told to him by Wing Commander F. F. E. Yeo-Thomas, by Bruce Marshall. *The Bookman*, May 1952, pp. 14-15. *See also* C2842.

C2818 [Review of] *The Pentameron*, by Giambattista Basile, translated by Sir Richard Burton, introduction by E. R. Vincent. *TLS*, 2 May 1952, p. 302. Unsigned.

C2819 [Review of] *Rockets, Missiles, and Space Travel*; second edition, by Willey Ley. *TLS*, 2 May 1952, p. 303. Unsigned.

C2820 At Pisa Once. *The Spectator*, 9 May 1952, pp. 620, 622. Review of *Byron, Shelley and their Pisan Circle*, by C. L. Cline.

C2821 Two Rare Plays. *TLS*, 9 May 1952, p. 316. Review of *Bonduca*, by John Fletcher; and *Wit and Science*, by John Redford, the Malone Society Reprints. Unsigned.

C2822 More About Cricket. *TLS*, 9 May 1952, p. 318. Review of *Next Man In*, by Gerald Brodribb; *Cricket*, by N. W. D. Yardley and J. M. Kilburn; and *Hedley Verity*, by Sam Davis. Unsigned.

C2823 "A Spirit, Yet a Woman Too". *Everybody's*, 10 May 1952, p. 15. On Sara Coleridge.

C2824 A Wordsworthian. *TLS*, 16 May 1952, p. 329. Leader on Lascelles Abercrombie. Unsigned.

C2825 [Review of] *Restless Consort: The Invasion of Albert the Conqueror*, by E. E. P. Tisdall. *TLS*, 16 May 1952, p. 329. Unsigned.

C2826 [Review of] *A History of Philosophy*, by Frank Thilly, revised by Ledger Wood. *TLS*, 16 May 1952, p. 335. Unsigned.

C2827 [Review of] *Straight Hit*, by Keith Miller and R. S. Whitington. *TLS*, 16 May 1952, p. 335. Unsigned.

C2828 [Review of] *Japan*, edited by Hugh Borton. *TLS*, 23 May 1952, p. 351. Unsigned.

C2829 Painter and Prebendary. *TLS*, 30 May 1952, p. 356. Review of *John Constable and the Fishers: A Record of a Friendship*, by R. B. Beckett. Unsigned.

C2830 [Review of] *The British Museum Quarterly*, Vol. 15. *TLS*, 30 May 1952, p. 366. Unsigned.

C2831 [Review of] *Unknown India: A Pilgrimage into a Forgotten World*, by Walther Eidlitz. *TLS*, 30 May 1952, p. 366. Unsigned.

C2832 [Review of] *1001 Questions Answered about Your Aquarium*, by Ida M. Mellen and Robert J. Lanier. *TLS*, 30 May 1952, p. 366. Unsigned.

C2833 THE WOOD'S EDGE. *Pegasus*, New York, Summer 1952, Vol. 1, No. 3, p. one.

C2834 A Poetical Petition. *West Country Magazine*, Summer 1952, Vol. 7, No. 2, pp. 96–97. On C. V. Le Grice.

C2835 [Review of] *Night Be My Witness*, by Walter J. Clapham. *The Bookman*, June 1952, pp. 6–7.

C2836 [Review of] *To Teach the Senators Wisdom*, by J. C. Masterman. *The Bookman*, June 1952, pp. 15–16.

C2837 [Footnote to] "Did You Once See Shelley Plain?" by Shane Leslie. *Keats-Shelley Memorial Bulletin, Rome*, [June] 1952, No. 4, p. 3. The footnote did not appear in the *Eton College Chronicle*, 1 June 1939 where Leslie's article was first published.

C2838 A Poet's Castle. *Keats-Shelley Memorial Bulletin, Rome*, [June] 1952, No. 4, pp. 4–8. On Castle Goring built by Sir Bysshe Shelley.

C2839 The Family of Edward Williams. *Keats-Shelley Memorial Bulletin, Rome*, [June] 1952, No. 4, pp. 49–51.

C2840 Fred Edgcumbe. *TLS*, 6 June 1952, p. 377. Letter signed E. Blunden. *See also* C2605 for earlier letters.

C2841 [Review of] *Austrian Holiday*, by S. P. B. Mais, with a diary by Gillian Mais. *TLS*, 6 June 1952, p. 383. Unsigned.

C2842 [Review of] *The White Rabbit*, from the story told to him by Wing Commander F. F. E. Yeo-Thomas, by Bruce Marshall. *TLS*, 6 June 1952, p. 383. Unsigned. *See also* C2817.

C2843 [Review of] *I Was a Monk*, by John Tettemer, edited by Janet Mabie. *TLS*, 13 June 1952, p. 394. Unsigned.

497

C2844   [Review of] *The Left Wing in Japanese Politics*, by Evelyn S. Colbert. *TLS*, 13 June 1952, p. 395. Unsigned.

C2845   Lost and Found. *TLS*, 20 June 1952, p. 405. Leader on *The Lost Literature of Mediaeval England*, by R. M. Wilson. Unsigned.

C2846   [Review of] *Cricket and the Clock: A Post-War Commentary*, by E. W. Swanton. *TLS*, 20 June 1952, p. 411. Unsigned.

C2847   [Review of] *Gentlemen Spies*, by Kurt Singer. *TLS*, 20 June 1952, p. 411. Unsigned.

C2848   In Old Japan. *Time and Tide*, 21 June 1952, pp. 685–686. Review of *The Japanese Discovery of Europe*, by Donald Keene.

C2849   [Review of] *The Journal of the Royal Society of Antiquaries of Ireland*, 1951, Vol. 81, Part 2. *TLS*, 27 June 1952, p. 426. Unsigned.

C2850   [Review of] *Notes and Records of the Royal Society of London*, May 1952, Vol. 9, No. 2. *TLS*, 27 June 1952, p. 426. Unsigned.

C2851   [Review of] *Who's Who in World Cricket*, by Roy Webber. *TLS*, 27 June 1952, p. 427. Unsigned.

C2852   [Review of] *Dead Cities and Forgotten Tribes*, by Gordon Cooper. *TLS*, 27 June 1952, p. 427. Unsigned.

C2853   Quatercentenary Celebrations, 1953. *The Blue*, July 1952, Vol. 69, No. 3, p. 171. Letter requesting further contributions for *The Christ's Hospital Book* (*see* B153). See also C2929, 3025, 3027.

C2854   [Review of] *People of the Deer*, by Farley Mowat. *The Bookman*, July/August 1952, pp. 3–4.

C2855   [Review of] *James Braid*, by Bernard Darwin. *The Bookman*, July/August 1952, pp. 13–14. Signed E.B.

C2856   THE SEASON REOPENS [*later* THE SEASON OPENS]. *Medical Bulletin*, July 1952, Vol. 1, No. 1, p. 7.

     Reprinted: *The Book of Cricket Verse*, 1953; and *Poems of Many Years*, 1957.

C2857   Confidante. *National and English Review*, July 1952, Vol. 139, No. 833, pp. 44–45. Review of *Dearest Isa: Robert Browning's Letters to Isabella Blagden*, edited by Edward C. MacAleer.

C2858   The Overflowing Sun. *The Spectator*, 4 July 1952, pp. 38, 40. Review of *Llewelyn Powys: A Selection from His Writings*, by Kenneth Hopkins.

C2859   Cricket Heroes. *TLS*, 4 July 1952, p. 440. Review of *W. G. Grace*, by Clifford Bax; and *Frank Woolley*, by Oliver Warner. Unsigned.

C2860 [Review of] *New Light on the Most Ancient East*, by V. Gordon Childe. *TLS*, 4 July 1952, p. 442. Unsigned.

C2861 [Review of] *The Ship's Compass: Including General Magnetism, Theory, Practice and Calculations . . . by G. A. A. Grant and J. Klinkert. *TLS*, 4 July 1952, p. 474. Unsigned.

C2862 [Review of] *Cricket's Secret History*, by Walter Hammond. *TLS*, 18 July 1952, p. 475. Unsigned.

C2863 A Lover of Books, J.-W. Dalby (1799–1880). *Études anglaises*, août 1952, Vol. 5, No. 3, pp. 193–201. Also issued separately as an offprint (*see* A116).

C2864 [Review of] *Avicenna, Scientist and Philosopher: A Millenary Symposium*, edited by G. M. Wickens. *TLS*, 1 August 1952, p. 506. Unsigned.

C2865 [Review of] *Storm and Stress*, by H. B. Garland. *TLS*, 1 August 1952, p. 506. Unsigned.

C2866 [Review of] *A Tribute to George Coffin Taylor: Studies and Essays, Chiefly Elizabethan*, by his Students and Friends, edited by Arnold Williams. *TLS*, 1 August 1952, p. 506. Unsigned.

C2867 [Review of] *Museless Musings*, by Ardaser Sorabjee N. Wadia. *TLS*, 1 August 1952, pp. 506–507. Unsigned.

C2868 [Review of] *Come and Fish*, by Michael Shephard. *TLS*, 1 August 1952, p. 507. Unsigned.

C2869 [Review of] *New Handbook of Freshwater Fishing*, by Lee Wulff. *TLS*, 1 August 1952, p. 507. Unsigned.

C2870 Japanese Classic. *TLS*, 8 August 1952, p. 513. Review of *The Tale of Genji*, by Lady Murasaki, translated from the Japanese by Arthur Waley. Unsigned.

C2871 [Review of] *Literature through Art*, by Helmut A. Hatzfeld. *TLS*, 15 August 1952, p. 538. Unsigned.

C2872 [Review of] *Britannica Book of the Year*, 1952. *TLS*, 15 August 1952, p. 539. Unsigned.

C2873 Poetical Profundities. *TLS*, 22 August 1952, p. 551. Review of *A Reading of George Herbert*, by Rosamond Tuve. Unsigned.

C2874 [Review of] *Wordsworth: Poems in Two Volumes*, 1807, second edition, edited by Helen Darbishire. *TLS*, 22 August 1952, p. 555. Unsigned.

C2875 [Review of] *League Cricket in England*, by Roy Genders. *TLS*, 22 August 1952, p. 555. Unsigned.

C2876 Japanese Print. *TLS*, 29 August 1952, Special Autumn Issue, p. xlviii. Written in collaboration with Tomop Abe. On Japan's young writers.

C2876 [Review of] *Men at Arms*, by Evelyn Waugh. *The Book-*
.1 *man*, September, 1952, p. 3.

C2877   [Review of] *Museum Pieces*, by William Plomer. *The Bookman*, September 1952, pp. 5-6.

C2878   [Review of] *The Aeneid of Virgil*, translated by C. Day Lewis. *The Bookman*, September 1952, p. 14.

C2879   The Real Robin Hood? *TLS*, 5 September 1952, p. 581. Second leader on the outlaw. Unsigned.

C2880   An Emancipated Woman. *TLS*, 5 September 1952, p. 582. Review of *Mary Wollstonecraft*, by Ralph M. Wardle. Unsigned.

C2881   [Review of] *Ballistics in the Seventeenth Century*, by A. R. Hall. *TLS*, 5 September 1952, p. 586. Unsigned.

C2882   [Review of] *The Tea Clippers: An Account of the China Tea Trade and Some of the British Sailing Ships* . . . by David R. MacGregor. *TLS*, 5 September 1952, p. 587. Unsigned.

C2883   [Review of] *Human Geography*, by Jean Brunhes, abridged edition by M. Jean-Brunhes Delamarre and Pierre Deffontaines, translated by Ernest F. Row. *TLS*, 5 September 1952, p. 587. Unsigned.

C2884   [Review of] *The Book of Cricket*, by Denzil Batchelor. *TLS*, 5 September 1952, p. 587. Unsigned.

C2885   Miss Brawne, Mrs. Lindon. *The Spectator*, 12 September 1952, pp. 336, 338. Review of *Fanny Brawne*, by Joanna Richardson.

C2886   Ascribed to Blake. *TLS*, 12 September 1952, p. 594. Review of *Genesis: The Seven Days of the Created World*, by William Blake. Unsigned.

C2887   Disputed Legacy. *TLS*, 12 September 1952, p. 597. Leader on *English Character and the English Literary Tradition*, by Malcolm Wallace. Unsigned.

C2888   [Review of] *The Trial of Gustav Rau, Otto Monsson and Willem Smith*, edited by G. W. Keeton and John Cameron; *The Trial of the Seddons*, edited by Filson Young; and *The Trial of William Palmer*, edited by George H. Knott, revised by Eric R. Watson. *TLS*, 12 September 1952, p. 602. Unsigned.

C2889   [Review of] *With the West Indies in Australia, 1951-52: A Critical Study of the Tour*, by A. G. ("Johnnie") Moyes. *TLS*, 12 September 1952, p. 603. Unsigned.

C2890   [Review of] *Quantock Country*, by Berta Lawrence. *TLS*, 12 September 1952, p. 603. Unsigned.

C2891   Oxford Team. *Nippon Times*, 22 September 1952, p. 8. Letter to Professor Kaoru Matsmoto, Sophia University, Tokyo.

C2892   [Review of] *The Dickensian*, September 1952, Vol. 48, Part 4. *TLS*, 26 September 1952, p. 634. Unsigned.

C2893 [Review of] *The Amateur Historian*, August/September 1952, Vol. 1, No. 1. *TLS*, 26 September 1952, p. 634. Unsigned.

C2894 1952 (In winter moonlight, thinking of many things). *Pegasus*, Autumn 1952, No. 4, p. twelve.

C2895 [Review of] *A Ray of Darkness*, by Margiad Evans. *The Bookman*, October 1952, pp. 11–12. Signed E.B.

C2896 [Review of] *Fear God and Dread Nought*, edited by Arthur J. Marder. *The Bookman*, October 1952, p. 12.

C2897 [Review of] *The Years with Mother*, by Augustus J. C. Hare. *The Bookman*, October 1952, pp. 14–15. Signed E.B.

C2898 [Review of] *A Book of Beauty*, by John Hadfield. *The Bookman*, October 1952, p. 16.

C2899 [Review of] *Arrow in the Blue*, by Arthur Koestler. *The Bookman*, October 1952, p. 21.

C2900 [Review of] *Miss Douglas of New York*, by Angus Davidson. *The Bookman*, October 1952, pp. 21–22.

C2901 [Review of] *The Devils of Loudun*, by Aldous Huxley. *The Bookman*, October 1952, pp. 22–23. Signed E.B.

C2902 Letters from London and Boston. 1. *Bulletin, Tokyo Woman's Christian College*, October 1952, Vol. 5, No. 9, p. 2. Part 2 is by A. K. Reischauer.

C2903 PICARDY IN AUTUMN [*later* PICARDY SUNDAY]. *Medical Bulletin*, October 1952, [Vol. 1, No. 2], p. 11.
Reprinted (revised): *A Hong Kong House*, 1962.

C2904 Monumentum. *TLS*, 10 October 1952, p. 661. Leader on the Oxford University Press's edition of Ben Jonson. Unsigned.

C2905 A Family History. *TLS*, 17 October 1952, p. 682. Review of *Four Generations in China, Japan and Korea*, by A. C. Hyde Lay. Unsigned.

C2906 [Review of] *The Art of Sinking in Poetry*, edited by Edna Leake Steeves. *TLS*, 24 October 1952, p. 698. Unsigned.

C2907 [Review of] *Freshwater Tropical Aquarium Fishes*, by G. F. Harvey and Jack Hems. *TLS*, 24 October 1952, p. 699. Unsigned.

C2908 Edmund Spenser's 'Faerie Queene'. *Everybody's*, 25 October 1952, p. 17. On the quatercentenary of his death.

C2909 [Review of] *The Works of Aristotle*, translated into English under the editorship of Sir David Ross, Vol. 12, *Select Fragments*. *TLS*, 31 October 1952, p. 715. Unsigned.

C2910 [Review of] *Eclipses of the Sun*, fifth edition, by Samuel Alfred Mitchell. *TLS*, 31 October 1952, p. 715. Unsigned.

C2911   [Review of] *Noursemen in England: The South African Cricket Tour, 1951*, by C. O. Medworth. *TLS*, 31 October 1952, p. 715. Unsigned.

C2912   [Review of] *The Mind of East Asia*, by Lily Abegg. *TLS*, 31 October 1952, p. 715. Unsigned.

C2913   [Review of] *The Man Whistler*, by Hesketh Pearson. *The Bookman*, November 1952, pp. 7–8.

C2914   [Review of] *Jan Christian Smuts*, by J. C. Smuts. *The Bookman*, November 1952, pp. 8–9.

C2915   [Review of] *Robert Browning: A Portrait*, by Betty Miller. *The Bookman*, November 1952, pp. 11–12.

C2916   [Review of] *Portraits*, by Sir Joshua Reynolds. *The Bookman*, November 1952, p. 14.

C2917   [Review of] *Wings of the Wind*, by Peter Stainforth. *The Bookman*, November 1952, pp. 14–15.

C2918   [Review of] *The Denton Welch Journals*, edited by Jocelyn Brooke. *The Bookman*, November 1952, p. 16.

C2919   [Review of] *The Face of England*, by H. E. Bates. *The Bookman*, November 1952, p. 17.

C2920   [Review of] *Collected Poems*, by Dylan Thomas. *The Bookman*, November 1952, p. 18. Signed E.B.

C2921   Tributes from a Kinship in Husbandry. *Wessex*, Midwinter 1952, No. 4, pp. 81–82. In memoriam Harold John Massingham. Arthur Bryant, Adrian Bell and others also contributed.

C2922   Three Famous Schools. *TLS*, 7 November 1952, p. 730. Review of *A History of Shrewsbury School, 1552–1952*, by J. Basil Oldham; *King Edward's School, Birmingham, 1552–1952*, by T. W. Hutton; and *A History of Sherborne School*, by A. B. Gourlay. Unsigned.

C2923   [Review of] *Journey to the Far Pacific*, by Thomas E. Dewey. *TLS*, 7 November 1952, p. 731. Unsigned.

C2924   SPIRIT-WIND (In the night, in the night the wild harp answered best;). *Everybody's*, 8 November 1952, p. 33.

C2925   War Graves in Italy: Southern Memorials to British Sacrifice [*later* War Cemeteries in Italy]. *The Times*, 8 November 1952, p. 7. Signed From Our Special Correspondent in Italy. The article entitled 'War Cemeteries in Italy' in the issue of 26 August 1952, p. 5 is not by Blunden.
Reprinted (revised): *Their Name Liveth*, [1954], Vol. 1, pp. 5–9.

C2926   Sir Edward Marsh. *TLS*, 21 November 1952, p. 761. Second leader on his eightieth birthday. Unsigned.

C2927   Poetry and Children. *TLS*, 28 November 1952, p. 777. Second leader on the conference arranged by the West Riding of Yorkshire Education Committee. Unsigned.

C2928   The Pick of the Year. *TLS*, 28 November 1952, p. 780.
Review of *The Bedside "Guardian": A Selection from
the Manchester Guardian, 1951-52*, edited by Ivor Brown;
and *Spectator Harvest*, with a foreword by Wilson Harris.
Unsigned.

C2929   Quatercentenary Celebrations, 1953. *The Blue*, December
1952, Vol. 70, No. 1, pp. 41-42. Letter appealing for
assistance with the Fortune Theatre production, *The Dede
of Pittie*, on the history of Christ's Hospital (*see* A118;
B154). *See also* C2853, 3025, 3027.

C2930   [Review of] *Midsummer Meadow*, by John Moore. *Bookman Annual*, Christmas 1952, p. 7.

C2931   [Review of] *The Elizabethan Woman*, by Carroll Camden.
Bookman Annual, Christmas 1952, p. 13.

C2932   [Review of] *They Came to the Hills*, by Claire Eliane
Engel. *Bookman Annual*, Christmas 1952, pp. 14-15.
Signed E.B.

C2933   [Review of] *Nepal Himalaya*, by H. W. Tilman. *Bookman
Annual*, Christmas 1952, p. 15.

C2934   [Review of] *Queen Victoria and her Prime Ministers*, by
Algernon Cecil. *Bookman Annual*, Christmas 1952, pp. 16-
17. Signed E.B.

C2935   [Review of] *The Private Papers of Douglas Haig, 1914-
1919*, edited by Robert Blake. *Bookman Annual*, Christmas
1952, p. 17.

C2936   Some Recent Poetry. *Bookman Annual*, Christmas 1952,
pp. 18-19. Review of *News from the Village*, by Gerald
Bullett; *The Enchanted Grindstone*, by Henry Morton
Robinson; *In Praise of Life*, by H. N. Spalding; *New Poems:
A P.E.N. Anthology*, edited by Clifford Dyment, Roy
Fuller, and Montagu Slater; *The Choir Speaks*, edited by
W. G. Bebbington and E. N. Brown; and *Key to Modern
Poetry*, by Lawrence Durrell.

C2937   [Review of] *The English Language*, by Ernest Weekley.
TLS, 5 December 1952, p. 805. Unsigned.

C2938   "Brewer". *TLS*, 12 December 1952, p. 819. Second leader
on *Dictionary of Phrase and Fable*, by Brewer. Unsigned.

C2939   [Review of] *The Year's Work in English Studies*, Vol. 31,
edited by Frederick S. Boas and Beatrice White. *TLS*, 12
December 1952, p. 826. Unsigned.

C2940   [Review of] *Climate and the British Scene*, by Gordon
Manley. *TLS*, 12 December 1952, p. 827. Unsigned.

C2941   Training a Prince. *TLS*, 19 December 1952, p. 831. Review
of *Windows for the Crown Prince*, by Elizabeth Gray
Vining. Unsigned.

C2942 A Renowned Correspondence. *TLS*, 19 December 1952, p. 838. Review of *Jane Austen's Letters to her Sister Cassandra and Others*, second edition collected and edited by R. W. Chapman. Unsigned.

C2943 [Review of] *Dickens the Dramatist: On Stage, Screen and Radio*, by F. Dubrez Fawcett. *TLS*, 19 December 1952, p. 842. Unsigned.

C2944 [Review of] Excerpt from the *General Catalogue of Printed Books in the British Museum: Dante*. *TLS*, 26 December 1952, p. 857. Unsigned.

C2945 [Review of] *Poetry*, October 1952, Vol. 81, No. 1. *TLS*, 26 December 1952, p. 858. Unsigned.

C2946 [Review of] *Maps and Diagrams: Their Compilation and Construction*, by F. J. Monkhouse and H. R. Wilkinson. *TLS*, 26 December 1952, p. 859. Unsigned.

C2947 [Review of] *Orpheus*, by Herbert H. Marks. *TLS*, 26 December 1952, p. 859. Unsigned.

C2948 [Review of] *An Epistle, in Verse, occasioned by the Death of James Boswell*, by Samuel Martin. *TLS*, 26 December 1952, p. 859. Unsigned.

1953

C2949 THE SUSSEX DOWNS. *Medical Bulletin*, January 1953, Vol. 1, No. 3, p. 31.

Reprinted: *Poems of Many Years*, 1957.

C2950 [Review of] *Mary II, Queen of England*, by Hester W. Chapman. *The Bookman*, January/February 1953, pp. 3-4. Signed E.B.

C2951 [Review of] *Blind White Fish in Persia*, by Anthony Smith. *The Bookman*, January/February 1953, pp. 12-13.

C2952 Hongkong. *TLS*, 2 January 1953, p. 10. Review of *Hong Kong*, by Harold Ingrams. Unsigned.

C2953 [Review of] The Faber Gallery of Oriental Art: *Japanese Colour Prints from Harunobu to Utamaro*, with an introduction and notes by Wilfrid Blunt; *Kangra Painting*, with an introduction and notes by W. G. Archer; and *Persian Painting of the Fourteenth Century*, with an introduction and notes by Douglas Barrett. *TLS*, 2 January 1953, p. 14. Unsigned.

C2954 [Review of] *British Authors before 1800: A Biographical Dictionary*, edited by Stanley J. Kunitz and Howard Haycraft. *TLS*, 2 January 1953, p. 14. Unsigned.

C2955 [Review of] *William Barnes, Linguist*, by Willis D. Jacobs. *TLS*, 2 January 1953, p. 14. Unsigned.

C2956 [Review of] *The Coasts of the Country: An Anthology of Prayer drawn from the Early English Spiritual Writers*, edited by Clare Kirchberger, with introduction by Godfrey Anstruther. *TLS*, 2 January 1953, p. 15. Unsigned.

C2957 [Review of] *Tropical Fish as a Hobby: A Guide to Selection, Care and Breeding*, by Herbert R. Axelrod, with contributions by Myron Gordon and James W. Atz. *TLS*, 9 January 1953, p. 30. Unsigned.

C2958 Conversations in St. James's Place. *The Spectator*, 16 January 1953, p. 74. Review of *Recollections of the Table-Talk of Samuel Rogers*, first collected by the Revd Alexander Dyce, edited by Morchard Bishop.

C2959 [Review of] *The Game Fishes of Africa*, by Hugh Copley. *TLS*, 16 January 1953, p. 47. Unsigned.

C2960 [Review of] *Keats-Shelley Memorial Bulletin*, No. 4. *TLS*, 23 January 1953, p. 61. Unsigned.

C2961 [Review of] *Andrews' and Dury's Map of Wiltshire, 1773*, a reduced facsimile. *TLS*, 23 January 1953, p. 62. Unsigned.

C2962 [Review of] *The Story of the Woodward Schools*, by K. E. Kirk. *TLS*, 23 January 1953, p. 62. Unsigned.

C2963 [Review of] *Passenger Liners of the Western Ocean*, by C. R. Vernon Gibbs. *TLS*, 23 January 1953, p. 63. Unsigned.

C2964 [Review of] *India in Test Cricket 1932–1952*, by D. W. Bacha. *TLS*, 30 January 1953, p. 79. Unsigned.

C2965 [Review of] *Naval Memorials in the United Kingdom 1939–1945: Introduction to the Registers*; and *The War Dead of the British Commonwealth and Empire: The Register of the Names of those who fell in the 1939–1945 War and have no other Grave than the Sea*, Part 1. *TLS*, 30 January 1953, p. 79. Unsigned.

C2966 [Review of] *Salute the Red Duster*, by A. B. Campbell, with a foreword by Lord Mountevans. *TLS*, 6 February 1953, p. 95. Unsigned.

C2967 Famous Love of the Brownings. *Everybody's*, 7 February 1953, pp. 18, 26.

C2968 Borrowed Passages. *TLS*, 13 February 1953, p. 106. Review of *The Kenkyusha Dictionary of English Quotations*, edited by Sanki Ichikawa, Masami Nishikawa, and Mamoru Shimizu. Unsigned.

C2969 [Review of] *Études anglaises*, November 1952, No. 4. *TLS*, 13 February 1953, p. 110. Unsigned.

C2970 [Review of] *The Murison Burns Collection*, compiled by Nancie Campbell. *TLS*, 13 February 1953, p. 110. Unsigned. *See also* the article on the collection in the issue of 9 January, p. 32.

C2971 [Review of] *Mahatma Gandhi*, by Haridas T. Muzumdar. *TLS*, 13 February 1953, p. 110. Unsigned.

C2972 [Review of] *The Use of Radar at Sea*, edited by F. J. Wylie. *TLS*, 13 February 1953, p. 111. Unsigned.

C2973 [Review of] *Directions concerning Matter and Stile of Sermons*, by James Arderne. *TLS*, 20 February 1953, Supplement: Religion and Philosophy, p. xvi. Unsigned.

C2974 [Review of] *The Archaeology of World Religion: The Background of Primitivism, Zoroastrianism, Hinduism . . .* by Jack Finegan. *TLS*, 20 February 1953, Supplement: Religion and Philosophy, p. xvi. Unsigned.

C2975 Massingham the Younger. *TLS*, 20 February 1953, p. 121. Second leader on H. J. Massingham. Unsigned.

C2976 [Review of] *Oxford*, Vol. XII, No. 1. *TLS*, 20 February 1953, p. 125. Unsigned.

C2977 [Review of] *Selected Papers*, by Ludwig Jekels, including two papers written in collaboration with Edmund Berger. *TLS*, 20 February 1953, p. 126. Unsigned.

C2978 Roget's Thesaurus. *TLS*, 27 February 1953, p. 138. Review of *Everyman's Thesaurus of English Words and Phrases*, revised from Peter Roget by D. C. Browning. Unsigned.

C2979 Academic Activities. *TLS*, 27 February 1953, p. 139. Review of *Proceedings of the British Academy*, 1949 and 1950. Unsigned.

C2980 [Review of] *Marlowe and Shakespeare: A Thematic Exposition of some of their Plays*, by H. Röhrman. *TLS*, 27 February 1953, p. 142. Unsigned.

C2981 IN HOKKAIDO: A LETTER IN VERSE, AND IN THE ROMANTIC MANNER. *Poetry Review*, January/March 1953, Vol. 44, No. 1, pp. 260–262.

Reprinted: *A Hong Kong House*, 1962.

C2982 [Review of] *Exploration Fawcett*, by P. H. Fawcett. *The Bookman*, March 1953, pp. 3–5.

C2983 [Review of] *The Early Victorian Woman*, by Janet Dunbar. *The Bookman*, March 1953, pp. 12–13. Signed E.B.

C2984 A Keats-Shelley Diversion. *Keats-Shelley Journal*, January 1953 [*i.e.* March 1953], Vol. 2, p. 121. On a match between the Hampstead Cricket Club and a Keats-Shelley Eleven. Also issued separately as an offprint (*see* B149).

C2985 An Educator. *TLS*, 6 March 1953, p. 153. Leader on S. T. Coleridge. Unsigned.

C2986 [Review of] *The Aryan Path*, January 1953, Vol. 24, No. 1. *TLS*, 6 March 1953, p. 158. Unsigned.

C2987 [Review of] *A Surgeon's Heritage*, by James Harpole. *TLS*, 6 March 1953, p. 158. Unsigned.

C2988 Quaint Old Tom Fuller. *Everybody's*, 7 March 1953, p. 17. Review of *The Worthies of England*, by Thomas Fuller, edited by John Freeman.

C2989 [Review of] *The Year's Work in Modern Language Studies*, 1950-1951, Vols. 12-13. *TLS*, 13 March 1953, p. 159. Unsigned.

C2990 [Review of] *Henry Vaughan*, by E. W. Williamson, Annual lecture broadcast in the Welsh Home Service on 8 January 1953. *TLS*, 13 March 1953, p. 174. Unsigned.

C2991 MY ROOM. *TLS*, 20 March 1953, p. 185. From the French of Marceline Desbordes-Valmore, 1786-1859, translated by Blunden. Unsigned.

First published: *Eastward*, [1950].

C2992 [Review of] *Christ's Hospital, Hertford: A History of the School against the Background of London and Horsham*, by Frances M. Page. *TLS*, 20 March 1953, p. 193. Unsigned.

C2993 [Review of] *The Voice of England: A History of English Literature*, second edition, by Charles Grosvenor Osgood. *TLS*, 20 March 1953, p. 193. Unsigned.

C2994 [Review of] *The Lilies and the Bees*, by Edward Grierson. *The Bookman*, April 1953, pp. 4-5. Signed E.B.

C2995 [Review of] *Shelley: The Last Phase*, by Ivan Roe. *The Bookman*, April 1953, pp. 7-8. *See also* C3002.

C2996 [Review of] *Elizabeth I and Her Parliaments*, by J. E. Neale. *The Bookman*, April 1953, pp. 8-10.

C2997 [Review of] *Gordon: The Story of a Hero*, by Lawrence and Elisabeth Hanson. *The Bookman*, April 1953, pp. 10-11.

C2998 [Review of] *A Mingled Yarn*, by H. M. Tomlinson. *The Bookman*, April 1953, pp. 12-13. Signed E.B.

C2999 [Review of] *Coleridge*, by Humphry House. *The Bookman*, April 1953, p. 14. *See also* C3004.

C3000 TO SPRING. *Medical Bulletin*, April 1953, Vol. 1, No. 4, p. 19.

C3001 A Writer of Dreams. *National and English Review*, April 1953, Vol. 140, No. 842, pp. 240-242. Review of *Forrest Reid: A Portrait and a Study*, by Russell Burlingham.

C3002 Shelley at Lerici. *The Spectator*, 3 April 1953, p. 424. Review of *Shelley: The Last Phase*, by Ivan Roe. *See also* C2995.

C3003 [Review of] *Growth and System of the Language of Dickens: An Introduction to a Dickens Lexicon*, revised edition, by Tadao Yamamoto; and *An Index to Tadao Yamamoto's Growth and System of the Language of Dickens*, compiled by C. Higashida and M. Masui. *TLS*, 3 April 1953, p. 226. Unsigned.

C3004   Wordsworth and Coleridge. *TLS*, 10 April 1953, p. 238. Review of *Wordsworth and Coleridge, 1795-1834*, by H. M. Margoliouth; and *Coleridge*, by Humphry House (*see also* C2999). Unsigned.

C3005   Two Old Plays. *TLS*, 10 April 1953, p. 238. Review of The Malone Society Reprints: *The Conflict of Conscience*, by Nathaniel Woodes (1581) and *When you see me, you know me*, by Samuel Rowley (1605). Unsigned.

C3006   Concise Biography. *TLS*, 17 April 1953, p. 253. Leader on *Thomas Fuller: A Seventeen-Century Worthy*, by S. C. Roberts. Unsigned.

C3007   [Review of] *The Nature of Culture*, by A. L. Kroeber. *TLS*, 17 April 1953, p. 258. Unsigned.

C3008   [Review of] *First Readings in Old English*, selected and edited by P. S. Ardern. *TLS*, 17 April 1953, p. 259. Unsigned.

C3009   Mr. Walter de la Mare. *TLS*, 24 April 1953, p. 269. Second leader on his eightieth birthday. Unsigned.

C3010   [Review of] *Tragedy and the Paradox of the Fortunate Fall*, by Herbert Weisinger. *TLS*, 24 April 1953, pp. 274-275. Unsigned.

C3011   [Review of] *The Monastic Agreement of the Monks and Nuns of the English Nation*, translated from the Latin with introduction and notes by Thomas Symons. *TLS*, 24 April 1953, p. 275. Unsigned.

C3012   Our Best-Loved Poet is 80. *Everybody's*, 25 April 1953, p. 12. On Walter de la Mare; includes review of *Walter de la Mare*, by Kenneth Hopkins.

C3013   [Review of] *Henry James: The Untried Years, 1843-1870*, by Leon Edel. *The Bookman*, May 1953, pp. 3-4.

C3014   [Review of] *Safety Last*, by W. F. Stirling. *The Bookman*, May 1953, pp. 9-10. Signed E.B.

C3015   [Review of] *Landsman Hay: The Memoirs of Robert Hay, 1790-1847*, edited by M. D. Hay. *The Bookman*, May 1953, pp. 10-11.

C3016   [Review of] *Journey into Wonder*, by M. J. Berrill. *The Bookman*, May 1953, p. 14.

C3017   [Review of] *Poèmes choisis*, by John Keats, traduction, préface et notes par Albert Laffay. *Études anglaises*, mai 1953, année 6, No. 2, pp. 161-163. In English.

C3018   Highgate Grove. *TLS*, 1 May 1953, p. 285. Second leader on the unveiling of the plaque in honour of Coleridge. Unsigned.

C3019   Cricket Verse. *TLS*, 1 May 1953, p. 288. Review of *The Book of Cricket Verse: An Anthology*, edited by Gerald Brodribb. Unsigned.

C3020 PRINCE AKIHITO POEM READ: SIX VERSES BY MR. E. BLUNDEN [*later* TO WELCOME PRINCE AKIHITO]. *Daily Telegraph*, 5 May 1953, p. 8. Read by the author at a dinner of the Japan Society of London in honour of Prince Akihito.

Reprinted: *Bulletin of the Japan Society of London*, June 1953, No. 10, p. 2. Signed E.B. Also issued separately as an offprint (*see* B155).

C3021 Immortals. *TLS*, 8 May 1953, p. 299. Review of *The Twelve Olympians*, by Charles Seltman. Unsigned.

C3022 [Review of] *Nietzsche and the French: A Study of the Influence of Nietzsche's French Reading on his Thoughts and Writings*, by W. D. Williams. *TLS*, 8 May 1953, p. 305. Unsigned.

C3023 [Review of] *All on a Summer's Day*, by Margaret Hughes, with a foreword by Neville Cardus. *TLS*, 8 May 1953, p. 306. Unsigned.

C3024 A Mysterious Mariner. *The Spectator*, 15 May 1953, pp. 634, 636. Review of *The Wake of the Bounty*, by C. S. Wilkinson.

C3025 Christ's Hospital Celebrations: "A Unique Foundation". *Times Educational Supplement*, 15 May 1953, p. 440. On the quatercentenary celebrations. Signed by a Special Correspondent. *See also* C2853, 2929, 3027. Also issued separately as an offprint (*see* A118.1).

C3026 Proper Studies. *TLS*, 15 May 1953, p. 317. Leader on *The Social Function of the University*, by Sir Hector Hetherington. Unsigned.

C3027 Bluecoat Birthday: Boys & Girls of Christ's Hospital through 400 Years. *The Times*, 18 May 1953, p. 9. On the quatercentenary celebrations. *See also* C2853, 2929, 3025.

C3028 [Review of] *The Development of English Humor*, Parts 1 and 2, by Louis Cazamian. *TLS*, 22 May 1953, p. 338. Unsigned.

C3029 THE WHITE-FLOWERING DAYS. *Sunday Times*, 24 May 1953, p. 6.

Reprinted: *A Garland for the Queen*, [1953].

C3030 [Review of] *The Advancement of Learning* (1649), by John Hall, edited by A. K. Croston. *TLS*, 29 May 1953, p. 354. Unsigned.

C3031 [Review of] *The Latin Epigram of Thomas More*, edited with translations and notes by Leicester Bradner and Charles Arthur Lynch. *TLS*, 29 May 1953, p. 354. Unsigned.

C3032   [Review of] *Laurence Nowell's Vocabularium Saxonicum*, edited by Albert A. Marckwardt. *TLS*, 29 May 1953, p. 354. Unsigned.

C3033   AS BOSWELL RECORDS. *Wine and Food*, Summer 1953, No. 78, p. 94.

Reprinted: *Poems of Many Years*, 1957.

C3034   Of Mountains and Men. *TLS*, 5 June 1953, p. 365. Leader on mountaineers. Unsigned.

C3035   Cambridge Men. *TLS*, 5 June 1953, p. 367. Review of *Alumni cantabrigienses*, Part 2: From 1752 to 1900, Vol. 5, compiled by J. A. Venn. Unsigned.

C3036   [Review of] *Art in the Western World*, third edition by David M. Robb and J. J. Garrison. *TLS*, 5 June 1953, p. 370. Unsigned.

C3037   [Review of] *Wordsworth's Imagery: A Study in Poetic Vision*, by Florence Marsh. *TLS*, 5 June 1953, p. 370. Unsigned.

C3038   [Review of] *That Grand Whig Milton*, by George F. Sensabaugh. *TLS*, 5 June 1953, p. 371. Unsigned.

C3039   [Review of] *The English Primers (1529-1545): Their Publication and Connection with the English Bible and the Reformation in England*, by Charles C. Butterworth. *TLS*, 5 June 1953, p. 371. Unsigned.

C3040   [Review of] *Challenge of the Unknown: Exploring the Psychic World*, by Louis Anspacher, with an introduction by Waldemar Kaempffert. *TLS*, 12 June 1953, p. 387. Unsigned.

C3041   [Review of] *Britannica Book of the Year*, 1953, edited by John Armitage. *TLS*, 19 June 1953, p. 403. Unsigned.

C3042   [Review of] *Scientific Explanation: A Study of the Function of Theory, Probability and Law in Science*, by Richard Bevan Braithwaite. *TLS*, 19 June 1953, p. 403. Unsigned.

C3043   EARLY IDEAS REMEMBERED [*later* EARLY IDEAS REAWAKENED]. *Medical Bulletin*, July 1953, Vol. 1, No. 5, p. 15.

Reprinted: *Poems of Many Years*, 1957.

C3044   [Review of] *Horace Odes and Epodes*, by A. Y. Campbell. *TLS*, 3 July 1953, p. 434. Unsigned.

C3045   [Review of] *Aristotle's Metaphysics*, by Richard Hope, newly translated. *TLS*, 3 July 1953, p. 434. Unsigned.

C3046   [Review of] *Game of a Lifetime*, by Denzil Batchelor. *TLS*, 3 July 1953, p. 435. Unsigned.

C3047   [Review of] *The South Africans in Australia 1952-1953*, by A. G. Moyes, with a foreword by Jack Cheetham. *TLS*, 3 July 1953, p. 435. Unsigned.

C3048   Plato in Arabic. *TLS*, 10 July 1953, p. 450. Review of *Plato Arabus*, Vol. 1, ediderunt Paulus Kraus et Richardus Walzer, Vol. 3, edidit et Latine vertit Franciscus Gabrieli. Unsigned.

C3049   [Review of] *Bromsgrove School through Four Centuries*, by H. E. M. Icely. *TLS*, 10 July 1953, p. 450. Unsigned.

C3050   [Review of] *Essays in the Conciliar Epoch*, by E. F. Jacob. *TLS*, 10 July 1953, pp. 450–451. Unsigned.

C3051   [Review of] *The Ancient Burial Mounds of England*, by L. V. Grinsell. *TLS*, 17 July 1953, p. 466. Unsigned.

C3052   [Review of] *Friar Bacon and Friar Bungay; John of Bordeaux, or The Second Part of Friar Bacon*, by Robert Green, edited by Benvenuto Cellini. *TLS*, 17 July 1953, p. 466. Unsigned.

C3053   [Review of] *The Life and Minor Works of George Peele*, by David H. Horne. *TLS*, 17 July 1953, p. 466. Unsigned.

C3054   [Review of] *Japanese Literature: An Introduction for Western Readers*, by Donald Keene. *TLS*, 17 July 1953, p. 466. Unsigned.

C3055   [Review of] *The Accidence of Ben Jonson's Plays, Masques and Entertainments*, by A. C. Partridge. *TLS*, 17 July 1953, p. 466. Unsigned.

C3056   [Review of] *Canadian Regions: A Geography of Canada*, edited by Donald F. Putnam. *TLS*, 17 July 1953, p. 466. Unsigned.

C3057   [Review of] *Contemporary Reviews of Romantic Poetry*, edited by John Wain. *TLS*, 24 July 1953, p. 482. Unsigned.

C3058   [Review of] *A Hundred Years of the West Sussex Gazette, 1853-1953*. *TLS*, 24 July 1953, p. 483. Unsigned.

C3059   [Review of] *Bentham and the Ethics of Today*, by David Baumgardt, with Bentham manuscripts hitherto unpublished. *TLS*, 24 July 1953, p. 483. Unsigned.

C3060   [Review of] *Jack Hobbs: Gentleman and Player*, by Pat Landsberg. *TLS*, 24 July 1953, p. 483. Unsigned. *See also* C3071.

C3061   [Review of] *Cricket My Pleasure*, by A. A. Thomson. *TLS*, 24 July 1953, p. 483. Unsigned. *See also* C3071.

C3062   [Review of] *The Tropical World: Its Social and Economic Conditions and its Future Status*, by Pierre Gourou, translated by E. D. Laborde. *TLS*, 24 July 1953, p. 483. Unsigned.

C3063   Here's a Book Worth Hundreds. *Everybody's*, 25 July 1953, p. 15. On Joseph Cottle the publisher of *Lyrical Ballads*, by Samuel Taylor Coleridge and William Wordsworth in 1798.

C3064 [Review of] *It Isn't Cricket*, by Sidney Barnes, introduction by Herbert W. Evatt. *TLS*, 31 July 1953, p. 499. Unsigned.

C3065 [Review of] *Too Late the Phalarope*, by Alan Paton. *The Bookman*, July/August 1953, pp. 4-5.

C3066 [Review of] *Vidocq*, by Philip John Stead. *The Bookman*, July/August 1953, p. 9.

C3067 [Review of] *The Tirpitz*, by David Woodward. *The Bookman*, July/August 1953, pp. 11-12.

C3068 [Review of] *Jungle Green*, by Arthur Campbell. *The Bookman*, July/August 1953, pp. 14-15.

C3069 Japanese Citizens. *National and English Review*, August 1953, Vol. 141, No. 846, pp. 116-117. Review of *Five Gentlemen of Japan*, by Frank Gibney. Signed E. Blunden. *See also* C3087.

C3070 Japanese Outlook. *The Spectator*, 7 August 1953, p. 157. Review of *Daughter of the Pacific*, by Yoko Matsuoka. *See also* C3087.

C3071 More for the Winter Evening. *The Spectator*, 14 August 1953, pp. 181-182. Review of *Cricket*, by John Arlott; *Best Cricket Stories*, chosen by E. W. Swanton; *Australian Bowlers*, by A. G. Moyes; *Bumper*, by Keith Miller and R. S. Whitington; *Cricket My Pleasure*, by A. A. Thomson; and *Jack Hobbs: Gentleman and Player*, by Pat Landsberg. *See also* C3060-1.

C3072 Ancient Poet. *TLS*, 14 August 1953, p. 522. Review of *The Poems and Poetical Fragments*, by Nicander, edited with a translation and notes by A. S. F. Gow and A. F. Scholfield. Unsigned.

C3073 [Review of] *The Rise of English Journalism*, by R. V. Symonds. *TLS*, 14 August 1953, p. 527. Unsigned.

C3074 [Review of] *delta*, edited by Rodney Banister and Peter Redgrove. *TLS*, 14 August 1953, p. 527. Unsigned.

C3075 [Review of] *Handwriting Analysis as a Pyschodiagnostic Tool: A Study in General and Clinical Graphology*, by Ulrich Sonneman. *TLS*, 21 August 1953, p. 538. Unsigned.

C3076 [Review of] *The Johannesburg Story*, by F. Addington Symonds. *TLS*, 21 August 1953, p. 538. Unsigned.

C3077 [Review of] *The Rose in Britain*, third revised edition, by N. P. Harvey. *TLS*, 21 August 1953, p. 538. Unsigned.

C3078 [Review of] *England*, revised edition, by Ralph William Inge. *TLS*, 21 August 1953, p. 539. Unsigned.

C3079 [Review of] *India in World Affairs, August 1947-January 1950: A Review of India's Foreign Relations from Independence Day to Republic Day*, by K. P. Karunakaran. *TLS*, 21 August 1953, p. 539. Unsigned.

C3080 [Review of] *Brush Script*, by Donald Stevens. *TLS*, 28 August 1953, p. 553. Unsigned.

C3081 [Review of] *The Unseen Beloved*, by E. H. W. Meyerstein. *TLS*, 28 August 1953, p. 554. Unsigned.

C3082 [Review of] *Colour and Light at Work*, by Robert F. Wilson, with a foreword by Sir Charles J. Mole. *TLS*, 28 August 1953, p. 554. Unsigned.

C3083 [Review of] *Bandoola*, by J. H. Williams. *The Bookman*, September 1953, pp. 10, 12.

C3084 [Review of] *Rum Jungle*, by Alan Moorehead. *The Bookman*, September 1953, pp. 16, 18.

C3085 The Poet as Critic. *Britain To-day*, September 1953, No. 209, pp. 41–42. Review of *Private View*, by Walter de la Mare.

C3086 [Review of] *A Study of Donne's Imagery*, by Kaichi Matsuura. *TLS*, 4 September 1953, p. 570. Unsigned.

C3087 Interpreters of Japan. *TLS*, 11 September 1953, p. 578. Review of *Five Gentlemen of Japan*, by Frank Gibney; and *Daughter of the Pacific*, by Yoko Matsuoka. Unsigned. *See also* C3069–70.

C3088 C.E.B. [*later* THE OLD SCHOOLMASTER; *and* C.E.B.]. *South China Morning Post*, 22 September 1953, p. 5. On the author's father.
Reprinted (revised): *New Poems 1954*, [1954]; and *Poems of Many Years*, 1957.

C3089 Greek Drama. *TLS*, 25 September 1953, p. 608. Review of *Three Plays*, by Euripides, translated by Philip Vellacott. Unsigned.

C3090 [Review of] *The Reason Why*, by Cecil Woodham-Smith. *The Bookman*, October 1953, pp. 1–3. Also issued separately as an offprint (*see* A119).

C3091 [Review of] *Decade of Decision*, by Fred Hoyle. *The Bookman*, October 1953, pp. 13–14. Signed E.B.

C3092 [Review of] *The Onslow Family*, by C. E. Vulliamy. *The Bookman*, October 1953, p. 14.

C3093 [Review of] *Leopardi*, by Iris Origo. *The Bookman*, October 1953, p. 18.

C3094 THE PASSER-BY (A thrush, I know not by what humour drawn). *Medical Bulletin*, October 1953, Vol. 1, No. 6, p. 10.
Reprinted: *A Hong Kong House*, 1962; and *A Selection from the Shorter Poems*, [1966].

C3095 [Review of] *We Bought an Island*, by Evelyn M. Richardson. *The Bookman*, November 1953, p. 15.

C3096   The Growth of English Literature. *English Student*, Tokyo
        and Osaka, November 1953, No. 11, pp. 26–31. In English
        and Japanese; translated by Ichirô Nishizaki, with notes.
        Abbreviated version.

        First published (in full): *Two Lectures in English Literature*,
        1948; and *Poetry and Science*, 1949.

C3097   Cricket Commemoration. *Keats-Shelley Memorial Bulletin*,
        Rome, [November] 1953, No. 5, p. xii. On the match be-
        tween the 'Friends of Keats and Shelley' and the Hampstead
        Cricket Club on 10 September.

C3098   The School of Shelley. *Keats-Shelley Memorial Bulletin*,
        Rome, [November] 1953, No. 5, pp. 11–19.

C3098   Some English Poets and the East. *South China Morning*
    .1 *Post*, 17 November 1953, pp. 7, 15. At head of title: A
        Literary Discourse. A talk to the Alumni of the University
        of Hong Kong.

C3099   HONG KONG: A POSSIBLE PRELUDE. *Hong Kong*
        Undergrad, December 1953, No. 1, p. 6.

C3100   A CHRISTMAS TALE: FROM "THE GOLDEN LEGEND".
        St John's Review, Hong Kong, December 1953, Vol. 20,
        No. 12, p. 297.

        First published: *Eastward*, [1950]; reprinted: *A Hong Kong*
        House, 1962.

C3101   Great Writers in Fairyland. *Folio Magazine*, Winter 1953,
        Vol. 7, No. 1, pp. 11–14.

C3102   The Literary Profession in England, 1953. *Peak*, Hong
        Kong, 30 December 1953, pp. [2–4].

1954

C3103   ON SHAKESPEARE'S WINTER'S TALE [*later* AUTO-
        LYCUS'S COUNTRY]. *Medical Bulletin*, January 1954,
        Vol. 2, No. 1, p. 14.

        Reprinted (revised): *A Hong Kong House*, 1962.

C3104   Tokyo. *This is Japan*, January 1954, No. 1, p. 115.*

C3105   EIGHT JAPANESE POEMS. *Encounter*, February 1954,
        Vol. 2, No. 2, p. 42. Translations of 17th and 18th cen-
        tury *haiku*.

C3106   Keats's Odes: Further Notes. *Keats-Shelley Journal*, Winter
        1954 [*i.e.* April or May 1954], Vol. 3, pp. 39–46. Also
        issued separately as an offprint (*see* A120).

C3107   THE FARMHOUSE FAMILY. *Medical Bulletin*, April
        1954, Vol. 2, No. 2, p. 51.

        Reprinted: *Poems of Many Years*, 1957.

C3108   COUNTRY FOOTBALL. *St John's Review*, Hong Kong, April 1954, Vol. 21, No. 4, p. 89.

C3109   An Inaugural Lecture from the Chair of English. *University of Hong Kong Supplement to the Gazette*, 1 April 1954, Vol. 1, No. 1, pp. 1-4.

C3110   "To the Editor". *Japan News*, 10 April 1954, Vol. 4, No. 1344, p. 1. Letter on contemporary Japan. Signature in autograph facsimile.

C3111   ON THE PROFESSION OF PHYSIC. *Elixir*, May 1954, p. 44.

C3112   THE UNIVERSITY. *Elixir*, May 1954, p. 45.

C3113   A Mirror for Literature: *The Times Literary Supplement*. *Rising Generation*, 1 May 1954, Vol. 100, No. 5, p. 240.*

C3114   A VIEW FROM THE DEPARTMENT OF ENGLISH [*later* A VIEW FROM A HONG KONG OFFICE; *and* VIEW FROM THE UNIVERSITY OF HONG KONG]. *The Union*, Hong Kong, 1953/4 [*i.e.* summer 1954], p. 15.

Reprinted: *Hong Kong Business Symposium*, 1957; and *A Hong Kong House*, 1962.

C3115   Most Sincerely Yours. *Medical Bulletin*, July 1954, Vol. 2, No. 3, pp. 86-90. With E.C.-J. [*i.e.* E. Clayton-Jones]. 'Notes on a complete series of hitherto unpublished letters from Leigh Hunt to his doctor written during the last illness of his son Vincent, 1851-52.'

C3116   A READER INTERRUPTED. *TLS*, 9 July 1954, p. 434.

C3117   Poet and Critic. *TLS*, 16 July 1954, p. 455. Review of *Coleridge, Opium and "Kubla Khan"*, by Elisabeth Schneider. Unsigned.

C3118   Douglas Grant's War Book. *TLS*, 6 August 1954, Special Autumn Number: Personal Preference, Appreciations, p. iii. Review of *The Fuel of the Fire*, by Douglas Grant. Unsigned. *See also* C2574.

C3119   Thomas Percy. *TLS*, 27 August 1954, p. 538. Review of *The Percy Letters: The Correspondence of Thomas Percy and David Dalrymple, Lord Hailes*, edited by A. F. Falconer. Unsigned.

C3120   "I Found the Poems in the Fields" [*later* Country Poets]. *TLS*, 29 October 1954, p. 688. Review of *The Rural Muse: Studies in the Peasant Poetry of England*, by Rayner Unwin. Unsigned. Also issued separately as an offprint (*see* A121).

Reprinted: *English Critical Essays: Twentieth Century*, Second Series, selected by Derek Hudson.

C3121 FOR A SPRING DANCE BY TAMAMI GOJO [*later* VOICE OF SPRING]. *Evening News*, Tokyo, 8 November 1954, p. -.

Reprinted: *Commemorative Performance*, 11 November 1954; *Elixir*, Hong Kong, December 1954, p. 36 [at head of title: Patterns for a Japanese Ballet; *see also* C2542]; and *A Hong Kong House*, 1962.

C3122 Engineering and Poetry. *Hong Kong University Engineering Journal*, December 1954, Vol. 18, pp. 18-22. Also issued separately as an offprint (*see* A125).

C3123 The Keats-Shelley Poetry Contests. *Notes and Queries*, December 1954, Vol. 199, p. 546. Signed E. Blunden. *See also* the 'Readers' Queries' section by Ben W. Griffith in the issue of August 1954, pp. 359-360.

C3124 TO OLIVER SIMON. *Signature*, 1954, New Series, No. 18, p. 4. Holograph facsimile.

C3125 On the Memorials in Poets' Corner. *Folio*, Winter 1954/5, pp. 3-7.

1955

C3126 Shakespeare's Doctors. *Medical Bulletin*, January 1955, Vol. 3, No. 1, pp. 3-6.

C3127 UNRECORDED. *Time and Tide*, 1 January 1955, p. 15.

Reprinted: *Poems of Many Years*, 1957.

C3128 VERSES ON BEHALF OF THE UNIVERSITY OF HONG KONG IN HONOUR OF THE VICE-CHANCELLOR DR. L. T. RIDE'S MARRIAGE WITH MISS VIOLET MAY MITCHELL ON 12 NOVEMBER 1954. *Malayan Undergrad*, 22 January 1955, p. 3.

First published: separate edition, 12 November 1954.

C3129 A Fragment of Byronism. *Études anglaises*, janvier/mars 1955, Vol. 8, No. 1, pp. 32-42. Also issued separately as an offprint (*see* A126).

C3130 On Individual Limitations. *Sanseido*, Tokyo, 25 February 1955, No. 2, pp. 2-5. In English and Japanese; translated by Sigeru Tomiyama.

C3131 Is Any Subject Left for New Writers? *Asahi Evening News*, 18 March 1955, p. 4.*

Reprinted: *Catholic Bulletin*, Hong Kong, January/February 1959, Vol. 3, No. 1, pp. 9-10.

C3132 The Family Physician in the 17th Century. *Elixir*, Spring 1955, pp. 15-19. Also issued separately as an offprint (*see* A127). *See also* "Signals" (C3147).

C3133 ANTIQUITIES. *Medical Bulletin*, April 1955, Vol. 3, No. 2, p. 57. Holograph facsimile.

Reprinted: *A Hong Kong House*, 1962.

C3134 Read, Mark Learn . . . *Hongkong Standard*, 20 April 1955, p. 7. Letter to Tweedledum, editor of the column 'This Hongkong of Ours'; on some poems submitted.

C3135 H-BOMB. *TLS*, 29 April 1955, p. 192.

Reprinted: *Poems of Many Years*, 1957.

C3136 West and East. *Youth's Companion*, May 1955, No. 5, pp. 6-9.

C3137 Impressions of the '55 Bui[l]ding. *Hôsei*, Tokyo, 1 May 1955, Vol. 5, No. 36, p. 47. In English and Japanese; translated by Makoto Sungû. On Hôsei University.

C3138 Returning to Hôsei University. *Hôsei*, Tokyo, 1 May 1955, Vol. 5, No. 36, p. 47. In English and Japanese; translated by Makoto Sungû. Holograph facsimile.

C3139 Lives of the Poets: If Dr Johnson had lived rather longer. *TLS*, 20 and 27 May 1955, pp. 276, 292. Title of second article: Short lives of Wordsworth and Coleridge in the style of Johnson. *See also* letters by David C. Rutter in the issue of 27 May, p. 285; R. W. King in 3 June, p. 301; and Gordon W. Dennis in 10 June, p. 323.

C3140 On Church Music. *Music & Worship*, Tokyo, June 1955, Vol. 1, No. 3, pp. 1-2.

C3141 Essayist and Editor. *TLS*, 24 June 1955, p. 344. Review of *The Englishman: A Political Journal*, by Richard Steele, edited by Rae Blanchard. Unsigned.

C3142 Occupation and Aftermath. *TLS*, 29 July 1955, p. 431. Review of *Typhoon in Tokyo*, by Harry Emerson Wildes. Unsigned.

C3143 A Cricketer's Bookshelf. *Books*, June/August 1955, No. 294, pp. 122-123.

C3144 MARVELL'S "HORTUS" [*later* ANDREW MARVELL'S *HORTUS* TRANSLATED]. *TLS*, 12 August 1955, p. 462.

Reprinted: *Eleven Poems*, [1966].

C3145 10 Years of Renaissance. *The Mainichi*, 16 August 1955, p. 8. On Hiroshima.

C3146 "How Should I Forget?". *Japan Quarterly*, July/September 1955, Vol. 2, No. 3, pp. 308-312. On Professor Takeshi Saito.

C3147 "Signals". *Elixir*, Autumn 1955, pp. 17-18. Signed E. B. On medical recipes. Also issued separately as an offprint (*see* A129). *See also* The Family Physician in the 17th Century (C3132).

C3148   WATER-MEADOW EVENING. *Medical Bulletin*, October 1955, Vol. 3, No. 4, p. 150.

Reprinted: *Poems of Many Years*, 1957.

C3149   Today—But Yesterday. . . . *This is Japan*, October 1955, No. 3, pp. 67–68. Wrapper dated 1956. On Tokyo.

C3150   Some Seventeenth-Century Latin Poems by English Writers. *University of Toronto Quarterly*, October 1955, Vol. 25, No. 1, pp. 10–22. Includes English translations by Blunden of Latin poems by Donne, Herbert, Crashaw and Milton. Also issued separately as an offprint (*see* A128).

C3151   A Chinese View of Spenser. *TLS*, 4 November 1955, p. 658. Review of *Allegory and Courtesy in Spenser: A Chinese View*, by H. C. Chang.

C3152   THE GRACE. *The Tatler*, 11 November 1955, p. 12.

C3153   Harriet Shelley's Brother-in-Law. *TLS*, 11 November 1955, p. 680. On R. F. Beauchamp. Signed From a Correspondent [*i.e.* Blunden and Henry Tyler].

C3154   A Retired Naval Man. *Elixir*, Christmas 1955, pp. 21–25. On William Vane. Illustrated by Prudence Rowe-Evans. Also issued separately as an offprint (*see* A132).

C3155   On a Portrait by Mrs. Leigh Hunt. *Keats-Shelley Memorial Bulletin, Rome*, [December] 1955, No. 6, pp. 7–12. Also issued separately as an offprint (*see* A130.1).

C3156   Christmas and Charles Dickens. *St John's Review*, Hong Kong, Christmas 1955, Vol. 22, No. 12, pp. 258–259.

C3157   Convention and Misrule. *TLS*, 2 December 1955, p. 723. Letter. *See also* centre page review in the issue of 23 September, p. 556.

C3158   GREETINGS: FROM THE LATIN OF JOHN SKELTON. *The Quill*, 1955, Vol. 1, p. [3].

C3159   A HONG KONG HOUSE. *The Quill*, 1955, Vol. 1, p. 21.

Reprinted: separate edition, 1959; *Edmund Blunden: Sixty-Five*, 1961; *A Hong Kong House*, 1962; and *The Midnight Skaters*, [1968].

1956

C3160   [The Charles Lamb Society Comes of Age]. *C.L.S. Bulletin*, January 1956, No. 128, p. 96. Letter in his capacity as Vice-President.

C3161   [Review of] *Japanese Masters of the Colour Print*, by J. Hillier; *Japanese Colour Prints from Harunobu to Utamaro*, introduction by William Blunt; and *Pageant of Japanese Art: Painting 2*, Vol. 2, edited by staff members of the Tokyo National Museum, with historical sketch and explanation of plates by Ichiro Kondô. *Journal of Oriental*

Studies, July 1955 [*i.e.* January 1956]. Vol. 2, No. 2, pp. 371–373. At head of page: Japanese Colour Prints. Also issued in an offprint of the reviews section of the journal (*see* B181).

C3162 [Review of] *A Story of Ukiyo-e*, by Ichitaro Kondo; and *Utamaro*, by Ichitaro Kondo. *Journal of Oriental Studies*, July 1955 [*i.e.* January 1956], Vol. 2, No. 2, pp. 385–386. Signed E.B. Also issued in an offprint of the reviews section of the journal (*see* B181).

C3163 [Review of] *Japanese Folk Tales*, by Kunio Yanagita, translated by Fanny Hagin Mayer. *Journal of Oriental Studies*, July 1955 [*i.e.* January 1956], Vol. 2, No. 2, p. 387. Signed E.B. Also issued in an offprint of the reviews section of the journal (*see* B181).

C3164 ECHO DE L'AUTRE GUERRE: A BALLAD OF THE SERGEANTS OF OTHER DAYS—AFTER VILLON AND D. G. ROSSETTI [*later* BALLAD OF THE SERGEANTS OF OTHER DAYS]. *Medical Bulletin*, January 1956, Vol. 4, No. 1, p. 10.

Reprinted: *A Hong Kong House*, 1962.

C3165 Towards a New Understanding of Japanese Culture. *Nishinihon Shimbun*, 3 January 1956, p. 8. In English and Japanese; translated by Tomoji Abe.

C3166 Invited to China: A Few Impressions. *The Mainichi*, 6 February 1956, p. 8; 7 February, p. 8; and 8 February, p. 8.

Reprinted: *Current of the World*, May 1956, Vol. 33, No. 5, pp. 2–22. In English and Japanese; translated anonymously.

C3167 Thackeray on His Contemporaries. *TLS*, 17 February 1956, p. 98. Review of *Contributions to the "Morning Chronicle"*, by William Makepeace Thackeray, edited by Gordon N. Ray. Unsigned.

C3168 AT THE GREAT WALL OF CHINA. *TLS*, 16 March 1956, p. 166.

Reprinted: *Poems of Many Years*, 1957; *A Selection of the Shorter Poems*, [1966]; and *A Selection from the Poems*, [1969].

C3169 When Cricketers Wore Belts. *Elixir*, Spring 1956, pp. 16–18.

C3170 APPEARANCES OF THE SEASON. *Medical Bulletin*, April 1956, Vol. 4, No. 2, p. 57.

Reprinted: *A Hong Kong House*, 1962.

C3171 Long Friendships. 3. *Books*, April/May 1956, No. 301, p. 88. On Walter de la Mare. The first two articles are by L. A. G. Strong and Frank Swinnerton.

Reprinted: *Tribute to Walter de la Mare*, 1974 (*see* B290).

C3172 My First Housemaster. *The Blue*, May 1956, Vol. 83, No. 2, pp. 72–77. On H. S. Goodwin.

C3173 Just a Victorian. *Rising Generation*, 1 May 1956, Vol. 102, No. 5, pp. 221–224. In English and Japanese; translated with notes by Torao Uyeda.

First published: *The Face of England*, 1932.

C3174 ARRIVAL AT A RIVER, IN JAPAN. *English*, Summer 1956, Vol. 11, No. 62, p. 53.

Reprinted: *A Hong Kong House*, 1962.

C3175 Poems of the New Japan. *TLS*, 22 June 1956, p. 378. Review of *Bread Rather than Blossoms*, by D. J. Enright. Unsigned.

C3176 THE SEASIDE HOUSE. *Medical Bulletin*, July 1956, Vol. 5, No. 3, p. 95.

Reprinted: *The Chimes*, Hong Kong, August 1964, p. 166 [with sub-title: Cheung Chau].

C3177 JAPANESE INN [*later* THE TEA-HOUSE]. *The Tatler*, 4 July 1956, p. 21.

Reprinted: *A Hong Kong House*, 1962; *A Selection of the Shorter Poems*, [1966]; and *A Selection from the Poems*, [1969].

C3178 Teaching English in Japan: Students' Penchant for Poetry. *Times Educational Supplement*, 10 August 1956, p. 1021.

C3179 Walter de la Mare. *Gakuen Shimbun*, 15 August 1956, pp. —.*

C3180 Handbook to Edward Thomas. *TLS*, 24 August 1956, p. 494. Review of *Edward Thomas*, by H. Coombes. Unsigned.

C3181 [untitled] (To all the honours that a hundred years) [*formerly* FOR THE CENTENARY OF MELBOURNE UNIVERSITY]. *University of Hong Kong Gazette*, 1 September 1956, Vol. 4, No. 1, p. 7. On the centenary celebrations of the University of Melbourne.

First published: 15 August 1956 (*see* B191).

C3182 CHRISTMAS INVITATION FOR 1756 [*later* sub-title added: PRE-TELEPHONE]. *The Tatler*, 9 November 1956, p. 12.

Reprinted: *A Hong Kong House*, 1962.

C3183 Lord Byron: Some Early Biographies. *Keats-Shelley Memorial Bulletin, Rome*, [December] 1956, No. 7, pp. 1–3. Also issued separately as an offprint (*see* A134).

C3184 ON THE AIR. *Spectrum*, Hong Kong, December 1956, No. 5, p. 1.

Reprinted (revised): *A Hong Kong House*, 1962.

C3185   Anniversaries and Commemorations. *Peak*, Hong Kong, 4 December 1956, pp. 4–5. Address to the Rotary Club of Hong Kong.

1957

C3186   Mr. Sassoon in Contemplative Mood. *TLS*, 4 January 1957, p. 11. Review of *Sequences*, by Siegfried Sassoon. Unsigned.

C3187   Seen from Japan. *TLS*, 1 February 1957, p. 66. Review of *Faulkner at Nagano*, edited by Robert A. Jelliffe. Unsigned.

C3188   A Poet's Enigma. *Rising Generation*, 1 March 1957, Vol. 103, No. 3, pp. 100–101. Review of *The Mask of Keats: A Study of Problems*, by Robert Gittings.

C3189   Evenings at Home and Abroad. *New Sundial Magazine*, April 1957, Vol. 1, No. 3, pp. 9–11. Signed E. Blunden.

C3190   JAMES CLARENCE MANGAN. *New Chapter*, May 1957, Vol. 1, No. 1, p. 3.

Reprinted: *A Hong Kong House*, 1962.

C3191   Edmund Blunden Writes . . . *Poetry Book Society Bulletin*, May 1957, No. 14, p. [1]. On early views as a poet.

C3192   Septuagenarian S.S. *Rising Generation*, 1 May 1957, Vol. 103, No. 5, pp. 213–214.*

C3193   Hunt the Examiner. *TLS*, 3 May 1957, p. 272. Review of *Leigh Hunt's Literary Criticism*, by Lawrence Huston Houtchens and Carolyn Washburn Houtchens. Unsigned.

C3194   A Japanese Garland. *TLS*, 3 May 1957, p. 274. Review of *Modern Japanese Literature*, edited by Donald Keene. Unsigned.

C3195   [Review of] *Drafts and Fragments of Verse*, by William Collins, edited by J. S. Cunningham. *Modern Language Review*, July 1957, Vol. 52, No. 3, pp. 421–422.

C3196   News of P. B. Shelley. *Rising Generation*, 1 July 1957, Vol. 103, No. 7, pp. 324–325. Review of *Shelley at Work: A Critical Inquiry*, by Neville Rogers.

C3197   [Review of] *Modern English Literature In Honour of Professor Rintaro Fukuhara*; and *Where Two Cultures Meet*, by Junesay Iddittie. *Journal of Oriental Studies*, June 1956 [*i.e.* August 1957], Vol. 3, No. 1, p. 147. Also issued in an offprint of the reviews section (*see* B199).

C3198   [Review of] *Hokusai (1760–1849)*, by Ichitaro Kondo. *Journal of Oriental Studies*, June 1956 [*i.e.* August 1957], Vol. 3, No. 1, pp. 147–148. Also issued in an offprint of the reviews section (*see* B199).

C3199   Roy Campbell: A Poet's Death. *Rising Generation*, 1 August 1957, Vol. 103, No. 8, p. 385.

C3200 Japanese Modernists. *Adam International Review*, [September] 1957, Year 25, No. 261, p. 3. On *The Poetry of Living Japan*, edited and translated by Professor Ninomiya and D. J. Enright. For VOICES IN TOKYO, p. 4 (*see* C2445).

C3201 Keats's Italian Biographer. *Rising Generation*, 1 October 1957, Vol. 103, No. 10, pp. 490-491. On *Keats*, by Michele Renzulli.

C3202 Introduction [to The Ballad of Reading Gaol]. *Elixir*, Winter 1957, Supplement, p. [iii]. Also issued in an offprint of the poem (*see* B202).

C3203 Inspiration, Vaccination, and Some Poets. *Elixir*, Winter 1957, pp. 13-16.

C3204 Books and Bookmen. *TLS*, 1 November 1957, p. 658. Review of *Talking of Books*, by Oliver Edwards. Signed review.

C3205 The Rosy Prime. *TLS*, 8 November 1957, p. 674. Review of *Nymphs and Rivers*, by Kenneth Hare. Unsigned.

C3206 TRAFFIC IN A GREY CITY. *The Postmaster*, December 1957, Vol. 2, No. 1, p. 8.

1958

C3207 [Review of] *Hokusai: Paintings, Drawings and Woodcuts*, by J. Hillier. *Journal of Oriental Studies*, July 1956 [*i.e.* January 1958], Vol. 3, No. 2, pp. 362-363. Also issued in an offprint of the reviews section (*see* B204).

C3208 A Classic Still. *Medical Bulletin*, January 1958, Vol. 6, No. 1, p. 23. Review of *Horace for Company*, by L. N. Jackson.

C3209 ECOLIER: THE SCHOLAR. *Catholic Bulletin*, January/ February 1958, Vol. 2, No. 2, p. 2. A translation of a poem by Paul Déroulède.

C3210 IN AN ALBUM, 1958. *National and English Review*, April 1958, Vol. 150, No. 902, Supplement: Life & Language: An Anthology of New Work by Contemporary Poets, p. 4.

C3211 Wandering Scholar-Poet. *TLS*, 30 May 1958, p. 299. Review of *The Percy Letters*, edited by David Nichol Smith and Cleanth Brooks, Vol. 3: *The Correspondence of Thomas Percy and Evan Evans*, edited by Aneirin Lewis. Unsigned.

C3212 Shelley at Work, I. *Essays in Criticism*, July 1958, Vol. 8, No. 3, pp. 336-337. On the review of *Shelley at Work*, by Neville Rogers in the issue of October 1957, Vol. 7, No. 4, pp. 428-439. Parts II and III are by the reviewer G. M. Matthews, and D. M. Davin. Also issued separately as an offprint (*see* B208).

C3213 Occasional Notes on China Reflected in English Writings. *Some Sino-British Club Lectures*, 1957-58 [*i.e.* August 1958], pp. 1-20. Delivered 4 January 1957.

C3214 HEINE IN THE EAST. *The Outlook*, Autumn 1958, New Series, No. 24, p. 4.

C3215 BRING YOUR MUSIC, *Music Magazine*, Hong Kong, September 1958, Vol. 4, No. 9, p. 11.

Reprinted: *Hong Kong Festival Programme*, October 1958.

C3216 Japan's Cultural Traditions. *Geographical Magazine*, October 1958, Vol. 31, No. 6, pp. 277-289.

C3217 The New Professor. *Today's Japan*, October 1958, Vol. 3, No. 10, pp. 9-10. On his appointment to the Chair of English Literature at Tokyo University in 1924.

C3218 Love and Friendship. *TLS*, 28 November 1958, p. 688. Review of *Edward Thomas: The Last Four Years: Book One of the Memoirs of Eleanor Farjeon*. Unsigned. Also issued separately as an offprint (*see* A139).

C3219 Godwin's Library Catalogue. *Keats-Shelley Memorial Bulletin, Rome*, [December] 1958, No. 9, pp. 27-29. Also issued separately as an offprint (*see* A140).

C3220 THE READER, NO READER. *The Quill*, Hong Kong, 1957/8, Vol. 3, p. 8.

Reprinted: *A Hong Kong House*, 1962.

1959

C3221 Lafacadio Hearn, Teacher. *Today's Japan*, January 1959, Vol. 4, No. 1, pp. 63-65.

C3222 Mrs Hani was Prometheus. *Gakuen Shimbun*, 25 January 1959, p. - .*

C3223 Island Colony. *TLS*, 6 February 1959, p. 73. Review of *A History of Hong Kong*, by G. B. Endacott. Unsigned.

C3224 IN HONOR OF ROYAL COUPLE [*later* IN HONOR OF CROWN PRINCE AKIHITO AND MISS MICHIKO SHODA, ON 10 APRIL 1959; *and* IN HONOUR OF ROYAL COUPLE]. *Japan Times*, 10 April 1959, p. 5.

Reprinted: *Student Times: The Japan Times Junior Weekly*, 10 April 1959, Vol. 9, No. 15, p. [1]; in English and Japanese; translated by Ichiro Ando; and *Poems on Japan*, 1967.

C3225 A Tourist to Tourists. *Etudes anglaises*, avril/juin 1959, Vol. 12, No. 2, pp. 97-99. On John Clare. Also issued separately as an offprint (*see* A141).

C3226 [Review of] *The Lloyd-Manning Letters*, edited by Frederick L. Beaty. *Etudes anglaises*, avril/juin 1959, Vol. 12, No. 2, p. 168. Signed E. Blunden.

C3227 A Comment on this Century. *Bulletin of the International House of Japan, Inc.*, Summer 1959, No. 4, pp. 17-23. Part of lecture given on 24 June at the International House; the text was not seen in proof by Blunden or Takeshi Saito.

C3228 MR. COLLINS AT MIYAJIMA 1959. *Asahi [Shimbun]*, Tokyo, 30 June 1959, p. - . In English and Japanese; translated by Rikutarô Fukuda. On William Collins, died 1759. Holograph facsimile of English.

Reprinted: *Britain: Life & Culture*, 20 November 1963, No. 1, p. 3; and *Poems on Japan*, 1967.

C3229 Fourth Visit: or, Japan up-to-date. *Albion*, Tokyo, 1 August 1959, No. 46, pp. 9-11.

C3230 Leigh Hunt Centenary. *The Blue*, September 1959, Vol. 86, No. 3, pp. 131-133.

C3231 Shakespeare's "Tempest". *Ronshu: Essays and Studies*, Tokyo, October 1959, Vol. 10, No. 2, pp. 1-12. A lecture delivered at the Tokyo Woman's Christian College. Also issued separately as an offprint (*see* A144).

C3232 Marianne Hunt: A Letter and Fragment of a Diary. *Keats-Shelley Memorial Bulletin, Rome*, [December] 1959, No. 10, pp. 30-32. Also issued separately as an offprint (*see* A146).

C3233 A Return to Japan. *Japan Quarterly*, October/December 1959, Vol. 6, No. 4, pp. 490-494. Above title: Through the Eastern Window.

C3234 The Obscure Webb(e). *TLS*, 18 December 1959, p. 748. On Cornelius Webb. Also issued separately as an offprint (*see* A147). *See also* letters by Joanna Richardson in the issue of 1 January 1960, p. 7; Alec Reid in 22 January, p. 49; and Albert Mordell in 19 February, p. 113.

C3234 .1 Charles Lamb. *Illustrated Weekly of India*, 20 December 1959, pp. - .*

1960

C3235 The Poet Hood. *Review of English Literature*, January 1960, Vol. 1, No. 1, pp. 26-34.

C3236 Psalmanazar. *Today's Japan*, 1955/60 [*i.e.* January 1960], Vol. 5, No. 1, pp. 29-32. On the author of *Formosa*.

C3237 The Literary Life. *The Tower*, February 1960, Vol. 10, No. 8, pp. 7-8. An address to the Rotary Club of Kowloon on 21 January 1960.

C3238 A Wessex Worthy. *Literary Repository*, [March] 1960, No. 2, pp. 1-3. On Thomas Russell. Also issued separately as an offprint (*see* A151).

C3239 "From the Past". *Today's Japan*, March/April 1960, Vol. 5, No. 3, pp. 29-32. Autobiographical notes.

C3240 [untitled poem] (Their spring-breeze from the greenwood moist and warm,). *Today's Japan*, March/April 1960, Vol. 5, No. 3, p. 33. Four lines of an unpublished sonnet written between 1913-1914, and included in 'Edmund Blunden, Poet' by Takeshi Saito, pp. 33-37. For A HONG KONG HOUSE, p. 39, THE BOURNE and THE MIDNIGHT SKATERS, p. 40, ZERO 1916 [*later* COME ON, MY LUCKY LADS; *and* ZERO], p. 41, and THE AUTHOR'S LAST WORDS TO HIS STUDENTS, p. 42 (*see* A1, 17, 26, 145).

C3241 The Romantics and Ourselves. *Studies in English Literature*, April 1960, Vol. 36, No. 2, pp. 217-228. Lecture delivered at the 31st General Meeting of the English Literary Society of Japan. Also issued separately as an offprint (*see* A149).

C3242 Wrong from the Start. *The Observer*, 26 June 1960, p. 26. Review of *Mons*, by John Terraine.

C3243 A CHINESE PAPERKNIFE [*later* CHINESE PAPERKNIFE]. *Eastern Horizon*, July 1960, Vol. 1, No. 1, p. [21]. At head of title: Three Poems from Hong Kong. Holograph facsimile. *See also* C3244-5.

Reprinted: *A Hong Kong House*, 1962; and *The Midnight Skaters*, [1968].

C3244 THE BUSY FLY. *Eastern Horizon*, July 1960, Vol. 1, No. 1, p. [22]. Holograph facsimile. *See also* C3243, 3245.

Reprinted: *A Hong Kong House*, 1962.

C3245 TWO OF US. *Eastern Horizon*, July 1960, Vol. 1, No. 1, p. [22]. Holograph facsimile. *See also* C3243-4.

C3245 Still Things Japanese. *Eastern Horizon*, July 1960, Vol. 1,
.1 No. 1, pp. 57-58. Review of *Meeting with Japan*, by Fosco Maraini. The 'Japanese Travelogue' to which reference is made in this issue did not appear.

C3245 China in English Literature. *Eastern Horizon*, August 1960,
.2 Vol. 1, No. 2, pp. 27-33, 57-58. Review of *Japanese Nô Drama*, Vol. 3.*

C3246 Moments in a Library. *Library Association Record*, August 1960, Vol. 62, No. 8, pp. 243-247. Also issued separately as an offprint (*see* A150).

C3247 Shakespeare Oddities. *Notes and Queries*, September 1960, New Series, Vol. 7, No. 9, pp. 334-335. On Shakespeare's last descendant. Signed E. Blunden.

C3248 [Review of] *Nymph in Thy Orisons: Poems*, by Wrenne Jarman [*later* Wrenne Jarman]. *Aylesford Review*, Winter 1960/61, Vol. 4, No. 1, pp. 31-32. St Albert's Press, Aylesford, Kent, publisher of *Nymph in Thy Orisons* published the review as an advertisement in, probably, November 1960.

Reprinted: *Poetry Review*, July/September 1961, Vol. 52, No. 3, pp. 145-146; and *Poems of Wrenne Jarman*, 1970 (as the Foreword; *see* B285).

C3249 Indications of Keats. *Keats-Shelley Memorial Bulletin, Rome*, [December] 1960, No. 11, pp. 1-5. Also issued separately as an offprint (*see* A152).

1961

C3249 An Oriental Paradise Lost. *Eastern Horizon*, New Year
.1 1961, Vol. 1, No. 6/7, pp. 31-33. With Claire Blunden.*

C3250 Out of Wessex. *TLS*, 20 January 1961, p. 44. Review of *William Barnes*, by William Turner Levy. Unsigned.

C3250 [Review of] *Poems of Solitude*, translated from the Chi-
.1 nese by Jerome Ch'en and Michael Bullock. *Eastern Horizon*, March 1961, Vol. 1, No. 9, p. 61.*

C3251 JAPAN BEAUTIFUL. *Chûgoku Shimbun*, Hiroshima, 3 March 1961, No. 24012, p. 9. In English and Japanese; translated by Mikio Hiramatsu. Holograph facsimile of English.

Reprinted: *A Hong Kong House*, 1962. *See also* D38.

C3252 Battle of the Somme. *TLS*, 19 May 1961, p. 303. Review of *The Big Push*, by Brian Gardner. Unsigned.

C3253 Off the Shelf. *The Times*, 6 July 1961, p. 17. One of a series entitled Pleasure in Reading.

C3254 To Do or Die. *The Times*, 20 July 1961, p. 15. Review of *The Donkeys*, by Alan Clark. Unsigned.

C3255 A Pride of Poets. *Sunday Telegraph*, 23 July 1961, p. 6. Review of *A Short History of English Poetry, 1340-1940*, by James Reeves.

C3256 Nature his Goddess. *Daily Telegraph*, 28 July 1961, p. 15. Review of *Collected Poems*, by Ralph Hodgson. *See also* C3265.

C3257 THE EXPLORER. *The Chimes*, August 1961, plate facing p. 2. Holograph facsimile.

C3258 AFTER 'ROMEO AND JULIET' PERFORMED BY THE MASQUERS, HONG KONG MARCH 1961. *The Chimes*, August 1961, pp. 62-64.

C3259 On 'Jude the Obscure'. *The Chimes*, August 1961, pp. 98-100.

C3260 On Keats' Ode to a Nightingale. *Notes on Literature*, [August 1961, No. 1], leaves 5-8. *Notes on Literature*, published by the British Council, Feature Articles Service, is issued free of charge through their overseas offices.

C3261 Percy Relics. *TLS*, 25 August 1961, p. 563. Review of *The Percy Letters: The Correspondence of Thomas Percy and George Paton*, Vol. 4, edited by A. G. Falconer. Unsigned.

C3262 Ships and Deep Friendships. *TLS*, 25 August 1961, p. 564. Review of *The Bluebells and Other Verse*, by John Masefield. Unsigned.

C3263 An Old-Fashioned Day. *This is Japan*, September 1961, No. 9, pp. 88–89.*

C3264 Felicities. *TLS*, 29 September 1961, p. 646. Review of *Poems and Pieces, 1911 to 1961*, by Francis Meynell. Unsigned.

C3265 A Sense of Strange Glories. *TLS*, 6 October 1961, p. 667. Review of *Collected Poems*, by Ralph Hodgson. Unsigned. *See also* C3256.

C3266 FOR THE CENTENARY OF RABINDRANATH TAGORE. *South China Morning Post*, 14 October 1961, p. 10.

Reprinted: *Cultural Forum*, New Delhi, November 1961, p. 3; and *A Hong Kong House*, 1962.

C3267 Keats's Editor. *Keats-Shelley Memorial Bulletin, Rome*, [December] 1961, No. 12, pp. 1–2. On H. W. Garrod. Also issued separately as an offprint (*see* A154).

C3268 On Regency Fiction: A Fragment. *Essays and Studies*, 1961, Vol. 14, pp. 52–65.

1962

C3269 Shelley. *Notes on Literature*, February 1962, No. 7, leaves 1–10. Contents: To a Skylark — Adonais — The Sensitive Plant. *See* note to C3260.

C3270 A Triumph of Pigs. *TLS*, 9 February 1962, p. 86. Review of *The Symbolic Pig: An Anthology of Pigs in Literature and Art*, by Frederick Cameron Sillar and Ruth Mary Meyler. Unsigned.

C3270 "A Song to David," 1763. *Ronshu: Essays and Studies*,
.1 Tokyo, March 1962, Vol. 14, No. 2, pp. 1–8.* A lecture delivered at the Tokyo Woman's Christian College. Also issued separately as an offprint (*see* A155.1).

C3270 A NEW CITY HALL (1962). *South China Morning Post*,
.2 3 March 1962, City Hall Supplement, p. v.*

C3271 [On the Charles Lamb Birthday Celebration]. *C.L.S. Bulletin*, May 1962, No. 165, p. 368. Letter signed E. Blunden.

C3272 The Post-War *Times Literary Supplement*. *Rising Generation*, 1 May 1962, Vol. 108, No. 5, pp. 246–247.

C3273 Eastern Anchorage. *TLS*, 8 June 1962, p. 427. Review of *Fragrant Harbour: A Private View of Hongkong*, by F. D. Ommanney. Unsigned.

C3274   Shakespeare's Precursor. *TLS*, 13 July 1962, p. 512. Review of *The Dramatic Works of George Peele: Edward I*, edited by Frank S. Hook; *The Battle of Alcazar*, edited by John Yoklavich. Unsigned.

C3275   Many-Sided T.E.L. *Daily Telegraph*, 20 July 1962, p. 16. Review of *Letters of T. E. Lawrence*, edited by A. W. Lawrence.

C3276   Tribute to Poets. *The Times*, 28 July 1962, p. 9. Letter on the report in the issue of 25 July, p. 15 on his address to the National Book League on some twentieth century poets. Quotations from the address appeared in *The Times*, 25 July, p. 15 (*see* E*b*26). On Alfred Noyes.

C3277   Hardy. *Notes on Literature*, August 1962, No. 13, pp. 1–8. Contents: "The Convergence of the Twain" — "The Darkling Thrush" — "Afterwards". *See* note to C3260.

C3277 .1   The Wessex Muse. *The Observer*, 5 August 1962, p. 14. Review of *The Poems of William Barnes*, edited by Bernard Jones.

C3278   Courtly Taste. *TLS*, 5 October 1962, p. 778. Review of *Japanese Court Poetry*, by Robert H. Brower and Earl Miner. Unsigned.

C3279   A Queer Time. *TLS*, 7 December 1962, p. 959. Review of *The Price of Glory: Verdun 1916*, by Alistair Horne. Unsigned.

C3280   The Spirit of Japan. *Asia Magazine*, 16 December 1962, p. 18. Review of *Japan: A Short Cultural History*, by G. B. Sansom; and *Two Minutes to Noon*, by Noel F. Busch.

C3281   George Edward Shelley, M.B.E. *Keats-Shelley Memorial Bulletin, Rome*, [December] 1962, No. 13, pp. 2–3. Also issued separately as an offprint (*see* A157).

1963

C3282   On from Hiroshima. *TLS*, 18 January 1963, p. 38. Review of *Mother and Son: A Japanese Correspondence*, by Isoko and Ichirô Hatano. Unsigned.

C3283   A Captain Courageous. *The Blue*, April 1963, Vol. 90, No. 2, pp. 111–113. Obituary tribute to J. H. E. Woods (Sir John Woods).

C3284   Memoirs of a Gunner. *TLS*, 12 April 1963, p. 251. Review of *As from Kemmel Hill*, by Arthur Behrend. Unsigned.

C3285   Leigh Hunt. *The Times*, 30 May 1963, p. 16. No. 9 of a series entitled Critics Who Have Influenced Taste; other contributors include Simon Nowell-Smith, G. S. Fraser, Douglas Grant, Agnes Latham, Dorothy R. Jones and Bonamy Dobrée.

Reprinted: *Critics Who Have Influenced Taste*, [1965].

C3285 Camoens. *Eastern Horizon*, July 1963, Vol. 2, No. 9, pp.
.1 24.29.* *See also* C3306.

C3286 Leigh Hunt the Leader Writer. *TLS*, 16 August 1963, p. 618. Review of *Leigh Hunt's Political and Occasional Essays*, edited by Lawrence Huston Houtchens and Carolyn Washburn Houtchens. Unsigned.

C3287 A Poet's Youth. *TLS*, 16 August 1963, p. 626. Review of *Journey from Obscurity: Wilfred Owen 1893-1918*, Vol. 1: *Childhood*, by Harold Owen. Unsigned.

C3288 Abeunt Studia in Mores (4 August 1963). *Gakuen Shimbun*, 25 September 1963, pp.   -   .*

C3289 English Studies in Japan. *Rising Generation*, 1 October 1963, Vol. 109, No. 10, pp. 574-576.*

C3290 THE PROPHETESS. *Study of English*, November 1963, Vol. 52, No. 11, p. 1. Holograph facsimile.

C3291 THE STONE GARDEN (KYOTO). *Study of English*, November 1963, Vol. 52, No. 11, pp. 10-11. In English and Japanese with notes; anonymous translation.
First published: *A Hong Kong House*, 1962; reprinted: *A Selection of the Shorter Poems*, [1966].

C3292 Authors to Whom I Return. *Study of English*, November 1963, Vol. 52, No. 11, pp. 14-21. In English and Japanese with notes; anonymous translation.

C3293 Barry Cornwall and Keats. *Keats-Shelley Memorial Bulletin, Rome*, [December] 1963, No. 14, pp. 4-7. Also issued separately as an offprint (*see* A160).

1964

C3294 David Leslie Murray (1888-1962). *Reports of the Royal Society of Literature*, 1961-62/1962-63 [*i.e.* January 1964], pp. 54-55. Obituary. *See also* E*b*27.

C3295 The Aims of Literature. *Rising Generation*, 1 January 1964, Vol. 110, No. 1, pp. 12-17.

C3295 [Review of] *Thought and Behaviour in Modern Japanese*
.1 *Politics*, by Masao Maruyama. *Eastern Horizon*, February 1964, Vol. 3, No. 2, p. 65.*

C3296 Legends from Japan. *TLS*, 20 February 1964, p. 151. Review of *Folktales of Japan*, edited by Keigo Seki, translated by Robert J. Adams. Unsigned.

C3297 A Poet of this Age: Wong Man. *Eastern Horizon*, March 1964, Vol. 3, No. 3, pp. 18-20.*

C3298 Japan Meets Europe —. *TLS*, 16 April 1964, p. 309. Review of *The Japanese Enlightenment: A Study of the Writings of Fukuzawa Yukichi*, by Carmen Blacker. Unsigned.

C3298 [Review of] *Suikaku Ihara: The Life of an Amorous Man.*
.1 *Eastern Horizon*, May 1964, Vol. 3, p. 59.*

C3299   Clare's Genius. *Chronicle & Echo*, 20 May 1964, p. 6. One of 'Four Views of John Clare' on the centenary of his death; the others being by Anne Tibble, James Fisher and Lord Brain.

C3300   IN REMEMBRANCE OF A SISTER. *Texas Quarterly*, Summer 1964, Vol. 7, No. 2, p. 40.

C3301   Poet of Common Objects. *Daily Telegraph*, 11 June 1964, p. 20. Review of *The Shepherd's Calendar*, by John Clare, edited by Eric Robinson and Geoffrey Summerfield; *The Later Poems of John Clare*, edited by Eric Robinson and Geoffrey Summerfield; *The Life of John Clare*, by Frederick Martin; and *Selected Poems of John Clare, 1793–1864*, edited by Leonard Clark.

C3302   A Victorian Garland. *Daily Telegraph*, 18 June 1964, p. 18. Review of *The Oxford Book of Nineteenth-Century English Verse*, chosen by John Hayward.

C3303   Shelley the Realist. *TLS*, 2 July 1964, p. 572. Review of *Shelley: Selected Poems and Prose*, chosen and edited by G. M. Matthews. Unsigned.

C3304   Foreword [to the issue dedicated to Blunden]. *The Chimes*, August 1964, p. 3. Holograph facsimile.

C3305   OVERHEARD. *The Chimes*, August 1964, p. 4. Holograph facsimile.

         First published: *New Poems 1957*, [1957].

C3306   Camoens. *The Chimes*, August 1964, pp. 9–18. A talk given in Macao to the English Society of the University of Hong Kong, December 1961. *See also* C3285.1.

C3307   A Snowdrop Discovered. *The Chimes*, August 1964, pp. 43–48. On Mary Robinson.

C3308   LISTEN. *The Chimes*, August 1964, p. 70.

C3309   A Hundred Years Ago: A Talk in the East in 1955. *The Chimes*, August 1964, pp. 98–107. For Warton Lecture on English Poetry: Romantic Poetry and the Fine Arts, pp. 143–165, and THE SEASIDE HOUSE, p. 166 (*see* C1899, 3176).

C3310   Nippophil. *TLS*, 6 August 1964, p. 701. Review of *Fenollosa*, by Lawrence W. Chisholm; and *The Chinese Written Character as a Medium for Poetry*, by Ernest Fenollosa. Unsigned.

C3311   'Ram Corps' was among its more polite nicknames. *Medical News*, London, 7 August 1964, p. twelve. Blunden 'remembers some of the RAMC staff he knew' during the 1914–1918 War.

C3312   Varieties of Poetry. *Daily Telegraph*, 13 August 1964, p. 18. Review of *73 Poems*, by E. E. Cummings; *Autumn Journal*, by Louis MacNeice; *The Leaves Darken*, by Sheila

Wingfield; *Recoveries*, by W. E. Henley; *Western Time*, by Keith Wright; *Breathing Space*, by Thomas Blackburn; *Wild Honey*, by Alistair Campbell; *The Rose in the Tree*, by Bryan Guinness; *Events and Wisdoms*, by Donald Davie; *Turning Point*, by Philip Callow; and *Telephone Poles*, by John Updike.

C3313 Critics Among the Romantics. *Daily Telegraph*, 20 August 1964, p. 18. Review of *Romantic Perspectives*, edited by Patricia Hodgart and Theodore Redpath.

C3314 FLIGHT OVER CHINA. *Eastern Horizon*, Hong Kong, September 1964, Vol. 3, No. 9, p. 31. At head of title: Verse Sketches in China, 1964. *See also* C3315–18.

C3315 IN THE HANDICRAFT ESTABLISHMENT. *Eastern Horizon*, Hong Kong, September 1964, Vol. 3, No. 9, p. 31. *See also* C3314, 3316–18.

C3316 YOUNG PIONEERS. *Eastern Horizon*, Hong Kong, September 1964, Vol. 3, No. 9, p. 32. *See also* C3314–15, 3317–18.

C3317 VILLAGE: KINDERGARTEN. *Eastern Horizon*, Hong Kong, September 1964, Vol. 3, No. 9, p. 32. *See also* C3314–16, 3318.

C3318 THE OPENED TOMB. *Eastern Horizon*, Hong Kong, September 1964, Vol. 3, No. 9, pp. 32–34. *See also* C3314–17.

C3319 Corduroy Country. *TLS*, 17 September 1964, p. 858. Review of *Apple Acre*, by Adrian Bell. Unsigned. Also issued separately as an offprint (*see* A161). *See also* C1929.

C3320 What Cat's Averse to Fish? *TLS*, 17 September 1964, p. 859. Letter signed Edmund Blunden and Francis Warner.

C3321 TWO SONNETS (first lines: Now over hill and dale in Shakespeare's England; *and* Replies as certain as the daffodil). *Review of English Literature*, October 1964, Vol. 5, No. 4, p. 45.

First published: *15 Poems for William Shakespeare*, June 1964.

C3322 Mr. Richard Cobden-Sanderson. *The Times*, 3 October 1964, p. 10. Obituary.

C3323 Survivors of the Somme. *TLS*, 8 October 1964, p. 911. Review of *The Somme*, by A. H. Farrar-Hockley. Unsigned.

C3324 One Owen at Sea. *TLS*, 8 October 1964, p. 916. Review of *Journey from Obscurity, Wilfred Owen, 1893–1918: Memoirs of the Owen Family*, Vol. 2: *Youth*, by Harold Owen. Unsigned.

C3325 [Review of] *Under Suffolk Sky*, by Allan Jobson. *TLS*, 8 October 1964, p. 925. Unsigned.

C3326 [Review of] *Basic Japanese for College Students*, by Tamako Niwa and Mayako Matsuda. *TLS*, 8 October 1964, p. 925. Unsigned.

C3327 Li by Li. *TLS*, 12 November 1964, p. 1023. Review of *Hong Kong Surgeon*, by Li Shu-fan. Unsigned.

C3328 John Taylor, 1781–1864. *Keats-Shelley Memorial Bulletin, Rome*, [December] 1964, No. 15, pp. 21–24. Also issued separately as an offprint (*see* A163).

C3329 Yarns Laureate. *TLS*, 31 December 1964, p. 1178. Review of *Old Raiger*, by John Masefield. Unsigned.

1965

C3330 Mary Lamb 1764–1847: A Bicentenary Tribute, 5th December, 1964. *C.L.S. Bulletin*, January 1965, No. 181, pp. 469–472.

C3331 Coleridge's Universe. *TLS*, 14 January 1965, p. 26. Review of *La Formation de la Pensée de Coleridge, 1772–1804*, by Paul Deschamps. Unsigned.

C3332 Into the Trenches. *TLS*, 4 February 1965, p. 84. Review of *The Lost Generation*, by Reginald Pound; and *General Jack's Diary, 1914–1918*, edited by John Terraine. Unsigned.

C3333 A. C. W. Edwards, 1881–1964 (Christmas Morning, 1964). *C.L.S. Bulletin*, March 1965, No. 182, pp. 481–482. Obituary. *See also* C3335.

C3334 [Review of] *Modern Japanese Novels and the West*, by Donald Keene; *Modern Japanese Stories: An Anthology*, edited by Ivan Morris; *Folk Legends of Japan*, by Richard M. Dorson; and *The Road to Inamura*, by Lewis Bush. *Journal of Oriental Studies*, 1959/60 [*i.e.* March 1965], Vol. 5, No. 1/2, pp. 252–253. Also issued in an offprint of the reviews section (*see* B259).

C3335 Alfred Cecil Wall Edwards, 1882–1964. *The Blue*, April 1965, Vol. 92, No. 2, pp. 77–79. Obituary. Signed E. Blunden. *See also* C3333.

C3336 Prologue [to Special Poperinge Number]. *Toc H Journal*, May 1965, p. 142. *See also* C3347.

C3337 The Poetry of Rupert Brooke. *Cambridge Review*, 12 June 1965, Vol. 86, No. 2104, pp. 483–484. On the fiftieth anniversary of his death.

C3338 Permanent Pens. *TLS*, 17 June 1965, p. 491. Review of *Soldier from the Wars Returning*, by Charles Carrington; and *A Passionate Prodigality*, by Guy Chapman (*see also* C1252). Unsigned.

C3339 A Poet's Miltonic View of Fame. *Western Mail*, 7 August 1965, p. 7. Review of *John Clare: Selected Poems*, edited by J. W. and Anne Tibble.

C3340 Story of a Heart. *TLS*, 19 August 1965, p. 713. Review of *Richard Jefferies: Man of the Fields*, by Samuel J. Looker and Crichton Porteous. Unsigned.

C3341 T. J. Hogg's Library. *Keats-Shelley Memorial Bulletin, Rome*, [September] 1965, No. 16, pp. 45–46. Also issued separately as an offprint (*see* A166).

C3342 An Author Dressed as Lamb. *Western Mail*, 4 September 1965, p. 10. Review of *Peppercorn Papers*, by Claude A. Prance.

C3343 Dr. Johnson's Friendships. *Western Mail*, 2 October 1965, p. 7.

C3344 Dean and Bookman. *TLS*, 28 October 1965, p. 968. Review of *C. H. Wilkinson 1888–1960*, Festschrift published by Oxford University Press. Unsigned.

C3345 Owens into War. *TLS*, 25 November 1965, p. 1055. Review of *Journey from Obscurity, Wilfred Owen: Memoirs of the Owen Family*, Vol. 3: *War*, by Harold Owen. Unsigned.

C3346 THE TURN OF THE CENTURY. *Kipling Journal*, December 1965, Vol. 32, No. 156, p. 3.

C3347 FREEDOM OF POPERINGE. *Toc H Journal*, December 1965, p. 380. On the occasion of the 'Jubileum Toc H' at Poperinge, 19–20 June 1965. Also issued separately as an offprint (*see* A167). *See also* C3336.

C3348 Dr. Johnson Illustrated. *Western Mail*, 4 December 1965, p. 9. Review of *Dr. Johnson and his World*, by Ivor Brown.

1966

C3349 Coleridge's Notebooks. *Review of English Literature*, January 1966, Vol. 7, No. 1, pp. 25–31.

C3350 Born to be Forgot. *TLS*, 6 January 1966, p. 9. Letter signed E. Blunden on the review of the reprint of *Modern English Biography*, by Frederick Boase in the issue of 23 December 1965, pp. 1189–1190. *See also* letter by Derek Hudson in the issue of 6 January, p. 9.

C3351 Child of American Parnassus. *Western Mail*, 5 February 1966, p. 7. On *Parnassus*, edited by R. W. Emerson.

C3352 1966: S.S. BECOMES AN OCTOGENARIAN. *Illustrated London News*, 19 February 1966, p. 22. Signed E.B. 19 i 66. Holograph facsimile. For HAMMOND (ENGLAND) A CRICKETER, p. 24, INLAND SEA, p. 24, WATCHING RUNNING WATER, p. 25 *see* A35; C635, 2316.

C3353   The Charles Lamb Annual Birthday Celebration, 12th February 1966: An Address by Professor Edmund Blunden, Guest of Honour. *C.L.S. Bulletin*, March 1966, No. 188, pp. 515-516.

C3354   Auden's Thanksgiving. *Daily Telegraph*, 10 March 1966, p. 20. Review of *About the House*, by W. H. Auden.

C3355   Gentleman of Kent. *Western Mail*, 26 March 1966, p. 8. Review of *Sir Roger Twysden, 1597-1672*, by Frank W. Jessup.

C3356   Nature as Masefield Saw It. *Western Mail*, 7 May 1966, p. 8. Review of *Grace Before Ploughing*, by John Masefield.

C3357   Unreturning Times. *TLS*, 15 September 1966, p. 850. Review of *Wearing Spurs*, by John Reith. Unsigned.

C3358   Englishman of Japan. *Western Mail*, 5 November 1966, p. 6. Review of *Collected Writings of Sanki Ichikawa*.

C3359   Poetry, Light and Dark. *Daily Telegraph*, 10 November 1966, p. 20. Review of *High and Low*, by John Betjeman; *The Mind Has Mountains*, by Elizabeth Jennings; and *The North Ship*, by Philip Larkin.

1967

C3360   AESCHYLUS: 'PROMETHEUS BOUND', A TRANSLATION. *Review of English Literature*, January 1967, Vol. 8, No. 1, pp. 9-38.

C3361   [Reading of Poetry]. *Littlemore Life*, 10 March 1967, No. 178, p. [9]. Letter on forthcoming talk signed E. Blunden.

C3362   [Review of] *Hardy of Wessex: His Life and Literary Career*, by Carl J. Weber; *Thomas Hardy: The Will and the Way*, by Roy Morrell. *Review of English Studies*, May 1967, New Series, Vol. 18, No. 70, pp. 223-225. Also issued separately as an offprint (*see* A172). *See also* C1871.

C3363   50 years dedicated to the graves of world wars. . . . *The Times*, 13 May 1967, p. 8. Review of *The Unending Vigil*, by Philip Longworth.

C3364   Sassoon—the Poet of Passchendale. *The Observer*, 3 September 1967, p. 4. Title on p. 1: My Friend Sassoon. On his death.

        Reprinted: *Siegfried Sassoon: A Memorial Exhibition*, 1969.

C3365   Poets and Pedagogues. *Daily Telegraph*, 7 September 1967, p. 21. Review of *Romantics at School*, by Morris Marples.

C3366   Eastern Aesthetics. *TLS*, 16 November 1967, p. 1079. Review of *Legend in Japanese Art*, by Henri L. Joly; *The Chinese Theory of Art: Translations from the Masters of Chinese Art*, by Lin Yutang; and *Brushwork of the Far East: Sumi-e Techniques*, by Sademi Yamada. Unsigned.

C3367   Friends of Samuel Johnson. *Johnson Society Transactions*,
December 1967, pp. 25-36. Presidential address.

1968

C3368   As It Was. *TLS*, 18 July 1968, p. 758. Review of *A Life
Apart*, by Alan Thomas. Unsigned.

C3369   Fifty Years Ago on Monday the First World War Ended.
Daily Express, 8 November 1968, p. 9.

1969

C3370   Wordsworth's Later Poems. *Essays by Divers Hands*, [February] 1969, New Series, Vol. 35, pp. 18-22. The Tredegar
Memorial Lecture delivered to the Royal Society of Literature on 24 March 1966. Also issued separately as an off-print (*see* A175). *See also* E*b*32.

D.

TRANSLATIONS INTO FOREIGN LANGUAGES

CHINESE

Periodicals

D1   [A POEM OF A FEW LINES OFFERED TO CHINESE AUTHORS ON CHRISTMAS DAY, 1955]. *Kwong Ming*, 31 December 1955, p. 4. In Chinese; translated by Yang Hsien-i.

D2   [William Blake: London's Wise Eye]. *Wen Huei Pao*, Hong Kong, 21 December 1957, p. 9. In Chinese; Blunden's holograph facsimile of concluding paragraph.

FRENCH

Book

D3   BIBLIOTHÈQUE DE STYLISTIQUE COMPARÉE | Sous la direction de A. MALBANC | [*rule*] IV [*rule*] | L. BONNEROT | *Professeur à la Sorbonne* | CHEMINS DE LA TRADUCTION | *DOMAINE ANGLAIS* | *DU FRANÇAIS A L'ANGLAIS* [*vertical rule*] *DE L'ANGLAIS AU FRANÇAIS* | *Notes et commentaires de* | L. LECOCQ et J. RUER [*vertical rule*] H. APPIA et H. KERST | *Maîtres-Assistants à la Faculté des Lettres* | *de Paris* | Avec la collaboration de | J. DARBELNET | *Agrégé de l'Université* | [*rule*] | DIDIER | 4 et 6, rue de la Sorbonne | PARIS

Small royal 8vo. vii, 306 pp. 9¼ X 6 in.

Published 1963; number of copies not ascertained. 22.50 francs.

Pp. 224–226 The Bluecoat School; Le Collège des Tuniques Bleues; in English and French; and a translation from Sussex.

Periodical

D4   Le camp dans le bois (Bataille de la Somme, 1916). *Fontaine*, Algiers, 1944, Vol. 37/40, pp. 373–374. In French and English; translated by the author. This special issue of *Fontaine* is entitled *Aspects de la Littérature anglaise de 1918 à 1940*.

GERMAN

Book

D5   Shelley (die dt. über. bes Iring. Kutscher u. Karl Bahnmüller). Düsseldorf, Frankfurt am Main, Meridian-Verlag, 1948. 475 pp.*

A translation by Iring. Kutscher and Karl Bahnmüller of *Shelley*.

Books

D6   [*within a triple rule:*] THIRTY LYRICS | EDITED WITH TRANSLATIONS | AND COMMENTS | *by* | TAKESHI SAITO | TOKYO | SANKAIDO

Crown 8vo. xii, 178, [100] pp. 8 plates. 7¼ × 5 in.

Published 18 July 1931; number of copies printed not ascertained.

Pp. 8-9 ALMSWOMEN, with translation on pp. [11-15]; pp. 32-33 THE AUTHOR'S LAST WORDS TO HIS STUDENTS, with translation on pp. 66-68; plate [2] holograph facsimile in English of ALMSWOMEN; plate [3] John Clare's Unpublished Poems Copied by Mr. Blunden.

D6
.1   [*within a rule*] IWANAMI BUNKO | 3787-3788 | [*rule*] | GIRUBATO HOWAITO | SERUBÔN HAKUBUTSUSHI | JÔKAN | JUGAKU BUNSHO YAKU | [*publisher's device*] | IWANAMI SHOTEN

Foolscap 8vo. 202 pp. front., and illus. 5⅞ × 4¼ in.

Buff paper wrappers; printed in brown; edges cut flush; gummed. Published 20 February 1949 in Tokyo; number of copies printed not ascertained. 80 yen.

A translation by Bunshô Jagaku of *The Natural History of Selborne*, Vol. 1, by Gilbert White.

Pp. 3-5 Introduction in Japanese.

D7   EIKOKU KINDAI SAMBUNSHÛ | FUKUHARA RINTARÔ YAKU-CHÛ | [*device*] | [*rule*] | KENKYÛSHA | 1953

Small crown 8vo. vi, 314 pp. 7 × 4¾ in.

Published in Tokyo 25 July 1953; 3000 copies printed. 250 yen.

There were reprints of 500 copies each in 1955, 1957, 1958 and 1960, and 1000 copies in 1962.

A collection of modern English prose.

Pp. 268-311 Wordsworth: Occasional Thoughts on his Poetry and Characteristics; with translation by Rintarô Fukuhara.

D8   MATSUSHIMA | [*illustration*] | HARU NO GODAIDÔ | [*at left:*] MIYAGIKEN | [*at right:*] MATSUSHIMACHÔ | MATSUSHIMA KANKÔKYÔKAI

[8] pp. (folded). illus., and plan. 7¼ × 10⅜ in.

Published January 1955; number of copies printed not ascertained. Not for sale.

A brochure for the Tourist Society in Matsushima, published by the Miyagi Prefecture, Matsushima.

P. [3] MATSUSHIMA; with translation by Shôgo Shiratori.

D9 EIBUNGAKU HANDO-BUKKU—"SAKKA TO SAKUHIN" SHIRIZU │ [rule] │ JOHN │ KEATS │ EDMUND BLUNDEN │ KIKUCHI WATARU YAKU │ KENKYÛSHA TOKYO

Demy 8vo. viii, 52, ii, 10 pp. front. $8\frac{1}{2} \times 5\frac{1}{2}$ in.

Published 20 June 1956; 4000 copies printed. 100 yen.

There were reprints of 500 copies each in 1960 and 1961, and 1000 copies in 1963, 1965, 1966, 1968, 1970, 1971 and 1972.

A translation by Wataru Kikuchi of *John Keats*, revised edition.

D10 [*within a double rule*:] KADOGAWA-SHINSHO │ SAYO-NARA NIPPON │ EDOMUNDO BRUNDEN │ TOMIYAMA SHIGERU YAKU │ [*illustration*] │ 116

Foolscap 8vo. 184 pp. $6\frac{7}{8} \times 4\frac{1}{8}$ in.

Published in Tokyo 30 July 1957; number of copies printed not ascertained. 110 yen.

A translation by Shigeru Tomiyama of *A Wanderer in Japan*.

D11 EISHI NO AJIWAI KATA │ WASEDA DAIGAKU KYÔJU BUNGAKUHAKASE │ OSHIMA SHÔTARÔ CHO │ [*illustration*]│ KENKYÛSHA

Small crown 8vo. viii, 212 pp. $7 \times 4\frac{3}{4}$ in.

Published in Tokyo 20 December 1957; 2000 copies printed. 230 yen.

There were 13 reprints of 1000 copies each between 1958 and 1972.

How to Appreciate English Poems, by Shôtarô Oshima.

Pp. 71-72 FROM A STUDY WINDOW [*formerly* FROM A STUDY TABLE]; pp. 76-78 A DREAM [*later* THE FOND DREAM]; with translations by Shôtarô Oshima.

D12 KYÔIN ZUIHITSU │ YASUO YAMATO

Demy 8vo. [2], iv, 138 pp. front. (port.) and 3 illus. $8\frac{1}{2} \times 5\frac{7}{8}$ in.

Published 1 October 1967 by Osaka Kyôiku Tosho; 1000 copies printed. 650 yen.

Essays and notes by Dr Yasuo Yamato.

Pp. 49-52 IN MEMORY OF ROBERT NICHOLS, and THE FLOWERS OF THE ROCK; with translations and notes by Yasuo Yamato.

D13 ATARASHII EISHI NO KANSHÔ │ WASEDA DAIGAKU KYÔJU BUNGAKUHAKASE │ OSHIMA SHÔTARÔ CHO │ KABASHIKIGAISHA HOKUSEIDÔ SHOTEN

Crown 8vo. xii, 200 pp. front. $7\frac{1}{8} \times 5$ in.

Published 20 November 1968; 1000 copies printed. 500 yen.
New Appreciation of English Poems, by Shôtarô Oshima.
Pp. 28-33 THE STONE GARDEN (KYÔTO); pp. 159-165
FOREFATHERS; with translations and notes by Shôtarô
Oshima.

Periodicals

D14 Eikoku seinen shijin. *Jiji Shinpo*, 15/31 March 1925, p.
     - . A translation by Takeshi Saito of Some Younger English
     Poets.*

D15 Daiichi inshô (Tôkyô). *Kitsune to Suisen*, 10 July 1930, Vol.
     2, pp. 12-14. A translation by M. Sakai of First Impressions,
     Tokyo.

D16 Came to Japan Again. *The Mainichi*, Tokyo, 4 January 1948,
     p. 2. In Japanese; anonymous translation.*

D17 Contemporary English Writers. *Asahi Shimbun*, Tokyo, 1
     March 1948, p. 2. In Japanese; translated by Koji Nishi-
     mura.*

D18 Haru no shôhon. *Asahi Shimbun*, Tokyo, 1 March 1948, p. 2.
     An anonymous translation of A SMALL PIECE OF SPRING.

D19 Harbour Sketch Written in Absence. *Gunzô*, Tokyo, 1 April
     1948, Vol. 3, No. 4, pp. 12-13. In Japanese; translated by
     Ichirô Nishizaki; holograph facsimile of title and autograph.

D20 Blunden no shi. *Aoyama Bungaku*, Tokyo, 5 April 1948,
     Vol. 21, No. 1, p. 37. A translation by Takeshi Saito of part
     of THE AUTHOR'S LAST WORDS TO HIS STUDENTS.

D21 Genaishi. *World Literature*, Kyoto, 10 April 1948, No. 20,
     pp. 56-58. A translation by Hikaru Saito of Poetry Today.

D22 Fukei to kokuminsei. *Ningen*, Tokyo, May 1948, Vol. 3,
     No. 5, pp. 42-44. A translation by Koji Nishimura of The
     Landscape and its National Character.*

D23 Eikoku bundan no genjô. *Sekai Bunka*, Tokyo, 1 May 1948,
     Vol. 3, No. 5, pp. 38-41. A translation by Tetsuo Okumura
     of English Literature Today: Address to the Japan PEN
     Club.

D24 Heiwa ga motarashita kôfuku. *Nihon Keizai Shimbun*, Tokyo,
     3 May 1948, p. 4. An anonymous translation of [Happiness
     which peace has brought].

D25 Chôrui no tame ni inoru. *World Literature*, Kyoto, 10 May
     1948, No. 21, p. 36. A translation by Takeshi Saito of A
     PRAYER FOR THE BIRDS.

D26 Shimese shinjitsu no sugata. *Nippon Dokusho Shimbun*,
     Tokyo, 2 June 1948, p. 1. An anonymous translation of
     Show the True Appearance.

D27 The Recent Literature of England: A Fragmentary Survey.
     Spirit of British & American Literature, Tokyo, 1 July 1948,

No. 1, pp. 127-134. In Japanese; translated by K. Iwata; holograph facsimile in English of opening paragraphs, p. 127.

D28   Nihon no bunka ni tsuite. *Sekai Shûhô*, Tokyo, 1 January 1949, Vol. 30, No. 1, pp. 22-23. A translation by Ichirô Nishizaki of On Japanese Culture.

D29   Daichi to kikai. *Seikatsu Bunka*, Tokyo, 1 October 1949, Vol. 10, No. 10, pp. 22-23. A translation by Ichirô Nishizaki of Great Earth and Opportunity.

D30   Kyôen. *Seikatsu Bunka*, Tokyo, 1 October 1949, Vol. 10, No. 10, p. 23. A translation by Ichirô Nishizaki of RIVAL FEASTS [*formerly* RIVAL APPETITES].

D31   Sengo no Nihon—Wakare no kotoba. *Nippon Dokusho Shimbun*, Tokyo, 15 March 1950, p. 1. A translation by Hikaru Saito of Post-War Japan—A Farewell Message.

D32   Friendly Correspondence. *Asahi Shimbun*, Tokyo, 27 January 1953, p. 6. In Japanese; translated by Tomoji Abe.*

D33   Oitaru dokusha yori no shisa. *Kyôto Shimbun*, Kyôto, 28 March 1955, p. 4. An anonymous translation of A Suggestion by an Old Reader.

D34   The Decade of Renascence [of Japan]. *The Mainichi*, Tokyo, 15 August 1955, p. 3. In Japanese; anonymous translation.*

D35   [untitled poem (That the glory of heaven be bright)]. *Prelude*, Hiroshima, 20 September 1959, No. 16, p. 38. An anonymous translation of the poem sent to the Poets Association of Hiroshima Prefecture.

D36   Nihon o saru ni nozomite. *Tôkyô Shimbun*, Tokyo, 26 February 1960, p. 4. A translation by Tetsuo Okumura of A Farewell Message—On Leaving Japan.

D37   Idainaru yume. *The Mainichi*, Tokyo, 16 March 1960, p. 4. An anonymous translation of part of a farewell lecture entitled A Great Dream.

D38   Uruwashi no Nippon. *Hokkai Times*, Sapporo, Hokkaidô, 1 January 1961, p. 32. A translation by Mikio Hiramatsu of JAPAN BEAUTIFUL, with an introduction. The poem also appeared in *Shinano Mainichi Shimbun*, Nagano, 1 January 1961, Issue 2, p. 17, and other newspapers later in January 1961.

D39   Seeing More of Japan. *Yomiuri Shimbun* [Evening Edition], Nagano, 17 September 1963, p. 7; and 18 September 1963, p. 7. 1, Two Remarkable Museums — 2, Things Unforeseen. In Japanese; translated by Mikio Hiramatsu.*

D40   Shakespeare. *Gakuto*, [Tokyo], June 1964, Vol. 61, No. 6, pp. 58-63. In Japanese; translated by Masaho Hirai.*

For other translations in Japanese *see* A90*b*, 102; B125, 131-3, 139, 171, 224, 232-3, 283.1; C2422, 2425, 2427, 2430, 2435-6, 2439, 2455-8, 2463, 2469, 2511, 2516, 2523, 2542, 3137-8, 3165, 3173, 3224, 3228, 3251, 3291-2; E*e*2-3.

LATIN

Book

D41   VERSIONS | AND | DIVERSIONS | SELECTED GREEK | AND LATIN COMPOSITIONS | BY | D. S. MACNUTT | *Master of the Classical Grecians* | *1928-1963* | Presented to him on his retirement by his colleagues | pupils and friends | CHRIST'S HOSPITAL | Privately printed for the Subscribers | 1964

Small royal 8vo. [xii], 40 pp. $9\frac{7}{8} \times 5\frac{3}{4}$ in.

Published *c.* 5 May 1964; probably 150 copies printed.

Pp. [i–iv] and [37–40] form end-papers.

Pp. 14-15 A CRICKET ADVICE, in English and Latin CONSILIVM LVSORIVM; first published in *Cricket Country*, 1944 (*see* A76).

PORTUGUESE

Periodical

D42   A morte de John Middleton Murry. *Diario de Lisbôa*, 8 January 1958, p. —. Translation of the article contributed to the British Council's Feature Articles Service.*

SWEDISH

Book

D43   KRIGETS VARDAG | AV | EDMUND BLUNDEN | ÖVER-SATT OCH FÖRSEDD MED INLEDNING AV | STEN SELANDER | [*monogram*] | STOCKHOLM | ALBERT BONNIERS FÖRLAG

Crown 8vo. 308 pp. $7\frac{3}{4} \times 5$ in.

Published *c.* 20 May 1931; 2500 copies printed. 7.50 Swedish crowns.

A translation by Sten Selander of *Undertones of War*; the poems are omitted.

E.

APPENDIX

QUOTED LETTERS IN BOOKS AND
                        PERIODICALS

Ea1   [Quotation from a letter 'from our Professor at Tokio' and
       from his latest poem commencing: 'The Samurai and Daim-
       yos depart,' in] Oxford Letter. *The Blue*, December 1924,
       Vol. 52, No. 2, p. 77. Signed W.T.B. *i.e.* W. T. Bryant. *See
       also* C480.

Ea2   Ishii, Haxon. *Twelve Poems*. Tokyo, Bunka-Insatsu-sha, 1925.
       Leaf 5; letter dated Tokyo, 24 July 1925.

Ea3   Beaumont, Cyril W. *The First Score*. London, The Beaumont
       Press, 1927. Pp. [72], 78, 81, 83-[84]; quotations from
       letters on the publication of *To Nature*, 1923; *Madrigals &
       Chronicles*, 1924; and *Masks of Time*, 1925. *See also* A14,
       17; B14.

Ea4   Bridges, Robert, ed. *S.P.E. Tract No. XXVIII, English Hand-
       writing*. [Oxford], Clarendon Press, 1927. Plate 37; holo-
       graph facsimile of letter to Robert Bridges, dated Tokyo, 19
       April 1927.

Ea5   Rota, Bertram, bookseller. *Catalogue No. 25, The Personal
       Library of John Gawsworth (Terence Ian Fytton Armstrong)
       . . . offered for Sale by Betram Rota*. London, 1933. Pp. 5-
       10 quotations from letters to Fytton Armstrong.

Ea6   Lucas, E. V. Post-Bag Diversions. London, Methuen, 1934.
       Pp. 195-196 quotations from letters dated 5 March 1929
       and 1 June 1930 on an imperfect copy of *Undertones of
       War*, and on Leigh Hunt. *See also* A28.

Ea7   Lamb, Charles. *The Letters of Charles Lamb*, to which are
       added those of his sister, Mary Lamb; edited by E. V. Lucas.
       [London], J. M. Dent & Methuen, 1935. 3 vols. Vol. 1,
       pp. xii-xiv quotation from letter on Mrs G. A. Anderson.
       See also C1474.

Ea8   Blunden, Edmund. (*From a Letter, written by Edmund Blun-
       den, about Mysticism and Poetry*.) [London, 1935]. [1] leaf;
       extracts from a letter to A. Allen Brockington on his *Mysti-
       cism & Poetry*, published by Chapman & Hall, dated 27
       December 1934, and printed by the addressee as an adver-
       tisement. Signed E. Blunden.

Ea9   From Mr. Edmund Blunden. *Studies in English Literature*,
       October 1936, Vol. 16, No. 4, pp. 632-633; extracts from
       two letters to Professor Takeshi Saito dated 29 August and
       7 September 1936.

Ea10   *Irene Brent, Diseuse*. London, Purbrook & Eyres, printer, [September, 1946]. Pp. [3-4]; quotation from letter, undated, on meetings at the Poets' Club. Signed E. Blunden.

Ea11   Ikeda, Yoste. *Songs of a Wanderer*. [Tokyo, 1948]. P. [7]; letter dated Tokyo, 22 February 1948. Signed E. Blunden.

Ea12   *Issatsukampon Shekusupia zenshû, Tsubouchi Shôyô yaku* [Prospectus for the forthcoming new edition of the complete works of Shakespeare, translated by Shôyô Tsubouchi, Waseda University, and published by Sôgensha]. First fold of page; holograph facsimile of letter to Dr Kawatake, dated Tokyo, 10 October 1949.

Ea13   [On Charles Lamb, dated Tokyo, 10 February 1950]. *Rising Generation*, 1 April 1950, Vol. 96, No. 4, p. 155. Signed E.B.

Ea14   Japan and Western Literatures. *International P.E.N. Bulletin of Selected Books*, May 1951, No. 4, p. 4; quotation from a letter, undated, to P.E.N., London.

Ea15   *The Case of Mr. Johnson Ball, Dismissed Principal of the County Technical School, Halesowen, Worcestershire*. [Halesowen, Reliance Printing Works, printers, October 1952]. P. 16; quotation from letter in support of Johnson Ball.

Ea16   Matsuoka, Yoko. *Daughter of the Pacific*. Melbourne, London, [etc.], William Heinemann, [1953]. Dust-jacket, lower cover; quotation about the author.

Ea17   Hong Kong. *The Blue*, May 1954, Vol. 71, No. 2, pp. 122-123; quotations from letters to J. C. Ledward dated 5 October 1953.

Ea18   Sixty Years a Teacher of English. *Asahi Evening News*, 9 June 1954, p. —; quotations from two letters to Professor Eishiro Hori on his retirement, one undated, the other dated 10 November 1950. These quotations were also issued separately as an offprint in which the quotations were reprinted on pp. 4-5.

Ea19   Gourdie, Tom. *Italic Handwriting*. London, New York, The Studio Publications, 1955. P. [27] holograph facsimile of letter dated 29 July 1952. Signed E. Blunden.

Ea20   Hassall, Christopher. *Edward Marsh, Patron of the Arts: A Biography*. [London], Longmans, [1959]. Pp. 469-471, 516, 529, 534 untitled verse (In far Gray's Inn, what time the frosty Bear), 541, and 599 including untitled verse (It is not growing like a Tree).

Ea21   *Kenkyûhôkoku yoshi Nihon Eibungakukai chûba dai-junikai taikai* [Résumés of Reports and Lectures at the English Literary Society of Japan (Central XII General Meeting) and the Thomas Hardy Society of Japan (III General Meeting) held at the University of Kanazawa on 24-25 October 1959]. Pp. 6, 14; letters to Professor Mamoru Osawa dated 28

December 1959 and 15 August 1959 on the Third General Meeting of the Thomas Hardy Society of Japan.

Ea22   Footsteps of the [Thomas Hardy] Society [of Japan]. *Bulletin of the Thomas Hardy Society of Japan*, 1959, No. 3, p. 6; letter to Professor Mamoru Osawa dated 28 December 1959. Signed E. Blunden. The section was also issued separately as an offprint.

Ea23   Edmund Blunden, Teacher, by Yoshitaka Sakai. *Today's Japan*, March/April 1960, Vol. 5, No. 3, pp. 59–61; quotations from Blunden's first address to students at the University of Tokyo in 1924, and note in Professor Sakai's copy of *The Poems on Various Subjects of Thomas Warton. See also* E*b*24.

Ea24   Edmund Blunden, Teacher, by Tamotsu Sone. *Today's Japan*, March/April 1960, Vol. 5, No. 3, p. 58; note in Professor Sone's copy of *The Poets and the Poetry of the Century*, Vol. 4, edited by A. H. Miles, dated 14 July 1927.

Ea25   News and Notes: Edmund Blunden. *Keats-Shelley Journal*, Winter 1960, Vol. 9, No. 1, p. 3; quotation from a letter to Neville Rogers on Keats and the cricket ball.

Ea26   Lawrence, A. W. ed. *Letters to T. E. Lawrence.* London, Jonathan Cape, 1962. Pp. 14–15; letter dated 2 August 1923.

Ea27   Letters from Poets: A Literary Reminiscence by Rupert Croft-Cooke. *Books & Bookmen*, September 1962, p. 35; quotation from a letter from Tokyo, [1925].

Ea28   Edmund Blunden: Seven holograph letters to his publisher C. W. Beaumont. G. F. Sims (Rare Books), Catalogue 63, Spring (February) 1966, Item 20, p. 4; quotations.

Ea29   Oakes, Philip. Written in the Sand. *Sunday Times Magazine*, 22 October 1967, p. 55; quotation from a letter to a friend of Sidney Keyes.

Ea30   Nowell-Smith, Simon. ed. *Letters to Macmillan.* London, Macmillan, 1967. P. 335; quotation from a letter to John Hassall, Christopher Hassall's father.

Ea31   [On the Hardy Festival]. *Bulletin of the Thomas Hardy Society of Japan*, 1968, No. 7, Hardy Festival Number, p. 72; letter to Keizo Oba dated 10 July 1968. Signed E. Blunden.

Ea32   [On *Reprinted Papers* and the *TLS*]. *Rising Generation*, 1 June 1974, Vol. 120, No. 3, p. 109; autograph letter to Torao Uyeda of Kenkyusha Ltd, Tokyo, dated 19 November 1950. Signed EB (E. Blunden).

E*b*1 The Literature of War. *The Blue*, April 1930, Vol. 57, No. 4, pp. 200-201. Summary of an address given to Christ's Hospital Club on 17 March.

E*b*2 "Westfront—1918" at the Film Society. *The Cherwell*, 13 February 1932, Vol. 34, No. 4, p. 82. Signed D.R.H. (E. B. abetting.). *See also* review of film (C1185).

E*b*3 Biography. *Hermes: Westfield College Magazine*, December 1932, p. 3. Note of public lecture given at Westfield College, University of London on 19 February 1932. *See also Report of Westfield College*, Session 1931-1932, p. 15.

E*b*4 University Japan Society. *Oxford Times*, 26 January 1934, p. 9. Summary of Blunden's address 'Glimpses of Japanese Literature: Sonnets and Haiku'.

E*b*5 Scots' Celebration in Oxford: Burns Night Dinner. *Oxford Times*, 26 January 1934, p. 32. Summary of the toast 'The Immortal Memory' proposed by Blunden.

E*b*6 "Should Autobiographies Be Forbidden?": Miss Brittain's Defence of the Form. *The Times*, 1 February 1934, p. 11; introducing as Chairman a lecture by Vera Brittain in aid of the Elizabeth Levett Memorial Fund.

E*b*7 Donnelly, Ian. *The Joyous Pilgrimage: A New Zealander's Impressions of 'Home'*. London, J. M. Dent, [1935]. Pp. 205-209 'Blunden of Merton'.

E*b*8 Lamb's Claim to a Public Monument. *Charles Lamb Society Monthly Bulletin*, February 1936, No. 8, pp. 2-3. Summary of an address 'Charles Lamb' given to the January meeting of the Society. *See also* E*f*5.

E*b*9 Keats House Reopened. *The Times*, 29 October 1945, p. 6. Quotation from speech to mark the ceremony.

E*b*9 .1 *The English Literary Scene 1948 (Summary)*. 4 pp. Pp. 2-3. Summary covering the years 1928-1948.*

E*b*9 .2 *New English Teaching Method*, by Tsuneo Aoki, [1948?]. [4] pp. Pp. [3-4]. Summary of an address 'Main Interests of English Literature'.

E*b*10 *Lectures in English Literature, by Mr. Edmund Blunden [at] the Keio-Gijuku University*, 1948. 4 pp. Summaries of lectures at the Keio-Gijuku University, 7-25 June 1948.

E*b*11 *Address to Tokyo Toritsu Daiichi Koto Gakko, by Edmund Blunden, 29 October 1948*. 4 pp. Address to the school on English literature.

E*b*12 *Speech at the Inauguration of Takeshi Saito as President of Tokyo Joshi Daigaku*, 6 November 1948. 2 pp. (mimeo.).

Reprinted: *English Poetry*, December 1949, No. 2, pp. 16, 21. *See also* E*b*18.

Eb13 *La Litterature française: Quelques Souvenirs par E. Blunden.* [Tokyo, 1949]. [ii], 10 pp. (mimeo.). Summary of an address to the Maison français-japonaise, Tokyo in the spring, 1949.

Eb14 *The Author and the Community: Synopsis of Lecture by Edmund Blunden for Tokyo English Teachers' Association, 21 May 1949.* 1 leaf.

Eb15 *A Synopsis of Lecture by Prof. Edmund Blunden; Education: The Student of English,* by Professor Kuranaga. 1 leaf. In commemoration of the 75th anniversary of Aoyama Gakuin on 16 November 1949. *See also* C2519.

Eb16 Where is anti-British feeling so rare as to be almost "the smart thing"? *Daily Mail,* 23 June 1950, p. 3. Quotation from an address to the Royal Empire Society.

Eb17 Memories of Literature. *Bristol Grammar School Chronicle,* December 1950, Vol. 26, No. 1, pp. 6–7. Note of an address given 'off the cuff' on 20 October 1950.

Eb18 *Gakuen Zuisô: Speeches and Essays on the Campus Life,* by Takeshi Saito, President, Tokyo Joshi Daigaku, with speeches by Dr Reischauer and Professor Blunden. Tokyo, Kenkyusha, 25 July 1952. [iv], 38 pp. (English text); xii, 220 pp. (Japanese text). Pp. 9–11 (English text) Speech at the Inauguration of Takeshi Saito as President, Tokyo Joshi Daigaku, 6 November 1948; plate facing p. 32 (Japanese text) FOR TOKYO JOSHI DAIGAKU: A HYMN [*formerly* COLLEGE SONG], holograph facsimile (*see* A98, 171; C2520). *See also* Eb12.

Eb19 Blunden's Apotheosis. *Manchester Guardian,* 23 September 1953, p. 1. On accepting the Chair of English Literature at Hong Kong University.

Eb20 The Comparison Between Local Undergraduates and those of England. *The Quill,* 1955, Vol. 1, p. 58. The first of five replies on the topic recorded by Brenda Wan.

Eb21 A Humourous Talk: The Trials and Tribulations of a Modern Novelist, The Birth of an Idea. *South China Morning Post,* 24 November 1955, p. 9. Quotation from speech introducing Alec Waugh at a British Council meeting in Hong Kong.

Eb22 No Daydreams in Peking: European Visitors' Impressions. *The Times,* 31 December 1955, p. 5. Quotation from speech on return to Hong Kong after a visit at the invitation of the Chinese Society for Cultural Relations.

Eb23 Poetry of Cricket: Action and Words at Westminster. *The Times,* 20 June 1957, p. 12. Quotation from speech at luncheon on the annual match between the National Book League and the Authors at Westminster School.

E*b*24 Edmund Blunden, Teacher. *C.L.S. Bulletin*, July 1960, No. 154, p. 286. Quotation from his first address as Professor of English Literature at Tokyo University. *See also* E*a*23.

E*b*25 Blunden on Poets. *The Guardian*, 23 July 1962, p. 6. Quotation while on leave from Hong Kong University.

E*b*26 Tribute to Poets of an Era. *The Times*, 25 July 1962, p. 15. Quotation from an address to the National Book League on some twentieth century poets. *See also* letter by Blunden in the issue of 28 July, p. 9 (C3276).

E*b*27 [On receiving the Companion of Literature]. *Reports of the Royal Society of Literature*, 1961–62/1962–63 [*i.e.* January 1964], pp. 40–41. Speech at a dinner held on 25 July 1963. *See also* C3294.

E*b*28 Clare's poems 'drama of the world of nature'. *Peterborough Standard*, 22 May 1964, p. 13. Summary of an address at Peterborough during the Clare Centenary Festival. *See also* B251.

E*b*29 Chairing the Bard. *The Observer*, 9 January 1966, p. 40. On the forthcoming election to the Chair of Poetry at Oxford.

E*b*30 Mr. Blunden Wins Oxford Poetry Chair by 236 votes. *The Times*, 7 February 1966, p. 5. On his election.

E*b*31 [Charles Lamb Centenary Address, at the Central Library, Hampstead, 7 November 1934]. *C.L.S. Bulletin*, March 1966, No. 188, p. 520. Quotations from the speech. Summaries of the speech appeared in the *Hampstead & St John's Wood Advertiser*, 15 November 1934, p. 6, and the *Hampstead & Highgate Express*, 17 November 1934, p. 7.

E*b*32 Blunden View of Wordsworth as Elder Statesman. *The Times*, 25 March 1966, p. 6. Quotation from an address, 'Wordsworth's Later Poems', to the Royal Society of Literature. *See also* A175; C3370.

E*b*33 'One Haunting Touch' Justifies Poem. *Daily Telegraph*, 1 June 1966, p. 15. Quotation from inaugural lecture as Professor of Poetry at Oxford University.

E*b*34 *Oratio creweiana*. [Oxford], 22 June 1966. 8 pp. Pp. 2–7 oration in Latin and English. Creweian Oration 'in commemoration of Benefactors to the University' delivered by Blunden as Professor of Poetry.

E*b*35 Prof. Blunden defends MA's powers. *Daily Telegraph*, 15 February 1967, p. 19. Quotation from comments on the proposal to deprive MA's of their power to elect candidates to the Chair of Poetry at Oxford University.

E*b*36 Skating On. *Sunday Times*, 3 March 1968, p. 13. On the Poet Laureateship and the Chair of Poetry at Oxford University.

TESTIMONIALS

Ec1   Application and Testimonials submitted by Claude Colleer
       Abbott, M.A., B.A., Ph.D., Lecturer in the English Depart-
       ment of the University of Aberdeen: A Candidate for the
       Professorship of English Language and Literature in the Dur-
       ham Colleges of the University of Durham. Pp. [12]. In-
       cludes testimonial from Blunden dated Merton College,
       Oxford, 11 June 1932; it also appeared with minor varia-
       tions in Dr Abbott's application as candidate for the Chal-
       mers Professorship of English Literature in the University of
       Aberdeen, dated Merton College, Oxford, 10 July 1937.

Ec2   [Testimonial of Mr J. L. N. O'Loughlin]. 1 leaf. Dated Mer-
       ton College, Oxford, 19 May 1937. O'Loughlin was a mem-
       ber of the English Faculty.

Ed   MUSIC SCORES, SOUND RECORDINGS

Ed1   *Among the Roses: Song with Pianoforte Accompaniment*,
       by Ivy Frances Klein; Words by Edmund Blunden. London,
       Augener, [1949]. 4 pp. [*later* ONE AMONG THE ROSES].

Ed2   *A Garland for the Queen: Songs for Mixed Voices*; [text
       and music score by Gerald Finzi]. London, Stainer & Bell,
       [1953]. P. xi THE WHITE-FLOWERING DAYS. See B157.

Ed3   *Gems from English Poetry*, read by Edmund Blunden. [Tok-
       yo], Kenkyusha, [1960]. 1 record, $6\frac{7}{8}$ in. (disc 45-RPM;
       ER14; 7EK-111). Buff envelope printed in tan. Booklet
       inserted (*see* B224). Side 1: The Violet — Before the Paling
       of the Stars — The Lamb — Lucy Gray. Side 2: The Blind
       Boy — THE TREE IN THE GOODS YARD — VOICES
       IN TOKYO — FROM THE FLYING-BOAT — HOMES AND
       HAUNTS.

Ed4   British Council tape recording of Blunden reading: FORE-
       FATHERS — THE MIDNIGHT SKATERS — CONCERT
       PARTY: BUSSEBOOM — THE SUNLIT VALE [*formerly*
       THE FAILURE] — REPORT ON EXPERIENCE — FAMI-
       LIARITY — THE AUTHOR'S LAST WORDS TO HIS
       STUDENTS — VALUES — SERENA — THE HONG KONG
       HOUSE — AT THE GREAT WALL OF CHINA — THOUGHTS
       OF THOMAS HARDY. *Catalogue of Tape Recordings*, No.
       752, dated 3 September 1964. Not for sale. Available in
       British Council overseas poetry rooms, British Institute of
       Recorded Sound, Durham, Hull and Leeds Universities, and
       the Lamont Library of Harvard University. *See also* Ed7.

Ed5   British Council tape recording: Edmund Blunden talks to
       John Press. *Catalogue of Tape Recordings*, No. 753, dated 3
       September 1964. Not for sale. *See* note to Ed4. *See also*
       Ee6.

Ed5 *Oh Fair to See: Seven Songs for High Voice and Piano;*
.1   Words by Various Poets; Music by Gerald Finzi. [London],
     Boosey & Hawkes, [1965]. Pp. 14-16 TO JOY — pp. 17-21
     HARVEST.

Ed6 *Poems by Edmund Blunden,* read by C. Day Lewis, Jill
     Balcon, Carleton Hobbs. London, Jupiter Recordings Ltd,
     [1966]. 1 record, 9⅞ in. (JUR OOB8). White sleeve printed
     in turquoise blue and navy-blue. Side 1: FOREFATHERS —
     ALMSWOMEN — HIGH ELMS, BRACKNELL — CLARE'S
     GHOST [*formerly* PHANTASIES] — THOUGHTS OF
     THOMAS HARDY — NO CONTINUING CITY — THE
     CHILD'S GRAVE — THE SUNLIT VALE [*formerly* THE
     FAILURE] — THE MIDNIGHT SKATERS — THE ZONNE-
     BEKE ROAD. Side 2: 1916 SEEN FROM 1921 [*formerly*
     FESTUBERT, 1916] — THE BRANCH LINE — A PROS-
     PECT OF SWANS — FOR THE COUNTRY LIFE [*formerly*
     THE MEANS] — TO THE NEW JAPAN [*formerly* WALK-
     ING IN TOKYO 1948] — A HONG KONG HOUSE —
     NATURE'S ADORNINGS [*formerly* NATURE'S DARING]
     — FARM BAILIFF — REPORT ON EXPERIENCE.

Ed7 *The Poet Speaks.* Record 10, Side 1: Edmund Blunden —
     Andrew Young — Edwin Muir — Geoffrey Grigson — John
     Wain — Danny Abse. London, Argo Record Company, 1968.
     1 record, 11⅞ in. (PLP 1090). White sleeve printed in olive
     green, grey and mauve. FOREFATHERS — THE AUTHOR'S
     LAST WORDS TO HIS STUDENTS, read by Blunden. *See
     also* Ed4.

Ee   INTERVIEWS

Ee0 Interview with Prof. Blunden by Akira Ohtomo. *Mita Cam-*
.1   *pus,* January/February 1948, No. 9, p. 3.

Ee1 Igirisu bungaku no genjô. *Yûkan Kyôto,* Kyôto, 27 May
     1948, p. 1. In Japanese. A discussion with Kenji Ishida, and
     others on 'Present Situation of English Literature'; reported
     by Hara.

Ee2 Interviewing Professor Blunden, by I. Nishizaki. *Youth's
     Companion,* July 1949, No. 7, pp. 28-32. In English and
     Japanese.

Ee3 An Interview with Prof. Edmund C. Blunden: On Life and
     Reading, interviewer Prof. Ichiro Nishizaki. *Study of English,*
     November 1963, Vol. 52, No. 11, pp. 4-9. In English and
     Japanese.

Ee4 Omedeto to a Gentle Poet. *Illustrated London News,* 19
     February 1966, p. 23. On his election as Professor of Poetry
     of Oxford University.

Ee5   Moraes, Dom. A Dream of Violence Among the Spires: Edmund Blunden. *Nova*, London, May 1966, pp. 128-129, 131. On his election to the Chair of Poetry at Oxford University.

Ee6   Orr, Peter, general editor. *The Poet Speaks: Interviews with Contemporary Poets conducted by Hilary Morrish, Peter Orr, John Press, and Ian Scott-Kilvert*; preface by Frank Kermode. London, Routledge & Kegan Paul, May 1966. Pp. 33-37 Edmund Blunden, interviewed by John Press. *See also* Ed5.

Ef   COMMUNICATIONS TO THE PRESS SIGNED BY BLUNDEN

Apart from his own Letters to the Press (including one of joint authorship), listed in Section C, Blunden signed the following communications to the Press:

Ef1   Sir William Watson: Testimonial Fund Opened. *The Times*, 3 November 1930, p. 9. Quotation from an appeal signed Abercrombie, Henry Ainley, and others including Blunden. The appeal, in the form of a letter, also appeared in the *Nation & Athenaeum*, 15 November 1930, pp. 233-234.

Ef2   National Extravagance. *The Listener*, 23 September 1931, p. 508. Letter signed Norman Angell, Harrison Barrow, and others including Blunden. On the reduction of expenditure on armaments. *See also* letter by H. Teitelbaum in the issue of 21 October 1931, p. 698.

Ef3   The Book Society. *The Spectator*, 12 March 1932, p. 368. Letter signed Hugh Walpole, George Gordon, Edmund Blunden, Clemence Dane, Sylvia Lynd, members of the Selection Committee. On criticism of the Committee.

Ef4   A Challenge. *The Isis*, 25 May 1932, p. 4. Letter signed N. A. M. Lindsay, Eric Akers-Douglas, and others including Blunden. On cricket.

Ef5   Charles Lamb Appeal sponsored by the Elian Society for the "Lamb Centenary Memorial Fund" for the erection of a commemorative tablet in bronze in Christ Church, Newgate Street. [4] pp. Signed J. M. Barrie, E. V. Lucas, Edmund Blunden. The appeal also appeared in *The Times*, 14 June 1934, p. 11 under the heading 'A Charles Lamb Memorial: Elian Society's Fund'. *See also* Eb8.

Ef6   A Roman Villa. *The Times*, 20 March 1935, p. 15. Letter signed E. Blunden, R. L. H. Lloyd, and others. On the preservation of the villa near Sudeley Castle, Gloucestershire.

Ef7   A Memory of Shelley. *The Times*, 8 December 1938, p. 12. Letter signed Sylva Norman, R. Glynn Grylls, Edmund Blunden. On the preservation of Boscombe Manor, Bournemouth.

Ef8   The Keats-Shelley Memorial. *The Times*, 24 July 1946, p. 5.
Letter signed Margaret Crewe, Chairman, and others includ-
ing Blunden on behalf of the Keats-Shelley Memorial House,
Rome. *See also* later appeal (Ef10).

Ef9   The Impasse in Far East. *The Times*, 25 March 1953, p. 9.
Letter signed Edmund Blunden, A. E. Coppard, and others.

Ef10   Keats-Shelley Memorial. *The Times*, 6 November 1967, p. 9.
Letter signed Edmund Blunden, Evelyn Shuckburgh and
Abinger on behalf of the Keats-Shelley Memorial House,
Rome. *See also* appeal leaflet, and earlier appeal (B276;
Ef8).

Ef11   Bury St Edmunds Abbey. *The Times*, 10 August 1968, p. 9.
Letter signed Angus Wilson, J. Betjeman, Edmund Blunden,
and others. On the proposed demolition of the houses in the
Abbey grounds.

Eg   CONTRIBUTIONS TO PERIODICALS OF UNCERTAIN AUTHORSHIP

The items listed below are either probably or may be by Blunden.
Some are signed B., E.B., or E.C.B. The initials E.B. were used by
Eric [Walter] Blom and Edwyn [Robert] Bevan, both of whom
were contributing to similar journals in the 1930s. Contributions by
Blom, the music critic, are reasonably easy to identify. Bevan's
articles on early history and religion would have been identifiable
had it not been that EB also reviewed books of a like nature. The
author of entries signed E.C.B. has not been identified. It has, therefore, been thought unwise to include any of the following which
carry these initials in Section C:

The Compleat Chymiste. *The Blue*, March 1915, Vol. 42, No. 5, pp.
112–117. Unsigned.

THE ELF IN AUTUMN. *The Blue*, March 1915, Vol. 42, No. 5,
pp. 117–118. Unsigned.

An Afternoon of Romance. *The Blue*, April 1915, Vol. 42, No. 6,
pp. 131–133. On a walk through Sussex byways. Signed Biberius
Mero.

The Joy as it Flies. *Nation & Athenaeum*, 4 June 1921, p. 367. Review of *Some Birds of the Countryside: The Art of Nature*, by
H. J. Massingham. Unsigned.

The Women Poets. *Nation & Athenaeum*, 26 November 1921, pp.
352, 354. Review of *A Book of Women's Verse*, edited with a
prefatory essay by J. C. Squire. Unsigned.

Assorted Poetry. *Nation & Athenaeum*, 3 December 1921, pp. 404–
405. Review of *Poems: 1916–1920*, by John Middleton Murry;
Music: Lyrical and Narrative Poems, by John Freeman; and *The
Island of Youth, and Other Poems*, by Edward Shanks. Unsigned.

Old London. *Nation & Athenaeum*, 16 September 1922, p. 800. Review of *Trivia: or, The Art of Walking the Streets of London*, by John Gay, edited by W. H. Williams. Unsigned.

"Multitudes, Multitudes." *Nation & Athenaeum*, 1 December 1923, pp. 347-348. Review of *The Collected Poems of John Masefield; A King's Daughter: A Tragedy*, by John Masefield; *The Poems of John Drinkwater*; and *Sonnets and Verse*, by Hilaire Belloc. Unsigned.

Fives. *The Blue*, December 1924, Vol. 52, No. 2, pp. 77-78. On Christ's Hospital v. Lancing College and v. The Masters. Unsigned.

The Vase and the Parterre. *Nation & Athenaeum*, 26 November 1927, p. 328. Review of *A Poet's Calendar*, by W. H. Davies; and *England Reclaimed*, by Osbert Sitwell. Unsigned.

Tradition and Imagination. *Nation & Athenaeum*, 5 October 1929, p. 18. Review of *The Collected Poems of Gerald Gould; The Bird-Catcher*, by Martin Armstrong; *The Epic of the Mountains*, by G. H. Woolley; *God's Trombones*, by J. W. Johnson; and *Poems*, by Gerda Dalliba. Unsigned.

What to Read about Coleridge, Lamb, and Leigh Hunt. *The Blue*, December 1929, Vol. 57, No. 2, pp. 54-56. Letter signed Wm. Rufus.

[Review of] *Melody and the Lyrics: From Chaucer to the Cavaliers. Fortnightly Review*, 1 December 1930, New Series, Vol. 218, p. 855. Signed E.B.

St. Hilda's Dramatic Society—'The Lilies of the Field'. *The Isis*, 11 November 1931, No. 833, p. 5. Dramatic review. Signed E.C.B.

Piglets in Majorca. *The Isis*, 11 May 1932, No. 847, pp. 10-11. Signed E.C.B.

The Visit of the Dolmetsches. *The Isis*, 1 March 1933, No. 867, p. 13. Signed E.C.B.

E.C.W. *The Blue*, November 1934, Vol. 62, No. 1, pp. 9-10. On the retirement of E. C. Wright after 32 years as the cricket coach. Unsigned.

[Review of] *The Ideals of the East and West*, by Kenneth Saunders. *The Adelphi*, December 1934, New Series, Vol. 9, No. 3, pp. 190-191. Signed E.B.

[Review of] *A Dictionary of American Slang*, by Maurice H. Weseen. *The Fortnightly*, May 1935, New Series, Vol. 137, p. 632. Signed E.B.

[Review of] *Darius the Mede and the Four World Empires in the Book of Daniel: A Historical Study of Contemporary Theories*, by H. H. Rowley. *Oxford Magazine*, 30 May 1935, Vol. 53, No. 21, p. 684. Signed E.B.

[Review of] *Green Gates*, by R. C. Sherriff; *Miss Lindsey and Pa*, by Stella Gibbons; and *Waterloo in Wardour Street*, by Eric Siepman. *The Fortnightly*, June 1936, New Series, Vol. 139, p. 763. Signed E.B.

Children's Books. *The Fortnightly*, December 1936, New Series, Vol. 140, p. 763. Review of *Ballet Shoes*, by Noel Streatfeild; *A Pony for Jean*, by Joanna Cannan; *August Adventure*, by M. E.

Atkinson; *Two Boys Go Sailing*, by Conor O'Brien; *Henry Against the Gang*, by T. H. Johansen; *Pigeon Post*, by Arthur Ransome; *The Musical Box*, by Clare Leighton; and *The Modern Struwwelpeter*, by Jan Struther and Ernest Shepard. Signed E.B.

[Review of] *Roman Britain and the English Settlements*, by R. G. Collingwood and J. N. L. Myres. *Oxford Magazine*, 11 March 1937, Vol. 55, pp. 514-515. Signed E.B.

Fairies Under Glass. *Oxford Magazine*, 11 May 1939, Vol. 57, No. 19, pp. 593-594. On an exhibition of fairy literature in the Bodleian Library. Signed B.

[On Charles Lamb and air raids]. *The Blue*, June 1941, Vol. 68, No. 5, p. 135. Letter signed Tithonus; with P.S. on Thomas Barnes, the cricketer.

Encyclopaedia Britannica; contribution signed E.C.Bn. Blunden is listed as a contributor to the 1955 edition, and his name is no longer listed by 1962; no article by him has been found; the Deputy Editor for London writes that Blunden appears to have contributed part of the article 'English Literature' in Vol. 8, pp. 571-611, and it is thought that he may have assisted with the two sections, 'The Romantic Period', and 'Twentieth Century', possibly to the Poetry sub-section of the latter; both these sections are signed, S_{N_N}, *i.e.* Sylva Norman.

Oriental Literary Times, Tokyo—some of the following pseudonymous or unsigned contributions may be by Blunden:

Notes by the Way. 15 January 1925, Vol. 1, No. 1, pp. 1-5.

The War and the Peace. —— —— pp. 17-19. Review of *Ten Years After: A Reminder*, by Sir Philip Gibbs.

Speculation and Circulation. —— —— pp. 20-21. Review of *The Development of Japanese Journalism*, by Kanesada Hanazono.

Sard Harker. —— —— pp. 24-25. Review of *Sard Harker: A Novel*, by John Masefield.

Notes by the Way. 1 February 1925, Vol. 1, No. 2, pp. 1-5.

Australia's Epic. —— —— pp. 23-24. Review of *The Story of Anzac from 4 May 1915 to the Evacuation*, by C. E. W. Bean.

Criticism Without Tears. —— —— pp. 24-26. Review of *The Critic's Armoury*, by Cyril Falls.

The Pedlar's Pack. —— —— pp. 26-30. Signed Quince.

—— 15 February 1925, Vol. 1, No. 3, pp. 83-88. Signed Quince.

Notes by the Way. 1 March 1925, Vol. 1, No. 4, pp. 91-96.

Thoughts in Solitude. —— —— pp. 104-108. Signed Peter Bell.

The Near Distance. —— —— pp. 114-116. Review of *Ding Dong Bell*, by Walter de la Mare.

The Daedal Earth. 15 March 1925, Vol. 1, No. 5, pp. 148-149. Review of *Tidemarks*, by H. M. Tomlinson.

A Dimmed Radiance. —— —— pp. 150-155. Review of *Lafcadio Hearn's American Days*, by E. L. Tinker.

Three English Poets. —— —— pp. 157-159. Review of *Airs*, by
E. N. da C. Andrade; *Wayfaring*, by William Force Stead; and
Miss Bedell, by Claude Colleer Abbott.
The Pedlar's Pack. —— —— pp. 159-163. Signed Quince.
Thoughts in Solitude. 1 April 1925, Vol. 1, No. 6, pp. 188-189.
Signed Peter Bell.
The Pedlar's Pack. —— —— pp. 196-199. Signed Quince in Con-
tents.

Nation & Athenaeum—it is also thought that many of the contributions to the two weekly features 'From the Publishers' Table' and
'A Hundred Years Ago' which appeared in 1921, and 'Reviews
and Magazines' in 1923-1924 were by Blunden.

E*h*   SOME BOOKS AND PERIODICALS
CONTAINING REFERENCE TO EB AND HIS WORKS

S.P.E. Tract No V, 1921 ("The Dialectical Words in Blunden's
Poems" by Robert Bridges)
More Books on the Table by Edmund Gosse, 1923 ("Georgian
Poetry")
Essays on Poetry by J. C. Squire, [1923] ("Mr Edmund Blunden")
H.W.M. a Selection from the Writings of H. W. Massingham, ed. H. J.
Massingham, 1925 ("Edmund Blunden")
Edmund Blunden: His Professorship and his Writings, Tokyo, 1927
(B23 above)
New Paths on Helicon by Henry Newbolt [1927]
Poetry at Present by Charles Williams, 1930 ("Edmund Blunden")
Sunday Mornings by J. C. Squire, 1930 ("The War in Memory")
Out of Soundings by H. M. Tomlinson, 1931 ("A Footnote to the
War Books")
Second Impressions by T. Earle Welby, 1933 ("Mr Blunden)
Points Second Series 1866-1934 by Percy H. Muir, 1934
Japanese Lady in Europe by Haruko Ichikawa, 1937
Eight for Immortality by Richard Church, 1941 ("Edmund Blun-
den: Agonist")
Reflections in a Mirror: second series by Charles Morgan, 1946
("Edmund Blunden's 'Thomasina' ")
Poets and Pundits by Hugh l'Anson Fausset, 1947 ("Edmund
Blunden's Later Poetry")
Essays and Reflections by Harold Child, 1948 ("Leigh Hunt and
his Work")
Poems 1943-1947 by C. Day Lewis, 1948 ("Lines for Edmund
Blunden on his Fiftieth Birthday")
Talking of Books by Oliver Edwards, 1957 ("Gold Medal")
English, Autumn 1957 ("The Poetry of Edmund Blunden" by
Margaret Willy)
Edmund Blunden by Alec M. Hardie, 1958; revised edition, 1971

Edmund Blunden, Sixty-Five, 1961 (B234 above)
Collected Poems by Kenneth Hopkins, 1964 ("Edmund Blunden, a Teacher")
English Poetry of the First World War by John H. Johnston, 1964
Heroes' Twilight by Bernard Bergonzi, 1965
A Woman Unashamed and other Poems by Paul Engle, 1965 ("Edmund Blunden on his Sixty-Fifth Birthday")
Writing Between the Lines by Derek Hudson, 1965 (B 258 above)
The Poetry of Edmund Blunden by Michael Thorpe, 1971
Out of Battle: the Poetry of the Great War by Jon Silkin, 1972
Poets of the First World War by Jon Stallworthy, 1974
Edmund Blunden: A Tribute from Japan, Tokyo, 1974 (B291 above)
The Great War and Modern Memory by Paul Fussell, 1975
The Poet as Teacher by W. C. Chau, *White Wall Review*, Toronto, 1976
A Proper Gentleman by Vernon Scannell, 1977
The Warden's Meeting: A Tribute to John Sparrow, 1977 ("Blunden revisions to *Undertones of War*" by Michael L. Turner)

INDEXES

INDEX OF TITLES OF POEMS

563

ANCRE SUNSHINE (In all his glory the sun was high and glowing) B279

AND AWAY (I sent her in fancy,) A156

AND STILL, THE DEAN (For this most gracious welcome let my rhyme) A106

AND THEN (Inconstancy, too rarely) A64, 68, 135

ANDREW MARVELL'S *HORTUS* TRANSLATED *see* MARVELL'S "HORTUS"

ANNOTATION, AN (Emblem of innocence and earling finding, *later* Emblem of early seeking, early finding,) A25, 35, 135; C704

ANONYMOUS DONORS (A myriad gifts, and whence? To whom) A52, 68

ANOTHER ALTAR (I am Forgetfulness. I am that shadow) A45, 68, 135; C1223

ANOTHER JOURNEY FROM BÉTHUNE TO CUINCHY (I see you walking) A28, 35

ANOTHER SPRING *see* SHEPHERD'S CALENDAR

ANTHEM PRELIMINARY TO THE MASSACRE (Let Shaw write Shakespeare into note) B81

ANTI-BASILISK (But for a Basilisk who somewhere cowers) A64, 68

ANTIQUITIES (To walk through Kent apple-orchards sacred with bloom) A156; C3133

APPARITION (I saw an angel white high over me,) A2-3

APPARITIONS IN SUMMER [*later* SUMMER HIEROGLYPHS] (An enchantment was on that day from the calm first hours) A45, 68; C1202

APPEAL (Mankind! — so said the voice to me;) A97, 176

APPEARANCES OF THE SEASON (The gander peers over the home-field wall,) A156; C3170

APRIL (Green grasses down in the valleys,) A1, 3

APRIL BYEWAY (Friend whom I never saw, yet dearest friend,) A10, 35; B6, 9; C82

ARCADIAN LAW; A NOTICE IN CHELTENHAM (Be prudent, husbandmen, and walk in awe;) A52, 68

ARGUMENT IN SPRING (What you have heard from countless friends) A45, 68

ARMISTICE: A MARCH (Still in deep winter, the war country lies) A168

ARRIVAL AT A RIVER, IN JAPAN (Soon the chanting that first I took) A156; C3174

ART AND NATURE *see* DOES THE SAME CAUSE ALWAYS PRODUCE THE SAME EFFECT?

ART OF POETRY, THE [i] EPITAPH (Astronomer lies here. His lucky star) A52

— [ii] SATIRE (Still must I listen? Must the B.B.C.) A52

— [iii] SLOGAN (Ye men of England, hear the clarion. If) A52

— [iv] PASTORAL (Roadhouse to roadhouse swell the strain,) A52

— [v] EPIC (Dinner is served. Eternity begins.) A52

— [vi] ANOTHER (When Greek meets Greek, then comes the tug of war,) A52

ART STUDENT'S OTHER CAREER, THE (Be still a Painter, even when you become) A106

"ART THOU GONE IN HASTE?" (That I might watch the bells of wild bloom swing) A17, 20, 35; C493

AS BOSWELL RECORDS ('Not to drink wine,' said The Rambler,) A135; C3033

ASIDE, AN (Now while the serious sort declare) A40, 45, 68

ASK OLD JAPHET ("That's as that may be, that is; what the Lord will, He bestoweth—) A64, 68

ASSAULTING WAVES (The north wind vexes the water pit out of a sky of stone, *later* The north wind vexes the gravel pit, shrill from a sky of stone,) A135; C2693

ASTEROPÆA [i] (Asteropæa, at the springing day,) A7

— [ii] (Thus she, the poor, proud child of the dead priest,) A7

AT A CATHEDRAL SERVICE ("The almond will soon be flowering," said she) A77, 135; C2007

AT CHRIST CHURCH, GREYFRIARS *see* LINES TO CHARLES LAMB

AT HARIHAN (Time has his kindlier moods; in these) A171; B178; C2497

AT MAPLEDURHAM *see* AT MAPLEDURHAM IN WAR-TIME

AT MAPLEDURHAM IN WAR-TIME [*later* AT MAPLEDURHAM] (In these old country nooks, it is far from plain to see) A89; C2442

AT MY WRITING TABLE (Unquestioning I follow—follow whom?) A67-8

AT RUGMER (Among sequestered farms and where brown orchards) A52, 68

AT SENLIS ONCE (O how comely it was and how reviving) A17-18, 28, 35, 43*b*, 108, 135, 174; C828

AT THE DEPARTURE FROM KYUSHU (Voices of many cities, many streams,) A106

AT THE GREAT WALL OF CHINA (Perched in a tower of this ancestral Wall,) A135, 169, 176; C3168; Ed4

AT THE SHRINE OF APOLLO (And now before the new-built shrine) A97; B109

AT WARNHAM ("I was a boy here. Every fence and brake) A68

ATHEIST, 1817, THE *see* ATHEIST: LORD ELDON THINKS OVER SHELLEY V. WESTBROOKE, THE

ATHEIST: LORD ELDON THINKS OVER SHELLEY V. WESTBROOKE, THE [*later* THE ATHEIST, 1817] (Almighty wisdom from whose vouchesafed Law) A40, 45, 68

AUBADE (Come with your hat [etc.]) A2-3

— (Marie, forth from your bed: my lady, wake!) A2-3

AUGURY (What sweeter sight can ever charm the eye) A20, 35, 135; B8

AUTHOR OF "THE GREAT ILLUSION", THE (Some men, we say, are sent before their time;) A35; B37

AUTHOR'S LAST WORDS TO HIS STUDENTS, THE (Forgive what I, adventuring highest themes,) A26, 31, 35, 108, 135; B291; D6, 20; Ed4, 7

AUTOLYCUS, AN [*later* AUTOLYCUS AGAIN: IN MEMORY OF B.D.] [*i.e.* Bert Daines] (I had a visitor, one of a host) A156; C2496

AUTOLYCUS AGAIN: IN MEMORY OF B.D. *see* AUTOLYCUS, AN

AUTOLYCUS'S COUNTRY *see* ON SHAKESPEARE'S 'WINTER'S TALE'

AUTUMN AFTERNOON (We rowed upstream one autumn afternoon,) A1, 3

AUTUMN IN THE WEALD (Come, for here the lazy night) A31, 35, 135; C883

AUTUMN MOMENT, THE (As the breeze flies through orchard branches now) A106

AUTUMN SONG (The violins that sob) A2-3

AVENUE, THE (Up the long colonnade I press, and strive) A10, 35; C237

AWAKENING, THE (Come happy wind and blow away care) C293

BAKER'S VAN, THE (Village children shouted shrill,) A20, 35

BALLAD OF THE SERGEANTS OF OTHER DAYS *see* ECHO DE L'AUTRE GUERRE

BALLAD OF TITLES, A (Lord Randall started up in's bed,) A65; C1661

BALLAST-HOLE, THE (Can malice live in natural forms,) A40, 45, 68; C1146

BARN, THE (Rain-sunken roof, grown green and thin) A4, 6, 8, 35, 135, 176; B23; C929

BATTALION IN REST, JULY, 1917 (Some found an owl's nest in the hollow skull) A17, 28, 35, 135; C506

BEAUTY IN THE MOUNTAIN (Lovely, lovely, lovely child,) A67–8

BEFORE A RAINY DAYBREAK (The opalescent) A1, 3

BEHIND THE LINE (Treasure not so the forlorn days) A10, 35, B13

BELLS (What master singer, with what glory amazed,) A20, 35

BELOVED RIVER, THE (Beside the vision of an ancient weir) A97, 156

BLACKTHORN BUSH IN SPRING, THE (This blackthorn bush in sunny whiteness) A89

BLEUE MAISON (Now to attune my dull soul, if I can,) A35, 135

BLIND LEAD THE BLIND, THE (Dim stars like snowflakes are fluttering in heaven,) A31, 35, 135

BLINDFOLD (From the mirror-hall of sleep) A14, 18; C53

BLUE BUTTERFLY see BLUE BUTTERFLY, THE

BLUE BUTTERFLY, THE [later BLUE BUTTERFLY] (Here Lucy paused for the blue butterfly—) A14, 20, 35, 174; C332

BLUEPRINT, THE (Will you then build us a house that will vie with the houses we know,) A89, 135; C2036

BOOKS (Man, the inventive, with his ceaseless power) A171; B178; C2523

BOURNE, THE (He made me go through still majestic halls,) A1, 3

BOY ON LEAVE, THE (So you have chosen, saying little, knowing) A77; C1926

BOY ON THE WAGON, THE (With what delight the south's large rain) A89, 135

BRANCH LINE, THE (Professing loud energy, out of the junction departed) A52, 68, 108, 135, 174; C1292; Ed6

BREAM FISHING (Along the Medway towpath, when the west) A1, 3

BRIDGE, A (Beyond the church there stands a bridge) A17, 20, 35, 174; C492

BRING YOUR MUSIC (Musical both in soul and skill, you own) B211; C3215

BRITISH MUSEUM BLUES (I WAIT FOR A BOOK) (Smells like sluggish smelly stoves,) C1735

BROCELIANDE (The demon wildwoods of Broceliande!) C41

BROOK, THE (Up, my jewel! let's away) A14, 20, 35, 174; C309

BROOK IN DROUGHT (The willow catkins fall on the muddy pool) A14, 20, 35

BUDDING MORROW, A (When I woke, the sapphire sky) A17, 20, 35; C471.1

BUILDING THE LIBRARY, NIGHT SCENE, TOKYO UNIVERSITY [later BUILDING THE LIBRARY, TOKYO UNIVERSITY] (Like men of fire, in painful night,) A26, 31, 35; B291; C604

BUILDING THE LIBRARY, TOKYO UNIVERSITY see BUILDING THE LIBRARY, NIGHT SCENE, TOKYO UNIVERSITY

BURIAL IN SPRING FROM THE FRENCH OF BRIZEUX (Fifteen years Louise had seen: a forest flower was young Louise,) C494

BUSY FLY, THE (A thin strange fly, silent to human hearing,) A156, C3244

BUT AT LAST (These images of quiet, these I should not call) A156

BUTTERFLY DANCE (Among the rest, four butterflies,) A89, 135

BUXTED (In Buxted-park the summer's rule) A89

BY CHANCTONBURY (We shuddered on the blotched and wrinkled down,) A7

BY ROAD [later BYROAD] (Who knows not that sweet gloom in spring,) A20, 35, 43b, 135; B23; C515

BY THE BELGIAN FRONTIER [*later* DIKKEBUSCH; *and* BY THE BEL-
GIAN FRONTIER] (Where youth in fires) A68; B91, C1787
BYROAD *see* BY ROAD
BYRONIANA *see* KIRKE WHITE AT WILFORD; *and* NEWSTEAD ABBEY

C.E.B. [*later* THE OLD SCHOOLMASTER; *and* C.E.B.; *i.e.* Charles Edmund
Blunden] (Are all your eighty years defined at last) A135; B168; C3088
CABARET TUNE (I can't go back to Then.) A64, 68
CALM RAIN, A ("Come, shy and almost-silent rain;) A45, 68, 135; C1203
CAMP IN THE WOOD, THE (Desperate wood, your skinny trees) A68
'CAN YOU REMEMBER—?' (Yes, I still remember) A64, 68, 108, 135; B289;
C1501
CANAL, THE (Where so dark and still *later* There, so dark and still) A10, 35;
B7; C195
CAPTAINCY (Osaka, of old majesty and new,) A171
CARFAX (Here's the great skill of the race—and whither bound?) A52, 68
CATHEDRALS (These have marched with towering Fame) A156, 169; B201
CATHERINE SINGS (The baby-girl was crowing—) A156
CHAFFINCH *see* CHAFFINCH ON SUBURBAN GROWTHS
CHAFFINCH ON SUBURBAN GROWTHS [*later* CHAFFINCH] ("Gone
down, sir, and whatever bird you speak to) A64, 68
CHANCE, THE *see* FRAGMENTS
CHANCE PLEASURES (Smiles from strangers met but once,) A68; C1736
CHANCES OF REMEMBRANCE ("Turn not from me;) A35, 135; C942
CHANGE, A (How lovely it was, when all that came my way) A68
CHANGE AND SONG (No, do not tell me; have I not conceded) A97, 135
CHANGING MOON (The green East hagged with prowling storm,) A8, 35;
C43
CHAPTERS OF LITERARY HISTORY: VERY LITTLE KNOWN (Led by
great WALPOLE, at th' accustomed Task) A52; C1327
CHARM, THE (The voice of innocence I heard) A25, 35; C703
CHAUCER'S CANTERBURY TALES ("An Idler too ther was, as I you tell,)
C1424
CHILD IN CHURCH, THE (How cold those tops of the sharp arches are!)
A156; C2500
CHILD'S GRAVE, THE (I came to the churchyard where pretty Joy lies)
A10, 35, 43*b*, 135, 174; B9; C2427; E*d*6
CHILDREN PASSING (How many deaths, extinctions what a host) A89;
C2443
CHIMES AT MIDNIGHT (Saints from the old world sounding on) A135, 176
CHIMNEY-SMOKE (You see it there, there in those trees,) A97
CHINESE PAPER-KNIFE *see* CHINESE PAPERKNIFE, A
CHINESE PAPERKNIFE, A [*later* CHINESE PAPER-KNIFE] (For the first
time ever, and only now,—) A156, 174; C3243
CHINESE PICTURE (Ascend this path, whose stairway windings gleam) A25,
35; C668
CHINESE POND (Chinese pond is quick with leeches:) A8; C44
CHRISTMAS EVE 1913 (The winter day wanes damp, and cold, and dim) A1,
3
CHRISTMAS EVE 1959 (The time comes round when all the faiths and fears)
A156; B291
CHRISTMAS INVITATION FOR 1756 [*later* sub-title added: PRE-TELE-
PHONE] (Rosanthe, while some doleful Bards commend) A156; C3182

[*later* ART AND NATURE] (Our landlord intending more custom to win) A43a; C857

DOG FROM MALTA, THE (He came from Malta, and Eumelus says) A45, 68

DOG ON WHEELS (This dog—not a real dog, you know,—) A156

DOOMED OAK FROM THE FRENCH OF ANATOLE FRANCE, THE [*later* sub-title added: AN IMITATION OF ANATOLE FRANCE] (In the warm wood bedipped with rosy day) A16, 25, 35; C513

DOVEDALE ON A SPRING DAY (Approach we then this classic ground:) A77

DR JOHNSON REVISITS A MILL STREAM AT LICHFIELD (It winds on still, the glassy brook) B247; C2745

DREAM, A [*later* THE FOND DREAM] (Here's the dream I love,) A135; C2473; D11

DREAM, A (Unriddle this. Last night my dream) A17, 20, 35

DREAM CITY (Moveth atween the spires and roofs) A1, 3

DREAM ENCOUNTERS (The measureless houses of my dreams,) A31, 35, 135; C849

DREAMER, THE (When most were flocking into town) A67-8; C1685

DRIED MILL POND, THE (Old Broadbridge Pond, once on a time so deep,) A10, 35; B6

DYING OF MICHAEL MAYE, THE (The clock-room door swung to: the sexton turned) A7

E.W.T., ON THE DEATH OF HIS BETTY [*i.e.* E. W. Tice] (And she is gone, whom, dream or truth,) A17, 28, 35, 135

EARLY AND LATE (How fondly still the Grecian form) A25, 35

EARLY IDEAS REAWAKENED *see* EARLY IDEAS REMEMBERED

EARLY IDEAS REMEMBERED [*later* EARLY IDEAS REAWAKENED] (What ghosts are these? What hope could bring) A135; C3043

EARLY YEAR, FUKUOKA, THE *see* FROM THE JAPANESE INN WINDOW

"EARTH HATH BUBBLES, THE" (Come they no more, those of ecstasies of earth,) A10, 35; C296

EASTERN TEMPEST [*later* TEMPEST; *and* EASTERN TEMPEST] (This flying angel's torrent cry) A26, 31, 35; B23; C620

ECCENTRIC, THE (His sleeping or his waking mind) A25, 35

ECHO DE L'AUTRE GUERRE [*later* BALLAD OF THE SERGEANTS OF OTHER DAYS] (Tell me now in what hidden way is) A156; C3164

ECHOES FROM 1914-18 [*later* TO A NATURE-LOVER] (Your cry is 'Back to Nature'; we) A68; C1835

ECLOGUE, THE (So talk ran on, and turning like a lane) A14, 20, 35; B10; C314

ECOLIER: THE SCHOLAR (Little boy, on your road to the School,) C3209

ECSTASY (One starry night, alone beside the sea,) A2-3

EIGHT JAPANESE POEMS (The labourer hoes on. — The tide goes out; — On the temple's great bell — Now the snows have gone — There's the first cart-load of the year, — The camellia-flower dropped, — I see — I have sold my cow.) C3105

ELEGY (The Chinese tombs,) A20, 35, 174; C478

ELEGY [*later* AN ELEGY; *and* ELEGY ON HIS MAJESTY KING GEORGE V] (To face the fortune of a scowling time,) A64, 68, 135; C1505

ELEGY, AN *see* ELEGY

ELEGY ON HIS MAJESTY KING GEORGE V *see* ELEGY

11TH R.S.R. (How bright a dove's wing shows against the sky) A10, 35, 135, 176

570

FAIRY GIFTS (In dreams I found silver and gathered it fast *later* In a dream [etc.]) A97; C2482

FAMILIARITY (Dance not your spectral dance at me;) A31, 35, 135; Ed4

FAMILY DISCOURSE, A (Let's go hunting whatever's in the picture.) A156

FANCY AND MEMORY (Adieu, young Fancy with the gipsy eye,) A45, 68, 135; C1174

FAR EAST (Old hamlets with your groves of flowers) A19, 26, 31, 35, 174; C555

FARM BAILIFF (Enter the man, right farmer's countenance: part) A89, 135, 174, 176; C2185; Ed6

FARM BEHIND BATTLE ZONE (Gentle, dark day, and country tracks) A68

FARM NEAR ZILLEBEKE, A (Black clouds hide the moon, the amazement is gone;) A10, 35, 135, 169, 176

FARMHOUSE FAMILY, THE (I ran along, I sang alone;) A135; C3107

FATE OF SERVILIUS, THE (As with the lyre, even so it is with life;) A23

FATHER WILLIAM AGAIN ("You are old, Father William," the youngster observed,) B70

FAVOURITE SCENE [etc.], A (Hauntest thou so my waking and my sleeping,) A25, 35

FESTUBERT, 1916 [*later* 1916 SEEN FROM 1921] (Tired with dull grief, grown old before my day,) A10, 35, 135, 174; B5-6; Ed6

FESTUBERT SHRINE, THE (A sycamore on either side) A35, 135

FESTUBERT: THE OLD GERMAN LINE (Sparse mists of moonlight hurt our eyes) A35, 135

FINE NATURE, THE (This fine nature clear) A77; B94; C1842

"FIRST IMPRESSION, A" *see* "FIRST IMPRESSION" TOKYO, A

"FIRST IMPRESSION" TOKYO, A [*later* "A FIRST IMPRESSION"] (No sooner was I come to this strange roof,) A18, 20, 26, 35, 135; B15; C481

FIRST RHYMES (In the meadow by the mill) A14, 20, 35, 174; C446

FIRST SNOW (By the red chimney-pots the pigeons cower,) A10, 35; C234

FIRST VISIT TO YASHIMA, A [*later* YASHIMA IN WINTER; *and* A FIRST VISIT TO YASHIMA] (Like a long roof, they say, and well they say, *later* Like a long roof, men say, [etc.]) A97, 122; B189; C2501

"FIRST WINTER, THE" (When first dark winter, wrapt in scudding clouds) C1

FLANDERS NOW *see* OLD BATTLEFIELDS

FLASHING FLINT, THE *see* FLASHING FLINT: FROM THE LATIN OF HENRY VAUGHAN, THE

FLASHING FLINT: FROM THE LATIN OF HENRY VAUGHAN, THE [*later* THE FLASHING FLINT] (O I confess, without a wound) A23; C500

FLIGHT OVER CHINA (This aircraft crossing China over China's chief domain) C3314

FLORILEGIUM, THE ("From Helicon's unfading hill) A77

FLOWER-GATHERERS, THE (Where a brook with lisping tongue) A20, 35; C522

FLOWERS, THE (They fade then; other flowers have faded,) A77, 135

FLOWERS OF THE ROCK *see* FLOWERS OF THE ROCK, THE

FLOWERS OF THE ROCK, THE [*later* FLOWERS OF THE ROCK] (Upon that cliff, that rock upright) A143, 156, 171; C2511; D12

FLOWERS WALKING (These have been much and well described) A89

FOND DREAM, THE *see* DREAM, A

FOR A MUSICIAN'S MONUMENT: G.F. [*i.e.* Gerald Finzi] (Twine buds and leaves with some full blooms, to dress) A156

FOR A SPRING DANCE BY TAMAMI GOJO [*later* VOICE OF SPRING] (Every feather of snow that floated,) A156; B171; C3121

FOR A WATER-COLOUR BY Y. NOGUCHI (Blue and cool and sacred rise) A171

FOR TAKESHI AND FUMIKO (We travelled far along the track) A171

FOR THE CENTENARY OF MELBOURNE UNIVERSITY (To all the honours that a hundred years) B191; C3181

FOR THE CENTENARY OF RABINDRANATH TAGORE (Out of the past what graciousness still grows,) A156; C3266

FOR THE COUNTRY LIFE see MEANS, THE

FOR THE EDUCATION INSTITUTE OF AICHI PREFECTURE (The iron drought, the soulless days) A171; B283.1

FOR THE ENGLISH GROUP IN ASAHIGAWA (To Shakespeare's spirit let us all, like one,) A171

"FOR THE FALLEN" (Some of us were unlucky;) A89

"FOR THERE IS NO HELP IN THEM" see 1919

FOR TOKYO JOSHI DAIGAKU: A HYMN see COLLEGE SONG

FOR YOSHITAKA SAKI (Though time our troubler is,) A171

FOR YUKUCHI NAKAMURA (You quoted Shelley and I dream,) A171

FOREFATHERS (Here they went with smock and crook,) A10, 18, 35, 108, 135, 174; B4, 23; C48; D13; Ed4, 6-7

FOREST, THE (Among the golden groves when June walketh there) A10, 35; C271

FORSAKEN MEMORIALS see NOUVELLES LITTÉRAIRES

FRAGMENT (Steal abroad, your time is come; doubt not once the new-blown hour.) A31, 35; C898

FRAGMENTS [later THE CHANCE] (Mind and soul a halting brook) A25, 35; C520

FRANK WORLEY, D.C.M. (There was no death but you would face it) A135

FREDDY FLAIL PROVES HIS POINT ("They're funny things, wild animals," said Flail,) A68

FREEDOM OF POPERINGE (Shall we not also join the friends) A167; C3347

FRESH THOUGHTS ON AN OLD POEM (With old Abou ben Adleem dwells the light,) A64, 68

FROM A STUDY TABLE [later FROM A STUDY WINDOW] (Wave at my window, my green friends,) C2475; D11

FROM A STUDY WINDOW see FROM A STUDY TABLE

FROM A TOKYO LAWN see TOKYO LAWN

FROM AGE TO AGE see ONLY ANSWER, THE

FROM OUR CORNER IN HONG KONG (Before day broke, the golden oriole) A168

FROM THE BRANCH LINE (Brightest of red roofs, glittering) A64, 68

FROM THE COTTAGE GARDEN (When the vine of the East is afruit with the day,) A1, 3

FROM THE FLYING-BOAT (Into the blue undisturbable main) A89, 135; B224; Ed3

FROM THE HILL-TOP (Early arises the merry May-morning, poising a melody on her lips,) A1, 3

FROM THE JAPANESE INN WINDOW [later THE INN WINDOW, FUKU-OKA; and THE EARLY YEAR, FUKUOKA] (Fierce came the snow—and is gone like a dream) A94, 97, 106; B178; C2513

FROM VERLAINE: LE CIEL EST, PAR-DESSUS LE TOIT (How blue the sky, how deep its calm) C502

FULFILMENT (Fulfilment is a puzzling goddess,) A77, 135

FULL BLOOM (This time of year the sparrow takes) A52, 68

FUR COAT (The heifer eyed us both and chose) A52, 68

GATE TO POETRY (Herein, we travel far) A171

GAVOTTE (The very blossoms danced to see) C25

GEOGRAPHER'S GLORY: OR, THE GLOBE IN 1730, THE *see* GEOGRA-
PHER'S GLORY: OR THE WORLD IN 1730, THE

GEOGRAPHER'S GLORY: OR, THE WORLD IN 1730, THE [*later* THE
GEOGRAPHER'S GLORY, OR, THE GLOBE IN 1730] (When through
the windows buzzed the thoughtless bee *later* [...] the way-lost bee) A31,
35; C873

GIANT PUFFBALL, THE (From what star I know not, but I found *later*
From what proud star I know not, [etc.] A10, 35; B9, C233

GIBBON: IN THE MARGIN *see* MAN GROWN SAFE

GIFT: FOR C.M.P., THE [*i.e.* Claire M. Poynting] (Were it my fortune, I
would bring you) A77

GIRL WITH SHAWL (Her arms were like the Nymphs,) A25; C700

GIRL'S INVOCATION, A (My Queen, Queen of Paphos; Venus; O hear.) A97

GLEANING (Along the baulk the grasses drenched in dews) A10, 18, 35, 135;
C51

GLIMPSE, A (White walls with their black outlines,) A171

GLIMPSE, THE (I'm not rejected then, my mind's delight) A14

GOD'S TIME (A gentler heaven steals over the hour,) A77, 135; B289; C1999

GODS OF THE EARTH BENEATH, THE (I am the god of things that burrow
and creep,) A5-6, 8, 35

GODS OF THE WORLD BENEATH, THE *see* GODS OF THE EARTH BE-
NEATH, THE

GODSTOW (Sparkling with west winds dancing along the tansies) A68; B91

GOING TO A LECTURE (The elm-tree, the willow there,) A171

GONE (What happened to The Gun? a fine gun it seemed,) A168

GOUZEAUCOURT: THE DECEITFUL CALM (How unpurposed, how inconsequential) A28, 35

GRACE, THE (It has been known how even in war) C3152

GREEK DEITY: INSCRIBED TO THE APOLLO SOCIETY, A (That we may
yet transcend the dark will of the storm) A89

GREETINGS: FROM THE LATIN OF JOHN SKELTON (Greetings to you,
even ten times more ...) C3158

[GREETINGS FOR NEVILLE ROGERS, 1954] (My Christmas Card O,)
B292

GROWN UP (I grudge a year, or hardly that,) A52, 68

GUARD'S MISTAKE, THE *see* SENTRY'S MISTAKE, THE

H-BOMB ("If they roosh on like this they'll ruin all,") A135; C3135

HALF A CENTURY (Sweet this morning incense, kind) A89, 135, 169, 176

HALTED BATTALION, THE *see* HALTED BATTALION: 1916

HALTED BATTALION: 1916, THE [*later* THE HALTED BATTALION]
(One hour from far away! each man we had *later* One hour from far
returns: Each man we had) A89, 135; C2285

HAMMOND (ENGLAND): A CRICKETER *see* HAMMOND OF ENGLAND

HAMMOND OF ENGLAND [*later* HAMMOND (ENGLAND): A CRICKE-
TER] (When of all games the wisest, loveliest game *later* Since our most
beautiful and subtle game) A89, 108, 135, 169; C2316

HAPPIEST, THE (How surpassingly happy the musician) A77

HAPPY MORN, THE *see* "HAPPY MORN, THE"

"HAPPY MORN, THE" [*later* THE HAPPY MORN] (Then: then the days
were dark,) A130, 156

HARBOUR SKETCH: WRITTEN IN ABSENCE (Nine fluffy sparrows in a
shrub) A89

IN A PARK AT KYOTO (Beneath the leaves I lie, and read, and glance) A97; B178; C2564

IN AN ALBUM, 1958 (The eye of eternity) C3210

IN BERKSHIRE (The frosty sunny morning makes) A64, 68; B76

IN CHILDHOOD (I'll take a journey out of our old house.) A68; C1828

IN DISAPPOINTMENT [*later* DESIRE AND DELIGHT] (Desire, the lovelier prophet of delight,) A45, 68, 135; C1207

IN FESTUBERT (Now everything that shadowy thought) A8, 35, 135

IN HELPSTON CHURCHYARD [*later* TO JOHN CLARE] (Rest there, dear dust, beneath the lichened stone,) A14; B13

IN HOKKAIDO: A LETTER IN VERSE, AND IN THE ROMANTIC MANNER (Lover of solitude and those wild tracks) A156; C2981

IN HONOR OF ROYAL COUPLE [*later* IN HONOR OF CROWN PRINCE AKIHITO AND MISS MICHIKO SHODA; *and* IN HONOUR OF ROYAL COUPLE] (To Akihito, Michiko–) A171; C3224

IN MAY 1916: NEAR RICHEBOURG ST. VAAST (The green brook played, talked unafraid) A68

IN MEMORIAM A.R.-I. YOKOHAMA, NOVEMBER 1938 [*i.e.* Arthur Rose-Innes] (Delay not; for the years advance) A68; C1748

IN MEMORY OF ROBERT NICHOLS (Truth is not less painful because " 'tis true," *later* Truth is not less aloof [etc.]; *and* Truth may not be less sharp [etc.]) A135; C2510; D12

IN MY TIME (Touched with a certain silver light) A64, 68; C1503

IN NAGASAKI HARBOUR (Among the hulls of shipping blue and red,) A106

IN REMEMBRANCE OF A SISTER (Dear other-times, and yet not far,) C3300

IN SUMMER [*later* THE ROTUNDA] (Out of the sparkling flood of green) A42, 45, 68; B57

IN THE FENS (We'll row up the fens as we've many a day done,) A14

IN THE HANDICRAFT ESTABLISHMENT (You'd call him a Professor in his way,) C3315

IN THE MARGIN (While few men praise and hardly more defend) A67-8, 135; B84, 291; C1677

IN WEST FLANDERS (Is it the light that makes the silence) A67-8, 135

IN WILTSHIRE SUGGESTED BY POINTS OF SIMILARITY WITH THE SOMME COUNTRY (Fairest of valleys, in this full-bloomed night,) A35; C895

IN ZUIGANJI TEMPLE (Here abide Tranquillity,) A171

INACCESSIBLE HOUSE, THE (No one will ever be living in that tall house,) A64, 68

INACCESSIBILITY IN THE BATTLEFIELD (Forgotten streams, yet wishful to be known,) A31, 35; C893

INCIDENT IN HYDE PARK, 1803 (The impulses of April, the rain-gems, the rose-cloud,) A40, 45, 68, 108, 135; C1101

INFANTRYMAN, AN (Painfully writhed the few last weeds upon those flatted uplands; *later* [. . .] houseless uplands,) A25, 35, 135, 174; C701

INHERITANCE (Ah what magic was that, and what the mystery,) A14, 20, 35

INLAND SEA *see* JAPANESE NIGHTPIECE

INN WINDOW, FUKUOKA, THE *see* FROM THE JAPANESE INN WINDOW

INSCRIBED IN WAR-BOOKS I (More rarely now the echo of these men) A45

— II *see* INSCRIPTION, AN

576

INSCRIPTION, AN [*later* INSCRIBED IN WAR-BOOKS II] (These marched towards Death, or what seemed he,) A45, 68; C1159

INTER ARMA (Being asked to conceive that the fortune of war now raging) A89

INTERNATIONAL FOOTBALL MATCH, AN (Some time the English name in sport was good,) A64, 68

INTERVAL (When cloudy evening shows) A17, 20, 35; C476

INTIMATIONS OF MORTALITY (I am only the phrase) A17, 20, 35, 135; C471

INTO THE DISTANCE (Silent they stand and into silence hoard) A52, 68

INTO THE SALIENT (Sallows like heads in Polynesia,) A35

INVIOLATE, THE (There on the white Pacific shore the pines) A26, 31, 35, 135

INVITATION [*later* POETRY'S INVITATION] (In happy hours, some hours, I spring;) A64, 68, 135; C1565

INVOCATION WRITTEN IN SPRING 1944 (Come, angel most beloved, come, most rejected;) A89, 135; C2438

ISLAND TRAGEDY, AN (Among the twinkling tree-tops on our hill—) A156

IVY BUSH, THE [*later* THE IVY BUSH IN AUTUMN] (See to this ivy bush what hundreds hurry,) A89; C2155

IVY BUSH IN AUTUMN, THE *see* IVY BUSH, THE

JAMES CLARENCE MANGAN (So after flights of years, the genius reappears;) A156; C3190

JANUARY EVENING SUSSEX, 1914 (The three days' frost wained, and was well-nigh spent;) A1, 3; C9

JANUARY FULL MOON, YPRES (Vantaged snow on the gray pilasters) A35

JAPAN BEAUTIFUL (What most we love we do not well express,) A156; B291; C3251, D38

JAPAN REVIVED ('O ship, the winds once more will bear you) A156

JAPANESE EVENING, A (Round us the pines and darkness) A35, 174

JAPANESE GLIMPSES [*later* THREEFOLD SCREEN] (Merrily under the trees they ran) A156; C2698

JAPANESE INN [*later* THE TEA-HOUSE] (When on the mountain side we saw the tea-house) A156, 169, 176; C3177

JAPANESE NIGHTPIECE [*later* INLAND SEA] (Here in the moonlit sea,) A26, 31, 35; C635

JIM'S MISTAKE (Leaning against the barrow which displayed) A67–8

JOURNEY (Along the relic of an ancient ride,) A10, 35; C291

JOY AND GRIEF (There is a joy in Spring,) A1, 3; C2

JOY AND MARGARET (My darling, what a power is yours) A89, 135

JUNE 1959, TO THE ENGLISH DEPARTMENT OF HIROSHIMA UNIVERSITY (And still, as Chaucer said, from the old fields come) A171

KEATS HOUSE, ROME (Here must the glory and the grief) B276

KESTREL FARM, 1796 (In the long loud lash of the rain and the wind,) A1, 3; C8

KILN, THE (Beside the creek where seldom oar or sail) A31, 35; C844

KIND STAR, THE (You must be as others are;) A67–8

KINGFISHER (The eastern God with natural blessing gleams) A35, 135; C887

KING'S ARMS HOTEL, KOBE JAPAN, THE [*later* THE KING'S ARMS, KOBE] (Elizabethan England, rise) A171; B140

KING'S ARMS, KOBE, THE *see* KING'S ARMS HOTEL, KOBE JAPAN, THE

KIRKE WHITE AT WILFORD [BYRONIANA, I] (Here came the mild boy loving loneliness) A89, 135; C2100

KISS, THE (I am for the woods against the world,) A40, 45, 68, 108, 135; C1100

"KNOW'ST THOU THE LAND . . . ?" (How that territory called them) A97

L.A. [*later* LASCELLES ABERCROMBIE] (It was not mine to know your younger strength,) A77, 108, 135; C1947

L.C. [*i.e.* Lily Chan] (Everything she does is delicate, —) A168

LA GIROUETTE (Sous la lune le plomb de la tourelle) A37

LA QUINQUE RUE (O road in dizzy moonlight bleak and blue,) A28, 35, 135

LANDSCAPE (In the vast senselessness) C533

LANE, THE (The weltering air, as warm as tears,) A7

LARK DESCENDING (A singing firework; the sun's darling;) A52, 68, 135

LASCELLES ABERCROMBIE *see* L.A.

LAST OF AUTUMN, THE (From cloudy shapes of trees that cluster the hills) A10, 35, 135

LAST RAY, THE (Now the world grows weak again, the sinewed woods are all astrain,) A20, 35, 135

LAST WORD, THE *see* MEMORIAL, THE

LATE AUTUMN (When Autumn with his shroud of leaves doth pay) A1, 3; C16

LATE LIGHT (Come to me where the swelling wind assails the wood with a sea-like roar) A64, 68, 135; B234

LATE STAND-TO, THE (I thought of cottages nigh brooks) A10, 35, 174; C303

LATER FLOWERS (Forgetful among his fancies, which once came to their best,) A156

LAWN: A FRAGMENT OF FAMILY HISTORY AT A HOUSE IN TOKYO, THE (The day was done: I mused alone,) A97

LECTURING (When I see hundreds of young faces turned) A106

LEISURE (Listen, and lose not the sweet luring cry,) A8, 35, 135; B2

LES HALLES D'YPRES (A tangle of iron rods and spluttered beams,) A35, 135

LET JOE DO IT (In the sharpness of need, the mind) A67-8

LIBERTINE (In summer-time when haymaking's there) A25, 35, 135

LIBERTY (What is lovelier than to be) A97

LIFE, BE KIND (Life, be kind to all these hastening) B273

LIFE'S UNITY, A (That sudden all-surviving voice) A156; B144; C2648

LINES TO CHARLES LAMB [*later* AT CHRIST CHURCH, GREYFRIARS] (Among all houses in haunted London) A63-4, 68, 135; B72

LISTEN (I too will listen, gladly will,) C3308

LITTLE SONG, THE (What others overtake in wit's advance) A156

LONDON: A DECEMBER MEMORY (With magic haste our spirits range) A68

LONELY LOVE (I love to see those loving and beloved) A64, 68, 135

LONG MOMENTS (A shadow lay along my wall) A52, 68, 135

LONG TRUCE, THE (Rooks in black constellations slowly wheeling) A14, 20, 35

LOOKING EASTWARD *see* SONG, A

LORET'S ODE (O All ye Courtiers and ye Cits) B12

LOST BATTALION, THE ("To dream again." That chance. There were no fences,) A52, 68

LOST NAME, THE (No ship perhaps again will ever bear) A77
LOVELIGHT (Such light calm moonrise never gave,) A77
LYRICAL BALLAD (It was the Spring, the pleasant Spring,) C1753

MAHATMA GANDHI (What garland for him now, Imagination,) C2490
MALEFACTORS (Nailed to those green laths long ago,) A8, 35, 135
MAN GROWN SAFE: ON RE-READING A FAVOURITE PASSAGE IN ED-
    WARD GIBBON [later GIBBON: IN THE MARGIN] (What would I give
    to have been) A77, 135; C1998
MAN IN THE STREET, THE (Journeying through the shade of sleep,) A77
MARCH, A (Come, let us weep once more for all the dead,) A156
MARCH BEE, THE (A warning wind comes to my resting-place) A10, 35; B7;
    C275
MARCH OF MIND, THE (In ancient days, just before all that want of har-
    mony) A52, 68, 135; C1243
MARCHING BACK TO PEACE 1916 (How came such minutes, such inimit-
    ables) A64, 68
MARKET TOWN (This drowsy day, were I only near,) A64, 68
MARRING, THE (When in the summer midnight some fierce cloud) A1, 3
MARVELL'S "HORTUS" [later ANDREW MARVELL'S HORTUS TRANS-
    LATED] (What power so sways the hearts of human-kind) A168; C3144
MASKS OF TIME (Then the Lark, his singing on a sudden done,) A17, 20, 35,
    135
MASQUERADE, THE (Here winds) A20, 35
MATCH, THE see PRISON, THE
MATSUSHIMA (Melodious is that name Matsushima;) A86, 97; B178, 189,
    291; C2563; D8
MAY DAY GARLAND, THE (Though folks no more go Maying) A10, 35,
    174; C262
MEADOW STREAM, THE (Young joy to me is as the miser's gold,) A35;
    C1030
MEADOWS FOR EVER, THE (It should not be changed. Are there not some
    things) B257
MEANS, THE [later FOR THE COUNTRY LIFE] (No sunbeam clearer) A77,
    174; B90; Ed6
MELANCHOLIA (Much has been writ of wraiths and ghostly things,) A1, 3
MEMORIAL, THE [later THE LAST WORD] (As in an elegy black Vesper
    holds) A40, 45, 68; C1139
MEMORIAL, 1914-1918, THE (Against this lantern, shrill, alone,) A45, 68,
    135; B53
MEMORY OF KENT, THE (Kentish hamlets gray and old,) A7
MENTAL HOSPITAL see TWO IN A CORNER; and POOR TOM'S WEL-
    COME
MESSAGE, THE [later PRELUSION; and THE MESSAGE] (Then in petals
    of the air,) A20, 35; C561
MICHIO MASUI ("When high romance" deserts the paths of men) A171
MIDNIGHT (The last-lighted windows have darkened,) A17, 20, 35; B23
MIDNIGHT SKATERS, THE (The hop-poles stand in cones,) A17-18, 20, 35,
    108, 135, 174, 176; B234; Ed4, 6
"MIGHTY FALLEN, THE" (Was this in truth that mighty lord's demesne?)
    B1
MILLSTREAM MEMORIES (Shattering remembrance, mercy! Not again)
    A156

NEARING YOKOHAMA, 15 AUGUST 1960 (Over these evening waters, snowy-crested,) A156; B291

NEVER AGAIN (Never again shall we go to the woods, for the laurels are felled.) A2–3

NEW CITY HALL (1962), A (Some still remember—though not many now) C3270.2

NEW MOON, THE (New-silver-crescented the moon forth came) A35

NEW SONG, A (So from slow silence, strange one, sing:) A156

NEW YEAR: OLD JAPAN (The boats are resting along the shore,) C2498

NEWSTEAD *see* NEWSTEAD ABBEY

NEWSTEAD ABBEY [*later* NEWSTEAD, BYRONIANA, II] (Past the mines and past the workshops) A89, 135; C2101

NIGHT PIECE (Spell of the mournful holy night) A14

NIGHT-PIECE, A ("Asleep; the pinnacles and precipices of the mountains,) A40, 45, 68, 135

NIGHT-SOUNDS ("The years are outfleeting us,"–) A89

NIGHT THUNDER IN WEST SUSSEX (The sweltering day went down to die) A1, 3

NIGHT-WIND *see* NIGHTWIND

NIGHTINGALES, THE (They went along the little wood,) A1, 3

NIGHTS BEFORE BATTLE (Moving through those nights) A64, 68

NIGHTWIND [*later* NIGHT-WIND] (Along the lifted line of sombre green) A25, 35; C542

1952 (In winter moonlight, thinking of many things) C2894

1919 [*later* "FOR THERE IS NO HELP IN THEM"] (She lies on that white breast she loves, and well) A25, 35; C521

1916 SEEN FROM 1921 *see* FESTUBERT, 1916

1966: S.S. BECOMES AN OCTOGENARIAN (Another era came while yet the last) C3352

NO CONTINUING CITY (The train with its smoke and its rattle went on,) A20, 35, 135, 174; Ed6

NOT SO DEAD (How old I grow, how out of date,) A64, 68

NOT UNUSUAL CASE, A (It may be so: their love was never fire,) A68, 135

NOUVELLES LITTÉRAIRES, OR INANI MUNERE [*later* FORSAKEN MEMORIALS] (Béranger's tomb, this picture tells me, dies) A156; C2773

NOVEMBER 1, 1931 (We talked of ghosts; and I was still alive;) A45, 68, 135

NOVEMBER HOUR, THE (Pausing in the churchyard here, I feel anew) A56

NOVEMBER MORNING (From the night storm sad wakes the wintry day) A10, 18, 35, 135; C45

NOW OR NEVER (Bright fleet slow shadow! puzzling guide,) A20, 35

NUN AT COURT, THE (With what voluptuous and distorted care) A35

OCCULT ENCOUNTER, AN (As I came down by Grosvenor-place) C1786

OCTOBER COMES (I heard the gray bird bathing in the rill,) A77; C1938

OCTOBER NIGHTFALL (The turbulence of wild and shattering thought) A1, 3

OCTOBER, 1914 (From the white cottage on the glimmering wold) A1, 3

OCTOGENARIAN ("Old we shall find him; eighty years) A77; C1967

ODE FOR ST. CECILIA'S DAY, AN (Delightful Goddess, in whose fashionings) A97, 156; B121

ODE TO AN INK-JAR (STEPHENS' INK) [*later* TO A BRITISH JAR [etc.]] (Dear patient Jar, whose function is no more *later* Concise brown jar, [etc.]) A100, 156; C2533

ODE TO THE MEMORY OF S. T. COLERIDGE, AN (While now the moonlight and the water-mist) C1841

OEDIPUS AT COLONUS (Woodlands, and hill-slopes, hid in olive-bowers,) A1, 3

OFFERING, AN (Mother of arts, and nature's child,) C2430

OLD AND THE NEW, THE (Let the dead leaves lie) A1, 3

OLD BATTLEFIELDS [*later* FLANDERS NOW] (There, before us no master action struck) A28, 35, 135; C606

OLD CHURCHYARD, THE (The old churchyard has many graves) A1, 3

OLD HOMES (O happiest village! how I turned to you,) A11, 20, 35, 135; C318

OLD MERTONIAN (Entering my room about midnight—I knew this would happen—) C1799

OLD PLEASURES DESERTED (Cobwebs and kisks have crept) A20, 35

OLD REMEDIES (The yardman, he with the coins on his watch-chain, stood) A35; C1004

OLD SCHOOLMASTER, THE *see* C.E.B.

OLD SONG, AN (Once again the Siren sang:) A156

OLD YEAR, THE (The moon was going down; the empty trees shook, sighing,) A14, 20, 35

OMEN (Now the day is dead, I cried,) A17, 20, 35; C496

OMINOUS VICTORIAN, AN *see* EMINENT VICTORIAN, AN

ON A BIOGRAPHICAL DICTIONARY (Proud is assembly, and the anthem proud) A31, 35; C796

ON A FLY-LEAF OF CHAUCER'S *WYF OF BATHE* (There are few places in the common path) A106

ON A JOURNEY, 1943 (The scythesman and the thatcher are not dead,) A77

ON A PICTURE BY DÜRER (Where found you, Dürer, that strange group of trees,) A64, 68; B76

ON A PICTURE OF H.I.H. PRINCE CHICHIBU (So once we saw him, and no more) A171

ON A SMALL DOG [etc.] (*Animula vagula blandula*, foundling dear,) A26, 31, 35

ON BLOOD TRANSFUSION [*later* TRANSLATED FROM THE JAPANESE OF H.M. EMPRESS NAGAKO] (The blood's supplied! and see,) (So that a multitude) A171; B227

ON CHARLES LAMB'S BIRTHDAY 1945 [*later* ON CHAS. LAMB'S [etc.]] (Speak, Elia, from afar, with eyes still bent) A97; C2108

ON J. BLANCO WHITE (As I have seen the golden-girded sun) A1, 3

ON LAMMA ISLAND MARCH 1961 TO S.G.D. [*i.e.* Professor S. G. Davis] (This quiet place is changing as all do.) A156

ON MR. PORTER'S ROOM OF PICTURES [*later* ON MR. FREDERICK PORTER'S [etc.]) (The Sun's your radiant painter, he) A35; B36

ON MYSELF (No more am I what I have been,) A2-3

ON READING "A BRIEF SURVEY" (Encampment and entrenchment, these) B214

ON READING A MAGAZINE EDITED BY OSCAR WILDE (Once on a time before I heard) A89, 135; C2068

ON READING OF MAHATMA GANDHI'S DEATH *see* TO THE MEMORY OF GANDHI

ON READING THAT THE REBUILDING OF YPRES APPROACHED COMPLETION (I hear you now, I hear you, shy perpetual companion,) A28, 35, 135

ON RECEIVING FROM THE CLARENDON PRESS [. . .] CHRISTOPHER SMART'S 'SONG TO DAVID' [*later* SONNET ON RECEIVING FROM THE CLARENDON PRESS [etc.]; *and* SONNET ON SMART'S "SONG TO DAVID"] (The Song itself! thus the majestic rhyme) A22, 25, 35

ON SHAKESPEARE'S 'WINTER'S TALE' [*later* AUTOLYCUS'S COUNTRY]
(What passed when fantasy ruled the hour) A156; C3103
ON SOME CROCUSES: AT TRINITY COLLEGE (Light and busy wings,
beating this bright air;) A45, 68
ON TEARING UP A CYNICAL POEM (Grand Justice, I have heard in awe
your speech.) A156; B212
ON THE AIR (I let the radio go. The hour was late.) A156; C3184
ON THE DEATH-MASK OF JOHN CLARE [*later* THE DEATH-MASK [etc.]]
(Kind was the hand that at the last) A17, 20, 35, 135
ON THE FIFTH ANNIVERSARY OF THE OPENING OF THE CITY HALL,
HONG KONG (Five years ago with happy auguries) B273.1
ON THE PORTRAIT OF A COLONEL *see* PORTRAIT OF A COLONEL
ON THE PROFESSION OF PHYSIC (When in my quiet time I have reviewed,)
C3111
ON TURNING A STONE (Trolls and pixies unbeknown) A8, 35; B1
ONCE ON A HILL (If only and only a turn of time would allow) A156
ONE AMONG THE ROSES *see* AMONG THE ROSES
ONE KIND OF ARTIST (Rainbows on flying foam, glitterings of high-sunned
cloud,) A77; C1887
ONLY ANSWER, THE [*later* FROM AGE TO AGE] (Retarded into history's
marble eyes) A52, 68, 108, 135; C1268
ONLY NOT INFINITE ("Only not infinite!" Sometimes drowsily) C2480
OPENED TOMB, THE (With a few modernizings, it is still the proud highway)
C3318
OPERA—A HYMN OF PRAISE, THE (Footlights, footlights, shedding light)
C463
ORIENTAL ORNAMENTATIONS [*later* ORNAMENTATIONS] (The curving
cranes with serpent necks) A26, 31, 35; C587
ORIENTAL TALE *see* THOUGHTS ON BOOKS
ORNAMENTAL WATER, THE (Limned in the lake the rosy portraiture) A77;
C1983
ORNAMENTATIONS *see* ORIENTAL ORNAMENTATIONS
ORNITHOPOLIS (Not your least glory, many-gloried Wren,) A25, 35, 135;
B23; C584
OSAKA IN RECONSTRUCTION (Men pass; and cities pass; and yet the years)
A85
OTANI WOMEN'S COLLEGE (Here amid juniors, seniors, all united) A171
OVER THE VALLEY (Trembling blue, blent grey or green) A156
OVERHEARD (There will always be gardens where somebody's fancy) B201;
C3305

PAGODA, THE (From the knoll of beeches peeping) A35
PAINTED WINDOW, A (Figured in gray and brown) A77
PARABLE (Wide as the world is, music abounds,) A31, 35, 135
PARAPHRASE, A (Mary with her white hands pressed) C276
PASSER-BY, THE (A thrush, I know not by what humour drawn) A156, 169;
C3094
—— (The listless year goes dimly down,) A25, 35
PAST AND PRESENT: A HYMN (Those spirits fallen too late in time) A64,
68
PAST AND PRESENT: A SECOND HYMN (Traversing the early starlight, and
the miles of shade,) A64, 68
PASTORAL, A (When the young year is sweetest, when the year) A20, 35
PASTORAL TO MADELINE, A (In sunbright years) A68, 135
PASTURE (Seagull, crow and wagtail) A64, 68

SONNET ON SMART'S "SONG TO DAVID" *see* ON RECEIVING FROM THE CLARENDON PRESS [etc.]

[SONNET] ON THE ENGLISH POETS NOW FORGOTTEN [i] (Dead poets, you that had a life of fame,) A7

— [ii] (I do not know for sure how much I dream,) A7

— [iii] (Often a thought breaks in upon my mind) A7

SOUTH ATLANTIC (Flitting from pulley-block to wheelhouse roof,) A52, 68; C1338

SOUTH-EAST ENGLAND IN 1944 [*later* "SOUTHERN ENGLAND" IN 1944] (In the green Indian-corn first evening airs are playing,) A89; B103; C2056

SOUTH-WEST WIND, THE (We stood by the idle weir,) A10, 35, 43*b*, 174; B7; C207

"SOUTHERN ENGLAND" IN 1944 *see* SOUTH-EAST ENGLAND IN 1944

SOUTHERN PILGRIM, A (Looking on Sussex from afar I find) A156; B203

SPEECH BY A HAMLET IN THE AMIENS DISTRICT (My humdrum life has been) A156

SPELL, THE (Loud the wind leaps through the night and fills the valley with his wings,) A14, 20, 35; C360

SPELL OF FRANCE, THE (Little enough of that wide country) A64, 68; C1609

SPIRE, THE (The moment holds me; pale cool fire) A64, 68

SPIRIT-WIND (In the night, in the night the wild harp answered best;) C2924

— (Sway those green worlds [etc.]) *see* UNEXPECTED VICTORY, THE

SPLEEN: FROM BAUDELAIRE (When the low and leaden sky crushes like a lid upon) C507

SPRING AND CRITICISM (The year gains fast; the pear-trees many buds) A67-8

SPRING GALE, THE (Sound, sound, immortal Tempest, through the dark,) A77, 135

SPRING NIGHT (Through the smothered air the wicker finds) A10, 35; C122

SPRING SONG (The loitering wilderness) A2-3

SPRING-TIME, DEATH (Now the snows are gone, and the green comes to the leas,) A97

STANE STREET (Mown, strown are the grayhead grasses,) A5-6, 35

STANZAS (Princess whom all Observers view) B12

STANZAS: MIDSUMMER 1937 (O England! lose not now, O never lose) A64, 68, 135

STARLING'S NEST, THE (I laughed; a joyful joke to see) A43

STATION ROAD (There's the new green verge at the woodside gleaning,) A89

STILL HOUR, THE (As in the silent darkening room I lay,) A14, 20, 35, 108; C444

STONE GARDEN (KYŌTO), THE (Signs and wonders fill) A156, 169; B291; C3291; D13

STORM: 1907, A (White on the tempest darkness, hardly stirring,) A156, 169, 176

STORM, THE (Sky beyond words! Elysian-field) A25, 35; C681

STORM AT HOPTIME (The hoptime came with sun and shower) A8

STORMY NIGHT *see* VOICE OF THE PAST, THE

STRANGE PERSPECTIVE (Happy the herd that in the heat of summer) A17-18, 20, 35, 135

STREAMSIDE, THE (I have been a pleasant ramble,) A1, 3

STROLLING PLAYERS (Break forth, some crashing clashing fiery genius, lead the way,) A68

589

STUDY, THE (While I sit penning plans of dead affairs,) A31, 35, 135
SUBTLE CALM, THE (Seas like Roman glass,) A64, 68
"SUITABLE ADVICE" (Fixing his pinchers on the snake,) A40, 45, 68
SUM OF ALL, THE (So rise, enchanting haunting faithful) A68, 108, 135; C1744
SUMMER HIEROGLYPHS *see* APPARITIONS IN SUMMER
SUMMER IDYLL, A (Came to the garden walks a swooning Breeze,) A1, 3; C5
SUMMER JOURNEY, THE (Even as we travelled, travel seemed) A171
"SUMMER PEACE" (White water-lilies hang their heads) A1, 3; C3
—— [ii] (Then hither come, smit with desire) A1, 3
SUMMER RAINSTORM *see* SUMMER RAINSTORM, THE
SUMMER RAINSTORM, THE [*later* SUMMER RAINSTORM] (Sweet conversations, coppice incantations *later* Sweet conversations, woodland incantations) A31, 35, 135; C877
SUMMER STORM [*later* SUMMER STORM IN JAPANESE HILLS] (This is the forecast storm, the rage) A102, 156, 169, 176
SUMMER STORM IN JAPANESE HILLS *see* SUMMER STORM
SUMMER'S FANCY, A (The time and place agree; each leaf has grown) A34, 45, 68
SUNDOWN (Throughout its blue-grey knolls of cloud the sky) A1, 3; C10
SUNKEN LANE, THE (Behind the meadows where the windmill stood) A35
SUNLIT VALE, THE *see* FAILURE, THE
SUNRISE IN MARCH, A (While on my cheek the sour and savage wind) A31, 35, 135; C734
SUPERSTITION RE-VISITED, A [*later* A SUPERSTITION REVISITED] (While on the lavender by the door) A25, 35; B26; C560
SUPERSTITION REVISITED, A *see* SUPERSTITION RE-VISITED, A
SURPRISE, THE (Shot from the zenith of desire) A52, 68, 135
SURVIVAL, THE (To-day's house makes tomorrow's road;) A35; B41; C992
SURVIVOR FROM ONE WAR REFLECTS DURING ANOTHER, A (Who, esteeming mankind) A97
SURVIVORS (1916), THE [*later* TWO VOICES] ("There's something in the air," he said,) A17, 28, 35, 135; C475
"SUSSEX AND FLANDERS" (From Brighton and Chichester, Horsham and Rye,) B77
SUSSEX DOWNS, THE (Calm and curious, kindly, great,) A135; C2949
SWAN, A MAN, A (Among the diad reeds, the single swan) A168
"SWEETEST MELANCHOLY" (The white moon shines among the woods:) A2-3
SYMPOSIUM (With thoughts of many times and places) A106

TAGORE'S PAINTINGS (So much he had already given) B246
TAILWAGGER, THE *see* TALE NOT IN CHAUCER, A
TAKAMATSU COUNTRYSIDE (Perpetual are these hills, these ways) A171
TALE NOT IN CHAUCER, A (In *France*, no matter what the Town, there stood) A43*b*, 45, 68; C1180
TEA-HOUSE, THE *see* JAPANESE INN
TEACHER, THE (We wish you all that life can give) A106
TELL YOUR FORTUNE (This was my pleasant dream, not ten days past:—) A64, 68; B74
TEMPEST *see* EASTERN TEMPEST
TEMPLE, THE (Truly you observed me; it was as you record,) A102
THAMES GULLS (Beautiful it is to see) A20, 35, 43*b*, 135; C486

THEIR VERY MEMORY (Hear, O hear!) A28, 35, 135, 174

THEOLOGY OVER THE GATE (We have no God, though old Miss Moon still seeks) A52, 68; C1359

"THERE IS A COUNTRY" (While thus the black night rushes down in rain) A14, 20, 35

THESE PROBLEMS (Strenuous to live the life for which he came,) A68

THIEPVAL WOOD (The tired air groans as the heavies swing over, the river-hollows boom;) A35

THINK OF SHELLEY [later A TOUCHSTONE] (I think of Shelley, and my own poor speed) A52, 68, 108, 135; C1272

THIRD YPRES: A REMINISCENCE (Triumph! how strange, how strong had triumph come) A10, 28, 35, 135, 176; B44

THOMASINE (No stranger yet no friendlier call) A77, 135

THORNY WINTER (Thorny winter! Old gods, save;) A156

THOSE WHO FIRST ENCOURAGED US (Sweet sing the verse, while this we sing:) A135; C2502

"THOU" (Comest thou so, my little child,) A97; C2483

THOUGHT FROM SCHILLER, A (Evening falls: to numbered night) A25, 35

THOUGHT OF H.I.H. PRINCE CHICHIBU, A (In Oxford he must be sought, along) A171

THOUGHT OF THE DOWNS, A (Come now, my love without whom nothing wakes) A52, 68, 135

THOUGHTS OF A ROMANTIC (Ten thousand miles from land are we,) A12

THOUGHTS OF THOMAS HARDY ("Are you looking for someone, you who came pattering) A77, 135, 174; B244.1; C1856; Ed4

THOUGHTS ON BOOKS: A SATIRE IN VERSE [later ORIENTAL TALE] (The library of Alexandria) A52, 68; C1230

THREEFOLD SCREEN see JAPANESE GLIMPSES

THRESHOLD (If I knocked in this dead night,) B10; C320

THUS FAR (In glades where frost is ambushed in the ferns,) A17, 20, 35; B23; C472

"THY DREAMS OMINOUS" (Blest is the man that sees or hears later [. . .] sees and hears) A20, 35; C516

TIGRANES (Tigranes the all-highest) A77

TIMBER (In the avenues of yesterday) A77, 174

TIME FOR NEW LEAVES (Come now, sweet creatures, come;) A97

TIME IS GONE, THE (The time is gone when we could throw) A10, 35, 174; B7

TIME OF ROSES (Clean flows the wind as from its grand source flowing) A14, 20, 35; C358

TIME TOGETHER (When you are by, I think of time as boys) A77, 135

TO . . . [later TO A SPIRIT] (Dear (thus I dare), how I have longed) A20, 35; C511

TO A BRITISH JAR CONTAINING STEPHENS' INK see ODE TO AN INK-JAR (STEPHENS' INK)

TO A FRIEND (I knew your power, I thought, and I was wrong:) A68

TO A NATURE-LOVER see ECHOES FROM 1914-18

TO A PLANNER (O well I know, and well I like, and warmly long to see) A89; C2014

TO A SPIRIT (Dear (thus I dare), how I have longed) see TO . . .

—— (The young spring night in all her virtue walks;) A25, 35

TO A WALTONIAN IN KYUSHU (If it had been our chance, centuries ago) A106

591

TO THE SOUTHDOWNS (Come, and defy or else forget) A52, 68; B63

"TO THE SOUTHDOWNS!" [later TO THE SOUTHDOWNS: AT THE YEARLY REUNION, 1939] (True, wars have not yet died out of the earth.) A68; B85

TO W.O. AND HIS KIND [i.e. Wilfred Owen] (If even you, so able and so keen,) A67-8, 135

TO WELCOME PRINCE AKIHITO see PRINCE AKIHITO POEM READ

TO WILFRED OWEN (Where does your spirit walk, kind soldier, now?) B90; C1798

TO YUKICHI NAKAMURA ("Tell it not here, it needs no saying,") A171

TOAD, THE ("I like my twilight walk as well as you,) A52, 68; C1300

TOGETHER [later AN ANCIENT PATH] (Rosy belief uplifts her spires) A25, 35, 135; C559

TOKYO: AN UNPUBLISHED PASSAGE FROM GOLDSMITH'S THE TRAVELLER? (The Muse still thoughtful into Nippon flies,) C479.

TOKYO LAWN [later FROM A TOKYO LAWN; and TOKYO LAWN (1948)] ("I'm a starling.") A100, 156; C2530

TOKYO LAWN (1948) see TOKYO LAWN

TOMKINS ("I could never do it, but my son perhaps can.) A100; C2532

TORAO TAKETOMO (To him whose own poetic power might yield) A171

TOUCHSTONE, A see THINK OF SHELLEY

TOURIST (NEAR KOMORO), THE (Perched upon the templed height) A85

TOWARDS THE FUTURE (Let us speak to those afar,) C2516

TOWER, THE (Stone ghost,) A43a, 108, 135

—— (I fell wishing that the room in which I was pent, later Wishing that the room where I darkened closely pent,) A89; B97

TOWN END see UNEASY QUIET

TRAFFIC IN A GREY CITY (Coming through Stamford town on a sleepy autumn day,) C3206

TRAGEDY (Two forms there are of tragedy: one makes) A7

TRANSCRIPTION, A ("This young man comes from your way, Tom.") A17, 20, 35; C466

TRANSLATED FROM THE JAPANESE OF H.M. EMPRESS NAGAKO see ON BLOOD TRANSFUSION

"TRANSPORT UP" AT YPRES (The thoroughfares that seem so dead to daylight passers-by) A35, 108, 135

TRAVELLERS, 193- see TRAVELLERS—1938

TRAVELLERS—1938 [later TRAVELLERS, 193-] (Bright insolent winds assail the shores) A77, 135; C1825

TREE IN THE GOODS YARD, THE (So sigh, that hearkening pasts arouse) A89, 135; B224; Ed3

TREES ON THE CALAIS ROAD (Like mourners filing into church at a funeral,) A35, 135

"TRENCH NOMENCLATURE" (Genius named them, as I live! what but genius could compress) A28, 35; B260

TRENCH RAID NEAR HOOGE (At an hour before the rosy-fingered) A28, 35; C505

TRIUMPH OF AUTUMN see TO AUTUMN

TRIUMPH OF THE POET, THE (Firmer than bronze here stands my monument,) A97

TRIUNE [later HAWTHORN] (Behind that hawthorn shade the grass will hardly grow, later Beneath that hawthorn [etc.]) A20, 35, 135, 174; B23; C557

TROUBLED SPIRIT, THE (Said God, Go, spirit, thou hast served me well) A10, 35

VOICES I HEARD ("Who are you afraid of?" "Spider Dick.") B110
VOICES IN TOKYO (Numberless voices needs must arise) A85, 89; B224; C2445; Ed3
VOLCANO, THE see SAKURAJIMA, A VOLCANO

W.S.: LAST PLAYS [*i.e.* William Shakespeare] (Immeasurable, and undiscoverable:) A156
WAGGONER, THE (The old waggoner drudges through the miry lane) A8, 18, 35, 43*b*, 135, 174; C33
WAITING THE WORD (Half lost between river and hill,) A64, 68; C1549
WALKING IN TOKYO 1948 [*later* TO THE NEW JAPAN] ("Come, little babe; come, silly soul,")A89, 174; B291; Ed6; p. xiii
WAR AUTOBIOGRAPHY (WRITTEN IN ILLNESS) (Heaven is clouded, mists of rain) A10, 35, 135; C307
WAR CEMETERY (Why are they dead? Is Adam's seed so strong) A68, 135; B68
WAR TALK: WINTER 1938 (They're talking of another war,) A68
WAR'S PEOPLE (Through the tender amaranthine domes) A31, 35
WARDER, THE see SHADOW, THE
WARNING TO TROOPS (What soldier guessed that where the stream descended) A20, 35, 135
WARTONS AND OTHER EARLY ROMANTIC LANDSCAPE POETS, THE see WARTONS AND OTHER EARLY ROMANTICS, THE
WARTONS AND OTHER EARLY ROMANTICS, THE [*later* THE WARTONS AND OTHER EARLY ROMANTIC LANDSCAPE POETS; *and* THE WARTONS AND OTHER LANDSCAPE POETS] (Mild hearts, and modest as the evening bell) A25, 35, 135; C676
WARTONS AND OTHER LANDSCAPE POETS, THE see WARTONS AND OTHER EARLY ROMANTICS, THE
WASTE GROUND (The wheat crowds close, the land falls sharp) A14, 20, 35; C359
WATCHERS, THE (I heard the challenge "Who goes there?") A28, 35, 135; B260; C632
WATCHING RUNNING WATER (How swift and smooth this water glinters past!) A35; C3352
WATER-MEADOW EVENING (After the great blue day, the assuring light) A135; C3148
WATER MOMENT (The silver eel slips through the waving weeds) A14, 18, 20, 35; C357
WATER-SPORT ("Come, all who hear our song" say Yalding bells,) A10, 35; C109
WATERFALL, THE see SONG, A (I haunt a waterfall)
WATERMILL, THE (I'll rise at midnight and I'll rove) A10, 35, 135; B7; C232
WATERPIECE, A (The wild rose-bush lets loll) A8, 35, 135; C32
WEATHERCOCK, THE (The turret's leaden carapace) A37; B57
WELCOME, THE (He'd scarcely come from leave and London,) A17, 28, 35
WESERLAND [*later* WESERLAND, 1939] (Here above the water-meads) A68; B91
WESERLAND, 1939 see WESERLAND
WHAT IS WINTER? see DAY IN DECEMBER, A
WHEN THE STATUE FELL: A GRANDFATHER'S TALE ("What was the strangest sight you ever saw?") A89

596

WHETHER LIVING BODIES HAVE ULTIMATE AIMS? (Vesey the Constable waddles the Town,) C858
WHITE-FLOWERING DAYS, THE (Now the white-flowering days) B157; C3029; Ed2
WICKED MILLER OF REDLANDS, THE (Not far from the lane is the broken mill) A4, 6
WILD CHERRY TREE (Here be rural graces, sylvan places,) A35
WILD CREATURES AT NIGHTFALL (Their houses are not lighted, nor do they) A156, 169
WILDERNESS (On lonely Kinton Green all day) A8, 35; C36
WILL-O'-THE-WISP (From chocked morass I leap and run) A10, 35; C304
WILLIAM ADAMS AT ITO [later TO THE CITIZENS OF ITO] (Here then, while Shakespeare yet was with us, came) A85; B189, 291; C2506
WILLIAM LILY'S RULES FOR SCHOOLBOYS see QUI MIHI
WINDOW IN GERMANY: AUGUST 1939, A (Still the mild shower grows on; amid the drops) A68; B92; C1775
WINNERS, THE (At summer's close, beneath a blackening sky,) A68
WINNOWER'S PRAYER TO THE WINDS, THE (Ye habitants of air,) A2-3
WINTER: EAST ANGLIA see WINTER PIECE
WINTER ENDING (Old weeds upthrust in pasture wide half cheat) A64, 68
WINTER NIGHTS (Strange chord! the weir-pool's tussling dance,) A27, 35, 135
WINTER PIECE [later WINTER: EAST ANGLIA] (In a frosty sunset) A14, 18, 20, 35, 135, 169, 176
WINTER-PROUD (With idle joy rippling the moon's green light) A43a
WINTER STARS (Fierce in flaming millions, ready to strike they stood,) A40, 45, 68; C1085
WINTER WALK, THE (Now while the winter wind at last,) A77, 135
WITH A SALMON (Accept this Salmon, that, when he had fought) A23
WOE TO THE DRUNKARDS: A JACOBEAN SERMON (What is the world about?) A64, 68
WOODLAND HOLIDAY KARUIZAWA, A (In solitude, we say— but good society) A97
WOOD'S EDGE, THE (All the winter through) C2833
WOULD YOU RETURN? (Poppies never brighter shone, and never sweeter smelled the hay,) A25, 35, 135; B_5; C591
WRITING A SKETCH OF A FORGOTTEN POET (Here this great summer day,) A64, 68, 135
WRITTEN IN THE WOMAN'S CHRISTIAN COLLEGE, TOKYO (I saw three graces under dark green boughs,) A168, 171

YASHIMA IN WINTER see FIRST VISIT TO YASHIMA, A
YELLOWHAMMER, THE (With rural admixture of shrill and sweet,) A35, 135
YEOMAN, A (This man that at the wheatstack side,) A17, 20, 35, 176; B15; C439
YEWS AND A BROOK (The crowding ghosts of many years) A1, 3
YOU NEVER STAY (Stay kingfisher, so fleet along) A67-8
YOUNG FIELDMOUSE (Beseechingly this little thing—) A135
YOUNG MARINERS, THE (The green boat was moored) A156
YOUNG PIONEERS (When we came to the hall we were made to feel grand;) C3316
YOUNG TRAVELLERS (By every brake, and every brook,) A43a
YUKICHI (You still invite, Yukichi; we) A171

ZERO [*later* COME ON, MY LUCKY LADS; *and* ZERO 1916] (O rosy red,
   O torrent splendour) A17, 28, 35, 135; B260
ZERO 1916 *see* ZERO
ZILLEBEKE BROOK (This conduit stream that's tangled here and there) A35
ZONNEBEKE ROAD, THE (Morning, if this late withered light can claim)
   A17, 28, 35, 135, 174; B44; C829; E*d*6
ZUDAUSQUES (How joyously the south's large rain) C1836

Behind that hawthorn shade the grass will hardly grow, [*later* Beneath that hawthorn [etc.]] (TRIUNE *later* HAWTHORN) A20, 35, 135, 174; B23; C557

Behind the meadows where the windmill stood (THE SUNKEN LANE) A35

Being asked to conceive that the fortune of war now raging (INTER ARMA) A89

Believe in the earth, explorer of the sky, (A VICAR IN REMEMBRANCE) A156

Beneath that hawthorn shade the grass will hardly grow, *see* Behind that hawthorn [etc.]

Beneath the leaves I lie, and read, and glance (IN A PARK AT KYOTO) A97; C2564

Béranger's tomb, this picture tells me, dies (NOUVELLES LITTÉRAIRES, OR INANI MUNERE *later* FORSAKEN MEMORIALS) A156; C2773

Beesechingly this little thing— (YOUNG FIELDMOUSE) A135

Beside his barn the country parson stood, (A SHADOW BY THE BARN) A40, 45, 68

Beside the broken tower I gaze for thee, [*later* Beside the lovely tower [etc.]] (RUIN) A25, 35; C621

Beside the creek where seldom oar or sail (THE KILN) A31, 35; C844

Beside the lovely tower I gaze for thee, *see* Beside the broken tower [etc.]]

Beside the vision of an ancient weir (THE BELOVED RIVER) A97, 156

Beyond the church there stands a bridge (A BRIDGE) A17, 20, 35, 174; C492

Black clouds hide the moon, the amazement is gone; (A FARM NEAR ZILLEBEKE) A10, 35, 135, 169, 176

Black ponds and boughs of clay and sulky sedge (MUFFLED) A20, 35, 135, 169

Blest is the man that sees and hears *see* Blest is the man that sees or hears

Blest is the man that sees or hears [*later* [. . .] sees and hears] ("THY DREAMS OMINOUS") A20, 35; C516

Blue and cool and sacred rise (FOR A WATER-COLOUR BY Y. NOGUCHI) A171

Book, lie you there: such borrowed wings *see* I'll read no more; man's mental wings

Boys on the beach where East and West yet meet, (A READER INTERRUPTED) C3116

Break forth, some crashing clashing fiery genius, lead the way, (STROLLING PLAYERS) A68

Brief were the hours and rapidly they flew, (THE DEAN) A106

Bright fleet slow shadow! puzzling guide, (NOW OR NEVER) A20, 35

Bright insolent winds assail the shores (TRAVELLERS, 1938 *later* TRAVELLERS, 193-) A77, 135; C1825

Brightest of red roofs, glittering (FROM THE BRANCH LINE) A64, 68

Bring all your bravery, miss no flower of the field; (TO SPRING) C3000

Bring to our song the thankful soul, (SCHOOL SONG) B194

Brisk in the forest the dead twigs snapped, (THE ELF IN AUTUMN) p. 556

Bronze noonlight domes the dim blue gloom (A VIGNETTE) A35

But for a Basilisk who somewhere cowers (ANTI-BASILISK) A64, 68

But have you read it, sir? (THE REJECTED'S REVENGE: A DRAMATIC FRAGMENT [etc.]) C1489

By every brake, and every brook, (YOUNG TRAVELLERS) A43*a*

By my old house a yew-tree stood, (TO KOICHI NAKANE) A171

By Herndyke Mill there haunts, folks tell, (THE SILVER BIRD OF HERNDYKE MILL) A5-6, 8, 35, 135

By the pasture pond alone (THE PASTURE POND) A10, 35, 135; C171
By the red chimney-pots the pigeons cower, (FIRST SNOW) A10, 35; C234

Calm and curious, kindly, great, (THE SUSSEX DOWNS) A135; C2949
Came to the garden walks a swooning Breeze, (A SUMMER IDYLL) A1, 3; C5
Can malice live in natural forms, (THE BALLAST-HOLE) A40, 45, 68; C1146
Child, of my school, whom well the wish beseems (QUI MIHI later WILLIAM
    LILY'S RULES FOR SCHOOLBOYS) A89; C2271
Chinese pond is quick with leaches: (CHINESE POND) A8; C44
Clear flows the wind as from its grand source flowing (TIME OF ROSES) A14,
    20, 35; C358
Cobwebs and kisks have crept (OLD PLEASURES DESERTED) A20, 35
"Come, all who hear our song" say Yalding bells, (WATER-SPORT) A10, 35;
    C109
Come, all who love the way of truth, (COLLEGE SONG later FOR TOKYO
    JOSHI DAIGAKU: A HYMN) A98, 171; B291; C2520
Come, and defy or else forget (TO THE SOUTHDOWNS) A52, 68; B63
Come, angel most beloved, come, most rejected; (INVOCATION WRITTEN
    IN SPRING 1944) A89, 135; C2438
Come, for here the lazy night (AUTUMN IN THE WEALD) A31, 35, 135;
    C883
Come happy wind and blow away care (THE AWAKENING) C293
Come hither, fisher maiden, (HEINE IN THE EAST) C3214
Come, let us weep once more for all the dead, (A MARCH) A156
"Come, little babe; come, silly soul,"– (WALKING IN TOKYO 1948 later TO
    THE NEW JAPAN) A89, 174; B291; Ed6; p. xiii
Come now, my love without whom nothing wakes (A THOUGHT OF THE
    DOWNS) A52, 68, 135
Come now, sweet creatures, come; (TIME FOR NEW LEAVES) A97
"Come, shy and almost-silent rain; (A CALM RAIN) A45, 68, 135; C1203
Come, tell me: of these two books lying here, (THE TWO BOOKS) A71, 77,
    135; C1896
Come they no more, those ecstasies of earth, ("THE EARTH HATH BUB-
    BLES") A10, 35; C296
Come to me where the swelling wind assails the wood with a sea-like roar
    (LATE LIGHT) A64, 68, 135; B234
Come, to the Shrine; the thousandth stair (SOMEWHERE EAST later AFTER-
    NOON IN JAPAN) A52, 68; C1248
Come with your hat thrown on your long black hair (AUBADE) A2–3
Come ye to my jubilee! (RONDEL) A2–3
Comest thou so, my little child, ("THOU") A97; C2483
Coming by the sluices (THE RIPPLE) B69; C1334
Coming through Stamford town on a sleepy autumn day, (TRAFFIC IN A
    GREY CITY) C3206
Coming to converse with gentle Diana (AFTER A MASQUE) A68
Concise brown jar, whose mystery seems no more see Dear patient Jar, [etc.]

Dance not your spectral dance at me; (FAMILIARITY) A31, 35, 135; Ed4
Dark, marvellous eyes she has, not small, (QUAM NON SINE AMORE VIDEO)
    A7
Dark War, exploding loud mephitic mines, (SOME TALK OF PEACE–) A52,
    68, 169, 176
Dead poets, you that had a life of fame, ([SONNET] ON THE ENGLISH
    POETS NOW FORGOTTEN [i]) A7

Dear other-times, and yet not far, (IN REMEMBERANCE OF A SISTER) C3300

Dear patient Jar, whose function is no more [*later* Concise brown jar, whose mystery seems no more] (ODE TO AN INK-JAR (STEPHENS' INK) *later* TO A BRITISH JAR [etc.]) A100, 156; C2533

Dear (thus I dare), how I have longed (TO . . . *later* TO A SPIRIT) A20, 35; C511

"Death!" he cried, and, leaden-eyed, (THE CONDEMNATION (HAMEL MILL)) C23

Deed and event of prouder stature (RETURN) A31, 35, 135; C777

Delay not; for the years advance (IN MEMORIAM A.R.-I. YOKOHAMA, NOVEMBER 1938) A68; C1748

Delightful Goddess, in whose fashionings (AN ODE FOR ST CECILIA'S DAY) A97, 156; B121

Desire, the lovelier prophet of delight, (IN DISAPPOINTMENT *later* DESIRE AND DELIGHT) A45, 68, 135; C1207

Desperate wood, your skinny trees (THE CAMP IN THE WOOD) A68

Dim stars like snowflakes are fluttering in heaven, (THE BLIND LEAD THE BLIND) A31, 35, 135

Dim through cloud veils the moonlight trembles down (ESTRANGEMENT *later* THE ESTRANGEMENT) A8, 35; C34

Dinner is served. Eternity begins. (THE ART OF POETRY. [v] EPIC) A52

Down our street when I was a boy I met with a friendly man (A SONG *later* LOOKING EASTWARD) A64, 68; B291; C1472

Dream not that all the mind's eye gleans (THE TUNE) A14; C342

Dream-like the little journey in the sun,— (NATURE'S BEAUTY: DURING A CRISIS OF WAR) A89, 135

Early arises the merry May-morning, poising a melody on her lips, (FROM THE HILL-TOP) A1, 3

Earth is a quicksand; yon square tower (IN A COUNTRY CHURCHYARD) A20, 35, 135; C512

Elia! and Edward Moxon! both together (untitled) C2509

Elizabethan England, rise (THE KING'S ARMS HOTEL, KOBE JAPAN *later* THE KING'S ARMS, KOBE) A171; B140

Emblem of early seeking, early finding *see* Emblem of innocence and early finding,

Emblem of innocence and early finding, [*later* Emblem of early seeking, early finding,] (AN ANNOTATION) A25, 35, 135; C704

Encampment and entrenchment, these (ON READING "A BRIEF SURVEY") B214

Enter the man, right farmer's countenance: part (FARM BAILIFF) A89, 135, 174, 176; C2185; E*d*6

Entering my room about midnight—I knew this would happen— (OLD MERTONIAN) C1799

Even as we travelled, travel seemed (THE SUMMER JOURNEY) A171

Even Many Years have now become still More; (untitled) A171

Evening falls: to numbered night (A THOUGHT FROM SCHILLER) A25, 35

Evening has brought the glow-worm to the green, (SHEPHERD) A10, 35, 135; C120

Every feather of snow that floated, (FOR A SPRING DANCE BY TAMAMI GOJO *later* VOICE OF SPRING) A156; B171; C3121

Everything she does is delicate,— (L.C.) A168

Fail me not, flying angel, when I come (RECURRENCE) A64, 68
Fairest of valleys, in this full-bloomed night, (IN WILTSHIRE) A35; C895
Far out upon the burning heath (HOLIDAY) A7
Far over cornfields to the rim of hills (A CHURCH) A77
Far up a valley, next a quarry deep (FABLE) A52, 68
Farewell, kind house on the hill; shine in remembrance till (THE SEASIDE HOUSE) C3176
Field flowers, hide the burying; (PRAYER OF THE TWO DEAD FORESTERS) A7
Fierce came the snow—and is gone like a dream (FROM THE JAPANESE INN WINDOW *later* THE INN WINDOW, FUKUOKA; *and* THE EARLY YEAR, FUKUOKA) A94, 97, 106; C2513
Fierce in flaming millions, ready to strike they stood, (WINTER STARS) A40, 45, 68; C1085
Fifteen years Louise had seen: a forest flower was young Louise, (BURIAL IN SPRING FROM THE FRENCH OF BRIZEUX) C494
Figured in gray and brown (A PAINTED WINDOW) A77
Firmer than bronze here stands my monument, (THE TRIUMPH OF THE POET) A97
Five years ago with happy auguries (ON THE FIFTH ANNIVERSARY OF THE OPENING OF THE CITY HALL, HONG KONG) B273.1
Fixing his pinchers on the snake, ("SUITABLE ADVICE") A40, 45, 68
Flashing far, tolling sweet, telling of a city fine (THE VANISHING LAND) A77, 135
Flitting from pulley-block to wheelhouse roof, (SOUTH ATLANTIC) A52, 68; C1338
Flowers in their trusting way (THE DELL) A89
Footlights, footlights shedding light (THE OPERA—A HYMN OF PRAISE) C463
For ever, says the stream, must I (A CORNER OF THE MEADOW) A43a
For now the bleak, unblossomed year (A SONG AGAINST HOPE) A7
For the first time ever, and only now,— (A CHINESE PAPERKNIFE *later* CHINESE PAPER-KNIFE) A156, 174; C3243
For this most gracious welcome let my rhyme (AND STILL, THE DEAN) A106
For what reason I never can tell, (ANCRE, 1916) A168
Forget the winter's tooth; the merry flames leap (untitled) A171
Forgetful among his fancies, which once came to their best, (LATER FLOWERS) A156
Forgive what I, adventuring highest themes, (THE AUTHOR'S LAST WORDS TO HIS STUDENTS) A26, 31, 35, 108, 135; B291; D6, 20; Ed4, 7
Forgotten streams, yet wishful to be known, (INACCESSIBILITY IN THE BATTLEFIELD) A31, 35; C893
Four singers with a Delphic seriousness (A QUARTET: "THE MIKADO" AT CAMBRIDGE) A31, 35; C721
Frances aged five is no such fool (THE READER, NO READER) A156; C3220
Friend whom I never saw, yet dearest friend, (APRIL BYEWAY) A10, 35; B6, 9; C82
From Brighton and Chichester, Horsham and Rye, ("SUSSEX AND FLANDERS") B77
From choked morass I leap and run (WILL-O'-THE-WISP) A10, 35; C304

From cloudy shapes of trees that cluster the hills (THE LAST OF AUTUMN) A10, 35, 135

From dark to fiery, mute to loud (SERENA) A89, 135; C2069; Ed4

From far away and long ago we bring (PROLOGUE [COMUS]) B184

From gaunt A.B.'s, and dialogue marine (PROLOGUE [SAVONAROLA])
A55

"From Helicon's unfading hill (THE FLORILEGIUM) A77

From shadows of rich oaks outpeer (THE PIKE) A8, 18, 35, 135, 174; C29

From the dark mood's control (THE RECOVERY) A40, 45, 68; C1152

From the knoll of beeches peeping (THE PAGODA) A35

From the mirror-hall of sleep (BLINDFOLD) A14, 18; C53

From the night storm sad wakes the winter day (NOVEMBER MORNING)
A10, 18, 35, 135; C45

From the white cottage on the glimmering wold (OCTOBER, 1914) A1, 3

From tower that seemed in sunset living stone, (THE RIVER HOUSE) A14;
C286

From what proud star I know not, but I found *see* From what star I know
not, [etc.]

From what star I know not, but I found *later* From what proud star I know
not, [etc.] (THE GIANT PUFFBALL) A10, 35; B9; C233

Fulfilment is a puzzling goddess, (FULFILMENT) A77, 135

Gay water-sprite, whose voice and look [*later* Watersprite whose [etc.]] (TO
TEISE, A STREAM IN KENT) A77, 135; C1840

Genius named them, as I live! what but genius could compress ("TRENCH
NOMENCLATURE") A28, 35; B260

Gentle, dark day, and country tracks (FARM BEHIND BATTLE ZONE) A68

Glide beneath those elms, lost lane, (RUE DES BERCEAUX) A64, 68

God hath made her wondrous fair, (RONDEL) A2-3

"Gone down, sir, and whatever bird you speak to (CHAFFINCH ON SUBUR-
BAN GROWTHS *later* CHAFFINCH) A64, 68

Graces in the air, or from earth or wave (AMONG ALL THESE) A77

Grand Justice, I have heard in awe your speech. (ON TEARING UP A CYNI-
CAL POEM) A156; B212

Gray lights of cloudy dawning on the sea, (CIRCE PENITENT) A4, 6

Green grasses down in the valleys, (APRIL) A1, 3

Greetings to you, even ten times more than are minutes in the day, (GREET-
INGS: FROM THE LATIN OF JOHN SKELTON) C3158

Had this been three long lives ago, (DEVELOPMENT) A68

Half dead with fever here in bed I sprawl, (SICK-BED) A8, 35; C50

Half lost between river and hill, (WAITING THE WORD) A64, 68; C1549

Happily through my years this small stream ran; (EPITAPH) A31, 35, 135;
C842

Happy St. Brandan, happy mariner, (THE UNFORTUNATE SHIPMATE)
A77; C1792

Happy the herd that in the heat of summer (STRANGE PERSPECTIVE) A17-
18, 20, 35, 135

Hark, the new year succeeds the dead, (II PETER ii 22) A17, 28, 35

Harmonious trees, whose lit and lissom graces (RUE DU BOIS) A20, 35, 135

Harold was as straight a youth (VILLAGE SONG) A68

Hauntest thou so my waking and my sleeping, (A FAVOURITE SCENE [etc.])
A25, 35

He came from Malta, and Eumelus says (THE DOG FROM MALTA) A45, 68

He made me go through still majestic halls, (THE BOURNE) A1, 3

He stumbles silver-haired among his bees, (THE VETERAN) A8, 35, 108, 135; C28

He who now speaks some verse to waking minds (ABOUT THESE GERMANS) A68; C1791

Hear, O hear! (THEIR VERY MEMORY) A28, 35, 135, 174

Heart of great hopes, and glance of eager day, (RESENTIENTS) A20, 35

Heaven is clouded, mists of rain (WAR AUTOBIOGRAPHY (WRITTEN IN ILLNESS)) A10, 35, 135; C307

He'd scarcely come from leave and London, (THE WELCOME) A17, 28, 35

Help to save the country-side, (SONG FOR THE SECRETARY OF A PRE-SERVATION LEAGUE) C1722

Her arms were like the Nymphs, (GIRL WITH SHAWL) A25; C700

Here abide Tranquillity, (IN ZUIGANJI TEMPLE) A171

Here above the water-meads (WESERLAND *later* WESERLAND, 1939) A68; B91

Here aloft I live, *see* High up here I live

Here amid juniors, seniors, all united (OTANI WOMEN'S COLLEGE) A171

Here be rural graces, sylvan places, (WILD CHERRY TREE) A35

Here Bunyan finds a home, a house of learning, (untitled) A171

Here by the river we would glady stay— (RINKOTEI) A106

Here came the mild boy loving loneliness (KIRKE WHITE AT WILFORD [BYRONIANA I]) A89, 135; C2100

Here come old friends of most who love the stage, (PROLOGUE SPOKEN BY BENDICK) B264

Here gathered in this kindly town (untitled) C2508

Here in the moonlit sea, (JAPANESE NIGHTPIECE *later* INLAND SEA) A26, 31, 35; C635

Here is Charles Lamb's first church, which modern war (untitled) A171

Here is strange darkling sullenness; for dully, (THE MOUTH OF THE MED-WAY) A1, 3

Here Lucy paused for the blue butterfly— (THE BLUE BUTTERFLY *later* BLUE BUTTERFLY) A14, 20, 35, 174; C332

Here must the glory and the grief (KEATS HOUSE, ROME) B276

Here on the sunnier scarp of the hill let us rest, (MONT DE CASSEL) A8, 35, 135

"Here pause," wrote Wordsworth in a yet dark time (TO OLIVER SIMON) C3124

Here then, while Shakespeare yet was with us, came (WILLIAM ADAMS AT ITO *later* TO THE CITIZENS OF ITO) A85; B189, 291; C2506

Here they went with smock and crook, (FOREFATHERS) A10, 18, 35, 108, 135, 174; B4, 23; C48; D13; Ed4, 6-7

Here this great summer day, (WRITING SKETCH OF A FORGOTTEN POET) A64, 68, 135

Here we have found our goddess; moor the boat (CONSTANTIA AND FRAN-CIS) A41, 45, 68

Here winds (THE MASQUERADE) A20, 35

Here's a dell that's sunny enough (THE SHADOW *later* THE WARDER; *and* THE SHADOW) A20, 35; B13; C319

Here's the dream I love, (A DREAM *later* THE FOND DREAM) A135; C2473; D11

Here's the great skill of the race— and whither bound? (CARFAX) A52, 68

Herein, we travel far (GATE TO POETRY) A171

High summer came: the tall hedge by the road (SONG OF SUMMER MID-NIGHT) A7

High up here I live [*later* Here aloft I live,] (MY ROOM) A97; C2991

His sleeping or his waking mind (THE ECCENTRIC) A25, 35

Horses, their heads together under a tree; (VILLAGE SKETCH) A64, 68, 135, 176; C1491

Hot pursuit has done its worst, and here stand we, (TO SYLVA ON THE MOUNTAINSIDE) A68

How blue the sky, how deep its calm (FROM VERLAINE: LE CIEL EST, PAR-DESSUS LE TOIT) C502

How bright a dove's wing shows against the sky (11TH R.S.R.) A10, 35, 135, 176

How came such minutes, such inimitables (MARCHING BACK TO PEACE 1916) A64, 68

How cold those tops of the sharp arches are! (THE CHILD IN CHURCH) A156; C2500

How fondly still the Grecian form (EARLY AND LATE) A25, 35

How is it with you, famous Time, (CHRONOMACHY OR ONE OF US IS NOT TIRED YET *later* A CHRONOMACHY) A68; C1762

How joyously the south's large rain (ZUAUSQUES) C1836

How like a large and cheerful family show (A VIEW FROM THE DEPART-MENT OF ENGLISH *later* A VIEW FROM A HONG KONG OFFICE; *and* VIEW FROM THE UNIVERSITY OF HONG KONG) A156; B196; C3114

"How lovely are the messengers that preach us the gospel of peace." (COM-PANY COMMANDER, 1917) A68

How lovely it was, when all that came my way (A CHANGE) A68

How many a morning at my first awaking (TO ETHELBERT WHITE [ii]) B116

How many deaths, extinctions what a host (CHILDREN PASSING) A89; C2443

How old I grow, how out of date, (NOT SO DEAD) A64, 68

How quietly the by-road turns away (A PATROL) A77

How shall this thing be done? (THE SCIENTISTS) A67-8

How surpassingly happy the musician (THE HAPPIEST) A77

How soon these little girls run round the lovely lake (untitled) A171

How sweet in infancy I found (DISTRESS) B105

How sweetly passed, but swiftly too, (SERENITY) p. xiv

How sweetly sound those western village bells (TO JOJUN DEGUCHI) A171

How swift and smooth this water glinters past! (WATCHING RUNNING WATER) A35; C3352

How that territory called them ("KNOW'ST THOU THE LAND . . . ?") A97

How unpurposed, how inconsequential (GOUZEAUCOURT: THE DECEIT-FUL CALM) A28, 35

I always thought to find my love (THE COVERT) A10, 35, 135

I am for the woods against the world, (THE KISS) A40, 45, 68, 108, 135; C1100

I am Forgetfulness. I am that shadow (ANOTHER ALTAR) A45, 68, 135; C1223

I am only the phrase (INTIMATIONS OF MORTALITY) A17, 20, 35, 135; C471

I am the god of things that burrow and creep, (THE GODS OF THE EARTH BENEATH) A5-6, 8, 35

I am the *Poems* of the late *Eliza Cook*, (AN EMINENT VICTORIAN *later* AN
OMINOUS VICTORIAN) A52, 68, 135; C1319
I ask but little; and I ask far more (THE DEEPS) A20, 35; C524
I came to the churchyard where pretty Joy lies (THE CHILD'S GRAVE) A10,
35, 43*b*, 135, 174; B9; E*d*6
I can't go back to Then. (CABARET TUNE) A64, 68
"I could never do it, but my son perhaps can. (TOMKINS) A100; C2532
I do not know for sure how much I dream, ([SONNET] ON THE ENGLISH
POETS NOW FORGOTTEN [ii]) A7
I encouraged you, you said; but you encourage me more. (TO T. KITAMURA)
A171
I fell wishing that the room in which I was pent, [*later* Wishing that the room
where I darkened closely pent,] (THE TOWER) A89; B97
I gather from a survey of ('SENTIMENTAL') A52, 68
I grudge a year, or hardly that, (GROWN UP) A52, 68
I had a visitor, one of a host (AN AUTOLYCUS *later* AUTOLYCUS AGAIN:
IN MEMORY OF B.D.) A156; C2496
I haunt a waterfall, (A SONG *later* THE WATERFALL) A77, 135; B101;
C1961
I have been a pleasant ramble, (THE STREAMSIDE) A1, 3
I have been young, and now am not too old; (REPORT ON EXPERIENCE)
A31, 35, 108, 135, 169, 174, 176; E*d*4, 6
I have sold my cow. (EIGHT JAPANESE POEMS [viii]) C3105
I hear from winters long ago (UP, UP!) A171
I hear you now, I hear you, shy perpetual companion, (ON READING THAT
THE REBUILDING OF YPRES APPROACHED COMPLETION) A28,
35, 135
I heard the challenge "Who goes there?" (THE WATCHERS) A28, 35, 135;
B260; C632
I heard the graybird bathing in the rill, (OCTOBER COMES) A77; C1938
I knew your power, I thought, and I was wrong: (TO A FRIEND) A68
I laughed; a joyful joke to see (THE STARLING'S NEST) A43
I let the radio go. The hour was late. (ON THE AIR) A156; C3184
"I like my twilight walk as well as you, (THE TOAD) A52, 68; C1300
I live still, to love still (SEERS) A156, 176
I looked across the fields and saw a light (THE ENGLISH POETS) A14, 20,
35, 174; C310
I love my hill, and you would love it too (THE HILL) A52, 68
I love to see those loving and beloved (LONELY LOVE) A64, 68, 135
I loved her in my innocent contemplation (NATURE DISPLAYED) A25, 35;
C674
I loved the cottage at first sight, (AMONG THE HILLS) A102; C2570
I picked this flower for you upon the hill, ("I PICKED THIS FLOWER")
A2-3
I ran along, I sang alone; (THE FARMHOUSE FAMILY) A135; C3107
I saw an angel white high over me, (APPARITION) A2-3
I saw the sunlit vale, and the pastoral fairy-tale; (THE FAILURE *later* THE
SUNLIT VALE) A35, 108, 135, 174; C899; E*d*4, 6
I saw three graces under dark green boughs, (WRITTEN IN THE WOMAN'S
CHRISTIAN COLLEGE, TOKYO) A168, 171
I see (EIGHT JAPANESE POEMS [vii]) C3105
I see you walking (ANOTHER JOURNEY FROM BÉTHUNE TO CUINCHY)
A28, 35

609

In *France*, no matter what the Town, there stood (A TALE NOT IN CHAU-
CER) A43*b*, 45, 68; C1180
In glades where forst is ambushed in the ferns, (THUS FAR) A17, 20, 35;
B23; C472
In Goro Katayama's page (untitled) B283.1
In happy hours, some hours, I spring; (INVITATION *later* POETRY'S INVI-
TATION) A64, 68, 135; C1565
In Horyuji all the world agrees (A SMALL OFFERING) A171
In human paths, delightful as they show, (THE AMBUSH) A64, 68; C1550
In Oxford he must be sought, along (A THOUGHT OF H.I.H. PRINCE CHI-
CHIBU) A171
In solitude, we say—but good society (A WOODLAND HOLIDAY: KARUI-
ZAWA) A97
In summer-time when haymaking's there (LIBERTINE) A25, 35, 135
In sunbright years (A PASTORAL TO MADELINE) A68, 135
In the avenues of yesterday (TIMBER) A77, 174
In the bright shallow of this broadened dyke, (MISUNDERSTANDINGS) A20,
35; C518
In the dusk a wind came on (A POEM DREAMED) A7; C14
In the evenings of Autumn, when sad sad mists crept out from the river (THE
DEAD BROTHER) A1, 3
In the gate of old Japan, where her modern life began (NAGASAKI OLD AND
NEW) A106
In the green Indian-corn first evening airs are playing, (SOUTH-EAST ENG-
LAND IN 1944 *later* "SOUTHERN ENGLAND" IN 1944) A89; B103;
C2056
In the long, loud lash of the rain and the wind, (KESTREL FARM, 1796) A1,
3; C8
In the meadow by the mill (FIRST RHYMES) A14, 20, 35, 174; C446
In the night, in the night the wild harp answered best; (SPIRIT-WIND) C2924
In the sharpness of need, the mind (LET JOE DO IT) A67–8
In the stubble blossoms (THE ESCAPE) A25, 35
In the vast senselessness (LANDSCAPE) C533
In the warm wood bedipped with rosy day (THE DOOMED OAK: FROM
THE FRENCH OF ANATOLE FRANCE) A16, 25, 35; C513
[In the woods bright, green outlines glitter (A SMALL PIECE OF SPRING)]
D18
In these old country nooks, it is far from plain to see (AT MAPLEDURHAM
IN WAR-TIME *later* AT MAPLEDURHAM) A89; C2442
In this small room it happens we have none (RANDOM TRIBUTES TO
BRITISH PAINTERS) B268
In winter moonlight, thinking of many things (1952) C2894
In you we see the spirit which attains (A SCHOLAR) A106
Inconstancy, too rarely (AND THEN) A64, 68, 135
Ingenious Beauty making love to Love, (THE ADORNED *later* THE ADORN-
ING) A156; C2679
Into the blue undisturbable main (FROM THE FLYING-BOAT) A89, 135;
B224; E*d*3
Is it the light that makes the silence (IN WEST FLANDERS) A67–8, 135
Is not this enough for moan (TO JOY) A14, 20, 35, 43*b*, 108, 135; C619;
E*d*5.1
It has been known how even in war (THE GRACE) C3152
It is a country, (THE PROPHET) A17, 28, 35
It is but open the door of this walled den, (THE IMMOLATION) A25, 35
It is not growing like a Tree (untitled) E*a*20

611

It is not in the shining, countless ways (THE FAIR HUMANITIES OF OLD RELIGION) A7

It is not wholly past, the time enrolled (HOMES AND HAUNTS) A89, 135; B108, 224; C2041; E*d*3

It may be so: their love was never fire, (A NOT UNUSUAL CASE) A68, 135

"It must be so; it is clearly meant:" *later* "It must be so: it is planned and meant"; (MOUNTAIN ONE NOVEMBER MORNING, THE *later* THE MOUNTAIN) A97; C2463

"It must be so: it is planned and meant: *see* "It must be so; it is clearly meant:"

It needs no word of ours: your fame (TO MR AND MRS HANI) A171; B143

It seemed the tranquil morning-landscape's mind (PICARDY IN AUTUMN *later* PICARDY SUNDAY) A156; C2903

It shall be written: (untitled) A171; B229

It should not be changed. Are there not some things (THE MEADOW FOR EVER) B257

It was not mine to know your younger strength, (L.A. *later* LASCELLES ABERCROMBIE) A77, 108, 135; C1947

It was the Spring, the pleasant Spring, (LYRICAL BALLAD) C1753

It winds on still, the glassy brook (DR JOHNSON REVISITS A MILL STREAM AT LICHFIELD) B247; C2745

Japanese friends and others all, (PROLOGUE [THE TAMING OF THE SHREW]) A165, 171; B261

Journeying through the shade of sleep, (THE MAN IN THE STREET) A77

"Jump to it," roared a thunderous voice; "Fall in," another bawled; ("AGE 200") A68; B82

Just see what's happening, Worley!—Worley rose (PILLBOX) A17, 28, 35; B260; C830

Keiko commanded, and we met (untitled) A171

Kentish hamlets gray and old, (THE MEMORY OF KENT) A7

Kikue-san, we here express (TO KIKUE-SAN) A106

Kind Usk, among thy flowers, whose wave (TO THE RIVER USK) A23

Kind was the hand that at the last (ON THE DEATH-MASK OF JOHN CLARE *later* THE DEATH-MASK [etc.]) A17, 20, 35, 135

Late into the lulling night the pickers toiled, (UNEASY PEACE) A35

Leaning against the barrow which displayed (JIM'S MISTAKE) A67-8

Learned in life, across white fields (EXPERIENCE TEACHES . . .) A52, 68

Led by great WALPOLE, at th' accustomed Task (CHAPTERS OF LITERARY HISTORY: VERY LITTLE KNOWN) A52; C1327

Leisurely over lea and grove and stream (SHELLS BY A STREAM) A77; B98; C1916

Let Shaw write Shakespeare into note, (ANTHEM PRELIMINARY TO THE MASSACRE) B81

Let the dead leaves lie (THE OLD AND THE NEW) A1, 3

Let us speak to those afar, (TOWARDS THE FUTURE) C2516

Let's go hunting whatever's in the picture. (A FAMILY DISCOURSE) A156

Life, be kind to all these hastening (LIFE, BE KIND) B273

Light and busy wings, beating this bright air; (ON SOME CROCUSES: AT TRINITY COLLEGE) A45, 68

Like a great bat's wing angled on the West (EVENING MUSIC) A26, 35

Like a long roof, men say, and well they say, *see* Like a long roof, they say, [etc.]

612

Like a long roof, they say, and well they say, [*later* Like a long roof, men say, [etc.]] (A FIRST VISIT TO YASHIMA *later* YASHIMA IN WINTER) A97, 122; B189; C2501

Like as the rose upon the branch in May (SONNET) A2-3

Like men of fire, in painful night, (BUILDING THE LIBRARY, NIGHT SCENE, TOKYO UNIVERSITY *later* BUILDING THE LIBRARY, TOKYO UNIVERSITY) A26, 31, 35; B291; C604

Like mourners filing into church at a funeral, (TREES ON THE CALAIS ROAD) A35, 135

Lily-white and rosy-red (RONDEL) A2-3

Limned in the lake the rosy portraiture (THE ORNAMENTAL WATER) A77; C1983

Listen, and lose not the sweet luring cry, (LEISURE) A8, 35, 135; B2

Little and great ones, young ones, old ones (VERSE) B12

Little boy, on your road to the School, (ECOLIER: THE SCHOLAR) C3209

Little enough of that wide country (THE SPELL OF FRANCE) A64, 68; C1609

Live in that land, fair spirit and my friend, (THE RESIGNATION) A25, 35, 135

Long have we travelled in the realms of fear (MODERN TIMES) A168

Look with what Titan majesty arise (CLOUD-LIFE) A25, 35

Looking from my upstairs window any night I saw (TWO OF US) C3245

Looking on Sussex from afar I find (A SOUTHERN PILGRIM) A156; B203

"Lord, how enchanting is the flow (A COUNTRY CHARACTER: HOMO UNIUS LIBRI) A77; C1881

Lord Randall started up in's bed, (A BALLAD OF TITLES) A65; C1661

Loud the wind leaps through the night and fills the valley with his wings, (THE SPELL) A14, 20, 35; C360

Lovely, lovely, lovely child, (BEAUTY IN THE MOUNTAIN) A67-8

Lover of solitude and those wild tracks (IN HOKKAIDO: A LETTER IN VERSE, AND IN THE ROMANTIC MANNER) A156; C2981

Love's a curious praiser ('VERY JEWELS IN THEIR FAIR ESTATE') A20, 35

Lucky and pretty Light! smiling on me (A MORNING PIECE: WRITTEN IN ABSENCE) A25, 35; C702

Man, the inventive, with his ceaseless power (BOOKS) A171; B178; C2523

Manda's twig-like arms (THE UNKNOWN QUANTITY) A20, 35

Mankind!—so said the voice to me; (APPEAL) A97, 176

Many the poems offered through the years (TO MR ITO, MAYOR OF MATSUSHIMA) A171

Many words may never find (untitled) A171

Map me the World, and watch you mark (RELIQUES) A20, 35

Marie, forth from your bed: my lady, wake! (AUBADE) A2-3

Mary, what news?— (untitled) A12

Mary with her white hands pressed (A PARAPHRASE) C276

Melodious is that name Matsushima; (MATSUSHIMA) A86, 97; B189, 291; C2563; D8

Men pass; and cities pass; and yet the years (OSAKA IN RECONSTRUCTION) A85

[Men seek the road of peace everywhere, (A POEM OF A FEW LINES OFFERED TO CHINESE AUTHORS)] D1

Merrily under the trees they ran (JAPANESE GLIMPSES *later* THREEFOLD SCREEN) A156; C2698

Mild hearts, and modest as the evening bell (THE WARTONS AND OTHER EARLY ROMANTICS *later* THE WARTONS AND OTHER EARLY ROMANTIC LANDSCAPE-POETS; *and* THE WARTONS AND OTHER LANDSCAPE POETS) A25, 35, 135; C676

Mind and soul a halting brook (FRAGMENTS *later* THE CHANCE) A25, 35; C520

Mirror of wall and tree, of cloud and star, (REFLECTIONS) A52, 68, 135, 169, 176

Moated and granged, recall the Gentry who (DEPARTED: OR, 'TIS TWENTY YEARS SINCE) A64, 68, 135; C1408

Moonlight and water mist (TO THE MEMORY OF COLERIDGE) A77, 135

Moonsweet the summer evening locks (AN EVENSONG *later* SHEEPBELLS) A8, 35, 135; C30

More rarely now the echo of these men (INSCRIBED IN WAR-BOOKS I) A45

Morning, if this late withered light can claim (THE ZONNEBEKE ROAD) A17, 28, 35, 135, 174; B44; C829; Ed6

Mother of arts, and nature's child, (AN OFFERING) C2430

Mourn, though no Lady Isabeau (EPITAPH) B12

Moveth atween the spires and roofs (DREAM CITY) A1, 3

Moving through those nights (NIGHTS BEFORE BATTLE) A64, 68

Mown, strown are the grayhead grasses, (STANE STREET) A5-6, 35

Much has been writ of wraiths and ghostly things, (MELANCHOLIA) A1, 3

Musical both in soul and skill, you own (BRING YOUR MUSIC) B211; C3215

My Christmas Card O, ([GREETINGS FOR NEVILLE ROGERS, 1954]) B292

My darling, what a power is yours (JOY AND MARGARET) A89, 135

My hesitant design it was, in a time when no man feared, (AFTER THE BOMBING) A89, 135

My humdrum life has been (SPEECH BY A HAMLET IN THE AMIENS DISTRICT) A156

My Queen, Queen of Paphos; Venus, O hear. (A GIRL'S INVOCATION) A97

My soul, dread not the pestilence that hags (PREPARATIONS FOR VICTORY) A17, 28, 35, 135

Nailed to these green laths long ago, (MALEFACTORS) A8, 35, 135

Never again shall we go to the woods, for the laurels are felled. (NEVER AGAIN) A2-3

New-silver-cresented the moon forth came (THE NEW MOON) A35

Nine fluffy sparrows in a shrub (HARBOUR SKETCH: WRITTEN IN ABSENCE) A89

No, do not tell me; have I not conceded (CHANGE AND SONG) A97, 135

No more am I what I have been, (ON MYSELF) A2-3

No one will ever be living in that tall house, (THE INACCESSIBLE HOUSE) A64, 68

No ship perhaps again will ever bear (THE LOST NAME) A77

No sooner was I come to this strange roof, (A "FIRST IMPRESSION" TOKYO *later* "A FIRST IMPRESSION") A18, 20, 26, 35, 135; B15; C481

No stranger yet no friendlier call (THOMASINE) A77, 135

No sunbeam clearer (THE MEANS *later* FOR THE COUNTRY LIFE) A77, 174; B90; Ed6

Not far from the lane is the broken mill (THE WICKED MILLER OF REDLANDS) A4, 6

'Not to drink wine,' said The Rambler, (AS BOSWELL RECORDS) A135; C3033

Not your least glory, many-gloried Wren, (ORNITHOPOLIS) A25, 35, 135; B23; C584

"Now all are gone, and I a moment pause, (NATURE AND THE LOST) A77

Now all the birds are flown, the first, the second brood (HIGH SUMMER) A10, 35, 135; C288

Now everything that shadowy thought (IN FESTUBERT) A8, 35, 135

Now golden-russet apples bend to ground (HOPES AND HARVESTS) A1, 3

Now here assembled, old and young, (HYMN) B240

Now out of rainy veils I come all calm, (VOICE OF AUTUMN) A156; B139; C2542

Now over hill and dale in Shakespeare's England (SONNET) B252; C3321

Now ragged clouds in the west are heaping, (EVENING MYSTERY) A10, 35, 135; B23; C283

Now the day is dead, I cried, (OMEN) A17, 20, 35; C496

Now the snows are gone, and the green comes to the leas, (SPRING-TIME, DEATH) A97

Now the snows have gone (EIGHT JAPANESE POEMS [iv]) C3105

Now the white-flowering days (THE WHITE-FLOWERING DAYS) B157; C3029; E d2

Now the wild strawberry has put forth his flower (EVENING WALKS) A43a

Now the world grows weak again, the sinewed woods are all astrain, (THE LAST RAY) A20, 35, 135

Now to attune my dull soul, if I can, (BLEUE MAISON) A35, 135

Now while the serious sort declare (AN ASIDE) A40, 45, 68

Now while the winter wind at last, (THE WINTER WALK) A77, 135

Now you can hardly prove (TO SYLVA) A52, 68

Now you shall see what once took great Queen Bess (PROLOGUE [TWELFTH NIGHT]) A197

Numberless voices needs must arise (VOICES IN TOKYO) A85, 89; B224; C2445; E d3

O All ye Courtiers and ye Cits (LORET'S ODE) B12

O 'ave you never 'eard the Tale (THE COOK'S STORY, OR NEVER NO MORE!) C18

O England! lose not now, O never lose (STANZAS: MIDSUMMER 1937) A64, 68, 135

O God in whom my deepest being dwells, (A PSALM) A14, 20, 35, 135

O happiest village! how I turned to you, (OLD HOMES) A11, 20, 35, 135; C318

O how comely it was and how reviving (AT SENLIS ONCE) A17-18, 28, 35, 43b, 108, 135, 174; C828

O I confess, without a wound (THE FLASHING FLINT: FROM THE LATIN OF HENRY VAUGHAN later THE FLASHING FLINT) A23; C500

O lightening love that makes drab lanes (THE VICTOR) A77, 135; C1927

O my stern mother, aye, to that name loved, (TO NATURE) A14, 20, 35; C354

O Nymph, that through the drowsy thicket fliest, (TO ECHO) A23

O road in dizzy moonlight bleak and blue, (LA QUINQUE RUE) A28, 35, 135

O rosy red, O torrent splendour (ZERO later COME ON, MY LUCKY LADS; and ZERO 1916) A17, 28, 35, 135; B260

'O ship, the winds once more will bear you (JAPAN REVIVED) A156

O the days when I was young! (THE SELF-IMPRISONED) A14

O well I know, and well I like, and warmly long to see (TO A PLANNER) A89; C2014

October gone, dank lies the land, and dreary; (THE RUNNERS) A1, 3; C6

Of men I met you were the quietest, (AN EMPTY CHAIR [CHAS. E.B.]) A156

'Of old, this sweet domestic touch (untitled) B293

Often a thought breaks in upon my mind ([SONNET] ON THE ENGLISH POETS NOW FORGOTTEN [iii]) A7

Old Broadbridge Pond, once on a time so deep, (THE DRIED MILL POND) A10, 35; B6

Old friend, I know you line by line, (A RECOGNITION *later* RECOGNITION) A17, 28, 35, 135

Old hamlets with your groves of flowers (FAR EAST) A19, 26, 31, 35, 174; C555

'Old Shakespeare?' said the Town, the clever Town (SEVENTEENTH-CENTURY FASHION) A156

Old town of France, the wish to walk (RHYMES ON BETHUNE, 1916) A68, 135

"Old we shall find him; eighty years (OCTOGENARIAN) A77; C1967

Old weeds upthrust in pasture wide half cheat (WINTER ENDING) A64, 68

Omicron, who with just and vigorous wit (untitled) C509

On a rainy June morning (untitled) A171

On lonely Kinton Green all day (WILDERNESS) A8, 35; C36

On the far hill the cloud of thunder grew (PERCH FISHING) A8, 35; B2, 9

On the roof-ridge stops the sparrow to enjoy his bit of bread, (RIVAL APPETITES *later* RIVAL FEASTS) A89, 135; C2178; D30

On the straggling scanty hedge out there (AINU CHILD) A102

On the temple's great bell (EIGHT JAPANESE POEMS [iii]) C3105

Once again the Siren sang: (AN OLD SONG) A156

Once I was only for the ladies bright, (HORACE RENOUNCES LOVE) A97

Once more above the gale that square dark tower (THE VOICE OF THE PAST *later* STORMY NIGHT) A52, 68; C1276

Once on a time before I heard (ON READING A MAGAZINE EDITED BY OSCAR WILDE) A89, 135; C2068

Once on a time might you or I (UNRECORDED) A135; C3127

Once we three in Nara walked (THE QUICK AND THE DEAD) A26, 31, 35, 135

One fell a'roaring lyke a bull, (untitled) B105

One hour from far away! each man we had [*later* One hour from far returns: Each [etc.]] (THE HALTED BATTALION: 1916 *later* THE HALTED BATTALION) A89, 135; C2285

One hour from far returns: Each man we had *see* One hour from far away! [etc.]

One starry night, alone beside the sea (ECSTASY) A2-3

"Only not infinite!" Sometimes drowsily (ONLY NOT INFINITE) C2480

Opening the narrow tottering door, alone (AFTER THREE YEARS) A2-3

Osaka, of old majesty and new, (CAPTAINCY) A171

Othello is our play and I appear, (PROLOGUE [OTHELLO]) B245

Our company is met once more, and you, (PROLOGUE [AS YOU LIKE IT]) A136; B206

Our great Charles Dickens in years long past (AFTER "ROMEO AND JULIET" [etc.]) C3258

Our landlord intending more custom to win (DOES THE SAME CAUSE ALWAYS PRODUCE THE SAME EFFECT? *later* ART AND NATURE) A43a; C857

Our play is old, and new, and from its glooms (PROLOGUE [ROMEO AND JULIET]) B231

Out of the centuries, Moji is making (MOJI ON THE SEA) A106; B135

Out of the night a miniature, (THE EXPLORER) C3257

Out of the past what graciousness still grows, (FOR THE CENTENARY OF RABINDRANATH TAGORE) A156; C3266

Out of the sparkling flood of green (IN SUMMER *later* THE ROTUNDA) A42, 45, 68; B57

Outside, the night, the lamps of distant farms (untitled) A171

Over the streams and roofs the moon rides high: (AIRCRAFT) A77; C1953

Over these evening waters, snowy-crested, (NEARING YOKOHAMA, 15 AUGUST 1960) A156; B291

Painfully writhed the few last weeds upon those flatted uplands; [*later* [. . .] houseless uplands,] (AN INFANTRYMAN) A25, 35, 135, 174; C701

Painfully writhed the few last weeds upon those houseless uplands, *see* Painfully writhed [. . .] flatted uplands

Passing; exposed to a strange new hour— (I JUST NOTICED . . .) A67–8

Past the mines and past the workshops (NEWSTEAD ABBEY *later* NEWSTEAD [BYRONIANA, II]) A89, 135; C2101

Pausing in the churchyard here, I feel anew (THE NOVEMBER HOUR) A56

Perched in a tower of this ancestral Wall, (AT THE GREAT WALL OF CHINA) A135, 169, 176; C3168; E*d*4

Perched upon the templed height (THE TOURIST (NEAR KOMORO)) A85

Perhaps no greater wonder than ('A MUSIQUE, SOLDIER') A64, 68

Perpetual are these hills, these ways (TAKAMATSU COUNTRYSIDE) A171

Physician, from the blest abodes of light (TO DR. I. LETTSOM) A52, 68

Pitch-dark night shuts in, and the rising gale *see* The pitch-dark night [etc.]

Poets there are whose songs are for the few: (SONNET *incorporated in* JANUARY EVENING SUSSEX, 1914) A1, 3; C9

Poppies never brighter shone, and never sweeter smelled the hay, (WOULD YOU RETURN?) A25, 35, 135; B25; C591

Pour forth, shrill sparkling brook, your deathless wave, (RELEASE) A25, 35

Presume not that grey idol with the scythe (A CONNOISSEUR) A31, 35, 135; C780

Princess, I dare be sure of this, (THE COMIC MUSE) B12

Princess whom all Observers view (STANZAS) B12

Professing loud energy, out of the junction departed (THE BRANCH LINE) A52, 68, 108, 135, 174; C1292; E*d*6

Proud is assembly, and the anthem proud (ON A BIOGRAPHICAL DICTIONARY) A31, 35; C796

Pull the curtains across; (AGE) A100; C2529

Rain-sunken roof, grown green and thin (THE BARN) A4, 6, 8, 35, 135, 176; B23; C929

Rainbows on flying foam, glitterings of high-sunned cloud, (ONE KIND OF ARTIST) A77; C1887

Receive, most modest scholar, this (A MODEST SCHOLAR) A106

Replies as certain as the daffodil (SONNET) B252; C3321

Rest there, dear dust, beneath the lichened stone, (IN HELPSTON CHURCHYARD *later* TO JOHN CLARE) A14; B13

Rest you well among your race, you who cannot be dead; (A.G.A.V.) A28, 35, 135

617

Retarded into history's marble eyes (THE ONLY ANSWER *later* FROM AGE TO AGE) A52, 68, 108, 135; C1268

'Rise from your grave, Charles Waterton,' (A PRAYER FOR THE BIRDS) A89, 135; C2431; D25

Roadhouse to roadhouse swell the strain, (THE ART OF POETRY. [iv] PASTORAL) A52

Rooks in black constellations slowly wheeling (THE LONG TRUCE) A14, 20, 35

Rosanthe, while some doleful Bards commend (CHRISTMAS INVITATION FOR 1756 *later* sub-title added: PRE-TELEPHONE) A156; C3182

Rosy belief uplifts her spires (TOGETHER *later* AN ANCIENT PATH) A25, 35, 135; C559

Round all its nooks and corners goes ("THE CROWN" *later* THE CROWN INN) A17, 20, 35, 135

Round us the pines are darkness (A JAPANESE EVENING) A35, 174

Said God, Go, spirit, thou hast served me well (THE TROUBLED SPIRIT) A10, 35

Saints from the old world sounding on (CHIMES AT MIDNIGHT) A135, 176

Sallows like heads in Polynesia, (INTO THE SALIENT) A35

Seagull, crow and wagtail (PASTURE) A64, 68

Seas like Roman glass, (THE SUBTLE CALM) A64, 68

Secret and soft as a summer cloud that blooms (THE UNQUIET EYE) A25, 35

See to this ivy bush what hundreds hurry, (THE IVY BUSH *later* THE IVY BUSH IN AUTUMN) A89; C2155

See what lovely hours you lost (AFTER ANY OCCASION) A68, 135

Seeking no more (PRESENT DISCONTENTS) A64, 68; C1574

Set in a circlet of silver rain, (THE RIVER HOUSE) A4, 6, 35

Shall we not also join the friends (FREEDOM OF POPERINGE) A167; C3347

Shall we upon de Troye or Mignard call (EPIGRAM ON THE PORTRAIT OF SCARAMOUCH) B12

Shattering remembrance, mercy! Not again (MILLSTREAM MEMORIES) A156

She lies on that white breast she loves, and well (1919 *later* "FOR THERE IS NO HELP IN THEM") A25, 35; C521

'She's off to Madagascar, (THE SHOP DOOR) A20

Shot from the zenith of desire (THE SURPRISE) A52, 68, 135

Shrill and small the wind in the reeds and sedges, (VERSES IN REMINISCENCE AND DELIGHT) A45, 68

Signs and wonders fill (THE STONE GARDEN (KYÔTO)) A156, 169; B291; C3291; D13

Silent they stand and into silence hoard (INTO THE DISTANCE) A52, 68

Since our most beautiful and subtle game *see* When of all games [etc.]

"Sir, I cannot profess to understand (CRICKET, I CONFESS) A64, 68, 108, 135, 169, 176

Sir, though I volunteered no jubilant ode (EMPIRE DAY) C2467

Sky beyond words! Elysian-field (THE STORM) A25, 35; C681

Smells like sluggish smelly stoves, (BRITISH MUSEUM BLUES (I WAIT FOR A BOOK)) C1735

Smiles from strangers met but once, (CHANCE PLEASURES) A68; C1736

So after flights of years, the genius reappears; (JAMES CLARENCE MANGAN) A156; C3190

So from slow silence, strange one, sing: (A NEW SONG) A156

So have you lived, that finer life may be; (untitled) A171
So much he had already given (TAGORE'S PAINTINGS) B246
So once we saw him, and no more (ON A PICTURE OF H.I.H. PRINCE CHI-
CHIBU) A171
So rise, enchanting haunting faithful (THE SUM OF ALL) A68, 108, 135;
C1744
So sigh, that hearkening pasts arouse (THE TREE IN THE GOODS YARD)
A89, 135; B224; E*d*3
So soon as the news reached Flanders— (AN ANCIENT, BUT JUBILANT BAL-
LAD 1696) A45, 68; C1208
So talk ran on, and turning like a lane (THE ECLOGUE) A14, 20, 35; B10;
C314
So that a multitude (ON BLOOD TRANSFUSION II *later* TRANSLATED
FROM THE JAPANESE OF H.M. EMPRESS NAGAKO II) A171; B227
So the fierce beauty of this princely play (THE EPILOGUE FOR KING JOHN)
A48
So there's my year, the twelvemonth duly told (HARVEST) A17, 20, 35, 135;
C483; E*d*5.1
So you have chosen, saying little, knowing (THE BOY ON LEAVE) A77;
C1926
Softly, ivy, steal upon (EPITAPH FOR SOPHOCLES) A40, 45, 68
Some day in England [SOME DAY IN ENGLAND] B125
Some found an owl's nest in the hollow skull (BATTALION IN REST, JULY,
1917) A17, 28, 35, 135; C506
Some men, we say, are sent before their time; (THE AUTHOR OF "THE
GREAT ILLUSION") A35; B37
Some of us were unlucky; ("FOR THE FALLEN") A89
Some pause (SIXPENCE TO THE RIVER) A64, 68, 135
Some said that the streets of Corymbe [*later* Some say [etc.]] (SOME SAID
... *later* A RECOLLECTION IN A FAR YEAR) A68; B90
Some say that in the streets of Corymbe *see* Some said [etc.]
Some still remember—though not many now (A NEW CITY HALL (1962))
C3270.2
Some time the English name in sport was good, (AN INTERNATIONAL
FOOTBALL MATCH) A64, 68
Some tune or phrase, some scene or face, (A REMEMBRANCE) A77
Soon the chanting that first I took (ARRIVAL AT A RIVER, IN JAPAN)
A156; C3174
Soon we shall know; and soon we shall not know, (untitled) A67
Sound, sound, immortal Tempest, through the dark, (THE SPRING GALE)
A77, 135
Sous la lune le plomb de la tourelle (LA GIROUETTE) A37
Sparkling with the west winds dancing along the tansies, (GODSTOW) A68;
B91
Sparse mists of moonlight hurt our eyes (FESTUBERT: THE OLD GERMAN
LINE) A35, 135
Speak, Elia, from afar, with eyes still bent (ON CHARLES LAMB'S BIRTH-
DAY 1945 *later* ON CHAS. LAMB'S [etc.]) A97; C2108
Spell of the mournful holy night (NIGHT PIECE) A14
Standing on the shaded knoll (A COUNTRY GIRL) A1, 3
Startling all spirits, dreams, and secrets (TO OUR CATCHMENT BOARD)
A67-8; C1754
Stay, kingfisher, so fleet along (YOU NEVER STAY) A67-8

Steal abroad, your time is come; doubt not once the new-blown hour. (FRAG-MENT) A31, 35; C898

Still in deep winter, the war country lies (ARMISTICE: A MARCH) A168

Still must I listen? Must the B.B.C. (THE ART OF POETRY. [ii] SATIRE) A52

Still the mild shower grows on; amid the drops (A WINDOW IN GERMANY: AUGUST 1939) A68; B92; C1775

Stone ghost, (THE TOWER) A43a, 108, 135

Strange chord! the weir-pool's tussling dance, (WINTER NIGHTS) A27, 35, 135

Strenuous to live the life for which he came, (THESE PROBLEMS) A68

Such light calm moonrise never gave, (LOVELIGHT) A77

Such surge of black wings saw I never homing (THE EVIL HOUR) A89; C2419

Suddenly the other side of this world wide, (THE VISITOR) A31, 35, 135; C881

Summers to be will shine on the new city, (SHINDO-SAN) A171

Suppose the heavens still dominate our day, (TO J.A.) A68

Sway those green worlds of leaves, dear summer ghost (THE UNEXPECTED VICTORY later SPIRIT-WIND) A52, 68; B65

Sweet conversations, coppice incantations [later [. . .] woodland incantations] (THE SUMMER RAINSTORM later SUMMER RAINSTORM) A31, 35, 135; C877

Sweet conversations, woodland incantations see Sweet conversations, coppice incantations

Sweet sing the verse, while this we sing: (THOSE WHO FIRST ENCOURAGED US) A135; C2502

Sweet this morning incense, kind (HALF A CENTURY) A89, 135, 169, 176

Swift away the century flies, (THE AFTERMATH) A14, 20, 35

Swift, sleekit, glamorous, our High Priestie (A.M.H. OUR LEADER AND IN-SPIRER) B249

"Tell it not here, it needs no saying," (TO YUKICHI NAKAMURA) A171

Tell me now in what hidden way is (ECHO DE L'AUTRE GUERRE later BALLAD OF THE SERGEANTS OF OTHER DAYS) A156; C3164

Ten thousand miles from land are we, (THOUGHTS OF A ROMANTIC) A12

That flying angel's torrent cry see This flying angel's [etc.]

That grey-green river pouring past, (THE EMBRYO) A20, 35; C523

That I might watch the bells of wild bloom swing ("ART THOU GONE IN HASTE?") A17, 20, 35; C493

That shower-silvery grass where the damson-flower drifted (ENTANGLE-MENT) A25, 35

That sudden all-surviving voice (A LIFE'S UNITY) A156; B144; C2648

[That the glory of heaven be bright (untitled)] D35

That we may both receive and give (A SONG FOR KWANSEI) A90, 171; B134

That we may yet transcend the dark will of the storm (A GREEK DEITY: INSCRIBED TO THE APOLLO SOCIETY) A89

That well you draw from is the coldest drink (THE COTTAGE AT CHIGA-SAKI) A52, 68, 135, 169, 176; C1284

That you have given us others endless means (MINORITY REPORT) A64, 68, 135, 169, 176

"That's as that may be, that is; what the Lord will, He bestoweth— (ASK OLD JAPHET) A64, 68

The hoptime came with sun and shower (STORM AT HOPTIME) A8

The impulses of April, the rain-gems, the rose-cloud, (INCIDENT IN HYDE PARK, 1803) A40, 45, 68, 108, 135; C1101

The iron drought, the soulless days (FOR THE EDUCATION INSTITUTE OF AICHI PREFECTURE) A171; B283.1

The labourer hoes on. (EIGHT JAPANESE POEMS [i]) C3105

The last-lighted windows have darkened, (MIDNIGHT) A17, 20, 35; B23

"The Last of the Fancy!" In Sendai! (untitled) B291

The leafiest trees we ever saw, (NEARING THE ANCRE BATTLEFIELD 1916) A64, 68

The library of Alexandria (THOUGHTS ON BOOKS later ORIENTAL TALE) A52, 68; C1230

The listless year goes dimly down, (THE PASSER-BY) A25, 35

The little gate-latch chinked and stopped, (HARDHAM) A7

The loitering wildness (SPRING SONG) A2–3

The manner of this death would make life seem (TO THE MEMORY OF GANDHI later ON READING OF MAHATMA GANDHI'S DEATH) A156; C2491

The meadows are all flooded, and the song (THE RIVER IN FLOOD) A1, 3

The measureless houses of dreams, (DREAM ENCOUNTERS) A31, 35, 135; C849

The moment holds me; pale cool fire (THE SPIRE) A64, 68

The Moon came up to the trysting-place (IDYLL) A1, 3

The moon seems creeping with retarded pace (UNEASY QUIET later TOWN END) A61, 64, 68

The moon was going down; the empty trees shook, sighing, (THE OLD YEAR) A14, 20, 35

The Muse still thoughtful into Nippon flies, (TOKYO: AN UNPUBLISHED PASSAGE FROM GOLDSMITH'S THE TRAVELLER?) C479

The north wind vexes the gravel-pit, shrill from a sky of stone, see The north wind vexes the waterpit out of a sky of stone,

The north wind vexes the waterpit out of a sky of stone, [later [. . .] the gravel-pit, shrill from a sky of stone,] (ASSAULTING WAVES) A135; C2693

The old churchyard has many graves (THE OLD CHURCHYARD) A1, 3

The old horse, clay-stained, comes to talk (HORSE AND COWS) A68

The old waggoner drudges through the miry lane (THE WAGGONER) A8, 18, 35, 43b, 135, 174; C33

The opalescent (BEFORE A RAINY DAYBREAK) A1, 3

The pike all tyranny and teeth (DEPOSED) C2705

The pitch-dark night shuts in, and the rising gale [later Pitch-dark night [etc.]] (PHANTASIES later CLARE'S GHOST) A8, 35, 108, 135, 174; C21

The quiet dew has paled the yellowing sward: (THE TWILIGHT FARM) A7

The rhyme shall yet again relate (untitled) A171

The river runs its never-ending round, (THE DESERTED MILL) A1, 3; C7

The same divinity that gnarls (untitled) A171

The scythesman and the thatcher are not dead, (ON A JOURNEY, 1943) A77

The sea hath its pearls (untitled) A171

The sighing time, the sighing time! (THE SIGHING TIME) A8, 35, 135

The silver eel slips through the waving weeds (WATER MOMENT) A14, 18, 20, 35; C357

The Song itself! thus the majestic rhyme (ON RECEIVING FROM THE CLARENDON PRESS [. . .] CHRISTOPHER SMART'S "SONG TO

DAVID" *later* SONNET ON RECEIVING FROM THE CLARENDON PRESS [etc.]; *and* SONNET ON SMART'S "SONG TO DAVID") A22, 25, 35

The Southern men, the King's defenders, (END OF THE FORTY-FIVE *later* AFTER THE FORTY-FIVE) A40, 45, 68; C1149

The stage was set, the house was packed, (CONCERT PARTY: BUSSEBOOM) A28, 35, 135; B260; Ed4

The starbeam lights, a touch, a breath (THE SECRET) A25, 35; C711

The station roofs curve off and line is lost (RAILWAY NOTE) A67-8

The stream runs on with speed and leisure too (PRODIGAL) A20, 35

The sun's noon throne is hid in hazy cloud ("A VIEW OF THE PRESENT STATE OF IRELAND") A35

The Sun's your radiant painter, he (ON MR. PORTER'S ROOM OF PICTURES *later* ON MR FREDERICK PORTER'S [etc.]) A35; B36

The swallow flew like lightning over the green (THE CORRECT SOLUTION *later* SOLUTIONS) A25, 35, 135; C539

The swallows come on swift and daring wings (THE DAIMYO'S POND) A18, 20, 26, 35; B23, 291; C480

The sweltering day went down to die (NIGHT THUNDER IN WEST SUSSEX) A1, 3

The thatched roofs green with moss and grass stand round, (VILLAGE GREEN) A10, 18, 35; C235

The thin strange fly, silent to human hearing, (THE BUSY FLY) A156; C3244

The thoroughfares that seem so dead to daylight passers-by ("TRANSPORT UP" AT YPRES) A35, 108, 135

The three days' frost waned, and was well-nigh spent; (JANUARY EVENING SUSSEX, 1914) A1, 3; C9

The tide goes out; (EIGHT JAPANESE POEMS [ii]) C3105

The time and place agree; each leaf has grown (A SUMMER'S FANCY) A34, 45, 68

The time comes round when all the faiths and fears (CHRISTMAS EVE 1959) A156; B291

The time grows perilous; forth she comes once more, (AN ANCIENT GODDESS) A35, 135

The time is gone when we could throw (THE TIME IS GONE) A10, 35, 174; B7

The tired air groans as the heavies swing over, the river-hollows boom; (THIEPVAL WOOD) A35

The train with its smoke and its rattle went on, (NO CONTINUING CITY) A20, 35, 135, 174; Ed6

The trunks of trees which I knew glorious green, (EPOCHS; *later* ERAS; *and* ACHRONOS) A17, 20, 35, 135; C499

The turbulence of wild and shattering thought (OCTOBER NIGHTFALL) A1, 3

The turret's leaden carapace (THE WEATHERCOCK) A37; B57

The very blossoms danced to see (GAVOTTE) C25

The village spoke: "You come again, (THE COMPLAINT) A25, 35, 135; C556

The violins that sob (AUTUMN SONG) A2-3

The voice of innocence I heard (THE CHARM) A25, 35; C703

The way was long, the church was cold, (untitled) A171

The weltering air, as warm as tears, (THE LANE) A7

The wheat crowds close, the land falls sharp (WASTE GROUND) A14, 20, 35; C359

623

The white moon shines among the woods: ("SWEETEST MELANCHOLY")
A2-3
The wild rose-bush lets loll (A WATERPIECE) A8, 35, 135; C32
The willow catkins fall on the muddy pool (BROOK IN DROUGHT) A14, 20,
35
The windmill in his smock of white (REUNION IN WAR) A10, 18, 35, 135;
B6; C165
The winter day wanes damp, and cold, and dim (CHRISTMAS EVE 1913) A1,
3
The wood-tops clattering, the green rains pattering, (A SACRILEGE) A7
The world rolls on, and wonders race in orbit,— (PROLOGUE [MIDSUMMER
NIGHT'S DREAM]) B239
The yardman, he with the coins on his watch-chain, stood (OLD REMEDIES)
A35; C1004
The year gains fast; the pear-tree's many buds (SPRING AND CRITICISM)
A67-8
"The years are outfleeting us,"— (NIGHT-SOUNDS) A89
The young moon, refreshed from her lynns of light, (MY WINDOW) A35
The young spring night in all her virtue walks; (TO A SPIRIT) A25, 35
Their houses are not lighted, nor do they (WILD CREATURES AT NIGHT-
FALL) A156, 169
Their spring-breeze from the greenwood moist and warm, (untitled) C3240
Then hither come, smit with desire (SUMMER PEACE [ii]) A1, 3
Then in petals of the air, (THE MESSAGE later PRELUSION; and THE MES-
SAGE) A20, 35; C561
Then it was faith and fairness, (THE AGE OF HERBERT AND VAUGHAN)
A25, 35, 108, 135; C675
Then the Lark, his singing on a sudden done, (MASKS OF TIME) A17, 20, 35,
135
Then: then the days were dark, ("THE HAPPY MORN") A130, 156
Then wallflowers, under lower windows, yield (COUNTRY CHARACTERS)
A68; C1767
There are faces here to-day, (TWENTY MILES FROM TOWN) A135
There are few places in the common path (ON A FLY-LEAF OF CHAUCER'S
WYF OF BATHE) A106
There are four officers, this message says, (ESCAPE) A17, 28, 35
There came before the Emperor Octavius— (A CHRISTMAS TALE: FROM
"THE GOLDEN LEGEND") A97, 156; C3100
There comes a day,— (TO ETHELBERT WHITE [i]) B45
There in a solitude of silence slips (ROSA MUNDI) A17, 20, 35; C473
There is a joy in Spring, (JOY AND GRIEF) A1, 3; C2
There is a mediaeval bridge that spans (TWYFORD BRIDGE) A1, 3
There lay the letters of a hundred friends (DEAD LETTERS) A13, 20, 35,
135; C347
There may be nights to come when I shall need (untitled) A171
There on the white Pacific shore the pines (THE INVIOLATE) A26, 31, 35,
135
There, so dark and still see Where so dark and still
There the puddled lonely lane, (DEATH OF CHILDHOOD BELIEFS) A10,
35, 174; C126
There was a conquering army of the East (PLUNDER) A1, 3
There was a ship, no lady, it was said, (EPITAPH) C452
There was no death but you would face it (FRANK WORLEY, D.C.M.) A135

There was winter in those woods, (RURAL ECONOMY (1917)) A14, 18, 28, 35, 135; C340

There were magicians when my life began (THE TURN OF THE CENTURY) C3346

There, where before no master action struck (OLD BATTLEFIELDS *later* FLANDERS NOW) A28, 35, 135; C606

There will always be gardens where somebody's fancy (OVERHEARD) B201; C3305

There's brilliant moss, there's ginko-fruit (A SABBATH) A106

"There's something in the air," he said, (THE SURVIVORS (1916) *later* TWO VOICES) A17, 28, 35, 135; C475

There's the first cartload of the year, (EIGHT JAPANESE POEMS [v]) C3105

There's the new green verge at the woodside gleaming, (STATION ROAD) A89

These dim-lamped cabins leaning upon the gulf of oceanic night (VILLAGE LIGHTS) A25, 35; C658

These have been much and well described (FLOWERS WALKING) A89

These have marched with towering Fame (CATHEDRALS) A156, 169; B201

These images of quiet, these I should not call (BUT AT LAST) A156

These marched towards Death, or what seemed he, (AN INSCRIPTION *later* INSCRIBED IN WAR-BOOKS II) A45, 68; C1159

'These,' one said who long ago is dead, (SENTENTIAE: IN MEMORIAM SAMUEL WILLIAMS B.A.) A156; B212

These, then, have triumphed. You have broken (VERSES TO H.R.H. THE DUKE OF WINDSOR) A60, 108

They fade then; other flowers have faded, (THE FLOWERS) A77, 135

They went along the little wood, (THE NIGHTINGALES) A1, 3

"They're funny things, wild animals," said Flail, (FREDDY FLAIL PROVES HIS POINT) A68

They're talking of another war, (WAR TALK: WINTER 1938) A68

Things beautiful, thoughts powerful, deeds commonplace or strange (IM-PROMPTU AFTER READING DR. JULIAN HUXLEY ON PROGRESS *later* IMPROMPTU UPON [etc.]) A97; C2457

Think not, because the winds rise chilly (SONG) A1, 3

Think not too glibly of their soft escape, (VICTORIANS) A67-8, 135

This aircraft crossing China over China's chief domain (FLIGHT OVER CHINA) C3314

This blackthorn bush in sunny whiteness (THE BLACKTHORN BUSH IN SPRING) A89

This conduit stream that's tangled here and there (ZILLEBEKE BROOK) A35

This dog—not a real dog, you know,— (DOG ON WHEELS) A156

This drowsy day, were I only near, (MARKET TOWN) A64, 68

This fine nature clear (THE FINE NATURE) A77; B94; C1842

This flying angel's torrent cry (EASTERN TEMPEST *later* TEMPEST; *and* EASTERN TEMPEST) A26, 31, 35; B23; C620

This is a scene that from my early years (untitled) A171

This is an ancient England in the new; (SIR WILLIAM TRELOAR'S DINNER [etc.] *later* SIR W. TRELOAR'S DINNER [etc.]) A31, 35

This is the forecast storm, the rage (SUMMER STORM *later* SUMMER STORM IN JAPANESE HILLS) A102, 156, 169, 176

This is your day, but can this be your year? (CLAIRE'S BIRTHDAY IN 1940) A77, 135

This man that at the wheatstack side, (A YEOMAN) A17 , 20, 35, 176; C439

This, then, is the school for the smallest; (VILLAGE: KINDERGARTEN) C3317

To Shakespeare's spirit let us all, like one, (FOR THE ENGLISH GROUP IN ASAHIGAWA) A171

To some, thoughts flying into futurity's cloud; (UNTEACHABLE) A20, 35; C482

To this house came (IT SHALL BE WRITTEN:) B229

To walk through Kent apple-orchards sacred with bloom (ANTIQUITIES) A156; C3133

To-day's house makes tomorrow's road; (THE SURVIVAL) A35; B41; C992

Too bold a light suits not all qualities; (SEEN IN TWILIGHT) A35

Too soon for us more happy days must end, (untitled) A171

Touched with a certain silver light (IN MY TIME) A64, 68; C1503

Tranquil enough they sit apart (TWO IN A CORNER [MENTAL HOSPITAL I]) A45, 68

Travellers from far away, we here have found (TO MRS HIRAI OF KIKUSUI HOTEL) A106

Traversing the early starlight, and the miles of shade, (PAST AND PRESENT: A SECOND HYMN) A64, 68

Treasure not so the forlorn days (BEHIND THE LINE) A10, 35; B13

Trembling blue, blent grey or green (OVER THE VALLEY) A156

Trenches in the moonlight, in the lulling moonlight (ILLUSIONS) A28, 35, 135, 169, 174, 176; C504

Triumph! how strange, how strong had triumph come (THIRD YPRES: A REMINISCENCE) A10, 28, 35, 135, 176; B44

Trolls and pixies unbeknown (ON TURNING A STONE) A8, 35; B1

"True, cousin; shaken times like these deny (MR CHARLES DEFENDS HIM-SELF) A40, 45, 68

True, wars have not yet died out of the earth. ("TO THE SOUTHDOWNS!") A68; B85

Truly you observed me; it was as you record. (THE TEMPLE) A102

Trust is a trembling thing; (TRUST) A25, 35; B23

Truth is not less aloof because ' 'tis true' see Truth is not less painful because " 'tis true,"

Truth is not less painful because " 'tis true," [later Truth is not less aloof be-cause ' 'tis true'; and Truth may not be less sharp because ' 'tis true,'] (IN MEMORY OF ROBERT NICHOLS) A135; C2510; D12

Truth may not be less sharp because ' 'tis true,' see Truth is not less painful because " 'tis true,"

"Turn not from me; (CHANCES OF REMEMBRANCE) A35, 135; C942

Turning aside from the Southgate, to take the monks' path through the marches, (SEGRAVE'S DEATH: A MARKET TOWN REMINISCENCE) A45; C1135

"Tuskin my name; and I am here to say (THE DEIST) A68

Twenty years had nearly passed since the war called Great had roared its last, (EXORCIZED) A68; C1716

Twilight became Cassandra. (THE PROPHETESS) C3290

Twine buds and leaves with some full blooms, to dress (FOR A MUSICIAN'S MONUMENT: G.F.) A156

Two buds we took from thousands more (HIGH ELMS, BRACKNELL) A89, 135, 174; Ed6

Two forms there are of tragedy: one makes (TRAGEDY) A7

"Two households, both alike in dignity,"— (PROLOGUE, THE SECULAR MASK; TOM THUMB THE GREAT) B89

Unbuild, unsquare, make nothing of this scrum (RESTORATION) B90

Under protecting mounds of ancient hills (HOUSING QUESTIONS *later* HOUSING QUESTION) A52, 68; B65
Under the burden of the tyrant War (THE SOLDIER'S BURDEN) A106
Under the bus wheel comes the tiny snail (THE SNAIL) A89; C2339
Under the evening lamp ("ENGLISH STUDIES") A106
Under the thin green sky, the twilight day, (COUNTRY SALE) A20, 35, 135, 174; B10; C321
Unfold the map of memories; let us wing (TO CLAIRE) A106
Unquestioning I follow—follow whom? (AT MY WRITING TABLE) A67-8
Unriddle this. Last night my dream (A DREAM) A17, 20, 35
Unspeedy friend, poor earth-child, whose sad eyes (THE HEDGEHOG KILLED ON THE ROAD) A89; C2338
Up, my jewel! let's away (THE BROOK) A14, 20, 35, 174; C309
Up the long colonnade I press, and strive (THE AVENUE) A10, 35; C237
Upon that cliff, that rock upright (THE FLOWERS OF THE ROCK *later* FLOWERS OF THE ROCK) A143, 156, 171; C2511; D12

Vantaged snow on the gray pilasters (JANUARY FULL MOON, YPRES) A35
Vesey the Constable waddles the Town, (WHETHER LIVING BODIES HAVE ULTIMATE AIMS?) C858
Village children shouted shrill, (THE BAKER'S VAN) A20, 35
Voice of Kyōto, tune of a continuous city (VOICE OF KYŌTO) A156, 169; B291
Voices of many cities, many streams, (AT THE DEPARTURE FROM KYU-SHU) A106

Walking the river way to change our note (A PROSPECT OF SWANS) A77, 135, 174; E*d*6
Wandering through time with Boswell, I arrived (A CORSCOMBE INHABI-TANT) A159
Warm-breathing deep perfume, a sun-breeze over Surrey (PINE-TREES) A156
Was this in truth that mighty lord's demesne? ("THE MIGHTY FALLEN") B1
Watersprite whose voice and look *see* Gay water-sprite, [etc.]
Wave at my window, my green friends, (FROM A STUDY TABLE *later* FROM A STUDY WINDOW) C2475; D11
We bless you, cicada, (TO THE CICADA) A40, 45, 68
We climbed the hill and passed the mill, (A CITY ON A HILL) A59, 64, 68; C1580
We come to Saga, here we find (SAGA MEMORY) A106
We happened on a theme so fine, (AFTER A DISCUSSION) A97
We have come to the farthest limit of the world (AESCHYLUS: 'PROME—THEUS BOUND', A TRANSLATION) C3360
We have no God, though old Miss Moon still seeks (THEOLOGY OVER THE GATE) A52, 68; C1359
We hear great things of you, young as you are, (TO JAPANESE STUDENTS: A SONNET) A97; C2458
We meet in life, long having met (SEIGO SHIRATORI AT MATSUSHIMA) A171
We peered at winter, (COATS OF ARMS) A7; C13
We rowed upstream one autumn afternoon, (AUTUMN AFTERNOON) A1, 3
We shuddered on the blotched and wrinkled down, (BY CHANCTONBURY) A7
We stood by the idle weir, (THE SOUTH-WEST WIND) A10, 35, 43*b*, 174; B7; C207

628

We talked of ghosts; and I was still alive; (NOVEMBER 1, 1931) A45, 68, 135

We travelled far along the track (FOR TAKESHI AND FUMIKO) A171

We wish you all that life can give (THE TEACHER) A106

We'll row up the fens as we've many a day done, (IN THE FENS) A14

Well, I suppose I am soon to be dead and done for; (COUNTRY CONVERSA-TION) A52, 68, 135; C1246

Well-travelled poet, whose clear sense discerned (TO THE AUTHOR) B87

Were all eyes changed, were even poetry cold, (THE DEEPER FRIENDSHIP) A31, 35, 135

Were it my fortune, I would bring you (THE GIFT: FOR C.M.P.) A77

What but a child expecting treats and gifts (DECORATIONS) A97

What garland for him now, Imagination (MAHATMA GANDHI) C2490

What ghosts are these? What hope could bring (EARLY IDEAS REMEM-BERED *later* EARLY IDEAS REAWAKENED) A135; C3043

What happened to The Gun? a fine gun it seemed, (GONE) A168

What happy place we travel through! (VILLAGE) A17, 20, 35; C455

"What hearest thou? (VOICES BY A RIVER) A25, 35; C558

What instruments of music have I heard, (TO SHERARD VINES) B20

What is lovelier than to be (LIBERTY) A97

What is the world about? (WOE TO DRUNKARDS: A JACOBEAN SERMON) A64, 68

What is this tyrant fate which dragged me here (SAM'L PEPYS: HIS PLAINT *later* SERIOUS CALL) A68; C1723

What master singer, with what glory amazed, (BELLS) A20, 35

What most we love we do not well express, (JAPAN BEAUTIFUL) A156; B291; C3251; D38

What others overtake in wit's advance (THE LITTLE SONG) A156

What passed when fantasy ruled the hour (ON SHAKESPEARE'S WINTER'S TALE *later* AUTOLYCUS'S COUNTRY) A156; C3103

What power so sways the hearts of human-kind (MARVELL'S "HORTUS" *later* ANDREW MARVELL'S *HORTUS* TRANSLATED) A168; C3144

What rarities you set before us (untitled) A171

What soldier guessed that where the stream descended (WARNING TO TROOPS) A20, 35, 135

What sweet voice do we hear along the dale? (DIALOGUE: VIATORES, AND A FRIEND OF ALAN PORTER, ESQ.) B43

What sweeter sight can ever charm the eye (AUGURY) A20, 35, 135; B8

What unkind power denies (RETURN TO JAPAN) A171

"What was the strangest sight you ever saw?" (WHEN THE STATUE FELL: A GRANDFATHER'S TALE) A89

What would I give to have been (MAN GROWN SAFE: ON RE-READING A FAVOURITE PASSAGE IN EDWARD GIBBON *later* GIBBON: IN THE MARGIN) A77, 135; C1998

What you have heard from countless friends (ARGUMENT IN SPRING) A45, 68

What's that over there? (PREMATURE REJOICING) A35, 135; B260

When all was grown to grim mid-night (PROPHETIC BALLAD FOR MCMXXXV) C1420

When Autumn with his shroud of leaves doth pay (LATE AUTUMN) A1, 3; C16

When first dark winter, wrapt in scudding clouds, ("THE FIRST WINTER") C1

When from Pagani's painted palace freed,– (untitled) B258

629

When Greek meets Greek, then comes the tug of war, (THE ART OF POETRY. [vi] ANOTHER) A52

When groping farms are lanterned up (A COUNTRY GOD) A8, 18, 35, 135; C26

"When high romance" deserts the paths of men (MICHIO MASUI) A171

When I began to write some schoolboy verse, (R. H. MOTTRAM) B277

When I see hundreds of young faces turned (LECTURING) A106

"When I was here in the War," he said, (UNLUCKY ALLUSIONS) A52, 68

When I was thirty-five, I think (TO THE COMPANY MET FOR MY BIRTH-DAY, 1961) A153, 156

When I woke, the sapphire sky (A BUDDING MORROW) A17, 20, 35; C471.1

When in my quiet time I have reviewed, (ON THE PROFESSION OF PHYSIC) C3111

When in the summer midnight some fierce cloud (THE MARRING) A1, 3

When lambs were come, who could be slow and sear? (SHEPHERD'S CALEN-DAR *later* ANOTHER SPRING) A20, 35; C517

When most were flocking into town (THE DREAMER) A67-8; C1685

When Mr. Doublet sang "Jerusalem" (TWO VILLAGE MINSTRELS) A100; C2531

When now at this stern depth and shade of soul *see* When, sunk to some stern depth and shade of soul,

When of all games the wisest, loveliest game [*later* Since our most beautiful and subtle game] (HAMMOND OF ENGLAND *later* HAMMOND (ENG-LAND): A CRICKETER) A89, 108, 135, 169; C2316

When on the green the rag-tag game had stopt (SHEET LIGHTNING) A10, 35, 135; B4; C46

When on the mountain side we saw the tea-house (JAPANESE INN *later* THE TEAHOUSE) A156, 169, 176; C3177

When, sunk to some stern depth and shade of soul [*later* When now this stern depth [etc.]] (PORTRAIT OF A COLONEL *later* ON THE PORTRAIT OF A COLONEL) A25, 35, 135; C705

When the cloudy evening shows (INTERVAL) A17, 20, 35; C476

When the low and leaden sky crushes like a lid upon (SPLEEN: FROM BAUDELAIRE) C507

When the vine of the East is afruit with the day, (FROM THE COTTAGE GARDEN) A1, 3

When the young year is sweetest, when the year (A PASTORAL) A20, 35

When these sweet strains of Elgar die, (A VARIATION) A156

When through the windows buzzed the thoughtless bee [*later* [. . .] the way-lost bee] (THE GEOGRAPHER'S GLORY: OR, THE WORLD IN 1730 *later* THE GEOGRAPHER'S GLORY: OR, THE GLOBE IN 1730) A31, 35; C873

When through the windows buzzed the way-lost bee *see* When through the windows [. . .] thoughtless bee

When war came something like a summer storm, (A SONNET AFTER LISTENING TO B.B.C. NEWS, 12 NOVEMBER 1963) A168

When we came to the hall we were made to feel grand; (YOUNG PIONEERS) C3316

When you are by, I think of time as boys (TIME TOGETHER) A77, 135

When you were young, you saw this puzzling scene:— (MONTS DE FLANDRE) A64, 68

Whence is such glory? who would dream (NATURE'S DARING *later* NATURE'S ADORNINGS) A89, 135, 174; B88; Ed6

Where a brook with lisping tongue (THE FLOWER-GATHERERS) A20, 35; C522

631

With coat like any mole's, as soft and black, (MOLECATCHER *later* MOLE CATCHER) A10, 35, 135, 174; C54

With half a hundred sudden loops and coils (THE HURRYING BROOK) A66-8, 135

With idle joy rippling the moon's green light (WINTER-PROUD) A43*a*

With magic haste our spirits range (LONDON: A DECEMBER MEMORY) A68

With May's tomthumb and daisy come, (RUSTIC WREATH) A14, 20, 35

With old Abou ben Adleem dwells the light, (FRESH THOUGHTS ON AN OLD POEM) A64, 68

With rural admixture of shrill and sweet, (THE YELLOWHAMMER) A35, 135

With thoughts of many times and places (SYMPOSIUM) A106

With what a sweet insistency (HONG KONG: A POSSIBLE PRELUDE) C3099

With what delight the south's large rain (THE BOY ON THE WAGGON) A89, 135

With what voluptuous and distorted care (THE NUN AT COURT) A35

Woodlands, and hill-slopes, hid in olive-browns, (OEDIPUS AT COLONUS) A1, 3

Writing of precious stones, the ancients draw (CLAIRISSIMA) A97

Ye habitants of air, (THE WINNOWER'S PRAYER TO THE WINDS) A2-3

Ye men of England, hear the clarion. If (THE ART OF POETRY. [iii] SLOGAN) A52

Ye who through wood, through river and through lea (SONNET) A2-3

Yes, I still remember ('CAN YOU REMEMBER?') A64, 68, 108, 135; B289; C1501

Yes, the strenuous world whirls on, (TO THE MEMORY OF VISCOUNT CARLOW) A89; C2437

"You are old, Father William," the youngster observed, (FARMER WILLIAM AGAIN) B70

You are welcome here, good friends. (PROLOGUE [DUCHESS OF MALFI]) B226

You must be as other are; (THE KIND STAR) A67-8

You quoted Shelley and I dream, (FOR YUKICHI NAKAMURA) A171

You see it there, there in those trees, (CHIMNEY-SMOKE) A97

You still invite, Yukichi; we (YUKICHI) A171

You'd call him a Professor in his way, (IN THE HANDICRAFT ESTABLISHMENT) C3315

Young joy to me is as the miser's gold, (THE MEADOW STREAM) A35; C1030

Your cry is 'Back to Nature'; we (ECHOES FROM 1914-18 *later* TO A NATURE-LOVER) A68; C1835

Yours is the modern Castle of Osaka. (untitled) A171

GENERAL INDEX

— *A Wreath for San Gemignano*, review, C2306
— ed., *Great French Romances*, review, C2231
— ed., *Poetry of the English-Speaking World*, C2416
Alexander, Russell George, *Poems*, review, C853
Alexander the Great, C1277
Alexandra, Queen, C535
Alias Shakeshafte, C2699
Allan, G. A. T., *Christ's Hospital*, review, C1649
Allen, G. C., *Modern Japan and its Problems*, review, C671
Allen, Hervey, *Toward the Flame*, review, C1381
Allen, Robert J., *The Clubs of Augustan London*, review, C1351
Allen, W. H., London, publisher, B187
Allen, Warner, *Gentlemen, I Give You Wine*, review, C1060
Allingham, Philip, *Cheapjack*, review, C1373
Allurements to Serenity, C1566
Altick, Richard D., *The Cowden Clarkes*, review, C2477
Amateur and Idler, C1992
Amateur Historian, The, Vol. 1, No. 1, review, C2893
America Collects Art, C580
American Comment, The, C2255
American Literature in England, C2439
American Philological Association, *Transactions and Proceedings*, Vol. LXXV, review, C2255
American Shogun, The, C2673
Among Many, C166
Among the English Poets, C2181
Among the Evangelicals, C2690
Among the Ghosts, C823
Among the Ruins, A102
Among These Rocks, C988
Analysts and Critics, C2182
Anatomy of Authorship, C2134
Ancient and Modern, C837
Ancient Holiday, An, A43
Ancient Poet, C3072
Ancient Race, An, C1542
Ancient School, An, C2747
And for Delight, C955
"And If We Fail—", C2677

"And Japanese Scenery?", C2455
And Still They Come, C468
Andersen, J. C., *The Laws of Verse*, review, C713
Anderson, Mrs. G. A., Ea7
Anderson, J. Redwood, *Paris Symphony*, review, C2416
— *To the Dyfrdwy, the River I Love*, review, C2641
— *The Vortex*, review, C715
Anderson, M. D., *Design for a Journey*, review, C1893
Andô, Ichirô, trans., C3224
Andrade, E. N. da C., *Airs*, review, p. 559
Andrae, Tor, *Mahommed, the Man and his Faith*, review, C1515
Andrew Young: Prospect of a Poet, B203
Andrews, Andrew, *The Blue Tunnyman*, review, C1451
Andrews, W. L., *Haunting Years*, letter, C1002
Anesake, Masaharu, *History of Japanese Religion*, review, C1013
Angell, Sir Norman, B37
— *The Steep Places*, review, C2402
Anglers and Fellow-Creatures, C2183
Anglo-German Review, C1760
Animal Stories, C180
Annals of the Fine Arts, C966
"Annals of the Fine Arts", C2435
Annan, Noel, *Leslie Stephen*, review, C2718
Anniversaries and Commemorations, C3185
Annotations's Aid, C2078
Annuals, The, C173, 177
Anodyne or Stimulant? C1381
Anonymous Table-Talker, An, C968
Another Convention, C686
Another Poor Indian, C1673
Another Problem, C1091
Another Victorian, C985
Anson, Sir Archibald, *About Others and Myself, 1745–1920*, review, C96
Anson, Harold, *Looking Forward*, review, C1687
Anspacher, Louis, *Challenge of the Unknown*, review, C3040
Antarctic Continent, Life and Adventure [etc.], The, C736
Anthologies, C519

Anthologies and Claimants, C300

Anthologies for Every Mood, C1577

Anthology Not Extinct, C807

Anthology of War Poems, An, B44

Anti-Antimacassar, C317

Anti-Babel, C1000

Antique Verse, C325

Antongini, Tom, *D'Annunzio*, review, C1689

Aoki, Tsuneo, *New English Teaching Method*, E*b*9.2

Aoyama Bungaku, Tokyo, C2449; D20

Aoyama Gakuin, E*b*15

Aoyama Trojan, Tokyo, C2684

Apperson, G. L., *English Proverbs and Proverbial Phrases*, review, C915

Appleton, Joan, A68

Appreciation of Literary Prose, The, A9

Arbuthnot, John, C1439, 1506

Archaeological Journal, The, Vol. 106, review, C2775

Archer, W. G., intro., *Kangra Painting*, review, C2953

Architectural Review, The, London, C1251

— October 1920, review, C155

Archon Books, Hamden, Connecticut, publisher, A32*c*, 49*c*; B27*c*

Ardern, P. S., *First Readings in Old English*, review, C3008

Arderne, James, *Directions concerning Matter and Stile of Sermons*, review, C2973

Aretz, Gertrude, *The Elegant Woman*, review, C1228

Argo Record Company, E*d*7

Argonaut Press, The, London, B51

Ariadne's Lover, C1260

Ariel Poems, The, A27; C643; 1167

Aristotle, *Metaphysics*, review, C3045

— *The Works of*, Vol. 12, review, C2909

Arkell, W. J., *The Geology of Oxford*, review, C2367

Arlott, John, *Cricket*, review, C3071

— *Of Period and Place*, review, C2067

Arms and Men, C2293

Armstrong, Edward A., *Shakespeare's Imagination*, review, C2283

Armstrong, Fytton, pseud. of Gaws-worth, John, *q.v.*

Armstrong, H. C., *Unending Battle*, review, C1421

Armstrong, Martin, *The Bird-Catcher*, review, p. 557

Arnold of Rugby, C712

Arnold, Matthew, A110; B56; C2492

— *The Scholar-Gypsy*, B56a; C1904

Arnold, William Harris, *Ventures in Book-Collecting*, review, C442

Arrival [in Japan], A102

Arrowsmith, J. W., Bristol, printer, A53

Art Gallery, A102

Art of Handwriting, C551

Art of Life Cultural Courses, The, A9

Arthur Skemp Memorial Lecture, A53

Aryan Path, The, Vol. 24, No. 1, review, C2986

As It Was, C3368

Asahi Evening News, Tokyo, C3131; E*a*18

Asahi Shimbun, The, Tokyo, C2542, 3228; D17–18, 32

Asahi-shimbun-sha, Tokyo, publisher, A102; B147

Asatarô, Miyamori, trans., *Masterpieces of Japanese Poetry Ancient and Modern*, review, C1551

Ashmead-Bartlett, E., *The Uncensored Dardanelles*, review, C720

Ashmun, Margaret, *The Singing Swan*, review, C1121

Ashton, Helen, *Letty Landon*, review, C2708

Asia Magazine, Hong Kong, C3280

Askwith, Betty, *First Poems*, review, C757

— *Keats*, review, C1860

Aspects de la Littérature anglaise de 1918 à 1940, D4

Aspects of Modern Poetry, C1316

Assorted Poetry, p. 556

Aston, Sir George, *Secret Service*, review, C1052

Astro-dramatic, C2152

At Pisa Once, C2820

At St. Helena, Napoleon in Exile, C685

At 7, Albemarle Street, C2330

Atami of the Past, A50; C592

Atarashii Eishi no Kanshô, D13

Athenaeum, The, London, C35–6,

Baker, Ernest A., *On Foot in the Highlands*, review, C1226

Baker, John Milton, *Henry Crabb Robinson of Bury, Jena*, [etc.], review, C1601

Baker, Philip Noel, and others, *Challenge to Death*, B68

Balcon, Jill, Ed6

Bald, R. C., *Donne's Influence on English Literature*, review, C1596

Ball, F. Elrington, *Swift's Verse*, review, C822

Ball, Johnson, Ea15

Ballad of Reading Gaol, The, B202; C3202

Balmain, Count, *Napoleon in Captivity*, review, C685

Balston, Thomas, *John Martin: His Life and Works*, review, C2421

Banville, Théodore de, A2–3

Bare Hills and Backcloths, The, C1251

Barea, Arturo, *Lorca*, review, C2019

Barfield, Owen, *Poetic Diction*, review, C713, 2802

Baring, Maurice, *The Lonely Lady of Dulwich*, review, C1391

Barn, The, A4, 6

Barnes, Joshua, C2175

Barnes, Sidney, *It Is'nt Cricket*, review, C3064

Barnes, Thomas, C1431, 1862, 1991, 2267

Barnes, Thomas, cricketer, p. 558

Barnes, William, C2040, 2275, 2955, 3250

— *The Poems of*, review, C3277.1

Barrett, Douglas, *Persian Painting of the Fourteenth Century*, C2953

Barrie, Sir James, *Allahakbarries C.C. 1899*, review, C2581

Barrow, R. H., *Slavery in the Roman Empire*, review, C742

Barry Cornwall & Keats, A160; C3293

Bartlett, Phyllis, *Poems in Process*, review, C2757

Bartlett, Vernon, *No Man's Land*, review, C936

Barton, Margaret and Sir Osbert Sitwell, eds, *Sober Truth*, review, C977

Bashford, H. H., *Lodgings for Twelve*, review, C1451

Basile, Giambattista, *The Pentameron*, review, C2818

Bataille de la Somme, 1916, D4

Batchelor, Denzil, *The Book of Cricket*, review, C2884

— *Game of a Lifetime*, B152; C3046 (review)

Bates, H. E., *Down the River*, review, C1659

— *The Face of England*, review, C2919

— *The Modern Short Story*, review, C1902

— *Through the Woods*, review, C1573

Bates, Katherine Lee, *From Gretna Green to Land's End*, review, C943

Bates, W. N., Jr, *Poetical Intoxication*, reviews, C1084, 1087

Bateson, F. W., ed., *The Cambridge Bibliography of English Literature*, B93

Batho, Edith C., *The Later Wordsworth*, review, C1335

Batsford, B. T., Ltd, London, B71a, 75a

Battalion History, A, A50

Batten, H. Mortimer, *Habits and Characters of British Wild Animals*, review, C179

Batterham, Eric N., *A Kite's Dinner*, review, C1666

Battiscombe, Georgina, *Charlotte Mary Yonge*, review, C1979

Battle for Crete, The, B222

Battle for Hong Kong, The, B180

Battle of the Somme, C3252

Battlefield, A43

Baudelaire, Charles, C507

Baumgardt, David, *Bentham and the Ethics of Today*, review, C3059

Bax, Clifford, *Antique Pageantry*, review, C290

— *Vintage Verse*, reviews, C2103, 2131

— *W. G. Grace*, review, C2859

Baxter, Herbert, ed., B1

Bayes, Walter, *Small Vehicles*, review, C1237

Bayley, Harold, *The Lost Language of London*, review, C1451

Bayly, H. W., ed., *What We Drink*, review, C1060

Beacon: A Monthly Review of Local Government in the Uckfield Rural District Council, The, Crowborough, C2331

639

Blue, The, Horsham (*cont.*)
346, 445, 462-3, 479, 503, 510,
527, 541, 589, 602-3, 608, 618,
1002, 1070, 1431-2, 1718, 1739,
2039, 2175, 2205, 2237, 2448,
2468, 2853, 2929, 3172, 3230,
3283, 3335; E*a*1, *a*17, *b*1; p. 556-
8
—— Editorial, C11, 15
Bluecoat Birthday, C3027
Blumenfeld, R. D., *What is a Journal-
ist?*, review, C986
Blunden, Catherine, A156
Blunden, Charles Edmund, A115,
135, 156; B168; C2744, 3088
Blunden, Claire, A77-8, 106, 135;
C3249.1
—— jt ed., B242
Blunden, Clare, A25
Blunden, G. A., A4-6, 11, 38; C318
Blunden, John, A25
Blunden, Joy, A8, 14, 20, 35, 43*b*,
89, 108, 135
Blunden, Margaret, A89, 135
Blunden, Mary, A20, 25
Blunden, Mary Daines, A8
Blunden Society in Japan, A171
Blunt, Reginald, ed., *Mrs. Montagu*,
review, C459
Blunt, Wilfrid, C76
—— *Japanese Colour Prints from
Harunobu to Utamaro*, reviews,
B181; C2953, 3161
Blyth, R. H., trans., *Senryu*, review,
C2504
Blyton, W. J., *English Cavalcade*, re-
view, C1602
Boas, Frederick S., *Christopher Mar-
lowe*, review, C1815
—— *An Introduction to the Reading
of Shakespeare*, review, C630
—— *An Introduction to Stuart Drama*,
review, C2209
—— *Songs and Lyrics from the Eng-
lish Playbooks*, review, C2179
Boase, Frederick, *Modern English
Biography*, C3350
Boase, T. S. R., *Reading and Listen-
ing*, review, C2664
Boat and Barge, C2215
Boden, F. C., *A Derbyshire Tragedy*,
review, C1441
Bodleian Quarterly Record,
C66

Bodley Head, The, London, publi-
sher, A174; B265, 284
Boinville, Mme de, and Cornelia,
C2441
Bois, Elie J., *Truth on the Tragedy
of France*, review, C1850
Bolton, Glorney, *The Tragedy of
Gandhi*, review, C1391
Bolton Public Libraries, C91
Bombing of Cities, C1809
*Bonadventure: A Random Journal of
an Atlantic Holiday, The*, A12,
108
Bone, Gavin, *Beowulf*, review, C2251
Bone, Gertrude, *Mr. Paul*, review,
C302
Bonnerot, Louis, *Matthew Arnold*,
review, C2492
—— and Mme, A47
Bonniers Förlag, Albert, Stockholm,
D43
Bonsal, Stephen, *Unfinished Business*,
review, C2049
Book-Collector's Quarterly, The, Lon-
don, C1071
Book Forgeries: "An Enquiry" Re-
Read, A82; C2284
Book of Cricket Verse, The, B150
Book of Narrative Verse, A, B38
Book of the Month, The, C1128
Book of the Queen's Dolls' House,
B13
Book of the Week, The, C377, 399
Book-Pastime and Book Science,
C654
Book Society, The, London, B102*a*,
106; E*f*3
Book Society Annual, London,
C1246, 1327, 1420-1, 1489,
1580-1, 1661, 1723-6, 1784-6,
1837-40, 1894-6, 1942-5, 1994-
8, 2065-7, 2176-8
Book Society Choice for November
[1953] A119
Book Society News, London, C1189,
1200-1, 1209-10, 1216-17, 1221-
2, 1227-8, 1230-1, 1236-7, 1244-
5, 1252-3, 1257-8, 1262-3, 1270-
1, 1279-80, 1285-6, 1293-4,
1299, 1303-4, 1307-8, 1314-15,
1325-6, 1336-7, 1340-1, 1347-9,
1356-8, 1366-8, 1373-5, 1382-4,
1391-3, 1397-9, 1405-7, 1413-
14, 1418-19, 1427-9, 1433-5,

Brady, Benjamin, jt ed., B19
Braga, J. M., compiler, *Hong Kong Business Symposium*, B196
Braithwaite, Richard Bevan, *Scientific Explanation*, review, C3042
Bramwell, James, *Beyond the Sunrise, and Other Poems*, review, C1404
Brantom, William, *Our Brave Boys*, review, C464
— *Various Verses*, review, C464
Brathwait, Richard, *Barnabae Itinerarium*, review, C1261
Braun, Thomas F. R. G., B257
Brave des Braves, Le, C1667
Brave Old World, C2063
Brawne, Fanny, C2885
— *Letters of . . . to Fanny Keats (1820–1824)*, review, C1589
Braybrooke, Neville and Elizabeth King, eds, *Translation (London)*, B109
Braybrooke, Patrick, *Thomas Hardy and His Philosophy*, review, C679
Brent, Irene, Ea10
Brereton, Frederick, compiler, *An Anthology of War Poems*, B44
Bret Harte, Selected Poems, B19
Breton, Nicholas, *A Mad World My Masters*, review, C889
— Prose, A39; C889
Brett-James, Norman G., *The Growth of Stuart London*, review, C1441
Brett-Smith, H. F. B., ed., *Peacock's Four Ages of Poetry*, review, C308
Brettell, N. H., *Bronze Freize*, review, C2556
Brewer's Dictionary of Phrase and Fable, C2938
Bridge Books, A177
Bridges, Elizabeth, *Sonnets from Hafez, and Other Verses*, review, C270
Bridges, Robert, A92; C568, 2286
— *Collected Essays, Papers, &c*, reviews, C647, 1084
— The Ideal Laureate, C969
— *New Verse*, review, C548
— ed., *S.P.E. Tract No. XXVIII, English Handwriting*, Ea4
Brief Candle, C2614
Brief Elegies, C2322
Brief Survey of Quaker Work Camps in Hong Kong, A, B214

Brightfield, Myron F., *Theodore Hook and His Novels*, review, C808, 811
Bringing Them Home, A50; C1071
Brinig, Myron, *Sons of Singermann*, reviews, C1194, 1199
Bristol, University of, A53
Bristol Grammar School Chronicle, Eb17
Britain: Life & Culture, [Tokyo], C3228
Britain To-day, London, C1861, 1981, 2001, 2020, 2027, 2058, 2081, 2086, 2099, 2141, 2189, 2220, 2264, 2315, 2351, 2360, 2380, 2406, 2417, 3085
Britannica Book of the Year, 1952, review, C2872
— *1953*, review, C3041
British Academy, London, *Proceedings*, C1899
— — 1942, C2188
— — 1945, C2553
— — 1948, review, C2777
— — 1949, 1950, review, C2979
British Book News, Supplement, A107
British Council, The, A107, 124, 137; D42; Ed4–5; p. xiv
British Council Series, A, C2638
British Craftmanship, C1964
British Embassy, Tokyo, C2207
British Envoy, A, C2194
British in Flanders, The, C949
British Landscape, C2045
British Literature of 1925 contrasted with [the] Victorian Age, C532
British Museum, *General Catalogue of Printed Books*: Dante, review, C2944
British Museum Quarterly, The, Vol. 15, review, C2830
British Operations in Norway, B174
British Rhine Army Dramatic Society, C88
British School, The, A43
British Society of Master Glass-Painters, *Journal*, Vol. 11, No. 1, review, C2767
British Sport, C752
Brittain, Vera M., *England's Hour*, review, C1849
— *The Testament of Youth*, review,

C1304
— ed., B4, 68b
Brizeux, C494
Broadhurst & Co., C. K., Southport, bookseller, C1180
Broadus, Edmund Kemper, *The Laureateship*, review, C306
Broch, Hermann, *Unknown Quantity*, review, C1471
Brockington, A. Allen, Ea8
Brodribb, C. W., *Poems*, B114
Brodribb, Gerald, *Cricket in Fiction*, review, C2642
— *Next Man In*, review, C2822
— ed., *The Book of Cricket Verse*, B150; C3019 (review)
Brogan, D. W., *The American Problem*, review, C2048
— *The English People*, review, C1957
Bronowski, J., *A Man Without a Mask*, review, C2026
Bronte, Charlotte, *The Spell*, review, C1157
— Emily, B205
Brook, Barnaby, *Wife to John*, review, C682
Brooke, Essex, *Vagabond Flag*, review, C1258
Brooke, Rupert, C3337
Brooke, Stopford A., *Naturalism in English Poetry*, review, C151
Brooker, J., Uckfield, A4–5
Broome, William, C2181
Brophy, John and Eric Partridge, *Songs and Slang of the British Soldier, 1914–1918*, reviews, C1015, 1045, 1173
Brower, Robert H., and Earl Miner, *Japanese Court Poetry*, review, C3278
Brown, Alec, trans., *The Voyage of the Chelyuskin*, review, C1471
Brown, Charles Armitage, *Life of Keats*, reviews, C1618, 1620
— *Narensky*, letter, C1674
— *Some Letters and Miscellanea of*, reviews, C1589, 1591
Brown, Harry, *Poems*, review, C2131
Brown, Hilton, *The Gold and the Grey*, review, C1563
— *Rudyard Kipling*, review, C2128
Brown, Ivor, *Dr. Johnson and His World*, review, C3348
— *A Word in Your Ear*, review,

C1931
— ed., *The Bedside "Guardian"*, review, C2928
Brown, John, *John Bunyan (1628–1688)*, reviews, C688, 799
Brown, Paul A., *The Development of the Legend of Thomas Becket*, review, C1078
Brown, Percy, *Round the Corner*, review, C1407
Brown, T. E., C985
Brown, T. Graham, *Brenva*, review, C2065
Browne, D. G., and E. V. Tullett, *Bernard Spilsbury*, review, C2740
Browne, G. F., *King Alfred's Books*, review, C205
Browning, Robert, A110
— *Dearest Isa: . . . Letters*, review, C2857
— *Famous Love of the Brownings*, C2967
Brunhes, Jean, *Human Geography*, review, C2883
"Brush Up Your English!", C1280
Bryan, J. Ingram, *The Civilization of Japan*, review, C657
Bryant, Arthur, *The England of Charles II*, review, C1421
— *The Years of Endurance*, review, C1943
— *The Years of Victory*, review, C2066
Bryant, W. T., Ea1
Buchan, Alastair and Oliver Villiers, *Twenty-Five Years, 1919–1944*, review, C2614
Buchan, Alice, *A Stuart Portrait*, review, C1421
Buchan, John, *Augustus*, review, C1652
— *Memory Hold-the-Door*, review, C1826
— *Montrose*, review, C785
Buchanan, George, *Words for Tonight*, review, C1515
Buck, Pearl S., *The Exile*, review, C1515
Buckland, A. R., *John Bunyan*, review, C728
Buddhist Paintings, A50; C530
Budge, Sir E. A. Wallis, *The Bandlet of Righteousness*, review, C851

Bull, Gerald, *Wayside Poems*, review, C137

Buller, E. Amy, *Darkness over Germany*, review, C1997

Bullett, Gerald, *George Eliot*, review, C2359

— *The Golden Year of Fan Chengta*, review, C2240

— *News from the Village*, review, C2936

— *Poems*, review, C2499

— ed., *The English Galaxy of Shorter Poems*, reviews, C1311, 1322

— ed., *The Jackdaw's Nest*, review, C1778

Bullock, Shan F., *After Sixty Years*, review, C1098

Bunin, Ivan, *Grammar of Love*, review, C1441

Bunka-Insatsu-sha, Tokyo, Ea2

Bunyan, John, A110

— *The Church Book of Bunyan Meeting, 1656–1821*, review, C800

— *The Pilgrim's Progress*, reviews, C722, 744, 799, 826

— The Spirit of, A39; C799

Burchardt, C. B., *Norwegian Life and Literature*, review, C151

Burdett, Osbert, *The Brownings*, review, C808

Burgess, Percy, *Who Walk Alone*, review, C1876

Burke, Thomas, *The Beauty of England*, review, C1294

— *English Inns*, C2008

Burlingame, Roger, *Of Making Many Books*, review, C2353

Burlingham, Russell, *Forrest Reid*, review, C3001

Burnet, John, *Essays and Addresses*, review, C916

Burnett, W. R., *Dark Hazard*, review, C1366

Burney, Fanny, *Evelina*, review, C961

Burns, W. N., *Tombstone, An Epic of Arizona*, review, C716

Burra, Peter, *Wordsworth*, review, C1518

[Burrage, Alfred M.], *War is War*, by Ex-Private X, review, C949

Burt, Struthers, *Entertaining the Islanders*, review, C1356

Bury, Adrian, *Two Centuries of British Water-Colour Painting*, review, C2569

Bury St. Edmunds, C922; Ef11

Busch, Noel, F., *Two Minutes to Noon*, review, C3280

Bush, Douglas, *Paradise Lost in Our Time*, review, C2272

Bush, Lewis, *The Road to Inamura*, review, C3334

Butler, A. S. G., *Recording Ruin*, review, C1944

Butler, E. M., *Sheridan*, review, C1112

Butler, Samuel, *Notebooks*, review, C2645

— Some Remarks on *Hudibras*, C724

Butterworth, Charles, C., *The English Primers (1529–1545)*, review, C3039

Butts, Mary, *The Macedonian*, review, C1277

Buxton, John, *A Marriage Song for the Princess Elizabeth*, review, C2416

— *Such Liberty*, review, C2044

By a Lonely Sea, B215

By Mossy Stones, C1386

By Whom? C2376

"Byble in Englyshe, The", C1699

Bynner, Witter, trans., *The Jade Mountain*, review, C948

Byrom, John, C2633

Byron, Lord, A99, 142

— A Fragment of Byronism, A126; C3129

— Some Early Biographies, A134; C3183

Byron, Robert, *The Byzantine Achievement, A.D. 330–1453*, review, C855

C.L.S. Bulletin see Charles Lamb Society Monthly Bulletin

C.M.P. [*i.e.* Claire M. Poynting *later* Claire Blunden] A77

Cairncross, John, B275

— *By a Lonely Sea*, B215

Cairo Anthology, A, C2118

Calais, C1516

Calder-Marshall, Arthur, *A Date With a Duchess*, review, C1641

Calendar of Modern Letters, London, C515–18

644

Callow, Philip, *Turning Point*, review, C3312

Callwell, C. E., *Stray Recollections*, review, C442

Cambridge, Elizabeth, *Hostages to Fortune*, review, C1285

Cambridge Bibliography of English Literature, The, B93

Cambridge History of English Literature, The, review, A46; C1253

Cambridge Men, C3035

Cambridge Review, Cambridge, C3337

Cambridge University Press, A49a; B79, 91, 93a, c, 96a

Camden, Carroll, *The Elizabethan Woman*, review, C2931

Came to Japan Again, D16

Cameron, Kenneth Neill, *The Young Shelley*, review, C2734

Cameron, Norman, *The Winter House*, review, C1498

Cammell, Charles Richard, *Poems Satirical and Miscellaneous*, review, C464

Camões, Luiz de, C3285.1, 3306

— *The Lusiads*, review, C2634

Camp dans le Bois, Le, D4

Campaign in North-West Africa, The, B193

Campaign in Sicily, The, B160

Campaign in Southern Italy: From Reggio to Rome, The, B170

Campaigns in North-East Africa and the Middle East, B163

Campbell, A. B., *Salute the Red Duster*, review, C2966

Campbell, A. Y., *Horace Odes and Epodes*, review, C3044

Campbell, Alistair, *Wild Honey*, review, C3312

Campbell, Arthur, *Jungle Green*, review, C3068

Campbell, H. F., *Caithness and Sutherland*, review, C248

Campbell, Kathleen, *An Anthology of English Poetry*, review, C918

Campbell, Nancie, *The Murison Burns Collection*, review, C2970

Campbell, Patrick, *A Short Trot with a Cultured Mind*, review, C2578

Campbell, Roy, C3199

— *Adamastor, Poems*, review, C982

— *Choosing a Mast*, review, C1167

— *The Georgiad*, review, C1170

— *The Gum Trees*, review, C1059

— *Mithraic Emblems*, review, C1581

— Political Poetry, C723

— *The Wayzgoose*, review, C673

Canadian Memorials, Western Front, C223

Canadian Prophet, C2381

Cannan, Gilbert, *Pugs and Peacocks*, review, C278

Cannan, Joanna, *A Pony for Jean*, review, p. 557

Canning, John, *Living History: 1914*, B278

Canning, R. Gordon, *Flashlights from Afar*, review, C115

Cape, Jonathan, London, publisher, A50, 58; B15a, 25a, 41a, 59, 84a, 92a, 94a, 98a, 101a; Ea26

Capek, Karel, *Travels in the North*, review, C1729

Capes, Renalt, *Poseidon*, review, C2387

Captain Courageous, A, C3283

Captain of Industry, C2214

Carberry, Eehna and Seumas and Alice Milligan, *We Sang for England*, review, C2617

Cardus, Neville, *Good Days*, review, C1421

Care of Churches, The, C2661

Careless Raptures: What the Birds Say, C327

Carew, Dudley, *To the Wicket*, review, C2234

Carmen, Arthur H., and Noel S. Macdonald, eds, *The Cricket Almanack of New Zealand*, review, C2652

Caroline Poet, C2700

Carpenter, Maurice and others, eds, *New Lyrical Ballads*, review, C2148

Carpenter, Rhys, *The Plainsman*, review, C188

Carr, Edward Hallett, *The Bolshevik Revolution*, C2587

Carr, J. L. ed., B267

Carrick, Edward, illus., A42

Carrington, Charles, *Soldier from the Wars Returning*, review, C3338

Carrington, Dorothy, *The Traveller's Eye*, C2345

Carson, Rachel, L., *The Sea Around Us*, review, C2730
Carswell, Donald, *Brother Scots*, review, C644
— ed., *Trial of Guy Fawkes*, review, C1391
Carver, P. L., *The Life of a Poet*, B271
Cary, H. F., C547
Cary, Joyce, *The Drunken Sailor*, review, C2416
Case, Robert Hope, *Reflections*, by R. Q., reviews, C715, 735
Case for the Archdeacon, The, C261
Cassagnac, Paul de, *French Wines*, review, C1060
Cassell & Company Ltd, London, B30
Cassell's Weekly, London, C367–8, 370, 372-3, 375, 377-8, 381, 383-4, 386-9, 391-2, 395-6, 399-400, 402-6, 408-10, 413-15, 417, 420-2, 424, 428-30, 432-3, 435, 437
Casson, Stanley, *Steady Drummer*, review, C1481
Casteret, Norbert, *Ten Years Under the Earth*, review, C1771
Castle of Indolence, The, B190
Casual Cavalier, The, C575
Catalogue of the Exhibitions . . . by Ethelbert White, B45
Catholic Bulletin; A Publication of the Hong Kong University Catholic Society, Hong Kong, C3131, 3209
Causley, Charles, *Poems in Pamphlet*, review, C2618
Caxton and After, C2289
Cazamian, Louis, C2187
— *The Development of English Humor*, review, C3028
— *La Poésie romantique anglaise*, review, C1783
Cecil, Algernon, *Queen Victoria and Her Prime Ministers*, review, C2934
Cecil, Lord David, *The Poetry of Thomas Gray*, review, C2196
— *Two Quiet Lives*, C2423
Céline, Louis-Ferdinand, *Journey to the End of the Night*, review, C1384
Celtic Unities, C835

Cemeteries in Belgium, B198
Cemeteries in Crete and the Dodecanese, B222
Cemeteries in Denmark, Iceland and the Faroe Islands, B177
Cemeteries in France, B172
Cemeteries in Germany, B195
Cemeteries in Greece, B221
Cemeteries in Hong Kong, B180
Cemeteries in Italy, B160, 170
Cemeteries in Norway and Sweden, B174
Cemeteries in Tunisia, B193
Centaur Press, London, B235a
Ceylon Observer, Colombo, C391
Cha-No-Yu, B125
Chairing the Bard, E*b*29
Challenge, A, E*f*4
Challenge, The, London, C342, 345
Challenge to Death, B68
Chalmers, W. S., *The Life and Letters of David Beatty, Admiral of the Fleet*, review, C2729
Chamberlin, William, *Japan Over Asia*, review, C1679
Chambers, E. K., *Arthur of Britain*, review, C661
— *Samuel Taylor Coleridge*, review, C1731
— *Sources for a Biography of Shakespeare*, review, C2242
Chambers, Ephraim, C1814
[Chambers, Jessie], *D. H. Lawrence*, by E. T., review, C1451
Chambers's Encyclopaedia, B270
Chang, H. C., *Allegory and Courtesy in Spenser*, review, C3151
Changes in England's Countryside, C2422
Channing School Founder's Day Service, B240
Chapbook (A Monthly Miscellany), The, reviews, C85, 246
Chaplin, Charles, C497
Chapman, Guy, *A Passionate Prodigality*, reviews, C1252, 3338
— ed., *Vain Glory*, review, C1636
Chapman, Hester W., *Mary II, Queen of England*, review, C2950
Chapman, R. W., *Cancels*, review, C1076
Chapman & Hall, London, publisher, C996
— *Universal Art*, review, C79

646

Christmas greetings cards, A19, 65–6, 71, 86, 94–5

Christmas Tradition, The, C487

Christophers, London, publisher, A15

Chronicle & Echo, Northampton, C3299

Chûgoku Shimbun, Hiroshima, C3251

Church, Richard, *The Glance Backward*, review, C1048

— *Green Tide*, review, C2092

— *The Lamp*, review, C2306

— *Twelve Noon*, review, C1517

— *Twentieth Century Psalter*, review, C1960

— and M. M. Bozman, eds, *Poems of Our Time, 1900–1942*, review, C2121

Churchill, Charles, A39; C1095

— *Poems*, review, C1318

Churchill, Sir Winston, *The Hinge of Fate*, review, C2672

— *Marlborough*, Vol. 4, review, C1711

— *The Unrelenting Struggle*, review, C1929

— *The World Crisis*, review, C617

Ciano, Count, *Diary 1939–1943*, review, C2348

Circling Year, The, C1355

Citizen Publishing Co. Ltd., Southend-on-Sea, B244

City Hall, Hong Kong, B273.1; C3270.2

City Hall Theatre, The, Hong Kong, B239, 245

City Literary Institute, Oxford, The, B34

City of Dreadful Night, The, B54

Civasaqui, José, B136, B224

Civic Hall Quarterly, Wolverhampton, C2338–9

Clapham, Sir Arthur, C2775

Clapham, Walter J., *Night Be My Witness*, review, C2835

Clare, John, A5, 14, 92, 108, 177; B14, 93; C39–40, 42, 52, 245, 265, 267, 279, 281, 361, 413, 615, 914, 1213–14, 2583, 2591, 3299

— Centenary, B251; E*b*28

— Notes and References, A21, 104; C545

— *The Later Poems of*, review, C3301

— *Poems*, ed. by A. Symons, review, C35

— —, ed. by J. W. Tibble, C1441, 1448 (reviews), 1444 (letter)

— *Poems Chiefly from Manuscript*, B3

— *Selected Poems of*, ed. by Leonard Clark, review, C3301

— —, ed. by Geoffrey Grigson, review, C2591

— —, ed. by J. W. and Anne Tibble, review, C3339

— *The Shepherd's Calendar*, review, C3301

— *Sketches in the Life of*, B48

— *A Tourist to Tourists*, A141; C3225

— *The Wood is Sweet*, B265

Clarendon Press, Oxford, A22; B107; E*a*4

Clark, A. M., *The Realistic Revolt in Modern Poetry*, review, C328

— *Studies in Literary Modes*, review, C2260

Clark, Alan, *The Donkeys*, review, C3254

Clark, Sir Kenneth, *The Gothic Revival*, review, C808

— lectures, C2410

Clark, Leonard, *Alfred Williams*, reviews, C2097, 2107

— *Tribute to Walter de la Mare*, B290

— ed., *Andrew Young*, B203

— ed., *Singing in the Street*, B288

Clark, Roy Benjamin, *William Gifford*, review, C1119

Clark Lectures, A49

Clarke, Austin, *The Collected Poems of*, review, C1541

— *Pilgrimage*, review, C835

Clarke, Charles and Mary Cowden, C2590

— The Cowden Clarkes, A108; C2104

Classic Still, A, C3208

Classic Verse, C2269

Classical Background, C2111

Claxton, William J., *The Mastery of the Air*, review, C178

Clayton-Jones, E., C3115

Clifford, Alexander, *Crusader*, review, C1944

Clifford Library, A43*a*

Cousins, E. G., *To Comfort the Signora*, review, C2643
Coutts, Francis, *Selected Poems*, reviews, C416, 419
Coventry Public Libraries, C128
Coward, Noel, *Present Indicative*, review, C1598
Coward, T. A., *The Birds of the British Isles*, Series, II, review, C181
Cowper, William, A92; C788, 1164, 2660, 2690
— *The Poems of*, review, C1165
— *The Poetical Works of*, review, C623
— *Selections from*, review, C1321
Cox, J. Stevens, A151, 158a, 159, 162
Crabbe, George, C1182-3
— *The Life of*, B120
Craddock, Harry, *Savoy Cocktail Book*, review, C1060
Craigie, Sir Robert, *Behind the Japanese Mask*, review, C2207
Craigie, Sir William A., *The Critique of Pure English*, review, C2299
— *A Dictionary of the Older Scottish Tongue*, review, C2239
Crane, Ronald S., ed., *A Collection of English Poems, 1660-1800*, review, C1267
Cranmer, Elsie Paterson, *The Conflict*, review, C464
Cranmer-Byng, L., and S. A. Kapadia, eds, *The Wisdom of the East Series*, review, C1435
Crawford, Robert, *In Quiet Fields*, review, C880
Creed of the Book, The, A108; C2163
Creese, A. R., C24
Cresset Press, The, London, B120
Cressey, George B., *Asia's Lands and Peoples*, review, C2812
Creweian Oration, E*b*34
Cricket Chroniclers, C2581
Cricket Commemoration, C3097
Cricket Country, A76
Cricket Festival, A, C2528
Cricket History, C2748
Cricket Heroes, C2859
Cricket Master, A, C2554
Cricket Verse, C3019
Cricket Verses, B142
"Cricket Won't be Druv", A108

Cricketer's Bookshelf, A, C3143
Cricketing Sketches, C2651
Cricketing Twins, C2671
Crime and its Echo, A, C696
Critic and Poet, C2286
Critic's Commentary, C2232
Critical Essays of To-day, B55
Critical Forum, The, B208
Critical Voluntaries, C1283
Criticism: Sidney to Arnold, A91
Criticism Without Tears, p. 558
Critics who have Influenced Taste, B263; C3285
Critics Among the Romantics, C3313
Crockett, L. Herndon, *Popcorn on the Ginza*, review, C2495
Crockford's Clerical Directory, C139
Croft-Cooke, Rupert, *Letters from Poets*, E*a*27
— *Some Poems*, review, C880
Cronin, A. J., *The Stars Look Down*, review, C1445
Cross Continent Co., Ltd, Tokyo, B213
Crosse, Gordon, ed., *Every Man's Book of Sacred Verse*, review, C448
Crowe, William, A158; C2181
Crowsley, Ernest G., C2108
Cruikshank, R. J., *The Double Quest*, review, C1515
— *The Moods of London*, review, C2721
Crump, Phyllis E., *Nature in the Age of Louis XIV*, review, C784
Crusade for Poetry, C2566
Cruse, Amy, *The Victorians and their Books*, review, C1455
Crutwell, C. R. M., *A History of the Great War*, review, C1413
Cultural Forum, New Delhi, C3266
Cultural Rôle of the University, The, B262
Culture: A Little Dialogue, A102
Culture through English, B126
Cummings, E. E., *The Enormous Room*, review, C765
— *73 Poems*, review, C3312
Cunard, Nancy, *Sublunary*, review, C419
Cundall, H. M., *The Norwich School*, review, C105
Curie, Eve, *Journey Among Warriors*, review, C1994

Curle, Richard, A162
Curling, Jonathan, *Janus Weather-cock*, review, C1692
Current Notes, C930
Current of the World, The, Tokyo, C2427, 3166
Current Thoughts in English Litera-ture, [Tokyo], C2519, 2561
Curtis, J., *The Mysterious Murder of Maria Marten*, review, C696
Curtis, Jean-Louis, *The Forests of the Night* review, C2585
Curtis, Lewis Perry, *The Politicks of Laurence Sterne*, reviews, C841, 848

Da Vinci, Leonardo, *The Drawings of*, review, C2236
Daedel Earth, The, p.558
Daedalus Press, Stoke Ferry, Nor-folk, B277
Daily Express, London, C3369
Daily Herald, London, C89, 110, 156, 193, 208, 215, 244, 255, 257, 259, 262, 264, 284, 292, 298, 329
Daily Mail, London, E*b*16
Daily News, London, C317, 322, 327, 331, 334, 351
Daily Telegraph, London, C672, 683, 685, 693, 708, 712, 719, 730, 733, 736, 742, 745-6, 749, 751, 759, 761, 768, 778, 783, 787, 795, 801, 804, 812, 817, 820, 822, 833, 839, 841, 843, 851, 855, 876, 878, 885, 903, 905, 911, [916, 1083, 1108, 1113-14, 1124-5, 1136, 1138, 1144, 1148, 1153, 1156, 1166, 3020, 3256, 3275, 3301-2, 3312-13, 3354, 3359, 3365; E*b*33, *b*35; p. xiv
Dalby, J.-W., A116, C871
Dale, Sir Thomas, *A True Relation of the State of Virginia*, review, C2789
Dalliba, Gerda, *Poems*, review, p. 557
Dane, C., *The Arrogant History of White Ben*, review, C1772
Dante, C60
Darby, H. C., *The Draining of the Fens*, review, C1804
— *The Medieval Fenland*, review, C1804

D'Arcy, M. C., *The Mind and Heart of Love*, review, C2227
Darley, George, A39; C821
Darling, F. Fraser, *Island Years*, re-view, C1819
Darling, Sir Malcolm, *Rusticus Loqui-tur*, review, C998
— *Wisdom and Waste in the Punjab Village*, review, C1407
Darlow, T. H., selector, *Christmas Poems*, review, C350
Darton, Harvey, *English Fabric*, re-view, C1488
Darwin, Bernard, *James Braid*, review, C2855
— *Pack Clouds Away*, review, C1885
Darwin, Charles, A99; C708
Darwin, Erasmus, C1171
Daryush, Elizabeth, *Verses, Third Book*, review, C1297
Daubney, Robert and Harold Cooper, eds, *Miscellany*, B65
Davenport, David, *Richard Plantage-net, and Other Poems*, review, C137
Davey, Norman, *Desiderum*, MCMXV-MCMXVIII, review, C124
Davidson, Angus, *King Lear*, review, C1690
— *Miss Douglas of New York*, re-view, C2900
Davie, Donald, *Events and Wisdoms*, review, C3312
Davies, Hugh Sykes, *Petron*, review, C1495
Davies, Idris, *Tonypandy*, review, C2131
Davies, Martin, *The British School*, review, C2324
Davies, Peter, London, publisher, B255*a*
Davies, Rhys, *Honey and Bread*, re-view, C1441
Davies, Sneyd, C605
Davies, Stuart, C90
Davies, W. H., C339
— *The Birth of Song*, review, C1564
— *Collected Poems: Second Series*, review, C374
— *The Collected Poems of*, review, C1406
— *Forty-Nine Poems*, review, C813
— *The Hour of Magic, and Other Poems*, review, C339

— *The Lovers' Song-Book*, review, C1331
— *Poems, 1930–31*, review, C1250
— *A Poet's Calendar*, review, p. 557
Davis, Sam, *Hedley Verity*, review, C2822
Davison, Edward L., *Poems*, review, C166
Dawkins, R. M., *The Monks of Athos*, review, C1515
Day, J. Wentworth, *Farming Adventure*, review, C1958
Day, John, *Gentleness and Nobility; Law Tricks*, review, C2674
Day Company, John, New York, B280
Day by Day, C2592
Daydream in Hokkaido, A102
Days Before the War, C537
De Bello Germanico, A33
De Bury, Richard, *The Philobiblon*, review, C2184
De Candole, Henry, *The Story of Henfield*, review, C2393
De la Mare, Walter, C601, 854, 2637, 3171, 3179
— *Alone*, review, C643
— *Behold, this Dreamer*, review, C1757
— *The Burning Glass and Other Poems*, reviews, C2172, 2189, 2192
— *Collected Poems*, review, C1909
— *Collected Poems and Verses*, review, C2018
— *Ding Ding Bell* review, p. 558
— *Down-Adown-Derry*, review, C350
— *Early One Morning in the Spring*, review, C1463
— 80th birthday, C3009, 3012
— *The Fleeting*, review, C1286
— The Friend of Life *later* Walter de la Mare, A108; C2172
— *Inward Companion*, reviews, C2573, 2593
— *Love*, review, C1977
— *Memoirs of a Midget*, review, C280
— *News*, review, C1059
— *Pleasures and Speculations*, review, C1823
— *Private View*, review, C3085
— *Poems, 1919–1934*, review, C1498

— *Time Passes*, review, C1945
— *To Lucy*, review, C1167
— *The Traveller*, review, C2351
— *Tribute to*, B123, 290
— *Winged Chariot*, reviews, C2689, 2691
— ed., *Come Hither*, review, C448
De Quincey, Thomas, A24
— 1785–1859, B18; C257
De Sola Pinto, Vivian, B266
De Selincourt, Ernest, *Wordsworthian and Other Studies*, review, C2380
Dean and Bookman, C3344
Deardon, Harold, *The Fire-Raisers*, review, C1392
Death of a Youth, B50
Decachord, The, London, C2108
Decade of Renascence, The, D34
Decline of Puritanism, The, C1038
Dede of Pittie, The, A118; B154; C2929
Dedicated to Elia, C346
Definitive Text, A, C826
Defoe, Daniel, C68, 979, 1632
— Bicentenary, A39; C1115
— Defoe's Great Britain, A39; C659
— *A Tour Thro' the Whole Island of Great Britain*, review, C659
Delafield, E. M., *The Provincial Lady in War-Time*, review, C1794
Delightes of the Schollar, C12
delta, review, C3074
"Delusive Fly, The", C412
Dent, J. M., & Sons Ltd, London, B99; Ea7, b7
Department of Scientific and Industrial Research, C81
Déroulède, Paul, C3209
Desbordes-Valmore, Marceline, C2991
Deschamps, Eustache, A2–3
Deschamps, Paul, *La Formation de la Pensée de Coleridge, 1772–1804*, review, C3331
Deutsch, Babette and Avrahm Yarmolinsky, eds, *Contemporary German Poetry*, review, C448
Devon Worthy, A, C450
Dewey, Thomas E., *Journey to the Far Pacific*, review, C2923
Dial Press, The, New York, B18, 244.1
Dialect Poems, C2275

654

Douglas, Keith, *Collected Poems*, B269
— jt ed., *Augury*, B90
Douglas, Norman, C2771
— *Looking Back*, review, C1349
Douglas, Ronald Macdonald, *Strangers Come Home*, review, C1441
Douie, Charles, *Beyond the Sunset*, review, C1458
Dove, Robert, C1739
Dowden, Edward, *The Life of Percy Bysshe Shelley*, review, C2670
Downing, F. A., A32
Downing, Rupert, *If I Laugh*, review, C1844
Doyle, Camilla, *Poems*, review, C448
Dramatic Fragment, A, C425
Draper, John W., *The Funeral Elegy and the Rise of English Romanticism*, review, C850
— *The Humors and Shakespeare's Characters*, review, C2152
Drayton, Michael, *Nimphidia*, review, C277
— *Polyolbion*, review, C330
Dreadful Note, B137
Dream Inn, The, C2008
Dream of Violence Among the Spires, A, Ee5
Dreams of Great Writers, C590
Dreiser, Theodore, *Chains*, review, C682
— *Moods Cadenced and Declaimed*, review, C853
Drennan, Professor, on words, C94
Drinkwater, John, *A Book for Bookmen*, review, C612
— *The Collected Poems of*, review, C1669
— *The Pilgrim of Eternity*, review, C576
— *The Poems of*, review, p. 557
— *Preludes, 1921-1922*, review, C341
— *Some Contributions to the English Anthology*, review, C324
— *Summer Harvest*, review, C1332
— ed. *The Way of Poetry*, review, C108
Drunken Barnaby, C1261
Dryden, John, B89, 184
Du Bellay, Joachim, A2-3
Du Maurier, Daphne, *The du Mauriers*, review, C1592

— *The Young George du Maurier*, review, C2712
Dublin Magazine, The, January-March 1947, review, C2327
Duchess of Malfi, The, B226
Duckworth, London, publisher, A10c, 12c-d, 20c
Duke, Winifred, *Six Trials*, review, C1336
Dukes, Sir Paul, *An Epic of the Gestapo*, review, C1827
Dumont-Wilden, L., *The Wandering Prince*, review, C1421
Dunbar, Janet, *The Early Victorian Woman*, review, C2983
Duncan, Ronald, *This Way to the Tomb*, review, C2251
Dunn, H. H., *The Crimson Jester*, review, C1357
Dunsany, Lord, *The Blessing of Pan*, review, C634
Durham University Journal, The, Vol. 38, No. 3, review, C2133
— Vol. 43, No. 2, review, C2635
Durnford, H. G., *The Tunnellers of Holzminden*, review, C157
Durrell, Lawrence, C2116
— *Key to Modern Poetry*, review, C2936
— *Prospero's Cell*, review, C2144
— and others, eds, *Personal Landscape*, review, C2118
Dutton, E. P., & Co., Inc., New York, B68b, 73b
Duvernois, Henri, *The Holidays*, review, C284
Dyer, George, C709
Dyer, John, C622
Dyment, Clifford, *First Day*, review, C1498
— and others, eds, *New Poems 1952*, B144

E.C.W. [*i.e.* E. C. Wright], p. 557
Earle, John, *Micro-Cosmographie*, review, C684
Early Drama, The, C2674
Early English Text Society, C2343
Ears and No Ears, C2664
East Africa Memorial, The, B179
Eastern Aesthetics, C3366
Eastern Anchorage, C3273
Eastern Empire, C855

Essayist and Editor, C3141

Essayists of the Romantic Period, A24, 117

Essays and Studies, by Members of the English Association, Oxford, London, C1376, 1584, 3268

— Vol. 18, review, C1283

Essays & Studies Presented to Dr. Sanki Ichikawa, B165·1

Essays by Divers Hands: Being the Transactions of the Royal Society of Literature, London, C1898, 3370

— New Series, Vol. 15, review, C1590

— — Vol. 22, review, C2225

Essays in Criticism, Oxford, C3212

Essays in Retrospect, C1557

Essays of the Year 1930–1931, B51

— review, C1178

Essays on the Eighteenth Century, B107

Estese, Elia, Indicator, C239

Estimates and Reminders, C649

Etchells, Frederick, and Hugh Macdonald, London, publisher, B29

Ethiopic Texts and Marvels, Christianity and Magic, C851

Eton College Chronicle, Windsor, C245

Études anglaises, Paris, C1609, 1783, 2863, 3017, 3129, 3225-6

— No. 4, review, C2969

Euripides, *Three Plays*, review, C3089

Evans, A. R., *The Sailor's Way*, review, C1421

Evans, A. W., *Warburton and the Warburtonians*, review, C1215

Evans, B. Ifor, *English Literature*, review, C2123

— *English Poetry in the Later Nineteenth Century*, review, C1288

Evans, Godfrey, *Behind the Stumps*, review, C2631

Evans, Margiad, *Autobiography*, review, C1989

— *A Ray of Darkness*, review, C2895

Evelyn, Elizabeth, *No Promise in Summer*, review, C2262

Evelyn, John, *The Early Life and Education of*, review, C266

Evening News, Tokyo, C3121

Evenings at Home and Abroad, C3189

Everybody's, London, C2473, 2496, 2570, 2583, 2612, 2633, 2745, 2823, 2908, 2924, 2967, 2988, 3012, 3063

Everybody's Books, C1614

Everyman, London, C907

Ewart, Wilfrid, *Scots Guard*, review, C1391

Ewers, John K., *Creative Writing in Australia*, review, C2199

Exchange Hotel Theatre, Tokyo, B137

Exchange of Ideas, C2546

Excluded Angel, An, C2298

Ex-Footballer, An, A43

Exhibition Dedicated to Youth, B148

Exhibition of Paintings by Pansy Ng, B230

Expensive Vision, An, C720

Experience and Record, A91

Experiment in Epic, An, C470

Expressions at the Market, A43

"Extempore Effusion", Wordsworth's Dead Friends, C1493

Extra Turn, The, A50; B52

Eye for London, An, C2411

Eyre, Frank and Charles Hadfield, *English Rivers and Canals*, reviews, C2206, 2215

Eyre & Spottiswoode, London, publisher, B40

Faber, Geoffrey, *The Buried Stream*, review, C1897

Faber & Faber Ltd, London, B73a, 108, 123, 269

Faber & Gwyer Ltd, London, A27

Fable of Comenius, The, C2701

Face of England, The, A43

Facts and Fixtures, C2652

Fading Voices, C1015

Fairbridge, Kingsley, *Veld Verse*, review, C707

Fairchild, Hoxie Neale, *The Noble Savage*, review, C769

Fairies Under Glass, p. 558

Fall In, Ghosts, A44, 108; B60

Fallas, Carl, *The Gate is Open*, review, C1719

Fallen Englishmen, A39; C1032

Falls, Cyril, C900
— *The Critic's Armoury*, review, p. 558
— jt compiler, B35
Family Album, C2420
Family History, A, C2905
Family Physician in the 17th Century, The, A127; C3132
Famous Case, A, C719
Famous Forest, A, C2180
Fan Tod, The, A43
Fantasies and Satires, C411
Fantastics, C1177
Fantasy, C449
Far Away and Long Ago, A102
Far Away and To-day, C2450
Far East, The, C2706
Farewell Message, A, D36-7
Farjeon, Eleanor, *A Collection of Poems*, review, C880
— *Edward Thomas*, review, C3218
Farley, Miriam S., *Aspects of Japan's Labor Problems*, review, C2655
Farm Labourer, C1808
Farmer, David, compiler, B283
Farmer, F. Rhodes, *Thirsty Earth*, review, C1407
Farming Memoirs, C2082
Farrar-Hockley, A. H., *The Somme*, review, C3323
Farrell, Fred A., *The 51st Division*, review, C184
Farrington, Benjamin, *Francis Bacon*, review, C2697
"Fastidious Brisk of Oxford", C2362
Father and Son, B120
Fausset, Hugh l'Anson, *The Condemned; The Mercy of God*, review, C356
— *Samuel Taylor Coleridge*, review, C577
— *Walt Whitman*, review, C1907
— *William Cowper*, review, C788
Favourite Studies in English Literature, A101
Fawcett, F. Dubrez, *Dickens the Dramatist*, review, C2943
Fawcett, P. H., *Exploration Fawcett*, review, C2982
Fear No More: A Book of Poems for the Present Time, B91
Fearey, Robert A., *The Occupation of Japan*, review, C2749
"Feast of Five, The", C19

Feist, Hans, *Ewiges England*, review, C2230
Felicities, C3264
Fender, P. G. H., *An ABC of Cricket*, review, C1616
Fenollosa, Ernest, *The Chinese Written Character as a Medium for Poetry*, review, C3310
Fermented Liquors, C1060
Few Not Quite Forgotten Writers, A, A173
Fiction: Chaucer to Dickens, A91
Field, Michael, *The Wattlefold*, review, C1055
Fielding, Henry, *Tom Thumb the Great*, B89
Fifth Visit to Japan, A, B291
15 Poems for William Shakespeare, B252
XVth-Century Bestiary, A, C761
Fifty Years Ago on Monday the First World War Ended, C3369
50 years dedicated to the graves of world wars [etc.], C3363
Find, The, A43, 108
Finegan, Jack, *The Archaeology of World Religion*, review, C2974
Fingleton, J. H., *Brown and Company*, review, C2748
Finzi, Gerald, A156; B157; Ed5·1
Firbank, Ronald, *The Princess Zoubaroff*, review, C226
Fireside Collaboration, A43
Firkins, O. W., *Jane Austen*, review, C172
First Address, A, A24; C477
First Asian Student Salon of Photography, B216
"First Catch Your Shakespeare", C2512
First Draft, A, C1588
First Englishman in Japan, The, B189
First Impressions, Tokyo, D15
First Poems, C287
First Steps in English Conversation, B233
Fischer, Louis, *The Life of Mahatma Gandhi*, review, C2600
Fisher, John, *Island of Refuge*, review, C1407
Fisher Unwin Ltd., T., London, B8
Fishing, B31
Fitzgerald, F. Scott, *Tender is the*

Night, review, C1407

Fitzgerald, M. H., *Herbert Edward Ryle*, review, C716

Fitzurse, R., *It Was Not Jones*, review, C715

Five Greatest Novels, The, C384

Fives, p. 557

Flashing Stream, The, B169

Flatman, Thomas, C622

Flecker, James Elroy, *Collected Prose of*, review, C336

— *Hassan*, review, C336

Fleg, Edmond, *The Wall of Weeping*, review, C880

Fleisher, Wilfrid, *Volcanic Isle*, review, C1911

Fleming, J. A., *Flemish Influence in Britain*, review, C949

Fleming, Peter, 'Two Lears', letter on, C1120

— and Derek Verschoyle, eds, *Spectator's Gallery*, B59

Fletcher, C. R. L., *The Great War, 1914–1918*, review, C57

Fletcher, John, *Bonduca*, review, C2821

Floodland, A43

Foch, Marshal, C1156

Folio, London *see Folio Magazine*, London

Folio Magazine, London, C3101, 3125

Folk-Songs of the Thames, C385

Follett, F. V., *A History of Worcester Royal Grammar School*, review, C2747

Follower of Cobbett, A, C2186

Follower of the Humanities, A, C916

Folly Bridge, B105

Fontaine, Algiers, D4

Foot, Edward Edwin, *Jane Hollybrand, and Other Original Poems*, review, C1235

Footman, David, *Pig and Pepper*, review, C1515

For the Record, C2229

For the Young Person, C2737

Ford, Ford Madox, *Great Trade Route*, review, C1587

Ford, George H., *Keats and the Victorians*, review, C2109

Ford, Newell F., *The Prefigurative Imagination of John Keats*, review, C2694

Ford, S. Gertrude, A7

Foreign Language Teaching [*Bulletin of the Institute for Research in Language Teaching*], Tokyo, C2451

Forest, Ellen, *Yuki-San*, reviews, C717, 722.1

Forester, C. S., *The General*, review, C1531

Form, London, C293

Forrest, Charles, *The Defendant Soul*, review, C865

Fortescue, Sir J. W., *The Last Post*, review, C1421

Fortnightly, The see Fortnightly Review

Fortnightly Review later *The Fortnightly*, London, C873, 893, 941, 948, 960, 1021, 1152, 1274, 1415, 1436, 1448, 1463, 1472, 1478, 1490, 1502, 1573, 1588, 1626, 1760, 1938, 2021; p. 557

Fortune Theatre, London, A118; B154

Forty Miles from London, C888

Foster, J. J., *Wessex Worthies*, review, C249

Four Cavaliers Assembled, C1155

Four Square Books, A28*i*

Four Strange Years: Anthology of the Great War, The, C1636

Four Years of War, C1727

Fourteenth Volume, The, C628

Fourth Estate, The, C2020

Fourth Visit: or, Japan up-to-date, B291; C3229

Fox, Adam, *Old King Coel*, review, C1668

Fracchia, Umberto, *Robino and Other Stories*, review, C1237

Fragment of Byronism, A, A126; C3129

Fragment of Truth, A, C566

Fragmentary Notes on the Painter-Poets, A104; C622

France, Anatole, C513

Frank, Leonhard, *In the Last Coach*, review, C1421

Fränkel, Hermann, *Ovid: A Poet Between Two Worlds*, review, C2139

Frankau, Pamela, *I Find Four People*, review, C1487

— *No News*, review, C1678

Frankland, Edward, *The Path of Glory*, review, C1441

— ed., *Up the Line to Death*, B260

Gardner, Edmund G., *Italian Literature*, review, C624

Garland, H. B., *Storm and Stress*, review, C2865

Garland, B279

Garland for the Queen, A, B157

Garland of Verse, A, C1504

Garnett, David, *War in the Air*, review, C1877

Garrod, H. W., A68, 154; C3267

— *Collins*, review, C818

— *Epigrams*, review, C2322

— *Keats*, review, C610

— *The Poetry of Collins*, review, C818

Garrod, H. W., *The Study of Poetry*, review, C1530

Garstang, Walter, *Songs of the Birds*, review, C327

Garvin, Viola, *Dedication*, reviews, C710, 726

Gascoyne, David, *Poems, 1937–1942*, review, C2019

Gauntlett, J. O., *Advanced English Course*, B175

Gavin, Catherine, *Edward VII*, review, C1895

Gawsworth, John, A42; B50; Ea5; p. XV

— ed., *Known Signatures*, B57

— ed., *The Muse of Monarchy*, review, C1611

Gay, John, C978

— *Rural Sports*, review, C978

— *Trivia*, review, p. 557

Gay and Grave, C284

Gelb, I. J., *A Study in Writing*, review, C2808

Gell, Hon. Mrs, *John Franklin's Bride*, review, C958

Gems from English Poetry, B224; Ed3

Genders, Roy, *League Cricket in England*, review, C2875

Generals and Ghosts, C1476

Genesis of Wuthering Heights, The, B205

Genius and Insanity, C1737

Genius and Merit, C757

Genji, Takahashi, *Advanced English Course*, B175

Gentle Pagan, A, C2360

Gentleman, David, illus., A174; B284

Gentleman of Kent, C3355

"Gentleman's Magazine, The", 1731–1907, A39; C1131

Geographical Improvements, A50

Geographical Maagazine, London, C3216

George, Daniel, *Pick and Choose*, review, C1577

Georgian Poetry 1920–1922, B9

Georgics in Prose, C1602

Gepp, E., *Essex Dialect Dictionary*, Supplement, review, C174

Gerhardi, William, *Of Mortal Love*, review, C1571

— *The Romanovs*, review, C1788

German Life and Letters, Oxford, C1645

Ghost of Soho, A, C2001

Ghosts [*or* Ghosts in Flanders], p. XVI

Ghosts and Grotesques, A50; C582

Ghyka, Matila, *Again, One Day*, review, C1552

Gibbings, Robert, *Coming Down the Wye*, review, C1942

— *Sweet Thames Run Softly*, review, C1837

Gibbon, Edward, A53, 99

— Captain Gibbon *later* An Infantry Officer, A39; C862

— *Journal to January 28th, 1763*, review, C862

Gibbons, Stella, *Miss Lindsey and Pa*, review, p. 557

Gibbs, C. R. Vernon, *Passenger Liners of the Western Ocean*, review, C2963

Gibbs, Lewis, *Earthquake in the Triangle*, review, C1407

— *Michael and His Angels*, review, C1498

Gibbs, Sir Philip, *Ten Years After*, review, p. 558

Gibney, Frank, *Five Gentleman of Japan*, reviews, C3069, 3087

Gibson, Ashley, *Postscript to Adventure*, review, C949

Gibson, Douglas, *The Singing Earth*, on, C2743

Gibson, James, ed., B289

Gibson, Wilfrid, *The Early Whistler*, review, C643

— Gibson for Schools, C578

— *The Golden Room*, review, C792

— *Leaves and Fruit*, review, C628

— *Selected Essays*, reviews, C747, 756

Göttingen Celebrations: Oxford's Abstention, C1613

Gough, Philip, illus., B146

Gould, Gerald, *The Collected Poems of*, reviews, C963; p. 557

— *The Journey*, review, C270

Gourdie, Tom, *Italic Handwriting*, Ea19

Gourlay, A. B., *A History of Sherborne School*, review, C2922

Gourou, Pierre, *The Tropical World*, review, C3062

Gow, A. S. F., *A. E. Housman*, review, C1568

Gowen, Herbert H., *An Outline History of Japan*, review, C671

Grabo, Carl, *The Meaning of "The Witch of Atlas"*, review, C1475

— *A Newton Among Poets*, review, C1116

Graham, Rigby, illus., B277

Graham, Stephen, ed., *The Tramp's Anthology*, review, C807

Graham, Virginia, *Consider the Years*, review, C2306

Graham, Walter, *English Literary Periodicals*, review, C1130

Grand Tour, B73

Grand Tour, C1464

Grant, Douglas, *The Fuel of the Fire*, reviews, C2574, 3118

— *James Thomson, Poet of "The Seasons"*, review, C2714

Grant, G. A. A., and J. Klinkert, *The Ship's Compass*, review, C2861

Granville-Barker, Helen, *The Locked Book*, review, C1577

Graphic, The, London, C25

Grass Widow, B244

Graves, Charles, *Life Line*, review, C1895

Graves, Nancy, A8

Graves, P. P., *The Pursuit (Hauran, Autumn 1918)*, review, C1067

Graves, Robert, A8; B7

— *The Feather Bed*, review, C425

— *Goodby to All That*, review, C924

— *Poems, 1926–1930*, review, C1137

— *To Whom Else*, review, C1137

— *Whipperginny*, review, C369

Gray, Thomas, A84

— *Correspondence of*, review, C1490

Great Administrator, A, C2611

Great Church of the Holy Trinity, Long Melford, A169, 176

Great Church of the Holy Trinity Long Melford, A164

Great Dream, A, D37

Great Earth and Opportunity, D29

Great Hurry, A43

Great Names, B18; C613 (review)

Great Names, C89, 156, 193, 257, 298, 329

Great Short Stories of the War, B40

Great Victorians, The, B56

Great Writers in Fairyland, C3101

Greater Tide, The, C2154

Grecian Muse, The, C2696

Grecian Urn, The, C995

Greek Drama, C3089

Green, F. E., *A History of the English Agricultural Labourer, 1870–1920*, review, C77

Green, F. Pratt, *This Unlikely Earth*, review, C2778

Green, H. M., *The Book of Beauty*, review, C906

— *A Midsummer Nights Dream*, review, C1596

Green, Matthew, *The Spleen*, review, C1543

Green, R. L., *Tellers of Tales*, review, C2208

Green, Robert, *Friar Bacon and Friar Bungay*, review, C3052

Green, Russell, *Passions*, review, C253

Greenaway, Kate, C1012

Greene, Graham, *Stamboul Train*, review, C1244

— ed., *The Old School*, review, C1391

Greenwell, Graham H., *An Infant in Arms*, review, C1456

Greenwood, Walter, *His Worship the Mayor*, review, C1391

Grennan, Margaret R., *William Morris*, review, C2197

Gretton, M. Sturge, *Burford Past and Present*, review, C57

Gribble, Leonard, intro., *Profiles from Notable Biographies*, A78

Grierson, Edward, *The Lilies and the*

Bees, review, C2994

Grierson, H. J. C., *The Flute, with Other Translations and a Poem*, review, C1187

— *Lyrical Poetry from Blake to Hardy*, reviews, C805, 837; p. XVI

Grieve, Hilda E. P., *More Examples of English Handwriting*, review, C2616

Grieve, Peter, *The Wilderness Voyage*, review, C2752

Griffith, Gwilym O., *John Bunyan*, review, C650

Griffith, Hubert, *Playtime in Russia*, review, C1451

Griggs, Earl Leslie, *Coleridge Fille*, review, C1863

— *Hartley Coleridge, His Life and Works*, reviews, C905, 912

— jt. ed., *Coleridge Studies*, B66

Grigson, Geoffrey, *Before the Romantics*, on, C2369, 2379

— *Visionary Poems and Passages*, review, C2083

— ed., *The Romantics*, review, C1952

Grinsell, L. V., *The Ancient Burial Mounds of England*, review, C3051

Gronow, Captain, *The Last Recollections of*, review, C1357

Groom, Bernard, *A Short History of English Words*, review, C1407

Growth of English Literature, The, A85, 93; C3096

Grylls, R. Glynn, *Mary Shelley*, reviews, C1675–6

Guardian, The, Manchester *see* Manchester Guardian

Guedalla, Philip, *The Duke*, review, C1153

— *Middle East 1940–1942*, review, C2071

— *Mr. Churchill: A Portrait*, review, C1894

Guest of Thomas Hardy, A162

Guinness, Bryan, *The Rose in the Tree*, review, C3312

Gunn, J., *Orkney*, review, C1226

Gunner on the Western Front, B75a

Gunther, John, *Inside Asia*, review, C1756

— *The Riddle of MacArthur*, review, C2673

Gunzô, Tokyo, D19

Gurner, Ronald, *Pass Guard at Ypres*, review, C949

Gurney, Ivor, *Poems*, B167

Guy and His Followers, C152

Gwynn, Denis, *The Irish Free State, 1922–1927*, review, C749

Gwynn, Stephen, *Oliver Goldsmith*, reviews, C1470, 1478

Haas, C. de, *Nature and the Country in English Poetry [etc.]*, reviews, C750, 766

Haberly, Loyd, *Anne Boleyn*, review, C1498

Hadfield, John, *A Book of Beauty*, review, C2898

— ed., *The Saturday Book*, B146, 268

Hadfield, Miles, *An English Almanac*, review, C2592

Hafiz, *Poems from the Divan*, review, C715

Hagberg, Knut, *Carl Linnaeus*, C2753 (review), 2785

Haggard, Lilias Rider, *I Walked by Night*, review, C1477

— *A Norfolk Notebook*, review, C2279

— and Henry Williamson, *Norfolk Life*, reviews, C1978, 1980

Hagreen, Philip, illus., B15

Haig, Douglas, Field-Marshal Lord, *The Private Papers of*, review, C2935

"Haig Strikes Again", C631

Haight, Elizabeth Hazelton, *More Essays on Greek Romances*, review, C2117

Haiku, Vol. 1, review, C2504

Hakluyt Society, C2309

Haldane, J. B. S., *Keeping Cool & Other Essays*, review, C1796

Hale, Constance, *Grass Widow*, B244

Halfway House, A45

Halkett, G. R., *The Dear Monster*, review, C1769

Hall, A. R., *Ballistics in the Seventeenth Century*, review, C2881

Hall, Bert and J. J. Niles, *One Man's War*, review, C897

Hall, John, *The Advancement of Learning*, review, C3030

Hall, P. Barbara, *Last Flight*, review, C1471

Hallam, Arthur Henry, C429

— *The Writings of*, review, C1982

Hambloch, Ernest, *British Consul*, review, C1672

— *Italy Militant*, review, C1859

Hamilton, George Rostrevor, *John Lord, Satirist*, review, C1357

— *Selected Poems and Epigrams*, review, C2131

— and John Arlott, eds, *Landmarks*, review, C2000

Hamilton, Hamish, London, publisher, B153

Hamilton, Mary Agnes, *Remembering My Good Friends*, review, C2066

Hamilton, W. H., *John Masefield: A Critical Study*, review, C335

Hamlet, and Other Studies, A96

Hammer, S. C., *Ludvig Holberg*, review, C102

Hammond, Walter R., *Cricket My Destiny*, review, C2287

— *Cricket's Secret History*, review, C2862

— *Cricketer's School*, review, C2554

Hampstead & Highgate Express, London, E*b*31

Hampstead & St John's Wood Advertiser, London, E*b*31

Han Suyin, *A Many-Splendoured Thing*, review, C2814

Hanazono, Kanesada, *The Development of Japanese Journalism*, review, p. 558

Hanchant, W., ed., *England is Here*, review, C1962

Handlist of English and Welsh Newspapers, Magazines and Reviews, review, C241

Hanging No Remedy, C1080

Hani, Y., A171; B143

Hani was Prometheus, Mrs, C3222

Hanighen, Frank C., and Anton Zischka, *The Secret War*, review C1441

Hanson, Lawrence, *The Life of S. T. Coleridge*, review, C1731

— and Elizabeth, *Gordon*, review, C2997

[Happiness which peace has brought], D24

Happy Island, The, A39; C330

Happy Voyager, C2695

Harada, Jiro, *The Gardens of Japan*, review, C729

Harbingers, The, A6

Harbour Sketch Written in Absence, D19

Harcourt, Brace and Company, Inc., New York, A29*b*; B15*b*, 25*b*, 41*b*, 84*b*, 92*b*, 94*b*, 98*b*, 101*b*

Hardie, Alec M., B249, 261

— ed., *The Castle of Indolence*, by James Thomson, B190

— 'and Keith C. Douglas, eds, *Augury*, B90

Hardie, Catherine Mackenzie, A73

Harding, R. Winboult, *John Bunyan*, review, C687

Harding, William Henry, *John Bunyan, Pilgrim and Dreamer*, review, C698

Hardy, Mrs, *The Later Years of Thomas Hardy, 1892–1928*, review, C980

Hardy, Thomas, A72, 84; B56, 118, 126, 270; C100, 136, 1698, 2373, 2680, 2762, 2809, 3277; E*a*31

— and His American Publisher, C626

— [and Max Gate], C2052

— *The Dynasts*, A99; C488 (Argument of)

— Guest of Thomas Hardy, A162

— [Hardy of Wessex], A70, 172; C1871, 3362

— Hardy's Earliest Verse, B119; C2394

— Hardy, Gosse and Bridges Fifty Years Ago, C568

— *Human Shows*, review, C548

— in America, C2259

— Notes on Visits to Thomas Hardy, *see* Thomas Hardy

— On 'Jude the Obscure', C3259

— *Pages from the Works of*, review, C335

— Thomas Hardy *later* Notes on Visits to Thomas Hardy, A108; B56

— *Yuletide in a Younger World*, review, C643

Hardy Annual, C2750

Hardy Society *see* Thomas Hardy Society of Japan

Hardyana, C679

Hare, Augustus J. C., *The Years with Mother*, review, C2897

Hare, Kenneth, *Nymphs and Rivers*, review, C3205

Harford, Lesbia, *The Poems of*, review, C1920

Hargest, James, *Farewell Campo 12*, review, C2169

Harlan, Aurelia Brooks, *Owen Meredith*, review, C2265

Harper & Brothers, New York & London, A31c, 32b, 35c; B27b, 97

Harper's Monthly Magazine, New York, C606

Harpole, James, *A Surgeon's Heritage*, review, C2987

Harrap & Co. Ltd, George G., London, B289

Harris, B., *In Quest of the Ashes*, review, C2675

Harris, Frank, *Oscar Wilde*, review, C1706

Harris, Wilson, foreword, *Spectator Harvest*, review, C2928

Harrison, Brian, ed., *University of Hong Kong: The First 50 Years 1911–1961*, B241

Harrison, Sir Edward R., *Harrison of Ightham*, review, C716

Harrison, G. B., *John Bunyan*, review, C744

— *A Second Elizabethan Journal*, review, C1108

— *Shakespeare*, review, C624

Harrison, G. H., A8

Hart, B. H. Lidell, *The Defence of Britain*, review, C1768

— *Europe in Arms*, review, C1607

— *Foch*, review, C1156

— *T. E. Lawrence: In Arabia and After*, review, C1358

— ed., *The Letters of Private Wheeler*, review, C2723

Hart-Davis, Rupert, London, publisher, A108a; B150, 203

Hart-Davis, Sir Rupert, A58, 135; pp. VII–XII

Harte, Bret, *Selected Poems*, B19

Hartley, L. P., *Night Fears*, review, C549

— *Simonetta Perkins*, review, C549

Hartman, Herbert, *Hartley Coleridge, Poet's Son and Poet*, reviews, C1132, 1134

Hartog, Sir Philip, *On the Relation of Poetry to Verse*, review, C597

Harvard Library Bulletin, Vol. 4, No. 3, review, C2582

Harvey, G. F., and Jack Hems, *Freshwater Tropical Aquarium Fishes*, review, C2907

Harvey, N. P., *The Rose in Britain*, review, C3077

Harvey, William, *The Anatomical Exercises of*, review, C733

Harvill Press, The, London, B189

Hashimi, M. I. ed., *The Government College Miscellany*, review, C2763

Haskell, Arnold L., *Balletomania*, review, C1421

— *Waltzing Matilda*, review, C1803

Haslam, George and others, eds, *Miscellany*, B76

Haslett, A. W., *Everyday Science*, review, C1578

— *Science in Transition*, review, C2396

Hassall, Christopher, *Devil's Dyke*, review, C1581

— *Edward Marsh*, Ea20

— and Denis Mathews, compilers, *Eddie Marsh*, B151

Hassall, John, Ea30

Hastings House, New York, publisher, A69b; B113b

Hatano, Isoka and Ichirô, *Mother and Son*, review, C3282

Hatzfeld, Helmut A., *Literature through Art*, review, C2871

Hay, Robert, *Landsman Hay*, review, C3015

Haycroft, Howard, *Murder for Pleasure*, review, C1924

Haydon, A. L., ed., *The Boy's Own Reciter*, review, C217

Haydon, Benjamin Robert, C691, 2246

— *Autobiography*, B24

Hayes, J. Gordon, *Antarctica*, review, C736

Hayley, William, C2181

Hayward, Gordon, *Avalanche*, review, C1622

Hayward, John, intro., *Poems, 1951*, review, C2735

Hayward, Richard, *In Praise of Ulster*, review, C1701

Hazlitt, William, A24, 101; C1976, 2001
—— 1778-1830, B18; C156
Head, Adrian, *Seven Words and the Civilian*, review, C2306
Head Master's Album, The, A131; B182
Headlam, Maurice, *A Holiday Fisherman*, review, C1391
Heard, Gerald, *These Hurrying Years*, review, C1357
Hearn, Lafcadio, C1138, 3221
—— *Essays on American Literature*, review, C939
—— *Glimpses of Unfamiliar Japan*, review, C657
—— *Lectures on Shakespeare*, review, C939
—— *Some New Letters and Writings of*, review, C544
—— *Some Strange English Literary Figures* [etc.], review, C656
Heath, Sir H. Frank and A. L. Hetherington, *Industrial Research and Development*, review, C2219
Heine, Heinrich, C903
Heinemann, William, C127
Heinemann Ltd, William, London, B88a, 228a, 262; Ea16
Helps to Teachers of English Literature, C2451
Helston, John, *Broken Shade*, review, C337
—— *High Road and Lonning*, review, C757
Henderson, W. B. Drayton, *The New Argonautica*, review, C762
Henley, W. E., *Recoveries*, review, C3312
Hennell, Thomas, illus., B104
—— *British Craftsmen*, review, C1964
—— *Poems*, review, C1597
—— *The Witnesses*, review, C1702
Henrey, Robert, *Letters from Paris, 1870-1875*, review, C1915
Henriques, Robert, *Captain Smith and Company*, review, C1963
Her Privates We, B255
Herbert, Dorothea, *Retrospections of*, review, C860
Herbert, George, A25
—— *Latin Poems*, A51; C1376
—— *The Temple*, review, C629
Herbert of Cherbury, Edward, Lord,

The Autobiography of, review, C739
Here's a Book Worth Hundreds, C3063
Herling, Gustav, *A World Apart*, review, C2722
Hermes: Westfield College Magazine, London, Eb3
Hermine, Empress, *Days in Doorn*, review, C716
Hero of "In Memoriam", The, C429
Herrick, Robert, A110; C2700
—— *Delighted Earth: A Selection* [etc.], review, C652
—— *The Poetical Works of*, review, C285
—— *Robert Herrick*, A39; C285
Herrmanns, Ralph, *Lee Lan Flies the Dragon Kite*, B243
Hertzler, Arthur E., *The Horse and the Buggy Doctor*, review, C1741
Hervey, Lord Francis, ed., *The History of King Edmund the Martyr* [etc.], review, C922
Hervey, George, *The Goldfish of China in the XVIII Century*, review, C2609
Hetherington, Sir Hector, *The Social Function of the University*, review, C3026
Hewitt, Graily, *Lettering*, review, C1046
Hewlett, Dorothy, *Adonais*, review, C1633
Hewlett, Maurice, *Extemporary Essays*, review, C365
Hexapoda, C2153
Hiawatha's Wedding Feast, B173
Hibbard, G. R., ed., *Renaissance and Modern Essays*, B266
"Hic et Ubique", C345
Hichens, Robert Peverell, *We Fought Them in Gunboats*, review, C2010
Hicks, Arthur C., and R. Milton Clarke, *A Stage Version of Shelley's Cenci*, review, C2164
High Hill Books, London, B258
Higham, F. M. G., *King James the Second*, review, C1421
Highgate Grove, C3018
Highway, The, London, C1254
Hilary Press, London, B285
Hillier, J., *Hokusai*, B204; C3207 (review)
—— *Japanese Masters of the Colour*

669

Hong Kong University Book Store, B225
Hong Kong University, English Poetry, B234
Hong Kong University Engineering Journal, Hong Kong, C3122
Hong Kong University Press, A155; B190, 200, 205, 215, 236, 241, 248, 253, 275, 287
Hongkong, C2952
Hongkong Standard, Hong Kong, C3134
Honour to the Swiss, C2226
Hood, Thomas, A110; C599, 3235
— Hood's Literary Reminiscences, A39; C952
Hook, Theodore, C808, 811
Hop Leaf, The, A43
Hope and Object, C2342
Hope-Nicholson, Hedley, *The Mindes Delight*, review, C807
Hopkins, Gerard Manley, A113
Hopkins, Kenneth, *English Poetry: A Short History*, B247
— *Walter de la Mare*, review, C3012
— compiler, *Edmund Blunden: A Selection of His Poetry and Prose*, A108
Hopkins, R. Thurston, *Thomas Hardy's Dorset*, review, C335
Hopkinson, Austin, *Religio Militis*, review, C638
Horace, *More Odes of*, review, C2119
— *Twenty-Five Odes of*, review, C2119
Horace Lends His Shield, C2116
Horatians, C2149
Horgan, Paul, *No Quarter Given*, review, C1466
Hori, Eishiro, Ea18
— *Complete Guide to English Conversation*, B232
— *First Steps in English Conversation*, B233
— *The Talk of the Town*, B17
Hori, Masato, trans., C2523
Hori, Naoyuki, B233
Hori, Yoshiaki, B233
Horizon, London, C2068-9
Horizon Press, New York, A108*b*
Hornby, Clifford, *Rural Amateur*, review, C1992
Horne, Alistair, *The Price of Glory*, review, C3279

Horne, David H., *The Life and Minor Works of George Peele*, review, C3053
Horne, R. H., *Orion*, reviews, C731, 773
Horrabin, J. F., illus., B18
Horrible Example, The, C964
Horsefeathers, film review, C1763
Horsnell, Horace, *The Horoscope*, review, C1357
Hôsei, Tokyo, C3137-8
Hosei University Press, The, A92
Hosken, James Dryden, *Shores of Lyonesse*, review, C448
Hotson, Leslie, *Shakespeare's Sonnets Dated, and Other Essays*, review, C2512
Houghton, Claude, *This Was Ivor Trent*, review, C1427
— *Transformation Scene*, review, C2300
Houghton, Lord, *The Life and Letters of John Keats*, review, C786
Houpt, Charles Theodore, *Mark Akenside*, review, C2117
House, Humphry, *Coleridge*, reviews, C2999, 3004
House in Richmond Park, A, C2054
Housman, A. E., *More Poems*, reviews, C1568, 1572
— *The Name and the Nature of Poetry*, reviews, C1288, 1296
— *A Shropshire Lad*, on, C2213
Housman, Laurence, *The Collected Poems of*, review, C1657
— *The Unexpected Years*, review, C1593
— *Victoria Regina*, review, C1421
— ed., *War Letters of Fallen Englishmen*, reviews, C1029, 1032
Houtchens, Lawrence Huston and Carolyn Washburn Houtchens, *Leigh Hunt's Literary Criticism*, review, C3193
"How Should I Forget?", C3146
How the Fens Were Drained, C1804
Howard, Sir Albert, *Farming and Gardening for Health or Disease*, review, C2130
Howard, Keble, *The Fast Gentleman*, review, C682
Howard, L. O., *History of Applied Entomology*, review, C1091
Howarth, R. G., *Minor Poets of the*

Joyce, Michael, *Ordeal at Lucknow*, review, C1713
"Judgments", A102
Judson, Alexander C., *The Life of Edmund Spenser*, review, C2320
Jugaku, Bunshô, trans., A90*b*, 97
— *A Bibliographical Study of William Blake's Note-Book*, B159
Jüngèr, Ernst, *The Storm of Steel*, review, C866
Junzaburo, Nishiwaki, *Advanced English Course*, B175
Jupiter Recordings Ltd, London, E*d*6
Just a Victorian, A43; C3173

Kabashikigaisha Hokuseidô, D13
Kadogawa-Shinso, D10
Kagoshima University, B207*b*
Kairyudo, Tokyo, publisher, A43*b*
Kansai University Bulletin, C2523
Karmendi, Ferenc, *Via Bodenbach*, review, C1441
Karunakaran, K. P., *India in World Affairs*, review, C3079
Katayama, Gorō, B283.1
Kavanagh, Patrick, *A Soul for Sale*, review, C2337
Kawade Shobō Kan, Tokyo, publisher, B161
Kawatake, Dr, E*a*12
Keary, C. F., *The Posthumous Poems of*, review, C419
Keats, John, A21, 24, 84, 99, 142; B16; C421, 1618, 1620, 1633, 2198, 3188, 3201; E*a*25
— Barry Cornwall and Keats, A160; C3293
— Beauty and Truth, C2694
— Friends of, C2477
— — The, A39; C786
— in America, C2347
— Indications of Keats, A152; C3249
— Keats and C. A. Brown, C938
— Keats and His Predecessors, B55; C869
— Keats and His Reviewers, C1411
— Keats and Shelley, C252
— "Keats Circle, The", C2487
— Keats, G. F. Mathew and Others, C1026
— Keats House, C2170-1
— Keats House, Rome, B276

— Keats's Editor, A154; C3267
— Keats's Friend Mathew, A54; C1499
— Keats's Friends, C1591
— Keats's Letters, 1931, A38, 104; C1150
— Keats's Odes: Further Notes, A120; C3106
— Keatsian Studies, C2582
— Lectures on Keats, C610
— *Letters of*, review, C1113
— New Sidelights on Keats, Lamb, and Others, C265
— Ode to the Nightingale, C3260
— *Poèmes Choisis*, review, C3017
— *The Poems and Verses of*, review, C1036
— *The Poetical Works of*, review, C1764
— *Selected Poems*, B176
— Severn After Keats, C1965
Keats House and Museum later *Keats House: A Guide to the House and Museum; and A Guide to Keats House and Museum*, B86
— reopened, E*b*9
Keats, Shelley & Rome: An Illustrated Miscellany, B130; C2465 (letter on)
Keats-Shelley Diversion, A, B149; C2984
Keats-Shelley Journal, New York, C2984, 3106; E*a*25
Keats Shelley Memorial Association, B130, 276
Keats-Shelley Memorial Bulletin, Rome, C2590, 2837-9, 3097-8, 3155, 3183, 3219, 3232, 3249, 3267, 3281, 3293, 3328, 3341
— No. 4, review, C2960
Keats-Shelley Memorial House, Rome, E*f*8, *f*10
Keats-Shelley Poetry Contests, C3123
Keats' View of Poetry, B33
Keats's Publisher, A58
Keen, Alan, "*In the Quick Forge and Working-House of Thought*, [etc.] ", review, C2699
Keene, Donald, *The Japanese Discovery of Europe*, review, C2848
— *Japanese Literature*, review, C3054
— *Modern Japanese Novels and the*

675

West, review, C3334
— ed., *Modern Japanese Literature*, review, C3194
Keeping Wicket, C2631
Keeton, G. W., and John Cameron, eds, *The Trial of Gustav Rau*, [etc.], C2888
Keio-Gijuku University, A101; E*b*10
Keith Douglas Collected Poems, B269
Kelling, Lucile and Albert Suskin, *Index Verborum Iuvenalis*, review, C2810
Kellow, Henry Arthur, *Queensland Poets*, review, C1044
Kelway, Ian, *Poet's Light*, review, C448
Kendall, S. G., *Farming Memoirs of a West Country Yeoman*, review, C2082
Kendon, Frank, *Poems and Sonnets*, review, C469
— *Tristram*, review, C1391
Kenkyūsha Dictionary of English Quotations, The, review, C2968
Kenkyūsha Geppō, Tokyo, C2534
Kenkyūsha Modern English Classics, A28*e*
Kenkyūsha Modern English Literature Series, A28*e*
Kenkyūsha Publishing Company, Ltd, Tokyo, A21, 28*e*, 84, 91, 104, 110, 142, 171; B22-3, 165.1,
Kenkyūsha Publishing Company, (*cont.*)
182, 186, 224, 291; C2534; D7, 9, 11; Ea32, *d*3
Kennedy, Ludovic, *Nelson's Band of Brothers*, review, C2728
Kennedy, Virginia Wardlow, *Samuel Taylor Coleridge*, review, C1468
Kennesswood Poet, The, C2386
Kent, Rockwell, *Salamina*, review, C1522
Kenward, J., *Summervale*, review, C1451
Kenyon, Katharine M., *A House that Was Loved*, review, C1891
Kermode, Frank, E*e*6
Kernan, Thomas, *Report on France*, review, C1906
Ketton-Cremer, R. W., *Horace Walpole*, review, C1811
Keyes, Sidney, E*a*29

— *The Collected Poems of*, review, C2135
— *The Cruel Solstice*, reviews, C2019, 2021
— Poets in the Storm, B129; C2135
Keynes, Sir Geoffrey, intro., *The Library of Edward Gibbon*, review, C1851
Keynes, Lord, C2268
Kidd, Benjamin, *A Philosopher with Nature*, review, C292
Kikuchi, Wataru, trans., D9
Kilburn, J. M., *In Search of Cricket*, review, C1616
Kimmins, Anthony, *Half-Time*, review, C2415
Kind of Allegory, A, C1011
Kindaishi No Shiteki Tembo, B161
King, Cecil, *H.M.S.: His Majesty's Ships and their Forebears*, review, C1830
King, R. W., *England from Wordsworth to Dickens*, review, C790
— *The Translator of Dante*, review, C547
King Coel, C1668
King's Theatre, Hong Kong, B185
Kingdom Come: The Magazine of War-time Oxford, Oxford, C1787, 1856
Kingdon-Ward, F., *A Plant Hunter in Tibet*, review, C1421
Kings of Thought, C2472
Kingsmill, Hugh, *Matthew Arnold*, review, C808
— *The Poisoned Crown*, review, C2030
— *Samuel Johnson*, review, C1326
— ed., *Parents and Children*, review, C1577
Kipling, Rudyard, *The Irish Guards in the Great War*, review, C380
Kipling Journal, The, London, C3346
Kirchberger, Clare, ed., *The Coasts of the Country*, review, C2956
Kircher, Rudolf, *Fair Play*, review, C752
Kirk, K. E., *The Story of the Woodward Schools*, review, C2962
Kirkhope, John, Bequest, C216
Kirschbaum, Leo, *The True Text of King Lear*, review, C2159
Kishimoto, G. S. I., ed., A43*b*
Kitamura, T., A171

Hawk, review, C2301

Lewis, Eiluned, *Morning Songs*, review, C2044

Lewis, Ernest, *In Search of the Gyr-Falcon*, review, C1705

Lewis, Sinclair, *Case Timberlane*, review, C2216

Ley, Willey, *Rockets, Missiles, and Space Travel*, review, C2819

Leyland, Peter, *The Naked Mountain*, on, C2743

Li by Li, C3327

Li Shu-fan, *Hong Kong Surgeon*, review, C3327

Liberal, The, C2626

Liberal Outlook in Japan, The, C2627

Library Association Record, London, C3246

Library of Congress, *American and English Genealogies in the*, review, C214

Library of the late Siegfried Sassoon, The, B293

Life Aboard a "Tramp", A50; C574

Life and Letters of a Great Russian, C399

Life & Letters Series, The, A50, 58

Life-Lyrics, C2680

Life of a Poet, The, B271

Life of Flowers, The, C2565

Life of George Crabbe, The, B120

Life of George S. Gordon, The, B106

Lifeboat, The, London, C452

Light Reading of the Elizabethans, The, C935

Lillyputian Fantasy, A, C280

Lily, William, C2271

Lindbergh, Anne Morrow, *Listen! the Wind*, review, C1726

Lindsay, Jack, *The Passionate Neat-herd*, review, C853

Lindsay, Philip, *Kings of Merry England*, review, C1515

Line upon Line, A50, 108

Linssen, E. F., compiler, *Nature Interlude*, review, C2640

Lippincott Company, J. B., Philadelphia, New York, B247*b*

Listener, The, London, C874, 1296, 1306, 1464, 1485, 1491, 1677, 1685, 1736, 1744, 2005, 2202, 2254, 2307, 2510, 2648, 2691; E*f*2

Literary Centenaries *see* Upon Literary Centenaries

Literary Criticism: Power and Gentleness, C498

Literary Discoveries, C2625

Literary England, C489, 501, 1449, 2452

Literary England Month by Month, C725, 741, 753, 764, 782, 789, 802, 810, 816, 838, 846, 859, 872, 884, 892, 901, 910, 920, 931, 940, 947, 959, 973, 993, 1003, 1020, 1031, 1043, 1057, 1072, 1081, 1094, 1102, 1110, 1118, 1129, 1133, 1140, 1143, 1151, 1161, 1168, 1176, 1181, 1191, 1196, 1204, 1211, 1218, 1224, 1232, 1239, 1247, 1255, 1259, 1264, 1273, 1281, 1287, 1295, 1301, 1305, 1309, 1328, 1339, 1342, 1350, 1360, 1369, 1377, 1385, 1394, 1400, 1409, 1416-17, 1430, 1437, 1442

Literary Exchange, A, C2281

Literary Exchanges, C2746

Literary Explorers, C2355

Literary Gossip, C75, 80, 87, 92, 98, 104, 117, 125, 132, 141, 148, 159, 163, 168, 175, 185, 191, 198, 203, 212, 218, 224, 243, 250

Literary History, C2253

Literary History and Criticism, C172, 205, 266, 305, 308, 335, 808

Literary Impostures, C526

Literary Life, The, C3237

Literary Modes, C2260

Literary Notes, C2440, 2446, 2459, 2461, 2471, 2474, 2479, 2488, 2503, 2515

Literary Occasions, C2432

Literary Periodicals, C1130

Literary Pocket-Book, A, C962, 967, 972, 981, 990, 997, 1014, 1017, 1023, 1034, 1039, 1042

Literary Profession in England, 1953, The, C3102

Literary Recreations, C273

Literary Repository, The, Beaminster, Dorset, C3238

Literary Researches, C2117

Literary Talk, C2716

Literature of War, The, E*b*1

Maclaren, Malcolm, *Khartoum Tragedy*, review, C1441

Maclean, Catherine Macdonald, *Born Under Saturn*, reviews, C1976, 2001

—— *Dorothy Wordsworth*, review, C1229

McLean, George, *Spirit of Delight*, review, C787

MacLeish, Archibald, *Poems*, review, C1498

McMenemy, William Henry, *A History of the Worcester Royal Infirmary*, review, C2383

Macmillan & Co. Ltd, London, A68*a*, 72*a*, 77*a*, 89*a*; B55, 95, 114; Ea30

Macmillan Company, The, New York, A45*c*, 49*b*, 68*b*, 72*b*, 77*b*, 89*b*, 93*b*, 96*b*, 228*b*

MacNeice, Louis, *Autumn Journal*, review, C3312

—— *Springboard*, review, C2067

MacNutt, D. S., *Versions and Diversions*, D41

Machault, Guillaume de, A2-3

Machines and Men, C2399

Mad Masters, The, A165; B261

Madan, Falconer, *Books in Manuscript*, review, C61

Madariaga, Salvador de, *Shelley and Calderón*, review, C266

Madrigals & Chronicles, B14; Ea3

Maeterlinck, Maurice, *The Magic of the Stars*, review, C960

Maginn, William, *A Story Without a Tail*, review, C737

Magoun, Francis Peabody, Jr, *Shrove Tuesday Football*, review, C1197

Maillart, Ella, *Forbidden Journey*, review, C1638

Main, Alexander, C2590

Mainichi, The, Tokyo, C2457, 2462, 3145, 3166; D16, 34, 37

Main Interests of English Literature, E*b*9·2

Mainly the Poets, C1498

Mais, S. P. B., *Austrian Holiday*, review, C2841

—— *The Home Counties*, review, C1984.

Maison français-japonaise, Tokyo, E*b*13

Majdalany, F., *The Monastery*, review, C2168

Making of a Novelist, The, A79; C2247

Malayan Undergrad, Organ of the University of Malaya Students' Union, C3128

Malim, Michael, *Island of the Swan: Mauritius*, review, C2781

Malory, Sir Thomas, C2210

—— *Le Morte d'Arthur*, review, C661

Malta Memorial, The, B165

Man and His Chances, C616

Man and Machine, C2012

Man and Nature, A91

Man of Feeling, The, C2136

Man of Letters, The, C2537

"Man So Various, A", C453

Manchester Guardian, Manchester, C921; E*b*19, *b*25

Mandach, André de, *Molière et la Comedie de Moeurs en Angleterre*, review, C2224

Mangan, James Clarence, A156; C3190

Manley, Gordon, *Climate and the British Scene*, review, C2940

Mann, Thomas, *The Young Joseph*, review, C1421

Manning, Frederic, *Her Privates We*, B255

Manning, Thomas, *The Letters of . . . to Charles Lamb*, review, C546

Manning-Saunders, Ruth, *Pages from the History of Zachy Trenoy*, review, C449

Mansbridge, John, *Here Comes Tomorrow*, review, C1972

Mansfield, Katherine, *The Letters of*, review, C798

—— *Poems*, review, C456

—— *The Scrapbook of*, review, C1780

Maraini, Fosco, *Meeting with Japan*, review, C3245.1

Marchant, Sir James, ed., *Toward Evening*, review, C1577

Marder, Arthur J., ed., *Fear God and Dread Nought*, review, C2896

Margaret of Sarawak, H.H. The Ranee, *Good Morning and Good Night*, review, C1421

Margoliouth, H. M., *Wordsworth and Coleridge, 1795–1834*, review, C3004

Marillier, H. C., *Christie's, 1766–1925*, review, C581

Massingham, H. J., A8; B187; C2921, 2975
— *Country Relics*, review, C1779
— *The English Countryman*, review, C1940
— *The Friend of Shelley*, review, C1007–8
— *In Praise of England*, review, C485
— *Men of Earth*, review, C1990
— *Remembrance*, review, C1925
— *Some Birds of the Countryside*, reviews, C292; p. 556
— *This Plot of Earth*, review, C2033
— *Untrodden Ways*, review, C410
— *The Wisdom of the Fields*, review, C2186
— *Wold Without End*, reviews, C1195, 1251
— ed., *English Country*, B67; C1407 (review)
— — *The Natural Order*, B104
— — *Poems About Birds*, B8; C348 (review)
— and Hugh Massingham, eds, *The Great Victorians*, B56
Massingham, H. W., A12; B187
Master Journalists, The, C2125
Master-Key, A, C595
Master-Poet, A, C2192
Masterly Series, A *later* A Poet on the Oxford Poets, A36; C1073
Masterman, J. C., *Marshal Ney*, review, C1667
— *To Teach the Senators Wisdom*, review, C2836
Masters, Edgar Lee, *Domesday Book*, review, C263
Masters, Henry and W. E. Masters, *In Wild Rhodesia*, review, C74
Masui, Michio, A171
Mathew, David, *The Naval Heritage*, review, C2074
Mathew, George Felton, A54; C1499
Matsmoto, Kaoru, C2891
Matsuoka, Yoko, *Daughter of the Pacific*, C3070, 3087 (reviews); Ea16
Matsushima, Miyagi Prefecture, D8
Matsuura, Kaichi, *A Study of Donne's Imagery*, review, C3086
Matthews, Kenneth, *Greek Salad*, review, C1451
Matthews, William K., *The Tricolour Sun*, review, C1595

Mattingley, Garrett, *Catherine of Aragon*, review, C1907
Maugham, F. H., *The Case of Jean Calas*, review, C719
Maugham, W. S., *Altogether*, review, C1397
— *The Summing Up*, review, C1670
Maurois, André, *Dickens*, review, C1421
Mawer, A. and F. M. Stenton, *The Place-Names of Sussex*, review, C1001
May, H. A. R., *Memories of the Artists' Rifles*, review, C949
May, J. Lewis, *Charles Lamb*, review, C1402
Mayo, Eileen, illus., A26
Mayr-Ofen, Ferdinand, *Ludwig II of Bavaria*, review, C1664
Mears, Helen, *Mirror for Americans: Japan*, review, C2454
Mechanisms of Poetry, C713
Medcalf, Stephen E., B257
Medical Bulletin, May & Baker, Dagenham, C2856, 2903, 2949, 3000, 3043, 3094, 3103, 3107, 3115, 3126, 3133, 3148, 3164, 3170, 3176, 3208
Medical News, London, C3311
Medieval Sources, C2273
Meditation, B206
Meditation upon Time, C2691
Medworth, C. O., *Noursemen in England*, review, C2911
Meek, H. G., *Johann Faust*, review, C964
Melbourne University, Centenary, B191; C3181
Mellen, Ida M., and Robert J. Lanier, *1001 Questions Answered about Your Aquarium*, review, C2832
Mellor, Bernard, ed., *The Poems of Sir Francis Hubert*, B236
— — *Wayside Poems of the Early Eighteenth Century*, B253
— — *Wayside Poems of the Seventeenth Century*, B248
— — *Wayside Sonnets 1750–1850*, B287
Melody and the Lyric: From Chaucer to the Cavaliers, p. 557
Melville, C. H., *Life of General the Right Hon. Sir Redvers Buller, V.C.*, review, C450

2344, 3038
— *Complete Poetical Works*, review, C2272
— *Comus*, B184
— Milton Regained, A81; C2272
— Tercentenary, C2150
Milward, Peter, ed., B291
Minchin, H. Cotton, ed., *The Legion Book*, B30
Mind's Eye, The, A50; C1370
Mind's Eye, The, C2083
Mirror for Literature, A, C3113
Mirror of the May-Day Age, A *later in* "A Wedding or a Funeral" A39; C316
Mirsky, Jeanette, *Northern Conquest*, review, C1421
Miscellanies, C614, 868
Miscellany, B65, 76
Miscellany of Poetry, A, B10
Misfits Drama Club, The, Tokyo, B264
Miss Warble, A50, 108; B2
Mists and Fogs, A43
Mita Campus, Ee01
Mitchell, Kate L., *India*, review, C1959
Mitchell, Samuel Alfred, *Eclipses of the Sun*, review, C2910
Mitchell, Violet May, A123; C3128
Mitsuoka, A., A171
Miyamori, Asatarō, trans., *An Anthology of Haiku*, review, C1274
Modern Biography, C484
Modern Book, The, C2385
Modern Books and Writers, C2656
Modern Devotional Poet, A, C2326
Modern Essays 1939-1941, B95
Modern Language Association of America, *Publications*, Vol. 64, No. 4, Part 1, review, C2328
Modern Language Review, The, Cambridge, C3195
— Vol. 42, No. 1, review, C2358
Modern Poetry, A note on, C1254
Modern Review, Calcutta, C2490-1
Moles, T. W., *Ballads and Narrative Poems*, review, C1575
Molière, C2224
Moments in a Library, A150; C3246
Moments of Revision, C623
Monash, General, *The War Letters of*, review, C1476
Monet, Claude, C144

Money-Coutts, Hugh, *The Broads, 1919*, review, C227
Monkhouse, F. J., and H. R. Wilkinson, *Maps and Diagrams*, review, C2946
Monro, Harold, *The Collected Poems of*, review, C1290
— *Elm Angel*, review, C1059
Montagu, George, Earl of Sandwich, *Boyhood*, review, C2769
Montague, C. E., *Fiery Particles*, review, C363
— *A Writer's Notes on his Trade*, review, C955
Montgomerie, William, *Squared Circle*, review, C1357
Montgomery, Elizabeth, illus., B41, 92
Month, The, London, C2483, 2500-2
Monthly Chronicle, The, C2685
Months, The, C923
Montrose, Duke of, C785
Monument of Mercy, B254
Monumentum, C2904
Moonlight Fancies, C2579
Moore, Eva, *Exits and Entrances*, review, C442
Moore, George, C672
— *The Making of an Immortal*, review, C672
Moore, John, *Brensham Village*, review, C2294
— *Midsummer Meadow*, review, C2930
Moore, Marianne, *Collected Poems*, on, C2743
Moore, T. Sturge, *Nine Poems*, review, C1079
— *The Poems of*, Vol. 1, review, C1179
Moorehead, Alan, *Rum Jungle*, review, C3084
Moorland Spirit, The, C379
Moorman, F. W., *More Tales of the Ridings*, review, C190
— *Tales of the Ridings*, review, C130
Moraes, Dom, Ee5
Moran, Lord, *The Anatomy of Courage*, review, C2099
Mordaunt, Elinor, *The Tales of*, review, C1421
More, Sir Thomas, *The Latin Epigrams of*, review, C3031
More About Cricket, C2822

Near London, C2264

Neill, Roy S., *Once Only*, review, C2378

Nelson, Horatio, Admiral, C1144

Nesbitt, George, *Benthamite Reviewing*, review, C1460

Neumann, Robert, *The Queen's Doctor*, review, C1532

Nevill, Ralph, *The World of Fashion, 1837–1922*, review, C442

Nevinson, C. R. W., *Paint and Prejudice*, review, C1663

Nevinson, H. W., *Fire of Life*, review, C1480

—— *In the Dark Backward*, review, C1348

New Adelphi, The, London *see Adelphi, The*, London

New Age, Tokyo, C2458

New and Old, C448

New and Recent Poetry, C2044

New Cambridge English Bibliography of English Literature, The, B93c

New Campus, B127.1

New Chapter: A Quarterly Magazine of Literature, London, C3190

New Country Conversations, C1212

New England Relics, C677

New English Library Ltd., London, A28*i*

New English Poems, B53

New English Review, The, London, C2100–1

New Forget-me-not, The, B31

New Japan, The, C2495

New Judgments, C2087

New Keepsake, The, B5, 52

New Literary Series, The, Sixth Book, review, C106

New Oxford Poetry, 1936, review, C1581

New Pocket Plan of the Cities of London and Westminster, review, C600

New Poems 1952, B144; C2936 (review)

—— 1954, B168

—— 1957, B201

—— 1958, B212

New Poet, A, C1269

New Professor, The, C3217

New Readers' Library, The, A10*c*, 12*c*, 20*c*

New Statesman, The, London, C474, 881, 883

New Statesman & Nation, The, London, C1100, 1132, 1185, 1207, 1370, 1793

New Sundial Magazine, The, South Croydon, Surrey, C3189

New Textbooks, C550

New Theatre, The, Oxford, A48

New War-Books, C897

New World English Course, The, Second Book, review, C106

"New World of Words, The", B165.1

New Year Greeting, A, C2456

New Zealand Essayist, A, C2147

Newbolt, Sir Henry, *A Child is Born*, review, C1167

—— *The Linnet's Nest*, review, C643

—— compiler, *An English Anthology*, review, C300

—— ed., *The Tide of Time in English Poetry*, review, C550

—— intro., *The Mercury Book of Verse*, review, C1128

Newman, Bertram, *Jonathan Swift*, review, C1626

News Chronicle, London, C2539

News-Letter, The, National Labour Party, London, C1242, 1269, 1424

News Notes, B149

Newton, A. E., *Amenities of Book-Collecting*, review, C131

Newton's Poet, C625

Ng, Pansy, B230

Nicander, *The Poems and Poetical Fragments*, review, C3072

Nichols, John, C2732

Nichols, Robert, A135; B217; C2510

Nicholson & Watson, Ivor, London, B56a

Nicholson, Norman, *Five Rivers*, review, C2044

—— *Old Man of the Mountains*, review, C2251

—— *William Cowper*, reviews, C2660, 2690

Nicolson, Alexander, *Gaelic Proverbs*, review, C2792

Nicolson, Sir Harold, *Dwight Morrow*, review, C1482

—— intro., *England*, review, C2034

Night Thoughts, C460

Nihon Keizai Shimbun, Tokyo, D24

690

On the Borders of Prose, C469
On the Keeping of Diaries, C377
On the Memorials in Poets' Corner, C3125
On the Poems of Henry Vaughan, A23; C585
"Once a Week Players", C134
Ondorisha, Tokyo, publisher, B133
One Battalion's War, C1352
'One Haunting Touch' Justifies Poem, E*b*33
One Hundred, C2624
One Hundred and One Chinese Poems, B275
One Hundred English Poems, B22
One Soldier's Faith, C638
Onions, Oliver, *A Case in Camera*, review, C215
Oracular Poets, The, C1064
Orbilius non plagosus, C129
Oriental Literary Times, Tokyo, C489-90, 494-5, 497, 500-2, 507; p.558-9
Oriental Paradise Lost, An, C3249.1
Origo, Iris, *Leopardi*, review, C3093
—— *War in Val D'Orcia*, review, C2319
Orion: A Miscellany, London, C2155
"Orion" Horne, C731
"Orion" Refreshed, C773
Orléans, Charles d', A2-3
Ormerod, James, *Tristram's Tomb*, review, C757
Orr, Peter, ed., *The Poet Speaks*, E*e*6
Orr, Robert Low, *Lord Guthrie: A Memoir*, review, C442
Ōru Yomimono, Bijitto, [Tokyo], C2430
Osaka Kyōiku Tosho, D12
Osawa, Mamoru, E*a*21-2
Osborn, E. B., *Nightcaps*, review, C460
Osborne, W. A., *Essays and Studies*, review, C2296
Osgood, Charles Grosvenor, *The Voice of England*, review, C2993
Oshima, Shôtarô, *Poems Among Shapes and Shadows*, B87
—— ed., *Eastward*, A97
—— trans., *Atarashi Eishi no Kansho*, D13
—— —— *Eishi no Ajiwai Kata*, D11
Other Ranks, B46
Other Words, C2299

Ould, Charles, *The Illustrated Gorilla and Other Tales*, review, C2382
Our Best-Loved Poet is 80, C3012
Our Curious Present, C573
Our English Heritage, B141
Our Library Table, C57
Our Lost Leader, C754
Ourselves and Germany, C1760
Out of China, C2391
Out of Town, C1984
Out of Wessex, C3250
Outlook: A Housey Magazine published at Christ's Hospital, The, [West Horsham], C276, 366, 3214
Outward Bound, No. 1, review, C119
Overflowing Sun, The, C2858
Oversights, C2373
Ovid, C2139
Owen, Harold, *Journey from Obscurity*, Vol. 1, review, C3287
—— —— Vol. 2, review, C3324
—— —— Vol. 3, review, C3345
Owen, Peter, London, publisher, B274
Owen, Wilfred, A67-8, 135; C617, 1364, 2229, 3287, 3324, 3345
—— *Poems*, C183 (review), 254 (letter on)
—— *The Poems of*, B47
Owl, The, London, C26, 446
Oxford, Vol. XII, No. 1, review, C2976
Oxford & Cambridge Miscellany, The, B1
Oxford Book of American Verse, The, review, C2610
Oxford Book of Christian Verse, review, C1820
Oxford Book of Eighteenth Century Verse, review, C623
Oxford Book of Greek Verse, C995
Oxford Book of Nineteenth Century English Verse, The, review, C3302
Oxford Book of Regency Verse, The, review, C805
Oxford Book of Sixteenth Century Verse, The, review, C1245
Oxford Chinoiserie, C2070
Oxford Dictionary of Christian Names, review, C2200
Oxford Group 1919-1920, The, C569
Oxford Magazine, Oxford, C1574,

Piggott, F. S., *Broken Thread*, review, C2535
Pike, Harry W., *The Wise Beasts of Hindustan*, review, C180
Pilgrim Trust, C2668
Pilley, Dorothy, *Climbing Days*, review, C1451
Pilsudski, Madame, *Memoirs of*, review, C1834
Pinafore, H.M.S., C463
Pioneers of Progress: Women, review, C72
Piper, John, illus., A164*b*
—— *British Romantic Artists*, review, C1941
Piper, Myfanwy, ed., *Sea Poems*, C2090
Pitt, Frances, *Wild Creatures of Garden and Hedgerow*, review, C95
Pitter, Ruth, B282
—— *A Mad Lady's Garland*, reviews, C1391, 1410
Plato in Arabic, C3048
Playing at Plays, C290
Plays: 1641-1700, C2244
Plays and Pictures, C999
Pleasure in Reading, C3253
Plomer, William, *Ali the Lion*, review, C1520
—— *The Child of Queen Victoria*, review, C1303
—— *The Dorking Thigh*, review, C2131
—— *Double Lives*, review, C1993
—— *The Family Tree*, review, C913
—— *Museum Pieces*, review, C2877
—— *Notes for Poems*, review, C803
—— *Paper Houses*, review, C834
—— *Visiting the Caves*, C1581
Plough and Pen, C2312
Plough Sunday 1946, B112
Plowman, Mark, *A Subaltern on the Somme*, review, C631
Poe, Edgar Allan, *Letters till Now Unpublished*, review, C611
Poem of Action, A, C1067
Poemata, C2238
Poems by C. W. Brodribb, B114
Poems by Ivor Gurney, B167
Poems, The, A35
Poems about Birds, B8
Poems among Shapes and Shadows, B87
Poems from the Dutch, C1187

Poems in Divers Humours, C1666
Poems 1913 and 1914, A1, 3
Poems 1930-1940, A68
Poems of Many Years, A135
Poems of 1936, C1582
Poems of Sir Francis Hubert, The, B236
Poems of the East, C312
Poems of the New Japan, C3175
Poems of This War, B96
Poems of Wilfred Owen, The, B47
Poems of William Collins, The, B29
Poems of Wrenne Jarman, B285
Poems on Japan, A171
Poems translated from the French, A2-3
Poet and Critic, C3117
Poet as Critic, The, C3085
Poet as Purser, A, C402
Poet Comes South, A, C2813
Poet Displayed, A, C1395
Poet Hood, The, C3235
Poet in the Storm, A, C2223
Poet-Journalist, C2145
Poet Laureate, The, C1539
Poet of Common Objects, C3301
Poet of East Anglia, C1681
Poet of Felicity, The, C2080
Poet of South Africa, A, C2368
Poet of this Age, A, C3297
Poet on Dartmoor, C1648
Poet on the Oxford Poets, A *see* Masterly Series, A
Poet Reviews His Journey, C2193
Poet Revises, The, C2757
Poet Speaks, The, Ed7, *e*6
Poet Who Taught Shorthand, C2633
Poet's Appreciation of a Critic *later* Mr. J. M. Murry and His Work, C391
Poet's Boyhood, A *see* Forty Miles from London
Poet's Castle, A, C2838
Poet's Characteristics, A, C854
Poet's Choice, B244·1
Poet's Collection, A, C2290
Poet's Enigma, A, C3188
Poet's Miltonic View of Fame, A, C3339
Poet's Prophecy, A, C907
Poet's Prose, C2252
Poet's Quotations, The, C2196
Poet's Reading, A, C1415
Poet's Variety, A, C2398

3206
Postscript, A *later* Aftertones, A50, 108; B30
Potter, Simeon, *The Outlook in English Studies*, review, C2299
Potter, Stephen, *Coleridge and S.T.C.*, reviews, C1451-2
Potter Press, Oxford, The A55; B81, 89
Pound, Ezra, *Seventy Cantos*, review, C2589
Pound, Reginald, *The Lost Generation*, review, C3332
—— *Turn Left for England*, review, C1770
Powell, Anthony, *Agents and Patients*, review, C1508
Powell, David, B265
Powell, Dilys, *Remember Greece*, review, C1873
Powell, Stewart, compiler, *British Newspapers and Periodicals, 1632-1800*, review, C2615
Power and Gentleness, C1165
Power and Serenity, C1079
Powley, E. B., *A Hundred Years of English Poetry*, review, C1093
Powys, Llewelyn, *A Selection from His Writings*, review, C2858
Powys, T. F., *The Left Leg*, review, C390
Practical Wordsworthian, A, C1132
Prance, Claude A., *Peppercorn Papers*, review, C3342
Praviel, Armand, *The Murder of M. Fualdes*, review, C427
Praz, Mario, ed., *English Miscellany*, review, C2546
Prewett, Frank. *Poems*, review, C287
Pre-Georgian, A, C416
Pre-Plywood Carpenters, C1650
Preedy, George R., *Autobiography of Cornelius Blake*, review, C1421
Prelude, Hiroshima, D35
Preservation of England, The, A39; C831
Press, John, Ed5
—— ed., *Commonwealth Literature*, B262
—— ed., *The Poet Speaks*, Ee6
Preston, Harry, *Memories*, review, C738
Preternatural History, C1233
Prevailing Paradise, The, C2022

Price, Lawrence Marsden, ed., *Inkle and the Yarico Album*, review, C1673
Price, Willard, *The Son of Heaven*, review, C2151
Price & Co., Horsham, printer, A1-3
Pride of Poets, A, C3255
Priestley, J. B., *Midnight on the Desert*, review, C1599
Priestley, Mary, *A Book of Birds*, review, C1656
"Prime Old Tusser", C437
Prince of Privateers, C693
Pritchett, V. S., *In My Good Books*, review, C1914
Professor and Poet, C2628
Professor and the Poet, The, C2314
Progress? C1070
Progress of Poesy, C1939
Progress of Poetry, The, C880
Prokosch, Frederic, *Chosen Poems*, review, C2019
Promise of Greatness, B280
Promise of May, The, C813
Proper Studies, C3026
Prophecy of War, C2608
Prose and Poetry, C371
Prose Election, A, C2726
Prose-Writer's Poems, C456
Protheroe, Ernest, *Earl Haig*, review, C716
Proud Title, A, C70
Pryce-Jones, Alan, *People in the South*, review, C1216
—— *The Spring Journey*, review, C1125
—— preface, *Little Innocents*, B58
Psalmanazar, C3236
Public and the War Book, The, C921
Public Opinion, London, C2653
Publications of 1930, The, C1099
Publishers and Authors, C2353
Pudney, John, *Ten Summers*, C2019
Pupin, Michael, *From Immigrant to Inventor*, review, C442
Purcell, Daniel, *Life Be Kind*, B273
Purdom, C. B., *Everyman at War*, review, C950
Purney, Thomas, *Works of*, reviews, C1298, 1306
Pursuits of Literature, C2738
Putnam, Donald F., *Canadian Regions*, review, C3056
Putnam's Sons, G. P., New York &

review, C2337
— *Invocations to Angels*, review, C813
Riddell, Agnes Rutherford, *Flaubert and Maupassant*, review, C205
Riddell, E., and M. C. Clayton, *The Cambridgeshires, 1914-1919*, review, C1352
Ride, Dr L. T., A123; C3128
Riding, Laura, *Love as Love, Death as Death*, review, C813
Rime of the Ancient Mariner, The, B49
Rising Generation, Tokyo, C477, 488, 570, 590, 755, 929, 1449, 2425, 2440-1, 2446, 2452, 2459, 2461, 2470-1, 2474, 2479, 2487-8, 2492, 2494, 2503, 2506-15, 3113, 3173, 3188, 3192, 3196, 3199, 3201, 3272, 3289, 3295; Ea13, a32
Robb, David M., and J. J. Garrison, *Art in the Western World*, review, C3036
Roberts, Bechhofer, *Bread and Butter*, review, C1515
Roberts, D. Kilham, ed., *The Author's Handbook for 1935*, review, C1441
— and others, compilers, *The Year's Poetry*, B69
Roberts, H. Harrington, *Memories of Four-score Years*, review, C147
Roberts, Harry, *English Gardens*, review, C2032
Roberts, Michael, ed., *Elizabethan Prose*, review, C1322
— *Faber Book of Modern Verse*, review, C1515
— *New Country*, review, C1275
— *New Signatures*, review, C1201
Roberts, R. Ellis, *H. R. L. Sheppard*, review, C1922
Roberts, S. C., *An Eighteenth Century Gentleman, and Other Essays*, review, C991
— *Thomas Fuller*, on, C3006
Robertson, Arnot, *Ordinary Families*, review, C1299
Robertson, H. R., *More Plants We Play With*, review, C182
Robertson, John W., *Edgar A. Poe*, review, C305
Robin, P. Ansell, *Animal Lore in English Literature*, review, C1233

Robin Hood, C2879
Robinson, The Late Mrs., *Memoirs of*, B39
Robinson, Edwin Arlington, *Roman Bartholow*, review, C448
— *Tristram*, review, C726
Robinson, Henry Crabb, C1601, 2202
— *Blake, Coleridge, Wordsworth, Lamb, &c.*, reviews, C352, 364
— *The Correspondence of . . . with the Wordsworth Circle (1808-1866)*, review, C665
— *Crabb Robinson on Germany, 1800-1805*, review, C839
— *Henry Crabb Robinson in Books and their Writers*, review, C1717
Robinson, Henry Morton, *The Enchanted Grindstone*, review, C2936
Robinson, Kenneth, *Wilkie Collins*, review, C2741
Robinson, Mary, C3307
Robinson, Ray, *From the Boundary*, review, C2651
Rodd, Sir J. Rennell, *Social and Diplomatic Memories, 1894-1901*, review, C442
Roe, F. Gordon, *Rowlandson*, review, C2370
Roe, Ivan, *Shelley*, reviews, C2995, 3002
Roeder, Ralph, *The Man of the Renaissance*, review, C1407
Rogers, Benjamin, *The Diary of*, review, C2649
Rogers, Neville, B292; Ea25
— *Shelley at Work*, B208; C3196 (review), 3212 (on)
— compiler, *Keats, Shelley & Rome*, B130; C2465
Rogers, P. G., *The First Englishman in Japan*, B189
Rogers, Samuel, *Dusk at the Grove*, review, C1441
— *Recollections of the Table-Talk of*, review, C2958
Rogerson, Sidney, *Twelve Days*, review, C1320
Roget's Thesaurus, C2978
Röhrman, H., *Marlowe and Shakespeare*, review, C2980
"Roll of Thespis, The", C1016
Rollins, Hyder E., *Keats' Reputation in America to 1848*, review,

Philosophy, review, C2302
[Russell, G. W.], Enchantment and Other Poems, review, C1082
— Midsummer Eve, review, C727
— Selected Poems, review, C1498
— Vale and Other Poems, review, C1122
Russell, Leonard, ed., English Wits, review, C1838
— The Saturday Book, B117
Russell, Richard Joel and Fred Bowerman Kniffen, Culture Worlds, review, C2805
Russell, Thomas, A151; C3238
Ruth Pitter: Homage to a Poet, B282
Rutherston, Albert, illus., A27
Rutland, William R., Thomas Hardy, review, C1698
Rutter, Joan, Here's Flowers, review, C1658
Ryan, A. P., ed., B262
Ryan, Desmond, Remembering Sion, review, C1367
Rye, Anthony, The Inn of the Birds, review, C2416
Rylands, George, Poems, review, C1192

S., D. A., The Knights of Dee, review, C464
S.G.D. [i.e. Professor S. G. Davis], A156
Sackville-West, Edward, A Flame in Sunlight, review, C1523
— The Sun in Capricorn, review, C1407
Sackville-West, V., Collected Poems, review, C1324
— The Dark Island, review, C1407
— The Eagle and the Dove, review, C1995
— Invitation to Cast Out Care, review, C1167
— King's Daughter, review, C913
— Sissinghurst, review, C1142
Sadleir, Michael, Blessington-D'Orsay, reviews, C1314, 2413
— Things Past, review, C2046
Saigo, Takamori, B207
St. Cecilia's Day Festival Concert, B121
St Cyres, Dorothy, The Holy City, review, C349
Saint Exupery, Antoine de, Wind,

Sand and Stars, review, C1777
St George's Gallery, London, B116
St. Hilda's Dramatic Society, p. 557
St James's Library, A76
St John's Review, Hong Kong, C3100, 3108, 3156
St Martin's Press, New York, A72c
St Martin's Review, London, C632, 909, 1203, 1627, 1791, 1828, 1835
St. Matthew's Day, C111
SS. Peter & Paul, Yalding, with S. Mary, Laddingford [Parish Magazine], Yalding, C2744
St. Peter's College Literary Society, Oxford, B281
Saintsbury, George, C2160
— A Last Vintage, review, C2537
Saito, Hikaru, trans., C2422, 2455; D21, 31
Saito, Takeshi, A43b, 84, 98b, 171; C2458, 2516, 3146; D14, 20, 25; Ea9, b12, b18
— Gems from English Poetry, B224
— Keats' View of Poetry, B33
— Thirty Lyrics, D6
Saito Takeshi Hakase Koki Shukuga Rombunshu, B186
Sakai, M., trans., D15
Sakai, Yoshitaka, A97, 171; Ea23
Sakamoto, Moriaki, trans. B207
Salaman, Nina, Songs of Many Days, review, C464
Salmon, Arthur L., Westward, review, C1519
Salt, Henry S., The Call of the Wild Flower, review, C331
Salter, Sir Arthur, Personality in Politics, review, C2404
Same War, The, C297
Sampson, John, In Lighter Moments, review, C1425
— ed., The Wind on the Heath, review, C1041
"Samson of Northamptonshire, The", C1214
Sanderson, Lord, Memories of Sixty Years, review, C1098
Sandford and Merton, C1266
Sangū, Makoto, B161
Sankaido, Tokyo, publisher, D6
Sanseido, Tokyo, C3130
Sansom, G. B., Japan, review, C3280
— Japan in World History, review,

703

D38
Shinkyo Shuppansha, Tokyo, publisher, B136
Shinosaki Shobō, Tokyo, publisher, B223
Ships and Deep Friendships, C3262
Shipton, E. E., *Nanda Devi*, review, C1515
Shiratori, Seigo, A171
Shiratori, Shogô, trans., D8
Shiroyama, B207
Shopkeepers, The, C1312
Short, Dorothy Dudley, ed., *Poet's Choice*, C1278, 1842
Shorter Oxford Dictionary, The, review, C1280
Shorter Poems, A91
"Should Autobiographies Be Forbidden?", E*b*6
Show the True Appearance, D26
Shu She-yu, *Heavensent*, review, C2687
Shūkan Asahi, Tokyo, C2542
Sichel, Walter, *The Sands of Time*, review, C442
Sicre, Ricardo, *The Tap on the Left Shoulder*, review, C2584
Sidgwick & Jackson, London, A8*a–b*; B271
Sidney, Sir Philip, A91–2
Siegfried Sassoon: A Memorial Exhibition, B283
Siepman, Eric, *Waterloo in Wardour Street*, review, p. 557
Sieveking, L. de G., ed., B1
Sigh, The, A43; C2433
"Signals", A129; C3147
Signature, London, C3124
Signature of Pain and Other Poems, The, B43
Signature Tune, The, C2120
Signed or Unsigned? C2165
Signs and Spirits, C2756
Sillar, Frederick Cameron and Ruth Mary Meyler, *The Symbolic Pig*, review, C3270
Simmons, Jack, *Southey*, review, C2085
Simon, Oliver, C3124
Simplicity, C341
Simpson, Charlotte A., *Rediscovering England*, review, C1089
Sims, Alan, *Well Shone Moone*, review, C353

Sims (Rare Books), G. F., E*a*28
"Sinbad", *Red Saunders*, review, C1421
Singer, Charles, *From Magic to Science*, review, C751
Singer, Kurt, *Gentlemen Spies*, review, C2847
Singing in the Streets, B288
Sino-British Club Lectures, C3213
Sisson, C. J., C2683
Sitwell, Edith, *Bucolic Comedies*, review, C393
— *The Collected Poems of*, review, C1021
— *Edith Sitwell's Anthology*, review, C1790
— *Five Variations on a Theme*, review, C1343
— *Gold Coast Customs*, review, C825
— *Green Song*, review, C2044
— *Jane Barston, 1719–1746*, review, C1167
— *Plants and Glow-worms*, review, C2019
— *The Pleasures of Poetry*, reviews, C1077, 1126, 1234, 1415
— and others, *Key Poets*, reviews, C2566, 2589
Sitwell, Sir Osbert, *England Reclaimed*, review, p. 557
— *Left Hand! Right Hand!*, review, C2084
— *A Letter to My Son*, review, C2051
— *Out of the Flame*, review, C411
— *The Scarlet Tree*, review, C2261
— *Sing High! Sing Low!*, review, C2028
Sitwell, Sacheverell, *Collected Poems of*, review, C1581
— *Dance of the Quick and the Dead*, review, C1559
— *Doctor Donne and Gargantua*, review, C1011
— *The Hundred-and-One Harlequins*, review, C338
— *Mauritania*, review, C1807
— *Poltergeists*, review, C1821
— *Two Poems, Ten Songs*, review, C934
Sixtieth Anniversary, Kwansei Gakuin University, B134
Sixty Years a Teacher of English,

Some Recent Poetry, C2067, 2936
Some Recent Scholarly Works, C2478
Some Remarks on Hudibras, C724
Some Seventeenth-Century Latin Poems, A128; C3150
Some Sino-British Club Lectures, C3213
Some Women Writers, A103; C2550
Some Younger English Poets, D14
Somerville, Boyle T., Commodore Anson's World Voyage, review, C1421
Somerville, E. Œ., and Martin Ross, The Irish R.M., review, C682
Somerville, J. C., C150
Somme Still Flows, The, A50; C874
Soñe, Tamotsu, A97; Ea24
Song to David, A, A155.1; B11; C3270.1
Songs from the Plays, C2179
Sonneman, Ulrich, Handwriting Analysis as a Psychodiagnostic Tool, review, C3075
Sons of Light, A92
Soul of a Race, C812
Soul of England, B71b
Sounkyo, A102
South China Morning Post, Hong Kong, C3088, 3098.1, 3266, 3270.2; Eb21
— Ltd, B196
Southdown Battalions Association, Annual Dinner, B63, 70, 74, 77, 82, 85, 166
Southern Illinois University Press, Carbondale, B235b
Southey, Robert, A24b
— The Doctor, &c., review, C1063
— Homage to Southey, review, C2059
— Journal of a Tour in Scotland in 1819, review, C927
— Letters from England, review, C2797
— Southey's "Doctor", A39; C1063
Spalding, H. N., In Praise of Life, review, C2936
Sparrow, John, Sense and Poetry, review, C1346
"Spasmodic", A, C337
Spectator, The, London, C286, 355, 364, 459, 542, 1120, 1212, 1214, 1220, 1233, 1241, 1250, 1265, 1268, 1275, 1291-2, 1302, 1320, 1334-5, 1344, 1354-5, 1378, 1452, 1455, 1474, 1479, 1523, 1535, 1540, 1549-50, 1565, 1576, 1589, 1601, 1618, 1635, 1647, 1659, 1667, 1675, 1717, 1737, 1764, 1879, 1939, 1941, 2051, 2398, 2475, 2494, 2498, 2677, 2772, 2796, 2820, 2858, 2885, 2958, 3002, 3024, 3070-1; Ef3
Spectator's Gallery, B59; C1293
Spectrum: The Magazine of the University of Hong Kong University Science Society, Hong Kong, C3184
Speculation and Circulation, p. 558
Spencer, Walter T., Forty Years in My Bookshop, review, C434
Spender, Stephen, Ruins and Visions, review, C1901
— World Within World, review, C2621
Spenser, Edmund, A24, 110; C2320, 2908, 3151
— 1552-1599, B18; C329
Spettigue, Jane, Nero, An African Mongrel, review, C180
Spewack, Samuel, B137
Speyer, Wilhelm, The Court of Fair Maidens, review, C1545
Sphere, The, London, C508
Sphinx Smiles, The, C2313
Spingarn, Lawrence, The Lost River, on, C2743
Spirit of British & American Literature, Tokyo, D27
Spirit of England, The, B95; C1829
Spirit of Japan, The, C3280
Spirit of the Classics, Greek Ideal and Romance, C911
"Spirit, Yet a Woman Too, A", C2823
Spiritual Persistence, C1590
Splendid Survey, A, C244
Spooner, Glenda, Victorian Glencairn, review, C1451
Spring Pie: A Pocket Miscellany, B111
Squire, H. F., and A. P., Pre-Victorian Sussex Cricket, review, C2748
Squire, Sir John C., A43a; B8, 286
— American Poems and Others, review, C407
— The Honeysuckle and the Bee, re-

view, C1605
— *Sunday Mornings*, review, C1024
— ed., *Apes and Parrots*, review, C807
— ed., *A Book of Women's Verse*, review, p. 556
Ssu Lang T'an Mu, B185
Stacke, H. FitM., *The Worcestershire Regiment in the Great War*, review, C897
Stainer & Bell, publisher, B157
Stainforth, Peter, *Wings of the Wind*, review, C2917
Staniland, Boston, C1516
Stanley, Arthur, ed., *The Out-of-Doors Book*, review, C1317
— *The Testament of Man*, review, C1577
Stark, Freya, *Winter in Arabia*, review, C1819
Stead, Philip John, *Vidocq*, review, C3066
Stead, William Force, A31
— *Festival in Tuscany*, reviews, C653, 673
— *The House on the Wold, and Other Poems*, review, C994
— *The Sweet Miracle and Other Poems*, review, C313
— *Verd Antique, Poems*, review, C73
— *Wayfaring*, review, p. 559
Steegman, Philip, *Indian Ink*, review, C1732
Steele, Richard, *The Englishman: A Political Journal*, review, C3141
— Richard Steele, A39; C891
Steen, Marguerite, *Matador*, review, C1347
— *William Nicholson*, review, C1975
Steeves, Edna Leake, ed., *The Art of Sinking in Poetry*, review, C2906
Steinbeck, John, *The Moon is Down*, review, C1913
Stephens, J., *Etched in Moonlight*, review, C686
Stephenson, H. W., *William Hazlitt and Hackney College*, review, C1092
Stern, G. B., *The Augs*, review, C1315
Sterne, Laurence, C841, 848
— *A Sentimental Journey*, B115
Stevens, Donald, *Brush Script*, review,

C3080
Stevens Cox's Literary Repository see Literary Repository, The
Stewart, Cecil, *Byzantine Legacy*, review, C2390
Stigand, C. H., *Equatoria, The Lado Enclave*, review, C438
Still Things Japanese, C3245.1
Stirling, W. F., *Safety Last*, review, C3014
Stobart, J. C., *The Glory that Was Greece*, review, C244
— *The Grandeur that Was Rome*, review, C244
Stokoe, F. W., *German Influence in the English Romantic Period, 1788–1818*, review, C596
Stonehill, C. A., and H. W., *Bibliographies of Modern Authors*, review, C567
Stories of the War, C178
Storm of Battle, The, C941
Story of a Heart, C3340
Story of a Surgeon, The, C987
Stothard, Thomas, C1718
Stovall, Floyd, *Desire and Restraint in Shelley*, review, C1206
Strachey, Lady, *Nursery Lyrics*, review, C350
Strachey, Lytton, B200
Strachey, Mrs St Loe, *The Frozen Heart*, review, C1479
Strand Magazine, London, C2115, 2156, 2252, 2316, 2407
Strang, Colin, jt ed., B96
Strang, Francis, *Town and Country in Southern France*, review, C1625
Strange and Stranger, C427
Stranger in Asahigawa, A102
Strauss, Ralph, *Sala*, review, C1930
Stray Notes in Lockhart's "Exhibitioners", C445
Streatfeild, Noel, *Ballet Shoes,* review, p. 557
Street, A. G., *From Dusk till Dawn*, review, C1949
Street, Lucie, ed., *I Married a Russian*, review, C2029
Stribling, T. S., *The Sound Wagon*, review, C1521
— *Unfinished Cathedral*, review, C1391
Strict and Free in Verse, C270
Strong, A. T., *A Short History of*

711

Towards a New Understanding of Japanese Culture, C3165
Tower: Official Monthly Bulletin of the Rotary Club of Kowloon, The, C3237
Tower Hill Memorial, The, B192
Town With a Past, A, C664
Townsend, John, C2205
Townshend, Frank, *Earth,* review, C880
Towpath and Track, C2206
Toyama, Shigeru, trans., C2469
Tracts for All Times, C655
Tracy, Honor, *Kakemono,* reviews, C2526-7
Tradition and Experiment, B34
Tradition and Imagination, p. 557
Tradition in Poetry, B34; C919
Tradition of L'Allegro, The, C636
Tragical Consequences, or a Disaster at Deal, B50
Training a Prince, C2941
Tranquility, C313
Transatlantic, New York, publisher, B88b
Translation (London), B109
Translator of Horace, A, C2119
Translators, C2311
Travel Books for the Pocket, C1226
Travels in Bohemia, C1478
Traz, Robert de, *Silent Hours,* review, C1421
Treasure Restored, A, C2233
Treaty Port, A102
Tredegar Memorial Lecture, C3370
Treece, Henry, *The Black Seasons,* review, C2131
Trees and Birds under Fire, C22
Trelawny Interpreted, A39; C1008
Trelawny, E. J., C1007-8
— *The Recollections of Shelley and Byron,* reviews, C1265, 1271
Trench Tour, C1320
Trevelyan, George Macauley, *English Literature and its Readers,* on, C2758
— *Must England's Beauty Perish?,* review, C831
Trevelyan, R. C., *Beelzebub and Other Poems,* review, C1504
— ed., *From the Chinese,* review, C2204
Tribune, London, C2174
Tribute from the Field, A, C20

Tribute to Poets, C3276
Tribute to Poets of an Era, Eb26
Tribute to Walter de la Mare, B123, 290
Tributes from a Kinship in Husbandry, C2921
Trilling, Lionel, *The Liberal Imagination,* C2646
Triumph of Pigs, A, C3270
Triumphant Captive, The, C765
Trollope, Anthony, *An Autobiography,* review, C397
Trotter, Jacqueline, ed., *Valour and Vision,* review, C448
Trouble at Twilight, A43
Trower, Philip, *Tillotson,* review, C2727
Troyer, Howard William, *Ned Ward of Grubstreet,* review, C2411
True Aristocracy, The, C669
True Prince, A, C2274
Trypanis, C. A., ed., *Medieval and Modern Greek Poetry,* on, C2696
Tschichold, Jan, *Chinese Color-Prints,* review, C2791
Tuohy, Ferdinand, *The Crater of Mars,* review, C866
Turbulent Priest, The, C1078
Turner, W. J., *Jack and Jill,* review, C1391
— *Landscape of Cytherea,* reviews, C401, 406
— *New Poems,* reviews, C726, 815
— ed., *The Englishman's Country,* B113
— ed., *Great Names,* B18; C613 (review)
Turquet-Milnes, G., *Poems,* review, C757
Tusser, Thomas, *Five Hundred Points of Good Husbandry,* review, C437
Tuve, Rosamond, *A Reading of George Herbert,* review, C2873
Twelve Poems, B277
Twenty Years After, C1022
Twenty Years with Aunt Judy, C2308
Two Anthologies, C1322
Two Blessings, B282
Two Blind Mice, B137
Two British Wars, C1861
221B, Baker Street, C2669
Two Japanese Songs on Blood Transfusion, B227

Two Japans, The, C657
Two Lectures on English Literature, A85
Two Masters of Irony, B200
Two Modern Poets, C815
Two Old Plays, C3005
Two on a Tower, C548
Two Poets, C1517
Two Rare Plays, C2821
Two Remarkable Museums, D39
Two Travelers, C485
Two Travellers, C438
Tyler, Henry, C3153
Tyrrell, Mabel L., *Monkey's Money*, review, C1434

Uchida, Mr & Mrs, C2508
Ulysses Bookshop, A37
Ullman, James Ramsey, *Mad Shelley*, review, C983
Undertones of War, A28; D43; Ea6
Undset, Sigrid, *The Axe*, review, C682
Unending Vigil, The, B272
Unguessed Poetry, An *see* Dickinson, Emily
Union, The, Hong Kong, C3114
Unesco, C2311
United Nations News, London, C2627
University Memories, C2541
University of Hong Kong: the First 50 Years 1911-1961, B241
University of Hong Kong Gazette, Hong Kong, C3181
University of Hong Kong Supplement to the Gazette, Hong Kong, A155b; C3109
University of Texas, Academic Center, B283
University of Toronto Quarterly, Toronto, C3150
Unlucky Romantic, An, C1058
Unpublished Letters, C1589
Unreturning Times, C3357
Unsigned Review, The, C2678
Untermeyer, Louis, *The Albatross Book of Living Verse*, review, C1310
Unwin, Rayner, *The Rural Muse*, review, C3120
Up the Line to Death, B260
Upcott, Dr, C27
Updike, John, *Telephone Poles*, re-

view, C3312
Upon Literary Centenaries, C394
Uppingham School, *Passages for English Repetition*, review, C106
Ura Senke School of Tea Ceremonials, B125
Urn Burial, A43
Ussher, Arland, *Postscript on Existentialism*, review, C2266
Uttley, Alison, *Country Things*, review, C2250
— *When All is Done*, B108
Uyeda, Torao, C3173; Ea32
Uyehara, Yukus, *Songs for Children, Sung in Japan*, review, C2504

Vaccari, Oreste and Enko Elissa, *A.B.C. Japanese-English Dictionary*, review, C2555
— *Pictorial Chinese-Japanese Characters*, review, C2555
Vachell, Horace Annesley, *Arising Out of That*, review, C1441
— *Fellow-Travellers*, review, C442
Vallentin, Antonina, *Leonardo da Vinci*, review, C1740
Vallins, George H., *Kent Ways*, review, C464
Van Doren, Mark, *John Dryden*, review, C205
Vanbrugh, Sir John, *The Complete Works of*, review, C683
Vandercook, John W., *Black Majesty*, review, C716
— *Dark Islands*, review, C1686
Vane, William, A132; C3154
Vansittart, Sir Robert, *The Singing Caravan*, review, C1256
Vare, Daniele, *The Last of the Empresses*, review, C1515
Varieties of Poetry, C3312
Vase and the Parterre, The, p. 557
Vaughan, A. J., A26
Vaughan, Henry, A23, 25, 92
Vaughan, Hilda, *The Soldier and the Gentlewoman*, review, C1200
Vaughan, Richard, *Moulded in Earth*, review, C2622
Velhagen & Klasing, Bielefeld, Leipzig, A28f
Venables, Robert, *The Experienced Angler*, review, C670
Venezy, Alice S., *Pageantry on the*

Shakespearean Stage, review, C2666

Venn, J. A., compiler, *Alumni cantabrigienses*, Part 2, review, C3035

Vercel, Roger, *Captain Conan*, review, C1462

Verga, Giovanni, *Cavalleria Rusticana*, review, C682

Verlaine, Paul, A2–3; C502

Versatile Victorian, C2489

Verschoyle, Derek, B59

Verse, C137

Verse and the Attention, C597

Versions and Diversions, D41

Very Old Blues, C1615

Veteran, A, C344

Victoria and Albert Museum, C143

Victorian Adventure, A, C1479

Victorian Editor, A, C2525

Victorian England, C1040

Victorian Garland, A, C3302

Victorian Muse, A, C1235

Victorian Reading, C1455

Vidler, Arnold G. A., A28, 35, 135; C462

Viking Press, New York, A78*b*; B47*c*

Village Character, C301

Village Chimneys, The A43

Village Cricket is His Theme, C2252

Village Diarist, A, C2649

Village Secrets, C2055

Village To-Day, The, C2023

Villiers, A. J., *The Last of the Wind Ships*, review, C1421

— *Sons of Sindbad*, review, C1832

Vines, Sherard, *The Pyramid*, B20; C616 (review)

— *Triforium*, review, C757

— *Yofuku*, review, C1114

Vining, Elizabeth Gray, *Windows for the Crown Prince*, review, C2941

Virginia in 1616, C2789

Visick, Mary, *The Genesis of Wuthering Heights*, B205

Vision of Faith, A, C349

Visionary Gleams, C1986

Visionary Painters, The, C1941

Vivante, Leone, *English Poetry* [*etc.*], review, C2536

Vivat! C497

Voice Apart, A, C374

Voices, London, C34, 41, 46, 122

Voices from the Past, C2184

Voices on the Green, B110

Voltaire, C2776

Volume of Verses, A, C2213

Volunteer Laureate, The, C1540

Voska, Emanuel Victor and Will Irwin, *Spy and Counter-Spy*, review, C1846

Votive Tablets, A39

Vulliamy, C. E., *The Onslow Family*, review, C3092

— *Ursa Major*, review, C2295

W.O. [*i.e.* Wilfred Owen], A67–8, 135

W.S. [*i.e.* William Shakespeare], A156

Wade, Aubrey, *The War of the Guns*, B75

Wade, Gladys I., *Thomas Traherne*, review, C2080

Wadia, Ardaser Sorabjee N., *Museless Musings*, review, C2867

Waggoner and Other Poems, The, A8

Wagner, F. W., A76

Wain, John, ed., *Contemporary Reviews of Romantic Poetry*, review, C3057

Wainewright, T. G., C396

Wainewright, Thomas, C1692–3

Wake, Eugenia, *Musical Chains*, review, C1637

Wakefield, Archdeacon, proceedings against, C261

Wakefield, Harold, *New Paths for Japan*, review, C2447

Waldman, Milton, *Elizabeth and Leicester*, review, C2060

Waldock, A. J. A., *Hamlet*, review, C1596

— *Thomas Hardy and The Dynasts*, review, C1596

— and others, *Some Recent Developments in English Literature*, review, C1596

Waley, Arthur, trans., *The Book of Songs*, review, C1655

— *Chinese Poems*, review, C2391

— *The Real Tripitaka*, review, C2782

Walker, George, *The Voyages and Cruises of*, review, C693

Walker, I. B., *James Thomson (B.V.)*, review, C2545

Walker, Thomas Capell, *Chateau-*

719

C3142

Wilhelm, Donald, *Writing for Profit*, review, C1028

Wilkinson, C. H., *Festschrift*, C3344

— *More Diversions*, review, C1988

— ed., *The King of the Beggars*, review, C1154

Wilkinson, C. S., *The Wake of the Bounty*, review, C3024

Wilkinson, Clennell, *Nelson*, review, C1144

— *Prince Rupert the Cavalier*, review, C1419

Wilkinson, John T., *Richard Baxter and Margaret Charlton*, review, C716

Wilkinson, L. P., *Horace and His Lyric Poetry*, review, C2149

"Will You Come to the Camp?" C1041

Willans, Geoffrey, *One Eye on the Clock*, review, C1996

Willey, Basil, *The 'Q' Tradition*, review, C2299

William Crowe, A158

Williams, Alfred, C2097, 2107, 2577

— ed., *Folk Songs of the Upper Thames*, review, C385

Williams, Arnold, ed., *A Tribute to George Coffin Taylor*, review, C2866

Williams, Charles, *Heroes and Kings*, review, C1107

— *James I*, review, C1398

— *The Region of the Summer Stars*, review, C2067

Williams, E. T., and Helen M. Palmer, eds, *The Dictionary of National Biography, 1951–1960*, B286

Williams, Edward, C2839

Williams, Harley, *Between Life and Death*, review, C2720

Williams, Iola A., *Byways Round Helicon*, review, C324

— *The Elements of Book-Collecting*, review, C654

Williams, J. H., *Bandoola*, review, C3083

Williams, Orlo, *The Good English-woman*, review, C172

Williams, Samuel, A156

Williams, Valentine, *The World of Action*, review, C1688

Williams, W. D., *Nietzsche and the French*, review, C3022

Williams-Ellis, Clough and others, eds, *Britain and the Beast*, review, C1631

Williamson, C. N., C135

Williamson, E. W., *Henry Vaughan*, review, C2990

Williamson, G. C., *Behind My Library Door*, reviews, C308, 335

Williamson, Henry, *The Labouring Life*, review, C1212

— *The Sun in the Sands*, review, C2098

— *Tales of a Devon Village*, review, C2143

— intro., *A Soldier's Diary of the Great War*, review, C833

Williamson, J. A., *Sir Francis Drake*, review, C2719

Williamson, Margaret, *Colloquial Language of the Commonwealth and Restoration*, review, C908

Wills, Helen, *Tennis*, review, C752

Wills and Testaments, A43, 108

Willy, Margaret, *Every Star a Tongue*, on, C2743

Wilmot, Chester, *The Struggle for Europe*, review, C2751

Wilmot, Martha and Catherine, *The Russian Journals of*, review, C1399

Wilson, Sir Arnold, *Walks and Talks Abroad*, review, C1529

Wilson, Donald Powell, *My Six Convicts*, review, C2659

Wilson, Elkin Calhoun, *Prince Henry and English Literature*, review, C2276

Wilson, G. F., *Yorkshire in Prose and Verse*, review, C894

Wilson, Sir James, trans., *Old Scotch Songs and Poems*, review, C667

Wilson, John G., London, publisher, B10

Wilson, Jonathan, *Poems*, review, C2251

Wilson, Mona, and others, *Grand Tour*, B73

Wilson, R. M., *The Lost Literature of Mediaeval England*, review, C2845

Wilson, Robert F., *Colour and Light at Work*, review, C3082

Wiltshire, Andrews' and Drury's Map of, review, C2961